The Irish Legal System

The Irish Legal System

Sixth Edition

RAYMOND BYRNE

BCL, LLM (NUI), Barrister-at-Law
Director of Research, Law Reform Commission

J PAUL MCCUTCHEON

BCL, LLM, LLD (NUI)
Professor of Law, University of Limerick

with

CLAIRE BRUTON

LLB (Dub), LLM (Lond), Barrister-at-Law

GERARD COFFEY

BA (UL), LLB, PhD (NUI)
Lecturer in Law, University of Limerick

with Foreword to the First Edition
by
Mr Justice Niall McCarthy
Judge of the Supreme Court of Ireland
1982–1992

Bloomsbury Professional

Published by
Bloomsbury Professional
Maxwelton House
41–43 Boltro Road
Haywards Heath
West Sussex
RH16 1BJ

Bloomsbury Professional
The Fitzwilliam Business Centre
26 Upper Pembroke Street
Dublin 2

ISBN: 978 178043 500 8
© Raymond Byrne & J Paul McCutcheon 2014
Bloomsbury Professional is an imprint of Bloomsbury Publishing Plc

British Library Cataloguing-in-Publication Data
A catalogue record for this book is available from the British Library

Typeset by Marlex Editorial Services Ltd, Dublin, Ireland
Printed and bound in Great Britain by
CPI Group (UK) Ltd, Croydon, CR0 4YY

Foreword to the First Edition

Mr Justice Niall McCarthy
Judge of the Supreme Court of Ireland
1982 – 1992

Shakespeare had a word for it - indeed, as was his practice, he had several words for it. In Henry VI Pt 2 one of the rabblement said – "The first thing we do, let's kill all the lawyers."[1]

This cry derived in part, at least, from ignorance. It is in the nature of man to fear what he does not understand. In Ireland, ignorance of the law is compounded by a suspicion and fear that springs from our history. The law, as it touched upon the average Irishman of a hundred years ago, was an instrument of oppression in the enforcement of either the criminal law or of taxation. The average Irishman seldom sought its help because the law was of little use to him; it was administered by the propertied classes for the propertied classes, it was the visible instrument of British rule through its buildings, local symbols of imperial might, and through its Judges and practitioners, garbed in ancient forms of dress and speaking an arcane language. Although the revolutionaries of 1916 proclaimed a republic and the author of the Constitution of 1937 often vouchsafed the State to be such, as it was proclaimed in 1948,[2] the structures, formal approach, and, most regrettably, attitudes of lawyers in Ireland remain English orientated. In a sense, this is not the fault of the lawyers of this generation because they inherited it from the last and the generation before that; but it is the fault of this generation because of a failure to examine and analyse the law, rather than take refuge in an unthinking and uncritical citation of precedent. Forensic forelock touching is as much a part of the cultural cringe that has beset our country as the mimicry of English accents and manners, but it may be more damaging in its long term effects. Whilst no lawyer of the last sixty years can escape his share of blame, some have sought at least to inform the public as to some of the intricacies of the legal system but none to the extent that this work seeks to do. Although one is mildly conscious of it at the Bar, it is really since I have sat on the Bench that I have become so aware of the degree to which the citation of precedent is made a substitute for reasoned argument and analysis of principle. Messrs Byrne and McCutcheon in this book, make a valiant effort to examine the doctrine of precedent recognising the vital distinction that it is the reason for the decision that is important, rather than the decision itself; that if the reason be good, it matters not in what Court such reason were used; if the reasoning be defective, then the leather binding of the Law Reports does not give it authenticity or merit. A recent exposure of defective reasoning is to be found in the robust language of Professor Glanville Williams in his article "The Lords and Impossible Attempts, or *quis custodiet ipsos custodes?*"[3]

---

1. Henry VI Pt 2 - Act IV - Scene II – line 86.
2. Republic of Ireland Act 1948.
3. (1986) Cambridge Law Journal 33.

In the memoirs of Lord Shandon, of which the type-script is in the King's Inns Library, that worthy did not spare even the great Chief Baron on this score. "There can be no question" he said "that his judgments were held in deserved respect, but his mind was of the type which I dislike though it was one which our legal system necessarily encourages with its slavish adherence to mere precedent. Palles not only had an immense knowledge of case law but his industry was colossal and one might always rely upon Palles's disinterring some forgotten authority which everyone else had failed to discover. Such men remind me of the contrapuntal musicians who by the application of purely empirical rules occasionally produce the most magnificent harmony. So it was with the Chief Baron. His method was always the same, that of piling up analogy on analogy but often to produce a most logical and coherent result. In the same way he worshipped technicality as if it were a fetish and even when he was fully conscious that the result at which he arrived was imminently unsatisfactory he was unable to burst the bonds of precedent and technicality. He was ably abetted - indeed often inspired in the matter of technicality by his Co-adjutor, Baron Fitzgerald who would subdivide the split hair that his Chief had divided."[4] Strong words indeed, but it is still at times refreshing to be referred to the earlier cases in which Judges appeared to be able to enunciate both principle and decision in a few pages whilst now, armed with the dictating machine gun, we sometimes get lost in a sea of words.

When the Supreme Court decided *Brogan v Bennett*[5] in June 1952, the report indicates that judgment was delivered on the day of hearing. The unfortunate Christopher Brogan had believed a pamphlet entitled "TB CONQUERED by Mr J H Bennett, Lamagh, Newtownforbes, of Kelly & Bennett, Divining Specialists, Longford. Tel: Longford 53", and requested some relatives to get in touch with Mr Bennett who undertook to cure Christopher Brogan and make him fit for work within three months, charging fees of £100 for a rich person and £20 for a poor person, into which category the unfortunate Christopher Brogan fell; as a result, he left Longford tuberculosis hospital and returned home where he took a medicine "prescribed" by Bennett for approximately five weeks and then died. His parents sued for damages for negligence and called evidence from the relatives who had interviewed Bennett, who "produced a bullet on the end of a string, and said he was going to X-ray the patient. He then caused the pendulum to oscillate and pronounced the case to be a fairly bad one. He purported to diagnose the exact percentage of impairment of all the main organs of the patient, and claimed that by means of his pendulum he could diagnose the ailments of a person at the other end of the world." When Kingsmill Moore J, sitting as a Judge of the High Court on Circuit, stated a case for the Supreme Court as to whether he could legally hold that the death of Christopher Brogan was caused by the wrongful acts, neglect, or default of the defendant within the meaning of those words as used in the Fatal Accidents Act 1846,[6] the Supreme Court unanimously, and without hesitation, answered - Yes. With enviable brevity, James Murnaghan J said at page 127:

---

4   Memoirs of Lord Shandon - type-script – p 183.
5   [1955] IR 119.
6   The relevant statute would now be the Civil Liability Act 1961.

"There are various kinds of skill which can be exercised. If a person professes to use skill for reward he is liable for negligence in not using that skill ... The defendant made elaborate claims of power and success. It was not unreasonable for the deceased to believe what he was told and it seems clear that he did believe it and that the defendant failed to fulfil the representations which he made, and he is therefore liable."

Is this much different from what it took the House of Lords innumerable pages to express in *Hedley Byrne and Company Limited v Heller and Partners Limited*?[7] You may search, however, the textbooks and find no reference to *Brogan v Bennett*. Every law student knows what happened to Mrs Donoghue to the extent, even, of the variety of spellings of her names[8] or whether or not there ever was a snail in the bottle although the way had been identified in *Heaven v Pender*[9] almost fifty years before.

This excursus on grinding a private axe is a feature of the writing of Forewords to legal textbooks. Partly it derives from a sense of frustration with the ignorance of the general public about the legal structures of the State. The man in the Cabra bus or, indeed, on the DART has little interest in the law except when it impinges on him directly - obviously in the enforcement of the criminal law and of taxation. His knowledge of the Constitution is mostly one of "rights" and seldom one of "duties". He is not to blame; he is taught nothing of these structures when he is at school or at any level of education unless he takes up the study of the law as an object in itself or as ancillary to some other discipline. The requirement of knowledge of the law in all its aspects is so great that, indeed, those who qualify to practise are often themselves ill equipped to examine and explain the underlying theory - the underlying principle. In this book the authors have set out to pierce that great curtain of ignorance; this book is directed towards the general public as well as to the student and practitioner; it is a book that requires concentration and study; it deserves both; although one may not agree with all of the authors' sentiments, it is right to pay tribute to their energy, research and initiative and, particularly, to their clarity of expression. The law is often the victim rather than the victor in the battle of words. If this book does, as I believe it can, create a more informed body of citizens who will recognise and accept that the law is a two-way traffic, their efforts will have been justly rewarded. If their readers can come to recognise that the Constitution is not merely a document to be quoted and misquoted when the electorate is much exercised about personal or family rights, but is also the fundamental law of the State governing our relationships with each other and with the State itself, their achievement will have been great.

Niall McCarthy,
9 July 1986.

---

7 [1964] AC 465.
8 *Donoghue v Stevenson* [1932] AC 562. [The case is sometimes incorrectly cited, using Mrs Stevenson's maiden name, as either *Donoghue (M'Alister) v Stevenson* or *M'Alister v. Stevenson*. See Lord Macmillan, 'The Citation of Scottish Cases' (1933) 49 LQR 1 - eds]
9 (1883) 11 QBD 503.

Preface

We have endeavoured to reflect the changes to the Irish legal system since the publication five years ago of the previous edition of this work in 2009. In the best of times it would have been optimistic to expect that the level of investment in process improvement and court infrastructure that we witnessed in the first decade of the century would or could be maintained. The drastic economic circumstances of the State between 2009 and 2013 (which it appears are beginning to improve in 2014) ensured that that did not happen, and the legal system, in common with all public services, has witnessed a significant reduction in expenditure with all the consequent challenges that this has involved.

While the overall impact of the reduced annual budget for the courts has correctly been described by the Chief Justice as at the edge of acceptability, there have been some positive developments to report. Notably, one of the most important infrastructural projects of the short-lived Celtic Tiger period, the Criminal Courts of Justice Complex at Parkgate Street in Dublin, made it through to successful completion before the budgetary axe fell. Whereas the courts complex in Green Street in Dublin (currently housing the Special Criminal Court) reflects the Victorian-era approach to the design of a criminal court, the Parkgate Street complex has been designed with the separate interests of the accused and witnesses in mind, as well as the needs of victims, and with a very 21st century eye on digital-era technology. In contrast, we have seen an ongoing rationalisation of the District Court system, including the closure of a number of court venues especially in rural and less populated areas. While the number of venues was in need of some reduction, there is a risk that an inherited concept of justice administered close to and within the community may be lost on the altar of enforced efficiency.

At the higher end of the court system, the compelling case for the establishment of a Court of Appeal has finally been accepted with the ratification by referendum of the Thirty-third Amendment to the Constitution Act 2013. This represents the most significant alteration to the court structure since the adoption of the Constitution in 1937, and it reflects the exponential growth in judicial workload since the 1960s and the concern that the Supreme Court has been expected to handle more cases annually than its UK or US counterparts, leading to a four-year waiting list for all but the most urgent appeals. As we write, the Court of Appeal Act 2014 has been enacted, six of the ten judges of the new Court have been appointed, albeit as judges-designate, and it is expected that the Court will be formally established by the end of 2014. We have sought to capture this important development in the relevant chapters of the text, but bearing in mind that it will take some time for the new Court to take over fully the backlog of Supreme Court civil appeals, as well as the current workload of the Court of Criminal Appeal, our discussion and observations are necessarily tentative and transitional in nature.

The State's 2010 Financial Agreement with the troika (the EU Commission, the European Central Bank and the International Monetary Fund), which amounted to a guaranteed ?70 billion "bailout" or loan, involved considerable conditions that not surprisingly included a strong element of structural economic reforms. These included commitments to reform competition law in general as well as related regulation of a number of professions. The Legal Services Regulation Bill 2011, which at the time of writing has made some progress through the Oireachtas, is one result of this aspect of the commitments made to the troika. The detailed contents of the 2011 Bill remain much-debated (to use a neutral phrase), and while the State "exited" the bailout in December 3013 the troika retains a continued interest in seeing its conditions fulfilled (especially as the loans have yet to be repaid). As a result, the 2011 Bill will be enacted in 2014 or 2015, perhaps with some of its most contentious provisions either much diluted or postponed.

Regardless of the final content of the 2011 Bill as enacted, the nature of the legal profession in the near and middle distance will be influenced not merely by such legislation but also by the increasingly international nature of legal services and the obvious effects of information and communications technology; and this has prompted a brief discussion in Chapter 3 of Richard Susskind's views on what the future holds.

The 2010 Agreement with the troika also contained a commitment to support the development of mediation as a dispute resolution mechanism (as recommended in a 2010 Law Reform Commission Report). This has been widely welcomed and, as we discuss in Chapter 8, a Mediation Bill is likely to be published in the near future. This would provide a clear legislative basis for a flexible mechanism that is controlled by the parties and which at the same time is likely to require some assistance from professional advisers.

It is noticeable that the superior courts have continued to demonstrate their fidelity to the principle of *stare decisis*, which we discuss in Chapter 12. It is refreshing to observe the techniques of case analysis being displayed so prominently by the current generation of judges, when some commentators might have dismissed those practices as outmoded. This is a trend that we had observed in the 5th edition and the continued articulation of the principle is a welcome reinforcement of judicial discipline, which as we have noted previously is essential to ensuring the legitimacy of judicial law-making. The importance of identifying the *ratio decidendi* of a case, the methods by which that is done and the incremental manner in which legal rules develop will continue to perplex current and future generations of law students, as they did that of the authors, but mastering them will provided a fuller understanding of our common law system.

The rise in the importance of legislation as a source of legal rules is equally significant and explains in part why we discuss it over two chapters, 13 and 14. Lawyers spend the greater amount of their time engaged in navigating the meaning of legislation for their clients, and indeed the majority of case law now involves the application and interpretation of statutory rules rather than "pure" common law. Hence the importance of a structured approach to the principles of statutory interpretation. We should also note the efforts that have been made to improve the state of the statute book, notably with the enactment of the Statute Law Revision Act 2007, which for the first time allowed us to know with accuracy the precise number of pre-1922 Public Acts that remain in force. More significantly, the online publication of the Legislation Directory on the electronic Irish Statute Book and the preparation by the Law Reform Commission of Revised Acts represents a significant change in the Irish legal landscape, making the law increasing accessible to lawyers and citizens alike.

While information technology has transformed legal practice and the court system, and has facilitated improvements to the statute book and the quality of legislation, it also poses the corresponding challenge of information overload. This is especially significant where case law is concerned, with the decisions of courts throughout the common law world being readily and speedily accessible from a wide variety of electronic sources. In the past, a small jurisdiction like ours was characterised by the paucity of reported and accessible case law but now we might be reaching a point where we have too much law! In this context the extra-judicial remarks of Clarke J regarding the citation of foreign precedent, noted in Chapter 12, merit deep and considered reflection.

Since 2009, a series of amendments and proposed amendments to the 1937 Constitution has also focused attention on the fact that we live in changing times. What was regarded until 2011 as a fundamental pillar of judicial independence, that judicial salaries could not be reduced, was swept away by a convincing majority of the voting public who may have felt that the judiciary should not be immune from the painful effects of the economic collapse. On the same day, the people rejected a proposal to confer greater investigative powers on Oireachtas Committees: a consolation prize for the judiciary, perhaps, that the people thus preferred the Supreme Court's view ten years earlier in *Maguire v Ardagh* (one of the few cases better known by its geographical origins, Abbeylara) that another great constitutional principle, the separation of powers, requires that elected politicians are not well placed to determine issues of individual reputation or liability. And in 2013, the people also expressed a preference to retain the second parliamentary chamber, Seanad Éireann. We note in Chapter 15 that as this edition is being prepared, the deliberations and recommendations of the Convention on the Constitution are likely to lead to referendums on further significant changes to the Constitution, ranging from a possible reduction in the voting age to 16, provision for same-sex marriage and abolition of the offence of blasphemy.

All of this is against the background that, as they have been since the 1960s, the courts are still being asked in constitutional litigation to adjudicate on complex social and moral questions, virtually all of which ultimately require political and legislative solutions. The debates of previous decades concerning access to contraception, which moved between the Oireachtas and the courts, were ultimately settled through legislative solutions. More difficult and challenging have been the debates over termination of pregnancy and abortion, where the constitutional position, as interpreted by the Supreme Court in 1992, was belatedly legislated for in the Protection of Life During Pregnancy Act 2013, but this remains a continuing matter for ongoing debate. Similarly, the moral, ethical and legal challenges posed by some end-of-life decisions, including whether assisted suicide should in some circumstances be lawful, were litigated as far as the Supreme Court in 2013 in *Fleming v Ireland*. That decision illustrated the limits of the judicial function and of constitutional case law. Both the High Court and Supreme Court in *Fleming* considered that the scope of the law of suicide was fundamentally a matter for the Oireachtas: a mirror image of the separation of powers analysis in the Abbeylara case.

The two previous editions were written in the challenging intervals between the initial rejection and subsequent adoption of, respectively, the Treaties of Nice and Lisbon. Happily, we have been spared an equivalent challenge in Chapter 16 of the current edition. The reforms brought about by the Treaty of Lisbon are now in place and the fractured and complicated arrangements that were in place prior to that Treaty have been replaced by more streamlined and coherent Treaty arrangements and governance structure. The potential reach of EU law and its penetration into the domestic legal system is far greater than could have been imagined in 1973 when Ireland acceded to what were then known as the European Communities. Who, for example, would have envisaged that EU action might determine the definition of criminal offences? Yet that is what was brought about by the Treaty of Lisbon which envisages the harmonisation of the definition of criminal offences that have a cross-border dimension, such as terrorism, trafficking in human beings and sexual exploitation of women and children, illicit drug trafficking, illicit arms trafficking, money laundering, corruption, counterfeiting of means of payment, computer crime and organised crime. In one respect this reflects current political reality that common European problems may yield common European solutions. Nevertheless, one of the key themes in the continued development of the EU is likely to be a pronounced tension between the competing demands of an expressed preference for European action and respect for national sovereignty.

Byrne and McCutcheon would like to record the enormous debt they owe to their contributing authors, Claire Bruton and Gerard Coffey; both the 5th edition and this one have benefitted greatly from their significant and fresh insights throughout the entire text. We are also both extremely grateful for the support of our colleagues in the School of Law, University of Limerick and in the Law Reform Commission. Claire Bruton would also like to thank Simon Donagh BL and Grainne Duggan BL for their assistance. We all express our renewed gratitude to the family of the late Mr Justice Niall McCarthy for their continued agreement to allow us use the text of the Foreword, which he contributed to the first edition of this text in 1986.

It is also a pleasure to acknowledge our publishers Bloomsbury Professional who ensured that our manuscript was edited to the highest standard, and whose patience ensured that we were allowed to add material that came to hand in September. We are especially grateful to Sandra Mulvey for her encouragement and tolerance, and to Tessa Robinson for reading and editing the entire manuscript with obvious care and attention to detail. Thanks are also due to Andrew Turner for producing the index and to Marian Sullivan for typesetting this book with such skill.

Raymond Byrne
Paul McCutcheon

30 September 2014

Contents

Foreword to the First Edition v
Preface ix
Contents xiii
Table of Cases xix
Table of Legislation xlv
Table of Statutory Instruments lxxxi
Table of Constitutional Articles lxxxvii
Table of European Legislation xciii
Table of International Treaties and Conventions xcvii

Chapter 1   Introduction to the Irish Legal System

[1]   Introduction 1
[2]   Law and Laws 3
[3]   The Irish Legal System as a Common Law System 4
[4]   Sources of Law 5
[5]   Divisions of the Law 10
[6]   Legal Personality 13
[7]   A Jurisprudential Overview 15
[8]   Law and Morality 20
[9]   The Rule of Law 25

Chapter 2   Development of the Irish Legal System

[1]   Introduction 29
[2]   Pre-Norman Ireland and the Brehon Law 29
[3]   The Arrival of English Law in Ireland 30
[4]   The Institutions of State in the United Kingdom
      (1800–1922) 39
[5]   The Emergence of a New State 49
[6]   The 1922 Constitution 50
[7]   The 1937 Constitution 57
[8]   A Revised Court System 64

Chapter 3   The Legal Profession

[1]   Introduction 69
[2]   Solicitors 87
[3]   Barristers 97
[4]   The Law Officers 109

[5]   Legal Education Generally 115
[6]   Other Professionals 121

Chapter 4   The Court System, the Judiciary and Administration of the Courts Service

[1]   Introduction 123
[2]   The Administration of Justice in Courts 126
[3]   The Need to Establish a Post-1937 Court System 142
[4]   The Court System in Ireland: Judicial Composition
       and Structure 144
[5]   Appointment and Qualifications 160
[6]   Judicial Independence and Judicial Ethics 179
[7]   Vacating of Judicial Office and Retirement 209
[8]   Court Officers and Administration 213
[9]   Management of the Court System 217

Chapter 5   The First Instance Jurisdiction of the Courts

[1]   Introduction 225
[2]   The Original Jurisdiction of the Courts in Civil Cases 238
[3]   The Original Jurisdiction of the Courts in Criminal Cases 260
[4]   Proposals for Fundamental Reform of the Court Structure 270

Chapter 6   Civil and Criminal Court Procedure

[1]   Introduction 277
[2]   Civil and Criminal Procedure Compared and Contrasted 277
[3]   Civil Procedure 284
[4]   Reform of the Civil Justice System: the UK Woolf
       Reforms and Judicial Case Management 305
[5]   Criminal Procedure 311
[6]   Court Procedure and Rules of Evidence 327
[7]   Judge and Jury 333

Chapter 7   The Appellate Jurisdiction of the Courts

[1]   Introduction 341
[2]   Appellate Jurisdiction in Civil Cases 346
[3]   Appellate Jurisdiction in Criminal Cases 357
[4]   Appellate Jurisdiction of Courts from Adjudicative Bodies 369
[5]   Analysis that led to Reforms of the Appellate Process 369
[6]   Appellate Jurisdiction of the EU Court of Justice 373

Chapter 8　Other Dispute Resolution Processes: Mediation, Arbitration, Administrative Adjudicative Bodies and Ombudsmen

[1]　Introduction 377
[2]　Mediation, Conciliation, the Courts and an 'Integrated' Civil Justice System 378
[3]　Arbitration 384
[4]　Administrative Law and the Emergence of Modern Government 387
[5]　Administrative Law and Adjudicative Bodies Generally 393
[6]　Coroners' Courts 402
[7]　Tribunals of Inquiry and Commissions of Investigation 404
[8]　Ombudsmen 407

Chapter 9　Access to Law

[1]　Introduction 413
[2]　The Constitutional Setting: Access to the Courts 413
[3]　Provision of State-Funded Legal Aid 418
[4]　State-Assisted Criminal Legal Aid 420
[5]　State-Assisted Civil Legal Aid 427
[6]　Court Fees 438
[7]　Legal costs 440
[8]　Protective Costs Orders 441

Chapter 10　Remedies and Enforcement in Civil and Criminal Matters

[1]　Introduction 443
[2]　Remedies in Civil Matters 443
[3]　Procedure for Enforcement of Court Orders 448
[4]　Enforcement in Criminal Matters 451
[5]　Contempt of Court 458
[6]　Judicial Review 460

Chapter 11　Law Reform

[1]　Introduction 463
[2]　Law Reform and A Legislative Code 463
[3]　Law Reform Commission 466
[4]　Other Law Reform Bodies 472
[5]　Judicial Decisions 474

Chapter 12   Precedent

[1]   Introduction 475
[2]   *Stare Decisis* in the Irish Courts 485
[3]   The *Ratio Decidendi* and *Obiter Dictum* 519
[4]   Precedent in Action: an Example 542

Chapter 13   Legislation

[1]   Introduction 563
[2]   Legislative Process 570
[3]   Legislative Product 586
[4]   Delegated Legislation 604

Chapter 14   Interpretation of Legislation

[1]   Introduction 629
[2]   The Principal Approaches 640
[3]   Aids to Interpretation 664
[4]   External Sources 694

Chapter 15   The Constitution and its Interpretation

[1]   Introduction 711
[2]   The 1937 Constitution 712
[3]   Fundamental Rights and Constitutional Judicial Review 723
[4]   Principles of Constitutional Interpretation 752
[5]   Report of Constitution Review Group, Reports of
       Oireachtas Committee on Constitution and
       Reports of Constitutional Convention 776
[6]   The Constitution and the European Convention on
       Human Rights 779

Chapter 16   European Union Law

[1]   Introduction 785
[2]   European Integration after 1945 788
[3]   The Three European Communities 789
[4]   From European Community to European Union 796
[5]   The Nature of European Union Law 812
[6]   Institutions of the European Union 828
[7]   The Form of European Union Laws 840
[8]   Implementation of European Union Law in Ireland 846

Chapter 17   International Law

[1]   Introduction 853
[2]   Sources of International Law 854
[3]   Ireland in International Law 856
[4]   The Council of Europe 858
[5]   The United Nations Organisation 862
[6]   The World Trade Organisation 869
[7]   International Law in Ireland 873
[8]   Private International Law 880

Bibliography 883

Index 911

Table of Cases

A

AA v Medical Council [2003] IESC 70 .... 7.25
A v Governor of Arbour Hill Prison [2006] IEHC 169, [2006] IESC 45,
    [2006] 4 IR 88 ....12.122, 15.75–15.77, 15.98
AA v Medical Council [2003] IEHC 611, [2003] 4 IR 302 (SC) 9.57
Aamand v Smithwick [1995] 1 ILRM 61 .... 14.107, 14.165
AB v Minister for Justice [2002] 1 IR 296 .... 7.28
Abrahamson v Law Society of Ireland [1996] 1 IR 403 .... 3.56, 15.80
ACC Bank plc v Brian Johnston & Co [2010] 4 IR 605 .... 12.173
AD v Ireland [1994] 1 IR 369 .... 6.04
Addie (Robert) and Sons (Collieries) Ltd v Dumbreck [1929] AC 358 .... 12.37
Adoption (No 2) Bill 1987, Re [1989] IR 656 .... 15.58
Aer Lingus Teo v Labour Court [1990] ILRM 485 .... 8.50
Agricultural Machinery Ltd v Ó Culacháin [1990] 1 IR 535 .... 14.73
Ahern v Bus Éireann [2011] IESC 44 .... 6.43
Airey v Ireland (1979) 2 EHRR 305 ....9.41–9.42, 9.60, 17.68
Allen & Hanbury Ltd v Controller of Patents, Designs and Trade Marks
    and Clonmel Healthcare Ltd [1997] 1 ILRM 416 .... 17.56
Allied Finance and Investments Ltd v Haddow [1983] NZLR 22 .... 12.164
Amministrazione della Finanze dello Stato v Simmenthal
    [1978] ECR 629 .... 14.62
An Blascaod Mór Teo v Commissioners of Public Works (No 2)
    [2000] 1 IR 1 .... 14.44, 14.163
Anisminic Ltd v Foreign Compensation Tribunal [1969] 2 AC 147 .... 12.104
Anns v London Borough of Merton [1978] AC 728 .... 12.149
Ansbacher (Caymen) Ltd, Re [2002] 2 ILRM 491 .... 4.28
AO v Minister for Justice, Equality and Law Reform [2003] 1 IR 1
    .... 15.19, 15.192
Article 26 and the Health (Amendment) (No 2) Bill 2004, Re
    [2005] IESC 7, [2005] 1 IR 105 .... 5.87, 15.126
Article 26 and the School Attendance Bill 1942, Re
    [1943] IR 334 .... 12.47–12.50
Ashford Castle Ltd v SIPTU [2006] ELR 201 .... 8.50
Ashville Investments Ltd v Elmer Contractors Ltd [1989] QB 488 .... 12.102
Atkinson v Carty [2005] 16 ELR 1 .... 5.56, 8.52
Attorney General (Fahy) v Bruen [1936] IR 750 ....7.17, 7.35, 8.25
Attorney General (Shaughnessy) v Ryan [1960] IR 181 .... 12.92
Attorney General (Society for the Protection of Unborn Children Ltd) v
    Open Door Counselling Ltd [1988] IR 593 ....3.121, 12.45, 15.176

Attorney General and Minister for Posts and Telegraphs v CIÉ
(1956) 90 ILTR 139 ....12.36
Attorney General v Edison Telephone Co (1886) 6 QBD 244 ....14.97
Attorney General v Hamilton (No 1) [1993] 2 IR 250 ....3.122
Attorney General v Leaf Ltd [1982] ILRM 441 ....14.125
Attorney General v McBride [1928] IR 451 ....2.68
Attorney General v Paperlink Ltd [1984] ILRM 343 ....15.58
Attorney General v Residential Institutions Board [2012] IEHC 492 ....12.63
Attorney General v Ryan's Car Hire Ltd [1965] IR 642 ....12.36, 12.40
....12.46, 12.72, 12.76
Attorney General v Scotcher [2005] 1 WLR 1867 ....6.153
Attorney General v Smith [1927] IR 564 ....7.47
Attorney General v X [1992] 1 IR 1 ....1.57, 3.122, 4.164, 12.106
....15.112, 15.147, 15.165, 15.177
Awoyomi v Radford [2007] EWHC 1671 (Admin), [2008] 3 WLR 34,
[2007] NLJR 1046 ....3.109

B

B (PML) v J(PH) (5 May 1992, unreported), HC 9.11
B v B [1975] IR 54 (decided in 1970) 7.25
Baker v The Queen [1975] AC 774 ....12.102
Bakht v Medical Council [1990] 1 IR 515 ....7.30, 14.149
Battle v Irish Art Promotion Centre Ltd [1968] IR 252 ....9.11
Beatty v Rent Tribunal [2006] 2 IR 191 ....12.157
Beatty v The Rent Tribunal & Another [2006] 2 IR 191 ....4.184
Beecham Group Ltd v Bristol Myers Co (13 March 1981,
unreported), HC 14.175
Behan v Allied Irish Banks plc [2009] IEHC 554 ....6.43
Behan v McGinley [2008] IEHC 181 ....3.108
Berns v Bethell [1982] Ch 294 ....12.102
Best v Wellcome Foundation Ltd [1993] 3 IR 421 ....7.11, 9.09
Blake v Attorney General [1982] IR 117 ....15.69, 15.102
Blehein v Minister for Health and Children [2004] 3 IR 610 (HC),
[2008] IESC 40 ....9.03
Bloomer v Incorporated Law Society of Ireland [1995] 3 IR 14 (HC),
(1997) 6 IJEL 220 (SC) 3.55
Blottner v Bestuur van de Niewe Algemene Bedrijfsvereniging
[1977] ECR 1141 ....14.88
Bonham's (Dr) Case (1610) 8 Co Rep 114(a) 14.111
Bosphorus Hava v Minister for Transport [1994] 2 ILRM 551 ....14.59
Bosphorus v Ireland (2006) 42 EHRR 1 ....17.36
Bourke v Attorney General [1972] IR 36 ....14.165, 14.175, 14.190
Bourne v Norwich Crematorium Ltd [1967] 2 All ER 576 ....14.128
Boylan v Dublin Corporation [1949] IR 60 ....12.72, 12.76
Boyle v Allen [1979] ILRM 281 ....5.66

Brady v Director of Public Prosecutions [2010] IEHC 231 .... 12.63
Brady v Donegal County Council [1989] ILRM 282 .... 9.02
Brasserie du Pêcheur SA v Federal Republic of Germany/Reg v
  Secretary of State for Transport, ex p Factortame Ltd
  [1996] 2 WLR 506 .... 16.205
Brennan v Attorney General [1983] ILRM 449 (HC), [1984]
  ILRM 355 (SC) 15.101
Brennan v Minister for Justice [1995] 1 IR 612 .... 4.15, 10.33
Brennan v Mullane [2014] IEHC 61 .... 12.63
Brosnan v Leeside Nurseries Ltd [1998] 2 IR 304 .... 14.70
Browne v Attorney General [1991] 2 IR 58 .... 15.103
Browne v Bank of Ireland Finance Ltd [1991] 1 IR 431 .... 7.07
Buchanan (James) Ltd v Babco Forwarding Shipping (UK) Ltd
  [1977] QB 208, [1978] AC 141 .... 14.58–14.59
Buckley v Attorney General [1950] IR 67 .... 14.141
Burke v Aer Lingus plc [1997] 1 ILRM 148 .... 14.42
Burke v Minister for Labour [1979] IR 354 .... 8.51, 13.149
Burt v Claude Cousins & Co [1971] 2 QB 426 .... 12.156
Butterly v Mayor of Drogheda [1907] 2 IR 134 .... 12.140
Byrne v Conroy [1998] 3 IR 1 .... 14.90–14.91, 14.107, 16.223
Byrne v Dublin City Council [2009] IEHC 122, [2012] IESC 18 .... 15.202, 15.205
  .... 17.72
Byrne v Ireland [1972] IR 241 .... 9.02, 15.31, 15.37, 15.66–15.71
  .... 15.87, 15.104, 15.116

C

Cahill v Governor of Military Detention Barracks, Curragh Camp
  [1980] ILRM 191 .... 9.11
Cahill v Sutton [1980] IR 269
  .... 6.07, 15.69, 15.88, 15.91–15.93, 15.101, 15.168
Campbell-Sharpe v Independent Newspapers (11 February 1998,
  unreported), SC 12.21
Campus Oil Ltd v Minister for Industry and Energy [1983] IR 82 .... 7.80
Campus Oil Ltd v Minister for Industry and Energy (No 2)
  [1983] IR 88 .... 10.14
Canada Southern Ry Co v International Bridge Co
  (1883) 3 App Cas 723 .... 14.156
Candler v Crane, Christmas & Co [1951] 2 KB 164 .... 12.104, 12.150
Canty v Private Residential Tenancies Board [2008] IESC 24 .... 7.28
Carmello v Casey [2007] IEHC 362, [2008] 3 IR 524 .... 6.43
Carmody v Minister for Justice, Equality and Law Reform
  [2005] IEHC 10, [2005] 2 ILRM 1, [2009] IESC 91
  [2009] 1 IR 635 .... 9.22, 15.206
Carrigaline [Community Television Broadcasting] Co Ltd v Minister
  for Transport [1997] 1 ILRM 241 .... 13.133

Carron v McMahon [1990] 1 IR 239 ....12.30, 12.53
Cassell & Co Ltd v Broome [1972] AC 1027 ....12.32
Cassidy v Minister for Industry and Commerce [1978] IR 297
....13.143, 13.145
Caulfield v Bourke [1980] ILRM 223 ....14.110
CC Bank plc v Brian Johnston & Co [2010] 4 IR 605 ....12.173
CC v Ireland (No 2) [2005] IESC 48, [2006] 4 IR 1 ....12.92, 15.76–15.77
....15.98, 15.110
Chahal v United Kingdom (1997) 23 EHRR 413 ....17.73
Chamberlain v Lai [2006] NZSC 70 ....3.110
Chemical Bank v McCormack [1983] ILRM 350 ....14.116
Chestvale Properties Ltd v Glackin [1993] 3 IR 35 ....14.115
Chief Adjudication Officer v Foster [1993] 2 WLR 292 ....14.180
City of London v Wood (1701) 12 Mod Rep 669 ....14.111
Cityview Press Ltd v An Chomhairle Oiliúna [1980] IR 381 ....13.123
....13.130, 13.142, 15.100, 16.124, 16.132
CK v CK [1993] ILRM 535 ....14.178
Clancy v Irish Rugby Football Union [1995] 1 ILRM 193 ....8.61
Clancy, Re [1943] IR 23 ....12.59
Clarke v County Registrar County Galway (14 July 2010) HC,
  The Irish Times, 15 July 2010 ....6.144
Clay v United States 403 US 698 (1971). 4.169
Cleary v Booth [1893] 1 QB 465 ....13.12
Clinton v An Bord Pleanála [2007] 1 IR 272 ....12.122
Close v Steel Co of Wales [1962] AC 367 ....12.36
CM v TM (No 2) [1991] ILRM 268 ....15.58
Coakley (Denis) & Co Ltd v Commissioner of Valuation
  [1991] 1 IR 402 (HC) 14.71
Coastal Line Container Terminal Ltd v SIPTU [2000] 1 IR 549 ....14.60
Coffey v Tara Mines Ltd [2008] 1 IR 436 ....9.11
Coleman v Clarke [1991] ILRM 841 ....7.11
Colgan v Independent Radio and Television Commission
  [1999] 1 ILRM 22 ....14.83
Collier v Hicks (1831) 2 B & Ad 663 ....9.10
Commission v Germany [1989] ECR 1263 ....16.68
Commission v Ireland, Case C-459/03, [2006] ECR I-4635 ....17.42
Commonwealth v Cooley (1830) HF & N 36 ....14.144
Condon v Minister for Labour [1981] IR 62...7.24
Connolly v Byrne [1997] IEHC 195 ....1.21
Connors v United Kingdom (2002) 35 EHRR 691 ....17.72
Conroy v Attorney General [1965] IR 411 ....5.93
Considine v Shannon Regional Fisheries Board [1994] 1 ILRM 499 (HC),
  [1998] 1 ILRM 11 (SC) 7.33, 12.89, 12.103, 12.116
Cooke v Walsh [1984] IR 710 ....13.126, 13.141–13.142
Coonan v Attorney General [2002] 1 ILRM 295 (HC) 3.124

Copeland v Smith [2000] 1 All ER 457 .... 3.90, 12.19
Corbett v DPP [2001] 3 IR 144 .... 14.146
Cork County Council v Shackleton and Murphy Construction
    [2008] 1 ILRM 185 .... 14.50
Cork County Council v Whillock [1993] 1 IR 231 .... 14.33, 14.95
Corley v Gill [1975] IR 313 .... 7.22, 12.42
Cormack v DPP [2009] 2 IR 208 .... 6.11
Corry v Lucas (1869) IR 3 CL 208 .... 12.147
Costa v ENEL [1964] ECR 585 ....16.88, 16.92, 16.104, 16.199
Costigan v Laois County Council [2000] IESC 7 .... 9.05
Cotter and McDermott v Minister for Social Welfare
    [1991] ECR I-1155 .... 16.204
Coughlan v Broadcasting Complaints Committee [2000] 3 IR 1 .... 15.113
Cowan v Freaghaile [1991] 1 IR 389 .... 4.61
Cowan v Trésor public [1989] ECR 195 .... 16.67, 16.74–16.75
Cowl v Plymouth City Council [2002] 1 WLR 803 .... 8.15
Cox (RD) Ltd v Owners of MV Fritz Raabe (1 August 1974,
    unreported) 4.39
Creaven v DPP [2004] 4 IR 434 .... 4.40, 4.70
Crilly v Farrington Ltd [2001] 3 IR 251 ....14.11, 14.19–14.21
    ....14.163–14.165, 14.183–14.188
Criminal Law (Jurisdiction) Bill 1975, Re [1977] IR 129
    ....2.78, 5.120, 14.116, 15.07
Croke v Ireland (21 December 2000) ECt HR 17.68
Croke v Smith [1995] IEHC 6... 14.94
Croke v Smith (No 2) [1998] 1 IR 101 .... 14.79
Cronin (Inspector of Taxes) v Strand Dairy Ltd (18 December 1985,
    unreported), HC 14.69, 14.73
Cronin v Cork and County Properties Ltd [1986] IR 559 .... 14.157
Cronin v Youghal Carpets (Yarns) Ltd [1985] IR 312 .... 14.157–14.159
Crotty v An Taoiseach [1987] IR 713 ....4.62, 4.168, 15.92
    ....15.104, 16.102–16.105, 16.152
Crowley v Ireland [1980] IR 102 .... 12.50
Cullen v Wicklow County Manager [1996] 3 IR 474 .... 14.74
Cumann Luthchleas Gael Teo v Windle [1994] 1 IR 525 .... 6.91, 6.98
Curtin v Clerk of Dáil Éireann [2006] IESC 14, [2006] 2 IR 556,
    [2006] 2 ILRM 99 .... 4.54, 4.152, 8.58
CW Shipping Co Ltd v Limerick Harbour Commissioners
    [1989] ILRM 416 .... 14.106, 14.123

D

D v Minister for Education [2000] 3 IR 62 .... 15.105
D v Minister for Education [2001] 4 IR 259 .... 15.106
D, Re [1987] IR 449 .... 5.80
D'Orta-Ekenaike v Victoria Legal Aid (2005) 223 CLR 1 .... 3.107–3.110

Dalton v Minister for Finance [1989] IR 269 ....7.25
Damache v DPP [2012] 2 IR 266 ....14.79
Danagher v Glentine Inns [2010] IEHC 214 ....6.43
Daniels v Heskin [1954] IR 73 ....12.168, 12.171
Davis v Johnson [1979] AC 317 ....12.58
Day v Savadge (1614) Hob 85 ....14.111
DB v Minister for Health [2003] 3 IR 12 ....14.36
de Búrca v Attorney General [1976] IR 38 ....1.44, 6.143, 11.28
....15.68, 15.98, 15.139
De Róiste v The Minister for Defence [2001] 1 IR 190 ....12.31
De Rossa v Independent Newspapers [1999] 4 IR 432 ....12.43
de Vere Decd, Re [1961] IR 224 ....12.60
Deane v Voluntary Health Insurance Board [1992] 2 IR 319 ....14.166
Deighan v Ireland [1995] 2 IR 56 ....4.185
Dekra Éireann Teo v Minister for the Environment [2003] 2 IR 270 ....8.62
Delap v Minister for Justice [1980–1998] IR Special Reports 46 ....13.68
Dellaway Investments Ltd v National Asset Management Agency
    [2011] 4 IR 1 ....3.122, 4.54, 4.62
Demirel v Stadt Schwäbisch Gmünd [1981] ECR 3719 ....16.69
Desmond v Brophy [1985] IR 449 ....12.87, 12.155
Desmond v Glackin (No 2) [1993] 3 IR 67 ....14.92, 15.86
Devrajan v KPMG [2006] IEHC 81 ....9.07
DF v Garda Commissioner [2013] IEHC 312 ....4.29
DF v McGarry [2007] IEHC 215 ....15.203
DG, an Infant, Re, OG v An Bórd Uchtála [1991] 1 IR 491 ....7.07
Dillane v Ireland [1980] ILRM 167 ....9.72
Dillenkofer v Germany [1996] ECR I-4845 ....16.129
Dillon v DPP [2008] 1 IR 383 ....15.62
Dillon v Minister for Posts and Telegraphs (3 June 1981,
    unreported), SC 14.128, 14.134
Dillon-Leetch v Calleary (No 2) (31 July 1974, unreported), SC 5.81
Doe v Armour Pharmaceutical Co Inc [1994] 1 ILRM 416 ....4.29, 17.84
Dolan v Corn Exchange [1975] IR 315 ....7.21–7.22
Dolan, Re [2007] IESC 26 ....5.80
Dolan, Re [2008] IEHC 264 ....5.80
Donegan v Dublin City Council [2008] IEHC 288, [2012] IESC 18 ....15.205, 17.72
Donnelly v Ireland [1998] 1 ILRM 401 ....15.103
Donnelly v Timber Factors Ltd [1991] 1 IR 553 ....4.120
Donoghue v Stevenson [1932] AC 562 ....1.43, 12.38, 12.87, 12.145, 12.159
Donovan v Landy's Ltd [1963] IR 441 ....12.37
Doran v Delaney [1998] 2 IR 61 ....11.28, 12.161, 12.165
Doran v Ireland [2003] ECHR 417 ....4.184, 6.11
Dowling v Ireland [1991] 2 IR 379 ....3.148, 14.82, 14.88
Doyle v An Taoiseach [1986] ILRM 693 ....7.80, 14.110, 16.113

Doyle v Bergin [2010] IEHC 531 .... 4.30
Doyle v Hearne [1987] IR 601 ....7.21–7.22, 12.42, 12.54
DPP (Ivers) v Murphy [1999] 1 IR 98 ....14.22, 14.32, 14.44, 14.49
DPP (Walsh) v Cash [2007] IEHC 108 .... 12.30
DPP v Best [2000] 2 ILRM 1 .... 12.46–12.50
DPP v Byrne [1994] 2 IR 236 .... 6.11
DPP v Corcoran [1996] 1 ILRM 182 .... 14.107
DPP v Doyle [1994] 2 IR 286 .... 6.93
DPP v Doyle [1996] 3 IR 579 .... 14.36
DPP v Flanagan [1979] IR 265 .... 14.24
DPP v Freeman [2009] IEHC 179 .... 12.12
DPP v Grey [1986] IR 317 .... 14.130
DPP v Haugh and Haughey [2000] 1 IR 184 ....4.62, 6.150
DPP v Independent Newspapers (Ireland) Ltd [2009] IESC 20
.... 15.136, 15.142
DPP v Keogh [1998] 1 ILRM 72 .... 14.107
DPP v McCreesh [1992] 2 IR 239 .... 14.105
DPP v Ni Chonduin [2008] 3 IR 498 .... 6.93
DPP v Ottewell [1970] AC 642 .... 14.34
DPP v Tivoli Cinema Ltd [1999] 2 IR 260 .... 14.106
DPP (Travers) v Brennan [1998] 4 IR 67... 7.14
DPP v Wexford Farmers' Club [1994] 1 IR 546 .... 14.30
Dublin City Council v Fennell [2005] 1 IR 604,
    [2005] 2 ILRM 288 ....1.20, 9.12, 15.202, 15.207
Dublin City Council v Gallagher [2008] IEHC 354,
    [2012] IESC 18 .... 17.72
Dublin County Council v Eighty Five Developments Ltd (No 1)
    [1993] 2 IR 378 .... 14.157
Dublin County Council v Grealy [1990] 1 IR 77 .... 14.113
Dublin Wellwoman Centre Ltd v Ireland [1995] 1 ILRM 408 .... 4.121
Dudgeon v United Kingdom (1981) 4 EHRR 149 .... 15.173, 17.66
Duff v Minister for Agriculture (No 2) [1997] 2 IR 22 .... 15.80
Duffy v Dublin Corporation [1974] IR 33 .... 14.131
Duffy v News Group Newspapers Ltd [1992] 2 IR 369 .... 4.53
Duggan v Dublin Corporation [1991] 1 IR 275 .... 14.132
Dunne v Minister for the Environment [2004] IEHC 304,
    [2007] 1 IR 194 (SC) 15.87
Dunne v National Maternity Hospital [1989] IR 91 ....7.30, 9.09, 9.15
Dunne v O'Neill [1974] IR 180 .... 12.61
Dunnett v Railtrack plc [2002] 2 All ER 850 .... 8.15
Dutton v Bognor Regis UDC [1972] 1 QB 373 .... 1.43
Dwyer (decd) (1908) 46 ILTR 147 .... 12.59

E

Eamonn Andrews Productions Ltd v Gaiety Theatre Productions Ltd
 [1973] IR 295 ....7.21
East Donegal Co-Operative Livestock Mart Ltd v Attorney General
 [1970] IR 317 ....12.50, 13.128, 14.78
Eastern Health Board v McDonnell [1999] 1 IR 174 ....14.79
Eccles v Ireland [1985] IR 545 ....5.120
Educational Co of Ireland Ltd v Fitzpatrick (No 2) [1961] IR 323 ....12.76
EF v Minister for Education [2007] IEHC 36 ....15.107
Electricity Supply Board v Gormley [1985] IR 129 ....8.25
Elwyn (Cottons) Ltd v Master of the High Court [1989] IR 14 ....12.93
Emergency Powers Bill 1976, Re [1977] IR 159 ....14.107, 15.100
Emmott v Minister for Social Welfare [1991] ECR I-4269 ....16.204
Employment Equality Bill 1996, Re [1997] 2 IR 321 ....15.102
Enright v Ireland [2003] 2 IR 321 ....14.110
Environmental Protection Agency v Neiphin Trading Ltd
 [2011] IEHC 6 ....12.63
EPI v Minister for Justice, Equality and Law Reform
 [2008] IEHC 23 ....17.73
Equal Status Bill 1997, Re [1997] 2 IR 387 ....15.102
ERT v Dimotiki Etairia Pliorforissis [1991] ECR I-2925 ....16.69
European Chemical Industries Ltd v Bell [1981] ILRM 345 ....10.15
European Fashion Products Ltd v Eenkhoorn [2001] IEHC 181 ....9.05
Evans v Secretary of State for the Environment Transport and the Regions
 [2003] ECR I-14447 ....16.129
Eviston v Director of Public Prosecutions [2002] 1 ILRM 134 ....6.100, 6.119
Exham v Beamish [1939] IR 336 ....12.72, 12.76, 12.148

F

Fallon v Gannon [1988] ILRM 193 ....12.157
Fanning v University College Cork [2007] 18 ELR 301 ....14.117
Farrell v Alexander [1975] 3 WLR 64 ....14.34
Fay v Tegral Pipes Ltd [2005] IESC 34 ....4.39
Feeney v Pollexfen & Co Ltd [1931] 589 ....12.140
FF v CF [1987] ILRM 1 ....14.177, 14.181
Finlay v Murtagh [1979] IR 249 ....12.74, 12.152, 12.154, 12.158, 12.159, 12.171
Finucane v McMahon [1990] 1 IR 165, [1990] 1 ILRM 505
 ....12.51, 14.86, 14.163
Fitzgerald v DPP [2003] 2 ILRM 537 ....7.34
Fleming v Ireland [2013] IEHC 2, [2013] IESC 19 ....4.54, 4.62, 15.193, 15.195
Flynn and Village Crafts v Irish Nationwide Building Society Ltd
 (31 July 1995, unreported), HC 14.179
Flynn v Denieffe [1989] IR 722 ....14.192
Flynn v Power [1985] ILRM 36 ....8.53
Foley v Independent Newspapers (Ireland) Ltd [1994] 2 ILRM 61 ....3.30

Fothergill v Monarch Airlines Ltd [1980] 3 WLR 209,
    [1981] AC 251 .... 12.85, 14.175
Foy v An t-Ard Chlaraitheoir [2002] IEHC 116,
    [2007] IEHC 470 .... 15.203, 15.207, 17.71
FP v Minister for Justice [2002] 1 IR 164 .... 15.103
Francovich v Italian Republic [1991] ECR I-5357 ...... 16.129, 16.172, 16.200, 16.222
Franklin v Gramaphone Ltd [1948] 1 KB 542 .... 14.108
Frescati Estates Ltd v Walker [1975] IR 177 .... 14.44, 14.106
Furniss v Dawson [1984] AC 474 .... 14.14

G

G v An Bord Uchtála [1980] IR 32 .... 4.19, 12.13, 12.50, 15.58, 15.174, 15.189
G v Director of Public Prosecutions [1994] 1 IR 374 .... 6.101
Gaffney v Gaffney [1975] IR 133 .... 12.76
Garvey v Ireland [1981] IR 75 .... 6.24
Garvey v Minister for Justice, Equality and Law Reform
    [2006] 1 IR 548 .... 12.104
Gavin v Criminal Injuries Compensation Tribunal [1997] 1 IR 132 .... 8.48
GE Capital Woodchester Homeloans Ltd v Faulkner Madden
    [2013] IEHC 540 .... 12.63
Geitling v High Authority [1960] ECR 423 .... 16.63
General Pickney: Yeaton v United States (1809) 9 US 281 .... 14.144
Geoghegan v Institute of Chartered Accountants in Ireland
    [1995] 3 IR 86 .... 4.15, 8.61
Geraghty v Embassy of Mexico [1998] ELR 310 .... 17.80
Gillen v Commissioner of An Garda Síochána [2012] IESC 3 .... 12.135
Gilligan and Zappone v Revenue Commissioners [2008] 2 IR 417 .... 15.138
Gilligan v Ireland [2001] 1 ILRM 473 .... 5.120
Gilligan v The Special Criminal Court [2006] 2 IR 389 .... 5.120
Gilmer v Incorporated Law Society of Ireland [1989] ILRM 590 .... 3.55
Gilroy v Flynn [2005] 1 ILRM 290 .... 6.11, 6.42, 6.57
GL Saunders Ltd (in liq), Re [1986] 1 WLR 215 .... 12.77
Glavin v Governor of Mountjoy Prison [1991] 2 IR 421 .... 4.85, 4.188
Gleeson v Feehan [1993] 2 IR 113 .... 12.87
Goodman International v Hamilton [1992] 2 IR 542 .... 4.15, 8.79
Goodwin v Bus Éireann [2013] IESC 56 .... 6.43
Goodwin v United Kingdom (2002) 35 EHRR 447 .... 17.71
Gorris v Scott (1874) LR 9 Ex 125 .... 14.28
Gough v Kinsella (1971) 105 ILTR 116 .... 14.159
Government of Canada v Employment Appeals Tribunal and Burke
    [1992] 2 IR 484 .... 17.80
Grace (John) Fried Chicken Ltd v Catering JLC [2011] IEHC 277,
    [2011] 3 IR 211 .... 8.51, 13.123, 13.149
Grace v Attorney General [2007] 2 ILRM 283 .... 15.87
Gavelkind, Case of (1605) Dav 49 .... 2.18

Grealis v DPP; Corbett v DPP [2001] 3 IR 144 ....14.142, 14.148
Green v McLoughlin [1991] 1 IR 309 (HC), (26 January 1995,
    unreported), SC 8.72
Greene v Minister for Agriculture [1990] 2 IR 17 ....14.58
Greene v Minister for Defence [1998] 4 IR 464 ....14.95
Gregory v Windle [1994] 3 IR 613 ....10.35
Grey v Pearson (1857) HL Cas 61 ....14.24
Grimes v Owners of SS Bangor Bay [1948] IR 350 ....4.40
Griswold v Connecticut (1965) 381 US 479 ....1.55

H

H v Director of Public Prosecutions [1994] 2 IR 589 ....6.100
H v H [1978] IR 138 .... 14.13, 14.22, 14.134
Hadmor Productions Ltd v Hamilton [1981] 3 WLR 139 ....14.175
Hall (Arthur JJ) & Co v Simons [2000] 3 All ER 673 ....12.157
Hall & Co v Simons [2000] 3 All ER 673 ....3.110
Hamilton v Hamilton [1982] IR 466 .... 12.54, 14.111–14.112
Hanafin v Minister for the Environment [1996] 2 IR 321
    .... 4.62, 5.23, 5.81, 15.114
Hanrahan v Merck, Sharpe & Dohme Ltd [1988] ILRM 629 ....4.168, 7.09
Harlequin Property (SVG) Ltd v O'Halloran [2013] 1 ILRM 124 ....12.30
Harrison v National Coal Board [1951] 1 All ER 1102 ....14.108
Harvey v Facey [1893] AC 552 ....14.39
Harvey v Minister for Social Welfare [1990] 2 IR 232 ....13.127–13.129
Haughey v Moriarty [1999] 3 IR 1 ....8.79
Haughey, Re [1971] IR 217 ....8.58, 15.58
Hay v O'Grady [1992] 1 IR 210 ....7.07
Hazylake Fashions Ltd v Bank of Ireland [1989] IR 601 ....12.167
Health Service Executive v Carroll [2012] 3 IR 1 ....14.03, 14.106
Heaney v Ireland [1996] 1 IR 580 ....15.103
Hedley Byrne & Co Ltd v Heller and Partners Ltd [1964] AC 465
    .... 12.104, 12.150, 12.159, 12.164–12.166
Hefferon Kearns Ltd (No 1), Re [1993] 3 IR 177 ....14.110, 14.114
Hegarty v Labour Court [1999] 3 IR 603 ....14.36
Heinulllian v Governor of Cloverhill Prison [2011] 1 ILRM 1 ....3.96
Herrington v British Railways Board [1972] AC 877 ....12.38
Hetherington, Re [1990] Ch 1 ....12.102
Heydon's case (1584) 3 Co Rep 7a 14.27
HI v Minister for Justice, Equality and Law Reform [2003] 3 IR 197 ....9.12
Hibernian Bank v Mansfield [1962] IR 454 ....1.21
Hoey v Minister for Justice [1994] 3 IR 329 ....4.168
Hogan v United Beverages Sales [2006] 17 ELR 274 ....8.53
Holland v Athlone Institute of Technology [2011] IEHC 414,
    [2012] 23 ELR 1 ....3.121
Holohan v Donohoe [1986] IR 45 ....4.39, 7.30
Home Office v Dorset Yacht Co Ltd [1970] AC 1004 ....12.149

Horgan v An Taoiseach [2003] 2 IR 468 .... 17.79
Howard v Commissioners of Public Works [1994] 1 IR 101
.... 14.13, 14.36, 14.180
Hunter v Nurendale Ltd [2013] IEHC 430 .... 9.75
Hutchinson v Minister for Justice [1993] ILRM 602 .... 17.13
Hynes Ltd v Independent Newspapers Ltd [1980] IR 204 .... 12.87
Hynes-O'Sullivan v O'Driscoll [1989] ILRM 349 .... 12.41, 12.142

I

I Congreso del Partido [1983] 1 AC 244 .... 17.80
I v United Kingdom (2003) 36 EHRR 53 .... 17.71
Iarnród Éireann v Ireland [1995] 2 ILRM 161 .... 12.87
Iarnród Éireann v Ireland [1996] 2 ILRM 500 .... 15.92
Illegal Immigrants (Trafficking) Bill 1999, Re [2000] 2 IR 360 .... 9.02, 15.103
Impact v Minister for Agriculture and Food [2008] ELR 181 .... 7.77
Independent Newspapers (Ireland) Ltd v Anderson [2006] 3 IR 341 .... 4.31
Industrial Services Ltd, Re [2001] 2 IR 118 .... 12.63
Inspector of Taxes v Arida Ltd [1992] 2 IR 155 .... 14.118
Inspector of Taxes v Kiernan [1981] IR 117 .... 14.15, 14.34, 14.68
.... 14.75, 14.109, 14.126, 14.158, 14.191
Internationale Handelsgesellschaft mbH v Einfuhr-und Vorratsstelle
    für Getreide und Futtermittel [1970] ECR 1125 .... 16.63, 16.90, 16.104
Ireland v United Kingdom (1979–1980) 2 EHRR 25 .... 17.23
Irish Agricultural Machinery Ltd v Ó Culacháin [1990] 1 IR 535
.... 14.72–14.75, 14.159
Irish Asphalt Ltd v An Bord Pleanála [1996] 2 IR 179 .... 7.28
Irish Bank Resolution Corp Ltd v Quinn Investments Sweden AB
    [2012] IESC 51 .... 10.49
Irish Commercial Society Ltd v Plunkett [1986] IR 258 .... 14.122
Irish Creamery Milk Suppliers Association Ltd v Ireland
    (1979) 3 JISEL 66 .... 7.80
Irish Leathers Ltd v Minister for Labour [1986] IR 177 .... 14.159
Irish Nationwide Building Society Ltd v Revenue Commissioners
    (2 October 1990, unreported), HC 14.125
Irish Penal Reform Trust v Governor of Mountjoy Prison
    [2005] IEHC 305 .... 15.92
Irish Press Plc v Ingersoll Publications Ltd [1994] 1 IR 176 .... 4.30
Irish Refining plc v Commissioner of Valuation [1990] 1 IR 568 .... 14.152
Irish Shell Ltd v Elm Motors Ltd [1984] IR 200, [1984] IR 511 .... 12.13
.... 12.72–12.76, 12.85
Irish Times Ltd v Ireland [1998] 1 IR 359 .... 4.31
Irish Trust Bank Ltd v Central Bank of Ireland
    [1976–7] ILRM 50 .... 12.61, 12.63
Izevbekhai v Ireland, No 43408/08, European Court of Human Rights,
    17 May 2011 .... 17.74

Izevbhekhai v Minister for Justice Equality and Law Reform
  (10 November 2006, unreported), HC 17.73

J

J (A Minor), Re [1991] Fam 33 ....15.187
Jarvis v Moy, Davies, Smith, Vanderell and Co [1936] 1 KB 399 ....12.153
JH, Re [1985] IR 375 ....14.86
Johnson and Kelly v Horace [1993] ILRM 594 ....12.87
Johnston v Chief Constable for the Royal Ulster Constabulary
  [1986] ECR 1651 ....16.65
Jones v Grove Turkeys Ltd [2011] IEHC 152 and Wall v DPP [2013] IESC 56 ....6.11
Jones v Gunn [1997] 3 IR 1 ....14.44, 14.114
Jones v Kaney [2011] UKSC 13 ....3.108
Jordan v Attorney General [2013] IEHC 625 ....15.51
Jordan v Minister for Children and Youth Affairs [2014] IEHC 327 ....5.81
Jordan v O'Brien [1960] IR 363 ....14.87
Jordan v United Kingdom (2003) 37 EHRR 52 ....6.102
Joyce v Brady [2011] IESC 36 ....9.23–9.26
JS v CS [1997] 2 IR 506 ....1.21

K

K(S) v Director of Public Prosecutions (26 February 2004,
  unreported), HC 12.31
Kadri v Governor of Wheatfield Prison [2012] IESC 27 ....12.64
Kavanagh v Government of Ireland [1996] 1 IR 321 ....5.120
Kavanagh v Government of Ireland [2007] IEHC 389 ....9.70
Kavanagh v Governor of Mountjoy Prison [2002] 3 IR 97 ....17.76–17.79
Kavanagh v Legal Aid Board [2001] IEHC 149 ....9.44
Kay v Goodwin (1830) 6 Bing 576 ....14.144
Keane v An Bord Pleanála [1997] 1 IR 184 ....14.98, 14.192
Keane v Electricity Supply Board [1981] IR 44 ....1.43, 12.149
Keane v Western Health Board and Ann Meehan [2007] 2 IR 555 ....14.129
Kearns v Dilleen [1997] 3 IR 286 ....14.109
Kearns v Manresa Estates Ltd (25 July 1975, unreported), HC 12.60
Keegan v de Burca [1973] IR 223 ....10.51
Keegan v Ireland (1994) 18 EHRR 342 ....17.68
Keenan Brothers Ltd, Re [1985] IR 401 ....12.85
Kehoe v CJ Louth & Son [1992] ILRM 282 ....12.157
Kelly (Dermot C) v Finbarr J Crowley [1985] IR 212 ....12.170
Kelly and Buckley v Ryan [2013] IEHC 321 ....6.91, 6.98
Kelly and Deighan, Re [1984] ILRM 424 ....4.185
Kelly v Haughey Boland & Co [1989] ILRM 373 ....12.154
Kelly v Ireland [1986] ILRM 318 ....7.51
Kelly v Scales [1994] 1 IR 42 ....14.110
Kellystown Co v Hogan [1985] ILRM 200 ....14.109

Kemmy v Ireland [2009] IEHC 178, [2009] 4 IR 74 .... 4.184–4.185
Kennedy v Ireland [1987] IR 587 .... 10.08, 15.58
Kennedy v Killeen Corrugated Products Ltd [2007] 3 IR 561 .... 4.197
Kenny v Quinn [1981] ILRM 385 .... 14.125
Kenny v Trinity College Dublin [2008] 2 IR 40 .... 4.53, 4.123
Kiberd v Hamilton [1992] 2 IR 257 .... 8.79
Kielthy v Ascon Ltd [1970] IR 122 .... 14.124
Kiely v Minister for Social Welfare [1977] IR 267 .... 14.117
Kimpton Vale Developments Ltd v An Bord Pleanála
    [2013] IEHC 442 .... 12.63
King v Attorney General [1981] IR 233 .... 15.62, 15.67, 15.91, 15.166
Kinsale Yacht Club (Trustees of) v Commissioner of Valuation
    [1993] ILRM 393, [1994] 1 ILRM 457 .... 14.13, 14.109, 14.192
Kirby v Burke and Holloway [1944] IR 207 .... 12.87, 12.147
Kirkwood Hackett v Tierney [1952] IR 185 .... 12.41
Kirwan v Minister for Justice [1994] 2 IR 417 .... 9.33, 9.44
Klench v Secretaire d'État à l'Agriculture et à la Viticulture
    [1986] ECR 3477 .... 14.88
Knetch v United States (1960) 364 US 361 .... 14.14
Kreil v Bundesrepublik Deutschland [2000] ECR I-69 .... 16.65
Kruse v Johnson [1898] 2 QB 91 .... 13.115
Kylemore Bakery Ltd v Minister for Trade, Commerce and Tourism
    [1986] ILRM 529 .... 13.10

L

L v Minister for Justice, Equality and Law Reform [2004] IEHC 81 .... 12.65
Larkins v National Union of Mineworkers [1985] IR 671 .... 10.20
Laurentiu v Minister for Justice [1999] 4 IR 26 .... 13.131, 13.136, 13.151, 16.132
Lavery v Member in Charge, Carrickmacross Garda Station
    [1999] 2 IR 268 .... 9.34
Law Society of Ireland v Competition Authority [2006] 2 IR 262 .... 15.206
Law Society v Walker [2007] 3 IR 581 .... 3.90
Lawlor v Flood [1999] 3 IR 107 .... 8.80, 14.15, 14.36, 14.47, 14.66
Lawlor v Members of the Tribunal of Inquiry into Certain Planning
    Matters and Payments [2008] IEHC 282 .... 8.81
Lawlor v Minister for Agriculture [1990] 1 IR 356 .... 14.57, 14.59
Lawrence v Texas (2003) 539 US 558 .... 1.55
Leontjava v Director of Public Prosecutions [2004] 1 IR 591 .... 13.135
Lewis Merthyr Consolidated Collieries, Re [1929] 1 Ch 498 .... 12.77
Li v Governor of Cloverhill Prison [2012] 2 IR 400 .... 14.128
Listowel Urban District Council v McDonagh [1968] IR 312 .... 13.147
Liversidge v Anderson [1942] AC 206 .... 12.104
Locabail Ltd v Bayfield Properties Ltd [2000] QB 451 .... 4.122
Logan v O'Donnell [1925] 2 IR 211 .... 12.140

Lommers v Minister van Landbouw, Natuurbeheer en Visserij
 [2002] ECR I-2891 ....16.65
London Street Tramways Co v London County Council
 [1898] AC 375 ....12.28, 12.36
London Transport Executive v Betts (Valuation Officer)
 [1959] AC 213 ....12.36
Lonergan v Morrisey (1947) 81 ILTR 130 ....14.30
Lopes v Minister for Justice, Equality and Law Reform
 [2014] IESC 21 ....12.31
Lotus case (1927), PCIJ Ser A No 10 ....14.116
Luke v The Inland Revenue Commissioners [1963] AC 557 ....14.54
Lynch v HSE [2010] IEHC 346 ....12.63
Lynham v Butler (No 2) [1933] IR 74 ....4.11

M

M v An Bord Uchtála [1977] IR 287 ....4.19, 11.28
M v M [1979] ILRM 160 ....7.07
Macauley v Minister for Posts and Telegraphs [1966] IR 345 ....9.02, 15.58
MacCurtain, Re [1941] IR 43 ....5.120
MacGabhann v Incorporated Law Society of Ireland [1989] ILRM 854 .....3.24
MacGairbhith v Attorney General [1991] 2 IR 412 (HC), (29 March 1995,
 unreported), SC 9.05, 9.69
Madden v Minister for the Marine [1997] 1 ILRM 136 ....14.47, 14.80
Madigan v Attorney General [1986] ILRM 136 ....15.103
Magee v Culligan [1992] 1 IR 223 .... 4.68, 4.118, 14.110
Maguire v Ardagh [2002] IESC 21, [2002] 1 IR 385
 ....4.54, 4.62, 8.58, 15.141–15.143
Maher v An Bord Pleanála [1999] 2 ILRM 198 .... 14.09, 14.60, 14.192
Maher v Attorney General [1973] IR 140 .... 12.142, 14.169, 14.175, 15.86
Mahon v Keena and Kennedy [2007] IEHC 348, [2009] IESC 64.................4.62, 8.76
Maloney v Ireland [2009] IEHC 291 ....6.07
Mandarim Records Ltd v Mechanical Copyright Protection Society
 (Ireland) Ltd [1999] 1 ILRM 154 ....14.103
Manning v Benson and Hedges Ltd [2004] 3 IR 556 ....4.39
Mannix (GJ) Ltd, Re [1984] 1 NZLR 309 ....9.11
Mapp v Gilhooley [1991] 2 IR 253 ....6.124
Mara v Hummingbird Ltd [1982] ILRM 498 ....7.05
Marbury v Madison (1803) 1 Cranch 137 ....15.116
Mareva Compania Naviera SA v International Bulkcarriers SA
 [1975] 2 Lloyd's Rep 509 ....10.11
Mason v Levy [1952] IR 40 ....14.31
Massey v United States (1934) 291 US 608 ....14.144
McAteer v Sheahan [2013] IEHC 417 ....12.63
McBrearty v Morris [2003] IEHC 154 ....8.81
McCabe v Lisney & Son Ltd [1981] ILRM 289 ....8.53

McCann Ltd v Ó Culacháin [1986] IR 196
....11.28, 14.47, 14.68–14.74, 14.109

McCann v Judge of Monaghan District Court [2009] IEHC 276 .10.23, 11.28, 15.206

McCann v Minister for Education [1997] 1 ILRM 1 .... 13.10, 13.80

McCarthy [1990] ILRM 84 .... 5.89

McCauley v McDermott [1997] 2 ILRM 466 .... 9.04

McCausland v Ministry of Commerce [1956] NI 36 .... 14.69

McCord v ESB [1980] ILRM 153 .... 13.08, 13.119

McCrystal v Minister for Children and Youth Affairs [2012] IESC 53 .... 5.81

McDaid v Sheehy [1991] 1 IR 1 .... 13.137

McDermott and Cotter v Minister for Social Welfare
[1987] ECR 1453 .... 16.204

McDonald v Bord na gCon (No 2) [1965] IR 217 .... 4.13–4.15

McFarlane v McFarlane [2004] 3 WLR 1480 .... 4.27

McGee v Attorney General [1974] IR 284 .... 1.38, 12.106
.... 15.58, 15.109, 15.138, 15.169–15.173, 15.177

McGimpsey v Ireland [1988] IR 567 (HC), [1990] 1 IR 110 (SC)
.... 14.116, 15.08, 15.16, 15.25, 15.92, 15.108

McGlinchey v Governor of Portlaoise Prison [1988] IR 671 .... 5.120

McGlinchey v Ireland [1990] 2 IR 215 .... 9.06

McGlynn v Clark [1945] IR 495 .... 12.140

McGonagle v McGonagle [1951] IR 123 .... 14.129–14.131

McGowan v Labour Court [2013] IESC 21 .... 13.122, 13.123, 13.149

McGrath v Commissioner of An Garda Síochána [1991] 1 IR 69 .... 12.104

McGrath v McDermott [1988] IR 258 ....14.14–14.15, 14.22, 14.35

McGurrin v Campion Publications Ltd (15 December 1993,
unreported), HC 14.192

McIlwraith v Fawsitt [1990] 1 IR 343 .... 4.184

McKenna v An Taoiseach [1995] 2 IR 10 .... 15.92, 15.113

McKenzie v McKenzie [1971] P 33 .... 9.10

McKeogh v Doe [2012] IEHC 95 .... 4.29

McKerring v Minister for Agriculture [1989] ILRM 82 .... 8.42, 13.10

McKinley v Minister for Defence [1992] 2 IR 333 .... 15.71

McLoughlin v Minister for Public Service [1985] IR 631 .... 14.169–14.173

McMahon v Attorney General [1972] IR 69 .... 14.175, 15.99

McMenamin v Ireland [1994] 2 ILRM 368 (HC),
[1997] 2 ILRM 177 (SC) 4.190

McMullen v Farrell [1993] 1 IR 123 .... 12.157

McMullen v Ireland, No 42297/98, 29 July 2004 (ECt HR) 4.184, 6.11

McNally v Ó Maoldomhnaigh [1990] 2 IR 513 .... 14.74

McNamara v Electricity Supply Board [1975] IR 1 .... 12.37–12.38, 12.42
....12.140–12.142, 12.149, 12.152

McNeill v The Commissioner of An Garda Síochána, Ireland
and the Attorney General [1997] 1 IR 469 .... 12.135

Meagher v Minister for Agriculture and Food [1994] 1 IR 329
.... 6.10, 12.106, 13.124, 13.155, 15.105, 16.112, 16.121, 16.127, 16.203
Melling v Ó Mathghamhna [1962] IR 1 ....5.93
Mellowhide Products Ltd v Barry Agencies Ltd [1983] ILRM 152 ....4.197
Melton Enterprises v Censorship of Publications Board [2003] 3 IR 623 ....4.15
Metropolitan Properties Ltd v O'Brien [1995] 1 IR 467,
  [1995] 2 ILRM 383 ....12.31, 12.87
MF v Legal Aid Board [1993] ILRM 797 ....9.54
MFM v WFB [1999] 1 IR 122 ....9.33
Michaels v Taylor Woodrow [2000] 4 All ER 645 ....12.21
Microsoft Corp v Brightpoint Ireland Ltd [2001] 1 ILRM 540 ....4.27, 10.11
Midland Bank plc v Cameron, Thom Peterkin and Duncan
  1988 SLT 611 ....12.164–12.165
Midland Bank v Hett, Stubbs & Kemp [1979] Ch 384 ....12.159
Midland Silicones Ltd v Scruttons Ltd [1962] AC 466 ....12.36
Miley v Flood [2001] 1 ILRM 489 ....8.80
Millar v Taylor (1769) 4 Burr 2303 ....14.175
Miller's Case (1764) 1 Black W 451 ....14.144
Minister for Agriculture and Food v Barry [2008] IEHC 216,
  [2009] 1 IR 215 ....12.87, 12.90
Minister for Finance v O'Brien [1949] IR 91 ....12.36, 12.72, 12.76
Minister for Industry and Commerce v Hales [1967] IR 50
  ....13.140, 14.26, 14.47, 14.105, 14.161, 14.175
Minister for Industry and Commerce v Hammond Lane Metal Co Ltd
  [1947] Ir Jur Rep 59 ....14.40
Minister for Industry and Commerce v Pim Brothers Ltd [1966] IR 154 ....14.38
Minister for Justice v Dundon [2005] 1 IR 261 ....14.36
Minister for Justice v Wang Zhu Jie [1993] 1 IR 426 ....7.17, 7.28, 7.35
Minister for Justice, Equality and Law Reform v Adams
  [2011] IEHC 366 ....12.30
Minister for Justice, Equality and Law Reform v Stapleton
  [2006] 3 IR 26 ....12.30
Minister for Social, Community and Family Affairs v Scanlon
  [2001] 1 IR 64 ....14.110
Miranda v Arizona 384 US 436 (1964) 9.34
Mixnam's Properties Ltd v Chertsey Urban District Council
  [1964] 1 QB 214 ....13.146
MMcC v JMcC [1994] 1 IR 293 ....12.78
Mogul of Ireland Ltd v Tipperary (North Riding) County Council
  [1976] IR 260 ....12.41–12.46, 12.71, 14.159
Monahan v Legal Aid Board [2008] IEHC 300 ....9.50
Montagu v Earl of Sandwich (1886) 32 Ch D 525 ....12.62
Montex Holdings Ltd v Controller of Patents [2000] 1 IR 577 ....14.36
Montgomery Decd, Re (1953) 89 ILTR 62 ....12.60
Moore v Attorney General [1930] IR 471 ....3.121

Moore v Attorney General [1934] IR 44 .... 2.18
Moore v Attorney General [1935] IR 472 .... 2.69–2.75
Morelle Ltd v Wakeling [1955] 2 QB 379 .... 12.130
Morrissey, Re [1944] IR 361 .... 12.59
Moy v Pettman Smith [2005] 1 All ER 903 .... 3.109
MP v AP [1996] 1 IR 144 .... 4.27
Mulcahy v Minister for the Marine (4 November 1994,
    unreported) HC 14.47
Mullen v Quinnsworth Ltd (No 2) [1991] ILRM 439 .... 7.11
Mullins v Hartnett [1998] 4 IR 426 .... 14.142
Murphy and McGrath v Minister for the Environment
    [2007] IEHC 185 .... 15.51
Murphy v Attorney General [1982] IR 241 .... 4.18–4.21, 12.84
    .... 15.67–15.72, 15.80, 15.101
Murphy v Bayliss (22 July 1976, unreported), SC 7.13
Murphy v Bord Telecom Éireann [1989] ILRM 53
    .... 14.61, 14.89, 16.187, 16.223
Murphy v DPP [2009] 3 IR 821 .... 6.11
Murphy v Dublin Corporation [1976] IR 143 .... 14.160
Murphy v Flood [2010] IESC 21, [2010] 3 IR 136 .... 3.121, 4.15
Murphy v GM [2001] IESC 33 .... 9.33
Murphy v Greene [1990] 2 IR 566 .... 9.04, 9.07
Murphy v Minister for Defence [1991] 2 IR 161 .... 7.25
Murphy v Minister for Justice [2001] 2 ILRM 144 .... 4.216, 9.70
Murphy v Minister for the Marine [1997] 2 ILRM 523 .... 14.88, 16.223
Murphy v Stewart [1973] IR 97 .... 15.58
Murray v Ireland [1985] IR 532 (HC), [1991] ILRM 465 (SC) 15.58
MV 'Kapitan Labunets' [1995] 1 IR 164 .... 12.85

N

N(K) v K [1985] IR 733 .... 15.151
Nathan v Bailey Gibson [1998] 2 IR 162 .... 14.60
National Authority for Occupational Safety and Health v Fingal County
    Council [1997] 2 IR 547 .... 14.129
Northern Bank Finance Corporation Ltd v Charlton [1979] IR 149 .... 7.25
National Irish Bank, Re [1999] 3 IR 145, [1999] 1 ILRM 321 .... 14.11, 14.179
National Union of Journalists v Sisk [1992] 2 IR 171 .... 14.86
Navan Tanker Services Ltd v Meath County Council [1998] 1 IR 166 .... 14.89
Nestor v Murphy [1979] IR 326 .... 10.17, 14.46, 14.48, 14.54, 14.58, 14.62–14.64
News Verlags GmbH v Austria (2000) 31 EHRR 8 .... 4.31
Nolan, Re [1939] IR 388 .... 12.59
Nold v Commission [1974] ECR 941 .... 16.64
Norris v Attorney General [1984] IR 36 .... 1.38, 4.59, 7.07
    .... 12.106, 15.61, 15.69, 15.110, 15.171–15.174, 17.66
Norris v Ireland (1988) 13 EHRR 186 .... 15.110, 15.173, 17.67

North Western Health Board v HW [2001] 3 IR 622 .... 15.192
Northern Bank Finance Corp Ltd v Charlton [1979] IR 149 .... 7.07, 12.152
Norwegian Loans case [1957] ICJ Rep 9 .... 17.39
NS v Anderson [2008] 3 IR 417 .... 17.63

O

Ó Beoláin v Fahy [2001] 2 IR 279 .... 13.66, 13.108
Ó Culacháin v Hunter Advertising Ltd [1990] 2 IR 431 .... 14.70, 14.74, 14.109
Ó Domhnaill v Merrick [1984] IR 151 .... 6.11, 12.100, 14.93
Ó Laighléis, Re [1960] IR 93 .... 12.49, 14.94, 17.64, 17.75–17.79
Ó Laochdha v Johnson and Johnson (Ireland) Ltd
    [1991] 2 IR 287 ....14.73, 14.75
Ó Machín v Ireland [2014] IESC 12 ....12.42–12.45
Ó Monacháin v An Taoiseach [1986] ILRM 660 ....4.69
O v Minister for Justice [2002] 2 IR 169 ....15.112
O'B v Patwell [1994] 2 ILRM 465 ....12.33
O'Brien v Bord na Móna [1983] IR 277 ....4.15
O'Brien v Brown 409 US 1 (1972) 4.20
O'Brien v Mirror Group Newspapers Ltd [2001] 1 IR 1 .... 12.21, 12.43, 12.53
O'Brien v Personal Injuries Assessment Board [2006] IESC 62,
    [2007] 1 IR 328, [2008] IESC 71, [2009] 3 IR 243 ....5.19
O'Byrne v Minister for Finance [1959] IR 1 ....4.179
O'Callaghan v Attorney General [1993] 2 IR 17 .... 6.153–6.159, 15.139
O'Callaghan v Disciplinary Tribunal [2002] 1 IR 1 ....3.59
O'Callaghan v Sullivan [1925] 1 IR 90 ....1.21
O'Connor v Carroll [1999] 2 IR 160 ....4.184
O'Connor v Power [2008] IEHC 179 ....3.111
O'Connor, Re [1930] IR 623 ....4.191
O'Donnell v Kilsaran Concrete Ltd [2001] 4 IR 183 ....12.154
O'Donnell v South Dublin County Council (11 January 2008,
    unreported), HC 17.70
O'Donnell v South Dublin County Council [2007] IEHC 204 ....15.107
O'Donnell v South Dublin County Council [2011] 3 IR 417 ....14.92
O'Donoghue v Legal Aid Board [2006] 4 IR 204 ....9.44
O'Donoghue v Minister for Health [1996] 2 IR 20 ....12.50
O'Donovan v Attorney General [1961] IR 114 ....4.21, 15.99
O'Donovan v Cork County Council [1967] IR 173 ....12.168–12.171
O'Dwyer v Cafolla Ltd (1950) 84 ILTR 44 ....14.125
O'Dwyer v Keegan [1997] 2 IR 585 ....14.48
O'Gorman (A) & Co Ltd v JES Holdings Ltd [2005] IEHC 168 ....12.31
O'H v O'H [1990] 2 IR 558 ....14.113
O'Keeffe v Kilcullen [2001] 3 IR 568 ....3.108
O'Leary v Cunningham [1980] IR 367...7.32
O'Leary v Wood Ltd [1964] IR 269 ....12.37
O'Neill v Minister for Agriculture [1997] 2 ILRM 435 ....13.10

O'Neill v Ryan and Ryanair Ltd (No 3) [1992] 1 IR 166 .... 4.30
O'Reilly and Judge v Director of Public Prosecutions
    [1984] ILRM 224 .... 5.117
O'Reilly v Cassidy (No 2) [1995] 1 ILRM 311 .... 4.122
O'Reilly v Cassidy [1995] 1 ILRM 306 .... 4.122
O'Reilly v Ireland, No 54725/00, 29 July 2004 .... 4.184, 6.11
O'Reilly v Lee [2008] IESC 21 .... 3.108
O'Reilly v Limerick Corporation [1989] ILRM 181 .... 1.44, 4.22, 15.122
O'Shaughnessy v Attorney General (16 February 1971,
    unreported), HC 9.39–9.43
O'Shea v Italian Embassy [2002] 13 ELR 276 .... 17.80
O'Sullivan v Leitrim County Council [1953] IR 71 .... 14.125
O'T v B [1998] 2 IR 321 .... 15.58–15.60
Offences against the State (Amendment) Bill 1940, Re
    [1940] IR 470 .... 12.48
Oliver, Re 333 US 257 (1948) 4.24
Orange Communications Ltd v Director of Telecommunications
    Regulation (No 2) [2000] 4 IR 159 .... 6.77, 8.64
Ostime v Australian Mutual Provident Society [1960] AC 459 .... 12.36

P

P v P [2006] IESC 76 .... 7.21
Park Hall School Ltd v Overend [1987] IR 1 .... 12.157
PC v Director of Public Prosecutions [2005] IEHC 103 .... 12.31
PD v Director of Public Prosecutions [2008] IESC 22 .... 6.11
Peilow v ffrench O'Carroll (1971) 105 ILTR 21 .... 4.54
People (Attorney General) v Bell [1969] IR 24 .... 5.105, 9.72, 14.24
People (Attorney General) v Conmey [1975] IR 341
    .... 7.28, 7.41, 7.57, 7.65, 12.129
People (Attorney General) v Coughlan (1968) 1 Frewen 325 .... 12.33
People (Attorney General) v Dermody [1956] IR 307 .... 12.33
People (Attorney General) v Doyle (1943) 77 ILTR 108 .... 5.120
People (Attorney General) v Doyle (1964) 101 ILTR 136 .... 12.30, 12.130
People (Attorney General) v Earls [1969] IR 414 .... 7.49
People (Attorney General) v Giles [1974] IR 422 .... 12.122
People (Attorney General) v Kennedy [1946] IR 517 .... 7.56, 14.127, 15.133
People (Attorney General) v McGlynn [1967] IR 232 .... 7.39, 14.25
People (Attorney General) v Mills (1955) 1 Frewen 153 .... 12.33
People (Attorney General) v Moore [1964] Ir Jur Rep 6 .... 12.67
People (Attorney General) v O'Brien [1965] IR 142 .... 12.123, 15.97
People (Attorney General) v O'Callaghan [1966] IR 501 .... 6.107, 15.97
People (Attorney General) v O'Dwyer [1972] IR 416 .... 12.85
People (Attorney General) v O'Neill [1964] Ir Jur Rep 1 .... 12.67
People (Attorney General) v Singer (1961) 9.08
People (DPP) v Barnes [2007] 3 IR 130 .... 3.113

People (DPP) v Bourke Waste Removal Ltd [2012] IECCA 66 ....9.72
People (DPP) v Buck [2002] 2 IR 206 ....9.34
People (DPP) v Cawley [2003] 4 IR 321 ....14.110
People (DPP) v Corbally [2000] IESC 38 ....7.46
People (DPP) v Doran (1987) 3 Frewen 125 ....6.157
People (DPP) v Farrell [1978] IR 13 ....14.107, 14.122
People (DPP) v Gilligan [1992] ILRM 769 ....14.135
People (DPP) v Gilligan (No 3) [2006] 3 IR 273 ....12.121
People (DPP) v Gormley [2014] IESC 17 ....9.35
The People (DPP) v Hannon [2009] 4 IR 147 ....7.53
People (DPP) v Healy [1990] 2 IR 73 ....9.34, 12.127
People (DPP) v Kavanagh (29 October 1997, unreported), SCC 14.140
People (DPP) v Keane [2007] IECCA 119 ....12.04, 12.64, 12.69
People (DPP) v Kelly [1982] IR 90 ....14.129–14.131
People (DPP) v Kelly (No 2) [1983] IR 1 ....14.30
People (DPP) v Kenny [1990] 2 IR 110 ....12.30, 12.109, 12.128
People (DPP) v Lynch [1982] IR 64 ....12.87, 12.125
People (DPP) v Marley [1985] ILRM 17 ....9.08
People (DPP) v McDonagh [1996] 1 IR 565 ....14.183, 14.190
People (DPP) v McDonagh [2001] 3 IR 411 ....3.111
People (DPP) v Nevin (April 2000) Central Criminal Court 4.31, 4.171
People (DPP) v O'Brien (Application of Dunne) (29 November 2010)
  Central Criminal Court 6.144
People (DPP) v O'Brien [2005] 2 IR 206 ....9.34
People (DPP) v O'Reilly [2009] IECCA 18 ....4.168
People (DPP) v O'Shea [1982] IR 384 ....7.57, 12.113, 15.130, 15.136, 15.142
People (DPP) v O'Shea (No 2) [1983] ILRM 592 ....12.113
People (DPP) v Pringle (No 2) [1997] 2 IR 225 (SC) 7.53
People (DPP) v Quilligan and O'Reilly [1986] IR 495
  .... 5.113, 7.58, 12.114, 14.180
People (DPP) v Quilligan and O'Reilly (No 2) [1989] IR 46 ....7.58, 12.114
People (DPP) v Quilligan and O'Reilly (No 3) [1993] 2 IR 305 ....6.95, 7.58
People (DPP) v Rock [1994] 1 ILRM 66 ....7.54, 12.33
People (DPP) v Shaw [1965] IR 142 ....12.128
People (DPP) v Shaw [1982] IR 1 ....5.105, 12.92, 12.123
People (DPP) v Sheedy [2000] 2 IR 184 ....4.130
People (DPP) v Shortt (No 2) [2002] 2 IR 696 ....7.53
People (DPP) v T (1988) 3 Frewen 141 ....14.129
People (DPP) v Tiernan [1988] IR 250 ....6.114
People (DPP) v Wall and McCabe 6.100
People (DPP) v Walsh [1980] IR 294 ....12.109
People (DPP) v WM [1995] 1 IR 226 ....4.28
People (DPP) v Z [1994] 2 IR 476 ....4.30

Pepper v Hart [1993] 1 All ER 42 .... 14.180
Phillips (Inspector of Taxes) v Bourne [1947] KB 533 .... 14.158
Pigs Marketing Board v Donnelly [1939] IR 413 .... 13.121
Piller (Anton) KG v Manufacturing Processes Ltd [1976] Ch 55 .... 10.11
Pine Valley Developments v Minister for the Environment
   [1987] IR 23 .... 13.79
PJ v JJ [1993] 1 IR 150 .... 14.13
Planning and Development Bill 1999, Re [2000] 2 IR 321 .... 15.103
Post Office v Estuary Radio Ltd [1968] 2 QB 740 .... 14.175
Power Securities Ltd v Daly [1984] IEHC 266 .... 8.24
Powerscourt Estates v Gallagher [1984] ILRM 123 .... 10.11
Powertech Logistics Ltd v Companies Act [2007] IEHC 43 .... 10.20
Prendergast (WJ) & Son Ltd v Carlow County Council
   [1990] ILRM 749 .... 5.65, 7.28
Pretty v United Kingdom (2002) 35 EHRR 1 .... 15.194
Pringle v Government of Ireland [2012] IESC 47 .... 12.91, 12.115
Pringle v Ireland [1994] 1 ILRM 467 .... 7.51
Pringle v Ireland [2012] IESC 1 .... 4.54
Pringle v Ireland [2012] IESC 47 .... 1.42, 16.110
Pullen v Dublin City Council [2008] IEHC 379 .... 9.12, 12.63, 17.72

Q

Quinlivan v Governor of Portlaoise Prison [1998] 2 IR 113 .... 14.141
Quinn (Application of) [1974] IR 19 .... 14.127
Quinn v Wren [1985] IR 322 .... 14.85
Quinn's Supermarket Ltd v Attorney General [1972] IR 1 .... 15.191
Quirke v Folio Homes Ltd [1988] ILRM 496 .... 1.44

R

R (Cooney) v Clinton [1935] IR 245 .... 2.63–2.68
R (Edwards) v Environment Agency [2013] UKSC 78 .... 9.75
R (Edwards) v Environment Agency (No 2) Case C-260/11
   (11 April 2013), ECJ 9.75
R (Kelly) v Maguire [1923] 2 IR 58 .... 2.104
R (Moore) v O'Hanrahan [1927] IR 406 .... 2.18
R (O'Brien) v Military Governor, North Dublin Union [1924] 1 IR 32 .... 2.68
R (Purdy) v Director of Public Prosecutions [2009] UKHL 45,
   [2010] 1 AC 435 .... 15.195
R Ltd, Re [1989] IR 126 .... 4.30
R v Bow Street Magistrate, ex p Pinochet (No 2) [2000] 1 AC 119 .... 4.122
R v Gibson (1887) 18 QBD 537 .... 6.132
R v MacKenzie (1820) Russ & Ry 429 .... 14.144
R v Ministry of Agriculture, Fisheries and Food, ex p Hedley Lomas
   (Ireland) Ltd [1996] ECR I-2553 .... 16.129
R v Mirza, R v Connor and Rollock [2004] 2 WLR 201 .... 6.153

R v Norman [1924] 2 KB 315 ....12.67
R v O'Connell (1845) 7 Ir Law Rep 261 ....3.90
R v Peters (1886) 16 QBD 636 ....14.192
R v R [1984] IR 296 ....5.59, 5.76, 5.127
R v R [2006] IEHC 359 ....15.112, 15.141
R v Secretary of State for the Environment, ex p Spath Holme Ltd
    [2001] 2 WLR 15 ....14.11
R v Stanley [1920] 2 KB 235 ....12.67
R v Swann (1849) 4 Cox CC 108 ....14.144
R v Taylor [1950] 2 KB 368 ....12.36
R v Warwickshire County Council, ex p Johnson
    [1993] 1 All ER 299 ....14.180
Rafferty v Crowley [1984] ILRM 350 .... 11.28, 13.57, 14.54–14.55
    ....14.63, 15.69
Rahill v Brady [1971] IR 69 ....14.21, 14.192
Ramsey (WT) Ltd v IRC [1982] AC 300 ....14.14
RD v McGuinness [1999] 2 IR 411 ....9.11
Regulation of Information (Services Outside the State for the Termination
    of Pregnancies) Bill 1995, Re [1995] 1 IR 1 .... 1.38, 1.57, 4.32, 15.147, 15.181
Reilly v Gill (1951) 85 ILTR 165 ....12.41
Revenue Commissioners v Doorley [1933] IR 750 ....14.15
Riggs v Palmer (1889) 22 NE 188 ....1.41
Riksskatteverket v Gharehveran [2001] ECR I-7687 ....16.129
Riordan v An Taoiseach [2001] 4 IR 463, [2001] IESC 83 ....9.07
Roberts Petroleum Ltd v Bernard Kenny Ltd [1983] 2 AC 192 ....12.21
Robertson v Fleming (1861) 4 Macq 167 ....12.159
Roche v Peilow [1985] IR 232 ....12.169
Roe v Blood Transfusion Service Board [1996] 1 ILRM 555 ....4.28
Roe v Revenue Commissioners [2008] IEHC 5, [2008] IR 328 ....4.28
Roe v Wade (1972) 410 US 113 .... 1.55, 4.29, 15.174
Rohan Construction Ltd v Insurance Corporation of Ireland plc
    [1988] ILRM 373 ....12.154
Rondel v Worsley [1969] 1 AC 191 ....3.107, 12.157
Rooney v Minister for Agriculture and Food [1991] 2 IR 539
    .... 13.10, 13.78–13.81
Rooney v Minister for Agriculture and Food [2001] 2 ILRM 37 ....4.122
Ross v Caunters [1980] Ch 297 ....12.159
Rowe v Law [1978] IR 55 ....14.163
Royal Dublin Society v Revenue Commissioners [2000] 1 IR 270 ....14.124
Russell v Fanning [1988] IR 505 ....12.30, 12.51, 14.86, 15.08
Rutili v Minister for the Interior [1975] ECR 1219 ....16.64
Ryan v Attorney General [1965] IR 294 .... 15.54, 15.58, 15.99
    .... 15.134, 15.166–15.173
Ryan v Director of Public Prosecutions [1989] IR 399 ....6.107
Ryan v Ireland [1989] IR 177 ....15.40

Ryan v Sheedy (1999) The Irish Times, 9 October 4.130
Ryan's Car Hire [1965] IR 642 .... 12.45
Ryanair Ltd v Labour Court [2007] 4 IR 199 .... 8.50

S

S v Landy (Legal Aid Board) (10 February 1993, unreported), HC 9.44
Saatchi & Saatchi Advertising Ltd v McGarry [1998] 2 IR 562 .... 14.109
Saif Ali v Sydney Mitchell & Co [1980] AC 198 .... 3.107, 12.157
Salomon v Commissioners of Customs and Excise
    [1967] 2 QB 306 .... 14.175
Savage v Director of Public Prosecutions [1982] ILRM 385 .... 5.117
Schrems v Data Protection Commissioner [2014] IEHC 351 .... 9.76
Securities Trust Ltd v Hugh Moore & Alexander Ltd
    [1964] IR 417 .... 12.150, 12.167
Sgarlatta v Commission [1965] ECR 215 .... 16.63
Shannon Realties v St Michel (Ville de) [1924] AC 185 .... 14.25
Shannon Regional Fisheries Board v An Bord Pleanála
    [1994] 3 IR 449 .... 14.09, 14.60, 14.192
Shaw v DPP [1962] AC 220 .... 1.49
Shelly v Mahon [1990] 1 IR 36 .... 4.85, 4.188
Shirley v A O'Gorman & Co Ltd [2012] 2 IR 170 .... 14.79
Short v Dublin County Council [1982] ILRM 117 .... 14.131
Shortt v Garda Commissioner [2007] IESC 9, [2007] 4 IR 587 .... 10.08
Simmons v Pennington & Son [1955] 1 WLR 183 .... 12.170
Simon and Tadea v Governor of Cloverhill Prison
    [2004] IEHC 392 .... 12.87
Sinnott v Minister for Education [2001] 2 IR 545
    .... 4.54, 4.55, 15.106, 15.125, 15.140
Sirros v Moore [1975] QB 118 .... 4.184
Society for the Protection of Unborn Children Ltd v Coogan
    [1989] IR 734 .... 3.121, 15.92, 15.176
Society for the Protection of Unborn Children Ltd v Grogan (No 5)
    [1998] 4 IR 343 .... 12.45–12.47
Solicitors Act 1954, Re [1960] IR 239 .... 3.58, 4.15, 13.57
Solomons, Re [1949] IR 3 .... 12.59
Somers v Erskine [1943] IR 348 .... 12.74, 12.153
Sorrell v Finch [1977] AC 728 .... 12.156
Sports Arena Ltd v O'Reilly [1987] IR 185 .... 7.14, 7.34
Stanley v Georgia (1969) 394 US 557 .... 1.55
State (Aer Lingus Teo) v Labour Court [1987] ILRM 373 .... 8.50
State (Boyle) v Neylon [1986] IR 551 .... 4.40, 5.103
State (C) v Frawley [1976] IR 365 .... 15.58
State (Clarke) v Roche [1986] IR 619 .... 4.15, 6.92, 11.28
State (Costello) v Bofin [1980] ILRM 233 .... 8.72

State (Creedon) v Criminal Injuries Compensation Tribunal
[1989] ILRM 104 ....8.47
State (D & D) v Groarke [1990] 1 IR 305 ....14.153
State (Dowling) v Kingston (No 2) [1937] IR 699 ....12.34
State (DPP) v Walsh [1981] IR 412 .... 4.185, 10.52, 14.92
State (Duggan) v Tapley [1952] IR 62 ....12.34
State (Elm Developments) v An Bord Pleanála [1981] ILRM 108 ....14.151
State (Ennis) v Farrell [1966] IR 107 ....6.91, 6.98
State (Foley) v Carroll [1980] IR 150 ....12.33
State (Harkin) v O'Malley [1978] IR 269 ....12.30, 12.130
State (Harrington) v Wallace [1988] IR 290 ....13.115
State (Hayes) v Criminal Injuries Compensation Tribunal
[1982] ILRM 210 ....8.47
State (Healy) v Donoghue [1976] IR 325 ....9.19, 9.39–9.43, 15.58–15.61, 15.70
State (Hunt) v Donovan [1975] IR 39 ....7.41
State (Kennedy) v Little [1931] IR 39 ....2.65
State (Kershaw) v Eastern Health Board [1985] ILRM 235 ....8.68
State (Killian) v Minister for Justice [1954] IR 207 ....4.46, 12.71
State (King) v Minister for Justice [1984] IR 169 ....4.168
State (Lynch) v Cooney [1982] IR 337 .... 4.49, 12.48, 12.71, 12.122
State (M) v Attorney General [1979] IR 73 ....15.58
State (McCarthy) v Lennon [1936] IR 485 ....2.65
State (McCormack) v Curran [1987] ILRM 225 ....5.117
State (McKeown) v Scully [1986] IR 524 ....8.72
State (Minister for Lands and Fisheries) v Judge Sealy [1939] IR 21 ....14.119
State (Murphy) v Johnson [1983] IR 235 ....14.17
State (Murray) v McRann [1979] IR 133 ....4.62
State (O'Connell) v Fawsitt [1986] IR 362 ....6.11
State (O'Connor) v Ó Caomhanaigh [1963] IR 112 ....14.96
State (O'Flaherty) v Ó Floinn [1954] IR 295 ....4.05
State (Quinn) v Ryan [1965] IR 110 .... 4.49, 12.34–12.36, 12.45
....12.71, 12.76, 12.102
State (Raftis) v Leonard [1960] IR 381 ....12.122
State (Rollinson) v Kelly [1984] IR 248 ....14.18
State (Royle) v Kelly [1974] IR 259 ....9.24
State (Ryan) v Lennon [1935] IR 170 .... 2.70–2.76, 15.171
State (Sheehan) v Government of Ireland [1987] IR 550 ....13.76–13.81
....13.139, 14.158
State (Sheerin) v Kennedy [1966] IR 379 ....12.106
State (Smith) v Governor of Mountjoy Gaol (1964) 102 ILTR 93 ....9.06
State (Smullen) v Duffy [1980] ILRM 46 ....8.61
State (Turley) v Ó Floinn [1968] IR 245 ....7.14
State (Walshe) v Murphy [1981] IR 275 .... 4.62, 4.78, 4.82, 10.56
State (Williams) v Kelly [1970] IR 259 ....4.54
Statens Control v Larsen [1978] ECR 1543 ....14.88

Stauder v City of Ulm [1969] ECR 419 .... 16.63
Stephens v Flynn [2008] IESC 4 .... 6.11
Stillman v Rushbourne (2014) NSWSC 730 .... 3.110
Stork v High Authority [1959] ECR 17 .... 16.63
Stuart (Carl) Ltd v Biotrace Ltd [1993] ILRM 633 .... 14.192
Stubbings v Webb [1993] 2 WLR 120 .... 14.180
Subramaniam v Public Prosecutor [1956] 1 WLR 965 .... 6.132
Sunday Times Ltd v United Kingdom (1979) 2 EHRR 245 .... 10.49
Sussex Peerage Case (1844) 11 Cl & Fin 85 .... 14.20

T

Takamore v Clarke [2011] NZCA 587 .... 1.19
Tanistry, Case of (1607) Dav 28 .... 2.18
Tate v Minister for Social Welfare [1995] 1 IR 419 .... 15.80, 16.205, 16.223
Taylor v Ryan (10 March 1983, unreported), HC 12.170
TD v Minister for Education [2001] 4 IR 259 .... 4.22, 4.54, 15.60, 15.125
Texaco (Ireland) Ltd v Murphy [1991] 2 IR 449 .... 14.35, 14.109
TF v Ireland [1995] 1 IR 321 .... 15.113
TH v DPP [2004] IEHC 76 .... 15.206
The People (DPP) v Nevin [2003] 3 IR 348 .... 4.31
Tilson Infants, Re [1951] IR 1 .... 12.35
Todd v Murphy [1999] 2 IR 1 .... 5.103
Tormey v Ireland [1985] IR 289 .... 4.53, 5.69, 5.102, 7.13, 7.33, 15.144
Tradax Ltd v Irish Grain Board Ltd [1984] IR 1 .... 3.148
Transactus Investments Ltd v Dublin Corporation [1985] IR 501 .... 8.55
Travers v Ryan [1985] ILRM 343 .... 9.09
Treacy's Application for Judicial Review, Re [2000] NI 330 .... 3.148
Tromso Sparebank v Beirne (No 2) [1989] ILRM 257 .... 12.77
Truloc Ltd v McMenamin [1994] 1 ILRM 151 .... 14.30
Tuck & Sons v Preister (1887) 19 QBD 629 .... 14.34
Tuohy v Courtney [1994] 3 IR 1 .... 9.02

U

UF (orse UC) v JC [1991] 2 IR 330 .... 1.21, 12.74, 12.137, 12.142
Ugbelase v Minister for Justice, Equality and Law Reform
    [2010] 4 IR 233 .... 12.87, 12.90, 12.95
United Bars Ltd, Re [1991] 1 IR 396 .... 12.77
United States Tobacco Co v Minister for Consumer Affairs
    (1988) 83 ALR 79 .... 9.12
United States Tobacco International Inc v Minister for Health
    [1990] 1 IR 394 .... 14.128
United States v Tynen 11 Wall 88 .... 14.144
Universal City Studios Incorporated v Mulligan (No 1)
    [1999] 3 IR 381 .... 14.103

Unwin v Hanson [1891] 2 QB 115 ....14.34
Ussher v Ussher [1912] 2 IR 445 ....1.21

V

Van Gend en Loos v Nederlandse Belastingadministratie
   [1963] ECR 1 ....16.82, 16.92, 16.104, 16.185, 16.199
Von Colson and Kamann v Land Nordrhein-Westfalen
   [1984] ECR 1891 ....14.89

W

Wadda v Ireland [1994] ILRM 126 ....14.178
Waldson v Junior Army and Navy Stores [1910] 2 IR 318 ....12.140
Wall v Hegarty [1980] ILRM 124 ....10.04, 11.28, 12.93, 12.158, 12.159, 12.166
Walsh v Minister for Justice, Equaliy and Law Reform
   [2010] 2 IR 463 ....14.20
Walsh v Minister for Local Government [1929] IR 377 ....12.122
Walsh v President of the Circuit Court and DPP
   [1989] ILRM 325 ....12.65
Warburton v Loveland (1828) 1 Hud & B 623 ....14.24
Ward of Court (No 2), Re [1996] 2 IR 79 ....1.38, 15.112, 15.185
Ward v Kinahan Electrical Ltd [1984] IR 292 ....5.45
Wavin Pipes Ltd v Hepworth Iron Co Ltd [1982] 8 FSR 32
   .... 12.58, 14.175, 14.175
Webb v Ireland [1988] IR 353 ....15.42
Weekes v Revenue Commissioners [1989] ILRM 165 ....8.67, 14.47
Welch v Bowmaker (Ireland) Ltd [1980] IR 251 ....14.129
Weston v An Bord Pleanála [2008] IEHC 71 ....12.87
Whelan v Kirby [2004] IESC 17, [2005] 2 IR 30. ....6.93
White v Dublin City Council [2004] 1 IR 545 ....9.02
Woods (Application of) [1970] IR 154 ....9.11
Worldport Ireland Ltd, Re [2005] IEHC 189 ....12.63
Worth Library, Re [1995] 2 IR 301 ....3.121
Wouters v Algemene Raad van de Nederlandse Orde van Advocate
   [2002] ECR I-1577 ....3.66
Wunder v Hospitals Trust (1940) Ltd 9.07

X

XY v Clinical Director of Saint Patrick's University Hospital [2012] IEHC 224 ...4.30

Y

Young v Bristol Aeroplane Co Ltd [1944] KB 718 ....12.58

Z

Z v A Government Department [2014] EUECJ C-363/12 (ECJ,
   18 March 2014) 7.77

Table of Legislation

Ireland Post-1922

Abattoirs Act 1988
  s 16 ....8.41
Adaptation of Enactments Act 1922 ....13.93
Adoption Act 2010 ....17.88
Agriculture Appeals Act 2001 ....8.46
Air Pollution Act 1987 ....16.217
Aliens Act 1935 ....13.134–13.135
  s 5(1) 13.135
      (e) 13.131
Altamont (Amendment of Deed of Trust) Act 1993 ....13.41, 13.45
Anglo-Irish Bank Corporation Act 2009 ....13.24, 13.57
Animal Remedies Act 1993 ....13.155, 16.126
  s 22 ....6.90
    (2) 6.10
Anti-Discrimination (Pay) Act 1974 .... 14.61, 14.89, 16.223
  s 2 ....14.62
   3 ....14.62
Arbitration Act 1954 ....8.21
Arbitration Act 1980 ....8.21
  s 5 ....8.22
Arbitration Act 1996 ....9.69
Arbitration (International Commercial) Act 1998 ....8.21, 17.87
Arbitration Act 2010 .... 3.158, 8.21–8.23, 17.87
Bail Act 1997 ....5.26, 6.107–6.109, 11.18
  s 2 ....6.108
Bank of Ireland Act 1929 ....13.41
Bank of Ireland Act 1935 ....13.41
Bankers' Books Evidence Act 1959 ....14.116
Bankruptcy Act 1988 ....5.78, 15.203
British-Irish Agreement Act 1999 .... 13.66, 15.11, 15.15

Broadcasting Act 1960
  s 18 .... 15.113
Building Societies Act 1976
  s 80 .... 14.54
Building Societies (Amendment) Act 1983 .... 11.28, 13.57, 14.55
Building Societies Act 1989
  s 31 .... 3.63
Capital Acquisitions Tax Consolidation Act 2003 .... 13.102
Capital Gains Tax Act 1975 .... 14.14
  s 12 .... 14.15
  33 .... 14.15
    (5) 14.15
Censorship of Publications Acts 1929 to 1967 .... 4.15
Central Bank Act 1989 .... 13.155
  s 15(5) 13.116
Central Bank and Financial Services Authority of Ireland Act 2004 ...... 8.89
Charities Act 2009 .... 8.34
Child Abduction and Enforcement of Custody Orders Act 1991 .... 9.54. 14.178
  s 1(2) 14.156
Child Abuse Act 2000 ....
Child and Family Agency Act 2013 .... 9.09
Child Care Act 1991 .... 13.55
  s 25 .... 9.09
  26 .... 9.09
  71 .... 6.10
Child Trafficking and Pornography Act 1998 .... 4.151, 5.25
Children Act 1997
  s 11 .... 9.09, 9.54
  13 .... 9.54
  28 .... 6.124
Children Act 2001 .... 10.43–10.44
  s 61 .... 9.09
  71 .... 5.99
  75 .... 5.99
  91 .... 9.09
  252 .... 4.25
City of Dublin (Extension of Boundaries) Order 1953 .... 13.41

Civil Law (Miscellaneous Provisions) Act 2008 ....3.59

s 14 ....4.69
27 ....4.29, 4.30
31 ....4.27
32 ....4.52, 4.68
34 ....3.58
40 ....3.60
54 ....6.144
64 ....6.145
78 ....9.52
80 ....9.51

Civil Law (Miscellaneous Provisions) Act 2011 ....9.75

s 3 ....9.52
54 ....9.59
64 ....4.63

Civil Law and Courts (Miscellaneous Provisions) Act 2013 ....8.73

Civil Legal Aid Act 1995 ....9.33, 9.45–9.47, 9.59, 9.64, 9.71, 17.68

s 4 ....9.45
5 ....9.44–9.45
9 ....9.45
10–11 ....9.46
24 ....9.48
25 ....9.47
26 ....9.52
   (2) 9.52
   (3)(b) 9.52
   (3A) 9.52
   (3B) 9.52
   (4) 9.47
27 ....9.47, 9.56
28 ....9.47
   (2) 9.53
   (3) 9.54
   (8) 9.56
   (9) 9.52, 9.57
      (c) 9.57
   (10) 9.58
29 ....9.49–9.53
   (2) 9.51
30 ....9.46
33–36 ....9.71

Civil Liability Act 1961 .... 11.09
  s 34 .... 12.140
    60 .... 13.139
      (1) 13.76
      (7) 13.76
Civil Liability and Courts Act 2004 .... 5.15, 5.20, 5.64, 6.31, 6.35, 6.51
  s 6–8 .... 5.20
    10 .... 6.31
    11 .... 6.52
    12 .... 6.53
      (1) 6.51
      (3) 6.53
    14 .... 6.34, 6.43
    22 (1) 10.07
    25 .... 6.34, 6.43
    26 .... 6.34, 6.43
    40 .... 4.27
      (3) 4.27
      (6) 4.27
    45 .... 5.63
    55 .... 4.184
    40A 4.27
Civil Liability (Assessment of Hearing Loss) Act 1998 .... 14.95
  s 3 .... 14.95
    4 .... 14.95
Civil Partnership and Certain Rights and Obligations of Cohabitants
  Act 2010 .... 5.23, 15.199
    Pt 15 .... 11.19
Civil Service Regulation (Amendment) Act 2005
  s 28–31 .... 3.124–3.128
Commission of Investigations Act 2004 .... 8.77
Committees of the Houses of the Oireachtas (Compellability, Privileges
  and Immunities of Witnesses) Act 1997
  s 3 .... 4.151
Communications Regulation Act 2002 .... 8.64
Companies Act 1963 .... 5.77, 12.171, 16.216
  s 60 .... 6.151
    99 .... 14.54
    205 .... 4.26, 4.30
    297A 14.114
Companies (Amendment) Act 1977 .... 16.216

Companies (Amendment) Act 1983 ....16.216
Companies (Amendment) Act 1990
  s 33 ....14.114
Companies Act 1990 ....4.28, 5.77, 8.54, 16.216
Companies (Miscellaneous Provisions) Act 2013 ....5.67, 5.77
Competition Act 1991 ....14.166
Competition Act 2002
  s 6 ....5.107
    7 ....5.107
Competition Acts 1991 and 1996 ....3.05, 16.221
Competition and Consumer Protection Act 2014 ....3.05, 5.24, 8.40
Comptroller and Auditor General Acts 1923 to 1998 ....2.82
Constitution (Amendment No 16) Act 1929 ....2.67, 2.70
Constitution (Amendment No 17) Act 1929 ....2.67
Constitution (Amendment No 22) Act 1933 ....2.67
Constitution (Amendment No 24) Act 1936 ....2.67
Constitution (Amendment No 27) Act 1936 ....2.67
Constitution of the Irish Free State (Saorstát Éireann) Act 1922 ....2.58, 2.59
  s 1 ....2.71
    2 ....2.71–2.72
    Sch 4.02
Constitution (Removal of Oath) Act 1933 ....2.67, 2.72
Constitutional Reform Act 2005 ....4.110
Consumer Credit Act 1995 ....5.24, 5.50, 5.61, 13.155–13.157
  s 13 ....5.94
    14 ....6.10
Consumer Information Act 1978 ....5.24
Consumer Protection Act 2007 ....5.24
Contractual Obligations (Applicable Law) Act 1980 ....17.86
Contractual Obligations (Applicable Law) Act 1991 ....17.88
Convalescent Home Stillorgan (Charter Amendment) Act 1958 ....13.41
Copyright Act 1963 ....14.103
Copyright and Related Rights Act 2000 ....5.25
Cork Harbour Act 1933 ....13.41
Coroners Act 1962 ....8.70–8.73
  s 26 ....8.72
    30 ....8.71
    40 ....8.70–8.72

Coroners (Amendment) Act 2005 .... 8.70–8.72

Corporation Tax Act 1976 .... 14.159

  s 17 .... 14.151
   24(2) 14.151
   54 .... 14.68
   Pt IV 14.69

Court of Appeal Act 2014 .... 4.34, 4.51, 4.53, 4.60, 7.18, 7.39

  s 6 .... 4.51

Court of Justice Act 1936

  s 34 .... 4.63
   35 .... 4.63

Court Officers Act 1926 .... 4.195–4.201

Courts (Establishment and Constitution) Act 1961 .... 4.03, 4.47–4.50
.... 4.78, 5.01, 12.36, 12.41, 12.48, 12.71

  s 1 .... 4.53
   1A 4.51
   2 .... 4.61
   3 .... 7.41
   4 .... 4.65
   5 .... 4.68
   6 .... 4.186
   25 .... 4.67
   48 .... 5.91
   22–24 .... 4.67
   Sch 3 .... 4.67

Courts (Supplemental Provisions) Act 1961 .... 4.03, 4.47, 4.69
.... 4.78–4.81, 4.86, 4.108, 4.114, 4.180, 5.01, 7.02

  s 1(2) 4.53
   4(1) 4.53
   (2) 4.61
   5(2) 4.80
   7(1) 4.53
   (3) 4.54, 12.55
   (4) 4.54
   (5) 4.53, 4.55
   8 .... 5.63, 5.70, 5.79
   (1) 4.61
   9 .... 5.63
   (1) 5.80
   (4) 5.80
   10 .... 5.63
   (1) 5.89

Courts (Supplemental Provisions) Act 1961 (contd)

(3) 4.61
(4) 4.141
11 ....5.105
(1) 5.105
(2)(b) 4.62
12 ....7.41
16 ....4.65
17(2) 4.80–4.81
18 ....4.187
20(1) 4.66
21 ....4.65
22 ....5.55–5.57, 5.63, 7.21
(1)(b) 5.56
23 ....7.21
24 ....5.58
25 ....5.102
(2) 5.106–5.108
28 ....4.68
29(2) 4.79
30(1) 4.188
32(1) 4.69
32A 4.40, 4.70
33 ....5.46
35(2) 4.69
36 ....4.69
(2) 4.141
39–42 ....4.69
45(1) 4.25, 4.30
46 ....4.182, 4.190
48 ....4.51, 4.68, 4.118, 4.187, 7.21
51 ....7.14, 7.34
52 ....7.13–7.17, 7.34–7.35
(2) 7.17, 7.35
54 ....10.35
55(2) 4.202
(3) 4.202
Sch 3 ....5.32, 5.55–5.63
Sch 4 ....5.55
Sch 6 ....4.69
Sch 8 ....4.195–4.201

Courts Act 1964
s 6 ....5.103

Courts (Supplemental Provisions) (Amendment) (No 2) Act 1968 ......4.182

Courts Act 1971 .... 3.71, 11.23

  s 6 .... 4.65
    7 .... 5.32
    13 .... 4.68

Courts Act 1977

  s 2 .... 4.66

Courts Act 1981 .... 5.69, 6.42

  s 2 .... 5.32
    5 .... 5.59
    6 .... 5.32
    17 .... 5.45
    18(1)(a) 4.53
    22 .... 4.197, 10.08
    31 .... 5.103, 15.144

Courts (No 2) Act 1986 .... 5.58, 10.22

  s 4 .... 5.48

Courts (No 3) Act 1986 .... 4.18, 11.28

Courts Act 1988 .... 3.104, 5.15, 6.142, 6.158

  s 1 .... 4.62
    5 .... 5.40

Courts (Supplemental Provisions) (Amendment) Act 1991 .... 4.190

Courts (Supplemental Provisions) (Amendment) Act 1999 .... 4.135

Courts (Supplemental Provisions) Act 1991 .... 4.190

Courts Act 1991 .... 5.03

  s 2 .... 5.32, 5.61–5.63
    4 .... 5.32, 5.46
    (c) 5.47
    14–15 .... 5.45
    16 .... 5.34
    21 .... 4.52, 4.68, 4.118
    (1)(a) 4.68

Courts Act 1996

  s 1 .... 4.52

Courts (Miscellaneous Provisions) Act 1997

  s 7 .... 7.45

Courts Act 1997

  s 1 .... 4.52

Courts (Supplemental Provisions) (Amendment) Act 1999 .... 4.136

Courts and Civil Law (Miscellaneous Provisions) Act 2011

  s 64 .... 7.66

Courts and Civil Law (Miscellaneous Provisions) Act 2013 ....4.27, 4.207
.... 5.01–5.03, 5.33, 5.47–5.56, 5.72, 6.32, 6.62, 6.151
 s 22 ....4.52–4.53
Courts and Court Officers Act 1995 ....3.07, 3.74, 4.53, 4.55–4.56, 4.73
....4.81, 4.98, 4.110, 4.147, 4.187, 4.196
....4.202, 5.15, 6.64, 6.127, 13.32, 13.49
 s 2 ....4.52
    4 ....4.02
    6 ....4.52
     (1) 4.52–4.53
     (2) 4.53
    7 ....4.53, 4.54, 12.55
    8 ....4.53
    9 ....4.52, 4.61
   10 ....4.52, 4.65
   11 ....4.52, 4.68–4.69
   12 ....4.102
   13 ....4.101–4.105
    (3) 4.104
   14 ....4.105
   16 ....4.106–4.107, 4.147
    (6) 4.109
    (7) 4.108
    (8) 4.110
   17 ....4.110
   18(3) 4.103
   19 ....4.108
   20 ....4.110
   21–22 ....4.105
   23 ....4.102
   24 ....4.11, 4.197, 11.23
   25(1) 4.197
    (2) 4.197
   28 ....4.81
   30 ....4.81
   32 ....5.103
   33 ....4.51, 4.65
   34 ....4.202
   36 ....4.66
   38–39 ....4.69
   46 ....5.45

Courts and Court Officers Act 1995 (contd)

47 .... 4.189

  (1) 4.187

  (2) 4.187

48 .... 4.147

49 .... 3.114, 5.23, 5.60, 5.76

50(1) 4.197

53 .... 5.60

Sch 1 .... 4.53

Sch 2 .... 4.202

Courts and Court Officers Act 2002 .... 4.84, 5.03, 5.33

s 4 .... 3.74, 4.81

8 .... 4.81, 4.108

11 .... 4.101

46 .... 4.184

Courts and Court Officers Act 2007

s 2 .... 4.61

3 .... 4.52, 4.65

Courts and Court Officers Act 2009 .... 4.202

Courts and Courts Officers Act 1995

Courts and Legal Services Act 1990 .... 3.38

Courts (No 2) Act 1997

s 2 .... 4.52

3 .... 4.53, 4.61, 4.151

Courts (No 3) Act 1986 .... 4.17, 6.92

s 3 .... 6.10

Courts of Justice Act 1924 .... 2.68–2.70, 2.111, 4.02–4.05, 4.40

.... 4.47, 4.78, 4.87, 4.189, 5.01, 5.31, 5.70

.... 5.122, 6.30, 7.02, 8.32–8.36

s 1(iii) 8.33

2(1) 8.35

3 .... 5.105

4 .... 4.52, 4.61

5 .... 4.52

6 .... 4.53, 4.61

7 .... 4.53

8 .... 7.38–7.41

9 .... 4.51

10 .... 4.73

11 .... 4.186

12 .... 4.187

13 .... 4.180

Courts of Justice Act 1924 (contd)

15	4.190
16	4.80
17	4.61
18	4.53
19(2)–(3)	5.89
20	12.04
24	4.62, 5.79
25	5.45
29	7.56, 12.122, 14.127, 15.133
30	7.41
31	7.41–7.45
32–33	7.45
34	7.47
37	4.52, 4.65
38	4.51
39	4.118
40	4.187
41	4.180, 4.190
44	4.66
45	4.186
46–47	4.65
48	5.32, 5.55
(i)	5.56
49	5.102
50	5.58
51	5.55
63	7.41–7.45
67	4.68
68	4.52
69	4.79
70	4.186
71	4.69
72	4.188
73	4.118
74	4.180
75	4.190
76	4.68
77	5.32, 5.46, 5.91
(a)	5.47
(ii)	5.53
77A	5.48
79	4.70
83	7.13, 7.34
84	7.13, 7.21

Courts of Justice Act 1924 (contd)

94 .... 4.62, 4.65
95 .... 6.159
99 .... 4.116
Sch Pt II 8.34

Courts of Justice Act 1926

s 4 .... 5.105

Courts of Justice Act 1928

s 5 .... 7.47
18 .... 7.33

Courts of Justice Act 1936

s 4 .... 4.53
5 .... 4.61
9(1) 5.80
14 .... 4.65
(1) 4.80
16 .... 7.22
31 .... 7.21
37 .... 7.21
38 .... 7.21
(1) 7.21
(3) 7.21–7.22
39 .... 7.21
51 .... 4.68
(1) 4.79
57 .... 7.13
58 .... 7.33

Courts of Justice (District Court) Act 1946

s 9 .... 4.61
20 .... 4.118
21 .... 4.141

Courts of Justice (District Court) Act 1949

s 2 .... 4.188

Courts of Justice Act 1947 .... 4.181

s 9 .... 4.65
(3) 4.51
10 .... 4.67
14 .... 4.65
15 .... 4.187
16 .... 7.22, 7.39

Courts of Justice Act 1953 ....4.181

  s 11 ....4.61

    16 ....4.66

    18 ....4.65

    21 ....4.69

Courts of Justice Act 1971 ....3.08

Courts Service Act 1998 .... 3.115, 4.05, 4.27, 4.205, 4.209

    .... 4.217, 4.221, 5.12, 5.125, 6.77, 8.16, 8.38, 11.24, 12.24

  s 11 ....4.218

    12 ....4.219

    21 ....4.220

Criminal Court Act 2006

  s 9 ....3.127

    10 ....3.127

Criminal Damage Act 1991 .... 5.25, 5.95, 5.115, 11.07, 13.103

  s 8 ....13.91

Criminal Evidence Act 1992 .... 5.26, 6.134, 13.55

  s 27 ....6.124

Criminal Justice (Administration) Act 1924 ....6.110

  s 9 ....3.125

Criminal Justice Act 1925 ....4.32

Criminal Justice Act 1951 .... 5.97, 6.104, 10.33

  s 8 ....14.130

  Sch 5.97

Criminal Justice Act 1960

  s 2 ....10.33

Criminal Justice (Legal Aid) Act 1962 .... 9.18–9.25, 9.33

    .... 9.39, 9.52, 9.72, 14.20, 15.70

  s 2–6 ....9.22

Criminal Justice Act 1964 ....9.18

Criminal Justice (Community Service) Act 1983 ....5.26, 10.39

Criminal Justice Act 1984 .... 5.26, 6.95, 6.127, 15.139

  s 5 ....9.34

    21–22 ....6.136

    25 ....6.159

Criminal Justice (Forensic Evidence) Act 1990 ....5.26

Criminal Justice Act 1990 ....6.82, 9.18

Criminal Justice Act 1993 ....5.26, 5.107, 7.56, 10.36
  s 2 ....7.48
    6 ....6.04
Criminal Justice (Public Order) Act 1994 ....5.25, 6.15, 11.18, 13.103
  s 1(3) 13.74
    8 ....15.67
   17 ....6.83
    (3) 6.83
   19 ....5.97, 5.136
  20–22 ....13.55
Criminal Justice Act 1994 ....5.25, 10.48
Criminal Justice (Drug Trafficking) Act 1996 ....5.25–5.28, 6.95–6.97
Criminal Justice (Miscellaneous Provisions) Act 1997 ....5.26, 6.104, 13.55
  s 6(1) 14.51
Criminal Justice Act 1999 ....4.28, 5.26
  s 41 ....5.136
  Pt 3 ....6.106
  Pt III 6.105, 11.23
Criminal Justice (Safety of United Nations Workers) Act 2000
  s 2 ....5.107
Criminal Justice (United Nations Convention Against Torture)
  Act 2000 ....5.107, 10.48
Criminal Justice (Theft and Fraud Offences) Act 2001 ....5.95–5.96, 6.104
  ....13.55, 13.103
  s 4 ....9.23
   14 ....6.111, 13.89
Criminal Justice Act 2006 ....5.25, 6.95
  s 21 ....7.55
   22 ....7.56, 15.133
  108 ....10.33
  167 ....13.103
  177 ....6.10
  180 ....4.40, 4.70
Criminal Justice Act 2007 ....5.25–5.26, 6.95–6.97, 7.60
  s 59 ....7.56
Criminal Justice (Amendment) Act 2009 ....5.113
Criminal Justice (Community Service) (Amendment) Act 2011 ....10.39
Criminal Justice Act 2011...5.25
Criminal Justice (Public Order) Act 2011 ....15.62

Criminal Justice (Withholding Information on Crimes against Children and Vulnerable Persons) Act 2012 ....13.55

Criminal Justice (Forensic Evidence and DNA Database System) Act 2014 ....5.26, 6.135, 11.19

Criminal Law Amendment Act 1935
  s 1(1) 15.76, 15.77
    2(2) 12.92
    17 .... 15.109, 15.138, 15.168

Criminal Law Act 1967
  s 58 ....6.84

Criminal Law (Jurisdiction) Act 1976 ....5.97, 6.104
  s 5 ....13.89

Criminal Law (Rape) Act 1981 ....6.120
  s 2(1) 14.183
    6 ....4.28

Criminal Law (Rape) Act 1990 ....6.120

Criminal Law (Rape) (Amendment) Act 1990 ....5.25, 5.107
  s 10 ....5.107
    11 ....4.28

Criminal Law (Sexual Offences) Act 1993 .... 1.57, 5.25, 13.55–13.56
    .... 15.110, 15.173, 17.68

Criminal Law (Suicide) Act 1993
  s 2 ....4.53, 15.193

Criminal Law (Incest Proceedings) Act 1995
  s 6 ....4.28

Criminal Law Act 1997 .... 5.97, 6.82–6.84

Criminal Law (Theft and Fraud Offences) Act 2001 ....11.07

Criminal Law (Insanity) Act 2006 .... 9.33, 11.10, 13.103

Criminal Law (Sexual Offences) Act 2006 ....5.25, 15.76

Criminal Law (Sexual Offences) (Amendment) Act 2007 ....5.25

Criminal Procedure Act 1967 .... 5.97, 6.103–6.105
  s 6 ....6.105
    12 ....6.105
    13(2)(b) 7.41
    34 ....7.54

Criminal Procedure (Amendment) Act 1973
  s 1 ....7.41

Criminal Procedure Act 1993 ....5.26, 7.47–7.52, 13.55
  s 2 .... 7.51
    3 .... 7.47
    7 .... 7.51
    9 .... 7.53
    11 .... 7.58
Criminal Procedure Act 2010 ....6.156, 7.45, 7.70
  s 31–32 .... 7.45
  Pt 3 .... 7.60
Dáil Éireann Courts (Winding-Up) Act 1923 .... 2.104
Daniel McGrath Foundation Act 1945 .... 13.41
Data Protection Act 1988 .... 17.29
Decimal Currency Act 1970
  s 9(1) 13.93
Defamation Act 2009 .... 8.95
  s 38 .... 6.09
Defence Act 1954 ....2.80, 5.110
Dentists Act 1985 .... 8.61
  s 38–40 .... 4.17
Derelict Sites Act 1990 .... 8.65
Disability Act 2005 .... 8.85
Diseases of Animals Act 1966 .... 13.78
  s 20 .... 13.79
    58 .... 13.79
Domestic Violence Act 1996 ....5.23, 5.49, 13.55
Dublin United Tramways (Lucan Electric Railway) Act 1927 .... 13.41
Dundalk Harbour and Port Act 1925 .... 13.41
Education Act 1998
  s 6 .... 13.17, 13.73
    28–29 .... 8.61
Electoral Act 1959 .... 15.99
Electoral Act 1963 .... 15.99
Electoral Act 1992
  s 132 .... 5.81
Electoral (Amendment) Act 1996 .... 13.36
Electricity Regulation Act 1999 .... 8.64
Electricity Supply Act 1927
  s 27 .... 8.25

Electricity Supply (Amendment) Act 1985 ....8.25
Emergency Powers Act 1976 ....15.100
Employment Act 1980 ....14.175
Employment Equality Act 1998 ....9.56, 15.102
   s 75 ....8.52
      77 ....5.56, 8.52
      83 ....8.52
      90 ....8.52
Employment Equality Acts 1998–2008 ....8.52
Enforcement of Court Orders (Amendment) Act 2009 ....10.23
Enforcement of Court Orders Acts 1926 and 1940 ....10.22–10.23
Enforcement of Court Orders (Amendment) Act 2009 ....11.28
Environment (Miscellaneous Provisions) Act 2011 ....9.74
Environmental Protection Agency Act 1992 .... 6.90, 8.54, 8.74, 16.217
Equal Status Act 2000 ....15.102
   s 44 ....6.10
Erasmus Smith Schools Act 1938 ....13.41
Ethics in Public Office Act 1995
   s 37 ....5.94
Euro Changeover (Amounts) Act 2001 ....13.93
European Arrest Warrant Act 2003 ....5.100, 7.13
European Communities Act 1972 .... 16.114, 16.209, 16.217
   s 1 ....16.115
      2 .... 14.62, 16.116–16.117
      3 ....5.95, 12.106, 13.124, 13.155, 15.105
         ....16.118–16.133, 16.210–16.215
      (2) 16.127
      4 ....13.153, 16.118
European Communities (Amendment) Act 1973 ....13.153, 16.119
European Communities (Amendment) Act 1986 ....16.105
European Communities (Amendment) Act 1993
   s 5(1) 16.126
European Communities (Amendment) Act 1995 ....16.119
   s 1 ....13.153
European Communities Act 2007 ....8.42, 16.214
European Communities (Amendment) Act 2012 ....16.115
European Communities Acts 1972–2012 ....8.42
European Communities (Confirmation of Regulations) Act 1973 ....13.153

European Convention on Human Rights Act 2003 ....1.20, 12.84, 14.92
.... 15.01, 15.202, 17.69–17.71, 17.75
  s 1(1) 15.204
    2 ....1.20, 14.92, 15.204, 17.70
      (1) 15.202
    3 .... 15.204, 17.70
    4 .... 1.20, 17.70
    5 .... 1.20, 15.206
    Sch 15.205
European Union Act 2009
  s 3 .... 16.116
Europol Act 1997 .... 16.60
Executive Authority (External Relations) Act 1936 ....2.67, 15.31, 15.34
Executive Powers (Consequential Provisions) Act 1937 .... 15.43
  s 2 .... 3.100
Explosive Substances Act 1883 .... 5.115
Extradition Act 1965 ....5.100, 11.09
  s 47(5) 7.13
    50 ....14.85, 14.90, 14.163
    Pt 3 .... 3.127
    Pt II 13.56
    Pt III 14.175
Extradition (Amendment) Act 1987 ....3.120, 3.127, 4.99
Extradition (European Convention on the Suppression of Terrorism)
  Act 1987 .... 17.29
Extradition (European Union Conventions) Act 2001 .... 7.13
Factories Act 1955 .... 14.108
Family Home Protection Act 1976 .... 14.58, 14.64
  s 3(1) 14.46
     9 .... 5.49
     10(5) 5.49
Family Law (Maintenance of Spouses and Children) Act 1976
  s 23 .... 5.49
Family Law Act 1995 .... 10.25
Family Law (Divorce) Act 1996 ....5.23, 15.114
  s 6–9 .... 8.12
     38 .... 5.60
Family Support Act 2001 .... 8.12
Fifteenth Amendment of the Constitution Act 1995 .... 2.78

Fifteenth Amendment of the Constitution Act 1996 .... 1.57, 15.03, 15.149

Fifth Amendment of the Constitution Act 1972 ....15.196

Finance Act 1971

  s 22 ....14.74

Finance Act 1975 ....14.159

  s 31 ....14.72

Finance Act 1976

  s 46 ....13.137–13.138

Finance Act 1980 ....15.75

  s 41(2) 14.69

    (8) 14.109

    42 ....14.73

    (2) 14.70

Finance Act 1982 ....15.103

  s 26 ....14.69

  Sch 2 ....14.69

Finance Act 1984 ....15.103

Finance Act 1989

  s 86 ....14.16

Finance Act 1990

  s 41(1)(b) 14.109

Financial Emergency Measures in the Public Interest Act 2009 ....4.174. 13.72

Financial Emergency Measures in the Public Interest (No 2) Act 2009 ....4.178

Financial Emergency Measures in the Public Interest Act 2010 ....4.174, 4.177

Financial Emergency Measures in the Public Interest (Amendment)

  Act 2011 ....4.64, 4.176

  s 3–6 ....4.178

Fines Act 2010 ....5.94, 10.28

Fines (Payment and Recovery) Act 2014 ....10.29

Fire Services Act 1981 ....8.54

  s 20 ....8.55

Firearms Acts 1925–1990 ....5.115

First Amendment of the Constitution Act 1939 ....15.82

Fisheries (Consolidation) Act 1959 ....13.102

  s 310 .... 7.33, 12.04, 12.116–12.119

Fisheries (Amendment) Act 1978 ....3.127

Free State (Constitution) Act 1922 ....2.57

Galway Harbour Act 1935 .... 13.41
Garda Síochána Act 2005 .... 5.28, 6.96, 8.93
  s 8 .... 6.91
Gas (Interim Regulation) Act 2002 .... 8.64
Geneva Conventions Act 1962 .... 5.107, 13.56
Genocide Act 1973 .... 3.127, 10.48, 13.56
Greyhound Industry Act 1958
  s 13 .... 13.113
    25 .... 13.113
    48 .... 13.113
Guardianship of Infants Act 1964 .... 5.49, 11.09
  s 3 .... 14.86
    28 .... 9.09, 9.54
Harbours Act 1946
  s 53(1) 14.106
Harbours Act 1953
  s 53(1) 14.123
Health Act 1947 .... 8.54
Health (Fluoridation of Water Supplies) Act 1960 .... 15.54–15.55, 15.59
Health Act 1970
  s 2 .... 13.142
    52 .... 13.142
    56 .... 13.142
    72 .... 13.126, 13.141
Health (Family Planning) Act 1979 .... 15.109
Health (Mental Services) Act 1981 .... 13.81
Health (Family Planning) (Amendment) Act 1985 .... 15.109
Health (Amendment) Act 1986
  s 2(1) 14.188
Health (Family Planning) (Amendment) Act 1992 .... 15.109
Health (Family Planning) (Amendment) Act 1993 .... 15.109
Health Act 2004 .... 8.36
Health Act 2008
  s 1(1) 14.155
Health Acts 1947–2007 .... 14.155
Hepatitis C Compensation Tribunal Act 1997 .... 9.62

Hire-Purchase (Amendment) Act 1960

   s 19 ....5.50, 5.61

Hire-Purchase Acts 1946–1980 ....5.50, 5.61

Holidays (Employees) Act 1961 ....13.140, 14.175

Hotel Proprietors Act 1963 ....5.50, 5.61

   s 10(1) 5.61

      (2) 5.50

Houses of the Oireachtas (Laying of Documents) Act 1966 ....13.151

Housing Act 1966 ....14.160

   s 62 ....17.72

Housing Act 1970

   s 13 ....17.72

Housing (Private Rented Dwellings) Act 1982 ....15.102

Housing Act 1988 ....15.62

Housing (Miscellaneous Provisions) Act 2002

   s 24 ....6.15

Human Rights Commission Act 2000

   s 5(6) 4.53

Housing (Miscellaneous Provisions) Act 2014

   Pt 2 ....17.72

Illegal Immigrants (Trafficking) Act 2000 ....15.103

   s 5 ....9.03

      (3)(a) 12.65

Imposition of Duties Act 1957

   s 1 ....13.136–13.138

    2 ....13.136

Income Tax Act 1918 ....14.34

Income Tax Act 1967 ....13.102, 14.34

   s 428(6) 14.118

    192–196 .... 15.72–15.75, 15.101

Indemnity Act 1923 ....2.63, 2.68

Industrial and Provident Societies (Amendment) Act 1978

   s 14(8) 14.122

Industrial Relations Act 1946 ....13.123, 13.149

   s 17 ....8.50

    42–43 ....13.123

    45 ....13.123

    Pt III 13.123

    Pt IV 8.51, 13.123

Industrial Relations Act 1990

   s 42 .... 13.09

     48 .... 13.123

Industrial Relations (Amendment) Act 2001 .... 8.50

   s 2(1) 8.50

     11 .... 8.50

Industrial Relations (Miscellaneous Provisions) Act 2004

   s 2 .... 8.50

Industrial Relations (Amendment) Act 2012 .... 8.51, 13.123

Infanticide Act 1949 .... 13.92

   s 1(4) 13.91

Institute of Chartered Accountants in Ireland (Charter Amendment)

   Act 1966 .... 13.41

Insurance (No 2) Act 1983 .... 13.24

Insurance (No 2) Act 1983 .... 13.57

Intermediate Education (Ireland) Acts 1878–1924 .... 13.09

International Criminal Court Act 2006 .... 5.107, 10.48, 17.49

International War Crimes Tribunal Act 1998 .... 10.48, 17.48

Interpretation Act 1937

   s 11(a)–(b) 14.30

      (g) 13.83

     21 .... 14.137

      (1)(e) 14.136

Interpretation (Amendment) Act 1993 .... 14.30

Interpretation (Amendment) Act 1997 .... 14.30–14.32, 14.140–14.148

   s 1 .... 14.145–14.146

     (3) 14.145–14.146

Interpretation Act 2005 .... 11.19, 14.30–14.31

   s 5 .... 14.32, 14.56

     6 .... 14.103

     7 .... 13.83

    14(1) 13.69

    18(g) 13.83

    22(3) 13.110

    27 .... 14.137

Intoxicating Liquor Act 2008

   s 22 .... 6.38

     Sch 2 .... 6.38

Irish Aviation Authority Act 1993 .... 8.54

Irish European Communities Act 1972 ....13.96

Irish Free State (Agreement) Act 1922 ....2.69, 2.103

Irish Free State (Saorstát Éireann) Act 1922 ....2.57

Irish Land Commission (Dissolution) Act 1992 ....2.43

Irish Nationality and Citizenship Act 1956 ....15.18

Irish Nationality and Citizenship Act 2004 ....15.19

Irish Sports Council Act 1999

  s 6(1)(c) 13.09

Judicial Separation and Family Law Reform Act 1989 .... 5.18, 5.59–5.60

  .... 11.18, 13.36, 13.49, 15.113

  s 5–8 ....8.12

    9 ....5.60

    29 ....14.113

    31(2) 5.60

    32 ....5.60

    33 .... 3.113, 5.60, 5.76

    45 ....3.113

Juries Act 1927 .... 6.143, 15.68, 15.98

Juries Act 1976 .... 6.144, 6.150, 8.70, 11.28, 15.68

  s 6 ....6.143

    7–8 ....6.144

    9 ....6.145–6.146

    11–12 ....6.148

    15 ....6.148

    17–19 ....6.151

    20–21 ....6.149

    34 ....6.148

    Sch 1 ....6.144

      Pt II 6.145–6.147

Jurisdiction of Courts and Enforcement of Judgments (European

  Communities) Act 1998 ....4.196

Jurisdiction of Courts and Enforcement of Judgments Act 1998 ....10.26

Jurisdiction of Courts and Enforcement of Judgments Act 2012 ....10.26

Labourers Act 1936 ....14.159

Land and Conveyancing Law Reform Act 2009 .... 11.05–11.07, 11.19

Landlord and Tenant Act 1931 ....14.159

Landlord and Tenant (Amendment) Act 1980 ....5.56

  s 3 ....5.64

Landlord and Tenant (Amendment) Act 1994 ....13.36

Landlord and Tenant (Ground Rents) (No 2) Act 1978 ....12.31

Larceny Act 1916 .... 13.90
Larceny Act 1990 .... 13.55
  s 3 .... 14.135
Law Reform Commission Act 1975 .... 11.11–11.15, 11.21
  s 14(1) 4.53, 4.61
    (a)(i) 4.53
Law Reform (Personal Injuries) Act 1958
  s 1 .... 12.140
Legal Aid, Sentencing and Punishment of Offenders Act 2012 .... 6.76
Legal Services Ombudsman Act 2009 .... 3.17, 3.141, 8.88
Liability for Defective Products Act 1991 .... 13.155
Licensing Acts 1833 to 2004 .... 5.58
Limerick Harbour Act 1926 .... 13.41
Limerick Harbour Tramways Act 1931 .... 13.41
Local Government and Public Health Provisional Order Confirmation
  Act 1953 .... 13.41
Local Government (Planning and Development) Act 1963 .... 14.44, 14.160
  s 82 .... 8.60
Local Government (Petitions and Disqualifications) Act 1974
  s 2 .... 5.66
Local Government (Water Pollution) Act 1977 .... 5.52, 5.62
  s 10 .... 5.52
Local Government (Water Pollution) Act 1990 .... 5.52, 5.62
Local Government (Planning and Development) Act 1992 .... 8.60
Local Government Reform Act 2014 .... 8.40, 15.199
Maintenance Act 1994 .... 9.54
Malicious Injuries Act 1981.. 8.47
  s 5 .... 14.133
  6 .... 14.132
Malicious Injuries (Amendment) Act 1986 .... 5.65, 8.48
Malicious Injuries Acts 1981 .... 5.65
Medical Practitioners Act 1978
  s 27(2)(d) 14.149
Medical Practitioners Act 2007 .... 8.61
Mental Health Act 2001 .... 9.03, 13.81
  s 74 .... 6.10

Mental Treatment Act 1945
  s 260 ....9.03
Methodist Church in Ireland Act 1928 ....13.41
Milk and Dairies Act 1935
  s 41 ....7.13
Minimum Notice and Terms of Employment Act 1973 ....14.159
Ministers and Secretaries Act 1924 ....8.32
  s 6 ....3.116–3.121
   9 ....3.116
Ministers and Secretaries (Amendment) Act 1977 ....8.36
Ministers and Secretaries (Amendment) Act 2011 ....8.40
Misuse of Drugs Act 1977 .... 13.69, 13.74, 13.82
  s 1 ....14.31
    5 ....13.14
   15(1) 13.14
   41(2) 13.75
   43(1) 13.75
    (2) 13.74
Misuse of Drugs Acts 1977 and 1984 ....5.95, 6.95
National Asset Management Agency Act 2009 ....4.54
National Disability Authority Act 1999
  s 10 ....13.09
National Minimum Wage Act 2000 ....8.51
National Standards Authority of Ireland Act 1996 ....8.54
Nineteenth Amendment of the Constitution Act 1998 .... 2.78, 2.97, 15.02
Non-Fatal Offences Against the Person Act 1997 .... 5.25, 5.95–5.96
  ....6.104, 11.07, 13.55, 13.103, 14.138–14.147
  s 24 ....13.12
   28(1) 14.144
Nuclear Test Ban Act 2008 ....17.43
Nurses and Midwives Act 2010 ....8.61
Occupiers' Liability Act 1995 ....11.18, 12.140
  s 4(2) 13.17
Offences Against the State Act 1939 .... 5.113, 5.114, 5.121, 6.95
  s 6 ....5.106
    7 ....5.106
    8 ....5.106
   30 ....12.114, 14.107, 14.122
   35 ....5.112

Offences Against the State Act 1939 (contd)
    36 .... 5.115–5.117
    39 .... 5.119
    44 .... 7.41–7.45
    46 .... 5.116
    Pt V 5.112, 5.118
Offences Against the State (Amendment) Act 1940 .... 17.64
Offences Against the State (Amendment) Act 1985 .... 13.24, 13.57
Offences Against the State (Amendment) Act 1998 .... 5.25, 5.115
    s 6 .... 5.115
    9 .... 5.115
    12 .... 5.115
Oireachtas (Allowances to Members) and Ministerial, Parliamentary and
    Judicial Offices (Amendment) Act 1977 .... 4.182
Oireachtas (Allowances to Members) and Ministerial, Parliamentary and
    Judicial Offices (Amendment) Act 1983 .... 4.182
Oireachtas (Allowances to Members) and Ministerial, Parliamentary,
    Judicial and Court Offices (Amendment) Act 1998
    Pt III 4.190
Oireachtas (Inquiries, Privileges and Procedures) Act 2013 .... 8.59
Ombudsman Act 1980 .... 8.84–8.86
    s 5 .... 8.85
    6   (3) 8.86
       (3A) 8.86
       (5) 8.87
    7   (1) 8.86
Ombudsman (Defence Forces) Act 2004 .... 8.92
Ombudsman (Amendment) Act 2012 .... 8.84–8.86
Ombudsman Acts 1980 to 2012 .... 8.84–8.86
Ombudsman for Children Act 2002 .... 8.91
Package Holidays and Travel Trade Act 1995 .... 5.24, 13.155
Patents Act 1964 .... 14.175
Patents Act 1992 .... 8.56
    s 96(7) 8.57
Pensions (Amendment) Act 2002 .... 8.90
Personal Injuries Assessment Board Act 2003 .. 5.03, 5.15–5.16, 5.33, 5.67, 5.73, 6.32
    s 7 .... 5.19
    14 .... 6.42
Personal Injuries Assessment (Amendment) Act 2007 .... 5.18

Personal Insolvency Act 2010 ....15.203

Personal Insolvency Act 2012 .... 4.65, 5.77, 10.24, 11.20

Pier and Harbour Provisional Order Confirmation Act 1932 ....13.41

Pigs and Bacon Act 1937 ....13.122

Planning and Development Act 2000 ....8.25, 15.103

  s 50–51 ....8.60

Planning and Development (Amendment) Act 2010

  s 32 ....10.56

Plebiscite (Draft Constitution) Act 1937 ....2.76

Poë Name and Arms (Compton Domvile Estates) Act 1936 ....13.41, 13.72

Prevention of Electoral Abuses Act 1923

  s 50 ....14.128

Prices Act 1958

  s 22A 13.143

Proceeds of Crime Act 1996 ....5.25, 9.33

Prosecution of Offences Act 1974 ....3.126, 6.99

  s 2 ....3.125

    (5) 3.126

    3(1) 3.125

    4 ....3.115

    5(1) 3.127

    7 ....3.128

Protection for Persons Reporting Child Abuse Act 1998 ....13.55

Protection of Animals (Amendment) Act 1965 ....13.49

Protection of Life During Pregnancy Act 2013 ....1.57, 15.174, 15.180

Provisional Government (Transfer of Functions) Order 1922 ....2.103

Public Health (Tobacco) Act 2002 ....14.03

Public Safety Act 1927 ....2.68

Public Service Management Act 1997 ....8.36–8.40

Public Service Management (Recruitment and Appointment) Act 2004 ....8.36

Public Service Pensions (Single Scheme and Other Provisions) Act 2012

  s 22...4.114, 4.165, 4.190

Radio and Television Act 1988 ....4.53

  s 10(3) 14.84

Railway Safety Act 2005 ....8.64

Redundancy Payments Act 1967 ....14.159

Referendum Act 1994 .... 15.51, 15.114

  s 42 .... 5.81

Refugee Act 1996 .... 8.66, 17.63

Regulation of Information (Services Outside the State for the
Termination of Pregnancies) Act 1995 .... 1.57, 15.112, 15.181

Rent Restrictions Act 1946 .... 14.87

Rent Restrictions Acts 1946 and 1960 .... 15.102

Republic of Ireland Act 1948 .... 15.33

  s 2 .... 15.33

   3 .... 15.33

Residential Tenancies Act 2004 .... 5.64

Restrictive Practices Act 1972

  s 12 .... 3.05

Road Traffic Act 1961

  s 3(4) 13.09

   49 .... 14.17–14.18

   103 .... 10.30

Road Traffic Acts 1961 to 2013 .... 5.95

Road Traffic Act 1968 .... 14.175

  s 44(2) 14.169

   Pt III 14.17

   Pt V 14.17

Road Traffic (Amendment) Act 1978

  s 23 .... 14.17

   Pt III 14.17

Road Traffic Act 1994

  s 43 .... 10.30

Road Traffic Acts 1994 and 1995 .... 13.66

Road Traffic Act 2004

  s 30 .... 5.94

Road Traffic Act 2010

  s 4 .... 6.92

Royal College of Surgeons in Ireland (Charter Amendment) Act 1965 .... 13.41

Royal College of Physicians of Ireland (Charter and Letters Patent
Amendment) Act 1979 .... 13.41

Royal College of Surgeons in Ireland (Charter Amendment) Act 2003 .... 13.41

Safety in Industry Act 1955 and 1980 .... 6.42, 6.52

Safety, Health and Welfare at Work Act 1989 .... 5.21, 13.55, 13.114, 14.108

Safety, Health and Welfare at Work Act 2005 ....5.21, 6.52, 8.54–8.55, 8.74, 10.47

  s 8 ....6.42, 6.52

    20 ....6.42, 6.52

    60 ....13.09

    82 ....6.10

    83 ....7.33

Sale of Goods and Supply of Services Act 1980 ....5.24, 13.07, 13.156

Sea Pollution Act 1991 ....17.89

Sea-Fisheries and Maritime Jurisdiction Act 2006

  s 39 ....3.127

    103 ....3.127

Second Amendment of the Constitution Act 1941 ....15.83

Select Committee on Legislation and Security of Dáil Éireann (Privilege
  and Immunity) Act 1994 ....4.96

Settled Land Act 1882

  s 63(1) 14.05

Sex Offenders Act 2001

  s 21 ....4.26

    Pt 6 ....6.120

Sexual Offences (Jurisdiction) Act 1996 ....13.36

Sixth Amendment of the Constitution Act 1979 ....4.19

Sligo Lighting and Electric Power Act 1924 ....13.41

Social Welfare Act 1952

  s 75 ....13.127–13.129

Social Welfare Act 1979

  s 7 ....13.129

Social Welfare (Consolidation) Act 1981 ....13.102

Social Welfare Act 1984 ....16.204

Social Welfare (Consolidation) Act 1993 ....13.102

Social Welfare Consolidation Act 2005 ....8.68, 13.102

Solicitors Act 1954 ....3.52, 3.58

  s 14 ....5.89

    26 ....3.53

    40 ....3.55, 3.143

    41 ....3.54

    50 ....3.63, 3.155

    71 ....3.75–3.76

Solicitors Act 1954 (contd)
73 .... 3.58
Pt IV 3.148
Solicitors (Amendment) Act 1960 ....3.52, 3.58–3.61, 4.17, 13.57
s 8(1A) 3.59
Solicitors (Amendment) Act 1994 .... 3.07, 3.52, 3.58–3.64, 8.88
s 4 .... 3.52
14B 3.60
42 .... 3.53
49 .... 3.143
50 .... 3.54
68 .... 3.34, 3.76
69 .... 3.75
70 .... 3.62
71 .... 3.68
80 .... 3.149
Solicitors (Amendment) Act 2002 .... 3.52
s 4 .... 3.75–3.76
20 .... 3.151
St Andrews Agreement 2004 .... 5.121
Stamp Duties Consolidation Act 1999 .... 13.102
Standards in Public Office Act 2001
s 22 .... 4.108
Status of Children Act 1987 .... 10.18
Pt IV 5.49
Statute Law (Restatement) Act 2002 .... 13.101, 13.107
Statute Law Revision Act 1983 .... 13.100
Statute Law Revision Act 2007 .... 11.05, 13.100
Statute Law Revision Act 2009 .... 13.100
Statute Law Revision Act 2012 .... 13.100
Statute Law Revision (Pre-1922) Act 2005 .... 13.100
Statute Law Revision (Pre-Union Irish Statutes) Act 1962 .... 13.100
s 2 .... 14.177
Statute of Limitations 1957 .... 14.93
s 11 .... 9.02
(2)(b) 15.88–15.89
Statute of Limitations Acts 1957 to 2000 .... 6.09
Statute of Limitations (Amendment) Act 1991 .... 13.55
Statute of Limitations (Amendment) Act 2000 .... 13.36

Statutory Instruments Act 1947 ....13.117
  s 1(1) 13.114
    2(1)(b) 13.117
Succession Act 1965 .... 11.09, 13.82, 13.103
  s 2...13.75
   90 ....13.83, 14.163
   124 ....13.83
Supreme Court Act 1981 ....2.112
Taxes Consolidation Act 1997 ....3.159, 8.67, 11.03, 13.102, 13.106, 15.75
  s 933 ....8.67
   941 ....8.67
   942 ....8.67
Thirty-Third Amendment of the Constitution (Court of Appeal) Act 2013 .....4.34–4.35
.... 4.43, 4.60, 4.77, 4.118, 7.01–7.02, 7.18, 7.26, 15.48
  s 2(2) 2.90
   5(2)(g) 12.106
Towns Improvement (Ireland) Act 1854
  s 1 ....14.34
Trade Marks Act 1996 ....8.56
  s 79(3) 8.57
Trade Union Act 1975
  s 2–4 ....14.86
Transfer of Sentenced Prisoners Act 1997 ....17.13, 17.29
Transport Act 1936 ....8.74
Treason Act 1939
  s 2–3 ....5.106
Tribunals of Inquiry Acts 1921–2004 ....8.81, 13.56
Tribunals of Inquiry (Evidence) Acts 1921 and 1979 ....4.15
Tribunals of Inquiry (Evidence) Acts 1921–2004 ....8.74, 8.79
Trinity College, Dublin (Charters and Letters Patent Amendment)
  Act 2000 ....13.41
Twenty-Eighth Amendment of the Constitution (Treaty of Lisbon)
  Act 2009 ....16.59
Twenty-Second Amendment of the Constitution Act 2001 ....9.18
Twenty-Third Amendment of the Constitution Act 2001 ....17.49
Twenty-Fourth Amendment to the Constitution Act 2001 ....6.82
Údarás na Gaeltachta (Amendment) Act 1999 ....13.66
Údarás na Gaeltachta (Amendment) (No 2) Act 1999 ....13.66

Unfair Dismissals Act 1977 .... 17.80

Unfair Dismissals Acts 1977 to 2007 .... 8.53

Valuation Act 1988 .... 8.65

Valuation Act 2001 .... 8.65

   s 39 .... 8.65

Value Added Tax Act 1972 .... 14.159

Value-Added Tax Consolidation Act 2010 .... 13.102

Worker Protection (Part-Time Employees) Act 1991

   s 8 .... 14.156

Ireland Pre-1922

Acquisition of Land (Assessment of Compensation) Act 1919 .... 8.25

Act of Settlement 1701 .... 4.118

Anglo-Irish Treaty 1921 .... 2.56, 2.72, 2.103, 4.162

Annual Revision of Rateable Property (Ireland) Amendment Act 1860

   s 7 .... 14.71

Ballot Act 1872 .... 14.175

Bankers' Books Evidence Act 1879 .... 14.116

Bill of Rights 1689 (1 Will III & Mary II, sess 2, c 2) 2.26

Children Act 1908

   s 23 .... 14.153

   37 .... 13.12

Conspiracy and Protection of Property Act 1875

   s 7 .... 5.115

Coroners (Ireland) Act 1846 .... 8.70

Criminal Law (Ireland) Act 1828 .... 13.71

Criminal Law (Sexual Offences) Act 2006

   s 2–3 .... 15.110

Crown Cases Act 1848 .... 7.38

Excise Management Act 1827

   s 27 .... 14.130

Forfeiture Act 1870 .... 6.82

Government of Ireland Act 1914 .... 2.44–2.46, 2.58

Government of Ireland Act 1920 .... 2.46, 2.55–2.57, 2.98–2.98, 2.103–2.108, 15.05

Grand Jury (Ireland) Act 1836

   s 135 .... 14.159

Irish Appeals Act 1783 .... 2.20

Irish Land Act 1903 ....2.43

Irish Land Act 1909 ....2.43

Land Law (Ireland) Act 1881 ....2.43

Land Law (Ireland) Act 1896 ....2.43

Larceny Act 1916 ....14.135

    s 23 ....13.89

     33 ....14.135

Local Government (Ireland) Act 1898

    s 16 ....13.113

Lunacy Regulation (Ireland) Act 1871 ....5.80

Malicious Damage Act 1861 ....5.115

Malicious Injuries (Ireland) Act 1853

    s 1 ....14.159

Merchant Shipping Act 1894 ....8.74

    s 638 ....14.99

Municipal Corporations Act 1840

    s 125–127 ....13.113

Oaths Act 1888 ....6.123

Offences Against the Person Act 1861

    s 38 ....5.97

     47 .... 6.82, 14.143–14.148

     50 ....15.180

     58 ....15.174, 15.180

     59 ....15.174

     60 .... 13.94, 15.110, 15.172–15.173, 17.66–17.67

     61 .... 15.110, 15.172–15.173, 17.66–17.67

Petty Sessions (Ireland) Act 1851 .... 2.53, 5.01, 6.92, 16.125

    s 10 .... 4.18, 6.10, 16.123

      (4) 6.10, 16.130

     29 ....12.34

Prevention of Crimes Act 1871

    s 15 ....15.63

Probation of Offenders Act 1907 ....10.34–10.37

    s 1 ....10.35

Punishment of Incest Act 1908

    s 5 ....4.28

Purchase of Land (Ireland) Act 1885 ....2.43

Purchase of Land (Ireland) Act 1891 ....2.43

Roman Catholic Relief Act 1793 .... 2.20, 2.95

Roman Catholic Relief Act 1829 .... 2.42

Solicitors (Ireland) Act 1898 .... 3.52

Summary Jurisdiction Act 1857 .... 2.53, 4.05, 5.01

  s 2 .... 7.14–7.17, 7.34–7.35

  4 .... 7.34

Supreme Court of Judicature (Ireland) Act 1877 .... 2.30–2.31, 2.47, 2.54

.... 2.112, 4.05, 5.01

  s 27 .... 5.77

Telegraph Act 1863 .... 14.97–14.99

Universities Act 1908 .... 14.117

Vagrancy Act 1824

  s 4 .... 15.62–15.67, 15.91

Valuation (Ireland) Act 1852 .... 15.101

United Kingdom

Access to Justice Act 1999 .... 3.40, 3.71, 3.156, 9.31–9.32, 9.50, 9.63

Act of Union 1800 .... 2.20, 2.26, 2.44, 3.147

  art 1 .... 2.20

  art 8 .... 2.20

Administration of Justice Act 1985 .... 3.156

Building Societies Act 1962

  s 32 .... 14.54

Civil Procedure Act 1997 .... 6.66

Contempt of Court Act 1981 .... 10.49

Courts Act 1971 .... 2.112

Courts and Legal Services Act 1990 .... 3.64, 3.72, 3.142, 3.156, 4.81

Criminal Appeal Act 1968 .... 7.51

Criminal Appeal Act 1995 .... 7.51

Criminal Defence Service Act 2006 .... 9.31

Criminal Justice Act 2003 .... 7.59–7.60

Crown Proceedings Act 1947 .... 15.39–15.41

Crown Proceedings (Armed Forces) Act 1987 .... 15.41

European Communities Act 1972 .... 13.96

Human Rights Act 1998 .... 1.16, 2.10, 15.156, 15.202, 15.205, 15.207

Judicature (Northern Ireland) Act 1978 .... 2.112

Justice Act (Northern Ireland) 2011 .... 3.71, 11.11

Law Commissions Act 1965 ....11.11

Legal Aid, Sentencing and Punishment of Offenders Act 2012 ....9.31, 9.63

Legal Services Act 2007 .... 3.38–3.41, 3.65, 3.68

Northern Ireland Act 1998 ....2.98

Northern Ireland Constitution Act 1973 ....2.98

Northern Ireland (Miscellaneous Provisions) Act 2006 ....2.98

Poyning's Act 1494 ....2.13, 2.20

Rape Act 1976 ....14.183

Safety at Work Act 1974 ....2.98

Second Statute of Westminster of 1285 ....2.50

Sexual Offences Act 1967 ....15.173

Suicide Act 1961 ....15.194

Supreme Court of Judicature Act 1873 .... 2.30–2.31, 2.112

Yelverton's Act 1781 ....2.19

Table of Statutory Instruments

Ireland

Aliens Order 1946 (SR&O 395/1946) 13.131

Circuit Court (Fees) Order 2008 (SI 201/2008) 9.66

Circuit Court Rules 2001 (SI 510/2001) 4.05, 6.01, 6.26, 6.61

    Ord 3 r 2 ....4.75

Circuit Court Rules (Mode of Address of Judges) 2006 (SI 274/2006) 4.75

Civil Legal Aid Regulations 1996 (SI 273/1996) 9.50–9.51

Civil Legal Aid Regulations 2002 (SI 8/2002) 9.50

Civil Legal Aid Regulations 2006 (SI 460/2006) 9.50

Civil Legal Aid Regulations 2013 (346/2013) 9.50

Civil Liability and Courts Act 2004 (Bodies Prescribed under Section 40)
    Order 2005 (SI 170/2005) 4.27

Civil Liability and Courts Act 2004 (Matters Prescribed under Section 40)
    Order 2005 (SI 339/2005) 4.27

Companies (Miscellaneous Provisions) Act 2013 (Section 2) (Commencement)
    Order 2014 (SI 285/2014)..5.67

Courts Acts 1981 (Interest on Judgment Debts) Order 1989 (SI 12/1989) 10.08

Courts and Civil Law (Miscellaneous Provisions) Act 2013 (Jurisdiction
    of District Court and Circuit Court) (Commencement) Order 2013
    (SI 566/2013) 5.03, 5.33

Courts (No 2) Act 1986 (Commencement) Order 1988 (SI 176/1988) 5.48

Courts (No 2) Act 1986 (Commencement) Order 1997 (SI 106/1997) 10.22

Courts Service Act 1998 (Second Schedule) (Amendment) Order 2004
    (SI 35/2004) 9.66

Courts (Supplemental Provisions) Act 1961 s 46) Order 1975 ....4.182

Courts (Supplemental Provisions) Act 1961 (Increase of Judicial Remuneration)
    Order 2001 (SI 44/2001) 4.182

Courts (Supplemental Provisions) Act 1961 (Section 46) Order 1989
    (SI 204/1989) 4.182

Courts (Supplemental Provisions) Act 1961 (Section 46) Order 1994
    (SI 273/1994) 4.182

Courts (Supplemental Provisions) Act 1961 (Section 46) Order 1998
(SI 73/1998) 4.182

Courts (Supplemental Provisions) Act 1961 (Increase of Judicial Remuneration)
Order 2007 (SI 841/2007) 4.182

Criminal Justice Act 1984 (Treatment of Persons in Custody in Garda
Síochána Stations) Regulations 1987 (SI 119/1987) 6.95

Criminal Justice (Legal Aid) (Tax Clearance Certificate) Regulations
1999 (SI 135/1999) 14.20

District Court (Civil Procedure) Rules 2014 (SI 17/2014) 6.62

District Court (Fees) Order 2008 (SI 202/2008) 9.66

District Court Rules 1948 (SR&O 431/1947), r 16 .... 4.203

District Court Rules 1997 (SI 93/1997) 4.05, 4.203, 5.47, 6.01, 6.26, 6.62, 13.68

    Ord 4 .... 4.76

    Ord A 5.51

District Court (Small Claims Procedure) Rules 1993 (SI 356/1993) 5.51

District Court (Small Claims Procedure) Rules 1991 (SI 310/1991) 5.51

District Court (Small Claims Rules) 2009 (SI 519/2009) 5.51

Emergency Powers (Scrap Lead) (Maximum Prices) Order 1945
(SR & O 212/1945)

    reg 3 .... 14.41

European Communities (Companies) Regulations 1973
(SI 163/1973) 16.119, 16.216

European Communities (Freedom to Provide Services) (Lawyers)
Regulations 1979 (SI 58/1979) 3.150

European Communities (Milk Levy) Regulations 1985 (SI 416/1985) 14.57

European Communities (Control of Oestrogenic, Androgenic, Gestagenic
and Thyrostatic Substances) Regulations 1988 (SI 218/1988) 16.121–16.129

European Communities (Control of Veterinary Medicinal Products
and their Residues) Regulations 1990 (SI 171/1990) 16.121

European Communities (General System for the Recognition of Higher
Education Diplomas) Regulations 1991 (SI 1/1991) 3.149

European Communities (Companies Group Accounts) Regulations 1992
(SI 201/1992) 16.216

European Communities (Rules on Competition) Regulations 1993
(SI 124/1993) 16.123

European Communities (Prohibition of Trade with the Federal Republic of
Yugoslavia (Serbia and Montenegro)) Regulations 1993
(SI 144/1993).. 14.59

European Communities (Accounts) Regulations 1993 (SI 396/1993) 16.216

European Communities (Unfair Terms in Consumer Contracts)
Regulations 1995 (SI 27/1995) 5.24, 13.07, 13.156

European Communities (Second General System for the Recognition of
Professional Education and Training) Regulations 1996 (SI 135/1996) 3.149

European Communities (Unfair Terms in Consumer Contracts)
(Amendment) Regulations 2000 (SI 307/2000) 13.07

European Communities (Lawyers Establishment) Regulations 2003
(SI 732/2003) 3.151

European Communities (Lawyers' Establishment) (Amendment)
Regulations 2004 (SI 752/2004) 3.151

European Communities (Award of Public Authorities' Contracts)
Regulations 2006 (SI 329/2006) 8.62

European Communities (Lawyers Establishment) (Amendment)
Regulations 2008 (SI 96/2008) 3.151

European Communities (Unfair Terms in Consumer Contracts)
(Amendment) Regulations 2013 (SI 160/2013) 13.07

Garda Síochána (Discipline) Regulations 1989 (SI 94/1989) 8.61

Health and Safety at Work (Northern Ireland) Order 1978 (SI 1039/1978) 2.98

Health Services Regulations 1971 (SI 105/1971)
reg 6 ....13.141

Industrial Relations Act 1990 (Code of Practice on Grievance and
Disciplinary Procedures) (Declaration) Order 2000 (SI 146/2000) 13.09

Local Government (Planning and Development) Regulations 1977 (SI 65/1977)
reg 36 ....14.151

Misuse of Drugs Act 1977 (Commencement) Order 1979 (SI 28/1979) 13.75

Recognition of Professional Qualifications Directive 2005/36/EC
Regulations 2008 (SI 139/2008)..3.149

Rules of the Circuit Court 1950 (SI 179/1950)
Ord 2 ....4.203
Ord 3 r 2 ....4.75
Ord 58 r 1 ....14.118

Rules of the Superior Courts 1986 (SI 15/1986) 4.05, 4.53, 6.01, 6.26
....6.35–6.42, 6.48, 6.57, 13.114
Ord 1A 6.31
Ord 4A r 3A 6.34, 6.41
Ord 27 ....6.57
Ord 31 r 29 ....6.59
Ord 49 r 1 ....4.62
Ord 63A 4.62, 5.78, 6.78
r 6(1)(b) 5.78, 6.78

Rules of the Superior Courts 1986 (SI 15/1986) (contd)
      r 14(7) 5.78, 6.79
      r 15(e) 5.78, 6.79
    Ord 118 .... 4.203
    Ord 119 r 1 .... 4.73
        r 2 .... 3.114
    App A 6.36
Rules of the Superior Courts (Commercial Proceedings) 2004 (SI 4/2004) 4.62
Rules of the Superior Courts (Commercial Proceedings) 2004
    (SI 2/2004) 6.78
Rules of the Superior Courts (Mode of Address of Judges) 2006
    (SI 196/2006) 4.73
Rules of the Superior Courts (No 4) (Chief Prosecution Solicitor) 2001
    (SI 535/2001) 3.128, 6.88
Rules of the Superior Courts (No 6) (Disclosure of Reports
    and Statements) 1998 (SI 391/1998) 6.59
Rules of the Superior Courts (Order 27) (Amendment) Rules) 2004
    (SI 63/2004) 6.57
Rules of the Superior Courts (Personal Injuries) 2005 (SI 248/2005) 6.31
Rules of the Superior Courts (Personal Injuries Assessment Board Act 2003)
    2004 (SI 517/2004) 6.34, 6.41
Rules of the Superior Courts (Robes of Bench) 2011 (SI No 524/2011) 3.114
Safety in Industry (Abrasive Wheels) Regulations 1982 (SI 30/1992) 6.42, 6.52
Safety, Health and Welfare at Work (General Application) Regulations
    2007 (SI 299/2007) 6.42, 6.52
Safety, Health and Welfare at Work (Signs) Regulations 1995
    (SI 132/1995) 13.114
Sea-Fisheries (Prosecution of Offences) Order 2009 (SI 314/2009) 3.127
Social Welfare (Overlapping Benefits) (Amendment) Regulations 1979
    (SI 118/1979)
    reg 4 .... 13.129
Social Welfare (Overlapping Benefits) Regulations 1953 (SI 14/1953)
    art 38 .... 13.129
Solicitors Acts 1954 and 1960 (Apprenticeship and Education) Regulations 1991
    (SI9/1991)
    reg 15 .... 3.55–3.55
      30 .... 3.56
Solicitors Acts 1954 and 1960 (Apprenticeship and Education)
    (Amendment) (No 2) Regulations 1992 (SI 360/1992) 3.55
Solicitors (Advertising) Regulations 2002 (SI 518/2002) 3.75–3.76, 3.88

Solicitors (Continuing Professional Development) Regulations 2007
(SI 807/2007) 3.145
State (Scheduled Offences) Order 1972 (SI 282/1972) 5.115
Succession Act 1965 (Commencement) Order 1966 (SI 168/1966) 13.75
Supreme Court and High Court (Fees) Order 2008 (SI 200/2008) 9.66

United Kingdom

Civil Procedure Rules 1998 (SI 1998/3132) 6.66, 6.70, 6.76, 8.15
  44(5)(3) 8.15
  r 1.4 ....8.15
Civil Proceedings Fees Order 2008 (SI 1053/2008) 9.69

Table of Constitutional Articles

Constitution 1922

Article
6 .... 2.63, 2.68
7 .... 2.63
8 .... 2.63
9 .... 2.63
50 .... 15.81
62 .... 2.76, 2.82
63 .... 2.82
64 .... 4.30
70 .... 2.63
72 .... 2.70
73 .... 2.64, 2.87, 2.91, 2.105, 12.36, 13.93, 15.46
64–73 .... 4.02
2A 2.67–2.70, 15.82

Bunreacht na hÉireann 1937

Article
2 .... 2.78, 15.02–15.06, 15.12–15.19, 15.35, 15.108, 15.149, 15.196
3 .... 2.78, 15.05–15.12, 15.21–15.35, 15.108, 15.149, 15.196
3.1 .... 15.22–15.26
3.2 .... 15.26
4 .... 15.30–15.33
5 .... 15.35, 16.109
6 .... 4.10, 4.35, 16.98
6.1 .... 15.35
8.1 .... 2.92
8.2 .... 2.92
9.2.1° 15.19
9.2.2° 15.19
12 .... 2.80, 4.53, 4.54
12.1 .... 2.80
12.10 .... 4.138
12.3.1° 5.83
13.4 .... 2.80
13.5 .... 2.80
13.9 .... 2.80, 4.77
14 .... 2.66
15 .... 13.122, 16.124
15.2 .... 1.15, 13.128, 13.132, 15.195, 16.98–16.103, 17.64

Bunreacht na hÉireann (contd)

15.4 .... 2.87, 15.45
15.5 .... 1.59, 14.110, 14.114, 15.51
15.6 .... 14.85
15.8 .... 15.51
15.10 .... 13.28
15.2.1° 1.15, 2.86, 12.142, 13.01, 13.109, 13.121, 13.130, 13.135, 15.45
16.2 .... 15.99
16.1.2° 15.51
16.1.4° 15.51, 15.99
16.2.3° 15.51
21 .... 13.21
22.1.1° 13.21
23 .... 13.20, 13.26–13.27
23.1.1° 13.20
24 .... 5.84, 13.22
24.1 .... 13.22
24.2 .... 15.83
25.3 .... 13.24
25.4 .... 15.83
25.2.1° 13.24
25.2.2° 13.24
25.4.1° 13.74
25.4.2° 13.24
25.4.3° 2.93
25.4.4° 13.66
25.4.5° 13.24
25.5.1° 2.93
25.5.2° 2.93
25.5.4° 2.94
26 .... 2.80, 4.49–4.53, 4.54, 5.84, 12.35, 12.46
.... 12.106, 13.25, 15.48, 15.69, 15.91, 15.100
26.1.3° 5.86
26.2.1° 5.85
26.2.2° 5.88
27 .... 13.26–13.27
28 .... 16.100
28.8 .... 13.28
28.12 .... 8.32
28.3.3° 15.82–15.83, 15.100
29 .... 15.10, 15.23, 15.29, 16.01, 16.99–16.104
.... 17.12, 17.49, 17.64, 17.79
29.1 .... 17.11
29.3 .... 1.20, 16.101, 17.11, 17.77–17.81
29.4 .... 16.101, 16.111, 16.114, 16.124, 17.13

Bunreacht na hÉireann (contd)

29.6 .... 1.20, 14.94, 16.102, 17.63, 17.76
29.8 ....15.29
29.4.10° 13.123
29.4.1° 15.31, 16.99, 17.12
29.4.2° 15.32, 16.100
29.4.3° 16.104–16.106, 16.152
29.4.5° 16.124–16.126, 16.134
29.4.6° 16.112–16.126, 16.134, 16.209
29.4.3° 1.17
29.7.2° 15.27
30 .... 2.81, 3.116–3.122
30.3 ....3.125
31 ....2.80
32A 7.18
33 ....2.82
34 .... 2.87–2.90, 4.36, 4.53, 4.61, 4.65, 4.68, 4.77
.... 4.187, 7.02, 7.27, 7.41, 7.57, 7.65, 7.71, 7.76
....................................8.27, 8.50, 8.58, 8.70, 8.79, 12.71, 15.28
.... 15.46, 15.98, 15.197, 16.98
34 –38 .... 4.03–4.06, 4.33
34–37 ....4.06
34.1 ....4.08–4.12, 4.17–4.23, 4.28, 4.46–4.47, 4.118, 9.02, 12.48, 15.51
34.2 .... 4.02, 4.34–4.36, 7.01, 7.26
34.3 ....4.35
34.4 ....2.89, 4.35, 7.02, 7.26–7.28, 12.36
34.5 .... 4.100, 4.116, 7.28
34.6 .... 4.36, 7.02, 7.26
34.3.1° 4.35, 5.68, 5.105, 7.13, 7.33, 15.144, 15.147
34.3.2° 2.88, 4.35, 5.57–5.59, 5.74, 15.48
34.3.3° 4.35, 5.88, 13.25
34.3.4° 4.40, 5.46, 5.54, 7.02, 7.13, 7.33, 7.41, 12.116–12.118
34.4.1° 5.72, 7.25
34.4.3° 7.17, 7.35, 7.58, 12.117–12.118, 15.49, 15.130–15.131
34.4.5° 12.106, 15.130
34.5.1° 4.116, 4.121
34.5.3° 12.117
34.3.3° 12.35
34A 4.34, 4.60, 7.18
35 .... 4.138–4.141, 4.149
35.1 ....4.77
35.2 .... 4.116, 4.184–4.185
35.3 ....4.116
35.4 .... 4.118–4.119, 4.152
35.5 .... 4.163, 4.174–4.183, 4.190

Bunreacht na hÉireann (contd)

35.4.1° 4.118
35.4.1° 4.150–4.151
36 .... 4.43, 4.52, 8.32
36.iii 4.78
37 .... 4.11, 4.197, 11.28, 15.145
37.1 .... 4.09–4.19, 4.23, 4.45
37.2 .... 4.19
38 .... 4.45, 6.81, 13.129, 15.131
39 .... 5.106
38.1 .... 4.188, 7.33, 10.52, 12.116–12.118, 15.51, 15.65, 15.97
38.2 .... 5.04, 5.90, 5.110
38.3 .... 5.109–5.112
38.4 .... 5.110, 5.119
38.5 .... 5.04, 5.100–5.104, 5.109, 6.143, 12.117, 12.130, 15.51
38.3.2° 5.112
38.4.1° 5.110
38.4.2° 5.110
39 .... 14.85
40 .... 15.134
43 .... 15.51
44 .... 15.51
40.1 .... 13.125, 15.51, 15.65–15.68, 15.98, 15.139, 15.157, 17.71
40.2 .... 15.51
40.3 .... 4.216, 6.04, 15.53–15.56, 15.59, 15.89, 15.99
.... 15.109, 15.117, 15.134, 15.157, 15.165–15.172
.... 15.183, 15.197, 15.202, 16.94
40.4 .... 6.107, 15.51, 15.65, 15.97
40.5 .... 15.51
40.6 .... 15.51
40.3.1° 15.60, 15.134, 15.182, 15.191
40.3.2° 15.134, 15.187, 15.194
40.3.3° 4.164, 15.111, 15.141, 15.165, 15.174–15.178
40.4.2° 9.02, 9.06, 9.08, 9.33, 10.54, 15.83, 17.64
40.4.4° 4.62
40.6.1° 15.62
40.6.1°(i) 15.200
40.6.1°(iii) 1.31, 14.86
41 .... 2.78, 14.87, 15.03, 15.51, 15.74, 15.101
.... 15.113, 15.149–15.151, 15.164–15.169, 15.196
41.1 .... 15.152
41.2 .... 15.150
41.3 .... 15.150
41.3.1° 15.150–15.151
41.3.2° 15.149–15.150

Bunreacht na hÉireann (contd)

42 ....15.51
42.1 ....14.86
42.4 ....15.106, 15.140
42A 15.51
43 .... 2.63, 15.101, 15.164
44 ....2.78
46 .... 2.85, 15.182–15.183
46.2 ....13.24
46.5 ....13.24
50 ....2.65, 2.72, 2.91, 12.36, 12.76, 15.71
50.1 ....2.87, 15.46
51 ....15.81
58 ....4.49
59 ....17.05
64.3.1° 4.60, 7.01, 7.18

Table of European Legislation

Treaties and Conventions

Anglo-Irish Agreement 1985 ....15.09, 15.16, 15.108
  1 .... 15.04, 15.09, 15.16
EAEC or Euratom Treaty 16.15
EC Treaty 16.02, 16.31–16.40, 16.156
  2 .... 16.20–16.23, 16.43, 16.49
  3 ....16.23–16.25
  3b 16.26
  7 ....16.21, 16.75
  7a 16.22
  11 ....16.51
  12 ....16.87, 16.185
  13 ....16.49
  141 (ex 119) 14.61–14.62, 16.223
  177 ....16.83, 16.204
  189 ....16.125
  234 (ex 177) 7.74, 9.56
  Preamble 16.18
European Coal and Steel Community Treaty 1951 ....16.15
European Convention on Extradition 14.165
German–Turkish Extradition Treaty of 1930 ....14.165
Good Friday Agreement 1998 ....5.121, 15.05, 15.11, 15.12, 15.29, 15.196, 15.202
Merger Treaty 16.39
Single European Act 1986 .... 15.92, 15.104, 16.01, 16.22
....16.41, 16.45, 16.68, 16.105, 16.152, 16.159, 16.178
Treaty Establishing a Constitution for Europe 16.58
Treaty Establishing the European Economic Community 16.02
Treaty of Amsterdam 16.27, 16.47–16.56, 16.161
Treaty of Lisbon 15.84, 16.29, 16.55–16.61, 16.111, 16.135
Treaty of Maastricht.. 16.02, 16.44–16.48, 16.60, 16.71
Treaty of Nice 2001 .... 16.53–16.53, 16.111, 16.161
Treaty on European Union 1992 ....16.02, 16.28
  6 ....16.48
    (1) 16.78
    (2) 16.80
  7 ....16.73
  13 ....16.73, 16.136

Treaty on European Union 1992 (contd)

14	16.155
(1)	16.154
15(1)	16.153
16	16.146
18(1)	16.139
(2)	16.139
(4)	16.142
(7)	16.142
19	16.164, 16.176
(1)	16.81
(2)	16.173
20	16.61, 16.111
49	16.48
275	16.116
K.3	3.153
Title VII	16.51

Treaty on the Functioning of the European Union 3.55, 9.56, 16.02
.... 16.60, 16.165, 16.173, 16.214

1	16.48
5(3)	16.29
6	16.48, 16.72
7	16.48
12	16.86
29	16.20
30	16.86, 16.185
48	16.151
82–89	16.60
101	16.221
102	16.221
157	14.61, 16.186, 16.223
238(1)	16.149
252	16.176
253	16.174
256	16.178–16.181
257	16.181
258	16.139, 16.166, 16.172, 16.199
259	16.166
260	16.166
263	16.167, 16.178
264	16.168
265	16.83, 16.117, 16.168–16.170, 16.178, 16.204
267	7.74–7.80, 16.170, 16.179
(3)	7.78

Treaty on the Functioning of the European Union (contd)

268 ....16.178
275 ....16.116
281 ....16.173
285 ....16.182
287 ....16.183
288 ....16.125, 16.188–16.195, 16.206–16.212, 16.215
290 ....16.189
300 ....16.144
340 ....16.178
375 ....16.116
328–334 ....16.61
Prot No 21 ....9.35

Secondary Legislation

Commission Decision 94/118/EC 16.206
Council Directive 76/207 ....16.65
Council Directive 77/249/EEC 3.150
Council Directive 79/7/EEC 16.204
Council Directive 80/987/EEC 16.200
Council Directive 85/358/ EEC 16.129
Council Directive 87/102/EEC 13.157
Council Directive 89/48/EEC 3.149
Council Directive 90/80/EEC 13.157
Council Directive 92/51/EEC 3.149
Council Directive 92/241/EEC 16.208
Council Directive 93/13/EEC 13.156
Council Directive 94/38/EC 3.149
Council Directive 95/43/EC 3.149
Council Directive 98/5/EC 3.151
Council Directive 2004/80/EC 8.48
Council Directive 2008/52/EC 8.06, 8.14
Council Directive 2012/29/EU 6.192, 6.121–6.122, 9.35
    art 4 ....6.121–6.122
    art 10 ....6.121
Council Directive 2012/29/EU 6.102
Council Directive 2013/48/EU 9.35
Council Regulation 17/62 ....16.210
Council Regulation 1371/84/EEC
    art 5 ....14.57

Council Regulation 4064/89/EEC 16.210

Council Regulation 990/93/EEC 14.59

Council Regulation 44/2001/EC (Brussels I Regulation) 10.26, 17.86

Council Regulation 2201/2003/EC (Brussels II Regulation) 10.26, 17.86

Table of International Treaties and Conventions

African Charter on Human and Peoples' Rights 1981 ....17.22

Agreement on Trade-Related Aspects of Intellectual Property Rights (TRIPS) 17.55

Agreement on Trade-Related Investment Measures (TRIMS) 17.55

American Convention on Human Rights 1969 ....17.22

Bretton Woods Agreement 1944 ....17.51

Brussels Conventions of 1968 and 1982 ....17.86

Charter of Fundamental Rights 16.57, 16.79

Convention establishing the International Criminal Court 1998 ....17.49

Convention for the Protection of Human Rights and Fundamental
    Freedoms 1950 ....1.16, 1.20, 4.184, 6.11, 6.102, 9.41
    ....12.84, 12.86, 14.92, 15.01, 15.103, 15.107
    ....15.156, 15.197, 15.202, 15.206–15.207, 16.11
    ....16.48, 16.71, 16.80, 17.07, 17.20–17.22, 17.27, 17.44, 17.64, 17.75
    art 2 ....17.21
       3 .... 17.21, 17.23, 17.73
      (8) 9.70
       4 ....17.21
       5 ....17.21, 17.64
       6 ....4.30, 4.184, 16.66, 17.21, 17.64
      (1) 9.41, 14.93–14.94
       7 ....17.21
       8 ....15.107, 15.194, 16.68, 17.21, 17.67, 17.72
       9 ....17.21
      10 .... 4.31, 15.200, 17.21
      11 ....17.21
      12 ....17.21
      13 .... 15.205, 16.66, 17.21
      14 ....17.21
    Prot 1 ....17.21
    Prot 4 ....17.21
    Prot 6 ....17.21
    Prot 7 ....17.21
    Prot 11 ....17.25
    Prot 14 ....17.25

Convention for the Protection of Individuals With Regard to the Automatic
    Processing of Data 1982 ....17.29

Convention on Access to Information, Public Participation in
Decision-Making and Access to Justice in Environmental
Matters 1998 .... 9.74–9.76
art 9 .... 9.74
Convention on Cybercrime 2001 .... 17.29
Convention on Protection of Children and Inter-Country Adoption
(The Hague, 1993) 17.88
Convention on the Elimination of All Forms of Discrimination 17.44
Convention on the Elimination of Discrimination against Women 17.44
Convention on the Law of the Sea 1982 .... 17.42
Convention on the Rights of Persons with Disabilities 17.44
Convention on the Rights of the Child 17.44
Convention on the Transfer of Prisoners (1983)
art 18.2 .... 17.13
18.3 .... 17.13
Convention on the Transfer of Sentenced Prisoners 1983 .... 17.13, 17.29
European Convention on Extradition 13.56
European Convention on the Suppression of Terrorism 1977 .... 17.29
General Agreement on Tariffs and Trade (1947) 17.07
Geneva Convention on the Status of Refugees 17.47
Genocide Convention 1948 .... 17.48
Hague (V) Convention on the Rights and Duties of Neutral Powers 1907 .... 17.79
International Convention for the Prevention of Pollution
from Ships (MARPOL) 1973 .... 17.89
International Covenant on Civil and Political Rights 1966 .... 17.44, 17.75
art 26 .... 17.76
International Covenant on Economic, Social and Cultural Rights 1966 .... 17.44
Oslo Convention banning cluster munitions 17.43
Ottawa Convention prohibiting the use of land mines 17.43
Protection of Children (Hague Convention) Act 2000 .... 17.88
Refugee Convention 1951 .... 17.63
Rome Convention on the Law Applicable to Contractual Obligations 17.86
Statute of the International Court of Justice
art 38(1) 17.05
UN Convention against Torture 17.48
UN Convention on the Rights of Persons With Disabilities 2006 .... 5.80, 9.09
UN Convention on the Rights of the Child 17.75

United Nations Charter (1946) 17.30

  1 ....17.30

  2 ....17.31–17.31

United Nations Convention against Torture 17.44

United Nations Genocide Convention 13.56

United Nations International Covenant on Civil and Political Rights (1966) 15.197

United Nations Model Law on International Commercial Arbitration 1985

  8 ....8.22

  18–27 ....8.23

  28–33 ....8.23

United Nations Model Law on International Arbitration 1985 ....17.87

Universal Declaration of Human Rights 17.44

Universal Declaration of Human Rights (1948)

  19 ....4.30

Vienna Convention on Contracts for the International Sale of Goods (1980) 17.87

Chapter 1

Introduction to the Irish Legal System

[1]   Introduction 1
[2]   Law and Laws 3
[3]   The Irish Legal System as a Common Law System 4
[4]   Sources of Law 5
[5]   Divisions of the Law 10
[6]   Legal Personality 13
[7]   A Jurisprudential Overview 15
[8]   Law and Morality 20
[9]   The Rule of Law 25

[1]   INTRODUCTION

[1.01] Popular perceptions of the law are derived from a variety of sources. From childhood thoughts which often view law in terms of policing (with the police being referred to as 'the law') to a diverse range of cultural sources, which include literature, cinema and television, certain images of the law and lawyers are conveyed. While these images might be distorted and do not conform to reality as understood by lawyers they do contain grains of truth. Cumulatively, they point to the law as involving a process which is authoritative in the sense that it is both normative and possesses mechanisms of enforcement. The cardinal characteristics of law are succinctly summarised by Raz:

> "The three most general and important features of the law are that it is normative, institu-
> tionalized, and coercive. It is normative in that it serves, and is meant to serve, as a guide for
> human behaviour. It is institutionalized in that its application and modification are to a large
> extent performed or regulated by institutions. And it is coercive in that obedience to it, and
> its application, are internally guaranteed, ultimately, by the use of force."[1]

[1.02] Later chapters will deal with the history of the Irish legal system, its institutions and the sources of law in which particular legal rules are located. At this stage it is sufficient to observe that those rules are found in various sources of law which are the product of different legal institutions such as the courts and the legislature.

[1.03] Our study is primarily functional in that it concentrates on the relationship between legal institutions and sources of law. We concentrate on the processes of law-making and adjudicating which are central to the legal system and which are the reality

---

1   *The Concept of a Legal System* (2nd edn, 1980), p 3.

of a lawyer's professional life. However, a more abstract examination would focus on what has been called the 'ideational'[2] source of law, that is the theoretical or conceptual source of the law. Such a source is essentially meta-legal and involves the notion of some underlying belief or theory which confers validity on the legal system and the laws which it produces. This might involve belief in a deity ('the will of God'), nature, human reason, a particular political philosophy or the consent of the people. This is to enter into the domain where the study of the law interacts with political science and philosophy.

[1.04] While our focus is, in the main, institutional, the broader dimension is important in two respects. The first is that it emphasises that law does not exist in isolation from a wider community of ideas and beliefs and that law-making in one way or another draws on them. Second, and more specifically, the Constitution of Ireland, which is the source of that important body of law known as constitutional law, spans both the institutional and ideational. As an element of the legal system, the Constitution is one of its institutions yet it is drafted in terms which are comparatively vague and aspirational, leaving it for the interpreter to ascertain its meaning in the light of its underlying values. This theme will be considered in greater depth in Chapter 15 on the Constitution.

[1.05] The law is one part of a set of processes – social, political, economic and cultural – which shape and direct the development of society. Like other mechanisms, the law seeks to govern human behaviour either by prohibiting identified forms of conduct or by attaching particular consequences to specified forms of behaviour. We are all familiar with the prohibitions on unlawful killing, injuring or depriving of property which are central to the criminal law. Equally, most of us are aware of the obligation to make recompense, by means of compensation, to those who are injured by our conduct, which is the focus of the civil law. But these prohibitions and obligations are shared with other normative systems such as morality, religion or etiquette. Moreover, these other systems with their implicit threats of damnation, divine retribution or social ostracism might be more effective in ensuring that people obey their various commands. However, what is distinctive about law is that it possesses a binding or obligatory quality which is enforceable, either by means of punishment or a re-adjustment of rights and liabilities. It is this quality, which we might call the force of law, that sets it apart from the other systems.

[1.06] It is important to be aware of the wider context in which the law operates. A distorted picture would be presented were attention focused exclusively on formal or institutional features to the exclusion of the broader panorama. To this end, socio-legal and realist analyses emphasise the connection between law and the society, in the broadest sense, in which it operates and observe the manner in which the structure and contents of the legal system are shaped by external phenomena. On this view, it would fly in the face of reality to ignore or disregard the extra-legal forces that contribute to the make-up of the legal system. A similar observation might be made about political science where it may be said that the descriptive (focusing on 'reality') provides a better

---

[2]   See generally, Goodrich, *Reading the Law* (1986), pp 4–13.

explanation than the normative or the legalistic. Despite the cogency of these views, it must be acknowledged that the law conditions human behaviour, to some extent at least, and the invocation of some form of legal structure is vital to virtually all societies.[3] It follows that an understanding of the formal legalistic process is as important to the full picture as are other perspectives.

[2] LAW AND LAWS

[1.07] The English language lacks the terminology to reflect the distinction made in Latin between *ius* and *lex*, in French between *droit* and *loi* and in German between *Recht* and *Gesetz*. The term 'law' is used to mean both the general body, or system, of law and individual rules of law.[4] The distinction was summarised by one commentator thus:

> "We commonly speak of both law and laws ... and these terms, though not used with precision point to two different aspects under which legal science may be approached. The laws of a country are thought of as separate, distinct, individual rules; the law of a country, however much we may analyse it into separate rules, is something more that the mere sum of such rules. It is rather a whole, a system which orders our conduct; in which the separate rules have their place and their relation to each other and to the whole; which is never completely exhausted by any analysis, however far the analysis may be pushed, and however much the analysis may be necessary to our understanding of the whole. Thus each rule which we call *a* law is part of the whole we call *the* law. Lawyers generally speak of *law*; laymen more often of *laws*."[5]

[1.08] This quotation encapsulates the focus of this work. As explained above, our concern is with the functioning of the legal system rather than particular individual rules. Indeed to the extent that we encounter individual rules of law, it is principally to illustrate some particular feature of the legal system. It is important to realise that a complete understanding of legal rules ('the laws') is necessarily based on an understanding of the legal system ('the law').[6] The latter explains the origin of the rules, their relationship with one another and their place in the overall system. However, while the law is composed of laws, it also embraces something more: the whole is greater than the sum of its parts. The manner in which laws are created and developed and the way they are interpreted and applied are part of the law, and that is our central concern.

---

[3]   See Blondel, *Thinking Politically* (1978), pp 20–21: 'Lawyers are unquestionably over-concerned with formal institutions; the criticisms levelled against them have much justification. But it is important to see why legal studies have played a large part in political analysis: reality, though not wholly governed by formal rules, is moulded by them to a large extent. Formal rules often constrain and therefore influence behaviour.'

[4]   See also, Allott, *The Limits of Law* (1980) where 'law' is used in three senses, each of which is represented by a different typeface. There 'law' is used to mean: (i) the general concept of legal institutions, as opposed to any occurrence of them; (ii) a particular legal system; and (iii) a particular rule in a legal system.

[5]   Geldart, *Introduction to English Law* (11th edn, 1995), p 1 (emphasis in original).

[6]   See Kelsen, *General Theory of Law and State* (1961), p 3: 'it is impossible to grasp the nature of law if we limit our attention to the single isolated rule.'

[1.09] One of the principal elements of a study of a legal system concerns the sources from which rules are derived. Those which are most readily identifiable are laws which have a distinct and separate origin, in other words laws which are specifically created. These laws bear the general title *legislation*, a term which denotes their origin as enacted laws. In the main, legislation consists of Acts of the Oireachtas (sometimes called *statute law*) and *delegated*, or *secondary*, *legislation*. Legislation accounts for large sections of the law as might be expected in an era where the state assumes the principal regulatory role in society. However, other laws have not been created in this manner but have emerged from or developed out of the legal system. By and large the origin of these laws consists of judicial decisions which have been delivered over centuries and which have incrementally grown to produce an identifiable body of law which is called the *common law*. Through the practice of *precedent*, by which a court is required to follow an earlier similar decision, judicial decisions are attributed the force of law. The common law shaped and defined the principal legal categories or subjects into which laws are placed – criminal law, contract law, law of torts, property law and the like. The essential principles and concepts which underlie these areas of the law were developed by the courts as common law rules and, despite the more recent enactment of legislative rules, the common law remains a significant component of the legal system. This is reflected in the fact that the Irish legal system is called a common law system.

[3]   THE IRISH LEGAL SYSTEM AS A COMMON LAW SYSTEM

[1.10] The Irish legal system belongs to a family of legal systems known as common law systems. The original common law system was that which was established in England by the Normans after the invasion of 1066. Being the first country colonised by the Normans after England, Ireland has aptly been described as providing the common law's first adventure.[7] Indeed, much of the history of the common law in Ireland is by and large a mirror image of that which occurred in England. In time the common law was introduced into each country which was colonised by the English or British and, with some exceptions, it is the system which is found in those countries which formerly made up the British Empire.[8] Thus 49 states of the United States of America (the exception is Louisiana, which was colonised by the French), the provinces of Canada (with the exception of Quebec, which also was a French colony), Australia, New Zealand, India, Nigeria and Kenya possess common law systems. In general, common law systems are associated with the Anglophone world. The other major family of systems consists of civil law systems, which operate in continental European countries and their former colonies.

[1.11] The label 'common law', in reference to a legal system, indicates both its English origin and its central feature, which is that it possesses an identifiable body of law called the 'common law'. As noted in the preceding section, this is the body of law which grew

---

[7]   Johnston, 'The First Adventure of the Common Law' (1920) 36 LQR 9.

[8]   Scotland, South Africa and Sri Lanka resisted the wholesale incorporation of the common law and have mixed systems.

out of centuries of judicial decisions and which has established the major categories into which legal rules are placed. The growth of this body of law has been gradual and has occurred since its initial establishment in England by the Normans in the 11th century. Historically, the common law accounted for the vast bulk of the law and it remains an important source of law. Decisions reached by the courts several centuries ago still enjoy the force of law and will do so until they are altered or replaced by some other legal rule. Common law is sometimes, inaccurately, referred to as case law, which reflects its significant feature, namely that it is made by judges, not legislators. It might be noted that the incremental development of the common law was essentially pragmatic. Since it depended on cases being brought before the courts by aggrieved parties, the law responded to actual rather than anticipated problems. In contrast, the law in a civil law system is now contained in comprehensive codes which are enacted by legislators and which attempt to provide for every legal contingency. In those systems case law, in French called *la jurisprudence* and in Italian *la giurisprudenza*, has a lesser significance and lacks the force of law.

[1.12] The term 'common law' bears another meaning. It refers to a body of law which was developed in the common law courts. In this sense it may be contrasted with *equity* which is a body of law which was developed in and administered by the Court of Chancery. At its inception the common law, through a rigorous adherence to precedent, was inflexible and, in particular, was incapable of reacting to provide a remedy for individual cases of injustice. As a result, aggrieved litigants who felt that they suffered an injustice at the hands of the common law courts petitioned the King for relief. In time, as the number of petitions increased, the task of deciding these petitions was assigned to the Lord Chancellor, the King's chief minister. The Lord Chancellor, who often was a cleric and came from a canon law background, determined these petitions on the basis of their individual merits in the Court of Chancery. Unlike the common law, equity was flexible, remedial and designed to meet the needs of individual justice. Eventually equity grew into a distinct body of law and by the beginning of the 19th century it had become as rigid as the common law which it was designed to supplement. Equity now exists as a distinct body of rules which is applied in conjunction with common law rules.

[4] SOURCES OF LAW

[1.13] Sources of law describe the legal origins of rules. They are understood in an institutional sense rather than a broader political or socio-legal sense. That is not to say that the latter are unimportant or that they are not areas worthy of study in their own right. However, from a lawyer's perspective a crucial feature of a legal system is that it identifies the origins of different rules and establishes their relationships to one another. A lawyer must know where to find particular rules which apply to the problem with which he or she is presented.[9] Of equal importance, the lawyer must know where different rules fit into an overall scheme and, if conflict arises, which is to prevail. Thus

---

9   See O'Malley, *Sources of Law: Introduction to Legal Research and Writing* (2nd edn, 2001).

the legal system sets out various sources of law within a hierarchical framework, so that some sources will prevail over others in the event of conflict. In the Irish legal system we can identify four principal sources of law.

Common law

[1.14] Common law[10] originally formed the core of the laws enforced by the system. It consists of the hundreds of thousands of decisions which have been delivered by the courts over the centuries and which, by virtue of the demands of the doctrine of precedent, enjoy binding force of law. The accumulation of these decisions over time allowed the common law to grow into a coherent body of law. To this day, significant areas of the law are governed by common law rules largely unaffected by rules derived from other sources.

Legislation

[1.15] Legislation[11] consists of laws enacted by a body that is invested with law-making power. Unlike the common law, legislation is specifically created and its origin is clearly identifiable in a particular exercise of law-making. Legislation was the mechanism by which common law rules were altered. In the past this was based on the doctrine of parliamentary supremacy, but now rests on Article 15.2 of the Constitution, which designates the Oireachtas as the sole law-making body in the state.[12] Statute law (Acts of the Oireachtas) is enacted by the Oireachtas, the national parliament. Delegated legislation is enacted by bodies or individuals that are conferred with that power by statute.

The Constitution

[1.16] The Constitution[13] came into force following a referendum held in 1937. The adoption of a written Constitution containing fundamental principles and guarantees of individual rights marked a break from the British tradition. The British Constitution was essentially unwritten and flexible and, at that time, English law lacked a concept of fundamental rights which were judicially enforceable.[14] The Irish Constitution is the basic law of the state and it takes precedence over other, inferior, sources of law. Indeed, rules which derive from those latter sources depend on the Constitution for their validity. A common law or legislative rule which conflicts with a provision of the Constitution is invalid and, consequently, has no legal effect. The Constitution establishes the state and

---

10 See generally Ch 12.
11 See generally Ch 13.
12 Article 15.2.1° reads: 'The sole and exclusive power of making laws for the State is hereby vested in the Oireachtas: no other legislative authority has power to make laws for the State.'
13 See generally Ch 15.
14 The position has changed significantly in the United Kingdom with the enactment of the Human Rights Act 1998, which incorporates the European Convention of Human Rights into its domestic law and invests courts with the power to consider the compatibility of national legislation with the provisions of the Convention.

its institutions, and it articulates in broad terms the fundamental principles on which the governance of the state is based. The Constitution may be amended only by popular referendum and in this respect it is considered to be rigid. Nevertheless, its provisions are amenable to interpretation, which function is entrusted to the courts which, given the manner in which it is drafted, enjoy a considerable discretion in this regard. Once the courts have determined the interpretation of a provision, it may only be overturned either by a later judicial decision or by a referendum. In practice the latter infrequently occurs, with the result that the courts enjoy extensive power in determining the meaning of the Constitution. Since the courts, under the guise of constitutional interpretation, have considered the validity of a wide range of laws which have a bearing on social and economic matters, the significance of the judicial role extends beyond the legal domain into the political. Decisions of the courts on matters of constitutional law have affected the formulation of economic and social policy. The growth of constitutional law and the accompanying role of the courts in the governance of the state have marked a significant legal development since 1922.

European Union law

[1.17] From the perspective of international organisations, a distinctive feature of the European Union is that it possesses its own legal system complete with a body of law[15] which is applicable and enforceable in each member state. The legal system is presided over by the Court of Justice of the European Union, which sits in Luxembourg. EU law enjoys supremacy over conflicting national law (including national constitutional provisions) both as a matter of EU law and of national law. From the EU law stance, supremacy is established in the Treaties which established the European Union and which require member states to accede to supremacy. It followed that accession to the European Union entailed yielding to EU law and, to this extent, national sovereignty was curtailed. In Ireland the Constitution was amended by the insertion of a new provision, Article 29.4.3°,[16] which reflected this arrangement. The effect of this amendment was to authorise the state's membership what at that time were three separate Communities; later amendments were adopted to facilitate more recent developments.[17] Within its sphere of competence, which is set out in the various Treaties, European Union law enjoys unquestioned supremacy. In practice, this has affected, in the main, the laws governing economic and social matters, and other areas of national law largely lay

---

15 See generally, Ch 16.

16 'The State may become a member of the European Coal and Steel Community (established by Treaty signed at Paris on the 18th day of April, 1951) the European Economic Community (established by Treaty signed at Rome on the 25th day of March 1957) and the European Atomic Energy Community (established by Treaty signed at Rome on the 25th day of March 1957). No provision of this Constitution invalidates laws enacted, acts done or measures adopted by the State necessitated by the obligations of membership of the Communities or prevents laws enacted, acts done or measures adopted by the Communities, or institutions thereof, from having the force of law in the State.'

17 See further paras **16.104–16.113**.

beyond the Communities' remit. Nevertheless, the course of European integration is such that the European Union has been invested with increased competence and, correspondingly, fewer areas of national law remain unaffected by EU law.

[1.18] Aside from the formal sources of law which are outlined in the preceding paragraphs other influences (or secondary sources) should be noted. These do not enjoy the force of law *per se* but might prove to be significant either because they are incorporated into law by a law-making act or they influence the interpretation of a law by an adjudicative body. These sources include custom, international law, canon law and commentaries and scholarly writing.

Custom

[1.19] With the establishment of the common law in both England and Ireland, the customary law which preceded it was progressively eliminated. In Ireland the common law competed with the native Irish customary law, the Brehon law, for a number of centuries before the latter was finally expunged in the early 17th century. However, custom still has a residual role and the common law has recognised and tolerated the existence of customs which are local or particular in nature. In this context, a custom is a habitual practice which by virtue of continuous practice and general acquiescence acquires legal force. The legal recognition of a custom is based on the assumed consent of those who are materially affected by its application.[18] The custom operates in circumstances which might otherwise be governed by a general common law rule. Two conditions must be satisfied before a custom may enjoy the force of law. One is that it is certain, reasonable and continuous. The other is that it exists in a particular locality in respect of some particular matter and other general matters are governed by the ordinary common law. The law does not recognise general customs which purport to extend throughout the state. The latter have either been eliminated or incorporated into, and become part of, the common law itself.

International law

[1.20] International law[19] is the body of law which governs states in their relationships with one another. It consists of a variety of sources including customary international law, treaties and international decisions of judicial bodies. In international law terms the Irish legal system is dualist: that is to become part of national law, an international measure must be specifically incorporated by a domestic legal instrument. This is reflected in Article 29.6 of the Constitution which requires an Act of the Oireachtas to incorporate treaties into domestic law.[20] Nevertheless, international law might prove to

---

18 The compatibility of the customs of indigenous people and the common law can arise in the New World; see eg *Takamore v Clarke* [2011] NZCA 587, denying legal status to a custom that authorised the use of force and had the potential to escalate into violence.

19 See generally, Ch 17.

20 'No international agreement shall be part of the domestic law of the State save as may be determined by the Oireachtas.'

be influential. Article 29.3 of the Constitution provides that the state 'accepts the generally recognised principles of international law as its rule of conduct in its relations with other States', a provision which might conceivably be invoked in domestic legal proceedings. The courts also adopt a presumption of compatibility with international law when interpreting legislation,[21] which indirectly might ensure that international legal obligations are matched by domestic provisions. An important international legal instrument is the European Convention on Human Rights (ECHR), which the state has ratified. The ECHR establishes a regime for the protection of the rights of the individual in signatory states and complaints are adjudicated by the European Court of Human Rights (ECt HR), which sits in Strasbourg. The state is expected, as a matter of international law, to give effect to ECt HR rulings but this is not yet enforceable in domestic law. One of the obligations undertaken by the state in the Good Friday Agreement of 1998 was to pass legislation incorporating the Convention and this was achieved with the enactment of the European Convention on Human Rights Act 2003. As a result, the Convention enjoys an enhanced profile in Irish domestic law.[22] The jurisprudence of the ECt HR has a greater purchase in domestic proceedings: Irish courts are now required to take judicial notice of declarations, decisions, advisory opinions and judgments of the ECt HR and to take 'due account' of the principles established by those instruments.[23] The courts are enjoined, where possible, to interpret national law in a manner that is compatible with the ECHR[24] and the superior courts are authorised to issue a declaration of incompatibility where a national law falls foul of the ECHR.[25]

Canon law

[1.21] Canon law is the law of the Christian Church. Originally it consisted of an unsystematic series of canons, but it became codified by the late medieval period. In general, canon law exists separately from the secular law of the state and does not enjoy the force of law. However, that is not to say that canon law is entirely irrelevant.[26] In

---

21 See paras **14.92–14.94**.

22 See *Dublin City Council v Fennell* [2005] 1 IR 604 at 608, *per* Kearns J: 'The 2003 Act … does not purport to incorporate the Convention directly into domestic law, but rather imposes an obligation that, when interpreting or applying any statutory provision or rule of law, a court shall, insofar as is possible, and subject to the rules of law relating to such interpretation and application, do so in a manner compatible with the State's obligations under the Convention provisions. The 2003 Act also provides that every organ of the State shall, subject to any statutory provision or rule of law, perform its functions in a manner compatible with the State's obligations under the Convention provisions. A party may also seek from the High or Supreme Court a declaration that a statutory provision or rule of law is incompatible with the State's obligations under the Convention provisions, and where such a declaration is made certain consequences as detailed in the Act then follow.' See further, Hogan, 'The European Convention on Human Rights Act 2003' (2006) 12(3) Eur PL 331.

23 European Convention on Human Rights Act 2003, s 4.

24 European Convention on Human Rights Act 2003, s 2.

25 European Convention on Human Rights Act 2003, s 5.

26 See Murdoch, 'Bell, Book and Candle' (December 2004) *Law Society Gazette* 8.

some circumstances, legal rules, especially in the area of marriage law, have been shaped by their canon law equivalents.[27] Moreover, in certain circumstances parties are free to choose which body of law governs their relationship and the courts will give effect to that choice. Thus, where the parties to a contract specify that it is to be governed by French law, an Irish court will apply that law in determining a dispute relating to that contract. In some cases it has been held that the canon law is the law chosen to govern the relationship in question and those cases have been resolved on the basis of canon law.[28]

Commentaries and scholarly writing

[1.22] In some instances the lack of a formal legal source might result in recourse being had to the writings of recognised commentators and scholars. For centuries the works of pre-eminent writers, such as Coke,[29] Hale[30] and Blackstone,[31] have been treated as being authoritative. These works were accorded a status which approached that of judicial decisions. It had been the practice to confine the citation of such works to those of deceased authors, on the assumption that posthumous reference invested them with an authority lacking during the authors' lifetimes, but this practice has been largely abandoned. The growth of the academic branch of the legal community has been accompanied by a commensurate volume of legal writing, consisting of textbooks, encyclopaedias, articles in scholarly journals and the like. Again these writings might be relied on but unlike those of the older jurists they are only 'persuasive' with courts being free to 'adopt' their conclusions as they consider appropriate.

[5] DIVISIONS OF THE LAW

[1.23] The sources of law do not exist as a homogenous whole but are broken down into various components or divisions (see Figure 1.1 at para **1.26**). These divisions have emerged over time with some having been recognised since the early years of the common law. The first distinction to be drawn is that between *substantive law* and *procedural*, or *adjectival*, *law*. Substantive law embraces the different legal subjects that confer rights and powers or impose obligations and liabilities. Procedural law refers to the bodies of rules concerned with the implementation of substantive law and consists of the law of civil and criminal procedure and the law of evidence.

[1.24] Substantive law may be further divided into *public law* and *private law*. The distinction between the two is not wholly clear-cut,[32] but broadly speaking public law is

---

[27] See eg *Ussher v Ussher* [1912] 2 IR 445; *UF v JC* [1991] 2 IR 330; *JS v CS* [1997] 2 IR 506.

[28] See *O'Callaghan v Sullivan* [1925] 1 IR 90; *Hibernian Bank v Mansfield* [1962] IR 454; *Connolly v Byrne* [1997] IEHC 195.

[29] *Institutes of the Law of England* 4 vols (1628–1644).

[30] *The History of the Pleas of the Crown* 2 vols (1736). The work was completed in 1676 but was not published until 1736.

[31] *Commentaries on the Laws of England* 4 vols (1765–1769).

[32] See Harlow, '"Public" and "Private" Law: Definition without Distinction' (1980) 43 MLR 1.

that which pertains to the state and its agencies or which is concerned with the public interest. Public law embraces the following:

- *Constitutional law*, which is the body of law that has grown out of the Constitution and affects the state in its most fundamental respects. It is concerned with the powers and functioning of the state and with the rights of the individual which are guaranteed by the Constitution.

- *Administrative law*, which is the body of law which governs the administration of the state and the operation of public authorities. It could be considered to be a cousin of constitutional law but, while the latter is concerned largely with issues of principle and policy, administrative law is concerned with 'questions of detail and … matters of function more than structure.'[33] The range of bodies which are subject to administrative law is broad and includes the executive, Ministers of State, semi-state bodies, the Gardaí, the Defence Forces, prison governors and statutory bodies.

- *Criminal law*, which defines conduct that is prohibited and provides punishment for breach of its prohibitions. In general, the investigation and prosecution of offences is a public matter and is undertaken by public agencies such as the Gardaí and the Director of Public Prosecutions, respectively.

[1.25] Private law is, in the main, concerned with relationships between private individuals and entities in which there is no significant public interest. It should be noted that public bodies are also subject to private law when they act in the same capacity as private bodies. It is more difficult to divide private law into individual subjects. It is convenient to employ two overlapping classifications. The first consists of the traditional legal subjects that form the 'core' of private law:

- *Contract law* is that body of law which governs voluntary relationships between two or more parties.[34] It identifies the agreements which the law considers to be binding, and provides for their interpretation and enforcement.

- The *law of torts* is concerned with private wrongs which usually result in injury to another. It includes a variety of wrongs such as assault, battery, false imprisonment, defamation and negligence. There is an obvious overlap with the criminal law and both bodies of law grew out of an undifferentiated law of wrongs that operated in the early days of the common law. Nowadays the purpose of the law of torts is to provide compensation for the injured party by the wrongdoer; the punishment of the wrongdoer is left to the criminal law.[35]

- *Property law* is the body of law which governs the ownership of property. It may be further divided into *real property* (in the main land and interests in land) and *personal property* (both tangibles and intangibles).

---

33 See Hogan and Morgan's *Administrative Law in Ireland* (4th edn, 2010), p 1; and paras **8.21–8.64**.

34 See Friel, *The Law of Contract* (2nd edn, 2000), p 1.

35 See McMahon and Binchy, *Irish Law of Torts* (4th edn, 2013), pp 5–7; Quill, *Torts in Ireland* (3rd edn, 2009), pp 2–6.

[1.26] The second subdivision of private law focuses on the areas of activity or social life around which distinctive and identifiable bodies of law have grown or been identified. Each of these bodies contains relevant elements of contract law, the law of torts and property law. These subjects, whose titles are self-explanatory, include *family law, company law, labour law, commercial law, intellectual property* and the like. These divisions and traditional core subjects have formed the basis for Legislative Codes in many common law jurisdictions.[36] Figure 1.1 sets out the foregoing divisions and classifications.

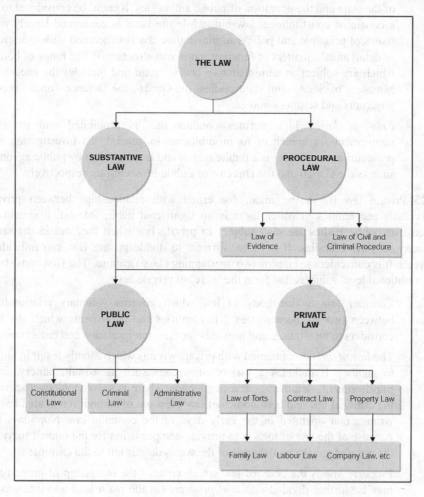

Figure 1.1

---

[36] See the discussion of statutory codes in paras **11.02** and **13.103**.

[1.27] It should be realised that the various subjects into which the law is divided overlap to a degree and that a legal problem might invoke several different bodies of law. For instance, an unlawful attack would result in criminal proceedings for assault initiated by the Gardaí or the Director of Public Prosecutions or, less frequently, by the victim as a private prosecutor in the District Court; but the same event might also be the subject of civil proceedings for the torts of assault and/or battery initiated by the victim. Moreover, a civil or private law dispute might embrace several different subjects. A client who suffers loss due to the negligent conduct of his or her solicitor would have a claim for both breach of contract and the tort of negligence.

Common expressions

[1.28] It will be obvious, at this stage, that vital terms such as 'common law' and 'civil law' are used in different senses which should be distinguished. It is helpful to set out the various meanings which such terms bear.

(i) Common law A general description of the Irish legal system and others of English origin	*Civil law* A general description of the legal systems of continental European countries
(ii) Common law Law developed by the courts; 'case law'	*Legislation* Law enacted by parliament ('statute law') or a delegated body ('delegated legislation')
(iii) Common law Law developed by the common law courts; a subset of common law sense (ii)	*Equity* Law developed in the Court of Chancery to supplement that developed in the common law courts
(iv) Civil law The secular law of the state; applicable to all	*Canon law* Church law; operates largely within the confines of that body
(v) Civil law Private law; one of the principal divisions of substantive law	*Public law* Law involving the public interest; one of the principal divisions of substantive law

Figure 1.2

[6] LEGAL PERSONALITY

[1.29] The law recognises different forms of legal personality. A legal person is an individual or entity to which, for the purposes of the law, the character of being a 'person' is attributed. It is obvious that human beings possess this capacity and they are known as *natural persons*. In addition, the law recognises artificial entities which possess legal personality. The most common such entity is a *corporation* which may be created by one of a number of devices. In the past corporations were created by royal charter, but this device is now redundant; examples of such corporations include universities, the Royal College of Surgeons and certain trading companies.[37] A second device is the creation of individual corporations by legislation; this is most commonly the case with 'semi-state' bodies such as the Electricity Supply Board. The third device, which is the most frequently employed nowadays, is the voluntary creation of a corporation by a number of individuals in the manner prescribed by the companies legislation which is applicable at the time. In each case the corporation is a separate legal entity from its members, and it continues in existence regardless of the fates of its individual members. Such corporations are sometimes known as *corporations aggregate*, a term which distinguishes them from *corporations sole*. The latter are essentially offices which are occupied by individuals, such as the President and Ministers of State, and are typically designated as such by legislation. The office is legally distinct from the holder and survives changes in its occupation – the legal incidents attach to the office rather than the individual. Thus, legal proceedings which are commenced against, for example, the Minister for Health will continue despite a new individual being appointed to that office.

[1.30] Like natural persons, corporations are, in general, subject to the law. They are capable of acting in their own capacity as 'persons', of owning property, entering into contracts, suing and being sued. On the other hand, there are certain transactions, such as marrying and making wills, which are unique to human persons and cannot be conducted by a corporation. But with that caveat in mind it can be said that corporations are subject to the general body of private law in much the same manner as natural persons. In respect of public law the matter is less straightforward. Corporations in general, unlike their individual members, do not enjoy the guarantees of constitutional rights. Moreover, the extent to which a corporation is subject to the criminal law is uncertain. It is only with some difficulty that a corporation can be punished, as unlike a human being it has 'no soul to damn, no body to kick.'[38] In other words the physical sanctions which were traditionally associated with the criminal law could not be enforced against an artificial person. Likewise, an artificial person lacks a conscience or moral sense which might be said to be affected by the condemnation which is implicit in criminal punishment. Moreover, the 'acts' of an artificial person lack the element of culpability which underlies most criminal offences.[39]

---

[37] In many cases royal charters have been supplanted by legislation.
[38] See Coffee, '"No Soul to Damn, no Body to Kick": an Unscandalised Inquiry into the Problem of Corporate Punishment' (1981) 79 Mich LR 386.
[39] See McAuley and McCutcheon, *Criminal Liability* (2000), pp 379–397.

[1.31] The right to form associations is guaranteed by the Constitution[40] but where such associations are not incorporated, the legal position is different from that of corporations. Unincorporated associations do not, in general, possess legal personality and are not considered to be distinct from their members. The property of the association is jointly held by each of the members, rather than by the association itself. Acts performed and transactions entered into on behalf of the group are considered to be the joint (all the members) and several (any particular member) responsibility of the members. In theory any individual member could be held liable for all the acts of the association in his or her own right. In some circumstances special legal provision has been made for certain categories of association, such as partnerships, charities and trade unions, each of which is governed by its own body of law.

[7]   A JURISPRUDENTIAL OVERVIEW

[1.32] We have already noted that this text does not examine in detail the more general political context within which legal principles and rules are made. Nonetheless, it is important to note that the latter do not evolve in an intellectual vacuum. Legislators and judges alike are influenced by intellectual and philosophical concepts in the formulation of principles and rules, and these concepts are examined as part of the study of jurisprudence, the science of law. While detailed consideration of these theories is beyond the scope of this work, a brief sketch of some major themes is warranted.

[1.33] For several centuries legal theory has been characterised by a division between positivist and natural law schools of analysis. Positivist theories contend that 'the existing state of the law should be considered without reference to intrusive moral or ethical criteria of identification.'[41] Such theories are descriptive rather than normative, concentrating on the 'is' rather than the 'ought'. Natural law theories, on the other hand, 'can be defined fairly accurately as that philosophy of law which emphasises the *continuity* of law with morality …'[42] and, in this regard, the distinction between the descriptive and the normative, which is crucial to positivism, is blurred.

[1.34] The positivist approach emerged in the intellectual environment of the Enlightenment and it sought to provide a purportedly 'scientific' explanation of law and legal phenomena. In the English-speaking world positivism can be traced to the philosopher Jeremy Bentham, best known for his utilitarian philosophy according to which political and legal arrangements were to be based on a principle of utility that seeks to maximise the benefits (or 'pleasures') of society, and to the jurist John Austin. In their principal jurisprudential works, *Of Laws in General* and *The Province of Jurisprudence Determined*, respectively, they conceived of a law as being a command issued by a sovereign which was backed by the threat of a sanction. A sovereign is a person or body to whom a political community pays obedience and, Austin added, is not

---

40   Article 40.6.1°.iii.
41   *McCoubrey and White's Textbook on Jurisprudence* (5th edn, 2012), p 41.
42   *McCoubrey and White's Textbook on Jurisprudence* (5th edn, 2012), p 13.

in the habit of obedience to another. This version of positivism concentrates on individual laws and tends to ignore the systemic context in which laws operate; at most an implicit view of a legal system can be discerned from their works.[43] More recent theories have addressed this defect, and other defects, in the views of Bentham and Austin and consider the phenomenon of legal systems.

[1.35] Modern positivism is associated with HLA Hart, who presented his theory in *The Concept of Law*. To Hart, law's central feature is its obligatory character, a feature that is to be understood in a legal, not a moral, sense. This notion of obligation informs Hart's views on the 'internal aspect' of rules. There should be what he called a 'critical reflexive attitude' that leads to an acceptance that the existence of a rule justifies the criticism that is levelled at deviant conduct. This is differentiated from:

> "... the external point of view, which limits itself to the observable regularities of behaviour, cannot reproduce ... the way in which rules function as rules in the lives of those who are normally the majority of society ... For them the violation of a rule is not merely the basis for the prediction that a hostile reaction will follow but a *reason* for hostility."[44]

[1.36] From an external viewpoint, we can observe that drivers typically stop at a red traffic light and predict what will happen based on this observation. However, it is only when we consider the 'internal aspect' that we can understand why drivers behave in this manner, namely because they understand themselves to be bound by a rule which obliges them so to act. Hart, however, recognised that a legal system consisted of more than rules imposing obligations. He considered duty-imposing rules to be 'primary' and observed that they were supplemented by 'secondary' rules. The latter consisted of 'rules of recognition' which establish the criteria by which rules are identified: 'rules of change' which facilitate the amendment and abolition of old rules; and 'rules of adjudication' which provide mechanisms for the resolution of disputes.

[1.37] The Austrian-born jurist Hans Kelsen sought to present an abstract theory that describes the structure and operation of any legal system. In the positivist tradition he excluded political, social and other contextual factors from consideration in his search for a 'scientific' explanation set out in his seminal work, *The Pure Theory of Law*. In his view law consists of norms, that is propositions about what ought to occur. However, the 'ought' with which Kelsen was concerned is very different from the ethical version which informs natural law analysis. A legal norm takes a general form: if a certain condition occurs a prescribed consequence ought to follow. This operates as an instruction to officials who enforce the law and validates the application of the relevant consequence. A legal system organises norms in a vertical structure, with each norm being validated by the prior one in the hierarchy until the basic norm, or *Grundnorm*, is reached. The *Grundnorm* is the point of ultimate legal authority, the apex of the pyramid so to speak. It should not be confused with the constitution, which is itself a legal norm. The *Grundnorm* operates at one remove by validating the constitution; in essence, it

---

43 See Raz, *The Concept of a Legal System* (2nd edn, 1980), pp 5–26.
44 *The Concept of Law* (1961), p 88 (emphasis in original).

amounts to a proposition concerning the validity of the constitution. The validity of legal development, including alterations to the constitution, is ultimately determined by reference to the *Grundnorm*. Where constitutional continuity is broken – as, for example, is the case where there is a revolution – a shift in *Grundnorm* results; a new proposition that authorises the changed legal order will emerge once that order has become effective.

[1.38] Natural law theories manifest a concern with the ethical dimension and seek to identify, or impose, normative limits to human positive law. A 'bad' law, however that might be defined, lacks moral authority and, it follows, there is no obligation to obey it. Natural law theories focus on the contents and purposes of the law, not just the formal criteria of identification of legal rules that are central to positive theories. The naturalism of Greek philosophy, represented in the works of Plato and Aristotle, was adopted by St Augustine and St Thomas Aquinas and recast in a Christian mould. For Augustine the will of God represented the highest law, the eternal law; positive law was presented as a mechanism to enforce the elimination of sinful conduct. In this scheme of things, right-thinking people are guided by the eternal law and, for them, positive law is largely irrelevant. In contrast, Aquinas accepted that positive law might have a wider role to play and that it might provide guidance for good conduct. However, in the Thomist scheme positive law is to be evaluated against higher sources, namely the 'divine law', derived from scripture, and 'natural law', which is the product of human reason which in turn rests on the eternal law. This version has influenced some Irish judges who have invoked natural law when interpreting the Constitution. Drawing on broad hortatory statements that speak of rights that are 'antecedent and superior' to positive law, those judges contended that this represented a constitutional endorsement of natural law; and their interpretation of natural law was one derived from the 'Christian and democratic' nature of the state.[45] The Supreme Court eventually rejected the idea that natural law took priority over the text of the Constitution[46] but it also accepted that, since the Constitution reflects religious and spiritual values, these remain important in the development of legal principles.[47]

[1.39] In the 16th and 17th centuries natural law theories took on secular overtones in the form of the social contractarian views of Thomas Hobbes and John Locke. For Hobbes the primary purpose of law and government was to preserve public peace and order. In his celebrated words 'the life of man [would be] solitary, poore, nasty, brutish and short'[48] in the absence of such a regime of governance. Locke considered that individuals possessed 'natural rights' and that the function of government was to provide the means to protect them. The collective views of Hobbes and Locke underpin

---

[45] *McGee v Attorney General* [1974] IR 284 (para **15.169**) and *Norris v Attorney General* [1984] IR 36 (para **15.172**).

[46] *Re the Regulation of Information (Services Outside the State for the Termination of Pregnancies) Bill 1995* [1995] 1 IR 1: para **15.181**.

[47] *Re a Ward of Court (No 2)* [1996] 2 IR 79: para **15.185**.

[48] *Leviathan* (1651), ch 13.

modern conceptions of democratic society, in particular in their insistence on a notion of government limited by the consent of the governed.

[1.40] While natural law thinking was eclipsed in the 18th and 19th centuries by the rise of positivism, a revival is evident.[49] In part, this return to natural law was stimulated by the 20th century experience of totalitarian states, particularly Nazi Germany and the Soviet Union, in which the abuse of law and legal form was widespread. Modern natural law, or perhaps more accurately post-positivist, theories share with classical naturalism a concern with ethical matters and the contents of the law. Modern theories include the procedural naturalism of Lon Fuller who established a set of procedural criteria, expressed negatively in the form of defects in law-making, which reflect the 'inner morality' of law,[50] and the work of John Finnis who has married the classical concern with ethical and procedural matters with the modern interest in human rights.[51]

[1.41] The importance of rights is also central to the work of Ronald Dworkin who, while not considering himself a natural law theorist, was avowedly anti-positivist.[52] In Dworkin's view legal rules are complemented by principles; the latter are general standards that might take priority over the mechanistic application of a particular rule. Thus, in a case where the question was whether a murderer could inherit under his grandfather's will in circumstances where he had murdered the latter the general principle that 'no man can profit from his own wrong' overrode statutory provisions which on a literal interpretation would allow him to succeed.[53] The important point from Dworkin's perspective is that the principle invoked is a legal standard not, as positivists like Hart would suggest, a policy based on essentially extra-legal considerations. In Dworkin's view a court presented with an unclear, or 'hard', case should resolve the decision by reference to legal principles rather than policies, which on this analysis refer to societal goals. An argument from principle justifies a decision 'by showing that [it] respects or secures some individual or group right.'[54] In this scheme of things the courts' function is to protect rights and while Dworkin would allow rights to be limited in the collective interest by the legislature the power so to act is circumscribed. In particular, 'the Government is [not] justified in overriding a right on the minimal grounds that would be sufficient if no such right existed.'[55]

[1.42] While the legal positivism of Bentham and Austin has been largely overtaken by theoretical developments in the 20th century[56] a more general legacy of utilitarianism may be observed. The close association between the utility principle and efficiency or

---

49   See George (ed), *Natural Law Theory* (1992).
50   *The Morality of Law* (1969).
51   *Natural Law and Natural Rights* (1980).
52   *Taking Rights Seriously* (1977).
53   The case Dworkin had in mind was *Riggs v Palmer* (1889) 22 NE 188.
54   *Taking Rights Seriously* (1977), p 82.
55   *Taking Rights Seriously* (1977), pp 191–192.
56   Nevertheless, O'Donnell J referred to Austin's notion of sovereignty outlined in *The Province of Jurisprudence Determined*, in his judgment in *Pringle v Ireland* [2012] IESC 47.

cost-effectiveness formed the basis for the Economic Analysis of Law, a school of jurisprudence which emerged in the 1970s and which is particularly associated with Richard Posner, then a Professor of Law and later a federal judge in the United States. Utilitarianism and the Economic Analysis of Law have a wide application;[57] they are of particular relevance to the legal regulation of business, exemplified in the mixed economies of many states, including Ireland, and expressed in many aspects of European Union law. They may also be of relevance in the resolution of liability in accident cases.[58] The concept of cost-effectiveness in the provision of state services has also been deployed in the context of proposals for reform of the Irish court system.[59]

[1.43] In certain areas of law, the combined influence of Christian thought and of utilitarianism can be seen. Thus, the neighbour principle developed by the House of Lords in *Donoghue v Stevenson*,[60] and adopted throughout the common law world, owes its origins, at least in part, to the biblical parable of the Good Samaritan. However, the later development of the neighbour principle, both in Britain and Ireland, seems to owe more to utilitarian concepts than to Christianity.[61]

[1.44] Other influential political theories have also featured in court decisions. Thus, the distinction between communitarian and distributive justice, developed by Aristotle, was used to describe the distinction between the role of the judiciary, who determine whether the rights of citizens have been breached by the state, and the executive and legislature, who have political responsibility for the distribution of state resources.[62] The growing concern for gender equality and gender studies has also been influential in constitutional litigation and in the wider area of law reform.[63] Finally, we should note that while at least one judge found 'much appeal' in the maxim of Karl Marx, 'From each according to his ability, to each according to his need', it was rejected as an appropriate aid to statutory interpretation.[64]

---

[57] See, eg, Posner, *Economic Analysis of Law* (7th edn, 2007) and Posner, 'Law and Economics in Common-Law, Civil-Law and Developing Nations' (2004) 17 *Ratio Juris* 166. Also Shavell, *Foundations of Economic Analysis of Law* (2004); Devlin, 'Law and Economics' 45 Ir Jur (ns) 165.

[58] See Carolan, 'Economic Analysis and the Law: An Introduction' (1995) 13 ILT 162.

[59] See *First Report of the Working Group on a Courts Commission: Management and Financing of the Courts* (Pn 2960, 1996), discussed at para **4.208**ff.

[60] *Donoghue v Stevenson* [1932] AC 562: see para **12.145**.

[61] For example, the judgment of Lord Denning MR (the highly influential former Master of the Rolls, judicial head of the civil division of the English Court of Appeal) in *Dutton v Bognor Regis UDC* [1972] 1 QB 373 and the decision of the Irish Supreme Court in *Keane v Electricity Supply Board* [1981] IR 44.

[62] *O'Reilly v Limerick Corporation* [1989] ILRM 181: see para **15.122**.

[63] *de Búrca v Attorney General* [1976] IR 38 (see para **15.139**). See also Connelly (ed), *Gender and the Law in Ireland* (1993), which focuses on the growing impact of women in the legal profession and the impact of gender equality studies in the formulation of laws.

[64] *Quirke v Folio Homes Ltd* [1988] ILRM 496 at 500 *per* McCarthy J, quoting Marx, *Critique of the Gotha Programme*.

[8] LAW AND MORALITY

[1.45] A major theme in jurisprudence is the relationship between law and morality. In general, and this is a very broad generalisation, given their formalistic concerns positivists have tended to disregard the link between the two. It is not that positivists consider morality unimportant and, indeed, Hart noted that a legal system contains what he called 'the minimum content of natural law'.[65] Rather from a positivist perspective considerations of morality raise questions about the contents of the legal system and, therefore, are political or social in nature, not legal. From the positivist perspective an immoral law is not denied its quality as law simply on that account. Natural law theories, being more concerned with the contents of the law and seeking to evaluate human law in the light of higher sources or aspirations, more readily lend themselves to a consideration of the morality of the law. From this perspective, human law is expected to conform to those standards and the law should be informed by moral considerations.

[1.46] The particular question that arises in this context is whether the law should be used to enforce a particular view of morality, a matter that has been the focus of debate between liberal and conservative commentators. The great 19th-century political philosopher John Stuart Mill tackled the issue from an individualist, libertarian perspective. He wrote that, 'the sole end for which mankind are warranted, individually or collectively, in interfering with the liberty of action of any of their number is self-protection.'[66] He argued that the right to limit individual freedom is confined: [67]

"… the only purpose for which power can rightfully be exercised over any member of a civilised community, against his will, is to prevent harm to others. His own good, either physical or moral, is not a sufficient warrant. He cannot rightfully be compelled to do or forbear because it will be better for him to do so, because it will make him happier, because, in the opinions of others, to do so would be wise or even right."

[1.47] Thus Mill would confine the power of a state to regulate to cases where harm to others is threatened – the so-called harm principle. It is clear that he would deny the state the right to act paternalistically, on its view of what is in the best interests of its citizens. Equally, the state is denied the entitlement to enforce a code of morality (unless the relevant regulation can be justified on the grounds of harm prevention). Although Mill proceeded to qualify his general statement of principle by acknowledging that the demands of a modern regulated society might warrant the restriction of personal freedom, the foregoing passage has been much-quoted and has become a slogan for the liberal cause.

[1.48] Mill's thesis was refuted by Sir James Fitzjames Stephen, arguably the pre-eminent criminal law judge in late Victorian England.[68] Stephen's principal concern was

---

65   *The Concept of Law* (1961), pp 189–195.
66   *On Liberty* (Cambridge Texts in the History of Political Thought 1989), p 13.
67   *On Liberty* (Cambridge Texts in the History of Political Thought 1989), p 13.
68   *Liberty, Equality, Fraternity* (1873).

with the contents of the criminal law. He contended that part of the law's purpose was to gratify 'the feeling of hatred' that the prospect of criminal conduct stimulates in the minds of right-thinking people. He recognised that the criminal law was concerned with the 'grosser forms of vice' and lesser forms, 'mere vice', fell beyond its remit. In this his views were not substantially different from those of Mill, and in the modern idiom would be accommodated within the principle of minimalism that is said to circumscribe the criminal law.[69] However, Stephen took the view that the criminal law as it existed at the time 'could hardly be regarded as imposing any restraint on decent people which is ever felt as such'. In other words, the range of prohibitions that the criminal law imposed could not properly be considered to amount to an inappropriate restriction of personal freedom. In his view, a number of factors could properly shape the criminal law, including the moral climate in which it operates, a concern for the 'incurable weakness of human nature' and societal revulsion at the 'grosser forms of vice'. These factors do not provide as apparently clear-cut a criterion as Mill's harm principle but instead they operate as broad guidelines to the outer limits of the criminal law.

[1.49] The question of law and morality was again the subject of debate in the 1960s between Professor Hart and Lord Devlin. The debate was stimulated by the publication in England, in 1957, of the Report of Wolfenden Committee,[70] which recommended the decriminalisation of male homosexual conduct and the regulation of prostitution-related activities, and the decision several years later in *Shaw v DPP*[71] in which the House of Lords held that conspiracy to corrupt public morals was an offence known to the law. To support its case for the liberalisation of the law, the Wolfenden Committee invoked the harm principle and suggested that there is a realm of private conduct that is no business of the law. In *Shaw* the House of Lords took a different approach and argued that one of the functions of the criminal law was to protect the public moral welfare. To this end, Lord Simonds opined that the courts enjoyed a residual power to recognise or create new offences in the interest of public morality.

[1.50] Devlin took issue with the central proposition in the Wolfenden Report.[72] He acknowledged that the harm principle could explain the core prohibitions of the criminal law (such as murder, rape, assault, theft) but, he suggested, that principle is not the sole criterion. In his view the principle does not explain the criminalisation of consensual conduct which by its nature does not cause harm to others and to this end he referred, *inter alia*, to the prohibition of voluntary euthanasia, suicide pacts, duelling, abortion and sibling incest. Those are acts which can 'be done in private and without offence to others and need not involve the corruption or exploitation of others … [t]hey can be

---

69   See Ashworth, *Principles of Criminal Law* (6th edn, 2009), pp 27–37.
70   *Report of the Committee on Homosexual Offences and Prostitution* (HMSO, 1957) Cmnd 257.
71   *Shaw v DPP* [1962] AC 220.
72   *The Enforcement of Morals* (1965).

brought within [the criminal law] only as a matter of moral principle.'[73] To Devlin a sense of public morality is vital to the integrity of society:

"... society means a community of ideas; without shared ideas on politics, morals, and ethics no society can exist. ... If men and women try to create a society in which there is no fundamental agreement about good and evil they will fail; if having based it on common agreement, the agreement goes, the society will disintegrate. For society is not something that is kept together physically; it is held by the invisible bonds of common thought ... A common morality is part of the bondage. The bondage is part of the price of society; and mankind, which needs society must pay its price."[74]

[1.51] Devlin went further and stated that '[m]orals and religion are inextricably linked' and that 'the moral standards of Western civilization are those belonging to Christianity.'[75] However, he did not contend that the Christian morals should be enforced through the mechanism of the criminal law. He made a more subtle point: for the purposes of the criminal law there was no discernible difference between 'Christian morals and those which every right minded member of society is expected to hold.'[76] He was careful to ensure that this notion of public morality would not become a vehicle for needless intolerance. The individual has rights which should be taken into account and '[n]othing should be punished by the law that does not lie beyond the limits of tolerance.'[77] In this respect he drew a distinction between conduct that is disliked by the majority and a 'real feeling of reprobation'; prohibition should be based on the latter not the former and the task of the lawmaker is to identify the boundary between the two. He also recognised that the limits of tolerance shift, thus acknowledging that conceptions of public morality evolve and develop. However, '[n]ot everything is to be tolerated. No society can do without intolerance, indignation, and disgust; they are the forces behind the moral law ...'[78]

[1.52] The liberal viewpoint was articulated by Hart who took Mill's dictum as his starting point.[79] However, he qualified this by accepting that it is permissible to legislate in order to protect the vulnerable from exploitation. In his view the rules that exclude the victim's consent in murder and assault can be explained as exercises in legal paternalism 'designed to protect individuals against themselves.'[80] This marks a significant dilution of the libertarian position suggested by the harm principle, as Hart indeed recognised, but he contended that paternalist regulation is an accepted fact of social life. The core of Hart's thesis is that society cannot be identified with a particular set of views on morality, a point that is at odds with Devlin's central theme. Moreover, he drew a

---

[73] *The Enforcement of Morals* (1965), p 7.
[74] *The Enforcement of Morals* (1965), p 10.
[75] *The Enforcement of Morals* (1965), p 4.
[76] *The Enforcement of Morals* (1965), p 23.
[77] *The Enforcement of Morals* (1965), pp 16–17.
[78] *The Enforcement of Morals* (1965), p 17.
[79] *Law, Liberty and Morality* (1963).
[80] *Law, Liberty and Morality* (1963), p 31.

distinction between questions of morality and of public decency, tacitly accepting that the law might permissibly prohibit conduct on the basis that it offends public decency.[81] However, true to his libertarian beliefs he rejected the notion that conduct might be prohibited on the ground that mere knowledge of its occurring might shock or cause offence to others:

"If distress incident to the belief that others are doing wrong is harm, so also is the distress incident to the belief that others are doing what you do not want them to do. To punish people for causing this form of distress would be tantamount to punishing them simply because others object to what they do; and the only liberty that could coexist with this extension of the utilitarian principle is liberty to do those things to which no one seriously objects. Such liberty is plainly nugatory. *Recognition of individual liberty as a value involves, as a minimum, acceptance of the principle that the individual may do what he wants, even if others are distressed when they learn what it is he does* – unless, of course, there are other good grounds for forbidding it. No social order which accords to individual liberty any value could also accord the right to be protected from distress thus occasioned."[82]

[1.53] The enforcement of sexual morality was its immediate context but the general terms in which the Hart–Devlin debate was conducted show that its scope is much broader and is relevant to other forms of behaviour: drug-taking, private use of pornographic material, gambling and animal cruelty are examples. A number of justifications might be invoked in support of prohibiting these activities, including a paternalistic determination of what is in an individual's best interests, public decency, public sentiment, feelings of revulsion as well as public morality. However, it is clear that prohibition in these cases cannot be brought within the harm principle, at least as that principle was classically articulated by Mill – the conduct in question occurs in private and does not, in any meaningful sense of the word, harm others.

[1.54] Nevertheless such is the enduring ideological appeal of the harm principle that it is frequently invoked to justify prohibitions. Thus it is said that drug-taking harms society in that drug users are liable to become a charge on the public purse: as a result of their conduct it is likely that they will rely on publicly-funded health and social welfare programmes. By the same token, the harm principle has been invoked in support of the imposition of stricter prohibitions of pornographic and violent literature and films: a link is said to exist between exposure to such materials and violence against women and children. However, this is to stretch the principle to such an extent that the reworked concept of harm becomes nebulous.[83] Hart implicitly acknowledged this difficulty in his

---

81 *Law, Liberty and Morality* (1963), p 45: 'Sexual intercourse between husband and wife is not immoral, but if it takes place in public it is an affront to public decency. Homosexual intercourse between consenting adults in private is immoral according to conventional morality, but not an affront to public decency, though it would be both if it took place in public.'

82 *Law, Liberty and Morality* (1963), p 47 (emphasis added).

83 See Harcourt, 'The Collapse of the Harm Principle' (1999) 90 J Crim L & Criminology 109; Ashworth, *Principles of Criminal Law* (6th edn, 2009), pp 27–31.

qualified adoption of Mill's proposition and his recognition that grounds other than harm, including paternalism and public decency, might justify legal prohibition. A further difficulty that Hart and others tend to overlook is that the concept of harm itself is 'morally loaded.'[84] The decision to classify a consequence (be it death, injury, loss of property, emotional hurt or whatever) as 'harm' with a view to its prohibition involves a societal value judgment that is essentially a moral evaluation.

[1.55] The years following the Hart–Devlin debate witnessed a general liberalisation of the criminal law, especially in regard to matters that might be considered to lie within the domain of private morality. This was achieved both by the enactment of reforming legislation and by judicial means, the latter in the form of recognising rights of autonomy and privacy. In Britain suicide and male homosexual conduct had been decriminalised and abortion legalised by the end of the 1960s. In the United States the Supreme Court held in a series of decisions that the right of privacy protected, *inter alia*, the use of pornographic materials in the home[85] and the use of contraceptives by married couples;[86] and in 1972, in a famous and still controversial decision, it held the right included the right to terminate a pregnancy.[87] More recently, the same Court struck down a state law that criminalised homosexual conduct.[88] These developments might be taken to amount to an endorsement of liberal position and a corresponding rejection of that associated with Devlin. Hart's thesis became the prevailing orthodoxy of the 1960s[89] and it still enjoys the ringing endorsement of commentators and theorists. Joel Feinberg took up the liberal cause in his four-volume work *The Moral Limits of the Criminal Law*.[90] He adopted the harm principle as it was articulated by Mill but would add the causing of hurt or offence to others, what he termed the 'offence principle', as a justification for the criminalisation. However, he contended that paternalism and moralism could not properly be invoked in support of penalising conduct.

[1.56] Like much else, legal theory is apt to be a matter of cultural fashion, and a renewed recognition of the cogency of Devlin's arguments is discernible.[91] His new supporters do not necessarily contend that the liberal reforms of the past 40 years should be undone. Rather they reject the proposition advanced by liberal theorists that the limits of the law can be fixed by reference either to a notion of harm or a principle of individual liberty. On this view of things the boundaries of the law are shaped, and

---

84 MacCormick, *Legal Right and Social Democracy* (1982), p 29.
85 *Stanley v Georgia* (1969) 394 US 557.
86 *Griswold v Connecticut* (1965) 381 US 479.
87 *Roe v Wade* (1972) 410 US 113.
88 *Lawrence v Texas* (2003) 539 US 558.
89 Lee, *Law and Morals* (1986), p 28.
90 *Harm to Others* (1984); *Offense to Others* (1985); *Harm to Self* (1986); *Harmless Wrongdoing* (1990).
91 See, eg, Dworkin, 'Devlin was Right: Law and the Enforcement of Morality' (1999) 40 Wm and Mary LR 927; Murphy, 'Moral Reasons and the Limitation of Liberty' (1999) 40 Wm and Mary LR 947; McAuley and McCutcheon, *Criminal Liability* (2000), pp 65–73.

always have been shaped, by an amalgam of factors that includes the concept of harm and a regard for personal freedom but also embraces paternalistic and moral concerns. The result is a much vaguer set of guidelines than the liberal position would provide but the central point is that 'there is no principled line following the contours of the distinction between immoral and harmful conduct such that only grounds referring to the latter may be invoked to justify criminalization.'[92]

[1.57] In an Irish context, where the views of the Catholic hierarchy weighed heavily with legislators in the post-Independence era,[93] the debate concerning the relationship between law and morality is especially relevant.[94] The Constitution had originally contained a reference to the 'special position' of the Catholic Church 'as the guardian of the Faith professed by the great majority of the citizens',[95] a provision that was eventually removed in 1972.[96] In recent years, the influence of the Catholic Church has been less marked. This can be seen, for example, in the enactment of legislation removing virtually all restrictions on the use of contraceptives,[97] the interpretation of the Constitution as permitting termination of pregnancy, at least in limited circumstances,[98] the passing of abortion information legislation (which the Supreme Court held is compatible with the Constitution),[99] and more recently the enactment of legislation permitting the termination of pregnancies in certain cases,[100] the decriminalisation of consensual sexual relations between homosexual men[101] and the narrow approval in a 1995 constitutional referendum of the removal of a ban on divorce.[102]

[9]   THE RULE OF LAW

[1.58] Underpinning the legal systems in most liberal democracies is the notion of the rule of law, sometimes referred to as the principle of legality. The values implicit in the rule of law transcend and permeate the various sources of law. Thus a particular principle might take legal effect as a common law rule, a section of an Act of the

---

92   Dworkin, 'Devlin was Right: Law and the Enforcement of Morality' (1999) 40 Wm and Mary LR 927 at 928.
93   See generally, Whyte, *Church and State in Modern Ireland*, 1923–1979 (2nd edn, 1980); Keogh, *The Vatican, the Bishops and Irish Politics 1919–39* (1986); Keogh, *Ireland and the Vatican: the Politics of Church–State Diplomacy* (1995); Lee, *Ireland 1912–1985* (1990).
94   See Clarke (ed), *Morality and the Law* (1982).
95   On its origins, see Keogh, 'The Constitutional Revolution: An Analysis of the Making of the Constitution', in Litton (ed), *The Constitution of Ireland 1937–1987* (1988).
96   See para **15.83**.
97   Health (Family Planning) Acts 1979–1993: see para **15.109**.
98   *Attorney General v X* [1992] 1 IR 1: see paras **15.177–15.180**.
99   Regulation of Information (Services outside the State for Termination of Pregnancies) Act 1995; *Re Article 26 and the Regulation of Information (Services outside the State for Termination of Pregnancies) Bill 1995* [1995] 1 IR 1.
100 Protection of Life During Pregnancy Act 2013.
101 Criminal Law (Sexual Offences) Act 1993.
102 Fifteenth Amendment of the Constitution Act 1996.

Oireachtas and a constitutional provision. Central to the rule of law is the idea of limited governmental power. The government of society functions according to legal rules which have been established in advance. Moreover, the separation of powers ensures a distribution of governmental power amongst different organs of state: the legislature, the executive and the judiciary. The relationship between the different organs is one of checks and balances, with no one organ enjoying supremacy at the expense of the others. The details of this governmental structure vary from one state to another but a crucial feature common to all democratic societies is the notion of limited power. This may be contrasted with systems where power is concentrated in the hand of one individual, such as a despot or dictator, or one entity, such as a political party or the bureaucracy.

[1.59] The rule of law insists that rights and obligations are prescribed in legal form and may be altered only in the matter permitted by law. Moreover, an individual is entitled to fair notice of the laws which govern his or her conduct. Several propositions flow from this. One is that laws must be enacted in advance and, correspondingly, retrospective laws, that is laws which apply to past events, are to be avoided. It is clear that it is fundamentally unfair to punish a person for an act which was lawful at the time it was performed but is later declared to be unlawful. The hostility to retrospective laws, encapsulated in the maxims *nullum crimen sine lege* and *nullum poena sine lege*,[103] is amplified in Article 15.5 of the Constitution which provides that '[t]he Oireachtas shall not declare acts to be infringements of the law which were not so at the date of their commission.' Moreover, the courts adopt a presumption against retrospection when interpreting legislation.[104] Fair notice also requires that the law be announced to those who are to be bound by it. It would be pointless to enact laws in advance if that exercise were not accompanied by measures to bring them to the attention of the public. This is an issue of accessibility and provision is made for the formal promulgation of legislation,[105] while judicial decisions are formally announced by their being delivered in court. However, a question of availability is also involved.

[1.60] It is necessary that laws are published in a manner which facilitates their being traced and located with comparative ease. Hence legislation is published by the Stationery Office[106] while law reports are published containing the most important judicial decisions.[107] Moreover, in the last decade or so those traditional paper sources have been supplemented by the dissemination of legal materials in electronic formats including the internet, websites, databases and CD-ROMs. A further question is that of intelligibility. Laws should be understandable and should not be formulated in opaque and unintelligible terms. Laws which are unduly vague fail in this regard and are potentially unconstitutional – in general laws should be formulated in precise terms

---

[103] Respectively, 'no crime without law' and 'no punishment without law'. O'Malley, 'Common Law Crimes and the Principle of Legality' (1989) 7 ILT 243.

[104] See paras **14.110–14.115**.

[105] See paras **13.24** and **13.117**.

[106] See para **13.24**.

[107] See para **12.14***ff*.

which are clear and do not admit of any ambiguity. However, there is a tension between the demands of intelligibility and precision. The drafting of laws with the desired precision is apt to lead to the use of lawyers' language, or 'legalese', and to render them less understandable by the general public. Whether this dilemma has been satisfactorily managed remains to be seen.[108] With these observations in mind, we may now proceed with our examination of the Irish legal system.

---

[108] See paras **13.96–13.99**.

Chapter 2

Development of the Irish Legal System

[1]   Introduction 29
[2]   Pre-Norman Ireland and the Brehon Law 29
[3]   The Arrival of English Law in Ireland 30
[4]   The Institutions of State in the United Kingdom (1800–1922) 39
[5]   The Emergence of a New State 49
[6]   The 1922 Constitution 50
[7]   The 1937 Constitution 57
[8]   A Revised Court System 64

[1] INTRODUCTION

[2.01] In this chapter we trace the historical development of the Irish legal system from its beginnings in the 12th century to the adoption of the Constitution in 1937.[1] In many respects the legal history of Ireland is also its political history, from the Anglo–Norman invasion of the 12th century to the creation of two separate jurisdictions on the island of Ireland in 1921 and 1922.

[2] PRE-NORMAN IRELAND AND THE BREHON LAW

[2.02] Prior to the arrival of the Anglo–Normans in the 12th century, Ireland was governed largely by a system of tribal 'royal' families or provincial chiefs. In the aftermath of the arrival of Christianity in the 5th century, Ireland may have been an 'island of saints and scholars', from which much learning made its way to mainland Europe, but it was also subject to considerable inter-tribal rivalry. Nonetheless, the Brehon law, a sophisticated indigenous system of law based primarily on custom, had developed. The system was administered by judicial figures known as Brehons, the equivalent of travelling justices, thought to have been successors to the pre-Christian Celtic druids. Many of the key elements of the Brehon system of law are to be found in the Irish law tracts, which were written down in the 7th and 8th centuries. These ancient sources of law have been the subject of scholarly research, beginning in the first half of the 19th century when they attracted the interest of prominent members of the antiquarian movement, most notably Eugene O'Curry and John O'Donovan who transcribed and translated large numbers of Brehon tracts. Their efforts paved the way

---

1   See Sinder, 'Irish Legal History: an Overview and Guide to the Sources' (2001) 93 *Law Library Journal* 231.

for the publication of *Ancient Law and Institutes of Ireland* in five volumes between 1865 and 1901. O'Curry and O'Donovan did not live to see that publication, which was undertaken under the auspices of the Brehon Law Commission, established by the British government in 1852. The 19th century also witnessed a more general revival of interest in Celtic civilisation, largely prompted by German scholars.[2] Brehon law scholarship continued into the 20th century,[3] with Professor Daniel A Binchy's years of labour culminating in the publication of a comprehensive multi-volume annotation of the extant ancient law tracts.[4] Although it has long been eclipsed by the English common law, the study of the Brehon law continues to the present and a body of scholarly work has been published in the past three decades.[5]

[3] THE ARRIVAL OF ENGLISH LAW IN IRELAND

[2.03] In theory at least, English law (or at least Anglo–Norman law) arrived in Ireland with the Anglo–Norman invasion of Wexford in 1169 led by Strongbow, Richard FitzGilbert, Earl of Pembroke.[6] In 1171, King Henry II visited Ireland, to some extent to reassert his royal authority. He landed at Waterford, where he held a Council. This was an important symbolic act because the King's Council, or *Curia Regis*, was the crucial decision-making body or group of advisers for the feudal Anglo–Norman kings. It is worth remembering that, at that time, the king enjoyed virtually absolute power, but the Council was the principal mechanism for acting in the king's absence, such as during the Crusades or some other foreign adventure. In its early manifestation, the Council comprised two departments, the Exchequer, headed by the Treasurer, and the Chancery, headed by the Chancellor, the chief adviser to the king. The Council later expanded to produce a court system, a Parliament and an executive or government, eventually

---

2   For example, Bourke, *The Aryan Origins of the Gaelic Race and Language: the Brehon Law Truth of the Pentateuch* (1876); Ginnell, *The Brehon Laws: a Legal Handbook* (1894).

3   For example, MacNeill, *Early Irish Law and Institutions* (1935); Thurneysen, *Studies in Early Irish Law* (1936).

4   Professor Binchy's *Corpus Iuris Hibernici* (1979) is a six-volume annotation of the surviving ancient Irish law tracts. The work has been described as 'a complete diplomatic text of all the major Irish legal manuscripts' but it was published without 'translation, indices, notes on the contents, or even clear identification of the individual tracts' thus limiting its appeal to scholars who are already familiar with the material: Simms, *Medieval Gaelic Sources* (2009), p 92.

5   See Kelly, *A Guide to Early Irish Law* (1988); Kelly, *Early Irish Farming: a Study Based Mainly on the Law Texts of the 7th and 8th Centuries AD* (1998); Charles-Edwards and Kelly (eds), *Bechbretha: an Old Irish Law Tract on Beekeeping* (1983); Breathnach, *Uraicecht na Ríar: the Poetic Grades in Early Irish Law* (1987); McLeod, *Early Irish Contract Law* (1996).

6   See Hand, *English Law in Ireland, 1290–1324* (1967); Brand, *The Making of the Common Law* (1992); Donaldson, *Some Comparative Aspects of Irish Law* (1957); Johnston, 'The First Adventure of the Common Law' (1920) 36 LQR 9; Moran, 'The Migration of the Common Law: Republic of Ireland' (1960) 76 LQR 69; Newark, 'The Bringing of English Law to Ireland' (1972) 23 NILQ 1; Sheehy, 'English Law in Medieval Ireland' (1960) 22 *Archivum Hibernicum* 167.

reducing the English monarch to a largely symbolic head of state. However, when Henry II landed at Waterford, the king was the indisputable holder of ultimate power and authority. The Waterford Council declared that 'the laws of England were by all freely received and confirmed.' However, this 12th century communiqué hardly reflected local realities and it was not until the early 17th century that it could be said that English law prevailed in the greater part of Ireland. While the landings of Strongbow and Henry II may have had immense symbolic significance, they did not have the immediate effect of transplanting English law to Ireland. That was a struggle that was to take several centuries and was not fully achieved until the whole island of Ireland had been subdued in the 17th century.

The development of the common law

[2.04] Because Ireland was the first recipient of the Anglo–Norman common law system, the development of the English system of law after the Norman invasion of 1066 must be referred to briefly.

[2.05] After 1066, the conquering kings began the process of extending control over the whole of England. The strength of the conquering army was the initial method of subjugating the native English but the Normans' real power lay in their aptitude for administration. To this end, their rule was characterised by the refinement and development of existing structures and laws rather than by innovation on their part. They established a centralised government that was focused on the king. The key to this was the introduction of the system of feudal tenure by which the possession of land (at the time the prime form of wealth) was determined by social hierarchy. The king granted large tracts of land to the principal nobles, who were known as 'tenants-in-chief', in return for 'services', usually in the form of providing personnel for the king's army. They were also liable to 'incidents' – payments made to the king on the occurrence of certain events. The tenants-in-chief granted land to sub-tenants, who in turn granted land to those further down in the social scale and the result was a pyramidal structure encompassing all the freemen of the kingdom. The cardinal feature of the feudal relationship was the personal bond between lord and tenant. Apart from the loyalty owed by all subjects to the king, each landowner swore an oath of fealty to his immediate superior in return for his lord's protection. In this way the king was provided with an army and revenue, vital in ensuring the stability of the state, while at the same time the bonds of personal loyalty were the cement that held the system together.

[2.06] To reinforce his authority, the king travelled around the kingdom 'holding court.' One of the king's functions was to hear complaints and consider petitions from his subjects but as time passed this role was transferred to officials delegated to act in the king's name, namely the justices. In time, a system of courts, manned by the king's justices, who acted with his authority, was established in Westminster, which was also to become the location of the English Parliaments. These courts and the later Parliaments originated as off-shoots of the royal power, or royal prerogative, originally exercised in the King's Council. As well as hearing cases brought to London, the king's justices travelled throughout the kingdom twice a year on what were called the 'Assizes'.[7] The primary function of these twice-yearly forays was to reinforce the king's rule. At the same time the itinerant justices ensured the application of a uniform body of law throughout the realm, a 'common law', replacing the variegated system of customary laws that existed prior to the Norman invasion. In the course of applying the common law the justices reviewed the older customary rules, absorbing those that were compatible into the body of the common law and rejecting the rest. Since the king was the ultimate source of all law at this stage in history, and there was no real parliamentary body to approve or enact laws, it followed that the king's judges had immense power and authority in the shaping of the law. The judicial role in the development of the law explains the continuing importance of judges within common law systems.

Separation of common law and civil law systems

[2.07] It is clear from English history that the judges were the first to apply rules of law within the kingdom. As centuries passed and the English system developed, the judges retained a central role in the creation of new legal rules. In effect, the judges came to have delegated to them the king's role in setting out the basic rules of law that were to be applied in the kingdom. As we have observed,[8] these rules came to be known collectively as the common law of England, and any system of law which is based to a large extent on the development of rules by judges is known as a common law system. By way of contrast, the legal systems which developed on the mainland of Europe were based on Roman law, the texts of which were rediscovered by continental scholars during the Middle Ages.[9] By this time, however, the English system had developed its own approach. The minimal amount of cross-fertilisation between mainland Europe and England at this crucial developmental stage thus resulted in quite different systems of law. Eventually the continental systems came to be characterised by their comprehensive codes that contain all the law on a particular subject. However, for centuries civil lawyers relied on Roman law, as adapted and modified to local conditions. Codification, in the modern sense, was a more recent development, which coincided with the emergence of the continental nation states in the late 18th and 19th centuries. The promulgation in 1804 by the Emperor Napoleon of the French codes, in common parlance known as the 'Napoleonic Code', is considered to mark the beginning of the 'age of codifications'.[10] Many of the historical differences between the common law and civil law systems, notably the relative paucity of comprehensive codes in common law

---

7   The practice of twice-yearly forays into the hinterland survives in the statutory arrangements for the High Court on Circuit: see para **4.63**.

8   See para **1.10**.

9   Scotland also developed a civil law system. It was only after the English and Scottish kingdoms were united in 1707 that England began to exercise full law-making powers for Scotland. Despite this, however, many elements of the Scottish legal system remain quite distinct from those in the rest of Britain.

10 Bellomo, *The Common Legal Past of Europe 1000–1800* (1995), p 9.

systems and the different roles of the judiciary in shaping the law, persist to the present day.[11]

The development of equity in the courts of chancery

[2.08] We have already referred to the separate development of the courts of common law and the chancery courts, the courts of equity.[12] In terms of the political structure of the medieval English kingdom, royal power was largely exercised through the King's Council. The head of the administrative or secretarial department of the Council, called the Chancery Department, was the Lord Chancellor who came to play a leading role in the court system. In order to initiate a claim in the king's common law courts, a litigant was required to file in the Chancery Department a document called a writ, in effect a summons issued in the king's name ordering the other party in the case to appear in court. The Chancery Department was, in effect, a clearing house for writs and it scrutinised the writ filed by a litigant to ensure that it came within one of the established forms of writ. If it did not, the common law courts would simply refuse to hear the matter. If this was the case, an appeal would lie to the king. In time, the king delegated the function of hearing such appeals to the Lord Chancellor, with full authority to decide the case according to 'the justice and equity' of the matter. To this end the Lord Chancellor's freedom to make decisions was not fettered by the rigidity that had come to characterise the common law courts.

[2.09] Ultimately, the Chancellor's Department began to deal with so many of these petitions from the common law courts that it developed into a separate court of law, which became known as the Court of Chancery, where the body of law known as equity was applied. The decisions of the Chancellor's Court were once described as being so free of common law rigidity that decisions as to the equity of a case were said to vary according to the length of the Chancellor's foot – a phrase that has been handed down over the centuries as a mark of disapproval of arbitrary judicial decisions. By the late 18th century, however, the growth of equity was such there were very few areas which had not been covered by previous cases and equity itself, like the common law, had acquired the rigidity associated with a system governed by a faithful adherence to precedent.

Parliaments and statute law as a source of law

[2.10] Although the concept of parliament as a law-making institution emerged much later than the development of the judicial law-giving function, it had become well-established in the medieval period as a method of curbing the absolute authority of the Crown and as an alternative source of legal rules, called statute law or legislation. However, the judges were slow to acknowledge that statute law could take priority over

---

[11] See generally, van Caenegem, *Judges, Legislators and Professors: Chapters in European Legal History* (1987); Robinson *et al*, *European Legal History: Sources and Institutions* (3rd edn, 2000).

[12] See para **1.12**.

the common law rules which had been in existence for many centuries. The acceptance by the judges of the superiority of statute law did not fully emerge until the reign of the Tudors in the 16th century. Ultimately, however, the judges accepted that parliament had full authority to overturn the common law, and that by and large remains the position in England to this day. Parliament, not the monarch, is the supreme and only source of laws, and the function of the judges is to interpret those laws. In British constitutional theory at least, the Westminster Parliament is unfettered and could enact a law that all blue-eyed babies be put to death.[13]

Judges as law makers

[2.11] The declaratory theory saw the common law as a seamless whole, elements of which were revealed by judges as they determined cases. On this view the judge did not make law, but merely announced what the law was. That is not to say that judges in English courts have no law-making function and it is now accepted that there is a creative dimension to adjudication that sometimes comes close to law-making. Where legislation has not yet been enacted to deal with a particular area of law, the judges therefore continue to be the primary sources of the law to be applied in such situations. Furthermore, in spite of the increased volume of legislation in recent years, a substantial amount of law remains as laid down by the common law.[14] However, even where legislation has been enacted to deal with a particular area, the judges have an important role in interpreting that law where a dispute arises as to its meaning.[15] In Ireland, the role of the judges is further enhanced by the Constitution as they are empowered to declare invalid any law passed by the National Parliament, the Oireachtas, as well as to modify any common law rule to meet constitutional requirements.[16]

The initial reception of English law into Ireland to 1494

[2.12] The Anglo–Norman invasion of Ireland resulted, at least initially, in the extension of English law to most of the eastern portion of the island of Ireland in what we have already seen was described as 'the first adventure of the common law'. The practical application of English rule arose, as with the Norman conquest of England in the previous century, from a combination of military and civil authority: the granting by Henry II of feudal land rights to Strongbow over most of the eastern province of Leinster and the appointment in 1172 of Hugh de Lacy as the first Justiciar of Ireland (the chief governor or representative of the King). In 1204 King John authorised the issuing of

---

13 However, as is the case in Ireland, European Union law takes precedence over British domestic law. The Human Rights Act 1998 (UK) establishes a system for reviewing the compatibility of legislation with the European Convention on Human Rights but it stops short of giving the courts the power to invalidate national legislation. These features represent slight but potentially significant inroads into the British constitutional doctrine of parliamentary supremacy.

14 See further Ch 12.

15 See further Ch 14.

16 See further Ch 15.

writs by the Justiciar, in effect directing the Irish courts to apply the common law. In 1226 Henry III ordered the Justiciar to adhere to the laws and customs of England, an instruction that was reinforced the following year by the sending of a 'Register of Writs' to Dublin.[17] The Register contained copies of all the writs issued by the English courts and its transmission across the Irish Sea represents the completion, in a formal sense at least, of the introduction of the common law into Ireland. The first recorded judicial appointment of an Anglo–Norman judge in Ireland is in 1221.[18] From that time onwards concerted efforts were made to ensure that persons versed in English law were appointed to the Irish courts in an effort to reinforce the uniform application of that body of law in Ireland.

[2.13] However, the influence of English law went into decline between 1300 and the end of the 15th century, during which time the original Norman invaders became 'more Irish than the Irish themselves' through inter-marriage with the native Irish noble families. Attempts were made to curb this decline by legislation, most notably the Statutes of Kilkenny of 1366, which sought to confirm the supremacy of English law and the supremacy of the English Parliament over any Irish Parliament.[19] In the 1480s, matters came to a head when a claim was made by certain Anglo–Norman merchants in Waterford that English legislation restricting trade did not apply to them. Although the courts initially decided in their favour, the final decision was that the English Parliament had full authority to legislate for Ireland.[20] Nonetheless, it was felt better to have the matter clarified and Henry VII dispatched Edward Poyning to Ireland as his Lord Deputy (the successor to the position of Justiciar) for this purpose. At a Parliament held in Drogheda in 1494, the Act, usually referred to as Poyning's Law, sought to restrict any Irish Parliament by providing that, henceforth:

> "no Parliament be holden hereafter in the said land [Ireland], but at such season as the King's lieutenant and counsail [the Privy Council] there first do certifie the King ... all such acts as them seemeth should pass ... and if any Parliament be holden in that land hereafter, contrary to the form and provision aforesaid, it be deemed void and of none effect in law."[21]

[2.14] Poyning's Law clearly established that, from 1495, any Parliament assembled in Ireland required the prior approval of the King's Lieutenant in Ireland and of the King's

---

[17] See Maitland, 'Notes and Documents: The Introduction of English Law into Ireland' (1889) 4 *English Historical Review* 516.

[18] See Ball, *The Judges in Ireland, 1221 to 1921* (1993), a two-volume work chronicling all known appointments to the Irish Bench prior to the establishment of the two jurisdictions in 1921 and 1922.

[19] See Richardson and Sayles, *The Irish Parliament in the Middle Ages* (1952).

[20] *Case of the Merchants of Waterford* (1483–4) YB Ric III f12; YB 1 Hen VII f2. 'YB' refers to the Yearbooks, the first form of law reports: see para **2.15.** On the background to the case, see Johnston, 'The English Legislature and the Irish Courts' (1924) 40 LQR 91.

[21] 10 Hen VII, c 4 (Irl), entitled 'An Act that no Parliament be holden in this Land until the Acts be certified in England'. The text of Poyning's Law is contained in *The Irish Statutes 1310– 1800* (1995), p 761.

Privy Council in London. This supremacy was underpinned by another Act passed at Poyning's Parliament in Drogheda, which provided:

> "That all estatutes, late made within the ... realm of England, concerning or belonging to the common and publique weal of the same, shall henceforth be deemed good and effectuall in the law, and over that be acceptyd, used, and executed within this land of Ireland in all points at all times requisite according to the tenor and effect of the same; and over that by authority aforesaid, that they and every of them be authorized, proved and confirmed in this said land of Ireland. And if any estatute or estatutes have been made within this said land, hereafter to the contrary, they and every of them by authority aforesaid be adnulled, revoked, voyd, and of none effect in the law."[22]

[2.15] The clear intention of the two Acts passed in 1494 was to affirm for Ireland the supremacy of English laws, but in subsequent centuries the Irish Parliaments sought to assert their independence from the English Parliament and occasionally purported to overstep the bounds set for them in 1494. In addition, some confusion (real or apparent) was expressed as to the precise meaning of the catch-all phrase 'concerning or belonging to the common and publique weal' contained in the second Act passed at Poyning's Parliament.[23]

[2.16] Moreover, whatever the formal terms of these Acts of 1494, the political reality was that English law in Ireland applied only so far as a military presence in support of the civil authorities assured this to be so. In 1494, English law was applied primarily in the eastern part of the island extending in an arc from Dublin known as 'the Pale' where the English settlers (and, to some extent, the native Irish)[24] were entitled to the benefit of the king's law. Outside the Pale, Brehon law continued to be applied, particularly in the western and northern parts of the country.[25]

The Tudor settlements or plantations

[2.17] The extension of English law outside the Pale to the greater part of Ireland only began in earnest under the Tudor monarchs. In the mid-16th century, Henry VIII proceeded with a large-scale 'surrender and re-grant' of land held by the native Irish

---

[22] 10 Hen VII, c 22 (Irl), entitled 'An Act confirming all the Statutes made in England'. See *The Irish Statutes 1310–1800* (1995), p 3. A note to the text states that the Drogheda Parliament was the first to use the English language for its Acts. Prior to this, most official texts were in Latin, and Latin remained the most common language for such official texts for some time thereafter.

[23] For an illuminating description of the difficulties associated with the scope of this Act passed at Poyning's Parliament, see Osborough's introductory essay to the 1995 reprint of *The Irish Statutes 1310–1800*.

[24] Within 'the Pale', the native Irish appeared to have the status of feudal villeins, and were known as *betaghs*. It was not until 1612 (11, 12, & 13, Jac I, c 5) that the Irish Parliament enacted that all natives of Ireland were 'taken into his Majestie's gracious protection, and doe now live under one law as dutiful subjects of our Sovereigne Lord and Monarch.'

[25] Sir William Blackstone observed: '[a]nd yet, even in the reign of queen Elizabeth [the first], the wild natives still kept and preserved their Brehon law.' 1 Bl Comm 99.

noble families, bringing them within the English landholding system. In addition, his break with the Church of Rome resulted in the extension to Ireland of the dissolution of the monasteries and the redistribution of church land. In the reign of Elizabeth I, a failed rebellion by the Irish noble families in Ulster ultimately led to the Flight of the Earls in 1607 and the consequent settlement or Plantation of Ulster, under which much of the land in Ulster formerly in the ownership of the departed Earls was granted to Scottish and English settlers. The events of the early 17th century continue to have a significant political influence almost 400 years later in the political debates on the future of the people who share the island of Ireland. The Flight of the Earls also removed from Ireland the remaining source of patronage for the Brehons, the jurists of the Brehon law system.

[**2.18**] The early 17th century also saw the courts in Ireland firmly accepting the dominance of the English laws of succession and, in turn, rejecting the Brehon systems of succession known as *tanistry* and *gavelkind*.[26] These decisions, linked to the further military conquest of Ireland in later years and centuries, signalled the death knell of the Brehon law as an influential body of law except in minor areas of law.[27] The middle of the 17th century saw the further conquest of Ireland by Oliver Cromwell's Commonwealth army between 1649 and 1652 and the resettlement of many of the Irish landowners in the western part of Ireland (made famous for Irish nationalists by the cry 'to Hell or to Connaught'). After the Restoration of the English monarchy under Charles II, the end of the 17th century saw the victory in 1690 at the Battle of the Boyne of the Protestant William of Orange over the Catholic James II and his Jacobite supporters, leading to the reassertion of a distinctly Protestant form of English rule in England and Ireland. While the accession of William III to the English throne was accompanied by his acceptance of limits on royal power in the Bill of Rights 1689,[28] the rights contained therein were confined to those of the Protestant faith. Those in England and (more numerously) in Ireland who chose the 'Papish' faith were excluded from full participation in the civil life of the kingdom through a series of legislative measures in the 18th century known collectively as the Penal Laws.

Grattan's Parliament and the Act of Union

[**2.19**] Despite the occasional assertion of independence from the Irish Parliaments of the Middle Ages, the 18th century saw an extension and clarification of the earlier Acts

---

26 *Case of Gavelkind* (1605) Dav 49 and *Case of Tanistry* (1607) Dav 28, both cases reported in a series of law reports collated by the then Attorney General for Ireland, Sir John Davies, later Chief Justice of the English Queen's Bench. See Prawlisch, *Sir John Davies and the Conquest of Ireland* (1985).

27 During the brief operation of the revolutionary Dáil Éireann Courts between 1919 and 1922, Brehon law was cited as a persuasive authority on a variety of matters: see further, para **2.102**. Since that time, Brehon law has been consulted in relation to certain fishery rights in *R (Moore) v O'Hanrahan* [1927] IR 406 and *Moore v Attorney General* [1934] IR 44.

28 1 Will III & Mary II, sess 2, c 2. The Bill of Rights remains a key element of the English Constitution to the present day.

passed during Poyning's Parliament, when the Irish Parliament passed Yelverton's Act 1781. This provided that all English statutes:

"for the settling and assuring [of] forfeited estates ... concerning commerce ... and ... the seamen of England and Ireland, ... the stile or calendar ... and ... the taking any oath or oaths ... or relate to the continuance of any office, civil or military or of any commission, or of any writ, process, or proceeding at law or in equity ... shall be accepted, used, and executed in this kingdom ..."[29]

[2.20] Ironically, just two years later, under the Irish Appeals Act 1783,[30] the Westminster Parliament repealed Poyning's Act and renounced its claim to legislate for Ireland.[31] For a brief time, between 1783 and 1800, the Irish Parliament in Dublin, known as Grattan's Parliament, enacted some legislation ameliorating the Penal Laws for the Catholic population, including a limited right to vote and admission to practice at the Bar.[32] This period also saw a growth in prosperity in Ireland and the creation of the great Georgian streets and squares of Dublin and other cities, most of which have survived to this day. However, the exclusive legislative powers of the Irish Parliament were short lived and, moreover, against the background of the American and French revolutions of the time, there was an unsuccessful but influential rebellion in parts of Ireland in 1798 against the existing regime. Shortly after this, and before another unsuccessful revolt in 1803, the Act of Union of 1800[33] disbanded the Dublin Parliament and established the Westminster Parliament as the sole legislative assembly for what was, until the establishment of the Irish Free State in 1922,[34] the United Kingdom of Great Britain and Ireland. Article 8 of the 1800 Act also 'carried over' the prior laws and court system into the new United Kingdom by providing that:

"all laws in force at the time of the union, and all courts of civil and ecclesiastical jurisdiction within the respective kingdoms, shall remain as now by law established within the same, subject only to such alterations and regulations from time to time as circumstances may appear to the parliament of the united kingdom to require ..."

[2.21] By establishing Westminster as the principal legislative body for Ireland (as well as the rest of the United Kingdom), the 1800 Act brought all major institutions of state –

---

[29] 21 & 22 Geo III, c 48 (Irl), entitled 'An Act for extending certain of the Provisions' of Poyning's Act 1494. See *The Irish Statutes 1310–1800* (1995), p 580.

[30] 23 Geo 3, c 28.

[31] The Irish House of Lords also reasserted its role as a judicial body during this period: see Lyall, 'The Irish House of Lords as a Judicial Body 1783–1800' (1993–1995) 28–30 Ir Jur (ns) 314.

[32] Roman Catholic Relief Act 1793, 33 Geo 3, c 21 (Irl). On the exclusion of Roman Catholics from the legal profession, see Kenny, 'The Exclusion of Catholics from the Legal Profession in Ireland, 1537–1829' (1987) 25(100) Ir Hist Stud 337.

[33] The Union was effected by identical Acts passed in London and Dublin: 39 & 40 Geo 3, c 67 and 40 Geo 3, c 38 (Irl). For the Irish Act, see *The Irish Statutes 1310–1800* (1995), p 723.

[34] Article 1 of the Act of Union had provided that the Union, which took effect on 1 January 1801, should be 'for ever'.

legislative, executive and judicial – firmly back within the control of the London administration.

[4] THE INSTITUTIONS OF STATE IN THE UNITED KINGDOM (1800–1922)

Separation of powers

[2.22] It is appropriate at this stage to mention that during the 19th century, the essential elements of the system of government familiar today began to take shape. The United Kingdom had not faced the revolutionary change that occurred in the United States of America or France in the late 18th century, though it was directly affected by both in the sense of losing a valuable colony and in suppressing an attempted revolution in Ireland in 1798. However, the pressure for substantial reform was felt in other less dramatic ways in the early decades of the 19th century. There was no Declaration of the Rights of Man or overthrow of an *ancien régime*, but there was real, if gradual, change in the relationship between the three branches of government – legislative, executive and judicial – which reflected the separation of the powers endorsed in revolutionary America and France.

[2.23] Important political thinkers, such as Jeremy Bentham and John Stuart Mill, as well as writers such as Charles Dickens, were influential in effecting significant law reform and modernisation of state institutions in the wake of the onset of the industrial revolution that marked the 19th century. Economic development and law reform went hand in hand.[35]

Legislature

[2.24] The legislative branch of government, embodied in parliament, had, of course, long before established its law-making function, taking over the powers exercised by the medieval King's Council. A critical element of its coming of age as a law-making body was the acceptance by the monarch of parliament's right to raise taxes. The early medieval parliaments of barons and earls grew into the House of Lords. Later, the House of Commons emerged to become the second half of what was now a bicameral legislature. By the mid-19th century, legislative proposals continued to require royal assent in order to become Acts of Parliament but this assent was, in practice, given as a matter of course once a Bill had been passed by both Houses of Parliament. Another aspect of the legislative power was the long-fought battle by the House of Commons to wrest real legislative control from the House of Lords. Without minimising its protracted nature, it was clear that, by the beginning of the 19th century, the House of Lords was starting to lose real power. However, it was not until 1911 that legislation was enacted to secure the primacy of the House of Commons, leaving the House of Lords with an advisory and delaying power only. Indeed, prior to 1911 a number of Home Rule

---

35 See McEldowney and O'Higgins, 'Irish Legal History and the 19th century' in McEldowney and O'Higgins, *The Common Law Tradition: Essays in Irish Legal History* (1990), p 203.

Bills[36] had failed to be enacted because of a negative vote in the House of Lords, even after they had been passed in the House of Commons.

Executive

[2.25] Executive authority, in the form of the power to declare war, to enter into international treaties and to administer the Departments and Ministries of State, had also been taken gradually from the king's immediate control. Thus, real executive power had in effect been transferred to the king's ministers. These were selected by the Houses of Parliament from their members, but increasingly as the 19th century progressed many of the more powerful ministers were members of the House of Commons, another indication of the shift in the balance of power between the two Houses. These ministers were presided over by a Prime Minister and increasingly they acted collectively through a Cabinet. In the wake of the Act of Union 1800, the Crown's principal representative in Ireland was now the Chief Secretary for Ireland, a member of the Cabinet in London. However, since the headquarters of the executive in Ireland was in Dublin Castle, it was the Under-Secretary of State, who resided more or less permanently in Dublin, who retained real control along with the Crown's official representative in Dublin, the Lord Lieutenant or Viceroy.

[2.26] These fundamental components of a constitutional monarchy were based on a combination of various laws (such as the Bill of Rights, the Act of Settlement and the Act of Union) and unwritten convention (such as the precise role of the Prime Minister), rather than on a single authoritative constitutional text, such as that which was adopted in the United States of America.[37] This constitutional arrangement became more firmly entrenched as the 19th century progressed and the shift of power from the monarch accelerated with the move towards a, more or less, popularly elected House of Commons.

Judiciary

[2.27] The third organ of government, the judiciary, also became the subject of considerable reform in the 19th century.[38] The medieval role of the Lord Chancellor in the administration of justice as head of the Chancery Department of the King's Council was transformed into that of overall head of the judiciary and, hence, the court system. The Lord Chancellor was the presiding judge in the Judicial Committee of the House of Lords, the final court of appeal in the United Kingdom. It might seem surprising that one of the Houses of Parliament was the final court of appeal in the kingdom, but this can be explained by the fact that it developed from the King's Council which ultimately held all power. A practical difficulty for the House of Lords as a court of law was that, until well into the 19th century, any member of the House was entitled, at least in theory, to sit in judgment in an appeal to the House of Lords acting in its judicial capacity.

---

36   See para **2.44**.
37   Strauss, 'Constitutions, Written and Otherwise' (2000) 19 *Law and Philosophy* 451.
38   See para **2.30**.

However, over time it became the practice that only legally qualified peers would hear such appeals and eventually legislation was enacted to ensure that the Judicial Committee comprised full-time judges only, the 'Law Lords', who were appointed to the House of Lords for this particular purpose. As a matter of convention, the Law Lords rarely participated in the legislative work of the House of Lords, though they might contribute to debates on Bills connected with the courts or the administration of justice generally.

[2.28] As well as presiding over the Judicial Committee of the House of Lords, the Lord Chancellor also acted in two other capacities which appear anomalous in the context of the separation of powers. The Lord Chancellor effectively was the chairman of the House of Lords acting in its legislative capacity as a House of Parliament. He also was a member of the British Cabinet, with a ministerial portfolio covering the regulation of the legal profession, the court system and connected issues. In this unique way, executive, legislative and judicial functions were concentrated in the one office.

[2.29] In the context of the appointment of the judiciary in Ireland, we have already mentioned that the Anglo–Norman kings had begun in 1221 to appoint lawyers versed in English law to the Irish Bench. Before and after the Act of Union of 1800, the London government continued to maintain close control over judicial appointments to the Irish courts, even if at this point Irish lawyers, including Catholics, were appointed in increasing numbers to the bench.

The Supreme Court of Judicature Acts 1873 and 1877

[2.30] By the 19th century it was becoming increasingly clear that the judicial system required significant reform. In particular, the phenomenon of parallel common law and equity courts, which emerged in the medieval period, no longer met the demands of an industrial and mercantile society. While in theory the courts dealt with separate subject matter the reality was very different and the boundaries between the two sets of courts were imprecisely defined. The two systems had become so complex that many years could be spent simply determining in which of the two systems a particular claim should be brought. Charles Dickens' *Bleak House*, with its savage caricature of the interminable litigation in the fictional wardship case *Jarndyce v Jarndyce*, played an important part in highlighting these anomalies in the system, and throughout the 19th century procedural reforms were introduced to ameliorate the worst flaws. However, it became clear that incremental reform was insufficient and that a more radical measure was necessary. This was achieved by the enactment of the Supreme Court of Judicature Act 1873 which governed the courts of England and Wales.[39] The equivalent measure for Ireland was passed four years later, the Supreme Court of Judicature (Ireland) Act 1877.[40] The important effect of the 1873 and 1877 Acts was that the administration of the twin systems of common law and equity was fused into a single unified court

---

[39]   36 & 37 Vict c 66.

[40]   40 & 41 Vict c 57.

system. Once a case was begun in the new court system, the court could apply either the rules of equity or of common law.[41]

[2.31] The 1873 and 1877 Acts established a unified court called the Supreme Court of Judicature, comprising the High Court of Justice, with original jurisdiction as well as power to hear appeals from courts of local jurisdiction, and the Court of Appeal, which was invested with appellate jurisdiction. The Judicial Committee of the House of Lords, presided over by the Lord Chancellor, retained its status as the ultimate court of appeal for Ireland. This essential framework remained the basis for the court system in the United Kingdom until 2009.[42] Indeed, in Ireland, a similar structure continues to apply.

[2.32] Under the 1877 Act, the High Court of Justice of Ireland sat in Dublin, and this court, housed in the Four Courts building, was the principal court for the island of Ireland. As well as fusing the courts of common law and equity into a unified court, the Judicature Acts also provided that the High Court of Justice was to be divided in turn into a number of divisions, which amalgamated and rationalised the many different courts that had developed from medieval times.

The Superior Courts

[2.33] The High Court of Justice established by the 1873 and 1877 Acts was the successor to the courts established in medieval times backed by the power and authority of the king. Because these courts acted on behalf of the king, and could trace their ancestry back to the King's Council, they were regarded as having certain inherent powers, simply by virtue of their being the royal courts. These included the power of the King's Bench Division to issue the prerogative writs[43] and the extension of this power over the whole kingdom. These courts came to be known as the superior courts of justice, in contrast to the inferior and local courts established over the centuries and whose powers were limited in some form or another, whether in terms of the type of case they were empowered to deal with or their geographical limits. We will return to the inferior and local courts below.[44]

[2.34] The four principal superior courts which had developed from the Middle Ages (which incidentally had given the title to the Four Courts building) were:

The Court of Exchequer

[2.35] This court emerged from the Exchequer Department of the King's Council presided over by the Treasurer, the other great adviser to the king along with the Lord

---

[41] See Keane, *Equity and the Law of Trusts in the Republic of Ireland* (1988) and Delany, *Equity and the Law of Trusts in Ireland* (4th edn, 2007).

[42] From 1 October 2009, the judicial business previously undertaken by the House of Lords transferred to a newly created Supreme Court of the United Kingdom. Its first members were existing Law Lords but justices appointed subsequently are not members of the House of Lords, thus cementing the separation between the judiciary and the legislature.

[43] See paras **2.37** and **10.53**.

[44] See paras **2.49–2.54**.

Chancellor. Originally, the Court of Exchequer dealt mainly with disputes by subjects concerning whether moneys were owed to the king's Treasury. It was presided over by a Chief Baron, the other judges being referred to as *puisne*[45] barons. Eventually, this court extended its jurisdiction by developing one of the 'fictions' of the law. The court was prepared to hear a civil case in which one party claimed that a debt owed to him by the other party would be used to discharge a debt owed to the Crown. As indicated, this device was ultimately used purely *pro forma* in order to ensure that the case would be heard by the Court of Exchequer. In the 19th century, the Irish Court of Exchequer also comprised a Lord Chief Baron and *puisne* barons, the last Chief Baron also being the longest-serving, Christopher Palles.[46]

The Court of Common Pleas

[2.36] This court was established to deal with 'common' disputes, that is disputes between private individuals or commoners, concerning what would be described today as civil claims. The Court comprised a Chief Justice of the Common Pleas and a number of *puisne* judges.

The Court of King's, or Queen's, Bench[47]

[2.37] This court was the third common law court to emerge from the *Curia Regis* and, in historical terms, remains more closely associated with the royal power and thus was regarded as being more important and influential. It dealt with criminal and civil matters, thus overlapping with the Court of Common Pleas. It also acted on behalf of the king's interest by exercising a supervisory jurisdiction over the inferior courts established over the years, through the mechanism of the prerogative writs.[48] The Court of King's Bench comprised the Chief Justice of the King's Bench and other *puisne* judges.

The Court of Chancery

[2.38] We have already noted that the Court of Chancery had developed from the Lord Chancellor's jurisdiction in equity. By the late 1860s, the Irish Court of Chancery comprised the Lord Chancellor of Ireland,[49] the Vice-Chancellor and the Master of the Rolls in Ireland.[50]

---

45 Pronounced 'puny'.
46 See further para **4.87**.
47 The title King's Bench or Queen's Bench varies, depending on whether the monarch is a king or queen.
48 See para **10.53**.
49 See O'Flanagan, *Lives of the Lord Chancellors of Ireland*, 2 vols (1810).
50 The Master of the Rolls had originally been keeper of the State Papers but later became a judicial office holder. The position remains in place in England, where the Master of the Rolls is the judicial head of the civil division of the Court of Appeal.

House of Lords

[2.39] Finally, although outside the realms of the four courts listed, it is convenient to reiterate here that the House of Lords, acting in its judicial capacity, was the final court of appeal for the kingdom.[51]

Other superior courts

[2.40] In addition to the foregoing courts, the following developed:

- the High Court of Admiralty, which dealt with maritime claims;
- the Landed Estates Court, which dealt with certain land matters;
- the Court of Bankruptcy and Insolvency;
- the Court of Probate, which dealt with cases arising from wills;
- the Court of Matrimonial Causes and Matters; and
- the Court for Crown Cases Reserved, which operated to some extent as a court for appeals in criminal matters before the right to appeal in such cases was established.

[2.41] The foregoing is not a comprehensive list, but it provides an indication of the complexity which had developed in the system up to the mid-19th century.[52] After the Judicature Acts, some further rationalisation of the court system was effected between 1897 and 1907, resulting in the High Court Divisions being reduced to two: the King's Bench Division and the Chancery Division (with two Judicial Commissioners of the Irish Land Commission also being High Court judges).

19th century land reform

[2.42] Returning to the impact of English law on Ireland in the early 19th century, further significant relaxation of the Penal Laws was effected, symbolised by the passing of the Roman Catholic Relief Act 1829,[53] more commonly known by its supporters as the Catholic Emancipation Act and generally associated with the Irish barrister and Member of Parliament Daniel O'Connell. Among other reforms brought about by the 1829 Act was the removal of the ban on Catholics being elevated to the Bench. In 1836, the first Irish Catholic was appointed to a senior judicial position.[54] However, O'Connell's wider campaign to repeal the Act of Union was not successful.

[2.43] While the relaxation of the Penal Laws was welcomed by what might be described as the Catholic establishment, an even greater political movement surrounded

---

51 See para **2.113**.
52 See further Osborough, 'The Irish Legal System, 1796–1877' in Costello (ed), *The Four Courts: 200 Years* (1996), p 33.
53 10 Geo 4, c 7.
54 Michael O'Loghlen, 'O'Connell's legal understudy', was appointed a Baron of the Court of Exchequer in 1836 and Master of the Rolls in 1837: see Ball, *The Judges in Ireland, 1221 to 1921* (1993), Vol II, p 274.

the plight of tenant farmers in Ireland in the 19th century, whose difficulties were exacerbated by the calamity of the Great Famine of the mid-1840s. Agitation for agrarian law reform became the focus of mass political action, exemplified by the Land League, founded in 1879 by Michael Davitt with Charles Stuart Parnell, the leader of the Irish Parliamentary Party at Westminster, as its president. Arising from the Land League's potent campaigning, considerable reform was effected through parliamentary methods by the Land Law (Ireland) Act 1881,[55] which established the Irish Land Commission and gave legal effect to the Ulster tenant right, encapsulated in the campaign slogan 'fair rent, free sale and fixity of tenure.' Later Acts passed between 1885 and 1909 also enabled tenant farmers to buy out their tenancies and purchase the freehold title to their land, with landlords being paid a land purchase bond rather than cash.[56]

The Home Rule movement

[2.44] Despite the significant land reforms,[57] the land agitation movement spilled over into the call by Irish nationalists for the repeal of the Act of Union of 1800 and, initially at any rate, the granting of limited Home Rule to Ireland. At Westminster, the Home Rule campaigns of the Irish Parliamentary Party received some support from Liberal Prime Minister Gladstone but met with opposition from Conservatives and Unionists. By the early years of the twentieth century, Unionist opposition to Home Rule (mainly concentrated in the province of Ulster and reflecting the Tudor Plantation or Settlement) solidified under the leadership of one of the leading barristers of the day, Sir Edward Carson. In 1914, the Irish Parliamentary Party, by now led by John Redmond, had secured the passing of the Government of Ireland Act 1914, the first Home Rule Act to be enacted. This provided for limited legislative powers for a Parliament of Ireland, subject to continuing overall control from Westminster, as well as an executive drawn from the Irish Parliament which would replace the executive headed by the Chief Secretary for Ireland that was appointed by London. However, the 1914 Act was suspended for the duration of World War I and, in any event, was to be amended to take account of Ulster Unionist opposition.

---

55   44 & 45 Vict, c 49.

56   These included the Purchase of Land (Ireland) Act 1885, 48 & 49 Vict, c 73; the Purchase of Land (Ireland) Act 1891, 54 & 55 Vict, c 48; the Land Law (Ireland) Act 1896, 59 & 60 Vict, c 47 (the latter two Acts known as the 'Balfour Acts'); the Irish Land Act 1903, 3 Edw 7, c 37 ('Wyndham's Act'); and the Irish Land Act 1909, 9 Edw 7, c 42 ('Birrell's Act'). The successors to the original Irish Land Commission and the associated land bond purchase scheme continued in operation in Northern Ireland until 1937, while its equivalent in the Republic of Ireland was only wound down in the late 1980s: see the discussion of the Irish Land Commission (Dissolution) Act 1992 by Humphreys, *Irish Current Law Statutes Annotated*.

57   The land purchase scheme, which extended to the entire island of Ireland, resulted in a much greater proportion of freehold farmers than is the case in England and Wales today, where 'absentee landlords' and tenant farmers remain common.

[2.45] From a nationalist perspective, two further events eclipsed the 1914 Act. Easter 1916 saw a nationalist rebellion or Rising in many parts of Ireland. While the Rising was a military failure and initially unpopular with the general populace, its crude suppression, including the execution of many of its leaders by the British authorities resulted in a significant swing towards militant nationalism, represented by the Sinn Féin Party, and away from the Irish Parliamentary Party. In the 1918 general election to the Westminster Parliament, Sinn Féin (many of whose candidates were still in prison or in hiding as a result of their participation in the 1916 Rising) almost completely supplanted the Irish Parliamentary Party. Rather than taking their seats in Westminster, Sinn Féin summoned a meeting in January 1919 of what, from the nationalist perspective, was the meeting of the first National Parliament, Dáil Éireann. From the British perspective, of course, this was a seditious assembly. The first Dáil adopted a declaration of independence and passed decrees establishing a Constitution, a Provisional Government and a court system.[58] Around the same time, a guerrilla-style armed campaign, commonly called the 'War of Independence', was conducted by nationalists against British rule. Attempts to suppress the nationalist rebellion ultimately failed and, by 1921, it was accepted by the British government that continued British rule was impossible in most parts of Ireland.

Government of Ireland Act 1920

[2.46] Prior to this, however, the Westminster Parliament passed the Government of Ireland Act 1920.[59] This amounted to a consolidated version of the 1914 Act, and it envisaged the establishment of two political units, Southern Ireland and Northern Ireland, with Dublin and Belfast as capitals. Significantly, Northern Ireland was to comprise six counties of Ulster – namely, Antrim, Armagh, Down, Fermanagh, Londonderry and Tyrone – with Southern Ireland comprising the remaining 26 counties. Each entity was to have a parliament, an executive chosen from the members of the respective parliaments, and a court system comprising a High Court and Court of Appeal, with a further layer added which envisaged a High Court of Appeal for Ireland to hear appeals from the Court of Appeal of Northern Ireland and the Court of Appeal of Southern Ireland. As with the 1914 Act, both parliaments would ultimately be subject to the Parliament at Westminster, and the Crown would continue to be represented by the Lord Lieutenant. The 1920 Act also held out the unlikely prospect of 'Irish union', provided the two parliaments voted for this.

[2.47] In paving the way for the separate court systems that would be required for the two jurisdictions that ultimately emerged in 1922, the Government of Ireland Act 1920 followed the model of the Judicature Act, with a Supreme Court of Judicature comprising a High Court of Justice and Court of Appeal. While the 1920 Act initially maintained, at least on paper,[60] a single court system for the island of Ireland for the

---

58   On the Dáil Éireann Courts, see para **2.101***ff*.
59   10 & 11 Geo 5, c 67.
60   See para **2.99**.

period up to 1922, the 1920 Act also envisaged that this would be split in two, with separate High Courts and Courts of Appeal for the two jurisdictions.

[2.48] By 1921, immediately before the two new political entities – the Irish Free State and Northern Ireland – came into being, the Supreme Court of Judicature in Ireland comprised a Court of Appeal of six judges and a High Court of Justice of twelve judges, the High Court being divided into a King's Bench Division of eight judges, a Chancery Division with four judges, with two other High Court judges, the Judicial Commissioners of the Irish Land Commission. It should be clear from the number of judges of the King's Bench Division (as well as the continued existence of a Chancery Division) that the bulk of civil and criminal business previously conducted by the pre-1877 courts had been absorbed into the King's Bench Division. It remains the case in England and Northern Ireland that the Queen's Bench Division deals with the vast majority of civil and criminal business of the High Court.

The Inferior Courts prior to 1922

[2.49] Before proceeding to discuss the arrangements made in 1921 and 1922 for the two jurisdictions established in Ireland, we should discuss the nature and development of a number of inferior and local courts which dealt with those less significant civil and criminal matters not dealt with in the High Court of Justice.

The Assize Courts

[2.50] We have already observed that the Assizes or sessions had developed early in the Norman legal system. They involved holding hearings of criminal and civil cases outside London where these had not already been heard at the sessions held by the courts at Westminster. This was an early feature of the administration of justice, and the Assizes, or *Nisi Prius* hearings,[61] avoided the inconvenience for those involved of having to travel to the capital. The judges of the Assize Courts were, in effect, travelling judges of what ultimately became the High Court of Justice. This finds a modern echo in the twice-yearly sittings of the High Court on Circuit.[62]

Quarter Sessions and Petty Sessions: Justices of the Peace

[2.51] Quite early in the development of the English legal system, officials who ultimately became known as Justices of the Peace (JPs) had emerged to hear less serious criminal matters than those heard at Assizes, and these Justices sat about four times a year in what were known as Quarter Sessions. Over the centuries, the jurisdiction of the

---

61   The Second Statute of Westminster of 1285 had provided that all civil matters were to be dealt with at Westminster '[u]nless the itinerant justices shall have come before into those parts'. As the Statute was enacted in Latin, the reference to the travelling justices not having heard the case would have involved the words '*nisi prius*' and so the Assize or hearings of the 'itinerant justices' came to be known as the *Nisi Prius* hearings.

62   See para **4.63**.

Justices of the Peace was extended by statute, but the more serious criminal offences, such as murder and offences connected with rebellion, were reserved for the Assizes.

[2.52] In addition to dealing with minor criminal matters, the Justices were also required to conduct preliminary hearings for the Assize Courts. These were held outside the Quarter Sessions dates, and were known as Petty Sessions. If the Justice of the Peace found that there was *prima facie* evidence to justify a trial, a document known as a 'bill of indictment' would be referred to a Grand Jury, whose function was to decide whether the bill was correct in form and whether it was supported by *prima facie* evidence. If they considered that this was the case, the bill of indictment became an indictment, triable by Petty Jury (which, in spite of its title, was the final decision-making body in the case) at the Assize hearing. Another important function conferred by statute on the Justice of the Peace was the power to require any person 'not of good fame' to agree to keep the peace and to be of good behaviour.[63] This power to 'bind to the peace' remains in place to this day.[64]

[2.53] In Ireland the sporadic outbreaks of rebellion and other disturbances led to the power to bind to the peace being used extensively as an instrument of control. For those who opposed the political connection with England, particularly in the 19th century, binding to the peace was considered a symbol of repression by an alien power. This was compounded by the fact that the Justices were, in general, part-time appointees and not necessarily qualified lawyers, raising the suspicion that they were prone to make decisions favoured by the political establishment rather than being capable of independent decision-making. The Dublin administration responded at least to some extent to the criticisms of the JP system with the appointment of paid Resident Magistrates (RMs) to deal with petty sessions matters outside Dublin.[65] Although this might be described today as being 'too little, too late' in the context of the overall political background, this had at least one lasting effect. The modern successor of the petty sessions courts, the District Courts, are presided over by full-time judges who are drawn from the ranks of practising lawyers.[66] Thus, what was the bitter experience of the 19th century for Irish nationalists has been remembered to that extent. Indeed, while the District Court system derives its validity from the Constitution, it should be noted that certain procedural aspects of the District Court's jurisdiction are to be found in pre-1922 legislation that remains in place.[67] In the legal systems of England and Northern Ireland, the modern day equivalent of Petty Sessions, the Magistrates Courts, continue to be presided over by part-time lay magistrates, but they are guided in matters of law by legally qualified Magistrate Court clerks.

---

[63] The jurisdiction was first conferred in 1361 by the statute 34 Edw III, c 1.

[64] See para **10.35**.

[65] The Sommerville and Ross *Irish RM* short stories set in the early 20th century cast a humorous eye on this aspect of the legal system.

[66] See para **2.106**.

[67] These include the Petty Sessions (Ireland) Act 1851 and the Summary Jurisdiction Act 1857.

County Courts

[2.54] The County Courts dealt with minor civil cases that would otherwise have overburdened the Assize hearings. The 1877 Act provided for the appointment of County Court judges, who also held the position of Chairman of Quarter Sessions. The document used to initiate a claim in the County Court was the civil bill, an initiating document unique to Ireland and not shared by the equivalent County Courts in England.[68] The civil bill still forms the basis for many claims initiated in the Circuit Court today, the approximate successor to the County Courts in this legal system.[69] In Northern Ireland and England, the County Courts remain in place, but only in Northern Ireland are claims initiated by the civil bill procedure.

[5] THE EMERGENCE OF A NEW STATE

[2.55] By the time it was enacted, the Government of Ireland Act 1920 had been overtaken by political events and was found to be unacceptable to Irish nationalists, now represented by Sinn Féin, who continued to press for a 32-county independent state. However, Ulster Unionists assented to the provisions of the 1920 Act. In May 1921, elections were held for the Parliaments of Northern Ireland and Southern Ireland. Although Sinn Féin had rejected the 1920 Act, the party used the electoral arrangements to renew its mandate. In Northern Ireland, Unionists won 40 of the 52 seats in the Northern Ireland House of Commons, while (in a largely uncontested election) Sinn Féin won 124 of the 128 seats in what to nationalists was the Second Dáil Éireann or, in terms of the 1920 Act, the House of Commons of Southern Ireland. The Parliament of Northern Ireland was opened in June 1921.

[2.56] A truce between the British forces and the Irish nationalists was agreed in July 1921 and the British recognised the Sinn Féin regime as the 'provisional government' of Southern Ireland and, in effect, transferred a large measure of control to what the nationalists regarded as the Cabinet of Dáil Éireann. After protracted negotiations, Articles of Agreement for an Anglo-Irish Treaty were signed by British and Irish plenipotentiaries in December 1921. While this provided for the establishment of the Irish Free State, with the possibility that it might comprise the entire island of Ireland, the Irish negotiators were forced to accept a number of concessions. The new state was to enjoy dominion status, on a par with the other British dominions, which at the time was considered to be something less than full sovereignty. The Crown was retained as head of state, represented in Dublin by a Governor General; members of the Oireachtas would swear an oath of loyalty to the Crown; and what amounted to an opt-out from the new state was granted to Northern Ireland. This opt-out was duly taken up by the Northern Irish Parliament in December 1921, thus cementing partition. After a bitter debate in Dáil Éireann, which resulted in a split within the Sinn Féin ranks followed by a

---

68 See Greer, 'The Development of the Civil Bill Procedure in Ireland' in McEldowney and O'Higgins, *The Common Law Tradition: Essays in Irish Legal History* (1990), p 27.

69 See para **6.61**.

Civil War that lasted until 1923, the Articles of Agreement (or 'The Treaty') were approved in January 1922. This paved the way for the creation of the Irish Free State.

[2.57] Under the post-1922 regime Northern Ireland remained part of what became the United Kingdom of Great Britain and Northern Ireland, while the Irish Free State became a member of the British Commonwealth. The Westminster Parliament passed the Irish Free State (Constitution) Act 1922,[70] which *inter alia* repealed the Government of Ireland Act 1920 in so far as the latter applied to Southern Ireland. The equivalent measure in the Irish Free State was the Constitution of the Irish Free State (Saorstát Éireann) Act 1922, which enacted into law the Constitution of the Irish Free State, in turn largely based on the 1921 Articles of Agreement. The Irish statute expressly provided that the new Constitution was subject to the provisions of the Treaty and that the latter would prevail in the event of conflict between the two documents. The adoption of a written constitution marked a tentative break from the British tradition and it proved to be a first step on the road towards the enactment of an indigenous instrument purged of any lingering vestiges of the old regime.[71]

[6] THE 1922 CONSTITUTION

[2.58] An understanding of the 1922 settlement must take account of the combination of legal theory and political ideology that typically underlies constitutional arrangements. From a British perspective, the Irish Free State was the successor to Southern Ireland as envisaged by the Government of Ireland Act 1920 and it followed that nothing more than an Act of Parliament was required to give effect to the modifications made to the 1920 arrangement by the Treaty and the 1922 Constitution – this was achieved by the Irish Free State (Constitution) Act 1922 [UK]. On this view ultimate control remained at Westminster, subject to whatever powers it conferred on the Irish Free State and the other states beginning to form the British Commonwealth of Nations. Irish nationalists had never accepted the 1920 Act or Southern Ireland as a political entity. From their perspective, the elections held in 1919, 1921 and 1922 were elections to a national assembly, Dáil Éireann, albeit that they had utilised the electoral machinery of the Government of Ireland Acts 1914 and 1920. Accordingly, a constitutional sequence emerges: the First Dáil of 1919, acting on behalf of the Irish people, was the source of all lawful authority in Ireland; the Second Dáil had approved the Treaty in 1921; and the Third Dáil, acting as a Constituent Assembly (a constitution-making assembly) had approved the 1922 Constitution of the Irish Free State.

[2.59] In blunt terms the British perspective sees Irish Independence as having been granted by Westminster, acting as Imperial Parliament, while the Irish viewpoint considers Independence to have been derived from the will of the Irish People as expressed in the mandate given to Dáil Éireann. While the distinction between the British and Irish legal perspectives is rooted in ideology and might appear obtuse, it was

---

70   13 Geo 5, sess 2, c 1.
71   See further, paras **2.76–2.98**.

to become a factor in the replacement of the 1922 Constitution in 1937.[72] The essential elements of the Treaty became law as the Constitution of the Irish Free State, enacted as a Schedule to the last Act passed by the Third Dáil and the first Act passed by the Oireachtas of the Irish Free State, the Constitution of the Irish Free State (Saorstát Éireann) Act 1922.

Institutions of State and fundamental rights

[2.60] The 1922 Constitution may be divided into two broad elements: an outline of the principal institutions of state and a description of certain fundamental rights of the citizens. Its text comprises a number of Articles, rather than the sections which characterise legislation.[73]

Separation of powers

[2.61] The 1922 Constitution prescribed a tripartite division or separation of powers, namely the executive, the legislature and the judiciary. This reflected developments in the political organisation of the state, particularly in the 19th century, which were noted above.[74] It also contained a number of controversial elements that divided Irish nationalists. Critically, the Treaty and the 1922 Constitution in effect excluded from the Irish Free State the six administrative counties which at the end of 1921 had formed Northern Ireland. Another limitation was that the dominion status accorded to the Irish Free State ensured that it remained within the British sphere of influence as a member of the British Commonwealth. There was a continued, albeit limited, British military presence in a number of ports of the Irish Free State (the Treaty ports).[75] However, the 1922 Constitution provided that the Irish Free State was not to be committed to active participation in any war without the consent of its legislature.

[2.62] On the organisation of the executive, there was a continued British political presence in the form of the Governor General, though this position was largely ceremonial. Real executive power lay with the Executive Council of the Irish Free State headed by the President of the Executive Council, in effect the Prime Minister of the Irish Free State. The Executive Council was to be elected from the legislative branch, which comprised the monarch (represented by the Governor General) and two Houses of the Oireachtas, Dáil Éireann (a Chamber of Deputies, directly elected by proportional representation) and the Senate (an indirectly elected Chamber whose membership was intended to include representatives of Southern Unionists). Members of the Oireachtas were required to swear an oath of fidelity to the British monarch. This requirement, together with the failure to achieve a 32-county Irish state, was a prime factor in the split

---

[72] See paras **2.69–2.75**.

[73] See para **13.82**.

[74] See para **2.22** *et seq*.

[75] Control of the ports was ultimately transferred to Ireland by agreement in 1938, and the small remaining numbers of British troops were then withdrawn.

within Sinn Féin in 1921 and the consequent Civil War.[76] As to the judicial branch, the 1922 Constitution provided for the establishment of a High Court, a Supreme Court and courts of local and limited jurisdiction.[77] A right of appeal from the Irish courts to the Judicial Committee of the Privy Council was also included.

Fundamental rights

[2.63] The enumeration of a number of fundamental rights of citizens was influenced by the Bill of Rights and the Declaration of the Rights of Man which had followed the 18th century revolutionary movements in the United States and France. This feature also reflected the dissatisfaction within Irish nationalism at the absence of legal protections for basic rights in the pre-1922 regime. Thus, Article 6 of the 1922 Constitution provided that no person could be deprived of liberty save in accordance with law and it also guaranteed the right to *habeas corpus*, subject to an exception for the actions of the military forces of the Irish Free State during a state of war or armed rebellion.[78] Article 7 contained a protection against entry into a person's dwelling unless authorised by law. Article 8 concerned freedom of conscience and of religious belief, while Article 9 dealt with freedom of expression, freedom of assembly and freedom of association. Other important provisions included Article 43, which prohibited the Oireachtas of the Irish Free State from enacting any retrospective criminal laws, while Article 70 contained a right to a criminal trial 'in due course of law'.

Continuity of laws

[2.64] Article 73 provided for the continuity of pre-1922 laws:

> "Subject to this Constitution and to the extent to which they are not inconsistent therewith, the laws in force in the Irish Free State (Saorstát Éireann) at the date of the coming into operation of this Constitution shall continue to be of full force and effect until the same or any of them shall have been repealed or amended by enactment of the Oireachtas."

[2.65] In *The State (Kennedy) v Little*,[79] O'Byrne J in the High Court observed that Article 73 was 'intended to set up the new State with the least possible change in previously existing law.' The courts indicated that Article 73 extended not merely to pre-1922 statute law but also pre-1922 common law.[80] However, it was also held that pre-1922 court decisions were not binding on the courts established under the 1922

---

[76] After the ending of the Civil War in 1923, many of those who had voted against the 1921 'Treaty' ultimately took their seats in Dáil Éireann after the 1927 General Election, as members of the Fianna Fáil Party led by Eamon de Valera. The oath of fidelity to the Crown was described at this stage as an 'empty formula'.

[77] See para **2.101**.

[78] On *habeas corpus* generally, see para **10.54**. Note also the retrospective and implicit amendment of Article 6 by the Indemnity Act 1923, discussed in *R (Cooney) v Clinton* [1935] IR 245: see para **2.68**.

[79] *The State (Kennedy) v Little* [1931] IR 39.

[80] For example, *The State (McCarthy) v Lennon* [1936] IR 485 (common law privilege against self-incrimination).

Constitution.[81] Nonetheless, the overall effect was that existing common law and statute law was carried over *in toto* into the Irish Free State subject to their being consistent with the Constitution itself.[82]

Amendment of the 1922 Constitution

[2.66] The 1922 Constitution provided for two methods by which its text could be amended. Article 14 required that a Bill to amend the Constitution be passed by the Oireachtas and then submitted to a referendum for approval by the electorate. However, Article 50 provided that, for eight years after it came into force, that is until December 1930, the Constitution could be amended by ordinary legislation, in other words by an Act of the Oireachtas, without the need for a referendum. As events transpired, no referendum to amend the 1922 Constitution was ever held, but its provisions were amended on many occasions between 1922 and 1936.[83]

[2.67] Article 50 was itself amended in 1929 to extend the period during which ordinary legislation could be employed to amend the constitutional text by a further eight years, thus extending this power until December 1938.[84] In 1931, an amending Act inserted Article 2A into the Constitution.[85] This lengthy and detailed provision authorised the Executive Council to establish special tribunals, staffed by military personnel, with extraordinary powers of detention, trial and sentence, up to and including the death penalty. The provisions of Article 2A were expressed to take priority over other Articles in the Constitution thus effecting the virtual abolition of fundamental rights, including *habeas corpus* and the right to jury trial. After Fianna Fáil came to power in 1932, almost all remaining traces of the 1921 Treaty were progressively removed. In 1933, legislation was enacted to remove both the oath of fidelity to the British monarch and the stipulation that amendments were limited by the terms of the 1921 Treaty.[86] In the same year, the right of appeal from the Supreme Court to the Privy Council was abolished.[87] In 1936, the Senate was abolished.[88] Later that year, King Edward VIII

---

81 See para **12.72**.

82 See also Article 50 of the 1937 Constitution, para **2.91**.

83 In total, 27 Acts expressly entitled 'Act to amend the 1922 Constitution' were passed between 1923 and 1936. Other Acts appeared to amend the Constitution by implication, such as the Indemnity Act 1923 discussed in *R (Cooney) v Clinton* [1935] IR 245. In addition the Constitution (Removal of Oath) Act 1933, although not expressed to be an Act to amend the Constitution, involved the removal of the oath of fidelity to the British monarch as well as any reference to amendments being limited by the terms of the 1921 Treaty.

84 Constitution (Amendment No 16) Act 1929. In the event, the 1937 Constitution came into effect before this period expired.

85 Constitution (Amendment No 17) Act 1929.

86 Constitution (Removal of Oath) Act 1933.

87 Constitution (Amendment No 22) Act 1933.

88 Constitution (Amendment No 24) Act 1936.

abdicated from the British throne and legislation was required to confirm this in each of the Commonwealth states and to provide for the succession. The response of the Irish Free State was to remove any remaining references to the Crown from the 1922 Constitution and to abolish the office of Governor General.[89] Legislation was also enacted to provide that the Executive Council was conferred with the power to enter into international treaties and to appoint diplomatic representatives. Any former role exercised by the monarch in these areas would henceforth be done only 'when advised by the Executive Council so to do'.[90] By the end of 1936, the constitutional constraints imposed by the 1921 Treaty had been all but completely removed.

[2.68] From the outset the courts, perhaps influenced by the British tradition in which parliament is supreme, were willing to facilitate legislative amendments to the 1922 Constitution, but they were to express significant reservations in later years. In 1924, the Court of Appeal of Southern Ireland[91] held in *R (Cooney) v Clinton*[92] that the 1922 Constitution could be amended by implication and retrospectively, subject to the proviso that it was within the terms of the 1921 Treaty; it was not necessary that a statute be expressed to be for the purpose of amending the Constitution. The court dismissed a challenge to the validity of the Indemnity Act 1923, which retrospectively validated the decisions of military courts, established under Article 6 of the 1922 Constitution to try those on the anti-Treaty side of the Civil War. The 1923 Act had been enacted in the immediate aftermath of the decision in *R (O'Brien) v Military Governor, North Dublin Union*,[93] in which the old Court of Appeal had held that a state of war or armed rebellion within the meaning of Article 6 of the 1922 Constitution did not exist at that time, August 1923; the Civil War had ended in May 1923 for most anti-Treaty forces.[94] The wider consequences of the decision were that, by virtue of the doctrine of implied amendment, ordinary legislation would, in effect, prevail over the 1922 Constitution in the event of conflict between the two. In 1928, the High Court held in *Attorney General v McBride*[95] that it was constitutionally permissible to provide that an Act of the Oireachtas, in this instance the Public Safety Act 1927,[96] was to prevail over the terms of the Constitution, without specifying which provisions of the 1922 Constitution were being amended.

89 Constitution (Amendment No 27) Act 1936.
90 Executive Authority (External Relations) Act 1936.
91 The Court of Appeal continued to operate until the establishment of the Supreme Court by the Courts of Justice Act 1924.
92 *R (Cooney) v Clinton* [1935] IR 245 (but decided in 1924).
93 *R (O'Brien) v Military Governor, North Dublin Union* [1924] 1 IR 32.
94 Although a state of widespread armed rebellion against the Free State no longer existed, sporadic violence continued, necessitating the continued operation of the military courts and their successors, the special tribunals established under Article 2A in 1931.
95 *Attorney General v McBride* [1928] IR 451.
96 The Act was passed in response to the murder of the then Minister for Justice, Kevin O'Higgins. The Act was the precursor to the provisions of Article 2A.

[2.69] In 1935, in *Moore v Attorney General*,[97] the Privy Council itself held that the abolition of the right of appeal to that court[98] lay within the powers of the Oireachtas of the Irish Free State as a member of the British Commonwealth. This was based primarily on the greater freedom granted by the Statute of Westminster 1931, a UK measure which had been enacted in the aftermath of an Imperial Conference of the Commonwealth Members. The Statute of Westminster 1931 provided that a Commonwealth State was empowered to enact legislation which conflicted with an Act of the Westminster Parliament, thus enhancing the legislative competence of Commonwealth Parliaments. In the case of the Irish Free State, this included the power to enact legislation that was at variance with the Treaty, which on the British view of things had been given legal effect by an Act of the Westminster Parliament, namely the Irish Free State (Agreement) Act 1922. From that perspective, therefore, the Irish Free State had been freed from any constraints imposed by the 1921 Treaty.

[2.70] However, by this time the Irish Supreme Court had taken a different, and ironically more restrictive, view of the powers of the Irish Free State. In *The State (Ryan) v Lennon*,[99] decided in December 1934, before the Privy Council decision in *Moore*,[100] the Supreme Court held, by a majority,[101] that it was permissible to override the right to trial in due course of law in Article 72 of the 1922 Constitution through the establishment of the special tribunals under Article 2A.[102] The court also accepted that the Oireachtas was entitled to extend the eight-year time limit for amending the 1922 Constitution by ordinary legislation.[103] However, the Supreme Court judges unanimously agreed that the Oireachtas could not enact any legislation that conflicted with the 1921 Treaty.

[2.71] The last point was based on the Irish perspective on the nature of the Third Dáil Éireann, acting in 1922 as a Constituent Assembly. Section 1 of the Constitution of the Irish Free State (Saorstát Éireann) Act 1922 had given legal force to the 1922

---

97   *Moore v Attorney General* [1935] IR 472. See Mohr, 'Law without Loyalty: the Abolition of the Irish Appeal to the Privy Council' (2002) 37 Ir Jur 187.
98   See para **2.62**.
99   *The State (Ryan) v Lennon* [1935] IR 170.
100 *Moore v Attorney General* [1935] IR 472.
101 Fitzgibbon and Murnaghan JJ; Kennedy CJ dissenting. Kennedy CJ, who had been the first Attorney General of the Irish Free State, a principal drafter of the 1922 Constitution and architect of the court system established by the Courts of Justice Act 1924, concluded that the establishment of the special tribunals conflicted not only with the 1921 Treaty but also with natural law, and on both grounds was invalid. While Fitzgibbon and Murnaghan JJ accepted that the Oireachtas was bound to adhere to the 1921 Treaty, they held that it did not prohibit the establishment of special tribunals. They rejected completely Kennedy CJ's view that legislation in conflict with natural law could be declared invalid. Kennedy CJ's views on the position of natural law were to re-emerge in the interpretation of the 1937 Constitution by a later generation of judges: see para **15.152** *et seq*.
102 See para **15.82**.
103 Achieved by the Constitution (Amendment No 16) Act 1929.

Constitution, which was scheduled to the 1922 Act. Section 2 gave legal effect to the 1921 Treaty, also scheduled to the 1922 Act. Section 2 provided that the Constitution was to be construed by reference to the Treaty and that:

> "if any provision of the said Constitution or of any amendment thereof or of any law made thereunder is in any respect repugnant to any of the provisions of the Scheduled Treaty, it shall, to the extent only of such repugnancy, be absolutely void and inoperative."

[2.72] Article 50 of the 1922 Constitution, which authorised amendments to the Constitution by ordinary legislation, echoed s 2 of the Act by providing that only amendments 'within the terms of the Scheduled Treaty' could be enacted. However, as already noted, in 1933, legislation was enacted to remove the oath of fidelity to the British monarch along with the stipulation that amendments be limited by the terms of the 1921 Treaty.[104] This legislation had repealed s 2 of the 1922 Act and deleted the words 'within the terms of the Scheduled Treaty' from Article 50.

[2.73] In *The State (Ryan) v Lennon*,[105] the Supreme Court stated that the Oireachtas was simply not empowered to remove the restrictions which had been imposed in s 2 of the 1922 Act by the Oireachtas, itself acting on behalf of the Irish People as a Constituent Assembly. From an Irish legal perspective, the Irish Free State drew its legitimacy from the Constitution-enacting vote of the Third Dáil in 1922, and s 2 of the 1922 Act had created a self-imposed straitjacket which the Oireachtas of the Irish Free State could not remove. While English law had moved on in the wake of the Statute of Westminster 1931, the Irish view was more restrictive.

[2.74] Since the court in *The State (Ryan) v Lennon* upheld the validity of the constitutional amendments directly in issue in the case, the views expressed on the deletion of s 2 of the 1922 Act are best considered to be *obiter* and strictly speaking were not binding on any later court.[106] Nonetheless, they indicated a judicial attitude on the competence of the Oireachtas of the Irish Free State to depart from the 1921 Treaty, a view that could scarcely be ignored.

[2.75] The competing constitutional evaluations, reflected in the very different decisions in *Moore*[107] and *The State (Ryan) v Lennon*,[108] resulted in what from an Irish perspective was an astonishing paradox. Irish legislative power was circumscribed by the terms of the Treaty, a limitation that Ireland imposed on itself in 1922. Moreover, this would cast constitutional doubt on many of the amendments made to the Constitution in the 1930s. On the other hand from the British view Ireland was considered by virtue of the Statute of Westminster 1931 to enjoy full legislative competence and to have had the capacity to amend its Constitution despite the terms of the Treaty. But, needless to say, it would

---

104 The Constitution (Removal of Oath) Act 1933: see para **2.67**.
105 *State (Ryan) v Lennon* [1935] IR 170.
106 See para **12.92**.
107 *Moore v Attorney General* [1935] IR 472.
108 *State (Ryan) v Lennon* [1935] IR 170.

have been politically impossible to base a claim for full legislative competence on a British statute. A different solution was required.

[7] THE 1937 CONSTITUTION

[2.76] The 1921 Treaty and the 1922 Constitution had been substantially dismantled by the end of 1936. Quite apart from the observations in *The State (Ryan) v Lennon*,[109] work had already begun on the preparation of an entirely new Constitution to replace, not merely to amend, the 1922 Constitution.[110] However, the Supreme Court decision emphasised the political desirability of enacting a new Constitution, based firmly on the Irish view of the constitutional settlement. In 1937, the Oireachtas of the Irish Free State, now comprising the Dáil alone, debated and approved the text of a new Constitution. Unlike in 1922, the Dáil did not enact the new Constitution, but referred it to a plebiscite or referendum of the electorate.[111] In July 1937, the draft Constitution was passed into law at the plebiscite and, in accordance with Article 62 of the Constitution itself, it came into effect on 27 December 1937 as the Constitution of Ireland. The Irish language title for the 1937 Constitution, *Bunreacht na hÉireann*, may be translated as the Basic Law of Ireland. Like the 1922 Constitution, its text comprises a number of Articles, rather than sections.

Institutions of state and fundamental rights

[2.77] In some respects, the Constitution of Ireland 1937 reflects the amended text of the 1922 Constitution. Like its 1922 predecessor, the 1937 Constitution may be divided into two component parts: an outline of the principal institutions of state and a description of certain fundamental rights of the citizens. However, vital differences exist in the detailed provisions.

Rhetoric of the 1937 Constitution

[2.78] Many provisions of the 1937 Constitution reflect the concerns of its principal architect, Eamon de Valera.[112] The text of the 1937 Constitution has been described as both 'law and manifesto', since it contains not only statements of basic legal principles but also general aspirations.[113] In their original version Articles 2 and 3 asserted that the

---

109 *The State (Ryan) v Lennon* [1935] IR 170.
110 In 1932, Fianna Fáil formed a minority government with the support of the Labour Party. In the 1933 General Election, Fianna Fáil won an absolute majority in Dáil Éireann. Since its foundation in 1924, Fianna Fáil had been committed to the removal from the 1922 Constitution of any trace of the 1921 Treaty. This led to a policy of its replacement by an entirely new Constitution.
111 Provided for in the Plebiscite (Draft Constitution) Act 1937.
112 See generally Keogh, 'The Constitutional Revolution: An Analysis of the Making of the Constitution', in Litton (ed), *The Constitution of Ireland 1937–1987* (1988).
113 Kelly, 'The Constitution: Law and Manifesto', in Litton (ed), *The Constitution of Ireland 1937–1987* (1988), p 208, citing the judgment of the Supreme Court in *Re the Criminal Law (Jurisdiction) Bill 1975* [1977] IR 129.

'national territory' of Ireland included the entire island of Ireland, a provision that was to remain politically controversial until its alteration in 1998.[114] Other provisions contained overtly religious statements which appeared to reflect the religious teachings of the Catholic Church to the exclusion of other religious faiths and the views of those with no religious beliefs.[115] The opening words of the preamble recite that the Constitution is enacted by the people of Ireland 'In the Name of the Most Holy Trinity'. Article 41, which contains guarantees of support for the family in society, has been criticised for its statement that women should not be required 'to engage in labour to the neglect of their duties in the home' and for the prohibition on divorce that was not removed until 1996.[116] We discuss later the overall ethos of the Constitution and its impact on constitutional judicial review.[117]

Separation of powers

[2.79] The basic tripartite separation of powers seen in the 1922 Constitution is retained in the 1937 Constitution, though with significant changes in the detail.

President of Ireland

[2.80] As might be expected, the 1937 Constitution contains no reference to the British Crown. The functions originally performed under the 1922 Constitution by the Governor General, such as the official promulgation of legislation, were, in effect, transferred by Articles 12 and 13 to the newly-established office of President of Ireland. While Article 12.1 provides that the President takes precedence over all other persons in the state, he or she is not formally designated as head of state.[118] The Presidency is not an office with executive powers, Article 13.9 providing that the majority of its functions, such as the appointment of judges, are performed on the advice of the government.[119] An important exception is the power to refer Bills to the Supreme Court under Article 26.[120] Article 13.4 vests supreme command of the Defence Forces in the President, but Article 13.5 provides that the exercise of this power must be regulated by law; the Defence Act 1954 in effect places actual command in the Minister for Defence. Thus, the President is titular commander-in-chief of the Defence Forces only. Provision is made in Article 12 for the direct election of the President, though where only one candidate is nominated no election is required. Article 31 established a Council of State to advise the President in the exercise of his or her powers, such as whether to refer Bills to the Supreme Court

---

[114] Nineteenth Amendment of the Constitution Act 1998; see further paras **15.11–15.29**.

[115] A reference in Article 44 to the 'special position' of the Catholic Church was removed by referendum in 1972. On the origins of Article 44, see Keogh, 'The Constitutional Revolution: An Analysis of the Making of the Constitution', in Litton (ed), *The Constitution of Ireland 1937–1987* (1988).

[116] Fifteenth Amendment of the Constitution Act 1995.

[117] See generally Ch 15.

[118] *The Report of the Constitution Review Group* (Pn 2632, 1996) recommended such a change.

[119] See para **4.77**.

[120] See para **5.84**.

under Article 26. Some suggestions have been made that the President's functions be expanded, though it seems improbable that this will be acted on.[121]

Executive power

[2.81] The Executive Council of the Irish Free State was replaced by the Government of Ireland, comprising the Taoiseach, that is prime minister, and other government ministers. Unlike its predecessor, the government is invested with the sole and exclusive power to exercise executive authority, without reference to any other external power such as the British Crown. Another innovative element is that Article 30 of the 1937 Constitution describes in broad terms the role of the chief law officer of the state, the Attorney General.[122]

Comptroller and Auditor General

[2.82] The office of Comptroller and Auditor General is dealt with in Article 33, which replaced comparable provisions in Articles 62 and 63 of the 1922 Constitution. The function of this office is to ensure that any state income is raised in accordance with the relevant legislation (the comptroller function) and spent in accordance with the vote of the Oireachtas (the auditor function). The Comptroller and Auditor General is appointed by the President on the nomination of Dáil Éireann and holds office on the same basis as members of the judiciary. The detailed functions of the Comptroller and Auditor General, which include examination of the spending of state bodies as well as government departments, are contained in the Comptroller and Auditor General Acts 1923 to 1998.

Legislative power

[2.83] Turning to the legislative branch, the 1937 Constitution provides that exclusive legislative power is vested in the Oireachtas, comprising the President and two Houses or Chambers, the directly-elected Dáil Éireann (or Chamber of Deputies) and the indirectly elected Seanad Éireann (or Senate). In this respect, there is a broad similarity with the 1922 Constitution in its original form. In terms of legislative powers, the Dáil is superior to the Seanad.[123]

Judicial power

[2.84] The provisions concerning the judicial branch, which we describe elsewhere in some detail,[124] are broadly similar to those in the 1922 Constitution.

---

121 See, eg, Mee, 'The Changing Nature of the Presidency: The President and the Government should be Friends' (1996) 14 ILT 2, 30.
122 See para **3.112**.
123 See para **13.20**.
124 See paras **4.33–4.40**.

Fundamental rights

[2.85] A significant feature of the 1937 Constitution is that it is superior to other sources of law, including statute law. Like the original text of the 1922 Constitution, the 1937 Constitution prohibits the Oireachtas from enacting any law which is in conflict with the provisions of the Constitution, including the fundamental rights of citizens which we discuss elsewhere.[125] Unlike the 1922 Constitution, this limitation on the Oireachtas cannot be overridden by ordinary legislation; a key feature of the 1937 Constitution is its entrenched nature. Article 46 of the Constitution provides that, from 1941 onwards, its provisions may not be amended by ordinary legislation; amendments may only be effected by popular referendum.[126] Moreover, the High Court and Supreme Court enjoy the power to declare invalid any law that conflicts with the provisions of the Constitution.

Restrictions on law-making authority of Oireachtas

[2.86] The 1937 Constitution places limits on the legislative authority of the Oireachtas. Article 15.2.1° appears to confer unlimited authority on the Oireachtas by providing:

> "The sole and exclusive power of making laws for the State is hereby vested in the Oireachtas: no other legislative authority has power to make laws for the State."

However, this must be read in conjunction with Article 15.4, which provides:

> "1° The Oireachtas shall not enact any law which is in any respect repugnant to this Constitution or any provision thereof.
>
> 2° Every law enacted by the Oireachtas which is in any respect repugnant to this Constitution or to any provision thereof, shall, but to the extent only of such repugnancy, be invalid."

[2.87] Article 15.4 deals with laws enacted by the Oireachtas after 1937. For laws in place prior to that, Article 50.1 states:

> "Subject to this Constitution and to the extent to which they are not inconsistent therewith, the laws in force in Saorstát Éireann immediately prior to the date of the coming into operation of this Constitution shall continue to be of full force and effect until the same or any of them shall have been repealed or amended by enactment of the Oireachtas."

This ensures continuity with laws enacted prior to the 1937 Constitution and echoes Article 73 of the 1922 Constitution.[127] However, Article 34 of the 1937 Constitution added a new dimension to these provisions.

---

[125] See para **15.51**.
[126] See para **15.81**.
[127] See para **2.64**.

60

The basis for constitutional judicial review

[2.88] Article 34 of the 1937 Constitution expressly confers on the High Court and Supreme Court the power to determine whether any law is valid having regard to the Constitution. Article 34.3.2° currently provides:

"Save as otherwise provided by this Article,[128] the jurisdiction of the High Court shall extend to the question of the validity of any law having regard to the provisions of this Constitution, and no such question shall be raised (whether by pleading, argument or otherwise) in any Court established under this or any other Article of this Constitution other than the High Court or the Supreme Court."

[2.89] Article 34.4 currently stipulates:

"3°   The Supreme Court shall, with such exceptions and subject to such regulations as may be prescribed by law, have appellate jurisdiction from all decisions of the High Court ...

4°   No law shall be enacted excepting from the appellate jurisdiction of the Supreme Court cases which involve questions as to the validity of any law having regard to the provisions of this Constitution."

[2.90] Thus, the High Court and, on appeal, the Supreme Court enjoyed exclusive jurisdiction to determine whether laws are valid or invalid on the ground that they were in conflict with any provision of the Constitution.[129] Article 34 will be amended to invest the new Court of Appeal with similar jurisdiction when that court is established.[130] The

---

128   This refers to the exclusive jurisdiction of the Supreme Court in referrals of Bills under Article 26: see para **5.84**.

129   O'Neill, 'The Effect of a finding that Legislation is Unconstitutional: The Approach of the Irish Supreme Court' (2007) 36 *Common Law World Review*, 220.

130   Thirty-third Amendment of the Constitution Act 2013, s 2(2). See also paras **4.34–4.39**. When the Court of Appeal is established the relevant provision of Art 34 will be amended to read:

34.3.2° Save as otherwise provided by this Article, the jurisdiction of the High Court shall extend to the question of the validity of any law having regard to the provisions of this Constitution, and no such question shall be raised (whether by pleading, argument or otherwise) in any Court established under this or any other Article of this Constitution other than the High Court, the Court of Appeal or the Supreme Court.

34.4.2° No law shall be enacted exempting from the appellate jurisdiction of the Court of Appeal cases which involve questions as to the validity of any law having regard to the provisions of the Constitution.

34.5.3° The Supreme Court shall, subject to such regulations as may be prescribed by law, have appellate jurisdiction from a decision of the Court of Appeal, if the Supreme Court is satisfied that –

i   the decision involves a matter of general importance, or

ii   in the interests of justice it is necessary that there be an appeal to the Supreme Court.

34.5.5° No law shall be enacted excepting from the appellate jurisdiction of the Supreme Court cases which involve questions as to the validity of any law having regard to the provisions of this Constitution.

most significant provisions in this respect are those which recognise basic or fundamental rights, similar to the Bill of Rights in the Constitution of the United States of America.[131]

Continuity of laws

[2.91] Like Article 73 of the 1922 Constitution,[132] Article 50 of the 1937 Constitution provided that the laws in the Irish Free State continued to have full force and effect unless they were inconsistent with the 1937 Constitution or were repealed by the Oireachtas established by that Constitution. While this carried forward pre-1922 laws as well as those of 1922 to 1937, the provisions of the 1937 Constitution concerning constitutional judicial review produced a different perspective on Article 50.[133]

English and Irish language text of Constitution

[2.92] Article 8.1 of the Constitution provides that the Irish language is the national language and the first official language,[134] while Article 8.2 states that the English language is recognised as a second official language. In fact, the English language is the mother tongue for the vast majority of the population of Ireland,[135] and the Irish language is the spoken and written language for a small number, mainly, though not exclusively, those living in certain western areas of Ireland, known as Gaeltacht areas.

[2.93] The 1937 Constitution was enacted as a dual language text, in English and Irish.[136] Article 25.5.1° provides that the Taoiseach may, from time to time, supervise the preparation of the latest text of the Constitution, as amended, which must be in both languages. Article 25.5.2° provides that a copy of every such text, when authenticated by the signatures of the Taoiseach and the Chief Justice, must be signed by the President of Ireland and enrolled for record in the office of the Registrar of the Supreme Court. Article 25.4.3° specifies that such a copy 'shall, upon such enrolment, be conclusive evidence of this Constitution'. Thus, the texts in both languages have, in general, equal status.

[2.94] Article 25.5.4° provides that, 'in case of conflict between the texts of any copy of this Constitution ... the text in the national language shall prevail.' The courts have emphasised that, in general, they will seek to avoid any conflict between the English and

---

131   Brennan, 'Why have a Bill of Rights' (1989) 9 OJLS 425; Macklem, 'Entrenching Bills of Rights' (2006) 26 OJLS 197.

132   See para **2.64**.

133   See para **15.47**.

134   See generally O'Malley, *The Status of the Irish Language – A Legal Perspective* (1990).

135   *Report of the Constitution Review Group* (Pn 2632, 1996), p 15.

136   See generally, Ó Cearúil, *Bunreacht na hÉireann: a Study of the Irish Text* (1999). The draft Constitution initially debated in the Oireachtas in 1937 was in the English language but it seems that an Irish language version of the text was prepared at the same time that the work of the main drafting committee was undertaken: see Hogan and Whyte, *JM Kelly: The Irish Constitution* (4th edn, 2003), p 385.

Irish language texts when attempting to interpret a particular constitutional provision. In most instances, the English language version is referred to first and, only if there is some doubt as to its meaning, the Irish language version is used to clarify or elucidate the meaning of the English language text.[137]

Further constitutional development

[2.95] Unlike its predecessor, the 1937 Constitution marked a clean break from the old order. References to the Crown, the oath, dominion status and appeals to the Privy Council – key elements of the Treaty settlement – were abandoned. As we have seen this was the culmination of a process of progressive amendment of the 1922 Constitution, engineered by the de Valera government in the 1930s. Moreover, the 1937 Constitution established the office of President, it contained a strengthened catalogue of fundamental rights and it expressly envisaged the judicial review of legislation. In this respect the new Constitution had the indicia of a republic but that term does not appear in the text. Matters changed in 1949 when the Republic of Ireland Act 1948 came into effect. That enactment provided that Ireland may be described as the 'Republic of Ireland'. However, since Article 4 of the Constitution of 1937 provides that the name of the state in the English language is Ireland, the official description preferred by successive governments since 1937 is 'Ireland'.[138] A further consequence was that Ireland formally withdrew from the British Commonwealth in 1949, although it had in effect been a non-participating member since 1937.

[2.96] Irish membership of the European Union has required a series of amendments to the Constitution. The obligations of membership involved the ceding of a measure of sovereignty and the subordination of national law to the European legal order. This was in conflict with the provisions of the Constitution as they stood at the time; hence the necessity to amend the Constitution. As the process of European integration deepened and the European Communities evolved into the European Union more recent developments have required further constitutional alteration in order that they be accommodated within the national legal system.[139]

[2.97] Under the Good Friday Agreement, which was signed in Belfast on 10 April 1998, the state undertook to abandon its territorial claim over Northern Ireland. This was brought about by amending Articles 2 and 3 of the Constitution with the territorial claim being deleted and being replaced by the principle of unity by consent.[140]

---

[137] See Hogan and Whyte, *J M Kelly: The Irish Constitution* (4th edn, 2003), pp 387–395.

[138] Given the variety of legislative and constitutional provisions touching on the subject, it is perhaps not surprising that Ireland is variously referred to as 'Southern Ireland', 'the Irish Free State', 'Éire' and 'the Republic of Ireland'.

[139] See further paras **16.104–16.113**.

[140] Nineteenth Amendment to the Constitution Act 1998. The amendment also facilitates the establishment of 'cross-border' institutions. See paras **15.11–15.29**.

The position in Northern Ireland

[2.98] It is appropriate at this stage briefly to note the position of Northern Ireland. Northern Ireland enjoyed legislative and executive competence under the Government of Ireland Act 1920. The Northern Irish Parliament (sitting at Stormont) functioned until 1972 when it was prorogued (disbanded) by the UK Parliament due to the violence that emerged in the late 1960s. Between 1972 and 1999, Westminster was the parliamentary body for Northern Ireland and the arrangements for the governance of Northern Ireland by means of this 'direct rule' were contained primarily in the Northern Ireland Constitution Act 1973 [UK]. Some legislation passed at Westminster, such as the 1973 Act itself, apply directly to Northern Ireland. However, most legislation during this period was enacted by means of Orders in Council, a form of secondary or delegated legislation that to all intents and purposes were functional equivalents of Northern Ireland Acts of Parliament.[141] Following the Good Friday Agreement, Northern Ireland regained legislative and executive powers. Westminster passed the Northern Ireland Act 1998 and, in the process, repealed the Government of Ireland Act 1920. An Assembly has been established and a 'power sharing' executive has been put in place. A number of important matters were reserved to the United Kingdom government. These include the politically sensitive areas of policing, prisons and criminal justice (although, under the Northern Ireland (Miscellaneous Provisions) Act 2006 [UK], these areas may be devolved to the Northern Executive) as well as matters of general UK concern such as international relations, taxation, national insurance and the regulation of financial services, telecommunications and broadcasting. The UK government continues to appoint a Secretary of State who has responsibility for Northern Ireland and represents its interests in the British cabinet.

[8] A REVISED COURT SYSTEM

[2.99] While the outcome in 1922 differed in a number of respects from that envisaged in the Government of Ireland Act 1920, it remained the case that two separate jurisdictions emerged in Ireland.[142] The Northern Ireland legal system retained the nomenclature of the 1877 and 1920 Acts, with the Supreme Court of Judicature for Northern Ireland comprising a High Court and Court of Appeal, the High Court being divided into the King's Bench and Chancery Divisions (with one Judicial Commissioner of the Irish Land Commission as an additional judge). As with the 1877 and 1920 Acts,

---

141 For example, the equivalent for Northern Ireland of the British Health and Safety at Work Act 1974 (1974, c 37) is the Health and Safety at Work (Northern Ireland) Order 1978 (SI 1039/1978), which is also given a parallel Northern Ireland 'Act' Number (1978, NI 9) to indicate that it is the equivalent of an Act.

142 On the general impact of the division in terms of legal systems, see Boyle and Greer, *The Legal Systems, North and South* (1983), a study prepared for the New Ireland Forum. See also Dickson, *The Legal System of Northern Ireland* (5th edn, 2005) and Dawson and Ors (eds), *One Hundred and Fifty Years of Irish Law* (1996).

a final appeal lay to the House of Lords. This underlined that Northern Ireland remained within the United Kingdom.

[2.100] In the Irish Free State, the nomenclature provided for in the Constitution of the Irish Free State broke with the 1877 and 1920 Acts, though the essential components remained. The superior courts[143] established by the 1922 Constitution were to comprise a High Court of Justice and a Supreme Court of Justice, the latter being the equivalent of the Court of Appeal of Southern Ireland envisaged by the 1920 Act. However, by contrast with the 1877 and 1920 Acts, a final appeal lay to the Judicial Committee of the Privy Council. This recognised that the Irish Free State had now stepped outside the United Kingdom into the emerging British Commonwealth of Nations.[144]

The revolutionary Dáil courts

[2.101] The transition from the pre-1922 to the post-1922 system was relatively straightforward for Northern Ireland, but matters were not as simple in the Irish Free State. The period between 1919 and 1921 was characterised by widespread insurrection and insurgency against British rule in many parts of Ireland. This had two consequences for the existing court system. It was increasingly difficult to operate the existing court system, whether in Dublin or the provinces. In addition, the parliamentary assembly of the Irish nationalists, Dáil Éireann, had passed decrees in 1920 establishing courts of Dáil Éireann.[145] These comprised:

> *Parish Courts*, which were to meet weekly to deal with minor civil and criminal matters;
>
> *District Courts*, which were to meet monthly to deal with more serious civil and criminal matters and to hear appeals from the Parish Courts;
>
> A *Circuit Court*, organised on the basis of four Circuits, and with unlimited civil and criminal jurisdiction, to hold three sessions per year, each Circuit to be presided over by a Circuit judge; and
>
> A *Supreme Court*, to sit in Dublin, composed of at least three judges, to operate both as a court of first instance and an appellate court.

[2.102] These Dáil Éireann Courts were to apply the law as it stood at January 1919, when the first Dáil Éireann sat, as amended by any subsequent Dáil decrees. English law

---

143 See para **2.62**.

144 This appeal mechanism, which required the permission of the Privy Council itself, was not often used and was in fact abolished by an amendment of the Free State Constitution in 1933: see para **2.67**. The Privy Council remains the final court of appeal from British Commonwealth states, though increasing numbers opted out of this arrangement as the 20th century progressed.

145 Nevertheless, republican activists had shown themselves to be quite adroit in using the official court structure; see Foxton, *Revolutionary Lawyers: Sinn Féin and the Crown Courts in Ireland and Britain 1916–1923* (2008).

textbooks were not to be cited, but the Brehon laws, referred to as 'the early Irish codes' could be used as persuasive precedents, as could decisions of civil law European courts and the principles of Roman law. These courts lacked validity from the point of view of the governing law and were suppressed by the British authorities in so far as this was possible. This was largely achieved in the Dublin area, but in the provinces the Parish and District Courts operated quite extensively between 1920 and 1922, thus providing a brief, if ultimately frustrated, revival of the Brehon laws in 20th-century Ireland.

[2.103] In the wake of the signing of 'The Treaty', in June 1922 the British formally handed over control of the court system provided for in the Government of Ireland Act 1920 to what English law regarded as the 'provisional government' of the Irish Free State.[146] It was ultimately decided, by two decrees of the Cabinet in July and October 1922, to abolish the Dáil Éireann Courts and to 'resurrect' the courts of the 1920 Act.

[2.104] After the establishment of the Irish Free State, the Dáil Éireann Courts (Winding-Up) Act 1923 conferred some retrospective legal validity on the decisions of the Dáil Éireann Courts. This was expressed to be subject to the overriding powers of a judicial commissioner appointed under the 1923 Act with authority to make final determinations arising out of any decision of the revolutionary courts. In effect, the abolition of the Dáil courts and the taking over of the 1920 Act court system represented a 'retreat from revolution'[147] and the courts established under the Constitution of the Irish Free State held that the decisions of the Dáil courts were void and of no legal effect.[148]

1923 Judiciary committee and Courts of Justice Act 1924

[2.105] In January 1923, the newly installed Executive Council of the Irish Free State appointed a Judiciary Committee to recommend the shape of the court system to be established under the 1922 Constitution. The terms of reference of the Committee appeared to give its members *carte blanche*, because it was authorised to make recommendations 'untrammelled by any regard to any of the existing systems of judicature' and the pre-1922 regime was described disparagingly as 'a standing monument of alien government'. However, it must be realised that the Committee was, in fact, limited by the essential outline contained in Article 73 of the Constitution of the Irish Free State, which envisaged a High Court of Justice and Supreme Court of Justice, together with 'courts of local and limited jurisdiction'.[149] The Report of the Judiciary Committee, published in May 1923, recommended a court system for the Irish Free State.

---

146 This was done by means of the Provisional Government (Transfer of Functions) Order 1922, an Order in Council made under the Irish Free State (Agreement) Act 1922, the Act passed at Westminster to give effect to the December 1921 Articles of Agreement.

147 For a discussion of the Dáil Éireann Courts, see Kotsonouris, *Retreat from Revolution* (1994).

148 See *R (Kelly) v Maguire* [1923] 2 IR 58.

149 See further, para **4.40**.

District Court

[2.106] The District Court was to replace the functions performed at Petty Sessions by the Justice of the Peace. The new Justices of the District Court would be full-time judges with legal experience. The court would have jurisdiction in minor civil and criminal matters.

Circuit Court

[2.107] The Circuit Court would also have a criminal and civil jurisdiction. On the civil side, it would replace the County Courts, while its criminal jurisdiction would mirror that of the Assizes in that it would try serious criminal matters, subject to certain 'reserved' offences. It would also hear appeals from the District Court in civil and criminal matters.

High Court

[2.108] As already noted, the Constitution of the Irish Free State 1922 required the establishment of a High Court. The Judiciary Committee recommended that it assume the functions exercised by the High Court of Justice of Southern Ireland under the Government of Ireland Act 1920. It would thus have a virtually unlimited civil jurisdiction (subject only to the matters to be dealt with in the District and Circuit Courts) and in criminal matters would deal with the most serious 'reserved' offences, such as murder. The High Court would be presided over by a President of the High Court.

Court of Criminal Appeal

[2.109] The Judiciary Committee also recommended the establishment of a Court of Criminal Appeal along the lines of the court of the same name established in England in 1907. This court would hear appeals from the Circuit Court and High Court in serious criminal matters, and a further appeal to the Supreme Court would be possible in cases involving points of law of exceptional public importance.

Supreme Court

[2.110] The Report was obliged to recommend that a final court of appeal entitled the Supreme Court be established. Its functions were to be virtually identical to those of the Court of Appeal of Southern Ireland under the 1920 Act. The Supreme Court would be presided over by the Chief Justice of Ireland, the most senior member of the judiciary in the state.

[2.111] The recommendations of the Committee were enacted in the Courts of Justice Act 1924. As we will see, while the Constitution passed in 1937 required the establishment of a 'new' court system in 1961, the arrangements put in place by the

1924 Act were repeated at that time,[150] and this layout of the system continues to the present day.[151]

Relevance of Pre-1922 system to Northern Ireland and English court systems

[2.112] The regime established by the 1873 and 1877 Acts continues to reflect the arrangements in place in Northern Ireland and in the courts of England and Wales. As will become clear in later chapters, decisions of the English courts, and to a lesser extent those of their Northern Irish counterparts, continue to be referred to in Ireland.[152] The current divisions of the English and Northern Ireland High Courts are identical, comprising the Queen's Bench Division, the Chancery Division and, since the passing by the Westminster Parliament of the Courts Act 1971 [UK] and its Northern Ireland equivalent the Judicature (Northern Ireland) Act 1978 [NI], the Family Division. The 1971 and 1978 Acts also replaced the ancient system of twice-yearly Assizes with the Crown Court, now also part of the Supreme Court of Judicature in those jurisdictions. The Westminster Parliament consolidated the changes first introduced by the 1873 Act in the Supreme Court Act 1981 [UK].

[2.113] For Northern Irish and English courts, the appeal system remains remarkably similar to that in the 1873 Act, with an appeal from the High Court to the Court of Appeal (whether that in Belfast or London) and the possibility of a further appeal to the House of Lords or, since October 2009, the newly created Supreme Court of the United Kingdom.

---

[150] See para **4.46**.
[151] See generally, Chs 4 and 7.
[152] See para **12.75** *et seq.*

Chapter 3

The Legal Profession

[1]   Introduction 69
[2]   Solicitors 87
[3]   Barristers 97
[4]   The Law Officers 109
[5]   Legal Education Generally 115
[6]   Other Professionals 121

[1]   INTRODUCTION

[3.01] In this chapter we discuss the many legal professionals who contribute in different ways to the operation of the Irish legal system. Principally, we look at the practising lawyers, solicitors and barristers. We also discuss the roles of the State's two law officers, the Attorney General and Director of Public Prosecutions, and also the Chief State Solicitor. The role of lawyers who are appointed as judges in the different courts is discussed elsewhere.[1] We also examine here the role of universities and other third level institutions in legal education. Finally, we outline how other professionals are involved in the legal system.

The two branches of the legal profession

[3.02] The legal profession in Ireland, as in England, Wales and Northern Ireland,[2] is divided into two branches, solicitors and barristers. This division was carried over from the arrangements which pertained prior to the creation of the two jurisdictions in Ireland in 1922.[3] As we will see, very few other common law jurisdictions continue with this division.

[3.03] The distinctions between the branches of the profession as they operate at present are quite significant. One essential starting point is that, in the vast majority of cases, a person with a legal problem must first consult a solicitor for legal advice. A barrister is not permitted to take instructions directly from a member of the public, except in a small

---

[1]   See para **4.79**.
[2]   While Scotland is part of the United Kingdom, its legal profession and legal system were organised on a separate basis even before the devolution of powers which occurred in 1998.
[3]   See Hogan, *The Legal Profession in Ireland 1789–1922* (1986) and Hogan and Osborough (eds), *Brehons, Sergeants and Attorneys: Studies in the History of the Irish Legal Profession* (1990) and O'Callaghan, *The Law on Solicitors in Ireland* (2000).

number of specific instances which we mention below. Again, broadly speaking, the solicitor tends to specialise in legal work which involves the preparation of cases for court rather than for advocacy in court. The barrister is, generally speaking, regarded as specialising in the preparation of cases for court as well as advocacy in court itself.

[3.04] The solicitor is, therefore, in the front line of dealing with the public and for most people their only contact with a lawyer is a visit to the office of the family solicitor in order, for example, to deal with legal problems related to the sale of a house (conveyancing) or the drafting of a will or with assistance with the drafting of commercial contracts in small-to-medium businesses. This is commonly referred to as non-contentious business, that is, it does not involve a court hearing or other dispute resolution such as arbitration. The local solicitor might also appear in court in relation to some contentious business, such as a summons regarding a road traffic offence. The picture of the solicitor as dealing primarily with conveyancing, wills and minor criminal matters is a common one, and indeed generally accurate. However, it must be borne in mind that, in the case of larger firms (which may have over 30 equity partners and employ hundreds of solicitors), a high level of legal advice, particularly in the commercial area, might call for an extremely wide range of legal services. These may include the need for legal advice in connection with competition law (such as mergers and takeovers), regulatory compliance (such as communications or aviation), banking and, for a firm's multi-national corporate clients, the ability to advise on the law across a number of jurisdictions, whether within the European Union or globally. The larger firms retain the need to advise such clients where they may be liable to civil litigation and, increasingly, arbitration, mediation or conciliation,[4] whether this arises from individuals or other private corporate bodies. In recent years, the large firms must advise corporate clients and senior managers on the risk of enforcement activity and criminal prosecution by regulatory bodies (such as the Revenue Commissioners, the Office of Director of Corporate Enforcement and, in the specific context of financial services, the Central Bank). It is important to note, however, that, despite what novels, films or TV series about lawyers might indicate, court-based work forms a small part of the legal activity of small or large legal firms. But all solicitors share in common the fact that they may do business directly with the public from a high street office. The barrister, on the other hand, may, in general, only give legal advice to a person, whether an individual or a corporate entity, after receiving instructions from a solicitor although some elements of 'direct professional access' have been in place for many years and at the time of writing (September 2014), the question of extending this remains a matter for debate. In general terms, direct professional access for barristers to non-members of the legal professional arises only for non-contentious business and in specialist areas such as taxation.

---

[4]   See Ch 8, below, on the increasing importance of mediation and conciliation.

Reform of the profession: Fair Trade Commission Report 1990 and Competition Authority Reports 2005 and 2006

[3.05] It will become clear from this and subsequent chapters that reform of the legal profession and the court system has been the subject of considerable debate since the 1980s. This has continued into the early 21st century, and has resulted in extensive reforms, which have already and will in the future affect the profession. The first significant investigation of the legal profession in Ireland was the Fair Trade Commission's *Report into Restrictive Practices in the Legal Profession*,[5] published in 1990. In 1984, the Commission had been requested by the then Minister for Industry, Trade, Commerce and Tourism (now known as the Minister for Jobs, Enterprise and Innovation) to undertake a wide-ranging inquiry into the legal profession and connected areas. It was required to examine any practices that might be causing increased costs to consumers of legal services or causing limited employment opportunities within the profess ions.[6] While the Commission was thus formally limited to a consideration of restrictive practices within the profession, its 1990 Report was extremely wide in scope. The recommendations in the Report resulted in substantial changes in the organisation of the profession and the courts in the late 1990s.

[3.06] A major conclusion of the Commission's 1990 Report was that the existing separation or division of the profession did *not* amount to a restrictive practice and therefore it did not need to be ended. Thus the Commission did not recommend 'fusion' into a unified legal profession. The Commission recommended, however, that nothing should be placed in the way of future fusion of the branches of the legal profession if that was desired.[7] Since the Report's publication in 1990, the legal profession in Ireland has done little to indicate that any such fusion will occur from within.

[3.07] Apart from the conclusion that the existence of the two branches was not a restrictive practice, the 1990 Report made significant recommendations on the reform of the profession and the vast majority of these have since been implemented either by legislation or voluntary changes within the legal profession. For solicitors, among the

---

5   Hereinafter the FTC Report. The Report runs to 334 pages.
6   The Commission's study was made under the Restrictive Practices Act 1972, s 12 by which studies into any trade or profession could be made to determine if practices in any trade or profession constitute a restrictive practice or might unreasonably restrict free and fair competition. The 1972 Act was replaced by the Competition Acts 1991 and 1996, and the 1991 Act replaced the Fair Trade Commission with the Competition Authority. The Competition Act 1991 and Competition (Amendment) Act 1996 were repealed by the Competition Act 2002 which, as amended, sets out the powers of the Competition Authority. The Competition and Consumer Protection Act 2014 provided for the amalgamation of the Competition Authority and the National Consumer Agency into the Competition and Consumer Protection Commission (this was part of a wider rationalisation of State agencies in recent years).
7   FTC Report, pp 71–3.

areas on which reform was recommended and subsequently implemented were the following:

- alterations to the legislation concerning advertising by solicitors;
- reform of the procedures where complaints of unprofessional conduct are made against solicitors, including the appointment of an independent adjudicator;
- extending to solicitors eligibility for appointment as judges of the higher courts, which previously had been restricted to barristers only.

These were implemented by the Solicitors (Amendment) Act 1994 and certain provisions of the Courts and Court Officers Act 1995.[8]

[3.08] The Commission had noted that although solicitors had been given the right of audience in the courts in the 1970s[9] – that is, their right to appear in the courts to represent clients – this had not been taken up by a significant section of the profession and it recommended that the Law Society engage in further efforts to promote the right of audience amongst solicitors. The Law Society has, since that time, engaged in significant efforts along those lines, including the provision of courses on litigation and advocacy.

[3.09] As to barristers, the areas on which reform was recommended by the 1990 Report and subsequently implemented were:

- limited changes which allow other professionals such as accountants 'direct professional access' to a barrister without the need to instruct a solicitor; and
- reform of the procedures where complaints of unprofessional conduct are made against barristers.

These were implemented by changes to the Bar Council's Code of Conduct for barristers and certain provisions of the Courts and Court Officers Act 1995.[10]

[3.10] The potential for a further review of the legal profession was re-opened in 2001 through the publication of a report on regulatory reform in Ireland by the Organisation for Economic Co-operation and Development (OECD).[11] This recommended that a number of professions, including the legal profession, be investigated from the point of view of whether they complied with OECD guidelines on competitiveness. The Report argued that the control of education and entry into the profession should be removed from the Law Society of Ireland and the Honourable Society of King's Inns, though it also accepted that close ties should be maintained with and to them in order to ensure quality of entrants and the content of education and training. This reopened an area not progressed since the 1990 Fair Trade Commission Report, namely the extent to which the Law Society and the King's Inns retain the 'monopoly' in the state to regulate entry into the profession.

---

8   We discuss the impact of the 1995 Act in Chs 4 and 5.
9   Under the Courts of Justice Act 1971: see para **3.71**.
10   We discuss the impact of the 1995 Act in Chs 4 and 5.
11   *Report on Regulatory Reform in Ireland* (April 2001).

[3.11] Following the 2001 OECD report, it became clear that further examination of the regulation of the legal professions was required. The government requested the Competition Authority to complete an examination of the issue of the regulation of the legal profession and, in addition, to complete a report concerning the reform of the legal profession in general.

[3.12] The Competition Authority produced two reports dealing with competition in legal services.[12] These reports examined the two professions in detail and made far-reaching recommendations for reform. The first, a 2005 Interim Report, essentially outlined key issues, provided a number of options for reform in the key issues and invited submissions from interested parties. The second, a 2006 Final Report, made recommendations based on a consideration of the issues and the submissions received. In its 2006 report, the Competition Authority concluded 'that the legal profession is in need of substantial reform. The profession is permeated with unnecessary and disproportionate restrictions on competition which should be removed so that consumers can benefit from greater competition in legal services.'[13]

[3.13] A number of key areas were highlighted by the Competition Authority as being in need of reform. These issues cover the legal profession, its regulation, structure, entry and education. Broadly speaking, the key issues examined in the Report were the monopoly on legal education in both branches of the profession; the business model of the legal profession, in particular, the fact that barristers cannot form chambers or partnerships; the absence of licensed conveyancers in Ireland (solicitors retaining a monopoly in this respect); the regulation of the legal profession by an independent body as opposed to self-regulation; the criteria in place for appointment as senior counsel; restrictions on advertising by barristers; switching of lawyers by clients; the ability to transfer between the two professions; and, finally, restriction on particular forms of part time employment for barristers.

[3.14] The key recommendation in the Competition Authority's 2006 Report was that the regulation of both branches of the legal profession and legal services should be overseen by a Legal Services Commission which would be an independent, transparent and accountable body. This recommendation entailed a move away from self-regulation of the legal profession. Self-regulation of the legal profession by the Bar Council and Law Society was seen to raise potential conflicts of interest between the interests of lawyers and the interests of consumers of legal services. It was envisaged that some regulatory functions could be transferred from the Legal Services Commission to the Bar Council and Law Society with the Legal Services Commission retaining a supervisory role.

---

12   Competition Authority, *Study of Competition in Legal Services: Preliminary Report* (February 2005) and Competition Authority, *Competition in Professional Services: Solicitors and Barristers* (December 2006). See Lysaght 'Competition Authority Report on Solicitors and Barristers' [2008] *Judicial Studies Institute Journal* 159.

13   *Competition in Professional Services* at p iii.

[3.15] The Report noted that the structures in place relating to when a client wished to change lawyers were in need of reform. In particular, in relation to solicitors, should a client wish to change solicitor, the solicitor has the right to withhold the file pending payment of all outstanding fees. The Competition Authority recommended that change be made, by way of legislation, to remove solicitors' rights over clients' files. As a result of the recommendations made by the Competition Authority a number of changes were introduced by the Law Society and Bar Council. Prior to 2006, a barrister was precluded from taking over a case from another barrister until the other barrister had been paid. This restriction was removed in 2006 by the Bar Council.

[3.16] After an examination of the issue, the Competition Authority concluded that the barriers faced by those seeking to transfer from one branch of the profession to the other were unduly difficult. It recommended that the Bar Council and the Law Society remove all unnecessary barriers for lawyers wishing to switch from one branch of the profession to the other. In August 2008 the Law Society ran its first Essentials of Legal Practice course over 17 days for those wishing to transfer from the barrister to solicitor profession.[14] This course has continued on an annual basis since that time. Similarly the rules for the transfer of a suitably qualified solicitor to become a barrister have been made more flexible. The Honorable Society of King's Inns now runs an annual Solicitor Transfer Course each summer for those wishing to transfer from the solicitor to barrister profession.

[3.17] The initial response to the 2006 Report was that a Legal Services Commission would not be established. Instead, the government and Oireachtas decided at that time that a Legal Services Ombudsman would be established to oversee complaints concerning both solicitors and barristers – this would involve the first occasion that complaints concerning barristers would be subject to independent review under a legislative framework (solicitors being already subject to independent review). As a result, the Legal Services Ombudsman Act 2009 was enacted, which envisaged the establishment of the office of the Legal Services Ombudsman to oversee the handling of complaints against barristers and solicitors by the Bar Council and Law Society. In fact, no Legal Services Ombudsman was ever appointed under the 2009 Act and the relatively limited reforms to the legal profession contained in the 2009 Act were superseded by the requirements of the 2010–2013 EU–IMF Framework of Financial Support Agreement for Ireland (often known as the EU–IMF 'bailout'), under which Ireland received almost €70 billion in low-interest loans to fund its fiscal deficit from 2011 to 2013 in return for complying with the conditions set out in the Framework Agreement.

[3.18] Among the many conditions in the Framework Agreement was reform of what were described as 'sheltered professions', that is, professions not perceived to be subject to the full range of competition principles, including the dental, legal and medical professions. These commitments to review the application of competition principles

---

14   See the (2008) 102(8) *Law Society Gazette* 49.

involved the reopening of the analysis in the Competition Authority Reports of 2005 and 2006, discussed above. Arising from the Framework Agreement, significantly more fundamental and radical reforms are proposed in the Legal Services Regulation Bill 2011. At the time of writing (September 2014) the 2011 Bill is still before the Oireachtas, although it passed Committee Stage in Dáil Éireann in 2014 and may be enacted by the end of 2014. While the state completed the main requirements of the 2010–2013 EU–IMF Framework Agreement in December 2013, the EU and IMF continue to monitor those commitments which have not been completed, including for example the need to enact the 2011 Bill.

[3.19] Among the main proposals in the 2011 Bill are:

- the establishment of an independent Legal Services Regulatory Authority, as envisaged in the Competition Authority Reports to deal with both legal professions and an independent complaints structure to deal with complaints about professional misconduct;

- the possible development and regulation by the Legal Services Regulatory Authority of alternative business structures (ABSs), which could include limited liability partnerships of solicitors and firms comprising solicitors and barristers;

- the possible development and regulation by the Legal Services Regulatory Authority of multi disciplinary practices (MDPs), which could include a firm comprising solicitors, barristers, accountants and other business advisers and consultants;

- the new Legal Service Regulator examining whether a new legal profession of conveyancers should be introduced in Ireland;

- the removal of restrictions on barrister partnerships;

- the removal of the monopoly on legal professional training for solicitors and barristers in Ireland;

- the removal of restrictions on direct access to barristers for legal advice;

- the establishment of an independent Legal Costs Regulatory Body, which would replace the current system of legal costs regulation involving Taxing Masters (in the High Court) and County Registrars (in the Circuit Court).

[3.20] While the Law Society and Bar Council have supported a number of the proposals in the 2011 Bill, they have raised serious objections to specific elements in the 2011 Bill as initiated, including:

- that the independence of the legal professions, and consequently the rule of law, would be undermined if, as envisaged by the 2011 Bill as initiated, the majority of the members of the Legal Services Regulatory Authority were to be appointed by the Minister for Justice which has the power to control all aspects of legal practice include training, entry to the professions and discipline;

- that the proposals for ABSs and MDPs could severely restrict access by small firms of solicitors to experienced barristers and could undermine the ability of the legal professions to provide truly independent legal advice to clients;[15]

- the Legal Services Regulatory Authority will introduce a new and high level of cost into the Irish legal system.

[3.21] At the time of writing (September 2014) it appears that significant changes will be made to the appointments process to the Legal Services Regulatory Authority before the 2011 Bill is enacted. As to the proposals for ABSs and MDPs, while the Law Society and Bar Council remain opposed to a greater or lesser degree to these, it appears that the government is committed to including some proposals along these lines. This may be influenced by the expectation by both the IMF and the EU that the enacted reforms would include provision for ABSs and MDPs. Whatever the detail of the Bill as finally enacted in 2014 or 2015, it is clear that significant reform, including external regulation in general and regulation of legal costs, is highly likely in the short and medium term future.

Numbers of practising lawyers and access to the profession

[3.22] There has been a significant increase in the number of practising solicitors since the 1960s, as Figure 3.1 illustrates.[16]

Year	Number
1960	1,335
1970	1,363
1975	1,655
1980	2,139
1983	2,788
1985	3,188
1987	3,360
1989	3,422
1996	4,100
2000	5,500
2006	7,242
2008	8,144
2014	9,000[17]

Figure 3.1

---

[15] There has also been criticism of certain elements of the 2011 Bill from other quarters. For example, in 2012 the American Bar Association and the Council of Bars and Law Societies of Europe wrote to the IMF arguing that the measures for legal reform in Ireland, Greece and Portugal threaten "one of the core principles of the legal profession: regulation independent from the executive branch of the state." See also the special edition of the *Law Society Gazette* of December 2011 where concerns were expressed at certain elements of the 2011 Bill by representatives of the International Bar Association (IBA) and the Council of Bars and Law Societies of Europe (CCBE).

[16] Source: 1990 FTC Report, p 80, Competition Authority Report, p 25 and Law Society.

[17] McDonald, 'Barristers Struggling to Survive as 180 quit in a year' (2014) *Irish Independent*, 11 March.

Similarly, there has been a substantial increase in the number of barristers in Ireland (with a small decrease between 2008 and 2012 which reflects the impact of the Great Recession), as Figure 3.2 of membership of the Law Library indicates.[18]

Year	Number
1968	217
1970	253
1975	292
1980	429
1983	481
1985	534
1987	638
1989	722
1996	900
2000	1,300
2006	1,665
2008	1,950
2014	2,225[20]

Figure 3.2

[3.23] The 9,000 solicitors in practice in 2014 were employed in 2,200 individual firms. The top six law firms in Ireland (the 'Big Six' firms) employed 1,247 solicitors. The next 14 largest firms collectively employed 736 practitioners. Thus, 22% of all practising solicitors were employed in just 20 law firms, that is, in 1% of the total number of firms. At the other end of the scale, 43% of firms have just one solicitor and 82% have three or less solicitors. This is representative of the position in the legal profession in many other comparable jurisdictions.[20]

The Code of Conduct of the Bar Council of Ireland prohibits barristers from forming firms or comparable arrangements such as chambers, which are common in the United Kingdom including Northern Ireland. This means that each practising barrister in the Republic of Ireland is self-employed and is a member of the independent referral bar. This long-standing tradition explains to a large extent the strong opposition of the Bar Council to the proposed reforms to business structures in the Legal Services Regulation Bill 2011, discussed above.

[3.24] This general increase in numbers since the 1960s has also created enormous pressures on the arrangements for the legal education of solicitors and barristers and ensuring that those who qualify have a reasonable future and the ability to earn a

---

18 Source: 1990 FTC Report, p 85, Competition Authority Report, p 25 and Bar Council of Ireland.

19 McDonald, 'Barristers Struggling to Survive as 180 quit in a year' (2014) *Irish Independent*, 11 March.

20 See Murphy, '22% of solicitors practised in just 1% of firms in 2013' *Law Society Gazette*, May 2014, p 7, available at lawsociety.ie.

livelihood. The balance between ensuring continued access to the profession and the need to assure entrants a reasonable standard of living for those who become qualified was discussed in detail in the 1990 Fair Trade Commission Report. The Commission recommended that the profession itself should not be entitled to determine the appropriate numbers to enter the profession, fearing that a 'quota' system might be against the public interest.[21] Rather, it was recommended that freedom of access, subject to proper standards of education, be the governing principle, with the market for professional services determining the number of practitioners. The Commission did, however, also recommend that, if necessary, a body might be established to determine if limits on entry were required in the future. At present, no such body has been established so that entry levels are not limited and, in effect, the market determines the numbers of practising solicitors.

[3.25] The Legal Services Regulation Bill 2011 envisages that the Legal Services Regulatory Authority will prepare and submit to the Minister for Justice a report on the number of persons admitted to practise as barristers and solicitors respectively during that year, and an assessment as to whether, having regard to the demand for the services of practising barristers and solicitors and the need to ensure an adequate standard of education and training for persons admitted to practise, the number of persons admitted to practise as barristers and solicitors in that year is consistent with the public interest in ensuring the availability of such services at a reasonable cost. As a result it seems likely that a re-examination of the issue of entry to the professions will take place in accordance with the terms of the 2011 Bill, when enacted.

[3.26] Figure 3.3, prepared for a report on personal injuries actions in the state and updated from the Competition Authority Report provides the following comparison between the number of lawyers in the state and in Britain.[22] This indicates that the number of solicitors in the state as a percentage of the population is lower than in Britain, whereas the opposite is true for barristers.

	Ireland	Britain
Population	3,606,952	52,247,525
Solicitors	4,900	95,521
Barristers	1,182	9,698
Population served per solicitor	736.11	546.97
Population served per barrister	3051.57	5387.45
Population served per lawyer per 1,000 population (2006)	2.1	2.5

Figure 3.3

---

21   Suggestions that a 'quota' system had been operated by the Law Society emerged in
      MacGabhann v Incorporated Law Society of Ireland [1989] ILRM 854, but this was contested
      by the Law Society. A declaration was made in the case that such a quota would be *ultra vires*
      the powers of the Law Society under the Solicitors Acts.
22   Source: *Second Report of the Special Working Group on Personal Injury Compensation*
      (2001), p 119 and Competition Authority Report, p 25.

Legal fees and costs

[3.27] In its 1990 Report, the Fair Trade Commission also examined whether the legal profession charges excessive fees for its services and whether it is feasible to place curbs on those fees, concluding that this was a matter on which it would not be appropriate to legislate. It was pointed out that such curbs would interfere with the market in legal fees and might be contrary to competition legislation. Nonetheless, s 46 of the Courts and Court Officers Act 1995 provides that 'scale fees' may be set by regulations for solicitors' costs and counsels' fees. This power has not yet been used. However, the Bar Council has, on a voluntary basis, accepted some changes to its own rules on the number of barristers who need to be briefed in certain cases, in particular personal injuries actions.[23]

[3.28] However, the level of fees charged by barristers has also been the subject of some public criticism in recent years. In 1996, considerable comment emerged concerning a total of £6.75m in legal fees awarded to solicitors and barristers who had been involved in a three-year tribunal of inquiry into the Irish beef industry, including fees of almost £1m for senior counsel engaged by one party to the tribunal.[24] Over the years, the fees earned by barristers working at tribunals in this jurisdiction have generated significant publicity.[25] In more recent years, a number of decisions of the Taxing Master (who measures legal costs in the event that costs cannot be agreed between the parties) have been reported in the media where significant reductions to the fees submitted by lawyers were made and on occasion criticism was made of the excessive legal fees charged.[26]

[3.29] In 2008, it was reported that senior counsel engaged by the state at a tribunal were paid €2,500 a day, while junior counsel earned €2,000 per day.[27] The income of barristers was discussed in detail by the Competition Authority. From figures they obtained from the Revenue Commissioners, they found that the average income for a junior counsel in 2002 was €120,893 and a senior counsel was €329,915.[28] It was also reported that the percentage of barristers who earn over €200,000 a year (12%) is proportionally greater than the percentage of pharmacists 6%, dentists 11%, medical consultants 7% and accountants 1.3% who earn over the same amount.[29]

---

[23] The *Second Report of the Special Working Group on Personal Injury Compensation* (2001), p 117 indicated that junior counsel only was briefed in 57% of cases surveyed, while one senior counsel was briefed in 17% of cases surveyed.

[24] See paras **8.74–8.81**.

[25] For example see (2008) *The Sunday Tribune*, 1 June; (2008) *The Sunday Times*, 25 July.

[26] For example see McDonald, 'Four Barristers won't appeal fee reduction' (2010) *Irish Independent*, 2 July.

[27] (2008) *The Sunday Tribune*, 1 June.

[28] Competition Authority Report, p 27.

[29] Competition Authority Report, p 27.

[3.30] Public commentary on legal fees has also resulted in at least one successful claim for libel by a senior member of the Bar. In *Foley v Independent Newspapers (Ireland) Ltd*,[30] the plaintiff had been appointed by a Government Minister as an inspector to investigate the affairs of a state company. Shortly after his appointment, he had agreed a daily fee with the relevant state authorities. The investigation took six months to complete and the plaintiff's fee amounted to £250,000. Although this had been based on the agreed fee, the plaintiff was criticised in a newspaper article for the level of fee charged. He successfully sued the newspaper and was awarded £30,000 damages for libel.

[3.31] Fees charged by solicitors have also been the subject of public debate in recent years. In the aftermath of alleged over-charging by solicitors in respect of certain claims, a Legal Costs Working Group was established in 2004[31] to examine ways of reducing legal costs. The 2005 Report of the Legal Costs Working Group examined the current basis for an award of legal costs in Ireland, namely, that 'costs follow the event', that is, that costs are awarded in favour of the successful party in litigation and must be paid by the losing party. The Legal Costs Working Group could see no reason for abandoning this principle. Accordingly, many of its recommendations relate to changing the process for the recovery of costs.

[3.32] The Report made two key recommendations:

- first, it recommended the establishment of a Legal Costs Regulatory Body, to formulate guidelines setting out the amounts of legal costs that would normally apply in respect of particular types of proceedings or steps within proceedings, to exercise regulatory functions and have a public information role; and

- second, it recommended the establishment of a Legal Costs Assessment Office to replace Taxing Masters, to assess legal bills.

[3.33] The Report also recommended the abandonment of the two-thirds rule, by which a junior counsel conventionally charges two-thirds of the rate of senior counsel. In September 2007, the Bar Council issued a direction which stated 'that it is not appropriate for a junior counsel to mark a brief fee of two thirds of the senior counsel's brief fee merely on the basis of this mathematical relationship'.[32] As a result, the two-thirds rule has been virtually eradicated. The Legal Costs Working Group also recommended that legal fees should be assessed on the basis of work undertaken by lawyers and not primarily on the current basis of the value of the case or size of the award. This is reflected in the Code of Conduct of the Bar of Ireland.

[3.34] The Group also recommended that barristers should, in future, as solicitors are under s 68 of the Solicitors (Amendment) Act 1994, be required to issue meaningful fee estimate letters in order that clients be fully aware of the legal costs entailed in any legal

---

30   *Foley v Independent Newspapers (Ireland) Ltd* [1994] 2 ILRM 61.
31   *Report of Legal Costs Working Group* (2005), available at www.justice.ie.
32   Bar Council Direction on the Two-Thirds Rule (September 2007).

services provided. A Ruling of the Professional Practice Committee of the Bar Council in January 2008 requires all barristers to issue fee estimates to solicitors or clients (in the case of direct professional access) 'as soon as practicable'. The Ruling included a draft fee estimate for guidance purposes. The ruling makes it clear that failure on the part of a barrister to furnish a fee estimate could constitute professional misconduct.

[3.35] In 2006, the Report of the Legal Costs Implementation Advisory Group set out how the recommendations of the 2005 Working Group Report would be implemented.[33] The 2006 Report recommended that the legal costs regulatory body should consist of three part-time commissioners and be given the task of drawing up appropriate guidelines governing the items of recoverable legal costs. The Implementation Group advocated a change to the 'global' approach to legal costs furnished by barristers and solicitors based on a flat instruction or brief fee. Instead they recommended that fees be generated on an hourly or daily rate.

[3.36] The Legal Services Regulation Bill 2011 will, when enacted, provide for the implementation of these recommendations, and the inclusion of reform of legal costs in the 2011 Bill also reflects the commitment to do so in the 2010–2013 EU–IMF Framework Agreement of Financial Support for Ireland discussed above. The 2011 Bill provides for the establishment of an independent Legal Costs Regulatory Body, which is intended to replace the current system of legal costs regulation involving Taxing Masters (in the High Court) and County Registrars (in the Circuit Court). The 2011 Bill also envisages more prescriptive regulation of individual fees, which reflects the analysis in the 2005 and 2006 Competition Authority Reports, which the EU–IMF Agreement endorsed. This reflects the need for transparency in the area of legal costs. Thus, it appears more likely that, at the least, hourly and daily fee rates will replace large up-front brief fees for both solicitors and barristers. It is also likely that solicitors firms in particular will be required by some corporate clients to move towards, for example, an annual fixed fee arrangement for legal services in order to reduce the overall costs to the client of legal services.[34]

[3.37] These also coincide with a growing concern that the high cost of legal services is a real barrier to effective access to justice for the majority of individuals in society. It is at least arguable that high legal fees mean that only the following groups are in a position to have access to legal services: (a) corporate entities such as private sector companies[35] and public bodies such as local authorities and central government agencies[36] who have sufficient resources to pay for legal services; (b) wealthy individuals whose resources allow them to engage legal services regardless of cost; (c)

---

33 *Report of the Legal Costs Implementation Advisory Group* (2006), p 5.
34 See the discussion below, para **3.47**, of Professor Richard Susskind's analysis of the future of the legal profession.
35 Subject to the increasing cost-consciousness of private sector bodies, including through the discussion below, para **3.50**, of in-house counsel as a method of legal cost containment.
36 Subject also to the reduction in State-funded legal aid since the financial crisis of 2008: see Ch 9.

extremely low income individuals whose income is very low and the subject matter of their dispute (such as family law or challenge to their immigration status) falls within the remit of the civil legal aid scheme; (d) individuals whose personal injuries claim is deemed sufficiently meritorious by a solicitor and counsel that it is taken on a deferred fee basis; (e) individuals with such an unusual public interest claim that a solicitor and counsel will take it on a pro bono basis; and (f) persons charged with criminal offences that come within the state-funded criminal legal aid scheme.[37] In this respect the proposed changes in the Legal Services Regulation Bill 2011 need not necessarily be seen as involving a narrow-focus attempt to reduce the fee income of individual lawyers but as an attempt to extend the range of persons in society (the "squeezed middle" who are ineligible for legal aid and not wealthy enough to be indifferent to cost) who would thereby be in a position to gain access to affordable legal services.

Reform of the Profession: UK and other influences

[3.38] It is notable that many recommendations from the Reports referred to, and the subsequent action taken on foot of them, mirror reforms which occurred towards the end of the 20th century and in the early part of the 21st century in the United Kingdom concerning the legal profession and the administration of justice. This began with the enactment of the Courts and Legal Services Act 1990, which substantially reorganised the provision of legal services in England, Wales and Northern Ireland. It introduced the prospect of solicitors gaining full rights of audience in the courts in England, Wales and Northern Ireland, through the introduction of solicitor advocates, though of course in this respect solicitors in Ireland had enjoyed this right since the early 1970s. The 1990 Act removed the solicitor's conveyancing monopoly, by allowing financial institutions to offer such a service through their own employed solicitors departments, subject to approval by the Legal Services Ombudsman in order to avoid potential conflicts of interest. In 2006, the Competition Authority recommended a similar provision in Ireland, and this is discussed in more detail below. The 1990 Act has been replaced by the British Legal Services Board Act 2007, which re-enacted the provisions discussed above.

[3.39] In 2004, an extensive review of the system of regulation of the legal profession in England and Wales was undertaken by Sir David Clementi for the then UK Department for Constitutional Affairs (now the British Ministry for Justice).[38] The main recommendation of the review was that a new Legal Services Board should be established as an independent body to oversee the regulatory activities of those bodies whose members offer legal services. The report envisaged that this change in the regulation of legal services would place the interests of the consumer at the centre of the regulatory system. This is now provided for on a legislative basis in the British Legal Services Act 2007 which implemented the recommendations in the Clementi Report.

---

[37]   See Ch 9.
[38]   Clementi, *Review of the Regulation System for Legal Services in England and Wales: Final Report* (Department of Constitutional Affairs, 2004).

The 2007 Act provides for the establishment of the Legal Services Board as regulator of legal services. The Legal Services Board was established in 2008[39] and its members comprise persons with experience in consumer issues, regulatory experience, the legal sector and public service. Its primary function is to drive improvements in regulation across the legal sector.

[3.40] Given the influence in Ireland of changes made in Britain since the 1990s, it is worth noting the impact of the UK Access to Justice Act 1999. The 1999 Act effected changes in the courts in England, Wales and Northern Ireland across a wide range of issues. On the organisation of the legal profession, it has, for example, introduced the principle of equal rights of audience for solicitors and barristers in the courts in England, Wales and Northern Ireland and this has been extended to include employed advocates, such as those employed by the Crown Prosecution Service (CPS). The 1999 Act also underlines the need to ensure the independence of advocates, including employed advocates, by providing that their overriding duty is to ensure that the administration of justice is served. Thus, nothing in their contract of employment could override the obligation to ensure that relevant evidence was not suppressed.

[3.41] The Clementi Report also recommended that a new independent Office for Legal Complaints, which would include a Legal Ombudsman, should be established as a single dispute resolution body for handling all complaints relating to the provision of legal services, whether by solicitors or barristers: this is also provided for in the British Legal Services Act 2007. The Legal Ombudsman[40] and the Office for Legal Complaints (which is the independent board appointed by the Legal Services Commission that oversees the Legal Ombudsman) began their work in 2010.

[3.42] It has been argued that the changes made by the UK 1999 and 2007 Acts, while retaining the formal distinction between solicitors and barristers, have sounded the first toll of the death knell for the divided profession; that it amounts to fusion by 'creeping changes'.[41] Indeed, it is notable that reports on the main professions in the United Kingdom, including the legal profession, were published in 2001 by the Office of Fair Trading and these made proposals for further reforms, including the extension of the right of audience to barristers in employment.[42] Similar recommendations were made by the Competition Authority and these are discussed below. There is, however, little indication to suggest that the formal division between barristers and solicitors is likely to end.[43]

---

[39]   See its website www.legalservicesboard.org.uk.

[40]   See its website www.legalombudsman.org.uk.

[41]   See Slapper and Kelly, *The English Legal System* (15th edn, 2014), Ch 16.

[42]   *Competition in Professions* (March 2001) and *Employed Barristers Rights to Conduct Litigation* (February 2001).

[43]   Malleson, *The Legal System* (3rd edn, 2007), p 191.

[3.43] A review of the legal services in Northern Ireland was completed in 2006 by the Legal Services Review Group ('the Bain Report').[44] The Bain Report took a very different view of whether complete independence is required in regulation of the legal profession and complaints made in relation to the legal profession. The Report concluded that regulation of the professions continues to be discharged by the professions themselves, subject to a supervisory role by a Legal Services Oversight Commissioner assisted by the Lord Chief Justice for Northern Ireland. Regarding complaints handling, the Bain Report acknowledged – given the public aspect involved – that it was necessary for the most wide-ranging reforms to be introduced. However, the report fell short of recommending a fully independent complaints system. Instead, because of the small amount of complaints against legal professionals in Northern Ireland, it recommended that complaints continue to be administered by the legal profession itself, subject to an increased lay participation, including a lay chair. It recommended that the Legal Services Oversight Commissioner monitor the regulation and complaints-handling system and ensure these responsibilities are discharged adequately by the legal profession. The Bain Report did not advocate any change to the business structure of the barrister and solicitor professions. At the time of writing (September 2014), the legal professions in Northern Ireland therefore continue to operate in a manner that resembles the position in the Republic. Finally, the report did not recommend the introduction of licensed conveyancers in Northern Ireland. In 2013, the Northern Ireland Department of Finance and Personnel published a draft Legal Complaints and Regulation Bill[45] which would implement the Bain Report recommendations.

[3.44] Further afield, there have been significant changes in other common law jurisdictions. In many of these, the distinction between solicitors and barristers has either been abolished or substantially reduced, and fusion of the legal profession has, in effect, occurred. In the United States, the single title attorney-at-law reflects the long-established fusion of the legal profession.[46] Similarly, though more recently, in Canada, New Zealand and most Australian states and territories, a person is now called as both a solicitor and barrister, although they practice as one or the other. In fact, virtually all the common law jurisdictions have abandoned the model of the divided profession and in this respect, Ireland together with England and Wales and Northern Ireland represent one of the last remaining outposts of the distinction.

---

44 Legal Services Review Group, *Legal Services in Northern Ireland: Complaints, Regulation, Competition* (TSO, 2006).

45 See O'Connell, "Comparative Research on Legal Complaints and Regulation" (Northern Assembly, Research and Information Service Research Paper, Paper 58/14, May 2014), available at www.niassembly.gov.uk.

46 In the United States the title 'solicitor' remains and is often associated with in-house lawyers in federal or state agencies. At federal level, the US Solicitor General represents the federal government in any litigation in the US Supreme Court, including constitutional cases. Prior to the establishment of the office of the Solicitor General in 1870, this function was performed by the US Attorney General.

Gender change in the Profession[47]

[3.45] Another notable change in the legal profession in recent decades is in its gender composition, which also reflects comparable changes in other liberal professions in Ireland. Until the 1960s, the overwhelming majority of practising lawyers, solicitors and barristers, were men. By 2013, the gender balance of the solicitors' profession was roughly 50/50, and in 2013, 63% of those who qualified as solicitors were women. The change in the composition of the barristers' profession has been more gradual. By 2013, 43% of practising barristers were women, and 45% of barristers with less than seven years experience were women. The recent nature of these changes is also reflected in the very high percentage of male senior counsel in 2013, 83% of a total of 354. In 2013, 60% of those in the final year at King's Inns were women students. It is predicted that, by 2024, women will constitute the greater majority of practising lawyers. This trend is reflected in the increase in number of female judges. The percentage of female judges is 30 per cent or higher in the Supreme, the Circuit and the District Courts. The High Court has a female representation rate of just over 12 per cent, following the appointment in 2013 of two women judges to the Supreme Court.[48]

[3.46] These changes were also reflected in the number of legal offices held by women. In 2013, the following law offices were held by women: Chief Justice, President of the District Court, the Attorney General, the Director of Public Prosecutions, and the Chief State Solicitor. In the private sector, women were in the managing partner position in three of the top 20 law firms. In the university law schools, a number of women have held or hold the position of head of the law school, though the number of women law professors in Ireland remains low.

Future of the Profession

[3.47] The reviews discussed above and consequent changes in the legislative regulation of the legal profession have been influenced by the increasing globalisation and commercialisation of professional services generally. Professor Richard Susskind has been an influential writer and adviser on the legal profession to many governments since the 1990s.[49] His analysis of the changing landscape of professional services generally and the emerging impact of information and communications technology (ICT) in the digital age has proved highly influential in the reform of the legal profession in a number of common law jurisdictions.

---

47 See generally Department of Justice, 'Towards Gender Parity in Decision-Making' (2013), ch 8.

48 See generally Department of Justice, 'Towards Gender Parity in Decision-Making' (2013), p 85.

49 His publications include Susskind, *The Future of Law: Facing the Challenges of Information Technology* (1997), Susskind, *The End of Lawyers? Rethinking the Nature of Legal Services* (2008) and Susskind, *Tomorrow's Lawyers: An Introduction to Your Future* (2013).

[3.48] Professor Susskind's analysis points out that professional service providers such as accountants, tax advisers and other related professionals are increasingly organised not as small or medium sized national firms but as part of multinational firms. In addition, the international accounting firms often engage in informal or formal partnerships with the international tax advice firms, or have actually merged with each other, in order to maximise the commercial benefits for their respective firms. The development of these closer relationships is also driven by an increasingly globalised services industry in which the clients of such service providers are often also multinational corporations who seek the most competitive service provider.

[3.49] This emerging landscape of how professional services are organised is already having an impact on the organisation of legal services, including in Ireland. As noted above, 22% of all practising solicitors in Ireland in 2013 were employed in just 20 law firms, that is, in 1% of the total number of firms. This indicates that Ireland reflects the increasing trend internationally towards concentration in a very small number of large firms. These large solicitor firms are, like their counterparts in other professional service providers, increasingly organised along cross-border lines. Indeed in recent years it is clear that English law firms who had no previous presence in Ireland have begun to establish in Ireland and, having attracted senior solicitors from existing solicitor firms, have grown rapidly to be among some of the top 20 firms in Ireland. Some solicitors firms have also begun to employ senior members of the Bar on a full-time in-house basis, rather than engage them on a fee-per-case basis. This has the potential for further blurring of the distinction between solicitors and barristers. It is important to note that this has occurred before the enactment of the Legal Services Regulation Bill 2011 so that in that respect the proposals in the 2011 Bill on alternative business structures may, by the time they are enacted, reflect existing arrangements rather than potential future ones.

[3.50] The changing landscape is also matched within the large (often also multinational) corporations who seek legal services. Many such companies now employ in-house counsel (which sometimes comprise a team of lawyers). The increase in in-house counsel had led to the Law Society running a course specifically to cater for such lawyers or aspiring lawyers. In-house counsel provide a large amount of legal service to the corporation; and in the event that the corporation needs further advice from an external firm of solicitors or from the Bar it is likely that in-house counsel will be especially familiar with the range of legal services available and the appropriate fee that could be expected. Professor Susskind has commented that another function of in-house counsel is to reduce the overall cost of legal services for the corporation. Most jurisdictions, including Ireland, have become increasingly regulated (in part a consequence of globalisation itself) and this has given rise to increased regulatory compliance costs, which involve, in part, legal advice. Thus, in-house counsel may request solicitors firms to move from hourly and daily charging (and large up-front brief fees, whether for solicitors or barristers) towards an annual fixed-fee arrangement for legal services in order to reduce the overall costs to the client (that is, a future of "less for more").

[3.51] The increased competition in the international services area has been reinforced by the emergence of the digital age in which new forms of service provision are facilitated by information and communications technology (ICT). Developments in ICT in coming years may result in the simplification of some legal processes, which is also likely to have an effect on who will provide these services and their cost. It may also affect the current model of the larger solicitors firms, potentially transforming the current arrangement of a relatively small number of senior equity partners and a large number of salaried solicitors into a model with a small equity-based firm that contracts out high-volume services to specialised firms, some but not all of which may be managed by lawyers. This outsourcing model, which has been long-used in, for example, customer support services (which gave rise to large customer contact specialist companies) would thus leave solicitors and barristers to engage in more specialised and customised legal services, especially for large corporate clients. Professor Susskind has projected that the legal profession is likely to be transformed significantly by these developments, but that it will survive on the basis that specialist legal advice will be required into the foreseeable future.

[2] SOLICITORS

[3.52] While originally connected to the barrister's branch of the profession, the solicitors ultimately developed into a distinct branch. The Incorporated Law Society of Ireland was formed in 1830 for the purpose of securing the independent existence of the solicitors as a branch of the profession and it was subsequently incorporated by Royal Charter in 1852. The Solicitors (Ireland) Act 1898 established for the first time that the Incorporated Law Society of Ireland was to have control over the education of students wishing to become solicitors as well as giving it important disciplinary powers over those who qualified as solicitors. The Society, which in 1994 was renamed the Law Society of Ireland, continues in this dual role and its activities are now regulated by statute, the Solicitors Acts 1954 to 2011.[50] The director general of the Law Society, its chief executive officer, also acts as the principal spokesperson in the media for the solicitor's branch of the profession.

Admission to the profession

[3.53] Before becoming a solicitor, most persons must serve a period of apprenticeship to an established solicitor. Prior to 1995, the minimum period for this was three years, but this was reduced to two years.[51] Obtaining a contract of apprenticeship, referred to as articles of indenture, became increasingly difficult from the mid-1980s onwards when

---

50   The Solicitors Act 1954, which consolidated the statutory regulation of this branch of the profession, has been amended in significant respects on three occasions: by the Solicitors (Amendment) Act 1960, the Solicitors (Amendment) Act 1994 and Solicitors (Amendment) Act 2002. Section 4 of the 1994 Act removed the word 'Incorporated' from the name of the Law Society of Ireland.

51   Solicitors Act 1954, s 26, as amended by Solicitors (Amendment) Act 1994, s 42.

the number of persons seeking admission to the profession increased dramatically. In recent years, the numbers seeking admission have increased to unprecedented levels leading to great difficulty in obtaining an apprenticeship, in particular given the lower number of apprenticeships available due to the effects of the recession on solicitors' practices.

[3.54] In addition to obtaining articles of indenture, most persons must also complete the courses of study organised by the Law Society at its headquarters in Blackhall Place, Dublin. A pre-condition to consideration for admission to these courses of study is that a prospective student must hold a university degree or its equivalent or be a barrister or equivalent; this is referred to as the preliminary examination requirement.[52] If a person meets these requirements, he or she must then complete the Society's final examination, which is divided into three segments, commonly referred to as FE-1, PPC I and PPC II.

[3.55] The FE-1 examination is the crucial examination in terms of the transition from university student to the Law Society's examinations. It comprises eight 'core subjects': company law, constitutional law, contract law, criminal law, equity, law of the European Union, property law, and tort law. Prior to 1995, pursuant to reg 15 of the Solicitors Acts 1954 and 1960 (Apprenticeship and Education) Regulations 1991,[53] the Law Society had granted exemptions from FE-1 to law graduates from the universities of the Republic of Ireland provided they had successfully completed these 'core' subjects in their law degrees.[54] The exemption in reg 15 of the 1991 Regulations was removed arising from *Bloomer and Ors v Incorporated Law Society of Ireland*.[55] The plaintiffs, law graduates of Northern Ireland universities, had sought parity with their counterparts from the Republic of Ireland. It was held by Laffoy J in the High Court that the exemption in reg 15 of the 1991 Regulations for law graduates from the universities in the Republic of Ireland was invalid because it was in conflict with the prohibition of discrimination on grounds of nationality in what is now the Treaty on the Functioning of the European Union (TFEU).[56] In light of the High Court decision, the Law Society stated that it would henceforth require all persons to sit the FE-1 examination rather than extend the prior exemption. However, pursuant to reg 30 of the 1991 Regulations, which empowers the Law Society to modify any requirement of the Regulations 'in exceptional circumstances,' it decided that the plaintiffs in *Bloomer* be granted an exemption from FE-1.[57]

---

52 Solicitors Act 1954, s 41, as amended by Solicitors (Amendment) Act 1994, s 50.
53 SI 9/1991, as amended by the Solicitors Acts 1954 and 1960 (Apprenticeship and Education) (Amendment) (No 2) Regulations 1992 (SI 360/1992). The Regulations are made under the Solicitors Act 1954, s 40, as amended.
54 Other aspects of the Law Society's arrangements had given rise to litigation in the 1980s: see *Gilmer v Incorporated Law Society of Ireland* [1989] ILRM 590.
55 *Bloomer and Ors v Incorporated Law Society of Ireland* [1995] 3 IR 14 (HC); (1997) 6 IJEL 220 (SC).
56 On European Union law, see Ch 16.
57 The effect of this was that the plaintiffs in *Bloomer* had achieved the objective of their proceedings, namely, exemption from FE-1. (contd.../)

[3.56] Later in 1996, in *Abrahamson and Ors v Law Society of Ireland*,[58] over 800 undergraduate law students in the Republic's universities[59] sought to restore the position prior to *Bloomer*, at least for those 'already in the system'. It was held by McCracken J in the High Court that, since reg 15 had been declared invalid in *Bloomer*, the 800 applicants in *Abrahamson* were no longer entitled to rely on the expectation that they would be exempt from FE-1. However, he also held that the position of the 800 applicants constituted 'exceptional circumstances' under reg 30 of the 1991 Regulations and directed the Law Society to consider granting them the exemptions they would have had if reg 15 had been valid. The Law Society subsequently decided that all law students attending the previously exempted law degrees at the time of the decision in *Abrahamson* were exempt from FE-1. Thus, students who began their law studies in universities in the Republic from the academic year 1996–97 have had no exemption from FE-1.

[3.57] The Professional Practice Course I (PPC I) and Professional Practice Course II (PPC II) courses and examinations are the principal courses conducted by the Law Society. They comprise courses primarily of a practical or vocational nature rather than academic in tone. PPC I involves 14 weeks' intensive full-time instruction followed by examination. If successfully completed, this is followed by 11 months' in-office training for the students as part of their apprenticeship. Finally, the PPC II course, the 'Advanced Course', comprises 11 weeks' further intensive full-time instruction, also followed by an examination. Once the PPC II has been completed, and the indentures have expired, the person is entitled to be admitted to the roll of solicitors.

Discipline and compensation

[3.58] After admission as a solicitor, every solicitor is subject to the disciplinary powers of the Law Society. Under the Solicitors Acts, the Disciplinary Tribunal of the Law Society may investigate an allegation of misconduct such as misappropriation of client funds by a solicitor and it may refer the matter to the President of the High Court. The President may take a number of courses of action, including suspending the solicitor from the roll of practising solicitors. The effect of this is that the solicitor may not practice for the period of the suspension. The President of the High Court also has power to lift the suspension. Under the Solicitors Act 1954 as originally enacted, the Disciplinary Committee was empowered to suspend a solicitor, but this power was held to be unconstitutional.[60] The Solicitors (Amendment) Act 1960 accordingly transferred the disciplinary function to the President of the High Court. Short of the drastic powers of suspension, the Solicitors (Amendment) Act 1994 conferred powers on the Law

---

57 (\...contd) The plaintiffs had already appealed the High Court decision to the Supreme Court, but the Law Society's decision rendered this moot. Consequently the Supreme Court judgment in *Bloomer* was concerned primarily with the question of costs, though the Court's formal order confirmed the High Court decision that reg 15 of the 1991 Regulations was invalid.

58 *Abrahamson and Ors v Law Society of Ireland* [1996] 2 IR 403.

59 See (1996) *The Irish Times*, 3 July, p 4.

60 *In re the Solicitors Act 1954* [1960] IR 239: see para **4.15**.

Society to investigate complaints against solicitors concerning, for example, overcharging and requiring repayment to clients if the complaints are upheld. Where such functions of the Law Society are delegated to a committee, the majority of the members of that committee must be lay members but the chairperson must be a solicitor.[61]

[3.59] An appeal lies to the High Court concerning any decision of the Law Society and, to ensure general confidence in the system, the 1994 Act required that a number of lay persons be members of the Disciplinary Tribunal and that an independent adjudicator oversee the operation of the Law Society's investigative powers. The Solicitors Disciplinary Tribunal is also amenable to judicial review thereby giving rise to a different option to seek to challenge a decision of the Tribunal. The Civil Law (Miscellaneous Provisions) Act 2008 inserted a new s 8(1A) into the Solicitors (Amendment) Act 1960 to allow the Law Society to make submissions to the High Court in relation to the Solicitors' Disciplinary Tribunal on the conduct of a solicitor. In *O'Callaghan v Disciplinary Tribunal and Ors*[62] a solicitor challenged the procedure involved in the Solicitor Disciplinary Tribunal contained in the 1960 and 1994 Acts. The tribunal had examined the complaints submitted against the applicant solicitor to decide whether a prima facie case had been made out requiring investigation, without the applicant being formally put on notice of the complaints. The applicant argued that this procedure breached his constitutional right to natural justice. The Supreme Court held that as the Law Society had notified the applicant of the complaint and had given him the opportunity to respond to it and the correspondence passing between the Law Society and the applicant was before the Disciplinary Tribunal when it was making its decision as to whether there was a prima facie case, all the requirements of natural justice were complied with.[63]

[3.60] The Law Society is also now empowered to be proactive in its monitoring of solicitors, allowing it to investigate alleged misconduct by a solicitor whether or not it has received a complaint in relation to that solicitor.[64]

[3.61] Connected with this is the requirement that all solicitors make payments, usually annually, to the statutory Compensation Fund established by the Solicitors (Amendment) Act 1960 to compensate clients of solicitors who have suffered loss arising from the wrongdoing (including fraud) of solicitors. The Compensation Fund amounts to a levy on all practising solicitors. Claims by solicitors' clients have increased dramatically since the 1970s, and the Solicitors (Amendment) Act 1994 introduced a general cap (set at €700,000 as of 2009 and subject to a 'grave hardship' clause) in any particular case. Prior to the 1994 Act, no cap on an individual claim existed. To

---

61 Civil Law (Miscellaneous Provisions) Act 2008, s 34, which amends the Solicitors Act 1954, s 73.

62 *O'Callaghan v Disciplinary Tribunal and others* [2002] 1 IR 1.

63 [2002] 1 IR 1, 8–9.

64 Civil Law (Miscellaneous Provisions) Act 2008, s 40 which inserts a new s 14B into the Solicitors (Amendment) Act 1994.

compensate for this, the 1994 Act also imposed requirements on solicitors to satisfy the Law Society that their personal professional indemnity cover is sufficient before the annual practising certificate is granted.

Practice: firms and incorporated practices

[3.62] In relation to practice as a solicitor, a significant feature of this branch of the profession is that solicitors may form a partnership as a firm of solicitors. As noted above, many such firms exist, particularly in the larger towns and cities, but there are also many 'sole practitioners', that is, one-person firms. Clearly, there are advantages in having a partnership and the larger firms are capable of providing a high level of expert advice to their clients. The Legal Services Regulation Bill 2011 envisages that provision will be made for solicitors to form incorporated practices that are equivalent to the formation of companies, subject to certain restrictions.[65]

Non-contentious business and conveyancing

[3.63] There are no express limits as to the areas of law in which solicitors may practice. In relation to non-contentious business (that is work not connected with court proceedings or analogous work such as arbitration), the drafting of wills and conveyancing are important areas for many solicitors. Indeed, under s 58 of the Solicitors Act 1954 solicitors enjoyed what was generally described as a 'conveyancing monopoly'.[66] Under s 58 as originally passed, a solicitor was the only professional person who could advise on the legal validity of title to land. The result was that the services of a solicitor were invariably required in relation to all land transactions, including the sale of houses. There was, of course, no legal prohibition on a purchaser checking that everything was in order in relation to the house being purchased, but in practice most purchasers would be advised to have the matter checked by a professional adviser. In any event, since the vast majority of house purchases in Ireland are made with the aid of a mortgage or other loan from a financial institution, it is generally a condition of the granting of the loan that title is checked by a professional person.

[3.64] The 1990 Report of the Fair Trade Commission recommended removal of the 'monopoly', following a similar move in Britain, and that financial institutions be empowered to provide such services. However, while this was initially proposed in the Solicitors (Amendment) Bill 1994, it was abandoned in the course of its passage through the Oireachtas and is thus not found in the Solicitors (Amendment) Act 1994. This was done on the expectation that solicitors would be required to show that fees charged for such services are not excessive, and the disciplinary arrangements in place in the 1994

---

65   The provisions in the 2011 Bill would, if enacted, supersede those in the Solicitors (Amendment) Act 1994, s 70, which have never been brought into force.

66   The Building Societies Act 1989, s 31 permits building societies to provide conveyancing services once the Minister for the Environment introduces regulations to bring the provision into effect. No such regulations have been implemented so the monopoly in the provision of conveyancing continues.

Act concerning overcharging, referred to above, must be seen in that light. As already mentioned, this contrasts with the position in Britain, where the conveyancing monopoly was abolished by the Courts and Legal Services Act 1990 [UK]. Impetus for change in this country has again been generated by the 2006 Report of the Competition Authority, which noted that England, Wales, Scotland, most Australian states and New Zealand have introduced specialist professionals called 'conveyancers'.[67] The argument that the introduction of such professionals would result in lower protection for consumers was rejected by the Competition Authority which stated that providing a high level of consumer protection does not require conveyancing to be limited to solicitors. Other jurisdictions have introduced detailed regulations for conveyancers which adequately protect the interests of consumers. The Competition Authority recommended that legislation be brought forward allowing for the creation of non-solicitor qualified persons to provide conveyancing. There would be a registration requirement with a suitable body charged with regulation in the area, and conveyancers would be required to have professional indemnity insurance, abide by a code of ethics and contribute to a compensation fund in order that a high degree of consumer protection be achieved.[68]

[3.65] The Legal Services Act 2007 in England and Wales legislated for a liberalisation of the legal profession in the introduction of alternative business structures into the legal profession.[69] The Clementi Report recommended that 'legal disciplinary partnerships' be permitted to be set up which would allow for a range of legal service providers to practice together as managers provided that non-lawyers in the partnership remained in the minority. These partnerships could be funded by non-lawyers. Clementi also suggested that multi-disciplinary partnerships, combining legal professionals with other professionals might be considered. The 2007 Act allows for the creation of multi-disciplinary partnerships and legal disciplinary partnerships as part of 'Alternative Business Structures'. These provisions created a large amount of criticism and concern from those within the legal profession.[70] Legal disciplinary practices (LDPs) have been permitted in England and Wales since 31 March 2009 and permit lawyers from the different disciplines to come together to provide legal services to third parties. LDPs permit firms to have up to 25% of non-lawyers or different kinds of lawyers as partners. The 2007 Act also allows for the introduction of Alternative Business Structures (ABS) for law firms and ABS allow for both lawyers and non-lawyers, such as accountants or estate agents, to share the management and control of the business, as well as allowing for external investment. ABS are different from LDPs as they allow for significant non-legal ownership and external investment. It is for this reason they have become known as 'Tesco Law'. These have been operational in England and Wales since October 2011. The 2007 Act provides that approved regulators (such as the Law Society and Bar Council) can apply for designation as licensing authorities for the new partnerships. The

---

[67]   Competition Authority Report (2006), p 73.
[68]   Competition Authority Report (2006), p 77.
[69]   See Slapper and Kelly, *The English Legal System* (15th edn, 2009), Ch 16.
[70]   See for example *Intendance Research, Brave New World: Impact of the Legal Services Act 2007* (2007).

Legal Services Board determines the suitability of designation of any applicants for licensing authorities. Any firms interested in applying for designation as one of the two alternative business structures will have to apply to the relevant licensing authority for a licence to operate. At the time of writing (September 2014), these provisions of the 2007 Act have been brought into force in England and Wales and, as already noted, the Legal Services Regulation Bill 2011 may provide for some equivalent provisions in Ireland.

[3.66] It is worth noting that the EU Court of Justice examined whether a prohibition by the Dutch Bar on a particular type of multi-disciplinary partnership between accountants and lawyers was justified or was anti-competitive.[71] The Court held that the ban was objectively justified because the accountancy profession in the Netherlands was not subject to the same requirements of professional conduct as the Netherlands Bar. Therefore, this suggests that had the accountancy profession been subject to the same stringent level of professional conduct as the Dutch legal profession, the ban on the creation of multi-disciplinary partnerships would have been anti-competitive.

[3.67] In addition to these areas of non-contentious practice, the larger firms of solicitors, primarily based in Dublin, are, for example, involved in the formation of private companies, the flotation of companies on the stock exchange, engaging tax advisers for clients and many other areas of commercial law. For these large firms, significant issues of concern include whether they should engage in strategic alliances with other professions, such as accountants and general business advisers. In recent years, it has become increasingly common for larger firms in other jurisdictions, such as the United Kingdom and the United States, to form multi-disciplinary firms or practices, encompassing accountants, lawyers and general business advisers. This reflects a concern to ensure that potential commercial clients can receive relevant advice from a single entity, rather than being required to engage separate firms. Within the legal profession, this development has given rise to concerns about the independence of legal advice being given in such contexts. Nonetheless, as already noted, it appears that the Legal Services Regulation Bill 2011 may provide for some equivalent provisions in Ireland.

[3.68] As we have seen, far reaching changes to business structures for solicitors firms operating in England and Wales have come about since the Legal Services Act 2007 and the coming into effect of legal disciplinary partnerships and multi-disciplinary partnerships and alternative business structures. These provisions also allow for practices composed of barristers and solicitors, and lawyers (both barristers and solicitors) and other professionals to be formed. It is worth noting that s 71 of the Solicitors (Amendment) Act 1994 allows for the Minister for Justice and Equality and the Minister for Jobs, Enterprise and Innovation to make regulations in respect of the sharing of fees between a solicitor and non-solicitor generated either from a partnership

---

[71]   *Wouters v Algemene Raad van de Nederlandse Orde van Advocate* [2002] ECR I-1577.

between them or an agency agreement concluded between them. At the time of writing (September 2014) no such regulations have been made. Barristers are prohibited from entering into partnerships with any professionals be they solicitors or other professionals but, as already noted, the Legal Services Regulation Bill 2011 envisages considerable reform and it remains to be seen whether this would include such fee sharing.

[3.69] The Competition Authority examined the issue of business structures of lawyers. The primary argument against changing legal professional business structures is that any change would impinge on the strict ethical requirements of both solicitors and barristers to provide independent legal advice. The Bar Council expressed concern at barristers being privy to the handling of client funds. The Competition Authority could see benefits flowing from the establishment of legal disciplinary practices, primarily that clients would have access to a one-stop shop with legal expertise, no longer having to pay a double mark-up to each branch of the legal profession. In relation to multi-disciplinary practices, the Law Society expressed the view that regulation of different professions working together would prove difficult. The Competition Authority saw the introduction of multi-disciplinary practices as providing benefits to consumers: in particular lower cost. It did, however, acknowledge that there were surrounding issues concerning access to justice and regulation in relation to the two forms of alternative business structures which require further consideration. It suggested that the Legal Services Commission would be best placed to engage in such consideration. Given the introduction of alternative business structures in England and Wales involving both branches of the legal profession and the increase in globalisation, it would not be surprising if the experience gained in the UK were to influence the introduction of comparable proposed changes to business structures in this state as envisaged in the Legal Services Regulation Bill 2011.

Contentious business, the right of audience and judicial appointments

[3.70] As indicated above, many solicitors do not become engaged in advocacy, except in some cases, civil and criminal, in the lower courts. In relation to proceedings in the High Court and Supreme Court in particular, the tendency remains for solicitors to instruct a barrister (counsel) to appear in court. Indeed, this also occurs frequently in Circuit Court and District Court cases. The solicitor's primary function in such circumstances is to prepare the papers in the case for the court hearing. This will include, in a civil case for example, writing on behalf of the client to the firm of solicitors for the other party in the case and obtaining reports from expert witnesses, such as medical consultants and engineers. The solicitor also liaises with the barrister in relation to what is required at the court hearing.

[3.71] Since the enactment of the Courts Act 1971, solicitors have, in fact, the same right to appear in any court, including the High Court and Supreme Court, as barristers. Prior to the 1971 Act this right, called the right of audience, was severely limited, but the 1971 Act provided for complete parity between the branches of the profession in Ireland in this respect.[72] Despite this, relatively few solicitors take full advantage of the right of audience, though in many instances they appear in the High Court and Supreme Court in relation to preliminary matters relating to a case and this has proved extremely convenient.

[3.72] Subject to a small number of exceptions, therefore, much of the advocacy and arguing of full cases in the High Court and Supreme Court remains in the hands of the Bar. The Fair Trade Commission, in its 1990 Report, expressed disappointment that this was the case and recommended that the Law Society should encourage its members to make fuller use of their right of audience.[73] Since 1990, the Law Society has engaged in significant efforts along those lines, including the provision of courses on litigation and advocacy. Nonetheless, the changes since 1990 would not appear to have been as significant as those in the United Kingdom. With the changes effected by the Courts and Legal Services Act 1990 [UK] and the Access to Justice Act 1999 [UK], many more solicitor advocates have emerged than is the case in Ireland. In addition, in England and Wales solicitors can be appointed as Queen's counsel (the equivalent of senior counsel in this state).

[3.73] The Competition Authority highlighted the low level of advocacy of solicitors in the higher courts in Ireland. Two main reasons were given for this: firstly, that solicitors are ineligible for the title of senior counsel, irrespective of their competency in court; and, secondly, that the Bar of Ireland Code of Conduct prevents a barrister from being led in a case by any person other than a barrister (or in exceptional cases, at the discretion of the Bar Council, a foreign lawyer). It recommended that the Bar Council of Ireland Code of Conduct be amended so as to allow solicitors to become senior counsel and also to allow solicitors to lead barristers.

[3.74] A related issue is the question of the suitability of solicitors for appointment as judges. Prior to 1995, solicitors were qualified for appointment to the District Court only. The enactment of the Courts and Court Officers Act 1995 for the first time provided for the direct appointment of solicitors to the Circuit Court. Since 2002, solicitors have been eligible for direct appointment to the High Court and Supreme Court.[74] In addition, a judge of the Circuit Court who has served two years can also be appointed to the High Court or Supreme Court. In 2002, Peart J was the first solicitor appointed to the High Court. Although a number of other solicitors have been appointed to the High Court, it is less common for judicial appointees to the High Court to come from the rank of solicitors. This has been criticised by the Law Society. In the United

---

72 The 1971 Act gave effect to the recommendations in the *13th Interim Report of the Committee on Court Practice and Procedure*, published in 1971. Since the enactment of the Access to Justice Act 1999 [UK], solicitors in Britain have enjoyed the same rights as their Irish counterparts and the Justice Act (Northern Ireland) 2011 provided for the same in Northern Ireland.

73 FTC Report, pp 131–2.

74 The Courts and Court Officers Act 2002, s 4. See also Carroll, 'The Right Stuff' (2007) 101(7) *Law Society Gazette* 32.

Kingdom, in 2009, Laurence Collins, a former solicitor advocate, was appointed as a Justice of the UK Supreme Court.

Advertising

[3.75] The 1990 Fair Trade Commission Report recommended that restrictions on advertising by solicitors, in particular any restrictions on fee advertising, be removed. Section 69 of the Solicitors (Amendment) Act 1994 gave effect to this by amending s 71 of the Solicitors Act 1954, which deals with the power of the Society to make regulations with respect to the professional practice, conduct and discipline of solicitors.[75] The Solicitors Act 1954, as amended, states that a solicitor shall not publish any advertisement which brings the profession into disrepute, is in bad taste, reflects unfavourably on other solicitors, is false or misleading, is published in an inappropriate place, claims a specialist knowledge superior to other solicitors or is contrary to public policy. Advertisements can only contain the solicitor's name, address and contact details, qualifications and experience, a factual description of the legal services provided by the solicitor, charges or fees. The Solicitors (Advertising) Regulations 2002 set out details of advertisements which are prohibited, for example those with phrases such as 'no win, no fee' or 'first consultation free'.[76]

The Competition Authority recommended that solicitors be permitted to advertise as specialists so as to allow consumers to identify a solicitor suitable to their needs and that the Legal Services Commission be empowered to monitor and analyse solicitors' advertising and promote reform where consistent with public policy.

Deferred fees and 'no foal, no fee' litigation

[3.76] In the past, many solicitors engaged in litigation, particularly involving personal injuries, on the basis that the client would not be charged a professional fee if the claim were unsuccessful. This is commonly referred to as the 'no foal, no fee' arrangement. While such practices have been criticised by those outside the legal profession as encouraging a proliferation of litigation, they have not been prohibited by legislation. However, s 68 of the Solicitors (Amendment) Act 1994 requires a solicitor to provide a client with a letter (commonly called a 'section 68 letter') which itemises the expected costs of the solicitor's legal services, and s 68 also prohibits a solicitor from charging a client on the basis of a percentage or proportion of any damages awarded to the client, except in cases relating to recovery of a debt or a liquidated demand. Section 68 clearly requires a solicitor to specify the expected cost to a client, but it does not prohibit the solicitor from deciding not to require the client to pay the fee in the event that the client loses the civil claim to which the fee is connected. In that respect such a deferred fee arrangement remains permissible. We consider this in more detail elsewhere.[77] Connected with deferred fee arrangements are the advertisements which solicitors are, since the 1994 Act, entitled to make. Section 4 of the Solicitors (Amendment) Act 2002

---

[75] The Solicitors Act 1954, s 71 was amended further by the Solicitors (Amendment) Act 2002, s 4.

[76] SI 518/2002.

[77] See para **5.39**, fn 84.

amended s 71 of the Solicitors Act 1954 to provide that no advertisement may refer to damages, outcomes or provision of legal services in connection with personal injury claims. In addition, the Solicitors (Advertising) Regulations 2002 expressly prohibit the use of 'no win, no fee' or 'no fee, no foal' in any advertisement by solicitors.

[3] BARRISTERS

[3.77] As mentioned already, the barristers' branch of the profession is generally also known collectively as 'the Bar'. Individually, they may be referred to as barristers or counsel.[78] The Bar is usually regarded as the senior branch of the profession, though like the solicitors' branch it has gone through many changes over the centuries, so its precise roots are difficult to trace. Again the English influence is important in this context. Originally, Inns of Court were established in London for the purpose of providing, amongst other things, for the education of those who wished to practice as advocates. A similar institution, the Honorable Society of King's Inns,[79] was established in Dublin and it remains the body which provides post-graduate legal training for those who wish to practice at the Bar, in a system parallel to the Law Society. Generally members of the Bar are also required to be members of the Law Library, situated in or near the Four Courts Building, Dublin. Disciplinary matters are regulated by the Bar Council of Ireland. Unlike the solicitors' branch, the Bar is in general not currently regulated by legislation but this is due to change with the impending enactment of the Legal Services Regulation Bill 2011, discussed above.

Admission to the profession

[3.78] The Honorable Society of King's Inns, situated in Henrietta St, Dublin,[80] at one time operated under Royal Charter granted in 1792, but this, it appears, was later revoked. The King's Inns therefore operates at present as a voluntary society, under the control of a body known as the Benchers of the Honorable Society of King's Inns. These Benchers include a number of members of the judiciary as well as senior members of the Bar. The Benchers exercise ultimate control over the courses of education provided by the King's Inns, which lead to the award of the degree of barrister-at-law.

[3.79] Prior to 2002, the number of places available annually on the barrister-at-law degree course of the King's Inns was limited to about 100. A minimum of 50% of the places were reserved for law graduates, 40% were reserved for holders of the King's Inns diploma in legal studies, a two-year diploma course for which lectures are provided in the Inns' own premises, and the remaining 10% of places were allocated by the

---

78 Thus many of the extracts from judgments in this text include phrases such as 'Counsel for the plaintiff has submitted ...'.

79 On its early history, see Hogan, *The Honorable Society of King's Inns* (Council of the King's Inns, 1987) and Kenny, *King's Inns and the Kingdom of Ireland: the Irish 'inn of court' 1541–1800* (1992).

80 The Society's premises also front onto Constitution Hill in Dublin. For a history see McCarthy, *'A Favourite Study' Building the King's Inns* (2006)

Education Committee of the King's Inns. Because of the restrictions on numbers, those holding a law degree were required to achieve a high second class honours degree to gain admission.

[3.80] A new regime was introduced in 2002 when admission to the King's Inns course became by means of entrance examination.[81] Holders of approved law degrees or the diploma in legal studies, who have passed the following 'core subjects,' namely, land law (including law of succession), law of equity and trusts, administrative law, company law, jurisprudence and law of the European Union, are eligible to sit the examination. The subjects examined at the time of writing (September 2014) are contract law, criminal law, Irish constitutional law, law of torts and the law of evidence.[82] Places on the barrister-at-law course are allocated in order of merit.

[3.81] Since 2004, the nature of the barrister-at-law degree has altered to be vocational in nature. Between 2004 and 2008 it was only available as a full-time one-year course. In October 2008, a two-year modular (part-time) barrister-at-law degree course commenced in addition to the one-year full-time course: this re-introduced a long-standing part-time course that had existed prior to 2004. The course is practical in nature focusing on important legal skills such as advocacy, negotiation, consultation and drafting, in addition to practice and procedure. In addition to completing the course of studies prescribed, the student of King's Inns must also 'keep commons' by dining in the Hall of the Honorable Society on 12 days in the academic year of the barrister-at-law degree course. The tradition of dining reflects a much earlier time when no precise course of academic study was prescribed for those wishing to become a barrister. Rather, by dining with established barristers the students would become familiar with the practice of the law in a more informal academic context.

[3.82] When a student has successfully completed the course of studies prescribed by the King's Inns, he or she is 'called to the Bar' in the Supreme Court, located in the Four Courts building Dublin, in the presence of the Chief Justice and, generally speaking, other members of the Supreme Court bench. The barrister then signs the roll of members of the Bar which is also located in the Four Courts. While at this stage, the person in question is a barrister-at-law, there are further additional requirements in place before the person may engage in paid legal work.

The Law Library

[3.83] The call to the Bar means that the person is admitted to practice as a barrister-at-law, or junior counsel. A significant feature of the Bar in Ireland is that barristers may not join together to form groups or 'chambers' of barristers as is the practice in England. Instead, most members of the Bar practice from what is called, simply, the Law Library. For over 200 years, the Law Library was housed in part of the Four Courts building in

---

81 See generally *Education Rules of the Honorable Society of King's Inns*.
82 These entrance exam subjects have altered a number of times since the introduction of entrance exams at King's Inns. See www.kingsinns.ie for up-to-date information.

Dublin and this is where the 'old' Law Library remains. In the wake of the creation of the two jurisdictions in Ireland in the 1920s, a similar 'Library' arrangement was made in Northern Ireland and continues to prevail in the Royal Courts of Justice, Belfast. Due to the expansion in numbers since the late 1980s in the Republic, additional accommodation was provided adjacent to the Four Courts in what is now referred to as the 'new' Law Library. In addition the Bar Council provides offices for rent by its members in two buildings, the Church Street Building and Distillery Building (including a legal research centre library), adjacent to the Four Courts. In 2010, the majority of the criminal courts located in the Four Courts were relocated to a new purpose-built Criminal Courts of Justice Complex about one mile from the Four Courts. Because of this, the Bar Council also provides accommodation for barristers in the Criminal Courts of Justice Complex.

[3.84] It has been a long-established requirement of the Bar that barristers be members of the Law Library in order to practice. The 1990 Report of the Fair Trade Commission regarded this as a restrictive practice and recommended that it should be removed, if necessary by legislation. However, in its response to the Report, the Bar Council and the members of the Law Library voted in 1991 to retain the existing requirement in the Code of Conduct concerning membership. The situation has changed since that time and currently the Bar Council Code of Conduct rather provides that it is "desirable" for all practising barristers to be members of the Law Library.[83]

[3.85] Before entering the Law Library, the barrister must ensure that an established barrister of at least seven years' standing has agreed to act as 'master' for the new member of the Law Library, the new member being referred to as a 'devil' (a more archaic word being 'tyro').[84] This, in effect, mirrors the apprenticeship for solicitors. The period of pupillage is generally 12 months. It has become common practice for barristers to complete a second year of devilling with a second master. During devilling, the master is expected to introduce the devil or pupil to the general practice of the Law Library, legal research, court work and to ask the devil to assist with drafting pleadings and other documents for court. The devil will assist the master in all aspects of the master's practice and will generally attend court and consultations with the master as a means of learning the role of the barrister.

[3.86] In the Law Library in Dublin, barristers are provided with accommodation and access to legal textbooks and IT facilities, on payment of an annual membership fee. The Four Courts building houses all the major courts in the state, including the High Court and Supreme Court as well as some other courts. After the relocation of the majority of the criminal courts to the Criminal Courts Complex, the courts at the Four Courts deals primarily with civil and constitutional cases. Not all members of the Bar practice on a permanent basis from the Four Courts or the Criminal Courts of Justice.

---

[83] Rule 8.2 of the Code of Conduct for the Bar of Ireland.
[84] Rule 8.8 of the Code of Conduct for the Bar of Ireland provides that in exceptional circumstances a barrister of less than seven years' practice can be entered onto the register of masters if approved by the Internal Relations Committee of the Bar Council.

Many barristers practice primarily outside Dublin, that is 'on circuit' and practice only occasionally in the courts in Dublin. For those who practice primarily in the Cork and Southern regions, many barristers in fact have chambers in Cork city, though generally these are not shared with other members of the Bar. In addition, a Bar Library has been provided adjacent to the courthouse in Cork City reflecting the growing amount of barristers practising in Cork.

[3.87] At present, unlike in many other jurisdictions, barristers in Ireland operate as sole traders and generally are members of the Law Library.[85] The Competition Authority examined the structure of the Bar in some detail. It first discussed the prohibition on groups of barristers who share facilities, premises and costs of practice, for example a secretary, to carry on their business as a partnership, or a group or holding themselves out as doing so. The Bar Council justified the restriction on the primary basis that it was necessary to avoid conflicts of interest. The Competition Authority recommended that barristers who operate in an informal group by sharing premises and running costs be permitted should they so wish to realise this efficiency by holding themselves out, by advertisement or otherwise as practising in a group. Similarly, the Competition Authority recommended that barristers be given the option to operate in partnerships which would allow shared costs, shared work, shared professional reputation and efficiency. Partnerships would also allow for clients to choose a partnership which matched their needs. The Competition Authority did not envisage the cessation of sole trader barristers, instead each barrister would be free to choose which alternative suited them.

[3.88] Following a recommendation from the Competition Authority, the Code of Conduct for the Bar of Ireland has been amended to allow barristers to engage in advertising. In March 2008, the Bar Council issued guidelines to members on the appropriate form and content of this advertising. These guidelines mirror very closely the content of the Solicitors (Advertising) Regulations 2002.

Discipline and conduct

[3.89] The general conduct of the members of the Bar is controlled by a non-statutory body, the Bar Council of Ireland.[86] The Council is elected annually by the members of the Bar, and a Chairman is also elected to chair the most important business committees and also to represent the Bar in, for example, discussions with government or for interview by the media. The Bar Council issues to each member a Professional Code of Conduct which is amended from time to time by the members themselves.

[3.90] The provisions of the Code of Conduct cover such matters as the requirement that a barrister accept only so much work as he or she can give adequate attention to within a reasonable time; the need to ensure confidentiality concerning client matters; the taking

---

85   For arguments for the abolition of the sole trader nature of the barrister profession see Devlin, 'Questioning the Sole-Trader Rule in the Barrister Profession' (2010) 45 Irish Jurist 123.

86   See www.barcouncil.ie.

of instructions from solicitors; the duty of the barrister to the courts, in particular not to mislead a court in any manner;[87] prohibitions on touting and advertising his or her services to the public; the precedence between barristers on the basis of call to the Bar and general conduct between members of the Bar; the relationship between barristers and the Law Library and Bar Council; specific rules on the duty of a barrister in criminal cases; the position of senior counsel; the charging of fees; and the position of overseas lawyers.

[3.91] Prior to 1991, complaints against members of the Bar, whether from the public, a solicitor, another barrister or a judge, were investigated by the Disciplinary Committee of the Bar Council. Where a barrister was found by the Disciplinary Committee to be in breach of the Code of Conduct, he or she was liable to disciplinary sanctions, including admonishments as well as suspension, and ultimately expulsion, from the Law Library. In addition, he or she could be reported to the Benchers of the King's Inns who appeared to retain the ultimate disciplinary sanction of disbarment, that is, removal of the person's name from the roll of members of the Bar.

[3.92] As the Fair Trade Commission noted in its 1990 Report, 'the constitutionality of the powers of neither the Bar Council nor the King's Inns has been challenged, unlike those of the Law Society.'[88] The Commission recommended that the Bar Council alone be responsible for discipline within the Bar and that it was not appropriate that the King's Inns be involved, particularly as many of its Benchers were members of the judiciary. Although the Commission recommended that legislation might be required on foot of this recommendation, non-statutory measures have, instead, been put in place on this point.

[3.93] In 1991, the Bar Council adopted substantial amendments to the Bar's Code of Conduct. Since then, allegations of breach of the Code are investigated by the Barristers Professional Conduct Tribunal pursuant to the Disciplinary Code for the Bar of Ireland. This Tribunal includes lay members, that is, persons who are not members of the Bar. The Tribunal has extensive powers to impose fines on members of the Bar found in breach of the Code of Conduct as well as issue admonishments and, suspend or exclude a member from the Law Library or recommend to the King's Inns that the barrister be disbarred. From 2007 to 2013 the Tribunal has imposed fines amounting to €30,000 in total, imposed three suspensions and made two recommendations for disbarment.[89] In 2012 a barrister was disbarred by King's Inns, following a recommendation from the Tribunal, for professional misconduct. It has been noted that the penalty of suspending a

---

87 See generally, the comments of Crampton J in *R v O'Connell* (1845) 7 Ir Law Rep 261 at 313, on the duties of the barrister and *Law Society v Walker* [2007] 3 IR 581 as to a solicitor. The duty not to mislead the court includes the duty to be aware of the most recent case law on a particular topic: see *Copeland v Smith* [2000] 1 All ER 457.

88 FTC Report, p 281.

89 McCann, Professional Conduct Tribunal, delivered at Bar Council CPD seminar on Ethics held on 22 April 2013.

barrister from the law library has increased in recent years.[90] Appeals from the Professional Practices Committee can be made to the Appeals Board, which is chaired by a Circuit Court judge and which also comprises a lay member.[91]

[3.94] As we have seen the Legal Services Regulation Bill 2011 proposes to transfer supervisory responsibility for dealing with complaints against barristers from the Bar Council to the Legal Services Regulatory Authority. When the 2011 Bill is enacted, further changes to the regulation of the Bar are likely in the medium to long term.

Instructions and direct access

[3.95] A barrister was, as already indicated, traditionally required to receive instructions from a solicitor and was prohibited by the Code of Conduct of the Bar from receiving instructions from other professionals or from members of the public. This prohibition on what is described as direct access was regarded as an essential element of the independence of the Bar and as essential to ensure the continued strength of the Bar as advocates. A corollary of this convention was that, once a barrister received instructions from a solicitor, he or she was obliged to accept the instructions unless it was in an area in which the barrister had no previous experience or expertise. This is known as the 'cab rank' rule.

[3.96] In the context of appearing in court, judges would also be loath to 'hear' counsel unless a solicitor was physically present in court to instruct the barrister. This rule was applied with greater or lesser strictness by different judges but, on many occasions, matters would be adjourned where a solicitor was not present in court with counsel. The Code of Conduct prescribes that barristers are, in general, to be attended by an instructing solicitor when they are in court subject to certain exceptions, most notably that of District Court or District Court appeals hearings where rather a barrister must be instructed by a solicitor.[92] These rules do not apply to statutory tribunals, such as employment tribunals, which are not courts. Another consequence of receiving instructions through a solicitor was that the solicitor was also responsible for ensuring that the barrister's fees were paid. The convention which followed was that a barrister could not sue for fees due, though this convention had not been put to the test in recent times, but most barristers continue to rely on a good relationship with their instructing solicitors to ensure collection of fees.

[3.97] The practice of requiring instructions from a solicitor and prohibiting direct access was examined in detail by the Fair Trade Commission in its 1990 Report. It considered that the blanket ban on direct access was a restrictive practice and should be deleted from the Professional Code of Conduct. However, it also considered that in

---

90 John Gleeson SC, 'The Barrister Professional Conduct Tribunal and its Disciplinary Procedure' delivered at the Bar Council Conference on Ethics held on 21 July 2008.

91 For an example, see (1993) *The Irish Times*, 31 July.

92 Clause 5.15 of the Code of Conduct of the Bar of Ireland. See also *Heinulllian v Governor of Cloverhill Prison* [2011] 1 ILRM 1.

certain instances, particularly concerning litigation, the continued involvement of solicitors was desirable. Thus, it accepted that a barrister could, in an individual case, refuse to accept direct instructions from a client and could insist that a solicitor be engaged. As a consequence, the Commission recommended that there should no longer be any statutory or other rules requiring the physical attendance of a solicitor in court to instruct a barrister. These recommendations of the Fair Trade Commission have not been implemented in full, and the Bar continues to defend restrictions on direct access on the basis that they are fundamental to the separation of the Bar from the solicitors' branch of the profession. However, a number of amendments to the Code of Conduct were made in 1990 to extend the circumstances in which direct access is permitted. These now include direct access from certain professionals (direct professional access), such as accountants, trade mark agent and others.[93] The advice sought in direct professional access circumstances is usually specialist, such as tax advice, and arises outside of any litigation.[94]

[3.98] Direct access to barristers by clients without the services of a solicitor is allowed only for approved bodies and then only for legal advice in non-contentious matters. Approved bodies may not have direct access to a barrister for the purposes of legal representation in court. The Competition Authority recommended that direct access be extended to all members of the public for legal advice. In respect of contentious matters it advocated that the Legal Services Commission be entrusted with undertaking research in the area of direct access. The Bar Council objected to direct access for barristers in contentious matters as it felt it would undermine the nature of objective legal advice given to clients and also affect the nature of the barrister profession which is not involved in the management of the affairs or funds of its clients. As already noted, the

---

93   The list of Approved Professional Bodies to which direct professional access applies includes the following: the Association of Chartered Certified Accountants (fellows and associates); the Institute of Chartered Accountants in Ireland (fellows and associates); the Royal Institute of Architects in Ireland (members); the Irish Association of Architects and Surveyors (corporate members); the Institution of Engineers of Ireland (fellows and ordinary members); the Institution of Taxation in Ireland (associates and fellows); the Irish Institute of Secretaries and Administrators (members); the Ombudsman for Credit Institutions; the Ombudsman for the Insurance Industry; and Oireachtas Committees. This list has been extended in recent years. For a full list of approved bodies for the purposes of Direct Professional Access, see the Bar Council website www.barcouncil.ie.

94   The list of approved professional bodies to which direct professional access applies includes the following: the Association of Chartered Certified Accountants (fellows and associates); the Institute of Chartered Accountants in Ireland (fellows and associates); the Royal Institute of Architects in Ireland (members); the Irish Association of Architects and Surveyors (corporate members); Engineers Ireland (fellows and ordinary members); the Institution of Taxation in Ireland (associates and fellows); the Irish Institute of Secretaries and Administrators (members); the Financial Services Ombudsman; and Oireachtas Committees. This list has been extended in recent years. For a full list of approved bodies for the purposes of direct professional access, see the Bar Council website www.barcouncil.ie.

proposals for reform in the Legal Services Regulation Bill 2011 may have an effect in the medium term on current arrangements.

Junior counsel and senior counsel

[3.99] A distinction exists within the Bar between junior counsel and senior counsel. The initial call to the Bar is to the ranks of junior counsel, sometimes referred to as the Outer Bar. The general rule is that a barrister will practice for a number of years as a junior counsel before considering whether to become a senior counsel. The move from junior to senior counsel is also referred to as 'taking silk', since by tradition the black gown worn by senior counsel is of silk rather than the poplin of junior counsel. Senior counsel are collectively referred to as the Inner Bar. The abbreviation 'SC' is often inserted after that of a 'senior', but 'JC' is never used to signify that a person is a member of the junior bar. The distinction between junior and senior counsel replaced the distinction between junior counsel and Queen's (or King's) counsel that preceded the establishment of the two legal systems on the island in the 1920s. In 1990, there were 112 senior counsel in the Law Library, representing about 15% of the total membership of 728.[95] In 2013, there were 354 senior counsel in the Law Library representing approximately 14% of the total Law Library membership.

[3.100] Progression from junior to senior counsel is not a simple matter of automatic 'promotion' after a specified number of years. Indeed, many eminent members of the Bar choose not to become senior counsel and remain as 'juniors' into their 70s and 80s. However, in general, most barristers consider 'taking silk' after about 15 years' practice, when they reach their late 30s or early 40s. Once a barrister decides to become a senior counsel, he or she applies to the Chief Justice and Attorney General for approval, but the actual appointment is made by the government,[96] acting on the advice of the Attorney General who also liaises with the Chairman of the Bar Council.

[3.101] There were at one point no strict rules setting out the criteria for granting an application to become a senior counsel, though as the Fair Trade Commission Report put it, '[a]pproval depends on considerations such as personal observation of the barrister's work in court, and his [or her] general reputation and standing'.[97] While approval is thus not automatic, it could be said that virtually no member of the Bar applies unless they have already made informal soundings amongst their colleagues or members of the Bar Council that they are 'qualified' to be approved. However there are no figures available as to the percentage of applicants who are successful in their application each year. The Fair Trade Commission was not attracted to some of the mystery and apparent secrecy surrounding the 'taking of silk' and recommended that the

---

95 FTC Report, p 85.

96 The government issues a formal letter patent to senior counsel under the Executive Powers (Consequential Provisions) Act 1937, s 2 carrying over a function formerly given to the monarch when issuing a letter patent to Queen's or King's counsel under the pre-1922 arrangements: see para **15.37**.

97 FTC Report, p 107.

government's function in the process be terminated and that the status be a less formal matter for the profession.[98] However, no action has been taken on this recommendation. It is certainly the case that the process in Ireland is less formal than that in England and Wales where applicants must attend an interview and recommendations for appointment are made by an independent panel set up by the English Law Society and Bar Council.[99]

[3.102] The Competition Authority again highlighted the issue in its 2006 Report and concluded that, as currently awarded, it could distort competition as the title of senior counsel does not amount to a reliable mark of quality. Concern was express at the lack of transparent criteria for awarding the title, that there was no ongoing monitoring of quality and no procedure for withdrawing the mark should quality be reduced. In order to achieve the goal of ensuring that the title of senior counsel provided an accurate indication of quality, the Competition Authority recommended that it be retained but that the government establish objective criteria for the awarding, monitoring and withdrawing of the title. As a result of these comments, applicants are now required to submit a detailed application form setting out details of their professional careers and contribution to the profession.

[3.103] In general, the functions of a junior counsel include the drafting and preparation of pleadings as well as conducting some cases in court, generally in the lower courts though not exclusively so. The senior counsel's functions, on the other hand, include scrutiny of draft pleadings which have been prepared by a junior counsel (called 'settling' pleadings) as well as the conduct of some of the more difficult legal cases in the High Court and Supreme Court. While a minority of senior counsel do not engage in court work, the majority of 'SCs' or 'silks' are known for their courtroom wizardry.

[3.104] A number of conventions developed over the years (many again pre-dating the 1920s) as to the circumstances in which junior and senior counsel would be retained in a case. An important example was that, in the vast majority of cases, a senior counsel was precluded from appearing in a case unless a junior counsel was also retained. In civil claims for personal injuries (colloquially called 'running down' cases because of the number of road traffic accidents involved) it was the convention that one junior and two senior counsel would be retained by each side. This 'two senior' rule was subject to some criticism and, since the passing of the Courts Act 1988 (which provided that High Court personal injuries cases should no longer be decided by a judge and jury, but by a judge alone and which had also indicated that the 'two senior' rule would be abolished by legislation unless abandoned 'voluntarily') the practice in many cases is to retain one junior and one senior counsel.[100]

---

[98] FTC Report, pp 122–123.
[99] See http://www.qcappointments.org.
[100] See further, para **5.37**.

Advocacy and the Bar

[3.105] The general picture of barristers, and in particular senior counsel, is of great orators and in many instances the most eminent practitioners are indeed extremely persuasive advocates and speakers.[101] This may be particularly important in cases heard before juries where the barrister is expected to 'tug the jury's heartstrings'. But apart from those barristers who specialise in criminal cases and also the civil cases which tend to receive a large degree of publicity (and which form the basis for most films or television series on the law) the reality of practice at the Bar is that much time is spent on 'paperwork', in other words the preparation of pleadings, advices and research in anticipation of a court hearing. Given that the vast majority of cases in which a barrister receives instructions are settled before a court hearing,[102] the true position is that advocacy plays a relatively minor part in the normal work of the practitioner. Of much greater practical importance is the ability to give advice on a legal problem and to draft documents which will begin the process of accelerating the satisfactory settlement of the legal problem presented, whether through a court hearing or otherwise.

[3.106] Ireland has, of course, produced well-known and brilliant advocates, including Daniel O'Connell and Sir Edward Carson, and it may be no coincidence that both were also well-known and successful politicians. The mixture of law and politics as a career continues to the present, a feature of most countries. Ireland has also produced its quota of anecdotal publications about life at the Bar, which tend to emphasise the moments of courtroom mirth.[103]

Advocacy and immunity from suit

[3.107] For many years, it was the case that the common law rules of negligence[104] were thought not to apply to the conduct by an advocate in court. Thus, in the leading English decision, *Rondel v Worsley*,[105] the House of Lords held that decisions made by a barrister in the course of litigation could not form the basis for any subsequent claim in negligence by a client; in effect, a barrister, or any other advocate, was immune from being sued in respect of such decisions. Of course, lawyers could be sued in negligence for other legal advice and activity, whether by clients or third parties.[106] It was argued that the immunity in respect of advocacy was justified on the ground that if the advocate

---

101 See the views of the former Chief Justice, Mr Justice Finlay, in an address to Law Society students 'Criminal Defence Advocacy' (1981) 1 *Crim Law Journal* 1 and his 1986 address at Fordham University School of Law 'Advocacy: Has it a Future?' published as a Supplement to the December 1986 issue of the *Irish Law Times*.

102 See paras **6.63–6.65**.

103 See Healy, *The Old Munster Circuit* (1981), Mackey, *Windward of the Law* (1965) and McArdle, *Irish Legal Anecdotes* (1995).

104 See generally, para **12.144**.

105 *Rondel v Worsley* [1969] 1 AC 191. The decision was followed in *Saif Ali v Sydney Mitchell & Co* [1980] AC 198.

106 See generally para **12.152**.

was liable to be sued for actions in the conduct of litigation he or she might be 'looking over their shoulder' and this would interfere with the advocate's duty to the court and thus damage the administration of justice. It was argued that, where very poor advocacy resulted in injustice, this could be remedied by using the appeal system in the courts. A further new argument has emerged in recent years as justification for retention of the immunity: the importance of finality in legal matters and that this would be undermined by abolishing the immunity.[107]

[3.108] In *Hall & Co v Simons*,[108] the UK House of Lords overruled its decision in *Rondel v Worsley* and decided that the blanket immunity should no longer be regarded as good law.[109] Subject to some restrictions, therefore, the law in the United Kingdom is that advocates can be sued in negligence where their advocacy fails to meet the standard of care normally expected in such circumstances. In 2011, this principle was extended to expert witnesses and the Supreme Court of England and Wales held that expert witnesses' immunity from suit for breach of duty should be abolished.[110] While no definitive decision has been made in Ireland on this point at the time of writing (September 2014), a number of judicial comments indicate that a blanket immunity is unlikely to survive.[111]

[3.109] The issue was again examined in the United Kingdom in *Moy v Pettman Smith*[112] where it was alleged that a barrister had negligently failed to give realistic advice as to the consequences for her client of rejecting a settlement offer made by a defendant health authority in clinical negligence litigation. As a result of rejecting this settlement offer, the client ultimately had to accept a lower figure when settling the case. The House of Lords ultimately held that the barrister was not liable in negligence in relation to her advice to reject the settlement and the adequacy of her explanation to her client. It saw the reality of the situation in which the advice was imparted, in this case at the door of the court. Lord Carswell who delivered the leading judgment stated that it 'would be surprising if every piece of advice were reasoned with as much comprehensive precision as may be applied in hindsight by an appellate tribunal which has had the benefit of extensive argument and leisurely reflection'.[113] He also stated that he would be 'slow to

---

[107] This justification was discussed by the High Court of Australia (the highest court in Australia) in *D'Orta-Ekenaike v Victoria Legal Aid* (2005) 223 CLR 1. See also Ryan and Ryan, 'A Bar to Recovery? Barristers, Public Policy, and Immunity from Suit' [2005] 10(6) *Bar Review* 209.

[108] [2000] 3 All ER 673.

[109] See English, 'Forensic Immunity Post-Osman' (2001) 64 MLR 300.

[110] *Jones v Kaney* [2011] UKSC 13.

[111] The *Hall* case was referred to in *O'Keeffe v Kilcullen* [2001] 3 IR 568, though the *O'Keeffe* case involved the immunity from suit of a witness, in that case an expert psychiatrist. In *Behan v McGinley* [2008] IEHC 181 and *O'Reilly v Lee* [2008] IESC 21, further doubts were expressed about a blanket immunity. See also Ryan and Ryan, 'A Bar to Recovery? Barristers, Public Policy, and Immunity from Suit' [2005] 10(6) *Bar Review* 209 and O'Halloran, 'Barristers' Immunity in the Twenty First Century' (2008) 26 ILT 304.

[112] *Moy v Pettman Smith* [2005] 1 All ER 903. See also *Awoyomi v Radford* [2007] EWHC 1671 (Admin), [2008] 3 WLR 34, [2007] NLJR 1046.

hold advocates to blame in cases such as the present if they concentrated on giving clear and readily understood advice to their clients about the course of action they recommend'.[114] It has been noted that in *Moy* the 'House of Lords has arguably signalled a note of caution about the bringing of negligence actions against barristers and has demonstrated the difficulties facing plaintiffs'.[115]

[3.110] The High Court of Australia has decided that the immunity from suit in negligence by barristers should be retained. In *D'Orta-Ekenaike v Victoria Legal Aid*[116] the Court concluded that the immunity could be justified because of the promotion of the administration of justice and the role played by the advocate in that process. In a case decided after the *D'Orta-Ekenaike* case, the Supreme Court of New Zealand held that the immunity for barristers in civil and criminal matters should be abolished.[117] In doing so, the Court decided that the approach taken by the House of Lords in *Hall & Co v Simons*[118] was to be preferred to that of the High Court of Australia in *D'Orta-Ekenaike*.

[3.111] Irish courts have referred cases of possible breaches of the Bar of Ireland Code of Practice to the Bar Council. In *The People (DPP) v McDonagh*[119] the Supreme Court deemed that the public interest necessitated such a referral due to the possible breaches of the Code of Practice by a barrister when he accepted a criminal case during a trial. In *O'Connor v Power*[120] the High Court furnished a copy of the judgment to the Chairman of the Bar Council due to counsel's 'persistent flouting of the ordinary rules of courtesy and behaviour in the conduct of litigation' which 'were quite unacceptable'.

Mode of dress

[3.112] A further long-standing distinction between the two branches of the legal profession relates to the mode of dress of a member of the Bar in court. Until 1996, barristers were required by statutory rules of court to wear a wig, usually made of horsehair, as well as a black gown over dark dress. The barrister's shirt, or blouse, has, generally speaking, a winged collar and, in place of a tie, the barrister wears a white band. These requirements were carried over from the rules of court which existed prior to the creation of the two jurisdictions in the 1920s. During the 1980s, the question of wearing wigs in court in particular became the subject of considerable debate.

---

113   [2005] 1 All ER 903, 921.
114   [2005] 1 All ER 903, 924.
115   Ryan and Ryan, 'A Bar to Recovery? Barristers, Public Policy, and Immunity from Suit' [2005] 10(6) *Bar Review* 209 at 209.
116   *D'Orta-Ekenaike v Victoria Legal Aid* (2005) 223 CLR 1. See more recently *Stillman v Rushbourne* (2014) NSWSC 730.
117   *Chamberlain v Lai* [2006] NZSC 70.
118   *Hall & Co v Simons* [2000] 3 All ER 673.
119   *The People (DPP) v McDonagh* [2001] 3 IR 411.
120   *O'Connor v Power* [2008] IEHC 179.

[3.113] In its 1990 Report, the Fair Trade Commission noted that while the issue was peripheral in many ways to its main recommendations it was important to a number of persons, particularly those who represented the consumers of legal services, who felt that the wig created an element of intimidation for those unaccustomed to appearing in court. The Bar Council indicated it had no firm views on the wearing of the wig, but that it would not like to see it disappear completely. The Commission also referred to some judicial criticisms of the continued wearing of wigs,[121] and noted that it had been prohibited in family proceedings.[122] It also pointed out that the continued wearing of wigs might have an inhibiting effect on solicitors representing their clients. The Commission also considered that, since judges also wore wigs, 'this may convey the impression of an association and a community of interest between the two'. The Commission therefore considered that 'it would be a sensible move towards a more modern profession if barristers no longer wore wigs'.

[3.114] While the prohibition of the wearing of wigs had been proposed in the Courts and Court Officers Bill 1995, ultimately, s 49 of the Courts and Court Officers Act 1995 provides only that the wearing of wigs by members of the Bar 'shall not be required' and thus is a matter for their own discretion and is no longer mandatory. As a result, the number of barristers deciding not to wear wigs is increasing in particular as judges are no longer required to wear wigs when presiding in court.[123] It should be noted that, for those appearing without a wig, the traditional gown, wing-collared shirt and tab remains in place. Finally, the requirements concerning mode of dress do not apply in relation to sittings of the courts during the Vacations or to barristers appearing in statutory tribunals such as the Employment Appeals Tribunal.[124]

[4] THE LAW OFFICERS

[3.115] We turn now to discuss the two law officers in the state. Prior to 1922, a number of lawyers, primarily barristers, were appointed to represent the government and to some extent the general public in matters of law and legal opinion. This tradition was carried

---

[121] The Commission referred to the paper delivered by the late Mr Justice McCarthy to the 1987 MacGill Summer School in which he had described the 'post-colonial servitude' of the Irish courts system. He described the continued wearing of wigs as 'absurd' and as 'comic' that women should wear what were originally male wigs. The Report noted that Mr Justice McCarthy also heard it had been suggested that wigs afforded a sense of protection against clients 'as if they were a form of forensic condom'. See also *The People (DPP) v Barnes* [2007] 3 IR 130 where the Court of Criminal Appeal commented *obiter* that an advocate is not required to wear a wig in court and that a trial judge should not comment on the presence or absence of a wig.

[122] Judicial Separation and Family Law Reform Act 1989, ss 33, 45.

[123] Rules of the Superior Courts (Robes of Bench) 2011 (SI No 524/2011) which inserted Ord 119, r 2 of the Rules of the Superior Courts 1986.

[124] On the Vacations, see para **4.203**.

over into the Irish Free State. The present law officers in the state are the Attorney General (which also incorporates the Chief State Solicitor's office) and the Director of Public Prosecutions.[125] In 1998, a report on the law officers was published which made a number of significant changes to the organisational structure of the office of the Attorney General and of the Director of Public Prosecutions and facilitated greater coordination of their functions.[126]

The Attorney General

[3.116] Article 30 of the Constitution of Ireland provides that the Attorney General is 'the adviser of the government in matters of law and legal opinion' and that he or she shall perform any additional functions conferred by law. Section 6 of the Ministers and Secretaries Act 1924[127] provides that the Attorney General was vested with the functions of the Attorney General for Ireland, that is the Attorney General in the pre-1922 era.

[3.117] Article 30 also provides that the Attorney General (sometimes referred to as 'the AG' or 'the Attorney') is appointed by the President of Ireland on the nomination of the Taoiseach. The Attorney General must retire from office on the resignation of the Taoiseach, thus indicating that the office has a close personal connection with the fate of the Taoiseach of the day. The position of Attorney General as principal adviser to the government and as a close confidante of the head of the executive also echoes the position of the Attorney General for Ireland in the pre-1922 era and indeed the title Attorney General was adopted by the first such legal adviser to the government, Hugh Kennedy, who later became Chief Justice.

---

[125] The phrase 'law officers' is also used in the Prosecution of Offences Act 1974, s 4 to refer to the present offices of Attorney General and Director of Public Prosecutions. The definitive account of the history and role of the law officers, in particular that of the Attorney General and the Director of Public Prosecutions, is Casey, *The Irish Law Officers: Roles and Responsibilities of the Attorney General and Director of Public Prosecutions* (1996).

[126] The *Report of the Review Group on the Law Offices of the State* (completed in June 1997 and published in February 1998) is not available on the Attorney General's website, www.attorneygeneral.ie. In 2000, the Attorney General's office published its first *Statement of Strategy 1999–2002* (which is available on the website) which sets out its strategic aims for the period in question. The publication of such a document, which includes a Mission Statement for the office and detailed discussion of how the strategy is to be implemented, reflects recent incorporation of private sector management thinking into the public sector. Some similar elements of customer service and discussion of 'stakeholders interests' is also evident in the proposals for reform of the courts service, which led to the enactment of the Courts Service Act 1998: see para **4.205**.

[127] The 1924 Act concerned the Attorney General of the Irish Free State, but it appears to be accepted that it has been 'carried forward' to apply to the Attorney General under the 1937 Constitution: see Casey, *The Irish Law Officers* (1996).

[128] An exception was the appointment in 1977 of John M Kelly, then government Chief Whip, as Attorney General. Professor Kelly had practised at the junior Bar in the early 1960s (contd.../)

[3.118] The Attorney General is, by convention, a practising member of the Bar and a senior counsel.[128] The Attorney General is also what is by convention referred to as 'the leader of the Bar', in other words he or she ranks as the most senior member of the Bar. This is largely a ceremonial position. While there is no rule requiring the Attorney to cease private practice while acting as Attorney, this has in fact been the case in recent years.

[3.119] As legal adviser to the government, the Attorney General scrutinises all draft legislation which any government department proposes to bring before the Oireachtas. This function is performed by the staff of the office of Parliamentary Counsel to the government in the Attorney General's office.[129] The Attorney also advises the government in an international context, for example in relation to the ratification of international agreements.[130]

[3.120] Prior to 1976, all serious criminal offences were prosecuted in the name of the Attorney General, but this function has, in most instances, been transferred to the Director of Public Prosecutions, whose functions we describe below. However, in an area connected with criminal law, extradition requests, the Attorney General was conferred with certain functions by the Extradition (Amendment) Act 1987, which is also discussed below, and these functions have since been transferred to the Director of Public Prosecutions.[131]

[3.121] Section 6 of the Ministers and Secretaries Act 1924 also provides that the Attorney General, as successor to the pre-1922 Attorney General for Ireland, is to represent the public 'in the assertion of or protection of public rights'. This provision refers to the traditional right of the Attorney General in England as the representative of the 'public interest' to oppose a particular legal claim that is being litigated. Thus, a claim by a person to be entitled to private fishery rights over a river and to exclude the public might be contested by the Attorney General on behalf of the general public.[132] In more recent years, the practice has developed for the Attorney General to furnish written submissions in proceedings where there is a public interest or where it is required to assist the Court on a particular issue.[133] A development of this was that the Attorney

---

[128] (\...contd) but had left the Bar having been appointed Professor of Jurisprudence and Roman Law at University College Dublin. In 1969, he was elected to Dáil Éireann. Immediately prior to his appointment as Attorney General, he also 'took silk' to become a senior counsel.

[129] Until 2000, the office of Parliamentary Counsel to the government was known as the office of the Parliamentary Draftsman. On legislative drafting generally, see para **13.58**.

[130] See generally Ch 17.

[131] In December 1994, the then government collapsed arising indirectly from the exercise of these functions: see paras **4.96–4.100**.

[132] See *Moore v Attorney General* [1930] IR 471. Similarly, the destination of an important library collection whose original home had ceased to exist: *Re the Worth Library* [1995] 2 IR 301.

[133] See for example *Murphy v Flood* [2010] IESC 21, [2010] 3 IR 136; *Holland v Athlone Institute of Technology* [2011] IEHC 414, [2012] 23 ELR 1.

General would 'lend' his or her title as a 'relator' in proceedings initiated by private citizens who might otherwise lack the necessary connection or standing concerning a particular legal point.[134]

[3.122] Although Article 30 of the Constitution recognises the political nature of the Attorney's role, as upholder of the general public good, the Attorney General acts independently of the government of the day. Indeed, this aspect of the role has given rise to a number of celebrated cases over the years.[135] In the context of the Constitution of 1937, the Attorney General is always the principal defendant in cases challenging the constitutionality of legislation and in this regard the function as upholder of the public interest is to argue for the constitutionality of any challenged legislation. In some instances, the Attorney has argued such cases in the High Court and Supreme Court[136] but in the majority of cases other senior counsel are chosen to appear in Court on the Attorney's behalf.

[3.123] A convention which applied until 1995 was that the Attorney General had 'first refusal' on any judicial vacancy that arose in the High Court or Supreme Court. Arising from a highly-publicised debate about this convention, it no longer applies.[137]

[3.124] Since the state is involved in much litigation, whether criminal or civil, there is a requirement of a permanent solicitor to represent the state and to instruct barristers on the state's behalf. This is the function of the Chief State Solicitor who is a civil servant and is solicitor to the Attorney General, the Director of Public Prosecutions as well as government departments and state bodies.[138] In 2001 the role of the Chief State Solicitor

---

134 Some of the litigation concerning abortion and the right to life of the unborn began as relator proceedings: see *Attorney General (Society for the Protection of Unborn Children Ltd) v Open Door Counselling Ltd* [1988] IR 593. In later proceedings concerning the same issue, the courts held that the 'relation' of the Attorney General was not required because of the general importance of the right to life of the unborn: *Society for the Protection of Unborn Children Ltd v Coogan* [1989] IR 734: see further para **15.96**.

135 In *Attorney General v X* [1992] 1 IR 1 (see further para **15.126**), another celebrated abortion-related case, the Attorney General successfully applied to the High Court for an injunction to restrain a 14-year-old girl from leaving the state for any purpose, but in particular with a view to obtaining an abortion in England. Although the injunction was set aside on appeal to the Supreme Court (on the ground that, in the particular circumstances where the girl had been raped and threatened to commit suicide if she was forced to carry the foetus to full term and give birth to the baby, she was not prohibited by the Constitution from obtaining an abortion) the Court confirmed that the Attorney General was perfectly correct to bring the matter to the courts and that, in fact, the Attorney could not have taken any other course. To the same effect, see *Attorney General v Hamilton (No 1)* [1993] 2 IR 250.

136 See for example *Dellaway Investments Ltd v National Asset Management Agency* [2011] 4 IR 1.

137 See paras **4.96–4.100**.

138 *A Report on the Organisation and Management Review of the Office of the Chief State Solicitor* (Deloitte & Touche, 1996), commissioned by the government, had found the Chief State Solicitor's Office to be seriously under resourced and thus not in a position to meet the demands placed on it effectively and efficiently. (contd.../)

in criminal matters was transferred to the Director of Public Prosecutions.[139] In addition to the Chief State Solicitor, solicitors in private practice were appointed to appear at local level on behalf of the state, and were referred to as state solicitors. They were usually paid an annual salary.[140] In 2005, the role of state solicitors was transferred to the Director of Public Prosecutions.[141]

The Director of Public Prosecutions[142]

[3.125] We have already mentioned that, prior to 1976, all serious criminal offences were prosecuted in the name of the Attorney General. Section 9 of the Criminal Justice (Administration) Act 1924 and Article 30.3 of the Constitution of Ireland 1937 provide that all serious crimes be prosecuted in the name of the People at the suit of the Attorney General. However, Article 30.3 of the Constitution also provides that this function may be carried out 'by some other person authorised in accordance with law to act for that purpose'. The office of the Director of Public Prosecutions (commonly referred to as 'the DPP' or 'the Director') was created by s 2 of the Prosecution of Offences Act 1974 against this background. The 1974 Act came into effect in 1976 when the first Director took up appointment. Section 3(1) of the 1974 Act provides:

> "Subject to the provisions of this Act, the Director shall perform all the functions capable of being performed in relation to criminal matters ... by the Attorney General immediately before the commencement of this section ..."

[3.126] The rationale behind the Prosecution of Offences Act 1974 was that it was felt that an officer, independent of an appearance of political connections, was required to discharge these functions, similar to the situation in England where the same office had already been established. Although the Director is appointed by the government, the office is that of a civil servant, so that the Director does not resign when a government falls, unlike the position of the Attorney General. This ensures an important element of continuity in the prosecution of offences. Section 2(5) of the 1974 Act also provides that the Director 'shall be independent in the performance of his [or her] functions'. The Director may be removed by the government, but only on consideration of a report into

---

[138] (\\...contd) In particular, it was found to lack sufficient solicitors and technical and other staff to support them. The Report recommended significant changes in the funding of the Chief State Solicitor's Office, and these were accepted and implemented by the government.

[139] See Rules of the Superior Courts (No 4) (Chief Prosecution Solicitor) 2001 (SI 535/2001). See also Loftus, 'Establishment of office of Chief Prosecution Solicitor' (2002) *Bar Review* 348. See also para **3.128**.

[140] A convention existed by which such state solicitors continued in office until 65 years of age, but could be continued in office until 70 years of age, on a basis similar to that for judges of the District Court. In recent years, a retirement age of 65 years applies. In at least one instance, an incumbent state solicitor who was not continued to the age of 70 years successfully claimed damages for loss of earnings: see *Coonan v Attorney General* [2002] 1 ILRM 295 (HC).

[141] See Civil Service Regulation (Amendment) Act 2005, ss 28–31.

[142] See www.dppireland.ie.

the Director's health or conduct made by a committee comprising the Chief Justice, a judge of the High Court and the Attorney General.

[3.127] The Attorney General had retained some functions in relation to certain criminal matters having an international dimension, but legislation has gradually removed these functions and transferred them to the Director of Public Prosecutions.[143] Section 5(1) of the Prosecution of Offences Act 1974 provides that the government may by order[144] declare that the Director's functions 'in relation to criminal matters' may be performed only by the Attorney General where the government is 'of opinion that it is expedient in the interests of national security to do so'. However, since the 1974 Act came into force no such order has been made.

[3.128] Section 7 of the 1974 Act provides that the Attorney General and the Director must ensure that the distribution of retainers to the panel of barristers retained by them to act on their behalf is done on the basis of a 'fair and equitable' distribution. Apart from indicating that there must be a fair distribution of business between those on the Attorney's or Director's panel of barristers, s 7 also implies that much of the work of both offices is, in fact, done by barristers in private practice rather than by barristers in the paid employment of the state. In relation to criminal prosecutions in this jurisdiction, therefore, there is no equivalent of salaried officials entitled 'public prosecutors' as is the case in many states of the United States of America and in the case of the Crown Prosecution Service (CPS) in England. In 1999, a report on the criminal prosecution system in the state concluded that a 'unified' prosecution such as exists in England should *not* be introduced in Ireland.[145] However, it recommended that the functions of the Chief State Solicitor in criminal matters (then part of the Attorney General's office) should be transferred to the Director of Public Prosecutions. This occurred in 2001.[146] In

---

143 International Criminal Court Act 2006, ss 9 and 10 provide that prosecutions for genocide and crimes against humanity (previously matters for the Attorney General under the Genocide Act 1973) are matters for the Director of Public Prosecutions. Sea-Fisheries and Maritime Jurisdiction Act 2006, ss 39 and 103 and the Sea-Fisheries (Prosecution of Offences) Order 2009 (SI 314/2009) provide that prosecutions for sea fisheries offences (previously matters for the Attorney General under the Fisheries (Amendment) Act 1978) are matters for the Director of Public Prosecutions. The Attorney General also had certain functions under the Extradition (Amendment) Act 1987, which inserted sections into Part 3 of Extradition Act 1965 (referred to at para **4.99**). Part 3 of the 1965 Act was repealed and replaced by the European Arrest Warrant Act 2003, s 42 of which refers to prosecutions by the Director of Public Prosecutions or the Attorney General, but the reference to the Attorney General in the 2003 Act appears to be redundant in light of the 2006 Acts and 2009 Order referred to above.

144 A form of secondary or delegated legislation: see para **13.109**.

145 The *Report of the Public Prosecution System Study Group* (1999) (the Nally Report) is available on the Attorney General's website, www.gov.ie/ag. The criminal prosecution system is further discussed in para **6.85**.

146 See Rules of the Superior Courts (No 4) (Chief Prosecution Solicitor) 2001 (SI 535/2001). See also Loftus, 'Establishment of office of Chief Prosecution Solicitor' (2002) *Bar Review* 348.

2005, the role of state solicitors was also transferred to the Director of Public Prosecutions.[147]

[5] LEGAL EDUCATION GENERALLY

Role of universities in legal education

[3.129] We have mentioned already that both the Law Society of Ireland and the Honorable Society of King's Inns provide courses of study leading to the admission of persons to the roll of solicitors and barristers, respectively. Admission to these 'professional courses' requires the candidates in question to have a high level of knowledge of the various 'core' subjects in law specified by both bodies.

[3.130] Most solicitors and barristers who have qualified in the past 25 years hold a law degree from one of the universities in the state. This was not always the case, and until the 1960s the state of law schools in Ireland was less than satisfactory. It was only in the 1960s, for example, that the universities increased the number of full-time law lecturers to a level which was capable of offering a law degree in the form in which it is recognised today. Up to that time, and continuing to the end of the 1960s, many of the lecturers were practitioners who divided their time between the universities and the courts.

[3.131] Because of the state of the law schools for much of the 20th century, many of the senior practitioners of the law – solicitors, barristers and judges – held general university degrees such as a BA and/or MA followed by the training provided by the Law Society or the King's Inns as the case may be. Whether this was an advantage or a disadvantage at the time is a matter of debate, but it is the case that many of the important decisions given by Irish judges up to recent years were delivered by persons whose university education did not include a law degree.

[3.132] The result of the change to full-time staff in the universities has been significant. As indicated, many students now follow a path from law degree through to professional qualification, although there are also a number who take a general degree followed by the equivalent of the King's Inns diploma in legal studies. A number of comparable courses are provided by the many other third level colleges that prepare students for the professional course entrance examination. The university law school sector has increased in size and importance since the 1970s in particular. Apart from the more professional contribution to legal education which has resulted from this, much of the increased level of publications on Irish law in recent years has been produced by the university sector. In addition, the number of private colleges awarding law degrees has increased in recent years.

---

[147] See Civil Service Regulation (Amendment) Act 2005, ss 28–31.

Fair Trade Commission Report

[3.133] Although the role of the universities has expanded in recent years, it is also the case that both the Law Society of Ireland and the Honorable Society of King's Inns have expanded and increased their investment in legal education since the 1980s. In this respect, it may be said that they have maintained a discreet distance from the universities as to the extent to which the universities should be involved in 'professional' courses in particular. In addition, they have also maintained some distance between themselves as professional law schools in terms of the distinctiveness of the courses provided to aspiring solicitors and barristers.

[3.134] The 1990 Report of the Fair Trade Commission on the Legal Profession considered in great detail the arrangements then in place concerning legal education and the respective roles of the universities and the professional law schools. Bearing in mind that the Commission did not recommend the fusion of the two branches of the legal profession, the Report did not recommend that the educational role of the Law Society or of the King's Inns should end. Nonetheless, the Commission made some radical proposals.[148]

[3.135] On the academic side, the Commission considered that knowledge of the basic or core elements of the law was essential for a person to progress to the vocational or professional stage of legal education. While a three- or four-year law degree was regarded by the Commission as the best indicator of academic competence, it also accepted that a qualification similar to the King's Inns diploma in legal studies should be acceptable, particularly as this would ensure that a certain number of persons from a non-law academic background would continue to be attracted to the legal profession. The Commission also considered that such a diploma route might also 'help widen the socio-economic background of entrants to the legal profession'. The Commission also considered that entry to the professional stage might be conditional on attaining a certain level of performance in the degree or diploma.

[3.136] As to the vocational element of legal education, the Commission recommended the establishment by the Minister for Justice 'as a matter of urgency' of an Advisory Committee on Legal Education and Training (ACLET) with a view to reviewing all aspects of legal education, including the academic university element and the vocational element. However, especially far-reaching was the Commission's recommendation that the proposed ACLET would be responsible for 'implementing a system of common vocational training', which would in effect require some amalgamation or rationalisation of the existing arrangements in the Law Society and the King's Inns. The Commission added that this might require the foundation of an Institute of Legal Education, independent of the Law Society, King's Inns and the universities but which could make use of the Law Society's and King's Inns premises. The Institute would arrange the vocational training of prospective solicitors and barristers, with the element of

---

[148] FTC Report, pp 117–120.

instruction comprising no more than 12 months, with a further period of pupillage of perhaps a year.

[3.137] Many of the radical elements of the Commission's recommendations appear to have been influenced by the existence of such a system in Northern Ireland. The Council of Legal Education for Northern Ireland, the equivalent of the Commission's proposed ACLET, is the governing body in Northern Ireland for all aspects of legal education. It is also responsible for the Institute of Professional Legal Studies, the equivalent of the Commission's proposed Institute of Legal Education. The Institute of Professional Legal Studies, situated in Queen's University Belfast but independent of that university, organises an integrated system of vocational education for intending solicitors and barristers.

[3.138] In 1993, an Advisory Committee on Legal Education and Training was indeed established, though this was not at the behest of the Minister for Justice. Rather the Law Society, the King's Inns, the universities and other third level institutions involved in legal education came together on a voluntary basis to examine legal education, primarily though not exclusively with a view to an examination of the vocational phase of legal education. This voluntary ACLET was chaired by Mr Justice Ronan Keane, then a judge of the Supreme Court, who became Chief Justice in 2000.

[3.139] In recent years both the Law Society and King's Inns developed their training courses for trainee solicitors and barristers respectively to be more vocational in nature with a key emphasis on practical learning in small groups. As previously discussed, in 2004, the King's Inns commenced a full-time vocational barrister-at-law degree based on the barrister vocational course run in the United Kingdom.

[3.140] In its 2006 report, the Competition Authority noted that the provision of education to trainee barristers is in effect capped at the level of capacity at which the King's Inns has for places on its barrister-at-law qualification course. It recommended that the role of the Law Society and the King's Inns in setting standards for the provision of education and entry to both branches of the profession be removed and be transferred to an independent body such as a Legal Services Ombudsman. In addition, the provision of legal education by both institutions and any other institution wishing to provide legal training to solicitors and barristers should be subject to approval by this independent body. The monopoly on the provision of and standards in legal education exercised by the Law Society and King's Inns was criticised by the Competition Authority. In particular, the absence of competition removes an incentive to keep costs down and this leads to inefficiency and further a monopoly reduces the incentive to be innovative which is not in the best interests of society. Accordingly it recommended that an independent body such as the Legal Services Commission set standards for the training of barristers and solicitors and approve institutions to provide such training.

[3.141] As we have seen, the government and the Oireachtas initially decided against the establishment of such a Commission and instead enacted the Legal Services Ombudsman Act 2009. As already noted the 2009 Act was never brought into force and the Legal Services Regulation Bill 2011 (which it is expected will be enacted by the end of 2014 or early 2015) envisages the establishment of a Legal Services Regulatory Authority which will be empowered to assess the admission policies of the Law Society and the Bar Council.

[3.142] Substantial changes were effected in England and Wales through the establishment of a statutory Advisory Committee on Legal Education and Conduct (ACLEC) under the Courts and Legal Services Act 1990 [UK], whose functions have been taken over by the Legal Services Board. In effect, these changes have established a standards-setting agency outside the English Law Society and Bar Council, though these bodies continue to exist and to organise and arrange professional education courses. The Legal Services Board has the power to direct the standards being set by these two professional bodies. The experience of the Legal Services Board is likely to influence the operations of the Legal Services Regulatory Authority due to be established under the Legal Services Regulation Bill 2011.

[3.143] In a much more modest way, under s 40 of the Solicitors Act 1954, as amended by s 49 of the Solicitors (Amendment) Act 1994, the Law Society of Ireland may provide, either on its own or in association with other institutions, educational courses for its own students and for students of other educational and training institutions. In addition, the Society is also empowered to join with other institutions in providing joint or common courses leading to a joint or common qualification. These provisions clearly have in mind some form of joint courses with the King's Inns, though not necessarily on the lines envisaged in the 1990 Report.

Continuing professional development (CPD)

[3.144] While the 1990 Report of the Fair Trade Commission did not deal with the question of continuing legal education (CLE), this is an area in which there has been considerable development in recent years, in common with most other professions, where continuing professional development (CPD) has become a major issue. It has become increasingly important for professional persons, whether doctors or lawyers, to provide themselves with 'refresher' courses on an ongoing basis in the practice of their profession. While in the past it was felt that this was a matter for each individual practitioner, it is increasingly a matter of good professional conduct that a professional person take a number of continuing education modules over a given period.

[3.145] The Law Society, the Bar Council and the King's Inns provide CPD modules. Similar requirements have been introduced for members of the Bench, again reflecting developments in best practice internationally.[149] Both the Law Society and the Bar

---

[149] See para **4.147**. See also O'Reilly, '21 years on: The Changing Face of CLE' (1999) *Law Society Gazette*.

Council require their members to attend a certain amount of hours of CPD per year. Failure of members to do so can amount to misconduct.[150]

Recognition of foreign qualifications

[3.146] It was the case for many years that lawyers qualified in any other jurisdiction had no right to practice as a solicitor or barrister in the state or to the more limited right of audience in the courts of the state, except where special leave was granted.

[3.147] The position of solicitors and barristers who qualified in Northern Ireland and in England was somewhat different to lawyers from other jurisdictions given the historical connections. Since the creation of the two jurisdictions on the island in the 1920s and the separation from the United Kingdom created by the Act of Union of 1800, there has been an element of continued connection between the branches of the profession in the jurisdictions, largely based on mutual or reciprocal arrangements to facilitate practice in the different jurisdictions.

[3.148] For the solicitor's branch, the mechanisms for recognition of qualifications from Northern Ireland and England are contained in Part IV of the Solicitors Act 1954, as amended by subsequent Acts. For the Bar, recognition is a matter for the Bar Council, but it remains the case that many who are called to the Bar in Dublin later seek admission to one of the Inns of Court in London or to the Bar of Northern Ireland. Indeed, some leading senior counsel have been called to the Inner Bar of Northern Ireland as Queen's counsel.[151] As to the more limited issue of rights of audience in the courts, it is also the case that members of the Bar of Northern Ireland or of England present arguments in the courts of this jurisdiction,[152] and *vice versa*.

[3.149] As to lawyers from other jurisdictions, membership of the European Union has resulted in substantial changes to the recognition laws. The Recognition of Professional Qualifications Directive 2005/36/EC Regulations 2008[153] provide a framework within which the Law Society and King's Inns are the designated bodies charged with the task of recognising professional qualifications in law obtained in EU member states. Provision is made for aptitude and proficiency tests and appeals lie to the High Court for any persons aggrieved by an adverse decision.

---

[150] See Solicitors (Continuing Professional Development) Regulations 2007 (SI 807/2007) and Ruling of the Professional Practice Committee of the General Council of the Bar of Ireland, 18 January 2008, together with the Code of Conduct for the Bar of Ireland.

[151] Prior to 2000, some media coverage of such an event had focused to focus on whether, at the granting of the letter patent for Queen's counsel, the recipient was required to swear an oath of allegiance to the British monarch. This requirement no longer applies. See *Re Treacy's and another's Application for Judicial Review* [2000] NI 330.

[152] For example *Tradax Ltd v Irish Grain Board Ltd* [1984] IR 1; *Dowling v Ireland, the Attorney General and Minister for Agriculture* [1991] 3 IR 379.

[153] SI 139/2008.

[3.150] The European Communities (Freedom to Provide Services) (Lawyers) Regulations 1979[154] also provide for limited recognition of professional qualifications in law in respect of any EU member state. The 1979 Regulations provide that any lawyer qualified in an EU member state has the right of audience in the courts, though this must be exercised in conjunction with a qualified barrister or solicitor of this jurisdiction. The Regulations do not permit such a person to provide conveyancing services or to prepare the documents required to obtain title in order to administer the estate of a deceased person.

[3.151] Further significant changes were required to facilitate implementation of a 1998 Establishment Directive.[155] This Directive provides that the relevant bodies, namely the Law Society and King's Inns, must make provision to facilitate practice by a lawyer on a permanent basis where that person has qualified in any other member state. In general, the lawyer may retain his or her title from their home state and may, in Ireland, give advice on the law of his or her home state, on European Community law, on international law and on the law of Ireland. While a general right of audience in the Irish courts is granted under the 1998 Directive, some exceptions are permitted, including the power to require that such a lawyer appear in some cases with a lawyer specialising in a particular area, such as criminal procedure. In addition, an exception for conveyancing is also provided for, as in the 1979 Regulations. The 1998 Directive was implemented by s 20 of the Solicitors (Amendment) Act 2002 and the European Communities (Lawyers Establishment) Regulations 2003.[156]

[3.152] Lawyers who are qualified outside of the European Economic Area (EEA) have to undertake exams either at the Law Society or King's Inns before they are eligible to practice as lawyers in Ireland even if they are qualified lawyers in their home country with extensive experience. The Competition Authority found the disparity in treatment between lawyers qualified in the EEA and outside the EEA as disproportionate and unduly restrictive. It recommended that a similar system to that for EEA qualified lawyers be introduced.

Exchanges between lawyers at EU level

[3.153] In addition to formal recognition of qualifications, the European Union has also been engaged in initiatives aimed at improving awareness of European law in the member states and in the exchange of information between lawyers in the member states. These have included the Grotius initiative,[157] launched under Article K.3 of the

---

[154] SI 58/1979, implementing Directive 77/249/EEC, as amended by SI 753/2004 to reflect the new accession states to the EU.

[155] Directive 98/5/EC. See MacEochaidh, 'Eurowatch' (1998) 3 *Bar Review* 193.

[156] SI 732/2003. The 2003 Regulations were amended by SI 752/2004 and SI 96/2008 to reflect the new accession states to the EU.

[157] Joint Action under Article J of the Treaty on European Union (OJ L287, 8.11.1996), p 3. This initiative ran from 1997 to 2000. Council Regulation (EC) No 290/2001 (OJ L43, 14.2.2001), p 1, continued the programme for 2001 pending a review of its scope.

Treaty on European Union (the Maastricht Treaty), which provided for Joint Action between the Member States in the field of Judicial and Home Affairs. This initiative led to a number of exchanges and conferences between lawyers in the member states. In addition, the Robert Schuman project[158] established an action programme to improve awareness of Community law within the legal professions. The Jean Monnet project aims at promoting teaching on European integration at university level. This has resulted in the funding of many Jean Monnet positions at lecturer and professorial level throughout the European Union.

[6] OTHER PROFESSIONALS

[3.154] As mentioned at the beginning of this chapter, persons other than solicitors and barristers are also involved in the operation of the law.

Law clerks

[3.155] Under s 58 of the Solicitors Act 1954, activities normally associated with solicitors may be done by any person employed by a solicitor if acting under the solicitor's directions. This provision allows law clerks, a group of persons employed by many solicitors' firms, to engage in much work connected with conveyancing and certain court work, in particular appearances in the Master's Court in the High Court.[159] Many law clerks have progressed to being fully qualified solicitors and special account of their experience in the law is made in this respect in the Solicitors Acts.

Legal executives

[3.156] In its 1990 Report on the Legal Profession, the Fair Trade Commission considered the emergence of 'para-legals' or legal executives, who have mirrored the emergence of para-medics in the field of medicine and similar persons in other professions.[160] The Commission did not consider that such persons should be accorded any special statutory recognition, as this might lead to a further divisions within the legal profession and, in any event, such persons could be accommodated under the existing 'employee' provisions of s 58 of the Solicitors Act 1954. By contrast, legal executives are a recognised additional form of legal staff in England and Wales, employed mainly in solicitors' firms but also in large companies where such persons perform a large deal of conveyancing work. This reflects the licensed conveyancing system introduced in England and Wales in the 1980s,[161] but which has not been followed in this jurisdiction, although the Competition Authority's 2006 Report, discussed above, recommended its introduction.

---

158 Decision No 1496/98/EC, OJ L196, 14.7.1998, p 24.
159 See para **4.196**.
160 FTC Report, pp 272–277.
161 Under the UK Administration of Justice Act 1985. See now the UK Courts and Legal Services Act 1990 and the UK Access to Justice Act 1999.

[3.157] The Irish Institute of Legal Executives (IILEX)[162] was formed in 1987 and was incorporated in 1992. The aim of IILEX is to provide a system of training and examination for legal executives and to afford a recognised professional qualification to those engaged in all areas of legal employment. The institute's members are employed in private practice, the legal departments of banks, public or local authorities or in industry and commerce. The primary purpose of the IILEX is to represent, promote and encourage persons identified as registered legal executives practicing in all legal areas of employment.

Other professions

[3.158] Engineers and architects may require detailed knowledge of, for example, patent and copyright law, building standards legislation and technical standards, and many textbooks are written for that audience. In addition, such professionals may serve as specialist arbitrators in hearings conducted under the Arbitration Act 2010 and as mediators or conciliators.[163]

[3.159] Other professionals such as accountants are likely to have more detailed knowledge of the practical operation of certain areas of law than even some barristers who specialise in particular areas. Accountants are likely to be familiar with the details of the Taxes Consolidation Act 1997 and other revenue legislation, as well as some aspects of company law. For this reason, they will also be given a good grounding in the basic principles of law associated with those areas of legislation in their university degrees and professional courses.

[3.160] In effect, such professional persons may be in the 'front line' of the application of the law in the sense that many disputes concerning legal rules may be dealt with informally without recourse to the courts, such as the application of a particular provision in taxation legislation. Moreover, even where a dispute cannot be resolved informally, they may encourage their clients to resolve differences by means other than litigation in the courts, in particular through mediation and conciliation.[164]

---

[162] See the IILEX website, www.iilex.ie.
[163] See Ch 8, below.
[164] See Ch 8, below.

Chapter 4

The Court System, the Judiciary and Administration of the Courts Service

[1]   Introduction 123
[2]   The Administration of Justice in Courts 126
[3]   The Need to Establish a Post-1937 Court System 142
[4]   The Court System in Ireland: Judicial Composition
        and Structure 144
[5]   Appointment and Qualifications 160
[6]   Judicial Independence and Judicial Ethics 179
[7]   Vacating of Judicial Office and Retirement 209
[8]   Court Officers and Administration 213
[9]   Management of the Court System 217

[1] INTRODUCTION

[4.01] In this chapter we discuss the organisation of the court system. Beginning with the provisions of the Constitution that establish the essential elements of the system, we then describe in more detail the main statutory provisions applicable. Following this, we discuss the role of the judiciary, which makes up the most visible part of the court system, including the judicial appointments procedure and issues concerning judicial conduct and ethics. Finally, we examine the arrangements for the administration of the courts service, including the role of the various court officers and officials.

This chapter should be seen as introductory to subsequent chapters that describe the original jurisdiction of the courts,[1] court procedure[2] and the appellate jurisdiction of the courts.[3]

[4.02] When Saorstát Éireann, the Irish Free State, was established in 1922, Articles 64 to 73 of the 1922 Constitution of Saorstát Éireann[4] provided the basic structure of the court system to be established in the new state. This broad outline was filled in by the detailed provisions of the Courts of Justice Act 1924. The 1924 Act made permanent

---

1   Ch 5.
2   Ch 6.
3   Ch 7.
4   The 1922 Constitution was enacted as a Schedule to the Constitution of The Irish Free State (Saorstát Éireann) Act 1922, the first Act passed by the Oireachtas of Saorstát Éireann.

provision[5] for the establishment, as well as a description of, the jurisdiction (that is, the principal functions) of the following courts: the Supreme Court; the Court of Criminal Appeal;[6] the High Court; the Circuit Court; and the District Court.[7]

[4.03] The 1922 Constitution was replaced in 1937 by the present Constitution of Ireland, *Bunreacht na hÉireann*. Articles 34 to 38 of the 1937 Constitution contain some new provisions concerning the court structure, but the essential elements of the existing system envisaged in 1922 remained in place. As we will see,[8] the 1937 Constitution required the establishment of a new court system, but this was not formally done until the passing of the Courts (Establishment and Constitution) Act 1961. This Act, together with the Courts (Supplemental Provisions) Act 1961,[9] provided for the establishment of, and prescribed the jurisdiction of the Supreme Court, the Court of Criminal Appeal,[10] the High Court, the Circuit Court, and the District Court. In 2013, Article 34.2 of the Constitution was amended to provide for the creation of a Court of Appeal with jurisdiction in both civil and criminal matters, thus incorporating the role of the Court of Criminal Appeal.[11]

[4.04] It should be observed that the two 1961 Acts largely involved a re-establishment of the pre-1961 court system that had been in place since the passing of the Courts of Justice Act 1924. Indeed, many provisions of the 1924 Act were carried over into the 'new' system by the Courts (Supplemental Provisions) Act 1961. In that sense, there was no complete break with the pre-1961 court system and it will become clear from this and subsequent chapters that certain provisions of the Courts of Justice Act 1924 remain the statutory basis for large elements of the courts' jurisdiction.

---

5   For the courts in operation prior to 1924, see paras **2.30–2.54**.
6   The Courts and Court Officers Act 1995, s 4, envisaged the abolition of the Court of Criminal Appeal and the transfer of its functions to the Supreme Court, but this was never brought into force and was superseded by the amendment made to Article 34.2 in 2013 which provided for the creation of a Court of Appeal with jurisdiction in both civil and criminal matters: see further paras **4.36**, **7.25** and **7.41** and Law Reform Commission, *Report on the Consolidation and Reform of the Courts Acts* (LRC 97-2010). See also para **7.71** on the 2009 Report of the Working Group on a Court of Appeal.
7   While the 1924 Act added the words 'of Justice' to each Court's formal name, the names as listed in the text were the usual descriptions given to the courts.
8   See para **4.46**.
9   The Courts (Establishment and Constitution) Act 1961 is a short Act providing for the formal establishment of the courts listed in the text. By contrast, the Courts (Supplemental Provisions) Act 1961, which was signed into law on the same date, is a lengthy Act since it describes the detailed jurisdiction of the various courts established under the Courts (Establishment and Constitution) Act 1961.
10   The Courts and Court Officers Act 1995, s 4, envisaged the abolition of the Court of Criminal Appeal and the transfer of its functions to the Supreme Court, but this was never brought into force and was superseded by the amendment made to Article 34.2 in 2013 which provided for the creation of a Court of Appeal with jurisdiction in both civil and criminal matters: see further, para **4.36**.
11   See further para **7.41**.

[4.05] Thus, the 1924 Act together with the two 1961 Acts are the principal legislative source of the jurisdiction of the courts[12] and they are supplemented by detailed statutory rules concerning the formal procedures to be followed in civil and criminal matters.[13] We will discuss these Acts in more detail later in this chapter.[14] For the present, we discuss the provisions of the 1937 Constitution concerning the court system.[15]

[4.06] As already indicated, Articles 34 to 37 of the 1937 Constitution (which are headed 'The Courts') provide an outline of the essential elements of the court system. Article 38 (which is included under the heading 'Trial of Offences') contains provisions regarding the jurisdiction and procedure of the courts in criminal matters. Although it can be said that the various Courts Acts fill in the detail contained in Articles 34 to 38, that detail must, like any legislation, conform to the basic framework established by the Constitution.

[4.07] In March 2001, the then Chief Justice, Keane CJ, delivered a lecture outlining his views as to how the current court system, which has not fundamentally altered since 1924, might be restructured with a view to improving its efficiency. In addition, the Law Reform Commission has made a number of recommendations for reform in this area.[16] We will discuss further these suggestions for reform elsewhere.[17]

---

[12]   Delany, *The Courts Acts 1924–1997* (2nd edn, 2000) is an excellent resource containing the annotated text of all Acts of relevance to the jurisdiction of the courts, from the Courts of Justice Act 1924 through to the Courts Service Act 1998. In addition to the Acts passed since 1924, a number of pre-1922 Acts, such as the Petty Sessions (Ireland) Act 1851, the Summary Jurisdiction Act 1857 and the Supreme Court of Judicature (Ireland) Act 1877, contain important provisions describing the jurisdiction of the courts in Ireland. There is a strong case for the consolidation of these Acts into a single Courts Act. In 2010, the Law Reform Commission published a *Report on the Consolidation and Reform of the Courts Acts* (LRC 97-2010), which includes a draft Courts (Consolidation and Reform) Bill containing the text of relevant provisions describing the jurisdiction of the courts, including pre-1922 and post-1922 provisions. At the time of writing (September 2014) the Government Legislation Programme, Autumn Session 2014, available at www.taoiseach.ie, indicates that the government proposes to publish a Courts (Consolidation and Reform) Bill to implement the Commission's 2010 Report.

[13]   The current rules of court for the High Court and Supreme Court are the Rules of the Superior Courts 1986 (SI 15/1986), as amended. The relevant rules for the other courts are the Circuit Court Rules 2001 (SI 510/2001), as amended and the District Court Rules 1997 (SI 93/1997), as amended. The leading decision as to what constitutes 'practice and procedure', the subject matter of such rules, is *The State (O'Flaherty) v Ó Floinn* [1954] IR 295.

[14]   See para **4.50**.

[15]   Because of the broad similarities between the 1922 and 1937 Constitutions in this respect, we will outline the relevant provisions of the 1937 Constitution only. For a detailed discussion of the provisions of the 1922 Constitution, see Kohn, *The Constitution of the Irish Free State* (1932).

[16]   Law Reform Commission, *Report on the Consolidation and Reform of the Courts Acts* (LRC 97-2010).

[17]   See para **5.122**.

[2] THE ADMINISTRATION OF JUSTICE IN COURTS

[4.08] Article 34.1 of the 1937 Constitution provides:

"Justice shall be administered in courts established by law by judges appointed in the manner provided by this Constitution, and, save in such special and limited cases as may be prescribed by law, shall be administered in public."

[4.09] Article 37.1, which should be read in conjunction with Article 34.1, provides:

"Nothing in this Constitution shall operate to invalidate the exercise of limited functions and powers of a judicial nature, in matters other than criminal matters, by any person or body of persons duly authorised by law to exercise such functions and powers, notwithstanding that such person or such body of persons is not a judge or a court appointed or established as such under this Constitution."

These provisions lie at the heart of the operation of the courts and other decision-making bodies in Ireland.

[4.10] Article 34.1 provides that 'justice' cannot be administered in any place other than a court which has been established in accordance with the Constitution, presided over by a properly appointed judge, and that, in general, the courts should operate in public.[18] Article 34.1 reiterates the basic 'separation of powers' principle contained in Article 6,[19] namely that the judicial power is to be administered separately from the two other arms of government, the legislature and the executive.

[4.11] However, Article 37.1 also authorises persons other than judges or courts to exercise 'limited' functions and powers of a judicial nature, except in criminal matters. Article 37.1 was intended to deal with the existing situation that there were a number of persons and bodies already given certain powers of a judicial nature and that these could continue, provided that they were 'limited' and did not deal with 'criminal matters'. It has been suggested that Article 37.1 was inserted into the 1937 Constitution to validate the functions of bodies such as the Land Commission[20] and the Master of the High Court.[21] It also allows for the establishment of certain specialist statutory bodies such as

---

18   The issue of the administration of justice in public is considered in paras **4.24–4.32**.

19   See paras **2.79–2.84**.

20   On the Land Commission generally, see para **2.43**. The Commission's powers, though limited to land-related matters, were extensive in the sense that it was empowered to acquire land compulsorily and to sell it to smallholders in order to create economically viable land holdings. The validity of its powers was challenged in *Lynham v Butler (No 2)* [1933] IR 74, where it was held that they were administrative rather than judicial in nature, and were thus not in breach of the equivalent in the 1922 Constitution of Article 34.1. Despite the *Lynham* case, Article 37.1 was intended to put the matter beyond doubt by legitimising the Land Commission's powers, and those of other similar bodies. It has been suggested, however, that Article 37.1 created more doubt than clarity: see generally Hogan and Whyte (eds), *JM Kelly: The Irish Constitution* (4th edn, 2003), pp 616 *et seq* and 1016 *et seq*.

the Private Residential Tenancies Board and the Labour Court that deal with specific statutory claims.

[4.12] What did Article 34.1 envisage when referring to the 'administration of justice'? This is an important question, because where a person or tribunal *other than* a duly appointed judge engages in the 'administration of justice', that person or tribunal acts in violation of the Constitution, and their decisions are thus invalid, unless they are 'limited' in the sense envisaged by Article 37.1. Indeed, there have been many cases over the years in which the courts have been asked to rule on whether certain persons or tribunals have been exercising powers in conflict with Article 34.1, and whether such powers are 'saved' by Article 37.1. The question is also important because it determines what issues are capable of being dealt with by the courts, what are called justiciable matters, and those which are not, which can be described as non-justiciable.[22]

Characteristic features

[4.13] In *McDonald v Bord na gCon (No 2)*,[23] the following five 'characteristic features' of an administration of justice within the meaning of Article 34.1 were suggested:

(1)   a dispute or controversy as to the existence of legal rights or a violation of the law;

(2)   the determination or ascertainment of the rights of parties or the imposition of liabilities or the infliction of a penalty;

(3)   the final determination (subject to appeal) of legal rights or liabilities or the imposition of penalties;

(4)   the enforcement of those rights or liabilities or the imposition of a penalty by the court or by the executive power of the state which is called in by the court to enforce its judgment;

(5)   the making of an order by the court which as a matter of history is an order characteristic of courts in this country.

[4.14] These factors have been very influential in the cases that have come before the courts, but it should be noted that they do not provide a definitive answer in all cases. In particular, the reference to whether as a matter of history the issue is one characteristically dealt with by courts has been criticised.[24]

---

21   The Courts and Court Officers Act 1995, s 24, expressly conferred on the Master limited functions and powers within the meaning of Article 37: see para **4.196**.

22   See para **4.20**.

23   *McDonald v Bord na gCon (No 2)* [1965] IR 217. This list reflects the comparable lists in definitions of judicial power in the cases cited to the High Court and Supreme Court in the *McDonald* case from other common law jurisdictions.

24   See Hogan and Whyte (eds), *JM Kelly: The Irish Constitution* (4th edn, 2003), pp 617 *et seq*.

[4.15] However, it may be useful to provide some examples of the matters dealt with by the courts through the years:

- in 1960, the Supreme Court held that, in striking a solicitor off the roll of solicitors, the Law Society of Ireland *was* exercising the judicial power and that this was not a limited power within the meaning of Article 37.1;[25]

- in 1965, the Supreme Court held that, in making an exclusion order against a greyhound trainer, Bord na gCon, the Greyhound Board, *was not* exercising the judicial power;[26]

- in 1982, the Supreme Court held that, in deciding whether to acquire land compulsorily, Bord na Móna, the Turf Development Board, *was not* exercising the judicial power;[27]

- in 1986, the Supreme Court held that, where a clerk of the District Court was required to be satisfied that a District Court summons was valid, the clerk *was* exercising the judicial power;[28]

- in 1992, the Supreme Court held that a tribunal of inquiry invested with the powers of the Tribunals of Inquiry (Evidence) Acts 1921 and 1979 *was not* exercising the judicial power;[29]

- in 1995, the High Court held that, in commuting (that is, reducing) fines imposed by a District Court judge in a criminal case, the Minister for Justice *was not* exercising the judicial power;[30]

- in 1995, the Supreme Court held that the Institute of Chartered Accountants in Ireland, in exercising its disciplinary powers, including the expulsion of members from the Institute, *was not* exercising the judicial power.[31]

- in 2003, the Supreme Court held that the Censorship of Publications Board, in prohibiting the sale or distribution of certain publications under the Censorship of Publications Acts 1929 to 1967, was exercising limited judicial functions within the meaning of Article 37.1.[32]

- in 2010 the Supreme Court held that the Tribunal of Inquiry into Certain Planning Matters and Payments was not exercising judicial powers; rather it had a fact-finding function, which it reported to the Oireachtas.[33]

[4.16] In the cases of Bord na gCon, Bord na Móna and the Institute of Chartered Accountants in Ireland, the decisions of the Supreme Court indicated that they were not

---

[25] *Re the Solicitors Act 1954* [1960] IR 239.
[26] *McDonald v Bord na gCon (No 2)* [1965] IR 217.
[27] *O'Brien v Bord na Móna* [1983] IR 277.
[28] *The State (Clarke) v Roche* [1986] IR 619.
[29] *Goodman International v Hamilton* [1992] 2 IR 542.
[30] *Brennan v Minister for Justice* [1995] 1 IR 612.
[31] *Geoghegan v Institute of Chartered Accountants in Ireland* [1995] 3 IR 86.
[32] *Melton Enterprises v Censorship of Publications Board* [2003] 3 IR 623.
[33] *Murphy v Flood* [2010] IESC 21, [2010] 3 IR 136.

prohibited by Article 34.1 from exercising their powers. However, the courts have made the point that such bodies, though they might be described as exercising administrative powers, must *exercise their powers in a judicial manner.* This requires such bodies to comply with certain principles of fair procedures, such as the obligation to give advance notice to affected parties, to conduct any hearings on the basis of allowing both sides an equal hearing and to ensure that those making decisions have not been affected by any bias.[34]

[4.17] In the case of the powers of the Law Society of Ireland and of District Court clerks, the consequences of the Supreme Court decisions were that alternative arrangements had to be put in place. The Solicitors (Amendment) Act 1960 provides that, while the Law Society remains the disciplinary body for solicitors, any decision to strike a person off the roll of solicitors must be made by the High Court.[35] This approach has been repeated in similar legislation for the different professions.[36] As to the functions of District Court clerks, the Courts (No 3) Act 1986 now provides that they are not required to make any judgment as to whether District Court summonses outline a criminal offence. The clerk simply processes the summons as an administrative matter; and any decision-making in relation to it is now performed by the relevant judge of the District Court, who is a judge appointed in accordance with Article 34.1 of the Constitution. Thus, even though the broad outline of the system has not changed in any substantial way, the form of the procedure has been altered.

[4.18] While the problems connected with the functions of District Court clerks were 'solved' by the 1986 Act, some difficulties might be noted. First, the decision invalidating the pre-1986 Act system meant that many thousands of summonses, in particular those under the Road Traffic Acts and including those relating to driving with an excess of alcohol, were declared invalid. Indeed, it proved impossible to issue new, valid, summonses in these cases as the six-month time limit for their issue[37] had, by then, expired. Second, what was the legal status of the hundreds of thousands of summonses issued between 1937 and 1986 in a manner that had been found, in 1986, to be in conflict with the Constitution? The Supreme Court decision in 1986 related to the particular summons being challenged in that case, but it could be argued that all previous summonses were equally invalid. While this is a complex problem, the short answer would appear to be that the courts are reluctant to make all their decisions fully retrospective and that the passage of time, and various other factors, would make the pre-1986 Act summonses immune from legal challenge.[38]

---

[34]   These principles of fair procedures are based on the common law principles of natural justice. See generally, Hogan and Morgan, *Administrative Law in Ireland* (4th edn, 2010) and Biehler, *Judicial Review of Administrative Action* (3rd edn, 2013).

[35]   See para **3.58**.

[36]   For example, the Dentists Act 1985, ss 38 to 40.

[37]   The time limit is set out in the Petty Sessions (Ireland) Act 1851, s 10. See further, para **6.09**.

[38]   See the discussion of *Murphy v Attorney General* [1982] IR 241, para **15.72**.

[4.19] There has been at least one instance where the suggestion that a particular body or tribunal was exercising powers contrary to Article 34.1 led to immediate remedial action. It was suggested, in the course of legal submissions in *M v An Bord Uchtála*,[39] that when making adoption orders An Bord Uchtála (now the Adoption Authority of Ireland), was exercising the judicial power under Article 34.1 and that such functions might not be 'limited' within the meaning of Article 37.1. While this suggestion was not translated into a definitive decision of the Supreme Court in the case,[40] the potential spectre of all adoptions being declared invalid led to the holding of a referendum to amend the Constitution in order to prevent even that possibility.[41] In this instance, the importance of ensuring that existing adoption orders were copper fastened was given a high priority, even though it seemed somewhat unlikely that courts would retrospectively invalidate those orders.

Justiciable and non-justiciable (political) controversies

[4.20] One other aspect of the 'administration of justice' is that the courts have also indicated that certain disputes are correctly the business of the courts, described as justiciable controversies, whereas others are more appropriate to the political realm, described as non-justiciable controversies. The distinction between justiciable and political or non-justiciable controversies is based on terminology developed under the 'cases and controversies' clause which forms part of the definition of judicial power in Article 3 of the United States Constitution. For example, the United States Supreme Court held that it had no function determining a dispute concerning the credentials of delegates at the Democratic Party's National Convention in 1972.[42]

[4.21] However, as with other aspects of Article 34.1, the precise boundary between justiciable and non-justiciable matters is difficult to draw. For example, the courts have declared invalid electoral laws where constituency boundaries have failed to comply with the provisions of the Constitution,[43] and have also declared invalid income tax laws where these have failed to comply with constitutional provisions.[44] Both these areas would generally be regarded as being very close to the legislative power and to involve questions of politics and public policy. In neither instance were the courts required to

---

39   *M v An Bord Uchtála* [1977] IR 287.
40   The High Court judge in the *M* case rejected the argument and the Supreme Court did not deal with the issue on appeal. In a later decision, *G v An Bord Uchtála* [1980] IR 32, Walsh J suggested that the Adoption Board was exercising administrative powers only, but no other Supreme Court judge expressed a view on the point. See Hogan and Whyte (eds), *JM Kelly: The Irish Constitution* (4th edn, 2003), p 1037.
41   The Sixth Amendment of the Constitution Act 1979 inserted Article 37.2 into the Constitution, which provides that no adoption is invalid by reason only of the fact that the order was made by a body or person other than a judge or court.
42   *O'Brien v Brown* 409 US 1 (1972).
43   *O'Donovan v Attorney General* [1961] IR 114.
44   *Murphy v Attorney General* [1982] IR 241.

make decisions about the allocation of public resources but it must be recognised that that outcome might be an indirect consequence.

[4.22] The courts have been more reluctant to become involved where their decisions would involve explicit decisions about how funds should be allocated, and they will generally not intervene but will allow the executive or legislative arms of government to make these difficult choices.[45] This is the case even where there is a clear breach of constitutional rights. *TD v Minister for Education*[46] involved one of a number of troubled youths who required specialised secure care facilities. However, the state was unable to provide such facilities. In the High Court, Kelly J ordered the relevant government ministers to provide the resources for such a facility and granted an order that the Minister for Education implement his policy to build the particular detention centre. The Supreme Court by a majority of 4:1 reversed this decision and concluded that a mandatory order directing the government to fulfil a legal obligation which would involve the expenditure of public funds would only be made in the most exceptional of circumstances, which the circumstances of the current case did not meet.

[4.23] In sum, therefore, Articles 34.1 and 37.1 provide that certain functions are exclusively a matter for the courts but that some limited functions may be dealt with by other persons or bodies. Those provisions also indicate that certain matters are justiciable and others not. The precise boundary between those matters which must always be assigned to the courts and those which may be conferred on other persons or bodies remains difficult to draw, but the principles adopted by the courts provide some useful indicators.

Administration of justice in public, with exceptions

[4.24] Article 34.1 of the Constitution provides that the courts must, in general, sit in public, 'save in such special and limited cases as may be prescribed by law'. A sitting other than in public is usually described as being *in camera*.[47] Where a case is heard *in camera*, members of the public as well as representatives of the media are excluded from the courtroom, attendance being restricted to the judge, the jury (if applicable), the court registrar or clerk, the parties to the proceedings and their legal representatives. Article 34.1 reflects a long-established antipathy to court proceedings being held in private.[48] This arose from the persecution associated with the Spanish Inquisition, the English Court of Star Chamber and the French monarchy's abuse of the *lettre de cachet*. Of course, Article 34.1 provides for certain legislative exceptions, but the courts have emphasised that the general rule should be public hearings.

---

45 See, eg, *O'Reilly v Limerick Corporation* [1989] ILRM 181 and para **15.122**.

46 *TD v Minister for Education* [2001] 4 IR 259 and see para **15.106**.

47 The phrase *in camera* indicates a court sitting 'in a box'. Some legislation refers to hearings 'in private' or 'in chambers'.

48 See the judgment of Black J in *Re Oliver* 333 US 257 at 268–270 (1948).

[4.25] Section 45(1) of the Courts (Supplemental Provisions) Act 1961 provides for a number of cases in which justice may be administered otherwise than in public. These are: applications of an urgent nature for *habeas corpus*, bail, prohibition or an injunction; family law cases (such as divorce, judicial separation or nullity cases); assisted decision-making and capacity cases;[49] and proceedings involving the disclosure of a secret manufacturing process.

[4.26] In addition, High Court proceedings under s 205 of the Companies Act 1963, where a company shareholder alleges oppression by the majority shareholders in the company, may be heard *in camera*. Section 205(7) of the 1963 Act provides that this may happen where the High Court is of the opinion that a public hearing 'would involve the disclosure of information the publication of which would be seriously prejudicial to the legitimate interests of the company.'[50]

[4.27] It is clear that the main justifications for excluding the public from such hearings are either the urgency of the case or the sensitivity of the material being discussed in court.[51] Any publication which would identify parties involved in *in camera* cases, or reveal sensitive information discussed in such hearings, would amount to contempt of court.[52] In view, however, of the importance of ensuring some element of transparency in the operation of the courts in matrimonial cases, it was recommended[53] that some form of media access be permitted. Thus, arrangements were put in place in 2001 to facilitate access by the media to the outcome of those cases, including the legal grounds on which

---

49 These are cases under the jurisdiction envisaged in the Assisted Decision-Making (Capacity) Bill 2013, which will replace the wards of court system. See also Children Act 2001, s 252, which provides that the anonymity of a child in any proceedings for an offence against a child or where the child is a witness in such proceedings must be protected.

50 See also the Sex Offenders Act 2001, s 21 provides that all proceedings under the 2001 Act (apart from any proceedings in relation to the contravention of a sex offender order) are heard in private.

51 While most states would provide for categories of cases to be heard in private, other jurisdictions, such as the United Kingdom and the United States, have removed the *in camera* rule for family law and such cases are heard in public. Thus, media reporting of divorce cases, particularly involving celebrities, is common in those countries. See, for example, *McFarlane v McFarlane* [2004] 3 WLR 1480. Similar coverage of divorce proceedings in Ireland is not possible.

52 The most common context in which such a contempt arises is where the media publishes a story identifying the parties involved in an *in camera* hearing, such as a divorce or judicial separation hearing. See generally McGonagle, *A Textbook on Media Law* (2nd edn, 2003). See also *MP v AP* [1996] 1 IR 144 and *Microsoft Corp v Brightpoint Ireland Ltd* [2001] 1 ILRM 540 (which included an order to erase any material from the parties' websites that might identify the subject matter of the case, until a final determination in the case). See also Ch 10.

53 By the Working Group on a Courts Commission in its *Working Paper: Information and the Courts* (November 1997). The Working Group, which also produced six reports during its existence between 1995 and 1998, led to the creation of the Courts Service under the Courts Service Act 1998: see further para **4.205**.

decisions are made by the courts.[54] These arrangements are on the basis that the continued anonymity of the parties involved is preserved. The normal contempt rules thus remained in place. The absolute nature of the *in camera* rule in family law cases received a large amount of consideration.[55] In 1994, the Law Reform Commission had expressed the view that it created 'an unhealthy atmosphere in which anecdote, rumour and myth inform the public's understanding of what goes on the family courts.'[56] Section 40(3) of the Civil Liability and Courts Act 2004 has amended the *in camera* rule in family law cases[57] and provides that a barrister, solicitor, researcher or specialist working in a particular area can prepare and publish a report of proceedings instituted under particular family law provisions.[58] Initially the Courts Service has engaged a number of barristers as researchers and publishes a regular magazine providing details of family law judgments and trends.[59] The parties were not identified in any manner. Subsequently a Child Care Law Reporting Project was established to report on the proceedings where the HSE seeks Care Orders or Supervision Orders in the District Court, whose decisions may be appealed to the Circuit Court.[60] Section 40(6) of the 2004 Act which allows for orders made and evidence given in *in camera* proceedings to be used in other specified hearings.[61] Section 40 of the 2004 Act was further amended by the Courts and Civil Law (Miscellaneous Provisions) Act 2013, and the 2013 Act inserted s 40A into the 2004 Act, in order to put in place similar arrangements for other family-related cases including cases involving children. As a result, since 2014 (when the 2013 Act came into force), the media have been in a position to report most family law proceedings in the courts, provided that the reporting does not identify any of the parties. The media have utilised the 2013 Act to report frequently on family law cases, in particular those in the District Court.

---

54   See (2000) *The Irish Times*, 26 October.

55   See for example, Coggans, 'The in camera rule time for change?' (2001) 4 (1) IJFL 1, Horgan, Shannon and Gallagher, 'Reform of the In Camera Rule – A Sensitive Balancing Act' (2002) *Bar Review* 278 and Walsh, 'Privacy's New Paradigm: The Rise and Reform of the In Camera Rule' (2005) 8(1) IJFL 10 and Egan, 'The *In Camera* Rule: A Barrier to Transparency or a Necessity in Irish Family Law?' [2012] IJFL 59.

56   Law Reform Commission, *Consultation Paper on Family Law Courts* (LRC CP-78 1994), para 7.09.

57   The Civil Liability and Courts Act 2004, s 40 reflects the recommendations made in the Sixth Report of the Working Group on a Courts Commission, *Conclusion with a Summary* (1998).

58   Civil Law (Miscellaneous Provisions) Act 2008, s 31 amended the Civil Liability and Courts Act 2004, s 40(3) so that the researcher can have access to any relevant documents in a family law case subject to any directions given by the court.

59   The Family Law Matters publications are available on the Courts Service website at www.courts.ie.

60   See Coulter, 'The Child Care Act in Practice: Some Emerging Issues from the Child Care Law Reporting Project' [2014] IJFL 35.

61   A number of statutory instruments set out the types of investigations or hearings to which s 40 applies. These include barrister professional conduct hearings and the professional practice committee of the Bar Council. See SI 170/2005 and SI 339/2005.

[4.28] In addition to these limited instances of proceedings being held otherwise than in public, a number of other restrictions apply in the context of criminal proceedings. In criminal proceedings on indictment, restrictions apply on the information that may be published concerning the defendant once proceedings have been initiated.[62] In prosecutions for rape and other sexual offences, the trial judge is required to exclude the general public, but *bona fide* representatives of the media as well as the court officers and those directly involved in the case can attend the hearing; and while the verdict and sentence (if any) must be pronounced in public, the names of the defendant and the complainant may only be published by the media where the court authorises this.[63] Similar restrictions apply in prosecutions for incest.[64]

[4.29] The requirement that justice be administered in public has also been interpreted as requiring that litigants in civil proceedings use their given names, thus preventing them from suing under assumed names.[65]

---

[62] Criminal Justice Act 1999. These restrictions apply until the hearing of the trial of the offence, when the evidence given in court may be reported, provided that the case is one that is heard in public.

[63] Criminal Law (Rape) Act 1981, s 6 as amended by the Criminal Law (Rape) (Amendment) Act 1990, s 11.

[64] Criminal Law (Incest Proceedings) Act 1995, s 6 replacing the Punishment of Incest Act 1908, s 5 in the wake of the decision of the High Court in *The People (DPP) v WM* [1995] 1 IR 226. In *Roe v Blood Transfusion Service Board* [1996] 1 ILRM 555, Laffoy J held that the plaintiff, Bridget McCole, was required to use her real name, rather than a pseudonym. The case involved a claim that the defendant had negligently supplied a blood transfusion product to the plaintiff, causing her to develop hepatitis C. See also *In re Ansbacher (Caymen) Ltd* [2002] 2 ILRM 491 where the applicants were solicitors for two of the parties who had been informed that their names were to appear in a report prepared under the Companies Act 1990. They sought an order directing that the application and any subsequent applications be heard *in camera*. McCracken J held that they were not entitled to such an order as their circumstances did not give rise to any exception to Article 34.1. See also *Roe v Revenue Commissioners* [2008] IEHC 5, [2008] IR 328 where Clarke J refused an application to bring proceedings using pseudonyms. The proceedings sought to prevent the Revenue Commissioners from publishing the applicants' names in its list of tax defaulters who had reached a settlement on their tax liability.

[65] For criticism of the *Roe/McCole* decision, see Byrne and Binchy, *Annual Review of Irish Law 1996* (1997), pp 139–142. By contrast, in a similar claim initiated by persons who had contracted HIV from infected blood products, pseudonyms were allowed, although this ruling had been made with the consent of the defendants: see *Doe v Armour Pharmaceutical Co Inc* [1994] 1 ILRM 416 (para **17.84**). In the United States, the use of assumed names is relatively common. The landmark decision in which the United States Supreme Court held that the right of privacy encompassed the right to terminate a pregnancy, *Roe v Wade* 410 US 113 (1972), involved the use of a pseudonym (the plaintiff, Norma McCorvey, later made her name publicly known). (contd.../)

[4.30] The priority given to public hearings in Article 34.1 was underlined by the Supreme Court in *Re R Ltd*,[66] which concerned proceedings under s 205 of the Companies Act 1963 instituted by the former chief executive of the airline Ryanair Ltd.[67] The company argued that the proceedings should be held *in camera* because its share price could be affected by some of the information that might emerge in evidence in the case. However, the Supreme Court ordered that the proceedings be held in public. Walsh J made the following comment in the course of his judgment:

"The issue before this Court touches a fundamental principle of the administration of justice in a democratic State, namely the administration of justice in public. [He then recited Article 34.1.] The actual presence of the public is never necessary but the administration of justice in public does require that the doors of the courts must be open so that members of the general public may come and see for themselves that justice is done."[68]

---

65   (\...contd) If the *McCole* case came before the courts now, a different result might arise. Section 27 of the Civil Law (Miscellaneous Provisions) Act 2008 provides that in any civil law proceedings in relation to the medical condition of a person, an application can be made to the court prohibiting the publication of any details which would identify the person as having that condition. Such an application can only be granted where the identification of that person with the condition would be likely to cause distress. It is likely that Mrs McCole would come within this category. The courts have, nonetheless, applied s 27 of the 2008 Act sparingly: see for example, *McKeogh v Doe* [2012] IEHC 95 and *DF v Garda Commissioner* [2013] IEHC 312.

66   *Re R Ltd* [1989] IR 126. See also *Doyle v Bergin* [2010] IEHC 531.

67   While the official title of the case in the law reports is *Re R Ltd*, it was widely known that the proceedings involved Ryanair Ltd. Indeed, on foot of the decision of the Supreme Court, there were a number of subsequent public hearings and judgments in this case where the full names of the parties are given: see, for example, *O'Neill v Ryan and Ryanair Ltd (No 3)* [1992] 1 IR 166. In a subsequent case on public hearings under s 205 of the Companies Act 1963, *Irish Press Plc v Ingersoll Publications Ltd* [1994] 1 IR 176, the full names of the parties were given in the judgment determining that the proceedings be in public. However, in *The People (DPP) v Z* [1994] 2 IR 476, an application for an *in camera* hearing under s 45(1) of the 1961 Act, the defendant was not named as it arose in a criminal prosecution for sexual assault on a young person and the anonymity of the defendant was preserved to protect the victim.

68   [1989] IR 126, 134. Walsh J noted that Article 64 of the 1922 Constitution of Saorstát Éireann had provided for public hearings without any apparent provision for exemptions. He also pointed out that the general requirement that justice be administered in public was included as a right in the Sixth Amendment to the United States Constitution and was also contained in many international declarations and conventions, such as Article 10 of the United Nations Universal Declaration of Human Rights (1948) and Article 6 of the Council of Europe Convention on Human Rights and Fundamental Freedoms (1950). See also *XY v Clinical Director of Saint Patrick's University Hospital* [2012] IEHC 224 on the reluctance of the courts to allow proceedings to be heard *in camera* even in cases involving important values such as medical confidentiality, family privacy and personal dignity. The Court protected the anonymity of the applicant by not naming her pursuant to s 27(1) of the Civil Law (Miscellaneous Provisions) Act 2008.

[4.31] Similarly, in *Irish Times Ltd v Ireland*,[69] the Supreme Court held that a trial judge had no general power to impose a ban on contemporaneous reporting of court proceedings. The case concerned an order made by a Circuit Court judge presiding over the trial of five persons, who were charged with importation and possession of illegal drugs. The judge made an order forbidding the media from reporting the evidence that would be given, while stating that the case was not being held *in camera*. However, the Supreme Court held that a contemporaneous ban on media reporting was not justified. The court accepted that, in general, any damage caused by improper reporting could be remedied by the trial judge by appropriate directions to the jury, or by the application of the contempt jurisdiction. The court held that if the press were prohibited from reporting contemporaneously the course of proceedings and the evidence given, the trial would lose the character of being one held in public. The courts have thus emphasised the importance of media reporting of court proceedings, but they do not accept that sensationalist or 'colour pieces' which might trivialise the proceedings are appropriate.[70]

[4.32] While there is a strong leaning in the Constitution towards hearings in public, until 1995[71] the courts in Ireland and England[72] invariably prohibited photographers or television cameras from court. While 'Court TV' may be a feature of certain parts of the

---

[69]   *Irish Times Ltd v Ireland* [1998] 1 IR 359. See also *Independent Newspapers (Ireland) Limited v Anderson* [2006] 3 IR 341.

[70]   During the course of a highly-publicised murder trial, *The People (DPP) v Nevin*, in the Central Criminal Court in April 2000 the trial judge, Carroll J, imposed reporting restrictions on the print media, prohibiting them from publishing 'colour pieces' which referred to the defendant's demeanour, dress, reading material or other similar matter. See McAleese, 'Reporting Restrictions', *Law Society of Ireland Gazette*, May 2000, who suggested that the restrictions imposed may be in conflict with Article 10 of the European Convention on Human Rights as interpreted by the European Court of Human Rights in *News Verlags GmbH v Austria* (2000) 31 EHRR 8. In *The People (DPP) v Nevin* [2003] 3 IR 348, the Court of Criminal Appeal upheld the reporting restrictions.

[71]   In April 1995, television video cameras from the state broadcasting service, Radio Telefís Éireann, were allowed to film the opening arguments in the Supreme Court hearing of *Re the Regulation of Information (Services Outside the State for the Termination of Pregnancies) Bill 1995* [1995] 1 IR 1. This was the first occasion in the history of the state that television cameras had been allowed to film any court in session: see McGonagle, *A Textbook on Media Law* (2nd edn, 2003), p 260. In 2004, RTÉ transmitted a documentary produced by Mint Productions entitled 'Legal Eagles' about the legal profession and its training. Television cameras were permitted into the Master's Court and the District Court during the making of the documentary and coverage of both courts was shown.

[72]   While there are no statutory restrictions in place in Ireland concerning cameras in court, permission to take pictures, whether still or video, was generally refused prior to 1995. In England, an express prohibition had been introduced in the Criminal Justice Act 1925.

[73]   The Law Reform Commission recommended, in its 1994 *Report on Contempt of Court* (LRC 47-1994) that an advisory committee on this question be established by the Minister for Justice. For a discussion of this area, see McGonagle, *A Textbook on Media Law* (2nd edn, 2003), pp 259–261. (contd.../)

United States of America, it seems unlikely that such a development will emerge in Ireland in the near future.[73]

Outline of the court system

[4.33] The basic structure of the system is outlined in Articles 34 to 38. A significant feature of those Articles is that they refer specifically to the High Court, Court of Appeal and Supreme Court. In addition, the Constitution envisaged the continuation of the existing system of other courts with 'local and limited jurisdiction' but these are not mentioned by name.

Courts of first instance and of appeal

[4.34] Article 34.2 of the Constitution, as amended in 2013,[74] states:
"The Courts shall comprise:
    i   Courts of First Instance;
    ii a Court of Appeal; and
    iii a Court of Final Appeal."

---

[73] (\...contd) Lambert, 'Cues, Cameras and Courtroom Actors: Resisting the Temptation of Courtroom Television Cameras' (1996) 14 ILT 13 and (1997) 15 ILT 176 discussed a questionnaire circulated to members of the judiciary, which indicated that there was continued resistance to cameras in Irish courts. Tottenham, 'Justice Should be Seen to be Done – On Television' (2003) 21 ILT 138, argues that a gradual approach, similar to that taken in relation to Oireachtas proceedings should be taken to the televising of court proceedings. Initially it could begin with court proceedings being broadcast on the radio which could then pave the way for experimental broadcasting of court proceedings on television, within boundaries set by the Supreme Court. Live streaming of proceedings in the UK Supreme Court is now the norm. See also Lambert, *Television Courtroom Broadcasting Effects* (2013).

[74] This is the text of Article 34.2 as amended by the Thirty-Third Amendment of the Constitution (Court of Appeal) Act 2013, which provided for the establishment of the Court of Appeal and which was approved by a referendum held in 2013. The text of Article 34.2 prior to 2013 read: 'The Courts shall comprise Courts of First Instance and a Court of Final Appeal.' Article 34A of the Constitution, also inserted by the Thirty-Third Amendment of the Constitution (Court of Appeal) Act 2013, provides:

    1 The Court of Appeal referred to in paragraph ii of Article 34.2 hereof ('the Court of Appeal') shall be established in accordance with this Article.

    2 As soon as practicable after the enactment of this Article, a law providing for the establishment of the Court of Appeal shall be enacted.

    3 That law shall require the Government to appoint by order a day ('the establishment day') on which the Court of Appeal shall be established by virtue of that law; an order of the Government as aforesaid shall operate to have that effect accordingly.

    4 This Article shall be omitted from every official text of this Constitution published after the establishment day.

The Court of Appeal Act 2014 provides for the establishment of the Court of Appeal in accordance with Article 34A; and at the time of writing (September 2014) it is envisaged that this may occur by the end of 2014. Article 64.3.1° of the Constitution, also inserted by the Thirty-Third Amendment of the Constitution (Court of Appeal) Act 2013, provides that after the Court of Appeal has been established, the Chief Justice may direct that appeals pending in the Supreme Court at that time may be transferred to the Court of Appeal for decision.

Article 34.2, even as amended in 2013, broadly continued the pre-2013 arrangements under which certain courts have first instance jurisdiction, that is, the power to hear and determine cases *ab initio*. It also now provides that, in addition to the Supreme Court as the Court of Final Appeal whose functions would not ordinarily involve hearing a case *ab initio* but would be empowered to make a definitive determination on issues of law, the Court of Appeal is now available to provide an intermediate function in appeals from the first instances courts.

The High Court, the Court of Appeal and the Supreme Court

[4.35] Article 34.3 and 34.4 describe the essential powers of functions of the High Court, the Court of Appeal and Supreme Court. Article 34.3.1° states:

> "The Courts of First Instance shall include a High Court invested with full original jurisdiction in and power to determine all matters and questions whether of law or fact, civil or criminal."

Article 34.3.2° provides:

> "Save as otherwise provided by this Article,[75] the jurisdiction of the High Court shall extend to the validity of any law having regard to the provisions of this Constitution, and no such question shall be raised (whether by pleading, argument or otherwise) in any court established under this or any other Article of this Constitution other than the High Court, the Court of Appeal[76] or the Supreme Court."

[4.36] Article 34.4 to Article 34.6 of the Constitution, as amended in 2013,[77] state:

> "4.1° The Court of Appeal shall—
>
> > i   save as otherwise provided by this Article, and
> >
> > ii with such exceptions and subject to such regulations as may be prescribed by law,
>
> have appellate jurisdiction from all decisions of the High Court, and shall also have appellate jurisdiction from such decisions of other courts as may be prescribed by law.
>
> 2° No law shall be enacted excepting from the appellate jurisdiction of the Court of Appeal cases which involve questions as to the validity of any law having regard to the provisions of this Constitution.
>
> 3° The decision of the Court of Appeal shall be final and conclusive, save as otherwise provided by this Article.

---

[75]   Article 34.3.3° provides that no court (thus including the High Court) shall have jurisdiction to question the validity of any law which is enacted after a reference to the Supreme Court pursuant to Article 26 of the Constitution. On Article 26 references, see paras **5.84–5.88**.

[76]   The reference to the Court of Appeal was added by the Thirty-Third Amendment of the Constitution (Court of Appeal) Act 2013, which provided for the establishment of the Court of Appeal and which was approved by a referendum held in 2013.

[77]   This is the text of Article 34.4 to Article 34.6 as amended by the Thirty-Third Amendment of the Constitution (Court of Appeal) Act 2013, which provided for the establishment of the Court of Appeal and which was approved by a referendum held in 2013.

5.1° The Court of Final Appeal shall be called the Supreme Court.

2° The President of the Supreme Court shall be called the Chief Justice.

3° The Supreme Court shall, subject to such regulations as may be prescribed by law, have appellate jurisdiction from a decision of the Court of Appeal if the Supreme Court is satisfied that—

    i   the decision involves a matter of general public importance, or

    ii in the interests of justice it is necessary that there be an appeal to the Supreme Court.

4° Notwithstanding section 4.1° hereof, the Supreme Court shall, subject to such regulations as may be prescribed by law, have appellate jurisdiction from a decision of the High Court if the Supreme Court is satisfied that there are exceptional circumstances warranting a direct appeal to it, and a precondition for the Supreme Court being so satisfied is the presence of either or both of the following factors:

    i   the decision involves a matter of general public importance;

    ii the interests of justice."

[4.37] These provisions indicate the importance of the High Court, the Court of Appeal and the Supreme Court in the court system. The High Court is conferred with 'full original jurisdiction in and power to determine all matters and questions whether of law or fact, civil or criminal'. This includes the power to decide whether any law is invalid having regard to the Constitution. The Court of Appeal is given full appellate jurisdiction from all High Court decisions, although the Supreme Court may also hear appeals, either by way of direct appeal from the High Court (a 'leapfrogging appeal' similar to that from the English High Court to the UK Supreme Court) or from the Court of Appeal. In both instances, such appeals are possible if the Supreme Court (not the High Court or the Court of Appeal) is satisfied that: (i) the decision involves a matter of general public importance, or (ii) in the interests of justice it is necessary that there be an appeal to the Supreme Court. Thus, after this 2013 amendment to Article 34 it is envisaged that the Supreme Court can exercise control over the flow of appeals to it.

[4.38] The specific reference to the High Court, the Court of Appeal (since 2013) and the Supreme Court is significant in a number of ways. Thus, it would seem clear that the High Court, the Court of Appeal nor the Supreme Court could be abolished by legislation unless the relevant provisions of the Constitution were themselves deleted. This gives a permanence to the High Court, the Court of Appeal and Supreme Court which other courts established by legislation cannot claim.

[4.39] Another effect is that, since the High Court is conferred with 'full original jurisdiction in and power to determine all matters and questions whether of law or fact, civil or criminal', its powers, and those of the Court of Appeal and Supreme Court on appeal, are not entirely dependent on the limits of the powers conferred by statute. While, as we will see,[78] statute law confers jurisdiction on the High Court in specific

---

78 See paras **5.71** and **5.75**.

instances, the 'full' jurisdiction it enjoys adds a further layer over and above this. Thus, judges of the High Court and Supreme Court will occasionally refer to the 'inherent' jurisdiction of the High Court or Supreme Court as a basis for making a decision which might not fit into an already established approach.[79] A similar claim may be made for the Court of Appeal. This is similar to the position of the King's (or Queen's) superior courts of record under the system which operated in Ireland prior to 1922.[80] The Court of Appeal and High Court that operated in the pre-1922 system did so with the authority of the monarch, and were for that reason said to possess certain 'inherent' powers arising from the royal prerogative, including powers over and above those actually conferred by statute law.[81] While such royal prerogative powers no longer apply in the post-1922 arrangements,[82] the 'full' jurisdiction conferred on the High Court, Court of Appeal and Supreme Court is similar. In contrast, the same kind of inherent powers simply cannot be claimed by judges of the other courts that are envisaged by the Constitution.

Courts of local and limited jurisdiction

[4.40] The courts other than the High Court, Court of Appeal and Supreme Court are provided for in Article 34.3.4° as follows:

> "The Courts of First Instance shall also include Courts of local and limited jurisdiction with a right of appeal as determined by law."

We have already seen that, in 1937, courts of local and limited jurisdiction – the Circuit Court and District Court – existed by virtue of the 1922 Constitution and the Courts of Justice Act 1924. Indeed, these were the successors of pre-1922 'inferior' courts, especially the County Courts and the Justices of Petty Sessions, who also had limited powers and functions.[83] Such courts have an important role in the court structure, by ensuring local and less expensive venues for people involved in litigation than would be the case were they required to initiate claims in the High Court.[84] Of course, the courts envisaged by Article 34.3.4° cannot be conferred with the 'full' jurisdiction already reserved for the High Court and Supreme Court. The use of the words 'local and

---

[79] See the discussion of *RD Cox Ltd v Owners of MV Fritz Raabe* (1 August 1974, unreported), SC, in Hogan and Whyte (eds), *JM Kelly: The Irish Constitution* (4th edn, 2003), pp 756–7. An example in connection with the Supreme Court is *Holohan v Donohoe* [1986] IR 45, where the Supreme Court held it could, in certain instances, substitute its own award of damages in place of that given in the High Court, even though such power of substitution was not provided for by statute. The High Court has utilised its inherent jurisdiction to strike out proceedings which it found to be an abuse of process or where there are delays in the proceedings which are found to be inordinate and inexcusable: see for example *Fay v Tegral Pipes Ltd* [2005] IESC 34 and *Manning v Benson and Hedges Ltd* [2004] 3 IR 556.

[80] On the nature of a court of record, see fn 111 below.

[81] On the pre-1922 system, see para **2.33**.

[82] On the question of prerogatives under the Constitution, see para **15.37**.

[83] See paras **2.49–2.54**.

[84] See *The State (Boyle) v Neylon* [1986] IR 551.

limited' indicate that there should be a geographical limit on the jurisdiction of a judge of the District Court or of the Circuit Court and that the nature of the cases (whether civil or criminal) would be relatively less serious than those in the High Court.[85]

[4.41] In addition, whether referring to the local and limited courts prior to 1922 or those contemplated by the 1937 Constitution, judges of the High Court and Supreme Court have often referred to the District Court or Circuit Court as 'creatures of legislation', indicating that such courts only have powers to the extent that they are actually granted by statute.[86]

Judicial appointment, independence and ethical conduct

[4.42] The Constitution provides for extensive protections for those appointed as judges, in particular those appointed as judges of the High Court, Court of Appeal and Supreme Court. We discuss the appointment and independence of judges later in the chapter, as well as the need to ensure that, while retaining their independence, their conduct in office conforms to high standards of ethical behaviour.[87]

Regulation of court business by law

[4.43] Article 36 of the Constitution is an important provision concerning the extent to which the general business of the courts may be regulated by statute law. It provides:

"Subject to the foregoing provisions of this Constitution relating to the Courts, the following matters shall be regulated in accordance with law, that is to say:

i. the number of judges of the Supreme Court, of the Court of Appeal,[88] and of the High Court, the remuneration, age of retirement and pensions of such judges,

ii. the number of the judges of all other Courts, and their terms of appointment, and

iii. the constitution and organisation of the said Courts, the distribution of jurisdiction and business among the said Courts and judges, and all matters of procedure."

---

85   See generally, *Grimes v Owners of SS Bangor Bay* [1948] IR 350 and *Creaven v DPP* [2004] 4 IR 434. *Creaven* concerned the validity of search warrants issued by a District Judge sitting in Dublin but temporarily assigned to District Area 12 which covered Co Clare where the house the subject matter of the search warrants was located. The Supreme Court held that the search warrants were invalid as the District Court jurisdiction is based on territorial limits. This situation has been altered by s 180 of the Criminal Justice Act 2006 which inserts a new s 32A into the Courts (Supplemental Provisions) Act 1961 that allows a District Judge to issue a warrant for arrest or a search warrant for a district outside the district in which he or she is sitting.

86   On the first instance jurisdiction of the Circuit Court and District Court, see Ch 5. On their appellate jurisdiction, see Ch 7.

87   See paras **4.116–4.160**.

88   The reference to the Court of Appeal was added by the Thirty-Third Amendment of the Constitution (Court of Appeal) Act 2013, which provided for the establishment of the Court of Appeal and which was approved by a referendum held in 2013.

.

[4.44] This provision recognises the reality that the matters referred to, such as the number of judges, their salaries and pensions as well as the distribution of business between the different courts, will be subject to change from time to time. As we shall see, the distribution of business between the courts has been the subject of much legislation since 1937, reflecting the need to respond to changing needs in society and the increased amount of civil and criminal matters coming before the courts.[89]

Criminal matters

[4.45] As we have seen already, Article 37.1 empowers persons or bodies other than courts to exercise limited functions and powers of a judicial nature, but not in relation to any criminal matters. This indicates that all criminal matters, even of a limited nature, must be dealt with in the courts. In addition, Article 38 sets out important general principles concerning the conduct of criminal trials in the courts. These include the requirement that criminal trials be held 'in due course of law', that minor offences may be tried in courts of summary jurisdiction, and that, subject to certain limited exceptions, a person charged with a non-minor offence cannot be tried without a jury. These provisions are considered elsewhere.[90]

[3]   THE NEED TO ESTABLISH A POST-1937 COURT SYSTEM

[4.46] One further consequence of the provisions contained in Articles 34 to 38 should be mentioned at this stage. In *The State (Killian) v Minister for Justice*,[91] the Supreme Court considered an aspect of Article 34.1 of the Constitution that had received little attention until then. The court held that, where Article 34.1 provided that 'Justice shall be administered in courts established by law', this should be read as 'Justice shall be administered in courts *to be established* by law'. The court thus concluded that the courts in operation at that time (including the Supreme Court itself) were not those referred to in Article 34.1 of the 1937 Constitution, but rather the courts referred to in Article 58, which provided for the continuance of the court system that operated under the 1922 Constitution. The effect of the *Killian* decision was the re-establishment of the court system by the enactment of new legislation.

Courts (Establishment and Constitution) Act 1961

[4.47] The Courts (Establishment and Constitution) Act 1961 was enacted to 'regularise' the position and to 'establish' the court system envisaged by Article 34.1. This short Act merely carried forward the existing court system which had been created by the Courts of Justice Act 1924 under the provisions of the 1922 Constitution. At the same time, the opportunity was taken in the Courts (Supplemental Provisions) Act 1961 to update and clarify the different jurisdictions of the courts. The Supplemental

---

89   See paras **5.07–5.34**. See also Law Reform Commission, *Report on the Consolidation and Reform of the Courts Acts* (LRC 97-2010).
90   See paras **5.90–5.97**.
91   *State (Killian) v Minister for Justice* [1954] IR 207.

Provisions Act, as subsequently amended, contains much of the detailed provisions on the current jurisdiction of the courts.

[4.48] In addition to being aware of the changes effected to the two Acts of 1961 since their initial passing, it is also necessary to refer to the jurisdiction of the courts prior to 1961, since both of the 1961 Acts refer to pre-1961 legislation conferring functions on the different courts. This includes references to the various jurisdictions conferred on the pre-1961 courts by the Courts of Justice Act 1924. In addition, since the 1924 Act had 'carried over' various pre-1922 jurisdictions, it is also necessary in some instances to consult pre-1922 legislation. This would, however, no longer be required if the consolidation of all the Courts Acts, both pre-1922 and post-1922, recommended in 2010 by the Law Reform Commission were enacted.[92]

The 'former' courts

[4.49] Aside from the jurisdictional alterations made by the 1961 Acts, it might be asked whether the establishment of a 'new' court system had any significant effect? Strictly speaking the courts established in 1961 are different entities to those that existed prior to that date. In the period between 1937 (when the Constitution came into effect) and 1961 the courts that operated were 'transitory' courts under Article 58 of the Constitution. This might, for example, justify the courts created by the 1961 Act treating the decisions of the pre-1961 courts as having less force as precedents than decisions of the courts established under the Courts (Establishment and Constitution) Act 1961[93] though it would seem that this has not happened.[94] However, it has become common practice to refer to the pre-1961 courts as, for example, 'the former Supreme Court', 'the former High Court' and so forth.[95] Other, more difficult, problems also arise in this context, such as whether the Supreme Court which operated prior to the 1961 Act was entitled to hear references of Bills from the President under Article 26 of the Constitution, though this has not arisen in any decision of an Irish court.[96]

---

[92] See Law Reform Commission, *Report on the Consolidation and Reform of the Courts Acts* (LRC 97-2010), which includes a draft Courts (Consolidation and Reform) Bill that incorporates, with a number of reforms, all pre-1922 and post-1922 Courts Acts. At the time of writing (September 2014) the Government Legislation Programme, Autumn Session 2014, available at www.taoiseach.ie, indicates that the government proposes to publish a Courts (Consolidation and Reform) Bill to implement the Commission's 2010 Report.

[93] This had been suggested in argument in *The State (Quinn) v Ryan* [1965] IR 110: see para **12.34**.

[94] See *The State (Lynch) v Cooney* [1982] IR 337 (Henchy J), para **12.48**.

[95] See *The State (Lynch) v Cooney* [1982] IR 337, para **12.47**.

[96] See Hogan and Whyte (eds), *Kelly: JM Kelly: The Irish Constitution* (4th edn, 2003), p 729.

[4]   THE COURT SYSTEM IN IRELAND: JUDICIAL COMPOSITION AND STRUCTURE

[4.50] We shall discuss in turn the judicial composition of each court established by the Courts (Establishment and Constitution) Act 1961, beginning with the Supreme Court. The other administrative arrangements necessary to ensure the effective running of the court system will be described later in the chapter.[97]

Judicial precedence, numbers and titles

[4.51] Section 9 of the Courts of Justice Act 1924, as amended by the Court of Appeal Act 2014, sets out the precedence between the judges of the Supreme Court, the Court of Appeal and the High Court. The Chief Justice ranks first, then the President of the Court of Appeal, then the President of the High Court, then the judges of the Supreme Court (in priority of appointment), then the judges of the Court of Appeal (in priority of appointment), then the judges of the High Court (also in priority of appointment). Section 9(3) of the Courts of Justice Act 1947 provides that the President of the Circuit Court takes precedence over all other Circuit Court judges and s 38 of the Courts of Justice Act 1924 provides that the Circuit Court judges rank among themselves according to priority of appointment.[98] No similar ranking is provided for in connection with District Court judges. However, since the President of the District Court is an *ex officio* judge of the Circuit Court,[99] this creates some form of precedence for the holder of that office. Provision is made on a similar basis for the Chief Justice who is an *ex-officio* judge of the High Court, the President of the High Court who is an *ex-officio* judge of the Supreme Court and the President of the Circuit Court who is *ex offio* a judge of the High Court.[100] The President of the Court of Appeal is *ex-officio* judge both of the Supreme Court and the High Court.[101]

[4.52] In accordance with Article 36 of the Constitution,[102] the number of judges of the different courts is fixed from time to time by legislation. Over the years, the number of judges has been substantially increased to reflect the increased workload in the different courts.[103] In 1924, the maximum permissible number of permanent judges in the different courts was 50, comprising three Supreme Court judges, six High Court judges, eight Circuit Court judges and 33 District Court Justices.[104] By 1997, this had more than

---

97   See para **4.204**.
98   The statutory provisions on precedence were carried forward by the Courts (Supplemental Provisions) Act 1961, s 48.
99   Courts and Court Officers Act 1995, s 33.
100 Section 1A of the Courts (Establishment and Constitution) Act 1961 as inserted by section 6 of the Court of Appeal Act 2014.
101 Section 1A of the Courts (Establishment and Constitution) Act 1961 as inserted by section 6 of the Court of Appeal Act 2014.
102 See para **4.43**.
103 See para **4.206**.
104 See Courts of Justice Act 1924, ss 5, 4, 37 and 68, respectively.

doubled to 112, comprising eight Supreme Court judges, 25 High Court judges, 28 Circuit Court judges and 50 District Court judges.[105] By 2008, this had further increased to eight Supreme Court judges (the Chief Justice and seven judges),[106] 36 High Court judges (the President of the High Court and 35 judges), 38 Circuit Court judges (the President of the Circuit Court and 37 judges) and 64 District Court judges (the President of the District Court and 63 judges).[107] With the establishment of the Court of Appeal (at the time of writing (September 2014), envisaged by the end of 2014), its 10 extra judges will be added to this list. It is worth noting that, in 2006, it was suggested that Ireland has the lowest level of judges per 100,000 population compared with other European states: in 2006 there were 3.1 judges in Ireland per 100,000 inhabitants, as compared with almost 12.1 in France and 28 in Germany and Greece.[108]

Supreme Court[109]

[4.53] The Supreme Court established in 1961 under Article 34 of the Constitution[110] is a superior court of record.[111] From 1961 to 1996, the court comprised five judges, the

---

105 See Courts and Court Officers Act 1995, ss 6, 9, 10 and 11, respectively. Section 9 of the 1995 Act has been amended by Courts Act 1997, s 1, and the Courts (No 2) Act 1997, s 2. Section 10 of the 1995 Act has been amended by Courts Act 1996, s 1. The Courts Act 1991, s 21 produced the change in title from 'Justice of the District Court' to 'Judge of the District Court'.

106 In 2013, two additional Supreme Court judges were appointed to address the four-year waiting list in the Court and pending the long-term solution to the backlog envisaged with the establishment of the Court of Appeal. When the Supreme Court backlog is dealt with, it is envisaged that the full complement of Supreme Court judges will return to eight. See the Courts and Civil Law (Miscellaneous Provisions) Act 2013, s 22 (which increased the number of judges to 10 (the Chief Justice and not more than 9 ordinary judges).

107 The Courts (Establishment and Constitution) Act 1961, s 1(2) as amended by s 6(1) of the Courts and Court Officers Act 1995 (Supreme Court judges), s 9 of the Courts and Courts Offices Act 1995 as amended by s 2 of the Courts and Court Officers Act 2007 (High Court), s 10 of the Courts and Court Officers Act 1995 as amended by s 3 of the Courts and Court Officers Act 2007 (Circuit Court) and s 11 of the Courts and Court Officers Act 1995 as amended by s 32 of the Civil Law (Miscellaneous Provisions) Act 2008 (District Court).

108 European Commission for the Efficiency of Justice, 'European Judicial Systems Edition 2008 (date 2006): Efficiency and Quality of Justice' (Council of Europe, 2008), 255. See also (2008) *The Irish Times*, 11 October. The ratio of judges to population was also highlighted by the Irish Council for Civil Liberties: *Justice Matters: Independence, Accountability and the Irish Judiciary* (ICCL, 2007), 92. This issue is especially acute when judicial vacancies arise and the shortage of judges has caused practical issues such as cancellation of court dates or the inability to assign courts to cases listed for hearing. This caused the President of the High Court (Kearns P) to comment publicly in 2014 that High Court lists were at "breaking point": see (2014) *Irish Independent*, 20 February.

109 The Supreme Court has a separate website: www.supremecourt.ie.

110 Courts (Establishment and Constitution) Act 1961, s 1(1) formally established the Supreme Court envisaged by Article 34 of the Constitution, replacing the former Supreme Court established by the Courts of Justice Act 1924, s 5.

111 Courts (Supplemental Provisions) Act 1961, s 7(1) replacing the former Supreme Court established by the Courts of Justice Act 1924, s 18. (contd.../)

Chief Justice,[112] who presides over the court, and four ordinary judges.[113] The Courts and Court Officers Act 1995 provided for an increase in the number of ordinary judges from four to seven, thus bringing the total membership of the Supreme Court to eight.[114] The additional three judges in 1995 were appointed to prepare for the transfer to the Supreme Court of the functions of the Court of Criminal Appeal, but this never occurred. In 2013, two additional judges were appointed to deal with a large backlog in

---

111 (\...contd) The concept of a court of record is of some antiquity. Originally, it referred to a royal court, with authority to impose fines and to imprison. It also was a court whose acts and proceedings were to be enrolled 'for perpetual memorial and testimony', the rolls thus being its permanent record. The authority of the monarch has been replaced by the authority conferred by Article 34 of the Constitution, but the concept of keeping records for perpetuity remains an important indication that a court has a permanent standing. The description of the Supreme Court and, we will see later, the High Court as 'superior' courts of record also reflects pre-1922 arrangements, where the Court of Appeal and High Court were the superior courts and the County Courts and Justices comprised the inferior courts: see paras **2.33** and **2.49**. It is notable also that the rules of court for the High Court and Supreme Court are titled the Rules of the Superior Courts 1986 (SI 15/1986).

112 The title in the Irish language is An Príomh-Breitheamh.

113 The Supreme Court established by the Courts of Justice Act 1924, s 5 comprised three judges, the Chief Justice and two ordinary judges. This reflected the composition of the Court of Appeal of Southern Ireland which it had replaced: see para **2.110**. The number of judges was increased to five by the Courts of Justice Act 1936, s 4. The Courts (Establishment and Constitution) Act 1961, s 1(2) provided that the Court comprised the Chief Justice and 'not ... less than four' ordinary judges. Section 1(2) of the 1961 Act was amended by the Courts and Court Officers Act 1995, s 6(1). The Courts (Supplemental Provisions) Act 1961, s 4(1) provided that the number of ordinary judges of the Court 'shall be four'. Section 4(1) was repealed by the Courts and Court Officers Act 1995, First Sch. Arts 12 and 26 of the Constitution and the Courts (Supplemental Provisions) Act 1961, s 7(5) (as amended by the Courts and Court Officers Act 1995, s 7) require that the Court comprise at least five judges in cases having a constitutional dimension (as to which see para **4.54**).

114 Courts (Establishment and Constitution) Act 1961, s 1(2) as amended by the Courts and Court Officers Act 1995, s 6(1), which increased the number of judges to eight (the Chief Justice and not more than seven ordinary judges), and by the Courts and Civil Law (Miscellaneous Provisions) Act 2013, s 22, which increased the number of judges to 10 (the Chief Justice and not more than nine ordinary judges). Note also that the Law Reform Commission Act 1975, s 14(1)(a)(i) as originally enacted, provided that, where a judge of the Supreme Court was appointed President of the Law Reform Commission, the number of ordinary judges of the Supreme Court would be five. From 1975 to 1985, Walsh J, at that time a Supreme Court judge, was the President of the Law Reform Commission and so the number of ordinary Supreme Court judges for that time was five. On the appointment of a High Court judge as President of the Law Reform Commission in 1986 (see para **11.13**) the Court continued to comprise six judges in all. In 1988, Henchy J resigned to take up the position of Chairman of the Independent Radio and Television Commission, established by the Radio and Television Act 1988. After that, the Supreme Court reverted to the 'normal' position of comprising five judges. The Law Reform Commission Act 1975, s 14(1) was amended by the Courts (No 2) Act 1997, s 3 (replacing the Courts and Court Officers Act 1995, s 6(2)) to take account of the increase in ordinary Supreme Court judges from four to seven. (contd.../)

Supreme Court appeals,[115] with the stated intention that when this backlog was reduced the number of judges would revert to eight and that a further backlog would be unlikely because of the envisaged establishment of the Court of Appeal in 2014.[116] The President of the Court of Appeal and the President of the High Court are also *ex officio* members of the Supreme Court.[117] The Chief Justice, as well as being the presiding judge, is responsible for the general organisation of the court's work.[118] Each ordinary judge is formally styled or titled 'Judge of the Supreme Court'.[119] In the event of the illness of a judge of the Supreme Court or where, for any other reason, a sufficient number of Supreme Court judges is not available to transact the court's business, the Chief Justice may request a High Court judge to sit as an additional judge of the Supreme Court.[120] A similar arrangement for judges of the Court of Appeal is provided for in the Court of Appeal Act 2014.

[4.54] In cases having what might be described as a constitutional connection, the Supreme Court sits as a five-judge or seven-judge court.[121] Articles 12 and 26 of the

114 (\...contd) Thus, in 2005 when McGuinness J was appointed President of the Law Reform Commission, the number of ordinary Supreme Court judges increased to eight (plus the Chief Justice). Similar provision was made in s 5(6) of the Human Rights Commission Act 2000 if a judge was appointed President of the Irish Human Rights Commission, but no comparable provision was included in the Irish Human Rights and Equality Commission Act 2014, which provided for the merger of the Irish Human Rights Commission and the Equality Authority into the Irish Human Rights and Equality Commission.

115 Courts (Establishment and Constitution) Act 1961, s 1(2) as amended by the Courts and Civil Law (Miscellaneous Provisions) Act 2013, s 22, which increased the number of judges to 10 (the Chief Justice and not more than nine ordinary judges).

116 On the Court of Appeal see para **4.34**ff, above, and immediately below.

117 Courts (Establishment and Constitution) Act 1961, s 1(3). See also the Courts of Justice Act 1924, s 6, and Court of Appeal Act 2014.

118 Courts and Court Officers Act 1995, s 8 modifying the Courts Act 1981, s 18(1)(a). Section 8 of the 1995 Act appears to be the first statutory recognition that the Chief Justice is responsible for the general organisation of the Court's work, though in practice this had always been the case.

119 The title in the Irish language is Breitheamh den Chúirt Uachtarach: the Courts (Establishment and Constitution) Act 1961, s 1(2) (as amended by the Courts and Court Officers Act 1995, s 6(1)).

120 Courts (Establishment and Constitution) Act 1961, s 1(4), replacing the Courts of Justice Act 1924, s 7. See, for example, *Tormey v Ireland* [1985] IR 289 (Barrington and Carroll JJ), *Duffy v News Group Newspapers Ltd* [1992] 2 IR 369 (Costello J) and *Kenny v Trinity College Dublin* [2008] 2 IR 40.

121 In 2001, the court sat for the first time as a seven-judge court, in *Sinnott v Minister for Education* [2001] 2 IR 545; see (2001) *The Irish Times*, 28 March. It also sat as a seven-judge court in *TD v Minister for Education* [2001] 4 IR 259 which concerned the failure by the state to provide appropriate residential facilities for the applicants who were troubled youths, *Maguire v Ardagh* [2002] 1 IR 385 which was concerned with the constitutionality of the Oireachtas Committee set up to investigate the fatal shooting of John McCarthy at Abbeylara, Co Laois by members of the An Garda Síochána, and (contd.../)

Constitution require that when the court performs its functions under those provisions,[122] the court must consist of not less than five judges. In addition, the relevant legislative provisions in place between 1961 and 1995 provided that the court also comprised five judges in cases involving the validity of any law having regard to the Constitution, but that, in any other case the Chief Justice, or in his or her absence the senior ordinary judge of the time being available, could direct that the court comprise three judges only.[123]

Simultaneous sittings in divisions

[4.55] Until 1995, the Supreme Court sat either in plenary session as a five-judge court or as a three-judge court, but never in divisions of three judges simultaneously. However, the Courts and Court Officers Act 1995 provided for the first time that the Supreme Court 'may sit in two or more divisions and they may sit at the same time'.[124] The 1995 Act affirmed the existing arrangement that the Court must comprise five judges in cases involving the validity of any law having regard to the Constitution,[125] but it amended the prior legislative arrangements for three-judge courts to read that, in any other case the

---

121 (\...contd) *Curtin v Clerk of Dáil Éireann* [2006] IESC 14, [2006] 2 IR 556, [2006] 2 ILRM 99 which was concerned with the constitutionality of the process put in place by the Oireachtas to facilitate the investigation of a Circuit Court judge prior to his possible impeachment by both Houses of the Oireachtas. *Dellaway Investments Ltd v National Asset Management Agency* [2011] 4 IR 1 considered the constitutionality of certain provisions of the National Asset Management Agency Act 2009. In *Pringle v Ireland* [2012] IESC 1 the Supreme Court rejected a claim that the EU Stability Mechanism Treaty involved a transfer of sovereignty to a degree that made it incompatible with the Constitution. In *Fleming v Ireland* [2013] IESC 19, the Supreme Court rejected a challenge to the ban on assisted suicide in s 2(2) of the Criminal Law (Suicide) Act 1993: see para **15.193**ff.

122 See fn 113.

123 See the Courts (Supplemental Provisions) Act 1961, s 7(3) and (4) (since amended by the Courts and Court Officers Act 1995, s 7, to provide for sittings of the court in divisions of three or five judges). The original provisions of the 1961 Act were discussed in *The State (Williams) v Kelly* [1970] IR 259 and *Peilow v ffrench O'Carroll* (1971) 105 ILTR 21. In the latter case, a Supreme Court judge had died before judgment was delivered and the Chief Justice directed that a re-hearing of the matter be heard by a three-judge Court.

124 Courts (Supplemental Provisions) Act 1961, s 7(3), as inserted by Courts and Court Officers Act 1995, s 7. Until the change effected by the 1995 Act, the physical location of the Supreme Court was a single courtroom in the Four Courts building, Dublin, which was almost exclusively set aside for the court. With the coming into force of the 1995 Act, there was a need for the first time to provide extra courtroom accommodation for simultaneous sittings of the Court.

125 Courts (Supplemental Provisions) Act 1961, s 7(5), as inserted by Courts and Court Officers Act 1995, s 7. As to whether it is constitutionally permissible for the court to sit as a five-judge court to deal with the constitutional validity of laws, to the possible exclusion of the remaining three judges provided for by the 1995 Act, see the doubts expressed in Kelleher, 'The Courts and Court Officers Act 1995 – the Main Provisions' (1996) 14 ILT 18. In 2001, the Court sat for the first time as a seven-judge court, in *Sinnott v Minister for Education* [2001] 2 IR 545: see (2001) *The Irish Times*, 28 March and fn 121 above.

Chief Justice (or in his or her absence the senior available ordinary judge) may direct that the court will comprise a division of five or three judges only.[126]

[4.56] This significant innovation allowing the Supreme Court to sit in divisions was intended to deal with two matters. First, it was aimed at relieving the increasing backlog of appeals to the Supreme Court. In 1996, the average delay in such appeals was between two and three years.[127] Second, it was introduced with a view to transferring to the Supreme Court the functions of the Court of Criminal Appeal. The combination of these two measures replaced an earlier proposal to retain the Court of Criminal Appeal and to create a Civil Court of Appeal which would have heard, for example, personal injuries appeals from the High Court, which comprised many of the appeals to the Supreme Court.[128] The provision that eventually materialised in the Courts and Court Officers Act 1995, namely, to combine the functions of the existing Court of Criminal Appeal with the suggested Civil Court of Appeal and to incorporate both within the jurisdiction of the Supreme Court, resulted from consultation between the government and the senior judiciary.[129] The amalgamation of the Court of Criminal Appeal and the Supreme Court did not, ultimately, proceed. Instead, the Court of Appeal has been established whose functions incorporate those of the Court of Criminal Appeal as well as having jurisdiction in civil matters.[130]

Collegiate court

[4.57] An important feature of the Supreme Court is that it is a collegiate court, in other words it always consists of a number of judges, not just one. From this point of view it is

---

126   Courts (Supplemental Provisions) Act 1961, s 7(4), as inserted by Courts and Court Officers Act 1995, s 7. The Courts and Court Officers Act 1995, s 7 re-numbered the Courts (Supplemental Provisions) Act 1961, s 7(3) and (4) as s 7(4) and (5) (with the consequential changes concerning five-judge and three-judge court as noted in the text) and also inserted a new s 7(3) which introduced the innovation that the Court may sit in two or more divisions which may sit at the same time.

127   *First Report of the Working Group on a Courts Commission* (Pn 2690, 1996), p 37. See further para **4.209**. At the time of the introduction of the referendum to establish the Court of Appeal (March 2013), it was reported that delays in appeals before the Supreme Court achieving hearing dates were approximately four and a half years: see (2013) *Irish Independent*, 3 March.

128   The proposal to create a Civil Court of Appeal was contained in the Courts and Court Officers Bill 1994, whose origins are discussed at para **4.96**. While this aspect of the 1994 Bill was not proceeded with, the bulk of its other provisions became the substance of the Courts and Court Officers Act 1995. As already noted, a constitutional referendum to establish a Court of Appeal, with jurisdiction in criminal and civil matters, was passed in 2013: see para **4.34**ff, above.

129   See 458 *Dáil Debates* c 1756. The changes effected in the 1995 Act had also been recommended in 1966 in the *7th Interim Report of the Committee on Court Practice and Procedure*.

130   On the Court of Appeal see para **4.34**ff, above, and immediately below.

different from most of the other courts discussed below.[131] Being a collegiate court presents two points of note which we discuss here briefly.

[4.58] First, as there is a common law convention that each judge on a collegiate court is entitled to express a view on the legal issues arising in a case, this means that in a court with five judges, a case may be decided by the views of three of the judges sitting. This has implications for the doctrine of precedent, and we discuss this elsewhere.[132]

[4.59] Second, as a collegiate body, how the judges of the Supreme Court arrange their workload, and in particular to what extent they exchange views after the hearing of a case but before their decision is announced in open court, must differ from the situation that applies where a case is dealt with by a lone judge. Very little has been published about this aspect of the court's work. What is known is that the judges of the Supreme Court meet in conference to discuss cases after they have been argued in court. The discussions at these conferences remain confidential, but it is clear from reading judgments delivered in the Supreme Court that drafts are circulated between the judges prior to the date when they are delivered in open court.[133]

Court of Appeal

[4.60] As already noted,[134] a constitutional referendum to establish a Court of Appeal, with jurisdiction in both criminal and civil matters, was passed in 2013 by the Thirty-Third Amendment of the Constitution (Court of Appeal) Act 2013. This implemented recommendations made in the 2009 *Report of the Working Group on a Court of Appeal*.[135] The Court of Appeal Act 2014 provides for the establishment of the Court of Appeal in accordance with Article 34A of the Constitution, inserted by the Thirty-Third Amendment of the Constitution (Court of Appeal) Act 2013.[136] At the time of writing (September 2014) it is envisaged that the Court of Appeal will be formally established by the end of 2014.[137] The Court of Appeal Act 2014 provides that the Court comprises 10 judges, the President of the Court of Appeal and 9 ordinary judges. The 2014 Act

---

[131] In some instances, the High Court comprises a three-judge Divisional Court, though this is the exception rather than the rule: see para **4.62**. The Special Criminal Court (para **5.110**) and Court of Criminal Appeal (para **7.41** (and the Court of Appeal when it is established, expected in 2014)) are also collegiate courts, but their decisions are announced by one member of the court only.

[132] See para **12.104**.

[133] See, eg, the judgment of McCarthy J in *Norris v Attorney General* [1984] IR 36 where he quotes extracts from the other judgments which had just been delivered. This clearly required advance circulation of the judgments between the judges.

[134] See para **4.34***ff*, above.

[135] Prn A8/0153, available at www.courts.ie.

[136] For the text of Article 34A see fn 74, above.

[137] Article 64.3.1° of the Constitution, also inserted by the Thirty-Third Amendment of the Constitution (Court of Appeal) Act 2013, provides that after the Court of Appeal has been established, the Chief Justice may direct that appeals pending in the Supreme Court at that time may be transferred to the Court of Appeal for decision.

also provides that the Court may sit in divisions of three judges each. During the Oireachtas debates on the 2014 Act it was indicated that two of these divisions would, at least initially, deal with civil appeals and that the other division would deal with criminal appeals. This reflects the reality of a large backlog of civil appeals in the Supreme Court, which was a key reason for the establishment of the Court of Appeal. Another important rationale was that by having in place a permanently constituted court to deal with criminal appeals, this could lead to a more consistent pattern of decision-making in criminal law matters, including sentencing, by comparison with the somewhat ad hoc nature of the composition of the Court of Criminal Appeal, which since its establishment in 1924 was composed of a judge of the Supreme Court and two judges of the High Court selected on a rotating basis from time to time.[138] The first President of the Court of Appeal is Mr Justice Seán Ryan, a senior High Court judge at the time of his appointment. Six other judges of the Court of Appeal were nominated from the existing judges of the High Court. At the time of writing (September 2014), the remaining three judicial positions in the Court (which comprises 10 judges in total) have not yet been filled.

High Court

[4.61] The High Court established in 1961 under Article 34 of the Constitution[139] is a superior court of record.[140] The Court comprises the President of the High Court[141] and such number of ordinary judges as may from time to time be fixed by Act of the Oireachtas.[142] The number of ordinary judges fixed in 1961 was not more than six[143] but since then this has been increased by a number of Acts[144] to be not more than 36.[145] The President of the High Court, as well as being the second most senior judge in the state,[146]

---

138   See the 2009 *Report of the Working Group on a Court of Appeal* Prn A8/0153, available at www.courts.ie.
139   Courts (Establishment and Constitution) Act 1961, s 2(1) formally established the High Court envisaged by Article 34 of the Constitution, replacing the Courts of Justice Act 1924, s 4.
140   Courts (Supplemental Provisions) Act 1961, s 8(1) replacing the Courts of Justice Act 1924, s 17, which had established the former High Court. On the concept of a court of record, see fn 111 above.
141   The title in the Irish language is Uachtarán na hArd-Chúirte.
142   Courts (Establishment and Constitution) Act 1961, s 2(2).
143   Courts (Supplemental Provisions) Act 1961, s 4(2). The High Court established by the Courts of Justice Act 1924, s 4 had comprised the President of the High Court and five ordinary judges and this was increased by one by the Courts of Justice Act 1953, s 11.
144   For the various increases between 1961 and 1997, see Delany, *The Courts Act 1924–1997* (2nd edn, 2000).
145   The Courts and Court Officers Act 1995, s 9 as amended by the Courts and Court Officers Act 2007, s 2. Note also that the Law Reform Commission Act 1975, s 14(1), as amended by the Courts (No 2) Act 1997, s 3, provides that, where a judge of the High Court is appointed President of the Law Reform Commission, the maximum number of ordinary judges of the High Court may be increased by one.
146   See para **4.51**.

is responsible for the general organisation of the High Court's work.[147] Each ordinary judge is formally styled or titled 'Judge of the High Court'.[148] The Chief Justice and the President of the Circuit Court are both *ex officio* additional judges of the High Court.[149] In the event of the illness of a judge of the High Court or where, for any other reason, a sufficient number of High Court judges is not available to transact the court's business, the Chief Justice, at the request of the President of the High Court, may request a Supreme Court judge to sit as an additional judge of the High Court.[150]

[4.62] Unlike the position that obtained prior to 1922, there are no formal separate divisions of the High Court, though administratively certain cases are in practice referred to particular judges.[151] The Commercial Court constitutes a form of the old division, on an administrative basis, of the business of the High Court.[152] Each High Court judge is empowered to hear and determine any case whether civil or criminal, in equity or at common law.[153] Under s 94 of the Courts of Justice Act 1924, a litigant in a High Court civil action was entitled to have the case determined by a judge and jury. This was extended to personal injuries actions arising from road traffic and work-related accidents. However, as a result of criticisms of the allegedly high levels of awards by juries in such cases,[154] s 1 of the Courts Act 1988 provided that personal injuries actions be heard by a High Court judge alone.[155] Juries in High Court civil actions are thus now confined to defamation cases and much less common actions such as assault, false imprisonment and malicious prosecution. In effect, therefore, in many civil actions 'the High Court' means 'a judge of the High Court'. We have already seen that, where the High Court hears major criminal matters, the Constitution requires that the court comprise a judge and jury.[156] In some instances, the President of the High Court may direct that a panel of two or more judges (usually three judges) shall sit to hear certain

---

147   Courts (Supplemental Provisions) Act 1961, s 10(3).
148   The title in the Irish language is Breitheamh den Ard-Chúirt: Courts (Establishment and Constitution) Act 1961, s 2(2).
149   Courts (Establishment and Constitution) Act 1961, s 2(3) and (4), replacing the Courts of Justice Act 1924, s 6 and the Courts of Justice (District Court) Act 1946, s 9.
150   Courts (Establishment and Constitution) Act 1961, s 2(5), replacing the Courts of Justice Act 1936, s 5. For an example, see *Cowan v Freaghaile* [1991] 1 IR 389 (O'Flaherty J).
151   On the divisions prior to 1922, see para **2.34**ff. On the administrative arrangements for chancery matters, see para **5.79**, and on the introduction of a Commercial Court in the High Court, see para **5.78**.
152   The Rules of the Superior Courts 1986, Ord 63A as inserted by the Rules of the Superior Courts (Commercial Proceedings) 2004 (SI 4/2004) which establishes the Commercial Court of the High Court.
153   Courts of Justice Act 1924, s 24.
154   See para **5.13**.
155   For criticism of the removal of juries in High Court personal injuries actions, see Kerr, *Annotation to the Courts Act 1988*, *Irish Current Law Statutes Annotated* (1988).
156   See para **4.45**. On juries see further para **6.142**.

cases. In this situation the panel of judges is known as a Divisional High Court, which reflects the pre-1922 concept of High Court Divisions.[157]

[4.63] The High Court ordinarily sits in Dublin,[158] but on a number of occasions each year, High Court judges (as well as such Supreme Court judges as may be assigned) sit in various venues around the country to hear appeals from the Circuit Court and also to determine cases at first instance. This is known as the High Court on Circuit which, until 2011,[159] involved twice-yearly Circuit appeals which could be traced to the *Nisi Prius* hearings which originated in the Anglo–Norman period.[160] In addition, the High Court has begun to sit in provincial locations to hear personal injuries, non-jury and criminal actions throughout the legal year.[161] This is due to the increase in number of High Court judges available to hear matters and also to clear backlogs of cases.

Research assistants/clerks

[4.64] One other aspect of the arrangements in the High Court and Supreme Court is worthy of note. Prior to 1993, the judges of the High Court and Supreme Court were entirely dependent on counsel to ensure that all aspects of a case had been dealt with at

---

[157] Article 40.4.4° of the Constitution provides that the President of the High Court may order a panel of three judges to sit in cases of inquiries into the validity of a person's detention in custody: see for example *The State (Murray) v McRann* [1979] IR 133. The Courts (Supplemental Provisions) Act 1961, s 11(2)(b) provides that the President may direct that two or more judges sit for the purposes of a criminal trial in the Central Criminal Court. It would appear, however, that no such Divisional Court has been convened for a criminal trial since 1961. Order 49, r 1 of the Rules of the Superior Courts 1986 (SI 15/1986) also provides that the President may order that two or more judges (usually three) sit to hear any civil case. Divisional Courts were convened for *Crotty v An Taoiseach* [1987] IR 713 (see para **16.106**), *The State (Walshe) v Murphy* [1981] IR 275 (see para **4.82**), *Hanafin v Minister for the Environment* [1996] 2 IR 321 (see para **15.114**), *Director of Public Prosecutions v Haugh* [2000] 1 IR 184 (see para **6.150**), *Maguire v Ardagh* [2002] 1 IR 385 (High Court), *Mahon v Keena and Kennedy* [2007] IEHC 348; *Dellaway Investments Ltd v National Asset Management Agency* [2011] 4 IR 1 and *Fleming v Ireland* [2013] IEHC 2.

[158] Virtually all sittings of the High Court that deal with civil cases take place in the Four Courts Building, Dublin, but on occasion other premises in Dublin, such as those of the Honorable Society of King's Inns or of the Law Society of Ireland, have accommodated such sittings. Since the opening in 2010 of the purpose-built Criminal Courts of Justice complex in Parkgate Street, Dublin, virtually all sittings of the Central Criminal Court (the High Court) and indeed of the Dublin Circuit Criminal Court have taken place in that complex.

[159] See the Court of Justice Act 1936, ss 34 and 35, which until 2011 required twice-yearly High Court appeals from the Circuit Court. As amended by s 64 of the Civil Law (Miscellaneous Provisions) Act 2011, ss 34 and 35 of the 1936 Act provide that such sittings take place not less than once a year. This was intended to ensure that such sittings would only occur where the number of appeals justified them, and also implemented a recommendation to this effect in the Law Reform Commission's *Report on the Consolidation and Reform of the Courts Acts* (LRC 97-2010), para 2.125.

[160] See para **2.06**.

[161] See www.courts.ie.

the hearing in court.[162] Once this had been completed, the judges were largely alone in their endeavours to research the legal issues arising. However, since 1993, the High Court and Supreme Court have had available the services of a number of judicial researchers to assist them in legal research generally and the difficult task of preparing their judgments.[163] This arrangement is based on the system that applies for those law graduates in the United States who 'clerk' for senior members of the judiciary, or for the equivalent *réfendaires* to judges of the EU Court of Justice, both of whom actively assist their judges in the preparation of judgments.[164] Thus, the advent of legal research assistants in the Irish courts (by 2000, there were 11) is a significant development.[165] In 2008, judicial assistants, known as judicial fellows, were appointed to assist High Court judges. In general, each judicial fellow is assigned to a particular area of court business: chancery, asylum, commercial and competition and work alongside an individual judge. Their role is to assist the judge to whom they are assigned with his or her judgments and workload. To this end, they sit in court for the duration of cases over which the judge to which they are assigned is presiding. They then prepare a draft summary of relevant facts and law and the submissions of parties for inclusion in the first draft of a judgment, along with further research if required.[166] The introduction of judicial fellows was aimed at shortening delays in the delivery of reserved judgments in the High Court. Following the 2009 Report of the Special Group on Public Service Numbers and Expenditure Programmes (also known as An Bord Snip Nua), and the subsequent enactment of the Financial Measures in the Public Interest (Amendment) Act 2011, new appointees as judges of the Supreme Court, High Court and Circuit Court are no longer entitled to the services of an individual usher or crier, but rather are provided with the services of a Judicial Assistant drawn from a panel of such persons on an "as required" basis.

---

[162] It had been the practice for many years in constitutional cases for counsel to be requested to submit detailed written submissions of the arguments to be addressed to the Supreme Court: see Collins and O'Reilly, *Civil Proceedings and the State in Ireland* (2004), p 248.This practice has now been extended to any civil proceedings in the High Court and Supreme Court where substantial legal issues arise and in all judicial review applications: *Practice Direction: Pre-trial Written Submissions on Legal Issues*, November 1993, cited in [2001] 3(1) *Practice and Procedure* 22. See also Practice Direction on Written Submissions lodged in the office of the Supreme Court SC05, Practice Direction on Appeals and Cases Stated in the Supreme Court SC13, available at www.courts.ie.

[163] This had been recommended in the *11th Interim Report of the Committee on Court Practice and Procedure* (1970).

[164] See para **16.174**.

[165] For a summary of the current role of the legal research assistants and their future role within a Judicial Council, see *Report of the Committee on Judicial Conduct and Ethics* (Pn 9449, 2000) discussed further in para **4.140**. See also Coonon, 'The Role of Judicial Research Assistants in Supporting the Decision Making Role of the Irish Judiciary' [2006] 6(1) *Judicial Studies Institute Journal* 171.

[166] See (2007) *The Irish Times*, 10 December and (2008) *The Irish Times*, 3 March.

Circuit Court

[4.65] The Circuit Court established in 1961 pursuant to Article 34 of the Constitution[167] is a court of record.[168] The court comprises the President of the Circuit Court[169] and such number of ordinary judges as may from time to time be fixed by Act of the Oireachtas.[170]

The number of ordinary judges fixed in 1961 was not more than eight[171] but since then this has been increased by a number of Acts to be not more than 37.[172] Since 1995, the President of the District Court is an *ex officio* member of the Circuit Court.[173] In addition, in the event of the temporary absence from duty for any cause of a judge of the Circuit Court or where, for any other reason, the business of the Circuit Court may fall into arrears, the government is empowered to appoint persons to act as 'temporary' Circuit Court judges, over and above the maximum provided for at the time.[174] Each ordinary judge is formally styled or titled 'Judge of the Circuit Court'.[175] In general, a Circuit Court judge sits alone to hear cases, except in those cases where the court hears serious criminal cases when a jury trial is required.[176] In 2013, six Specialist Judges of the Circuit Court were appointed pursuant to the Personal Insolvency Act 2012 to deal with insolvency applications. These six Specialist Judges were previously serving County Registrars. The 2012 Act restricted applications for the positions to serving County Registrars.

[4.66] The Circuit Court is organised on a regional basis, with the state currently divided into eight Circuits, namely the Cork, Dublin, Eastern, Midland, Northern, South East,

---

167   Courts (Establishment and Constitution) Act 1961, s 4(1) formally established the Circuit Court as a Court of First Instance envisaged by Article 34 of the Constitution, replacing the Circuit Court established by the Courts of Justice Act 1924, s 37.

168   Courts (Supplemental Provisions) Act 1961, s 21, replacing the Courts of Justice Act 1924, s 47. On the concept of a court of record, see fn 111 above.

169   The title in the Irish language is Uachtarán na Chúirte Chuarda.

170   Courts (Establishment and Constitution) Act 1961, s 4(2).

171   Courts (Supplemental Provisions) Act 1961, s 16. The Circuit Court established by the Courts of Justice Act 1924, s 37 comprised eight judges in all, the office of President being created by the Courts of Justice Act 1947, s 9 in relation to the 'former' Circuit Court and s 14 of the 1947 Act also providing for an additional ordinary judge. The Courts of Justice Act 1953, s 18 provided for another judge, bringing the total to the number that obtained in 1961.

172   The Courts and Court Officers Act 1995, s 10 as amended by Courts and Court Officers Act 2007, s 3.

173   Courts and Court Officers Act 1995, s 33.

174   Courts of Justice Act 1936, s 14, replacing the Courts of Justice Act 1924, s 46. On the constitutionality of the similar power in respect of 'temporary' District Court judges, see n 172 below. In recent years, this power has not been exercised.

175   The title in the Irish language is Breitheamh den Chúirt Chuarda: Courts (Establishment and Constitution) Act 1961, s 4(2).

176   See para **5.101**. The Courts Act 1971, s 6 abolished the right to a jury in the trial of a civil action in the Circuit Court, thus effectively rendering otiose the elements of the Courts of Justice Act 1924, s 94 in so far as they concerned civil actions in the Circuit Court.

South West and Western Circuits.[177] At least 10 judges, including the President of the Circuit Court, are permanently assigned by the government to the Dublin Circuit, at least three to the Cork Circuit and the remaining Circuits are assigned one judge each.[178] Where practicable, a person assigned as a judge to a Circuit where the Irish language is in general use should possess enough knowledge of the language to enable proceedings to be conducted without the aid of an interpreter.[179] Each Circuit outside Dublin incorporates a number of towns in which the Circuit Court judge sits on dates specified in advance on a yearly basis.[180]

[4.67] While the government determines the number and size of Circuits and the assignment of judges to those Circuits, the President of the Circuit Court is responsible for the general organisation of the Circuit Court's work, including the allocation of dates for the sittings of the court in the different Circuits.[181] Underlining the 'local' element of the Circuit Court, a Circuit Court judge may only exercise jurisdiction in the Circuit to which he or she is assigned.[182] This geographical limitation of the Circuit Court's jurisdiction in different areas is a feature shared with the District Court.

District Court

[4.68] The District Court established in 1961 under Article 34 of the Constitution[183] is a court of record.[184] The court comprises the President of the District Court[185] and such number of other judges as may from time to time be fixed by Act of the Oireachtas.[186] The number of other judges fixed in 1961 was not more than 34[187] but since then this has

---

177 Courts of Justice Act 1953, s 16 carried forward by the Courts (Supplemental Provisions) Act 1961, s 20(1).

178 Courts Act 1977, s 2 as amended by Courts and Court Officers Act 1995, s 36.

179 Courts of Justice Act 1924, s 44. There is a similar requirement concerning judges of the District Court: see fn 194 below. On the Irish language generally, see paras **2.92–2.94**.

180 For a full list of the Circuits and the towns they serve, see the website of the Courts Service: www.courts.ie.

181 Courts of Justice Act 1947, s 10.

182 In civil matters, see the Courts (Establishment and Constitution) Act 1961, ss 22–24 and the Third Sch. In criminal matters, see s 25 of the 1961 Act.

183 Courts (Establishment and Constitution) Act 1961, s 5(1) formally established the District Court as a Court of First Instance envisaged by Article 34 of the Constitution, replacing the former District Court established by the Courts of Justice Act 1924, s 67.

184 Courts Act 1971, s 13. The former District Court established by the Courts of Justice Act 1924, s 67 had not been conferred with the title of a 'court of record', though s 13 of the 1971 Act would seem to have merely given effect to the existing *de facto* position: see Delany, *The Courts Act 1924–1997* (2nd edn, 2000). On the concept of a court of record, see fn 111 above.

185 The title in the Irish language is Uachtarán na Chúirte Dúiche.

186 Courts (Establishment and Constitution) Act 1961, s 5(2).

187 Courts (Supplemental Provisions) Act 1961, s 28. The District Court established by the Courts of Justice Act 1924, s 67 comprised not more than 33 Justices, there being no office of President of the District Court at that time.

been increased by a number of Acts to be not more than 63.[188] In addition, in the event of the temporary absence from duty for any cause of a judge of the District Court or where, for any other reason, the business of the District Court may fall into arrears, the government is empowered to appoint persons to act as 'temporary' judges of the District Court, over and above the maximum provided for at the time.[189] Each judge is formally styled or titled 'Judge of the District Court'.[190] In all cases, whether civil or criminal, a judge of the District Court sits alone.

[4.69] The District Court is, like the Circuit Court, organised on a regional basis, with the state currently divided into 24 District Court Districts, comprising the Dublin Metropolitan District and 23 other Districts.[191] The President of the District Court must be assigned by the government to the Dublin Metropolitan District.[192] A number of the other District Court judges are permanently assigned to the Dublin and Cork Districts and the remaining District Court Districts are assigned one judge each.[193] Where practicable, a person assigned as a judge to a District where the Irish language is in general use should possess enough knowledge of the language to enable proceedings to

---

[188] Courts and Court Officers Act, s 11 as amended by the Civil Law (Miscellaneous Provisions) Act 2008, s 32.

[189] Courts of Justice Act 1936, s 51 replacing the Courts of Justice Act 1924, s 76. The constitutionality of this power, as carried over by the Courts (Supplemental Provisions) Act 1961, s 48 was upheld in *Magee v Culligan* [1992] 1 IR 223 on the ground that it was a valid regulation of the business of the courts under Article 36 of the Constitution: see para **4.42**. However, in recent years, the power has not been exercised.

[190] The title in the Irish language is Breitheamh den Chúirt Dúiche: the Courts (Establishment and Constitution) Act 1961, s 5(2)(b) as amended by the Courts Act 1991, s 21(1)(a). As originally enacted, s 5(2)(b) provided that the title of each judge was 'Justice of the District Court' but s 21 of the 1991 Act amended this to 'Judge of the District Court'. This was intended primarily to ensure that judges of the District Court were seen as no less judges than their counterparts in the other courts. The older term 'Justice' reflected the pre-1922 position where the Justice of the Peace (see para **2.53**) might not have the legal training now required of a District Court judge. The change effected by the 1991 Act only applied to the English language title, the Irish language style remaining 'Breitheamh den Chúirt Dúiche'.

[191] Courts of Justice Act 1953, s 21 carried forward by the Courts (Supplemental Provisions) Act 1961, s 32(1). These 23 districts outside Dublin are further divided into over 200 District Court Areas. In recent years there has been an ongoing review of district venues, sittings and business by the Courts Service. This has resulted in a number of changes to venues in districts.

[192] Courts (Supplemental Provisions) Act 1961, s 35(2)

[193] The arrangements for assigning judges of the District Court, contained primarily in the Courts (Supplemental Provisions) Act 1961, ss 39–42, and the Sixth Sch as amended by the Courts and Court Officers Act 1995, ss 11, 38 and 39 are less prescriptive than for the Circuit Court. By virtue of amendments to the Sixth Sch of the Courts (Supplemental Provisions) Act 1961 by the Civil Law (Miscellaneous Provisions) Act 2008, s 14, the President of the District Court is empowered to temporarily assign judges of the District Court for periods of up to six months to any district.

be conducted without the aid of an interpreter.[194] The government determines the number and size of District Court Districts and the assignment of judges to those Districts, and the President of the District Court is responsible for the general organisation of the District Court's work, including the allocation of dates for the sittings of the court in the different Districts.[195]

[4.70] Again, as with the Circuit Court, a judge of the District Court may only exercise jurisdiction in the District to which he or she is assigned.[196]

Mode of address and notation

[4.71] Brief mention will be made of the statutory requirements as to addressing a judge and the manner of noting a judge's name in written form. This is, to some extent, a companion to correct citation of names of cases and law reports.[197] The correct mode of address of a judge should, however, be regarded as somewhat more serious.[198]

Judges of the High Court and Supreme Court

[4.72] We have already seen that the Supreme Court comprises the Chief Justice, who is the president of the court, and ordinary judges, each ordinary judge being formally styled or titled Judge of the Supreme Court.[199] The Court of Appeal to be established in 2014 will comprise a President and nine ordinary judges, each ordinary judge being formally styled or titled Judge of the Court of Appeal. We have also seen that the High

---

[194] Courts of Justice Act 1924, s 71. There is a similar requirement concerning judges of the Circuit Court: see fn 179, above. Section 71 of the 1924 Act does not require proceedings in Irish speaking areas to be held in the Irish language, but substantial efforts must be made to facilitate a person who wishes to give evidence in the Irish language: see *Ó Monacháin v An Taoiseach* [1986] ILRM 660. On the Irish language generally, see paras **2.92–2.94**.

[195] Courts (Supplemental Provisions) Act 1961, s 36. In addition, the President is empowered to hold meetings with the other judges of the District Court, not more than twice yearly, concerning the discharge of the Court's business, including the avoidance of undue divergences in the exercise by the judges of the Court's jurisdiction and the general level of fines and other penalties. Each judge of the District Court must attend these meetings if convened, unless unable to do so owing to illness or other unavoidable cause. There is no equivalent for such judicial conferences in relation to the other courts, though such meetings are held on an informal basis. If a Judicial Council is established, such arrangements will be formalised: see *Report of the Committee on Judicial Conduct and Ethics* (Pn 9449, 2000) discussed further in para **4.140**.

[196] Courts of Justice Act 1924, s 79 as amended. For the various amendments and restrictions affecting s 79, see Delany, *The Courts Acts 1924–1997* (2nd edn, 2000). See *Creaven v DPP* [2004] 4 IR 434 and Criminal Justice Act 2006, s 180 which inserts a new s 32A into the Courts (Supplemental Provisions) Act 1961. See fn 85 above.

[197] See para **12.19**.

[198] For the correct notation to be used in correspondence, see the *Institute of Public Administration Directory*, published annually by the IPA.

[199] See para **4.53**.

Court comprises the President of the High Court and ordinary judges, each ordinary judge being formally styled or titled Judge of the High Court.[200]

[4.73] The modes of address for the judges of the High Court and Supreme Court are prescribed separately in rules of court.[201] The current rules of court[202] specify that the Chief Justice and the President of the High Court shall be addressed in Irish or English by their respective title and the other judges of the Superior Courts shall be addressed, in court, individually, in Irish, as 'A Bhreithimh' or, in English, as 'Judge'. In addition, judges of the Superior Courts may be referred to, in Irish, as 'An Chúirt' or, in English, as 'The Court.' In practice, when solicitors or counsel appear in the High Court or Supreme Court, they generally use one of two alternative modes of address. The first is 'The Court', the mode provided for in the current rules of court, as in the following: 'If the Court pleases, might I make the following application.'

[4.74] When writing a High Court or Supreme Court judge's name, the following is correct: 'Mr Justice Hardiman' or 'Hardiman J' (note that 'Hardiman J' reads as 'Mr Justice Hardiman' and not 'Hardiman Jay'). When addressing a High Court or Supreme Court judge directly, but not in court, the correct mode of address is: 'Judge Hardiman', but, perhaps confusingly, when introducing a judge the method is: 'Mr Justice Hardiman'. Thus, at a public meeting, the person who proposes a vote of thanks might say: 'I would like to thank on your behalf Mr Justice Hardiman for his presence this evening' and then turn to the judge and say to him directly 'Thank you Judge Hardiman'. Special notations exist for the Chief Justice and President of the High Court. 'The Chief Justice, Mrs Justice Denham' is usually noted as follows: 'Denham CJ', while 'the President of the High Court, Mr Justice Kearns' is usually noted thus: 'Kearns P'.

Judges of the Circuit Court

[4.75] We have already seen that the Circuit Court comprises the President of the Circuit Court and ordinary judges, each ordinary judge being formally styled or titled Judge of the Circuit Court.[203] As with the High Court and Supreme Court, the mode of address is

---

[200] See para **4.61**.

[201] Courts of Justice Act 1924, s 10. See also Rules of the Superior Courts (Mode of Address of Judges) 2006 (SI 196/2006).

[202] Order 119, r 1 of the Rules of the Superior Courts 1986 (SI 15/1986) as amended by the Rules of the Superior Courts (Mode of Address of Judges) 2006 (SI 196/2006). In the course of the Oireachtas debate on the Courts and Court Officers Act 1995, it was proposed that the use of the form of address 'My Lord' be abolished as no longer being appropriate. While there was general acceptance of this point, it was decided to retain the discretion concerning modes of address with the Superior Courts Rules Committee, as provided in the 1924 Act: see 459 *Dáil Debates* c 1219–22 (12 December 1995). However, the Oireachtas members appeared to be under the impression that these informal modes were actually provided for in the current 1986 Rules, whereas they are a matter of long-standing convention. The change to the rules as we have seen came in 2006.

[203] See para **4.65**.

prescribed separately in rules of court.[204] The current rules of court[205] specify that the mode of address for the President of the Circuit Court is by his title in Irish or English, while judges of the Circuit Court are addressed individually, in Irish, as 'A Bhreithimh' or, in English, as 'Judge'. The rules also provide that judges of the court may be referred to, in Irish, as 'An Chúirt' or, in English, as 'The Court'. Previously, a judge of the Circuit Court was referred to as 'A Thiarna Bhreithimh' or 'My Lord'.[206] The written notation for the President of the Circuit Court, as an *ex officio* judge of the High Court, is 'the President of the Circuit Court, Mr Justice Groarke, or 'Groarke J'. When addressing any other judge of the Circuit Court in direct conversation outside of court, the correct form of address is 'Judge McCartan'. A similar notation is used in the written form.

Judges of the District Court

[4.76] We have already seen that the District Court comprises the President of the District Court and other judges, and that each judge is formally styled or titled Judge of the District Court.[207] The President of the District Court may be referred to thus 'the President of the District Court, Judge Horgan'. The mode of address provided for in the current rules of court is 'A Bhreithimh' or 'Judge'.[208] Both inside and outside court, therefore, the correct mode of address is 'Judge'.

[5] APPOINTMENT AND QUALIFICATIONS

[4.77] Article 35.1 of the Constitution provides:

"The judges of the Supreme Court, the Court of Appeal,[209] the High Court and all other Courts established in pursuance of Article 34 hereof shall be appointed by the President."

While the formal appointment of judges is made by the President through the presentation of seals of office to those appointed, this power is, by virtue of Article 13.9, exercised 'only on the advice of the Government', so that, in fact the real power of appointment rests with the government.

Formal qualifications

[4.78] The Courts of Justice Act 1924 had set out various minimum qualifications for appointment as judges and these were, in large part, repeated in the Courts (Supplemental Provisions) Act 1961 for the courts established by the Courts

---

204 Courts of Justice Act 1924, s 38.
205 Order 3, r 2 of the Circuit Court Rules 2001 as amended by Circuit Court Rules (Mode of Address of Judges) 2006 (SI 274/2006).
206 Order 3, r 2 of the Rules of the Circuit Court 1950 (SI 179/1950).
207 See para **4.68**.
208 Order 4 of the District Court Rules 1997 (SI 93/1997).
209 The reference to the Court of Appeal was added by the Thirty-Third Amendment of the Constitution (Court of Appeal) Act 2013, which provided for the establishment of the Court of Appeal and which was approved by a referendum held in 2013.

(Establishment and Constitution) Act 1961. Although the Constitution does not expressly deal with qualifications, it has been held that the criteria set out in the Courts (Supplemental Provisions) Act 1961 are within the contemplation of Article 36.iii, which provides that the 'constitution' of the courts shall be regulated in accordance with law.[210] The formal qualifications vary according to the Court to which a person is to be appointed. At the time of writing (September 2014), the Department of Justice is engaged in a review of the judicial appointments process.[211]

[4.79] Beginning with the District Court, s 29(2) of the Courts (Supplemental Provisions) Act 1961 provides that a person 'who is for the time being a practising barrister or solicitor of not less than ten years' standing' is qualified for appointment as a judge of the District Court.[212] A similar requirement applies to the appointment of persons as judges of the District Court on a temporary basis.[213]

[4.80] In relation to the other courts, until 1996 only members of the Bar had been qualified for appointment. Thus, s 17(2) of the Courts (Supplemental Provisions) Act 1961 as originally enacted provided that only a practising barrister of at least ten years' standing was qualified to be appointed as a judge of the Circuit Court, with a similar requirement applying to the appointment of persons as judges of the Circuit Court on a temporary basis.[214] And s 5(2) of the 1961 Act provided that only a person who is for the time being a practising barrister of 12 years' standing may be appointed as a judge of the High Court or Supreme Court.[215] From this it is clear that only practising barristers of the relevant years standing were qualified to be appointed to the Circuit, High or Supreme Courts. To that extent, therefore, all the important judgments which had developed the law until 1996 were written by judges who had been practising barristers prior to their appointment.

[4.81] For many years, solicitors had pressed for an amendment to the Courts (Supplemental Provisions) Act 1961 so that they could be qualified for appointment to the Circuit Court as well as the High Court and Supreme Court.[216] Ultimately, a

---

210   See *The State (Walshe) v Murphy* [1981] IR 275.

211   In January 2014, the judiciary (the Judicial Appointments Review Committee) made a preliminary submission to the Department as part of the public consultation on the review of the judicial appointments process, available at www.supremecourt.ie: see para **4.112**. Both the Law Society and the Bar Council also made submissions. For further observations on the current judicial appointment procedure see Department of Justice, 'Towards Gender Parity in Decision-Making' (2013), ch 8.

212   This replaced Courts of Justice Act 1924, s 69 which had required six years' standing only.

213   Courts of Justice Act 1936, s 51(1).

214   Courts of Justice Act 1936, s 14(1).

215   Replicating the Courts of Justice Act 1924, s 16 though the 1924 Act provided that holders of certain pre-1924 judicial offices were qualified for appointment to the new courts.

216   See the Fair Trade Commission's *Report of Study into Restrictive Practices in the Legal Profession* (1990), pp 296–9. To a large extent, the broad recommendations in the 1990 Report were implemented in the 1995 Act. On the 1990 Report generally, see para **3.05**.

significant change was effected in the Courts and Court Officers Act 1995. Section 30 of the 1995 Act amended s 17(2) of the 1961 Act by providing that, in addition to a practising barrister of ten years' standing, a practising solicitor of ten years' standing is qualified for appointment as a judge of the Circuit Court.[217] As to appointment to the High Court and Supreme Court, s 28 provides that a judge of the Circuit Court of two years' standing is qualified for appointment as a judge of the High Court or Supreme Court. Since 2002, solicitors have been eligible for appointment to the High Court and Supreme Court.[218] In July 2002, the first ever solicitor was appointed to the High Court, Mr Justice Michael Peart. The number of practising solicitors who have been appointed to the High Court is considerably lower than practising barristers and this has been highlighted by the Law Society. It has been argued that the requirement in s 8 of the 2002 Act that the potential appointee must have appropriate experience of superior court practice and procedure could reduce the number of solicitors eligible for appointment.[219] The Courts and Court Officers Act 1995 also effected a significant amendment by providing that service as a judge of the EU Court of Justice, as a judge of the EU General Court (previously called the Court of First Instance) or as an Advocate-General of the EU Court of Justice are to be deemed practice at the Bar for the purposes of appointment.[220]

---

[217] The first appointments of solicitors to the Circuit Court were made in July 1996.

[218] Courts and Court Officers Act 2002, s 4. See also Carroll, 'The right stuff' (2007) 101(7) *Law Society Gazette* 32. The 2002 Act gave effect to the recommendations contained in the *Report of the Working Group on Qualifications for Appointment as Judges of the High Court and Supreme Court* (1999). The Report rejected the possibility that barristers or solicitors who were not engaged in practice, such as members of the academic community with such qualifications, could be appointed as judges. The Report concluded that only those engaged in practice would have the necessary skills required for judicial appointment. It is worth noting that, since the enactment of the Courts and Legal Services Act 1990 [UK], non-practising lawyers are eligible for appointment to the British bench. Baroness Hale, formerly Professor Brenda Hoggett, was appointed to the English High Court in 1993, having previously been a Law Commissioner and leading academic. She became the first woman member of the Judicial Committee of the House of Lords (and then became a judge of the UK Supreme Court on its establishment in 2009 and in July 2013 was appointed Deputy President of the Supreme Court). In other European jurisdictions, it is also common for judges to be chosen from the ranks of the academic community. It is unlikely, given the views expressed in the 1999 Report, that such a development will occur in Ireland in the near future. McMahon J, a judge of the High Court until 2012, had formerly been a Professor of Law in University College Cork and is also the author (and co-author) of leading textbooks on Irish law. He had, however, been a practising solicitor for a number of years prior to his appointment to the Bench. At the time of writing (September 2014), the Department of Justice is engaged in a review of the judicial appointments process, see para **4.111**.

[219] Carroll, 'The right stuff' (2007) 101(7) *Law Society Gazette* 32, 33.

[220] In the immediate aftermath of the passing of the 1995 Act, Barrington J, who had been a judge of the EU General Court (then called the Court of First Instance), was appointed to the Supreme Court. (contd.../)

[4.82] The meaning of some of the relevant legislative phrases was considered by the High Court in *The State (Walshe) v Murphy*.[221] Although the court dealt with the qualifications of a person being appointed as a judge of the District Court, we have seen that the basic qualifications are quite similar for all the courts, so that the decision is relevant to all appointments. The prosecutor in *Walshe* had been charged with offences under the Road Traffic Acts and been convicted in May 1981 by the respondent, who had been appointed a temporary judge of the District Court in April 1981. The respondent had been called to the Bar in 1962 and from that time had practised at the Bar for over eight years until April 1971, when he took up a post as legal assistant in the Attorney General's office until 1973, and from then until his appointment as a judge in 1981 was an examiner in the Land Commission. The prosecutor claimed that his conviction was invalid and should be quashed on *certiorari* on a number of grounds, including the argument that the respondent was not 'a practising barrister of ten years' standing' when he had been appointed a judge. The High Court agreed.

[4.83] As to 'ten years' standing', the court examined whether this referred to ten years between a person's call to the Bar as a barrister and appointment as a judge (in which case the respondent would have been qualified) or referred to ten years' practice as a barrister (in which case the phrase 'practising barrister' would have to be examined in more detail). The court accepted that there was some ambiguity in the legislation in this respect, so that it should look to the presumed or apparent intention of the legislature.[222] Delivering the main judgment,[223] Finlay P stated:

> "I have no doubt that the apparent intention of the legislature was to provide a minimum standard of competence and skill for the person eligible for appointment as a Justice of the District Court."[224]

[4.84] He concluded that the court would be failing to implement that intention if it interpreted 'ten years' standing' as meaning simply the lapse of time from call to the Bar, without regard to the period during which the person practised law before appointment as a judge. The court therefore concluded that it was necessary for a person to have practised as a barrister for ten years before appointment, though the court did *not* interpret the legislation as requiring that 'those ten years must have immediately

---

220 (\...contd) Although Barrington J had been a judge of the High Court prior to being appointed a judge of the EU General Court, and before that had been a practising senior counsel, there was a doubt over whether the 1961 Act required a person to have been in practice and/or have been a judge of the Irish courts *immediately* prior to being appointed to the Bench. Section 28 of the 1995 Act remedied this particular difficulty, thus paving the way for Barrington J to be appointed to the Supreme Court.

221 *State (Walshe) v Murphy* [1981] IR 275.

222 On interpretation in cases of ambiguity, see para **14.34**.

223 The Court was a three-judge Divisional Court comprising Finlay P, Gannon and Hamilton JJ. Finlay P delivered the main judgment in the case, the other two judges concurring. On Divisional Courts, see para **4.62**.

224 [1981] IR 275, 289.

preceded the date of the appointment or that there must have been a continuous period of ten years.'[225]

[4.85] As to the term 'practising barrister', Finlay P stated that, although not defined in the legislation, it had a generally accepted meaning:

> "That meaning ... refers to a person who, having the degree of barrister-at-law and having been called to the Bar, offers himself on hazard to take work (whether as an advocate or as an adviser) from persons who, through the agency of a solicitor, seek his services in the field in which he practises."[226]

He held that a person employed in the Attorney General's office or in the Land Commission 'could not be said to be on hazard and offering himself as a barrister to the world at large.' On this basis, the court concluded that the respondent had not been a 'practising barrister' on his appointment and the applicant's conviction was quashed on *certiorari*.[227]

Informal aspects of the appointments process: political allegiances

[4.86] As already indicated, while the formal appointment of all judges is made by the President, the reality is that, since this power is exercised on the advice of the government, it is the government who has final control over judicial appointments. And while the Courts (Supplemental Provisions) Act 1961, as amended, indicates that only barristers or solicitors of a number of years standing will be appointed, this does not provide a full picture of the appointments procedure. As discussed below, connections with political parties prior to appointment remain a matter of debate and, at the time of writing (July 2014), a review of the appointments process is being undertaken by government. This has given rise to considerable debate as to the transparency of the appointments process and the influence of political connections.[228]

[4.87] In general, many of those appointed to judicial office have had connections, to some extent or another, either with the political party or parties whose members form the government of the day or have become known to the government in some other way. This, indeed, had been the case prior to 1922. During the 19th century, many of the

---

[225] [1981] IR 275, 289. This view was formally incorporated into the relevant legislation with the enactment of the Courts and Court Officers Act 2002.

[226] [1981] IR 275, 290.

[227] While the Court did not consider the effect of this decision on the other convictions handed down by the respondent, it would seem that they would be equally invalid: see *Shelly v Mahon* [1990] 1 IR 36 and *Glavin v Governor of Mountjoy Prison* [1991] 2 IR 421, discussed at fn 407 below.

[228] The judiciary's January 2014 preliminary submission to the Department as part of the public consultation on the review of the judicial appointments process, available at www.supremecourt.ie, discussed the need for reform of the appointments process because of the perception that political considerations formed part of the process: see para **4.112**. The Law Society and the Bar Council also made written submissions. All three submissions recommend amendments to the current judicial appointments procedure.

barristers appointed to the Irish Bench had either been MPs in the Westminster Parliament or served as Attorney General or some other law officer in Ireland. This indicated the connection between political activity and judicial appointment, and it must be said that this arrangement was similar to that in the remainder of what was the then UK.[229] Of course, the situation concerning Ireland was complicated by the growing movement for Home Rule and, later, the movement for the creation of an independent state, and judicial appointments became part of this wider political picture. By the time the Irish Free State was established in 1922, many of those who had been appointed to the Bench would not have shared the political outlook of those who now determined judicial appointments. Nonetheless, the new government did appoint some judges who had been part of the pre-1922 regime to the new court system established by the Courts of Justice Act 1924.[230]

[4.88] In a study conducted in 1969,[231] the system of judicial appointment established in the post-1922 era was described as follows:

"A general consensus exists that there are no promises of judgeships for party service and this same consensus holds that no appointments are made of those unqualified for the judicial posts ... This is not to say that the best person available is always named but that usually those named are of judicial calibre.

However, there is the very realistic point that, with rare exceptions, a person named as judge will be one who is favourably regarded by the Government perhaps out of gratitude for past services either to the party or to the State. Even in the rare instance where an adherent of the opposition party is named this may well be of indirect advantage of the Government party in that such a 'non-partisan' appointment projects an image of objectivity to the public with concern for the quality of the courts rather than considering only political and partisan factors.

A judicial appointment does not 'just happen'. It is in a very real sense the finest and the most desirable appointment that the Government can make. It is a status appointment. The choice is not made casually ... The 'inner circles' of the party and of the Government always

---

[229] See Delany, *The Administration of Justice in Ireland* (4th edn, 1975), p 74. On the circumstances surrounding the appointment of Chief Baron Palles, see Delany, *Christopher Palles* (1960), pp 75–85.

[230] Of the three judges of the new Supreme Court in 1924, (Charles) O'Connor J had been Master of the Rolls in the pre-1922 Court of Appeal. Of the six judges in the new High Court, four had been members of the pre-1922 regime: Wylie J had been a member of the pre-1922 High Court, both O'Shaughnessy and Johnson JJ had been members of the lower courts and Hanna J had been a law officer. See Delany, *The Administration of Justice in Ireland* (4th edn, 1975), p 75.

[231] Bartholomew, *The Irish Judiciary* (1971). This study was the result of a 1969 survey of judges and other persons in Ireland conducted by Professor Bartholomew, the then Professor of Government and International Studies at the University of Notre Dame, Indiana, during a residency in the Faculty of Law, University College, Dublin. The study, described by the author as being in part 'a mildly behavioural investigation of judges as persons' was a pioneering one in the Irish context.

have in mind potential appointees for judicial vacancies before they actually occur ... The Minister for Justice makes up a list of prospects and presents it in Cabinet meeting. The 'list' may contain a single name. The Ministers may add names to this list. Persons on it may be politically active or politically neutral.

Some judges have thought that their work as a counsel in 'State cases' has helped their cause, that this gave them an opportunity to get to know the Taoiseach. Others have had members of the Government as clients and the personal friendship resulting helped. Another judge pointed out that his uncle was a friend of influential persons. One judge said simply that he met the Minister for Justice through a member of parliament and proceeded to tell the Minister that he was interested in an appointment. Persons who feel that they have a chance to be appointed commonly put in an application for the post.

No formal vote is taken at the Cabinet meeting; an informal agreement on a particular person evolves. If the Taoiseach ... has a favourite, that man[232] will get the appointment. Certainly no one has ever been named judge over the objections of the Taoiseach.[233] The person chosen is then formally consulted and his consent secured. Then the President, who has not been consulted on the appointment, is told the name of the appointee and the formal appointment is made by the President ...

A former Taoiseach made the statement that 'all things being equal' a person's politics is controlling in such appointments. All Irish governments have to a greater or lesser degree been politically motivated in the making of judicial appointments. The English used judges as patronage and the new government after independence named judges that agreed with its aims."[234]

[4.89] As this account notes, there was certainly a political element to judicial appointments for many years. It must, of course, be borne in mind that those appointed to judicial office were required to meet the qualification standards specified in legislation and that, on their appointment, they were required to be independent in their decisions.[235] Nonetheless, the system has been criticised from time to time. In response to specific matters that arose in 1994,[236] in 1995 the Judicial Appointments Advisory Board was established to provide for some elements of transparency in the process. As noted above, at the time of writing (September 2014) the judicial appointments process is again under review, which is discussed below.

---

[232]   At the time the author was writing, the only woman member of the judiciary was District Justice Eileen Kennedy: see Bartholomew, *The Irish Judiciary* (1971), p 40. The first woman High Court judge, Carroll J, was appointed in 1980. The first woman Supreme Court judge, Denham J, was appointed in 1992, having been a judge of the High Court since 1991. The first woman judge of the Circuit Court, Judge McGuinness, was appointed in 1994. In 1996, she became McGuinness J on her appointment to the High Court; in 2000, she was appointed a judge of the Supreme Court.

[233]   See, however, the discussion of the nomination of the President of the High Court in 1994, discussed at para **4.96**.

[234]   Bartholomew, *The Irish Judiciary* (1971), pp 32–36.

[235]   See para **4.116**.

[236]   See para **4.96**.

[4.90] In 2004 a comprehensive study was completed on the backgrounds of Superior Court Judges.[237] Of the Superior Court judges, 62% interviewed stated that at the time of their appointment to judicial office they had no affiliations with a political party. The author noted that this was a considerable increase from the 12% of Superior Court judges in the 1969 study who stated that they had no political affiliation at the time of their appointment.[238] However, in the 2004 study, a number of judges stated that despite having no affiliation with a political party at the time of their appointment, they might still be regarded by their colleagues or the media to be a member of a particular political party.

Allegiances, ideology and class

[4.91] Two other aspects of the 1969 study are worthy of note. First, while it indicated that political *allegiances* in general played a part in appointments, it also noted that political *ideology*, in the sense of liberalism or conservatism, seemed to have played little part. This would appear to reflect the general lack of a 'left–right' political divide in the state. However, it is of interest that, in 1969, 43% of the judges interviewed in the study characterised themselves as liberals, with about 13% professing conservatism.[239] As to the Supreme Court, the study's author stated:

"On the current Supreme Court there appears to be an interesting 3-1-1 division on a 'liberal', 'centrist', 'conservative' basis."[240]

[4.92] This view that the Supreme Court of the 1960s had a broadly 'liberal' perspective would appear to be supported by academic commentators in Ireland who have addressed this point.[241] This also reflected the general development of Irish society in the 1960s, based on a departure from political isolationism that had characterised Ireland up to the 1950s.[242] It would seem that judicial appointments were also seen by those in government as an element of the modernisation of Irish society.[243] The 2004 study asked judges what their ideology was in the same terms as those used by Bartholomew in 1969, 'liberal, centre, or right of centre'. The author of the 2004 study remarked that the

---

237 Carroll, 'You Be the Judge: A Study of the Backgrounds of Superior Court Judges in Ireland in 2004 Part I' [2005] 10(5) *Bar Review* 153 and Carroll, 'You Be the Judge Part II' [2005] 10(6) *Bar Review* 182.

238 [2005] 10(5) *Bar Review* 182 at 183.

239 Bartholomew, *The Irish Judiciary* (1971), p 37. The terms 'liberal' and 'conservative' were not further defined by the author.

240 Bartholomew, *The Irish Judiciary* (1971), p 37. The judges of the Supreme Court at the time were: Ó Dálaigh CJ, Walsh, Budd, Fitzgerald and McLoughlin JJ.

241 See further, para **15.121**.

242 For a general discussion, see Coakley and Gallagher, *Politics in the Republic of Ireland* (4th edn, 2005).

243 Walsh J stated that, on his appointment to the Supreme Court in 1962, the then Taoiseach, Mr Seán Lemass, had indicated that, where the opportunity arose, there was a case for the Supreme Court to engage in active development of the 'Fundamental Rights' provisions of the 1937 Constitution. See Sturgess and Chubb (eds), *Judging the World* (1988).

judges found these terms difficult to define and inapplicable in the Irish context. Therefore of the judges who did classify themselves as having an ideological viewpoint or outlook did so reluctantly and with reservations: 31% classified themselves as liberal and 24% as centrist.[244]

[4.93] The other point worthy of note concerned the background of the judges. The 1969 study made this comment:

"None of the Irish judges has been of humble family origin. On the contrary almost two-thirds came from admittedly upper middle class social and economic backgrounds and almost all of the remainder from middle class. A number of the judges attended private preparatory schools ... A goodly number were 'born to the law', that is, more came from families where the father was a lawyer than where the father had any other occupation. Overall more than half of the judges have lawyers somewhere in their family relationship ... After law the chief paternal occupation was business on the managerial level, civil service, medicine and farming ... With this family background the encouragement and finances for the necessary education for law were readily available. Also from such families may well have come the proper attitudes of civic responsibility and social consciousness that produced 'men of the law.'"[245]

[4.94] The 2004 survey was a comprehensive one and its conclusions on the type of person who is most likely to be a judge of the Superior Courts in Ireland as at 2004 showed that:

"The person who is most likely to be a judge of the Superior Courts in Ireland in 2004 is male, was born in Dublin and grew up in an urban setting. He lived in Dublin and was a practising Senior Counsel at the time of his appointment. He did not necessarily come from a legal family background. He attended a private secondary school and studied at University College Dublin and obtained a Bachelor of Arts degree. His first self-supporting job was as a barrister and he has never worked in any other capacity. He was first appointed to the Court between 1995 and 1999 and had no judicial experience prior to his current appointment. He was appointed after he was forty-five, but most likely after he was fifty. He describes himself as middle class but believes it is very difficult to define or apply a social class structure to the Irish context. His family was not involved in politics but he himself was involved in a political party at some point in his career, either as a student or local supporter. He was never a member of a political party. He had no political party affiliation at the time of his appointment and has no political party sympathy now. He is Roman Catholic and of pure Irish ethnicity. He views himself as liberal but does not believe there is any room for ideology in the Courts. He believes he was appointed to the judiciary because of his professional status, but thinks that his particular legal speciality and political connection may have been important contributing factors."[246]

---

[244] Carroll, 'You Be the Judge: A Study of the Backgrounds of Superior Court Judges in Ireland in 2004 Part I' [2005] 10(5) *Bar Review* 153, 171.

[245] Bartholomew, *The Irish Judiciary* (1971), pp 41–2.

[246] Carroll, 'You Be the Judge: A Study of the Backgrounds of Superior Court Judges in Ireland in 2004 Part I' [2005] 10(5) *Bar Review* 153, 154.

An important difference between the 1969 and 2004 studies was the proportion of Superior Court judges that believed their gender had been a factor in their appointment: 14% of Superior Court judges interviewed in the 2004 study stated that they had been appointed because they were women.[247] At the time of the 1969 survey, there were no women judges of the Superior Courts, by the time of the 2004 survey this had increased to 13.5% of judges of the Superior Courts.

[4.95] The 2004 survey also examined whether the Judicial Appointments Advisory Board had had any effect on the tradition pattern of judicial appointments based on politics. Those surveyed recognised the purpose of the Judicial Appointments Advisory Board in seeking to reduce the political element of appointments but commented that while the JAAB provides an important seeking process, they found it only to be a cosmetic change when it came to the impact of the new system on the tradition pattern of judicial appointments based on politics.[248] This perspective is echoed in the review of the appointments process being carried out at the time of writing (September 2014), discussed below.

Appointment of President of High Court in 1994

[4.96] For many years, the question of judicial appointments would not have been a subject for debate in the wider media, but certain events in 1994 brought the issue into sharp focus and led, in part, to the establishment of a Judicial Appointments Advisory Board.[249] The background to this should be noted.[250]

[4.97] In early 1994, the then Attorney General, Mr Harold Whelehan SC, expressed an interest to the then Taoiseach, Mr Albert Reynolds, in being nominated to the Presidency of the High Court if a vacancy should arise. It was known that the then Chief Justice, Thomas Finlay, would reach retirement age in September 1994 and that a judicial vacancy would therefore arise. Mr Reynolds gave Mr Whelehan an informal commitment that he would support his candidacy for the High Court in the event of a

---

247   Carroll, 'You Be the Judge: A Study of the Backgrounds of Superior Court Judges in Ireland in 2004 Part I' [2005] 10(5) *Bar Review* 153, 172.

248   Carroll, 'You Be the Judge Part II' [2005] 10(6) *Bar Review* 182, 188.

249   The shortcomings of the system by which appointments were entirely within the hands of the government had been criticised by a number of writers since the foundation of the state: see Delany, *The Administration of Justice in Ireland* (4th edn, 1975), pp 76–7. In 1990, the Fair Trade Commission, *Report of Study into Restrictive Practices in the Legal Profession*, p 299, had explicitly recommended the establishment of a Judicial Appointments Advisory Board (on the Report generally, see para **3.05**). While the 1990 Report was, ultimately, implemented in the 1995 Act, the events of 1994 may be regarded as the immediate catalyst.

250   This account is based largely on the *Report of the Sub-Committee on Legislation and Security* (Pn 1478, 1995). This Report was published on foot of resolutions passed by Dáil Éireann and the enactment of the Select Committee on Legislation and Security of Dáil Éireann (Privilege and Immunity) Act 1994, authorising the Committee to inquire into certain events in November 1994, including those discussed in the text.

vacancy arising. This would appear to have been partly influenced by the informal convention that the Attorney General had 'first refusal' on any judicial vacancy.[251]

[4.98] During the summer of 1994, there was considerable publicity in the various media to the effect that the then Tánaiste and leader of the Labour Party, Dick Spring, was not prepared to assent to the nomination of Mr Whelehan.[252] In September 1994, the then President of the High Court, Liam Hamilton, was nominated by the government to fill the vacancy in the post of Chief Justice arising from the retirement of Mr Justice Finlay and this created a vacancy in the Presidency of the High Court. There were continuing disagreements over the appointment of Mr Whelehan, and an informal committee comprising four government ministers was established to end the continuing impasse. At a meeting between the Taoiseach and Tánaiste on 9 October 1994, the elements of a Courts Bill to effect substantial reform of the court system as well as to amend the arrangements for future judicial appointments were agreed. It appeared for a time that this meeting had produced a compromise, with the appointment of Mr Whelehan to go ahead in return for the changes to be contained in the Courts Bill.[253]

[4.99] However, almost simultaneously, in October 1994 there were media reports, including a documentary on Ulster Television, indicating that there had been a seven-month delay in the Office of the Attorney General in the processing of an application for the extradition to Northern Ireland of a Catholic priest, Fr Brendan Smyth, to face charges of sexual assault on children.[254] The government requested Mr Whelehan, as the Attorney General, to prepare a report on this delay for discussion at Cabinet. The report was circulated to ministers before the Cabinet meeting, but it appeared that the Labour Party ministers did not consider that it adequately explained the delay in dealing with the extradition request, and they reluctantly came to the conclusion that they could not support the nomination of Mr Whelehan as President of the High Court.[255]

[4.100] On 11 November 1994, the Cabinet formally discussed Mr Whelehan's report, and the Labour Party ministers then withdrew from the meeting. Mr Whelehan's nomination as President of the High Court was then put to and approved by the remaining ministers (in the absence of the Labour Party ministers) and later that day, he was formally appointed by the President of Ireland to his position as President of the

---

[251] See para **3.120**.

[252] Some of the newspaper coverage is included in the material in Appendix 3 of the *Report of the Sub-Committee on Legislation and Security*, pp 735–45.

[253] This became the basis for the Courts and Court Officers Bill 1994, which was presented to Dáil Éireann by the then Minister for Justice in November 1994. However, the 1994 Bill lapsed on the fall of the government later that month. An amended version of the 1994 Bill became the Courts and Court Officers Act 1995.

[254] The Attorney General had been conferred with certain functions in extradition cases by the Extradition (Amendment) Act 1987. These functions have since been transferred to the Director of Public Prosecutions: see para **3.127**.

[255] See letter from Mr Spring to Mr Reynolds in the *Report of the sub-Committee on Legislation and Security*, p 725.

High Court, and he made his declaration as President of the High Court on 15 November 1994.[256] However, arising from subsequent developments, on 17 November 1994 Mr Whelehan resigned as President of the High Court[257] on the same day as a motion of no confidence in the government was passed by Dáil Éireann. While the wider political aspects of these events are outside the scope of this book,[258] it can be said that they were the genesis, at least in part, of the establishment of a Judicial Appointments Advisory Board.[259]

Judicial Appointments Advisory Board

[4.101] Section 13 of the Courts and Court Officers Act 1995 provides for the appointment of a Judicial Appointments Advisory Board (JAAB) for the purposes of 'identifying persons and informing the Government of the suitability of those persons for appointment to judicial office.' Since 2002, the JAAB must submit an Annual Report to the Minister for Justice and Equality.[260]

[4.102] Section 12 of the Courts and Court Officers Act 1995 defines 'judicial office' as being: 'the office of ordinary judge of the Supreme Court, ordinary judge of the High Court, ordinary judge of the Circuit Court or judge of the District Court (other than the President of the District Court).' Thus, the remit of the JAAB excludes the offices of Chief Justice, President of the High Court, President of the Circuit Court and President of the District Court, though in relation to these offices, the government is subject to some limitations in that it is required to 'have regard first' to the qualifications and suitability of existing judges.[261]

[4.103] The JAAB consists of 10 persons:

- the Chief Justice, who chairs the JAAB,
- the President of the High Court,
- the President of the Circuit Court,
- the President of the District Court,
- the Attorney General,[262]

---

[256] On the declaration required by Article 34.5 of the Constitution, see para **4.116**.

[257] In a statement issued to the media, Mr Whelehan stated that he was resigning as President of the High Court in order to avoid any potential damage to the administration of justice: see (1994) *The Irish Times*, 18 November. Mr Whelehan subsequently recommenced his practice at the Bar: see further fn 419 below.

[258] For an informal account of the events, written by the government press secretary of the day, see Duignan, *One Spin on The Merry-Go-Round* (1995).

[259] See also fn 249 above.

[260] Courts and Court Officers Act 2002, s 11. The annual reports of the Judicial Appointments Advisory Board are available on the Courts Service website www.courts.ie.

[261] Courts and Court Officers Act 1995, s 23.

[262] Section 18(3) specifies that where the Attorney General wishes to be considered for appointment for judicial office, he or she shall withdraw from any deliberations of the board concerning his or her suitability for office.

- a practising barrister nominated by the Chair of the Council of the Bar of Ireland,

- a practising solicitor nominated by the President of the Law Society of Ireland, and

- not more than three persons appointed by the Minister for Justice who are engaged in or have appropriate knowledge or experience of commerce, finance or administration or persons who have experience as consumers of the services provided by the courts.[263]

[4.104] The nominated solicitor and barrister and the three members appointed by the Minister remain on the JAAB for a three-year term,[264] thus indicating that it has a continuing presence and is thus not empanelled only where a judicial vacancy arises. It may also be noted that the three members appointed by the Minister introduce the first formal mechanism by which non-lawyers are involved in judicial appointments. This reflects the 'lay' involvement in the Council of the Bar of Ireland and of the Law Society of Ireland.[265]

[4.105] Section 14 of the Courts and Court Officers Act 1995 empowers the JAAB to adopt its own procedures, and in this respect it may: advertise for applications for judicial appointment; require applicants to complete application forms; consult persons concerning the suitability of applicants to the JAAB; invite persons, identified by the JAAB, to submit their names for consideration by it; and arrange to interview applicants who wish to be considered for judicial appointment. The JAAB thus has extensive powers to identify those persons suitable for appointment in accordance with its function under s 13 of the 1995 Act.[266] The JAAB has not conducted interviews of candidates. In its 2013 Annual Report, the view was expressed by the JAAB that there was no necessity for interviews as there would be practical obstacles to holding them and sufficient information was given in the application documentation for the JAAB to perform its functions. The JAAB also stated that the merits of the named persons recommended to the Government for appointment were not required under its remit which reinforced its view that there was no requirement for interviews.[267]

---

263 The first board took office in 1996 on the appointment of the three members nominated by the Minister for Justice and advertisements later appeared in national newspapers seeking applications for consideration by the board. The first appointments under this procedure were also made in 1996 to fill the judicial positions created by the 1995 Act.

264 Courts and Court Officers Act 1995, s 13(3), which also provides that such persons are eligible for re-appointment.

265 See paras **3.58** and **3.93**.

266 Section 21 of the 1995 Act also provides for staffing for the board, while s 22 is a standard provision that the expenses incurred by the board shall be paid out of moneys provided by the Oireachtas.

267 JAAB, *Annual Report 2013* (2014) at p 15.

[4.106] Section 16 of the Courts and Court Officers Act 1995 specifies that a person who wishes to be considered for judicial appointment:

"shall so inform the [JAAB] in writing and shall provide the [JAAB] with such information as it may require to enable it to consider the suitability of that person for judicial office, including information relating to education, professional qualifications, experience and character."

[4.107] Section 16 of the 1995 Act also specifies that, where the Minister for Justice requests, the JAAB must submit to the Minister the name of each person who has informed it of his or her wish to be considered for judicial office. In general, the JAAB is required to recommend at least seven names from the list it submits, but this can be a lesser number where there are multiple vacancies for which there are less than the requisite multiple of seven whom the JAAB considers it can recommend. The JAAB must also provide the Minister with particulars of education, professional qualification, experience and character of the persons whom it recommends. However, the JAAB cannot submit the list of recommended candidates in any sort of preference based on merit.[268]

[4.108] A person who is recommended for judicial appointment by the JAAB must comply with the relevant qualifications set out in the Courts (Supplemental Provisions) Act 1961.[269] In addition, s 16 provides that the JAAB must not recommend a person unless, in its opinion, the person:

(a) has displayed in his or her practice as a barrister or solicitor, as the case may be, a degree of competence and a degree of probity appropriate to and consistent with the appointment concerned. This includes having regard to the 'nature and extent of the practice of the person concerned insofar as it relates to his or her personal conduct of proceedings in the Supreme Court and the High Court whether as an advocate or as a solicitor instructing counsel in such proceedings or both',[270]

(b) is suitable on grounds of character and temperament,

(c) is otherwise suitable, and

---

[268] This was criticised by the Irish Council for Civil Liberties in its Report *Justice Matters: Independence, Accountability and the Irish Judiciary* (ICCL, 2007), p 51. See also Gwynn Morgan, 'Selection of Superior Court Judges' [2004] ILT 42 and Carroll, 'You Be the Judge Part II' [2005] 10(6) *Bar Review* 182 who recommend that the list of names to be recommended to the government be limited to three. This recommendation was reiterated by the Irish Council for Civil Liberties in its 2007 Report at p 72. See also Ward, 'Independence, Accountability and the Irish Judiciary' [2008] JSIJ 1 and Feenan, 'Judicial Appointments in Ireland in comparative perspective' [2008] JSIJ 34.

[269] See paras **4.77–4.85**.

[270] Courts and Court Officers Act 1995, s 16(7) as amended by the Courts and Court Officers Act 2002, s 8. See also Carroll, 'The right stuff' (2007) 101(7) *Law Society Gazette* 32, 33 who argues that this requirement may inhibit the number of solicitors eligible for appointment.

(d) undertakes in writing to the JAAB his or her agreement, if appointed to judicial office, to take such course of training or education, or both, as may be required by the Chief Justice or the President of the court to which the person is appointed,[271]

(e) in addition, the JAAB cannot recommend a person to the Minister unless the person has furnished to it a relevant tax clearance certificate.[272]

The JAAB has stated that, having received guidance from counsel, it regards these requirements as a minimum standard, but having these qualities is not sufficient for a person to be appointed.[273]

In 2007, the Irish Council for Civil Liberties completed a report on the Irish judiciary concentrating on the issues of independence and accountability. One of its primary criticisms of the current method of judicial appointments was that the criteria used by the JAAB in deciding whether to recommend candidates to the Minister lacked transparency, meritocracy and precision and were imprecise.[274] It recommended that such criteria be transparent and well-defined.[275]

[4.109] It must be remembered that, ultimately, the Constitution requires such appointments be made by the President acting on the advice of the government. This is recognised in s 16(6) of the 1995 Act, which provides:

> "In advising the President in relation to the appointment of a person to judicial office the Government shall firstly consider for appointment those persons whose names have been recommended to the Minister pursuant to this section."

[4.110] Thus, while the recommendations of the JAAB are undoubtedly of considerable importance,[276] the final decision rests with the government. In addition, we have already noted that the functions of the JAAB do not extend to appointments to the offices of Chief Justice, President of the High Court, President of the Circuit Court and President of the District Court.[277] One other limitation is that the JAAB's recommendation function does not apply where the government proposes to 'promote' a sitting judge.[278] These limitations aside, the changes effected by the Courts and Court Officers Act 1995

---

271 Sections 16(7) and 19 of the 1995 Act.
272 Standards in Public Office Act 2001, s 22.
273 Annual Report 2007 of the Judicial Appointments Advisory Board (2007) available at www.courts.ie.
274 Irish Council for Civil Liberties, *Justice Matters: Independence, Accountability and the Irish Judiciary* (ICCL, 2007), 51.
275 Irish Council for Civil Liberties, *Justice Matters: Independence, Accountability and the Irish Judiciary* (ICCL, 2007), 72.
276 Courts and Court Officers Act 1995, s 16(8) provides that appointments made under the procedure envisaged by the Act must be published in *Iris Oifigiúil*, the Official Gazette, and the notice must include a statement, if that is the case, that the name of the person was recommended by the board to the Minister. This would appear to be an 'encouragement' to the government to advise the appointment of recommended persons only.
277 See para **4.102**.

created a degree of openness in the appointments procedure[279] which did not apply until the JAAB's establishment.[280] This is not to say that the appointments procedure is now free from political controversy. Indeed, reflecting increasing political and media interest in this area,[281] there have been suggestions that appointments have been delayed until candidates acceptable to the government party or parties have been on the list of candidates sent to government by the JAAB.[282] It is also noteworthy that the Irish Council for Civil Liberties did not recommend the introduction of an independent judicial appointments commission similar to that in England and Wales to replace the JAAB.

[4.111] Against this background, at the time of writing (September 2014) the government is engaged in a review of the judicial appointments process. In December 2013, the Department of Justice and Equality initiated a public consultation process seeking views on the appointments process. The Department stated that, in particular, it sought views on how the judicial appointments process might be enhanced, both generally and specifically in relation to the following:

- eligibility for appointment;
- the need to ensure and protect the principle of judicial independence;
- promoting equality and diversity;
- the role of the Judicial Appointments Advisory Board, including its membership and its procedures.

It is notable that the Department also stated that 'any changes advocated must be capable of implementation within the current relevant provisions of the Constitution'.[283]

[4.112] In response to this the Chief Justice and the Presidents of the High, Circuit and District Courts decided that they should establish a Judicial Appointments Review

---

278 Section 17 of the 1995 Act. The Irish Council for Civil Liberties in its Report *Justice Matters: Independence, Accountability and the Irish Judiciary* (ICCL, 2007) criticised this lacuna and recommended that the Judicial Appointments Advisory Board be involved in the promotion process. See also Gwynn Morgan, 'Selection of Superior Court Judges' [2004] ILT 42.

279 Section 20 of the 1995 Act provides that the proceedings of the board and all communications to it are confidential and shall not be disclosed except for the purposes of the Act.

280 On the procedure for judicial appointment in the United Kingdom, see Slapper and Kelly, *The English Legal System* (9th edn, 2009). The Constitutional Reform Act 2005 established the Judicial Appointments Commission (UK), which is an independent body set up to select candidates for judicial office on merit, through fair and open competition. See Malleson, *The Legal System* (3rd edn, 2007), ch 17.

281 The controversy over the appointment of the President of the High Court in 1994, discussed above, was followed in 1999 by the circumstances surrounding the resignation of the Supreme Court judge, Hugh O'Flaherty, and High Court judge Cyril Kelly, discussed below.

282 See generally, Coakley and Gallagher, *Politics in the Republic of Ireland* (4th edn, 2005) and (2000) *The Irish Times*, 18 September and 11 October.

283 'Public consultation on a review of procedures for appointment as a Judge', available at www.justice.ie (posted on the website on 6 December 2013).

Committee, to provide a forum for the judiciary to formulate submissions following consultation with all of the judges, detailed research and study. In January 2014, the Judicial Appointments Review Committee published a detailed preliminary submission on the review.[284] The submission made the following 16 recommendations:

"1. The present system of judicial appointments is unsatisfactory. The opportunity should now be taken to appoint a high level body to carry out research, receive submissions and within a fixed timescale develop comprehensive detailed proposals in a structured, principled and transparent way to make a radical improvement in the judicial appointments process in Ireland. In advance of any such comprehensive review there are a number of steps which can and should be taken immediately:

2. As a matter of principle, political allegiance should have no bearing on appointments to judicial office. Early acceptance of this principle is essential to a transformation of the appointments process.

3. The merit principle should be established in legislation.

4. A properly resourced judicial education system should be established without delay with a mandate to provide education to members of the judiciary on all matters bearing on the administration of justice.

5. The creation of a Judicial Council is a much needed reform to support the judiciary. A Judicial Council should be established forthwith, with responsibility for representation of the judiciary, an independent disciplinary process, judicial education, and the judicial involvement in the appointment process. However, judicial appointments need not be part of a Judicial Council but can be conducted by a committee as envisaged in the European Network of Councils for the Judiciary 'Dublin Declaration' of May 2012.[285]

6. The key to reforming the judicial appointments system rests on reform and development of the Judicial Appointments Advisory Board.

7. The process of judicial appointments should first and foremost enhance the principle of judicial independence, upon which the rule of law in our democracy is built.

8. The Committee believes that all judges should be capable of performing and be seen to perform the full functions of their colleagues of the same court jurisdiction. Variations and inconsistency lead to lack of clarity and confusion where such should be avoided.

9. The number of candidates for a single judicial post submitted by the Judicial Appointments Board for Governmental decision should be reduced to three. Where there are multiple vacancies in a Court, the number of candidates should be increased by no more than the number of additional vacancies.

---

[284] Judicial Appointments Review Committee, *Preliminary Submission to the Department of Justice and Equality's Public Consultation on the Judicial Appointments Process*, available at www.supremecourt.ie (posted on the website on 30 January 2014). The submission was supported by the Association of Judges in Ireland, the representative body for judges in Ireland: see www.aji.ie.

[285] On the establishment of a Judicial Council, see para **4.138**.

10. Where it is proposed to fill a judicial position by promotion, including the positions of Chief Justice and Presidents of the other Courts, the candidates should also be subject to the advisory process of the Judicial Appointments Advisory Board. Applications from serving judges to advance between different courts should be processed through application to the Judicial Appointments Advisory Board.

11. The Judicial Appointments Advisory Board should be empowered to rank candidates and to designate any particular candidate as 'outstanding'.

12. The Judicial Appointments Advisory Board should be specifically empowered to inform the Government when it considers that there are either no, or no sufficient candidates of sufficient quality.

13. The Judicial Appointments Advisory Board requires adequate financial resources to enable it to carry out its functions. A reformed appointments system will require adequate resources. It is recommended that there be consultation with the Judiciary on this matter.

14. The current statutory minimum periods of practice as a barrister or solicitor for appointment to all Courts should be extended to fifteen years.

15. It is essential that high quality experienced candidates are attracted to the bench. Recent changes to pension provisions, both public and private, as they apply to entrants to the judiciary, may have little fiscal benefit to the State, yet create a wholly disproportionate disincentive to applicants for judicial posts, and deter high quality applicants from seeking appointment. It is desirable that such provisions should be immediately reviewed to assess the benefit if any to the State, and assessing their impact on the quality of candidates for appointment to the judiciary.

16. The current requirement for Judges of the District Court to apply for yearly renewal from age 65 to age 70 should be abolished. Judges of all jurisdictions should have the same retirement age on judicial appointment."

The Law Society[286] and the Bar Council[287] also made written submissions. Both recommended that the JAAB conduct a detailed evaluation of each candidate in order that suitable candidates for judicial posts are selected on a meritorious basis and that the names of candidates provided by the JAAB are ranked.

[4.113] At the time of writing (September 2014) reform of the judicial appointments process remains a matter of significant debate. Although the current review is limited to the present constitutional arrangements under which the government makes the final decision to nominate a person to the President for appointment, it appears that the judiciary's submission on this matter seeks the maximum level of reform within that context. The need for reform is also expressed in the submissions provided by the Law Society and Bar Council.

---

[286] Law Society, *Consultation on the Review of Procedures for Appointment of Judges: Submissions of the Law Society* (January 2014) available at www.lawsociety.ie.
[287] Bar Council, *Submissions on the Procedure for Appointment as a Judge* (January 2014).

Other informal aspects

[4.114] As noted, the Courts (Supplemental Provisions) Act 1961 lays down minimum qualifications, and the terms of reference of the Judicial Appointments Advisory Board provide further information on the appointments process. Other informal aspects of the appointments process remain to be mentioned. Thus, while the 1961 Act refers to 10 and 12 years' practice, in most instances up to recently those appointed to the Bench have considerably longer experience, and the average age of judges on appointment is in the mid-50s.[288] In more recent years, the age of judges appointed to the Bench has been considerably younger, with a number of appointees being in their early to mid forties. The reason for the younger appointees is likely to be the alteration to the years of service requirement for judges to avail of their full entitlement to a judicial pension being increased from 15 years to 20 years for those appointed to the Supreme Court, High Court and Circuit Court.[289] Another important convention is that, in most instances, only senior counsel, as opposed to junior counsel, are considered for appointment to the High Court and Supreme Court.[290] It has also been a long-standing convention that at least one judge of the Supreme Court is not a Roman Catholic, while a number of judges in the other courts are also from other religious faiths, including the Church of Ireland, the Presbyterian Church and the Jewish community. More recently, the convention has grown that judicial appointments reflect a gender balance in proportion to the increasing number of women at senior levels in the profession.

[4.115] As to progression from the High Court to the Supreme Court, there is a general tendency for judges appointed to the High Court to be considered for later appointment to the Supreme Court on the retirement of a Supreme Court judge, but no clear rules exist in this respect either and a number of appointments to the Supreme Court have been made directly from the ranks of senior counsel.[291] As to the Circuit Court, many of the appointments up to 1996 were also from the ranks of the inner Bar. Prior to the 1990s, Circuit Court judges were rarely 'promoted' to any of the higher courts. An exception to both of these conventions was McWilliam J, who was first appointed to the Circuit Court at a time when he was a junior counsel, and was appointed to the High

---

288   There have been some notable exceptions, such as Walsh J, Denham J and Hardiman J, who were appointed judges in their 40s. In July 1996, a number of judges appointed to the Circuit Court were in their 30s.

289   Section 22 of Public Service Pensions (Single Scheme and Other Provisions) Act 2012. Concerns have been raised at the introduction of this measure by the Association of Judges in Ireland which expressed the view that it will have considerable consequences for both quality and experience of future candidates for appointment to the Bench.

290   Ms Justice Dunne who was appointed to the Supreme Court in 2013 did not take silk prior to her appointment to the Circuit Court in 1996. She was appointed to the High Court in 2004.

291   In 1982, Niall McCarthy SC was appointed a judge of the Supreme Court. In 2000, Adrian Hardiman SC was appointed a judge of the Supreme Court. In 2010, Donal O'Donnell SC was appointed a judge of the Supreme Court.

Court in 1977. Since the 1990s it appears that such upward judicial progression has become more common.[292]

[6]   JUDICIAL INDEPENDENCE AND JUDICIAL ETHICS

[4.116] Whatever the genesis of a person's appointment to judicial office, the Constitution underlines the independence of office once a person is appointed.

First, Article 34.5.1° requires all judges to make the following declaration on their appointment:

> "In the presence of Almighty God I _____ do solemnly and sincerely promise and declare that I will duly and faithfully and to the best of my knowledge and power execute the office of Chief Justice (or as the case may be) without fear or favour, affection or ill-will towards any man, and that I will uphold the Constitution and the laws. May God direct and sustain me."[293]

Both Article 35.2 and 35.3 underline this declaration by providing that:

> "2.   All judges shall be independent in the exercise of their judicial functions and subject only to the Constitution and the law.
>
>   3.   No judge shall be eligible to be a member of either House of the Oireachtas or to hold any other office or position of emolument."

[4.117] Another practical element in the independence of the judges of the High Court and Supreme Court is made explicit in the Constitution: a judge may only be removed from office for 'stated misbehaviour or incapacity' after resolutions of impeachment have been passed in both Houses of the Oireachtas. The impeachment requirement is of long standing, but in recent years it has been recognised that there is a need to have in place some other mechanism, short of impeachment, which would deal with improper or

---

[292]   By way of example, in 1996, Circuit Court judges Moriarty and McGuinness were appointed to the High Court; and in 2000, McGuinness J was appointed to the Supreme Court. Similarly, in 2013 Dunne J was appointed to the Supreme Court, having originally been appointed to the Circuit Court and, later, to the High Court. Significantly, Ms Justice Dunne did not take silk prior to her appointment as a Judge of the Circuit Court. The possibility of a greater degree of judicial promotion had been discussed in the Fair Trade Commission's *Report of Study into Restrictive Practices in the Legal Profession* (1990), pp 296–9. Bartholomew, *The Irish Judiciary* (1971), p 39, had suggested that a formalised system of promotions might lead some judges to 'look over their shoulder' and become more deferential towards the government of the day. It should be noted that the Judicial Appointments Advisory Board does not currently have any function in such promotions. In the 2014 submission of the judiciary to the review of the appointments process, discussed above, it was recommended that the JAAB be given such a role. In that event, it may be that this would minimise the risk identified by Bartholomew.

[293]   This replaced the declaration provided for in the Courts of Justice Act 1924, s 99. The *Report of the Constitution Review Group* (Pn 2632, 1996) (on which see generally para **15.196**) and the *Fourth Progress Report of the All-Party Oireachtas Committee on the Constitution, The Courts and the Judiciary* (1999) recommended that the following be added to Article 34.5: 'A judge may omit the religious references.'

unethical behaviour falling short of 'stated misbehaviour or incapacity'. This has led to calls for the introduction of a Judicial Council.[294]

Removal for stated misbehaviour or incapacity

[4.118] On the issue of removal from office, Article 35.4.1° provides:

> "A judge of the Supreme Court, the Court of Appeal[295] or the High Court shall not be removed from office except for stated misbehaviour or incapacity, and then only upon resolutions passed by Dáil Éireann and Seanad Éireann calling for his removal."

Similar protection, though in statutory form only, has been extended to judges of the Circuit Court[296] and District Court.[297] Like the provision in Article 34.1 concerning the administration of justice in public, these protections reflect the lessons of history and the need to ensure that the judiciary is independent of the current political climate. For the judiciary in the higher courts of Great Britain and Ireland, such provisions date back to 1701[298] and similar protections exist under many constitutions.[299]

---

[294] On the establishment of a Judicial Council, see para **4.139**ff.

[295] The reference to the Court of Appeal was added by the Thirty-Third Amendment of the Constitution (Court of Appeal) Act 2013, which provided for the establishment of the Court of Appeal and which was approved by a referendum held in 2013.

[296] Courts of Justice Act 1924, s 39 which was carried forward by the Courts (Supplemental Provisions) Act 1961, s 48 provides: 'The Circuit Judges shall hold office by the same tenure as the Judges of the High Court and the Supreme Court.' This is taken to mean in particular that the dual resolution required by Article 35.4 of the Constitution applies to the removal of a Circuit Court judge: see Hogan and Whyte (eds), *JM Kelly: The Irish Constitution* (4th edn, 2003), p 1007. The Irish Council for Civil Liberties has recommended that in order to eliminate any uncertainty consideration should be given to providing District Court and Circuit Court judges with security of tenure by the Constitution. See Irish Council for Civil Liberties, *Justice Matters: Independence, Accountability and the Irish Judiciary* (ICCL, 2007), 55.

[297] Courts of Justice (District Court) Act 1946, s 20 which was carried forward by the Courts (Supplemental Provisions) Act 1961, s 48 provides (as adapted by the Courts Act 1991, s 21): 'District Judges shall hold office by the same tenure as the Judges of the Supreme Court and the High Court.' See the comments on s 39 of the 1924 Act, above. This protection greatly extended the tenure of judges of the District Court by comparison with that contained in the Courts of Justice Act 1924, s 73. It would seem that the requirement for a resolution by both Houses does not apply to a temporary judge of the District Court, as the 1946 Act excludes a temporary judge from its definition of judge: see the High Court judgment of Lynch J in *Magee v Culligan* [1992] 1 IR 223, cited in Delany, *The Courts Acts 1924–1997* (2nd edn, 2000). A similar exclusion may not apply to temporary judges of the Circuit Court, s 39 of the 1924 Act containing no similar limitation.

[298] The Act of Settlement 1701 provided that judges of the higher courts held office for life 'subject to a power of removal by Her Majesty by both Houses of Parliament'. Similarly, in 1782, the Irish Parliament in Dublin ('Grattan's Parliament') passed An Act for securing the Independency of Judges, and the impartial administration of Justice, 21 & 22 Geo III, c 50. (contd.../)

[4.119] The question of removal of a judge, sometimes referred to as impeachment, had never been given serious consideration between 1937 and 1999, and so the phrase 'stated misbehaviour or incapacity' had not been interpreted by the courts. It has been suggested that the word 'incapacity' suggests medical unfitness for office, in the sense that the judge in question was suffering from a physical or other disability such as a stroke or mental illness.[300] The words 'stated misbehaviour' would appear to include both misbehaviour off the bench, such as a conviction for a serious criminal offence,[301] as well as misbehaviour on the bench, such as accepting a bribe, and most commentators would accept that such eventualities are unlikely to occur.[302] Misbehaviour might embrace more general matters, such as a judge's endorsement of a particular political party's views. Such a problem has not arisen.

Judicial conduct and ethics in individual cases

[4.120] In terms of behaviour falling short of misbehaviour or incapacity, a judge is required to comply with the basic principles of natural justice or fair procedures,[303] namely *audi alteram partem* and *nemo judex in causa sua*. These principles essentially require a judge to hear both sides fairly and impartially and without bias or even the appearance of bias. The requirement to hear both sides fairly would be breached if, for example, a judge became actively engaged in the proceedings by excessive interruption of the legal representatives in their submissions or examination of witnesses; in effect, both sides must be given an equal opportunity to present their case.[304] The rule against bias means that a judge should not be involved in any matter in which he or she has an

---

[298] (\...contd) This Act provided that all commissions of judges would 'continue and remain in full force during their good behaviour ... notwithstanding the demise of the King (whom God long preserve)', that all salaries would be continued while their commissions remained in force, and that removal of a judge could only be by the King 'upon the address of both houses of Parliament': see *The Irish Statutes, 1310-1800* (1995 reprint), p 582.

[299] For example, Article III of the US Constitution, Articles 64 and 65 of the French Constitution, Article 97 of the German Basic Law.

[300] Hogan and Whyte (eds), *JM Kelly: The Irish Constitution*, (4th edn, 2003), pp 551–2.

[301] Hogan and Whyte (eds), *JM Kelly: The Irish Constitution*, (4th edn, 2003), p 552, fn 20 suggest that a conviction for an offence under the Road Traffic Acts would not come within the definition of 'stated misbehaviour', but that a series of convictions for drink-related driving offences might. In 1993, it was reported that a High Court judge (Carney J) had apologised for seeking a drink in a Dublin hotel after closing hours: see (1993) *The Irish Times*, 9 March, p 1. It could not be suggested that this behaviour came within Article 35.4 of the Constitution.

[302] The most recent (!) and only instance of an impeachment since 1701 was in 1830 when Sir Jonah Barrington was dismissed for mishandling funds of wards of court. Charles Dickens' *Bleak House*, in describing the fictitious litigation of *Jarndyce v Jarndyce*, largely concerned the (mal)administration of the wardship jurisdiction in 19th century England. See, however, the *Curtin* case, para **4.150**.

[303] See para **8.29**.

[304] See *The People (DPP) v MacEoin* [1978] IR 27 and *Donnelly v Timber Factors Ltd* [1991] 1 IR 553.

interest, whether financial or otherwise, or where he or she may have previously expressed a view on the issue in question or where he or she may have advised one of the parties involved in the case. In such a situation, the judge should recuse himself or herself from adjudicating on the matter where it might appear that he or she might be influenced.

[4.121] Thus, in *Dublin Wellwoman Centre Ltd v Ireland*,[305] the Supreme Court held that the High Court judge Carroll J ought not adjudicate in a case concerning access to information on abortion as she had previously, as chairwoman of the Second Commission on the Status of Women, written a letter to the Taoiseach expressing the support of the Commission for the right of access to abortion counselling and information services. Speaking for the Supreme Court, Denham J pointed out that there had been no suggestion that this letter would have resulted in any actual bias on the part of Carroll J in adjudicating the points of law at issue in the case; rather a judge should offer to recuse himself or herself where there was even an *appearance* of bias. This test of the appearance of bias rather than actual bias is consistent with the constitutional declaration in Article 34.5.1° to execute the judicial office 'without fear or favour, affection or ill-will'. The decision in *Dublin Wellwoman* indicates the high standards of impartiality thus required.

[4.122] A similar issue arose in a high-profile case in Britain in 1998, in which the extradition of the former Chilean President Pinochet was sought. The extradition application was supported by the human rights organisation, Amnesty International. When the case was heard in the House of Lords, one of the law lords, Lord Hoffmann, had not revealed that he and his wife were members of Amnesty International. It was later held that Lord Hoffmann should have recused himself from the case.[306] It has been held that a judge is not required to recuse himself merely on the ground that he represented one of the parties involved in a case where the previous case involved different issues.[307] Equally it has been held that the mere fact that a judge's daughter appeared as counsel for one party did not require that judge to recuse himself where no objection had been made by any of the parties in the proceedings. However, the matter would be viewed differently where the relationship between the judge and counsel became 'inextricably entangled' with other factors in the case such that it could give rise to a fear, in the mind of a reasonable person, that the outcome would be affected.[308] In these circumstances the issue of perceived bias on the part of a judge is dealt with within the court system by way of appeal to a higher court or by means of judicial review.[309]

---

[305] *Dublin Wellwoman Centre Ltd v Ireland* [1995] 1 ILRM 408.

[306] See *R v Bow Street Magistrate, ex p Pinochet (No 2)* [2000] 1 AC 119. See also *Locabail Ltd v Bayfield Properties Ltd* [2000] QB 451.

[307] See *Rooney v Minister for Agriculture and Food* [2001] 2 ILRM 37, which also discussed the case law in detail.

[308] See *O'Reilly v Cassidy* [1995] 1 ILRM 306 and *O'Reilly v Cassidy (No 2)* [1995] 1 ILRM 311, in which the particular circumstances gave rise to a reasonable apprehension of bias.

[309] On the appeal system, see Ch 7, and on judicial review, see Ch 10.

[4.123] In *Kenny v Trinity College Dublin*,[310] the plaintiff objected to the building of a development of new student residences. In 2003, the Supreme Court granted an application by the defendant to have the proceedings struck out for disclosing no reasonable cause of action. The court's judgment was given by Murray J. In 2007, the plaintiff applied to have the previous order set aside as he had become aware that Murray J's brother was a partner in the architectural firm which had designed the development in question. The Supreme Court overturned its previous decision on the grounds that a reasonable person would have perceived there to have been bias even though the judge's brother was not directly involved in the subject matter of the litigation.

Impeachment and the 'Sheedy affair' 1999

[4.124] It has been recognised that both major misconduct and lesser improprieties require a more transparent and accountable process, and this has resulted in significant proposals for reform which are likely to be implemented in the near future. The impetus for reform in the area of judicial conduct and discipline lay in events that became public in early 1999, when the question of judicial impeachment became a live issue. The issue came to the fore again in 2002. While the process was not activated in 1999, a Supreme Court and High Court judge resigned in circumstances where it appeared that impeachment was imminent. In April 1999, O'Flaherty J resigned as a judge of the Supreme Court, Kelly J resigned as a judge of the High Court and Mr Michael Quinlan resigned as a Circuit Court County Registrar. These resignations arose from what became known as the 'Sheedy Affair', which received extensive publicity during 1999. The resignations arose against the following background.[311]

[4.125] As a result of a casual encounter with an acquaintance, O'Flaherty J was given an outline of the facts of a case, *People (DPP) v Sheedy*. The defendant had been sentenced to a term of four years imprisonment in October 1997 by Judge Matthews in the Circuit Criminal Court, having pleaded guilty to a charge of dangerous driving causing death. O'Flaherty J considered that the facts outlined to him were somewhat similar to those in *People (DPP) v McDonald*, which also concerned a conviction for dangerous driving causing death and in which the Court of Criminal Appeal, over which he had presided, had reduced a custodial sentence. O'Flaherty J suggested to the people he met that it might be possible for the *Sheedy* case to be re-listed before the Circuit Court and suggested that they should instruct their legal advisers to apply to the Court to have the case re-listed. Shortly after this meeting, in October 1998, O'Flaherty J requested the County Registrar, Mr Michael Quinlan, to visit him in his chambers for the purpose of confirming that such a course of action was feasible.

---

[310] *Kenny v Trinity College Dublin* [2008] 2 IR 40.
[311] This account is based largely on the *Report on the role of the judiciary* prepared by the then Chief Justice, Liam Hamilton, 14 April 1999. See also Byrne and Binchy, *Annual Review of Irish Law 1999* (2000).

[4.126] O'Flaherty J mentioned the *Sheedy* case to the County Registrar, indicating that it had been brought to his attention and that he had suggested that it might be possible to have it re-listed in the Circuit Court. He informed the County Registrar that his only interest in the matter arose from the fact that he had suggested that it might be possible for the case to be re-listed and wished to have such possibility confirmed. He gave the County Registrar a copy of the judgment in the *McDonald* case and the County Registrar agreed to look into the matter.

[4.127] As a result of the conversation with O'Flaherty J, the County Registrar contacted the solicitor now on record for Mr Sheedy (the solicitors who appeared at the 1997 hearing had come off record). The County Registrar advised the solicitor that, if he received instructions to do so, he could make an application before a judge of the Circuit Court who might or might not be willing to hear, and deal with, the application in question and recommended that the application, if it was being made, should be made before the judge in Court 24 of the Dublin Circuit Criminal Court. At the time of the original sentencing, the judge in that Court was Judge Matthews, but the presiding judge at this stage was Judge Cyril Kelly. An application to have the case re-listed was subsequently made. The County Registrar also informed O'Flaherty J that the case was being re-listed.

[4.128] The re-listed hearing occurred in November 1998. The Chief State Solicitor's office had been informed shortly before the hearing date that the case had been re-listed, and a solicitor from the Chief State Solicitor's office was present in court when the list was read over. However, the case, which was listed as No 19 of the cases to be dealt with, was heard by Judge Kelly as case No 9, and at this stage the solicitor from the Chief State Solicitor's office was not in court, having probably gone out of court to deal with a telephone call. Hamilton CJ's report stated that, based on the transcript of the re-listed hearing before Judge Kelly, it can have lasted for minutes only. Before either party had any opportunity to make any submissions, the report stated that Judge Kelly announced that he had had the benefit of a 'psychology report' and that he had grave concerns in relation to the mental condition of the accused 'at the moment'. He then stated: 'so I will suspend the balance of his sentence, own bond of three years to be of good behaviour.'

[4.129] Judge Kelly's decision was made on the basis of the medical and psychological reports on Mr Sheedy's state of health which had been available to Judge Matthews at the October 1997 hearing. It would appear that no new reports had been prepared for the November 1998 hearing, though Judge Kelly later had a conversation with counsel for Mr Sheedy in which he indicated that a new medical report be prepared which would be placed on the court file of the case. Between the time Judge Kelly made the release order and the date of the Chief Justice's report into the matter, Judge Kelly had been appointed a judge of the High Court.

[4.130] In February 1999, the Director of Public Prosecutions made an application for judicial review to the High Court challenging the validity of Judge Kelly's order for release. This application did not proceed to a full hearing, because Mr Sheedy consented to an order quashing the order for release made by Judge Kelly and agreed to surrender himself and to return to prison, with a view to appealing against the severity of the sentence imposed by Judge Matthews.[312]

[4.131] By this time, the matter had become the subject of considerable public discussion and disquiet. The Chief Justice's report stated that this disquiet and concern 'was shared by the members of the judiciary'. He contacted the President of the High Court and they both began a series of enquiries which culminated in the report published in April 1999. Hamilton CJ's report into the circumstances of the re-listing accepted that there were a number of unanswered questions concerning the matter, such as the question of whether sufficient notice had been given to the Chief State Solicitor and the hearing of the case out of sequence, but that these could only be answered in a different form of inquiry. His report was based on the agreed circumstances, as outlined, in particular as to whether the re-listing had come about from inappropriate judicial intervention and whether the hearing in November 1998 had been properly conducted.

[4.132] The Chief Justice accepted that O'Flaherty J had become involved in the case 'in a spirit of humanitarian interest'. However, he could not share O'Flaherty J's belief that a judge of the Supreme Court, having called the County Registrar, an official of a lower court, to his chambers could expect that anything said by him would be received by the official as if it had come from a private individual. He was satisfied therefore that the case might not have been re-listed in the way it was but for the intervention of O'Flaherty J. He therefore concluded that 'Mr Justice O'Flaherty's intervention was inappropriate and unwise, that it left his motives and action open to misinterpretation and that it was therefore damaging to the administration of justice.'

[4.133] As to Mr Justice Cyril Kelly, the Chief Justice's report noted that, in October 1997, Judge Matthews had made an order to the effect that he would review the sentence in October 1999. Such orders are regularly made, generally with a view to possible suspension of the remainder of the sentence. In November 1997, on an *ex parte* application of the defendant, Judge Matthews had removed this review clause from the October 1997 order. The Chief Justice's report stated that, at that stage the function of the Circuit Court in the matter was complete and the only manner of attack on Judge Matthews' order was by way of appeal to the Court of Criminal Appeal or by an application for judicial review in the High Court. The report stated that, apart from the most exceptional circumstances, there was no means of re-opening the matter in the Circuit Court. Contrary to Judge Kelly's belief, there was no practice in the Circuit Court whereby a Circuit Court judge could review, in a criminal case, the final order of a judge of equal jurisdiction who was available or was likely to become available. The

---

[312] In *People (DPP) v Sheedy* [2000] 2 IR 184, the Court of Criminal Appeal (Denham, Geoghegan and McGuinness JJ) reduced the sentence imposed from four years to three years. Civil proceedings arising from the death caused by the defendant were also dealt with in the High Court earlier in the same month as the Court of Criminal Appeal decision: see *Ryan v Sheedy* (1999) *The Irish Times*, 9 October.

report stated that, '[i]nsofar as Judge Kelly thought that such a practice existed he was mistaken. Insofar as he followed such an alleged practice himself, he was wrong.'

[4.134] The Chief Justice stated that the two psychological reports on the court file had both been before Judge Matthews when imposing sentence in 1997 and that there was no up-to-date psychological report on the file and no information on the file from which Judge Kelly could have deduced the mental condition of the accused 'at the moment'. Moreover, the report stated, by announcing his decision without allowing either party to make prior submissions concerning the case, Judge Kelly had deprived himself of any opportunity to learn from proper sources what the present condition of the accused was.

[4.135] Hamilton CJ stated that, in the circumstances, Judge Kelly should not have entered on a review of a sentence imposed by one of his colleagues. The report also stated: 'I conclude moreover that, having entered on the review, he failed to conduct the case in a manner befitting a judge.' The report also stated: 'In these circumstances, I concluded that Judge Kelly's handling of this matter compromised the administration of justice.'

The Chief Justice's report concluded with the following remarks:

> "In conclusion, I must, and do, emphasise that I, as Chief Justice, have no jurisdiction, whether under the provisions of the Constitution or any Act passed by the Oireachtas, to make any recommendations arising out of the facts in this case and, I do not, for this reason, propose to do so."

Although the Chief Justice's report made no formal recommendations, the conclusions that the actions of both judges had compromised the administration of justice were influential in the ultimate decision of both judges to resign their judicial posts shortly after its publication. [313]

[4.136] The Chief Justice's report did not deal with the consequences for Mr Quinlan of his involvement in the matter. This was the subject of a separate inquiry conducted by the Department of Justice, Equality and Law Reform.[314] This report concluded that Mr Quinlan had not in any way behaved corruptly, because he did not know Mr Sheedy. Instead, he appeared to proceed to implement what he took to be the wishes of O'Flaherty J. But the report concluded that he fell below the standards of what would be expected of a senior official in the courts by listing the case before a judge other than the judge who had dealt with sentencing originally. While the enquiry did not appear to conclude that this, of itself, would amount to misconduct, the report was critical of Mr Quinlan's initial failure to reveal the background to the re-listing when he was originally contacted about the matter, as part of the official-level inquiry conducted by the Department, on the Minister's instructions. In this respect, in particular, the report

---

[313] See (1999) *The Irish Times*, 19 April (resignation of Mr Justice O'Flaherty) and 21 April (resignation of Mr Justice Cyril Kelly). The Courts (Supplemental Provisions) (Amendment) Act 1999 provided for the relevant pension entitlements.

[314] *Report of the Department of Justice, Equality and Law Reform Arising from the Early Release from Prison of Philip Sheedy*, 19 April 1999.

concluded that his conduct 'fell very far short of what can reasonably be expected of a senior official and on the face of it amounted to misbehaviour.' Again, while this report did not, in terms, require Mr Quinlan to submit his resignation, he resigned as County Registrar shortly after its publication.[315]

[4.137] The judicial resignations occurred against a political background where it appeared highly likely that impeachment proceedings against the two judges would have been carried in both Houses of the Oireachtas. Media reports indicated that all political parties represented in the Oireachtas would have been united in passing articles of impeachment, particularly in light of the conclusion in Hamilton CJ's report that the actions involved had 'compromised the administration of justice'.[316] In the event, most commentators saw the resignations as averting a major conflict between the judiciary and the other branches of government. Some observers subscribed to the view that the event turned into personal tragedies for the judges and registrar but the predominant opinion was that their resignations were necessary to restore some degree of public confidence in the administration of justice. The 'Sheedy Affair' also prompted the more general consideration in some quarters that the options of resignation and impeachment were blunt instruments and that the system was ill-equipped to deal with the various types of judicial misbehaviour that might arise, which could range from a minor error of judgment through to the form of misconduct envisaged by Article 35. Nevertheless, given the findings in the Chief Justice's report it is not certain that the 'Sheedy Affair' itself could have been satisfactorily resolved by lesser measures than the resignation or impeachment of the judges in question.

Judicial conduct and ethics after Sheedy: proposed Judicial Council

[4.138] Immediately in the wake of the 'Sheedy Affair', the Department of Justice announced a series of measures intended to restore confidence in the administration of justice. In particular, attention was focused on ensuring that the highest standards of ethical behaviour by the judiciary be applied. Indeed, the issue of judicial conduct had already been discussed prior to the Sheedy Affair, but since the events of 1999 it has taken on a greater prominence. The 1996 *Report of the Constitution Review Group*[317] had concluded that the judicial impeachment procedure in Article 35 lacked clarity and that the simple majority vote in the Houses of the Oireachtas should be replaced by the two-thirds majority that applies to removal of the President under Article 12.10. It also recommended that judicial conduct generally should be regulated by the judiciary itself within the legislative framework of a Judicial Council embracing all the courts, and that amendments should be made to Article 35 of the Constitution to facilitate this. This aspect of the 1996 Report was considered by the All-Party Oireachtas Committee on the

---

315   See (1999) *The Irish Times*, 21 April. The Courts (Supplemental Provisions) (Amendment) Act 1999 provided for the relevant pension entitlements.
316   See (1999) *The Irish Times*, 19 April.
317   (Pn 2632, 1996), p 184. On the Constitution Review Group generally, see para **15.196**.

Constitution in 1999, after the resignations in the Sheedy affair, and the same conclusions were reached. [318]

[4.139] In the meantime, the *Sixth Report of the Working Group on a Courts Commission* had been submitted to the government in late 1998, though it was only published after the resignations in the 'Sheedy Affair'. [319] The Report outlined a number of options on future arrangements to regulate judicial ethics and conduct generally. It recommended the establishment by the Chief Justice of a Committee on Judicial Conduct and Ethics. The Minister for Justice and the government accepted this recommendation and the Committee was established by the then Chief Justice, Liam Hamilton, in May 1999, in the immediate wake of the 'Sheedy Affair'.

[4.140] In December 2000, the *Report of the Committee on Judicial Conduct and Ethics* was submitted to the Minister for Justice and was published in January 2001. [320] Its central recommendation was the establishment of a Judicial Council, largely on the lines of the arrangements in place in New South Wales. [321] The proposed Judicial Council would be empowered to deal with three areas: judicial conduct and ethics; judicial studies and publications; and judicial remuneration and conditions of work generally.

[4.141] The Report concluded that the existing provisions for dealing with concerns about judicial misconduct, namely impeachment, were inadequate. The Report noted that other instances of judicial misconduct, falling short of the 'misbehaviour' currently regulated by Article 35, merited some form of investigation. The proposed Judicial Council, of which all judges would be members, would be the mechanism for dealing with such matters. The Report noted that existing legislation dealt with this in a limited manner, confined to judges of the District Court. [322] In such cases, a number of avenues are available.

[4.142] First, the Minister for Justice may request the Chief Justice to appoint a Supreme Court or High Court judge to investigate the condition of health or inquire into the conduct of a judge of the District Court, and to report the result of the investigation or inquiry to the Minister. [323] Second, where the Chief Justice is of opinion that the conduct of a judge of the District Court has been such as to bring the administration of

---

[318] All Party Oireachtas Committee on the Constitution, *Fourth Progress Report: The Courts and the Judiciary*, November 1999.

[319] *Sixth Report of the Working Group on a Courts Commission: Conclusion with Summary* (Pn 2690, 1998). On the Working Group generally, see para **4.209**.

[320] *Report of the Committee on Judicial Conduct and Ethics*, Pn 9449, December 2000. The Report includes a wide comparative analysis of similar arrangements in other jurisdictions, including the United Kingdom, Canada, the United States, New Zealand and New South Wales. It also includes the text of papers delivered at a conference on judicial accountability organised by the Committee in May 2000.

[321] *Report of the Committee on Judicial Conduct and Ethics*, p 52.

[322] See Courts of Justice (District Court) Act 1946, s 21; Courts (Supplemental Provisions) Act 1961, s 10(4); and Courts (Supplemental Provisions) Act 1961, s 36(2). See *Report of the Committee on Judicial Conduct and Ethics*, pp 7–9.

justice into disrepute, the Chief Justice may interview the judge privately and inform him or her of that opinion. Third, the President of the District Court may investigate the conduct of a judge of the District Court where it appears the judge's conduct is prejudicial to the prompt and efficient discharge of the business of that court. In none of these situations is any sanction stipulated.

[4.143] The Report recommended that all members of the judiciary would automatically become members of the Judicial Council. It would carry out its functions through a board and three committees. The board of the Council would consist of the Chief Justice, the Presidents of the High Court, the Circuit Court and the District Courts, four ordinary judges, one from each of these courts to be elected by their colleagues, and a co-opted judge. The three committees would be: a Judicial Conduct and Ethics Committee, a Judicial Studies and Publications Committee and a General Committee. They would have the same structure and representation as the board.

Judicial Conduct and Ethics Committee

[4.144] The Report recommended that a complaint against a judge made by a member of the public or of the legal profession would be considered by the Judicial Conduct and Ethics Committee. The Report noted that, in other jurisdictions where similar procedures exist, most complaints by members of the public could be dealt with informally at this stage, because many arise due to misunderstandings, a lack of information or a failure in communication as to what occurred in court. Where some explanation of what occurred was thought necessary, the complainant would be informed that the judge would issue a statement to that effect, usually at a sitting of his or her court. There might be cases where no action was required, either because the complaint disclosed no inappropriate behaviour, or where an appeal or judicial review was the more appropriate response.

[4.145] Where the complaint was of a serious nature, and could not be disposed of informally or through the appeal mechanism in the courts, it would be dealt with by a panel of inquiry. This would comprise three members, two of them judges nominated by the committee and a lay person drawn from a panel of three 'people of standing in the community' appointed by the Attorney General. The Report emphasised the importance of lay participation in this process, referring to the benefits of such a procedure in the

---

323 Such an inquiry was held in 1957, and on that occasion the judge resigned. A similar inquiry was established in 2000, whose terms of reference were: 'To inquire into the conduct of District Judge Donnchadh Ó Buachalla in relation to the propriety of his handling of the licensing of the premises known as Jack White's Inn having regard to his acquaintance with its licensee, Mrs Catherine Nevin, and in relation to the discharge of his judicial functions in cases involving two Gardaí against whom complaints had been made by Mrs Catherine Nevin.' The inquiry was conducted in public by Murphy J, a judge of the Supreme Court. The Report of the Inquiry was published in December 2000 and concluded that there had been no impropriety by the judge, but that he had made some errors of judgement in the manner in which he had handled the application, particularly by not recusing himself from hearing the application in view of his acquaintance with Mrs Nevin.

New South Wales and Canadian systems. The Report concluded that there should be no representative of the legal profession on the panel of inquiry.[324] The Report indicated that the panel might have the same powers as those applicable under current legislation where the conduct of a District Court judge is being investigated. Where misconduct was established by the panel of inquiry, it could recommend that one of three courses of action be taken. The first is a private reprimand by the Conduct and Ethics Committee to the judge. The second is a public reprimand by the Conduct and Ethics Committee to the judge. The third is a recommendation by the Conduct and Ethics Committee to the Attorney General that the government consider the tabling of a resolution in both Houses of the Oireachtas calling for the removal of the judge from office for stated misbehaviour or incapacity.

[4.146] The Report acknowledged that any sanctions from the Conduct and Ethics Committee would be moral in nature, rather than legal. Thus, these arrangements would not affect the constitutional position that only the Oireachtas can remove a judge from office. Nonetheless, by putting in place these new measures, it was hoped that it would reinforce the concept of judicial accountability. The Report also stated that the Conduct and Ethics Committee could establish a general code of ethics, which would be given to all new members of the judiciary.

Judicial Studies Committee

[4.147] The Judicial Studies Committee would be responsible for judicial training and education and for the publication of a journal. It would supercede the existing Judicial Studies Institute, which was established in 1996 with a view to providing continuing education for all judges.[325] The Judicial Studies Institute was established against the background of the Courts and Court Officers Act 1995, which introduced for the first time a mandatory requirement that candidates for judicial appointment undertake to agree to take any course of training or education as may be required by the Chief Justice or the President of the court to which the person is appointed.[326] While such training and continuing education is not mandatory for those appointed prior to 1996, the Judicial Studies Institute has held a series of seminars since its establishment for all members of the judiciary, ranging from seminars on specific areas of law to the relationship between the judiciary and the media. It is envisaged that the proposed Judicial Studies Committee would develop this further, and would provide courses of training for members of the judiciary on specific areas of law, as well as other general topics, such as equal treatment of litigants. It would also publish 'bench books', which would include

---

[324] *Report of the Committee on Judicial Conduct and Ethics*, pp 54–55. The Law Society of Ireland in particular had argued that such representation was required.

[325] *Report of the Committee on Judicial Conduct and Ethics*, Ch 6. The training of judges reflects the general need for continuing professional development (CPD) within all professions, including the legal profession: see para **3.144**.

[326] Courts and Court Officers Act 1995 Act, s 16. Section 48 of the 1995 Act provides that such training and education may be funded by the Minister for Justice.

specimen directions for criminal trials and guidelines on sentencing.[327] The current Judicial Studies Institute established under the 1995 Act has developed the *Judicial Studies Institute Journal* aimed at the judiciary.[328] Since 2001, the legal journal has been published twice yearly and the articles are concerned with contemporary legal issues of interest to the judiciary. Indeed, members of the judiciary have published a number of articles in the journal since its inception. It was noted in 2007 that there is a need for judicial studies for the judiciary to be available on a more structured basis, allowing for enhanced judicial studies for the judiciary to be provided by the government as a matter of urgency.[329] With the establishment of the Interim Judicial Council in 2011, the Judicial Studies Institute was replaced by the Judicial Studies Committee of the Judicial Council and was tasked with similar functions to the Judicial Studies Institute.

General Committee

[4.148] The General Committee would be responsible for keeping under review questions of remuneration and the working conditions of judges. Any reports presented by the Committee to the board would, where appropriate, be referred to the Attorney General, the Minister for Justice or the Courts Service.

Response to the Report

[4.149] In response to the Report, the government indicated that it would bring forward the necessary constitutional amendment to Article 35 and enact the necessary legislation to place the Judicial Council on a statutory basis. Indeed, the Twenty-Second Amendment to the Constitution Bill was published in 2001 with a view to having the issue put to a referendum in June 2001. However, the proposal was withdrawn in May 2001 when the Opposition parties disagreed with the connected proposal in the Twenty-Second Amendment Bill that the impeachment procedure would, in future, require a two-thirds vote in the Oireachtas, rather than the current position where a simple majority suffices. The opposition parties were also concerned about elements of the detail concerning the proposed Judicial Council.[330] Subsequent events involving Circuit Court Judge Brian Curtin postponed any developments in this area until 2010.

The Curtin case: 2002–2005

[4.150] In 2002, for the first time since the foundation of the state, the impeachment of a sitting judge was considered. In January 2002, a Circuit Court judge, Judge Brian Curtin, was charged with possessing child pornography. In June 2004 he was acquitted

---

[327] *Report of the Committee on Judicial Conduct and Ethics*, p 56. The equivalent British Judicial Studies Board also publishes, for example, guidelines on damages in personal injuries actions.

[328] See www.jsijournal.ie.

[329] Irish Council for Civil Liberties, *Justice Matters: Independence, Accountability and the Irish Judiciary* (2007), 73.

[330] See 535 *Dáil Debates*, 1 May 2001 (Second Stage debate on 22nd Amendment to the Constitution Bill 2001) and 2 May 2001 (further debate on 22nd Amendment withdrawn on Order of Business). See also (2001) *The Irish Times*, 3 May.

of the offence as the judge presiding over his trial in the Circuit Court ruled that a search warrant authorising the search of Judge Curtin's house and seizure of a personal computer was invalid. This meant that the seizure of the computer was unconstitutional and evidence obtained from Judge Curtin's personal computer was inadmissible. Following Judge Curtin's acquittal steps were initiated to bring about his possible impeachment. Initially both Houses of the Oireachtas adopted a new procedure to allow for investigations into judicial conduct. Then the government moved two motions: the first calling for the removal of Judge Curtin from office pursuant to Article 35.4.1° and the second establishing a Joint Committee of the Houses of the Oireachtas for the purposes of investigating and receiving evidence in relation to Judge Curtin's conduct. The Dáil suspended the first motion to allow for the Joint Committee to begin its investigation into the judge's conduct.

[4.151] In order to facilitate the investigation by the Joint Committee and to allow it to take evidence, the Oireachtas amended s 3 of the Committees of the Houses of the Oireachtas (Compellability, Privileges and Immunities of Witnesses) Act 1997 to render judges compellable witnesses in investigations into their behaviour. In addition, the Child Trafficking and Pornography Act 1998 was amended to exempt both Judge Curtin and the Oireachtas Committee from any criminality by reason of the possession or distribution of child pornography in relation to actions pursuant to the investigation. Under the first of these powers, the Joint Committee ordered that Judge Curtin produce his computer for inspection by the Joint Committee. Judge Curtin challenged this request, the inquiry process and s 3 of the 1997 Act. The main arguments advanced in the legal challenge by Judge Curtin were as follows: firstly, that the procedures adopted by the Houses of the Oireachtas were inconsistent with Article 35.4.1° since it was not necessary to prove the charges against him before the Houses of the Oireachtas considered the impeachment resolution (rather the Joint Committee merely reported to both Houses of the Oireachtas and did not make findings of fact), secondly, the requirement in s 3 of the 1997 Act, which compelled judges to give evidence, was unconstitutional as it infringed judicial independence and, finally, it was unlawful for the Joint Committee to order him to produce his personal computer.

[4.152] When the challenge came on appeal from the High Court to the Supreme Court, the court acknowledged the legal significance of the case before it, being 'one of the few occasions in the annals of legal history that such a proposal [removal of a judge] had been considered by a court and the first time since the foundation of the State'.[331] The Supreme Court refused the applicant's claim and held, firstly, that it was permissible for the Houses of the Oireachtas to vest the Joint Committee with the power to report without making findings of fact. Secondly, the Supreme Court held that s 3 of the 1997 Act did not amount to an unlawful invasion of the independence of the judiciary, noting that the power in Article 35.4 of the Constitution to commence the process of

---

[331] *Curtin v Clerk of Dáil Éireann* [2006] IESC 14, [2006] 2 IR 556, 588, [2006] 2 ILRM 99, 106. See also Bruton and Sheehy Skeffington, 'Case note: *Curtin v Dáil Éireann and others*' [2006] ISLR 255.

impeachment against a judge included the purpose of ensuring the fitness and integrity of the judiciary. Finally, the Supreme Court held that the Joint Committee's direction to the applicant to produce his personal computer was legitimate so as to allow the Joint Committee to undertake the functions vested in it by the Houses of the Oireachtas.

[4.153] After the Supreme Court's decision, the Joint Committee re-commenced its hearings and obtained possession of Judge Curtin's personal computer. It also commissioned an expert report on his personal computer. In November 2006, legal representatives on behalf of Judge Curtin applied for a further adjournment of hearings by the Joint Committee due to Judge Curtin's ill health. When the Joint Committee refused the adjournment, Judge Curtin's legal advisers tendered his resignation from office of Circuit Court judge. Although ultimately no impeachment proceedings were initiated against Judge Curtin, the controversy surrounding his acquittal and subsequent moves by both Houses of the Oireachtas indicated the significant procedural and practical difficulties with the mechanism for removal of judges. The Irish Council for Civil Liberties noted that:

> "the *Curtin* case illustrates the defective nature of current judicial accountability mechanisms in Ireland in that the inquiry into his behaviour was not processed expeditiously with the result that no impeachment took place. However, at least the Supreme Court has provided clarity and established that, judges can be held to account in this way and are entitled to fair procedures rights."[332]

[4.154] A survey of judges in 2007 indicates that there was general support amongst the judiciary for the recommendations made in the *Report of the Committee on Judicial Conduct and Ethics* and an eagerness to see a judicial accountability mechanism put in place.[333] The Minister for Justice, Equality and Law Reform has established a Working Group made up of a representative of the Chief Justice and a representative of the Minister to examine the details of the legislative proposals that might be put in place.[334] The delay in advancing matters from the Report was highlighted by the Irish Council for Civil Liberties, who recommended that the government move to introduce legislation as a matter of urgency.[335] It was also recommended in that report that a code of ethics for the judiciary be devised.

Scheme of Judicial Council Bill (2010)

[4.155] Despite an apparent general commitment to establish a Judicial Council, specific progress has been extremely slow. Nonetheless, after discussions between the judiciary and government, the Scheme of a Judicial Council Bill, in effect a draft Bill,

---

[332] Irish Council for Civil Liberties, *Justice Matters: Independence, Accountability and the Irish Judiciary* (2007), 70.

[333] Irish Council for Civil Liberties, *Justice Matters: Independence, Accountability and the Irish Judiciary* (2007), 72.

[334] See (2008) *The Irish Times*, 17 April.

[335] Irish Council for Civil Liberties, *Justice Matters: Independence, Accountability and the Irish Judiciary* (2007), 72.

was published in 2010.[336] The Scheme broadly reflects the recommendations made in 2000 as to its composition and functions. Thus, Head 3 of the Scheme provides for the establishment of a Judicial Council of all serving members of the judiciary which shall be independent in its functions with its own seal, and Head 8 provides for a nine-member board of the Judicial Council.

[4.156] Head 5 sets out the functions of the Judicial Council as being to maintain and promote:

- excellence in the exercise by judges of their judicial functions,
- high standards of conduct among judges,
- the efficient and effective use of judicial resources,
- continued education among judges, and
- respect for the independence of the judiciary.

Head 11 makes provision for the establishment of Committees of the Council, and Head 16 for the appointment of a secretary to the Council.

[4.157] On judicial conduct, Head 20 provides for a Judicial Conduct Committee comprising eight judges and three lay members appointed by the government, which would be independent in the performance of its functions. Head 21 sets out the functions of the Judicial Conduct Committee, to include:

- the consideration and investigation of complaints,
- the preparation and submission to the board of the Council of draft guidelines concerning judicial conduct and ethics, and
- the making of regulations setting procedures for the consideration and investigation of complaints to be laid before both Houses.

Head 23 provides for the appointment of three designated members of the Judicial Conduct Committee to act as referees, one being a lay member.

Head 26 would empower the Judicial Conduct Committee to refer matters for informal investigations under, or alternatively, formal investigation by a panel of inquiry (comprising two judges and one lay member) to be established under Head 27.

[4.158] Head 30 would allow recommendations to be made by the panel of inquiry as may be considered necessary to safeguard the administration of justice, such as:

- issuing advice to the judge concerned,
- recommending a course of action the judge should follow, for example, that the judge attend a specified course,
- issuing a recommendation to the President of the Court of which the judge is a member,
- issuing a recommendation for procedural or organisational change, or
- issuing a reprimand.

---

336 Scheme of a Judicial Council Bill, available at www.justice.ie.

Head 31 provides that the carrying into effect of these recommendations would be for determination by the Judicial Conduct Committee.

Head 34 provides that the physical or mental health condition of a judge may also be a matter of investigation.

[4.159] On judicial studies and support, Head 12 of the Bill provides for the establishment of a Judicial Studies Institute, which would be responsible for the facilitation of the continuing education of judges including:

- the preparation and distribution of bench books,
- the publication of material relevant to its function,
- the organisation of relevant conferences, seminars and meetings,
- the provision of training for judges in relation to IT, and
- the dissemination of information on sentencing.

Head 13 of the Scheme provides for the establishment of Judicial Support Committees for the Supreme, High, Circuit and District Courts.

[4.160] In November 2011, an interim Judicial Council was established by the judiciary in anticipation of the establishment of a statutory Judicial Council along the lines envisaged in the Scheme of the Judicial Council Bill that was published in 2010. The interim Judicial Council made submissions to the Department of Justice on an earlier draft of the heads of the Judicial Council Bill. In addition the Interim Judicial Council established a sub-committee with a view to the preparation of draft guidelines concerning judicial conduct and ethics. At the time of writing (September 2014), it appears that a formal Judicial Council Bill will be published in 2014 or 2015.[337]

Independence, public criticism and the place of the judiciary in society

[4.161] As a corollary to the concept of judicial independence, there has been an implicit convention pre-dating the 1937 Constitution, and indeed the establishment of the state in 1922, that judges do not generally become involved in any matter of public controversy. Indeed, until recent years, a judge would not give interviews to the media while he or she was a sitting judge, particularly in relation to a case in which the judge had been involved. In a sense, the view was that judges made decisions, but that any political implications of such decisions were matters for the executive and legislative branches of government, and the judiciary should stand aloof.[338]

---

[337] At the time of writing (September 2014) the Government Legislation Programme, Autumn Session 2014, available at www.taoiseach.ie, indicates that the government proposes to publish a Judicial Council Bill in 2014 or 2015.

[338] Eg, see the interview with Mr Justice O'Higgins, former Chief Justice, (1991) *The Irish Times,* 7 and 8 October. This was given after Mr Justice O'Higgins had retired as a judge of the Court of Justice of the EU. Similarly, in December 2007 after her retirement from the Supreme Court, Mrs Justice Catherine McGuinness was interviewed on RTÉ Radio 1 by Marian Finucane.

[4.162] Many writers on the law would agree that there have been a number of highly influential judges over the years who, as individuals, have had a significant impact on the development of the law.[339] These individuals would have been the subject of autobiographies and biographies were it not for the conventional reticence attaching to holders of judicial office. The result has been that judicial autobiographies are a rarity in Britain and Ireland,[340] and any biographies have largely involved judges of an earlier era.[341] In their absence, students of law have had to be content largely with collections of anecdotes.[342]

---

[339] Thus, of the Irish judges of the 19th century, Christopher Palles, the last Lord Chief Baron, stands out, both for the length of his judicial tenure of almost 50 years stretching from the mid-19th century virtually to the establishment of the Irish Free State and also that his judgments continue to be cited as authority in many common law jurisdictions. In the 20th century, there have been a number of judges in Ireland who have contributed greatly to the development of Irish law, in particular constitutional law. Among these were Hugh Kennedy, the first Attorney General of the Irish Free State, an important architect of the 1924 court system and the first Chief Justice. George Gavan Duffy, who had been Roger Casement's solicitor in his treason trial and a member of the delegation that had signed the 1921 Anglo–Irish Articles of Agreement, was later a distinguished President of the High Court. Later, the developments both in the interpretation of the Constitution and of Irish law in general were associated with Cearbhall Ó Dálaigh (Chief Justice, judge of the European Court of Justice and then President of Ireland), Thomas O'Higgins (government minister and later Chief Justice and judge of the Court of Justice), Thomas Finlay (Chief Justice), Kenny J, Kingsmill Moore J, Walsh J and Henchy J. This list is inevitably selective and also excludes those many brilliant advocates who brought to the courts innovative submissions without which the law might not have developed as it did. Among these advocates who did not go on to become members of the judiciary might be mentioned Mr Thomas Connolly SC and Mr Séan McBride SC (who had also been a Minister for External Affairs).

[340] Exceptions in Britain include Lord Denning's *My Family Story* (1981). The only autobiography written by a member of the High Court or Supreme Court since 1922 is O'Higgins, *A Double Life* (1996), an autobiography of the former Chief Justice Thomas O'Higgins, who had previously been a leading politician and government Minister. Lindsay, *Memories* (1992) is an extended memoir by a former government minister and Master of the High Court.

[341] See Delany, *Christopher Palles* (1960) and Golding, *George Gavan Duffy* (1982). Other important biographical collections include Ball, *The Judges in Ireland 1221–1921*, 2 vols (1993 reprint). An exception to the convention that only long-distant judges are recognised in biography is Mathews (ed), *Immediate Man: Cuimhní ar Chearbhall Ó Dálaigh* (1983). In addition, *festschrifts* in honour of Irish judges of the recent past have been published. These include O'Reilly (ed), *Human Rights and Constitutional Law* (1992) (in honour of Walsh J), Curtin and O'Keeffe (eds), *Constitutional Adjudication in European Community and National Law* (1992) (in honour of O'Higgins CJ) and the 1990–1992 volume of the *Irish Jurist* (in honour of Professor John Kelly). Durcan, *Daddy, Daddy* (1990) includes a series of poems on the poet's relationship with his father, a former President of the Circuit Court.

[342] See para **3.106**.

[4.163] It is, perhaps, not surprising that, in an era of media power and rapid changes in Irish society in recent years, this convention should begin to break down.[343] Thus, in 1987 the then President of the High Court, Liam Hamilton (later Chief Justice), agreed to appear on an edition of an RTÉ television series, *Open File*, in which various influential public figures were questioned about their work. In that instance, Mr Justice Hamilton was questioned by a two-person panel, one a lecturer in law in University College Dublin and the other a well-known investigative journalist. Such a programme would have been unthinkable ten years previously.[344] Similarly, in 1986 there was a significant level of public discussion arising from a judicial inquiry conducted into what became known as the 'Kerry Babies Case'.[345] The High Court judge who conducted that inquiry, Lynch J, responded to adverse comments on the inquiry's report which had appeared in the current affairs magazine *Magill*.[346] In 2009, controversy arose when the judiciary were excluded from a pension levy introduced by the Oireachtas to which virtually all public servants were subjected. The judiciary had been excluded on the basis of legal advice from the Attorney General that their inclusion might infringe Article 35.5 of the Constitution (which at that time prohibited any reduction in judicial remuneration but, as discussed below, this was amended in 2011). Despite this exclusion, in May 2009 the Chief Justice, Murray CJ, arranged with the Revenue Commissioners for the judiciary to make equivalent voluntary payments. Media reports in June 2009 indicated that 'only' 19 of the 148 judges had made voluntary contributions under this scheme. The Chief Justice responded publicly to these media reports,[347] stating that they were 'unfair and misleading' because the judges had been given until the end of 2009 to make the contributions, and he expected there would be 'strong and continuous participation' by the judiciary in the scheme. The Chief Justice's statement noted that 'the judiciary do not normally make public statements even where criticism of judges was involved', but that this was an exceptional circumstance which justified making a public statement on the issue. In former times, the judiciary's response to public criticism would be to ignore the matter, or to bring a claim for defamation against the publication, or initiate contempt of court proceedings.[348] The trend of judges making public statements about issues which concern them has continued through the vehicle of the Association of Judges in Ireland, a representative

---

[343] On extra-judicial comments by judges see Kennedy, 'Extra Judicial Comments by Judges' [2005] 5(1) *Judicial Studies Institute Journal* 199.

[344] It is notable that, also in 1987, the then British Lord Chancellor, Lord Mackay, had removed the so-called 'Kilmuir rules' of 1955, which had imposed strict rules on when the judiciary should communicate with the media. Since 1987, the British judiciary has been much freer to speak on matters of public interest, including making adverse criticism of government proposals for law reform of which the judiciary disapproves. To date, the Irish judiciary has not been publicly critical of law reform proposals from government. In 2001, Keane CJ initiated a public debate on reform of the court structure: see para **5.122**.

[345] *Report of the Tribunal of Inquiry into the 'Kerry Babies Case'* (Pl 3514, 1985).

[346] *Magill*, March 1986.

[347] (2009) *The Irish Times*, 23 June.

[348] On contempt of court, see paras **10.49*ff*.

body for judges established in 2011.[349] For example the AJI made a public statement expressing concerning at the implications of the introduction of a legislative provision which increased the necessary service for judges of the Supreme Court, High Court and Circuit Court to retire and be entitled to a full judicial pension.[350]

[4.164] In 1992, the public comments of O'Hanlon J, then a High Court judge, on proposed changes in Irish law on abortion attracted considerable media attention and adverse comment.[351] The removal of O'Hanlon J as a judge did not arise from such comments, but it underlined the difficulties involved, even in the 'age of communication', when judges become embroiled publicly in matters on which they, and other members of the community, hold strong views.[352] In this changing situation, it is inevitable that the tone of comment on the work of the judiciary, whether from the academic and wider legal community or from the media, will become more robust, replacing what in the past would have been quite deferential and indeed reverential comment.

[4.165] It has also become increasingly common for judges to speak publicly at conferences or to university societies on topics of legal significance. For example, in 2001, the then Chief Justice, Mr Justice Ronan Keane delivered a paper to the University College Cork Law Society on the topic of 'The Irish Legal System in the 21st Century: Planning for the Future' in which he was critical of the court system in general.[353] In recent years, extra-judicial comments have garnered significant controversy. In early 2004, Mr Justice Carney was due to speak at a conference in Dublin on the issue of criminal justice system. It is believed that his paper would have dealt with the sittings of

---

[349] www.aji.ie. On the issue of Judges speaking publicly about issues see Lord Neuberger (of the Supreme Court of England and Wales), 'The Third and Fourth Estates: Judges, Journalists and Open Justice', lecture, 28 August 2014.

[350] Section 22 of Public Service Pensions (Single Scheme and Other Provisions) Act 2012.

[351] In *Attorney General v X* [1992] 1 IR 1 (see para **15.177**) the Supreme Court had held that Article 40.3.3° appeared to authorise abortion in limited circumstances. The case generated enormous publicity and controversy. O'Hanlon J publicly stated that he disagreed with the decision of the Supreme Court and that any attempt to amend the Constitution or to legislate for abortion would be contrary to natural law and therefore prohibited: see (1993) 11 ILT 8. By the time O'Hanlon J had made his comments, the government had committed itself to amending the Constitution and/or introducing legislation on the topic. O'Hanlon J was, at that time, also President of the Law Reform Commission (see para **11.13**). The Taoiseach of the day wrote to Mr Justice O'Hanlon objecting to the fact that he had made these views public and also purported in this letter to terminate his appointment as President of the Law Reform Commission. In reply, O'Hanlon J made a public statement to the effect that the purported termination had no legal effect, but he also simultaneously withdrew from the position as President of the Law Reform Commission, in effect resigning. See Hogan and Whyte (eds), *JM Kelly: The Irish Constitution* (4th edn, 2003), p 552, fn 21. He later instituted proceedings against the state for damages arising from these events, which were settled in 1998, reportedly for £100,000: see (1998) *The Irish Times*, 19 June.

[352] See further, paras **15.177–15.180**.

[353] See para **5.115**.

the Central Criminal Court in Limerick the previous year. The *Irish Times* reported that the then Chief Justice, Mr Justice Keane, who was to chair the conference, was not prepared to attend the conference if the paper was delivered. Mr Justice Carney did not speak at the conference.[354] In 2007, a lecture delivered by Mr Justice Carney to the University College Cork Law Society gained a large amount of publicity and further re-opened the debate on the type of topics which are suitable for extra-judicial comments by judges. The controversy surrounding the lecture by Mr Justice Carney centred on his comments regarding the use of victim impact evidence in a murder trial he had presided over.[355] In 2008, Mr Justice Carney's comments again made at a lecture at University College Cork attracted widespread media interest. The *Irish Times* reported that Mr Justice Carney told the lecture that knife crime is 'out of control' and that cases coming before the courts had doubled in a very short period of time.[356] In 2014, a radio interview given by Mr Justice Barry White a week after he retired as a High Court judge attracted some critical comments.[357] It is now increasingly common for judges to speak at public events and conferences.

[4.166] Legal publishing in Ireland, in particular academic legal writing, has only emerged in any real sense since the late 1970s and early 1980s, and many textbook writers have focused on 'black letter' law, describing the essential legal rules applicable to a particular subject area. The 1990s also saw the emergence of studies that focus on the societal context within which law operates.[358]

[4.167] More general socio-legal studies of the British judiciary have appeared in recent years and these include Professor Griffith's *The Politics of the Judiciary*[359] and Professor Lee's *Judging Judges*.[360] Both books provide a wider analysis of the political context in which the judiciary operate than have appeared to date in Ireland. Professor Lee's book suggested, for example, that in the age of the media, the courts may need to consider agreeing to hold media briefings in relation to their more important decisions. Indeed, it

---

354   See Kennedy, 'Extra Judicial Comments by Judges' [2005] 5(1) *Judicial Studies Institute Journal* 199, 202 and (2004) *The Irish Times*, 1 March.

355   See (2007) *The Irish Times*, 11 October.

356   (2008) *The Irish Times*, 12 June.

357   (2014) *The Irish Times*, 16 September, commenting on interview on RTÉ Radio One, *Today with Seán O'Rourke*, 15 September 2014, available at www.rte.ie.

358   These include Duncan (ed), *Law and Social Policy* (1987); Whelan (ed), *Law and Liberty in Ireland* (1993); O'Mahony, *Crime and Punishment in Ireland* (1993); Connelly (ed), *Gender and the Law in Ireland* (1995); and Quinn et al (eds), *Justice and Legal Theory in Ireland* (1995). In his Foreword to McMahon and Binchy, *A Casebook on the Irish Law of Torts* (1983), Mr Justice Walsh, the then senior ordinary judge of the Supreme Court, suggested that the decision-making process of collegiate courts 'should be studied under the rubric of small group sociology'.

359   (5th edn, 1997).

360   1988 (1989 paperback edition containing additional material).

would appear that some moves in this direction are likely to result arising from the creation of the Courts Service in 1999.[361]

[4.168] As for the approach of the media in general, there has been a steady stream in recent years of best-selling books describing 'famous trials', both criminal and civil.[362] Earlier pioneering work by the journalist Nell McCafferty during the 1970s on the Dublin District Court was collected as *In the Eyes of the Law*.[363] The descriptions of the people who came into contact with the law at this level of the criminal justice system reflected poorly on the overall system. The following provides a flavour of her vivid descriptions:

"The gowns and wigs may imply majesty, though they too are faded and torn sometimes. The Dublin District Courts themselves have the trappings of sadness ... Within the court itself, no room. Three hard benches, and the unlucky ones line the walls. It gets too hot, too cold, too stuffy, too noisy, too quiet. Even the gardaí don't know how to use the microphones. The Justice is irritated. Justice is flawed. The solicitor arrives late. Justice is delayed. The lists are long and the bailsmen have to come back next day. People don't know what to do and other people are too busy to help them. Tempers flare, spirits flag, and the long hopeless grind grinds on. Around in the High Court, planning permission is debated in leisure, and the dignity befitting high finance."

The conditions described there might be thought to reflect a bad day in Dickensian times, but conditions in the courthouses of Ireland in the late 20th century led to a number of court proceedings in which the Minister for Justice was ordered to comply with statutory obligations concerning the maintenance of courthouses.[364]

---

[361] See para **4.217**.

[362] Collections of 'famous criminal trials' include Deale, *Beyond any Reasonable Doubt?* (2nd edn, 1990) and Reddy, *Murder Will Out: A Book of Irish Murder Cases* (1990). Dunne and Kerrigan, *Round Up the Usual Suspects* (1984) and Joyce and Murtagh, *Blind Justice* (1984) deal with the 'Sallins Train Robbery case' of the mid 1970s. The 'Arms Trial' of 1970 is discussed in McIntyre, *Through the Bridewell Gate* (1971) and Kelly, *Orders for the Captain?* (published by the author, 1971). See also Williams, *The General* (1994), an account of the life of an alleged 'godfather' of crime. As to civil cases, Crotty, *A Radical's Response* (1988) is an account of the background to *Crotty v An Taoiseach* [1987] IR 713 (see para **16.105**) written by the plaintiff. Two other books of note are Kerrigan, *Nothing But the Truth* (1990), an account of *Dunne v National Maternity Hospital* [1989] IR 91 (see para **7.30**, fn 52), and O'Callaghan, *The Red Book* (1992), an account of *Hanrahan v Merck, Sharpe & Dohme Ltd* [1988] ILRM 629: see para **7.09**. See also Friel, *The Suspect: The Story of Rachel O'Reilly's Murder* (2007) an account of *The People (DPP) v O'Reilly* [2009] IECCA 18.

[363] (1981).

[364] The poor physical condition of many courthouses in the state had given rise to litigation initiated by members of the legal profession seeking orders requiring the relevant state agencies to carry out their statutory duties concerning their upkeep: see *The State (King) v Minister for Justice* [1984] IR 169 (decided in 1975) and *Hoey v Minister for Justice* [1994] 3 IR 329. See also para **4.214**.

[4.169] The criticism of courthouse conditions in *In the Eyes of the Law* is exceptionally mild by comparison with the more wide-ranging criticism of judicial performance to be found, for example, in the United States. Possibly the most controversial book published in this respect was *The Brethren*.[365] This 'inside' account of the workings of the United States Supreme Court from 1969 to 1975 clearly required the active assistance of some of the law clerks who are assigned to assist the Supreme Court justices. *The Brethren* discussed, for example, how the US Supreme Court apparently reached its unanimous 8-0 decision in *Clay v United States*.[366] This was a case in which Muhammad Ali (his birth name was Cassius Clay), one of the greatest professional heavyweight boxers of all time, appealed his conviction for his refusal to be drafted into the US army during the Vietnam War. He claimed that he was exempted on the ground of conscientious objection, which he had based on his Black Muslim religious faith. This ground was rejected and his conviction was upheld by the federal Fifth Circuit Court of Appeals. On further appeal, the US Supreme Court unanimously reversed the conviction.

[4.170] The discussion of the case in *The Brethren* described what it suggested was the internal discussion that led to this conclusion. The book stated that Justice Marshall had recused himself because he had been US Solicitor General when the case began, and the remaining eight justices had initially voted 5 to 3 to uphold Ali's conviction. Justice Harlan, who had been assigned by Chief Justice Burger to write the majority opinion, actually changed his vote after reading material on Black Muslim religious thinking which one of his law clerks had given him. Justice Harlan's change of mind thus tied the Court at 4–4 at this point, which would have resulted in Ali's conviction being upheld. At a further conference discussion of the Court, Justice Stewart put forward a basis on which Ali's conviction could be reversed on the relatively narrow ground that the government had failed to specify precisely why Ali's conscientious objection claim had been denied. This, according to *The Brethren*, ultimately gained the support of all the eight justices. Those who voted to reverse the conviction included Chief Justice Burger, who would have had little personal sympathy for Ali's claim to be exempted but who may also have taken the view that a split decision by the Court might have weakened its authority.

[4.171] In the 1980s, the then leading political affairs journal, *Magill* (at that time edited by Colm Tóibín, who later became a well-known fiction writer), published a lengthy article on the leading two Supreme Court judges of that time, Mr Justice Brian Walsh and Mr Justice Seamus Henchy.[367] This article could be described as the only equivalent Irish version of *The Brethren*, combining detailed analysis of decisions of the Supreme Court and commentary on the personalities of the two judges themselves. Since then, no

---

[365] Woodward and Armstrong, *The Brethren* (1979).
[366] *Clay v United States* 403 US 698 (1971).
[367] Tóibín, 'Inside the Supreme' *Magill* February 1985, pp 8–35.

similar account of the work of Irish judges has been published in Ireland.[368] Nonetheless, there has been a perceived increase in the number of 'colour' pieces published on the workings of the courts and judiciary in recent years. Journalists who write 'colour' pieces for their newspapers are now increasingly deployed to write 'sketches' of the judiciary, in some instances veering close to breaching the rules on contempt of court.[369]

[4.172] Similarly, as a result of a number of high-profile cases concerning the state's inability to provide secure accommodation for troubled adolescents, substantial profiles of Mr Justice Peter Kelly (then a High Court judge) appeared in the early years of this century, making him one of the best-known judges in Ireland at that time.[370] The public lectures delivered by Mr Justice Paul Carney, referred to already, have also attracted considerable media attention.

[4.173] The strong reputation of judges as being independent and forensic has also led to them being appointed to chair tribunals of inquiry, commissions of investigation and other ad hoc committees.[371] This is also common in many other jurisdictions where judicial inquiries similarly have a high reputation. In Ireland this has also increased the public and media profile of those judges, particularly where the published reports are seen to have uncovered past wrongdoings. While much of this media attention has been positive from the judiciary's perspective, it has been suggested that such high-profile and politically sensitive work may ultimately prove to be double-edged. The judiciary have been highly regarded for most of the history of the state, but the coverage surrounding the 'Sheedy affair' in 1999 and the Curtin case between 2002 and 2005 illustrated that the judiciary, like all other state institutions, enjoy no immunity from adverse publicity. Thus, it has been argued that judicial involvement in such high-profile activity, outside the core function of the administration of justice, may run the risk of damaging public confidence in the judiciary.[372] Nonetheless, it is clear that judges are likely to continue to be called on to chair sensitive public inquiries and investigations, primarily because of their reputation for integrity. In addition, it is also clear that judges can make an invaluable contribution to the debate on the legal system. As a result it has been recommended that a Code of Ethics be drafted for the judiciary and that provisions be included on extra-judicial comments and carrying out additional duties such as

---

368 There are two possible explanations for this: first, journalistic concerns that an Irish version of *The Brethren* could be defamatory or in contempt of court, and second that, in a small society, many of the points that might form the content of such a book are passed by word of mouth, perpetuating the 'oral traditions' of Irish life. Of course, in terms of fiction, the performance of the judiciary and the court system has, for many generations, been subjected to public scrutiny. Banville, *The Book of Evidence* (1992) examined aspects of the criminal mind and is said to have been based on a true story.

369 See the discussion of *People v Nevin*, fn 70 above.

370 See para **4.22**.

371 See ch 8 on such tribunals and commissions.

372 See Kennedy, 'Extra Judicial Comments by Judges' [2005] 5 (1); *Judicial Studies Institute Journal* 199 at 202 and *The Irish Times*, 1 March 2004 and *The Irish Times*, 11 October 2007.

chairing tribunals and commissions.[373] We can expect the Judicial Council, when established on a statutory basis, to consider the issue of extra-judicial comments by judges.

Judicial Salaries

[4.174] Until 2011, Article 35.5 of the Constitution had provided:

"The remuneration of judges shall not be reduced during their continuance in office."

This constitutional guarantee that judicial pay would not be reduced during a judge's term of office has been regarded as an important provision to underpin the judiciary's independence by ensuring that they did not feel that they were in any way 'obliged' to the government of the day, by contrast with members of the judiciary in the distant past who might have considered that their continued remuneration was dependent on making decisions that did not offend those in authority. In the wake of the Great Recession that emerged in 2007, the pay of virtually all civil servants and public servants was reduced under the Financial Emergency Measures in the Public Interest Acts 2009 to 2010, often referred to as FEMPA. Because of Article 35.5, these pay reductions could not, and did not, apply to the judiciary. Nonetheless, the then Chief Justice, Murray CJ, arranged a voluntary arrangement under which the judiciary could return a percentage of their pay that was in line with the FEMPA reductions. It was reported that over 90% of the judiciary participated in this voluntary arrangement. The government decided, however, that the voluntary arrangement was not sufficient to deal with this matter and a referendum to amend Article 35.5, set out in the Twenty-Ninth Amendment of the Constitution (Judge's Remuneration) Bill 2011, was therefore put to a vote of the people.

[4.175] Given the historical significance of Article 35.5, regarded as a bulwark of judicial independence against political interference, it was not surprising that there was considerable opposition voiced from the legal community. This included a letter to the print media from six former Attorneys General (which also voiced objection to the proposed extension of investigatory powers to Oireachtas Committees, and whose objections in this respect appear to have influenced greatly the rejection of that proposal in a referendum held on the same day as the vote on the reduction in judicial pay). Indeed, bearing in mind the conventional reluctance by the judiciary to comment on matters of public controversy, there were even some adverse comments made to the print media from (unattributed) representatives of the judiciary. Nonetheless, the amendment to Article 35.5 was approved by 79% of those who voted in the referendum.

[4.176] After the changes effected in 2011, Article 35.5 now provides:

"1° The remuneration of judges shall not be reduced during their continuance in office save in accordance with this section.

---

373 Irish Council for Civil Liberties, 'Justice Matters: Independence, Accountability and the Irish Judiciary' (ICCL, 2007) at 60.

2° The remuneration of judges is subject to the imposition of taxes, levies or other charges that are imposed by law on persons generally or persons belonging to a particular class.

3° Where, before or after the enactment of this section, reductions have been or are made by law to the remuneration of persons belonging to classes of persons whose remuneration is paid out of public money and such law states that those reductions are in the public interest, provision may also be made by law to make proportionate reductions to the remuneration of judges."

Following the changes made to Article 35.5, the Financial Emergency Measures in the Public Interest (Amendment) Act 2011 provided for the application of the FEMPA 2009 to serving members of the judiciary. During the Oireachtas debate on the 2011 Act, the Minister for Public Expenditure and Reform commented that the terms of the amended Article 35.5:

"were very carefully crafted from a legal and constitutional perspective in order to ensure that the ongoing independence of the Judiciary in carrying out its functions on a daily basis is maintained. This is as it should be. It would be a blow to our status as a constitutional democracy if there was even the perception, no matter how remote the possibility might be, of Government influence over decisions by judges on cases. In approaching this issue, that constitutional imperative was an absolute priority for the Government."[374]

The Minister noted that, prior to the amendment to Article 35.5, serving members of the judiciary together with the President were not subject to the provisions of the previous three FEMPA Acts. The 2011 Act provided that they are subject to the measures in those Acts from 1 January 2012. The 2011 Act also provided for a 10% reduction in pay for new judicial appointments from its enactment. This reflected a 10% reduction in pay from 1 January 2011 for new entrants into entry grades in the public service.

[4.177] In addition, the 2011 Act amended the Financial Emergency Measures in the Public Interest Act 2010 and imposed a higher reduction rate of 20% on public service pensions above €100,000. Pensions in excess of €60,000 had already been adjusted downwards by 12%. The Minister for Public Expenditure and Reform pointed out in the Oireachtas debates on the 2011 Act that the Attorney General had advised that pension entitlements are vested property rights which had already been earned, but the Minister also indicated that it was felt that the emergency financial circumstances referred to in the Preambles to these Acts would allow the reduction to withstand challenge. The Minister noted in this respect that two safeguards were contained in all the Financial Emergency Measures in the Public Interest Acts: first, the measures must be publicly reviewed annually; and second, the Minister may consider and may grant claims for exemption or modification if it is considered just and equitable to do so.

[4.178] Following the amendment to Article 35.5 of the Constitution on judicial remuneration, ss 3 and 4 of the 2011 Act apply the reductions in salary applied to other public servants through the application of the pension related deduction to serving judges, and ss 5 and 6 apply the reduction in salary effected through the provisions of

---

[374] For consideration of the issue after the constitutional referendum see O'Dowd, "Judges in Whose Cause? The Irish Bench After the Judges Pay Referendum" (2012) Irish Jurist 102.

the Financial Emergency Measures in the Public Interest (No 2) Act 2009. The net effect of the provisions of the 2011 Act resulted in reductions for serving judges ranging from 16% in the case of a judge of the District Court to 23% in the case of the Chief Justice.

[4.179] In addition to the provision for pay reductions in certain circumstances now provided for in Article 35.5, it had previously been determined that judges are liable to income tax on their salaries, which may also affect net pay. In *O'Byrne v Minister for Finance*,[375] the Supreme Court held that the original text of Article 35.5 did not preclude the deduction of income tax from the gross salary of a judge, provided that such deductions were similar to those for other persons having the same income level. In the *O'Byrne* case, the widow of Mr Justice John O'Byrne, who had been a judge of the High Court and later the Supreme Court from 1926 to 1954, claimed that subjecting a judge's salary to income tax was in conflict with Article 35.5. This claim was, however, rejected in the Supreme Court, by a 3:2 majority. The three judges in the majority stated that Article 35.5 must be read with Article 35.2 as protecting the independence of the judges from governmental interference. In this light, the court held that to require a judge to pay income tax like other citizens could not be described as an attack on judicial independence.

[4.180] The salaries of the judges are fixed from time to time by legislation. At the beginning of the 19th century, judicial salaries were very high by the standards of the day. Thus, prior to 1832, the Lord Chancellor of Ireland enjoyed an annual salary of £10,000, when it was reduced to £8,000. The salary of the Lord Chief Justice of Ireland was fixed at £5,000 in 1877, with ordinary High Court judges receiving about £3,500.[376] The establishment of the Irish Free State in 1922 saw a reduction in salaries from the old regime, and it would seem that judicial salaries were pegged at about half that of their English counterparts.[377] It is worth noting that, by 2008, the salaries of senior Irish judges and their English counterparts had approached par again.[378]

The following salaries were fixed in 1924:

- Chief Justice: £4,000
- Supreme Court judges (and High Court President): £3,000
- High Court judges: £2,500
- Circuit Court judges: £1,700
- District Justices: £1,000 to £1,200.[379]

---

[375] *O'Byrne v Minister for Finance* [1959] IR 1.

[376] See Delany, *The Administration of Justice in Ireland* (4th edn, 1975), p 74.

[377] See File S 15010 C, National Archives of Ireland, in the files relating to what became the Courts (Supplemental Provisions) Act 1961.

[378] For example, the Chief Justice's salary in 2008 was €281,656 while the UK's Lord Chancellor earned £230,400. The President of the High Court's salary was €261,538 and the Master of the Rolls earned £305,700. Taking currency differences into account, these salaries are very similar, but as a result of the changes made in 2011, the Irish judiciary salary levels fell below their British counterparts.

[379] Courts of Justice Act 1924, ss 13, 41 and 74.

[4.181] There were modest increases in 1947 and 1953,[380] but in June 1957 all the judges of the High Court and Supreme Court sent a memorandum to the government indicating that they considered that their salaries had fallen well below comparable salaries in the public sector and making unfavourable comparisons with their English and Northern Ireland brethren. It is also notable that the judges suggested that the imposition of income tax on their salaries was in breach of Article 35.5 of the Constitution, an issue which was, at the time, pending before the Supreme Court in the *O'Byrne* case and on which the Supreme Court ultimately held in effect against themselves, albeit by a 3:2 majority. While the government considered that, in general, judicial salaries were appropriate some further increases were made on the re-organisation of the courts in 1961.

[4.182] Further increases were effected in the 1960s,[381] and by 1975 judicial salaries ranged from £14,210 in the case of the Chief Justice to £6,757 for District Justices.[382] In 1977, judicial salaries were linked to other senior office holders in the public sector.[383] By the 1980s, it was accepted that these salaries had fallen well behind what was appropriate, with the potential effect this might have on attracting people of high calibre to these positions. Recommendations of the Review Body on Higher Remuneration in the Public Sector resulted in major increases taking effect in 1989 and 1990. The changes effected between 1990 and 2008 are summarised in the following table. In general, the salaries of the judiciary, as with most higher civil servants and politicians, had almost tripled between 1990 and 2008.

	1990[384]	1995[385]	1998[386]	2000[387]	2001[388]	2008[389]
	£	£	£	£	£	€
Chief Justice	72,356	95,920	104,535	120,293	132,955	
President of High Court	64,927	86,109	94,132	108,321	119,722	261,538
Supreme Court judges	62,274	82,840	90,597	104,254	115,227	245,445
High Court judges	57,498	76,300	83,426	96,002	106,107	231,366

---

380 Courts of Justice Act 1947 and Courts of Justice Act 1953.

381 Between 1961 and 1968, judicial salary changes required an Act amending the levels specified in s 46 of the 1961 Act. The Courts (Supplemental Provisions) (Amendment) (No 2) Act 1968 amended s 46 by specifying that further changes could be effected by Orders rather than an amending Act.

382 Courts (Supplemental Provisions) Act 1961 (s 46) Order 1975.

383 The arrangements for judicial salaries were brought under the general umbrella of those for government ministers and members of the Oireachtas by the Oireachtas (Allowances to Members) and Ministerial, Parliamentary and Judicial Offices (Amendment) Act 1977. See also the Oireachtas (Allowances to Members) and Ministerial, Parliamentary and Judicial Offices (Amendment) Act 1983.

	1990[384]	1995[385]	1998[386]	2000[387]	2001[388]	2008[389]
Circuit Court judges	45,825	56,680	65,650	75,548	83,500	168,998
District Court judges	38,397	46,870	54,540	62,762	69,368	140,831

Figure 4.1

[4.183] After the changes made in the wake of the amendment to Article 35.5 in 2011, the current salaries of various judges are as follows:

	Appointed before 2012	Appointed after 2012
Judge of the Supreme Court	€219,191	€197,272
Judge of the High Court	€206,618	€172,710
Judge of the Circuit Court	€156,248	€140,623
Judge of the District Court	€136,124	€122,512

Figure 4.2

It has been noted that in Northern Ireland a senior judge earns 11 times the average annual salary and in the Republic of Ireland it is more than seven times.[390] An argument

---

384   Courts (Supplemental Provisions) Act 1961 (Section 46) Order 1989 (SI 204/1989), giving effect to Report No 30 of the Review Body. The 1989 Order provided for three phased increases of 40%, 30% and 30% respectively over the period July 1989 to October 1990.

385   Courts (Supplemental Provisions) Act 1961 (Section 46) Order 1994 (SI 273/1994), giving effect to Report No 35 of the Review Body. The 1994 Order provided for a 50% increase over that contained in the 1990 Order with effect from April 1994 and a further 50% increase from May 1995. The Explanatory Note to the 1994 Order also stated that these figures would be further uprated in 1996 and 1997 to take account of the Programme for Competitiveness and Work, agreed between the social partners in 1994.

386   Courts (Supplemental Provisions) Act 1961 (Section 46) Order 1998 (SI 73/1998), giving effect to Report No 37 of the Review Body.

387   Courts (Supplemental Provisions) Act 1961 (Increase of Judicial Remuneration) Order 2001 (SI 44/2001), giving effect to Report No 38 of the Review Body.

388   Courts (Supplemental Provisions) Act 1961 (Increase of Judicial Remuneration) Order 2001 (SI 44/2001), giving effect to increases under the Programme for Prosperity and Fairness, the agreement made in 2000 between the social partners.

389   Courts (Supplemental Provisions) Act 1961 (Increase of Judicial Remuneration) Order 2007 (SI 841/2007).

390   European Commission for the Efficiency of Justice, 'European Judicial Systems Edition 2008 (2006): Efficiency and Quality of Justice' (Council of Europe, 2008), 15. See also (2008) *The Irish Times*, 11 October.

in favour of maintaining high salaries for the members of the judiciary is to dissuade against bribery and corruption.[391] A 2014 survey by the European Commission for the Efficiency of Justice (CEPEJ), based on 2012 figures, found that newly appointed Irish judges (even after the recent pay cuts) are the second highest paid judges in Europe.

Immunity from suit and contempt of court

[4.184] In addition to the provisions of the Constitution concerning judicial independence, certain common law principles have been accepted as consistent with the independence recognised in Article 35.2.[392] Thus, the common law recognised that a judge was absolutely immune from any claims arising from any acts of the judge in his or her judicial capacity, such as a claim in negligence or a claim that words spoken by a judge were defamatory.[393] In *McIlwraith v Fawsitt*,[394] the Supreme Court upheld the traditional common law rule that in judicial review proceedings, no order for costs should be made against a member of the judiciary where the decision was made *bona fide*. This traditional immunity is subject to any relevant provisions of the European Convention on Human Rights and would be affected indirectly by the Bill to establish a Judicial Council in as much as the latter will establish a mechanism by which judges will be made accountable.[395] It has recently been recommended that judges should enjoy

---

[391] Irish Council for Civil Liberties, *Justice Matters: Independence, Accountability and the Irish Judiciary* (ICCL, 2007), 57. For a discussion on similar arguments in the United States, see Posner, *How Judges Think* (2008).

[392] See Hogan and Whyte (eds), *JM Kelly: The Irish Constitution*, (4th edn, 2003), pp 999–1003.

[393] See McMahon and Binchy, *Irish Law of Torts* (4th edn, 2013) and *Sirros v Moore* [1975] QB 118. In the *Sirros* case, the defendant judge had wrongly ordered a person's detention; it was held that no civil action for damages could be taken as a result, because the judge had acted in good faith (*bona fide*) in his judicial capacity. This general approach was applied by McMahon J in *Kemmy v Ireland* [2009] IEHC 178, [2009] 4 IR 74, in which there is a detailed survey of the case law and literature on the immunity. The principle was extended to statutory bodies exercising adjudicative duties in the public interest: see *Beatty v The Rent Tribunal & Another* [2006] 2 IR 191.

[394] *McIlwraith v Fawsitt* [1990] 1 IR 343. See also *O'Connor v Carroll* [1999] 2 IR 160.

[395] For example, it may be argued that failure to give judgment within a reasonable time period is in breach of Article 6 of the Convention. On the proposed Judicial Council, see paras **4.140–4.160**. Note that s 46 of the Courts and Court Officers Act 2002 as amended by s 55 of the Civil Liability and Courts Act 2004 provides that that where judgment in proceedings is not delivered within two months from the date from which the judgment was reserved, the President of the Court shall list the proceedings before the relevant judge. On this date, the judge is required to specify the date on which he or she will deliver judgment in the proceedings. See *Doran v Ireland* Application No 50389/99, 31 July 2003, *McMullen v Ireland* Application Number 42297/98 and *O'Reilly v Ireland* Application Number 54725/00, 29 July 2004 which were successful claims against the state for the breach by Ireland of its responsibility to ensure that cases are dealt with within a reasonable length of time. See also Delany 'The Obligation on the Courts to Deal with Cases within a "Reasonable Time"' (2004) 22 ILT 249.

personal immunity from civil suits for monetary damages for improper acts or omissions in the exercise of their judicial functions.[396]

[4.185] The common law courts had also developed the concept of contempt of court to protect their independence. Under the common law principles of contempt, where a judge became aware of any interference with the administration of justice, he or she could order the arrest of the alleged offender (contemner), try the charges and impose sentence. Since contempt of court has not been regulated by statute in Ireland, there is no limit to the sentence that a judge may impose.[397] Ordinarily, of course, a prosecution would be initiated by the state authorities and would require a jury trial. However, in *The State (Director of Public Prosecutions) v Walsh*,[398] the then Chief Justice referred to Article 35.2 as supporting the common law power of a judge to punish a contempt in the face of the court without the need to await the institution of criminal proceedings by the executive arm of government or to have a jury trial.[399] In a later case, *Re Kelly and Deighan*,[400] two people had been imprisoned for contempt in this way by the High Court, but the Supreme Court had held that, in the particular circumstances, it had not been necessary for the High Court judge to exercise the jurisdiction to imprison summarily. However, in *Deighan v Ireland*,[401] the High Court dismissed a claim for damages against the state by one of those who had been imprisoned in the *Kelly and Deighan* case, primarily on the ground that to allow such a claim would undermine the independence of the judiciary.

[7] VACATING OF JUDICIAL OFFICE AND RETIREMENT

Vacating of judicial office

[4.186] Although no provision is made in the Constitution for the vacating of a judicial office, other than where the judge is removed or reaches retirement age, this is dealt with by statute. A vacating of office can occur either where the judge is appointed to another judicial office or where the judge resigns office 'in writing under his hand addressed to the President and transmitted to the Taoiseach'.[402] The latter form of vacating of office amounts, in effect, to a voluntary retirement.

---

[396] Irish Council for Civil Liberties, *Justice Matters: Independence, Accountability and the Irish Judiciary* (ICCL, 2007), 103.

[397] Proposals for statutory reform in this area are contained in the Law Reform Commission's 1994 *Report on Contempt of Court* (LRC 47-1994).

[398] *The State (Director of Public Prosecutions) v Walsh* [1981] IR 412.

[399] On contempt of court generally, see paras **10.49**ff.

[400] *Kelly and Deighan, Re* [1984] ILRM 424.

[401] *Deighan v Ireland* [1995] 2 IR 56. See also *Kemmy v Ireland* [2009] IEHC 178, [2009] 4 IR 74.

[402] Courts (Establishment and Constitution) Act 1961, s 6 replacing the Courts of Justice Act 1924, ss 11, 45 and 70.

Retirement ages

[4.187] Between 1924 and the end of 1995, the age of retirement for High Court and Supreme Court judges was 72,[403] and this retirement age continues to apply to judges appointed prior to 1996.[404] For judges appointed to the High Court and Supreme Court since the Courts and Court Officers Act 1995 came into operation in December 1995, the retirement age is 70. For a Circuit Court judge the age of retirement is also 70 years.[405]

[4.188] For a District Court judge, the general retirement age is 65.[406] However, a judge of the District Court who is about to reach 65 may be continued in office on a year-to-year basis until the age of 70 if he or she applies for such continuation to a Committee comprising the Chief Justice, the President of the High Court and the Attorney General. In order to continue the judge in office, the Committee (after consultation with the Minister for Justice) must be satisfied that the judge 'is not suffering from any disability which would render him unfit to continue to discharge efficiently the duties of his office'.[407]

---

[403] Courts of Justice Act 1924, s 12 as applied by the Courts (Supplemental Provisions) Act 1961, s 48.

[404] Courts and Court Officers Act 1995, s 47(1) introduced the 70 years of age retirement for judges appointed after the Act came into effect, which was 15 December 1995. Section 47(2) provides that 72 continues to be the retirement age for judges appointed before the 1995 Act came into force and s 47(3) provides that the 72 years retirement age also applies to any person who holds judicial office before the Act came into force in any of the courts established under Article 34 of the Constitution or in the Court of Justice of the European Communities or of the Court of First Instance attached thereto.

[405] Courts (Supplemental Provisions) Act 1961, s 18. Courts of Justice Act 1924, s 40 had also specified 70 as the retirement age, though between 1947 and 1961, the retirement age had been set at 72: Courts of Justice Act 1947, s 15.

[406] Courts (Supplemental Provisions) Act 1961, s 30(1). Courts of Justice Act 1924, s 72 had provided for a retirement age of 70 years for District Court judges appointed to Dublin and Cork, but a 65 age of retirement for other judges of the District Court.

[407] Courts of Justice (District Court) Act 1949, s 2. In *Shelly v Mahon* [1990] 1 IR 36 and *Glavin v Governor of Mountjoy Prison* [1991] 2 IR 421, the Supreme Court held to be invalid a summary conviction and a sending forward for trial on indictment made by a judge whose continuance in office had not complied with s 2 of the 1949 Act. An error had been made concerning the judge's true age, and he had, in fact, reached 65 before he had sought continuance in office under the 1949 Act. When the error was discovered, the Courts (No 2) Act 1988 was passed with a view to validating retrospectively his decisions for the periods when he had not been validly continued in office. However, the 1988 Act also expressly provided that the validation was without prejudice to any constitutional rights of citizens. In the *Shelly* and *Glavin* decisions, the Supreme Court held that the 1988 Act could not retrospectively validate any decisions that affected the rights of persons to a trial 'in due course of law', as required by Article 38.1 of the Constitution and thus the two decisions in question were held invalid.

[4.189] While these retirement ages are higher than the general 65 years retirement age for many occupations in the public sector,[408] a retirement age for judges of the higher courts did not exist prior to 1924[409] and was a novelty introduced by the Courts of Justice Act 1924. In Britain, retirement ages for judges of the High Court and above were not introduced until the 1940s. In the United States, there is no retirement age for justices of the Federal Supreme Court, who continue to hold office for life. In 2005, Chief Justice Rehnquist died in office at the age of 80. Indeed one of the current Justices of the US Supreme Court, Scalia J, is aged 78 at the time of writing (September 2014).

Pensions

[4.190] Pension provision for retired judges and judges who have otherwise vacated their office is made by legislation.[410] In 1991,[411] pension entitlements already available to other public servants were extended to the judiciary and other court officers.[412] The effect is that some level of pension is payable after five years of service.[413] In *McMenamin v Ireland*[414] certain elements of the pension provisions for District Court judges were found to be in conflict with Article 35.5 of the Constitution, largely arising from the effects of inflation since the provisions had been introduced in 1961. Amending legislation was enacted in 1998 to remedy the deficiencies.[415] As already

---

[408] It had been suggested in the Oireachtas debate on what became s 47 of the Courts and Court Officers Act 1995 that a 65 year retirement age be introduced for all judges, but this was resisted on the ground that the reduction from 72 to 70 had effectively introduced a common age of retirement for all judges (subject to the particular arrangements for judges of the District Court). It was also pointed out that, since many judges are appointed in their 50s, a retirement age of 65 would provide them with relatively little time to develop as a judge. See *Select Committee on Legislation and Security*, L5–11 (7 December 1995), cc 675–81.

[409] Thus, the Last Chief Baron, Christopher Palles, resigned judicial office in 1916 at the age of 85. He died in 1920. Lefroy CJ had been appointed Lord Chief Justice of Ireland in 1852, when he was 76, resigning judicial office in 1866 at the age of 90. Earlier that year he had successfully resisted suggestions in a House of Commons debate that he and the then Chancellor of Ireland (Blackburne LC, a mere 83) were unable to carry out their judicial functions. Lefroy CJ died in 1869.

[410] Courts (Supplemental Provisions) Act 1961, s 46 replacing the Courts of Justice Act 1924, ss 15, 41 and 75. See generally Delany, *The Courts Acts 1924–1997* (1999).

[411] Courts (Supplemental Provisions) (Amendment) Act 1991.

[412] The court officers covered by the Courts (Supplemental Provisions) Act 1991 are the Master of the High Court, Taxing Masters and County Registrars. On court officers generally, see para **4.193**.

[413] The Courts (Supplemental Provisions) Act 1991 had a substantial retrospective content and was applied to appointments going back to the 1970s. This led to some criticism expressed as the Act was being passed. For reaction, see the comments of the former Chief Justice, O'Higgins CJ, (1991) *The Irish Times*, 24 April. For media comment on the pension received by Judge Brian Curtin, who resigned as judge of the Circuit Court after five years in office, see (2006) *The Irish Times*, 14 November.

[414] *McMenamin v Ireland* [1994] 2 ILRM 368 (HC); [1997] 2 ILRM 177 (SC).

[415] Part III of the Oireachtas (Allowances to Members) and Ministerial, Parliamentary, Judicial and Court Offices (Amendment) Act 1998: see Byrne and Binchy, *Annual Review of Irish Law 1998* (1999), p 127.

noted, reductions in pension entitlements were made in the wake of the amendment in 2011 to Article 35.5. For judges appointed to the Supreme Court, High Court or Circuit Court from 2012, the necessary service for such judges to retire and be entitled to a full judicial pension has increased to 20 years.[416]

Retired judge may be precluded from appearing in court

[4.191] A long-established convention is that a retired judge does not practice in a court of equal or lower jurisdiction to that in which he or she sat as a judge.[417] In *Re O'Connor*,[418] the Supreme Court held that Sir James O'Connor, who had been a Lord Justice of Appeal in the pre-1922 Irish Court of Appeal, was entitled to be admitted to the roll of solicitors, but only on the condition that he refrain from practising in the courts. The court took the view that it would affect the administration of justice were a former judge to appear in court as an advocate in circumstances where he might be required to challenge some of his decisions as a judge or, at the least, fail to support them in argument.

[4.192] This convention, as affirmed in the *O'Connor* case, continues to be applied. Thus, former High Court and Supreme Court judges would be barred from practice on their retirement in those courts, creating an effective ban on practice in Ireland.[419] Former Circuit Court judges could appear in the High Court and Supreme Court as advocates,[420] while former District Court judges could appear in the Circuit Court as well as the High Court and Supreme Court, but not the District Court.[421] These rules do not apply to retired judges appearing in other jurisdictions. It was reported in 2013 that Ms Justice Macken, who had retired from the Supreme Court in 2010, had reapplied for admission to the Law Library in order to take up a position in a London based Chambers.[422] This convention does not, of course, prevent a former judge from being engaged as a mediator, or as a practitioner in another jurisdiction. Thus, a former judge of the Irish courts who has been called to the English or New York bars would not be precluded from practising in London or New York.

---

[416] Section 22 of Public Service Pensions (Single Scheme and Other Provisions) Act 2012.

[417] See the discussion in Bartholomew, *The Irish Judiciary* (1971), pp 6–7. The convention is included in the Code of Conduct of the Bar of Ireland.

[418] *Re O'Connor* [1930] IR 623.

[419] In the case of Mr Harold Whelehan SC, who had been President of the High Court for a matter of days in late 1994 (see para **4.100**), a General Meeting of the Bar of Ireland subsequently approved a resolution that, because of the shortness of his judicial tenure, he should be permitted to appear as counsel in any court.

[420] Mr Frank Roe SC, former President of the Circuit Court, resumed his practice at the Bar on his retirement in the late 1980s.

[421] Former District Court Justice Mr Robert Ó hUadhaigh recommenced his practice at the Bar after his retirement in the 1980s.

[422] (2013) *Irish Independent*, 26 August.

[8]   COURT OFFICERS AND ADMINISTRATION

[4.193] The judiciary represents the public face of the court system and, subject to the power of juries where they sit, the judges make the final decisions in virtually all situations. However, the administration of the court system rests largely with public servants who fall under the general heading of court officers. As we discuss below, the volume of work in the different courts, both in civil and criminal matters, has greatly increased since the 1960s. This, in turn, has placed great strains on the court system that has been in place since 1924. We note elsewhere that, in response to this, additional judges have been appointed to the different courts from time to time[423] and that other procedural changes have attempted to streamline court procedure.[424]

[4.194] Despite these changes, it has been increasingly recognised that more fundamental reform was required, and in 1996 recommendations were made by a Working Group on a Courts Commission which, if implemented, would effect a fundamental shift in the overall management of the court system. Before turning to the general background to those recommendations and their potential impact, we outline the functions of the various court officers engaged in the administration of the court system.

Court Officers in the High Court and Supreme Court

[4.195] The principal officers and offices attached to the High Court and Supreme Court are:

- the Master of the High Court,
- the Central Office,
- Registrars of the High Court,
- the Taxing-Masters' Office (to be replaced by the Office of Legal Costs Adjudicator under the Legal Services Regulation Bill 2011), and
- the Registrar of the Supreme Court.[425]

---

[423] See para **4.52**.

[424] See para **5.12**ff.

[425] See the Court Officers Act 1926 and the Eighth Schedule to the Courts (Supplemental Provisions) Act 1961 for a complete list. In addition to the offices and officers considered in the text are the following: the Probate Office (which deals with the administration of estates), the Office of the Official Assignee in Bankruptcy, the Examiner's Office (with responsibility for many chancery matters, including company law cases), the Accountant's Office (which is responsible for any moneys lodged in court) and the Office of the Wards of Court (responsible for those persons whose affairs are administered by the Court after an application to Court based on their inability to look after their own interests).

Master of the High Court

[4.196] Prior to the passing of the Courts and Court Officers Act 1995, the Master of the High Court was largely confined to exercising powers conferred by rules of court.[426] These functions include:

- granting orders for extension of time for various matters;[427]

- in civil claims initiated by special summons,[428] ensuring that the legal documentation is correct (that 'the papers are in order') before it is forwarded to a High Court judge;

- giving judgment in non-contested cases, for example where a claim for a sum in default of a loan is made by a bank and there is no defence to the claim or no real defence; and

- hearing applications for the enforcement of certain orders of courts of European Community member states.[429]

[4.197] The Master continues to exercise these functions, but the Courts and Court Officers Act 1995 added significantly to the scope of the powers of the office of Master. The 1995 Act provides that:

- the Master is empowered to exercise limited functions of a judicial nature within the scope of Article 37 of the Constitution;[430]

- the Master may exercise all the powers of a High Court judge in *ex parte* applications or applications on notice and in applications for judgment by consent or in default of appearance or defence: in effect, the Master may enter final judgment in these cases, whereas up to the passing of the 1995 Act, a decision by a High Court judge was required;[431]

---

[426] Court Officers Act 1926 and the Eighth Schedule to the Courts (Supplemental Provisions) Act 1961. Although the 1961 Act appeared to envisage more substantial functions being conferred on the Master, the office had, until 1995, been largely confined to powers conferred by rules of court: see Barron and Ford, *Practice and Procedure in the Master's Court* (2nd edn, 1998).

[427] See paras **6.58** and **6.60**.

[428] See para **6.30**.

[429] Jurisdiction of Courts and Enforcement of Judgments (European Communities) Act 1998.

[430] Courts and Court Officers Act 1995, s 24. The 1995 Act gave belated effect to the principal recommendations in the *16th Report of the Committee on Court Practice and Procedure* (1972): see Barron and Ford, *Practice and Procedure in the Master's Court* (2nd edn, 1998). On Article 37 of the Constitution, see para **4.09**.

[431] Courts and Court Officers Act 1995, s 25(1). Section 25(2) also contains a list of matters excluded from the Master's jurisdiction, such as any matter of a criminal nature and certain civil matters such as judicial review proceedings or any matter relating to the custody of children. See also *Kennedy v Killeen Corrugated Products Ltd* [2006] IEHC 38.

— in a case for a debt or a liquidated sum where an application is made for judgment in default of defence, the Master may award interest on the sum claimed.[432]

Central Office

[4.198] The Central Office of the High Court is essentially the administrative headquarters of the High Court.[433] All High Court business, both civil and criminal, is initiated and processed through the Central Office and is then transmitted, where relevant, either to the Master of the High Court or a High Court judge. While we have already noted that there are no formal divisions of the High Court,[434] the various civil and criminal matters are, from an administrative point of view, processed by the Central Office to the appropriate judge or judges who have been appointed by the President of the High Court to deal with particular matters.

Registrars of the High Court

[4.199] A number of Central Office staff members are nominated from time to time to be Registrars for the High Court.[435] In effect, a Registrar is the essential administrative assistant to a judge and will sit in court with the judge, usually in front of the judge facing the well of the court. A Registrar's functions include the drawing up of the formal court order which represents the official record of the decision for the purposes of the parties in the case. This formal order is what is presented by one party to any other person to prove in law that a particular decision was made in the case by the court. The judge will, of course, be required to approve the wording of an order but, in most cases, it is the Registrar who is responsible in the first place and may well liaise personally with the lawyers for the two parties to ensure that the wording of the order reflects their understanding of the decision of the judge. Consent matters such as adjournments in procedural matters or the setting of dates in certain High Court lists are heard by a Deputy Master (who is also a Court Registrar) in the interests of efficiency.

Taxing Master's Office (Office of Legal Costs Adjudicator)

[4.200] The principal function of the Taxing Master is to determine whether legal costs being sought by parties to proceedings in the High Court are appropriate. Under the

---

[432] Courts and Court Officers Act 1995, s 50(1). The power to award interest on claims in general was conferred on High Court judges by the Courts Act 1981, s 22. In *Mellowhide Products Ltd v Barry Agencies Ltd* [1983] ILRM 152, Finlay P held that s 22 of the 1981 Act did not confer on the Master any power to award interest, though he commented that he saw no logical reason why the Master should not be given this power. Section 50 of the 1995 Act gave effect to this recommendation.

[433] Court Officers Act 1926 and the Eighth Schedule to the Courts (Supplemental Provisions) Act 1961.

[434] See para **4.62**.

[435] Court Officers Act 1926 and the Eighth Schedule to the Courts (Supplemental Provisions) Act 1961.

Legal Services Regulation Bill 2011, the Taxing Master's functions will be transferred to the Office of Legal Costs Adjudicator. We consider these functions elsewhere.[436]

Registrar of the Supreme Court

[4.201] The Registrar of the Supreme Court is specifically assigned to the Chief Justice in order to carry out the administrative functions relevant to the functions of the Chief Justice and of the Supreme Court.[437]

Court Officers in the District Court and Circuit Court

[4.202] In the Circuit Court, the system is administered through County Registrars who also have considerable administrative support teams.[438] The Courts and Court Officers Act 1995 conferred additional powers on County Registrars, comparable (but not identical) to those conferred by the 1995 Act on the Master of the High Court.[439] In the District Court, the administrative side of the court system is the responsibility of District Court clerks.[440] The Courts and Court Officers Act 2009 provided for the establishment of Combined Court Offices which now provide support across different courts, for example, combined court offices for the District Court and Circuit Court.

Court sittings and vacations

[4.203] Four terms are fixed for the sitting of the High Court and Supreme Court.[441] The Michaelmas Term runs from the first Monday in October to 21 December; the Hilary Term begins on 11 January (or, if this falls on a Saturday or Sunday, the following Monday) and ends two weeks before Good Friday; the Easter Term runs from the Monday after Easter week and ends on the Thursday preceding Whit Sunday; and the Trinity Term begins on the Wednesday following Whitsun week and ends on 31 July. The periods outside term time are referred to as Vacation periods and the period between 31 July and the first Monday in October is called the Long Vacation. The Supreme Court does not, in general, sit outside term time. As for the High Court, business continues to be transacted outside term time, though at a reduced level. In recent years the High Court sits on a regular basis in September and certain matters can be listed for hearing during this month such as claims involving personal injuries, garda compensation, commercial, asylum, insolvency, non jury, judicial review, family law and child abduction. In the past there was relatively little court activity during the Long Vacation but nowadays a substantial amount of both administrative and judicial activity

---

[436] See para **5.42**.
[437] Court Officers Act 1926 and the Eighth Schedule to the Courts (Supplemental Provisions) Act 1961.
[438] Court Officers Act 1926 and the Courts (Supplemental Provisions) Act 1961, s 55(2).
[439] Section 34 of and Second Schedule to the Courts and Court Officers Act 1995.
[440] Court Officers Act 1926 and the Courts (Supplemental Provisions) Act 1961, s 55(3).
[441] Rules of the Superior Courts 1986 (SI 15/1986), Ord 118.

continues during this period.[442] Similar terms operate for the Circuit Court,[443] but the District Court sits for much longer terms, generally the same as for other public institutions.[444]

[9]   MANAGEMENT OF THE COURT SYSTEM

[4.204] We have already mentioned that, in 1996, recommendations were made which may have a significant impact on the manner in which the court system will be managed in the 21st century. Since the establishment of the Irish Free State in 1922, the budget and management of the courts had primarily been in the hands of the Department of Justice, with a number of other state agencies as well as local authorities being responsible for connected issues such as the upkeep and maintenance of courthouses. The court system operates in quite a different social context in the 21st century than at the beginning of the 20th century, and we have already seen how the judges have, to some extent, responded to change.[445] At a wider level, the workload of the courts had expanded greatly, but while additional judges and administrative personnel were appointed from time to time, the overall management and administration had not changed to reflect the many additional pressures placed on the system. We will outline below the extent of the growth in court business and some of the important procedural and substantive changes made, particularly in recent years, to deal with this.

[4.205] In addition to these changes, the manner in which the court system itself is managed has been the subject of substantial debate. Against a background of dissatisfaction concerning the inability of the court system to cope with the demands placed on it as well as problems with the physical condition of courthouses in the state,[446] a Working Group on a Courts Commission was appointed by the government in 1995 to make recommendations on how the court service should be managed. We outline the contents of the first report of that Working Group below and the subsequent establishment of the Courts Service under the Courts Service Act 1998,[447] but we first consider the growth in the workload of the courts and the various responses to date to this phenomenon.

---

[442] As to whether the courts should sit for longer periods, see the Fair Trade Commission *Report of Study of Restrictive Practices in the Legal Profession* (1990), p 299. See also the *Sixth Report of the Working Group on a Courts Commission: Conclusion and Summary* (November 1998).

[443] Rules of the Circuit Court 1950 (SI 179/1950), Ord 2.

[444] District Court Rules 1948 (SR&O 431/1947), r 16 provided that judges of the District Court were entitled to six weeks' holiday in the year. No similar provision is contained in the District Court Rules 1997 (SI 93/1997), which replaced the 1948 Rules, though this remains the practice.

[445] See para **4.163**.

[446] See para **4.168**.

[447] See para **4.217**.

The growth in civil and criminal cases from the 1960s to 1990s

[4.206] Figures 4.2 and 4.3 indicate the overall increase in a number of civil and criminal matters in the period 1965 to 1994. They do not represent all civil or criminal cases in the periods referred to, but have been chosen to indicate some general trends.[448]

Civil Cases	1965	1975	1981	1986	1994
High Court Plenary Summons	2,576	4,767	13,307	12,101	7,594
High Court Summary Summons	1,245	3,150	9,059	4,230	1,476
Circuit Court Ordinary Civil Bills	11.262	19,102	31,758	23,625	11,731
District Court Civil Proceedings	52,625	67,912	63,927	141,01	134,613

Figure 4.3

Criminal Cases	1965	1975	1981	1986	1994
Circuit Court criminal hearings/trials on indictment	480	1,008	1,300	1,356	1,513
Circuit Court criminal appeals	3,149	6,854	7,725	9,707	14,663
District Court: summary and indictable charges	219,197	422,809	676,078	648,442	541,758

Figure 4.4

[4.207] These figures underline the significant increase in the volume of business assigned to the courts in the 30-year period from 1965 to 1994. Even if we take these figures as representing merely the number of forms to be filed in the different courts, there has been a great increase in work generated. However, the data also represent an increase in the volume of cases actually disposed of by the courts in those years. Of course, in some areas, it is also clear that the graph has not always been on the increase, but the general trend is upwards. The trend upwards in the number of sets of proceedings issued continues to date. In 2012, there were 26,063 sets of proceedings instituted in the High Court by way of petition, summons or originating notice of motion. This figure increased to 26,422 in 2013. In the Circuit Court, 34,993 Civil Bills were instituted in 2012 and this increased to 37,808 in 2013. In the District Court, there was a decrease in civil summonses issued between 2012 and 2013: in 2012, 119, 231 civil summonses, were issued and in 2013 this figure was 110,179.[449] With the increase

---

[448] The sources for the figures for both civil and criminal matters were: *Statistical Abstract 1966, Statistical Abstract 1976, Statistical Abstract 1982–85, Statistical Abstract 1986, Statistical Abstract 1995* (all published by the Stationery Office, Dublin).

[449] *Annual Report of the Courts Service 2013* (2014) at p 42.

in the monetary jurisdiction of the Circuit Court and District Court in civil matters, we can expect less proceedings to be instituted in the High Court over the coming years.[450]

[4.208] This general increase gives rise to complex issues that affect the manner in which the business of the courts is determined. At a very simple level, if the number of civil or criminal cases increases in a given period, there may be a need to appoint more judges and administrative staff to process those cases. In addition, changes in society in recent years have been reflected in legislative changes, which in turn have increased the range and complexity of the type of cases coming before the courts. We discuss these in some detail elsewhere.[451]

Reforming the management of the court system

[4.209] Given that the court system has had to cope with enormous growth in civil and criminal litigation, with changes in the type of cases being heard and with consequent substantive and procedural changes in court practice, it is hardly surprising that the *First Report of the Working Group on a Courts Commission* dealt with the general management of the court system.[452] The Working Group's Report recommended the establishment of a state agency, the Courts Service, with a chief executive officer to be responsible for day-to-day budgetary allocation, subject to overall control by the Department of Justice. This proposal was accepted by the government[453] and the Courts Service was established in 1999, under the Courts Service Act 1998. The establishment of the Courts Service brought the state into line with similar systems established in the United Kingdom (where separate services were established for England and Northern Ireland), Australia and New Zealand.

[4.210] Against the background of the constitutional provisions concerning the courts, the Working Group's Report emphasised the importance of an efficient management system and the need to provide a high quality service to the public:

"An effective court system should provide a high level and quality of service to the public with the minimum of waste and effort. The service which is provided in the court system is the means by which the public obtain justice. An inefficient service impedes justice. In

---

[450] The Courts and Civil Law (Miscellaneous Provisions) Act 2013 increased the monetary jurisdiction of the District Court in civil matters from €6,384 to €15,000 and the Circuit Court from €38,092 to €75,000 in all civil matters except personal injuries matters, the jurisdiction for which was increased to €60,000.

[451] On the changing nature of civil and criminal matters coming before the courts, see paras **5.25–5.28**.

[452] *First Report of the Working Group on a Courts Commission: Management and Financing of the Courts* (Pn 2690), April 1996, hereinafter the First Working Group Report. The Working Group, which produced six reports during its existence between 1995 and 1998, was chaired by Denham J.

[453] (1996) *The Irish Times*, 22 May, p 8.

addition the Courts Service is of importance in commerce and the business community. Commerce is at a disadvantage if the system is inefficient or ineffective."[454]

This passage indicates a fundamental shift in the philosophy of the courts system, requiring it to take account of the concepts of quality, service and competitiveness more associated up to then with the private sector. While the Working Group's Report does not point in the direction of a privatised or 'pay-per use' justice system, there can be no doubt of a move from 'court system' to 'court service'.

[4.211] The Working Group's Report pointed that, prior to the establishment of the Irish Free State, the Lord Chancellor had overall responsibility for the courts system, but that, since 1922, the majority of such management functions had been transferred to the Minister for Justice. The Report noted that, since the Lord Chancellor had legislative, executive and judicial roles,[455] the judiciary had been represented 'at the highest level' of decision-making, whereas since 1922 it had become separated from this aspect of decision-making. Although the Report accepted the need to ensure that the establishment of the Courts Service would not breach the principle of the separation of powers, it also noted that the constitutional requirement of judicial independence was impaired if there was 'an absence of adequate administrative infrastructure and resources'.[456]

[4.212] The Working Group pointed out that the existing administrative structure was operated by eight separate sectors, although most had links with the Department of Justice.[457] The Report described this arrangement as 'cumbersome, unwieldy and outmoded'.

[4.213] The Report went on to discuss in detail the deficiencies which this structure had created.[458] Thus, on the administrative side of the system, there was no clear management structure with accountability and responsibility and no adequate performance measurements were in place for the 800 persons who staffed the different courts, so that there was minimum planning beyond day-to-day procedural matters. In addition, no strategic plan or annual reports on the work of the courts existed, there was minimum training and development of staff and there was a lack of professional management to support training and development needs. Allied to this, there was a lack of financial or statistical information on the courts in any understandable format.

[4.214] Moreover, there was no clear reporting structure with regular channels of communication between the various people involved in the system, including a lack of

[454] First Working Group Report, p 17.
[455] On the roles of the Lord Chancellor, see para **2.28**.
[456] First Working Group Report, p 18.
[457] The eight sectors referred to in the First Report were: the Department of Justice; the Presidents of each Bench of judges; the Circuit Court Registrars and District Court Clerks; High Court Registrars; Supreme Court Registrars; the Office of Public Works; local authorities; and Sheriffs: First Working Group Report, p 24.
[458] First Working Group Report, pp 35–6.

an organisational relationship between the Department of Justice and court staff. This poor level of communications had restricted initiatives for change and there was a fragmentation in the administrative systems between the different courts. The Report also stated that there was an apparent remoteness of the administrative system from the judiciary. The Report found that no structure existed to respond to the needs of court users, nor was there an information service to the public in general; that many existing courthouses were inadequate and lacked dignity; and there were substantial delays in bringing both civil and criminal matters to the different courts.

[4.215] The First Report of the Working Group also provided the first global information on the overall financial costs of the court system as well as information on the resources required to upgrade and maintain the physical condition of courthouses. The Report estimated that the cost of the courts system, including salaries, building work, pensions, administration, legal aid, law reporting and witness expenses was about £46.77m in 1995, up from £24.73m in 1990. This cost did not include the day-to-day cost of providing and maintaining court accommodation outside Dublin, as these figures had not been available to the Working Group. The court system earned an estimated income of £10.3m in 1995, largely from fees imposed on the filing of court pleadings,[459] and this was similar to the amount raised in 1990. Because of the rise in costs between 1990 and 1995, the net cost of the court system to the state had thus risen from £13.8m in 1990 to £36.4m in 1995. This sum, rounded up by the Working Group to £40m, represented 0.28% of total government expenditure (estimated at just over £14bn) for 1996. This compared with estimated government spending of about £2bn each in the Departments of Education and Health. The Report noted that given the number of personnel involved (about 1,000), the state was receiving good value for is investment. However, the Report also considered that reform could produce further benefits for the state.

[4.216] While a policy of self-financing would be inappropriate having regard to the constitutional right of access to the courts,[460] the Report noted that certain reforms could increase state income from the courts. Thus, a Commercial Court managed by judges with specially trained registrars could facilitate speedier litigation, with consequent

---

[459] On pleadings, see para **6.23**.

[460] See para **9.02**. It is notable that the UK Courts Service has begun to charge daily fees for some litigation and intends to recover the full cost of the court service, including the cost of judges, for all litigants in civil cases in the future: see Slapper and Kelly, *The English Legal System* (7th edn, 2004), p 67. In *Murphy v Minister for Justice* [2001] 2 ILRM 144 (see also para **9.70**), the Supreme Court held that reasonable charges for court services were not in breach of the right of access to the courts under Article 40.3 of the Constitution. Indeed, delivering the unanimous decision of the Court, Murphy J appeared to envisage 'full cost' charges being imposed on commercial entities in commercial disputes, as opposed to individuals. He commented that 'the concept of the entire cost of the judicial system being borne out of tax, including tax imposed on modest incomes, to exonerate substantial commercial organisations would seem absurd in principle and offensive in practice': [2001] 2 ILRM 144, 149.

benefits to business and commerce as well as the state through the generation of more court fees.[461]

The Courts Service

[4.217] Against this background the Working Group recommended the establishment of an independent statutory state agency, to be called the Courts Service, to manage a unified court system.[462] The recommendations of the Working Group were implemented in the Courts Service Act 1998, which came into effect in 1999.[463] The general functions of the Court Service include the following:

- management of the courts system, including staff and its administration;
- preparation of three-year plans for the courts service;
- preparation of its annual budget for submission to the Minister for Justice;
- management of the budget;
- publication of annual performance reports;
- the provision, management and maintenance of suitable court buildings, both in terms of physical suitability and matters such as improved public address systems;
- the provision of secretarial, research and other administrative services to the judiciary;
- the establishment of a communications system between staff and judges;
- provision of a public information system on the court service, including the introduction of a Charter for Court Users and improved communication with the various media.

[4.218] As recommended by the Working Group, the Courts Service comprises a board, representing the judiciary, the legal profession and court users, together with a full-time chief executive officer. Section 11 of the Courts Service Act 1998 provides that the board of the Courts Service comprises 17 members. The Chief Justice (who is also chair) and the Presidents of the High Court, Circuit Court and District Court are members of the board or nominate another judge in their place. One of the ordinary judges of each court is also elected to serve on the board by his or her judicial colleagues. In addition the Chief Justice nominates a further judge to the board in respect of his or her expertise or experience in a specific area.

[4.219] The other members of the board are: the chief executive of the Service, a practising barrister nominated by the Chairman of the Bar Council, a practising solicitor nominated by the President of the Law Society, a member of the staff of the Service, an

---

461 First Working Group Report, p 34.

462 First Working Group Report, pp 42–53.

463 After the acceptance of the First Report's recommendations, the Working Group was asked to set out in detail the arrangements envisaged in the proposed Courts Service. This was done in the Third Report of the Working Group, *Towards the Courts Service* (November 1996).

officer of the Minister for Justice, a person nominated by the Minister to represent consumers of services provided by the courts, a person nominated by the Irish Congress of Trade Unions and a nominee of the Minister with knowledge and experience of commerce, finance or administration. Section 12 of the Courts Service Act 1998 provides that, apart from the *ex officio* members of the board, membership will be for a renewable term of three years. Section 13 confers responsibility on the board of the Courts Service for the policy of the Service and overseeing the implementation of that policy by the chief executive. It requires the board to have regard to the best use of the resources of the Service and any government or ministerial policy or objective relating to the functions of the Service. There are also a number of standing committees established that deal with particular areas in which the courts service is involved: finance, audit, buildings and family law court development and these committees contain members who are not members of the Courts Service.[464]

[4.220] The chief executive of the Courts Service has the equivalent rank of the secretary general of a government department and has day-to-day responsibility for the management of court staff, who now operate in a unified, single stream and were redesignated as civil servants. The Courts Service is accountable to the Oireachtas through the Minister for Justice for issues concerning finance and administration, and its funding is audited by the Comptroller and Auditor General. It is not accountable to the Oireachtas for judicial decisions, as this would be in breach of the separation of powers provided for in the Constitution. Section 21 of the Courts Service Act 1998 requires the chief executive to attend before an Oireachtas Committee at the request in writing of the committee to account for the general administration of the Service. It is expressly provided that the chief executive will not be required to account for any judicial or quasi-judicial matter.

[4.221] The First Report of the Working Group was the first fundamental assessment of the court system since the foundation of the state, and the implementation of its recommendations in the Courts Service Act 1998 involved a profound change in the entire ethos of the court system. Even the title 'Courts Service' indicated a shift towards a customer or consumer-based approach, requiring the incorporation of modern business management methods into an element of the public sector steeped in tradition. In November 2000, the first three-year plan for the Courts Service was published, including targets to be achieved across a wide range of areas.

[4.222] The plan noted that the budget for the Service had doubled in the past few years to £60m per annum. The plan set specific targets for each section of the Courts Service. It also laid out criteria against which the tasks of improvement can be measured. The service had drawn up specific plans and advances in areas such as information technology, access to court buildings and supplying the public with information about how the courts system operates. The work of the service over its lifetime up to 2003 concentrated on fulfilling government policy to enable people to contract their business

---

[464]   See The Courts Service, *Annual Report 2007* (2008), p 14.

with the state via 'e-commerce'. This 'e-government' initiative has seen the payment of fines and the lodging of pleadings online. It is now possible for small claims forms to be transmitted electronically to the District Court Office. In addition, a criminal court case management system became operational in 2004 which allows for the tracking of these cases during their lifetime.[465]

[4.223] The strategic plan for the period 2002–2005 mainly provided for furthering of staff training and to ensure that the Courts Service and its ancillary services were user friendly. The strategic plan for the period 2005–2008 provided that the users of the courts would be provided with a high quality service (which included further development on electronic delivery of services), the timely and efficient support of court cases and court business (in particular to identify and assist with backlog of cases), working with members of the judiciary to ensure that matters coming before the courts are dealt with efficiently, the fostering of public understanding in the courts system (include outreach to schools and the provision of information to the pubic), the provision of modern buildings and facilities (in particular the criminal courts complex in Dublin) and the most efficient use of resources.

[4.224] The Courts Service's *Strategic Plan 2011–2014*[466] reiterates the aims of improving access to the courts and improving the public's understanding of the courts. The Plan also noted that it had been prepared at a time (2011) when the state's fiscal position in the wake of the Great Recession was exceptionally difficult. In 2014 the Chief Justice noted at the launch of the Courts Service's Annual Report 2013 that its budget had been reduced by 42% since 2008, from €100 million to €57.8 million. She commented that any further or continued reduction 'will cause a great and lasting damage to our courts system'.[467]

---

[465] See The Courts Service, *Annual Report of the Courts Service 2004* (2005) at p 5.
[466] Available on the Courts Service website, www.courts.ie.
[467] See Gartland, '"Lasting damage" to courts if budget cut again – Chief Justice' (2014) *The Irish Times*, 24 July.

Chapter 5

The First Instance Jurisdiction of the Courts

[1]   Introduction 225
[2]   The Original Jurisdiction of the Courts in Civil Cases 238
[3]   The Original Jurisdiction of the Courts in Criminal Cases 2602
[4]   Proposals for Fundamental Reform of the Court Structure 270

[1]   INTRODUCTION

[5.01] In Chapter 4, we described the essential elements of the court system in Ireland created by the Courts (Establishment and Constitution) Act 1961. In this chapter, we outline the present first instance, or original, jurisdiction of the courts in civil and criminal matters. In other words, this chapter outlines the basis on which one determines which court is designated by law to hear a particular civil or criminal case in the first place.[1] The most significant legislative source of jurisdiction are the many Courts Acts, including the Courts of Justice Act 1924, the Courts (Supplemental Provisions) Act 1961 and the Courts and Civil Law (Miscellaneous Provisions) Act 2013. In addition to the Acts passed since 1924, a number of pre-1922 Acts contain important provisions describing the jurisdiction of the courts in Ireland, including the Petty Sessions (Ireland) Act 1851, the Summary Jurisdiction Act 1857 and the Supreme Court of Judicature (Ireland) Act 1877. In 2010 the Law Reform Commission published a *Report on the Consolidation and Reform of the Courts Acts,*[2] including a draft Courts (Consolidation and Reform) Bill, which brings together the pre-1922 and post-1922 provisions in over 240 Acts concerning the jurisdiction of the courts. At the time of writing (September 2014), it appears the government is committed to implementing this through a consolidating Courts Bill.[3] This 2010 Report represents a response to a number of proposals made in the first decade of the century for reform of the jurisdiction of the courts, which began with proposals made in 2001 by the then Chief Justice, Mr Justice Ronan Keane.[4]

---

1   In Ch 7, we describe the appellate jurisdiction of the courts.
2   LRC 97-2010, available at www.lawreform.ie.
3   The *Government Legislation Programme, Autumn 2014*, available at www.taoiseach.ie, proposes the publication of a Courts (Consolidation and Reform) Bill to implement the Commission's 2010 Report.
4   See para **5.122**.

Basis of jurisdiction in civil claims

[5.02] In the case of a civil claim for damages, the question as to which court is designated by law to hear the case may be simply a matter of the amount of damages being claimed. In other civil claims, where damages are not the primary claim, the question may be resolved by reference to the subject matter of the claim, such as whether it involves an application to wind up a company.

A brief outline containing select examples of the original jurisdiction of the courts in civil cases is contained in Figure 5.1.

[5.03] The monetary level of jurisdiction of the courts for civil claims was considerably changed by the Courts and Civil Law (Miscellaneous Provisions) Act 2013, which came into force in 2014. Prior to 2014, the monetary levels had remained at the levels set in the Courts Act 1991. The 1991 Act had set the monetary jurisdiction limits for civil matters in the Circuit Court at €38,092 (£30,000) and for the District Court at €6,384 (£5,000). These amounts had been significantly eroded by inflation to the extent that the High Court was dealing with claims which were relatively modest in value and in many cases the legal costs involved would have considerably outweighed the value of the proceedings. The Courts and Court Officers Act 2002 had provided for an increase of the monetary jurisdiction of the Circuit Court from €38,092 to €100,000 and of the District Court from €6,384 to €20,000. These were never brought into force, because no commencement order had been made to bring them into effect. This was largely because the government accepted the recommendation in the 2002 *Report of the Motor Insurance Advisory Board* that the jurisdiction of these courts in personal injuries actions should remain unchanged and that, instead, the Injuries Board recommended in the 2002 Report should be established and, in effect, provide for a system that would avoid court-based litigation for most personal injuries actions. The Injuries Board was established by the Personal Injuries Assessment Board Act 2003.[5] The 2006 *Report of the Legal Cost Implementation Advisory Group* recommended that the changes proposed in the 2002 Act should be brought into force, but would not apply to personal injuries claims.[6] The Courts and Civil Law (Miscellaneous Provisions) Act 2013 provided for a general increase in the monetary jurisdiction limits to €75,000 for the Circuit Court and €15,000 for the District Court. As to personal injury actions, the monetary jurisdiction of the Circuit Court is restricted to €60,000. The lower amount for the jurisdiction of the Circuit Court in personal injuries proceedings was adopted to deal with concerns relating to possible inflation of awards and a consequent effect on insurance costs. These changes came into effect in 2014.[7]

---

5   On the 2003 Act, see para **5.15**.
6   Legal Costs Implementation Advisory Group, *Report of the Legal Costs Implementation Advisory Group* (Pn A7/0027, 2006), p 26.
7   The Courts and Civil Law (Miscellaneous Provisions) Act 2013 (Jurisdiction of District Court and Circuit Court) (Commencement) Order 2013 (SI 566/2013) brought the increased monetary limits into force on 3 February 2014.

```
┌─────────────────────────────────────────────────────────┐
│        Original Jurisdiction of Courts in Civil Cases     │
│                    SUPREME COURT                          │
│                   (5 or 7 Judges)                         │
│            • Reference of Bill by President               │
│                                                           │
│                    HIGH COURT                             │
│      (High Court judge; jury in some instances)           │
│            • Full original jurisdiction                   │
│            • Damages claimed: over €75,000 (in Personal   │
│              Injuries claims: over €60,000)               │
│            • Constitutional cases                         │
│            • Judicial review                              │
│            • Company winding-up                           │
│                                                           │
│                    CIRCUIT COURT                          │
│                 (Circuit Court judge)                     │
│            • Subject matter similar to High Court         │
│            • Damages claimed: €15,000–75,000 (PI:         │
│              €15,000–€60,000)                             │
│            • New intoxicating liquor licence              │
│            • Judicial separations and nullity             │
│                                                           │
│                    DISTRICT COURT                         │
│                (District Court judge)                     │
│            • Excluded from hearing some matters           │
│            • Damages claimed: €15,000 or less             │
│            • Intoxicating liquor licence renewal          │
│            • Maintenance for spouses and children         │
└─────────────────────────────────────────────────────────┘
```

Figure 5.1

Basis of jurisdiction in criminal cases

[5.04] Jurisdiction in criminal cases depends, in the first instance, on whether the offence charged is classifiable as summary or indictable. Summary offences are also known as 'minor' offences, the term used in Article 38.2 of the Constitution. As we discuss elsewhere,[8] Article 38.2 provides that minor offences may be tried summarily, which in practice means in the District Court. Indictable offences, to which the right to trial by jury attaches with some exceptions under Article 38.5, are tried in one of the 'higher' criminal courts. A brief outline of the courts' criminal jurisdiction is provided in Figure 5.2 below.

[5.05] In the more detailed discussion of the original jurisdiction of the courts that follows, we deal first with the jurisdiction of the courts in civil cases, beginning with, at

---

8   See paras **4.45** and **5.90**.

the lower end of the court system, the District Court, and ending with a discussion of the original jurisdiction of the Supreme Court. We then proceed to discuss the original jurisdiction of the courts in criminal matters.

[5.06] As it would be almost impossible to provide a comprehensive treatment of all statutes that affect the courts' jurisdiction, what follows is a description of the principal legislative provisions. It should be realised that the general framework thereby established is supplemented by many statutes that confer jurisdiction in individual instances on particular courts. We provide some examples of such legislation for illustrative purposes.

Original Jurisdiction of Courts in Criminal Cases
CENTRAL CRIMINAL COURT
(High Court)
(High Court judge and jury)
- Murder, attempted murder, conspiracy to murder
- Rape, rape offences

CIRCUIT COURT
(Circuit Criminal Court)
(Circuit Court judge and jury)
- Indictable offences other than those triable in Central Criminal Court

SPECIAL CRIMINAL COURT
(Three judges, no jury)
- Scheduled offences
- Non-scheduled offence, DPP certifies

DISTRICT COURT
(District judge, no jury)
- Minor/summary offences

Figure 5.2

The annual activity of the courts

[5.07] The Annual Reports of the Courts Service provide a general overview of the annual activity of the courts in both civil and criminal matters.[9] In recent years, the courts in Ireland have dealt with more than 500,000 criminal matters annually. In addition, over 150,000 civil cases have been initiated each year, as well as over 20,000 family law cases and more than 1,000 judicial review cases.

[5.08] Of the 500,000 criminal matters, over 400,000 are summary criminal cases dealt with in the District Court (over 300,000 being road traffic offences). The Circuit Criminal Court deals with 6,000 prosecutions on indictment (for example, theft and

---

[9] On the growth of the activity of the courts between the 1960s and 1990s, see para **4.206**.

drugs offences) and the High Court (Central Criminal Court) deals with 100 trials on indictment (primarily, murder and rape cases).

[5.09] Of the 150,000 civil cases initiated annually (other than family law cases), in the region of 80,000 are issued in the District Court (almost 30,000 involving enforcement of contract debt, and just under 4,000 involving the small claims procedure). The Circuit Court deals annually with over 40,000 civil claims (of which over 10,000 have involved enforcement of contract debt, and up to 7,000 concerned personal injuries claims). The High Court deals annually with up to 27,000 civil claims (of which in the order of 5,000 involve enforcement of contract debt, and over 7,000 concern personal injuries claims).

[5.10] Family law cases total 20,000 annually. Cases concerning custody, access and domestic violence are dealt with in the District Court and involve about 15,000 annually (almost 10,000 concern domestic violence). Divorce and judicial separation cases, dealt with in the Circuit Court and High Court, total in the region of 5,000 annually. The High Court also deals each year with many constitutional cases, as well as up to 1,000 judicial review cases, which concern challenges to decisions of courts and adjudicative bodies (in recent years, over 40% of these have involved immigration and asylum cases).

[5.11] In terms of the courts dealing exclusively with appeals (which we discuss in Chapter 7), the Court of Criminal Appeal deals with over 300 appeals annually. The Supreme Court, which is the final court of appeal in the state and deals with many complex cases (including constitutional cases), disposes of between 300 and 400 appeals each year.

Development of the business of the courts

[5.12] The description of the courts' jurisdiction should be seen against the background of the reform of the management of the court service effected by the Courts Service Act 1998, as recommended by the Working Group on a Courts Commission, which we discussed in Chapter 4.[10] In order to put the present first instance jurisdiction of the courts in context, we begin by outlining the development of the business of the courts in recent years. This has influenced both the appointment of additional judges to the courts as well as the distribution of business between the courts. In relation to civil claims, we refer to the impact of the alterations to personal injuries claims, increased family law cases and the emergence of consumer claims. On the criminal side, we refer to the impact of increases in criminal business generally. The examples we have chosen are not exhaustive. To these could be added the growing number of judicial review cases being initiated in the High Court.

---

[10] See para **4.209**.

Civil claims: personal injuries actions and the Personal Injuries Assessment Board

[5.13] During the 1980s and 1990s there was a substantial increase in the number of personal injuries actions in the courts,[11] many of them concerning accidents on the road, in supermarkets or at work. There was, however, a great deal of disagreement about what should be done to deal with this phenomenon. One side of the argument concerning this 'compo culture', as it is colloquially described, might include the following points. It is said that the increase in claims has been fuelled by the increase in the number of solicitors since the early 1980s who, in an increasingly competitive business environment, encourage litigation by promising a 'free first consultation' and a commitment to process personal injuries cases on a 'no foal, no fee' basis.[12] Court awards, alleged to be excessive and in any event well above European norms, are also said to lead potential litigants to believe that a financial bonanza awaits them in court. It is also alleged that the fees charged by some members of the legal profession in such cases are somewhat inflated. In addition, it is alleged that insurance companies may settle too many claims, thus further encouraging future claims. Finally, there has been some criticism of the fact that personal injuries awards involve a once-off lump sum payment to a plaintiff, much of which is calculated on the basis that interest earned on the capital sum should enable the plaintiff to obtain whatever medical and other treatment and facilities he or she requires. By contrast, in the United Kingdom, it is possible to have annual, staged payments of awards called periodic payment orders rather than a once-off lump sum award.

[5.14] This picture is contested by a number of people involved in the area. Thus, it is said that many employers fail to take appropriate precautions to prevent accidents, and that there exists a 'negligence culture'. It is also said that, in the absence of a comprehensive civil legal aid system,[13] solicitors are obliged to engage in a 'no foal, no fee' approach to personal injuries claims. The legal profession also vehemently denies that fees charged are excessive, pointing to the high level of legal fees in other states. As to excessive court awards, they are higher than in some comparable cases in the United Kingdom, though there has been a closer correlation in recent years. As for settling cases, insurance companies argue that they would fight in full any cases where a defence would be available, and that claims are settled where it is clear to fight the case (unsuccessfully) in court would result in further costs being incurred, causing in turn ever higher insurance premiums. On the question of staged or interim payments of

---

[11] The *First Report of the Working Group on a Courts Commission* (Pn 2690), p 37, stated that personal injuries actions accounted for over 86% of the plenary summons actions put down for trial in the High Court in recent years. In the 1994–95 period, of the 9,603 plenary summonses issued, 5,453 were set down for trial, of which 4,682 were personal injury actions. On the Working Group generally, see further para **4.209**.

[12] See para **5.39** for discussion of the 'no foal, no fee' arrangement.

[13] On civil legal aid generally, see paras **9.37–9.54**.

awards, at the time of writing (September 2014), it is expected that legislation to provide for periodic payment orders will be enacted in the near future.[14]

[5.15] It remains the case that this matter involves complex policy disputes in which agreement is difficult to find.[15] Despite this, various solutions have been attempted to deal with the problem since the late 1980s in particular. These included the abolition in 1988 of the statutory right to have High Court personal injuries actions heard by a jury as well as the introduction of restrictions on the number of counsel who might be briefed in such cases.[16] Legislation providing for procedural changes to facilitate earlier settlements, as well as for additional judicial appointments to clear the backlog of civil litigation, was also enacted in the mid-1990s.[17] More fundamental and far-reaching reform was introduced in the early years of this century, based on the 2001 *Report of the Advisory Group on Personal Injuries*[18] and the 2002 *Report of the Motor Insurance Advisory Board* (the MIAB Report).[19] These reports led to the enactment of the Personal Injuries Assessment Board Act 2003 and the Civil Liability and Courts Act 2004. In 2001, on foot of the report of the advisory group it had commissioned, the government announced it intended to establish a Personal Injuries Assessment Board aimed at encouraging litigants to settle claims at an early stage and thus reduce the costs associated with personal injuries claims. The 2001 report indicated that of the many personal injuries cases settled in Ireland, a large proportion was settled 'at the door of the court', that is, on the day the case was due to be heard. Consequently, the report also found that the costs involved in such settlements (in addition to the actual settlement payment to the plaintiff), such as the costs of obtaining medical and other expert reports as well as the legal fees involved, were quite high. The report stated that this contrasted with earlier settlements in comparable cases in Britain. The report concluded that a Personal Injuries Assessment Board (PIAB) should be established to facilitate earlier settlements which might involve reduced administrative and legal costs. The Personal Injuries Assessment Board (which now uses the shorter title 'Injuries Board') was established under the Personal Injuries Assessment Board Act 2003.[20] The purpose of

---

[14]   The *Government Legislation Programme, Autumn Session 2014*, available at www.taoiseach.ie, proposes the publication of a Civil Liability (Amendment) Bill to implement the recommendations in the 2010 *Report of the Working Group on Medical Negligence and Periodic Payments*, available at www.courts.ie, which also included a detailed draft Civil Liability (Amendment) Bill to implement these recommendations.

[15]   For a summary of the debate, see for example Fitzgerald, 'The Compo Culture' (1996) *Business and Finance*, 16 May. On the level of settlements, see para **6.64**.

[16]   This was effected by the Courts Act 1988: see further, para **4.62**.

[17]   Courts and Court Officers Act 1995.

[18]   *Second Report of the Advisory Group on Personal Injuries* (Department of Enterprise and Employment, 2001).

[19]   Final Report of the Motor Insurance Advisory Board (Department of Enterprise, Trade and Employment, 2002).

[20]   See www.injuriesboard.ie and generally Quigley and Binchy (eds), *The Personal Injuries Assessment Board: Implications for Legal Practice* (First Law, 2004); Nolan, 'The Personal Injuries Assessment Board Act 2003: A Critical Analysis' (2004) 9(1) *Bar Review* 7.

the 2003 Act is to provide for the assessment of damages for personal injuries without the need to have recourse to the courts.

[5.16] The 2003 Act provides that all personal injuries matters (excluding those arising out of the provision of health care, advice or treatment) are first to be referred to the Injuries Board for assessment. 'Personal injuries' means any disease or impairment of a physical or mental condition. The Injuries Board was a response to the high insurance and legal costs of recent years which had crept into personal injuries litigation. The 2002 *Report of the Motor Insurance Advisory Board* into motor insurance in Ireland highlighted these costs in compensation awarded in personal injuries.[21] It was also felt that there was no real incentive to control these costs. There was also a view that injuries were exaggerated and this needed to be actively discouraged. Every personal injuries claim covered by the 2003 Act must be submitted to the Injuries Board and not to court. The Injuries Board is empowered to make an assessment of damages on the assumption that liability is not in question The objective is to divert as many cases as possible from the courts and to achieve a more prompt and inexpensive settlement. The assessment may not take place if the defendant disputes liability or if he or she refuses to submit the claim to assessment.

[5.17] Each claim is submitted using a standard application form, medical assessment form, receipts and vouchers for any financial loss and a set fee. The Board then notifies the defendant who has 90 days to consent to the assessment. Before making an assessment the Board may require an independent medical assessment of the claimant. Where there is failure to respond by the defendant, this is regarded as consent. Where the defendant objects to the assessment of damages, the Board issues an 'authorisation' which allows the injured party to bring legal proceedings to the appropriate court. A person may proceed to bring court proceedings[22] if: the claim does not fall within the scope of the Personal Injuries Assessment Board Act 2003; or if the action is one to which the 2003 Act applies but the respondent does not consent to an assessment; or the Injuries Board refuses to deal with the claim; or where the claimant or respondent declines to accept the assessment.

[5.18] The Personal Injuries Assessment (Amendment) Act 2007 provides that, where a claimant rejects an Injuries Board assessment and where he or she fails in any subsequent legal proceedings to obtain more, he or she will not be entitled to costs. This was designed to encourage plaintiffs to accept assessments from the Injuries Board to divert more cases out of the courts. The 2007 Act also provides that no legal costs are to be allowed for the making of an application to the Injuries Board. The introduction of the Injuries Board attracted a large amount of criticism from both branches of the legal

---

21 *Final Report of the Motor Insurance Advisory Board* (Department for Enterprise, Trade and Employment, 2002).

22 Delany and McGrath, *Civil Procedure in the Superior Courts* (2nd edn, 2005), p 632.

profession.[23] For example, the then Chairman of the Bar Council stated publicly that the 2003 Act could lead to members of the public being less likely to engage professionals as these costs would not be met by the Injuries Board while the respondents with insurance would be able to avail of full representation, medical and engineering advice from the outset.[24] The Law Society expressed concern at the lack of provision for legal costs for vulnerable applicants.[25] In 2007, the Injuries Board announced that it would pay for legal costs and expenses in 'exceptional cases', such as for those with literacy difficulties, foreign nationals or those with diminished capacity.[26]

[5.19] This concession came in the wake of the decision of the Supreme Court in *O'Brien v Personal Injuries Assessment Board*,[27] in which it was decided that the refusal of the Injuries Board to deal directly with the applicant's solicitor, despite the applicant's wishes that it did, had been in breach of s 7 of the 2003 Act, which provides that the Act does not affect the right of any person to seek legal advice in respect of his or her claim. The importance of the proceedings for legal practitioners is evident from the fact that the Law Society was successfully joined in the proceedings as *amicus curiae*.

[5.20] Other changes to deal with personal injuries actions also arose from the 2002 *Report of the Motor Advisory Board* (MIAB).[28] The Civil Liability and Courts Acts 2004, which was the second major legislative response to the 2002 *MIAB Report*, enacted a wide range of alterations to personal injuries litigation. Sections 6 and 7 of the 2004 Act reduced the general limitation period for bringing personal injuries actions from three to two years. Section 8 of the Act provides that, within two months of the alleged incident, a plaintiff must write to the proposed defendant what is known as a letter of claim and this must give details of the claim and intention to institute proceedings (the statutory version of a 'solicitor's letter'). Failure to serve such a notice can have later cost implications for the plaintiff. A personal injuries summons must also contain a number of details, rather than general terms as was the case prior to the 2004

---

23 See, for example, (2003) *The Irish Times*, 19 November; Maguire, 'The Personal Injuries Assessment Board Act 2003: A Barrister's Perspective' in Quigley and Binchy (eds), *The Personal Injuries Assessment Board: Implications for Legal Practice* (2004); and Murphy, 'The PIAB: A Solicitor's Perspective' in Quigley and Binchy (eds), *The Personal Injuries Assessment Board: Implications for Legal Practice* (2004).

24 Maguire, 'The Personal Injuries Assessment Board Act 2003: A Barrister's Perspective' in Quigley and Binchy (eds), *The Personal Injuries Assessment Board: Implications for Legal Practice* (2004), p 30.

25 Murphy, 'The PIAB: A Solicitor's Perspective' in Quigley and Binchy (eds), *The Personal Injuries Assessment Board: Implications for Legal Practice* (2004), p 19.

26 See (2007) *The Irish Times*, 27 October.

27 *O'Brien v Personal Injuries Assessment Board* [2006] IESC 62, [2007] 1 IR 328, [2008] IESC 71, [2009] 3 IR 243.

28 *The Final Report of the Motor Insurance Advisory Board* (Department for Enterprise, Trade and Employment, 2002) and The Committee on Court Practice and Procedure, *29th Interim Report Inquiry to Examine All Aspects of Practice and Procedure Relating to Personal Injuries Litigation* (2004).

Act. The 2004 Act also provides that both claimants and defendants must swear an affidavit verifying that any factual assertions they have set out in the pleadings are accurate. If a court subsequently finds that these assertions are fraudulent or exaggerated, this can result in a criminal conviction and a sentence of imprisonment of up to 10 years and/or a fine of up to €100,000.

[5.21] On the preventative side of traffic-related accidents and claims, 'crackdowns' on speeding and drink driving have occurred, as well as more stringent legislative provisions and penalties for traffic offences.[29] Improvements in the standards of roads in the state have also occurred. As to accidents arising in the workplace, legislation was enacted to encourage accident prevention in all places of work.[30]

[5.22] It is clear that the landscape of personal injuries litigation in this country has been much changed in recent years with the two aims of lessening legal costs and punishing those who bring fraudulent claims. The decrease in the number of personal injuries cases initiated in the High Court in the immediate aftermath of the introduction of the Personal Injuries Assessment Board was stark. In 2004, there were 15,399 personal injuries claims initiated in the High Court, but by 2005 this had decreased to 746 cases.[31] The number of High Court personal injuries cases has steadily increased from the 2005 level: in 2006 there were 2,673 cases,[32] in 2007 there were 5,951 cases and in 2008 there were 6,466 cases initiated in the High Court. These figures are consistent with the view of the Injuries Board that two-thirds of all personal injuries matters are being disposed of without recourse to the courts. Annually, the Injuries Board processes over 20,000 applications, issuing up to 8,000 awards.[33] However in recent years the number of personal injuries claims instituted in the High Court has continued to creep up: in 2012 8,791 and in 2013 9,561 such claims were instituted.[34] Although these levels have not returned to the pre Injuries Board level, they indicate that the Injuries Board has not proved to be the death knell of personal injuries litigation in Ireland that had been suggested by legal practitioners when the Injuries Board first came into operation.

Civil claims: family law

[5.23] There has also been an enormous increase in the amount of what is described as family law business conducted by the courts since the 1960s. In particular, proceedings

---

[29] Notably through various Road Traffic Acts, enacted since the 1990s, which have: reduced the permitted blood-alcohol level for a person driving a motor vehicle, increased the penalties involved, introduced a wide-ranging penalty points system (under which drivers could lose their licences where they accumulate a certain number of penalty points), introduced mandatory alcohol testing and restricted the use of phones while driving, including texting and accessing social media sites while driving.

[30] Safety, Health and Welfare at Work Act 2005, replacing the Safety, Health and Welfare at Work Act 1989.

[31] *Annual Report of the Courts Service 2005* (2006), p 94.

[32] *Annual Report of the Courts Service 2006* (2007), p 102.

[33] See www.injuriesboard.ie.

[34] *Annual Report of the Courts Service 2013* (2014), p 43.

arising from marital breakdown in the state have increased substantially, again requiring changes to reflect this reality. Thus, in the 1980s, legislation was enacted to update the law concerning judicial separation and to provide for a more informal court atmosphere, such as dispensing with the wearing of the traditional wigs and gowns worn by judges and barristers.[35] Other changes have been effected to update the mechanisms for protecting women, in particular, from violent spouses[36] and also to improve arrangements for ensuring that awards of maintenance can be enforced against recalcitrant spouses.[37] In 1995, a referendum to remove the constitutional prohibition on divorce was narrowly approved and, after an unsuccessful challenge to the result of the referendum, [38] legislation to give effect to this change was enacted in 1996.[39] In 2010, legislation was enacted providing for civil partnership and a limited form of protection for cohabitants.[40] As with the increase in civil claims in general, a further response was the appointment of additional judges to the different courts. Although substantial changes have thus been made to reflect the increase in family-related cases, a substantial backlog of such cases had built up in the early 1990s. The majority of family law cases are dealt with in the District Court and Circuit Court. For example, in 2013 there were 3,609 applications for divorces as compared with 3,482 in 2012. There were 11 applications for divorce in the High Court and 3,598 in the Circuit Court.[41] The District Court deals with very important matters such as applications for guardianship and orders dealing under domestic violence legislation. Further reform to deal with this area was recommended and some of these recommendations were implemented.[42]

Civil claims: consumer and small claims

[5.24] A feature of the second half of the 20th century was the exponential growth of the 'consumer society'. Reflecting the growth in commercial transactions involving consumers, a substantial body of legislation has been enacted to ensure greater protection for individuals who enter into cash or credit-based agreements. This has included legislation to protect against unfair and misleading commercial practices,[43] increased protection in contracts for the sale of goods and supply of services[44] as well as

---

[35] See the Judicial Separation and Family Law Reform Act 1989. On the wearing of wigs generally by barristers, see Courts and Court Officers Act 1995, s 49, discussed at para **3.114**.

[36] Domestic Violence Act 1996.

[37] Family Law Act 1995.

[38] *Hanafin v Minister for the Environment* [1996] 2 IR 321.

[39] Family Law (Divorce) Act 1996.

[40] Civil Partnership and Certain Rights and Obligations of Cohabitants Act 2010. At the time of writing (September 2014), a referendum on marriage equality is scheduled to be held in 2015.

[41] *Annual Report of the Courts Service 2013* (2014) at p 31.

[42] See Law Reform Commission, *Report on Family Courts* (1996) and *Sixth Report of the Working Group on a Courts Commission* (1998) and Ch 4.

[43] For example, the Consumer Protection Act 2007, replacing and repealing previous legislation such as the Consumer Information Act 1978.

[44] For example, Sale of Goods and Supply of Services Act 1980, the Package Holidays and Travel Trade Act 1995 and the European Communities (Unfair Terms in Consumer Contracts) Regulations 1995 (SI 27/1995).

protective measures involving all forms of consumer credit, whether involving hire-purchase, leasing, credit cards or mortgages.[45] In addition, regulatory agencies such as the Competition and Consumer Protection Commission (which incorporated the Competition Authority and the National Consumer Agency)[46] were established in order to ensure that such protective legislation became widely known and accepted by the market operators.[47] However, consumer groups also pointed out that, where an individual's complaint could not be resolved by direct complaint to a retailer, the court system represented an expensive and forbidding place of resort. Thus, in keeping with many other states, a less formal system for dealing with what are called small claims has been developed, operating through the District Court.[48] This procedure is designed to handle consumer claims and business claims cheaply and efficiently.

Criminal cases

[5.25] We have already described how there has been an enormous increase in the criminal business of the courts, leading to increased judicial and administrative personnel.[49] There has been substantial public debate about the causes of crime and also the appropriate responses to the increase, both in terms of society and the court system. In brief terms, the response can be broken into two general categories. First, there has been recognition of the need to update the general criminal law. In recent decades there has been a substantial body of legislation enacted to update the criminal law concerning such areas as drug trafficking,[50] sexual offences,[51] other non-fatal offences,[52] public order,[53] organised crime,[54] computer crime.[55] and white collar crime.[56] In 2013/2014 a lengthy trial (48 days) of former directors of Anglo Irish Bank took place in the Circuit Court where the accused were charged with the provision of loans contrary to section 60 of the Companies Act 1963 to investors known as the Maple 10 to assist them to buy

---

45 Consumer Credit Act 1995.
46 See the Competition and Consumer Protection Act 2014, which forms part of a wider rationalisation of state bodies: see para **8.40**.
47 Non-statutory arrangements, such as the voluntary Codes of Practice operated by the Advertising Standards Authority of Ireland, also play an important role in this area: see para **13.13**.
48 See para **5.51** and McHugh, *Small Claims Court in Ireland: A Consumer Guide* (2003).
49 See paras **4.206** and **5.07**.
50 For example, the Criminal Justice Act 1994 and the Criminal Justice (Drug Trafficking) Act 1996.
51 For example, the Criminal Law (Rape) (Amendment) Act 1990, the Criminal Law (Sexual Offences) Act 1993, the Child Trafficking and Pornography Act 1998, the Criminal Law (Sexual Offences) Act 2006 and the Criminal Law (Sexual Offences) (Amendment) Act 2007.
52 Non-Fatal Offences against the Person Act 1997.
53 Criminal Justice (Public Order) Act 1994.
54 For example, the Proceeds of Crime Act 1996, Offences against the State (Amendment) Act 1998 and the Criminal Justice Act 2006 and Criminal Justice Act 2007.
55 Criminal Damage Act 1991 and Copyright and Related Rights Act 2000.
56 Criminal Justice Act 2011.

shares in Anglo in 2008. These types of white collar cases are likely to increase in the courts in the future.

[5.26] As to the procedures to be followed in criminal matters, legislation has been passed to facilitate detention of persons in garda custody for up to 24 hours in most cases[57] but up to 7 days in certain cases[58] and provide for majority verdicts in criminal trials;[59] to restrict bail pending trial;[60] to facilitate forensic testing of accused persons (including taking DNA samples, due to be supplemented by a DNA Database);[61] to alter significantly the preliminary examination procedure in indictable offences[62] and other aspects of procedure;[63] to facilitate video-link evidence in certain cases, especially sexual offences;[64] to ensure that sentencing takes account of the impact of the crime on the victim; to provide for appeals against lenient sentences and the payment of compensation to victims of crimes;[65] to provide for alternatives to imprisonment, such as community service;[66] and also to facilitate the investigation of possible miscarriages of justice.[67]

[5.27] A significant prison-building programme has been in place since the late 1990s in response to the argument that a 'revolving door' policy had operated in which the sentences of the courts were not carried into effect in the manner intended.

[5.28] Most of these matters are legislated against the background of strong debate on either side. For example, the changes to the bail laws required a constitutional amendment followed by legislation and there was a good deal of controversy about the need for such changes.[68] The particular problem of increased drug-related crime has led to the introduction of seven-day detention of suspects in garda custody, subject to some

---

57 Criminal Justice Act 1984.
58 Criminal Justice Act 2007.
59 Criminal Justice Act 1984, as amended by the Criminal Justice Act 2006 and Criminal Justice Act 2007.
60 Bail Act 1997: see para **6.107**.
61 Criminal Justice (Forensic Evidence) Act 1990, which is to be repealed and replaced by the Criminal Justice (Forensic Evidence and DNA Database System) Act 2014, which also provides for the establishment of a DNA Database, as recommended in the Law Reform Commission's *Report on the Establishment of a DNA Database* (LRC 78-2005).
62 Criminal Justice Act 1999: see para **6.106**.
63 Criminal Justice (Miscellaneous Provisions) Act 1997.
64 Criminal Evidence Act 1992.
65 Criminal Justice Act 1993.
66 Criminal Justice (Community Service) Act 1983. See also the Scheme of a Criminal Justice (Community Sanctions) Bill published in 2014 (para **10.40**). In 2014, the Department of Justice and Equality published a *Report of a Strategic Review of Penal Policy* available at www.justice.ie, which may lead to further policy and legislative developments in the future.
67 Criminal Procedure Act 1993.
68 For a discussion written prior to the referendum, see O'Mahony, 'The Proposed Constitutional Referendum on Bail: An Unholy Grail?' (1995) 13 ILT 234.

judicial control.[69] This, in turn, has given rise to suggestions that the criminal justice system in Ireland should move from its common law accusatorial tradition to embrace the civil law inquisitorial system employed in many other European states.[70] At a wider level, the general role of the gardaí has also been the subject of debate, particularly the changing nature of policing in an increasingly urbanised community and the use of developments such as 'Community Watch' programmes. The general legislative structure of the gardaí was fundamentally reformed in the Garda Síochána Act 2005. The 2005 Act sets out clear roles and responsibilities for the Garda Commissioner and the Minister for Justice; it provides for joint policing committees at local level, and for the recruitment of reserve members (unpaid part-time members); it provides for an independent Garda Síochána Ombudsman Commission to investigate complaints; and it also provides for a Garda Síochána Inspectorate with standard-setting functions for the gardaí. A number of these changes were also influenced by recommendations made in a series of reports of a tribunal of inquiry into the activities of some gardaí in Donegal.[71] As with the civil side of the work of the courts, many of these matters continue to be debated and substantial disagreement exists about the appropriate way forward. At the time of writing (September 2014), in the wake of further controversies concerning the absence of transparent independence of the gardaí from political influence, the Government has proposed that an independent police authority (comparable to the Northern Ireland Police Board) may be established.

[5.29] In summary, both in terms of the civil and criminal workload of the courts, substantial legislative changes in recent years have reflected the many changes in society in Ireland and this will undoubtedly continue into the future. The overall picture is of a system that has changed dramatically in recent years.

[5.30] We discuss below some of the changes effected over the years to the courts since 1924, primarily those altering the distribution of business between the courts. As already mentioned, in order to take account of the increase in volume of work, there have been substantial increases in the number of judges in the various courts. We can now proceed to discuss the first instance jurisdiction conferred on the different courts.

[2]   THE ORIGINAL JURISDICTION OF THE COURTS IN CIVIL CASES

Changes in the monetary limits

[5.31] As we already noted, a major factor in describing the original jurisdiction of the different courts in civil matters is the different level of damages that may be awarded. The general monetary jurisdiction of the different courts has been altered from time to time since the passing of the Courts of Justice Act 1924. These changes have, in large part, reflected the need to respond to changes in the value of money arising from

---

69   Criminal Justice (Drug Trafficking) Act 1996.
70   See further on this, para **6.138**.
71   See the eight reports of the Tribunal of Inquiry into complaints concerning some Gardaí of the Donegal Division, available at www.morristribunal.ie.

inflation and the consequent need to ensure an even distribution of business between the different courts.

[5.32] Thus, in 1924, the District Court was confined to a maximum award of £25 in damages[72] while the Circuit Court was confined to an award of £300.[73] The effect of this was that any claim in excess of £300 would be dealt with in the High Court. These limits have been substantially changed since 1924. By 1971, the general jurisdiction of the District Court had been raised to £250[74] and that of the Circuit Court to £600.[75] In 1981, the jurisdiction of the District Court was raised to £2,500[76] and that of the Circuit Court to £15,000.[77] In 1991, the District Court's jurisdiction was raised to €6,384[78] and the Circuit Court's to €38,092.[79]

[5.33] Prior to 2014, the monetary level of jurisdiction of the courts for civil claims remained at the level set in 1991. The Courts and Court Officers Act 2002 had provided for an increase of the monetary jurisdiction of the Circuit Court from €38,092 to €100,000 and of the District Court from €6,384 to €20,000. These were never brought into force, because no commencement order had been made to bring them into effect. This was largely because the government accepted the recommendation in the 2002 *Report of the Motor Insurance Advisory Board* that the jurisdiction of these courts in personal injuries actions should remain unchanged and that, instead, the Injuries Board recommended in the 2002 Report should be established, which would, in effect, provide for a system intended to avoid court-based litigation for most personal injuries actions. The Injuries Board was established by the Personal Injuries Assessment Board Act 2003.[80] The 2006 *Report of the Legal Cost Implementation Advisory Group* recommended that the changes proposed in the 2002 Act should be brought into force, but that these would not apply to personal injuries claims.[81] The jurisdictional levels of the courts set in 1991 had been significantly eroded by inflation to the extent that the High Court was dealing with claims which were relatively modest in value and in many cases the legal costs involved would have considerably outweighed the value of the proceedings. The Courts and Civil Law (Miscellaneous Provisions) Act 2013 provided for a general increase in the monetary jurisdiction limits to €75,000 for the Circuit

---

72 Courts of Justice Act 1924, s 77.
73 Courts of Justice Act 1924, s 48.
74 Courts Act 1971, s 7 amending Courts of Justice Act 1924, s 77.
75 Courts Act 1981, s 2 amending the Courts (Supplemental Provisions) Act 1961, the Third Schedule.
76 Courts Act 1981, s 6 amending Courts of Justice Act 1924, s 77.
77 Courts Act 1981, s 2 amending the Courts (Supplemental Provisions) Act 1961, the Third Schedule.
78 Courts Act 1991, s 4, amending the Courts of Justice Act 1924, s 77.
79 Courts Act 1991, s 2, amending the Courts (Supplemental Provisions) Act 1961, the Third Schedule.
80 On the 2003 Act, see para **5.15**.
81 Legal Costs Implementation Advisory Group, *Report of the Legal Costs Implementation Advisory Group* (Pn A7/0027, 2006), p 26.

Court and €15,000 for the District Court. As to personal injury actions, the monetary jurisdiction of the Circuit Court was raised to €60,000. The lower amount for the jurisdiction of the Circuit Court in personal injuries proceedings was adopted to deal with concerns relating to possible inflation of awards and a consequent effect on insurance costs. These changes came into effect in 2014.[82] Since 2014, therefore, claims in excess of €75,000 (for personal injury actions, in excess of €60,000) are heard in the High Court.

[5.34] It is notable that the 2013 Act, like all its predecessors, altered the courts' monetary jurisdiction by primary legislation. However, s 16 of the Courts Act 1991 provides that variations to the monetary jurisdiction of the courts may be made by way of statutory order by the government. Section 16 of the 1991 Act specifies that any such variation may only be made 'having regard to changes in the value of money generally in the State' since any previous alteration. In addition, any order to be made under s 16 must be laid before each House of the Oireachtas and requires a positive resolution in both Houses before it can come into effect. The power in s 16 of the 1991 Act has never, to date (2014), been used. In any event, an order under the 1991 Act also requires a vote in both Houses of the Oireachtas.

Monetary limits and the relative seriousness of a claim

[5.35] The changes in the monetary limits have an important practical consequence for litigants and practising lawyers. The intention in 1924 when the £25 limit for the District Court and the £300 limit for the Circuit Court were set was that the District Court should deal with relatively minor civil claims, that the Circuit Court would deal with relatively more serious claims and that the High Court should be confined to serious claims, in the sense that it is concerned with claims involving large sums of money or which involve complex legal issues. This is also reflected in the general content of the various procedural rules of court, in particular those governing the preparation of the formal documents or pleadings required to initiate and process a civil claim.

[5.36] The requirements for a District Court claim are relatively informal by comparison with those for the Circuit Court, while those for the High Court are more complex than those for either the Circuit or District Court.[83] However, the effect of inflation since the 1960s in particular has been that, if the monetary limits set in 1924 had been left unaltered the High Court would have been left to deal with virtually all civil claims, even those involving a modest claim for £301 arising from a traffic accident where a car was scratched. Hence the changes in the monetary limits to ensure the courts deal with the kinds of cases intended for them in 1924. The changes made in 2014 to the monetary limits, the first since 1991, can be seen as an overdue response to ensure that the original intention behind these limits was restored.

---

[82]   The Courts and Civil Law (Miscellaneous Provisions) Act 2013 (Jurisdiction of District Court and Circuit Court) (Commencement) Order 2013 (SI 566/2013) brought the increased monetary limits into force on 3 February 2014.

[83]   See para **6.26**.

Monetary limits and the award of costs

[5.37] The importance of changing monetary limits is especially obvious when the circumstances surrounding a commonplace civil action, such as a claim for damages for personal injuries, are considered. There are two points to be noted here.

[5.38] First, it is clear that, the more serious the injury, the more care will be needed to prepare the case for court. This will require more advice from, for example, medical experts as to the extent of a person's injuries as well as a prognosis on the long-term effects of the injuries. Another feature of many personal injuries cases is the need to prove negligence, thus necessitating an expert view from, for example, an engineer to give a view on the state of a road or the appropriateness or otherwise of safety precautions in a place of work.

[5.39] A second connected issue is the cost of a civil action and who is required to pay for the experts and lawyers engaged in the case. In general terms, where a party (whether the plaintiff or defendant) is successful in his or her civil claim, the court will order that the losing party must pay the successful party's legal costs – this is referred to as the rule that 'costs follow the event'.[84] In general, the court order for costs should cover most of the expenses incurred by the successful party, in particular the fees charged by the solicitor and (where briefed) the barristers who appeared for that party. Traditionally, it has been practice for more lawyers to be involved in a High Court civil action than for one in the Circuit Court or the District Court.

[5.40] As a general rule of thumb, the parties in a High Court civil claim would each engage a solicitor who, in turn, would brief one junior counsel and at least one senior counsel.[85] In a Circuit Court civil action one would expect to find each party being

---

84   The losing party must also pay their own costs, including the fees charged by their lawyers as well as any other professional fees. This system that 'costs follow the event' is quite different from that in the United States of America, where both parties in civil claims are, in general, required to discharge the fees incurred by their professional advisers, regardless of the outcome of their claim. Thus, a successful party in a civil claim in the United States will, in general, pay a percentage of their award to their lawyer, the precise percentage (ranging from 20% to 50% of the award) usually being agreed in advance. This system of fee-paying has been criticised as encouraging litigation and 'ambulance chasing' by lawyers. The system has, traditionally, been regarded as unethical in the United Kingdom and Ireland, though it should be distinguished from the 'no foal, no fee' arrangement in which the lawyer will agree to initiate a claim for a plaintiff on the basis that a fee will only be charged if the claim is successful (in which case, it is the losing defendant who pays the fee). The 'no foal, no fee' alludes to the traditional rule of veterinary surgeons. This type of arrangement is not regarded as unethical within the legal profession, though it has been the subject of much criticism from outside the profession, where it is equated with the United States system of percentage fees.

85   The almost invariable practice of engaging one junior counsel and two senior counsel (the 'two senior' rule) in High Court civil actions was common until 1988, but has to some extent been discontinued since then, arising from calls to restrict legal costs in High Court actions, in particular personal injuries actions. The Courts Act 1988, s 5 empowers the Minister for Justice to make rules restricting the number of counsel in respect of whom costs would be allowed, but voluntary self-regulation by the Bar in this area since 1988 has meant that no rules have been made under s 5 of the 1988 Act.

represented by a solicitor and, usually, junior counsel, while in a District Court action the general rule would be to find the parties represented by a solicitor alone.[86] In general also it should be said that in a High Court civil action it is more likely that there will be a need for professional witnesses to provide evidence to the court, particularly in a personal injuries action where expert opinion evidence of negligence and expert opinion medical evidence of the extent of injuries will be required.

[5.41] It should be clear from these different arrangements that the costs of a High Court civil action will be more expensive (for the losing party) than a Circuit Court or a District Court action. The changes in the monetary jurisdictions of the different courts has, in part, reflected the change in the value of money; it would clearly be wrong for the District Court to be limited to the £25 limit set in 1924 so the changes are a clear attempt to ensure that the civil claims dealt with in the District Court reflect the intention that the District Court deal with relatively minor civil claims, that the Circuit Court deal with relatively more serious claims and that the High Court should be confined to serious claims, in the sense that it deals with claims involving large sums of money or which involve complex legal issues. In addition the listing of cases in the District Court and Circuit Court, in particular outside of Dublin, does not facilitate the hearing of long cases whereas more time is allocated to High Court claims which reflects the relatively complex nature of the proceedings which come before that Court.

Regulation of legal costs

[5.42] If there is a dispute between the parties concerning the level of fees charged in a case (in particular those charged by the lawyers and expert witnesses in a case), the losing party may require that these be reviewed. At the time of writing (September 2014), this is done by an officer attached to the courts, in the High Court by the Taxing Master, in the Circuit Court by the County Registrar. This is referred to as the taxation of costs. As discussed in Chapter 3, the 2005 *Report of the Legal Costs Working Group* recommended that the office of Taxing Master be transferred to a newly established Legal Costs Assessment Office.[87] On foot of this the Legal Services Regulation Bill 2011 (currently, September 2014, before the Oireachtas) proposes to establish a Legal Costs Office to replace this system. The question whether a particular fee charged was appropriate or indeed whether it was appropriate, for example, for a solicitor to have briefed one or more barristers, will be a matter for the Legal Costs Office (replacing the Taxing Master or the County Registrar) to consider. For the lawyers and professional witnesses involved in a claim, it is important to know whether their fees 'will tax', that is whether the losing party must pay the fee involved.

[5.43] Only what are referred to as 'party and party' costs will be allowed, which essentially involves those costs which are regarded as necessary for the conduct of the

---

[86] It should also be noted, however, that solicitors have had a legal right of audience in all the courts since 1971 and would thus be entitled to represent a party to an action in all the courts: see para **3.71**. What is described here is the general practice.

[87] *Report of Legal Costs Working Group* (2005), discussed in paras **3.31–3.34**, above.

action. These are to be contrasted with what are referred to as 'solicitor and client' costs, which might be described as fees arising from the use of more lawyers or experts than were necessary for the correct conduct of the action. In any case challenging costs, the losing party in an action will argue that many items being claimed were 'solicitor and client' costs, while the successful party will attempt to argue that all items should be regarded as 'party and party' costs.

[5.44] In addition to the issue of whether one or two or three counsel should have been retained, a significant point of dispute on taxation will be the size of the fee charged, in particular by barristers.[88] Many efforts have been made over the years to ensure that the costs associated with civil litigation are appropriate to the seriousness of the claim. In this respect, various provisions have been included in the Courts Acts that have altered the monetary jurisdiction of the courts, that only certain costs 'will tax' and that the level of fees to be charged by lawyers and others involved in a claim are appropriate to the seriousness of the case. The most recent provisions on this aspect of court procedure deal with a number of connected issues.

[5.45] First, the powers of judges to 'remit' a case to a lower court where the case has been initiated in a higher court have been strengthened.[89] Second, there are provisions to limit the costs where the total sum actually awarded falls short of the thresholds currently laid down for the different courts,[90] for example where in a High Court claim very much less than €75,000 (since 2014) is actually awarded, or where less than €15,000 (since 2014) is awarded in a Circuit Court claim. Third, the possibility of introducing statutory levels of fees to regulate the legal profession has been provided for.[91] All these provisions are intended to ensure or persuade lawyers and litigants that

---

[88] For example, in a High Court civil claim, where a solicitor engaged one junior and one senior counsel. It is a traditional rule that the fee set by the senior counsel will influence that set by the junior counsel. Assume that the senior counsel sets a 'brief fee' of €2,000 and a daily fee of €750 and that the case concluded after two days, the senior counsel's fee would come to €3,500. Traditionally, the junior counsel's fee for the case would be in the region of two-thirds of that charged by senior counsel (the 'two-thirds' rule), and would therefore come to an additional €2,250. The total fees for both counsel would therefore be in the region of €5,750. The 'two-thirds' rule was criticised by the Fair Trade Commission in its 1990 Report on the Legal Profession and the Competition Authority. As a result, the Bar Council issued a ruling that the practice be discontinued (see generally para **3.05**). As a result the 'two-thirds rule' has been virtually eradicated and junior counsels' fees do not reflect the fees of the senior counsel briefed on the case. On fees generally, see para **3.27***ff*.

[89] Courts of Justice Act 1924, s 25 as amended, deals with the remittal of a case initiated in the High Court to either the Circuit Court or District Court. Its constitutionality was upheld in *Ward v Kinahan Electrical Ltd* [1984] IR 292. On the operation of s 25 of the 1924 Act, as amended, see Delany, *The Courts Acts 1924–1997* (2nd edn, 2000). Courts Act 1991, s 15 introduced for the first time the power of the Circuit Court to remit a case to the District Court. On s 15 of the 1991 Act, see Delany, *The Courts Acts* (2nd edn, 2000) and Delany and McGrath, *Civil Procedure in the Superior Courts* (2nd edn, 2005), pp 235–241.

[90] See the Courts Act 1981, s 17 as amended by the Courts Act 1991, s 14.

[91] Courts and Court Officers Act 1995, s 46. See generally, Kelleher, 'The Courts and Court Officers Act 1995 – The Main Provisions' (1996) 14 ILT 18 and para **3.27**.

the appropriate court is chosen for the particular case in which they are involved. There are also provisions to allow settlement offers to be opened to the Court if the award made by the Court is less than the settlement matter and in certain cases plaintiffs can be penalised on costs for having rejected a settlement offer by having the costs of the defendant awarded against them even if they win their cases.[92]

The District Court

[5.46] As we have already seen,[93] the District Court is a court of local and limited jurisdiction within the meaning of Article 34.3.4° of the Constitution and, broadly, the successor to the jurisdiction exercised at Petty Sessions.[94] As a 'creature of statute', therefore, the simple rule is that the jurisdiction of the District Court is restricted to whatever has been expressly conferred on it by legislation.[95] It is not possible to provide a complete listing of all civil matters with which the District Court deals, so what follows are the principal features of its original civil jurisdiction.

(a) General and monetary jurisdiction

[5.47] In cases of contract, breach of contract and tort (except libel, slander, seduction,[96] slander of title, malicious prosecution and false imprisonment)[97] and in proceedings brought on behalf of the state or a local authority to recover a debt due to the state or local authority, the District Court is empowered to award damages not exceeding €15,000 (since 2014).[98] In addition, where the parties to a District Court action consent in writing, the District Court is conferred with jurisdiction in excess of this limit.[99] Significantly the District Court has no jurisdiction in equity and cannot hear cases where equitable reliefs such as declarations or specific performance are sought.

---

92 Provisions such as those allowing for lodgements or making of Calderbank offers.

93 See para **4.40**.

94 See paras **2.49–2.54**.

95 The main jurisdiction-conferring provision is s 77 of the Courts of Justice Act 1924, carried forward by the Courts (Supplemental Provisions) Act 1961, s 33 and amended from time to time, most recently by the Courts Act 1991, s 4. For the changes effected to s 77, see Delany, *The Courts Acts 1924–1997* (2nd edn, 2000).

96 Seduction here refers to a claim by an employer arising from the loss of services of an employee, eg, during the pregnancy of an unmarried woman employee.

97 The exempted categories of torts contained in brackets are 'reserved' for the Circuit Court and High Court: see para **5.55**.

98 Courts of Justice Act 1924, s 77(a)(i), (iii) and (v) carried forward by the Courts (Supplemental Provisions) Act 1961, s 33, and amended from time to time, most recently by the Courts and Civil Law (Miscellaneous Provisions) Act 2013.

99 Courts Act 1991, s 4(c). See the District Court Rules 1997 (SI 93/1997). This was recommended by the Committee on Court Practice and Procedure in its fifth interim report. See Committee on Court Practice and Procedure, *Fifth Interim Report: Increase of Jurisdiction of the District Court and Circuit Court* (Stationary Office, PR 8936, 1966).

(b) Renewal of intoxicating liquor licences

[5.48] In 1924, the District Court was conferred with the jurisdiction to grant certificates of renewal to the holder of a spirit and other intoxicating liquor licence.[100] Up to 1988, the holder of an intoxicating liquor licence was required to apply each year to the District Court to obtain a certificate stating that (s)he was a fit person to continue to hold a licence.[101] Since 1988,[102] a licence-holder may now obtain a renewal of most liquor licences from the Revenue Commissioners without the need to produce a District Court certificate. An application to the District Court is now required only in certain instances, such as where there is an objection lodged to the licence renewal.

(c) Family proceedings

[5.49] In family law proceedings, the District Court has a limited jurisdiction. Thus, it is not given jurisdiction to grant a decree of divorce, judicial separation or nullity, such matters being reserved for the Circuit Court and High Court.[103] However, where judicial separation proceedings have already been initiated, the parties may apply to the District Court for variation of maintenance. In such circumstances, the court is empowered to award maintenance to a spouse up to a maximum of €500 per week and to a maximum of €150 per week per child.[104] The court also has jurisdiction concerning the disposal of household chattels, up to a value of €15,000, in proceedings under s 9 of the Family Home Protection Act 1976.[105] The District Court also deals with important family law matters such as proceedings for guardianship,[106] maintenance orders[107] and proceedings under domestic violence legislation such as where barring or safety orders are sought.[108] These are among the most common civil law matters which come before the District Court.

---

[100] Courts of Justice Act 1924, s 77(A).

[101] The licensing session of the District Court occurred in November of each year.

[102] Courts (No 2) Act 1986, s 4, which was brought into effect in 1988: Courts (No 2) Act 1986 (Commencement) Order 1988 (SI 176/1988).

[103] See para **5.59**.

[104] Family Law (Maintenance of Spouses and Children) Act 1976, s 23 as amended by the Courts and Civil Law (Miscellaneous Provisions) Act 2013. The effect of the Status of Children Act 1987, Pt IV is that the same rules as to maintenance now apply regardless of whether the parents of the child are married.

[105] The jurisdiction is conferred by s 10(5) of the 1976 Act, as amended by the Courts and Civil Law (Miscellaneous Provisions) Act 2013.

[106] Guardianship of Infants Act 1964.

[107] Family Law (Maintenance of Spouses and Children) Act 1976.

[108] Domestic Violence Act 1996.

(d) Commercial and consumer protection: general

[5.50] The District Court is empowered to deal with civil claims under the Hotel Proprietors Act 1963[109] and the Consumer Credit Act 1995,[110] again with limits of €15,000 as to the amount of damages that may be awarded.

(e) Commercial and consumer protection: small claims

[5.51] We have mentioned already[111] that, in line with other states, a procedure for dealing with small claims initiated by consumers has been introduced and is administered principally by clerks of the District Court.[112] It operates as a service provided by District Court offices and is designed to handle consumer claims and business claims cheaply and quickly. The procedure had been introduced on a pilot basis by the District Court (Small Claims Procedure) Rules 1991[113] and was extended to the entire state by the District Court (Small Claims Procedure) Rules 1993.[114] The small claims procedure is now set out in Ord 53A of the District Court Rules 1997.[115] The rules provide for an initial application to the appropriate Small Claims Registrar (a clerk of the District Court) who is empowered to attempt to reach a compromise between the parties in dispute, described as the claimant and respondent. Only where the Small Claims Registrar fails to effect a resolution of the claim is it referred to the Small Claims Court for determination. It is worth noting that the application can be made online.[116] A fee of €25 for the entire procedure is laid down in the rules. In the event of continued dispute, the matter may be referred to a judge of the District Court for resolution. A 'small claim' is defined in Ord 53A as one involving a claim not exceeding €2,000[117] which comes within the categories mentioned in that rule. The first category concerns consumer contracts (since 2010, defined to include disputes between businesses) such as the retail purchase of goods, but not a claim arising from an alleged breach of a hire-purchase or leasing agreement. The second category is a 'minor' property damage claim in tort ('minor' not being further defined, but obviously subject to the €2,000 overall ceiling) provided the claimant is not a corporate body and excluding personal injuries claims. The third category is a claim by a tenant for the return of rent deposit or any sum known as 'key money' unless the claim is a dispute which can be referred to the Private Residential Tenancies Board.

---

109 Hotel Proprietors Act 1963, s 10(2) as amended by the Courts and Civil Law (Miscellaneous Provisions) Act 2013.

110 The 1995 Act replaced the Hire-Purchase Acts 1946 to 1980. The Hire-Purchase (Amendment) Act 1960, s 19 as amended by the Courts Act 1991, s 6 had conferred jurisdiction on the District Court in relation to proceedings under the Acts of 1946 to 1980.

111 See para **5.24**.

112 McHugh, *Small Claims Court in Ireland: A Consumer Guide* (2003).

113 SI 310/1991.

114 SI 356/1993.

115 Ord 53A was inserted by the District Court (Small Claims Rules) 2009 (SI 519/2009).

116 See www.CSOI.ie (Courts Service Online).

117 Ord 53A was inserted by the District Court (Small Claims Rules) 2009 (SI 519/2009).

(f) Environmental matters

[5.52] The District Court is empowered to deal with claims for damages arising under the Local Government (Water Pollution) Acts 1977 and 1990, again limited to a maximum award of €15,000 in damages.[118]

(g) Land and equity matters

[5.53] Unlike the Circuit Court, the District Court has no jurisdiction to determine title to property or in other connected matters generally described as the equity jurisdiction. In this area, the District Court is limited to cases of ejectment for non-payment of rent or overholding in any class of tenancy, provided that the rent does not exceed €15,000 per annum.[119]

The Circuit Court

[5.54] Like the District Court, the Circuit Court is a court of local and limited jurisdiction within the meaning of Article 34.3.4° of the Constitution[120] and is thus empowered to deal only with those matters which have been expressly assigned to it by legislation. Again, broadly speaking, it is the successor to the County Courts and Courts of Quarter Sessions.[121] As with our description of the jurisdiction of the District Court, what follows is a selection of the original civil jurisdiction of the Circuit Court.

(a) General and monetary jurisdiction

[5.55] In terms of general subject matter, the Circuit Court is, pursuant to s 22 of the Courts (Supplemental Provisions) Act 1961, conferred with the same jurisdiction as that exercised by the High Court in over 20 different areas, which are listed in the Third Schedule to the 1961 Act.[122] The jurisdiction of the Circuit Court thus extends to all claims in contract or tort, including those which are outside the jurisdiction of the District Court, namely libel, slander, seduction, slander of title, malicious prosecution and false imprisonment.[123] It should be noted, however, that this concurrent jurisdiction of the Circuit Court is limited in two significant respects.

---

[118] Local Government (Water Pollution) Act 1977, s 10 as amended by the Courts and Civil Law (Miscellaneous Provisions) Act 2013.

[119] Courts of Justice Act 1924, s 77(a)(ii) as amended by the Courts and Civil Law (Miscellaneous Provisions) Act 2013.

[120] See para **4.40**.

[121] See para **2.54**.

[122] Section 22 of, and the Third Schedule to, the Courts (Supplemental Provisions) Act 1961 involved a complete restatement of the Circuit Court's jurisdiction, radically changing the provisions of the Courts of Justice Act 1924, s 48 as amended, which they replaced.

[123] See para **5.47**. Section 22 of the Courts (Supplemental Provisions) Act 1961 and the Fourth Schedule to the Courts (Supplemental Provisions) Act 1961 (replacing a similar provision in the Courts of Justice Act 1924, s 51) also expressly conferred jurisdiction on the Circuit Court concerning other matters dealt with prior to 1924 by Recorders, County Court judges and Chairmen and Courts of Quarter Sessions.

[5.56] In the first place, the Circuit Court is limited to an award of damages (since 2014) of €75,000 (for personal injury actions, €60,000).[124] However, it should also be noted that, as in the case of a civil claim in the District Court, the parties to a Circuit Court action can, if both of them consent, confer unlimited jurisdiction on the court.[125] In addition, the Circuit Court has exclusive and unlimited jurisdiction in applications for new commercial tenancies.[126] When the Circuit Court is dealing with a claim for discrimination on the grounds of gender, it is empowered to award unlimited compensation.[127]

[5.57] In the second place, the jurisdiction of the Circuit Court is limited in the sense that, where exclusive jurisdiction is given to another court over certain matters, the Circuit Court is necessarily precluded from hearing such cases at first instance. Thus, although s 22 of the Courts (Supplemental Provisions) Act 1961 confers extensive jurisdiction on the Circuit Court concurrently with the High Court, Article 34.3.2° of the Constitution confers exclusive jurisdiction on the High Court in cases involving the constitutional validity of any law.[128] In terms of exclusive jurisdiction conferred by legislation, we have already seen that the District Court has been conferred with the jurisdiction concerning the renewal of intoxicating liquor licences.[129]

(b) New intoxicating liquor licences

[5.58] The Circuit Court has exclusive jurisdiction to grant (or refuse) applications for new intoxicating liquor 'on-licences', within the meaning of the Licensing Acts 1833 to 2004.[130] This is not affected by the Courts (No 2) Act 1986 which, as we saw, has limited the jurisdiction of the District Court in relation to renewals of licences.

(c) Family proceedings

[5.59] The Circuit Court has a much more extensive jurisdiction in family proceedings than the District Court.[131] Section 5 of the Courts Act 1981 conferred on the Circuit Court the jurisdiction to award a decree of divorce *a mensa et thoro*, since 1989 referred

---

124 Courts (Supplemental Provisions) Act 1961, Third Schedule, as amended by the Courts and Civil Law (Miscellaneous Provisions) Act 2013.

125 Courts (Supplemental Provisions) Act 1961, s 22(1)(b) replacing a similar though not identical provision in the Courts of Justice Act 1924, s 48(i). This consent must be in writing and in the form prescribed for this purpose by the Circuit Court Rules 2001. On the consent jurisdiction of the District Court see para **5.47**.

126 Landlord and Tenant (Amendment) Act 1980.

127 Employment Equality Act 1998, s 77. For example see *Atkinson v Carty* [2005] ELR 1 where the plaintiff was awarded €102,750 as compensation for sexual harassment.

128 See para **5.74**.

129 See para **5.48**.

130 Courts (Supplemental Provisions) Act 1961, s 24 replacing the Courts of Justice Act 1924, s 50. On licensing law generally see Cassidy, *The Licensing Acts 1833–1995* (1996).

131 For the District Court's limited jurisdiction in this area, see para **5.49**.

to as judicial separation.[132] While the intention of the 1981 Act seemed to be to have all such cases heard in the Circuit Court, it was held in *R v R*[133] that the High Court retained a concurrent jurisdiction in relation to these areas by virtue of the inherent jurisdiction conferred on the High Court by Article 34.3.2° of the Constitution.[134] This decision resulted in some judicial separation cases being heard in the High Court, while others were assigned to the Circuit Court.

[5.60] Further substantial substantive and procedural changes were effected in this area by the Judicial Separation and Family Law Reform Act 1989 and, in deference to the decision in *R v R*, s 31(2) of the 1989 Act conferred concurrent jurisdiction on the Circuit Court and High Court in judicial separation proceedings. Section 32 of the 1989 Act also provides that, when dealing with family law matters, the Circuit Court is described as the 'Circuit Family Court', and, in an attempt to make the court atmosphere more suitable to such cases, s 33 of the 1989 Act also provided that judges, barristers and solicitors involved in such cases shall not wear wigs or gowns.[135] Section 53 of the Courts and Court Officers Act 1995 conferred jurisdiction on the court in nullity cases for the first time and s 38 of the Family Law (Divorce) Act 1996 confers jurisdiction on the court in divorce cases (also concurrently with the High Court). We should note that while s 9 of the 1989 Act deals with the precise issue raised in *R v R*, that decision casts a constitutional shadow over the legislation conferring exclusive jurisdiction on the Circuit Court relating to landlord and tenant and malicious injuries.[136] However, these exclusive powers remain in operation unless they are successfully challenged in a constitutional action.

(d) Commercial and consumer protection

[5.61] The Circuit Court, like the District Court, is empowered to deal with civil claims under the Hotel Proprietors Act 1963[137] and the Consumer Credit Act 1995,[138] but subject to the higher limits of €75,000 (since 2014) as to the amount of damages that may be awarded.

---

132 See the Judicial Separation and Family Law Reform Act 1989.

133 *R v R* [1984] IR 296.

134 See para **5.76**.

135 While the Courts and Court Officers Act 1995, s 49 (see para **3.111**) provides that the wearing of wigs by counsel is now generally optional, s 33 of the 1989 Act is clearly more wide-ranging in the family law context.

136 See paras **5.64–5.65**.

137 Hotel Proprietors Act 1963, s 10(1) as amended.

138 The Consumer Credit Act 1995 replaced the Hire-Purchase Acts 1946 to 1980. The Hire-Purchase (Amendment) Act 1960, s 19 and the Courts (Supplemental Provisions) Act 1961, the Third Schedule, as amended by s 2 of the 1991 Act had conferred jurisdiction on the Circuit Court in relation to proceedings under the Acts of 1946 to 1980.

(e) Environmental matters

[5.62] The Circuit Court, like the District Court, is empowered to deal with claims for damages arising under the Local Government (Water Pollution) Acts 1977 and 1990, but again subject to the higher limit of €75,000 (since 2014) as to the amount of damages that may be awarded.

(f) Land and equity suits

[5.63] As to issues involving title to land and certain actions for ejectment, the Circuit Court has jurisdiction where the rateable valuation of the land does not exceed €254.[139] When an order commencing s 45 of the Civil Liability and Courts Act 2004 is made, the basis of the jurisdiction of the Circuit Court in land and equity matters will alter from the current archaic concept of 'rateable value' to the more modern concept of 'market value'. When this provision is commenced, the Circuit Court will have jurisdiction over land and equity matters where the market value of the land does not exceed €3,000,000. In cases involving the grant of probate or the administration of an estate, the dissolution of a partnership, the specific performance of contracts, the partition or sale of land or an action concerning property claiming an injunction (all of which are commonly referred to as equity matters or equity suits), the court has jurisdiction where the subject matter does not exceed €75,000 (since 2014).

(g) Landlord and tenant

[5.64] The Circuit Court has been conferred with extensive jurisdiction concerning landlord and tenant cases.[140] This includes jurisdiction to determine claims for new leases, whether business or private and, unlike other matters, this jurisdiction applies regardless of the amount of rent payable or the value of the property in question.[141] However, where a claim is made concerning arrears of rent, the court's jurisdiction is again limited by the requirement that the subject matter does not exceed €75,000. The Private Residential Tenancies Board (established by the Private Residential Tenancies Act 2004) deals with consumer disputes arising between landlords and tenants. In relation to land and equity matters the jurisdiction of the Circuit Court is where the rateable valuation of any land involved is not greater than £254. As already mentioned, this will change to jurisdiction based on the market value of the property when the relevant provisions of the Civil Liability and Courts Act 2004 are commenced.[142]

---

139 Courts (Supplemental Provisions) Act 1961, s 22 and references 8, 9, and 10 of the Third Schedule, as amended by the Courts Act 1991, s 2.

140 For the limited jurisdiction of the District Court, see para **5.53**.

141 Landlord and Tenant (Amendment) Act 1980, s 3. See generally Wylie, *Landlord and Tenant Law* (2nd edn, 1998).

142 Courts (Supplemental Provisions) Act 1961, s 22 and references 11, 12 and 13 of the Third Schedule, as amended by the Courts Act 1991, s 2, Civil Liability and Courts Act 2004, s 45.

(h) Malicious injuries

[5.65] Exclusive jurisdiction was conferred on the Circuit Court by the Malicious Injuries Acts 1981 and 1986. Up to 1986, the Circuit Court heard many thousands of cases each year in which owners of property sought compensation from local authorities for damage to their property if it was caused maliciously. The cost to local authorities was enormous. Under the Malicious Injuries (Amendment) Act 1986, a claim may now only be made where the damage is caused in the course of a riot or arising from the activities of an unlawful organisation or an organisation advocating the use of violence related to Northern Ireland. The 1986 Act has, therefore, led to a large decrease in the number of malicious injuries cases in the Circuit Court.[143]

(i) Local government election petitions

[5.66] The Circuit Court is also the nominated court for the purposes of petitions challenging the validity of an election to a local authority.[144]

(j) Company law and personal insolvency

[5.67] The jurisdiction of the Circuit Court has been expanded to empower it to deal with certain company law restructuring or insolvency matters. This approach was taken to enable small companies to have access to the Circuit Court in order to save the expense of having to proceed to the High Court. The Companies (Miscellaneous Provisions) Act 2013 allows small private companies to apply to the Circuit Court to have an examiner appointed. It came into operation in July 2014.[145]

As noted, the Personal Insolvency Act 2012 made provision for a maximum of 8 new specialist judges to facilitate the speedy consideration of personal insolvency applications in the Circuit Court.[146] In 2013, 6 specialist judges were appointed, all of whom were former County Registrars. The Circuit Court has jurisdiction to deal with applications under the 2012 Act for proposals concerning personal debts which are below €2.5 million. This system is equivalent to the examinership protection provided to companies. Any application under the 2012 Act which exceeds this figure must be approved by the High Court. The 2012 Act allows individuals to come to a non-judicial solution to debt problems by way of agreeing to a restructuring arrangement of their debts. The High Court or Circuit Court is then required to approve any Personal insolvency arrangement (PIA) and debt settlement arrangement (DSA).

---

[143] For an example of post-1986 litigation, see *WJ Prendergast & Son Ltd v Carlow County Council* [1990] ILRM 749. The Malicious Injuries (Amendment) Bill 1996 proposed to repeal in full all remaining provisions of the malicious injuries code, but it lapsed after the 1997 General Election and was not re-introduced.

[144] Local Government (Petitions and Disqualifications) Act 1974, s 2. See *Boyle v Allen* [1979] ILRM 281.

[145] Companies (Miscellaneous Provisions) Act 2013 (Section 2) (Commencement) Order 2014 (SI 285/2014).

[146] Paragraph **4.63**.

The High Court

[5.68] Under Article 34.3.1° of the Constitution,[147] the High Court is vested with 'full original jurisdiction in and power to determine all matters and questions whether of law or fact, civil or criminal'. This marks the High Court as different from the District Court and Circuit Court, the courts of local and limited jurisdiction, and it reflects the position of the High Court prior to 1922 as a court possessing inherent powers, and as having substantial supervisory functions in relation to the inferior courts.[148] While Article 34.3.1° appears to give the High Court full jurisdiction in all cases, this has not generally been taken quite as literally as it appears. Thus, the lower courts can be assigned functions over certain matters, as described in the preceding sections – otherwise there would be no point in having other courts, and the Constitution itself envisages such other courts. In this context, Article 34.3.1° has been interpreted as having a two-fold effect.

[5.69] First, Article 34.3.1° has the effect that the High Court retains some jurisdiction, whether by way of appeal or by its traditional supervisory role of judicial review,[149] though first instance jurisdiction in certain areas may be given to the local and limited courts. This is the effect of the decision of the Supreme Court in *Tormey v Ireland*.[150] Second, there is some doubt as to whether a lower court can validly be given exclusive jurisdiction over an entire subject matter. We have already noted that, in *R v R*,[151] it was held that the High Court still retained its 'full' jurisdiction under Article 34.4.1°, even where the Courts Act 1981 had appeared to confer exclusive jurisdiction on the Circuit Court in certain family law cases.

[5.70] Bearing in mind these difficulties, therefore, the jurisdiction of the High Court is as provided for in legislation, subject to whatever the Constitution, by implication, has additionally (or concurrently) reserved to the High Court. This reality is reflected in s 8 of the Courts (Supplemental Provisions) Act 1961, which provides that the court shall have 'such original and other jurisdiction as is prescribed by the Constitution'. Section 8 of the 1961 Act goes on to specify that the High Court is invested with such jurisdiction as was vested in the former High Court under the Courts of Justice Act 1924.

[5.71] What follows, therefore, is what is generally understood in practice to be the current jurisdiction of the High Court.

(a) General monetary jurisdiction

[5.72] The effect of the Courts and Civil Law (Miscellaneous Provisions) Act 2013 is that (subject to the unlimited consent jurisdiction of the Circuit and District Courts) the High Court is the appropriate court to hear cases involving claims for damages in excess

---

147 See para **4.35**.
148 See para **2.33**.
149 On judicial review, see Ch 10.
150 *Tormey v Ireland* [1985] IR 289: see para **15.144**.
151 *R v R* [1984] IR 296. See para **5.59**.

of €75,000, or for personal injuries actions, in excess of €60,000.[152] No legislation has set an upper ceiling on the damages which may be awarded by the High Court, and indeed any such attempt might very well conflict with Article 34.4.1° of the Constitution.

[5.73] The result of the €60,000 threshold for personal injuries actions is that serious personal injuries cases will remain matters to be heard in the High Court because, between the sum of money required to provide for medical treatment in the future as well as compensation for the actual pain and suffering involved, the €60,000 threshold is passed in cases where an injury has long-term effects. Nonetheless, a significant number of personal injuries actions are, from 2014 onwards, likely to be heard in the Circuit Court.[153] Of course, as the Injuries Board established by the Personal Injuries Assessment Board Act 2003 – and other non-litigation processes – now deals with the assessment of damages in the majority of claims that were previously litigated, a large amount of personal injuries cases have, in one way or another, been taken out of the courts. As well as personal injury cases, many of the more significant civil claims between business undertakings, such as those involving building or other contracts, are heard in the High Court, again as the monetary consequences of breaches in such cases are likely to exceed €75,000.[154] Where a commercial case involves a value in excess of €1 million, the High Court's Commercial Court (in effect an administratively separate list of such cases) has been in place since 2004 to provide a fast-track procedure to deal more effectively with such claims.[155]

(b) Constitutional cases

[5.74] As already mentioned,[156] Article 34.3.2° confers on the High Court the exclusive function of determining the constitutional validity of legislation. No other court, other than the Court of Appeal (to be established in 2014) and the Supreme Court on appeal from the High Court, may make such a determination.

(c) Judicial review

[5.75] As already indicated, the High Court's 'full' jurisdiction extends to the general supervision of the 'inferior' or 'local and limited' courts as well as other decision-making statutory tribunals by means of judicial review. While this jurisdiction might not

---

152 These 'floors' of €75,000 and (for personal injuries actions) €60,000 are based on the maximum limit imposed by the Courts and Civil Law (Miscellaneous Provisions) Act 2013 on the jurisdiction of the Circuit Court: see para **5.56**.

153 On the background to changes in the monetary jurisdiction, see paras **5.31–5.34**.

154 Many consumer contract cases are, correspondingly, likely to be heard in the Circuit Court, such claims unlikely to exceed the €75,000 threshold.

155 The Commercial Court List was established by the Rules of the Superior Courts (Commercial Proceedings) 2004 (SI 2/2004), and implemented recommendations in the Twenty-Eighth Report of the Committee on Court Practice and Procedure (2003), available at www.courts.ie: para **5.78**.

156 See para **4.37**. On constitutional adjudication generally, see Ch 15.

easily fall into the civil jurisdiction of the court, it is important to note its place in the court's functions.[157] This has become an increasingly important part of the court's business, both in criminal matters on review of the lower courts and in civil matters where decisions of administrative bodies are challenged. In recent years, the number of judicial reviews of administrative decisions concerning the asylum process constituted a large proportion of the judicial reviews dealt with in the High Court.[158]

(d) Family proceedings

[5.76] We have noted that in *R v R*[159] it was held that the High Court retained a concurrent jurisdiction with the Circuit Court in relation to family law matters by virtue of the 'full' jurisdiction conferred on the court by Article 34.3.2° of the Constitution.[160] As a result, some divorce, judicial separation and nullity cases are heard in the High Court, while others are assigned to the Circuit Court. As with the Circuit Court, and in an attempt to make the court atmosphere more suitable to such cases, s 33 of the Judicial Separation and Family Law Reform Act 1989 provides that High Court judges, barristers and solicitors involved in family proceedings shall not wear wigs or gowns.[161]

(e) Company and personal insolvency

[5.77] The Companies Act 1963 designated the High Court as the court with exclusive jurisdiction in connection with the winding up of companies established under the 1963 Act. The Companies Act 1990 conferred exclusive jurisdiction on the High Court concerning the appointment of an examiner to a company but the Companies (Miscellaneous Provisions) Act 2013 introduced a less expensive examinership process in the Circuit Court for small and medium sized enterprises. At the time of writing (September 2014) the Companies Bill 2012, which consolidates and reforms the Companies Acts 1963 to 2013, is before the Oireachtas. As to personal insolvency, the Personal Insolvency Act 2012 introduced a non-judicial process for resolving personal insolvency matters, broadly the equivalent of examinership where proposals regarding debts of in excess of €2.5 million are considered by the High Court. The 2012 Act also amended the Bankruptcy Act 1988, the judicial process for dealing with personal insolvency, the equivalent of liquidation.

---

[157] On the growth of administrative bodies, see Ch 8.

[158] The *Annual Report of the Courts Service 2007* (2008), p 92 reports that in 2007 there were just over 1,000 applications for judicial reviews concerning asylum applications. While there has been a decrease in the number of applications for judicial reviews concerning asylum applications, in 2013 they constituted 40% of all judicial review applications received by the High Court so that they remain a significant part of the judicial review cases which come before the High Court. See *Annual Report of the Courts Service 2008* (2009), p 72 and the Annual Report of the Courts Service 2013 (2014) at p 31.

[159] *R v R* [1984] IR 296, discussed at para **5.59**.

[160] See para **4.35**.

[161] While the Courts and Court Officers Act 1995, s 49 (see para **3.114**) provides that the wearing of wigs by counsel is now generally optional, s 33 of the 1989 Act is clearly more wide-ranging in the family law context.

(f) The Commercial Court[162]

[5.78] In 2004, the Commercial Court, an administratively separate list of commercial cases valued in excess of €1m, was established.[163] However unlike other lists, an application has to be made for a case to be admitted into the Commercial Court list and the High Court judge hearing the application has discretion to refuse to admit any set of proceedings. If the application for admission to the Commercial Court is refused, the case remains in one of the other administrative divisions of the High Court such as Chancery or Non Jury. The Commercial Court aims to encourage the speedy resolution of large-scale commercial litigation using judicial case management (a concept championed in the reports on civil justice prepared by Lord Woolf in England and Wales in the 1990s).[164] A wide variety of pre-trial procedures are used in the Commercial Court, primarily to encourage the early identification of the matters at issue between the parties. In addition, the judge is empowered either on his or her own decision or if requested by the litigants to adjourn the matter for a period of up to 28 days to allow the parties to consider whether to refer the proceedings to mediation, conciliation or arbitration.[165] The judge may also direct that a case management conference be held prior to the date of trial of the case. The purpose of a case management conference is to ensure that the 'proceedings are prepared for trial in a manner which is just, expeditious and likely to minimise the cost of the proceedings'[166] and it is usually held two to four weeks prior to trial.[167] In addition, it is common for a pre-trial conference to be held between the lawyers for the parties involved and the judge. At a pre-trial conference, the judge seeks to ascertain what steps need to be taken to prepare the case for trial, the likely length, arrangements for witnesses (including video conferencing) and other arrangements for trial. At a pre-trial conference, the judge may give directions for arrangements necessary for trial and if no date for trial has been set, duly set a date. In order that matters are expedited to trial, there are possible cost sanctions for parties who delay a matter.[168] In 2012 215 cases were admitted into the Commercial Court list and this decreased to 169 in 2013.[169]

---

[162] See, Dowling, *The Commercial Court* (2nd edn, 2012); and Kelly, 'The Commercial Court' (2004) 9(1) *Bar Review* 4.

[163] The Commercial Court List was established by the Rules of the Superior Courts (Commercial Proceedings) 2004, SI 2/2004, and implemented recommendations in the Twenty-Seventh Report of the Committee on Court Practice and Procedure, *A Commercial Court in Ireland* (2003), available at www.courts.ie.

[164] See paras **6.66–6.74**.

[165] Rules of the Superior Courts, Ord 63A, r 6(1)(b)(xiii).

[166] Rules of the Superior Courts, Ord 63A, r 14(1).

[167] Dowling, *The Commercial Court* (2007), p 301.

[168] Order 63A, r 15(e).

[169] *Annual Report of the Courts Service 2013* (2014) at p 43.

(g) Equity and chancery

[5.79] Subject to the concurrent jurisdiction of the Circuit Court in claims concerning land,[170] the High Court has jurisdiction over the kind of claims concerning land and land ownership which were dealt with in the Chancery Division of the High Court prior to 1922.[171] While there are currently no divisions within the High Court,[172] in practice such chancery matters are channelled in administrative terms quite separately from other cases and will be heard by judges whose expertise lies in this area. Company law cases are also dealt with by the High Court chancery judges. Any proceedings where equitable relief is sought, such as specific performance or injunctive relief, are allocated to the Chancery list of the High Court. It is a common feature for certain interlocutory reliefs to be sought to protect the interests of one of the parties prior to the hearing of the proceedings, such as an injunction restraining the termination of employment of an employee and restoring him or her to salary, and these applications are listed in the Chancery list of the High Court.

(h) Capacity decisions (replacing wardship)

[5.80] The Assisted Decision-Making (Capacity) Bill 2013, which at the time of writing (September 2014) is before the Oireachtas, proposes to bring the state into line with most other jurisdictions by providing for a non-judicial process for assisting relevant persons in their decision-making. The 2013 Bill follows a 2006 Report of the Law Reform Commission which recommended the replacement of the wardship jurisdiction of the High Court with a process for adult guardianship, including the establishment of the Office of Public Guardian.[173] The enactment of the 2013 Bill would involve a significant contribution to ensuring that the state could ratify the 2006 UN Convention on the Rights of Persons With Disabilities. Until the 2013 Bill is enacted, the only process in place in this respect is the jurisdiction of the High Court concerning the judicial protection of wards of court which prior to 1922 had been exercised by the Lord Chancellor of Ireland and the Lord Chief Justice of Ireland and, between 1924 and 1936, by the Chief Justice.[174] This involves conferring the status of a ward of court on a person

---

[170] See para **5.63**.

[171] Courts of Justice Act 1924, s 24 as carried over by the Courts (Supplemental Provisions) Act 1961, s 8. Section 27 of the Supreme Court of Judicature (Ireland) Act 1877, which remains in force, provides that the rules of common law and equity are to be applied concurrently in the courts.

[172] See para **4.62**.

[173] Law Reform Commission, *Report on Vulnerable Adults and the Law* (LRC 83-2006). See also *In Re Dolan* [2007] IESC 26 and *In Re Dolan* [2008] IEHC 264.

[174] Courts (Supplemental Provisions) Act 1961, s 9(1) describes this as the jurisdiction in 'lunacy and minor matters'. This phrase derives from the Lunacy Regulation (Ireland) Act 1871, the relevant legislation for the exercise of what is also described as the *parens patriae* jurisdiction: see *Re D* [1987] IR 449. Section 9(4) of the 1961 Act provided that the words 'ward of court' or 'person of unsound mind' should be substituted for the word 'lunatic' in the 1871 Act. (contd../)

who is not capable of managing his or her affairs, whether because he or she is a minor[175] or by reason of mental illness or a brain injury. The High Court is thus empowered to administer any property of the person in question as well as determine other important issues concerning the fate of the person.[176]

(i) Oireachtas election and referendum petitions

[5.81] The High Court is designated as the court to which petitions may be brought challenging the validity of any election to the Oireachtas[177] or of any referendum result.[178]

The Supreme Court

[5.82] The Supreme Court is primarily an appellate court.[179] There are, however, two provisions of the Constitution which allow for the court to hear matters at first instance. In addition, certain first instance jurisdiction is conferred personally on the Chief Justice.

(a) Incapacity of President

[5.83] First, Article 12.3.1° provides that the question of whether the President of Ireland has become 'permanently incapacitated' must be 'established to the satisfaction

---

174 (\...contd) Courts of Justice Act 1924, s 19(1) had conferred the wardship jurisdiction on the Chief Justice, but this was transferred to the High Court by the Courts of Justice Act 1936, s 9(1). The court may be addressed by the guardian ad litem who represents the interests of the ward of court generally through solicitors and counsel.

175 At the time of writing, for example, if a person under 18 years of age is involved in a traffic accident that does not involve a brain injury, and subsequently is awarded a sum of money in civil proceedings, that person may be made a ward of court and the High Court will administer the money in question until the person reaches the age of majority. This process is not likely to survive the enactment of the Assisted Decision-Making (Capacity) Bill 2013. In earlier times, in so far as the wardship jurisdiction applied to young people it largely concerned those who were 'expectant heirs' whose property might become involved in excessively complex litigation in the Chancery Division of the High Court, presided over by the Lord Chancellor. The abuses of this wardship jurisdiction were pilloried in Charles Dickens' *Bleak House*.

176 In *In re a Ward of Court (No 2)* [1996] 2 IR 79, the High Court and, on appeal, the Supreme Court made orders authorising the withdrawal of a feeding tube to a 42-year-old woman, the ward of court referred to in the title of the case, who had been in a near-persistent vegetative state (near-PVS) for over 20 years. The person in question died shortly after the removal of the tube. The case became a *cause celebre* as the 'right to die' case: see para **15.185**.

177 Electoral Act 1992, s 132. See *Dillon-Leetch v Calleary (No 2)* (31 July 1974, unreported), SC.

178 Referendum Act 1994, s 42. See *Hanafin v Minister for the Environment* [1996] 2 IR 321 (para **15.114**). See also *McCrystal v Minister for Children and Youth Affairs* [2012] IESC 53 and *Jordan v Minister for Children and Youth Affairs* [2014] IEHC 327.

179 See para **7.02**.

of the Supreme Court consisting of not less than five judges'. This issue has not arisen for decision since 1937.

(b) Reference of Bills by President

[5.84] The other first instance function of the Supreme Court has been of more practical importance. Pursuant to Article 26 of the Constitution, the President of Ireland may, after consultation with the Council of State, refer a Bill passed by both Houses of the Oireachtas to the Supreme Court which is required to pronounce on whether the Bill, or any provision of the Bill, is repugnant to the Constitution. Article 26 provides that this reference power applies to any such Bill other than the following three types: a Money Bill, a Bill whose consideration by Seanad Éireann was abridged under Article 24 of the Constitution,[180] or a Bill containing a proposal to amend the Constitution.

[5.85] For the purpose of such a reference, Article 26.2.1° provides that the court must consist of at least five judges who must consider every question referred to it by the President. In practice, the President refers a single question: whether a Bill is repugnant to the Constitution. Article 26.2.1° also provides that the court shall hear arguments addressed by or on behalf of the Attorney General and by counsel assigned by the court. The Attorney General will argue for the validity of the Bill, while counsel assigned by the court will argue that the Bill is repugnant to the Constitution. Having heard these arguments, the court is required by Article 26.2.1° to give its decision in open court 'as soon as may be, and in any case not later than sixty days after the date of the reference'. This two-month deadline requires the court to give priority in its lists to Article 26 references.

[5.86] Article 26.1.3° prohibits the President from signing a Bill referred to the Supreme Court pending the pronouncement of the court's decision, and Article 26.3.1° prohibits the President from signing into law any Bill which is held by the court to be in any respect repugnant to the Constitution. If, however, the court finds there is no repugnancy, Article 26.3.3° requires the President to sign the Bill into law 'as soon as may be' after the date of the court's decision.

[5.87] At the time of writing (September 2014), there had been 15 references to the court under Article 26 of the Constitution.[181] It should be remembered that, while the Article 26 reference procedure has proved useful, the vast majority of litigation concerning the Constitution has arisen where a person initiates a case in the High Court alleging that enacted legislation, or some other instrument, or even the activity of private citizens, contravenes the rights contained in the Constitution. Thus the Article 26 procedure remains, and will remain by comparison, relatively insignificant as far as the

---

180   See para **13.22**.
181   The most recent was in 2005. See *In Re Article 26 and the Health (Amendment) (No 2) Bill 2004* [2005] IESC 7. A full list is available at www.supremecourt.ie.

development of constitutional law is concerned. Two difficulties with the Article 26 reference procedure have been noted in this respect.[182]

[5.88] First, the Supreme Court has, over the years, expressed some disquiet at being required, on an Article 26 reference, to consider the validity of a Bill 'in a vacuum', that is, without the benefit of a factual context within which to judge the application of the proposed legislation. Second, Article 34.3.3° of the Constitution provides that where the court upholds the constitutionality of a Bill on an Article 26 reference, the validity of what would then become an Act on being signed by the President cannot be questioned in any court. This immunity from further constitutional challenge at any time in the future builds a degree of inflexibility into the Article 26 procedure which has also not been regarded as appropriate.[183] A third difficulty was that Article 26.2.2° had provided that the decision of the majority of the judges shall be the decision of the court and that the decision was to be pronounced by one judge from the majority and that no other opinion, whether assenting or dissenting, was to be disclosed. This 'one-judgment' rule was an exception to the common law tradition of separate judgments in a collegiate court,[184] though a single judgment in such cases is a feature of the civil law systems. The 'one judgment' rule had been criticised by a number of commentators over the years[185] and it was deleted from the Constitution as part of the 2013 constitutional amendment which provided for the establishment of the Court of Appeal. [186]

(c) Functions exercised by Chief Justice

[5.89] Certain functions exercised prior to 1922 by the Lord Chancellor of Ireland and the Lord Chief Justice of Ireland were transferred to the Chief Justice in 1924, including certain matters concerning the admission of persons to the roll of solicitors.[187] In addition, the Chief Justice has exclusive jurisdiction to appoint notaries public and commissioners to administer oaths.[188]

---

182 See Casey, *Constitutional Law in Ireland* (3rd edn, 1998). Professor Casey also notes the existence of similar consultative provisions in other Constitutions.
183 The *Report of the Constitution Review Group* (Pn 2632, 1996) recommended the 'immunity' be removed: on the Report generally, see para **15.196**.
184 On the convention of delivering separate judgments, see para **12.104**.
185 The *11th Interim Report of the Committee on Court Practice and Procedure* (1970) criticised the one judgment rule as inhibiting the development of alternative rules and recommended that Article 26.2.2° be amended accordingly. A similar recommendation was made in the *Report of the Constitution Review Group* (1996): see generally para **15.196**. See also Hogan and Whyte (eds), *Kelly: The Irish Constitution* (4th edn, 2003), p 530.
186 See generally para **12.106**.
187 Courts of Justice Act 1924, s 19(2) since replaced by the Solicitors Act 1954, s 14 and the Courts (Supplemental Provisions) Act 1961, s 10(1)(a).
188 Courts (Supplemental Provisions) Act 1961 s 10(1)(b), replacing the Courts of Justice Act 1924, s 19(3). On the appointment of notaries public, see *Re McCarthy* [1990] ILRM 84.

[3] THE ORIGINAL JURISDICTION OF THE COURTS IN CRIMINAL CASES

[5.90] As with civil matters, the distribution of criminal business between the courts has altered over the years. In general, the issue of which court deals with criminal matters revolves around whether the criminal charge brought may be classified as minor, within the meaning of Article 38.2 of the Constitution. As we have already seen,[189] minor offences may be tried by courts of summary jurisdiction, such as the District Court. By a process of elimination, therefore, other criminal matters, involving major criminal offences, can only be dealt with by the Circuit Court and the High Court (the Central Criminal Court), or the Special Criminal Courts when they are in operation.

The District Court

[5.91] We have seen that the District Court is a court of local and limited jurisdiction.[190] In criminal matters, it can also be described as a court of summary jurisdiction.[191] Since Article 38.2 of the Constitution provides that minor criminal offences may be tried by courts of summary jurisdiction,[192] the District Court is empowered to hear and determine minor criminal offences, that is, what can generally be categorised as less serious criminal offences, such as assault, drink-driving, minor larcenies and criminal damage. While such offences are generally regarded as less serious than, say, murder or rape, they constitute, in terms of numbers, the largest portion of criminal cases heard in the state. In that sense, the District Court is the busiest, and therefore perhaps the most significant, criminal court in the state.[193]

(a) Minor offences in general

[5.92] Although Article 38.2 of the Constitution provides that minor offences may be tried in the District Court, it does not provide a definition of what distinguishes a minor from a non-minor offence. This has, however, been dealt with by way of decisions of the courts which have provided a framework against which to consider whether an offence, either at common law but more particularly where created by legislation, is minor and may be tried in the District Court.

[5.93] In *Melling v Ó Mathghamhna*[194] and *Conroy v Attorney General*[195] the Supreme Court indicated that two factors in particular were important:

---

189 See para **4.45**.
190 See para **4.40**.
191 Courts of Justice Act 1924, s 77 carried forward by the Courts (Establishment and Constitution) Act 1961, s 48.
192 See para **5.04**.
193 See para **5.07** on the annual activity of the courts.
194 *Melling v Ó Mathghamhna* [1962] IR 1.
195 *Conroy v Attorney General* [1965] IR 411.

(1)   the primary consideration is the severity of the punishment authorised by law, whether imprisonment or a fine; and

(2)   a secondary consideration is the moral quality of the acts required to constitute the offence in question, thus indicating that certain offences such as murder, manslaughter and rape could never be regarded as minor offences.

[5.94] As a result of these decisions, the general 'rule of thumb' in legislation creating criminal offences triable summarily has been to limit the maximum prison sentence permissible to 12 months. In relation to fines, a limit of £1,000 was common until 1994, but since then fines of up to €5,000 are provided for on summary conviction.[196] The Fines Act 2010 provided for the index linking of all District Court fines to ensure that their monetary value was brought up to date. This implemented recommendations made by the Law Reform Commission in 1991.[197] The 2010 Act also provides that the maximum fines that may be imposed in the District Court are now placed in five classes based on the amount of the fine: class A is a fine of up to €5,000, class B is a fine of up to €4,000, class C is a fine of up to €2,500, class D is a fine of up to €1,000 and class E is a fine of up to €500.

(b) Specific instances of minor offences

[5.95] In light of these factors, the range of offences with which the District Court deals includes the following:

–   most offences under the Road Traffic Acts 1961 to 2013, including parking offences, speeding, and what is generally described as drunken driving;[198]

–   possession of controlled drugs under the Misuse of Drugs Acts 1977 and 1984, where there is no evidence of intention to supply these to others;[199]

–   minor robberies and thefts under the Criminal Justice (Theft and Fraud Offences) Act 2001;[200]

---

[196]   Two Acts passed in the same month in 1995 demonstrated the changing pattern. The Ethics in Public Office Act 1995, s 37 provided that, on summary conviction, a person who commits an offence under that Act was liable to a fine not exceeding €1,308 and/or imprisonment for a term not exceeding six months. By contrast, the Consumer Credit Act 1995, s 13 provided that, on summary conviction, a person who commits an offence under that Act was liable to a fine not exceeding €900 and/or imprisonment for a term not exceeding 12 months. The Road Traffic Act 2004, s 30 provided on conviction of the offence of supply of a motor vehicle to a minor, a person was liable to a fine on summary conviction of up to €3,000. All these fines are amended in accordance with the index-linking formula in the Fines Act 2010: see Byrne, 'Class A to Class E: Are you ready for the Fines Act 2010?' (2011) 29 ILT 271, 287.

[197]   Law Reform Commission, *Report on the Indexation of Fines* (1991).

[198]   See Pierse, *Road Traffic Law: Annotated Legislation* (2011) and de Blacam, *Drunken Driving and the Law* (3rd edn, 2003).

[199]   See Charleton, *Controlled Drugs and the Criminal Law* (1986).

[200]   See McGreal, *The Criminal Law (Theft and Fraud Offences) Act 2001* (2003).

- simple assaults and other similar offences contained in the Non-Fatal Offences Against the Person Act 1997;[201]

- criminal damage under the Criminal Damage Act 1991;[202]

- summary offences under Regulations made pursuant to s 3 of the European Communities Act 1972.[203]

(c) Indictable offences triable summarily ('hybrid' and 'either way' offences)

[5.96] Most statutory criminal offences are nowadays created as 'hybrid' offences, that is, they may be tried either summarily or on indictment. For example, many of the offences in the Non-Fatal Offences Against the Person Act 1997 and in the Criminal Justice (Theft and Fraud Offences) Act 2001 are such offences. Whether an offence is dealt with summarily or on indictment is primarily a matter for the Director of Public Prosecutions, although a judge of the District Court may decline to deal with a case summarily if he or she considers that the case is not minor in nature and requires a trial on indictment.

[5.97] Such 'hybrid offences' now greatly outnumber the 'either way' offences listed in the Schedule to the Criminal Justice Act 1951.[204] The Schedule to the 1951 Act specifies certain offences which, although they may be tried on indictment in one of the higher criminal courts, can be dealt with in the District Court. For these scheduled offences to be tried in the District Court, two (and in some instances three) conditions must be fulfilled. First, the judge of the District Court must be satisfied that the offence is one fit to be tried summarily. This requires the judge to examine the factual circumstances relating to the particular alleged offence and then to decide whether those circumstances make the offence a minor or a non-minor offence. Second, the accused must be informed of the right to have the case tried before a jury, and the accused must not object to having the case tried in the District Court. In this context, the accused will be aware that if the case is heard in the District Court the maximum sentence which may be imposed will be no greater than 12 months' imprisonment. Generally speaking, in the offences mentioned in the Criminal Justice Act 1951, a maximum sentence of two years' imprisonment is possible in a higher court. In some instances, a third condition, the consent of the Director of Public Prosecutions, is also required. In certain cases, this consent is only required where there is damage to property over a certain limit. An example of where the consent is required without reference to any property damage is assault with intent to resist arrest.[205]

---

[201] See Charleton, *Offences Against the Person* (1992).

[202] The offence of criminal damage replaced, *inter alia*, the old offence of arson, but the 1991 Act also introduced offences connected with computer 'hacking'.

[203] See para **16.118**.

[204] As amended by the Criminal Procedure Act 1967, the Criminal Law (Jurisdiction) Act 1976 and the Criminal Law Act 1997.

[205] This is an offence under the Criminal Justice (Public Order) Act 1994, s 19 replacing the Offences against the Person Act 1861, s 38.

(d) The Children's Court: persons under the age of 18[206]

[5.98] Section 71 of the Children Act 2001 specifies that when the District Court deals with minor offences alleged against children, those under 18 years of age, or applications for orders relating to a child where the attendance of the child is necessary, it is known as the Children's Court. The Children's Court sits in a different building or room from the ordinary courts. It can deal with indictable matters with the exclusion of manslaughter and any offence within the jurisdiction of the Central Criminal Court when the judge is satisfied that the offence is a minor offence fit to be tried summarily and the child consents to it being so tried.[207]

(e) Sending forward indictable offences for trial

[5.99] Another important function of the District Court in criminal matters is to act as a 'clearing house' for non-minor, indictable, criminal cases which cannot be tried summarily. In general, such indictable offences will be sent for trial in the other criminal courts only after they have been dealt with in the District Court. We examine this procedure elsewhere.[208]

(f) Extradition applications

[5.100] Applications for the extradition of a person to face criminal charges in another jurisdiction previously were dealt with at first instance by the District Court.[209] These are now exclusively within the jurisdiction of the High Court.[210]

The Circuit Court

[5.101] The Circuit Court is empowered to hear many serious criminal offences, that is those which are tried on indictment. Since Article 38.5 of the Constitution provides that non-minor criminal offences must, in general, involve trial with a jury,[211] it follows that a significant feature of the Circuit Court as a criminal court is that it comprises a Circuit Court judge sitting with a jury.[212]

(a) General

[5.102] The Circuit Court is empowered to deal with all indictable offences which the High Court may hear, except for certain specified offences which are exclusively within the jurisdiction of the High Court. These 'reserved offences' include treason, murder,

---

[206] See Walsh, *Juvenile Justice* (2003).

[207] Children Act 2001, s 75.

[208] See para **6.105**.

[209] Under the Extradition Act 1965, as amended.

[210] European Arrest Warrant Act 2003. See also Farrell and Hanrahan, *The European Arrest Warrant in Ireland* (2011).

[211] See para **5.04**.

[212] In practice, the Circuit Court when sitting as a court of first instance to deal with serious criminal offences is described as the Circuit Criminal Court, though this has no formal status.

attempted murder and conspiracy to murder.[213] In addition to these exempted offences, the High Court has, since 1991, been conferred with exclusive jurisdiction in relation to other offences, notably rape and aggravated sexual assaults.[214]

(b) Restrictions on transfers of trial

[5.103] A first reading of s 25 of the Courts (Supplemental Provisions) Act 1961 might indicate that many serious criminal offences, such as manslaughter, robbery and other serious offences against the person and against property, would be tried in the Circuit Court. However, until 1981, the position was more complicated because, under s 6 of the Courts Act 1964, the prosecution or the accused could apply for a transfer of the trial to the High Court, such transfer being mandatory when requested. Many such transfer applications were granted in practice, thus generating an increased workload for the High Court. In 1981, the right of transfer in s 6 of the 1964 Act was abolished, and replaced by s 31 of the Courts Act 1981, which provided for a limited right of transfer from any Circuit Court outside Dublin to the Dublin Circuit Court. Challenges on constitutional grounds to s 31 of the 1981 Act were rejected in *Tormey v Ireland*[215] and *The State (Boyle) v Neylon*.[216] Section 31 of the 1981 Act was itself replaced by s 32 of the Court and Court Officers Act 1995, which now provides that any such transfer from a Circuit Court outside Dublin to the Dublin Circuit Court is entirely a matter for the discretion of the Circuit Court judge to whom the application is made. The constitutionality of s 32 of the 1995 Act was upheld in *Todd v Murphy*.[217]

[5.104] The effect is that, since 1981 to a large extent and even more so since 1995, the provisions of may now be relied on as reflecting what happens in practice, namely that the High Court generally only hears the 'reserved' offences, while the Circuit Court generally hears all other serious indictable offences, such as manslaughter, robbery and other serious offences against the person and against property. The Working Group on the Jurisdiction of the Courts recommended changes to allow for cases to be transferred between the Circuit Court and the Central Criminal Court.[218] These are discussed below.

The High Court

[5.105] As we have already noted in the context of the civil jurisdiction of the High Court, Article 34.3.1° of the Constitution invests the court with full original jurisdiction in all matters, whether civil or criminal.[219] And since Article 38.5 of the Constitution provides that non-minor criminal offences must, in general, involve trial with a jury,[220]

---

[213] Courts (Supplemental Provisions) Act 1961, s 25, replacing the generally similar Courts of Justice Act 1924, s 49. For the full list of these 'reserved offences', see para **5.106**.

[214] For the full list of these additional 'reserved offences', see para **5.107**.

[215] *Tormey v Ireland* [1985] IR 289: see para **15.145**.

[216] *State (Boyle) v Neylon* [1986] IR 551.

[217] *Todd v Murphy* [1999] 2 IR 1.

[218] Working Group on the Jurisdiction of the Courts, *The Criminal Jurisdiction of the Courts* (Stationery Office, 2003): see para **5.134**.

[219] See para **5.68**.

[220] See para **5.04**.

the High Court as a criminal court comprises a High Court judge sitting with a jury. When exercising its first instance criminal jurisdiction, the High Court is known as the Central Criminal Court.[221]

[5.106] Section 25(2) of the Courts (Supplemental Provisions) Act 1961 provides that the High Court has exclusive jurisdiction to deal with the following 'reserved offences':

> 'treason (an offence defined by Article 39 of the Constitution, with some further details being dealt with in the Treason Act 1939);
>
> an offence under ss 2 or 3 of the Treason Act 1939, namely encouragement or misprision of (concealing knowledge of) treason, respectively;
>
> offences under ss 6, 7 or 8 of the Offences against the State Act 1939, namely offences relating to the usurpation of the functions of government, obstruction of government and obstruction of the President, respectively;
>
> murder, attempted murder and conspiracy to murder; and
>
> piracy.[222]

[5.107] In addition to these reserved offences, the High Court has, since 1961, been conferred with exclusive jurisdiction in the following categories of offences:

- offences under the Geneva Conventions Act 1962;
- rape, aggravated sexual assault and attempted aggravated sexual assault, as defined in the Criminal Law (Rape) (Amendment) Act 1990;[223]

---

[221] Courts (Supplemental Provisions) Act 1961, s 11(1), replacing the definition in the Courts of Justice Act 1924, s 3 and the jurisdiction conferred by the Courts of Justice Act 1926, s 4. This name was used in the 1923 *Report of the Judiciary Committee* (see para **2.108**) and was borrowed from its English counterpart which, in addition to being described as the Central Criminal Court, is also known by the place in London where it sits, the Old Bailey. The *6th Interim Report of the Committee on Court Practice and Procedure* (1966) recommended that the title 'Central Criminal Court' be abolished and that the Court be known simply as 'The High Court'. The then Chairman of the Committee, Walsh J, later drew attention to this point in *The People (Attorney General) v Bell* [1969] IR 24, noting that the Constitution had given the High Court one name, whether dealing with civil or criminal matters, thus casting some doubt on the validity of the designation in s 11 of the 1961 Act. No action has been taken on these views, and the High Court as a criminal court continues to be referred to as the Central Criminal Court, whether in newspaper reports or by members of the judiciary, even Walsh J, when he was the senior ordinary judge of the Supreme Court: see *The People (DPP) v Shaw* [1982] IR 1, 26.

[222] Offences by an accessory before or after the fact are also included: s 25(2) of the Courts (Supplemental Provisions) Act 1961.

[223] Criminal Law (Rape) (Amendment) Act 1990, s 10. The effective transfer of jurisdiction in rape and other serious sexual assault cases from the Circuit Court to the High Court, as well as the other substantive amendments in the 1990 Act were made, in part, on foot of the recommendations of the Law Reform Commission. (contd.../)

- offences under the Criminal Justice (United Nations Convention Against Torture) Act 2000;

- the offence of murder under s 2 of the Criminal Justice (Safety of United Nations Workers) Act 2000;

- offences under ss 6 and 7 of the Competition Act 2002 (abuse of dominant position and anti-competitive agreements); and

- offences under the International Criminal Court Act 2006 (genocide and crimes against humanity).

[5.108] As already indicated, the effect of s 25(2) of the 1961 Act is that, aside from these offences, the Circuit Court has full jurisdiction to deal with indictable offences.[224]

Special Criminal Courts

[5.109] The title 'Special Criminal Courts' provides two clues as to the nature of these particular courts.[225] First, they are courts that function in relation to criminal trials only. As to being 'special', the courts derive their legal standing from Article 38.3 of the Constitution.

(a) Constitutional setting: non-jury court

[5.110] While Article 38.5 of the Constitution contains a general right to trial with a jury concerning criminal charges,[226] this is expressly stated to be subject to Article 38.2 (minor offences),[227] Article 38.3 (special criminal courts) and Article 38.4 (military courts).[228] This indicates that a feature of trial by special criminal courts is the absence of a jury.

---

[223] (\...contd) The transfer of jurisdiction reflected in large part concern over the perceived low sentencing level for such offences in the Circuit Court. On the general background, see Fennell's Annotation to the 1990 Act, *Irish Current Law Statutes Annotated*. The sentencing issue was also a major catalyst in the enactment of the Criminal Justice Act 1993: see para **5.26**.

[224] See para **5.102**. The Chief Justice, Keane CJ, in his suggestions for reform of the court structure made in 2001 (see para **5.126**), doubted the logic of limiting the jurisdiction of the High Court in this way.

[225] See generally, Hogan and Walker, *Political Violence and the Law in Ireland* (1989) and O'Malley, *The Criminal Process* (2009).

[226] See para **5.04**.

[227] See para **5.04**.

[228] The military tribunals provided for under Article 38.4.1° concern the trial of offences during a state of war or armed rebellion. As they do not deal with what might be described as 'ordinary' criminal law, their functions and powers are not considered here. Article 38.4.2° deals with trial by court-martial, which is regulated by the Defence Act 1954. See generally, Hogan & Whyte (eds), *JM Kelly: The Irish Constitution* (4th edn, 2003), pp 1215–**1220**.

[5.111] Article 38.3 states:

> "1° Special courts may be established by law for the trial of offences in cases where it may be determined in accordance with such law that the ordinary courts are inadequate to secure the effective administration of justice, and the preservation of public peace and order.
>
> 2° The constitution, powers, jurisdiction and procedure of such special courts shall be prescribed by law."

[5.112] The relevant law enacted in accordance with Article 38.3 is contained in Pt V of the Offences against the State Act 1939. Section 35 of the 1939 Act provides that Pt V comes into force (and special criminal courts may thus be established) only where the government makes and publishes a proclamation declaring that it 'is satisfied that the ordinary courts are inadequate to secure the effective administration of justice and the preservation of public peace and order'.[229] As can be seen, this formula is taken verbatim from Article 38.3 of the Constitution. Part V of the 1939 Act also provides for the matters referred to in Article 38.3.2° of the Constitution, namely the composition of the special criminal courts as well as providing for the detailed procedures by which they are to operate.

[5.113] Underlying the establishment of special criminal courts is a belief that the operation of the ordinary courts, and in particular the independent functioning of juries, might be undermined by the activities of subversive organisations. The background to the enactment of the 1939 Act was the issuing of 'proclamations' by the IRA to the effect that it had become the Government of the Republic and an expected increase in violent activity on their part.[230] Nevertheless, while concern over subversive crime lies behind the establishment of special criminal courts their jurisdiction is not so confined and extends to non-subversive, or 'ordinary', crime.[231] The jurisdiction of the Special Criminal Court was expanded in 2009 by the Criminal Justice (Amendment) Act 2009 which made provision for the use of the Special Criminal Court for the hearing of particular organised crime offences unless the Director of Public Prosecutions directs otherwise. The basis for the expansion of the jurisdiction of the Special Criminal Court to try such offences was the assertion that the ordinary courts were inadequate to deal with organised crime. As a result of the 2009 Act, a number of high profile alleged gangland members have been tried before the Special Criminal Court in recent years.

(b) Scheduled offences and transfer of trials

[5.114] One of the important features of the Offences Against the State Act 1939 as far as special criminal courts is concerned is that it is possible to have cases transferred from the ordinary criminal courts, that is, the District Court, the Circuit Court and the High Court. This can be effected in one of two ways.

---

229 This proclamation must be published in *Iris Oifigiúil*, the Official Gazette: s 35(6) of the 1939 Act.
230 See 74 *Dáil Debates*, cols 1283–1292.
231 *The People (DPP) v Quilligan* [1986] IR 495.

[5.115] First, s 36 of the Offences Against the State Act 1939 provides that certain lists of offences may be specified by the government by statutory order as offences which the ordinary courts are to be deemed inadequate to deal with within the terms of Article 38.3 of the Constitution. These offences are referred to as 'scheduled offences' and are transferred automatically to the special criminal courts.[232] The current list of scheduled offences is:

- any offence under the Criminal Damage Act 1991 (replacing the Malicious Damage Act 1861);
- an offence under s 7 of the Conspiracy and Protection of Property Act 1875;
- any offence under the Explosive Substances Act 1883;
- any offence under the Firearms Acts 1925 to 1990;
- any offence under the Offences against the State Act 1939 itself;[233] and
- certain offences under the Offences against the State (Amendment) Act 1998.[234]

This list reflects the primary concern with subversive crime and it is notable that other serious offences, such as murder, rape and robbery are not scheduled.

[5.116] Second, even where an offence is not a scheduled offence, such as murder, s 46 of the 1939 Act provides that an individual trial may be transferred to a special criminal court where the Director of Public Prosecutions issues a certificate stating that in his opinion the ordinary courts are inadequate to secure the effective administration of justice and the preservation of public peace and order. Once such a certificate is issued the case must be transferred by the ordinary court to a special criminal court.

[5.117] The combined effect of ss 36 and 46 of the 1939 Act is that all serious criminal offences may be transferred from the ordinary courts and tried by special criminal courts, including the offences 'reserved' to the High Court, such as murder,[235] or the other serious offences such as robbery that might be tried in the Circuit Court.[236] The courts have indicated that they will be extremely reluctant to invalidate such a transfer even where the accused person claims he has no connection with any terrorist-type organisation.[237]

---

[232] Such cases can, however, also be transferred back to the ordinary courts under the 1939 Act.

[233] These five categories are listed in the Offences against the State (Scheduled Offences) Order 1972 (SI 282/1972).

[234] The scheduled offences under the Offences against the State (Amendment) Act 1998 are those in ss 6 to 9 and 12, namely: directing an unlawful organisation; possession of articles for purposes connected with certain offences; unlawful collection of information; and training persons in the making or use of firearms. The 1998 Act was enacted in the wake of a bombing in Omagh in 1998, in the aftermath of the signing of the Belfast Agreement.

[235] See para **5.106**.

[236] See para **5.95**.

[237] See *Savage v Director of Public Prosecutions* [1982] ILRM 385, *O'Reilly and Judge v Director of Public Prosecutions* [1984] ILRM 224 and *The State (McCormack) v Curran* [1987] ILRM 225.

(c) Special criminal courts in operation

[5.118] Special Criminal Courts do not exist on a permanent basis but only where Pt V of the Offences against the State Act 1939 is in force. Part V has been in operation on two separate occasions. The first was at the outset of World War II in 1939. The special criminal courts continued to operate until 1946, when in effect they ceased to function, though the government proclamation bringing Pt V of the 1939 Act into force was not actually revoked and the special criminal courts were revived in 1961 to deal with a number of offences connected with what was termed the 'border campaign' of that time. The 1939 proclamation was revoked in 1962 and thus Pt V of the 1939 Act ceased to be in force. In 1972, a new government proclamation was issued bringing Pt V of the 1939 Act into force, and a single special criminal court was established. That court has continued to operate from 1972 to the present, dealing with cases primarily connected with subversive activities and other offences largely, though not exclusively, related to Northern Ireland.[238]

(d) Composition of courts

[5.119] The Special Criminal Court established in 1972 differed in a number of respects from the previous manifestations of World War II and the early 1960s. First, only one such court was established. However, the most significant difference was the composition of the court. Section 39 of the Offences Against the State Act 1939 provides that a person may be appointed as a member (in effect, a judge) of a special criminal court if he or she is a judge of the High Court, or the Circuit Court, or the District Court, a barrister or solicitor of not less than seven years' standing or an officer of the defence forces not below the rank of commandant. All members of special criminal courts sitting between 1939 and 1972 were defence forces officers.[239]

[5.120] However, since 1972 the Special Criminal Court has comprised three judges of the ordinary courts, usually one High Court judge, one Circuit Court judge and one judge of the District Court, with the High Court judge presiding. Any of these three might either be a sitting or retired judge. This change in composition from previous special criminal courts could largely be attributed to queries as to the constitutional validity of a person being tried with an ordinary criminal offence before officers of the defence forces. Numerous challenges to the constitutional validity of special criminal courts have been made, but all of these have been unsuccessful.[240] However, the

---

238 A number of offences connected with 'organised' drugs activity have also been transferred from the ordinary courts to the Special Criminal Court. These have included high-profile murder and drugs-related charges in the late 1990s connected with the murder of the investigative journalist Veronica Guerin in 1996.

239 Military tribunals, operating under Article 38.4, were also in existence separately at that time.

240 Two such challenges concerned the courts established in 1939: *Re MacCurtain* [1941] IR 43 and *The People (AG) v Doyle* (1943) 77 ILTR 108. As to the court established in 1972, see *Re the Criminal Law (Jurisdiction) Bill 1975* [1977] IR 129; *Eccles v Ireland* [1985] IR 545; *McGlinchey v Governor of Portlaoise Prison* [1988] IR 671; *Kavanagh v Government of Ireland* [1996] 1 IR 321 and *Gilligan v Ireland* [2001] 1 ILRM 473; *Gilligan v The Special Criminal Court* [2006] 2 IR 389.

continued operation of the Special Criminal Court has been repeatedly criticised at international level, particularly by the United Nations Human Rights Committee.[241] The Special Criminal Court was also criticised again following the explanation of its jurisdiction in 2009 to cover organised crime. [242]

[5.121] The 2002 *Report of the Committee to Review the Offences against the State Acts 1939–1998 and Related Matters* [243] considered whether there was a continued need for the Special Criminal Court in light of the 1998 Belfast (Good Friday) and 2004 St Andrews Agreements, under which a devolved administration was established in Northern Ireland. A majority of the Committee recommended its retention, with minor modifications, having regard to the continued threat posed by terrorism and organised crime. In addition, it recommended that a resolution establishing the court should lapse automatically after three years unless the Oireachtas passed a resolution continuing it in force (a 'sunset clause'). It also recommended the amendment of the 1939 Act so that it would no longer be possible to have members of the defence forces sit as judges of the court. These recommendations have not yet been implemented.

[4] PROPOSALS FOR FUNDAMENTAL REFORM OF THE COURT STRUCTURE

Keane CJ's 2001 lecture on the future of the courts system

[5.122] In 2001, the then Chief Justice, Keane CJ, delivered a public lecture sketching out a potentially fundamental reform for the court structure which, as he pointed out, had remained essentially unchanged since the enactment of the Courts of Justice Act 1924.[244] The basic landscape of the courts since then has been the three-tier system discussed in detail in this chapter, comprising the District Court, the Circuit Court and the High Court. Keane CJ made a number of suggestions for reform of the court system. This lecture was followed by the establishment of a Working Group on the Jurisdiction of the Courts, which published a report in 2003 on the *Jurisdiction of the Courts in Criminal Matters*. In 2010, the Law Reform Commission published a *Report on the Consolidation and Reform of the Courts Acts*.[245] In view of these ongoing developments, we end this chapter with an outline of the 2001 lecture and subsequent developments.

---

[241] See Fottrell, 'Reporting to the UN Human Rights Committee – A Ruse by Any Other Name?' (2001) 19 ILT 61.

[242] See for example criticism by the Irish Council for Civil Liberties and the Irish Human Rights Commission (now the Irish Human Rights and Equality Commission).

[243] Committee to Review the Offences Against the State Acts 1939–1998 and Related Matters, *Report of the Committee to Review the Offences Against the State Acts 1939–1998 and Related Matters* (Stationery Office, 2002).

[244] *The Irish Courts System in the 21st Century: Planning for the Future*, Lecture delivered to the Law Society, University College Cork, 23 March 2001 (2001) 6 *Bar Review* 321.

[245] LRC 97-2010, available at www.lawreform.ie.

[5.123] In his 2001 lecture, Keane CJ began by outlining the overall objectives of the courts:

"As to the objectives, it would probably be generally agreed that it is the duty of the State to provide the citizens with a system of civil and criminal justice that is accessible to all and which functions in a manner that is impartial, open and expeditious."

This outline reflects the overall objectives specified by Lord Woolf in his reports in the 1990s on civil justice in the United Kingdom, which led to fundamental reform of the UK civil justice system.[246] Indeed, Keane CJ went on to assess in brief terms to what extent the current system met these objectives.

[5.124] In his lecture, Keane CJ concluded that there were, in 2001, 'considerable difficulties in the administration of justice in Ireland'. He also noted that the position varied across the country and that, in some venues, judges were underworked. He suggested that this could be for a variety of reasons: 'a larger demographic base, a more efficient judge, more efficient local practitioners.' Whatever the reasons, he commented that the statistics masked a 'disquieting feature of the present system,' namely, that some judges were endeavouring to dispose of their crowded lists by holding protracted daily sessions, sometimes sitting late into the evening. While Keane CJ did not question the dedication and professional commitment of the judges concerned, this 'gives rise to anxiety as to the quality of justice being dispensed in courts where fatigue must inevitably set in for both judges and practitioners.'

Indeed, Keane CJ provided an insight into the effect this had on requests by the judiciary for additional judges. He noted:

"When appeals are made by the Presidents of the different jurisdictions for more judges, the reply sometimes given by the executive is that judges in some areas sit for only part of the day. That merely emphasises that the present system is not merely under-resourced: it is failing to make the most efficient use of such resources as are available."

[5.125] Keane CJ then referred to a number of other jurisdictions of comparable size in Europe, North America, Australia and New Zealand, where two-tier systems were emerging to replace three-tier systems. Indeed, the states referred to reflect the type of comparative surveys made by the Working Group on a Courts Commission in its recommendations which led to the Courts Service Act 1998[247] and by the Committee on Judicial Conduct and Ethics, which proposed the establishment of a Judicial Council.[248]

[5.126] Keane CJ then gave examples of what he said were 'a number of anomalies and irrational features of the present system'. Thus, he stated that there appeared no reason why the High Court (Central Criminal Court) could not deal with major crimes such as manslaughter, fraud, the importation and sale of drugs, robbery with violence and kidnapping, which currently are dealt with exclusively in the Circuit Court. Equally, he

---

[246] See para **6.66**.

[247] See para **4.209**.

[248] See para **4.138–4.160**.

considered that there was no reason why the Circuit Court was precluded from trying murder and rape cases. In the civil law area, he accepted that the anomalies were not so immediately apparent, but commented that they were nonetheless striking.

[5.127] He stated that cases which are currently within the jurisdiction of the Circuit Court might produce complex issues of law and/or fact but that the procedures are markedly different from those in the High Court. In addition, he noted that there was no right of appeal to the Supreme Court – the only appeal is to the High Court whose decision is final. Thus, he noted, points of law of major importance may not be decided at the Supreme Court level, unless what he described as 'the protracted and cumbersome procedure of a case stated is invoked'. He also noted that, as a result of the decision in *R v R*[249] the High Court and the Circuit Court have concurrent jurisdiction to grant divorces, judicial separations and decrees of nullity 'with no guidance to the hapless litigants in choosing the court in which to institute the proceedings'. He suggested that virtually the entire family law jurisdiction should be vested in the revamped District Court, including the divorce jurisdiction.[250]

[5.128] The anomalies he identified led Keane CJ to conclude that they derived from the three-tier system of courts of first instance, unlike most of the other systems which he had examined and in which a two-tier system is the norm. He then gave his broad outline of a new system:

> "A rationally designed Irish system would consist, at the first instance level, of a District Court with a significantly enhanced civil jurisdiction and an expanded High Court to which would be transferred all the existing civil and criminal jurisdiction of the Circuit Court."

[5.129] Under such a system, he said, the High Court would remain a unified court of first instance with unlimited original civil jurisdiction and exclusive criminal jurisdiction in serious crime, but would sit as a regional court. He thought that major constitutional and judicial review cases and commercial/chancery cases would be tried by the High Court in Dublin. To avoid any tendency for a two-tier High Court to emerge, he stated that it would be necessary for all the High Court judges to sit in rotation in the different regions, including Dublin. He also considered that these proposals would not require any amendment of the Constitution, since a court of local and limited jurisdiction in the form of the District Court would remain (though it is notable that the Constitution speaks of 'courts of local and limited jurisdiction').

[5.130] Keane CJ suggested that this new system would then be accompanied by a two-tier appeal structure. We examine his proposals in this area elsewhere.[251] Keane CJ also queried whether certain aspects of the courts' current jurisdiction should be retained. He commented:

---

[249] *R v R* [1984] IR 296: see para **5.59**.
[250] This aspect of the Chief Justice's lecture gave rise to criticism from family law practitioners who argued that this appeared to 'devalue' this area of civil law.
[251] See para **7.62**.

"The vesting of some statutory jurisdictions in the courts also calls urgently for reappraisal. Local authorities are now entrusted with the grant of permissions and licences in areas of enormous importance, such as planning and the environment generally. The retention by the District Court and the Circuit Court of a licensing jurisdiction in the case of alcohol can be seen, in this context, as an anachronistic survival which is also wasteful of judicial resources."

[5.131] This is a particularly sensitive area, because Keane CJ raised the prospect here of other areas being removed from the remit of the courts. If licensing could be removed, could the removal of personal injuries actions be resisted? Since 2001, of course, the Personal Injuries Assessment Board, discussed earlier in this chapter, has provided a kind of half-way house to the court system for much personal injuries litigation. The whole question of 'ouster' of the courts is a difficult one, and clearly Keane CJ did not mean his comments to be the final word on the matter.

[5.132] Central to Keane CJ's proposals were that any changes would be aimed at improving the efficiency and effectiveness of the court system in delivering improved access to justice, where possible at a local level. He also noted that the number of judges in Ireland appeared to be below the average in other comparable European states, although he accepted that the appointment of additional judges would not, per se, improve the efficiency of the courts. Thus, his central argument was that a structural reform was required.

[5.133] Keane CJ considered that the changes he suggested might also help reduce the overall cost of litigation and thus improve access to justice. Although outside the general terms of his lecture, he also acknowledged that improvements might be required in the whole area of legal aid, but he did not elaborate on this.[252] Keane CJ recognised that the suggested structure he outlined would involve an enormous change in the current arrangements and suggested that a Working Group along the lines of the Working Group on a Courts Commission should be established to examine the court system and to recommend changes. This is exactly what happened.

Working Group on the Jurisdiction of the Courts

[5.134] The Working Group on the Jurisdiction of the Courts, chaired by Fennelly J, was established under the auspices of the Courts Service in the aftermath of Keane CJ's 2001 lecture. Its terms of reference empowered it to make recommendations which, in the opinion of the Working Group, were desirable in the interests of the fair, expeditious and economic administration of justice.

[5.135] The Working Group published its report on the criminal jurisdiction of the courts in 2003.[253] In terms of the jurisdiction of the District Court, it concluded that the maximum sentencing powers of the District Court as to imprisonment (12 months)

---

[252] See Ch 9.
[253] Working Group on the Jurisdiction of the Courts, *The Criminal Jurisdiction of the Courts* (Stationery Office, 2003).

should not be reduced. The Working Group recommended an increase to €10,000 in the level of fines that could be imposed in the District Court.

[5.136] The Working Group also examined 'either way' offences (indictable offences which can either be tried in the District Court or be sent for trial by jury in the Circuit Court, and where the accused has some role in determining venue) and 'hybrid offences' (offences where the Director of Public Prosecutions has the sole discretion as to whether the offence is tried summarily or sent forward for trial in the Circuit Court). The Working Group highlighted the inconsistent manner in which 'either way' and 'hybrid offences' are created. For example, the Working Group noted that the offence of assaulting a police officer[254] is an either way offence and accordingly attracts a right of election to the accused, whereas the similar offence of harming, threatening or menacing persons assisting the gardaí[255] is hybrid in nature and therefore no right of election is available to the accused. The Working Group recommended that this inconsistency be rectified by providing for a right of election to the accused in all cases where a summary trial or trial by jury are optional.[256]

The Working Group also considered the issue of appeals in criminal matters, both summary and on indictment. The Group recommended against any extension of the existing limited right of the prosecution to appeal sentences given in the District Court. The Working Group discussed the criminal trial process in general and made recommendations relating to a number of procedural matters. The Working Group did not publish any report on the civil jurisdiction of the courts.

Law Reform Commission's 2010 Report on Consolidation and Reform of the Courts Acts

[5.137] Subsequently, the Law Reform Commission completed a project on the consolidation and reform of the Courts Acts. This was a joint project involving the Commission, the Courts Service and the Department of Justice and Equality. In 2010 the Commission published a *Report on the Consolidation and Reform of the Courts Acts*,[257] including a draft Courts (Consolidation and Reform) Bill, which brings together the pre-1922 and post-1922 provisions concerning the jurisdiction of the courts, currently contained in over 240 Acts. At the time of writing (September 2014), it appears the government is committed to implementing this Report through a consolidating Courts Bill.[258] The Commission's project complemented the previous work of the Working Group on the Jurisdiction of the Courts and reiterated many of that

---

254 Criminal Justice (Public Order) Act 1994, s 19.
255 Criminal Justice Act 1999, s 41.
256 Working Group on the Jurisdiction of the Courts, *The Criminal Jurisdiction of the Courts* (Stationery Office, 2003), p 76.
257 LRC 97-2010, available at www.lawreform.ie.
258 The *Government Legislation Programme, Autumn Session 2014*, available at www.taoiseach.ie, proposes the publication of a Courts (Consolidation and Reform) Bill to implement the Commission's 2010 Report.

Group's recommendations and incorporated them into the draft Bill appended to the Report.

[5.138] In addition to the consolidation of pre-1922 and post-1922 legislation on the jurisdiction of the courts, the draft Courts (Consolidation and Reform) Bill appended to the 2010 Report incorporates a diverse number of reforms, including reforms related to: the case stated procedure; the '*in camera*' rule; fixed charge penalties; appeals in civil and criminal matters; the rules of courts committees; and the summons procedure in summary criminal cases.

[5.139] As already noted a number of these reflect the views expressed in the 2003 *Report of the Working Group on the Jurisdiction of the Courts*. They also echo the fundamental principles set out by Keane CJ in his 2001 lecture, in particular the need for reform to improve access to justice. It is notable, however, that neither the Working Group nor the Commission proposed a change from the existing three-tier court system to the two-tier system suggested by Keane CJ.

Chapter 6

Civil and Criminal Court Procedure

[1]   Introduction 277
[2]   Civil and Criminal Procedure Compared and Contrasted 277
[3]   Civil Procedure 284
[4]   Reform of the Civil Justice System: the UK Woolf Reforms and
       Judicial Case Management 305
[5]   Criminal Procedure 311
[6]   Court Procedure and Rules of Evidence 327
[7]   Judge and Jury 333

[1]   INTRODUCTION

[6.01] In this chapter we outline some of the basic rules of civil and criminal court procedure which are set out in statutory rules of court[1] and some conventions of practice. We will see that there are many differences between these rules and conventions concerning civil procedure on the one hand and criminal procedure on the other. It is thus important to distinguish between the two. Nonetheless, there are a number of common principles which it is also important to bear in mind.

[2]   CIVIL AND CRIMINAL PROCEDURE COMPARED AND
         CONTRASTED

Private law and public law

[6.02] A critical distinction between civil and criminal procedure is the nature of disputes with which they are concerned and the mechanism by which they are initiated. Civil procedure tends to involve what are described as private law disputes. Typical

---

[1]   The relevant rules for the different courts are the District Court Rules 1997 (SI 93/1997), the Circuit Court Rules 2001 (SI 510/2001) and the Rules of the Superior Courts 1986 (SI 15/1986), the latter covering the High Court, the Supreme Court and the Court of Criminal Appeal. Each set of Rules has been amended substantially from time to time, largely to take account of changes to substantive law effected by Acts of the Oireachtas. On the legislative authority to make rules of court, see para **4.05**. For more detail on the rules for the different courts see Delany and McGrath, *Civil Procedure in the Superior Courts* (3rd edn, 2012), Dowling and McDonnell, *Civil Procedure in the Circuit Court* (2nd edn, 2013) and Dowling and Savage, *Civil Procedure in the District Court* (2009).

examples of such 'private' disputes would be personal injuries claims arising from traffic accidents or accidents in the workplace, claims for breach of contract, including commercial contracts, and family proceedings, where the proceedings are initiated by one or other of the parties themselves, generally by consulting lawyers who will act as the agents of the parties in processing the claim through the court system. By contrast, criminal procedure deals with the processing of some activity regarded as a wrong against society or the public in general, hence its description as a public law matter. Criminal prosecutions are typically initiated by a state authority, such as the Director of Public Prosecutions or the Garda Síochána. It is possible for criminal prosecutions to be initiated by a private individual,[2] but this is a rare occurrence. There are some exceptions to this neat categorisation, for example, judicial review proceedings[3] fall into the civil law arena but are part of public law.

Compensation and punishment

[6.03] The purpose of a civil claim is, in general,[4] to seek compensation or some other form of remedy such as an injunction or declaration.[5] In contrast, a key purpose of criminal proceedings is to punish a person, for example by means of a monetary fine to be paid to the state or a sentence of imprisonment.

[6.04] The general rule is that a fine is paid by the offender to the state rather than the victim, and this has traditionally been one way to emphasise the distinction between criminal and civil proceedings; in a civil claim, any award of damages is to be paid to the 'victim/plaintiff'. This traditional distinction may be contrasted with the arrangements in place for many years in civil law legal systems in which compensation to the victim may be dealt with in tandem with criminal proceedings. This concept has now been incorporated into Irish law.[6]

---

2   See paras **6.85** and **6.91**.
3   For discussion of judicial review, see para **10.53**.
4   However, for discussion of aggravated or punitive damages in civil cases, see para **10.08**.
5   For the different remedies in civil proceedings, see paras **10.02** and **10.17**.
6   Criminal Justice Act 1993, s 6 provides that a court may order a convicted person to pay compensation to 'any person ... who has suffered [any personal] injury or loss' arising from the commission of an offence. Section 6 is, however, limited in the sense that it allows for compensation awards to the victims of offenders who are of some means, but provides no redress to victims of impecunious offenders. A non-statutory criminal injuries compensation scheme was established in 1972 and administered by the Criminal Injuries Compensation Tribunal, but its parameters were severely restricted in 1986, since when only special damages, such as medical expenses or loss of earnings, may be claimed; general damages for the pain and suffering involved cannot be claimed. In *AD v Ireland* [1994] 1 IR 369, it was held that this 1986 alteration to the 1972 Scheme was not in conflict with the right of bodily integrity of victims of crime contained in Article 40.3 of the Constitution. Thus, the victim of an impecunious offender currently remains without an effective remedy after the 1993 Act. In recent years there have been a number of high profile cases where a remedy of compensation was applied in lieu of a custodial sentence and this has attracted criticism. See Cahillane, "Need for Sentencing Guidelines in Ireland" [2013] ICLJ 11.

[6.05] As to the sentence of imprisonment, while its primary intention is to punish the offender, other purposes of the sentence have also been referred to through the years. A simple purpose served by the sentence was to exact retribution on behalf of society: a kind of judicially authorised or sanitised revenge. In addition, at one time a cardinal principle of imprisonment was the concept that the offender would be reformed or rehabilitated into society by means of hard labour, some elements of craft training and an element of education (including religious instruction). Similarly, the element of deterrence, both of the offender and more generally of others who might be tempted to commit criminal acts, has been an avowed basis for imprisonment. More recently, after widespread disenchantment with what were seen as the failures of the earlier models of reform and rehabilitation, minimalist and negative concepts such as 'secure custody' came into vogue, with imprisonment being seen as an end in itself, and any attempt at rehabilitation was seen as a futile exercise. In Ireland, it may be said that a mixture of all of these elements permeates current thinking on 'crime and punishment'.[7]

Titles of the parties

[6.06] The titles allocated to parties in civil and criminal matters also appear to reflect the distinction between compensation and punishment. In a civil claim, the person initiating the claim is, in general, called a 'plaintiff' (whether a company or an individual) while the party against whom the claim is brought is called the 'defendant'. In some instances, such as family cases, the parties may be described as 'petitioner' and 'respondent' or, in a case of judicial review, 'applicant' and 'respondent'. In a criminal matter the parties are referred to as the 'prosecution' (or 'prosecutor' in the case of an individual) and 'defendant' or 'accused'.

Standing: *locus standi*

[6.07] It is a general rule that those involved in civil or criminal litigation must have a direct interest in the outcome of the proceedings. The law requires that the parties to litigation have the standing, or *locus standi*, to initiate a case. In many instances, the parties clearly meet the requirement of standing and it is not in issue. For example, in a very common type of civil proceeding, the personal injuries action, the plaintiff will typically be a person claiming damages (monetary compensation) for injuries which the plaintiff alleges were caused by the defendant. Both parties are clearly directly involved in the dispute. Similarly, in a contract claim, the plaintiff and defendant will typically be in dispute about the terms of an agreement they have made. In a criminal case, the parties are the prosecution, representing the general public (the People), and the accused or defendant, the alleged perpetrator. Again, in such cases, the question of standing is not in issue here. In other cases, the question of standing may become significant. Thus, in judicial review and constitutional actions, the person initiating the case must establish

---

[7]   See further, O'Mahony, *Crime and Punishment in Ireland* (1993) and O'Malley, *Sentencing Law and Practice* (2nd edn, 2006).

that his or her rights and entitlements have been directly affected by the actions being challenged. In a constitutional case, for example, the plaintiff must establish that his or her rights have been directly affected by any law being challenged as unconstitutional. The courts will thus not allow a person to bring a claim of unconstitutionality merely because they allege that the law might infringe some other person's rights. The person who initiates this kind of 'test case' will be prevented from proceeding because they lack *locus standi*.[8]

Notification of both sides

[6.08] An essential requirement of fair procedures in all legal systems is that before a case may proceed to court certain documents must be drafted, then filed in court and a copy given to the other party to the court proceedings. This basic requirement of advance notice from one side to the other applies in both civil and criminal cases, although the precise mechanisms by which this is achieved are substantially different in civil and criminal matters. As we will see below, in civil matters the documents are usually called pleadings (of which there are many types), while in criminal matters the documents include a summons and an indictment.

Time limits

[6.09] For civil proceedings, various time limits for the initiation of proceedings are laid down in legislation, notably in the Statute of Limitations 1957, as amended.[9] In some cases the relevant time limit for the initiation of proceedings is set out in the relevant piece of legislation relating to the particular cause of action without any reference to the Statute of Limitations.[10] In the case of the most common claims the limitation periods vary from two years to six years. It is important to note that these time limits refer to the period between the occurrence of the event in question, the actionable wrong, and the lodging of the initial document notifying the other party of the claim; that is 'the clock starts' at the time of the event and a person has two years or six years, as the case may be, from that time to initiate the claim. It may very well be that a further year or more years elapse before the case comes, if ever, to hearing.[11]

[6.10] As to criminal proceedings, a distinction should be drawn between summary prosecutions and prosecutions on indictment. Since 1851, the general rule for summary prosecutions is that proceedings must be initiated within six months of the date of the

---

8   See the discussion of *Cahill v Sutton* [1980] IR 269 in para **15.93**. See also *Maloney v Ireland* [2009] IEHC 291.

9   The Law Reform Commission has recommended the introduction of a more streamlined 'core limitations' law: see *Report on the Limitation of Actions* (LRC 104-2011). On limitation of actions generally see also Canny, *Limitation of Actions* (2010).

10 See for example s 38 of the Defamation Act 2009.

11 As to the settlement of proceedings prior to a court hearing and the role of the Injuries Board in personal injuries claims, see para **6.64**.

alleged offence,[12] though in recent years a period of one year has been more common,[13] with some legislation allowing up to two years.[14] As for prosecutions on indictment, by tradition the common law provided for no limitation period and this convention has been maintained.

[6.11] In connection with civil proceedings as well as summary criminal matters and prosecutions on indictment, it is possible, however, that delay in proceeding with a case will cause the courts to prohibit the case from proceeding to hearing for being an abuse of process. In recent years, the courts have ordered civil and criminal cases to be discontinued where there has been unreasonable delay in proceeding and, equally if not even more importantly, where that delay causes prejudice to the other parties in the case.[15] Thus, even where the requirements of a limitation period have been met (as in civil proceedings or summary prosecutions) or where no limitation apparently exists (as with prosecutions on indictment), the courts may order that the case not proceed because of the prejudicial effects of delay. This view is based on the general principle that a fair hearing is not possible if one party has been unduly prejudiced by delay. It is important to bear in mind that it is not the mere fact of delay, but whether prejudice has resulted from any delay that would cause a case to be stopped in this way.

Civil and criminal proceedings from a single event

[6.12] While the purposes of civil and criminal proceedings are different, it is important to note that both a civil compensation claim and a criminal prosecution can arise from

---

12   Petty Sessions (Ireland) Act 1851, s 10; Courts (No 3) Act 1986, s 3.

13   For example, s 71 of the Child Care Act 1991, s 44 of the Equal Status Act 2000, s 74 of the Mental Health Act 2001 and s 82 of the Safety, Health and Welfare at Work Act 2005. Section 10(4) of the 1851 Act was further restricted by s 177 of the Criminal Justice Act 2006 which provides that it does not apply to many indictable offences that are tried summarily in the District Court.

14   For example, Animal Remedies Act 1993, s 22(2) and s 14 of the Consumer Credit Act 1995. For justification of such longer periods, see *Meagher v Minister for Agriculture* [1994] 1 IR 329: see para **16.121**.

15   See *Ó Domhnaill v Merrick* [1984] IR 151; *The State (O'Connell) v Fawsitt* [1986] IR 362; *Director of Public Prosecutions v Byrne* [1994] 2 IR 236; *Gilroy v Flynn* [2005] 1 ILRM 290; *Stephens v Flynn* [2008] IESC 4; *PD v Director of Public Prosecutions* [2008] IESC 22; *Cormack v DPP* [2009] 2 IR 208; *Murphy v DPP* [2009] 3 IR 821; *Jones v Grove Turkeys Ltd* [2011] IEHC 152 and *Wall v DPP* [2013] IESC 56. See also *Doran v Ireland* Application No 50389/99, 31 July 2003, *McMullen v Ireland* Application No 42297/98 and *O'Reilly v Ireland* Application No 54725/00 29 July 2004 in which the state in effect conceded that, under the European Convention on Human Rights, it was obliged to compensate litigants for failing to ensure that cases are dealt with within a reasonable length of time. See also Delany, 'The Obligation on the Courts to Deal with Cases within a "Reasonable Time"' (2004) 22 ILT 249 Burke-Murphy, 'Delay in the Irish Courts as viewed from Strasbourg – *McFarlane v Ireland*' (2011) 29 ILT 30; Cox, 'Dismissal of an Action on the Grounds of Delay or Want of Prosecutions: Recent Developments' [2012] DULJ 121 and Law Reform Commission, *Report on Limitation of Actions* (LRC 104-2011), ch 4.

just one event. Take a traffic accident between two cars as an example. The Garda Síochána may be involved in bringing a criminal prosecution against the driver of one of the cars: this is the criminal side of the accident. Quite separately, a person injured in that accident might bring a civil claim for damages against the driver of one of the cars. The criminal prosecution and the civil compensation claim will be dealt with in separate proceedings, but they originate in the one event.

[6.13] There are, of course, instances where a dispute will clearly involve only a civil claim, for example, where one company claims that another company is in breach of the terms of a building contract. Nonetheless, it is important to bear in mind that, in many cases, one event may give rise to separate civil and criminal proceedings.

Individuals and corporate bodies

[6.14] In civil disputes, claims can be initiated by individuals against individuals, as would be the case in a traffic accident, though any insurance companies would also be closely involved in the case. Claims may also be initiated by individuals against corporate bodies, such as limited liability companies or other corporate bodies such as local authorities, or vice versa. Claims may also be initiated by one corporate body against another. As for criminal prosecutions, the most common instances are where an individual is prosecuted, but prosecutions of corporate bodies are also common, particularly for 'regulatory' crimes such as breaches of environmental or health and safety legislation.

Describing the case and its processing

[6.15] The description of the processing of civil and criminal litigation is, in general, distinct, though some similarities of expression are also used. Civil proceedings are initiated by a plaintiff, while criminal proceedings are initiated by the prosecution (or prosecutor). The continuation of the cases may, however, be described in similar tones. The criminal case will almost always be 'prosecuted' by the prosecution; on occasion, however, lawyers may refer to 'prosecuting' a civil claim with all due speed or 'to the full extent of the law'.[16] The court hearing for both civil and criminal cases is usually referred to as a 'trial', though 'trial of the action' is used in connection with civil claims only.

---

16 It is regularly asserted that, since trespassing is a civil matter, the sign 'Trespassers will be prosecuted' is an inappropriate notice to post on one's property. However, the sign is quite acceptable if it is understood as a truncated version of 'Take notice. That any person or persons audaciously presuming to trespass on this property, will be punished with the utmost severity of private chastisement, and prosecuted with the utmost rigour of the law', as in the case of Mr Boythorn's rather elaborate sign in Charles Dickens' *Bleak House*. See also now the various offences in the Criminal Justice (Public Order) Act 1994 as amended by s 24 of the Housing (Miscellaneous Provisions) Act 2002.

Different courts

[6.16] We have already seen that the arrangements by which civil cases and criminal cases are allocated to the different courts is quite different.[17] Similarly, in virtually all civil claims, the case will be decided by a judge, whereas in serious criminal trials a trial by judge and jury is very common.

Outcomes described

[6.17] The different outcomes in civil and criminal matters are also described using different terminology. For example, where the plaintiff loses a personal injuries claim, it is said that the defendant is not liable, whereas if the prosecution loses a criminal case the defendant is found not guilty or is acquitted. Where the plaintiff is successful in a personal injuries claim, the defendant is found liable, whereas if a criminal prosecution is successful, the defendant is found guilty of an offence.

Burdens of proof

[6.18] One further critical distinction between civil and criminal cases is the question of the burden of proof. In general, in a civil case any particular issue as well as the overall question of liability is determined by establishing the issue or the question of liability on the balance of probabilities, while in a criminal case all issues and the question of guilt must be proved beyond reasonable doubt. While in many instances it may be that this distinction will not lead to different results, the possibility of that occurring should not be discounted.

[6.19] Take the example of the traffic accident already referred to. Let us assume that both civil and criminal proceedings resulted from the accident. In general, the criminal proceedings will come to trial in the District Court long before any civil proceedings. Again, let us suppose that the driver of one car is charged with careless driving and that the driver of the other car (appearing as a witness for the prosecution) testifies that the defendant had been driving on the wrong side of the road, but that the defendant then testifies that she had been driving on the correct side of the road. This obviously presents a clear conflict of evidence for the trial judge. In order to find the defendant guilty of careless driving, the judge must be satisfied beyond reasonable doubt that the defendant was indeed driving on the wrong side of the road. The judge might be prepared to convict in the example given, and indeed that would happen in many instances; but if the judge has a reasonable doubt about the question, the benefit of that doubt must be given to the defendant. Thus, even if the judge considers that it is more likely than not that the defendant was driving on the wrong side of the road, the judge should find the defendant not guilty.

[6.20] Assuming then that the defendant in the criminal case is found not guilty and that, some time later, the same incident becomes the subject of a civil claim in the High Court.[18] On this occasion, we might suppose that the person who gave evidence for the

---

[17] See Ch 5.

prosecution in the criminal case is the plaintiff in the civil action. Again, the same evidence is given. On this occasion, the High Court judge, faced with precisely the same evidence, must decide whether the defendant had been negligent and thus liable to pay damages to the plaintiff. Here, the judge would be perfectly entitled to conclude that, although it is by no means certain that the defendant was on the wrong side of the road, this was, on the balance of probabilities, the more likely explanation for the accident. In this instance, the balance of probabilities test comes down to saying that one party's version of events is more likely (or more believable) than that of the other.

[6.21] Some people may object to what appear to be conflicting outcomes in the two cases. The explanation for this state of affairs is that the consequences of a guilty verdict in the criminal case (fine and possible imprisonment) demand a high standard of proof, and that a lesser standard of proof is acceptable in civil cases where the consequences are less drastic (payment of damages to the plaintiff in circumstances where the defendant is likely to be insured). Moreover, a criminal conviction involves a moral condemnation that is not usually entailed in a determination of civil liability.

[3]   CIVIL PROCEDURE[19]

[6.22] As we have already noted, it is important for both sides to be fully informed of the basic outline of the legal case being made by the other side so that there can be no complete surprises when and if the case comes to court. This is achieved by requiring both sides to furnish written documents outlining their cases to each other. In civil matters, these documents are called pleadings.

Pleadings

[6.23] It important to note that there is a major difference between pleadings and what is sometimes called pleading on behalf of a client in court. Pleadings are formal written documents, their intention being to state the claim being made by the plaintiff or defendant. Pleading in court forms part of the great oral tradition of advocacy, although it must be said that full-blooded rhetorical pleading is not as common as film and television might lead us to believe. In fact, a barrister is much more likely to be found at a laptop (or a dictaphone) composing the words of pleadings than regaling a court in the manner of the lawyers of popular fiction.

[6.24] The language used in pleadings might be described as arcane and severe rather than informal. Barristers will, in general, use phrases that are well established in legal practice rather than adopt a more contemporary mode of expression. The reason for such caution lies in the fact that at one time it was the case that even the slightest deficiency in the pleadings could result in a case being dismissed by a court. This can still occur on occasion[20] and the fear of such a calamitous result for a client has meant

---

18   This assumes any personal injuries incurred would bring the case within the jurisdiction of the High Court. See also the discussion of the Injuries Board in Ch 5.

19   See generally, Delany and McGrath, *Civil Procedure in the Superior Courts* (3rd edn, 2012).

that barristers take a particularly cautious approach to the wording of pleadings (and the potential fear that poorly drafted pleadings could lead to a negligence claim against the drafting barrister). Consequently, pleadings are written in language which might appear more at home in the 19th century, but this is based on the notion that erring on the side of caution is a better course than attempting to draft pleadings which are a delight to read.

[6.25] The consequences of a failure to 'plead accurately' can be illustrated with a simple example. Take a personal injuries action in which the initial pleadings were filed in court 18 months after the accident to which they relate. If the barrister has failed to state a basic legal ground on which the case either stands or falls, the matter may be dismissed by the court. But the defect might not be discovered until, perhaps, a year later, that is two and a half years after the accident. It may then be impossible to recommence proceedings because the relevant time limit under the Statute of Limitations 1957, as amended, may have expired.[21] This explains why pleadings tend to be over-inclusive documents which attempt to cover every possible ground on which the plaintiff or defendant might have a cause of action.

Level of formality in the different courts

[6.26] It may also be noted here that the requirements of the rules of court differ from one court to another. The most complex rules of court so far as all aspects of procedure and pleadings are concerned are those which apply in the High Court and Supreme Court, namely the Rules of the Superior Courts 1986. The requirements for the Circuit Court, set out in the Circuit Court Rules 2001, and for the District Court, contained in the District Court Rules 1997, are significantly less complex. Substantial changes are made from time to time in the rules of court in the light of new insights into problems

---

20 In *Garvey v Ireland* [1981] IR 75, the plaintiff had been dismissed as Commissioner of the Garda Síochána by the government. He brought proceedings claiming that the dismissal was invalid on the ground that the government had acted in breach of the principles of fair procedure in failing to inform him at the time of the basis on which the dismissal was being made. The government defended the case on the basis that it was entitled to dismiss a Commissioner without disclosing the basis for a dismissal, but the Supreme Court decided in favour of the plaintiff on this point. The government then stated that it had intended that this point be decided without prejudice to its intention to introduce evidence that indicated the plaintiff had in fact been given the basis for his dismissal and that, in the circumstances, it should be allowed to alter its pleadings to reflect that intention. However, the Supreme Court declined to allow the government to amend its pleadings at that late stage in the case: see (1979) *The Irish Times*, 26 April, p 13. This case must be seen in the context of the general wide discretion for courts to amend proceedings at any stage in the proceedings (even at the trial of the action in certain circumstances) where it is in the interests of justice that the real issues in controversy between the parties are before the court and no irreparable prejudice is caused to the opposing party. See generally Delany and McGrath, *Civil Procedure in the Superior Courts* (3rd edn, 2012), pp 289–311.

21 See para **6.09**.

which have come to light in litigation or where new legislation has been enacted to deal with a particular problem.

[6.27] We will provide in what follows a brief description of the course of civil proceedings in the High Court. This should not be taken in any way as a definitive account of a typical High Court case, but it typifies the language that appears in pleadings which, as indicated above, is a staple of the practice of law.

High Court pleadings

[6.28] Under the Rules of the Superior Courts 1986 (which in essence updated but continued in force the system of practice which had developed in the court system by the end of the 19th century), there are three basic forms of initiating documents for the broad range of civil cases which are dealt with by the High Court. These documents are all given the title summonses. In addition the 1986 Rules provide for initiating documents called petitions, which are used in relation to family law and company law matters. Yet another form of procedure is provided for in relation to seeking orders for judicial review.[22] For present purposes, we will concentrate on the summonses only.

[6.29] The first of the initiating documents is called the *summary summons*, which is the appropriate document used in relation to claims for what is called a liquidated sum of money, that is a sum of money which can be readily calculated. A typical case in which a summary summons may be issued is where a bank claims that, on default of a loan given by the bank, a customer owes a certain sum of money. Obviously, there may be complex calculations as to the rate of interest payable in order to calculate the precise sum owing on the date when the case comes to court, but once the sum can be calculated by reference to rates of interest which were agreed when the loan was taken out, then the summary summons procedure is the appropriate initiating document in the High Court. The procedure is designed to enable a plaintiff to obtain judgment against a defendant expeditiously where the plaintiff's claim is easily quantifiable and the defendant does not have a valid defence.

[6.30] The second form of initiating document is the *special summons*, which is used primarily for legal disputes relating to land. An example is a claim by a building society for possession of property on foot of a mortgage on which a person has defaulted. These special summonses will be dealt with by what are, in effect, the chancery judges of the High Court. Although as we have seen the divisions of the High Court were abolished on the passing of the Courts of Justice Act 1924, the administrative arrangements within the court system still exist by which such cases are directed towards particular judges who deal on a regular basis with these areas of law.[23]

[6.31] The third initiating document in the High Court is the *plenary summons*. This is used in connection with all other civil cases which are not appropriate for either a summary or special summons; in effect, it is the residual 'catch all' High Court

---

22 See para **10.53**.
23 See para **4.62**.

summons. The plenary summons is used, for example, in relation to any claim in which a full hearing requiring oral evidence under oath is anticipated. It is also used where the amount of damages claimed cannot be reduced to a liquidated sum of money. Although an experienced barrister, whether junior or senior, may have an accurate estimation of the amount of damages (compensation) that might be recoverable, there is no definitive system for calculating in advance the precise sum of money which should be awarded in damages, so that a summary summons would not be appropriate in such a case. Other cases in which a plenary summons is appropriate include defamation actions.

Prior to 2004, personal injuries matters were initiated using a plenary summons. The Civil Liability and Courts Act 2004 introduced a statutory variation of this, the personal injuries summons.[24] The main change made by the 2004 Act was to require that both the plaintiff and the defendant provide more detailed information to each other in the documents filed in a personal injuries action.

The personal injuries summons in action

[6.32] When a barrister receives instructions in relation to a personal injuries action, it is clear that the personal injuries summons procedure is the appropriate path to take.[25] The first document must be filed by the plaintiff in the action, who invariably is the person who has been injured. The example we will use is of a person who has been injured in the eye by fragments of glass flying from an abrasive wheel (which is a rotating wheel used to grind metals and other materials such as glass) while working for a company which manufactures glass. The barrister will, as indicated, know that this injury is quite serious and, although the medical prognosis for the employee may not be fully known at the time the barrister is first instructed, it will be regarded as in most cases as being sufficiently serious to warrant being brought in the High Court. In other words, the barrister will make an estimate that the level of damages which might be received by the employee would be over €60,000, the level set by the Courts and Civil Law (Miscellaneous Provisions) Act 2013 as the 'floor' for the High Court.[26] This estimate will be made on the basis of an assumption that the employee was not in any way to blame for the accident in question or if the employee was to blame, the apportionment of blame does not bring the value of the claim below that of the High Court jurisdiction. If

---

24 Civil Liability and Courts Act 2004, s 10. The relevant changes to the Rules of Court are contained in Ord 1A of the Rules of the Superior Courts 1986, inserted by the Rules of the Superior Courts (Personal Injuries) 2005 (SI 248/2005). In 2014, the Department of Jobs, Enterprise and Innovation commenced a public consultation on the operation and implementation of the Personal Injuries Acts 2003–2007. Some reform may therefore be expected in this area.

25 We assume for this discussion that an assessment of damages by the Injuries Board has been refused by the parties or that the claims is one to which the Personal Injuries Assessment Board Act 2003 does not apply. See generally Ch 5, above, and Delany and McGrath, *Civil Procedure in the Superior Courts* (3rd edn, 2012), pp 953–954.

26 See para **5.72**.

an assessment was made by the Injuries Board, the barrister will take note of this in determining the court in which to institute proceedings.

Personal injuries summons, plenary summons and indorsement of claim

[6.33] The first part of a personal injuries summons contains the defendant's name, the address at which he or she ordinarily resides (if this is known to the plaintiff), the defendant's occupation (if this is known to the plaintiff), the plaintiff's name, the address at which he or she ordinarily resides, his or her occupation, date of birth and PPS number. In non-personal injuries matters, such as a defamation or breach of contract claim, the first document is the plenary summons itself which contains little more than the names of the parties and a brief outline of the claim being made by the plaintiff.

[6.34] The indorsement in the personal injuries summons is not a separate document (it is where a plenary summons is used). It is part of the personal injuries summons itself, is entitled 'indorsement of claim' and must set out in numbered paragraphs full and detailed particulars of the nature of the claim and each allegation making up the claim, the injuries allegedly suffered by the plaintiff caused by wrongs of the defendant, the acts of the defendant which allegedly caused the wrong, each instance of negligence of the defendant and a schedule of full particulars of all items of special damage (out-of-pocket expenses, for example medical expenses) incurred by the plaintiff. Where the proceedings have been authorised by the Injuries Board to proceed to court, the indorsement of claim must contain a statement confirming this and outlining the reference number of the authorisation and date on which it was granted.[27] Both parties in a personal injuries action are also required to swear a verifying affidavit as to the truthfulness of the assertions or allegations in the pleadings.[28] If it subsequently transpires that the contents of the pleadings are untrue, the party concerned may be guilty of an offence.[29]

[6.35] The personal injuries summons consists of standard form pages, the basic contents of which are set out in Appendix CC to the Rules of the Superior Courts 1986 (inserted in 2005 in the wake of the Civil Liability and Courts Act 2004). The first page of the personal injuries summons is as follows:

---

[27] Order 4A, r 3A inserted by the Rules of the Superior Courts (Personal Injuries Assessment Board Act 2003) 2004 (SI 517/2004).

[28] Civil Liability and Courts Act 2004, s 14.

[29] Civil Liability and Courts Act 2004, s 25. Section 26 of the 2004 Act also provides that if a person has sworn an affidavit of verification that is knowingly false or misleading, the court is required to dismiss the proceedings unless this would result in an injustice.

THE HIGH COURT

2014 No. 10,000P

Between   **Raymond Byrne**   Plaintiff

and   **McCutcheon Glass Company Limited**   Defendant

To the defendant McCutcheon Glass Company Limited

of 23 Glass Lane, in the City of Dublin.

This personal injuries summons requires you to enter an Appearance in person or by solicitor in the Central Office, Four Courts, Dublin 7 in the above action within eight days after the Summons has been served on you (exclusive of the day of such service)

And TAKE NOTICE that if you do not enter an appearance the plaintiff may proceed in this action, and judgment may be given in your absence

BY ORDER,   The Honourable Susan Denham

Chief Justice of Ireland,

the 31st day of March two thousand and fourteen.

N.B.—This summons is to be served within twelve calendar months from the date hereof, unless the time for service has been extended by the Court.

The defendant may appear to this summons by entering an appearance either personally or by solicitor at the Central Office, Four Courts, Dublin.

Figure 6.1

[6.36] In a plenary summons, the indorsement of claim consists of three standard form pages, the basic contents of which are set out in Appendix A to the Rules of the Superior Courts 1986. It may be noted that the summons is, in effect, a call by order of the Chief Justice to the defendant to answer the claim by the plaintiff in the case. This form of initiating document has medieval roots, because it reflects the form of the old writs issued by the Lord Chancellor's Department on the authority of the monarch.[30]

[6.37] The number '2014 No. 10,000P' which appears at the top of the personal injuries summons (or a plenary summons) is the official file or record number for the case and is of great administrative importance. It identifies the case for the court officials who receive any further pleadings which are delivered in the case as well as identifying the case should it proceed to court hearing. The personal injuries summons is brought to the Central Office of the High Court in the Four Courts, usually by the solicitor for the plaintiff and, if it appears to be in the correct format set out in the Rules of the Superior

---

[30] See para **2.08**.

Courts 1986, it will be accepted by the officials of the High Court Central Office. The personal injuries summons will then be given its official court number and the fact that a personal injury summons has been issued will be entered in the Central Office records. These records include sufficient space to record any subsequent pleadings. Once the summons has been entered in the Central Office records, it is officially stamped, in accordance with the requirements of the 1986 Rules. It then becomes an official court document which may be served on the defendant. In fact the original summons is retained by the court officials, and the plaintiff's solicitor will serve on the defendant what is called a certified copy of the original summons.

[6.38] In a plenary summons, but not in a personal injuries summons, the second page contains a space for a brief outline of the plaintiff's claim, called the 'general indorsement of claim'. The relevant outline for our example might be as follows:

The Plaintiff's Claim is for Damages for Breach of Contract.

Figure 6.2

This may seem especially uninformative but it is merely the first stage in what becomes later an increasingly complex and, sometimes, long drawn-out process. With a personal injuries summons, the indorsement of claim incorporates the statement of claim from the plenary summons procedure. Therefore only one document is served in personal injuries matters; in other plenary matters, for example claiming breach of contract, the plenary summons is served first and then the statement of claim. In personal injuries matters, only the personal injuries summons is served.

[6.39] In addition to the general indorsement of claim, this part of the summons will also include a verification that the summons was served on the defendant. In the case of an individual, this is usually done at his or her residence, but in our example where a company is being sued as employer, service will take place at its registered place of business. Finally, the plenary summons also contains a space for the insertion of the place of residence of the plaintiff and where court documents in response to the summons may be served.

[6.40] The filing of the plenary summons or personal injuries summons has a great significance for the law on the limitation period for bringing claims to court. If a plenary summons is correctly issued within the two-year limitation period for personal injuries actions, that is sufficient under the Statute of Limitations 1957 (as amended), which does not require that the case comes to hearing before a court within two years. Once the plenary summons is issued within that time the Statute is complied with and it does not matter that the case is heard long after the two-year period has expired.[31]

[6.41] The indorsement in a personal injuries summons is to be entitled 'indorsement of claim' and must set out in numbered paragraphs full and detailed particulars of the nature of the claim and each allegation making up the claim, the injuries allegedly suffered by the plaintiff caused by wrongs of the defendant, the acts of the defendant

---

[31] See para **6.09**.

which allegedly caused the wrong, each instance of negligence of the defendant and a schedule of full particulars of all items of special damage (out-of-pocket expenses, for example medical expenses) incurred by the plaintiff. Where the proceedings have been authorised by the Injuries Board to proceed to court, the indorsement of claim must contain a statement confirming this and outlining the reference number of the authorisation and date on which it was granted.[32] An example of a personal injuries summons is provided at para **6.39** below.

[6.42] Once the plenary summons or personal injuries summons is duly issued and served on the defendant, it is up to the defendant to respond. As the first page of the summons indicates, there is an obligation to enter an appearance within eight days of being served with the documents. In fact this requirement is not an absolute obligation and in many instances an appearance might not be entered for a number of weeks. If the plaintiff attempted to obtain a decision from the High Court nine days after serving a plenary summons on the defendant, the court would be most unlikely to grant such judgment without giving the defendant an opportunity of defending the case. In fact many of the time limits specified in the Rules of the Superior Courts 1986 for various stages of the court procedure are not adhered to, and it is usually a year or even longer before all the relevant documents are served on both sides so that the stage is reached when the case is ready for hearing. However considerable delays in moving proceedings along could lead to the proceedings or pleadings being struck out for delay or want of prosecution.[33]

PERSONAL INJURIES SUMMONS

THE HIGH COURT

2014 No. 10,000P

Between   **Raymond Byrne**   Plaintiff

And   **McCutcheon Glass Company Limited**   Defendant

INDORSEMENT OF CLAIM

The Plaintiff's claim is for the reliefs set out herein for personal injuries suffered by the plaintiff as follows:

1. The Plaintiff is a maintenance fitter and resides at 2 Sunnybank Terrace, in the City of Dublin. At the time of the said accident the plaintiff was the servant and or agent of the defendant acting in course of his employment and was employed under a contract of employment with the Defendant.

---

[32] Order 4A, r 3A inserted by the Rules of the Superior Courts (Personal Injuries Assessment Board Act 2003) 2004 (SI 517/2004).

[33] See also Delany and McGrath, *Civil Procedure in the Superior Courts* (3rd edn, 2012), pp 287–289. (contd.../)

2. The defendant are a limited liability company having their registered place of business at 23 Glass Lane, in the City of Dublin and was at all material times was the employer of the plaintiff.

WRONG ALLEGED AGAINST THE DEFENDANT AND THE CIRCUMSTANCES GIVING RISE TO THE SAID WRONG

3. On or about the 23rd day of May 2013, the plaintiff suffered severe personal injury, loss, distress and damage while working at an abrasive wheel in the premises of the said defendants when he was struck in the eye by a fragment of glass which projected from the said abrasive wheel.

PARTICULARS OF THE ACTS OF THE DEFENDANT CONSTITUTING THE WRONG

4. The said personal injury, loss, distress and damage were caused solely by virtue of the negligence, breach of duty, including statutory duty, of the defendants, their servants or agents in or about the care, management and control of the said premises and more particularly the said abrasive wheel.
5. In addition, the plaintiff will rely on the matters pleaded in paragraph 3 of the Personal Injuries Summons.

PARTICULARS OF NEGLIGENCE AND BREACH OF DUTY INCLUDING STATUTORY DUTY

[*In this section the barrister will include the details of the manner in which it is alleged that the employer was in breach of some obligations which are owed by an employer to an employee in respect of safety in the workplace. The particulars might be as follows:*]

The defendant, its servants or agents, were guilty of negligence and or in breach of duty including statutory duty in that:

1. They failed to provide the plaintiff with a place of work which was reasonably safe in all the circumstances.
2. They failed to provide the plaintiff with plant and machinery which was reasonably safe in all the circumstances.
3. They failed to provide the plaintiff with a system of work which was reasonably safe in all the circumstances.
4. They failed to provide the plaintiff with co-workers who were in all the circumstances reasonably competent.

---

[33] (\...contd) and the comments of Hardiman J concerning case management in *Gilroy v Flynn* [2005] 1 ILRM 290.

5. They exposed the plaintiff to a danger of which they knew, or ought reasonably to have known.

6. They exposed the plaintiff to danger from the said abrasive wheel of which they knew or ought reasonably to have known.

7. They failed to provide the plaintiff with any, or any adequate, training or supervision in relation to the use of the said abrasive wheel.

8. They were in breach of statutory duty and in particular of the provisions of the Safety in Industry Acts 1955 and 1980, the Safety in Industry (Abrasive Wheels) Regulations 1982, sections 8 and 20 of the Safety, Health and Welfare at Work Act 2005 and Chapter 2 of the Safety, Health and Welfare at Work (General Application) Regulations 2007.

As a result of the said accident, the Plaintiff suffered personal injury, loss, damage, inconvenience and expense.

PARTICULARS OF THE INJURIES TO THE PLAINTIFF OCCASIONED BY THE WRONG OF THE DEFENDANT

Particulars of Personal Injuries

[*In this portion of the Personal Injuries Summons the barrister would insert information as to the extent of the eye injury which would be gleaned from the medical reports obtained by the plaintiff's solicitor. This could be in the form of a number of points relating to the immediate impact of the glass fragments, the extent to which this affected the eye immediately as well as some indication as to the prognosis. In addition, the particulars might add: 'Further adverse sequelae cannot be ruled out', a phrase which allows for subsequent medical information to be taken into account in the claim.*]

RELIEFS CLAIMED:

AND THE PLAINTIF CLAIMS:

1. Damages for severe personal injury, loss, damage, inconvenience, distress, and damage arising as a result of the negligence and breach of duty, including statutory duty, on the part of the Defendant;

2. Interest pursuant to the Courts Act 1981;

3. The costs of the proceedings

4. Such further or other order as this Honourable Court shall deem fit.

SCHEDULE

PARTICULARS OF SPECIAL DAMAGE

[*In this section the plaintiff will insert those items such as medical expenses and loss of earnings to date which are available. Some aspects of these claims may, however, be left over for further detailing later in the proceedings.*]

AUTHORISATION

By way of certificate bearing authorisation number PL0933985640328 and dated the 15 March 2014, the Personal Injuries Assessment Board authorised the Plaintiff to bring proceedings in respect of the above entitled claim, pursuant to section 14 of the Personal Injuries Assessment Board Act 2003.

This summons was issued by the Plaintiff whose personal details are as follows:

1. The address at the Plaintiff ordinarily resides is 2 Sunnybank Terrace in the City of Dublin.
2. The Plaintiff's occupation is a maintenance fitter;
3. The Plaintiff's date of birth is 10 May 1987
4. The Plaintiff's personal public service number is 48474642B

[*The names of counsel for the plaintiff will appear here.*]

Figure 6.3

Verifying affidavit in personal injuries matters

[6.43] Parties to personal injuries matters are required to swear a verifying affidavit to verify the truthfulness of the assertions or allegations in the pleadings.[34] If it subsequently transpires that the contents of the pleadings are untrue, the party concerned may be guilty of an offence.[35] A plaintiff is thus required to swear an affidavit verifying any assertions or allegations made in any pleading or further information provided to the defendant. A verifying affidavit must be lodged not later than 21 days after service of the personal injuries summons, or later if the parties so agree or the court directs.[36] Similarly a defendant is required to swear a verifying affidavit and again this must be lodged not later than 21 days after the service of the defence or later if the parties so agree or the court directs. A verifying affidavit could be in the following form:

---

[34]   Civil Liability and Courts Act 2004, s 14.
[35]   Civil Liability and Courts Act 2004, s 25. Section 26 of the 2004 Act also provides that if a person has sworn an affidavit of verification that is knowingly false or misleading, the court is required to dismiss the proceedings unless this would result in an injustice. This applies to plaintiffs only and there is no equivalent sanction where false or misleading evidence is given or adduced by a defendant. See further McMahon and Binchy, *Law of Torts* (4th edn, 2013), ch 44; *Carmello v Casey* [2007] IEHC 362, [2008] 3 IR 524; *Behan v Allied Irish Banks plc* [2009] IEHC 554; *Danagher v Glentine Inns* [2010] IEHC 214; *Ahern v Bus Éireann* [2011] IESC 44 and *Goodwin v Bus Éireann* [2013] IESC 56.
[36]   Civil Liability and Courts Act 2004, s 14.

THE HIGH COURT

2014 No. 10,000P

Between   **Raymond Byrne**   Plaintiff

And   **McCutcheon Glass Company Limited**   Defendant

I, Raymond Byrne of 2 Sunnybank Terrace in the City of Dublin, the plaintiff in the above-entitled proceedings, aged eighteen years and upwards MAKE OATH and say as follows:

1. I beg to refer to the contents of the personal injuries summons delivered herein on behalf of the plaintiff on the .....4 day of April 2014 * [upon which this affidavit is endorsed] * [and upon a true copy of which marked "A" I have signed my name prior to the swearing hereof].

2. The assertions, allegations and information contained in the said personal injuries summons which are within my own knowledge are true. I honestly believe that the assertions, allegations and information contained in the said personal injuries summons which are not within my own knowledge are true.

3. I am aware that it is an offence to make a statement in this affidavit that is false or misleading in any material respect and that I know to be false or misleading.

SWORN by RAYMOND BYRNE

This ..... day of 2014

At .... in the City of Dublin

Before me a Practising Solicitor/

Commissioner for Oaths and I know

The Deponent

Figure 6.4

Appearance

[6.44] As indicated, in response to the plenary summons or personal injuries summons, the defendant must enter an 'appearance'. The appearance is a very brief document which is, quite simply, an instruction to the court that an appearance should be entered for the defendant and that the defendant intends to defend the claim. The appearance typically indicates the solicitor representing the defendant and the address at which further pleadings may be served, usually the solicitor's office. The claim is then back in the plaintiff's hands.

Statement of claim

[6.45] In a plenary summons claim, the next document to be filed by the plaintiff is, usually, the 'statement of claim', which provides in much more detail the circumstances surrounding the accident which is the subject matter of the case. The statement of claim is in a standard format as with the plenary summons, but in this instance the amount which must be filled in by the plaintiff is considerably greater.

[6.46] It is clear that the language of the statement of claim is cautious, to what might appear to be an excessive degree. In particular, a degree of overlap in the statement of particulars is evident and, indeed, some might consider the eight paragraphs to be unduly repetitive. The point of this seemingly arcane mode of drafting is to ensure that this aspect of the statement of claim is comprehensive, even at the expense of being over-inclusive. In this context, especially having regard to the Statute of Limitations 1957 (as amended), it is better to be safe than sorry.

[6.47] It may be noted also there are also references to legislation, both primary and secondary, in claiming a breach of duty. In this respect, we should note that the primary purpose of the legislation in question is to prevent accidents and ill-health in the factory context by setting down standards which, if broken, may result in a criminal prosecution. However, a barrister will be aware that these statutory provisions are also actionable, that is they may be used in support of a civil claim for personal injuries if it can be shown that the injury in question is attributable, at least in part, to a failure to observe a statutory requirement. This is known as breach of statutory duty.[37]

[6.48] In response to the statement of claim, the defendants' approach may become more complex. One possible step is for the defendants to file a pleading known, simply, as the *defence*. But they may not be happy with several aspects of the plaintiff's statement of claim. A defendant is entitled, under the Rules of the Superior Courts 1986, to seek further information from the plaintiff in respect of the claim being made. This is called 'seeking further and better particulars' of the claim by way of a notice for particulars and it is a commonly adopted procedure in personal injuries actions. The format of the claim for particulars is, usually, a letter to the solicitors for the plaintiff which lists the points in respect of which more detail is required from the plaintiff by way of reply to the particulars sought. For example, the precise circumstances of the incident in which the glass fragment struck the plaintiff may be sought; the details of medical expenses, if these are not specified; and the precise terms of the legislative provisions in respect of which the defendants are alleged to be in breach.

Defence

[6.49] Having received satisfactory replies to these queries or particulars (in the absence of which the matter may be brought by way of motion to the High Court for a judge to

---

37   See McMahon and Binchy, *Law of Torts* (4th edn, 2013), Ch 21.

determine whether the replies were in fact adequate) the defendants may then file a defence in response to the statement of claim in a non-personal-injuries matter.

[6.50] The defence in a non-personal-injuries matter indicates even further perhaps the somewhat stilted style of prose in which lawyers must engage, at least in written form. A cardinal rule of a defence in civil proceedings excluding personal injuries matters is that each and every claim by the plaintiff must be denied. If the case goes to court, the plaintiff will then be obliged to prove each of the allegations contained in the statement of claim. If the defendant does not deny a particular claim made by the plaintiff, this is regarded as having been admitted by the defendant. By denying each allegation the defendant is forcing the plaintiff to prove the elements of the claim, a matter of some tactical importance.

[6.51] In personal injuries claims, since the enactment of the Civil Liability and Courts Act 2004, it is no longer possible for a defendant to file a defence that involves a blanket denial of all of the claims made by the plaintiff in his or her personal injuries summons. Section 12(1) of the 2004 Act states that a defence to a personal injuries summons is required to specify: (a) the allegations specified or matters pleaded in a personal injuries summons of which the defendant does not require proof; (b) the allegations specified or matters pleaded in a personal injuries summons of which the defendant requires proof; (c) the grounds upon which the defendant claims that he is not liable for any injuries suffered by the plaintiff; and (d) where the defendant alleges that some or all of the personal injuries suffered by the plaintiff were caused in whole or in part by the plaintiff's own acts, the grounds upon which he or she so alleges. The 2004 Act also states that the defence must also include full details of each allegation or denial included. An example of a defence in a personal injuries claim is provided at figure 6.5.

[6.52] The defendant is entitled to make a request for further information from a plaintiff in a personal injuries action, and where such a request is made the plaintiff is required to provide the defendant with the following information: (a) particulars of any personal injuries action brought by the plaintiff in which a court made an award of damages; (b) particulars of any personal injuries action brought by the plaintiff which was withdrawn or settled; (c) particulars of any injuries sustained or treatment administered to the plaintiff which would have a bearing on the personal injuries to which the action relates; (d) the name of any person from whom the plaintiff received such treatment.[38]

---

[38] Civil Liability and Courts Act 2004, s 11.

PERSONAL INJURIES DEFENCE

THE HIGH COURT

2014 No. 10,000P

Between   **Raymond Byrne**   Plaintiff

And   **McCutcheon Glass Company Limited**   Defendant

TAKE NOTICE that the Defence of the Defendant to the claim of the Plaintiff made by Personal Injuries Summons dated 16 May 2014 is as follows:

1. The Defendant does not require proof of the following allegations specified or matters pleaded in the personal injuries summons:

   (a) paragraphs 1 and 2 the description of the parties is admitted;

   (b) The PIAB Authorisation;

   (c) That the Plaintiff was at all material times employed by the Defendant.

2. The Defendant requires proof of the following allegations specified or matters pleaded in the personal injuries summons:

   (a) The matter pleaded in paragraph 3 of the Personal Injuries Summons.

   (b) That the said accident occurred as a result of the negligence and breach of duty including breach of statutory duty of the Defendant herein, his servants or agents and the Plaintiff shall be put on full proof thereof.

   (c) That the premises are a factory within the meaning of the Safety in Industry Act 1955 and 1980, as alleged or at all, or that the provisions of the Safety, Health and Welfare at Work Act 2005 or of the Safety, Health and Welfare at Work (General Application) Regulations 2007 are applicable to the alleged accident the subject matter of these proceedings, as alleged or at all.

   (d) That the Defendant was in breach of the Safety in Industry Act 1955 and 1980, the Safety in Industry (Abrasive Wheels) Regulations 1982, sections 8 and 20 of the Safety, Health and Welfare at Work Act 2005 and Chapter 2 of the Safety, Health and Welfare at Work (General Application) Regulations 2007.

   (e) The particulars of personal injuries.

   (f) The nature, circumstances and sequence of events of the said accident alleged by the Plaintiff.

   (g) The particulars of breach of duty including statutory duty.

    (h)   The particulars of special damage pleaded in the Personal Injuries Summons.

    (i)   The relief claimed by the Plaintiff.

3.   The grounds upon which the Defendant claims that it is not liable for any injuries suffered by the Plaintiff are as follows:

    (a)   The defendant denies that it or its servants or agents acted negligently or in breach of duty, including statutory duty as alleged or at all.

    (b)   The Plaintiff did not suffer or sustain the alleged or any personal injuries, loss, damage and expense and the particulars thereof are denied as if same were set forth individually and denied seriatim.

    (c)   The incident the subject matter of these proceedings and any personal injury, loss or damage suffered by the Plaintiff were caused or contributed to by his own negligence.

4.   The grounds upon which the Defendant claims that some or all of the injuries suffered by the Plaintiff were occasioned in whole or part by the Plaintiff's own acts are as follows:

    (a)   The plaintiff failed to wear eye wear supplied and as required of all employees.

    (b)   The plaintiff operated the abrasive wheel in a negligent and improper manner.

    (c)   The plaintiff failed to have regard for his own safety.

    (d)   Failed to carry out the task required of him in accordance with instructions given to him.

    (e)   Failed to avoid the incident in question.

    (f)   Carried out his work in a careless manner.

    (g)   Having performed the routine task he was engaged in at the material time on numerous occasions previously, he failed to perform the same in a safe and careful manner on the occasion in question.

    (h)   Failed to use his work skill, care and experience which same could reasonably be expected of him.

    (i)   Without prejudice to all of the foregoing the Defendants hereby expressly reserve the right to furnish further grounds upon which it claims that it is not liable for any injuries suffered by the Plaintiff.

5.   The Plaintiff is not entitled to the reliefs sought or any relief.

[*The names of counsel for the defendant will appear here.*]

Figure 6.5

Defence and counterclaim

[6.53] In certain other cases the defendant may go on the offensive by claiming that the plaintiff was at fault. For example, in a dispute over the sale of a car the plaintiff might be the seller who brings a claim for breach of contract against the buyer for non-payment. The buyer might not only put in a defence to such a claim but also counterclaim against the seller on the basis that the car was defective causing the buyer to incur the expense of renting another car. If the defendant's case is believed the court may award the defendant damages to compensate him or her for the rental costs, in addition to dismissing the plaintiff's claim. This indicates that the defendant may, in a civil case, turn the tables completely. Section 12 of the Civil Liability and Courts Act 2004 states that counterclaims in personal injuries actions must state the defendant's PPS number and the injuries which the defendant attributes to the wrongs committed by the plaintiff. Full particulars must be given of all items of special damage (such as loss of business) in respect of which the defendant is making a claim, the acts of the plaintiff constituting the wrong and the circumstances relating to each allegation of negligence by the plaintiff.[39]

Pleadings closed

[6.54] When the parties have served all the pleadings which they consider necessary on each other it is said that the pleadings have closed and the case is now ready to be placed in the list of cases for which dates for hearing may be assigned generally in order of priority with specially fixed cases appearing first in the list of cases. There is a specific listing basis for personal injuries cases apart from those which are specially fixed. These cases are assigned for a hearing to a particular judge on a random basis by way of a draw and not in the sequence they appear in the *Legal Diary*. On a regular basis the list of cases which are due for hearing on a specified date or dates are published in a document called the *Legal Diary*, which is published on a daily basis on the Courts Service website (www.courts.ie) while the High Court is sitting.

[6.55] As to the delay between the closing of pleadings and receiving a date for hearing, considerable public disquiet has existed since the early 1980s due to the considerable time lag involved. We discuss this phenomenon elsewhere.[40]

Reply and further pleadings

[6.56] The above examples of pleadings have dealt only with the statement of claim and defence in a High Court plenary summons action and a personal injuries action. They do not provide a comprehensive view of what the pleading process may involve or the length of time spent prior to a case coming to hearing in relation to the presentation of evidence for either side. In addition to the statement of claim and defence, parties may wish to serve on each other further pleadings. Thus, where in a particular case a

---

[39]   Civil Liability and Courts Act 2004, s 12(3).
[40]   See para **4.214**.

completely new issue is raised in the defence, the plaintiff may serve on the defendant a *reply*. And in response to the reply, the defendant may issue a *rejoinder*. This could be followed by a *surrejoinder* from the plaintiff, and the process could, conceivably, continue on indefinitely. However, in most cases the reply will mark the close of pleadings.

Pre-trial remedies

[6.57] There are a number of pre-trial remedies available to either side in a High Court civil action. As mentioned previously, a party may apply to court where there has been failure to comply with some time limit specified by the Rules of the Superior Courts 1986, such as in failing to enter an appearance within eight days from service. But, as also indicated, the court is unlikely to enter judgment in favour of the plaintiff without giving the defendant an opportunity of putting the other side of the case and explaining the delay. In keeping, however, with a more general movement internationally towards active case management by the courts to prevent unnecessary delays in civil litigation, the Rules of the Superior Courts 1986 were amended in 2004 to encourage more timely filing of pleadings.[41] There are many occasions in the course of a case proceeding through the court system in which such applications will come before the court. These are always brought by way of motion to the court, and must be on notice to the other side in the case. In most cases, these motions involve one side being given a specific period of time within which to file the relevant documents in the Central Office.

[6.58] Subject to certain exceptions, either party is entitled under the Rules of the Superior Courts 1986 to obtain possession of documents within the control of the other party. This process is known as the *discovery of documents*.[42] In some instances this may simply amount to the exchange of originals which were in the possession of each party, and in such a case there will be no dispute as to the scope of discovery. Over the years, however, there have been many examples of cases in which documents obtained by discovery ('discovered' being used in a somewhat unusual manner in this context) have been the key to success in a case. As indicated, there are limits to what may be sought on discovery. For example, communications from a legal adviser which were obtained by a party at a time when court proceedings were either contemplated or were already started are privileged from discovery. In addition, a party cannot simply come to court on a 'fishing expedition', claiming that the other side has unnamed documents which would help the applicant's case; the discovery application must be in relation to a specified document or there must be some, albeit limited, basis on which something concrete can be identified. In order for discovery to be granted by the High Court (in a case of a dispute over which discovery will be provided by one of the parties to the proceedings),

---

[41]   Order 27 of the Rules of the Superior Courts 1986, as substituted by the Rules of the Superior Courts (Order 27) (Amendment) Rules) 2004 (SI 63/2004). See also Delany and McGrath, *Civil Procedure in the Superior Courts* (3rd edn, 2012), pp 287–289 and the comments of Hardiman J concerning case management in *Gilroy v Flynn* [2005] 1 ILRM 290.

[42]   See Abrahamson, Dwyer and Fitzpatrick, *Discovery and Disclosure* (2nd edn, 2013).

the Court has to be satisfied that the documents are relevant to the issues in the proceedings and discovery is necessary to dispose fairly of the matter or for saving costs.[43]

[6.59] Up to the time of the coming into force of the Rules of the Superior Courts 1986, discovery could only be obtained by one party from another party to the proceedings, but now discovery may be obtained from a person who is not involved in the court proceedings provided that that non-party has relevant information.[44] Since 1997, in personal injuries actions, such as the example given in this chapter, both parties are required to disclose to each other and exchange relevant medical and other expert reports that have a bearing on the case. [45] This process requires the parties to disclose to each other any report or statement from any expert intended to be called to give evidence of medical or para-medical opinion in relation to an issue in the case or from any other expert of the evidence intended to be given by that expert in relation to an issue in the case. This process of disclosure of documents overrides some of the privileges available under the discovery rules; many such documents will be directly relevant to the strength or weakness of the plaintiff's or defendant's case, but must nonetheless be given to the other party.

[6.60] There are other pre-trial remedies which are also available to either party in High Court civil proceedings, such as *interrogatories*, by which one party may pose formal questions for answer by another party to proceedings in order further to identify an issue in dispute. The general rule concerning such interrogatories is that the question must be posed in such a way as to admit of a 'yes' or 'no' reply.

Circuit Court: Civil Bill

[6.61] The procedure in civil cases in the Circuit Court is, as indicated earlier, somewhat less complex than in the High Court, bearing in mind the fact that the court tends to deal with cases of lower monetary value, even if they may very well be important for those involved in the case. The basic originating document in the Circuit Court is the 'civil bill', the document used in the County Courts prior to 1922.[46] The civil bill contains the equivalent of the High Court statement of claim from the plaintiff. In response, the Circuit Court Rules 2001 provide for the defendant filing a defence, which is in similar terms to the High Court defence. The procedure for personal injuries actions in the Circuit Court is largely the same as for those initiated in the High Court. There is no further provision for pleadings in the Circuit Court.

---

43 Delany and McGrath, *Civil Procedure in the Superior Courts* (3rd edn, 2012), p 402.

44 Order 31, r 29 of the Rules of the Superior Courts. See also Delany and McGrath, *Civil Procedure in the Superior Courts* (3rd edn, 2012), pp 423–429.

45 Rules of the Superior Courts (No 6) (Disclosure of Reports and Statements) 1998 (SI 391/1998). See Pierse, 'Disclosure of Reports and Information in Personal Injuries Litigation: the 1998 Rules' (1999) 17 ILT 42.

46 See para **2.54** and generally Law Reform Commission, *Report on Consolidation and Reform of the Courts Acts* (LRC 97-2010), para 1.11.

District Court: Claim Notice

[6.62] In the District Court, until 2014 the originating document was called the 'civil summons'. In 2014, arising from the increase of the monetary civil jurisdiction of the District Court to €15,000 by the Courts and Civil Law (Miscellaneous Provisions) Act 2013, the District Court Rules 1997 were comprehensively reformed.[47] Since 2014 the main initiating document in the District Court is the 'claim form' and the person initiating a civil claim in the District Court is referred to as a claimant, rather than a plaintiff. This change in title reflects comparable changes in the United Kingdom in the 1990s in the wake of Lord Woolf's Reports, discussed below,[48] and the recommendations by the Law Reform Commission in 2010 to simplify the titles of parties in civil proceedings.[49] The claim form contains a brief description of the civil case made by the claimant. The District Court Rules 1997 also provide for the making of a defence and counterclaim (prior to 1997, this had not been possible). In essence, since 1997 the procedure in the District Court has become quite similar to that applicable in the Circuit Court. The procedure for personal injuries actions is largely the same as that in the High Court and Circuit Court, including that, since 2014, the initiating document is called a personal injuries summons (and since the enlargement of the monetary jurisdiction of the District Court in 2014, such actions may become more common in the District Court).

Compromise or settlement

[6.63] The preceding pages have outlined the formal process required to initiate a civil claim in the different courts. However, it is important to note that the vast majority of cases initiated each year will not require a court hearing – many are in fact compromised or settled before they are due to be heard in the different courts. Indeed, there are countless instances of disputes in which proceedings might not have been initiated but in which a formal letter from a potential plaintiff's solicitor (the well-known 'solicitor's letter') will produce a favourable response from a potential defendant. Of the cases in which such approaches do not produce the desired result, many will be settled quite early on, largely because the initiation of proceedings is sufficient to induce an offer of settlement from the defendant. But even where a case has progressed though all the stages referred to above and has been set down for hearing in court, a settlement is quite common even on the day the case is due to be heard – a settlement 'at the door or steps of the court'. In view of the negotiating skill of Irish people in general, and the wish of both parties to maximise their negotiating position, this is hardly surprising.

[6.64] Until recently, there had been relatively little detailed research done on the rate of settlements in civil litigation in Ireland. Surveys conducted by the Irish Business and

---

[47] The amendments are in the District Court (Civil Procedure) Rules 2014 (SI 17/2014).

[48] See para **6.66**.

[49] See Law Reform Commission, *Report on Consolidation and Reform of the Courts Acts* (LRC 97-2010), paras 2.02–2.07. The Commission's recommendations, incorporated into the draft Courts (Consolidation and Reform) Bill appended to the Report, would apply to all courts.

Employer's Confederation (IBEC) concerning personal injuries claims initiated against employers had indicated that less than 15 per cent of claims initiated result in a full court hearing, thus indicating that the vast majority are settled or compromised at some stage.[50] We refer elsewhere to the substantial legislative changes made in the 1980s and 1990s to encourage the more efficient conduct of such cases, whether in terms of encouraging earlier settlements or facilitating speedier hearings for those which are not destined to be settled.[51]

[6.65] The IBEC findings were generally underpinned by a report on personal injury compensation published in 2001.[52] This report indicated that of the many personal injuries cases settled in Ireland, a large proportion were settled 'at the door or steps of the court', that is, on the day the case was due to be heard. Consequently, the report also found that the costs involved in such settlements (in addition to the actual settlement payment to the plaintiff), such as the costs of obtaining medical and other expert reports as well as the legal fees involved, were quite high. The report stated that this contrasted with earlier settlements in comparable cases in Britain. The report concluded that a Personal Injuries Assessment Board (PIAB) should be established to facilitate earlier settlements which might involve reduced administrative and legal costs. As we have seen, the Injuries Board was established in 2003 on the basis of this recommendation.[53] The introduction of the Personal Injuries Assessment Board (known as the Injuries Board) has further facilitated the settlement of personal injuries claims without recourse to the courts. In 2013, the Injuries Board facilitated direct settlement of approximately 10,000 claims outside of the claims where formal assessment awards are made by the Injuries Board.[54] A Central Bank inspection of personal injury settlements made by insurance companies in 2011 confirmed that 70% of cases are either settled directly between the parties or through the formal awards made by the Injuries Board.[55]

---

[50] For example, in its survey *Employer/Public Liability Claims for Personal Injury* (1993), which examined over 2,000 claims notified to IBEC member companies between 1989 and 1992, it found that 7% of these claims had gone to a court hearing, though a further 45% of the claims had yet to be finalised. In its most recent such survey, *IBEC National Survey of Personal Injuries Claims 2000* (2001), which surveyed 2,900 claims notified to IBEC member companies between 1995 and 1999, it found that 5% of these claims had gone to a court hearing, with a further 40% of the claims yet to be finalised. Even assuming that a greater proportion of the claims to be finalised were more likely to result in full court hearings, the figure of 15% referred to in the text seems justified.

[51] See para **5.13** and the provisions of the Courts and Court Officers Act 1995.

[52] See the *Second Report of the Special Working Group on Personal Injury Compensation* (2001), available at www.deti.ie.

[53] See Ch 5.

[54] Injuries Board, *Annual Report of the Injuries Board 2013* (2014) at p 4.

[55] Central Bank, *Themed Inspection into Third Party Personal Injuries Claims* (October 2011).

[4] REFORM OF THE CIVIL JUSTICE SYSTEM: THE UK WOOLF REFORMS AND JUDICIAL CASE MANAGEMENT

[6.66] In addition to the reforms discussed above, the Irish civil procedure system has been to some extent influenced by the radical, and arguably revolutionary, changes made in the late 1990s in the United Kingdom civil justice system. The UK reforms are based on various reports on civil justice prepared in the mid-1990s by Lord Woolf, the former Lord Chief Justice and former Master of the Rolls (in effect, the head of the civil judiciary in England and Wales).[56] These had been prepared against the background of widespread dissatisfaction with the English civil process system, in particular its complexity and apparently consequent delays. The Woolf reports led to the enactment of the Civil Procedure Act 1997 (UK), which in turn led to radically new rules of court, the Civil Procedure Rules (CPR) 1998 (UK), which came into effect in 1999. The intention behind these changes was to streamline civil procedure in all the courts, to improve efficiency and reduce delays. The objectives of the Woolf reports were to improve access to justice and reduce the cost of litigation; to reduce the complexity of the rules and modernise terminology; and to remove unnecessary distinctions of practice and procedure between the different courts.

[6.67] The Woolf reports identified many problems within the pre-1998 English civil justice system. Litigation was too expensive, in that costs often exceeded the value of the claim and the system was too slow in bringing cases to a conclusion and uncertainty as to the cost and duration of litigation ensued. Inequalities existed between litigants who were wealthy and those who were not and the system was incomprehensible to many litigants. The system was too fragmented since there was no clear overall responsibility for the administration of civil justice. Litigation was overly adversarial with cases being run by the parties and not by the courts and, in this context, the rules of court were often ignored by the parties and not enforced by the courts.

[6.68] Woolf identified the principles which should underpin the civil justice system. The system should be *just* in the results it delivers. It should be *fair* and be seen to be so by ensuring that litigants are afforded an equal opportunity, regardless of their resources, to assert or defend their legal rights; by providing every litigant with an adequate opportunity to state his or her case and to answer that of his or her opponent; and by treating like cases alike. Procedures and costs should be *proportionate* to the nature of the issues involved. The civil process should deal with cases with reasonable *speed*, it should be *understandable* to those who use it and be *responsive* to their needs. It should provide as much *certainty* as the nature of particular cases allows. It should be *effective* with adequate resources and proper organisation.

---

56   Lord Woolf, *Access to Justice, Interim Report* (1995) and Lord Woolf, *Access to Justice, Final Report* (1996).

[6.69] In implementing these principles, the 1998 CPR rules of court involve a number of new features:

– *Pre-Action protocols*: to provide a clear framework for both parties to follow, to resolve or at least clarify a dispute before the issue of a claim. These have been developed for specific areas of litigation, for example personal injuries, professional negligence, judicial review and defamation.

– *Case control to ensure efficiency of cases*: This involves the progress of cases by way of a computerised diary monitoring system to ensure are matters dealt with promptly. Parties are encouraged to co-operate with each other.

– *Part 36 offers*: to enable claimants, as well as defendants, to make offers to settle.

– *Single joint experts*: to reduce costs and promote co-operation between the parties.

– *Judicial case management*: to ensure cases are dealt with justly.

– Defended cases are allocated to one of three tracks:

– *Small claims track*: for personal injury cases up to £1,000 and all other cases up to £5,000.

– *Fast track*: intended for cases above the small claims limit and not exceeding £15,000. Cases are to be run according to fixed timetables leading to trial in 20–30 weeks. The trial would be expected to last one day or less with limits on oral and expert evidence.

– *Multi-track*: for cases over £15,000 and those cases which were too complex for the fast track. Case management by judicial teams is a feature of the multi-track and there is either standard or tailor-made directions as appropriate.

– *Costs*: to increase certainty and proportionality, there are fixed costs for cases on the fast track. Costs orders are to better reflect the conduct of the successful party and the outcome of individual issues. Costs orders can also penalise a party for poor conduct in the proceedings such as failing to conform to time limits.

– *Rules of Court*: to reduce complexity there is now a single set of rules, the CPR, for the High Court and the County Courts (that is, all the civil courts).

– *ADR*: the use of alternative dispute resolution is encouraged. [57]

– *Time limits*: there are fixed times for serving proceedings and costs sanctions where these time limits are breached.

[6.70] A key feature of the English 1998 CPR rules of court is that claimants (no longer called plaintiffs) file the same documents regardless of the court in which they initiate their claim. A claim is initiated using a *claim form*, a multi-purpose document replacing the various summonses and petitions which had existed in English courts for many centuries (and which, as has been indicated, remain part of the current rules of court in

---

[57]   On ADR, see paras **8.04***ff.*

Ireland). There is an emphasis in the CPR on requiring legal advisers to use plain English in the statement of case which must be filed by the claimant to indicate the precise nature of the claim (the term 'pleadings' is not used in the CPR rules of court). The rules are kept under regular surveillance and review. In October 2013 the 66th update to the rules was introduced.

[6.71] In addition to removing much archaic language from the rules of court, the CPR introduced a radical concept in UK civil litigation: judicial case management. In essence, judicial case management involves judges becoming actively involved in the civil litigation process, rather than being a passive observer of the parties. The Final Woolf report defined judicial case management as:

> "... the court taking the ultimate responsibility for progressing litigation along a chosen track for a pre-determined period during which it is subjected to selected procedures which culminate in an appropriate form of resolution before a suitably qualified judge. Its overall purpose is to encourage settlement of disputes at the earliest appropriate stage; and, where trial is unavoidable, to ensure that cases proceed as quickly as possible to a final hearing which is itself of strictly limited duration."

[6.72] The criticism made in the Woolf reports of the pre-1998 UK civil process was that the courts were not in control of the process but were largely dependent on whether the litigants themselves chose to process a claim with reasonable speed (the same arguments may be made of the current civil process system in Ireland). The conclusion reached was that many of the delays in the civil process system were due to the absence of any overall control of litigation and that a key element in overcoming this was to give effective control of the process to the judges. Judicial case management is now mandatory under the 1998 CPR rules of court for the 'multi-track' cases where the damages claimed is over £15,000, and such claims are now under the control of a designated judge. The judge is involved in active 'tracking' of a case from its initial stages, including where necessary requiring the parties to attend judicial case conferences in which the progress, or delays, in a case are discussed. Amongst other things, more stringent sanctions for non-compliance with agreed dates for progressing a claim are specified in the CPR, including 'wasted costs orders' which in effect provide that lawyers will not be awarded their costs for delays associated with, for example, failure to file a relevant document.

[6.73] The Woolf Reforms have not been given uncritical approval and the claims that they would lead to cheaper civil litigation have been challenged.[58] A common complaint is that the reforms have had the effect of 'front loading' the time and money spent on a case before it came it court.[59] Another criticism is aimed at the costs sanctions in the CPR. Lord Woolf had asserted that the pre-1998 delays in the civil justice system had been in the interest of lawyers, but the question has been raised as to whether it is

---

58 Kelly and Slapper, *The English Legal System*, (15th edn, 2014), p 363.
59 Zander, *The State of Justice* (1999), Ch 2.

legitimate to penalise the actual litigants for the failure of their legal representatives to meet the strict time limits in the CPR.[60]

[6.74] Whether the reforms in UK civil procedure have translated into the stated objective of improving the efficiency of the court system and making justice more accessible to those involved in litigation has been considered by a number of bodies. In 2001, the UK Lord Chancellor's Department (now the UK Ministry of Justice) published the first progress report on the Woolf reforms, indicating that they had appeared to have resulted in some reduction in litigation and increased use of ADR. Judicial case management was regarded as having produced positive results.[61] Research completed in 2005 concluded that case management conferences were one of the most beneficial aspects of the new system and that the culture of litigation had altered significantly so that there was better cooperation between the parties and the parties and the courts.[62] The then Master of the Rolls, Lord Phillips, commented that the Woolf Reforms 'have been effective in changing the whole ethos of litigation' but that 'there was still a problem with the cost of civil litigation – it is extremely expensive ... Although the Woolf Reforms hoped to reduce costs, this hasn't happened.' [63] Research demonstrates that the introduction of the Woolf Reforms has led to a reduction in the number of civil actions begun in in the English courts. In 2003, the number of claims dealt with by the English High Court fell by 24 per cent from the previous year.[64] In 2008, Slapper and Kelly stated:

> "Overall it could be argued the Woolf Reforms can be seen as a triumphant step in the right direction as they have resulted in a wider proportion of society being able to achieve greater access to justice especially where the problem of a relatively small nature and can be dealt with quickly and cheaper in the lower courts. However, the reforms may not be so good where, for example, the problem involves complex commercial issues and or where a matter goes to appeal as costs rack up very quickly with the parties requiring the assistance of solicitors, barristers and experts and with the length of time it can take to resolve the more complex case."[65]

[6.75] Further reforms in English civil procedure have arisen from the 2010 Report *Review of Civil Litigation Costs*,[66] prepared by Lord Justice Jackson, a judge of the English Court of Appeal. Among the reforms recommended in the Jackson Report were that:

---

60 Malleson and Moules, *The Legal System* (4th edn, 2010), p 101.
61 *Emerging Findings – an early evaluation of the Civil Justice Reforms* (2001), available at www.justice.gov.uk.
62 Peysner and Semeviratne, *The Management of Civil Cases: The Courts and Post-Woolf Landscape* (Department for Constitutional Affairs, 2005).
63 Rothwell, 'Lord Phillips attacks expensive litigation and pledges to resist politicians' (2005) *Law Society Gazette*, 13 October.
64 Malleson and Moules, *The Legal System* (4th edn, 2010).
65 Kelly and Slapper, *The English Legal System* (15th edn, 2014), p 363.
66 Available at http://www.judiciary.gov.uk/.

- For fast track personal injury cases, a dual system be introduced (at least for now), whereby costs are fixed for certain types of case, and in other cases there is a financial limit on costs recoverable (£12,000 to be the limit for pre-trial costs).

- A Costs Council should be established to undertake the role of reviewing fast track fixed costs.

- Lawyers should be able to enter into contingency fee agreements with clients for contentious business, provided that: the unsuccessful party in the proceedings, if ordered to pay the successful party's costs, is only required to pay an amount for costs reflecting what would be a conventional amount, with any difference to be borne by the successful party; and the terms on which contingency fee agreements may be entered into are regulated, to safeguard the interests of clients.

- As to 'qualified one way costs shifting', where the claimant will not be required to pay the defendant's costs if the claim is unsuccessful, but the defendant will be required to pay the claimant's costs if it is successful, there should be further consultation on which categories of litigation should involve this qualified one way costs shifting.

- As to case management, a number of measures to enhance the courts' role and approach to case management should be made, including: where practicable allocating cases to judges who have relevant expertise; ensuring that, so far as possible, a case remains with the same judge; standardising case management directions; and ensuring that case management conferences and other interim hearings are used as effective occasions for case management, and do not become formulaic hearings that generate unnecessary cost

- Further use of IT and eWorking should be rolled out across the High Court in London and (suitably adapted) across all County Courts and District Registries

[6.76] While the Jackson Report was not as wide-ranging as the Woolf Review of the 1990s, it has also led to significant reforms, notably in the area of legal costs and legal fees in civil cases. Many of these reforms were implemented in the English Legal Aid, Sentencing and Punishment of Offenders Act 2012 (usually referred to as LASPO) and in further amendments to the CPR. A number of these reforms remain contested by British practitioners and commentators, notably the effect they may have on access to justice by those with limited means and it involves public sector cutbacks.[67] It is therefore likely that the Jackson reforms will prove much more contentious than their predecessor, the Woolf reforms of the 1990s.

---

67 See for example the Law Society Gazette of England and Wales, 5 September 2013 and Barton, 'Access to Justice – Balancing the Risks' Adam Smith Institute (August 2010).

[6.77] The essential concepts involved in the Woolf reforms were discussed in this state by the Working Group on a Courts Commission.[68] The Working Group held a conference in 1997 on the use of judicial case management in other jurisdictions, including the proposals for reform then being considered in the United Kingdom.[69] It took the view that consideration should be given to the introduction of judicial case management in Ireland. However, it also recognised that, with the establishment of the Courts Service in 1999, this was more appropriately a matter for the Courts Service itself to consider.[70] The key principles involved in judicial case management have begun to be applied to a greater or lesser extent in Ireland[71] and they were introduced in the Rules of Court that established the Commercial Court as a division of the High Court in 2004. The wider reforms involved in the Woolf reports have yet to be introduced in a comprehensive manner as a mandatory requirement in all civil litigation in Ireland, but the positive experience with the Commercial Court may prove influential.

Case management and the Commercial Court[72]

[6.78] The Commercial Court, established as a specialist list in the High Court in 2004[73] aims, through judicial case management, to facilitate the speedy and effective resolution of commercial litigation (currently limited to commercial claims that exceed €1m in value). It was established on foot of recommendations by the Committee on Court Practice and Procedure that a Commercial Court be provided to allow for the speedy resolution of commercial disputes and allow for the use of modern technology in court proceedings.[74]

A wide variety of pre-trial procedures are available in the Commercial Court, primarily to encourage the early identification of the matters at issue between the

---

[68] *Second Report of the Working Group on a Courts Commission: Case Management and Court Management* (1996). The Working Group, which produced six reports during its existence between 1995 and 1998 and led to the enactment of the Courts Service Act 1998 (see para **4.209**), was chaired by Denham J, a judge of the Supreme Court.

[69] See *Working Paper: Conference on Case Management* (1997). The Working Paper, which includes the text of the papers delivered at the conference, is available on the Courts Service website, www.courts.ie.

[70] *Sixth Report of the Working Group on a Courts Commission: Conclusion with Summary* (Pn 2690, 1998). The report is available on the Courts Service website, www.courts.ie.

[71] In a lecture delivered in March 2001 on the future of the court structure (see para **5.115**), the then Chief Justice, Keane CJ, noted that 'the introduction of case management techniques is under active consideration' in the High Court. In his judgment in *Orange Communications Ltd v Director of Telecommunications Regulation (No 2)* [2000] 4 IR 159 at 202, Keane CJ commented that the 51 days the case occupied in the High Court and 17 days in the Supreme Court was due in part to the absence of appropriate case management structures.

[72] Dowling, *The Commercial Court* (2nd edn, 2012).

[73] Rules of the Superior Courts (Commercial Proceedings) 2004, (SI 2/2004) inserted a new Ord 63A (Commercial Court) into the Rules of the Superior Courts 1986.

[74] Committee on Court Practice and Procedure Twenty-Seventh Interim Report, *A Commercial Court in Ireland* (2003).

parties. In addition, the presiding judge may, either on his or her initiative or if requested by either party, adjourn the matter for a period of up to 28 days to allow the parties to consider mediation, conciliation or arbitration.[75]

[6.79] The presiding judge may also direct that a case management conference be held before the date set for hearing the case. The purpose of a case management conference is to ensure that the 'proceedings are prepared for trial in a manner which is just, expeditious and likely to minimise the cost of the proceedings'[76] and it is usually held two to four weeks before the hearing date.[77] In addition, it is common for a pre-trial conference to be held between the lawyers for the parties and the judge. At a pre-trial conference, the judge attempts to ascertain what steps need to be taken to prepare the case for trial, the likely length, arrangements for witnesses (including video conferencing) and other arrangements for trial. At a pre-trial conference, the judge may also give directions for arrangements necessary for trial and, if no date for trial has been set, set a date. To ensure that matters are expedited, the Rules of Court provide for possible cost sanctions (clearly influenced by the UK Woolf reforms) for parties who engage in unnecessary delay.[78]

[5] CRIMINAL PROCEDURE[79]

[6.80] Having discussed the procedures for processing civil claims, we can now proceed to outline the essential elements of criminal procedure. As already mentioned, a crucial distinction is that most criminal prosecutions are initiated by a state agency, such as the Director of Public Prosecutions or the Garda Síochána.

Summary trial and trial on indictment

[6.81] For many centuries in Ireland, there have been two different procedural methods by which a criminal case comes to trial. The first method, used for less serious criminal cases, is by way of summons, leading to a summary trial. The second method, used in relation to more serious offences, is by way of indictment, leading to a trial on indictment. We have already seen that Article 38 of the Constitution provides that, except in connection with minor offences, a person charged with a criminal offence is entitled to a trial with a jury.[80] Since trial on indictment has traditionally involved trial by jury, the effect of Article 38 is that serious criminal matters are heard in the Circuit Criminal Court or the Central Criminal Court, while minor cases are, in general, heard in the District Court by way of summary trial. We have also seen that the penalties

---

75 Order 63A, r 6(1)(b)(xiii) of the Rules of the Superior Courts.
76 Order 63A, r 14(7) of the Rules of the Superior Courts.
77 Dowling, *The Commercial Court* (2007), p 301.
78 Order 63A, r 15(e).
79 See generally Ryan and Magee, *The Irish Criminal Process* (1983) and Walsh, *Criminal Procedure* (2003).
80 See para **4.45**.

provided for on foot of a trial on indictment are greater than on a summary prosecution, again reflecting constitutional requirements.[81]

[6.82] The distinction drawn in the Constitution between minor offences and offences requiring a jury trial did not fit easily with the older common law categorisation of criminal offences, felonies and misdemeanours. In general, felonies were the more serious offences but there were exceptions. Thus, murder was a felony as was assault with intent to rob, but assault occasioning actual bodily harm was a misdemeanour at common law and under s 47 of the Offences against the Person Act 1861. Moreover, some relatively serious offences, such as obtaining by false pretences and fraudulent conversion, were misdemeanours. Over time the distinctions between felonies and misdemeanours evaporated with the important exception that, at common law, there was a power of arrest without warrant for felony but not for misdemeanour; an arrest warrant was required in respect of a misdemeanour.[82] The concepts of felony and misdemeanour were abolished by the Criminal Law Act 1997 which introduced the concept of an 'arrestable offence'.[83]

[6.83] Since the 1950s, where new criminal offences had been created by statute in Ireland, the distinction between felonies and misdemeanours had tended to be disregarded in the drafting of the legislation. Instead, the penalties attaching to the offence were specified by reference to whether the charge was to be brought by way of summons or indictment. For example, s 17 of the Criminal Justice (Public Order) Act 1994 created an offence of demanding money with menaces. Section 17(3) of the 1994 Act provides:

"A person guilty of an offence under this section shall be liable—

    (a)   on summary conviction to a fine not exceeding €2,500[84] or to imprisonment for a term not exceeding 12 months or to both,

    (b)   on conviction on indictment to a fine[85] or to imprisonment for a term not exceeding 14 years or to both."

---

[81]   See para **5.90**.

[82]   Originally, felonies carried the death penalty, though the number of felonies for which this was true gradually reduced in number. The death penalty was formally abolished for all offences in Ireland by the Criminal Justice Act 1990 and all references in the Constitution to the death penalty were removed in 2001 by the Twenty-Fourth Amendment to the Constitution Act 2001. Conviction for felony also involved forfeiture of property to the Crown, which was abolished by the Forfeiture Act 1870. Certain other disabilities applied under the 1870 Act, which were ultimately removed by the Criminal Law Act 1997 when the concept of felony was abolished.

[83]   See para **6.84**.

[84]   Amended by s 22 and Sch 2 of the Intoxicating Liquor Act 2008.

[85]   The effect of this is that the person would be liable to an unlimited fine.

[6.84] The disregarding of the felony-misdemeanour distinction reflected the introduction in Britain in 1967[86] of the concept of an 'arrestable offence', an offence which carried a possible sentence of imprisonment of five years and for which a member of a police force could arrest without warrant. As indicated, the Criminal Law Act 1997 abolished the outdated distinction between felonies and misdemeanours and introduced the concept of 'arrestable offence' into Irish law, that is an offence which carries a possible sentence of imprisonment of five years and for which a member of the Garda Síochána may arrest without warrant.

Prosecution system: not a unified system

[6.85] The criminal prosecution system in Ireland is currently divided between a number of state agencies. In the vast majority of cases, investigations into crime, both minor and serious, are conducted by the Garda Síochána. In minor cases, the garda who investigated a minor offence also becomes the prosecutor in court, though in some instances the case is presented by counsel in private practice, instructed by the Chief State Solicitor or a state solicitor. In serious cases, such as murder, the offences are investigated by the Garda Síochána and their files on the case are then sent to the Director of Public Prosecutions who determines whether a criminal prosecution is initiated; the Chief State Solicitor or local state solicitor[87] then briefs counsel in private practice for the prosecution itself. In England and Wales the Crown Prosecution Service now employs barristers on a salaried and full-time basis to act as prosecutors and such barristers cannot continue in private practice.

[6.86] By contrast to this arrangement, where the various functions are spread through a number of state agencies, a unitary criminal prosecution system has existed in Britain since the 1980s in the form of the Crown Prosecution Service (CPS), and similar regimes operate in the United States of America in the form of the District Attorney system. In essence, a unitary prosecution system means that all criminal prosecutions, whether minor or serious, are 'vetted' by a lawyer before they proceed. In practice, the arrangements in Ireland are that, in minor offences, the Garda Síochána and the local state solicitor determine whether a case proceeds to court, though in many instances this may occur in the name of the Director of Public Prosecutions without any direct involvement from the office of the Director. In recent years, approximately 500,000 minor offences have been initiated annually in this manner. A more direct link between the gardaí and the Director of Public Prosecutions operates where serious charges such as murder or rape are being considered.

[6.87] In 1999, the Nally Report, the *Report of the Public Prosecution System Study Group*,[88] concluded that a unitary prosecution system should *not* be introduced in the state. Although the report accepted that there were some attractions in a unitary

---

86   Criminal Law Act 1967, s 58.

87   See para **3.124**.

88   The Study Group was chaired by Dermot Nally, former Secretary to the government, and hence the Group's Report is also known as the Nally Report.

prosecution system, it also noted that the advent of the CPS in Britain had not been universally acclaimed and that it had been bedevilled with communications difficulties from its inception, particularly between CPS headquarters and the various police forces it dealt with. The report concluded that there was little to be gained in terms of efficiency in transferring the 500,000 minor criminal offences from the control of the Garda Síochána and local state solicitors to a unified, centralised, prosecution system.

[6.88] It recommended, however, that there was a need for increased investment in the current system and that improvements in communication between all the agencies involved in the process be continued. On the administrative side, it also made a significant recommendation, namely that the criminal procedure functions of the Chief State Solicitor's Office be transferred from the Attorney General to the Director of Public Prosecutions. This recommendation, which was accepted by the government, goes some way towards a unified system, particularly in relation to prosecutions on indictment, while leaving the arrangements for minor prosecutions largely unchanged. The recommendation that the functions of the Chief State Solicitor in criminal matters should be transferred to the Director of Public Prosecution was implemented in 2001.[89]

[6.89] The Nally Report focused exclusively on the criminal prosecution system, and did not consider such questions as whether the current arrangements concerning the organisation of criminal defence, including criminal legal aid, should be changed. These are discussed elsewhere.[90]

Summary prosecution[91]

[6.90] In general, the initiation of many of the less serious crimes, such as road traffic offences, is a matter for a member of the Garda Síochána. Other minor offences created by legislation may be prosecuted by other regulatory authorities, for example the Environmental Protection Agency in relation to offences under environmental protection legislation[92] or the Minister for Agriculture in connection with the use of prohibited growth promoters in animals.[93]

[6.91] In addition, at common law, any person is empowered to initiate and prosecute a criminal charge by means of a private prosecution. Such a person has the rather ungainly title of *common informer* and indeed the Garda Síochána frequently operate under this banner in the absence of specific statutory authorisation for initiating prosecutions. This common law right of private prosecution has not, it seems, been affected by the Constitution of Ireland 1937.[94] Section 8 of the Garda Síochána Act 2005 provides that

---

89   See Rules of the Superior Courts (No 4) (Chief Prosecution Solicitor) 2001 (SI 535/2001). See also Loftus, 'Establishment of office of Chief Prosecution Solicitor' [2002] *Bar Review* 348.
90   See paras **9.17***ff*.
91   See generally Coonan and O'Toole, *Criminal Procedure in the District Court* (2011).
92   See generally, the Environmental Protection Agency Act 1992 and Scannell, *Environmental and Land Use Law* (2006).
93   Animal Remedies Act 1993, s 22.

any garda may institute summary prosecutions in the name of the Director of Public Prosecutions (DPP). The DPP may give particular or general directions to the gardaí in relation to prosecutions, which members of the Garda Síochána are required to follow. Such directions may exclude the prosecution of specific types of offences, or prosecutions in specific circumstances, or the conduct of proceedings beyond a particular stage. The DPP may take over the conduct of proceedings from a garda at any stage.

[6.92] In relation to a summary prosecution, the procedure is relatively straightforward. A summons is issued by a person authorised by legislation, such as a District Court clerk,[95] on application (sometimes called the complaint) by, for example, a member of the Garda Síochána. A summons for the drink-driving offence under the Road Traffic Acts might be in the following form.

District Court Area of	District No.1
Paul McCutcheon	Prosecutor
Raymond Byrne	Accused

WHEREAS on the 1st day of May 2014 an application was made to this office by the above named Prosecutor for the issue of a summons to you, of

3 Sunny Bank Terrace, in the City of Dublin

(in court area and district aforesaid) alleging the following offence(s):

that you did on the 1st day of January 2014, at Main Road, Barrystown, in the city of Dublin drive a mechanically propelled vehicle, registration No. 131 D 1234567, when there was in your bloodstream a quantity of alcohol in excess of 50 milligrammes of alcohol per 100 millilitres of blood, contrary to Section 4 of the Road Traffic Act 2010.

THIS IS TO NOTIFY YOU that you will be accused of the said offence at a sitting of the District Court for the court area and district aforesaid to be held at Barrystown on the 1st day of June 2014 at 10.00 a.m.

AND TO REQUIRE YOU to appear at the said sitting to answer the said accusation.

Dated this 5th day of May 2014.

Figure 6.6

---

94 See *The State (Ennis) v Farrell* [1966] IR 107; *Cumann Luthchleas Gael Teo v Windle* [1994] 1 IR 525; and *Kelly and Buckley v Ryan* [2013] IEHC 321. See Hogan and Whyte (eds), *JM Kelly: The Irish Constitution* (4th edn, 2003), pp 575–578.

95 See the Courts (No 3) Act 1986, enacted to overcome the difficulties under the Petty Sessions (Ireland) Act 1851 identified in *The State (Clarke) v Roche* [1986] IR 619: see para **4.15**.

[6.93] Thus, a summons alleges that a named person has committed an offence, in this case driving a motor vehicle with an amount of alcohol in excess of that permitted under s 4 of the Road Traffic Act 2010. The summons contains the allegation of the offence together with information as to the registration number of the vehicle, the owner of the vehicle (who, if the driver, is also the person charged) and the date and location of the alleged offence. This summons is then the basis for the charge being brought to the District Court. There may be other evidence, such as the results of the test conducted by the Medical Bureau of Road Safety on the urine or blood sample which must be provided by the driver of the vehicle under the Road Traffic Acts. The summons is, however, the basic document on which the criminal trial in the District Court will take place and, in general, no further information will be furnished by the prosecution to the defence.[96]

Prosecution on indictment

[6.94] As to trials on indictment the procedure is more complex, both in terms of how they are initiated and in how they proceed. We have already discussed the criminal prosecution system and the arrangements where offences are instituted by the Director of Public Prosecutions, largely on the basis of files prepared by the Garda Síochána.

[6.95] In connection with their investigative functions, the Garda Síochána have been conferred with extensive legislative powers of arrest and detention.[97] While the courts are reluctant to acknowledge that the gardaí have an express right to question those arrested and held in custody, this has in effect been conceded, subject to certain safeguards to the right to silence.[98] The right to silence, although indirectly diluted through the effect of the various powers of arrest and detention,[99] remains a key formal feature of the common law accusatorial system, by contrast with the inquisitorial system

---

[96] In exceptional cases, the concept of fair procedures under the Constitution may require that the prosecution furnish the defence with the information on which it proposes to run the case in the District Court, including witness statements: see *Director of Public Prosecutions v Doyle* [1994] 2 IR 286; *Whelan v Kirby* [2004] IESC 17, [2005] 2 IR 30. There is no reference to disclosure in the District Court Rules, and the power of the District Court to make orders for inspection and the power to make such orders arises as a matter of fair procedures as provided for in the Constitution. See *DPP v Ni Chonduin* [2008] 3 IR 498.

[97] For example, the Offences against the State Act 1939, the Misuse of Drugs Acts 1977 and 1984, the Criminal Justice Act 1984, the Criminal Justice (Drug Trafficking) Act 1996, the Criminal Justice Act 2006 and the Criminal Justice Act 2007.

[98] See the Criminal Justice Act 1984 (Treatment of Persons in Custody in Garda Síochána Stations) Regulations 1987 (SI 119/1987). On the constitutional protections available to persons in custody, see *The People (DPP) v Quilligan and O'Reilly (No 3)* [1993] 2 IR 305.

[99] It is sometimes stated by the police themselves that confessions obtained by the Garda Síochána at one time accounted for about 80% of successful criminal prosecutions.

of the civil law jurisdictions of Europe where investigating magistrates are entitled to require answers to questions put to those charged with offences.[100]

[6.96] Although a common law system such as Ireland's professes to be accusatorial rather than inquisitorial, it had been suggested that the extensive powers conferred on the Garda Síochána correspond to the powers of investigating magistrates in the civil law jurisdictions, and that the safeguards in place in Ireland until recently were not sufficient to prevent vulnerable people from wrongly confessing to crimes.[101] In the wake of the findings of a tribunal of inquiry into the conduct of gardaí in the Donegal area, the Garda Síochána Act 2005 contains a much-amended independent complaints system, the Garda Síochána Ombudsman Commission, to which further amendments are under consideration at time of writing (July 2014).[102]

[6.97] It nonetheless remains that, consistent with the common law tradition, the Garda Síochána continue to investigate while the courts deliberate on guilt or innocence, but in recent years there has been some debate on whether the existing system should be substantially remodelled on civil law lines or whether some form of 'intermediate' system be introduced. The Criminal Justice (Drug Trafficking) Act 1996 and the Criminal Justice Act 2007 provide for such an intermediate system, with increased powers of detention in connection with serious drugs offences and other offences connected with organised groups, subject to judicial control if the detention is intended to proceed beyond four days.

[6.98] As already indicated, in general the decision whether to prosecute is in the hands of the Director of Public Prosecutions. In addition, at common law, a common informer may initiate a private prosecution. As far as trials on indictment are concerned, it would appear that a private prosecution can be brought as far as the point in the District Court of the return for trial by the judge of the District Court,[103] but that the matter is in the hands of the Director of Public Prosecutions thereafter.[104]

[6.99] The office of the Director of Public Prosecutions was created by the Prosecution of Offences Act 1974. Up to the 1974 Act, prosecutions on indictment were initiated by the Attorney General and, while the Attorney General retains some functions in criminal matters, the Director of Public Prosecutions now takes the lead role in this respect.[105]

[6.100] In general the Director of Public Prosecutions, like any other prosecuting authority such as the Garda Síochána, has a discretion as to whether to prosecute in an individual case. Where the Director decides not to prosecute, the courts are reluctant to

---

[100] See generally, Van den Wyngaert *et al*, *Criminal Procedure Systems in the European Community* (1993).

[101] See, eg, Irish Council for Civil Liberties, *Interrogation Endangers the Innocent* (1993).

[102] See para **5.28**, above.

[103] Until 2001, known as the preliminary examination, see para **6.105**.

[104] See *The State (Ennis) v Farrell* [1966] IR 107; *Cumann Luthchleas Gael Teo v Windle* [1994] 1 IR 525 and *Kelly and Buckley v Ryan* [2013] IEHC 321.

[105] See para **3.101** on the 1974 Act.

interfere with that decision or order a prosecution to proceed,[106] although a decision to prosecute after an initial decision not to prosecute could be challenged.[107] Until 2000, the general reasons behind the decisions of the Director as to whether to prosecute were not published. Indeed, the Director had, in general, refused to comment on individual cases.[108]

[6.101] In 2000, the Director published for the first time the general factors taken into account in deciding whether to prosecute.[109] The most significant is whether, on the basis of the file presented to the Director by the Garda Síochána, there is sufficient evidence to indicate that a conviction is likely.[110] The second factor is whether the public interest lies in favour of a prosecution. These two factors will in most instances coincide, but in exceptional cases the public interest may militate against a prosecution even where there is some evidence that a conviction is likely. The Director's decision is, in effect, final and as the law stands at present no private prosecution can proceed beyond the District Court without the Director's consent.[111]

---

[106] See *H v Director of Public Prosecutions* [1994] 2 IR 589, where the Supreme Court refused to order the Director to proceed with a prosecution for sexual offences which the applicant alleged her husband had committed against their children and which the Director had already decided not to prosecute.

[107] See *Eviston v Director of Public Prosecutions* [2002] 1 ILRM 134, where the Director had initially decided not to prosecute the applicant, who had been involved in a fatal traffic accident, but later initiated charges after the victim's family had written to the Director seeking an internal review. Such an internal review is part of the *Victims' Charter* introduced in 1999: see para **6.112**. In *Eviston*, the High Court quashed the decision to prosecute.

[108] A notable exception was the statement published in November 1999 arising from the Director's investigation into *The People (DPP) v Wall and McCabe*, in which the defendants had been charged with and convicted of rape. The first defendant was a Roman Catholic nun and the case attracted widespread media coverage. In the immediate aftermath of the conviction, doubts were cast on the reliability of the evidence given by a prosecution witness. The Director's investigation into the case revealed that the witness had been called in the case despite instructions to the contrary from the Director's office. The Director subsequently did not oppose the defendants' appeal to the Court of Criminal Appeal and apologised in court for the errors that had led to their convictions: see (1999) *The Irish Times*, 23 November.

[109] *Annual Report of the Director of Public Prosecutions 1999*.

[110] This generally involves the simple question as to whether the evidence involved is sufficiently credible that a jury would be likely to convict, but in recent years the Director has also been required to consider whether, if there is a very long lapse between the crime and the initiation of the prosecution, the right to a speedy trial and to fair procedures can be upheld. This has occurred, for example, in the context of child sexual abuse cases which, typically, only come to light many years after the event: see, for example, *G v Director of Public Prosecutions* [1994] 1 IR 374.

[111] The publication of these general factors, which had become common in other jurisdictions, can be traced to some criticism of decisions of the Director during the 1990s, specifically in connection with the non-prosecution of some child sexual abuse cases. (contd.../)

[6.102] Since 2000, there has been a shift in thinking internationally about whether public prosecutors such as the Director of Public Prosecutions should provide reasons in some individual cases as a matter of policy. In 2008, after an extensive consultation exercise, the DPP published a *Report on Prosecution Policy on the Giving of Reasons for Decisions*.[112] The report states that reasons will, initially, be given in connection with alleged offences where a death has occurred including murder, manslaughter, infanticide, fatalities in the workplace and fatal road traffic accidents. This policy was implemented by the DPP and reasons for decisions not to prosecute are provided on request to the families of victims in fatal cases occurring after 22 October 2008. Reasons for decisions not to prosecute or discontinue a prosecution are furnished on request to parties closely connected with the deceased, including members of the deceased's family or household, their legal or medical advisers or social workers acting on their behalf. The DPP indicated that reasons will only be supplied in circumstances where it is possible to do so without causing any injustice. Thus, where potential witnesses or other persons are exposed to an injustice, or where the identity of confidential sources would be revealed, reasons would not be supplied.

The DPP's office has reported that the number of such requests has been quite low and in fact in 2013 17 requests for such information were received.[113] It was expected that in 2010, the DPP would evaluate the process and may extend the policy to other areas, including sexual offences but this was superseded by the EU Directive establishing standards on the rights, support and protection of victims of crime, which must be transposed into Irish law by November 2015.[114] This Directive includes the right of victims to receive information in relation to any decision not to proceed with or to end an investigation or not to prosecute the alleged offender. This is a far more encompassing right for victims than the policy in place with the Office of the DPP.

It is notable that the policy change initiated in 2008 came after the decision of the European Court of Human Rights in *Jordan v United Kingdom*[115] where the court held that the failure of the DPP for Northern Ireland to give reasons for the non-prosecution of members of the security forces who had killed a member of the public was a violation

---

[111] (\...contd) The *1999 Annual Report* included a survey of sex offence files carried out by the Director's office. This indicated that prosecutions were brought in 56% of cases where files were received. In almost half the cases where no charge was brought it was because there was insufficient evidence. Other reasons given for not prosecuting in sex offence cases were: the injured party withdrew the complaint or refused to make a statement; a child's parents refused to allow the child to give evidence; or the injured party was too young and the culprit was cautioned by the gardaí.

[112] Office of the Director of Public Prosecutions, *Report on Prosecution Policy on the Giving of Reasons for Decisions* (Office of the Director of Public Prosecutions, 2008), available at www.dppireland.ie.

[113] Office of the Director of Public Prosecutions, *Strategy Statement of the DPP 2013–2015* (2013) and *Annual Report of the Office of the DPP 2013* (2014) at p 15.

[114] Directive 2012/29/EU.

[115] *Jordan v United Kingdom* (2003) 37 EHRR 52.

of the right to life of the person involved under the European Convention on Human Rights. The 2012 EU Directive on Victims, Directive 2012/29/EU, also imposes a general obligation, subject to limitations, to provide victims with reasons for not prosecuting.[116]

The role of the District Court

[6.103] Once the decision is made to prosecute a person he or she will be brought before the District Court and formally charged. Where the accused is charged with an indictable offence, the Criminal Procedure Act 1967 provides in general for two options: one is that the judge of the District Court may be empowered to deal with the case summarily; the other is that the judge ensures that certain procedures are followed before sending the case forward for trial on indictment.[117]

(a) Indictable offences triable summarily

[6.104] We have already seen that most statutory criminal offences are nowadays created as 'hybrid' offences, that is, they may be tried either summarily or on indictment. For example, many of the offences in the Non-Fatal Offences Against the Person Act 1997 and in the Criminal Justice (Theft and Fraud Offences) Act 2001 are such offences. Whether an offence is dealt with summarily or on indictment is primarily a matter for the Director of Public Prosecutions, although a judge of the District Court may decline to deal with a case summarily if he or she considers that the case is not minor in nature and requires a trial on indictment. In addition the District Court will not have the jurisdiction to try an either way offence unless the accused has been informed of his right to be tried with a jury and does not object to being tried summarily. Such 'hybrid' offences' now greatly outnumber the 'either way' offences listed in the Schedule to the Criminal Justice Act 1951,[118] which specifies certain offences which, although they may be tried on indictment in one of the higher criminal courts, can be dealt with in the District Court. These are referred to as indictable offences triable summarily, or 'either way' offences. The offences mentioned include assault causing actual bodily harm, controlled drugs for personal use, handling stolen property and obtaining goods by false pretences.[119]

(b) Sending indictable offences forward for trial

[6.105] If the indictable offence cannot be dealt with summarily, the Criminal Procedure Act 1967 originally required a preliminary examination by a judge of the District Court

---

[116] See para **6.121**.

[117] One other option is that the accused may plead guilty in the District Court to an offence which cannot be tried summarily in the District Court, in which case the judge of the District Court will send the case forward to the Circuit Criminal Court for sentencing only.

[118] As amended by the Criminal Procedure Act 1967, the Criminal Law (Jurisdiction) Act 1976 and the Criminal Justice (Miscellaneous Provisions) Act 1997.

[119] For further see para **5.96**.

before the case could proceed to trial.[120] The preliminary examination was the successor to the grand jury system by which depositions from all relevant witnesses would be heard by a jury (or until the 1967 Act by the judge of the District Court) and then formally committed to writing before the case could proceed to trial.[121] In place of this, s 6 of the 1967 Act requires that the prosecution must provide to the defence all the evidence which the prosecution intends to use at trial. This material, colloquially called the 'book of evidence', includes a statement of the charges, a list of the witnesses it is proposed to call at trial and their statements and a list of exhibits (such as photographs) and any other relevant material such as forensic evidence, including genetic fingerprinting (DNA evidence). Until 2001 it was permissible under s 7 of the 1967 Act for the defence to examine any prosecution witness by way of sworn deposition, though in most instances this did not take place,[122] and most cross-examination was left to the trial itself.

[6.106] The concept of a 'preliminary examination' and the associated right to cross-examine was abolished under Pt 3 of the Criminal Justice Act 1999,[123] which came into effect in 2001. While the phrase 'preliminary examination' is no longer part of the criminal process, it remains the case after the 1999 Act came into effect that the accused cannot be sent forward for trial until the book of evidence has been served. Under the original provisions of the 1967 Act, where the book of evidence was served, the District Court judge decided whether a sufficient case had been presented to the court in order to justify sending the case forward for trial; and in rare instances this power had been exercised to refuse to send the case forward for trial. The 1999 Act abolished this right, so that service of the book of evidence will automatically lead to the case being sent forward. The case will then be sent forward to either the Circuit Criminal Court or the Central Criminal Court.[124]

Bail

[6.107] For many years, an accused person was usually entitled to bail, thus being at liberty up to the time of the trial. The judicial thinking behind this was that, regardless of the seriousness of the offence or the number of charges, the presumption of innocence and the right to liberty under Article 40.4 of the Constitution entitled a person to be free

---

[120] The Criminal Procedure Act 1967, s 12, provided that the accused may waive the right to a preliminary examination. This became redundant when Pt III of the Criminal Justice Act 1999 came into effect in October 2001.

[121] See para **2.52**. The grand jury system survives in other common law jurisdictions, such as the United States of America.

[122] This can be put down in most instances to a tactical decision that the defence did not wish to indicate to the prosecution any possible line of defence that may be taken at trial.

[123] It was accepted during the passage of the 1999 Act that this was contrary to the views expressed in the *Twenty-Fourth Report of the Committee on Court Practice and Procedure: Preliminary Examination of Indictable Offences* (1997): see Byrne, 'The Criminal Justice Act 1999' (2000) 18 ILT 190.

[124] See para **5.102**.

pending trial unless he or she was likely to 'evade justice', either by failing to appear in court or interfering with potential witnesses. Thus, courts were precluded from refusing bail merely because a person was facing a very serious charge or there was a likelihood of his or her committing further offences if released.[125] There was considerable political disquiet at what were perceived as excessively permissive bail rules, notably in connection with robbery and burglary charges, where it had been argued that 'professional criminals' engaged in serial robberies and burglaries while on bail in order to build a 'nest egg' when convicted. The evidence for this assertion was strongly contested,[126] but a constitutional amendment to Article 40.4 of the Constitution was effected in 1996 which paved the way for restrictions on granting the right to bail. The Bail Act 1997, enacted in the wake of the 1996 constitutional amendment, provides that a court may now refuse bail where a person is charged with a serious offence 'if the court is satisfied that such refusal is reasonably considered necessary to prevent the commission of a serious offence by that person'.[127]

[6.108] In deciding on a bail application, s 2 of the 1997 Act states that the court must take into account:

"(a) the nature and degree of seriousness of the offence with which the accused person is charged and the sentence likely to be imposed on conviction;

(b) the nature and degree of seriousness of the offence apprehended and the sentence likely to be imposed on conviction;

(c) the nature and strength of the evidence in support of the charge;

(d) any conviction of the accused person for an offence committed while he or she was on bail;

(e) any previous convictions of the accused person including any conviction the subject of an appeal (which has neither been determined nor withdrawn) to a court; and

(f) any other offence in respect of which the accused person is charged and is awaiting trial."

[6.109] These factors impose much more stringent criteria than applied prior to the Bail Act 1997. As a result, it was anticipated that many more persons would be refused bail, and thus a major prison-building programme was put in train by successive governments in the late 1990s.

---

[125] See *The People (Attorney General) v O'Callaghan* [1966] IR 501; *Ryan v Director of Public Prosecutions* [1989] IR 399.

[126] See para **5.26**.

[127] The Act defines 'serious offence' to include: murder; manslaughter; rape and other serious sexual assaults; other offences against the person, such as assault causing harm, harassment, false imprisonment and child abduction; sexual offences; some public order offences; various explosives and firearms offences; theft offences; some road traffic offences, such as dangerous driving causing death and taking a vehicle without authority ('joyriding'); various forgery offences; various offences against the state; and drug trafficking offences.

Form of indictment

[6.110] The form of most indictments is specified in the Criminal Justice (Administration) Act 1924, a measure that greatly simplified the procedural requirements regarding an indictment.[128] The Act also provides that defects in the indictment may be remedied at any time provided that this does not cause an injustice to the defendant.

[6.111] An indictment for the offence of robbery might be in the following form.

The People (at the suit of the Director of Public Prosecutions) v Raymond Byrne

Circuit Criminal Court, Dublin

Raymond Byrne is charged with the following offence:

[*Statement of offence*]

Robbery, contrary to s 14 of the Criminal Justice (Theft and Fraud Offences) Act 2001.

[*Particulars of offence*]

Raymond Byrne on the 1st day of May 2014 at Glass Lane, in the city of Dublin, robbed Paul McCutcheon of a sum of money in cash.

Figure 6.7

[6.112] The core of the indictment is the statement of the offences, or counts, which are charged. As can be seen from the example given, each count is in two parts: the statement of the offence and the particulars of the offence. The statement of the offence describes the offence in relatively straightforward language, and where the offence is one created by statute it is necessary to specify the legislation, as amended if appropriate. The particulars of the offence then set out the circumstances in which it is alleged that the defendant committed the offence, but these are not always as specific as the particulars in a civil pleading. In the above example, the date and place of the robbery may be specified. However, in the case of murder, the precise date may be unknown so that the particulars may state 'on a date unknown'. This is an acceptable form of particulars.

Arraignment

[6.113] It is not until an accused has been brought before the court of trial that the formal reading of the indictment is made. This is called the arraignment, and involves the calling of the person before the court, reading the indictment and asking the accused

---

128   See Ryan and Magee, *The Irish Criminal Process* (1983), Appendix B and also the Draft Indictments included in Charleton, *Offences Against the Person* (1992).

whether he or she pleads guilty or not guilty. If the accused pleads not guilty at this stage,[129] a jury is empanelled to hear the case.[130]

Guilty plea

[6.114] If the accused has pleaded guilty, the trial judge will impose sentence on the accused. Many factors may lead the accused to plead guilty, though in general the crucial factor may be the expectation that a lesser sentence will be imposed by the judge than would be the case if the accused pleads not guilty but is then found guilty after a full trial. In effect, a plea of guilty carries a discount on what the normal sentence might otherwise be. A person facing a possible five-year sentence after a full trial might thus expect a sentence of three years' imprisonment on a guilty plea. Such discounting will apply even where the offence is particularly serious, such as rape. Where the accused pleads guilty in such a case, the court will generally allow some discount on the basis that the person against whom the offence was committed has been spared the ordeal of giving evidence and having to re-live the rape itself.[131]

[6.115] The decision to plead guilty may also be linked to an informal 'plea bargain' with the prosecution, by which the accused might decide to plead guilty to certain charges in return for the prosecution not proceeding with others. Again, the prosecution may decide to accept a plea to save witnesses the ordeal of testifying or to save the substantial cost to the public of a long criminal trial. Clearly, there are many difficult issues that arise in connection with plea bargaining in general, whether for the accused, prosecution counsel or defence counsel. Plea-bargaining is a subject that has resulted in much debate in the United States, both in academic circles and in the wider media, though it is rarely discussed in Ireland, so to that extent any debate on its use remains somewhat speculative.[132]

Adversarial system and the role of the victim in criminal proceedings

[6.116] The system of court procedure that operates in common law systems is adversarial in nature. This means that the judge in a case plays the role of impartial referee between two sides in the contest that takes place in the courtroom.[133] The two sides, and their lawyers, play what has been described as a 'mutually antagonistic role', but this simply means that each side presents and argues its side. This adversarial system operates in both civil claims and criminal prosecutions, but it is particularly clear in the criminal context. In effect, the case is conducted between the prosecution, representing

---

129 The accused may withdraw a plea of guilty entered in the District Court and plead not guilty in the trial court.

130 On the right to trial with a jury, see para **4.45**.

131 See *The People (DPP) v Tiernan* [1988] IR 250.

132 See Ryan and Magee, *The Irish Criminal Process* (1983), pp 283–7, for a general discussion of some of the issues involved.

133 On the constitutional obligation of impartiality, see paras **4.120–4.123**.

the People, and the defendant or accused. In this model, the victim is not a party to the proceedings. In criminal trials other than murder, the victim is, at most, a witness.

[6.117] In recent years, it has been recognised that the adversarial model fails to address fully the needs of the victim. Various complaints have been made that the concerns of victims have not been taken into account in the criminal prosecution system. For example, in many instances, neither the victim nor his or her family are fully informed of the course of any criminal prosecution and they might become aware that a case has not been proceeded with only when they see the accused in their locality; they might not be informed of the date of trial until served with a witness summons to appear to give evidence; in certain types of cases, in particular rape and serious sexual assaults they are often subjected to such rigorous cross-examination in court that the experience has been described as more traumatic than the offence itself. Arguments have been advanced that victims should be represented separately in court by their own lawyers and that this should be funded by the state in the same manner as it funds the legal defence costs of accused persons.

[6.118] Substantial changes in practice in recent years have gone some way towards meeting some of these points. In 1997, a booklet entitled *Charter for Victims of Crime* was published by the Department of Justice, which contained some general information on the procedures to be followed to involve victims in the criminal procedure process. In 1999, the Department published a Revised Victims Charter.[134]

[6.119] Among the matters included in the charter are:

"– the commitment by the gardaí to afford equal priority to the investigation of all crime, irrespective of the gender, race, ethnic origin, sexual orientation or membership of any minority group of the victim;

– provision within the Office of the Director of Public Prosecutions for an internal review of decisions in appropriate cases on receipt of a request from interested parties;[135]

– the establishment of national victim liaison officers within the Garda Síochána and Prison Service, ensuring that a victim will be informed of the following: when a suspect has been charged with the crime following the investigation (and, where relevant, when a decision has been taken not to prosecute); whether bail has been granted; the date on which any court proceedings are expected to commence; whether it is likely that the victim will be required to give evidence; the outcome of the proceedings and effect on the victim;

– the provision of dedicated facilities for victims and their families within all new or refurbished court buildings;

– subject to the permission of the victim, victim impact statements are to be taken into account in the context of the early release of offenders from prison;

---

[134] The 1999 Charter is available on the Department's website, www.justice.ie.
[135] For an example of such an internal review, which gave rise to judicial review proceedings, see *Eviston v Director of Public Prosecutions* [2002] 1 ILRM 134, and para **6.100**.

– in cases involving serious crimes against the person, procedures for the notification by the gardaí to the victim of the release from prison of an offender."

[6.120] In the specific context of sexual assault cases, another major issue of contention is that victims should be accorded separate legal representation in court. In 1988, the Law Reform Commission[136] had expressed doubts as to the constitutionality of separate legal representation for victims/complainants in rape and other serious sexual assault cases, on the ground that it would alter the balance of the criminal process and deprive the accused of a trial in due course of law. A limited form of legal advice for victims, falling short of representation in court, was initiated in 1990, under the civil legal aid regime.[137] Part 6 of the Sex Offenders Act 2001 introduced separate legal representation for complainants in rape and other serious sexual assault cases in the specific context where an application is made by the defendant to adduce evidence or to cross-examine the complainant about his or her past sexual experience. Under the Criminal Law (Rape) Acts 1981 and 1990, the sexual history of a complainant may only be introduced into a trial by permission (leave) of the trial judge. Since such applications are made in the absence of the jury, the government was advised that the limited form of representation provided for in the 2001 Act did not present constitutional difficulties.

[6.121] More radical reform of the criminal justice process is required to implement the 2012 EU Directive on the rights, support and protection of victims of crime, Directive 2012/29/EU. The 2012 Directive must be implemented by 16 November 2015. The 2012 Directive considerably strengthens the rights of victims and their family members to information, support and protection as well as their procedural rights when participating in criminal proceedings. It also includes provisions that will ensure that professionals are trained in victims' needs and to encourage cooperation between EU Member States and awareness-raising on victims' rights. Thus, Article 4 of the 2012 Directive requires that the victims must be offered the following information, without unnecessary delay, from their first contact with a competent authority in order to enable them to access the rights set out in the Directive:

(a) the type of support they can obtain and from whom, including, where relevant, basic information about access to medical support, any specialist support, including psychological support, and alternative accommodation;

(b) the procedures for making complaints with regard to a criminal offence and their role in connection with such procedures;

(c) how and under what conditions they can obtain protection, including protection measures;

(d) how and under what conditions they can access legal advice, legal aid and any other sort of advice;

(e) how and under what conditions they can access compensation;

---

[136] *Report on Rape and Allied Offences* (LRC 24-1988).
[137] See para **9.52.**

(f)   how and under what conditions they are entitled to interpretation and translation;

(g)   if they are resident in a member state other than that where the criminal offence was committed, any special measures, procedures or arrangements, which are available to protect their interests in the member state where the first contact with the competent authority is made;

(h)   the available procedures for making complaints where their rights are not respected by the competent authority operating within the context of criminal proceedings;

(i)   the contact details for communications about their case;

(j)   the available restorative justice services;

(k)   how and under what conditions expenses incurred as a result of their participation in the criminal proceedings can be reimbursed.

In addition, Article 10 of the 2012 Directive provides:

"Member States shall ensure that victims may be heard during criminal proceedings and may provide evidence."

[6.122] While many of the provisions in Article 4 reflect the arrangements in the non-statutory Victims Charter, the right under Article 10 to be heard during criminal proceedings goes far beyond the traditional view of the victim as a passive participant in the criminal justice process. In addition, of course, from 2015 these provisions will be set out in the form of statutory rights of victims. This will no doubt require a reconsideration of the role of the victim in the adversarial process between the prosecution and the accused. A triangulation of interests has been referred to involving the prosecution, the accused and the public interest in the outcome of the case: the victim represents in some respects a very personal perspective of the public interest, which the 2012 Directive has now set out in terms of a rights-based analysis.

[6]   COURT PROCEDURE AND RULES OF EVIDENCE[138]

Evidence under oath

[6.123] The basis for many court hearings, whether civil or criminal, is that evidence to the court is given under oath.[139] This is, of course, the requirement in most legal systems, and its origins reflect the religious basis of much of our law. The oath originally had both a spiritual and temporal aspect, but in the context of this book the temporal aspect has more significance. Giving false evidence under oath constitutes the crime of perjury and although prosecutions and convictions for perjury are relatively rare they still constitute as much of a deterrent as any other criminal sanction.

---

138   See generally, McGrath, *Evidence* (2005). In 2014, the Law Reform Commission expects to publish a *Report on the Law of Evidence*, which will include the consolidation of existing pre-1922 and post-1922 Evidence Acts together with reform of the hearsay rule, of documentary and electronic evidence and the rules on expert evidence.

[6.124] In civil and criminal cases, all testimony must in general be given under oath. There are exceptions for children, that is, persons under the age of 14, who may give unsworn evidence.[140]

Oral and written testimony

[6.125] A feature of many court proceedings in common law systems is that testimony is given orally rather than in writing. The adversarial system has long regarded oral testimony to be highly probative, that is, carrying great value in relation to proving a particular assertion. The reason for this lies in the fact that the oral testimony is tested in court – the judge (and where relevant the jury) will have an opportunity to see the reaction of the witness and to test the veracity of the evidence given on that basis.

[6.126] However, while the general rule is that all evidence must be sworn, this does not necessarily require that the evidence be given orally. Sworn evidence may be given in writing, in the form of an affidavit, which is a document that is sworn in solemn form by a witness before a Commissioner for Oaths. Any untrue statements contained in an affidavit are equally subject to the crime of perjury as evidence sworn orally in court. In addition, the rules of the Commercial Court allow for witness statements to be admitted as evidence in chief of a particular witness who is then subject to cross-examination by the opposing party.

[6.127] Despite certain legislative changes,[141] it remains the case that the common law court hearing is characterised by oral evidence and oral presentations by the lawyers involved in the proceedings, whether civil or criminal. Some limits on the length of oral presentation in civil cases have been set in recent years in Ireland, but more fundamental changes along the lines of the Woolf reforms in the United Kingdom have yet to

---

139 Currently regulated by the Oaths Act 1888. The Law Reform Commission, in its 1990 *Report on Oaths and Affirmations* (LRC 34-1990) recommended the replacement of the oath with a solemn statutory declaration. Under the 1888 Act, the oath is generally based on swearing using a religious text, such as a Bible, but it also provides for the option of making an affirmation. The latter requires a witness to state that he or she has no religious beliefs. The Law Reform Commission considered that the current arrangements for taking oaths by reference to a religious text may be unduly narrow, to the exclusion of certain religions. It also considered that the requirement that a witness declare that he or she had no religious beliefs before making a statutory declaration constituted a breach of privacy. At the time of writing (September 2014), no legislative action has been taken on this 1990 report. In many other jurisdictions, such as the United Kingdom, witnesses have the option of taking an oath or affirming, the latter without any requirement to state whether the witness has or has not any religious beliefs.

140 See the Criminal Evidence Act 1992, s 27 (criminal proceedings) and the Children Act 1997, s 28 (civil proceedings). The 1997 Act removed the anomaly that children could give unsworn testimony in criminal cases but not in civil cases. See *Mapp v Gilhooley* [1991] 2 IR 253 for the position prior to the 1997 Act.

141 Criminal Justice Act 1984; Courts and Court Officers Act 1995.

emerge.[142] In criminal trials, defence lawyers are unlikely to agree to the admission of crucial evidence without challenge. This would particularly be the case where there is a doubt about the admissibility of that evidence; it might be, for example, that a crucial witness who handled certain evidence might not be available for the trial. By the same token defence counsel will not readily forego the opportunity to test the reliability of evidence proffered by the prosecution.

Rules of evidence

[6.128] The law of evidence has developed over many centuries in an attempt to regulate what may be used for the purpose of proving facts in court. Virtually all court cases require proof of facts, for example that a person was driving a car, that a contract was entered into, that a confession or inculpatory statement admitting to a crime was made. Evidence of a fact is whatever assertion or other matter tends to prove a fact, and the rules of evidence determine whether certain assertions or other matters are admissible in a court of law. We deal here only with a limited number of the rules of evidence to illustrate some of its important features: a more extensive discussion is outside the scope of this work.[143]

[6.129] The general intention behind the rules of evidence is to ensure that any evidence given is reliable and will provide the best opportunity for a true and fair verdict, whether in a civil or criminal trial. While the general rules of evidence are identical for civil and criminal proceedings, it may be that they are applied more vigorously in criminal trials than in civil trials, but even in civil trials the rules of evidence remain important.

[6.130] The general law of evidence can be summed up by the principle that all evidence that is sufficiently relevant to an issue is admissible, while all evidence that is not sufficiently relevant should be excluded. There are two major exceptions to the relevancy principle, namely that evidence of hearsay and evidence of opinion are, in general, inadmissible. The rules against hearsay and against opinion evidence are therefore known as exclusionary rules of evidence. However, to indicate the complexity of the rules of evidence, a number of exceptions to both these exclusionary rules have been developed, so that in certain instances hearsay and opinion evidence is admissible. The most common example of admissible hearsay is the confession or inculpatory admission, and opinion evidence is regularly used in civil and criminal cases where it is given by an expert witness. Because of their importance, we will discuss briefly hearsay and opinion evidence.

Hearsay

[6.131] A common definition of hearsay is that it consists of evidence of a fact not actually perceived by a witness with his or her own senses. In general, the rule against

---

142   On the Woolf reforms in the UK, see para **6.66**.
143   See generally Tapper, *Cross and Tapper on Evidence* (12th edn, 2010); Keane and McKeown, *The Modern Law of Evidence* (10th edn, 2014); McGrath, *Evidence* (2005); and Fennell, *Law of Evidence in Ireland* (3rd edn, 2009).

hearsay requires that witnesses may only assert the truth of facts or events of which they are aware and are thus prevented from asserting the truth concerning facts or events of which they have no direct knowledge. However, the rule does not always prevent the 'reporting' by a witness of what another person said; what is in general prohibited is giving the evidence of another person and asserting that the statement by the other person is true.

[6.132] An example of an inadmissible hearsay statement arose in a case where a person had been charged with unlawful wounding by throwing a stone at a person.[144] The victim of the wounding gave evidence that a woman had said to him immediately after the stone had been thrown, '[t]he man who threw the stone went in there', pointing to the defendant's house. The victim's repeating of this woman's statement was inadmissible hearsay because it had been introduced with a view to asserting that the woman's statement was true. By contrast, in a case where a person was charged with unlawful possession of firearms and the defendant was relying on the defence of duress,[145] it was held that he should be allowed to give evidence of threats made to him by a group of alleged terrorists. In that case, the reported threats were admissible because the purpose of referring to them was to establish that they had been made rather than that they were true. No doubt the distinction is a fine one, but what the defendant said about the reported threats is not a question of admissibility of the evidence but about the weight to be attached to it; in that case, the real question is whether the evidence, and the persons giving it, are believable.

[6.133] An effect of the hearsay rule is that, in general, a witness will not be allowed testify to the truth of something where the direct witness has not been called to prove the truth of the fact stated. This has led courts to exclude what might otherwise appear to be reliable evidence. Thus, in a drink driving prosecution, blood or urine samples to establish the blood-alcohol level of the driver must be taken by a registered medical practitioner. Failure to comply with a direction from a registered medical practitioner to supply a blood or urine sample is, itself, an offence. In any subsequent prosecution for refusal to comply with a direction, the evidence of the person who demanded the sample is crucial.

[6.134] How is it proved that the person who later gives evidence in court of requesting the sample and being refused, and who asserts that he or she is a registered medical practitioner, is in fact what they claim to be? Surely the answer is: if he or she is on the register of medical practitioners that is conclusive. However, a register (whether in the form of a computer printout or any other form) is hearsay in the sense that it is a record of information. If the person who entered the information originally (the registrar at the time of registration) is unavailable to testify that he or she entered that information, then the register would be inadmissible hearsay as it amounts to an assertion concerning the truthfulness of its contents. This particular hearsay problem has been dealt with by

---

[144] *R v Gibson* (1887) 18 QBD 537.

[145] *Subramaniam v Public Prosecutor* [1956] 1 WLR 965.

legislation,[146] but it illustrates the difficulty of the hearsay rule in a society where computerised records are relied on in many different contexts but where the hearsay rule may render them inadmissible in the absence of special legislation. In addition to such statutory exceptions, we have already mentioned that numerous exceptions to the hearsay rule have been developed at common law, such as the rule allowing the admissibility of confessions in criminal cases. Further reform of this area may be necessary in the near future.[147]

Opinion evidence

[6.135] Another exclusionary rule is that which prevents the admissibility of opinion evidence, to which there are a number of exceptions. The most significant exception is that 'expert' witnesses are permitted to give evidence of their opinion on certain matters within their area of expertise. In a civil claim for negligence, for example, a medical consultant may express an opinion as to whether a medical procedure was performed in accordance with current standards of medical practice. In many criminal prosecutions, the evidence of a forensic scientist as to whether the results of certain DNA fingerprinting can connect the defendant to the crime may be crucial.[148] By contrast with the 'expert' witness, the 'ordinary' witness may not express an opinion on any evidence they give.

Legislative alterations to the rules of evidence

[6.136] In addition to the legislative amendments to overcome the extremities of the hearsay rule, in recent years legislation has been enacted to encourage certain items to be agreed in advance of court proceedings, in order to facilitate more efficient discharge of business and prevent unduly lengthy court hearings. Thus, ss 21 and 22 of the Criminal Justice Act 1984 provide for proof of certain matters by way of formal statement and formal admission. It should be noted that these statements and admissions are not sworn statements and they do not relate in any way to the admission of confessions as evidence. Similarly, rules of court have been made which provide that in civil proceedings concerning personal injuries certain documents, such as medical reports, must be exchanged prior to court hearings rather than requiring both sides to call medical consultants in court to confirm the information contained in their reports.[149]

---

146 Criminal Evidence Act 1992.

147 The Law Reform Commission, in its *Report on the Rule against Hearsay in Civil Cases* (LRC 25-1988) proposed a number of significant changes limited to civil claims. The Commission expects to publish in 2014 a *Report on the Law of Evidence* which will include reform of hearsay in civil and criminal proceedings: see fn 138, above.

148 On the establishment of a limited DNA database, see Law Reform Commission, *Report on the Establishment of a DNA Database* (LRC 78-2005), which also discusses the existing wide use of DNA testing in criminal trials since the 1990s. On foot of this, the Criminal Justice (Forensic Evidence and DNA Database System) Act 2014 provides for the establishment of a limited DNA database.

149 See para **6.59**.

The sequence of witnesses

[6.137] The adversarial system requires that witnesses are called in a certain sequence to give their evidence, rather than there being a free-for-all. In a civil case, the witnesses for the plaintiff are called by the plaintiff's advocate to give evidence. After examination by the plaintiff's lawyer (which is called examination-in-chief), the witness for the plaintiff may then be cross-examined by the lawyer appearing for the defendant. A similar procedure operates in relation to the witnesses for the defendant, if any. In civil cases it is quite common for all parties to give evidence. A similar procedure of examination-in-chief and cross-examination applies to criminal prosecutions, with the prosecution being required to present its witnesses first. However, in a criminal trial the defendant is not obliged to go into evidence.

The accusatorial nature of criminal trials

[6.138] The procedure in criminal cases is governed to a large extent by the accusatorial nature of the common law criminal justice system. Under the accusatorial approach (as opposed to the inquisitorial system of civil law criminal justice systems),[150] where a person is charged with having committed a crime, this must be established by independently gathered evidence and without resorting to evidence from the defendant.

[6.139] This approach is also regarded as an important expression of the presumption of innocence, another central feature of the common law system of criminal justice. The presumption of innocence is modified somewhat by allowing the prosecution to rely on confessions or incriminating statements made by the accused person to, for example, a member of the Garda Síochána while the accused was in custody under a lawful arrest.

[6.140] Under the accusatorial system, the presumption of innocence means that the defendant is entitled to refuse to give evidence in a criminal trial and, at the end of the evidence for the prosecution, the case may go to the jury who must make a decision without reference in some instances to the defendant's version of events. The defendant is entitled to be acquitted by the jury if the prosecution has failed to prove its case beyond a reasonable doubt. This means that even if the jury considers that the prosecution has made a case which requires some explanation from the defendant, the defendant is still entitled to be found not guilty if there is a reasonable doubt in their mind.

[6.141] It may be noted that in a civil law system operating the inquisitorial system, the accused person may be asked a number of questions by an investigating judge, which the accused person is, in general, obliged to answer. While this is quite different from the position in Irish law, it would be a caricature of the civil law system to describe it as operating a presumption of guilt. Indeed, the extensive use of confessions evidence in

---

150 It should be borne in mind that it is only in criminal proceedings that the civil law systems apply an inquisitorial approach in which judges take an active investigative role. In civil proceedings, the civil law courts apply the adversarial model, and in such cases the judge plays the non-interventionist role familiar to common law systems.

the common law world has led some commentators to note that formal procedural safeguards in the civil law system may, in certain respects, give greater protection to the accused person's state of innocence.[151]

[7] JUDGE AND JURY[152]

[6.142] Some comments on the function of the judge and jury in civil and criminal cases are appropriate. As we have already seen,[153] juries in civil cases are quite unusual since the enactment of the Courts Act 1988, only being retained in a limited number of High Court cases. In criminal cases, the jury is present in serious trials in the Central Criminal Court and the Circuit Court (the Special Criminal Court is a non-jury court that deals with serious crimes, usually connected with organised groups).

Representative nature of jury

[6.143] The Juries Act 1927 provided that juries were to be drawn principally from panels of property (that is, land) owners, and indeed the level of property which qualified a person for jury service varied from one area of the state to another. The effect of the 1927 Act was that it effectively excluded women from jury service, as very few women qualified under the property-owning requirement. In its *Second Interim Report*, published in 1965, the Committee on Court Practice and Procedure recommended that jury service be available to all adult citizens, including women.[154] This and other important reforms to the jury selection process were due to be implemented in the Juries Bill 1975, and this was given added momentum when later in 1975 in *de Búrca v Attorney General*,[155] the Supreme Court found the 1927 Act to be in breach of the requirement in Article 38.5 of the Constitution requiring a jury trial. In particular, the court found that the property qualifications and effective barring of women from juries deprived such juries of the representative character, that is trial by a representative cross-section of the community, which was essential to the concept of a jury contained in Article 38.5. As a result of the *de Búrca* case, s 6 of the Juries Act 1976 now provides that jury members are to be drawn primarily from the electoral roll, that is persons over the age of 18 who are registered to vote in elections to Dáil Éireann. This means that persons living in Ireland who are not Irish or British citizens are not currently entitled to be jury members. The introduction of the 1976 Act has resulted in an increasing number of young people and women forming the juries which sit in criminal and civil cases.

---

[151] See generally, Van den Wyngaert *et al*, *Criminal Procedure Systems in the European Community* (1993).

[152] See generally, Devlin, *The Judge* (1979). On the relative demise of the jury, see Casey, 'Jury Reform' (2000) 18 ILT 122.

[153] Para **4.62**.

[154] The minority report to the 1965 Report of the Committee contains a dissent regarding the place of married women which no longer reflects reality.

[155] *de Búrca v Attorney General* [1976] IR 38.

Unqualified, ineligible, disqualified and excused persons

[6.144] The Juries Act 1976 also provides that certain persons are not qualified, are ineligible or are otherwise disqualified to sit on juries. Section 6 of the 1976 Act provided that persons on the electoral register for general elections over the age of 70 were not qualified to serve on juries. The age limit was removed by s 54 of the Civil Law (Miscellaneous Provisions) Act 2008, so that every citizen aged 18 or upwards on the electoral register for general elections is qualified to serve as a juror. Section 7 of the 1976 Act provides that certain named persons listed in Pt I of the First Schedule to the Act are ineligible to serve. These include the President of Ireland, judges or former judges, coroners, the Attorney General and members of his staff, the Director of Public Prosecutions and members of his staff, barristers and solicitors practising as such, court officers, court stenographers, members of the Garda Síochána, prison officers, probation officers, persons employed in a forensic science laboratory and members of the Defence Forces. As a result of another amendment to the 1976 Act made by the 2008 Act, there is no longer a blanket ban on persons who have a reading incapacity or an enduring impairment. The 2008 Act amended the 1976 Act so that such persons are ineligible only where it is not practicable for them to perform the duties of a juror.[156] Similarly, the provision in the 1976 Act to the effect that a person with a hearing impairment was unfit to serve on a jury was removed by the 2008 Act.[157] Section 8 of the 1976 Act provides that a person is disqualified from jury service if he or she at any time has been sentenced to a term of imprisonment for five years or more or, within the preceding 10 years, to a term of imprisonment of three months.

[6.145] Section 9 of the Juries Act 1976 authorises a County Registrar to excuse any person from jury service, provided the person meets certain criteria. Certain persons listed in Pt II of the First Schedule to the Act are excusable as of right. These include members of either House of the Oireachtas, members of the Council of State, the Comptroller and Auditor General, the Clerk of Dáil Éireann, the Clerk of Seanad Éireann, a person in Holy Orders, a regular minister of any religious denomination or community, a vowed member of a religious order living in a monastery, convent of other religious community, whole-time students, ships masters, aircraft pilots and persons

---

[156] Prior to 2008, the First Schedule to the 1976 Act stated that persons 'who because of insufficient capacity to read, deafness or other permanent infirmity' were unfit to serve on a jury.

[157] See *Clarke v County Registrar County Galway* (14 July 2010) HC, *The Irish Times*, 15 July 2010 where the High Court quashed a decision of the County Registrar to excuse the applicant, who was deaf, from jury duty. However the High Court did not find Ms Clarke was eligible for service as it was likely an interpreter to assist would be required and this would breach the rule of secrecy of jury deliberations. By contrast in *The People (DPP) v O'Brien (Application of Dunne)* (29 November 2010) Central Criminal Court, Carney J was satisfied the concerns over the presence of an interpreter in the jury room could be "met by an appropriate oath being taken by the signer in which he would submit himself to the same obligations of confidentiality as rest on the other jurors." See Law Reform Commission, Report on Jury Service (LRC 107-2013) pp 51–52.

aged 65 and upwards.[158] The list also includes the following professional persons if actually practising: doctors, dentists, nurses, midwives, veterinary surgeons and pharmacists. Various other categories are excusable as of right provided that it is certified that their functions cannot reasonably be postponed or performed by another person. The latter include a member of the staff of either House of the Oireachtas, Heads of government departments and other civil servants, chief executive officers and employees of local authorities, health boards and harbour authorities, school teachers and university lecturers.

[6.146] In addition, s 9 of the Juries Act 1976 also excuses as of right, persons who have served on a jury within the preceding three years or who have been excused by a judge at the conclusion of a previous period of service for a period that has not ended. It also provides that the County Registrar or the trial judge may also excuse any other person if satisfied there is 'good reason' for so excusing the person. Finally, s 9(8) provides that, at the conclusion of a case 'of an exceptionally exacting nature', the trial judge may excuse the jury members from jury service 'for such period as the judge may think fit'.

[6.147] In 2013, the Law Reform Commission in a *Report on Jury Service*[159] recommended significant reform of the jury selection system. Among the recommendations in the Report are that jury panels should be based on the electoral registers for Dáil, local and European elections, which would allow not only Irish citizens but also EU citizens and other long-term residents to be selected for jury service. The Commission's Report estimated that this would add about 200,000 persons to those qualified for jury service. The Report also recommended that jurors should be able to read, write, speak and understand English to the extent that they can carry out their functions and they should be reminded of this when summoned for jury service. The Report also recommended that the provisions in Pt II of the First Schedule to the Juries Act 1976 on excusal from jury service 'as of right' for many professionals and public servants should be repealed, and should be replaced instead by an individualised excusal 'for good cause'.

Selection of jury

[6.148] Section 11 of the Juries Act 1976 requires each County Registrar to draw up a panel of jurors for each court from the Dáil Éireann (General Election) electoral roll: this is referred to as empanelling of jurors. Section 12 provides that each person on the panel is then summoned to appear in court on a named date and any dates thereafter. Failure to appear on the date or dates in question is an offence, for which penalties are specified in s 34 of the Act. Section 15 provides that, on the date set for selection of a jury or juries from the panel, the method of selection is by 'balloting in open court'. This generally involves the selection of names from a box and each name is called out in court.

---

[158] As amended by Civil Law (Miscellaneous Provisions) Act 2008, s 64.
[159] *Report on Jury Service* (LRC 107-2013), available at www.lawreform.ie.

[6.149] Jury members may be challenged by any party in civil or criminal proceedings. Such challenges can be either 'without cause shown', that is where no reason to the objection is given, or 'for cause shown', where a reason must be advanced. Section 20 of the Juries Act 1976 provides that, in both civil and criminal cases, seven jurors may be challenged without cause, while s 21 provides that there is no limit to the number that may be challenged for cause.[160] It may be noted that the often lengthy pre-trial challenges to jurors in civil and criminal trials which occasionally occur in the courts of the United States of America are not a feature of jury trials in this jurisdiction or in those of the United Kingdom.

[6.150] In *Director of Public Prosecutions v Haugh and Haughey*,[161] the Director successfully challenged an order made by the first respondent, a judge of the Circuit Court, concerning a questionnaire which had been prepared for distribution to potential jurors in the pending trial of the second respondent. The second respondent was a former Taoiseach who had been charged with obstructing the activities of a tribunal of inquiry which had investigated him. The tribunal of inquiry had attracted extensive publicity and it was argued that the second respondent could not obtain a fair trial arising from the adverse comment on his activities in the various media. His defence lawyers argued that, to overcome the potential prejudice, a questionnaire should be distributed to potential juries which would include questions concerning their general knowledge of the second respondent and of the tribunal of inquiry in question. The respondent trial judge agreed to have such a questionnaire distributed, but the High Court held that this would constitute an unacceptable interference with the normal rules concerning jury selection under the Constitution and the Juries Act 1976. The High Court concluded that any alleged prejudice from the adverse media publicity concerning the second respondent could be dealt with at the trial in the more conventional form of appropriate directions from the judge to the actual jury selected that they must base their decision on the evidence presented in court. The court may have been influenced in this approach by the potential for the lengthy pre-trial jury selection process to be found in the United States. For the time being, at least, such processes remain unlikely to be adopted in Ireland.[162]

---

[160] In the United Kingdom, the Crown acknowledges that it also engages in the practice of 'jury vetting', by which the criminal records of potential jurors are examined prior to trial, with a view to excluding unsuitable jurors: see Slapper and Kelly, *The English Legal System* (8th edn, 2008). The Law Reform Commission's *Report on Jury Service* (LRC 107-2013), paras 6.34–6.42, discussed vetting of jury lists in Ireland.

[161] *Director of Public Prosecutions v Haugh and Haughey* [2000] 1 IR 184.

[162] The Law Reform Commission's *Report on Jury Service* (LRC 107-2013), paras 3.40–3.63, discussed this issue, including the arrangements for challenging jurors in the United States such as scientific jury selection (SJS) and the use of 'profilers'. The Commission favoured the approach taken in *Director of Public Prosecutions v Haugh and Haughey*. The Commission also noted, at para 3.55 fn 71, that the depiction in crime fiction of the effect of SJS (for example in John Grisham's *The Runaway Jury* (1996)) may not be as significant in real US trials as other mundane factors such as the choice of trial venue and the potential jury panel.

[6.151] The number of jury members in civil and criminal cases is not formally stated as 12, but this has been the tradition for many centuries.[163] Sections 17 to 19 of the Juries Act 1976 prescribe the form of oath or affirmation required of each jury member. In a criminal case, each jury member must swear as follows:

"I will well and truly try the issue whether the accused is (or are) guilty of the offence (or the several offences) charged in the indictment preferred against him (or her or them) and a true verdict give according to the evidence."

[6.152] In a civil claim, the oath required is as follows:

"I will well and truly try all such issues as shall be given to me to try and true verdicts give according to the evidence."

[6.153] Having been sworn, a foreman is selected by the jury members. The foreman acts as an informal chairperson of the jury. It should be noted that the deliberations of the jury are confidential and judges have often emphasised the secrecy of jury deliberations, even after a trial has been completed.[164]

Judge to direct jury on legal issues

[6.154] One of the judge's principal functions in a jury trial is to ensure that no inadmissible evidence is introduced and that the lawyers do not breach any of the relevant procedural rules. In addition, the judge must direct the jury on any points of law that arise. In civil cases, it may be to explain to the jury what in law amounts to defamation, while in a criminal case it may be to explain the ingredients of the offence of murder so that they can arrive at a proper verdict. At the end of the case in a civil or criminal case, it is also conventional for the judge to summarise the evidence given in court and indicate to the jury its obligation to arrive at a verdict in accordance with the evidence and not on the basis of any impression they might have obtained from any

---

[163] In 2013, the Juries Act 1976 was amended by the Courts and Civil Law (Miscellaneous Provisions) Act 2013 to provide for a 'super jury' of 15 for lengthy trials (to be reduced to 12 by balloting out any excess members at the end of the trial). This implemented a recommendation in the Law Reform Commission's *Report on Jury Service* (LRC 107-2013), and it was first used in 2014, in *The People (DPP) v Fitzpatrick, McAteer and Whelan* (a Circuit Criminal Court trial in which two of the defendants were found guilty of charges of providing loans contrary to s 60 of the Companies Act 1963, a so-called white collar crime). See also the provisions on majority verdicts, para **6.159**.

[164] For example, the judgment of O'Flaherty J in *O'Callaghan v Attorney General* [1993] 2 IR 17. While newspaper interviews with jury members remain a rarity in Ireland, there have been some cases where the confidentiality of the jury room has been broken in recent years. See Casey, 'The Sanctity of Jury Deliberations, Prejudice and Human Rights' (2001) 11(4) ICLJ 16, *R v Mirza, R v Connor and Rollock* [2004] 2 WLR 201 and *Attorney General v Scotcher* [2005] 1 WLR 1867. The Law Reform Commission's *Report on Jury Service* (LRC 107-2013), p 107 referred to an English case where a juror who contacted the defendant during the course of the trial through her Facebook account was convicted of contempt of court and sentenced to a term of imprisonment.

other source. In summary, therefore, the judge rules on the law while the jury determines the facts and returns its verdict.

Judge directing verdict

[6.155] In some instances the role of legal arbiter also allows the judge a more significant function. For example, in a civil case, if the judge considers that there is no basis on which the jury could find for the plaintiff the judge may withdraw the case from the jury and enter judgment for the defendant. The plaintiff can, of course, appeal such a decision. Once the judge allows the case to go to the jury, he or she cannot, however, instruct them to find for the plaintiff or defendant; that is a matter for the jury.

[6.156] In a criminal trial, the equivalent rule allows the judge to withdraw a case from the jury and direct them to find the accused not guilty, where the judge has arrived at the conclusion that no jury could reasonably convict the defendant. By contrast with a civil case, the prosecution has no power to appeal such a direction to the jury to find the accused not guilty.[165] Once the judge decides to let the case go to the jury, he or she cannot direct the jury to find the accused guilty; again, that is a matter for the jury.

[6.157] Anecdotal evidence from practitioners would appear to indicate that some judges will 'sway' a jury in a particular direction, whether in civil or criminal cases. While hard evidence on this is difficult to come by, there have been some instances in which, for example, a trial judge who emphasised the strength of the prosecution case in a criminal trial was held not to have overstepped the line into the jury's domain.[166] However, more common are cases where convictions are overturned where they appear to have resulted from overly robust directions by the trial judge to the jury.

Scope of jury's decision-making

[6.158] In the Irish legal system the jury in a civil case is empowered not merely to determine the liability issue but also to determine the level or quantum of damages to be awarded to a successful plaintiff. Of course, any such verdicts are subject to appeal. Nonetheless, the allegedly widely varying levels of such awards in personal injuries cases was one of the grounds on which it was provided in the Courts Act 1988 that jury trial in such civil cases be significantly curtailed.[167] As for criminal trials, we have already seen that the jury determines whether a person is convicted or acquitted; but it is for the trial judge in a criminal trial, rather than the jury, to determine the appropriate sentence to be imposed on the convicted person. This may be contrasted with other common law systems, in which certain sentencing decisions are within the province of the jury; thus, in certain states of the United States of America, juries determine whether the death penalty should be imposed in the particular circumstances of a capital case.

---

[165] See para **7.54**, subject to the limited modification of the double jeopardy rule in the Criminal Procedure Act 2010, discussed in para **7.60**.

[166] See, eg, *The People (DPP) v Doran* (1987) 3 Frewen 125.

[167] See para **4.62**.

Majority verdicts

[6.159] In a civil action, s 95 of the Courts of Justice Act 1924 provides that the verdict may by reached by a majority of nine of the 12 members. In a criminal case, s 25 of the Criminal Justice Act 1984, which introduced majority verdicts in criminal cases for the first time, provides that a verdict may be given where 10 of the members are agreed on the verdict. Special safeguards are built into the 1984 Act requiring the trial judge, *inter alia*, to be satisfied that the jury has considered the case for a reasonable period of time, and not less than two hours.[168]

Trial by judge alone

[6.160] Since 1988, in most civil cases the judge sits alone, without a jury.[169] In addition, criminal cases coming before the Special Criminal Court are dealt with by three judges. In these cases the judge (or judges) is (or are) both the legal arbiter and the person (or persons) with the responsibility to arrive at the verdict.

---

[168] The constitutional validity of s 25 was upheld in *O'Callaghan v Attorney General* [1993] 2 IR 17.

[169] See para **4.62**.

Chapter 7

The Appellate Jurisdiction of the Courts

[1]   Introduction 341
[2]   Appellate Jurisdiction in Civil Cases 346
[3]   Appellate Jurisdiction in Criminal Cases 357
[4]   Appellate Jurisdiction of Courts from Adjudicative Bodies 369
[5]   Analysis that led to Reforms of the Appellate Process 369
[6]   Appellate Jurisdiction of the EU Court of Justice 373

[1]   INTRODUCTION

[7.01] In Chapter 5 we described the original or first instance jurisdiction of the courts in civil and criminal matters. It is also a feature of the court system that the decisions of a court may be appealed to a higher court. Mirroring the approach in Chapter 5, we first discuss the appellate jurisdiction of the courts in civil cases and then proceed to the appellate jurisdiction in criminal cases. We then note that an extensive appellate jurisdiction arises in connection with appeals from adjudicative bodies other than courts.[1] As also noted in Chapter 5, in 2010 the Law Reform Commission published a *Report on the Consolidation and Reform of the Courts Acts*,[2] including a draft Courts (Consolidation and Reform) Bill, which as far as appellate jurisdiction is concerned took account of the 2009 Report that recommended the establishment of a Court of Appeal.[3] In Chapter 4, we noted that this recommendation was implemented in 2013, and that Article 34.2 of the Constitution now provides for a Court of Appeal with jurisdiction in both civil and criminal matters, thus incorporating the role of the Court of Criminal Appeal.[4] At the time of writing (September 2014) it is envisaged that the Court of Appeal will be established by the end of 2014. We therefore discuss in this chapter the effect of the Court of Appeal. Finally, we also consider the arrangements under which

---

[1]   On the functions of such bodies, see Ch 8.
[2]   LRC 97-2010, available at www.lawreform.ie.
[3]   *Report of the Working Group on a Court of Appeal* (2009), available at www.courts.ie.
[4]   Article 34.2 as amended by the Thirty-Third Amendment of the Constitution (Court of Appeal) Act 2013, which provided for the establishment of the Court of Appeal and which was approved by a referendum held in 2013. Article 64.3.1° of the Constitution, also inserted by the Thirty-Third Amendment of the Constitution (Court of Appeal) Act 2013, provides that after the Court of Appeal has been established, the Chief Justice may direct that appeals pending in the Supreme Court at that time may be transferred to the Court of Appeal for decision.

the Court of Justice of the European Union may hear appeals from the courts in Ireland as well as from other adjudicative bodies.[5]

Constitutional setting

[7.02] In relation to the courts of local and limited jurisdiction, Article 34.3.4° of the Constitution provides that they are to have 'a right of appeal as may be determined by law'. As discussed in Chapter 4, the establishment of the Court of Appeal has a significant effect on the appeals process. Article 34.4 to Article 34.6 of the Constitution, as amended in 2013,[6] indicate the importance of the High Court, the Court of Appeal and the Supreme Court in the court system. The High Court is conferred with 'full original jurisdiction in and power to determine all matters and questions whether of law or fact, civil or criminal'. This includes the power to decide whether any law is invalid having regard to the Constitution. The Court of Appeal is given full appellate jurisdiction from all High Court decisions, but the Supreme Court may also hear appeals, either by way of direct appeal from the High Court (a 'leapfrogging appeal' similar to that of the UK Supreme Court) or from the Court of Appeal. In both instances, such appeals are possible if the Supreme Court (not the High Court or the Court of Appeal) is satisfied that (i) the decision involves a matter of general public importance, or (ii) in the interests of justice it is necessary that there be an appeal to the Supreme Court. Thus, after this 2013 amendment to Article 34 it is envisaged that the Supreme Court can exercise control over the flow of appeals to it. These general provisions have been greatly amplified by the Courts of Justice Act 1924 and the Courts (Supplemental Provisions) Act 1961, and other legislative provisions that were carried over from before the establishment of the state in 1922.[7]

Two forms of appeal

[7.03] The forms of appeal may be divided into two general types, full rehearings (*de novo* hearings) and appeals on points of law.

De novo hearing

[7.04] First, there are some instances where either party may seek to have the case, whether it is civil or criminal, reheard in full in a higher court. This is called a hearing *de novo*, and as its name signifies, this form of appeal involves a complete rehearing of the case to the extent that it is as if the first hearing in the lower court had not taken place at all. In other words, the hearing *de novo* is conducted as if it was a first instance hearing. Such appeals are possible in connection with cases heard at first instance in the District Court or the Circuit Court. It follows that, in a *de novo* hearing in the Circuit Court on appeal from the District Court, the case will be heard 'from start to finish' including any

---

5   On European Union law, see Ch 16.

6   See the text of Article 34.4 to Article 34.6 at para **4.36**, as amended by the Thirty-Third Amendment of the Constitution (Court of Appeal) Act 2013, which provided for the establishment of the Court of Appeal and which was approved by a referendum held in 2013.

7   Notably, the Summary Jurisdiction Act 1857.

oral evidence from witnesses. The advantage of a *de novo* hearing is that it is an opportunity for a 'second bite at the cherry' in the Circuit Court. There are, however, some limits on the appellate court's powers in such instances. In particular, while the Circuit Court may reach a decision different to that in the District Court, its jurisdiction is confined to that which is conferred on the District Court. Thus, in civil matters it is subject to the general €15,000 ceiling that operates (since 2014) in the District Court, while in criminal matters its sentencing powers are also confined to those in the District Court.

Appeal on point of law

[7.05] The second form of appeal is an appeal on a point of law. This is a more limited form of appeal, and involves a resolution by the higher appeal court of some issue of law rather than a complete rehearing of the entire case. Two important and connected points should be noted concerning the functions of an appellate court when hearing an appeal on a point of law. It is clear that a complete rehearing must be different in certain respects to a hearing on a point of law. The difference is in relation to the finding of facts made by the court whose decision is under appeal. The appellate court does not hear any witnesses, but is generally given a transcript of the evidence as taken by the stenographer at the trial hearing or, in certain cases, a note of the evidence taken by the solicitors involved in the case under appeal. In examining the transcript the appellate court will, of course, be able to ascertain whether the findings of fact made by the trier of fact (the trial judge or jury as the case may be) have some foundation in the evidence which was given. But once there is a foundation in the evidence given, the appellate court will not generally interfere with the findings of fact made in the lower court.[8]

[7.06] The rationale for that arrangement is that the trier of fact will have had an opportunity to see the witnesses give their evidence and to detect the nuances of human reaction to examination and cross-examination which may not be obvious in a transcript. A range of non-verbal factors that might feature in the evaluation of a witness testimony cannot be conveyed in the transcript: demeanour, body language, eye contact and the confidence with which questions are answered are matters that a trier of fact will take into account in deciding whether to believe a witness. The appellate court will, therefore, leave intact what are called the primary findings of fact. There is, however, another category of findings which the appellate court does have certain control over; these are what are called secondary findings. These are the findings that arise by way of inference from the primary findings, and they do not depend on an assessment of the witness's candour in giving evidence.

Findings of primary fact

[7.07] The trier of fact might decide to rely on the evidence of one particular witness and not accept the evidence of another. This is, in effect, a finding of primary fact which will, in general, not be interfered with by an appellate court, even if, looking at the

---

[8] See generally *Mara v Hummingbird Ltd* [1982] ILRM 498.

transcript, it feels that the evidence of the witness whose testimony was not accepted appeared plausible. If the issue is one of credibility and there are two possible versions of what happened but the trial judge relies on one instead of another, the appellate court will not generally interfere with that decision.[9] However, there are some exceptional circumstances in which an appellate court would reverse the findings of primary fact. This would only arise where the evidence in the trial court was so overwhelmingly in one direction that the trier of fact, in relying on evidence that was in the other direction, came to conclusions that could not be upheld.[10]

Findings of secondary fact

[7.08] By contrast to findings of primary fact, the trier of fact may draw a particular inference from the evidence given; this is a finding of secondary fact. On an appeal, the appellate court may consider that this inference is not warranted in the circumstances and in that situation the secondary finding can be overturned and a different conclusion reached.

[7.09] This was the position in *Hanrahan v Merck Sharp & Dohme Ltd.*[11] In that case, the plaintiffs, who were dairy farmers, had sued the defendant, a pharmaceutical company, claiming that emissions from the company's factory had caused them, and their farm animals, to suffer a number of respiratory illnesses. The plaintiffs relied on various items of evidence to support this claim, including that of local people who testified as to noxious smells in the vicinity of the defendant's factory at the same time that they saw animals in distress. Other evidence included the opinion of a specialist in respiratory illnesses who had treated John Hanrahan, one of the plaintiffs, and who testified that, in his opinion, if there were fumes and chemicals present in the atmosphere the balance of probabilities favoured the conclusion that John Hanrahan's lung disease could be attributed to a toxic substance. In its defence, the company accepted that the plaintiffs and their animals had suffered illness but claimed that these were not connected with the factory. The company presented detailed scientific evidence of readings taken on the plaintiffs' farm which aimed to show in particular that, while there were greater concentrations of certain acid vapours in the plaintiffs' soil, any emissions were well within accepted guidelines and could not have affected the health of the plaintiffs or their farm animals.

[7.10] The High Court judge concluded that the plaintiffs had failed to prove their case. As to the specialist's opinion, the judge noted that the plaintiffs' family doctor had not been called to give evidence on their behalf and, in his view, this omission weakened the

---

9   See *Northern Bank Finance Corp Ltd v Charlton* [1979] IR 149, where the Supreme Court declined to overturn findings of primary fact by the High Court trial judge in that case. See also *Browne v Bank of Ireland Finance Ltd* [1991] 1 IR 431; *Hay v O'Grady* [1992] 1 IR 210.
10   See *M v M* [1979] ILRM 160 and *Norris v Attorney General* [1984] IR 36, *per* Henchy J; *In Re DG, an Infant; OG v An Bórd Uchtála* [1991] 1 IR 491.
11   *Hanrahan v Merck Sharp & Dohme Ltd* [1988] ILRM 629. For an account of the case, see O'Callaghan, *The Red Book* (1992).

specialist's opinion. On the illness and abnormalities in their animals, the judge concluded that the company's scientific evidence indicated that there was no connection between the emissions and these illnesses. The plaintiffs appealed to the Supreme Court[12] and were largely successful in having the High Court decision reversed. The Supreme Court took the view that the High Court judge should have given less priority to the abstract *ex post facto* scientific evidence and given more weight to the direct sensory evidence of locals and the opinion expressed by the specialist. Delivering the only judgment in the Supreme Court, Henchy J stated:[13]

> "[T]he scientific evidence ... even if accepted in full ... only shows what *could* or *should* have happened in the way of damage by toxic emissions. In the light of what *did* happen in the way of toxic damage, I consider that the defendant's evidence could not be held to rebut the plaintiff's case. Theoretical or inductive evidence cannot be allowed to displace proven facts. It was proven as a matter of probability that John Hanrahan suffered ill-health as a result of toxic emissions from the factory ... And there was a volume of uncontroverted evidence given by eyewitnesses that animals were seen and heard to be ill and in distress at a time when the observer was experiencing foul chemical smells or weeping eyes or irritated skin, which could have been caused only by the factory. It would be to allow scientific evidence to dethrone fact to dispose of this claim by saying, as was said in the judgment under appeal, that there was 'virtually no evidence in this case of injury to human beings or animals which had been scientifically linked to any chemicals emanating from the defendants factory."

On this basis, the Supreme Court was prepared to draw different inferences from the evidence and arrive at a different conclusion to that of the High Court judge in this case.[14]

[7.11] Similarly, where the trier of fact has drawn factual inferences from agreed evidence and there are no questions concerning the candour or the plausibility of the witnesses who gave the evidence, the Supreme Court may be prepared to reverse the findings of the High Court judge.[15]

---

12   With the projected establishment of the Court of Appeal in 2014, such appeals would be to the Court of Appeal, which is likely to take a similar approach.

13   [1988] ILRM 629, 644–645. Finlay CJ and Hederman J concurred with the judgment delivered by Henchy J.

14   Since the Supreme Court found in the plaintiff's favour, it remitted the case to the High Court for an assessment of damages. The case was ultimately settled without a further court hearing: see O'Callaghan, *The Red Book* (1992).

15   See *Mullen v Quinnsworth Ltd (No 2)* [1991] ILRM 439; *Coleman v Clarke* [1991] ILRM 841; *Best v Wellcome Foundation Ltd* [1993] 3 IR 421.

[2] APPELLATE JURISDICTION IN CIVIL CASES

Claim initiated in the District Court

[7.12] For claims heard at first instance in the District Court, both forms of appellate options are available. Either party may obtain a hearing *de novo* in the Circuit Court, and the decision of the Circuit Court is, in general, final and may not be further appealed. Alternatively, either party may appeal on a point of law to the High Court, in which case a further appeal on a point of law to the Supreme Court is also possible. We should also note that, in the context of a claim involving European Union law, an appeal to the EU Court of Justice may also arise, but we discuss that issue separately.[16]

Hearing de novo in Circuit Court

[7.13] In general, an appeal lies to the Circuit Court from all decisions of the District Court in civil matters,[17] subject to quite limited exceptions.[18] Under the present statutory arrangements, therefore, virtually all decisions of the District Court in civil claims may be appealed for a *de novo* hearing in the Circuit Court.[19] However, it would seem that, provided some form of appeal mechanism remains open, such as an appeal on a point of law, it would be permissible to restrict the present generous arrangements for *de novo* appeals.[20] The decision of the Circuit Court judge on appeal from the District Court is 'final and conclusive and not appealable'.[21]

---

16   On the appellate jurisdiction of the EU Court of Justice, including the likelihood of a case begun in the District Court being referred to it, see para **7.74**.

17   Courts of Justice Act 1924, s 84 as amended by the Courts of Justice Act 1936, s 57.

18   For example, Milk and Dairies Act 1935, s 41.

19   Although the Courts of Justice Act 1924, s 84 does not expressly state that the appeal to the Circuit Court involves a *de novo* hearing of the case, s 83 of the 1924 Act (since replaced by the Courts (Supplemental Provisions) Act 1961, s 52) provided for an appeal on a point of law by case stated from the District Court to the High Court. This indicated an intention to provide for a different form of appeal in s 84. See Delany, *The Courts Acts 1924–1997* (2nd edn, 2000), p 40.

20   In *Murphy v Bayliss* (22 July 1976, unreported), SC, the court held that, although the Extradition Act 1965, s 47(5) precluded a hearing *de novo* in the Circuit Court after a District Court hearing under the section, this did not prohibit an appeal on a point of law by way of case stated to the High Court. O'Higgins CJ commented that a provision which prevented some type of appeal would seem to be in conflict with Article 34.3.4° of the Constitution. In respect of the European Union area, the Extradition (European Union Conventions) Act 2001 and the European Arrest Warrant Act 2003 have largely replaced the 1965 Act but it continues to apply in respect of extraditions to and from non-EU states.

21   Courts of Justice Act 1924, s 84 as amended by the Courts of Justice Act 1936, s 57. The finality of the Circuit Court's decision on appeal may be subject to judicial review by the High Court under Article 34.3.1° of the Constitution: see *Tormey v Ireland* [1985] IR 289: para **15.144**.

Appeal on point of law by case stated to High Court

[7.14] The second form of appeal, an appeal on a point of law, lies from the District Court to the High Court. The form in which the appeal on a point of law takes place is by means of a case stated. Such an appeal can be made by either party while the case is still in progress in the District Court, referred to as a consultative case stated,[22] or else at the end of the District Court hearing, when the judge has made a final determination in the case.[23] Either party to the civil proceedings can request the judge of the District Court to refer any question of law to the High Court for determination in this way, and the point of law must be so referred unless the judge considers the request frivolous.[24] The refusal to state a case may be subject to judicial review.[25] The judge of the District Court must have heard sufficient evidence to make findings of fact on the basis of which the questions of law set out in the consultative case stated can be decided.[26]

[7.15] In form, a 'case stated' consists of a written document which includes the question or questions of law for determination by the High Court. A case stated will contain a recitation of the facts as found by the District Court judge and will end with a question being posed, which must allow of a 'Yes' or 'No' answer. The question or questions will be put in the following manner: 'On the basis of the foregoing findings of fact, was I correct in law in concluding that ... ?' The question is put in the first person because, in formal terms, it is put to the High Court by the judge of the District Court. However, in practice the content of the case stated document is prepared by agreement between the lawyers representing both parties and this document is then presented to the judge to be 'signed and stated'.

[7.16] The case stated is then transmitted to the High Court, where a hearing on the point or points of law raised will occur. At this hearing, there will be no oral evidence, there being only arguments by both parties concerning the points of law raised. The High Court judge will then give his or her decision on the points of law raised, in effect giving a 'Yes' or 'No' answer to each question posed in the case stated. On the basis of these answers, the case is returned to the District Court for a final determination in the matter, which must of course be in accordance with the view expressed by the High Court. Since the 'case stated' mechanism involves the remittal of the case from the High Court to the District Court, it may be said that the case remains in the District Court at all times, since the formal final order will be made by the judge of the District Court who sent the case stated to the High Court. In that respect, the case stated differs from the *de novo* hearing; where the Circuit Court makes a decision on appeal after a *de novo*

---

22 Courts (Supplemental Provisions) Act 1961, s 52 replacing the Courts of Justice Act 1924, s 83.

23 Summary Jurisdiction Act 1857, s 2 as extended by the Courts (Supplemental Provisions) Act 1961, s 51. In this instance, the application for the cases stated must be made within 14 days of the decision of the District Court.

24 See *Sports Arena Ltd v O'Reilly* [1987] IR 185.

25 See *The State (Turley) v Ó Floinn* [1968] IR 245.

26 See *DPP (Travers) v Brennan* [1998] 4 IR 67.

hearing, the final court order is made in the Circuit Court and the case is not in any way returned to the District Court. The High Court is permitted to remit the case back to the District Court (in the case of a case stated reference) with the benefit of the opinion of the High Court on the issues raised in the questions referred. It would appear that a decision of a District Court Judge made after, and in consequence of, a High Court order may be appealed to the Circuit Court.[27]

Further appeal on point of law to Court of Appeal

[7.17] One important difference may be noted between the consultative case stated from the District Court and the case stated where there has been a final determination in the District Court. On a consultative case stated, the decision of the High Court can be appealed from the High Court to the Supreme Court, but only where the High Court judge grants leave (that is, permission) to appeal.[28] By contrast, on a case stated to the High Court after a final determination of the District Court, a further appeal lies to the Supreme Court without the need to seek leave to appeal from the High Court.[29] For this reason, the appeal by way of case stated after a final determination is more commonly used.[30]

[7.18] As already noted,[31] a constitutional referendum to establish a Court of Appeal, with jurisdiction in criminal and civil matters, was passed in 2013 by the Thirty-Third Amendment of the Constitution (Court of Appeal) Act 2013. This implemented recommendations made in the 2009 *Report of the Working Group on a Court of Appeal*.[32] At the time of writing (September 2014) the Court of Appeal Act 2014 has been enacted and provides for the establishment of the Court of Appeal in accordance with Article 34A of the Constitution, inserted by the Thirty-Third Amendment of the Constitution (Court of Appeal) Act 2013.[33] It is envisaged that the Court of Appeal will be formally established by the end of 2014.[34] The Court of Appeal Act 2014 provides that such further appeals will in future be to the Court of Appeal, rather than the Supreme Court as at present.

---

[27] Collins and O'Reilly, *Civil Proceedings and the State* (2nd edn, 2004) at para 1–22.

[28] Courts (Supplemental Provisions) Act 1961, s 52(2). In *Minister for Justice v Wang Zhu Jie* [1993] 1 IR 426, this restriction was held to be within the limitations on the Supreme Court's appellate jurisdiction envisaged by Article 34.4.3° of the Constitution.

[29] Summary Jurisdiction Act 1857, s 2 as extended by the Courts (Supplemental Provisions) Act 1961, s 52. See *Attorney General (Fahy) v Bruen* [1936] IR 750.

[30] See Ryan and Magee, *The Irish Criminal Process* (1983), p 417.

[31] See para **4.34***ff*.

[32] Prn A8/0153, available at www.courts.ie.

[33] For the text of Article 32A see Ch 4, fn 74.

[34] Article 64.3.1° of the Constitution, also inserted by the Thirty-Third Amendment of the Constitution (Court of Appeal) Act 2013, provides that after the Court of Appeal has been established, the Chief Justice may direct that appeals pending in the Supreme Court at that time may be transferred to the Court of Appeal for decision.

[7.19] Figure 7.1 provides an outline of the appeal process from the District Court.

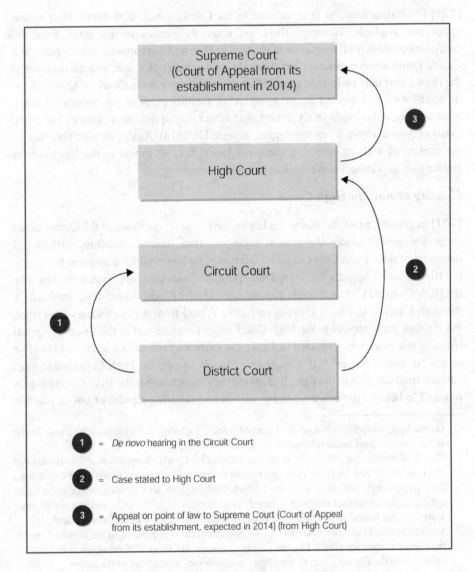

Appeals from the District Court: Civil
Figure 7.1

Claim initiated in the Circuit Court

[7.20] For claims heard at first instance in the Circuit Court, both forms of appellate option are available. However, there are some differences in the detail from the equivalent procedures that operate in relation to District Court appeals. Either party to a Circuit Court action may obtain a hearing *de novo* in the High Court, and the decision of the High Court may be further appealed in some instances to the Court of Appeal (from its establishment, expected in 2014, replacing for this purpose the Supreme Court). Alternatively, either party in a Circuit Court action may appeal on a point of law to the Court of Appeal (from its establishment, expected in 2014). Again, we note here that, in the context of a claim involving European Union law, an appeal to the EU Court of Justice may also arise, but we discuss that issue separately.[35]

Hearing de novo in High Court

[7.21] In general, an appeal lies to the High Court from all decisions of the Circuit Court in civil matters.[36] Under the present statutory arrangements, therefore, virtually all decisions of the Circuit Court in civil claims may be appealed for a *de novo* hearing in the High Court.[37] Appeals from non-Dublin Circuit Court cases are, in general, heard by the High Court on Circuit,[38] while appeals from Dublin Circuit Court cases are heard in the High Court in Dublin.[39] There is no further appeal from the High Court as of right, but if either party applies to the High Court judge for an appeal to the Court of Appeal (from its establishment, expected in 2014), the judge may refer any question of law if he or she 'so thinks proper'.[40] If a question of law is so put, the High Court judge must adjourn final decision in the case. It is not entirely clear whether the High Court judge is required to hear all the evidence in the case before referring a point of law or whether

---

[35]   On the appellate jurisdiction of the Court of Justice, including the likelihood of a case begun in the Circuit Court being referred to the Court of Justice, see para **7.74**.

[36]   Courts of Justice Act 1936, s 38 as carried forward by Courts (Supplemental Provisions) Act 1961, ss 22, 23 and 48 is the principal provision concerning appeals to the High Court from the Circuit Court. See also s 37 of the 1936 Act, which deals with appeals from Circuit Court actions in which no oral evidence is heard. In addition, s 31 of the 1936 Act deals with other instances, not falling within ss 37 or 38, where a decision of the Circuit Court is final.

[37]   Unlike the Courts of Justice Act 1924, s 84, which concerns appeals from the District Court to the Circuit Court (see para **7.13**), the Courts of Justice Act 1936, s 38 expressly states that the appeal from the Circuit Court to the High Court involves a rehearing of the action.

[38]   On the arrangements for the High Court on Circuit, see para **4.63**.

[39]   Courts of Justice Act 1936, s 38(1).

[40]   Courts of Justice Act 1936, s 38(3). Courts of Justice Act 1936, s 39 provides that appeals from the Circuit Court to the High Court are final and not appealable. The constitutionality of this section was upheld in *Eamonn Andrews Productions Ltd v Gaiety Theatre Productions Ltd* [1973] IR 295. See also *P v P* [2006] IESC 76.

this procedure can be utilised in a manner similar to a consultative case stated, that is before all the evidence in the case has been given.[41]

Appeal on point of law by case stated to Supreme Court

[7.22] The second form of appeal, on a point of law, lies from the Circuit Court to the Court of Appeal (from its establishment, expected in 2014). As with the appeal from the District Court to the High Court, the appeal is by way of case stated. If a question of law is so put, the Circuit Court judge must adjourn final decision in the case.[42] It is not clear, however, whether the Circuit Court judge is required to hear all the evidence in the case before referring a point of law to the Court of Appeal (from its establishment, expected in 2014), or whether this procedure can be utilised in a manner similar to a consultative case stated, that is before all the evidence in the case has been given.[43] The form of the case stated is similar to that where the District Court refers a point of law to the High Court on case stated.[44] As in that situation, the Court of Appeal (from its establishment, expected in 2014) gives its decision on the questions of law posed and the case is remitted to the Circuit Court for a final determination in accordance with the answers provided.

---

[41] The majority decision of the Supreme Court in *Dolan v Corn Exchange* [1975] IR 315 suggests that all evidence must be heard by the High Court judge before the question of law is posed for the Supreme Court, thus precluding the High Court from making further findings of fact when the case is returned. However, this view is at variance with the later majority decision of the Supreme Court in *Doyle v Hearne* [1987] IR 601: see fn 43.

[42] Courts of Justice Act 1947, s 16.

[43] We have already noted that, in relation to the similarly worded provisions of the Courts of Justice Act 1936, s 38(3), the majority decision of a three-judge Supreme Court in *Dolan v Corn Exchange* [1975] IR 315 suggests that all evidence must be heard by a High Court judge before a question of law is posed for the Supreme Court, thus precluding the High Court from making further findings of fact when the case is returned. A similar view on the Courts of Justice Act, s 16 was expressed by another three-judge Supreme Court in *Corley v Gill* [1975] IR 313. However, a later 3:2 majority decision of a five-judge Supreme Court in *Doyle v Hearne* [1987] IR 601 held that the correct interpretation of s 47 was that a Circuit Court judge could adjourn final determination in a case at any time and was not required to wait until all evidence had been heard. Although there is a clear difference of opinion between the *Doyle* majority and the majorities in both *Dolan* and *Corley*, the majority in *Doyle* did not expressly overrule the previous Supreme Court decisions. See also Delany, *The Courts Acts 1924–1997* (2nd edn, 2000), pp 87–88 and 119–121.

[44] See para **7.15**.

[7.23] Figure 7.2 provides an outline of the appeal process from the Circuit Court.

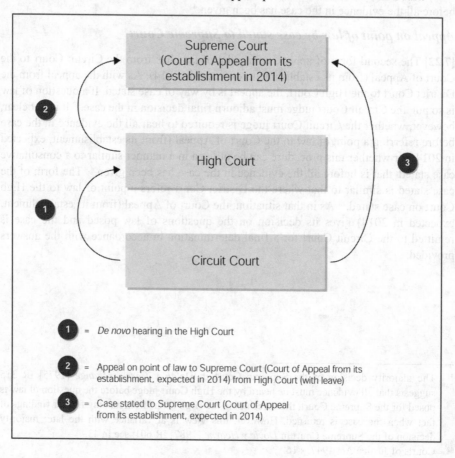

Appeals from the Circuit Court: Civil

Figure 7.2

Claim initiated in the High Court

[7.24] For claims heard at first instance in the High Court, only one type of appeal is possible, namely an appeal on a point of law. This arises from the fact that the only court available to which an appeal may be made is the Supreme Court, which only hears appeals on points of law, and this will remain the position with the Court of Appeal, which is expected to be established in 2014. In general, the Supreme Court will not permit the bringing of an appeal against a decision or ruling of the High Court made in the course of proceedings which are still ongoing before that court.[45] Again, we note

---

45   For an exception to this see *Condon v Minister for Labour* [1981] IR 62.

here that, in the context of a claim involving European Union law, an appeal to the EU Court of Justice may also arise, but we discuss that issue separately.[46]

Appeals on point of law to Supreme Court (and Court of Appeal when established)

[7.25] The Supreme Court, being the 'Court of Final Appeal' under Article 34.4.1° of the Constitution (subject to the jurisdiction of the EU Court of Justice), is not in general a court that hears cases at first instance.[47] It is therefore confined to hearing points of law: there are no witness boxes in the Supreme Court.[48] The same general position applies for appeals to the Court of Appeal when it is established, expected in 2014, because the Court of Appeal is not a court of first instance in any situation; it will remain the case, though, that the Supreme Court will be the only court of final appeal under Article 34.4.1° of the Constitution.

[7.26] Article 34.4 to Article 34.6 of the Constitution, as amended in 2013,[49] state:

"4.1° The Court of Appeal shall—

i save as otherwise provided by this Article, and

ii with such exceptions and subject to such regulations as may be prescribed by law,

have appellate jurisdiction from all decisions of the High Court, and shall also have appellate jurisdiction from such decisions of other courts as may be prescribed by law.

2° No law shall be enacted excepting from the appellate jurisdiction of the Court of Appeal cases which involve questions as to the validity of any law having regard to the provisions of this Constitution.

3° The decision of the Court of Appeal shall be final and conclusive, save as otherwise provided by this Article.

---

46 On the appellate jurisdiction of the Court of Justice, including the likelihood of a case being referred by the Supreme Court to the Court of Justice, see para **7.74**.

47 For the exceptional instances in which the Supreme Court is a court of first instance, see para **5.82**.

48 See generally *Northern Bank Finance Corporation Ltd v Charlton* [1979] IR 149; *AA v Medical Council* [2003] IESC 70. In exceptional circumstances, however, the Supreme Court may hear additional evidence, though even in such circumstances this would generally be in written form. On the principles applied by the Court, see *B v B* [1975] IR 54 (decided in 1970); *Dalton v Minister for Finance* [1989] IR 269; *Murphy v Minister for Defence* [1991] 2 IR 161.

49 This is the text of Article 34.2 as amended by the Thirty-Third Amendment of the Constitution (Court of Appeal) Act 2013, which provided for the establishment of the Court of Appeal and which was approved by a referendum held in 2013.

5.1° The Court of Final Appeal shall be called the Supreme Court.

2° The President of the Supreme Court shall be called the Chief Justice.

3° The Supreme Court shall, subject to such regulations as may be prescribed by law, have appellate jurisdiction from a decision of the Court of Appeal if the Supreme Court is satisfied that—

   i   the decision involves a matter of general public importance, or

   ii in the interests of justice it is necessary that there be an appeal to the Supreme Court.

4° Notwithstanding section 4.1° hereof, the Supreme Court shall, subject to such regulations as may be prescribed by law, have appellate jurisdiction from a decision of the High Court if the Supreme Court is satisfied that there are exceptional circumstances warranting a direct appeal to it, and a precondition for the Supreme Court being so satisfied is the presence of either or both of the following factors:

   i   the decision involves a matter of general public importance;

   ii the interests of justice."

[7.27] These provisions indicate the importance of the High Court, the Court of Appeal and the Supreme Court in the court system. The High Court is conferred with 'full original jurisdiction in and power to determine all matters and questions whether of law or fact, civil or criminal'. This includes the power to decide whether any law is invalid having regard to the Constitution. The Court of Appeal is given full appellate jurisdiction from all High Court decisions, although the Supreme Court may also hear appeals, either by way of direct appeal from the High Court (a 'leapfrogging appeal' similar to that from the English High Court to the UK Supreme Court) or from the Court of Appeal. In both such instances, such appeals are possible if the Supreme Court (not the High Court or the Court of Appeal) is satisfied that (i) the decision involves a matter of general public importance, or (ii) in the interests of justice it is necessary that there be an appeal to the Supreme Court. Thus, after this 2013 amendment to Article 34 it is envisaged that the Supreme Court can exercise control over the flow of appeals to it. It is also clear that, even after the amendments made in 2013, the Supreme Court retains jurisdiction to hear appeals from the High Court in constitutional cases, though in some instances these may be heard in the Court of Appeal instead (if the Supreme Court decides that it is not necessary to hear such a case because, for example, it does not appear to raise an entirely novel point).

[7.28] Article 34.4 and 34.5 also envisage that, apart from constitutional cases, appeals may, in general, be brought from all decisions of the High Court and of the Court of Appeal, but this is 'subject to such regulations as may be prescribed by law'. Although exceptions to the Court of Appeal's and the Supreme Court's jurisdiction can therefore be made, it would hardly be constitutional to enact a law that confined either Court's jurisdiction to constitutional cases. Indeed, the Supreme Court has made plain, in connection with the comparable pre-2013 constitutional provisions, that any exception to its appellate jurisdiction must be provided for in clear statutory language.[50] At present, it can be said therefore that virtually all decisions initiated in the High Court may be appealed to the Supreme Court, with a number of limited exceptions. This will continue for the Court of Appeal when it is established. For the Supreme Court, however, it is important to note that the amendments made in 2013 provide for the first time that the question as to whether the Supreme Court deals with a specific case will primarily be a matter for the Supreme Court itself to decide. This is a key change, bringing the Supreme Court into line with other comparable final courts of appeal in other jurisdictions, such as the UK Supreme Court and the US Supreme Court.

Liability and quantum

[7.29] Where a civil case involves a claim for damages, a typical appeal to the Supreme Court (and to the Court of Appeal when it is established in 2014) would involve the issue of liability (for example whether the defendant was in breach of a duty of care to the plaintiff in the circumstances which arose) and/or the issue of quantum (whether the amount of compensation awarded was correct). The appeal on liability is very like the appeal on points of law already discussed, and the appellate court enjoys a wide discretion in relation to the legal issues involved, subject of course to the constraints of precedent.[51] On the question of quantum, the appellate court's function in an appeal is limited to deciding whether the amount was within an acceptable range of damages; if so then the appeal will be dismissed even if the appellate court might, as a court of trial (looking at the matter originally, sometimes referred to as *res integra*), have awarded less (or more).

[7.30] Where the appellate court allows the appeal on the liability question, it may order a re-trial of the action in the High Court, which would normally be presided over by a different High Court judge. In effect, therefore, a successful appeal results in a hearing *de novo* in the High Court.[52] Where the appellate court considers that the quantum of

---

[50] See, eg, *The People (Attorney General) v Conmey* [1975] IR 341; *WJ Prendergast & Son Ltd v Carlow County Council* [1990] ILRM 749; *Minister for Justice v Wang Zhu Jie* [1993] 1 IR 426; *Irish Asphalt Ltd v An Bord Pleanála* [1996] 2 IR 179; *AB v Minister for Justice* [2002] 1 IR 296; and *Canty v Private Residential Tenancies Board* [2008] IESC 24. See also Delany, 'Regulation of the Supreme Court's Appellate Jurisdiction must be Clear and Unambiguous' (2002) 20 ILT 73.

[51] See Ch 12.

[52] See, eg, *Dunne v National Maternity Hospital* [1989] IR 91. Where a re-hearing is ordered, the second trial of the action may take quite a different course. For example, in the second hearing in the *Dunne* case, new witnesses had come forward arising from the publicity attaching to the case, which was a claim in negligence against the defendant hospital. For an account of the re-hearing in this case, which did not proceed to final decision and was ultimately settled without admission of liability, see Kerrigan, *Nothing But the Truth* (1990).

damages awarded in the High Court was excessive, it may, instead of ordering a re-trial on the issue, assess the correct level of damages itself.[53]

[7.31] Figures 7.3 and 7.4 provide outlines of the appeal process from the High Court: Figure 7.3 outlines the process *prior* to the establishment of the Court of Appeal, and Figure 7.4 outlines the process *after* the establishment of the Court of Appeal.

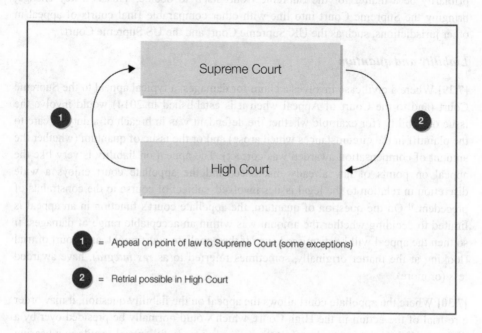

Supreme Court

High Court

1 = Appeal on point of law to Supreme Court (some exceptions)

2 = Retrial possible in High Court

Appeals from the High Court: Civil
(prior to establishment of Court of Appeal)
Figure 7.3

---

[53] See *Holohan v Donohoe* [1986] IR 45 and *Bakht v Medical Council* [1990] 1 IR 515. This approach is identical to that where the Supreme Court reviews findings of primary and secondary fact by a High Court judge: see paras **7.07–7.11**.

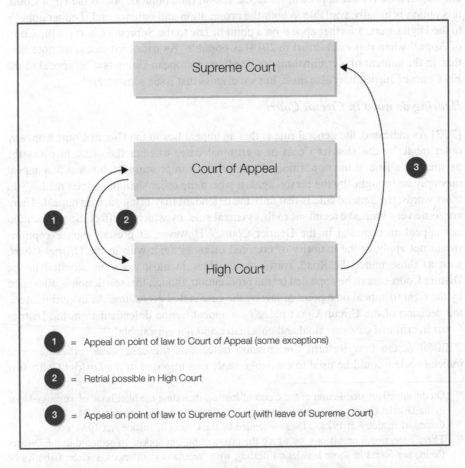

Supreme Court

Court of Appeal

High Court

1 = Appeal on point of law to Court of Appeal (some exceptions)

2 = Retrial possible in High Court

3 = Appeal on point of law to Supreme Court (with leave of Supreme Court)

**Appeals from the High Court: Civil (after establishment of Court of Appeal)
which is expected by the end of 2014
Figure 7.4**

[3]   APPELLATE JURISDICTION IN CRIMINAL CASES

Summary trials: District Court

[7.32] In respect of the criminal trials conducted summarily in the District Court, both forms of appellate options are available, subject to an important proviso. In general, a hearing *de novo* in the Circuit Court is available only in the event of a conviction in the District Court, and is thus generally only available to the defendant. Therefore if a judge of the District Court acquits an accused or makes no order, an appeal is not available to the prosecutor.[54] As with civil cases, the decision of the Circuit Court is, in general, final

---

54   *O'Leary v Cunningham* [1980] IR 367.

and may not be further appealed. As to the appeal on a point of law to the High Court, this option is usually available to both the prosecution and defence and if either appeals to the High Court, a further appeal on a point of law to the Supreme Court (to the Court of Appeal when it is established in 2014) is possible. As with civil cases, we note here that, in the context of a criminal matter involving European Union law, an appeal to the EU Court of Justice may also arise, but we discuss that issue separately.[55]

Hearing de novo in Circuit Court

[7.33] As indicated, the general rule is that an appeal lies to the Circuit Court from any order made by the District Court in a criminal case, whether the order involves the payment of a fine or the imposition of a sentence of imprisonment, but that this appeal may only be brought 'by the person against whom the order shall have been made'.[56] In other words, the general rule is that only the defendant may bring such an appeal. There are some very limited exceptions to this general rule, by which in effect the prosecution can appeal an acquittal in the District Court.[57] However, at present such exceptions would not apply to the majority of criminal offences dealt with in the District Court, such as those under the Road Traffic Acts. Thus, in most cases an acquittal in the District Court cannot be appealed by the prosecution, though this restriction is alleviated by the right to appeal on a point of law by the case stated procedure. As in civil matters, the decision of the Circuit Court judge[58] on appeal by the defendant from the District Court in criminal cases is 'final and conclusive and not appealable'.[59]

In 2006, the Law Reform Commission noted that the case stated procedure and judicial review could be used to challenge sentences imposed in the District Court that

---

[55]   On the appellate jurisdiction of the Court of Justice, including the likelihood of a criminal trial in the District Court requiring a reference to the Court of Justice, see para **7.74**.

[56]   Courts of Justice Act 1928, s 18, as amended by the Courts of Justice Act 1936, s 58.

[57]   These exceptional provisions, by which the prosecution can appeal an acquittal in the District Court, are found in some legislation dealing with 'regulatory' offences, such as fisheries or safety at work. Thus, the Fisheries (Consolidation) Act 1959, s 310 provides for an appeal by the prosecution against any District Court dismissal of a summons brought under the Act. In *Considine v Shannon Regional Fisheries Board* [1994] 1 ILRM 499 (HC); [1998] 1 ILRM 11 (SC), it was claimed that s 310 was invalid because it was in conflict with the requirement in Article 38.1 that criminal trials be 'in due course of law'. However, the High Court and Supreme Court dismissed the claim, agreeing with the defendants' contention that s 310 of the 1959 Act was valid under Article 34.3.4° of the Constitution, which provides that the appellate jurisdiction of the courts of local and limited jurisdiction may be 'determined by law'. On the use of precedent in the *Considine* case, see para **12.116**. To the same effect as s 310 of the 1959 Act, see the Safety, Health and Welfare at Work Act 2005, s 83.

[58]   Note that the Circuit Court, when hearing an appeal from the District Court in criminal matters, comprises a Circuit Court judge alone. It is only where the Circuit Court exercises its first instance criminal jurisdiction that it comprises a judge and jury: see para **5.101**.

[59]   Courts of Justice Act 1928, s 18 as amended by the Courts of Justice Act 1936, s 58. The finality of the Circuit Court's decision on appeal may be subject to judicial review by the High Court under Article 34.3.1° of the Constitution: see *Tormey v Ireland* [1985] IR 289.

are considered to be unduly lenient. On this basis, it concluded that it was not necessary to introduce an appeal *de novo* for such situations.[60]

Appeal on point of law by case stated to High Court

[7.34] As in civil cases, an appeal on a point of law by case stated lies to the High Court from decisions of the District Court in criminal matters and the relevant statutory provisions apply equally to criminal proceedings. Thus, in criminal cases the appeal can be made either while the criminal case is still in progress in the District Court, referred to as a consultative case stated,[61] or at the end of the District Court hearing, when the judge has made a final determination in the case.[62] Either the prosecution or defence can request the judge of the District Court to refer any question of law to the High Court for determination in this way and the point of law must be so referred unless the judge considers the request frivolous.[63] The form of the case stated has been referred to earlier.[64]

Further appeal on point of law to Supreme Court (to Court of Appeal when it is established)

[7.35] Again, as in civil cases, on a consultative case stated, the decision of the High Court can be appealed from the High Court to the Supreme Court (to the Court of Appeal when it is established in 2014), but only where the High Court judge grants leave to appeal.[65] By contrast, on a case stated to the High Court after a final determination of the District Court in a criminal case, a further appeal lies to the Supreme Court (to the Court of Appeal when it is established in 2014) without the need to seek leave to appeal from the High Court.[66] As stated in relation to civil cases, for this reason the appeal after a final determination is more commonly used.[67]

---

[60] Law Reform Commission, *Report on Prosecution Appeals and Pre-Trial Hearings* (LRC 81-2006).

[61] Courts (Supplemental Provisions) Act 1961, s 52 replacing the Courts of Justice Act 1924, s 83.

[62] Summary Jurisdiction Act 1857, s 2 as extended by the Courts (Supplemental Provisions) Act 1961, s 51. In this instance, the application for the case stated must be made within 14 days of the decision of the District Court.

[63] The 'frivolous' test does not apply where the appeal is sought under the 1857 Act by the Attorney General, the Director of Public Prosecutions, a Government Minister, a Minister for State or the Revenue Commissioners, s 4 of the 1857 Act making a case stated mandatory in such cases: see *Sports Arena Ltd v O'Reilly* [1987] IR 185. The constitutionality of this provision was upheld by the Supreme Court in *Fitzgerald v DPP* [2003] 2 ILRM 537.

[64] See para **7.15**.

[65] Courts (Supplemental Provisions) Act 1961, s 52(2). In *Minister for Justice v Wang Zhu Jie* [1993] 1 IR 426, this restriction was held to be within the limitations on the Supreme Court's appellate jurisdiction envisaged by Article 34.4.3° of the Constitution.

[66] Summary Jurisdiction Act 1857, s 2 as extended by the Courts (Supplemental Provisions) Act 1961, s 52. See *Attorney General (Fahy) v Bruen* [1936] IR 750.

[67] See para **7.17**.

[7.36] Figure 7.5 provides an outline of the appeal process from the District Court in criminal matters.

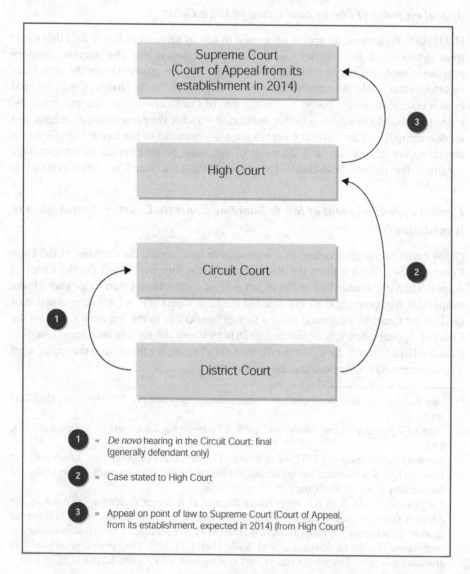

1 = *De novo* hearing in the Circuit Court: final (generally defendant only)

2 = Case stated to High Court

3 = Appeal on point of law to Supreme Court (Court of Appeal, from its establishment, expected in 2014) (from High Court)

Appeals from the District Court: Criminal
Figure 7.5

Trials on indictment

[7.37] Whereas we have seen that the appeal system from the District Court in civil and criminal matters is, broadly, similar, the appeal system concerning criminal trials on indictment involves a noticeable divergence from any arrangements in civil matters. We have seen that trials on indictment, which concern the most serious criminal offences, are conducted in the Circuit Court, the Central Criminal Court (the High Court) and (when they are in operation) Special Criminal Courts.[68]

[7.38] Prior to 1924,[69] there was no mechanism for appeal by a convicted person against a guilty verdict of a jury in a criminal trial. The available options required either a reference by the trial judge of the conviction to an appeal court or the intervention of the prosecution.[70] With the establishment of a Court of Criminal Appeal in 1924,[71] the convicted person was granted the right of appeal against conviction, in essence an appeal on a point of law. On the other hand, where the verdict of the trial court was 'not guilty' the prosecution was not allowed to appeal against the acquittal. However, it was entitled to appeal on a point of law 'without prejudice' to the verdict in the particular case.[72] On the separate question of the sentence imposed in the court of trial, both the prosecution and defence are entitled to appeal – the prosecution where the sentence is considered unduly lenient, the defence if it is considered too severe.

[7.39] The appellate system that operates at the time of writing (September 2014) is that the Court of Criminal Appeal hears appeals against conviction or sentence from the Circuit Court, the Central Criminal Court and Special Criminal Courts. A further appeal to the Supreme Court is possible (by leave).[73] As already noted,[74] a constitutional referendum to establish a Court of Appeal, which is to have jurisdiction in criminal and civil matters, was passed in 2013. At the time of writing (September 2014) the Court of Appeal Act 2014 has been enacted and it is envisaged that the Court of Appeal will be formally established by the end of 2014.

[7.40] As the Court of Appeal has not at the time of writing been established (although it is expected by the end of 2014) our description of the appeal system primarily focuses on the current arrangements with the Court of Criminal Appeal, but with appropriate modifications to take account of the proposed Court of Appeal. Consistent with our previous approach, we note here that, in the context of a criminal matter involving

---

68   See para **7.68**.
69   See generally, Ryan and Magee, *The Irish Criminal Process* (1983), p 419.
70   A conviction could either be referred by the trial judge to the Court for Crown Cases Reserved under the Crown Cases Act 1848 or the prosecution could apply for a writ of error which, if granted, would result in a re-trial: see also para **2.40**.
71   Courts of Justice Act 1924, s 8.
72   See, however, para **7.60**.
73   We have seen (para **7.22**) that the Courts of Justice Act 1947, s 16 empowered the Circuit Court to refer any point of law before it to the Supreme Court. In *The People (Attorney General) v McGlynn* [1967] IR 232, it was held that, in the context of a trial on indictment, s 16 of the 1947 Act does not apply between the time the defendant is put in charge and when the jury delivers its verdict. The effect is that s 16 of the 1947 Act has little application in practice to trials on indictment.
74   See para **4.34***ff*.

European Union law, an appeal to the EU Court of Justice may also arise, but we discuss that issue separately.[75]

Court of Criminal Appeal (Court of Appeal when established)

[7.41] The Court of Criminal Appeal, established in 1961 pursuant to Article 34 of the Constitution,[76] is a superior court of record.[77] The court is summoned by direction of the Chief Justice and comprises three judges, one Supreme Court judge (either the Chief Justice or another Supreme Court judge nominated by the Chief Justice) and two judges of the High Court (again, both nominated by the Chief Justice).[78] In *The People (Attorney General) v Conmey*,[79] the Supreme Court rejected a challenge to the constitutionality of the Court of Criminal Appeal. As already indicated, the court is empowered to conduct appeals against conviction or sentence from trials in the Circuit Criminal Court,[80] the Central Criminal Court[81] and any Special Criminal Court.[82] In an appeal against conviction, the Court of Criminal Appeal and, on further appeal, the Supreme Court, has three options: to dismiss the appeal, to quash the conviction and release the defendant, or to quash the conviction and order a re-trial.

---

[75] On the appellate jurisdiction of the Court of Justice, including the likelihood of a trial on indictment giving rise to an issue requiring a reference to the Court of Justice, see para **7.74**.

[76] Courts (Establishment and Constitution) Act 1961, s 3(1) formally established the Court of Criminal Appeal, replacing the Court of Criminal Appeal established by the Courts of Justice Act 1924, s 8.

[77] Courts (Supplemental Provisions) Act 1961, s 12, replacing the Courts of Justice Act 1924, s 30. On the concept of a court of record, see para **4.53**.

[78] Courts (Establishment and Constitution) Act 1961, s 3(2), replacing the Courts of Justice Act 1924, s 8.

[79] *The People (Attorney General) v Conmey* [1975] IR 341. See the discussion of this case at para **12.130** in connection with its status as a precedent.

[80] Courts of Justice Act 1924, s 63, carried forward by the Courts (Supplemental Provisions) Act 1961, s 12. In *The State (Hunt) v Donovan* [1975] IR 39, the High Court and, on appeal, the Supreme Court held that s 63 only applied where the defendant had been tried on indictment in the Circuit Court. In that case, the defendant had pleaded guilty to an indictable offence in the District Court and, under the Criminal Procedure Act 1967, s 13(2)(b), had been sent forward for sentencing in the Circuit Court. He sought to appeal to the Court of Criminal Appeal against the sentence imposed in the Circuit Court, but it was held that s 63 did not apply to him as he had not been tried on indictment. The High Court and Supreme Court held that this restriction was not in conflict with the Constitution, noting that Article 34.3.4° allowed appeals from the Circuit Court to be determined by law. Nonetheless, the Criminal Procedure (Amendment) Act 1973, s 1 passed after the *Hunt* case, provides that an appeal against sentence may be made in the circumstances that arose in the *Hunt* case. For criticism of the *Hunt* decision, see Delany, *The Courts Acts 1924–1997* (2nd edn, 2000).

[81] Courts of Justice Act 1924, s 31 carried forward by the Courts (Supplemental Provisions) Act 1961, s 12.

[82] Offences against the State Act 1939, s 44 carried forward by the Courts (Supplemental Provisions) Act 1961, s 12.

[7.42] As already noted, when the Court of Appeal is established (expected in 2014) it will comprise three divisions of three judges each. It is also envisaged that two of these divisions will deal with civil appeals and that the other will deal with criminal appeals. This reflects the reality of the backlog of civil appeals in the Supreme Court, which was a key reason for the establishment of the Court of Appeal. Another important rationale was that by having in place a permanently constituted court to deal with criminal appeals this could lead to a more consistent pattern of decision-making in criminal law matters, including sentencing, by comparison with the somewhat ad hoc nature of the composition of the Court of Criminal Appeal.

[7.43] Figure 7.6 provides an outline of the appeal process from trials on indictment.

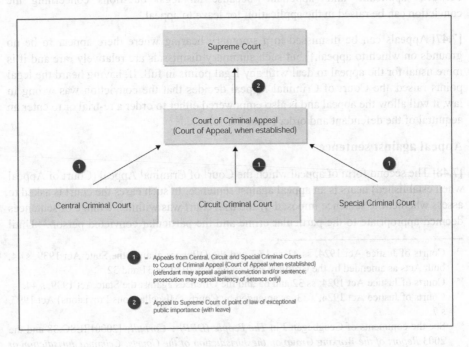

Appeals in Indictable Offences

Figure 7.6

[7.44] We now turn to discuss in more detail the procedure in appeals from trials on indictment.

Appeal against conviction

[7.45] A person convicted on indictment in the Circuit Court, High Court (Central Criminal Court) or a special criminal court may appeal that conviction to the Court of Criminal Appeal (Court of Appeal when established, expected in 2014). Prior to 2010, such an appeal formally required leave or permission of the trial court, but this formality was removed by the Criminal Procedure Act 2010.[83] The appeal against conviction is on the basis that the trial court made some error of law or the trial has been unsatisfactory.[84] It is thus primarily an appeal on a point of law and is based on a transcript or recording of the trial.[85]

[7.46] Prior to 2010, because most cases heard on appeal from trials on indictment were for leave to appeal a refusal by the trial court of a certificate of leave to appeal, the convicted person was referred to as the 'applicant', rather than the 'appellant', since he or she was applying for leave to appeal. However, as with any appeal involving points of law, both the prosecution and defence lawyers would have argued the relevant legal points involved in the appeal. Thus, nothing of substance turned on the distinction between 'applicant' and 'appellant' because all legal questions concerning the conviction can be raised in the application for leave to appeal.[86]

[7.47] Appeals can be dismissed in a summary hearing where there appear to be no grounds on which to appeal,[87] but such summary dismissals are relatively rare and it is more usual for the appeal to deal with any legal points in full. If, having heard the legal points raised, the Court of Criminal Appeal decides that the conviction was wrong in law, it will allow the appeal and is also empowered either to order a re-trial or to enter an acquittal of the defendant and order his or her release.[88]

Appeal against sentence

[7.48] The second form of appeal which the Court of Criminal Appeal (Court of Appeal when established) hears is an appeal against sentence. In such cases the court is asked to assess whether the sentence imposed by the trial court was within the range of sentences deemed appropriate to the particular crime and the particular convicted person.[89] Until

---

[83]   Courts of Justice Act 1924, ss 31 and 63 and the Offences against the State Act 1939, s 44, both Acts as amended by the Criminal Procedure Act 2010, ss 31 and 32.

[84]   Courts of Justice Act 1924, ss 32 and 63 and the Offences against the State Act 1939, s 44.

[85]   Courts of Justice Act 1924, s 33, as amended by Courts (Miscellaneous Provisions) Act 1997, s 7.

[86]   See the comments of Geoghegan J in *The People (DPP) v Corbally* [2000] IESC 38 and the 2003 *Report of the Working Group on the Jurisdiction of the Courts: Criminal Jurisdiction of the Courts*, para 643, cited in the Law Reform Commission's *Report on the Consolidation and Reform of the Courts Acts* (LRC 97-2010), para 2.12.

[87]   The power to dismiss summarily was introduced by the Criminal Procedure Act 1993.

[88]   Criminal Procedure Act 1993, s 3 replacing the Courts of Justice Act 1924, s 34 and the Courts of Justice Act 1928, s 5. Section 5 of the 1928 Act had conferred the power of re-trial, after it had been held in *Attorney General v Smith* [1927] IR 564 that s 34 of the 1924 Act did not allow this to be done. Section 3 of the 1993 Act has further extended the court's powers on appeal, in particular with a view to reviewing new evidence where there is a suggestion of a miscarriage of justice: see further para **7.51**.

[89]   On sentencing principles generally, see O'Malley, *Sentencing Law and Practice* (2nd edn, 2005).

1993, only the convicted person could bring an appeal concerning sentence, an appeal against severity of sentence; but it is now possible for the prosecution to initiate an appeal on the leniency of the sentence.[90]

[7.49] Prior to 1993, where the appeal had been initiated by the defendant, it would seem that he or she had the choice of appealing: (a) against conviction and sentence; or (b) against conviction only; or (c) against sentence only. Thus, where an appeal against conviction only was made and where this had been unsuccessful, the sentence given in the trial court would not be altered.[91] Where the convicted person appealed against the severity of sentence it was possible for the sentence to be increased, though this was quite unusual. From the convicted person's point of view, of course, the purpose of such an appeal was to have the sentence reduced and that outcome was certainly more common than an increased sentence.

[7.50] However, as already indicated, it is now possible for the prosecution to initiate an appeal against the leniency of the sentence imposed in the trial court. Thus, the ability of the convicted person to appeal against conviction only, leaving the sentence imposed in the trial court 'immune' from interference, has been affected to some extent by the right of the prosecution to appeal against leniency. As stated already, the principle to be applied in such an appeal is similar to that in an appeal by the convicted person, namely, whether the sentence imposed was within the range deemed appropriate to the offence and the individual circumstances of the defendant.

Appeals concerning miscarriages of justice

[7.51] The Criminal Procedure Act 1993 introduced a statutory mechanism to review a conviction which it is claimed has resulted in a miscarriage of justice.[92] Section 2 of the 1993 Act provides that the application to the Court of Criminal Appeal (Court of Appeal when established) is made by the convicted person.[93] This mechanism was introduced against the background of well-publicised cases of miscarriages of justice, both in England and Ireland, many dating back to the 1970s. Prior to 1993, the appellate jurisdiction had limited the ability of appellate courts to engage in *de novo* fact-finding concerning the basis for a conviction under appeal. In an attempt to circumvent the

---

90   Criminal Justice Act 1993, s 2.

91   See *The People (Attorney General) v Earls* [1969] IR 414.

92   Criminal Procedure Act 1993, s 2. The provision of such an appeal was recommended by the Committee to Inquire into Certain Aspects of Criminal Procedure, which was set up in 1989 in the wake of the Birmingham Six and Guildford Four cases in the UK and the Nicky Kelly case in Ireland. See Walsh, *Criminal Procedure* (2002), p 1213.

93   Under the Criminal Procedure Act 1993, s 7, the Minister for Justice is empowered to establish a committee to inquire into miscarriages of justice. Under the review procedure in the United Kingdom, first introduced by the Criminal Appeal Act 1968 (UK), the British Home Secretary (in Northern Ireland, the Secretary of State for Northern Ireland) initially had the sole power to refer a case to the Court of Appeal. The Criminal Appeal Act 1995 (UK) conferred these powers on an independent referrals body, the Criminal Cases Review Commission. The Scottish Criminal Cases Review Commission deals with Scottish cases.

limitations of the appellate system, some convicted persons had sought, in civil proceedings, to re-open issues determined in their criminal trial, but in those cases the courts had held that the majority of these matters were *res judicata* and could not be re-examined.[94]

[7.52] The Criminal Procedure Act 1993 provides, in effect, for a full hearing in the Court of Criminal Appeal (Court of Appeal when established) in connection with any conviction on indictment where the convicted person 'alleges that a new or newly-discovered fact shows that there has been a miscarriage of justice in relation to the conviction or that the sentence imposed is excessive'.[95] It is thus different from the conventional appeal based on a transcript since it is likely that the court will examine 'new' evidence, which in the normal course would not be admissible on appeal.

[7.53] Where the court allows an appeal against conviction, s 9 of the Criminal Procedure Act 1993 provides that the court may issue a certificate to the effect that a miscarriage of justice has occurred.[96] Such a certificate is a pre-condition to the successful applicant seeking monetary compensation for the miscarriage of justice. It has been held that whether a certificate under s 9 should be issued is not a criminal matter but a civil matter in which the onus is on the successful applicant to establish to the court, on the balance of probabilities (the civil standard of proof), that a miscarriage of justice occurred.[97]

Appeal by prosecution without prejudice to verdict

[7.54] Section 34 of the Criminal Procedure Act 1967 originally empowered the Director of Public Prosecutions to appeal on a point of law to the Supreme Court arising out of a trial on indictment in which the accused person was found not guilty. This form of appeal was without prejudice to the outcome of the trial, so that even if the Supreme Court found that there was an error of law in the trial, the person found not guilty could be re-tried. In effect, the procedure under s 34 of the 1967 Act was to clarify the law for future cases.[98]

[7.55] Section 34 was amended in 2006 to provide that the Attorney General or the Director of Public Prosecutions (where he or she is the prosecuting authority in the trial) may, without prejudice to the person tried on indictment and acquitted, refer a question of law arising during the trial to the Supreme Court for determination.[99] This

---

[94] See, eg *Kelly v Ireland* [1986] ILRM 318; *Pringle v Ireland* [1994] 1 ILRM 467. On this case law, see generally, Byrne and Binchy, *Annual Review of Irish Law 1992* (1994), pp 493–494.

[95] Criminal Procedure Act 1993, s 2(1)(b). One of those persons who had been faced with the *res judicata* difficulty took advantage of the new procedure in the 1993 Act: *The People (DPP) v Pringle* [1995] 2 IR 547 (CCA), [1997] 2 IR 225 (SC).

[96] For successful appeals see *The People (DPP) v Shortt (No 2)* [2002] 2 IR 696 and *The People (DPP) v Hannon* [2009] 4 IR 147.

[97] *The People (DPP) v Pringle (No 2)* [1997] 2 IR 225 (SC).

[98] An example of such a reference is *The People (DPP) v Rock* [1994] 1 ILRM 66.

[99] Criminal Justice Act 2006, s 21.

implemented a recommendation made in 2003 by the Working Group on the Jurisdiction of the Courts.[100] The Supreme Court is required to ensure that the identity of the accused person is not revealed during the appeal. In this regard, in 2006, the Law Reform Commission recommended that no reference whatsoever be made in the appeal to any person or any place which would be likely to lead to the identification of the acquitted person and also that the Supreme Court ensure that the identity of the accused not be revealed.[101]

Appeal by leave to the Supreme Court

[7.56] In 1946, in *The People (Attorney General) v Kennedy*,[102] the Supreme Court held that a prosecution appeal against an order of the Court of Criminal Appeal quashing a conviction did not lie to the Supreme Court. The Supreme Court found that the wording of s 29 of the Courts of Justice Act 1924 was not sufficiently clear and unequivocal to confer such a right of appeal on the prosecution. A mere 60 years later, in 2006, this position was amended so that the prosecution may bring a 'without prejudice' right of appeal to the Supreme Court in relation to a point of law arising in respect of a decision of the Court of Criminal Appeal (Court of Appeal when established).[103] This reflected recommendations by the Law Reform Commission and the Working Group on the Jurisdiction of the Courts that prosecution appeals on indictment should be extended to allow for a 'without prejudice' prosecution appeal which would not overturn an acquittal but would correct any legal errors for future cases.[104]

Appeal against acquittals and the double jeopardy rule

[7.57] As already indicated, the arrangements concerning appeals in respect of trials on indictment are restricted to appeals against convictions by the defendant, subject to the 'without prejudice' right of appeal for the prosecution. In the 1970s and 1980s, however, a series of cases established a right of appeal against acquittals, in the case of trials in the Central Criminal Court, thus having the potential to remove the common law principle of double jeopardy, under which a person who has been acquitted on indictment may not be placed on trial a second time for the same offence. In *The People (Attorney General)*

---

100 Working Group on the Jurisdiction of the Courts, *The Criminal Jurisdiction of the Courts* (2003).

101 Law Reform Commission, *Report on Prosecution Appeals and Pre-Trial Hearings* (LRC 81-2006).

102 *The People (Attorney General) v Kennedy* [1946] IR 517.

103 Courts of Justice Act 1924, s 29, as amended by the Criminal Justice Act 2006, s 22 and the Criminal Justice Act 2007, s 59. The 2007 Act provided that s 29 of the 1924 Act, as amended, does not affect the power of the DPP to seek a review of unduly lenient sentences under the Criminal Justice Act 1993.

104 Law Reform Commission, *Consultation Paper on Prosecution Appeals in Cases brought on Indictment* (LRC CP-19-2002) and Working Group on the Jurisdiction of the Courts, *The Criminal Jurisdiction of the Courts* (2003).

v Conmey[105] the Supreme Court had held that, by virtue of Article 34 of the Constitution, a right of appeal to the Court existed in respect of all verdicts of the Central Criminal Court, which of course is the High Court exercising its criminal jurisdiction. In *The People (DPP) v O'Shea*[106] the Supreme Court held that this right of appeal applied equally to the prosecution and the defence. Thus, in addition to acknowledging a right of appeal against conviction from the Central Criminal Court to the Supreme Court, the court held that, where a person had been found not guilty in the Central Criminal Court, the prosecution could appeal the acquittal to the Supreme Court.

[7.58] In a later case, The *People (DPP) v Quilligan and O'Reilly*,[107] the Supreme Court found that the acquittal of the two accused had been made on the basis of an error of law, and made an order allowing the appeal. However, the court did not subsequently order a re-trial on the charges in question.[108] Since the Supreme Court had held that this jurisdiction arose under Article 34.4.3° of the Constitution, it was permissible to remove the right of appeal by legislation. This was, indeed, effected by s 11 of the Criminal Procedure Act 1993, so that the right of appeal against an acquittal was removed. In 2001, the Director of Public Prosecutions argued that a 'with prejudice' right of appeal against acquittals should be available in order to appeal against the type of acquittal in the *O'Shea* case, an acquittal directed by a trial judge, though not against acquittals arrived at by the jury.[109]

[7.59] In the United Kingdom, the (UK) Criminal Justice Act 2003 provides for the re-opening of criminal prosecutions in certain circumstances where 'new and compelling' evidence has come to light after an acquittal. The 2003 Act thus reverses the common law double jeopardy principle. The 2003 Act arose against the background of the acquittal of a number of defendants who had been charged with the murder of a young man, Stephen Lawrence, in 1993. The report of the inquiry into the case, the Macpherson Report,[110] was severely critical of the police investigations into the death of Stephen Lawrence and also recommended that the double jeopardy rule be altered to

---

[105] *People (Attorney General) v Conmey* [1975] IR 341. See the discussion of this case at para **12.130** in connection with its status as a precedent.

[106] *People (DPP) v O'Shea* [1982] IR 384. See also the discussion of this case at para **12.109**.

[107] *People (DPP) v Quilligan and O'Reilly* [1987] IR 495.

[108] In *The People (DPP) v Quilligan and O'Reilly (No 2)* [1989] IR 46, the Supreme Court, by a 3:2 decision, held that a re-trial should not be ordered in this case. Only two of the judges (Henchy and Griffin JJ) held that re-trials should never be ordered. The third judge in the majority, Hederman J, merely decided not to order a re-trial in the particular case: see para **12.114**. The defendants were later tried on other charges which had some connection with the original charges on which they were acquitted and, ultimately, the conviction of one of the defendants was upheld: see *The People (DPP) v Quilligan and O'Reilly (No 3)* [1993] 2 IR 305, discussed in Byrne and Binchy, *Annual Review of Irish Law 1992* (1994), pp 234–239.

[109] See (2001) *The Irish Times*, 21 May.

[110] *The Stephen Lawrence Inquiry, Report of An Inquiry by Sir William Macpherson of Cluny* (Cm 4262-I, 1999).

allow certain trials to be re-opened. The 2003 Act was also influenced by the campaign for removal of the double jeopardy principle by the mother of a woman, Julie Hogg, who had been murdered in 1989 and in respect of whose death an individual, Billy Dunlop, had been acquitted after two jury trials ended in disagreement. Subsequently, he appeared to admit to the murder and pleaded guilty to perjury and was sentenced to imprisonment. After the 2003 Act came into force in 2005, he was charged again with her murder, to which he pleaded guilty in 2006, and he was sentenced to life imprisonment with a minimum tariff of 17 years.[111]

[7.60] In Ireland, the 2007 *Final Report of the Balance in the Criminal Law Review Group*[112] (some of whose recommendations were implemented in the Criminal Justice Act 2007) recommended the introduction of prosecution appeals against acquittals and re-opening of cases along the lines of the UK 2003 Act. This recommendation was implemented in the Criminal Procedure Act 2010, Pt 3 of which contains provisions broadly comparable to those in the UK 2003 Act. At the time of writing (September 2014), no such prosecution appeal has been initiated under Part 3 of the 2010 Act.

[4] APPELLATE JURISDICTION OF COURTS FROM ADJUDICATIVE BODIES

[7.61] We note here that the District Court, the Circuit Court, the High Court, the Court of Appeal (to be established in 2014) and the Supreme Court have each been conferred with different appellate jurisdiction, both in the form of *de novo* hearings and appeals on points of law, from various adjudicative bodies, tribunals and Ministers where these exercise administrative or decision-making functions. We discuss a number of these elsewhere.[113] This appellate jurisdiction should be distinguished from the judicial review jurisdiction exercised exclusively by the High Court.[114]

[5] ANALYSIS THAT LED TO REFORMS OF THE APPELLATE PROCESS

2001 Lecture of Keane CJ

[7.62] We have noted in detail elsewhere that in 2001, the former Chief Justice, Keane CJ, delivered a lecture advocating wide-ranging changes in the court structure, in particular suggesting that the three-tier first instance system of District Court, Circuit Court and High Court be replaced by a two-tier system of District Court and High Court.[115] This two-tier system would then be accompanied by a two-tier appeal structure, he suggested. Keane CJ noted that, by comparison with other jurisdictions he had briefly

---

111 (2006) *The Times*, 7 October.
112 The Review Group was chaired by Gerard Hogan SC. The Report is available at www.justice.ie.
113 See Ch 8.
114 See generally, para **10.53**.
115 See para **5.122**.

surveyed, Ireland was unusual in that the Supreme Court fulfilled all the functions of final courts of appeal in other jurisdictions, not merely in cases involving important points of law and in constitutional cases, but in all cases decided by the High Court, with the exception of the limited range of cases where the right of appeal was excluded by statute.

[7.63] He noted that the result was that the Supreme Court regularly hears appeals in cases which are of no general public importance (personal injuries actions, for example, though Keane CJ did not specify any examples) 'leading to inevitable delays' in the hearing of those cases which are of public importance. Keane CJ was of the view that:

"It would be far more satisfactory if a permanent Court of Appeal existed which sat in both civil and criminal divisions and which heard appeals from the High Court in all civil cases and cases of serious crime. That court in turn could grant leave to appeal to the Supreme Court where it was satisfied that a point of law of public importance was involved."

[7.64] Keane CJ emphasised that because the Court of Criminal Appeal had, since 1924, consisted of three judges chosen *ad hoc* for a particular list of cases, this had led to 'serious inconsistencies in the jurisprudence of that court and, in particular, in the all important area of sentencing'. As already noted, his proposal for a permanent Court of Appeal to deal with civil and criminal matters has been accepted, and the Court of Appeal is expected to be established in 2014.

[7.65] Keane CJ considered that no constitutional amendment would be required to introduce the Court of Appeal, since the Supreme Court had already upheld the establishment of the Court of Criminal Appeal in its present form.[116] This view was not shared in the 2009 *Report of the Working Group on a Court of Appeal* and, as discussed above, the Court of Appeal is being established on foot of a 2013 constitutional amendment to Article 34.

[7.66] Keane CJ also commented that the existing appeals structures from the District Court to the Circuit Court and the Circuit Court to the High Court were 'clearly defective'. He stated:

"In the case of appeals from the Circuit Court to the High Court, the hearing of such appeals outside Dublin by the High Court on Circuit is a seriously wasteful use of judicial resources. Members of the High Court, and, on occasions, the Supreme Court, frequently travel to the appointed venues to find that there is virtually no work for them to do. This is at a time when there are huge lists of cases to be dealt with in the High Court and it is constantly asked to supply judges to deal with other work of public importance, such as tribunals and other enquiries."

This view was supported by the Law Reform Commission in its *Report on the Consolidation and Reform of the Courts Acts*.[117] Section 64 of the Courts and Civil Law (Miscellaneous Provisions) Act 2011 has given effect to this analysis by conferring on the

---

116   See *The People (Attorney General) v Conmey* [1975] IR 341, para **7.41**.
117   LRC 97-2010, at paras 2.119–2.125, available at www.lawreform.ie.

President of the High Court a discretion to determine whether such twice yearly sittings, which originated in the medieval assize sittings, are required in practice.

[7.67] Another feature of the present appeal system which Keane CJ thought was particularly unsatisfactory was that every civil appeal from the District Court to the Circuit Court and the Circuit Court to the High Court is by way of rehearing. He considered that this was particularly unfortunate in family law cases:

"However much judges may endeavour to soften the adversarial nature of the proceedings, increased bitterness and tension is often engendered by the hearing and these difficulties are exacerbated if one party decides to appeal, since there then must be another confrontation at the next level."

[7.68] He suggested that, with improved information technology in the courts in the immediate future,[118] an appeal on a transcript to the proposed Court of Appeal would be more satisfactory. This view has not yet been supported by any subsequent reviews or legislative initiatives.

Working Group on the Jurisdiction of the Courts

[7.69] As noted in Chapter 5, the Working Group on the Jurisdiction of the Courts was established in the aftermath of Keane CJ's 2001 lecture. Its 2003 report on the criminal jurisdiction of the courts considered a number of issues relating to the appellate jurisdiction of the courts in criminal matters.[119] The report concluded that there should be no alteration to the current very limited circumstances in which the prosecution may appeal from a decision of the District Court.[120] The report also examined the composition of the Court of Criminal Appeal and agreed with Keane CJ's view that its constantly changing composition prevented it from establishing clear and consistent principles of criminal law. The report recommended that a group of judges be assigned to the court to hear appeals for a defined period of at least two years. This group of judges should include two Supreme Court and at least six High Court judges. As noted above, this analysis was superseded by the decision to establish a permanent Court of Appeal to deal with the civil and criminal matters.

[7.70] The report also discussed the issue of leave or permission to appeal to the Court of Criminal Appeal. It was noted that in most cases leave to appeal to the Court of Criminal Appeal is refused by the trial judge. When the leave to appeal is dealt with by the Court of Criminal Appeal it treats the application for leave to appeal as the actual hearing of the appeal proper. This reality led to the recommendation that the leave to appeal requirement in indictable criminal matters be abolished, as it does not serve the

---

118 See para **4.223**.
119 Working Group on the Jurisdiction of the Courts, *The Criminal Jurisdiction of the Courts* (2003).
120 Working Group on the Jurisdiction of the Courts, *The Criminal Jurisdiction of the Courts* (2003), pp 84–85.

purpose of filtering out unmeritorious appeals. As already noted, this was implemented in the Criminal Procedure Act 2010.

2009 Report on Court of Appeal

[7.71] In 2006, a Working Group was established to consider whether it is necessary to establish a court of civil appeal. The Working Group was chaired by Denham J, who had written extra-judicially that a Court of Appeal would be 'more efficient and effective and assist in the establishment of consistent jurisprudence'.[121] The core recommendation made in the 2009 Report of the Working Group[122] was that a full time Court of Appeal should be established, ideally with a permanent panel of judges, to deal with both criminal and civil matters. This would be similar to the English Court of Appeal. The Report concluded that, to avoid any uncertainty on its status, the Court of Appeal should be established on a constitutional basis. The proposed Court of Appeal would function above the level of the High Court but below the Supreme Court. As well as dealing with civil appeals, it would also be conferred with the existing jurisdiction of the Court of Criminal Appeal. The Report noted that a Court of Appeal was required in particular because of the increase in litigation in the High Court. The Report noted that, in 1971, there were nine High Court judges, while by 2007 this had increased to 36. This had led to an increasingly high volume of appeals coming before the Supreme Court when compared with other states. Thus, in 2007 the Supreme Court finalised 229 cases compared with 82 in the UK House of Lords (now the UK Supreme Court), 74 in the US Supreme Court and 27 in the Supreme Court of New Zealand.[123] The Report noted that, as a result, the average waiting time in 2009 for ordinary, that is, non-urgent, appeals in the Supreme Court was 30 months. The Report stated that this delay could potentially cause Ireland to be viewed as an unattractive destination for commercial activities.[124] The Report noted that a large number of civil appeals coming before the Supreme Court did not involve any novel points of law or constitutional importance and were in the nature of 'error correction'. The Report concluded that such appeals were inappropriate for the Supreme Court and were more suitable for an intermediate Court of Appeal.[125] The establishment of an intermediate Court of Appeal would thus allow for the Supreme Court to deal with cases of public importance as in the UK Supreme Court and the US Supreme Court. The Court of Appeal would, therefore, deal with the majority of appeals in civil and criminal cases and the Supreme Court would only hear appeals where leave to appeal was given by the Court of Appeal or leave to appeal directly to the Supreme Court was furnished by a lower court. As noted, this analysis was accepted and the Court of Appeal is scheduled to be established in 2014 on foot of the amendments made in 2013 to Article 34 of the Constitution.

---

[121] Denham, 'Proposal for a Court of Appeal' [2006] 6 Judicial Studies Institute Journal 1, 9.

[122] *Report of the Working Group on a Court of Appeal* (2009), available at www.courts.ie.

[123] *Report of the Working Group on a Court of Appeal* p 39.

[124] *Report of the Working Group on a Court of Appeal* p 45.

[125] *Report of the Working Group on a Court of Appeal* pp 45–46.

Law Reform Commission 2010 Report on Consolidation and Reform of the Courts Acts

[7.72] As noted in Chapter 5, in 2010 the Law Reform Commission published a *Report on the Consolidation and Reform of the Courts Acts*,[126] including a draft Courts (Consolidation and Reform) Bill, which brings together the pre-1922 and post-1922 provisions concerning the jurisdiction of the courts currently contained in over 240 Acts. In connection with the appellate jurisdiction of the courts, the Commission recommended that the appeal by way of case stated be abolished and that the consultative case stated only should be retained. The Commission considered that the appeal by way of case stated, which is available at the end of the proceedings, was catered for through the ordinary appeal mechanism.

[7.73] The Commission also recommended that all civil appeals be by way of leave by the court that hears the matter at first instance and that, where such leave is granted, the appeal in the higher court be dealt with by way of transcript of the original trial and on written submissions of the parties. This recommendation is particularly notable given that the Courts Service is currently rolling out electronic recording in courtrooms throughout the state. At the time of writing (September 2014), it appears the government is committed to implementing the 2010 Report through a consolidating Courts Bill, although the extent to which that Bill will reflect all the Commission's recommendations is not known at the time of writing. [127]

[6] APPELLATE JURISDICTION OF THE EU COURT OF JUSTICE

[7.74] In this section of the chapter we examine certain aspects of the appellate jurisdiction of the EU Court of Justice pursuant to art 267 of the Treaty on the Functioning of the European Union (TFEU) (formerly art 234 of the EC Treaty).[128] We discuss elsewhere the jurisdiction of the EU Court of Justice under the TFEU to hear and determine points of European Union law on a reference to it by any court or tribunal of the member states.[129] In essence, such a reference is similar to a case stated, in that a court or tribunal may refer a point of law to the EU Court of Justice, which gives a ruling on the point of law and remits the case to the court or tribunal of the member state for final determination of the point of law in issue. What we examine here is the scope of the 'courts or tribunals' to which the TFEU refers and also the question whether there

---

[126] LRC 97-2010, available at www.lawreform.ie.

[127] The *Government Legislation Programme, Autumn Session 2014*, available at www.taoiseach.ie, proposes the publication of a Courts (Consolidation and Reform) Bill to implement the Commission's 2010 Report.

[128] The EC Treaty became the TFEU after the coming into force of the EU Lisbon Treaty in 2009: see ch16. See also Fahey, *Practice and Procedure in Preliminary References to Europe: 30 years of Article 234 EC Caselaw from the Irish Courts* (2007).

[129] On European Union law generally, see Ch 16.

is an obligation or merely a discretion to refer questions of EU law to the Court of Justice.

[7.75] Before we consider these points, it should be reiterated that, since European Union law is part of domestic law, each court or tribunal envisaged by art 267 of the TFEU is required to apply EU law, including the decisions of the Court of Justice, without the need for a reference to the court. Put another way, all decisions of the EU Court of Justice on any area of EU law are binding precedents which must be followed in the domestic courts.

Courts and tribunals

[7.76] The courts envisaged by art 267 of the TFEU are those established pursuant to Article 34 of the Constitution, and whose jurisdiction has been discussed in this chapter. Thus, the Supreme Court, the Court of Appeal, the High Court, the Circuit Court and the District Court – and, when they are in operation, the Special Criminal Courts – are empowered by the TFEU to refer points of EU law for determination by the Court of Justice. At the time of writing (September 2014) all but the Special Criminal Courts (and, of course, the Court of Appeal, which is scheduled to be established in 2014) have exercised this power, but the majority of the cases referred to the EU Court of Justice are civil claims originating in the High Court.[130] An examination conducted in 2007 of the number of referrals made by Irish courts between 1973 and 2003 demonstrates that the overall number of referrals from Irish courts is amongst the lowest when compared with other small-sized countries.[131]

[7.77] As to the tribunals envisaged by art 267 of the TFEU, this poses more difficulties, though a good starting point would be the case law of the courts in Ireland as to what constitutes a tribunal, person or body with adjudicative powers that must be exercised judicially.[132] Among the tribunals or bodies that would be included are the Labour Court, the Employment Appeals Tribunal, the Equality Tribunal, the Appeals Commissioners, the Social Welfare Appeals Officers, the Adoption Authority of Ireland, An Bord Pleanála (the Planning Appeals Board), the Medical Council and other similar professional bodies established by legislation.[133] A number of Irish quasi-judicial and

---

[130] See McMahon and Murphy, *European Community Law in Ireland* (1989), p 225.

[131] See Fahey, *Practice and Procedure in Preliminary References to Europe: 30 years of Article 234 EC Caselaw from the Irish Courts* (2007), p 14.

[132] See para **4.16**.

[133] See McMahon and Murphy, *European Community Law in Ireland* (1989), p 226. On adjudicative bodies generally, see Ch 8. For example, see *Impact v Minister for Agriculture and Food* [2008] ELR 181 where the Labour Court made a preliminary reference pursuant to Art 267 TFEU to the EU Court of Justice.

administrative bodies have referred questions to the EU Court of Justice.[134] As is the position with referrals from courts, it appears that when compared with other jurisdictions, the number of such referrals is very low.[135]

Mandatory or discretionary references

Mandatory references

[7.78] Article 267(3) of the TFEU provides:

> "Where any such question [that is, of European Union law] is raised in a case pending before a court or tribunal of a Member State, against whose decisions there is no judicial remedy under national law, that court or tribunal shall bring the matter before the Court."

The mandatory tone of art 267(3) may be contrasted with art 267(2), which provides:

> "Where such a question [that is, of European Union law] is raised before any court or tribunal of a Member State, that court or tribunal may, if it considers that a decision on the question is necessary to enable it to give judgment, request the Court to give a ruling thereon."

[7.79] It is thus clear that a court or tribunal 'against whose decisions there is no judicial remedy under national law' must refer a point of EU law to the Court of Justice, whereas any other court or tribunal may refer such a point if considered necessary. It has been made clear by the Court of Justice itself that the courts or tribunals under a mandatory obligation to refer include those whose decisions cannot be appealed, and not merely the final courts of appeal in the member states. Thus, the Circuit Court on appeal *de novo* from the District Court and the High Court on appeal *de novo* from the Circuit Court may come within this mandatory provision, the Court of Appeal (to be established in 2014) may do so and the Supreme Court certainly does.[136]

Discretionary references

[7.80] In the case of the courts or tribunals that enjoy a discretion to invoke the jurisdiction of the Court of Justice the approach taken is that it is preferable to decide the case on a basis other than EU law where that is possible, thus avoiding the need for a reference.[137] This is similar to the rule by which the courts seek to avoid constitutional questions where a case can be decided on some other ground.[138] Once a court or tribunal

---

[134] See for example the reference made by the Equality Tribunal in *Z v A Government Department* [2014] EUECJ C-363/12 (judgment of EU Court of Justice, 18 March 2014).

[135] Fahey, *Practice and Procedure in Preliminary References to Europe: 30 years of Article 234 EC Caselaw from the Irish Courts* (2007), pp 37–40.

[136] See McMahon and Murphy, *European Community Law in Ireland* (1989), p 227.

[137] *Irish Creamery Milk Suppliers Association Ltd v Ireland* (1979) 3 JISEL 66.

[138] See para **15.86**.

has made a decision to refer the case to the Court of Justice, the reference must proceed ahead and not even the Supreme Court will interfere.[139] Finally, even where an art 267 reference has been made, the courts may ultimately hold that the matter can be decided on issues other than EU law.[140]

---

[139] *Campus Oil Ltd v Minister for Industry and Energy* [1983] IR 82.

[140] *Doyle v An Taoiseach* [1986] ILRM 693. McMahon and Murphy, *European Community Law in Irel*and (1989), p 288 criticise the approach of the Supreme Court in *Doyle* where the court declined to address the Community law issue, even after what is now an Art 267 reference, and where the High Court, whose decision was appealed to the Supreme Court, had applied the court's ruling in making its decision. See also Fahey, *Practice and Procedure in Preliminary References to Europe: 30 years of Article 234 EC Caselaw from the Irish Courts* (2007), p 49, to the effect that although *Doyle* has not been disapproved in subsequent case law, neither has it been followed in subsequent case law.

Chapter 8

Other Dispute Resolution Processes: Mediation, Arbitration, Administrative Adjudicative Bodies and Ombudsmen

[1] Introduction 377
[2] Mediation, Conciliation, the Courts and an 'Integrated' Civil
     Justice System 378
[3] Arbitration 384
[4] Administrative Law and the Emergence of Modern
     Government 387
[5] Administrative Law and Adjudicative Bodies Generally 393
[6] Coroners' Courts 402
[7] Tribunals of Inquiry and Commissions of Investigation 404
[8] Ombudsmen 407

[1] INTRODUCTION

[8.01] In previous chapters we discussed the court system, which remains the ultimate forum for the resolution of legal disputes, whether civil or criminal.[1] It must also be recognised that, for civil disputes in particular, effective access to the courts is difficult because of the costs involved in litigating a claim.[2] In this chapter, we focus on other adjudicative mechanisms for resolving disputes, primarily disputes of a non-criminal type. In recent years, voluntary dispute resolution processes – notably mediation and conciliation – have emerged as methods of resolving civil disputes. When they emerged first in the 1970s, they were referred to under the heading alternative dispute resolution (ADR). We note the emergence of the 'integrated' model of civil justice, which envisages mediation and conciliation as primary models for resolving civil law disputes, with the court system as the 'last resort' where other dispute resolution methods have failed. Mediation and conciliation have joined the longer-established arbitration procedure as a mechanism for resolving disputes outside the court process.

[8.02] The increased reach of government during the 20th century and into the 21st century has also led to an increase in what has been described as the regulatory state. In

---

1   See Chs 4–7.
2   On the provision of state-supported civil legal aid and criminal legal aid see Ch 9, below.

377

particular, there has been a growth in the exercise of quasi-judicial powers by various adjudicative bodies in connection with the regulation of, for example, financial services and the various forms of media and telecommunications and this exercise has included the awarding, and withdrawal, of licences. The area of law describing the regulation and control of these adjudicative bodies is administrative law.[3] In addition, specialist tribunals, dealing with such diverse matters as employment and social welfare disputes, have been established – many in recent years.

[8.03] Commissions of investigation and tribunals of inquiry, primarily aimed at establishing facts and inquisitorial in nature, are other mechanisms used to determine major disputes of public importance and are also discussed in this chapter. The chapter concludes with a discussion of the various ombudsmen established in recent years; these provide important means, often free to users, to resolve civil disputes especially consumer disputes that would otherwise involve litigation that, for the costs reasons mentioned, would be out of reach of many individuals.

[2] MEDIATION, CONCILIATION, THE COURTS AND AN 'INTEGRATED' CIVIL JUSTICE SYSTEM

[8.04] The Law Reform Commission, in its 2010 *Report on Alternative Dispute Resolution: Mediation and Conciliation*,[4] noted that in recent years, voluntary dispute resolution processes, notably mediation and conciliation, have emerged as methods of resolving civil disputes. When they emerged first in the 1970s, they were referred to as alternative dispute resolution (ADR). While the abbreviation ADR may have begun to appear almost anachronistic, the emergence of mediation and conciliation indicated some difficulties with the more formal court system and arbitration routes, and thus indicated they were seen as more effective 'alternatives' to these long-established dispute resolution mechanisms.

[8.05] It is important to note briefly the key distinctions between mediation and conciliation. In mediation, parties to a dispute select an independent party to assist them in reaching a mutually acceptable negotiated settlement. By contrast, with conciliation, the independent party appointed by the agreement of the parties takes a more interventionist approach in bringing the parties together to agree a settlement. If the parties are unable to reach a mutually agreeable settlement, the conciliator might issue a recommendation: this is not binding on the parties because either is free to reject it.

[8.06] The Law Reform Commission also noted in its 2010 Report that a fundamental aspect of mediation and conciliation is that they are both "interest-based dispute resolution processes" in that they address parties' emotions, and seek creative solutions to the resolution of the dispute. This means they are focused "on clarifying the parties'

---

3   See Hogan and Morgan, *Administrative Law in Ireland* (4th edn, 2010) and Delany, *Judicial Review of Administrative Action: A Comparative Analysis* (2nd edn, 2009).

4   Law Reform Commission, *Report on Alternative Dispute Resolution: Mediation and Conciliation* (LRC 98–2010).

real motivations or underlying interests in the dispute with the aim of reaching a mutually acceptable compromise which meets the real interests of both parties."[5] This is very different to the adversarial court process where the interests of the parties are secondary to the application of binding legal principles and rules. Mediation and conciliation are also both voluntary and non-binding in nature, under the control of the parties rather than an adjudicator (such as a judge or arbitrator) and based on confidentiality of the process.[6] This is also very different from the adversarial process involved in court-based litigation or arbitration.

[8.07] In many respects, it is important to note that the concept of voluntary dispute resolution processes is not new, and many societies have developed such informal and non-adversarial processes for resolving disputes.[7] Nonetheless, the more recent emergence of mediation and conciliation represent a different emphasis on alternatives to adversarial processes. The Law Reform Commission,[8] reflecting the international literature on this area, has described ADR as a broad spectrum of structured processes which are fundamental to any modern civil justice system in providing greater access to individualised justice for all citizens. In this respect ADR should not be seen as a separate entity from the court-based arrangements for civil justice but rather should be seen as complementing court-based arrangements and thus as an integral part of a more complete and entire system of justice.

[8.08] There is another fundamental difference between ADR processes and the adversarial court-based process. The adversarial nature of the court system means that in a contested claim there is a clear winner and a clear loser. Courts are also limited in terms of the civil remedies that have been developed over the centuries, notably through awarding monetary compensation called damages. These two limitations of the court-based system may in fact be counter-productive in terms of resolving some disputes. For example, in a marriage breakup where children are affected, an adversarial approach may adversely affect those children, and mediation is therefore preferable. Similarly, two companies who have a dispute over payment under a building contract may not wish to engage in a "winner takes all" dispute because they also wish to retain an ongoing working relationship for future building contracts: again, mediation rather than litigation is preferable.

---

5   Law Reform Commission, *Report on Alternative Dispute Resolution: Mediation and Conciliation* (LRC 98–2010) at para 2.22.

6   Law Reform Commission, *Report on Alternative Dispute Resolution: Mediation and Conciliation* (LRC 98–2010), ch 3. The Commission's Report notes that these principles are also included in the 2008 EU Directive on Mediation in Civil and Commercial Matters, 2008/52/EC which deals with mediation involving cross-jurisdiction disputes only.

7   See Barrett, *A History of Alternative Dispute Resolution* (2004) and Law Reform Commission, *Consultation Paper on Alternative Dispute Resolution* (LRC CP 50–2008), pp 20–34.

8   Law Reform Commission, *Report on Alternative Dispute Resolution: Mediation and Conciliation* (LRC 98–2010), ch 1.

[8.9] In the same way, a large group of parents who suddenly discover that organs of their children were retained by a hospital for many years without proper consent may not wish simply to obtain monetary compensation in a civil claim. They may be more interested in receiving an apology, in being involved in the development of informed consent procedures for the future and perhaps seeing a memorial to the babies being built in the grounds of the hospital. It is not possible to obtain these types of non-financial remedies through litigation but they are precisely the kind of imaginative outcomes that are possible through a well-organised mediation in which the parents would be involved in finding a solution that is restorative in a way that monetary compensation is not.[9]

[8.10] These non-adversarial restorative principles were also applied in Ireland in the 2013 *Magdalen Commission Report*.[10] This non-statutory Commission, chaired by Quirke J, had been established by the government to advise on the establishment of a scheme, to operate on a non-adversarial basis, for the benefit of up to 1,000 surviving women of over 10,000 in total who had been admitted to and worked in Magdalen Laundries between the 1930s and 1970s.[11] While the women had been subjected to degrading and exploitative working conditions in these laundries, it would have been difficult for them to bring successful civil claims for compensation, including because the claims were probably statute barred.[12] The Commission's terms of reference also

---

[9]   The English Centre for Effective Dispute Resolution (CEDR) organised a successful mediation involving over 1,000 claimants in the wake of the discovery that Liverpool's Alder Hey Children's Hospital had for many years retained the organs of babies for research purposes without informed consent: see the discussion in Law Reform Commission, *Report on Alternative Dispute Resolution: Mediation and Conciliation* (LRC 98–2010), para 3.132.

[10] *Magdalen Commission Report* (May 2013), available at www.justice.ie. The Commission formally comprised Mr Justice Quirke (President of the Law Reform Commission and former judge of the High Court). The Report noted, at paras 1.02–1.11, that Mr Justice Quirke was assisted by a small advisory group, and by a group of over 40 women barristers who volunteered to interview the women who were the focus of the Commission's work, those who had been sent to Magdalen laundries. The work of this group of volunteer barristers was recognised in 2014 as the largest single exercise in *pro bono* legal work in Ireland: see www.irishlawawards.ie.

[11] The Magdalen Commission had been established in the wake of the *Report of the Inter-Departmental Committee to establish the facts of State involvement with the Magdalen Laundries* (February 2013) (the McAleese Report), available at www.justice.ie. The McAleese Report had established that State institutions had been directly involved in the admission of women to Magdalen laundries. This had previously been contested by government representatives in response to groups representing the Magdalen women. The *Magdalen Commission Report* stated, para 3.03: "The consultation process conducted by the Commission suggested that a large number of young girls and women who were admitted to the Magdalen laundries were degraded, humiliated, stigmatised and exploited (sometimes in a calculated manner)."

[12] *Magdalen Commission Report*, para 5.06, fn 1, citing five obstacles to bringing any civil claims and noting that similar obstacles had been identified in a 2010 review of comparable Australian schemes.

stated that the scheme was "to contribute to a healing and reconciliation process."[13] Having regard to these terms of reference, the *Magdalen Commission Report* applied the ADR principles described in the Law Reform Commission's 2010 Report. It was also influenced in this respect by an analysis, based on restorative principles, of comparable schemes in Australia.[14] The ex gratia scheme recommended in the 2013 Report included a significant element of monetary compensation, but this was based on restorative principles rather than the criteria that apply in awarding damages in civil claims. The Report explained the restorative aspects as follows:[15]

> "Firstly, the monetary payments are intended to assist the Magdalen women who have endured suffering through no fault of theirs. The payments therefore form an important and sincere part of the recognition of past State failures. Secondly, by avoiding any adversarial process, the needs and interests of the Magdalen women and of Irish society generally are also met, because the voluntary nature of the offer of payments contributes to the process of on-going reconciliation to which the other aspects of the Scheme also contribute."

[8.11] In addition to these monetary elements, the scheme recommended in the 2013 Report also reflected ADR principles because it recommended that the general scheme for Magdalen women would include free access to health care for them and the establishment of a dedicated unit to assist them to obtain the health, monetary and other benefits to which they would be entitled. This unit would also be required to acquire, maintain and administer "any garden, museum or other form of memorial" which the women had requested. The Report also recommended that this unit would be established only after the Scheme's administrator "has first consulted with and received written submissions from an advisory body or committee representing the needs and interests of the Magdalen women."[16]

[8.12] Both mediation and conciliation have grown in use in recent years in Ireland. For example, arrangements have been in place in the employment context for many years, where mediation and conciliation services are a key element in ensuring reasonable industrial relations between employers and employees.[17] In the context of family law, solicitors have been obliged for a number of years to advise their clients of the options of reconciliation, mediation or a negotiated settlement as alternatives to litigation.[18] The Family Mediation Service was established by the Department of Social Protection in 1986 as a pilot service and was established on a statutory footing by the Family Support Act 2001. Under the relevant 2004 Rules of Court that established the Commercial Court in the High Court, the judge is empowered to adjourn proceedings to allow

---

13   *Magdalen Commission Report*, para 1.01.
14   *Magdalen Commission Report*, para 5.07, citing Winter, 'Australia's Ex Gratia Redress' (2009) 13(1) AILR 49, at p 54.
15   *Magdalen Commission Report*.
16   *Magdalen Commission Report*, para 5.21 (5th Recommendation).
17   See paras **8.49***ff*.
18   Judicial Separation and Family Law Reform Act 1989, ss 5–8; Family Law (Divorce) Act 1996, ss 6–9.

mediation and conciliation to take place. This reflects long-established judicial practice. In 2008, in *Charlton v Kenny*,[19] a land dispute between two high-profile litigants (the plaintiff was a well-known solicitor and the defendant a well-known radio and television personality), the presiding High Court judge intervened before the parties went into the witness box to suggest they attempt mediation. The parties agreed to do so and ultimately the matter was settled to their mutual satisfaction.

[8.13] For consumer complaints, such as retail transactions for the sale of goods, we have already seen that a Small Claims Court procedure has been initiated on a statutory basis, administered by clerks of the District Court.[20] Although operated within the court structure, the small claims procedure was established with a view to ensuring informality in the resolution of such complaints. Since 2006, the Small Claims Court has been operating an online dispute resolution procedure which allows for claims to be lodged online. In addition, for cross-border consumer disputes, the European Consumer Centre provides ADR mechanisms for redress.[21] In October 2001, the European Commission and member states established the European Extra Judicial Network to assist consumers to resolve their cross-border disputes through the vehicle of ADR schemes. This system operates across EU member states through clearing houses located in each member state. The European Consumer Centre is the European clearing house for Ireland. It provides advice to aggrieved consumers by intervening on their behalf with the relevant trader in the other EU member state.

[8.14] The increasing use of ADR in civil and commercial matters has been recognised by the EU in its 2008 Directive on Certain Aspects on Mediation in Civil and Commercial Matters.[22] The objective of the 2008 Directive is to promote the amicable settlement of disputes by encouraging the use of mediation by ensuring a balanced relationship between mediation and judicial proceedings. The Directive foresees the need for EU member states to provide a suitable legislative scheme to deal with key aspects of civil procedure and mediation. The Directive applies to mediation in cross-border disputes involving civil and commercial matters but also provides that member states can apply its provisions to their internal mediation processes. The Directive sees mediation as being encouraged by the courts to settle disputes coming before them. Consistent with the voluntary nature of mediation the Directive does not provide that mediation is compulsory.

[8.15] These developments reflect those in the United Kingdom. In 1994, the then Lord Chancellor appointed Lord Woolf to review the civil justice system with a view to increasing its efficiency and accessibility. He published two reports[23] which led to the

---

19 See Law Reform Commission, *Consultation Paper on Alternative Dispute Resolution* (LRC CP 50-2008), p 292.

20 See para **5.51**.

21 www.eccdublin.ie/.

22 Directive 2008/52/EC.

23 Woolf, *Access to Justice Interim Report* (1995) and Woolf, *Access to Justice Final Report* (1996).

introduction of the Civil Procedure Rules 1998 (CPR).[24] The CPR place ADR at the centre of civil litigation in the United Kingdom. The responsibility for active case management and encouragement of the use of ADR vests with the courts.[25] The judiciary in the UK have strongly encouraged the use of ADR in civil litigation. In a number of court decisions, it was indicated that should a party unreasonably refuse to submit to ADR, it may be subject to costs sanctions.[26] This has been further strengthened by the introduction of an amendment to the CPR which provides that should a party not comply with a court's direction that the parties submit to ADR, that party may be liable to cost sanctions.[27]

[8.16] Indeed, the reform of the Courts Service through the enactment of the Courts Service Act 1998 may also be seen against the background of the perceived inefficiency of existing arrangements in relation to other comparable arrangements, such as ADR.[28] The changes effected by the Woolf Reforms in the United Kingdom[29] were also driven by a concern to ensure that the civil justice process was efficient and accessible for users.

[8.17] It might be thought that the civil court system is 'in competition' with other adjudication mechanisms, such as arbitration and ADR. It certainly may be the case that the perceived inefficiency of the civil court process had, until the establishment of the Commercial Court list in the High Court in 2004, driven commercial litigants towards the ADR mechanisms, especially arbitration. It does not follow, however, that the courts should be in the business of becoming more efficient and creating a wider small claims procedure and establishing specialist commercial courts designed to deal efficiently with commercial disputes[30] merely to 'attract back' potential commercial 'customers' from the competition. Indeed, in the United Kingdom, the opposite is the case.

[8.18] In the wake of the Woolf civil justice reforms in the United Kingdom, the British government indicated that the next steps in the process were intended to ensure that legal disputes between individuals and corporate bodies should be resolved without having to use the court system. In other words, the court system should be the last resort where mediation, conciliation and arbitration have failed to resolve a dispute. This 'integrated' approach to civil justice also emphasises that in a 'knowledge society' there is a clear need to communicate to citizens their rights and entitlements under law, including increased emphasis on this within the education system.[31] The establishment in Britain

---

24 See further Ch 6.
25 CPR, r 1.4.
26 See *Cowl v Plymouth City Council* [2002] 1 WLR 803 and *Dunnett v Railtrack plc* [2002] 2 All ER 850.
27 CPR, r 44(5)(3).
28 See para **4.216**.
29 See para **6.66**.
30 See *First Report of the Working Group on a Courts Commission: Management and Financing of the Courts* (Pn 2690, 1996), p 34 (and paras **4.216** and **5.78** above), which discussed the rationale for the establishment of the Commercial Court within the High Court.

of a Community Legal Service (CLS), building on the long-established Citizens Advice Bureaux (CABs), is part of this process. In the medium term, it is envisaged that the law will become a resource available to all citizens in an easily accessible (web-based) form, with dispute resolution available online. It remains to be seen whether this wider vision will be fully realised in Ireland, but the Courts Service has been engaged in information technology initiatives which aim to introduce some of the innovations in technological terms which the integrated approach implies.[32]

[8.19] In its 2010 *Report on Alternative Dispute Resolution: Mediation and Conciliation* the Law Reform Commission recommended the introduction of a general legislative framework for mediation and conciliation, and appended a draft Mediation and Conciliation Bill to the Report.[33] We have already seen that the Commission sees mediation and conciliation forming an integrated part of a complete overall civil justice system, complementing the approach that is available through the courts system. The government accepted the thrust of the Commission's recommendations and, in 2012, it published the Scheme of a Mediation Bill which was largely based on the draft Bill in the Commission's 2010 Report. The government's Scheme of a Bill was referred for pre-legislative scrutiny to the Oireachtas Committee on Justice, Defence and Equality, which also supported the introduction of a Mediation Act. [34] At the time of writing (September 2014), it is expected that a government-backed Mediation Bill will be published in 2015. These developments, including the possible enactment of a Mediation Act, are likely to provide a further fillip to the growing emergence of mediation and conciliation as general civil dispute resolution processes.

[3] ARBITRATION

[8.20] As we have already noted, arbitration is a long-established form of dispute resolution, commonly used for commercial contract disputes, notably those arising from building contracts, insurance contracts and holiday contracts.[35] In addition, arbitration is regularly used to resolve disputes concerning compensation after the compulsory acquisition of land. Arbitration has also become increasingly significant against the background of commercial 'globalisation' since the 1980s. With the increase in international trade, it is common for many companies to require that any disputes be

---

[31] See the Report *Civiljustice.2000: A vision of the Civil Justice System in the Information Age* (2000), published by the then Lord Chancellor's Department (now the British Ministry of Justice).

[32] See para **4.222**.

[33] See generally Law Reform Commission, *Report on Alternative Dispute Resolution: Mediation and Conciliation* (LRC 98-2010).

[34] Joint Committee on Justice, Defence and Equality, *Report on hearings in relation to the Scheme of the Mediation Bill* (2012), available at http://www.oireachtas.ie/parliament/media/committees/justice/mediation-bill-report.pdf.

[35] See generally Forde, *Arbitration Law and Practice* (1994); Stewart, *Arbitration: Commentary and Sources* (2003) and Dowling-Hussey and Dunne, *Arbitration Law* (2008).

referred to arbitration in a particular location whose procedures are known to them, such as London or Dublin, rather than be resolved in the courts of the state in which they are trading. Thus, arbitration has both a national and international aspect.

[8.21] The principal advantages of arbitration over litigation include: the choice of an expert adjudicator, whether an architect, engineer or lawyer, as opposed to the imposition of a particular judge who may have no particular expertise in the area; procedural flexibility, subject to the essential rules of fair procedures; choice of location, procedure and applicable law; enforcement of arbitral awards internationally; the possibility of a speedy decision; and confidentiality through a hearing in private.[36] The Arbitration Act 2010[37] applies the UN Model Law on International Commercial Arbitration to all arbitrations, both domestic and international.[38] The 2010 Act sets out much of the procedural and legal requirements concerning a reference to arbitration, the conduct of the arbitration itself and the role of the courts. It has been noted that the incorporation of the UN Model Law into Irish law 'will have the effect of standardising and streamlining the manner in which arbitrations are conducted.'[39]

[8.22] As indicated, arbitration may arise automatically from the terms of a contract that includes an arbitration clause. These clauses are found increasingly in many commercial contracts. The Arbitration Act 2010 continues the long-standing position that where such an arbitration clause appears in a contract, any attempt to bring court proceedings without referring the matter to arbitration must be stayed on the application of the other party. Under the Arbitration Act 1954, the court had a discretion as to whether to grant a stay, but the 2010 Act, like its statutory predecessor in s 5 of the Arbitration Act 1980, severely limited this discretion.[40]

---

[36] Forde, *Arbitration Law and Practice* (1994), pp 3–4 and Dowling-Hussey and Dunne, *Arbitration Law* (2008) pp 19–23. On delays in the court system and proposals for reform, particularly in the commercial area, see paras **4.216** and **5.78**. Any reforms in the court system could not, of course, compete with the confidentiality of arbitration, or most of the other adjudicative bodies discussed in this chapter.

[37] The 2010 Act replaced and repealed the Arbitration Acts 1954 and 1980, which had regulated domestic arbitration, and the Arbitration (International Commercial) Act 1998, which had implemented the 1985 UN Model Law on International Commercial Arbitration, but had limited its application to international arbitrations. See Dowling-Hussey and Dunne, *Arbitration Law* (2008), pp vii–xv and Ó hOisín, 'Developing Ireland as a premier centre for international dispute resolution' (2008) *The Irish Times*, 30 June.

[38] In June 2001, the American Arbitration Association (AAA) opened an International Centre for Dispute Resolution in Dublin. At the time of the launch, it was indicated that international arbitration cases for the AAA had grown from 194 in 1996 to 510 in 2000. The AAA also had 54 cooperative agreements with international arbitral institutions in 39 other countries.

[39] Dowling-Hussey and Dunne, *Arbitration Law* (2008), p ix.

[40] Forde, *Arbitration Law and Practice* (1994), pp 23–8 and Dowling-Hussey and Dunne, *Arbitration Law* (2008), pp 104–106. Dowling-Hussey and Dunne note at p xiv that Article 8 of the UN Model Law is very similar to s 5 of the 1980 Act in relation to the obligation on the court to stay proceedings except in limited circumstances.

[8.23] Although an arbitration is held in private, the procedure is adversarial in nature and the arbitrator must act in an impartial manner, much like a judge in court. It is common for the rules of evidence, such as those governing hearsay, to be applied by arbitrators. In addition, the 2010 Act also lays down procedural requirements concerning the conduct of the arbitration and the arbitral award; these could be described as a detailed application of the rules of natural justice and fair procedures referred to at the outset of this chapter.[41]

[8.24] The Arbitration Act 2010 also provide for mechanisms by which the courts may become involved in resolving difficult points of law. It is stipulated that the arbitrator may refer points of law to the High Court by way of consultative case stated and a further appeal lies to the Supreme Court.[42] While the courts will provide such guidance as is requested, they are less likely to interfere with an arbitral award once it has been made. In line with courts in other jurisdictions, the courts have indicated that they are reluctant to interfere with the findings of an arbitrator.[43] This is based on a policy of encouraging arbitration as an alternative to litigation and the view that excessive interference would undermine the entire basis of arbitration.[44]

[8.25] In addition to the 2010 Act, legislation may establish particular arbitration schemes. These are common in the context of determining the level of compensation payable on the compulsory acquisition of land associated with planning, road construction and similar public civil engineering works. The most significant legislation in this respect remains the Acquisition of Land (Assessment of Compensation) Act 1919, which provides for the appointment of a property arbitrator where disputes concerning compulsory acquisition of land arises, for example by a local authority under a compulsory purchase order (CPO).[45] The scheme in the 1919 Act has been extended to the exercise of similar powers under other legislation.[46] It has also been extended to claims for compensation arising from refusal of planning permission.[47] Under the 1919 Act, as amended, an appeal lies by way of case stated to the High Court. Although the

---

41 See also Articles 18–27 of the UN Model Law on the conduct of arbitration proceedings and Articles 28–33 on the making of arbitration awards and termination of proceedings.

42 See Dowling-Hussey and Dunne, *Arbitration Law* (2008), pp 291–296.

43 For example, the High Court will be very reluctant to direct an arbitrator to state a case where the arbitration has refused to do so and this has been appealed by one or both of the parties to the arbitration. See the comments of Murphy J in *Power Securities Ltd v Daly* [1984] IEHC 266 and Dowling-Hussey and Dunne, *Arbitration Law* (2008), pp 291–294.

44 Forde, *Arbitration Law and Practice* (1994), pp 115–6.

45 See Galligan and McGrath, *Compulsory Purchase and Compensation in Ireland: Law and Practice* (2nd edn, 2013).

46 See, eg, Electricity Supply (Amendment) Act 1985, required by the decision in *Electricity Supply Board v Gormley* [1985] IR 129, which had found unconstitutional the Electricity Supply Act 1927, s 27, which contained no provision for compensation.

47 Planning and Development Act 2000.

1919 Act would appear to preclude further appeal, it seems that a further appeal lies to the Supreme Court.[48]

[4] ADMINISTRATIVE LAW AND THE EMERGENCE OF MODERN GOVERNMENT

[8.26] Administrative law encompasses the manner in which various adjudicative bodies are subject to legal control, but it also includes the role of the courts. The courts may become involved by means of appeals from such bodies, whether by way of a *de novo* hearing or an appeal on a point of law. In addition, the High Court may be involved through the mechanism of judicial review, the modern successor to the prerogative writs of the medieval Anglo–Norman courts.[49] There has been an exponential growth in recent years of administrative law litigation, largely evidenced by the increase of judicial review cases in the High Court. This growth mirrors the increased complexity of government and the range of adjudicative bodies it has generated.

[8.27] We have already seen that the extensive powers conferred on various adjudicative bodies, including the state bodies, have been questioned on the ground that they were exercising elements of the judicial function reserved to the courts by Article 34 of the Constitution. A challenge to the powers of the Land Commission was rejected on the ground that they were essentially administrative, as opposed to judicial. Similar conclusions were reached concerning Bord na gCon, the Greyhound Board, in making an exclusion order against a greyhound trainer, and in the case of Bord na Móna, the Turf Development Board, when deciding whether to acquire land compulsorily. The powers of the Law Society of Ireland to remove solicitors from the Roll of Solicitors and of clerks of the District Court in issuing summonses in criminal matters were declared to be invalid, requiring amending legislation, while doubts about the validity of adoption orders made by the statutory predecessor to the Adoption Authority of Ireland, An Bord Uchtála, precipitated an amendment to the Constitution.[50] Assuming that the powers exercised by the bodies discussed in this chapter are not liable to challenge under Article 34, they are nonetheless subject to judicial control.

The obligation to act judicially

[8.28] Although the bodies discussed in this chapter may not be exercising judicial power, they must act judicially when engaged in an administrative action affecting an individual. The obligation to act judicially requires that they act *intra vires* (that is,

---

[48] See *Attorney General (Fahy) v Bruen* [1936] IR 750; Pye, 'Appeals to the Supreme Court in Planning Compensation Cases' (1987) 5 ILT 252 and Galligan and McGrath, *Compulsory Purchase and Compensation in Ireland: Law and Practice* (2nd edn, 2013).

[49] On judicial review, see Ch 10.

[50] See para **4.19**.

within their powers)[51] and, subject to certain limitations,[52] comply with basic rules of natural justice or fair procedures.

[8.29] Although the rules of fair procedure are less formal than the rules of procedure and evidence of a court of law,[53] they require that a decision-making body be unbiased (*nemo judex in causa sua*) and that all sides involved have an opportunity to prepare their case and be treated in an even-handed manner, whether by oral hearing or by correspondence (*audi alteram partem*). Where such a body has been established under statute, it is sometimes provided that their decisions are subject to appeal to the courts, either by *de novo* hearing or on a point of law only. Where the statutory schemes do not provide for such appeals, they are subject to judicial review by the High Court.[54] Finally, where such bodies have been established outside a statutory framework, some may be amenable to judicial review, while the decisions of other non-statutory adjudicative bodies may be challenged in the courts using private law remedies such as injunctions.[55]

19th and 20th century development of government

[8.30] We have already noted that during the 19th century the essential elements of the system of government familiar today began to take shape.[56] The 19th century was also characterised by substantial law reform, including the overhauling of the administration of justice through the Judicature Acts 1873 and 1877, which replaced the complex network of courts that had developed since medieval times. The entire apparatus of state, from central to local government, was updated. To achieve these changes, older institutions were reformed and many entirely new executive bodies were established. In the Irish context, the Land Commission was one such body.[57]

[8.31] In effect, the 19th century saw an increase in the role and influence of the executive branch in the state, and this greatly accelerated during the second half of the 20th century and into the early 21st century. The outcome is that a great number of adjudicative bodies, or administrative bodies, emerged to administer the systems put in place by the Oireachtas and government, including bodies established to deal with employment disputes and social welfare claims. Before outlining the role and functions

---

[51] The corollary is that they must not act *ultra vires*, that is, outside their powers.

[52] Although we will see that coroners' inquests are inquisitorial in nature (paras **8.70–8.73**), the basic principles of fair procedures must be observed.

[53] See Ch 6.

[54] See para **10.53**.

[55] The judicial review procedure extends to decision-making bodies of a statutory or quasi-statutory nature, and this expresses the limit of administrative law, which is part of public law. Bodies exercising similar functions outside a statutory context are not amenable to judicial review but are subject to challenge using private law remedies, such as declarations and injunctions: see Ch 10.

[56] See para **2.22**.

[57] See para **2.43**.

of the adjudicative bodies generated by the expanding state, the essential elements of government organisation are outlined.

The organisation of government in Ireland

[8.32] Article 28.12 of the Constitution provides that the organisation and distribution of business amongst Departments of State and the designation of members of the government to be ministers in charge of those departments is to be regulated by law. This corresponds to the provisions of Article 36 on the regulation by law of the business of the courts.[58] The functions of ministers are described in the Ministers and Secretaries Act 1924, as amended. This Act effected the transition from the pre-1922 arrangements for the executive, which the Courts of Justice Act 1924 had done for the court system.

[8.33] By way of example of the allocation of business, s 1(iii) of the Courts of Justice Act 1924, which deals with the Department of Justice (now called the Department of Justice and Equality) provides:

"There shall be established ... (iii) The Department of Justice which shall comprise the administration and business generally of public services in connection with law, justice, public order and police, and all powers, duties and functions connected with the same ... and shall include in particular the business, powers, duties and functions of the branches and officers of the public service specified in the Second Part of the Schedule to this Act, and of which Department the head shall be, and shall be styled, an t-Aire Dlí agus Cirt or (in English) the Minister for Justice."

[8.34] The Second Part of the Schedule to the 1924 Act provides:

"Particular Branches of Administration Assigned to an Roinn Dlí agus Cirt (The Department of Justice)

Courts of Justice and the Offices thereof ...

Police.

The General Prisons Board for Ireland and all Prisons.

The Registrar of District Court Clerks.

The Public Record Office.

The Registry of Deeds.

The Land Registry.

The Commissioners of Charitable Donations and Bequests for Ireland."[59]

[8.35] Section 2(1) of the 1924 Act provides that each minister:

"shall be a corporation sole under his style or name ... and may sue and ... be sued under his style or name ... and may acquire, hold and dispose of land for the purposes of the functions, powers or duties of the Department of State of which he is head ..."

---

[58] See para **4.43**.

[59] The functions of the Commissioners were transferred to the Charities Regulatory Authority, established in 2014 under the Charities Act 2009.

The designation of the minister as a 'corporation sole' indicates that the style or name 'Minister for Justice and Equality' has a separate legal identity from the individual who is the minister at any given time, just as a limited liability company has a separate legal identity from the individuals who manage, or are shareholders in, that company.[60] The ministers are assisted by deputy ministers, called 'ministers of state',[61] who are generally delegated responsibility for particular functions within the department, but subject to the minister's overall control.

[8.36] As the Courts of Justice Act 1924 states, a minister is the head of the Department of State with ultimate responsibility for its activities. However, the full-time staff of the departments comprise the Civil Service, whose appointment is regulated and whose terms and conditions are regulated by the Public Service Management (Recruitment and Appointment) Act 2004. The day-to-day management of a department's functions is in the hands of the Secretary General of the department.[62] The Secretary General is a permanent civil servant and thus remains within the Civil Service where there is a change of government. In fact, party political activity is prohibited for all high-ranking civil servants. There are almost 30,000 people employed in the civil service. This figure is confined to persons employed within government departments and does not include over 250,000 employed in the wider public service, including those employed in about 100 state bodies established by legislation,[63] such as approximately 100,000 employed in the health care sector by the Health Service Executive (HSE),[64] those in the Defence Forces, the Prison Service, An Garda Síochána (the police force), teachers, and local authority staff, whose salaries are also ultimately paid by government (whether central or local) out of state funds.

[8.37] It is clear, even from this brief overview, that the government has enormous influence in the state. Whether at central government or local government level, its influence extends to the control of a great deal of economic activity, including the establishment and overall control of the various state bodies; the stimulation of investment in industry; awarding of public works contracts, such as road building, by government departments and local authorities; funding by government departments of social welfare programmes, the health service, the education service, the police service and the courts service;[65] ministerial licensing of numerous economic activities, from oil

---

[60] See para **1.29**.
[61] The Ministers and Secretaries (Amendment) Act 1977 introduced the title 'Minister of State', replacing the title 'Parliamentary Secretary', the title for deputy Ministers between 1924 and 1977.
[62] The Public Service Management Act 1997 introduced the title 'Secretary General' to replace the title 'Secretary'.
[63] See the OECD, *OECD Public Management Reviews: Ireland Towards an Integrated Public Service* (2008), p 22. A number of previously state-owned bodies, such as Bord Telecom Éireann, the telecommunications body, which employed over 10,000 people, were privatised in the late 1990s.
[64] Established by the Health Act 2004, which amalgamated the former health boards into the HSE.
[65] On the Courts Service, see para **4.217**.

exploration to livestock marts; the establishment and continued funding of state agencies and inspectorates to regulate such disparate matters as public health, environmental safety and competition in the public and private sectors; and the involvement of the state indirectly in the control of professions, including the legal profession, through legislation and other executive influence.[66]

Recent reforms in government

[8.38] In recent years, there has been much debate internationally about the role of the state, in particular the executive, in the economy. These economic and political debates are largely outside the scope of this text. However, their impact is being felt within the legal system, through, for example, the establishment of the Courts Service in 1999, thus separating day-to-day management of the courts from the Department of Justice and Equality, though it continues to be funded by the government.[67] This reflects an overall pattern of reform of the state sector, including the creation of similar semi-autonomous state bodies concerning public services and utilities, such as transport, the postal service, telecommunications and the generation, supply and distribution of electricity.

[8.39] In some respects, the 'liberalisation' of these sectors is required by European Union law,[68] but the demands of international competitive market forces also weigh heavily. Ultimately, many of these bodies and other commercial undertakings formerly in public ownership have been privatised, that is sold to private investors, including individuals as well as investment undertakings. This has occurred in the telecommunications and airline sector in Ireland. Again, the debate about the scale of privatisation is outside the scope of this text, but should nonetheless be borne in mind.

[8.40] In parallel with these developments, the general reorganisation and reform of the Civil Service began with the Public Service Management Act 1997, with more responsibility and accountability being transferred to civil servants. More reform has occurred in the context of critiques by influential international bodies such as the Organisation for Economic Cooperation and Development (OECD).[69] This has included

---

66 On the role of government in the legal profession, see discussion of the 1990 Fair Trade Commission Report and 2006 Competition Authority Report in Ch 3.

67 See para **4.217** on the Courts Service Act 1998, which came into effect in 1999.

68 See Ch 16.

69 See the OECD, *OECD Public Management Reviews: Ireland Towards an Integrated Public Service* (2008), which had been commissioned by the Irish government. In response, the government published a Framework for Sustainable Economic Renewal *Building Ireland's Smart Economy* (December 2008), available at www.taoiseach.gov.ie. This Framework Document committed the government to further public sector reform in the context of developing a 'Smart Economy'. In the wake of the EU–IMF Financial Support Agreement for Ireland (usually known as the 'EU–IMF Bailout'), which was in place between December 2010 and December 2013, further significant public service reform and rationalisation of state bodies was carried out: see para **8.40**. In parallel, a Department of Public Expenditure and Reform was established under the Ministers and Secretaries (Amendment) Act 2011.

the amalgamation and rationalisation of many State bodies, such as the amalgamation of the Competition Authority and the National Consumer Agency into the Competition and Consumer Protection Commission, under the Competition and Consumer Protection Act 2014. Similarly, the number of local authorities was greatly reduced under the Local Government Reform Act 2014. While privatisation may to some extent dilute the overall powers of government and ministers, it is also a feature of privatisation that the privatised utilities are subject to continued administrative control through the establishment of standard-setting regulatory bodies.

Examples of ministerial adjudicative powers

[8.41] The policy functions of a government minister as political head of a Department of State are not subject to judicial control.[70] However, many administrative powers and functions conferred on ministers must be exercised judicially in accordance with the rules of fair procedures. Such functions include the important power to award licences for certain undertakings, ranging from oil exploration to livestock marts. The statutory schemes for the exercise of such powers may provide for an appeal to the courts. Thus, s 16 of the Abattoirs Act 1988 provides that an appeal lies to the Circuit Court from a refusal of an abattoir licence by the Minister for Agriculture. In the absence of such an arrangement, the powers are subject to judicial review and must be exercised in accordance with fair procedures. In recent years, a large number of judicial review cases have involved challenges to the Minister for Justice's decisions in relation to the asylum process.

[8.42] Similarly, ministers have increasingly been granted powers by the Oireachtas to promulgate secondary or delegated legislation. This generally involves laying down detailed statutory rules on matters covered in general terms in primary legislation.[71] The exercise of such delegated power must not be *ultra vires* the rule-making authority conferred by the Constitution or by the primary legislation or otherwise in breach of the principles of fair procedures.[72] The substantial law-making powers conferred on Ministers by the European Communities Acts 1972–2012 include the power to amend primary legislation, a provision that in other circumstances would be unconstitutional[73] (and, since the enactment of the European Communities Act 2007, to create indictable offences using these regulation-making powers). In addition to such statutory powers, ministers exercise comparable functions under a range of non-statutory schemes. The exercise of decision-making powers under non-statutory schemes is subject to judicial control, by means of private law remedies such as a claim for damages.[74]

[8.43] However, not all functions of the government or of the adjudicative bodies referred to in this chapter are amenable to traditional forms of legal control, such as

---

[70] See para **8.32**.
[71] See para **13.109**.
[72] See paras **13.121–13.158**.
[73] See paras **16.118***ff*.
[74] *McKerring v Minister for Agriculture* [1989] ILRM 82.

appeals to the courts or judicial review. A distinction may be drawn in this respect between policy and administration. Where the government and the bodies it has created are engaged in policy making, judicial control is less likely. Thus, the balance to be struck between government grant aid for investment by foreign companies and indigenous companies is a matter of policy which is more a matter for political debate than debate in courts. Similarly, where the Minister for Justice and Equality and officials in the department propose a new approach to crime prevention, such a proposed policy is a matter for political debate rather than a matter to be challenged in court.

[8.44] By contrast, where government ministers and the other bodies described here are engaged in an administrative decision that affects an individual, such a decision is amenable to judicial control and may become a matter for debate in court. The distinction between policy and administration is not clear-cut, since many policy matters may spill over into administration. Thus, if government policy on grant aid were to operate in an arbitrary manner, an affected party might be entitled to challenge this in the courts. Similarly, if the crime policy of government involved a breach of constitutional rights, this could also be challenged.[75] In this chapter, we focus primarily on those administrative decisions that are amenable to judicial control.

[5] ADMINISTRATIVE LAW AND ADJUDICATIVE BODIES GENERALLY

[8.45] In addition to the adjudicative functions exercised by government ministers, many other adjudicative bodies have been established by legislation or government decision whose decisions are amenable to judicial review. In this section, we provide a brief overview of some of these; in view of the increased range and scope of the modern state, it is impossible to provide a complete listing of such adjudicative bodies. We have listed these adjudicative bodies in alphabetical order.

Agriculture

[8.46] The Agriculture Appeals Office established by the Agriculture Appeals Act 2001 provides an appeals process for farmers who are dissatisfied with decisions of the Department of Agriculture, Fisheries and Food regarding their entitlements under certain schemes.

Criminal injuries compensation

[8.47] We have already seen that the Malicious Injuries Acts 1981 and 1986, operated through the Circuit Court, provide a mechanism for compensating persons whose property has been damaged maliciously, such as in the course of a riot.[76]

Different arrangements have been put in place to deal with compensation for personal injuries suffered in similar circumstances. In 1974, the government published a non-

---

75 On the distinct nature of constitutional judicial review, see para **15.47**.

76 See para **5.65** discussing the Malicious Injuries Acts 1981 and 1986. The Malicious Injuries (Amendment) Bill 1996 proposed to repeal in full the 1981 and 1986 Acts, but it lapsed before it was debated in the Oireachtas.

statutory Scheme of Compensation for Injuries Inflicted Criminally, which established the Criminal Injuries Compensation Tribunal.[77] Similar schemes, though operating on a statutory basis, had been in place in Britain and Northern Ireland for many years.[78] The tribunal determines the level of compensation payable to a person who has suffered injuries in the course of a criminal act such as an assault or a riot. While the 1974 Scheme is not statutory, the courts have held that its decisions are subject to judicial review.[79]

[8.48] Prior to 1986, the tribunal was empowered to award general damages for the pain and suffering of any personal injuries suffered and any special damages such as loss of earnings.[80] However, in 1986 the relevant terms of the 1974 Scheme were amended, removing the power of the tribunal to award general damages.[81] This was done primarily as a means of limiting the cost to the state of criminal injuries compensation, confining it to awards for loss of earnings.[82] Since 2006, the tribunal has been designated as a transmitting and receiving authority for the state for the purposes of Directive 2004/80/EC relating to compensation to crime victims in cross-border situations. This means that an individual who suffers injury as a result of a crime which occurred in another EU member state can apply to the state where the incident occurred (the Receiving Authority) through the Criminal Injuries Compensation Tribunal (Transmitting Authority). The tribunal provides assistance to the person submitting the claim such as translation, including obtaining necessary documentation to process the claim. When the claim is finalised, the tribunal transmits the application directly to the authority in the member state where the crime was committed, which is then responsible for the application and paying out of compensation.

Employment

[8.49] Most states have established statutory bodies with extensive powers to deal with issues arising in the employment context. Some such bodies are empowered to investigate and mediate in industrial relations disputes with a view to a negotiated settlement where other means have failed. Others have been established to make findings similar to a court of law, such as determining whether a dismissal was in breach of statutory requirements.

---

[77] *Scheme of Compensation for Personal Injuries Criminally Inflicted* (Prl 3658, 1974). The Scheme has been amended a number of times since 1974.

[78] On the Northern Ireland scheme, see Dickson, *The Legal System of Northern Ireland* (3rd edn, 1993).

[79] See, eg, *The State (Hayes) v Criminal Injuries Compensation Tribunal* [1982] ILRM 210; *The State (Creedon) v Criminal Injuries Compensation Tribunal* [1989] ILRM 104.

[80] On damages, see para **10.03**.

[81] These changes should be linked to the limitations introduced to the malicious injuries statutory code by the Malicious Injuries (Amendment) Act 1986: see para **5.65**.

[82] See *Gavin v Criminal Injuries Compensation Tribunal* [1997] 1 IR 132.

[8.50] In the first category, that is mediation and conciliation, are the Labour Court and the Labour Relations Commission.[83] Neither body is a court exercising the judicial power under Article 34; rather their function is for the settlement of disputes that require the input of personnel who specialise in mediation between employers and employees. Both comprise representatives of employers, trade unions and other persons with expertise in the area of industrial relations. The Labour Relations Commission provides a conciliation service for individual disputes and also prepares codes of practice on industrial relations generally.[84] Where mediation in the Labour Relations Commission has failed, the Labour Court may investigate a dispute and is empowered to make decisions and issue recommendations to the parties. These are not always binding, but the parties may decide in advance of a Labour Court hearing that the court's recommendations will be accepted and implemented by both sides. The Industrial Relations (Amendment) Act 2001 empowers the Labour Court (at the request of a trade union) to investigate and make binding determinations on disputes where a number of pre-conditions are met.[85] Generally, no appeal lies to the courts from decisions of the Labour Court, but they are subject to judicial review.[86] However, because determinations of the Labour Court under the Industrial Relations (Amendment) Act 2001 are binding, an appeal on a point of law from such determinations lies to the High Court.[87] Rights Commissioners, who may be used to assist in the settlement of disputes, are attached to the Labour Court.

[8.51] The Labour Court is also empowered to set minimum wages for certain low-pay sectors, through Joint Labour Committees (JLCs).[88] The Labour Court gives effect to the proposals of the JLCs in the form of statutory orders, which is a form of delegated legislation. If, in making such an order, the Labour Court fails to comply with the principles of fair procedures referred to earlier, the order is liable to be declared invalid in the courts.[89]

---

[83] See Forde, *Industrial Relations Law* (1991), pp 34–40.

[84] These may be adopted by the Minister for Jobs, Enterprise and Innovation in statutory form: see para **13.09**, fn 10.

[85] Industrial Relations (Amendment) Act 2001, s 2(1), as amended by Industrial Relations (Miscellaneous Provisions) Act 2004, s 2.

[86] Industrial Relations Act 1946, s 17. See, eg, *The State (Aer Lingus Teo) v Labour Court* [1987] ILRM 373; *Aer Lingus Teo v Labour Court* [1990] ILRM 485 and *Ryanair Ltd v Labour Court* [2007] 4 IR 199.

[87] Industrial Relations (Amendment) Act 2001, s 11. See *Ashford Castle Ltd v SIPTU* [2006] ELR 201.

[88] Industrial Relations Act 1946, Pt IV. In *John Grace Fried Chicken Ltd v Catering Joint Labour Committee* [2011] IEHC 277, Part IV of the 1946 Act was declared unconstitutional because it conferred excessive legislative powers on the JLCs. The Industrial Relations (Amendment) Act 2012 was enacted in response, which provides for limits on the wage-setting powers of JLCs. Arising from this, a new JLC system was established in 2014.

[89] See *Burke v Minister for Labour* [1979] IR 354, discussed at para **13.149**. The JLCs continue in existence notwithstanding the enactment of the National Minimum Wage Act 2000.

[8.52] The Office of the Director of Equality Investigations, established in 1999,[90] took over functions formerly exercised by Equality Officers of the Labour Relations Commission. The Director's officers are empowered to make determinations in certain matters, notably in relation to equal pay and other aspects of discrimination at work under nine grounds of discrimination. It is worth noting that it is open for a claimant who alleges discrimination on grounds of gender to institute discrimination proceedings pursuant to the Employment Equality Acts 1998 to 2008 in the Circuit Court, which has unlimited jurisdiction in such cases.[91] Appeals from such determinations lie to the Labour Court and to the Circuit Court and, on a point of law, to the High Court.[92]

[8.53] The Employment Appeals Tribunal hears and determines cases in which an employee claims that he or she has been unfairly dismissed by an employer within the meaning of the Unfair Dismissals Acts 1977 to 2007.[93] The tribunal comprises three people, a solicitor or barrister who chairs the hearing, a representative of an employer's organisation and a representative of the trade union movement. The tribunal's procedures are adversarial in nature, though the rules of evidence might not be applied as strictly as in a court. An appeal lies from the Employment Appeals Tribunal to the Circuit Court, which conducts a full *de novo* re-hearing, and a further appeal and re-hearing may be had in the High Court.[94] At the time of writing (September 2014) the Workplace Relations Bill 2014 proposes the replacement of these adjudicative bodies with a single workplace Relations Commissioner.

Inspectorates: national and local

[8.54] Various Acts have established inspectorates or other comparable bodies both at national and local level to enforce standards established by such legislation. At national level, legislation has established the Health and Safety Authority,[95] the Environmental Protection Agency,[96] the Irish Aviation Authority[97] and the National Standards Authority of Ireland.[98] At a more local level, larger local authorities are required to appoint fire officers to ensure compliance with fire safety legislation[99] and environmental health officers to enforce food safety legislation in retail outlets.[100] Similarly, inspectors may be appointed on an *ad hoc* basis to investigate the dealings of companies pursuant to the

---

90   Employment Equality Act 1998, s 75.
91   Employment Equality Act 1998, s 77, as amended. For example, see *Atkinson v Carty* [2005] 16 ELR 1 where the plaintiff was awarded €102,750 as compensation for sexual harassment.
92   Employment Equality Acts 1998–2008, ss 83, 90.
93   Redmond, *Dismissal Law in Ireland* (2nd edn, 2007).
94   See *McCabe v Lisney & Son Ltd* [1981] ILRM 289; *Flynn v Power* [1985] ILRM 36; *Hogan v United Beverages Sales* [2006] 17 ELR 274.
95   Safety, Health and Welfare at Work Act 2005.
96   Environmental Protection Agency Act 1992.
97   Irish Aviation Authority Act 1993.
98   National Standards Authority of Ireland Act 1996.
99   Fire Services Act 1981.
100   Health Act 1947.

Companies Act 1990 (at the time of writing, September 2014, the Companies Bill 2012, which will consolidate and reform company legislation, is before the Oireachtas).

[8.55] In many instances, the statutory schemes establishing these agencies or inspectorates provide that an appeal lies to the courts in respect of decisions made by them. For example, s 20 of the Fire Services Act 1981 empowers a fire authority to serve a 'fire safety notice' on the owner of a potentially dangerous building, which the Act defines as a building likely to be a source of injury were a fire to occur in it. The notice can prohibit the use of the building to which it relates. Failure to observe the contents of the fire safety notice is a criminal offence. In addition, s 20 of the 1981 Act provides that an owner on whom such a fire safety notice has been served may appeal to the District Court. On such appeal, the judge of the District Court can either confirm or annul the fire safety notice. A further appeal on a point of law lies to the High Court by way of case stated.[101] In addition to such statutory arrangements, the administrative decisions of such inspectorates and agencies,[102] as opposed to their policy decisions, are amenable to judicial review.

Intellectual property

[8.56] Under a series of Acts, the Controller of Patents, Designs and Trade Marks is authorised to make important determinations in the area of intellectual property law. Thus, the Patents Act 1992 empowers the Controller to decide to whether certain inventions are entitled to be registered as patents and thus attract the statutory protections available under the 1992 Act. Similarly, the Trade Marks Act 1996 gives the Controller the power to determine whether certain symbols, drawings, marks and shapes connected with commercial products and services are entitled to the protection given under the 1996 Act.

[8.57] Section 96 of the Patents Act 1992 provides that an appeal lies to the High Court against most decisions of the Controller, such as refusal of a patent registration and that, on such appeal, the court may exercise any power of the Controller. This amounts to a hearing *de novo*. Section 96(7) of the 1992 Act provides that a further appeal on a point of law lies to the Supreme Court. Slightly different arrangements apply under the Trade Marks Act 1996. As with the 1992 Act, s 79 of the 1996 Act provides that an appeal lies to the High Court from a determination by the Controller, and that, on such appeal, the court may exercise any power of the Controller. However, s 79(3) of the 1996 Act provides that any further appeal to the Supreme Court on a point of law requires the leave of the High Court. Thus, there is no appeal to the Supreme Court as of right under the 1996 Act.

---

[101] See *Transactus Investments Ltd v Dublin Corporation* [1985] IR 501. Similar functions are conferred on the District Court by the Safety, Health and Welfare at Work Act 2005.

[102] See para **10.53**.

Oireachtas Committees

[8.58] Until recently, the Oireachtas had rarely established committees with powers to compel attendance of witnesses in a manner akin to a court. By contrast, such committees have become a feature of the United Kingdom Parliament in recent years and have been a feature of the Federal Congress of the United States for even longer. While such committees have occasionally proved controversial, they are also seen as part of the modernisation of Oireachtas procedures. Where such Oireachtas Committees have been established, the courts have made clear that the rules of fair procedures must be complied with and there must be no attempt to interfere with the judicial power reserved to the courts under Article 34 of the Constitution.[103]

In 2002, in *Maguire v Ardagh*,[104] the Supreme Court placed significant limits on the powers of Oireachtas Committees. The case concerned a Joint Oireachtas Committee set up to investigate the fatal killing by the members of the Garda Síochána of John McCarthy in Abbeylara, Co Longford. The Joint Oireachtas Committee was empowered to examine the effectiveness, appropriateness and reasonableness of the garda operation, the preparedness of the gardaí for the situation and the amount of force used. The Supreme Court held that the Oireachtas had no power to establish a committee that might make a finding of unlawful killing such as the Joint Committee appeared to envisage. The Supreme Court concluded that it would be constitutionally permissible for the Oireachtas to undertake certain types of inquiries but not of the nature proposed because it would have significant adverse effects on the rights of those persons appearing before it. In 2006, the Supreme Court rejected a challenge by a Circuit Court judge to the process put in place by the Oireachtas to begin a process of investigation prior to his possible impeachment.[105]

[8.59] In 2011, a proposal to amend the Constitution to confer wide-ranging quasi-judicial powers on Oireachtas Committees, in effect to overturn the decision in *Maguire v Ardagh*, was rejected in a referendum.[106] In the wake of this, the Houses of the Oireachtas (Inquiries, Privileges and Procedures) Act 2013 was enacted to consolidate the existing legislation in this area and to confer extensive fact-finding powers on Oireachtas Committees consistent with the constitutional limits prescribed in *Maguire v Ardagh*. The 2013 Act confers powers on virtually all Oireachtas Committees to compel the attendance of witnesses. The 2013 Act, like its statutory predecessors is seen as providing a more efficient, and less expensive, method of investigating issues of major public importance than that entailed in establishing judicial tribunals of inquiry or even

---

[103] *Re Haughey* [1971] IR 217 and *Maguire v Ardagh* [2002] IESC 21, [2002] 1 IR 385.

[104] *Maguire v Ardagh* [2002] 1 IR 385.

[105] *Curtin v Clerk of Dáil Éireann* [2006] 2 IR 556, [2006] 2 ILRM 99. The background to the case is discussed in Ch 4 above.

[106] The proposal was contained in the Thirtieth Amendment of the Constitution (Houses of the Oireachtas Inquiries) Bill 2011. This proposal was rejected on the same date that the Twenty-Ninth Amendment of the Constitution (Judges' Remuneration) Bill 2011 was approved: see para **4.174**.

a commission of investigation.[107] Indeed, an inquiry into tax evasion using the powers in the pre-2013 legislation on Oireachtas Committees, conducted by the Oireachtas Public Accounts Committee (PAC) in 1999–2001 was regarded as a highly successful use of the pre-2013 legislation.[108]

Planning and development

[8.60] The planning appeals board, An Bord Pleanála, is empowered to hear appeals from either the granting or refusing of planning permission by a planning authority. Prior to 1994, an appeal on a point of law lay to the High Court from the decisions of An Bord Pleanála, but this was removed and its decisions may now be challenged only on judicial review.[109]

'Private' adjudicative bodies

[8.61] We have seen that, in the legal profession, disciplinary tribunals have important decision-making powers in respect of members of the profession, which have an extremely important effect on that person's professional life.[110] Such tribunals are quite common within the professions, whether established by legislation[111] or otherwise.[112] In addition, such bodies are common within other statutory settings, such as schools,[113] and non-statutory settings, such as sporting associations.[114] Where such bodies are established by statute, the courts may be directly involved, as in the case of the disciplinary bodies for solicitors. In other instances, the decisions of such bodies are subject to judicial control either by means of judicial review or other private law remedies.

Public supply, works and services contracts

[8.62] Both central and local government are responsible for the procurement of many major public supply, public works and public services contracts, including the provision

---

107 See para **8.74**.
108 Public Accounts Committee, *Final Report of Sub-Committee on Certain Revenue Matters: Parliamentary Inquiry into DIRT* (2001).
109 Local Government (Planning and Development) Act 1963, s 82, as amended by the Local Government (Planning and Development) Act 1992. See now the Planning and Development Act 2000, ss 50 and 51. For appeals in arbitration connected with refusal of planning permission, see para **8.25**.
110 See paras **3.58** and **3.89**.
111 See the Medical Practitioners Act 2007; Dentists Act 1985; Nurses and Midwives Act 2010; and Garda Síochána (Discipline) Regulations 1989.
112 For barristers see para **3.89**; for accountants, see the Charter of the Institute of Chartered Accountants in Ireland. The constitutional validity of the Charter was upheld in *Geoghegan v Institute of Chartered Accountants in Ireland* [1995] 3 IR 86.
113 See the Education Act 1998, ss 28, 29. Prior to the 1998 Act, the non-statutory arrangements were subject to judicial review: see *The State (Smullen) v Duffy* [1980] ILRM 46.
114 See *Clancy v Irish Rugby Football Union* [1995] 1 ILRM 193; McCutcheon, 'Judicial Scrutiny of Sports Administration' (1995) 14 ILT 171.

of catering facilities, road building and the provision of professional services. Arising from European Community law requirements, the procurement procedures for such contracts must be open to bidding by undertakings from across the European Union. Where the appropriate procedures are not followed, an appeal lies to the High Court, which may quash any contract awarded in breach of Community law requirements.[115]

Public utilities: regulation of privatised economic sectors

[8.63] As already mentioned,[116] a feature of many EU member states in recent years has been the privatisation of former state-owned public utilities, in particular those in the telecommunications, electricity and transport sectors. Where such privatisation has occurred, the relevant legislation has included arrangements for the continued regulation of the sector by means of a state agency with substantial decision-making powers that can be described as quasi-judicial.

[8.64] Thus, in the telecommunications industry, now largely privatised and outside direct government control, the Commission for Communications Regulation[117] was established to set down licensing and other controls (including technical standards) that were formerly administered directly by government.[118] Thus, the decision of the Director of Telecommunications Regulation (since replaced by the Commission for Communications Regulation) to grant a mobile telephone licence to a particular company is an adjudicative decision which may give rise to complex judicial review proceedings.[119] Similar arrangements have been put in place for the energy, water and railway sectors.[120]

---

[115] European Communities (Award of Public Authorities' Contracts) Regulations 2006 (SI 329/ 2006). See also *Dekra Éireann Teo v Minister for the Environment* [2003] 2 IR 270.

[116] Para **8.39**.

[117] The Commission for Communications Regulation was established by the Communications Regulation Act 2002.

[118] Another facet of privatisation is that consumer complaints, which formerly were within the remit of the Ombudsman (see para **8.84**), are now dealt with by the Commission for Communications Regulation. On the approach to handling consumer complaints, see the Commission for Communications Regulation's website at www.comreg.ie.

[119] See *Orange Communications Ltd v Director of Telecommunications Regulation* [2000] 4 IR 159, 202. The case, which was at hearing for 51 days in the High Court and 17 days in the Supreme Court, was a challenge to the decision of the Director to award the third national mobile telephone licence to Meteor Mobile Communications Ltd. The applicant company was successful in the High Court, but the Supreme Court reversed this decision and the Director's original decision was re-instated. In his concluding remarks on the case, Keane CJ regretted that the case had not been subjected to judicial case management prior to the High Court hearing. On case management generally, see paras **6.66**ff.

[120] The Commission for Electricity Regulation was established by the Electricity Regulation Act 1999. Its name and remit was altered by the Gas (Interim Regulation) Act 2002 so it is now the Commission for Energy Regulation and its remit now includes the regulation of the natural gas sector and the standards and charges for water services provides by Irish Water. The Railway Safety Commission was established by the Railway Safety Act 2005, which is entrusted with responsibility for railway safety on passenger trains and, in certain circumstances, freight trains.

Rating and valuation

[8.65] The Valuation Tribunal[121] is empowered to hear applications in relation to the rateable valuation which has been placed on property by a local authority. The rateable valuation is the sum specified by a local authority as the basis for calculating the rates which the local authority may charge as a property tax on business premises in its functional area. The tribunal succeeded to the jurisdiction formerly exercised by the Circuit Court in this respect. The tribunal also deals with appeals against determinations of market value on derelict sites made by local authorities under the Derelict Sites Act 1990. In light of that history, it is not surprising, perhaps, that the procedures in the tribunal are similar to those in a courtroom and that in many instances counsel are retained to appear before the tribunal. An appeal by way of case stated lies from a determination of the tribunal to the High Court and a further appeal on a point of law lies to the Supreme Court.[122]

Refugees Appeal Tribunal

[8.66] The Refugee Appeals Tribunal, established by the Refugee Act 1996, is empowered to hear appeals from asylum seekers whose applications for refugee status have not been recommended by the Office of the Refugee Applications Commissioner. The tribunal sits with one member who is a trained barrister or solicitor and, following an oral hearing or consideration of the decision of the Officer of the Refugee Applications Commissioner, the member decides whether to affirm or set aside the original recommendation of the Office of the Refugee Applications Commissioner.

Revenue

[8.67] The Taxes Consolidation Act 1997, as amended, specifies a statutory scheme for the resolution of disputes concerning taxation. Initially, an assessment of tax is made by an Inspector of Taxes, a civil servant who is an officer of the Revenue Commissioners. If a taxpayer is dissatisfied with such an assessment, an appeal lies to the Appeal Commissioners, who are independent of the Revenue Commissioners and are empowered to conduct a full hearing concerning liability to tax, including any points of law that may arise. The procedure before the Appeal Commissioners is essentially adversarial, but the formal rules of evidence may not be applied as strictly as in a court. If either the Inspector of Taxes or the taxpayer is dissatisfied with the determination of the Appeal Commissioners, an appeal by way of *de novo* hearing in the Circuit Court lies.[123] A further appeal by way of case stated lies to the High Court and to the Supreme Court. Alternatively, an appeal by case stated from the Appeal Commissioners lies to the High Court and this may be appealed by another case stated to the Supreme Court.[124]

---

121 See the Valuation Act 2001, which repealed the Valuation Act 1988.
122 Valuation Act 2001, s 39.
123 Taxes Consolidation Act 1997, s 942.
124 Taxes Consolidation Act 1997, ss 933, 941, 942.

In addition, we may note that County Registrars and Sheriffs are empowered under the 1997 Act to seize a person's property where the person is in default in respect of tax which has been lawfully levied by an Inspector of Taxes.[125]

Social welfare

[8.68] The Social Welfare Consolidation Act 2005 provides that where an individual is refused a particular allowance or benefit under the social welfare legislation, an appeal may be made to an Appeals Officer of the Department of Social Welfare. Unlike the situation with respect to taxation matters, there is no direct appeal mechanism from an Appeals Officer to the court system. However, an aggrieved person may seek judicial review where, for example, it is alleged that the procedures adopted were unfair or that the Appeals Officer misapplied the law.[126]

Reform

[8.69] As we have seen, each of the various government departments or bodies has individual and stand-alone appeals from its decisions. It has been argued that such a multitude of appeals is inefficient and can lead to inconsistency in standards and rules applied throughout the various appeals forums.[127] In order to alleviate these difficulties and to introduce efficiency and cost effectiveness into the appeals system, it has been suggested that a single appeals panel be established to deal with all appeals from the various government departments and bodies.

[6] CORONERS' COURTS

[8.70] Perhaps the closest form of adjudicative bodies to the courts discussed in earlier chapters are the coroners' courts. Coroners have an ancient common law pedigree as quasi-judicial officers, but their functions are now regulated by the Coroners Act 1962.[128] They conduct inquests, in public,[129] into any violent, suspicious or otherwise unexplained death. The inquests are presided over by medical practitioners, though many of these also possess legal training. The Coroners Act 1962 prescribes the

---

125 See, eg, *Weekes v Revenue Commissioners* [1989] ILRM 165.

126 See, eg, *The State (Kershaw) v Eastern Health Board* [1985] ILRM 235. On reforms to the appeal mechanisms, see Cousins, *The Irish Social Welfare System: Law and Social Policy* (1995), p 116.

127 Commins, 'An Analysis of the Rationale for the Introduction of a Unified Appeals System in Ireland' (2007), available at www.socialwelfareappeals.ie/pubs/study07.pdf.

128 See generally, Farrell, *Coroners: Practice and Procedure* (2000).

129 Prior to the Coroners Act 1962, the Coroners (Ireland) Act 1846 authorised a coroner to order that a dead body be brought to the nearest convenient tavern, public house or house licensed for the sale of intoxicating liquor and the owner of such premises was required to allow the body to be deposited there until the inquest had taken place. The 1846 Act, which replicated a similar statutory regime for the rest of the United Kingdom, was repealed by the 1962 Act, which requires a body be removed to a convenient mortuary or morgue pending the holding of the inquest in public.

procedure under which inquests must be held and the circumstances in which a coroner's jury must be summoned by the coroner.[130] Section 40 of the 1962 Act provides that a jury is necessary where the coroner is of opinion that:

- the deceased came by his or her death by murder, infanticide or manslaughter;

- other statutory provisions require the holding of an inquest;

- the death was caused by accident, poisoning or disease of a type notifiable to a minister or government inspector;

- the death occurred from the use of a vehicle in a public place; or

- the death occurred in circumstances the continuance or recurrence of which would be prejudicial to the health and safety of the public.

[8.71] The coroner's court has some appearances of an ordinary court, in that it sits in public, it is presided over by a professional person, witnesses give their evidence under oath and there is often a jury. However, it differs markedly from an ordinary court in that it is essentially an inquisitorial body rather than an adversarial one. In this respect, the coroner determines which witnesses are called and the sequence in which they give evidence and he or she also has wide discretion as to who may be represented at the inquest. In addition, the findings that a coroner and jury may make are severely limited by the Coroners Act 1962. Section 30 of the 1962 Act precludes the giving of a verdict which would involve the implication of either civil or criminal liability on the part of the deceased. Indeed, inquests are generally stayed pending the conclusion of any criminal proceedings.

[8.72] Where an inquest is opened and An Garda Síochána inform the coroner that criminal proceedings are contemplated, the inquest is then adjourned.[131] In that respect, it is confined to determining 'who, how, when and where', that is, to determining who the deceased person was, as well as how, when and where he or she died. In effect, the Coroners Act 1962 limits the coroner or inquest jury to the following types of verdicts: death from natural causes, death by reason of accident or misadventure, death by the deceased's own act[132] or an 'open verdict', where the other verdicts are inappropriate. In the United Kingdom, coroners' courts have been authorised by statute to make findings of suicide, but this is not permissible under the 1962 Act.[133] Section 40 of the 1962 Act allows a jury to make a finding of murder, manslaughter or infanticide, but this is

---

130 The jury panels for coroners' courts are identical to those for courts operating under Article 34 of the Constitution and are governed by the Juries Act 1976: see para **6.142**. However, the procedure for selecting a coroners' jury is less formal. A coroners' jury may consist of six members, rather than the 12 associated with ordinary courts. In Britain and Northern Ireland, the jury ranges from 7 to 11 in number. Note also the changes introduced by the Coroners (Amendment) Act 2005, discussed below.

131 The former procedure by which the inquest is adjourned indefinitely (*sine die*) is not permissible: *The State (Costello) v Bofin* [1980] ILRM 233.

132 Generally, the phrase 'when the balance of the mind was disturbed' is included in the verdict.

133 *The State (McKeown) v Scully* [1986] IR 524.

confined to third-party involvement in the death.[134] The limitations contained in the 1962 Act have been criticised in recent years, and significant proposals for reform were published in 2000.[135] In 2005, the Coroners (Amendment) Act 2005 was enacted to deal with two critical issues: the limitation in s 26 of the Coroners Act 1962 that only two medical witnesses could give evidence at an inquest and the criminalising of non-attendance of a juror or witness served with a summons to attend an inquest.

[8.73] The Coroners Bill 2007, which is at the time of writing (September 2014), before the Oireachtas, proposes comprehensive reform of the legislative framework for coroners and will replace the Coroners Act 1962. The 2007 Bill proposes to widen the scope of an inquest from investigating the proximate medical cause of death, to establishing in what circumstances the deceased met his or her death. This extension was recommended by the 2000 Coroners Review Group. The 2007 Bill also proposes to establish a full-time Coroners Service. The 2007 Bill also provides for legal aid in proceedings before a coroner where a person has died in state custody or certain institutional care situations. This proposal stems from a number of judgments of the European Court of Human Rights which have held that there must be provision for legal aid in cases where there is an involvement of the state in the circumstances of death. In view of ongoing delay in enacting the 2007 Bill, the 1962 Act was amended by the Civil Law and Courts (Miscellaneous Provisions) Act 2013 to provide legal aid in coroners' inquests.

[7]   TRIBUNALS OF INQUIRY AND COMMISSIONS OF INVESTIGATION

[8.74] Many of the statutory adjudicative bodies referred to in this chapter have a permanent status, in the sense that the legislation establishing them provides for an indefinite life span, subject to the power of the Oireachtas to repeal the legislation under which they were established. The Oireachtas also has power to establish tribunals of inquiry to investigate certain matters of public importance. In addition, the Oireachtas may resolve that such a tribunal be invested with the powers contained in the Tribunals of Inquiry (Evidence) Acts 1921–2004.[136] In many cases a tribunal of inquiry may also be given the power to make recommendations with a view to preventing the future occurrence of the matter which gave rise to its establishment. This may include making suggestions for law reform.

[8.75] In recent decades, such tribunals have been established to inquire into the circumstances surrounding an explosion on an oil tanker which resulted in substantial

---

[134]   *Green v McLoughlin* [1991] 1 IR 309 (HC); (26 January 1995, unreported), SC.

[135]   *Review of the Coroner Service* (2000), available at www.justice.ie.

[136]   Similar, though less extensive, powers are also contained in particular legislation, eg Merchant Shipping Act 1894, Transport Act 1936, Safety, Health and Welfare at Work Act 2005 and Environmental Protection Agency Act 1992.

loss of life,[137] a St Valentine's Day fire at a disco resulting in almost 50 deaths,[138] the collapse of a homicide prosecution in a particular case,[139] allegations relating to the beef processing industry in the state,[140] the infection of large numbers of people in the 1970s and 1980s with contaminated blood products,[141] the payment of moneys to politicians,[142], including to a former Taoiseach (the Moriarty tribunal),[143] and possible collusion by members of An Garda Síochána or the state in the fatal shootings of two RUC Officers in 1989 (the Smithwick Inquiry).[144]

[8.76] Other tribunals in recent years have inquired into the infection with HIV and Hepatitis C of persons with haemophilia (the Lindsay Tribunal), into planning matters and payments to politicians and other persons (originally the Flood Tribunal, later the Mahon Tribunal), into complaints concerning some gardaí of the Donegal Division (the Morris Tribunal) and into the siege and shooting of John McCarthy in Abbeylara, County Longford (the Barr Tribunal). Each of the tribunals attracted considerable media discussion and debate concerning the issues being inquired into. In particular, the high cost of these tribunals and a number of leaks of reports to the media received a high level of media attention.[145]

[8.77] In 2003, the Law Reform Commission recommended the enactment of legislation providing for a private low-key inquiry which would focus on the wrong or malfunction in the system rather than on individual wrongdoers and which would operate as a preliminary to, or in many cases, as an alternative to, a full-scale tribunal of inquiry.[146] The recommendation was implemented in the Commission of Investigations Act 2004. The first commission of investigation established by virtue of the 2004 Act was the Commission established to investigate certain aspects of the Dublin and Monaghan Bombings 1974 (the MacEntee Commission), which published its report in April 2007.

[8.78] Because commissions of investigations have been regarded as more efficient than some of the tribunals of inquiry established in recent years, they have become the

---

[137] *Report of the Tribunal of Inquiry into the Disaster at Whiddy Island, Bantry, Co Cork* (Pl 8911, 1979).

[138] *Report of the Tribunal of Inquiry on the Fire at the Stardust, Artane, Dublin* (Pl 853, 1982).

[139] *Report of the Tribunal of Inquiry into 'the Kerry Babies case'* (Pl 3514, 1985).

[140] *Report of the Tribunal of Inquiry into the Beef Processing Industry* (Pn 1007, 1994).

[141] *Report of the Tribunal of Inquiry into the Blood Transfusion Service Board* (1997).

[142] *Report of the Tribunal of Inquiry into Payments to Politicians (Dunnes Stores)* (Pn 4199, 1997).

[143] *Report of the Tribunal of Inquiry into Payments to Politicians*, available at www.moriaty-tribunal.ie.

[144] *Report of the Smithwick Tribunal of Inquiry*, available at www.smithwicktribunal.ie.

[145] For example, see (2008) *The Sunday Tribune*, 1 June; (2004) *The Sunday Times*, 25 July; Cassidy, 'Hole in my Bucket' [2008] 101(5) *Law Society Gazette* 32 and *Mahon v Keena and Kennedy* [2009] IESC 64.

[146] Law Reform Commission, *Consultation Paper on Public Inquiries Including Tribunals of Inquiry* (LRC CP 22-2003).

preferred model of investigation into matters of public concern. At the time of writing (September 2014), therefore, it seems unlikely that tribunals of inquiry will be established to deal with such issues, at least not in the foreseeable future. Nonetheless, we describe briefly below the nature and powers of tribunals because they have been the subject of significant case law which has analysed their powers. In this context it is notable that commissions of investigation established under the 2004 Act have comparable powers, a significant difference being a statutory presumption in the 2004 Act that they conduct their investigations in private whereas the Tribunal of Inquiries Acts contain a statutory presumption of public hearings.

[8.79] A tribunal established under the Tribunals of Inquiry (Evidence) Acts 1921–2004 has powers similar to those of a court, including power to compel attendance of witnesses and of referral to the High Court where a person refuses to give evidence or is otherwise in contempt of the tribunal.[147] Indeed, in all instances where a tribunal has been established in recent years, it has been chaired by a judge. The courts, however, have rejected a number of challenges to the constitutionality of such tribunals, and have concluded that they are not engaged in exercising the judicial power reserved to the courts by Article 34 of the Constitution. It has also been held that they do not make determinations that pre-empt any pending or future civil or criminal proceedings and that their essential role is limited to one of 'fact finding'.[148] In that sense, such a tribunal is essentially inquisitorial in nature.

[8.80] However, because civil or criminal proceedings may emerge from the deliberations of tribunals, the procedures adopted by them have tended to conform quite closely to those of a court. Thus, it is common practice to grant any interested party the right to be legally represented at the tribunal. Typically, this would involve a solicitor who would instruct junior and senior counsel. In view of the presence of legal representation, tribunals of inquiry also tend to apply the rules of evidence as nearly as possible in the circumstances.[149] This has included the use of pre-hearing discovery of documents from any potential witness, which has in turn led to challenges to the scope of such discovery orders.[150] Another feature of legal representation is that tribunals have taken on an adversarial nature, despite their inquisitorial function. Thus, any witness before a tribunal is likely to be cross-examined by all other parties represented at the tribunal.

[8.81] It has also become established practice for such parties to be awarded their costs of appearing before the tribunal, thus requiring the state to defray these costs.[151] This has

---

[147] See *Kiberd v Hamilton* [1992] 2 IR 257.

[148] See *Goodman International v Hamilton* [1992] 2 IR 542; *Haughey v Moriarty* [1999] 3 IR 1.

[149] See *Goodman International v Hamilton* [1992] 2 IR 542.

[150] See, for example, *Haughey v Moriarty* [1999] 3 IR 1; *Lawlor v Flood* [1999] 3 IR 107; *Miley v Flood* [2001] 1 ILRM 489.

[151] This does not, however, require the state to provide in advance, the cost of the legal representation. See *McBrearty v Morris* [2003] IEHC 154 and *Lawlor v Members of the Tribunal of Inquiry into Certain Planning Matters and Payments* [2008] IEHC 282.

resulted in substantial costs being incurred by the state where such tribunals have been established.[152] A 2009 report by the Comptroller and Auditor General estimated the costs of the Mahon, Moriarty and Morris tribunals of inquiry to be in the region of €434m by the time of their completion.[153] Given the significant public disquiet about the cost of tribunals in recent years, it is as already mentioned unlikely that any tribunals will be established in the near future. At the time of writing (September 2014), nonetheless, the Tribunals of Inquiry Bill 2005, which is currently before the Oireachtas, proposes to replace the Tribunals of Inquiry Acts 1921–2004 with a more focused legislative framework for future tribunals, including significant reform of the management of tribunals and restrictions on the levels of costs likely to be involved. The 2005 Bill is based on recommendations made by the Law Reform Commission.[154] In addition, the Commission of Investigations Act 2004 provides an alternative to tribunals of inquiry in cases where it is more appropriate for wrongs in the system to be examined rather than taking an individualised approach.

[8.82] Statutory commissions have also been established on an *ad hoc* basis. In 2009, an *ad hoc* statutory commission to inquire into historical child sexual abuse issued a damning 3,500 page report on widespread physical and sexual abuse of children in industrial schools covering a period from the 1940s to the 1990s.[155]

[8] OMBUDSMEN

[8.83] Judicial control of adjudicative bodies, whether by statutory appeal, judicial review or other private law remedies, has greatly increased in recent years. However, recourse to the courts involves considerable expense and while corporate bodies may be prepared to challenge adjudicative decisions in this way, such a route may be beyond the means of many individuals, particularly in light of the limitations to the state-funded civil legal aid scheme.[156] In addition, while the decisions of some adjudicative bodies may be appealed to the courts, in many instances judicial review is the only available remedy. In this respect, judicial review does not provide a comprehensive means of

---

152 See further para **3.29**.
153 Comptroller and Auditor General, *Special Report 63: Tribunals of Inquiry* (December 2008).
154 See Law Reform Commission, *Report on Public Inquiries Including Tribunals of Inquiry* (LRC 73-2005).
155 *Report of the Commission to Inquire into Child Abuse* (in five volumes, 2009), available at www.cica.ie. This was established under the Commission to Inquire into Child Abuse Act 2000. The powers conferred on the Commission resembled those of a tribunal of inquiry, though it was not an inquisitorial tribunal. The Commission was initially under the direction of Miss Justice Laffoy, who returned to the High Court in 2003 after her resignation from the Commission. She was replaced by Mr Justice Sean Ryan, judge of the High Court. The Commission was made up of two committees: a confidential committee which provided a forum for victims of abuse to recount their experience on a confidential basis and an investigative committee which allowed victims to recount their experiences and have their allegations of abuse examined.
156 See Ch 9.

remedying faulty decision-making; it is limited to correcting *ultra vires* decisions and those which do not comply with fair procedures.

The Ombudsman (Parliamentary Commissioner)

[8.84] As part of the reform of the executive branch and the wider public sector, a more informal review mechanism has been introduced in the state. This borrows from the Scandinavian model of the Parliamentary Commissioner or Ombudsman. The Ombudsman Acts 1980 to 2012 provide that the Ombudsman, who is independent in the performance of her functions, may investigate any decision or failure to act which occurs 'in the performance of administrative functions' by most government departments and a wide range of other state bodies specified in the Acts, where such decision or failure to act 'may have adversely affected a person.'[157] The Ombudsman is empowered to investigate any such decision or failure to act where it was:

- taken without proper authority,
- taken on irrelevant grounds,
- the result of negligence or carelessness,
- based on erroneous or incomplete information,
- improperly discriminatory,
- based on an undesirable administrative practice, or
- otherwise contrary to fair or sound administration.

[8.85] While certain matters are excluded from the Ombudsman's remit,[158] the scope of the office's powers is wide and was greatly expanded in 2012 to include virtually all bodies funded by the state.[159] The Ombudsman is empowered to investigate what has been termed 'maladministration' or, put another way, to promote principles of good administration in the public service.

---

[157] Ombudsman Act 1980, as amended by the Ombudsman (Amendment) Act 2012, which introduced into the 1980 Act the concept of 'reviewable agency' over which the Ombudsman is empowered to investigate decisions or failure to act by such agencies. A list of the reviewable agencies, and those to be excluded, is provided in the Schedules to the 1980 Act, as inserted by the 2012 Act.

[158] Ombudsman Act 1980, s 5 excludes, eg, decisions in respect of which an appeal lies to the courts and decisions connected with national security, including the power of pardon and the administration of prisons.

[159] The Health Act 2004 expanded the remit of the Office of the Ombudsman into the area of large public voluntary hospitals: see Annual Report of the Office of the Ombudsman 2007, ch 4. Similarly, the remit of the Ombudsman was expanded under the Disability Act 2005 to include complaints in relation to compliance by public bodies with the 2005 Act. The effect of the changes made by the Ombudsman (Amendment) Act 2012 is to include bodies whose actions affect significant numbers of people and bodies set up in recent years whose functions were formerly carried out by government departments that were within the remit of the Ombudsman.

[8.86] The role of the Ombudsman is similar to that of a judge[160] in that he or she is empowered to investigate matters and make 'findings'. However, a key distinction is that the Ombudsman Acts 1980 to 2012 provide that there is no power to make determinations that are binding on those to whom they are directed. Rather, it is provided that if the Ombudsman finds that a decision has adversely affected a person, he or she may 'recommend ... that ... specified measures be taken to remedy, mitigate or alter' the adverse effect of the decision.[161] This regularly involves a recommendation to pay monetary compensation to the person adversely affected. If the response of the body to a 'finding' or recommendation is 'not satisfactory', the Ombudsman may make a formal report to this effect to both Houses of the Oireachtas. This may also be included in the annual report which the Ombudsman is required to make to both Houses of the Oireachtas. The Ombudsman is vested with extensive powers. The Office of the Ombudsman is empowered to demand any information, document or file from a body within its remit and can require any official to give information about a complaint.[162]

[8.87] Thus, the ultimate sanction of the Ombudsman is not a fine or contempt of court, but the adverse publicity for a government department or local authority if it became known that they had failed to take account of any recommendation. It would seem that this 'sanction' has proved sufficiently persuasive in the vast majority of cases. Indeed, the Ombudsman has suggested in the past that the absence of a formal power to make binding determinations prevented the initiation of judicial review of the powers of the office, especially in its early years.[163] The Ombudsman is also empowered to present a special report to the Houses of the Oireachtas should a public body fail to act on any of the recommendations made by her following the investigation of a dispute.[164]

Other Ombudsmen

[8.88] The establishment of the office of Ombudsman has led to the creation of similar offices in a wide range of areas not covered by the Ombudsman Acts 1980 to 2012. Thus, the independent adjudicator provided for in the Solicitors (Amendment) Act 1994 performed a similar function for the solicitor's branch of the legal profession. This may be replaced by the Legal Services Regulatory Authority, due to be established under the Legal Services Regulation Bill 2011, which is currently before the Oireachtas. This would replace the proposed Legal Services Ombudsman provided for in the Legal Services Ombudsman Act 2009, which was not brought into force.[165]

---

160 The Ombudsman Act 1980 provides that the Ombudsman is appointed by the President, is to be paid the same salary as that of a High Court judge and may only be removed from office for stated misbehaviour or incapacity on resolutions passed by both Houses of the Oireachtas.

161 Ombudsman Act 1980, s 6(3). Section 6(3A) of the Ombudsman Act 1980, as inserted by the Ombudsman (Amendment) Act 2012, provides that the Ombudsman may make a general recommendation to any of the bodies within his or her remit where, following an investigation, it is considered necessary to do so.

162 Ombudsman Act 1980, s 7(1).

163 *Annual Report of the Ombudsman 1995* (Pn 2590, 1996), p 7.

164 Ombudsman Act 1980, s 6(5).

165 See para **3.17**.

[8.89] The recognition of the benefits of an ombudsman-type model for various sectors has been apparent with the creation of a number of new ombudsmen in recent years. It was previously the case that a number of offices similar in nature to the office of the Ombudsman were established on a non-statutory basis. For example, the Insurance Ombudsman of Ireland and the Ombudsman for Credit Unions were in existence since the early 1990s. Towards the end of the 1990s it was felt that a statutory ombudsman scheme for all providers of financial services with enhanced statutory powers was necessary. The Financial Services Ombudsman was created by the Central Bank and Financial Services Authority of Ireland Act 2004.[166] It deals independently with unresolved complaints from consumers about their dealings with all financial service providers including banks, building societies, insurance companies, mortgage intermediaries, hire purchase providers and health insurance companies. The service is free to eligible consumers who include all natural persons, limited companies with a turnover of €3m or less, and unincorporated bodies such as clubs and charities.

[8.90] The office of the Pension Ombudsman was established in 2002 by the Pensions (Amendment) Act 2002 to investigate and decide on all complaints and disputes involving occupational pension schemes and Personal Retirement Savings Accounts (PRSAs).[167]

[8.91] In 2002, the office of the Ombudsman for Children was established pursuant to the Ombudsman for Children Act 2002.[168] The Ombudsman for Children is empowered to hear complaints from children (or adults on their behalf) against public organisations, schools or hospitals.

[8.92] The Ombudsman for the Defence Forces was established by the Ombudsman (Defence Forces) Act 2004.[169] The Ombudsman for the Defence Forces is charged with investigating complaints by members and former members of the defence forces which have not been adequately addressed by the internal military complaints process.

[8.93] The Garda Síochána Ombudsman Commission (GSOC) was established by the Garda Síochána Act 2005.[170] GSOC is empowered to investigate complaints against members of An Garda Síochána, to investigate any matter (even where no complaint has been made) where it appears to GSOC that a member of the force may have committed an offence or behaved in a way that would justify disciplinary proceedings, and to investigate any practice, policy or procedure of An Garda Síochána with a view to reducing the incidence of related complaints. Any member of the public who is directly affected by or who witnesses conduct by a member of An Garda Síochána that is alleged to constitute misbehaviour can refer a complaint.

---

[166] www.financialombudsman.ie/.

[167] www.pensionsombudsman.ie/.

[168] www.oco.ie/.

[169] www.odf.ie/.

[170] www.gardaombudsman.ie/.

[8.94] At the time writing (September 2014), the Garda Síochána (Amendment) Bill 2014 proposes to empower GSOC to receive complaints from serving members of An Garda Síochána concerning other members. This arises from serious allegations made in 2008 by a serving member which a report published in 2014 concluded had not been fully investigated.[171] As recommended in this report, a commission of investigation is to be established to investigate the manner in which these allegations were dealt with. It also appears at the time of writing that an independent Garda Authority, along the lines of the Northern Ireland Policing Authority, may be established.

[8.95] In 2007, the Office of the Press Ombudsman was established.[172] A Code of Practice agreed by the Press Council allowed for complaints of any breaches of the Code of Practice to be referred to the Office of the Ombudsman. The Office of the Press Ombudsman was placed on a statutory footing under the Defamation Act 2009. The aim of the Office of the Press Ombudsman is to provide members of the public with an accessible, fast and free method of resolving any complaints about newspapers and periodicals which allegedly breach the Code of Practice. It works closely with the Press Council of Ireland, which was established to regulate the press in Ireland. For example, in 2008, the Office of the Press Ombudsman referred two complaints to the Press Council as they were considered complex and difficult.[173] In 2008, the Press Council and the Office of the Press Ombudsman received a total of 372 complaints.[174] It is common for certain articles to receive a multiplicity of complaints; for example in 2008, one article generated 44 separate complaints, while another caused 15 separate complaints to be submitted. The most common ground for articles to be submitted was that of truth and accuracy.

---

[171] *Report by Sean Guerin SC on a Review of the Action Taken by An Garda Síochána Pertaining to Certain Allegations Made by Sergeant Maurice McCabe*, available at http://www.merrionstreet.ie/wp-content/uploads/2014/05/Final-Redacted-Guerin-Report1.pdf.

[172] www.pressombudsman.ie/.

[173] *Annual Report of the Press Council of Ireland and Office of the Press Ombudsman 2008* (2009), p 10.

[174] *Annual Report of the Press Council of Ireland and Office of the Press Ombudsman 2008* (2009), p 30.

Chapter 9

Access to Law

[1] Introduction 413
[2] The Constitutional Setting: Access to the Courts 413
[3] Provision of State-Funded Legal Aid 418
[4] State-Assisted Criminal Legal Aid 420
[5] State-Assisted Civil Legal Aid 427
[6] Court Fees 438
[7] Legal costs 440
[8] Protective Costs Orders 441

[1] INTRODUCTION

[9.01] In previous chapters, we described the jurisdiction of the courts and various adjudicative bodies that have decision-making powers concerning a variety of legal disputes. In this chapter, we describe the arrangements that have been put in place to ensure access to the courts and, to some extent, the other adjudicative bodies. We begin by examining the constitutional background to the right of access to the courts. We then discuss the position of persons who represent themselves in litigation without engaging the services of lawyers, including the circumstances in which they may be assisted by lay persons in the presentation of their case. We then discuss the provision for access to legal aid and advice in both criminal and civil matters for those who wish to engage their own legal representation but without the means to do so. We also discuss the extent to which court fees and other legal costs involved in litigation are compatible with the Constitution. Finally, we discuss the use of protective costs orders as a mechanism to provide access to justice.

[2] THE CONSTITUTIONAL SETTING: ACCESS TO THE COURTS

[9.02] We have already seen that Article 34.1 requires that, in general, justice be administered in public.[1] This general principle emphasises that the courts should be accessible to all. The Constitution expressly confers a right of access to the courts in Article 40.4.2°, which is the modern version of the *habeas corpus* procedure by which a person has the right to have an inquiry into the validity of his or her imprisonment. The courts have also held that the right of access to the courts is an implicit or unenumerated

---

1 See para **4.24**.

413

personal constitutional right under Article 40.3.[2] On this basis, the courts have held unconstitutional the requirement that proceedings against state bodies required the permission or fiat of the Attorney General before they could be initiated.[3] It has also been held that the immunity of the Crown from suit, which existed prior to the establishment in 1922 of the Irish Free State, is incompatible with the Constitution.[4] Similarly, the imposition of a two-month limitation period for initiating civil proceedings, without any possibility of extending that time to take account of exceptional circumstances, has been held to be an unreasonable restriction on the right to litigate.[5] At the other end of the spectrum, a six-year limitation period for tort actions in s 11 of the Statute of Limitations 1957 was held to be constitutionally permissible by the Supreme Court in *Tuohy v Courtney*.[6] The Supreme Court held that the common interest in protecting defendants from old claims outweighed any injustice or hardship caused.

[9.03] The courts have also held that access to the courts may be subject to some restrictions. For example, the Supreme Court upheld the constitutionality of s 5 of the Illegal Immigrants (Trafficking) Act 2000, which requires an applicant seeking judicial review of a decision or order made under the 2000 Act to demonstrate 'substantial grounds' that the decision or order should be quashed.[7] The High Court and, on appeal, the Supreme Court, held unconstitutional s 260 of the Mental Treatment Act 1945, which required the leave (permission) of the High Court before a negligence claim concerning the committal of a person to a psychiatric hospital could be initiated.[8] It is notable that, by the time this constitutional challenge had been heard by the High Court and Supreme Court, s 260 had been repealed by the Mental Health Act 2001. Both the High Court and Supreme Court held that the requirement that any application under s 260 of the 1945 Act had to demonstrate substantial grounds for contending that the person against whom the negligence proceedings would be initiated acted in bad faith or without reasonable care, unduly affected his or her right of access to the courts.

[9.04] It would seem that a pre-condition to proceedings, or partial curtailment of the right of access, is not unconstitutional.[9] Similarly, while unduly restrictive limitation

---

[2]   On unenumerated rights, see para **15.53**.

[3]   *Macauley v Minister for Posts and Telegraphs* [1966] IR 345.

[4]   *Byrne v Ireland* [1972] IR 241, discussed further at para **15.37**.

[5]   *Brady v Donegal County Council* [1989] ILRM 282, *per* Costello J in the High Court. On appeal, the Supreme Court did not deal with this point. Similarly, in *White v Dublin City Council* [2004] 1 IR 545 the Supreme Court declared invalid a rigid two-month time limit for challenging certain planning decisions as there was no possibility for any extension of this time limit. By contrast, *In Re the Illegal Immigrants (Trafficking) Bill 1999* [2000] 2 IR 360, the Supreme Court upheld a 14-day time limit for seeking judicial review of certain immigration decisions as the court was empowered to extend this time for good and sufficient reason.

[6]   *Tuohy v Courtney* [1994] 3 IR 1.

[7]   *In Re the Illegal Immigrants (Trafficking) Bill 1999* [2000] 2 IR 360.

[8]   *Blehein v Minister for Health and Children* [2004] 3 IR 610 (HC), [2008] IESC 40.

[9]   *Murphy v Greene* [1990] 2 IR 566.

periods may be in conflict with the Constitution, it would be contrary to the proper administration of justice to allow an exceptionally old or 'stale' civil or criminal case to be litigated.[10] In addition, where a point has already been determined in the courts, a litigant may also be debarred from bringing further proceedings on the ground that the matter has already been litigated and that the issue is *res judicata*.[11] To raise the matter again would be an abuse of the process of the court and contrary to the proper administration of justice. The right of access to the courts is not, therefore, unrestricted, but may in some instances be limited or curtailed.

Parties representing themselves

[9.05] It is sometimes said that 'the man who represents himself has a fool for a client', but there have been many instances in which those involved in litigation, whether criminal or civil, have represented themselves with success. While we have seen that the procedures involved in litigation are complex,[12] some consumers of the court system have been confident enough to represent their own interests rather than engage the services of a solicitor or counsel. In such cases, the courts are generally more accommodating to the personal litigant (also referred to as the 'unrepresented litigant' or the 'litigant *pro se*'), and the formal rules concerning pleadings or of criminal procedure are unlikely to be applied with the same rigour as would be the case where a qualified lawyer is involved.[13] However, it appears that a person representing himself does not have the right to a state-funded law library.[14]

[9.06] Where a convicted prisoner applies to the High Court under Article 40.4.2° of the Constitution seeking an inquiry into the validity of his or her imprisonment, the courts have emphasised their duty to investigate all possible grounds that might affect the legality of the detention and not merely those raised by the prisoner.[15] However, in line with the view that the right of access to the courts is not unrestricted, the courts may be less tolerant where a series of applications are made under Article 40.4.2° and it appears that the prisoner is merely repeating grounds which have already been rejected in previous applications or court proceedings.[16]

---

[10] See para **6.11**. See also the reforms proposed in the Law Reform Commission's *Report on Limitation of Actions* (LRC 104-2011).

[11] For the controversy this gave rise to in 'miscarriage of justice' cases, see para **7.51**. For a discussion of the principles surrounding the doctrine of *res judicata* see *McCauley v McDermott* [1997] 2 ILRM 466.

[12] See Ch 6.

[13] See Delany and McGrath, *Civil Procedure in the Superior Courts* (3rd edn, 2012); *European Fashion Products Ltd v Eenkhoorn* [2001] IEHC 181; and *Costigan v Laois County Council* [2000] IESC 7.

[14] See *MacGairbhith v Attorney General* [1991] 2 IR 412 (HC), (29 March 1995, unreported), SC.

[15] *The State (Smith) v Governor of Mountjoy Gaol* (1964) 102 ILTR 93.

[16] *McGlinchey v Ireland* [1990] 2 IR 215.

[9.07] A similar general principle of latitude applies in other civil litigation conducted by personal litigants, subject to the principle that there must be some finality in litigation. The order made by a court to dismiss proceedings on the basis that they amount to an abuse of process is sometimes referred to as a 'Wunder Order', after a litigant of the 1960s and 1970s whose proceedings against the same defendant gave rise to at least ten decisions of the High Court and Supreme Court.[17] Essentially, a Wunder Order restrains a person from instituting further proceedings against the parties in the earlier proceedings without first obtaining permission from a court.[18]

[9.08] In the absence of official statistics on the percentage of civil and criminal matters conducted personally, only a general assessment can be made. It would appear, however, that in civil matters, personal litigants are relatively common in family proceedings. In criminal cases, personal representation is very unusual, owing perhaps to the long-standing availability of state-funded legal aid. However, there have been cases in which personal litigants have successfully defended themselves in jury trials on indictment and in subsequent appeals.[19] A number of applications under Article 40.4.2° of the Constitution by convicted prisoners also appear to have been made personally.

Proceedings involving young persons and adults whose capacity is in question

[9.09] There is wide-ranging provision made in law by which those, for example, under 18 years of age (children or minors) or adults whose capacity is called in question[20] are assisted by others in civil and criminal matters. Thus, personal injuries actions involving a person under 18, or an adult whose decision-making is being assisted in some form, may be initiated by a 'next friend', such as a parent.[21] In child care and guardianship proceedings, a court may appoint a guardian *ad litem* (a litigation guardian), that is, a person who represents the interests of the child separately from the views expressed by the child's parents or the Child and Family Agency.[22] The court may also join a child to

---

17 See *Wunder v Hospitals Trust (1940) Ltd*, the judgments dating from 1 April 1966 to 10 June 1975: cited by McCarthy J in *Murphy v Greene* [1990] 2 IR 566.

18 Delany and McGrath, *Civil Procedure in the Superior Courts* (3rd edn, 2012), pp 428–432. See also *Riordan v An Taoiseach* [2001] 4 IR 463, *Riordan v An Taoiseach* [2001] IESC 83 and *Devrajan v KPMG* [2006] IEHC 81.

19 See *The People (AG) v Singer* (1961) 1 Frewen 214; *The People (DPP) v Marley* [1985] ILRM 17.

20 The Assisted Decision-Making (Capacity) Bill 2013 (which derives from the Law Reform Commission's 2006 *Report on Vulnerable Adults and the Law* (LRC 83-2006)), proposes a legislative framework on assisted decision-making and capacity that would be consistent with the 2006 UN Convention on the Rights of Persons With Disabilities. When enacted it would also provide for an empowering and protective national institutional structure, including the Office of the Public Guardian: see para **5.80**.

21 See, eg, *Dunne v National Maternity Hospital* [1989] IR 91; *Best v Wellcome Foundation Ltd* [1993] 3 IR 421.

22 Established by the Child and Family Agency Act 2013.

any child care and guardianship proceedings and appoint a solicitor on behalf of the child.[23] In criminal matters involving persons under 18, the presence of a child or young person's guardian is generally required, both during police questioning and, later, in any court hearing.[24]

Parties assisted by lay persons: 'McKenzie friends'

[9.10] In some cases a litigant might wish to be assisted by another lay person. In 1970, in *McKenzie v McKenzie*,[25] the English Court of Appeal re-affirmed a statement that was originally made in 1831:

> "Any person, whether he be a professional man or not, may attend as a friend of either party, may take notes, may quietly make suggestions, and give advice; but no one can demand to take part in the proceedings as an advocate, contrary to the regulations of the court as settled by the discretion of the justices."[26]

[9.11] The *McKenzie* case gave rise to the phrase 'McKenzie friend' to describe a person who may assist a personal litigant in civil and criminal court proceedings.[27] A 'McKenzie friend' may not in general speak on behalf of the personal litigant, or indeed any other litigant.[28] This is also currently the case in respect of those giving advice to a complainant in a sexual assault case, but the right to separate legal representation will be introduced in the near future.[29] Similarly, an application under Article 40.4.2° of the Constitution may be initiated on behalf of the person alleged to be in unlawful custody by any person who has a bona fide interest in the question, but the initiator may not present the case in court.[30] There may, however, be exceptional circumstances where such third parties would be permitted to address the court[31] and, in exceptional cases, the

---

23   Child Care Act 1991, ss 25, 26; Guardianship of Infants Act 1964, s 28 (inserted by Children Act 1997, s 11).

24   See *Travers v Ryan* [1985] ILRM 343; Children Act 2001, ss 61 and 91. See generally, Walsh, *Juvenile Justice* (2005).

25   *McKenzie v McKenzie* [1971] P 33.

26   *Collier v Hicks* (1831) 2 B & Ad 663 at 669, quoted in Delany and McGrath, *Civil Procedure in the Superior Courts* (3rd edn, 2012).

27   Delany and McGrath, *Civil Procedure in the Superior Courts* (3rd edn, 2012), *RD v McGuinness* [1999] 2 IR 411 and Walsh, 'Privacy's New Paradigm: The Rise and Reform of the In Camera Rule' [2005] 1 IJFL 10.

28   *Battle v Irish Art Promotion Centre Ltd* [1968] IR 252; *RD v McGuinness* [1999] 2 IR 411.

29   See para **9.43**.

30   *Application of Woods* [1970] IR 154; *Cahill v Governor of Military Detention Barracks, Curragh Camp* [1980] ILRM 191.

31   See *B (PML) v J(PH)* (5 May 1992, unreported), HC, where Budd J cited with approval the decision of the New Zealand Court of Appeal in *Re GJ Mannix Ltd* [1984] 1 NZLR 309 to this effect, though in the particular circumstances of the case (a family case), he held that the case was not an 'exceptional' case requiring the 'friend' to address the court. For a discussion, see Noctor, 'The Presence of McKenzie Friends in *in Camera* Proceedings' (1999) 17 ILT 214, discussing *RD v McGuinness* [1999] 1 IR 411.

courts have an inherent jurisdiction to allow an unqualified advocate to represent another litigant.[32] But apart from the litigant, the right of audience in the courts, that is, the right to address the courts, is reserved to solicitors and barristers unless there are exceptional reasons.[33]

[9.12] It has also become more common for an interested party to be appointed as an *amicus curiae* (literally, a 'friend of the court') to participate in proceedings with legal arguments and support materials.[34] Generally such a party does not present evidence. In *HI v Minister for Justice, Equality and Law Reform*[35] the Supreme Court adopted the following definition of an *amicus curiae*: 'a person, whether a member of the bar not engaged in the case or any other bystander, who calls the attention of the court to some decision, whether reported or unreported, or some point of law which would appear to have been overlooked.' The Irish Human Rights and Equality Commission, by virtue of its statutory functions, has been appointed as an *amicus curiae*.[36]

[3] PROVISION OF STATE-FUNDED LEGAL AID

[9.13] In light of these examples, it is clear that a personal litigant may present his or her case in court, may be facilitated by a 'friend' and will be given more latitude by the courts than a person with a legal qualification. In that sense, the adage 'the law, like the Ritz Hotel, is open to all' can be said to be accurate. However, it remains the case that most litigants would, if given the choice, prefer to have their case prepared by a professional lawyer. This raises the question of who is to pay for the advice tendered by solicitors and barristers.

[9.14] We have discussed elsewhere the concern that the high cost of legal services is a real barrier to effective access to justice for the majority of individuals in society, and that high legal fees mean that only some groups are in a position to have access to legal services. These are: (a) corporate entities such as private sector companies[37] and public bodies such as local authorities and central government agencies[38] who have sufficient

---

[32] See *Coffey v Tara Mines Ltd* [2008] 1 IR 436, where the High Court permitted the wife of the plaintiff to represent him in proceedings before the courts. The High Court (O'Neill J) acknowledged that it was an exceptional case and due to the health difficulties suffered by the plaintiff he would not be able to represent himself which would cause a grave injustice.

[33] See para **3.71**.

[34] See Delany, 'Joining Co-Defendants and Amici Curiae – Recent Developments' (2007) 25 ILT 237.

[35] *HI v Minister for Justice, Equality and Law Reform* [2003] 3 IR 197, 200, quoting the Australian case *United States Tobacco Company v Minister for Consumer Affairs* (1988) 83 ALR 79.

[36] See, for example, *Dublin City Council v Fennell* [2005] 1 IR 604 and *Pullen v Dublin City Council* [2008] IEHC 379.

[37] Subject to the increasing cost-consciousness of private sector bodies, including through the discussion in paras **3.36** and **3.50** of in-house counsel as a method of legal cost containment.

[38] Subject also to the reduction in state-funded legal aid since the financial crisis of 2008: see paras **9.25** and **9.59** below.

resources to pay for legal services; (b) wealthy individuals whose resources allow them to engage legal services regardless of cost; (c) extremely low income individuals whose income is both very low and the subject matter of their dispute (such as family law or challenge to their immigration status) falls within the remit of the civil legal aid scheme; (d) individuals whose personal injuries claim is deemed sufficiently meritorious by a solicitor and counsel that it is taken on a deferred fee basis; (e) individuals with an unusual public interest claim that a solicitor and counsel will take on a *pro bono* basis; and (f) persons charged with criminal offences that come within the state-funded criminal legal aid scheme.[39] In this respect the proposed changes in the Legal Services Regulation Bill 2011, notably the establishment of a Legal Costs Regulatory Body,[40] need not necessarily be seen as involving a narrow-focus attempt to reduce the fee income of individual lawyers but as an attempt to extend the range of persons in society (the 'squeezed middle' who are ineligible for legal aid and not wealthy enough to be indifferent to cost) who would thereby be in a position to gain access to affordable legal services. The discussion in the remainder of this chapter should therefore be seen against this background.

[9.15] Separately from the proposed new arrangements for regulating legal costs, the question is whether access to law is limited to those who can afford it or whether and to what extent public provision should be made in this regard. For many years it has been a tradition of the legal profession to engage in a certain percentage of work without charge, or at least without the expectation of payment; this is referred to as *pro bono* work.[41] While this remains a feature of legal practice in the state today, its origins lie in a sense of 19th century philanthropy. In a society where market forces may place pressure on such traditions, it is difficult to avoid the conclusion that justice may not be fully served without state intervention.

[9.16] It has become accepted in most states that a person facing a serious criminal charge, but who is unable to pay for the services of professional legal advisers, should have such advice provided by the state. In civil claims, a similar conclusion has been reached, though this is a more recent phenomenon. In both instances, the test of whether a person should qualify for 'free legal aid' is whether justice would be defeated if such assistance were not provided. To this end the state has established two legal aid schemes, one for criminal cases and the other for civil cases.

---

39 See **9.17** below.

40 See **3.36**.

41 This would include cases in which litigants are engaged in a highly complex civil case which would not come within the 'no foal, no fee' arrangement (see para **3.76**). The solicitors and counsel may be engaged in such a case for many months, or years, without any expectation of payment, though if they are ultimately successful the losing party will be obliged to pay the costs incurred to the successful party. In the meantime, the (ultimately successful) litigant of limited means may have incurred substantial costs other than legal fees. See, eg, Kerrigan, *Nothing But the Truth* (1990), an account of the medical negligence claim *Dunne v National Maternity Hospital* [1989] IR 91 (see para **7.30**, fn 52).

[4]   STATE-ASSISTED CRIMINAL LEGAL AID

Legal aid at trial

[9.17] Prior to 1962, a person accused of a criminal offence could only expect to be provided by the state with the assistance of a lawyer where the charge carried the death penalty. In all other cases the defendant was left to instruct, and pay for, his or her own lawyer. Indeed, even in capital cases prior to 1962, it was not uncommon for the defendant to be represented by junior counsel while the prosecution was represented by senior and junior counsel.[42]

[9.18] The Criminal Justice (Legal Aid) Act 1962 fundamentally altered this picture. The 1962 Act introduced a system of legal aid applicable to all serious criminal cases. It provides that legal aid must be granted where an application is made by a defendant and it appears to a judge of the District Court (or the trial court) that (a) the defendant's means are insufficient to enable him or her to obtain legal aid from his or her own resources; and (b) by reason of 'the serious nature of the offence or of exceptional circumstances, it is essential in the interests of justice that the person should have legal aid in the preparation and conduct' of his or her defence and any necessary appeal against conviction. This two-fold test in the 1962 Act conferred a certain element of discretion on the judge making the determination, although the Act also provided that legal aid was mandatory on a charge of murder, which at the time carried the death penalty.[43]

[9.19] The decision of the Supreme Court in *The State (Healy) v Donoghue*[44] marked an important development in the operation of the 1962 Act. Here, the prosecutor, aged 18, had been charged with breaking and entering a building, to which he pleaded guilty in the District Court. He was virtually illiterate, having left school at 13. He did not apply for legal aid under the 1962 Act and he was not informed by the respondent judge of the terms of the 1962 Act. Shortly after his appearance on the breaking and entering charge, he was charged in the District Court with larceny, also before the respondent judge. On this charge, he applied for and was granted legal aid under the 1962 Act. The next appearance in court was on the breaking and entering charge, for which he was sentenced to three months' detention by the respondent judge. Finally, he appeared before the respondent for sentence on the larceny charge, but by this time the solicitor assigned to him had withdrawn from the case due to a dispute in the legal profession about the operation of the scheme in the 1962 Act. The respondent judge, who refused an application by the prosecutor to have the case adjourned because of the withdrawal of the solicitor, sentenced him to six months' detention on the larceny charge. The

---

[42]   See generally Greer, 'Legal Services and the Poor in Ireland' (1969) 4 Ir Jur (ns) 270.

[43]   The death penalty was restricted to a limited category of 'capital' murders in the Criminal Justice Act 1964 and was abolished by the Criminal Justice Act 1990. All remaining references to the death penalty in the Constitution were removed in 2001 with the approval in a referendum of the Twenty-Second Amendment of the Constitution Act 2001.

[44]   *State (Healy) v Donoghue* [1976] IR 325.

prosecutor then applied for judicial review of his convictions,[45] seeking to have them quashed on the basis that he had been deprived of a trial in due course law under Article 38.1 of the Constitution.

[9.20] In the High Court, Gannon J held that the larceny sentence should be quashed because the respondent judge had already made a determination under the Criminal Justice (Legal Aid) Act 1962 that the prosecutor required legal representation. However, Gannon J would have allowed the breaking and entering sentence to stand since he did not consider that the 1962 Act or the Constitution required the judge to inform an accused person of his right to apply for legal aid. On appeal to the Supreme Court, it was held that both sentences were invalid. O'Higgins CJ stated:[46]

> "No one can be compelled to accept legal aid, and a person charged is entitled to waive his right in this respect and to defend himself ... However, if a person who is ignorant of his right fails to apply and on that account is not given legal aid then, in my view, his constitutional right is violated. For this reason it seems to me that when a person faces a possible prison sentence and has no lawyer, and cannot provide for one, he ought to be informed of his right to legal aid. If the person charged does not know of his right, he cannot exercise it; if he cannot exercise it, his right is violated."

[9.21] This passage emphasises the need to inform an accused person of his or her right to legal representation and that, without this, any subsequent trial, even where a person has pleaded guilty, would violate constitutional requirements. Of course, O'Higgins CJ also noted that the right to a lawyer applied where there is the possibility of a sentence of imprisonment and that a person may also waive the right to be represented. On the question of waiver, the court should take account of the circumstances of the defendant, as in the *Healy* case, where the prosecutor's lack of education should have led the court to conclude that he would be unable to defend himself adequately. Indeed, Griffin J made the point that '[v]ery few laymen, when charged in court where their liberty is in jeopardy, can present adequately their own cases, much less identify and argue legal questions.'[47]

[9.22] Thus, notwithstanding the instances mentioned already, where a person may choose to defend himself the general principle to be applied is that, where a person runs the risk of being imprisoned, he should be informed of his right to legal aid and that, unless he is capable of conducting his own defence, he should be provided with legal representation. In *Carmody v Minister for Justice, Equality and Law Reform*,[48] the plaintiff challenged the constitutionality of s 2 of the Criminal Justice (Legal Aid) Act 1962, which provides that an accused person is only entitled to a legal aid certificate in respect of a solicitor in a criminal matter dealt with in the District Court. Sections 3, 4, 5

---

45   On judicial review, see para **10.53**.
46   [1976] IR 325, 352.
47   [1976] IR 325, 357.
48   *Carmody v Minister for Justice, Equality and Law Reform* [2005] IEHC 10, [2009] IESC 91, [2009] 1 IR 635.

and 6 of the 1962 Act, which deal with free legal aid in relation to a trial on indictment, provide for an entitlement to counsel as well as a solicitor. The High Court and, on appeal, the Supreme Court held that s 2 of the 1962 Act was not unconstitutional. In the High Court, Laffoy J stated:

> "The fact that there may, in terms of lawyers, be a numerical imbalance or a divergence of legal qualification between the prosecution team and the defence team does not disadvantage the accused person to the extent that his guarantee to a fair trial is imperilled unless the lawyer defending him cannot do so effectively. In my view it has not been shown that such is the case."

[9.23] In *Joyce v Brady*[49] the Supreme Court reiterated the constitutional dimension to criminal legal aid. In this case the applicant had been charged with the 'either way' offence of theft under s 4 of the Criminal Justice (Theft and Fraud Offences) Act 2001. The prosecution decided to proceed with the charge in the District Court, which may have been influenced by the fact that this was the applicant's first offence and the circumstances of the theft did not involve any aggravating factors. The applicant had applied on several occasions for legal aid under the 1962 Act, but these were not considered because he had not filed a statement of means. When he did, the respondent judge who was dealing with the application for legal aid asked the prosecuting garda whether, if the applicant was convicted, he was 'at risk' of facing a sentence of imprisonment. The garda replied no, considering the circumstances of the case. On this basis, the respondent refused legal aid. On judicial review, the Supreme Court held that the judge had not dully taken account of the constitutional right to a fair trial which was the key framework against which the 1962 Act was to be considered. The Supreme Court accepted that, as the state carried the burden of funding criminal legal aid, it was entirely appropriate that there should be an enquiry as to a person's means before legal aid was granted. Nonetheless, the Court considered that, in this case, legal aid should have been granted especially as the applicant was a first time offender and that professional legal assistance would give greater assurance that a fair trial would result.

Management and funding of the criminal legal aid system

[9.24] The Criminal Justice (Legal Aid) Act 1962 refers to legal assistance being 'assigned' by the court, rather than being chosen by the defendant. Those assigned are chosen from the panel of solicitors and barristers who inform the Law Society of Ireland and the Bar Council of Ireland of their willingness to act in cases covered by the 1962 Act. While the courts are entitled to refuse to assign a solicitor who is not on the panel or who has withdrawn from the panel,[50] in the majority of cases the solicitor nominated by a particular defendant will be assigned to represent him or her.

[9.25] In effect, the current regime under the Criminal Justice (Legal Aid) Act 1962 is that an accused of limited means who is facing a serious criminal charge is entitled to be

---

49   *Joyce v Brady* [2011] IESC 36.
50   *The State (Royle) v Kelly* [1974] IR 259.

provided with the solicitor and barrister of his or her choice. Under current arrangements, the criminal legal aid scheme is based exclusively on a fee-per-case basis, with the fees being set by means of regulations made under the 1962 Act. These fees are revised from time to time, generally on the basis of representations to the Department of Justice from the Law Society and the Bar Council. On a number of occasions the scheme has collapsed due to the withdrawal of solicitors or barristers on the ground that fees have not been increased on a satisfactory basis. It must be said that the fees contained in the regulations made under the 1962 Act would be less than payable if 'market rates' were charged by solicitors and barristers. Of course, from the government's perspective, the cost of the criminal legal aid scheme is a matter for concern and the cost of funding it has been rising in recent years. The total cost of the scheme doubled between 2004 and 2008, increasing from €26.7 million in 2004 to €53 million in 2008.[51] In the wake of the global and national financial crisis that began in 2008, which necessitated the 2010–2013 EU–IMF 'bailout' of Ireland, the state imposed a general 10% reduction in criminal legal aid fees in order to reduce the overall cost. As a result, while the total cost was €56.5 million in 2010, this had been reduced to €50.5 million in 2013.

[9.26] At the time of writing (September 2014), it is expected that a Criminal Legal Aid (Amendment) Bill will be published with a view to setting out more specific criteria on which legal aid is considered and granted under the 1962 Act. Any such Bill will need to have regard to the constitutional dimension to criminal legal aid, as reiterated in *Joyce v Brady*.[52]

[9.27] The question arises whether the current system, under which solicitors and barristers in private practice charge fees per case, should be replaced by a public defender system such as exists in the United States where salaried lawyers employed by the state are assigned to accused persons of limited means without any real choice. In 1996, a Criminal Legal Aid Review Committee was appointed to examine the criminal legal aid scheme, and to consider the introduction of a public defender system. In its first report, published in 2000,[53] the Committee concluded that the current arrangements should, in general, remain and that a public defender system should not be introduced. This mirrors the view taken in a 1999 report that a unitary public prosecution system should not be introduced.[54]

[9.28] The Committee stated that the element of choice under the existing scheme is one of its greatest strengths, and creates conditions for independence, client confidence and trust. It has been argued that the public defender system does not provide complete

---

51 See (2009) *The Irish Times*, 2 March.

52 *Joyce v Brady* [2011] IESC 36.

53 *First Report of the Criminal Legal Aid Review Committee* (2000). The report is available on the Department of Justice's website, www.justice.ie.

54 The introduction of a unitary prosecution system, along the lines of the UK Crown Prosecution Service (CPS), was rejected in the Nally Report on the Public Prosecution System (1999): see para **6.87**.

access to justice for poor people, on the ground that public defenders may either be relatively inexperienced or are faced with such an excessive case load that they are unable to defend their clients' interests fully. It has been suggested that the public defender system may encourage a greater use of 'plea bargaining' than is consistent with justice. By contrast, the criminal legal aid regime in Ireland allows indigent defendants to engage highly qualified solicitors and counsel to defend them in court.

[9.29] In its first report, the Criminal Legal Aid Review Committee also concluded that, from an administrative perspective, the current system was streamlined and cost-effective. It referred to a 1994 Department of Finance report which found that the use of full-time salaried solicitors, barristers and support staff to provide criminal legal aid would be 70 per cent more expensive than the current scheme. The cost of providing a full public defender service, which would entail employing 21 senior counsel, 58 junior counsel and 42 support staff for them, along with between 141 and 202 solicitors and 163 support staff for them, would be between £22.8m and £27.2m, excluding PRSI. The Committee therefore concluded that the current scheme was less expensive than any of the alternative models considered and recommended its retention.

[9.30] In its final report in 2002,[55] the Committee recommended that a duty solicitor scheme, which would require solicitors in private practice to be available on a rota basis to provide assistance to defendants, should not be introduced. The main reasons for this were that the introduction of a duty solicitor would not lead to cost saving or vindicate the rights of the defendant in any better way than the existing arrangements. The Committee also examined whether the criminal legal aid system should be altered to allow for contracting out of legal aid services to particular law firms or individuals on the basis of an agreed amount of work at a particular fee. This system is particularly prevalent in the United States of America and has been introduced in the United Kingdom. After completing an analysis of the systems in the United Kingdom and the United States, the Committee concluded that the provision of criminal representation by way of contracting out would not result in a similar quality of representation or higher representation being supplied at a lower cost, the important principle of choice of legal representation would be removed and there was no evidence that any administration burden or cost would be removed by introducing a contracting-out system of legal aid.

[9.31] By contrast, a public defender service was introduced in the UK by the Access to Justice Act 1999 through the establishment of the Legal Services Commission, which was replaced by the Legal Aid Agency, established under the British Legal Aid, Sentencing and Punishment of Offenders Act 2012. The Legal Aid Agency manages the criminal legal aid budget and is required to achieve efficiencies in its use, which it is also mandated to do with the civil legal aid budget.[56] The Legal Aid Agency oversees another agency, the Public Defender Service (the PDS, established in 2001), which to

---

55 *Criminal Legal Aid Review Committee: Final Report* (2002), available at www.justice.ie.
56 The Legal Aid Agency is also responsible for managing the civil legal aid budget, replacing the British Legal Aid Board: see para **9.63**. Its website is www.justice.gov.uk/about/laa.

some extent mirrors the Crown Prosecution Service (CPS). The Public Defender Service is empowered to enter into contracts for the provision of criminal defence services either with firms in private practice or with salaried defenders employed by non-profit-making organisations. The UK Criminal Defence Service Act 2006 altered the arrangements for the grant of public funding for representation in criminal proceedings in the United Kingdom. It provides that the power to grant rights to representation is now conferred on the Legal Aid Agency instead of the court.

[9.32] In addition, the UK Access to Justice Act 1999 enabled the Legal Aid Agency (as successor to the Legal Services Commission) to establish a public defender service to provide for legal services through lawyers in its own employment. The Public Defender Service was established following a UK Government White Paper which found evidence from other countries which suggested that properly funded defenders can be more cost-effective and provide a better service than lawyers in private practice.[57] The Public Defender Service is the first salaried criminal provider in England and Wales and the Legal Aid Agency directly employs a staff of solicitors and administrators. Lawyers provide independent legal advice and representation on criminal matters and are available 24 hours a day to provide such advice to people in police custody and represent clients in criminal courts.[58] This fundamental change in the criminal legal aid regime in the United Kingdom was introduced, at least in part, in an attempt to limit the ever-increasing cost of funding the criminal legal aid system. Through the introduction of the Public Defender System, the Legal Aid Agency has for the first time introduced a system of criminal defence through salaried employees directly employed by it. One of the main reasons for its introduction was to ensure that value-for-money criminal defence services were provided to the public.[59] As already mentioned, the 2002 final report of the Criminal Legal Aid Committee rejected a similar system for Ireland, and the Irish arrangements continue to involve lawyers being engaged on a fee-per-case basis, rather than a salary.

Legal aid scheme for judicial review

[9.33] A non-statutory legal aid scheme also exists in connection with applications for criminal matters which are not covered by the 1962 Act (criminal legal aid) or the Civil Legal Aid Act 1995 (discussed below). This non-statutory scheme covers certain judicial reviews, bail applications, extraditions and applications under Article 40.4.2° of the Constitution (*habeas corpus*). Under this scheme the state meets the costs of legal representation where the High Court certifies that legal representation is required, and it was first announced in 1967 in the course of an application by a convicted prisoner under Article 40.4.2° of the Constitution.[60] The Criminal Legal Aid Review Committee

---

[57] *White Paper on Modernising Justice* (1998, Cm 4155, HMSO), para 6.18.
[58] See Slapper and Kelly, *The English Legal System* (9th edn, 2009), p 584.
[59] Slapper and Kelly, *The English Legal System* (9th edn, 2009), p 584.
[60] *Application of Woods* [1970] IR 154. Until 2012, this was known as the Attorney General's Scheme. In 2012, responsibility for the scheme was transferred to the Legal Aid Board.

recommended that the elements of the non-statutory scheme be placed on a statutory footing and brought within the ambit of the Criminal Legal Aid Scheme.[61] At the time of writing (September 2014), this general recommendation has not been implemented in legislative form but continues to operate on an administrative basis. It has also been held that a person found guilty but insane in a criminal trial was entitled to legal aid to be represented at hearings which consider whether to release such a person from detention in hospital.[62] This has now been placed on a statutory basis in the Criminal Law (Insanity) Act 2006. In addition, there is a non-statutory legal aid scheme available for respondents in Proceeds of Crime Act 1996 proceedings.[63]

Access to a lawyer in Garda custody

[9.34] Until 2014, it had been argued unsuccessfully in a number of cases that the right to legal aid should be extended to the pre-trial stage of the criminal process, where a person is in garda custody. In *The People (DPP) v Healy*,[64] the Supreme Court held that, where a person makes a reasonable request for access to a solicitor during questioning, the gardaí must themselves make reasonable efforts to secure the attendance of a solicitor. A number of other pre-2014 decisions had held that there was not a requirement on the gardaí to inform the person in custody of his or her right to request access to a solicitor, [65] unlike the position in the United States where an arrested person must be read their '*Miranda*' rights.[66] Section 5 of the Criminal Justice Act 1984 had imposed a limited statutory obligation on the gardaí to inform a person detained in custody of the right to consult a solicitor. In 2000, provision was made for the first time for payment to solicitors in respect of legal advice in police custody.[67] The Criminal Legal Aid Review Committee recommended that an administrative scheme be provided for legal aid for persons detained in garda stations[68] and this has been put in place.

---

[61] *Criminal Legal Aid Review Committee: Final Report* (Stationery Office, 2002), p 66. The report is available at www.justice.ie.

[62] *Kirwan v Minister for Justice* [1994] 2 IR 417.

[63] See *MFM v WFB* [1999] 1 IR 122 and *Murphy v GM* [2001] IESC 33.

[64] *People (DPP) v Healy* [1990] 2 IR 73.

[65] See *Lavery v Member in Charge, Carrickmacross Garda Station* [1999] 2 IR 268; *People (DPP) v Buck* [2002] 2 IR 206; *People (DPP) v O'Brien* [2005] 2 IR 206; and Daly, 'Does the Buck Stop Here: An Examination of the Right to Pre-Trial Legal Advice in the Light of *O'Brien v DPP*' (2006) 28 DULJ 345.

[66] The position in the United States, following the decision of the Supreme Court in *Miranda v Arizona* 384 US 436 (1964), is that police are obliged to inform an arrested person of his/her right to legal counsel during police questioning. Failure to 'Mirandise' an arrested person renders any statement or confession made during police questioning inadmissible in evidence.

[67] The scheme is available on the Department of Justice's website, www.justice.ie.

[68] *Criminal Legal Aid Review Committee: Final Report* (2002), p 59. The report is available at www.justice.ie.

[9.35] In 2014, in *The People (DPP) v Gormley*[69] the Supreme Court made it clear that it was likely to decide in a future case that the failure to inform a detained person of his or her right to have a solicitor present during questioning would be in breach of the Constitution. This unusual indication of its future approach was influenced by relevant case law of the European Court of Human Rights and by the adoption of the 2013 EU Directive on the Right of Access to a Lawyer,[70] even though at the time of its adoption Ireland (as well as Denmark and the United Kingdom) had opted not to be bound by the Directive (using the opt-out procedure in Protocol No 21 to the TFEU). Article 3.3 of the 2013 Directive provides that 'accused persons have the right for their lawyer to be present and participate effectively when questioned'. At the time of writing (September 2014) it remains an open question whether the state will opt in to the 2013 Directive. In any event, in the wake of the Supreme Court decision in the *Gormley* case the Director of Public Prosecutions issued a directive in 2014 that gardaí must permit a solicitor to be present during garda questioning. It has been noted that this direction involves a fundamental change in pre-trial criminal procedure and it is clear that it needs to be underpinned by legislation.[71] It is also likely that a new form of garda caution, which would be comparable in effect to the US *Miranda* caution, will need to be developed.

[9.36] In the United Kingdom the Legal Aid Agency (the successor to the Legal Services Commission) provides legal aid for persons in police custody, either by access to a duty solicitor or the client's own solicitor in certain circumstances. In addition, legal advice can be provided through the Public Defender Service to people in police custody.

[5] STATE-ASSISTED CIVIL LEGAL AID

[9.37] As already mentioned, the advent of state-assisted civil legal aid is a more recent phenomenon than its counterpart in criminal cases. Thus, in the United Kingdom, a limited form of criminal legal aid was first introduced in 1903, while civil legal aid was first introduced on a statutory basis in 1949.

FLAC

[9.38] The tradition within the legal profession of engaging in *pro bono* work was considerably expanded by the establishment in 1969 of the Free Legal Advice Centres (FLAC).[72] This was founded by law students who established law centres where members of the public could seek advice on a wide range of legal problems, including housing, social welfare and family law. The centres are staffed on a voluntary basis by law students, and practising lawyers also make their services available free of charge. In a limited number of instances, FLAC has supported test cases in these areas. FLAC continues to provide legal services to the public, and it now operates in addition to the

---

69   *The People (DPP) v Gormley* [2014] IESC 17.
70   Directive 2013/48/EU on the right of access to a lawyer in criminal proceedings.
71   See Robinson, 'Key Changes to Criminal Law get the Silent Treatment' (2014) *The Irish Times*, 19 May.
72   The website of FLAC is flac.ie

state-assisted scheme of civil legal aid and advice which it had campaigned for over many years. FLAC also continues as an influential campaigning organisation, including in the context of reform of the law on personal debt and, through its associated entity PILA (Public Interest Litigation Alliance), on the need for reform in the context of litigation that has a general public importance, notably through protective costs orders (PCOs), discussed below.

Committee on Civil Legal Aid and the Airey case

[9.39] In *O'Shaughnessy v Attorney General*,[73] the High Court rejected an argument that the Criminal Justice (Legal Aid) Act 1962 was unconstitutional because it failed to make provision for civil legal aid. O'Keeffe P held that the methods by which the personal rights of a citizen were to be vindicated were exclusively a matter for the Oireachtas. Most judges would not share this view today and it is probable that the remarks made in *O'Shaughnessy* will have to be revised in the light of the more recent decision in *The State (Healy) v Donoghue*.[74]

[9.40] Arising from representations made by FLAC and other organisations, the then government appointed a Committee on Civil Legal Aid and Advice to make recommendations for the introduction of a scheme of civil legal aid. The Committee reported in 1977, recommending that in the medium term a statutory scheme be established, with an interim non-statutory scheme to be put in place immediately.[75]

[9.41] In the meantime, proceedings had been initiated against the state alleging that the absence of a scheme was in breach of the Council of Europe's Convention on Human Rights and Fundamental Freedoms.[76] In *Airey v Ireland*,[77] the plaintiff had sought to initiate judicial separation proceedings in the High Court, but had apparently been unable to secure legal assistance to process the matter further. The European Court of Human Rights held in the *Airey* case that the state could be in breach of the right of access to the courts under Art 6(1) of the Convention where the complexity of the legal issues involved in a case prevented effective access. The court did not conclude that a state-assisted legal aid scheme was required for all litigants, and it pointed out that simplification of procedures was another mechanism for securing effective access.

[9.42] The requirement to secure effective access, the court stated:

"may sometimes compel the State to provide for the assistance of a lawyer when such assistance proves indispensable for an effective access to court either because legal representation is rendered compulsory, as is done by the domestic law of certain contracting

---

[73]   *O'Shaughnessy v Attorney General* (16 February 1971, unreported), HC.
[74]   *The State (Healy) v Donoghue* [1976] IR 325.
[75]   *Committee on Civil Legal Aid and Advice: Report to Minister for Justice* (Prl 6862, 1977). The Committee had been chaired by Pringle J, a High Court judge.
[76]   See generally Ch 17.
[77]   *Airey v Ireland* (1979) 2 EHRR 305.

States for various types of litigation, or by reason of the complexity of the procedures or of the case."[78]

[9.43] Because of the complexity of the plaintiff's judicial separation case, the court concluded that her rights under the Convention had been violated. This represents a rejection of the approach in *O'Shaughnessy v Attorney General*,[79] but the qualified, rather than absolute, nature of the right of access reflects the judgment in *The State (Healy) v Donoghue*.[80]

Non-statutory civil legal aid scheme

[9.44] In response to the *Airey*[81] case, and the recommendations of the Committee on Civil Legal Aid, the government introduced a non-statutory scheme for civil legal aid in 1979,[82] which was amended from time to time. Under the scheme, a legal aid board was established to oversee its administration and a number of law centres were opened, staffed by solicitors, to provide legal advice and legal aid, including the initiation of court proceedings for those of limited means. The civil legal aid scheme was criticised for a number of years on the grounds that it was inadequately funded by the state. While the terms of the scheme appeared to be wide-ranging, the effect of the shortfall in funding was that it was confined, in reality, to family law cases and that even in this limited area substantial arrears in responding to need had developed.[83] In the early 1990s, extra state funding was obtained for the scheme, and it was ultimately accepted that the scheme be placed on a statutory footing. This development was influenced in part by the realisation that the 1979 scheme failed to meet an increasing number of international agreements that required the provision of civil legal aid.[84] In addition, the courts had indicated that the failure to provide effective civil legal aid might, in some circumstances, breach the constitutional right of access to the courts.[85] In *Kavanagh v Legal Aid Board*[86] the plaintiff claimed that a wait of almost 20 months to have her legal aid application processed amounted to a breach of statutory duty. Butler J dismissed the claim, on the basis that, while the Legal Aid Board has a statutory duty to provide legal aid and advice, this is 'subject to Board's resources'.[87] In *O'Donoghue v Legal Aid*

---

[78] *Airey v Ireland* (1979) 2 EHRR 305, para 26.

[79] *O'Shaughnessy v Attorney General* (16 February 1971, unreported), HC.

[80] *The State (Healy) v Donoghue* [1976] IR 325.

[81] *Airey v Ireland* (1979) 2 EHRR 305.

[82] *Scheme of Civil Legal Aid and Advice* (Prl 8543, 1979).

[83] See Whyte, 'And Justice for Some' (1984) 6 DULJ (ns) 88; *The Closed Door; A Report on Civil Legal Aid Services in Ireland* (FLAC, 1987).

[84] See Cousins, 'Access to the Courts' (1992) 14 DULJ (ns) 51.

[85] *S v Landy (Legal Aid Board)* (10 February 1993, unreported), HC, where Lardner J held that the mother of a child whom a health board wished to make a ward of court was entitled to legal aid to be represented in the proceedings. See also Whyte, 'The Future of Civil Legal Aid in Ireland' (2005) 10(4) *Bar Review* 111.

[86] *Kavanagh v Legal Aid Board* [2001] IEHC 149.

[87] Civil Legal Aid Act 1995, s 5.

Board[88] the plaintiff was successful in her claim for damages against the state arising out of a delay of 25 months in providing her with legal aid. Kelly J, who followed the decision in *Kavanagh*, held, however, that the Board's statutory duty had been breached. Kelly J applied two other decisions[89] and held that the plaintiff's constitutional right to civil legal aid derived from her constitutional right of access to the courts and fair procedures, which had been breached by the delay in granting legal aid to the plaintiff.

Civil Legal Aid Act 1995

[9.45] The Civil Legal Aid Act 1995, which came into force in 1996, consolidated the 1979 scheme in statutory form and took account of the international obligations on the state concerning civil legal aid. The 1995 Act established the Legal Aid Board as a separate legal entity, in effect a state body.[90] The Board, consisting of a chairperson and 12 other members, is appointed by the Minister for Justice and Equality. Two members of the Board must be barristers, two must be solicitors and two must be members of the staff of the Board.[91] The principal functions of the Board are to provide, within its resources, legal aid and advice in civil cases to persons who satisfy the eligibility criteria of the 1995 Act, and to disseminate information concerning its services.[92] The Board must publish an annual report of its activities.[93]

[9.46] The Board has a chief executive, who is a civil servant,[94] and it may appoint full-time staff to carry out its functions. The full-time staff members are located in law centres.[95] A proportion of the staff are solicitors, who may be designated as civil servants, but the Civil Legal Aid Act 1995 provides that this designation shall not occur unless staff representatives are consulted.[96] This preserves the position prior to the 1995 Act that administrative staff were designated as civil servants, but that solicitors were not; such solicitors thus enjoyed the full standing of solicitors under the Solicitors Acts.[97] In addition, the Board is authorised to establish a panel of solicitors and barristers in private practice who are willing to provide legal aid and advice under the Act.[98] These are similar to the panels for criminal legal aid.[99]

---

[88]   *O'Donoghue v Legal Aid Board* [2006] 4 IR 204.
[89]   *Stevenson v Landy* (10 February 1993, unreported), HC and *Kirwan v Minister for Justice* [1994] 2 IR 417.
[90]   The website of the Legal Aid Board is legalaidboard.ie.
[91]   Civil Legal Aid Act 1995, s 4.
[92]   Civil Legal Aid Act 1995, s 5.
[93]   Civil Legal Aid Act 1995, s 9.
[94]   Civil Legal Aid Act 1995, s 10.
[95]   Civil Legal Aid Act 1995, s 30.
[96]   Civil Legal Aid Act 1995, s 11.
[97]   See para **3.71**.
[98]   Civil Legal Aid Act 1995, s 30.
[99]   See para **9.24**.

[9.47] While the title of the Civil Legal Aid Act 1995 refers to legal aid, it covers both legal advice and legal aid. Legal advice is defined in wide terms in s 25 to include any oral or written advice given to a person by a solicitor or barrister on the application of the law of the state. In the normal course of events, therefore, advice is limited to Irish law, but s 26(4) authorises the Board to grant advice concerning the law of another state if it deems this appropriate. This is particularly significant in the context of civil disputes involving citizens of other European Union member states.[100] Legal aid is defined in s 27 of the Act as representation by a solicitor or barrister in the categories of civil proceedings covered by s 28 of the Act as well as relevant preparatory work.

[9.48] The Civil Legal Aid Act 1995 sets out two basic tests of eligibility for legal aid: a 'merits' test and a 'means' test. For legal advice, the means test only applies. The merits test is laid down in s 24; this provides that a person shall not be granted legal aid unless, in the Board's opinion, a reasonably prudent person who could afford to engage such services would be likely to do so and where a solicitor or barrister would be likely to advise such a person to obtain such services at his or her own expense.

[9.49] The means test is contained in s 29, which provides that a person cannot receive legal aid or advice unless (a) he or she satisfies the requirements concerning financial eligibility specified in the Act and in any Regulations made under the Act; and (b) pays a contribution to the Board towards the cost of any legal aid or advice, the level of contribution to be laid down in Regulations made under the Act. The key financial eligibility question is the level of disposable income of the applicant (that is, gross income, less items such as income tax, mortgage repayments, rent, social insurance, health insurance contributions and other items to take account of, such as dependent children) and, where applicable, disposable capital (excluding the value of any home). The Act does not specify any particular sum as a ceiling above which a person is disqualified from receiving legal aid or advice from the Board; this is a matter for Regulations to be made under the Act.

[9.50] The qualifying capital and disposable income figures are reviewed from time to time. The current (September 2014) disposable income limit is contained in the Civil Legal Aid Regulations 1996,[101] as amended.[102] Under the 1996 Regulations, as amended, a person's annual disposable income must be less than €18,000. The minimum contribution for legal advice is €30 if a person's disposable income is less than €11,500. If a person's disposable income exceeds €11,500, the amount is calculated on the basis of one-tenth of the difference between their disposable income and €11,500, subject to a maximum of €150. The minimum income contribution for legal aid is €130 where a person's disposable income is less than €11,500. The maximum contribution for legal

---

[100] The EU Commission is empowered to ensure that appropriate legal aid facilities are provided where such trans-boundary legal disputes arise.

[101] SI 276/1996 made pursuant to s 29 of the Civil Legal Aid Act 1996. On s 29 of the Civil Legal Aid Act 1996, see *Monahan v Legal Aid Board* [2008] IEHC 300.

[102] 1996 Regulations as amended by the Civil Legal Aid Regulations 2006 (SI 460/2006) and the Civil Legal Aid Regulations 2013 (SI 346/2013).

aid is €1,675. Any capital disposable income may be taken into account in determining eligibility for civil legal aid, but not legal advice. If an applicant's disposal capital income exceeds €100,000 (prior to 2013, this was €320,000), they will not be eligible for legal aid. FLAC has recommended that the financial eligibility criteria for civil legal aid be measured on an annual basis against the national poverty proofing standards.[103] FLAC also criticised the removal in 2002 of allowances for loan repayments, life assurance, health insurance and travel to and from work from the 1996 Regulations in calculating disposable income for the purposes of civil legal aid.[104]

[9.51] The 1996 Regulations also provide that the Board is empowered, in certain circumstances, to grant legal aid or advice without reference to the means of an applicant.[105] Section 29 of the Civil Legal Aid Act 1995 had empowered the Legal Aid Board to waive any contribution or accept a lower contribution from an applicant. This has been amended, so that the Legal Aid Board can only waive any contribution or accept a lower contribution where failure to do so would cause 'undue hardship' to the applicant.[106]

Criteria for obtaining legal advice

[9.52] Section 26 of the Civil Legal Aid Act 1995 allows the Board to provide legal advice if the applicant satisfies the means test in s 29 of the Act and any Regulations made under the Act. Section 26(2) confirms that legal advice may not deal with a criminal law matter, unless it concerns how legal aid can be obtained under the Criminal Justice (Legal Aid) Act 1962. The Legal Aid Board may also provide legal advice to a complainant who is a witness in serious sexual offences such as rape, aggravated sexual assault and incest[107] or who is a victim of human trafficking.[108] Legal advice may also be provided by the Board in respect of the excluded categories of civil matters referred to in s 28(9) of the Act.[109]

---

103 FLAC, *Access to Justice: a Right or Privilege? A Blueprint for Civil Legal Aid in Ireland* (2005), p 64, available at www.flac.ie.

104 These allowances were removed by the Civil Legal Aid Regulations 2002 (SI 8/2002).

105 See also the Civil Legal Aid Act 1995, s 29(2), as inserted by the Civil Law (Miscellaneous Provisions) Act 2008, s 80.

106 Civil Legal Aid Act 1995, s 29, as amended by the Civil Law (Miscellaneous Provisions) Act 2008, s 80.

107 Civil Legal Aid Act 1995, s 26(3A) as inserted by the Civil Law (Miscellaneous Provisions) Act 2008, s 78.

108 Civil Legal Aid Act 1995, s 26(3B) as inserted by the Civil Law (Miscellaneous Provisions) Act 2011, s 3.

109 Civil Legal Aid Act 1995, s 26(3)(b) as amended by the Civil Law (Miscellaneous Provisions) Act 2008, s 78. See para **9.57**, below on the excluded categories.

Criteria for obtaining legal aid

[9.53] Section 28(2) of the Civil Legal Aid Act 1995 lays down the essential criteria under which the Board grants legal aid, by means of a legal aid certificate. A certificate must be granted if, in the Board's opinion:

(a)   the applicant satisfies the financial eligibility criteria in s 29 of the Act;

(b)   the applicant has as a matter of law reasonable grounds for instituting, defending or being a party to the proceedings for which legal aid is sought;

(c)   the applicant is 'reasonably likely to be successful in the proceedings';

(d)   the proceedings for which legal aid is sought are the most satisfactory means of achieving the result sought by the applicant; and

(e)   having regard to all the circumstances (including the probable cost to the Board, measured against the likely benefit to the applicant), it is reasonable to grant the application.

[9.54] Section 28(3) provides that factors (c) and (e) will not apply where the proceedings in question concern the welfare of a child, including custody or access or a sex offender order. The first of these was inserted to give effect to the decision of the Supreme Court in *MF v Legal Aid Board*,[110] in which the court held that the test of reasonable likelihood of success in the equivalent of s 28(2) in the non-statutory scheme was appropriate only in disputes *inter partes*. A similar provision was added in respect of guardianship applications.[111] In addition, s 28(5) provides that legal aid shall be provided by the Board where the state is obliged by international obligations to do so. In this respect, it refers expressly to international child abduction and custody cases,[112] those involving international enforcement of maintenance orders[113] and where a guardian *ad litem* is appointed.[114]

[9.55] FLAC has criticised the current means of assessment for civil legal aid as being unduly 'bureaucratic' as it consists of a three-tier test: principle test, merits test and means test. Instead, FLAC has recommended that the assessment for eligibility for civil legal aid should be the same as that for criminal legal aid: the client's need to access legal services.[115]

Legal aid in courts and prescribed tribunals

[9.56] Section 27 of the Civil Legal Aid Act 1995 provides that legal aid may, with some exceptions,[116] be given in connection with any civil proceedings in any court, from the

---

110   *MF v Legal Aid Board* [1993] ILRM 797.

111   Children Act 1997, s 13.

112   Child Abduction and Enforcement of Custody Orders 1991.

113   Maintenance Act 1994.

114   Guardianship of Infants Act 1964, s 28 as inserted by the Children Act 1997, s 11.

115   FLAC, *Civil Legal Aid in Ireland: Forty Years on* (2009), p 16, available at www.flac.ie.

116   See para **9.57**.

District Court to the Supreme Court. Proceedings brought to the EU Court of Justice under art 267 of the Treaty on the Functioning of the European Union (TFEU) (formerly art 234 of the EC Treaty) may also be legally aided. In general, the Board will grant legal aid in the lowest court having jurisdiction in the matter.[117] In addition, the Board may be authorised by ministerial order to provide legal aid for proceedings in any prescribed court or tribunal. During the Oireachtas debates leading to the enactment of the 1995 Act, it was proposed that it apply immediately to hearings in the Employment Appeals Tribunal, but this was resisted on the grounds of excessive costs. However, a commitment was given that the required ministerial order would be made if the budgetary situation so allowed.[118] No such order has been made to date (July 2014). In the context of employment discrimination within the scope of the Employment Equality Act 1998, the Irish Human Rights and Equality Commission operates a system of free legal advice to complainants. The exclusion of employment tribunals from the provision of legal aid has been criticised on the basis that, in such cases (as with other tribunal cases) persons appearing before such tribunals often have limited income, yet their legal situation may involve complex areas of law.[119] Appeals to the Social Welfare Appeals Tribunal are also excluded from the civil legal scheme. These exclusions have also been criticised by FLAC, who noted that these tribunals are a common means by which many poor people will attempt to access justice.[120] The Irish Human Rights and Equality Commission also operates a statutory scheme to grant legal assistance in connection with legal proceedings involving human rights issues. The remit of the Legal Aid Board has been extended to include the provision of legal aid and advice to those seeking refugee status in the state through the Refugee Legal Service, and this now accounts for a substantial proportion of the Board's activities.[121] The Refugee Appeals Tribunal is the only tribunal in which civil legal aid for legal advice and legal aid is permitted.

Excluded matters

[9.57] Section 28(9) of the Civil Legal Aid Act 1995 prohibits the Board from providing legal aid in the following categories of cases:[122]

    (a)   defamation claims;

    (b)   disputes concerning rights and interests in or over land;[123]

    (c)   civil matters covered by the small claims procedure;[124]

---

[117] Civil Legal Aid Act 1995, s 28(8).

[118] Select Committee on Legislation and Security, L5, No 4, cols 269–72 (12 July 1995).

[119] Whyte, 'The Future of Civil Legal Aid in Ireland' (2005) 10(4) *Bar Review* 111, 113.

[120] FLAC, *Civil Legal Aid in Ireland: Forty Years on* (2009), p 5, available at www.flac.ie. By contrast, the civil legal aid scheme in England and Wales expressly covers social welfare and employment issues.

[121] See para **9.59**.

[122] See *AA v Medical Council* [2003] IEHC 611, [2003] 4 IR 302 (SC).

[123] Family law proceedings concerning land and landlord and tenant disputes concerning residential property are not excluded: Civil Legal Aid Act 1995, s 28(9)(c).

[124] See para **5.51**.

(d)   licensing;[125]

(d)   conveyancing;

(e)   election petitions;

(f)   claims made in a representative, fiduciary or official capacity;

(g)   claims brought by a person on behalf of a group of persons to establish a precedent on a particular point of law ('test cases');

(h)   any other group or representative action.

[9.58] This list largely reiterates the categories that were excluded from the non-statutory scheme. However, a proposal to exclude claims concerning debt collection was removed during the debate on the Act in the Oireachtas.[126] Another divergence from the non-statutory scheme is that the Minister for Justice and Equality is authorised by s 28(10), subject to the consent of the Minister for Finance, to make an order removing any of the excluded categories. As is the case with the possible extension of the Act to claims in the Employment Appeals Tribunal, any removal of the excluded categories would depend on the general government budgetary position.[127] In the meantime, test cases and defamation actions contemplated by those of limited means will continue to require the goodwill of members of the legal profession to proceed to court.[128]

Management and funding of the civil legal aid scheme

[9.59] By 1995, the staff of the Legal Aid Board established by the 1979 non-statutory scheme comprised 75 solicitors and 126 administrative staff. By 2007, the Legal Aid Board had a staff of 284, of which 109 were solicitors.[129] In 2007, the Legal Aid Board provided legal services to approximately 18,000 individuals (an increase of 500 from 2006).[130] In 2007, approximately 2,650 individuals registered with the Refugee Legal Service.[131] In 1999, the funding for the Board's activities was almost £12 million; by 2007 this had increased to just over €24m (an increase from a figure of just under €22m in 2006). In 2007, the budget for the activities of the Refugee Legal Service was approximately €8.6m.[132] The Legal Aid Board reported that in 2007, only one of its centres was unable to meet its objective of providing legal services to applicants within four months as it had a six-month waiting time.[133] In the wake of the global and national financial crisis that began in 2008, which necessitated the 2010–2013 EU–IMF 'bailout'

---

125   Where hardship may arise, licensing disputes are not excluded: Civil Legal Aid Act 1995, s 28(9)(c).

126   458 *Dáil Debates*, cols 451–452 (15 November 1995).

127   455 *Dáil Debates*, col 770.

128   For criticism of these exclusions, see Phelan, 'The Civil Legal Aid Bill 1995: A Critique' (1995) 13 ILT 109.

129   *Annual Report of the Legal Aid Board 2007*, p 7.

130   *Annual Report of the Legal Aid Board 2007*, p 8.

131   *Annual Report of the Legal Aid Board 2007*, p 9.

132   *Annual Report of the Legal Aid Board 2007*, p 10.

133   *Annual Report of the Legal Aid Board 2007*, p 10.

of Ireland, the cost of civil legal aid came under scrutiny. As with the reduction in criminal legal aid fees, discussed above, funding for the Legal Aid Board has been reduced since 2008. As a result, in 2009 the Board's budget for all its activities was €40.5 million, but this fell to €37.06 million in 2011 and in 2013 to €36.5 million. The figure for 2013 included the cost of the Family Mediation Service, which was transferred to the Board at the end of 2011.[134]

[9.60] This comes against the background that the Civil Legal Aid Act 1995 is primarily used to provide legal aid and advice in family law areas of civil dispute, such as divorce, judicial separation, custody and guardianship. The focus on family law disputes reflects the origins in the *Airey*[135] case of the non-statutory scheme which preceded the 1995 Act. But, it seems indefensible that, for example in 2007, 8,121 of all legal advice cases in which the Board was involved were family law proceedings, the remainder consisting of 707 child care cases and 552 other civil matters.[136] It is difficult to believe that other civil litigation, such as personal injuries claims, are being conducted by people of much greater wealth than those who are engaged in family law litigation. This lack of diversity in the work of the board has been described as 'worrying'.[137] The reality, of course, is that the Legal Aid Board is constrained in the type of cases it can fund by the budget allocation which the government of the day is prepared to set aside. Given that the budget for civil legal aid has increased year on year, despite its de facto limitation to family law cases, it is not surprising that the political commitment may not exist to fund personal injuries actions, many of which are brought against the state or state agencies.

[9.61] It would appear that the state is prepared to leave personal injuries litigation to be determined by market forces and, in particular, by the informal 'merits test' which is implicit in 'deferred fee' arrangements, namely that lawyers will not take on such cases unless there is a reasonable prospect of success.[138] While lawyers may be prepared to pursue many relatively simple personal injuries actions on this basis, they may be less likely to pursue complex claims without some payment in advance from the client, if for nothing else to fund expert witness reports. These are precisely the kind of difficult cases which the limited budget of the Legal Aid Board is unable to fund. Under the UK civil legal aid regime, such cases are often part-funded on the basis that expert witness reports are funded by the scheme, but the legal fees are left, in effect, until the case is finalised; if the plaintiff is successful, his or her legal advisers will then be paid by the defendant. This has meant that at least some personal injuries actions, including major multiple actions, such as asbestos-related claims and claims following major disasters, have been part-funded under the United Kingdom civil legal aid scheme.

---

[134] Civil Legal Aid Act 1995, as amended by the Civil Law (Miscellaneous Provisions) Act 2011, s 54.

[135] *Airey v Ireland* (1979) 2 EHRR 305.

[136] *Annual Report of the Legal Aid Board 2007*, p 13.

[137] FLAC, *Access to Justice: a Right or Privilege? A Blueprint for Civil Legal Aid in Ireland* (2005), p 3, available at www.flac.ie.

[138] On the 'deferred fee' ('no foal, no fee' in all but name), see para **3.76**.

[9.62] In the absence of a properly funded regime in Ireland, litigants have largely depended on the 'no foal, no fee' arrangement or on *pro bono* work by lawyers. For victims of some major accidents and other disasters, there is a real risk that, in any event, civil claims would be a fruitless exercise because potential defendants may not have the resources to meet the large awards that would be made. In such cases in Ireland, political lobbying has resulted in some *ad hoc* 'no-fault' compensation schemes being established, by which awards are funded by the state. In the 1980s, such a scheme was established for the victims of a fire on St Valentine's Day 1981 at a Dublin discotheque, the 'Stardust'. Similar schemes were established in the 1990s for those people infected with HIV and Hepatitis C from contaminated blood products which had been distributed in the state.[139] Such schemes operate on the premise that payments will mirror those which would have been obtained in civil litigation, but are made on an *ex gratia* basis, that is without any admission of liability. The Stardust scheme was established on a non-statutory basis, but the more recent schemes have used a legislative framework.[140] In 2013, a scheme of redress based on restorative principles was developed for women who had been admitted to and worked in Magdalene laundries between the 1930s and 1970s. This scheme contained a number of innovative elements, including provision for health care and that a memorial should be erected to commemorate the Magdalene women (in addition to the more traditional element of *ex gratia* payments to compensate the women for their time in the laundries).[141]

[9.63] Because of the increased costs of funding civil legal aid in the United Kingdom, considerable efforts have also been made to bring further efficiencies into the civil legal aid scheme, mirroring those for the criminal legal aid scheme. The British Access to Justice Act 1999 (UK) provided for the establishment of the Legal Services Commission to replace the British Legal Aid Board. The Legal Services Commission was replaced by the Legal Aid Agency, established under the British Legal Aid, Sentencing and Punishment of Offenders Act 2012. The Legal Aid Agency manages the civil legal aid budget and aims to achieve efficiencies in its use, similar to the approach for the criminal legal aid budget.[142] In particular, it manages the activities of the Community Legal Service (CLS), whose general aim is to ensure that civil disputes are resolved without the need to engage in expensive court-based litigation. This is part of the 'integrated' approach to civil justice which we have discussed elsewhere.[143]

---

[139] All of these had also been the subject of tribunals of inquiry: see para **8.75**.

[140] For example, Hepatitis C Compensation Tribunal Act 1997.

[141] The Scheme was based on the *Magdalen Commission Report* (2013), available at www.justice.ie, discussed at para **8.10**.

[142] The Legal Aid Agency is also responsible for managing the criminal legal aid budget: see para **9.32**.

[143] See para **8.18**.

Review of Civil Legal Aid

[9.64] In 2005, FLAC published a review of 25 years of the operation of the state civil legal aid scheme.[144] Overall, the report found that the civil legal aid scheme was not meeting its stated aims. It found the civil legal aid scheme to be 'overburdened, under resourced and limited'.[145] It also was of the view that the system of civil legal aid did not place the needs of the applicant at the centre of the decision whether to grant legal aid. One of its recommendations, which has been implemented, was for the removal of the value of the family home from the calculation of capital for the purposes of means testing for legal aid.[146] FLAC also recommended that the Civil Legal Aid Act 1995 be amended to provide that legal aid will always be required where it is necessary to vindicate human rights. It is at least arguable that, given the scheme established by the Irish Human Rights Commission to provide assistance in the area of human rights, a degree of legal aid is already provided in this respect. FLAC also recommended the codification in a single piece of legislation of the right of access to the courts and legal aid.

[9.65] In 2009, FLAC was 40 years in operation. To coincide with this, it conducted a study,[147] which found that the legal problems it dealt with in north inner-city Dublin involved local authority housing (77.5% of the organisations), social welfare (also 77.5%) and domestic violence (72.5%). FLAC highlighted that only one of these areas, domestic violence, is covered by the civil legal aid scheme. It recommended that the designated areas of civil legal aid and those expressly excluded from the Civil Legal Aid Act 1995 be re-considered.

[6] COURT FEES

[9.66] In addition to the cost of retaining a solicitor and barrister, another significant cost factor in civil litigation in particular is the requirement that fees be paid on all pleadings and other court documents.[148] The precise rates of fees are set from time to time by statutory orders made by the Minister for Justice.[149] At the time of writing (September 2014), the fee on a High Court originating summons is €125, for setting

---

144 FLAC, *Access to Justice: a Right or Privilege? A Blueprint for Civil Legal Aid in Ireland* (2005) available at www.flac.ie.

145 FLAC, *Access to Justice: a Right or Privilege? A Blueprint for Civil Legal Aid in Ireland* (2005), p 4 available at www.flac.ie.

146 FLAC, *Access to Justice: a Right or Privilege? A Blueprint for Civil Legal Aid in Ireland* (2005), p 64 available at www.flac.ie.

147 FLAC, *Civil Legal Aid in Ireland: Forty Years on* (2009), available at www.flac.ie.

148 Court fees are collected by the Courts Service: see Courts Service Act 1998 (Second Schedule) (Amendment) Order 2004 (SI 35/2004).

149 See, for example, the Schedules to the Supreme Court and High Court (Fees) Order 2008, SI 200/2008, the Circuit Court (Fees) Order 2008 (SI 201/2008) and the District Court (Fees) Order 2008 (SI 202/2008).

down an action for trial it is €120, while the fee for filing a notice of appeal to the Supreme Court is €125.[150] In the Circuit Court, the fee for issuing a Civil Bill is €65.

[9.67] In 2013, the net cost of running the Courts Service was €57.8 million, compared with €59.1 million in 2012 and €100 million in 2008. Total current expenditure (including payroll and public private partnership payment for the Criminal Courts of Justice complex) was €96.55 million compared with €100.3 million in 2012, capital expenditure was €8.1 million compared with €7.3 million in 2012. Court fees in 2013 amounted to €42.16 million (out of a total income, including pension levy, of €46.8 million) compared with court fees in 2012 of €43.72 million (out of a total income of €48.5 million in 2012).[151]

[9.68] Fees are not charged in family proceedings or in judicial review proceedings concerning criminal matters. While the fees may not appear excessive and constitute a low percentage of the full cost of going to court, they may represent a disincentive for those who are unable to avail of state-assisted civil legal aid and in proceedings to which the scheme does not apply.

[9.69] In 1972, the Committee on Court Practice and Procedure[152] recommended the abolition of all court fees on the ground that they might constitute an unreasonable bar to the right of access to the courts. Other recommendations in relation to how court fees could be reduced were also made. It is clear that not all fees have been abolished, though certain categories, such as family law and criminal judicial review proceedings, are now exempt. The issue of principle remains unresolved, though some judges have expressed doubts about the constitutional validity of court fees in certain cases.[153] This argument may be particularly strong in its application to individual litigants, but perhaps the reason for the retention of fees in general is that in many instances the 'bill' is paid either by insurance companies (for example, in respect of personal injuries actions) or by large corporate entities (for example, in a complex contract case or judicial review). Indeed, it is notable that in the UK court fees are set at a level as far as possible that reflects the full costs of the process.[154] In 2008 the UK Ministry of Justice announced its intention to introduce daily hearing fees in large commercial cases.[155]

---

[150] The precise rate of court fees are provided on the Courts Service website at www.courts.ie.

[151] *Annual Report of the Courts Service 2013* (2014), pp 7 and 65, available at www.courts.ie.

[152] *Seventeenth Interim Report of the Committee on Court Practice and Procedure: Court Fees* (Prl 2699, 1972).

[153] See *MacGarbhith v Attorney General* [1991] 2 IR 412 (HC), (29 March 1995, unreported), SC.

[154] The most recent list of fees is contained in the Civil Proceedings Fees Order 2008 (SI 1053/2008). For example, a court fee of £360 becomes payable where proceedings are commenced to recover a sum of money exceeding £15,000 but not exceeding £50,000, and £400 for proceedings commenced in the High Court for the recovery of land.

[155] Ministry of Justice, *Civil Court Fees 2008: Consultation Paper* (2008), available at www.justice.gov.uk. At present where a judge of the English Commercial Court is appointed as an arbitrator under the Arbitration Act 1996, a fee of £1,800 per day or part day is payable. See Civil Proceedings Fees Order 2008 (SI 1053/2008).

[9.70] In *Murphy v Minister for Justice*,[156] the Supreme Court held that reasonable charges for court services were not in breach of the right of access to the courts under Article 40.3 of the Constitution.[157] Delivering the unanimous decision of the court, Murphy J appeared to envisage 'full cost' charges being imposed on commercial entities in commercial disputes, though not on individuals. He commented that:

> "[T]he concept of the entire cost of the judicial system being borne out of tax, including tax imposed on modest incomes, to exonerate substantial commercial organisations would seem absurd in principle and offensive in practice."

Clearly, the UK Ministry of Justice has indicated an intention to move in the direction of charging a full commercial rate, and it remains to be seen whether this model will be followed in Ireland,[158] but the views expressed in the *Murphy* case may be a straw in the wind.

[7] LEGAL COSTS

[9.71] Another direct cost of litigation is the fees which must be paid to the lawyers involved in civil and criminal cases. We discuss elsewhere the general principles concerning costs in civil litigation in this jurisdiction, including the rule that 'costs follow the event'.[159] In those civil cases to which the Civil Legal Aid Act 1995 applies, the state may also be required to bear the cost of the plaintiff's and/or defendant's legal representation.[160]

[9.72] In criminal cases covered by the Criminal Justice (Legal Aid) Act 1962, the costs of both the prosecution and defence are borne by the state. In criminal cases not covered by the 1962 Act, it is only in rare instances that a court will award costs to either side. Where the prosecution is successful and the defendant is found guilty, the state is generally required to pay its own costs. The defendant will also have to pay his or her legal advisers' fees. In some cases where the defendant is acquitted, the trial judge has a

---

[156] *Murphy v Minister for Justice* [2001] 2 ILRM 144, 149.

[157] See also *Kavanagh v Government of Ireland* [2007] IEHC 389, where Smyth J examined the text of Art 3.8 of the European Convention on Human Rights which states: 'Each party shall ensure that persons exercising their rights in conformity with the provisions of this Convention shall not be penalised, persecuted or harassed in any way for their involvement. This provision shall not affect the powers of national courts to award reasonable costs in judicial proceedings.' Smyth J stated that art 3 was 'concerned to ensure that the cost of entry upon litigation i.e. court fees are not prohibitively expensive.' See also the discussion of Protective Costs Orders, para **9.73**.

[158] In *First Report of the Working Group on a Courts Commission: Management and Financing of the Courts* (Pn 2690, 1996), p 34 (see para **4.209**), the Working Group leaned against full cost charges.

[159] See para **5.39**.

[160] See the Civil Legal Aid Act 1995, ss 33–36 on costs in successful and unsuccessful actions involving legally-aided persons.

discretion to award costs against the state.[161] In a summary prosecution in the District Court, rules of court provide that costs may never be awarded against a member of the Garda Síochána acting as prosecutor, and this special exemption has been held to be constitutionally valid.[162]

[8] PROTECTIVE COSTS ORDERS

[9.73] It is clear that legal costs operate as a barrier for many in accessing the courts in those instances that are not legally aided under the 1995 Act, and subject to the limited instances where lawyers take a claim on a *pro bono* basis. An alternative method developed to address this is the concept that costs might be capped at a fixed level in advance of the litigation. This is known as a protective costs order (PCO).[163]

[9.74] This concept was incorporated into the 1998 Convention on Access to Information, Public Participation in Decision-Making and Access to Justice in Environmental Matters. This Convention, often known as the Aarhus Convention, was developed by the United Nations Economic Commission for Europe (UNECE). Article 9 of the Convention provides that any court-based process required to challenge a decision that is in breach of the rights in the Convention must be 'not prohibitively expensive'. This aspect of the Aarhus Convention was implemented in the Environment (Miscellaneous Provisions) Act 2011, which provides for the making of a protective costs order (PCO).

[9.75] In a reference from the UK Supreme Court to the EU Court of Justice, *R (Edwards) v Environment Agency*,[164] the Court of Justice held that the test of what is 'not prohibitively expensive' is not purely subjective and must not exceed the financial resources of the person concerned nor 'appear to be objectively unreasonable' in order to ensure that the public plays an active role in protecting and improving the quality of the environment. Following this decision, the UK Supreme Court held, in *R (Edwards) v Environment Agency (No 2)*,[165] that an order for costs of £25,000 was appropriate. In *Hunter v Nurendale Ltd*[166] the High Court (Hedigan J) applied the principles set out by the EU Court of Justice in the *Edwards* case and made a PCO under the 2011 Act. The High Court did not specify in advance a specific cap on costs but it noted that the applicant 'has no assets'. The Court also stated that the following procedure should be followed in future applications: (a) the applicant should set out what broadly the expenses involved in such an application would be; (b) the applicant should set out a

---

[161] See *The People (AG) v Bell* [1969] IR 24 and *The People (DPP) v Bourke Waste Removal Ltd* [2012] IECCA 66.

[162] See *Dillane v Ireland* [1980] ILRM 167.

[163] In 2010, the Public Interest Law Alliance (PILA, an affiliate of FLAC) published a Report on this issue *The Costs Barrier and Protective Costs Orders*, available at www.pila.ie.

[164] *R (Edwards) v Environment Agency (No 2)* Case C-260/11 (judgment of the EU Court of Justice of 11 April 2013).

[165] *R (Edwards) v Environment Agency* [2013] UKSC 78.

[166] *Hunter v Nurendale Ltd* [2013] IEHC 430.

broad statement of his or her financial situation; (c) the applicant should set out the reasons why there is a reasonable prospect of success; (d) the applicant should set out clearly what is at stake for him or her and for the protection of the environment; (e) the applicant should deal with any possible claim of frivolous proceedings, should that arise; and (f) the applicant should deal with the existence of any possible legal aid scheme or any contingency arrangement in relation to costs that may have been made with their solicitors.

[9.76] In *Schrems v Data Protection Commissioner*[167] the High Court (Hogan J) made a PCO in a case that did not involve the Aarhus Convention. The applicant was an Austria-based law student who challenged a decision of the Data Protection Commissioner in which he had declined to deal with the applicant's complaint over the transfer by the social network company Facebook of data from Europe to its US parent company. The Court noted that having regard to previous decisions of the courts on costs in similar cases involving important constitutional issues, it was unlikely to make a costs order against the applicant in any event. The Data Commissioner accepted that the case raised legal questions of public importance and agreed they justified a PCO. The Commissioner sought an order capped at €55,000, which was the sum the applicant had raised as a member of a fund-raising group involved in bringing over 20 other similar complaints concerning Facebook to other data protection authorities in Europe. The High Court set the amount of the PCO at €10,000. The Court noted that the applicant, a post-graduate law student in his 20s on the cusp of his career, was somebody who was very likely to be exercised by the prospect of incurring legal costs. The Court also took into account that the €55,000 from public fund raising was not entirely under the applicant's control and that it was also being used to fund many other comparable complaints.

[9.77] While it is unlikely that future PCOs will be fixed at the €10,000 set in the *Schrems* case it is clear that the judiciary is becoming increasingly conscious of the barriers posed by high legal costs to effective access to justice. The changes to the general regulation of legal costs proposed in the Legal Services Regulation Bill 2011[168] are also likely to have a significant impact in the future.

---

[167] *Schrems v Data Protection Commissioner* (16 July 2014) HC. The details of the order made in the case are available at www.pila.ie.

[168] On the 2011 Bill see para **3.36**.

Chapter 10

Remedies and Enforcement in Civil and Criminal Matters

[1] Introduction 443
[2] Remedies in Civil Matters 443
[3] Procedure for Enforcement of Court Orders 448
[4] Enforcement in Criminal Matters 451
[5] Contempt of Court 458
[6] Judicial Review 460

[1] INTRODUCTION

[10.01] In this chapter we examine the different remedies and enforcement mechanisms available in civil and criminal matters. As to civil cases, we examine the basis on which the following remedies are awarded: damages (monetary compensation), injunctions and specific performance. We also outline the different enforcement mechanisms to ensure compliance with court orders in civil matters. As to criminal matters, we review the purposes of fines and imprisonment and examine alternative enforcement mechanisms such as probation, community service orders and the emergence of restorative justice. We also discuss enforcement mechanisms used by regulators in connection with corporate offences. We then examine contempt of court, a long-standing jurisdiction employed by the courts to ensure compliance with their orders in both civil and criminal matters. Finally, we examine judicial review, also available as a remedy in civil and criminal matters.

[2] REMEDIES IN CIVIL MATTERS

[10.02] Before the courts will grant any remedy in a civil matter, the plaintiff must establish that some recognised legal wrong has been committed, for example, a breach of contract or a recognised tort such as negligence.[1] We do not consider here the necessary ingredients required by the law to establish that a remediable wrong has occurred.

---

1. On the overlap between contract and other areas of liability see Phillips, 'The Concurrence of Remedies in Contract and Tort' (1977) 12 Ir Jur (ns) 234; Carey, 'Concurrent Liability in Contract and Tort Part I' (2001) 8(8) CLP 183; and Carey, 'Concurrent Liability in Contract and Tort Part II' (2001) 8(9) CLP 214.

443

Damages

[10.03] An award of damages, that is monetary compensation, is the most common form of remedy sought in civil claims. The essential principle underlying an award of damages is that the sum awarded is to be a compensatory amount which places the injured person in the position he or she was, so far as money can do so, before the legal wrong was committed.

[10.04] This is a relatively straightforward matter in a negligence case concerning financial loss. Thus, in *Wall v Hegarty*[2] the plaintiff claimed that the defendants, solicitors, had negligently prepared his uncle's will, causing it to be declared invalid; that as a result he had lost an expected inheritance of £15,000; that the defendants' solicitors had owed him a duty of care in the preparation of the will; that they had failed in this duty, through their carelessness; and that they should therefore be required to compensate him in the sum of £15,000. The High Court agreed that the defendants owed the plaintiff a duty of care and were in breach of that duty. The plaintiff was awarded £15,000 damages, the court having concluded that a loss had been sustained. In this instance, the award of damages satisfies the principle that the plaintiff be restored to his position prior to the wrong, or *restitutio in integram*.

[10.05] This principle cannot, however, be applied in full in all cases. Where a person has received personal injuries, even the most skilled surgeon may not be capable of repairing the damage. In such a case, the award of damages reflects an attempt to compensate for the loss suffered. Similarly, in defamation cases, an award of damages is designed to compensate the plaintiff for the hurt and loss of reputation arising from the publication of a false statement.

[10.06] In a personal injuries claim, such as arises from a road traffic accident, damages are awarded under two headings, *special damages* and *general damages*. Special damages refers to pecuniary losses such as medical expenses or loss of earnings, including loss of earnings in the future after the trial of the action. The calculation of such future loss generally requires evidence from an actuary. General damages refers to non-pecuniary loss and this, in turn, is usually broken into three components: pain and suffering, loss of amenities and loss of expectation of life. The element of pain and suffering includes the immediate pain of the accident and continuing and future discomfort and pain such as the effects of future arthritis. Loss of amenities refers to the loss of the use of a limb; in this respect damages may be increased if the plaintiff is unable to participate in sports or other activities which he or she enjoyed prior to the accident. Loss of expectation of life refers to the damages awarded for any reduction in life expectancy. As we have already seen, in this jurisdiction, damages are awarded on the basis of a one-off lump sum award, rather than 'staged' or periodic payments, although these may be introduced in the future.[3]

---

[2]   *Wall v Hegarty* [1980] ILRM 124: see para **12.153**.
[3]   See para **6.14**.

[10.07] As we have seen in Ch 5, a great many personal injuries claims are now referred in the first place to the Injuries Board (Personal Injuries Assessment Board) and not directly to the courts. If the Injuries Board makes an assessment of general damages for pain and suffering, it will do so using the Book of Quantum which provides general guidelines as to the amounts that may be awarded or assessed in respect of specified types of injury within particular ranges.[4] The Book of Quantum provides guidance to the Injuries Board (and if the matter proceeds to court, the court dealing with the matter)[5] on the compensation levels for particular injuries based on ranges of damages.[6]

[10.08] While the general principle is that an award of damages is intended to compensate a person for actual loss, so far as money can do so, there are exceptional circumstances where exemplary or punitive damages may be awarded. These include circumstances where there has been a conscious and deliberate violation of rights or where the court is satisfied that the wrongdoer intended to make a profit over and above what would be awarded to the injured party. In this jurisdiction such exemplary damages are, usually, relatively modest.[7] Under s 22 of the Courts Act 1981, a court awarding damages may also order the payment of interest[8] on all or part of that sum from the date of the cause of action to the date of the judgment.

Injunction

[10.09] The injunction was a remedy developed by the courts of equity[9] to prevent one party from acting in such a way as to interfere with the rights of another. It supplements the damages remedy available at common law. An injunction is an order of the court that directs a person to do or refrain from doing a specified act. Thus, a plaintiff who complains that the defendant has trespassed on his land in all likelihood will seek an injunction to restrain the defendant from further acts of trespass. In a case such as this damages may not be an adequate remedy, especially if the trespasser does not have any assets to meet the award.

---

4   See para **5.15** and Maguire, 'The Personal Injuries Assessment Board' (2001) 7(1) *Bar Review* 39; Nolan, 'The Personal Injuries Assessment Board Act 2003' (2004) 9(1) *Bar Review* 7; and O'Dwyer, 'New Procedures for Personal Injuries Claims' (2004) 9(6) *Bar Review* 199.

5   Civil Liability and Courts Act 2004, ss 22(1) provides that the court shall have regard to the Book of Quantum when assessing damages in a personal injuries action. However, s 22(2) provides that this provision shall not prevent a court from having regard to other matters when assessing damages in a personal injuries action.

6   The Book of Quantum (2004) is available at www.injuriesboard.ie.

7   See, for example, *Kennedy v Ireland* [1987] IR 587. An unusual example of an extremely large award is *Shortt v Garda Commissioner* [2007] IESC 9, [2007] 4 IR 587. See generally McMahon and Binchy, *Law of Torts* (4th edn, 2013) and Quill, *Torts in Ireland* (3rd edn, 2009).

8   The rate of Courts Act interest is currently set at 8% per annum. See Courts Acts 1981 (Interest on Judgment Debts) Order 1989 (SI 12/1989).

9   See generally, para **2.08** and Delany, *Equity and the Law of Trusts in Ireland* (4th edn, 2007) and Kirwan, *Injunctions Law & Practice* (2008).

[10.10] The injunction may also be used to prevent some future action which the applicant fears; this is referred to as a *quia timet* injunction. It may take the form of a mandatory injunction, by which the court orders a person to do something, for example, requiring a builder to use materials as agreed in the specifications of a building contract. Another form is the prohibitory injunction, by which a person is prohibited from doing something, as in the 'cease and desist' order used in the case of the trespasser.

[10.11] Once awarded after a full court hearing, an injunction has effect in perpetuity, that is for all time; this is referred to as a perpetual injunction. However, not all cases require a permanent injunction of this nature and, indeed, many situations are of such urgency that to wait for a full court hearing would render meaningless an application for a perpetual injunction. For example, where a person has left one company to become an employee of a rival company, it may very well be pointless for a lawyer to advise the first company that, in two years' time, when the case may come to court, the employee may be ordered by injunction not to pass on any trade secrets to the new employer. At that stage the secrets may have already been passed on and the first company may be out of business. In such circumstances, the injunction may be used as a holding order to 'freeze' the position of the parties until a full court hearing.[10]

[10.12] In the example given, the first company may apply to court, without notice to the rival company, for an *interim injunction*. The application without notice is referred to as an *ex parte* application, since only one party appears in court, contrary to the normal principle of the adversarial system that both parties should appear. The company applying for relief will outline to the court the background to the case; it will indicate that it intends to institute proceedings against its former employee and the rival company; it will present to the court the relevant initiating documents, which may include a claim for damages and/or a perpetual injunction, with a view to the court approving their issue without the normal notification requirements; and it will then apply for an interim injunction to preserve the status quo of the parties until the hearing of the intended action.

[10.13] Having heard the application, the judge may grant an interim injunction, in this case prohibiting the former employee from passing trade secrets to the rival company.

---

[10] The injunction obtained to 'freeze' financial assets, where a bank is ordered not to reduce the assets in a specified bank account below a certain level pending the outcome of an action, is generally referred to as a Mareva injunction (after one of the first English cases in which it was discussed, *Mareva Compania Naviera SA v International Bulkcarriers SA* [1975] 2 Lloyd's Rep 509): see *Powerscourt Estates v Gallagher* [1984] ILRM 123 and Kirwan, *Injunctions Law & Practice* (2008), pp 279–307. A similar type of remedy is the Anton Piller Order (also after one of the first English cases in which it was discussed, *Anton Piller KG v Manufacturing Processes Ltd* [1976] Ch 55), which allows one party to take documents and other items from a named premises; such orders are used, for example, in video piracy and internet fraud cases, but should be distinguished from discovery orders, discussed at para **6.58**. On Anton Piller Orders see *Microsoft Corporation v Brightpoint Ireland Ltd* [2001] ILRM 540 and Kirwan, *Injunctions Law & Practice* (2008), pp 319–334.

Once this court order has been granted, it carries the full authority of the courts, and failure to obey its terms would constitute contempt of court.[11] However, since it is obtained on the basis of one party's presentation without having heard the other side, an interim injunction has a limited life-span, generally 24 to 48 hours. In addition, the company obtaining the injunction must also undertake to serve the injunction on those affected by it; notify them when the next stage of the proceedings, an application for an interlocutory injunction, will take place; and undertake to the court to pay any damages to the affected parties in the event that the injunction should not have been granted in the first place.

[10.14] The next phase of the proceedings is the application for an *interlocutory injunction*, which takes place at the end of the 24- to 48-hour life of the interim injunction. At the interlocutory application, both parties are in court to present their case. However, the court does not make a final determination on the merits of the case, such as whether any restriction in the employee's contract prohibiting him from joining another company is valid.[12] Rather, the court considers two factors: whether the applicant has made out a stateable legal case in connection with the claim it has instituted and whether the balance of convenience favours granting an injunction.[13]

[10.15] On the question of a stateable case, the court need only be satisfied that the applicant has some legal grounds on which to institute proceedings, but not necessarily that these will be successful.[14] The issue of the balance of convenience requires the court to consider, on the one hand, the position where an interlocutory injunction has been granted but the restriction on the former employee is found to be invalid at the final hearing and, on the other, that where an interlocutory injunction is refused but at the final hearing the restriction is found to be valid.

[10.16] The balance of convenience generally favours the award of an interlocutory injunction in the example given. The courts will typically take the view that the consequences of refusing an injunction may be that the company seeking the injunction will have gone out of business before the case comes to hearing and that an award of damages is unlikely to be a sufficient remedy. In contrast, while the former employee might have his employment opportunities improperly restricted, this could be adequately remedied by an award of damages. The court is also likely to be influenced by the requirement that, if an interlocutory injunction is granted, the employer must continue the undertaking to pay any damages to the former employee and the rival company in the event that the restriction is ultimately found to be invalid.

---

[11] See para **10.49**.
[12] Such restrictions are referred to as covenants in restraint of trade: see generally Clark, *Contract Law in Ireland* (6th edn, 2008) and Kirwan, *Injunctions Law & Practice* (2008).
[13] See *Campus Oil Ltd v Minister for Industry and Energy (No 2)* [1983] IR 88.
[14] See *European Chemical Industries Ltd v Bell* [1981] ILRM 345.

Specific performance

[10.17] This is another equitable remedy developed to give a more effective remedy than damages in breach of contract cases. Specific performance is an order requiring the person in breach of contract to perform it according to the terms agreed. To obtain an order for specific performance, the court must be satisfied that damages would be an insufficient remedy and that there has been no undue delay or other matter which might disentitle the applicant to the remedy. In addition, there are certain types of contracts for which the remedy will not, usually, be granted. These include contracts of personal service, such as employment contracts. The remedy of specific performance is a particularly valuable remedy in connection with contracts for the sale of land.[15]

Declaration

[10.18] Where a plaintiff does not seek any of the remedies discussed above, he or she may apply to court for a *declaration*. This was another remedy developed by the courts of equity with a view to determining the rights or status of a person. Thus, at the time when a person's rights might be dependent on a determination of whether he or she was illegitimate,[16] the declaration was the appropriate remedy to seek. In this jurisdiction, the declaration is commonly used in constitutional claims, where for example the plaintiff seeks a declaration that a particular statutory provision is invalid on the ground that it is in conflict with a right contained in the Constitution.[17]

[3] PROCEDURE FOR ENFORCEMENT OF COURT ORDERS

[10.19] A number of well-established procedures exist for the enforcement of monetary awards by courts and we discuss these briefly here. A key method is for the person in whose favour an award has been made, the judgment creditor, to seek a further court order authorising the property of the defaulter, including goods, to be seized and then sold. An order for *fieri facias* (commonly referred to as a *fi fa* order) may be issued by the High Court authorising a County Registrar (in Dublin, the County Sheriff) to cause to be made (*fieri facias*) a sufficient sum out of the defaulter's assets to discharge the debt. The *fi fa* order authorises the seizure of goods.

[10.20] Another enforcement method is the garnishee order, which assigns the judgment creditor any debt owed to the defaulter by a third party. A well-charging order may be obtained by a judgment creditor in order to 'attach' the court award to any real property that is owned by the judgment debtor. The judgment creditor may also seek to have a

---

[15]   See, eg, *Nestor v Murphy* [1979] IR 326, discussed at para **14.46** and generally Delany, *Equity and the Law of Trusts in Ireland* (4th edn, 2007) and Farrell, *Irish Law of Specific Performance* (1994).

[16]   Many of the distinctions between the rights of a person born within marriage and one born outside marriage had been abolished prior to the abolition of the status of illegitimacy by the Status of Children Act 1987.

[17]   See Ch 15.

receiver appointed by way of equitable execution to intercept any income and profits before they reach the defaulter. This would be used in large debt situations.[18] In contempt of court cases, which we discuss below, committal for contempt may be accompanied by an application for sequestration of assets. Sequestration authorises the sequestrators to take possession of all property and assets in the possession of the individual or organisation in contempt of court and to manage that property and assets until the contempt has been purged.[19]

[10.21] One of the most difficult and controversial methods of enforcing a court order is an order for the possession and sale of land. Such an order might be obtained by a financial institution where there is default on a loan or mortgage and may often follow a well-charging order. As the folk memory of forced evictions remains vivid for many people, there have been occasions where land is placed for auction by court order but in which no bids have been made. In such circumstances, a bank attempting to recover a debt in relation to land may enter into an arrangement with the defaulting landowner under which the land is auctioned or otherwise sold without being categorised as a court sale.

[10.22] The Enforcement of Court Orders Acts 1926 and 1940, as amended by the Courts (No 2) Act 1986,[20] empower the District Court to require a person in default of a court order to make payments in accordance with a schedule of payments arrived at by the court after an assessment of the defaulter's means. If the defaulter continues to default on such payments, he or she may be attached for contempt of court[21] and lodged in prison for such failure. It may be noted, however, that a person may not be sent to prison for inability to pay a debt, but only for wilful refusal to pay a debt within his or her means: the distinction between those who 'won't pay' as opposed to 'can't pay'. While prisons might have been constructed in the early days to house debtors, imprisonment for debt is no longer a feature of the legal landscape. Nonetheless, a number of people continue to be imprisoned for wilful refusal to pay a debt, and this has been criticised by a United Nations Committee as an anachronism in the 21st century, which may result in the repeal of this legislation.[22] A 2002 report commissioned by the Department of Justice, Equality and Law Reform highlighted the deprived backgrounds from which people imprisoned for failure to pay civil debt came, and the adverse

---

18 For attachment of earnings in family proceedings, see para **10.25**.
19 In *Larkins v National Union of Mineworkers* [1985] IR 671 an application was refused to appoint sequestrators to funds held in an Irish bank on behalf of the British NUM, who were in contempt of an order of the English High Court. See also *In Re Powertech Logistics Ltd: Airscape Ltd v Powertech Logistics Ltd* [2007] IEHC 43.
20 The Courts (No 2) Act 1986 came into force in 1997: Courts (No 2) Act 1986 (Commencement) Order 1997 (SI 106/1997).
21 See para **10.49**.
22 See O'Flaherty, 'Implementation of the International Covenant on Civil and Political Rights' (1993) 11 ILT 225, 231.

consequences which such imprisonment had for their social welfare benefits and future employment prospects.[23]

[10.23] In *McCann v Judge of Monaghan District Court*,[24] Laffoy J held that the relevant provisions of the Enforcement of Court Orders Acts 1926 and 1940, which allowed the plaintiff's imprisonment for failure to pay arrears of €5,865 on a debt without the need for her presence in court were in breach of the Constitution. In response, the Oireachtas enacted the Enforcement of Court Orders (Amendment) Act 2009, which amended the relevant provisions of the 1926 and 1940 Acts to ensure the presence of the debtor before any court orders are made. The amendments made include: the power of a District Court judge to fix a new date for hearing if there is no appearance by the debtor; permitting the judge to request that the debtor and creditor attempt to resolve the matter by mediation; and provision for legal aid for debtors against whom instalment orders have been made.

[10.24] While the changes made by the 2009 Act addressed the specific issues raised in the *McCann* case, it was clear that a wider solution to the law on debt and its enforcement was required. This became clearer because of the enormous increase in personal debt arising from the global and financial crisis that emerged in 2008 and consequent job losses and income reductions. The Law Reform Commission's 2010 *Report on Personal Debt Management and Debt Enforcement*[25] recommended the enactment of a statutory non-judicial personal insolvency regime that would reflect the realities of a modern consumer society. The enactment of such legislation was among the many conditions attached to the 2010–2013 EU–IMF Financial Support Agreement for Ireland (the EU–IMF 'bailout') and this was enacted in the Personal Insolvency Act 2012, which established the Insolvency Service of Ireland (ISI) in 2013.

[10.25] The recommendations in the Commission's 2010 Report on modernising the general debt enforcement regime have not been implemented at the time of writing (September 2014). Pending this, other legislation in specific areas intended to facilitate the enforcement of court awards has a more modern approach. In the context of awards of maintenance to spouses and children, the Family Law Act 1995 provides for improved mechanisms aimed at ensuring that such awards are complied with; this includes attachment of earnings of defaulting spouses, by which the employer is required to pay a specified sum direct to the spouse and children in whose favour the maintenance order was made.

[10.26] A number of statutory provisions give effect to international agreements concerning enforcement in this jurisdiction of the orders of foreign courts. For example, the Jurisdiction of Courts and Enforcement of Judgments Acts 1998 and 2012 give

---

23 Redmond and Nexus Research Co-operative, 'Imprisonment for Fine Default and Civil Debt: Report to the Department of Justice, Equality and Law Reform' (2002), available at www.justice.ie.

24 *McCann v Judge of Monaghan District Court and Ors* [2009] IEHC 276.

25 *Report on Personal Debt Management and Debt Enforcement* (LRC 100-2010).

effect to international Conventions on the Enforcement of Judgments in Civil and Commercial Matters, including in a number of non-EU states.[26] Such legislation is part of private international law, or the conflict of laws.[27]

[4] ENFORCEMENT IN CRIMINAL MATTERS

[10.27] Before the enforcement mechanisms referred to below arise for consideration, it must be established that a criminal offence has been committed. We do not consider here the necessary ingredients required by the law to establish that a criminal offence has been committed.[28]

Fines and imprisonment

[10.28] We have already considered the principal enforcement mechanisms in criminal matters, namely fines and imprisonment, which characterise the punitive nature of criminal law.[29] A financial penalty in criminal matters is generally associated with minor offences, such as the lesser road traffic offences (for example, speeding or parking in prohibited areas), and corporate offences (such as those under financial services legislation, competition legislation or safety and health legislation). Until 2010, a specific monetary fine would be laid down in legislation and might be revised from time to time. The Law Reform Commission recommended in 1991 that a more systematic approach involving indexing old fines to take account of inflation was required.[30] This was ultimately implemented in the Fines Act 2010, which provides for the indexing of all pre-2010 fines so that their monetary levels are brought up to date. It also provides that, for all post-2010 legislation the maximum fines that may be imposed in the District Court are placed in five classes based on the amount of the fine: class A a fine of up to €5,000; class B a fine of up to €4,000; class C a fine of up to €2,500; class D a fine of up to €1,000; and class E a fine of up to €500.

[10.29] The Fines Act 2010 had also contained provisions which were intended to ensure that fewer individuals would be committed to prison for default of payment of

---

[26] See Byrne and Binchy, *Annual Review of Irish Law 2012* (2013), pp 64–69 and pp 110–114. These Conventions are complemented, in connection with enforcement within and between EU member states, by the Brussels I Regulation (2000), which is concerned with the enforcement of civil and commercial judgments across borders and Brussels II Regulation (2003), which applies to the enforcement of cross-border family law proceedings. See Smith de Bruin, *Transnational Litigation: Jurisdiction and Procedure* (2008) and Broderick, 'Recognition and Enforcement of Foreign Judgments' (2008) 15(8) CLP 188.

[27] See generally, Binchy, *Irish Conflict of Laws* (1988); Smith De Bruin, *Transnational Litigation: Jurisdiction and Procedure* (2008); and para **17.82** below.

[28] See generally, McAuley and McCutcheon, *Criminal Liability* (2000), Charleton, Bolger and McDermott, *Criminal Law* (1999) and Hanly, *An Introduction to Irish Criminal Law* (2nd edn, 2006).

[29] See para **6.03**.

[30] Law Reform Commission, *Report on the Indexation of Fines* (LRC 37-1991).

fines imposed either summarily or on indictment. These provisions were not brought into force because they were regarded as not sufficiently comprehensive. They were replaced by the provisions in the Fines (Payment and Recovery) Act 2014. The 2014 Act provides that an individual who is unable to make payment of the fine imposed can apply to court for payment by way of instalment. At the time a court is imposing a fine, the 2014 Act also provides that it must take account, where practicable, of the financial circumstances of the person concerned, including their dependents. The 2014 Act also provides that the court may impose a community service order on an individual in lieu of a fine not paid by its due date of payment.[31] The 2014 Act also provides that non-payment of a fine can be enforced in a similar manner to that of a civil debt[32] and the court can appoint a receiver where a fine imposed on indictment has not been paid by its due date. The 2014 Act provides that, as a last resort, a defendant who has failed to make payment of the fine imposed on conviction on indictment can be imprisoned but it is envisaged that this will in the future be a highly unlikely occurrence.

[10.30] Another development is the increasing use of fixed penalties (or 'on-the-spot' fines as they are commonly called), a mechanism by which a penalty may be imposed without the need for a court hearing; if the fixed financial penalty is paid by the offender, no prosecution will ensue.[33]

[10.31] The deprivation of liberty through imprisonment is a long-established law enforcement mechanism. The philosophy behind imprisonment has changed over the years, and has included a number of aims: deterrence, punishment, reformation, rehabilitation and incapacitation.[34] The issue of sentencing practice and apparent inconsistency in the application of relevant legislation, particularly in rape and sexual assault cases, has been a cause of considerable public debate and academic argument.[35]

---

[31] This option was discussed in Redmond and Nexus Research Co-operative, 'Imprisonment for Fine Default and Civil Debt: Report to the Department of Justice, Equality and Law Reform' (2002), pp 52–53, available at www.justice.ie.

[32] On enforcement of civil debts see para **10.19**.

[33] See for example the Road Traffic Act 1961, s 103, as amended by Road Traffic Act 1994, s 43. See also Law Reform Commission, *Report on Consolidation and Reform of the Courts* (LRC 97-2010), paras 2.89–2.91 in which the Commission recommended that the criteria for putting in place fixed charge notice systems should be set out in criminal procedure legislation and that an appeal process also be provided in respect of offences that are punishable by a fixed penalty.

[34] See Law Reform Commission, *Report on Mandatory Sentences* (LRC 108-2013), paras 1.20– 1.31. See also Byrne, Hogan and McDermott, *Prisoners' Rights* (1981), Ch 1; McDermott, *Prison Law* (2000), Ch 1.

[35] For an overview, see O'Malley, *Sentencing: Law and Practice* (2nd edn, 2006) and Law Reform Commission, *Report on Mandatory Sentences* (LRC 108-2013), paras 1.102–1.133. On legislative changes aimed at improving consistency and providing for appeals against lenient sentences, see para **7.48**.

Assuming that a Judicial Council is established to monitor judicial conduct and ethics,[36] it is likely that part of its remit will be to ensure consistency in sentencing.

[10.32] The Irish Sentencing Information System (ISIS) was established in 2006 to provide information on a broad range of sentences handed down in respect of offences dealt with in the Circuit Criminal Court.[37] Prior to its introduction, there was a dearth of reliable information on sentencing practice for judges in Ireland.[38] ISIS is a steering committee whose purpose is to ensure that information on sentences handed down in indictable cases is added to a database which can then be searched by judges. Between 2010 and 2012, ISIS had not been updated but in 2013 it was reactivated and published three detailed reports that analysed sentencing in cases of rape, manslaughter and robbery.[39] This re-emergence of ISIS is an important indication that the development of sentencing guidance remains a live issue.

[10.33] The actual imposition of the sentence of imprisonment is a matter for the courts, but its execution is a matter for the executive branch, the government. In this respect, the executive determines in most instances the actual length of time served by a person in prison. Legislation authorises the Minister for Justice to remit sentences of imprisonment, that is, to reduce the sentence imposed in court.[40] In addition, the Minister is empowered to release prisoners from prison without affecting the sentence imposed by means of a form of parole known as temporary release.[41]

It remains to consider the other enforcement mechanisms deployed in criminal matters.

---

[36]   See para **4.155**.

[37]   See Conroy and Gunning, 'The Irish Sentencing Information System' [2009] 1 JSIS 37; and Law Reform Commission, *Report on Mandatory Sentences* (LRC 108-2013), paras 1.114–1.115. The ISIS website is www.irishsentencing.ie.

[38]   O'Malley, *Sentencing: Law and Practice* (2nd edn, 2006), p 65. O'Malley had recommended the creation of a sentencing information system (pp 65–66).

[39]   These are available at www.irishsentencing.ie.

[40]   Criminal Justice Act 1951. See *Brennan v Minister for Justice* [1995] 1 IR 612, noted at para **4.15**.

[41]   Criminal Justice Act 1960, s 2. Criminal Justice Act 2006, s 108 provides that prisoners who are on temporary release may be made subject to electronic tagging. The Parole Board was established on an administrative basis in 2001 and it reviews cases of prisoners with long sentences and advises on their release on temporary release, in effect parole. The Annual Reports of the Parole Board are available at the website of the Department for Justice and Equality, www.justice.ie. The government has indicated that it intends to place the Parole Board on a statutory basis, and this has been supported by the Law Reform Commission: see *Report on Mandatory Sentences* (LRC 108-2013), paras 3.85–3.86.

Community sanctions: probation, binding to the peace and community service

[10.34] The Probation of Offenders Act 1907 allows the court to impose a probation order on an offender in certain circumstances.[42] A probation order is a formal warning to a person that if he does not keep the peace and abide by the conditions imposed by the court for a specified period, he is liable to be brought before the court for punishment.[43] The Probation of Offenders Act 1907 allows for two orders: a conditional discharge and an absolute discharge. The 1907 Act applies to corporate bodies as well as individuals and absolute discharges of companies are applied in 'regulatory' offences in the District Court.[44]

[10.35] The conditional discharge applies in any court where a person has been convicted of the offence, but the court considers that it is 'inexpedient', having regard to all the circumstances, to inflict any punishment other than a nominal punishment. Section 1 of the 1907 Act provides that the court may order a conditional discharge of the defendant, by which the defendant is required to enter into a recognisance, that is a bond or agreement, to be of good behaviour during a period not exceeding three years and, if in breach of probation during that period, to appear in court to be sentenced. The conditional discharge involves the supervision of the person by a probation officer, who is a civil servant within the Probation and Welfare Service of the Department of Justice. This jurisdiction may be compared with the power of the District Court under s 54 of the Courts (Supplemental Provisions) Act 1961 to bind a person to keep the peace, in succession to the former justices of the peace.[45]

[10.36] The absolute discharge applies only in the District Court. While the judge of the District Court will have concluded that the offence has been proved, an absolute discharge has the advantage for the person charged that no conviction is recorded or entered. Because of this aspect to an absolute discharge, probation orders are more frequently associated with the District Court. The Criminal Justice Act 1993 permits the District Court to make a compensation order in favour of an injured party despite the absence of a formal conviction.

[10.37] In many instances an absolute discharge in the District Court is also accompanied by a Court Poor Box payment.[46] This requires the defendant in a criminal

---

42 On probation generally see Law Reform Commission, *The Court Poor Box: Probation of Offenders* (LRC 75-2005); O'Malley, *Sentencing: Law and Practice* (2nd edn, 2006), pp 470–477; and Walsh, *Criminal Procedure* (2002), pp 1046–1050.

43 Walsh, *Criminal Procedure* (2002), p 1046.

44 For example, in a number of cases in 2007, health and safety offences involving corporate bodies were dealt with under the Probation of Offenders Act 1907. See *The Annual Report of the Health and Safety Authority* (2007) available at www.hsa.ie.

45 See para **2.52**. In *Gregory v Windle* [1994] 3 IR 613, it was held that the power was not in conflict with the Constitution of 1937.

46 Law Reform Commission, *Report on the Court Poor Box: Probation of Offenders* (LRC 75-2005).

case to make a payment to a charity generally on the basis that no conviction will be recorded. The Law Reform Commission recommended, in its 2005 *Report on the Court Poor Box: Probation of Offenders*, that the essential elements of the Court Poor Box should be placed on a statutory basis in the context of a modern replacement of the Probation of Offenders Act 1907.[47]

[10.38] In addition, the Commission examined the types of discharges available under the Probation of Offenders Act 1907 with a view to their reform. It recommended that a new system be established with two orders: a full dismissal with no conviction and no conditions attached, and a conditional dismissal where no conviction is recorded when the conditions attached to it are complied with. The Commission recommended that the types of conditions which could be attached include a financial reparation order (a statutory form of the Court Poor Box), a recognisance to keep the peace and be of good behaviour for up to three years. The Commission recommended that, if the conditions attached to a conditional discharge were not met, the person could be prosecuted for the original offence.

[10.39] The Criminal Justice (Community Service) Act 1983 introduced a regime common in many other states. The 1983 Act empowers any court, other than a special criminal court, to make a community service order in respect of any person over 16 years of age convicted of an offence for which a sentence of imprisonment might otherwise be imposed. The 1983 Act, as amended by the Criminal Justice (Community Service) (Amendment) Act 2011, now provides that a judge 'shall' (the 1983 Act had originally provided 'may') consider community service in place of a sentence of imprisonment. A community service order obliges the convicted person to complete between 40 and 240 hours' unpaid work under the supervision of a probation officer. The 1983 Act requires that such an order shall not be made unless the convicted person consents and the court is satisfied, having considered the convicted person's circumstances, that he or she is suitable to perform the work indicated in the community service order. The court must also explain to the convicted person that failure to perform the community service is itself an offence under the Act.[48]

[10.40] In 2014, the Department of Justice published the Scheme of a Criminal Justice (Community Sanctions) Bill.[49] This proposes the first comprehensive reform of this area of criminal procedure since the foundation of the state and would provide for the repeal and replacement of the Probation of Offenders Act 1907. It would also implement the 1999 *Final Report of the Expert Group on the Probation and Welfare Service* and of the Law Reform Commission's 2005 *Report on the Court Poor Box: Probation of Offenders*.

---

[47] Law Reform Commission, *Report on the Court Poor Box: Probation of Offenders* (LRC 75-2005), p 4.

[48] For an appraisal of the operation of the system see Walsh and Sexton, *An Empirical Study of Community Service Orders in Ireland* (1999).

[49] Available at www.justice.ie.

The effect would be to increase greatly the range of community alternatives to imprisonment in the District Court in particular.

Compensation orders

[10.41] We have referred elsewhere to the jurisdiction to make compensation orders in criminal matters.[50]

Restorative justice principles

[10.42] The concept of restorative justice has become an increasing part of the criminal justice landscape in this state. Restorative justice projects involve a wide variety of programmes and initiatives which involve the participation of victims, offenders and the wider community with a view to repairing the harm caused as a result of criminal wrongdoing.[51] Restorative justice recognises that the adversarial nature of the traditional criminal justice system excludes the victim and the offender from any meaningful participation in the process. In order to rectify this imbalance, restorative justice allows for the victim, offender and those affected to participate in a process aimed at providing the most suitable solution.[52] One of the most accepted definitions of restorative justice is '... a process whereby parties with a stake in a specific offence collectively resolve how to deal with the aftermath of the offence and its implications for the future.'[53] Internationally, restorative justice initiatives have been used in a wide variety of offences, from minor offences such as criminal damage to more serious offences such as theft and assault.

[10.43] In Ireland, restorative justice has been used in the juvenile diversion project which was placed on a statutory footing by the Children Act 2001. For example, a juvenile offender can be cautioned for an offence if he or she admits responsibility for their actions; he or she may be required to offer an apology directly to the victim and perhaps perform some form of reparation. A number of projects for adult offenders currently operate on a non-statutory pilot basis in the District Court. For example, the Nenagh Community Reparation Project offers adult offenders the opportunity to make reparation to the victim of the offence and to the community. The process involves the offender, victim and panel members, who all meet to attempt to draw up a reparation contract. This process runs alongside the traditional criminal justice system and, if the reparation contract is implemented, it is presented to the judge of the District Court who adjourns the matter pending successful completion of the contract. Should the contract be fulfilled on the terms agreed, the case is usually dismissed on the adjourned date.[54]

---

[50] See para **6.04**.

[51] See generally *Report of the National Committee on Restorative Justice* (2009).

[52] Joint Committee on Justice, Equality, Defence and Women's Rights, *Report on Restorative Justice* (2007), p 1.

[53] Marshall, *Restorative Justice* (1999), p 5.

[54] Law Reform Commission, *The Court Poor Box: Probation of Offenders* (LRC 75-2005), p 64.

[10.44] The benefit of a restorative justice system is to allow the offender to take responsibility for his or her actions, having commonly heard the views of the victim, and should he or she do so, it is unlikely that he or she will re-offend. The victim and the community are permitted to participate in the process and this assists with achieving an appropriate solution to the offence outside of the traditional criminal justice system. Head 9 of the Scheme of the Criminal Justice (Community Sanctions) Bill,[55] which as noted above was published in 2014 by the Department of Justice, proposes to provide for a limited and specific restorative justice approach in relation to District Court criminal proceedings for minor offences committed by adults (in addition to the existing provisions on restorative justice for those under 18 in the Children Act 2001). If enacted it would deal with cases such as minor assaults or minor criminal damage where the offender accepts responsibility for the wrongdoing, offers to make reparation, for example, by paying for medical expenses or repairs to a vehicle, and is subject to the important requirement that the victim is willing to accept the reparation.

[10.45] It is important to note that the increasing emphasis on community sanctions, such as probation and community service orders, and the limited incorporation of restorative justice principles in the Scheme of the Criminal Justice (Community Sanctions) Bill, indicates a significant, if tentative, movement towards viewing imprisonment as a sanction of last resort. It is notable that this tendency has appeared at a time when, in the wake of the global and national financial crisis that emerged in 2008, the state has sought various ways to reduce costs. It is clear that by contrast with the high cost of imprisonment the cost to the state of imposing community-based sanctions is significantly lower. The evidence from the international literature that such sanctions may also be more beneficial to the minor offender and to society may have been less influential.

Enforcement for corporate offences and by regulators

[10.46] We referred earlier to legislation directed primarily at corporate entities, such as financial services legislation, environmental protection legislation and occupational safety legislation.[56] While such legislation creates offences and accompanying penalties, including fines and imprisonment, it also typically involves other enforcement mechanisms which do not fall neatly into the civil–criminal categorisation.

[10.47] The regulatory bodies with responsibility in these areas are given wide-ranging powers to ensure compliance with the relevant legislative requirements. These can include setting standards through statutory codes of practice that can be taken into account in any regulatory enforcement action.[57] Many regulators are also empowered to issue enforcement notices where the regulator is of the view that a corporate entity is contravening or has contravened any relevant statutory provisions. The notice may include directions as to how the entity can comply with the relevant statutory duties and may specify a completion date. The relevant legislation usually provides that failure to

---

[55]   Available at www.justice.ie.
[56]   See para **8.37**.

457

comply with such an order is an offence, and a defaulter may also be in contempt of court. In some instances, such as in the case of the Revenue Commissioners and the Central Bank of Ireland, the regulator may be empowered to impose financial sanctions directly on a regulated corporate entity.

Transnational enforcement

[10.48] As with enforcement of civil law on a transnational basis, recent statutory provisions give effect to international agreements concerning enforcement of crimes committed on an international basis. These include the Criminal Justice Act 1994 (dealing with the 'money laundering' elements of international drug trafficking),[58] the International War Crimes Tribunal Act 1998,[59] the Criminal Justice (United Nations Convention Against Torture) Act 2000 and the International Criminal Court Act 2006 (dealing with the crime of genocide, replacing the Genocide Act 1973).[60]

[5] CONTEMPT OF COURT

[10.49] Contempt of court concerns the manner in which the courts punish a person for any action that involves an interference with the administration of justice. In this jurisdiction, contempt of court remains regulated by common law principles developed by the courts. In *Irish Bank Resolution Corp Ltd v Quinn Investments Sweden AB*[61] the Supreme Court acknowledged that the current law is in need of reform, and Hardiman J referred to the 'amorphous' nature of the current law on contempt. Indeed, because contempt of court law is based almost exclusively on case law it may be difficult to argue that it is fully compatible with the European Convention on Human Rights.[62] 62

---

57 See generally Connery and Hodnett, *Regulatory Law in Ireland* (2009), which discusses in detail the regulatory powers available to many of the sectoral economic regulators, such as the Commission for Communications Regulation (ComReg), the Commission for Energy Regulation (CER) and the Irish Aviation Authority (IAA). On the powers of the Health and Safety Authority under the Safety, Health and Welfare at Work Act 2005 see Byrne, *Safety, Health and Welfare at Work Law in Ireland* (2nd edn, 2008).

58 See also para **5.25**.

59 This deals with the tribunals established to deal with the war crimes committed in the former Yugoslavia and Rwanda in the 1990s. The jurisdiction of the International Criminal Court has been accepted into Irish law by the Twenty-Fourth Amendment to the Constitution, passed by referendum in 2001, and the International Criminal Court Act 2006 deals with its jurisdiction in detail, as well as setting out in Irish law the relevant domestic offences, such as genocide: see para **17.49**.

60 See para **5.107**.

61 *Irish Bank Resolution Corp Ltd v Quinn Investments Sweden AB* [2012] IESC 51.

62 In *Sunday Times Ltd v United Kingdom* (1979) 2 EHRR 245 the European Court of Human Rights held that aspects of the UK law on contempt of court which, like Irish law, was based on case law, were in breach of the European Convention on Human Rights because they lacked clarity in their application. (contd.../)

Civil contempt and criminal contempt

[10.50] Two forms of contempt have developed: civil contempt and criminal contempt. Civil contempt consists of the defiance of a court order, such as refusal to obey an injunction. Criminal contempt consists of any action intended to prejudice the due course of justice or which brings the administration of justice into disrepute. This includes contempt *in facie curiae*, that is in the face of the court, such as disrupting court proceedings; scandalising the courts, which includes the making of totally unfounded criticisms of the courts; breaching the *sub judice* rule, that is prejudicing pending court proceedings; subjecting a party to court proceedings to comment which ridicules that party, such as publishing scandalous material while their case is in progress; and other interferences with the administration of justice, such as threatening a witness.

Procedure in civil contempt

[10.51] Where a civil contempt is alleged to have occurred it is a matter for the person who obtained the court order that has been disobeyed to bring this to the attention of the court in question. The court may then order that the contemner, the person in contempt, be attached for contempt, that is, brought before the court. When the person comes before the court he or she may inform the court that he or she is prepared to obey the court order, and that is generally the end of the matter. Otherwise, the judge will order that the person be lodged in prison 'until he doth purge his contempt'. The effect of this is that the person must remain in prison until he or she is prepared to come before the court to apologise and to undertake to obey the court order in the future. Until that is done the person may not be released under any circumstances, except by order of the court. It is a term of imprisonment unlike any other, therefore, with no time limit. It has been described as coercive, rather than having the punitive element of a sentence of imprisonment on foot of a conviction in criminal matters.[63] Sequestration of assets may also accompany the civil contempt procedure.[64]

Procedure in criminal contempt

[10.52] A prosecution for criminal contempt may be initiated by the Director of Public Prosecutions in the manner we described elsewhere.[65] However, reflecting its medieval

---

[62] (\...contd) As a result, the UK Contempt of Court Act 1981 was enacted to regulate aspects of the law on contempt of court; see Miller, *Contempt of Court* (3rd edn, 2000). The Law Reform Commission, in its *Report on Contempt of Court* (LRC 47-1994) made proposals for legislation in this area, in order to ensure that the law in Ireland meets constitutional requirements as well as obligations arising from the European Convention on Human Rights (see para **17.21**). See generally, McGonagle, *A Textbook on Media Law* (2nd edn, 2003), pp 184–227. At the time of writing (September 2014), the Commission's 1994 Report has not been implemented and the law on contempt of court is again under consideration in the Commission's 4th Programme of Law Reform: see para **11.17**.

[63] See *Keegan v de Burca* [1973] IR 223.

[64] See para **10.20**.

[65] See para **6.94**.

origins, a prosecution may also be initiated by a judge, including the judge before whom an *in facie* contempt has occurred. Indeed, a judge may order a disruptive person to be arrested, initiate the prosecution, try the case without a jury and impose sentence. However, in light of the requirements of the Constitution, the Supreme Court has suggested that, in the absence of exceptional circumstances requiring the immediate protection of the administration of justice, the courts should be reluctant to initiate a prosecution without the intervention of the Director of Public Prosecutions and the procedural protections associated with a trial in due course of law pursuant to Article 38.1.[66]

[6] JUDICIAL REVIEW

[10.53] We have noted elsewhere that the medieval Anglo–Norman court of the King's Bench developed the prerogative writs as a means of ensuring that inferior courts and other adjudicative bodies complied with certain basic requirements of the common law.[67] In the aftermath of the foundation of the Irish Free State in 1922, these were transformed into the state side orders and, in 1986, became orders for judicial review.[68] In keeping with their pre-1922 origins, the jurisdiction in judicial review is vested in the High Court. While substantial procedural changes were effected in 1986, the original titles of the former prerogative and state side orders remain in place.

[10.54] The Anglo–Norman courts had developed a number of prerogative writs. *Certiorari* is used to quash the decision of a lower court or tribunal which has been found to have acted outside its powers. *Mandamus* is directed to a court or tribunal ordering it to fulfil a lawful obligation which it is not carrying out. An order of prohibition is directed at a court or tribunal, preventing it from exercising its powers, either completely or until certain conditions have been met. *Habeas corpus* is the remedy which requires production of a person in court in order to determine whether the person is validly detained, for example in police custody or in prison. Of the four prerogative writs developed by the common law, only the *habeas corpus* remedy has been overtaken by the Constitution. Article 40.4.2° provides for a procedure for inquiring into the legality of a person's detention. For this reason, it is felt that the old writ of *habeas corpus* may be obsolete, though many judges continue to use the Latin phrase when referring to an application under Article 40.4.2°.[69]

---

[66] See *The State (DPP) v Walsh* [1981] IR 412.

[67] See para **2.37**.

[68] See generally Delany, *Judicial Review of Administrative Action* (2nd edn, 2008) and de Blacam, *Judicial Review* (2nd edn, 2009). The detailed procedure for judicial review is set out in the Rules of the Superior Courts 1986, Ord 84 (SI 15/1986), as amended. The changes made by the 1986 Rules were based largely on the Working Paper of the Law Reform Commission *Judicial Review of Administrative Action: The Problem of Remedies* (1979), available at www.lawreform.ie.

[69] See generally Hogan and Whyte, *JM Kelly: The Irish Constitution* (4th edn, 2003), p 1684.

[10.55] Judicial review should be distinguished from an appeal on a point of law from a lower court or tribunal. An appeal on a point of law concerns the issue involved in the lower court's decision, while judicial review is concerned with the authority of the lower court or tribunal to enter into an adjudication in the first place (its jurisdiction) or the procedures followed by it in the course of the adjudication. We consider constitutional judicial review elsewhere.[70]

[10.56] We have noted elsewhere that judicial review thus involves determining whether the court or tribunal acted *intra vires* (that is, within its powers) or *ultra vires* (that is, outside its powers) and whether it complied with the basic rules of natural justice or fair procedures, in particular that it be unbiased (*nemo judex in causa sua*) and give all sides involved an opportunity to prepare their case and be afforded an even-handed hearing, whether an oral hearing or by correspondence (*audi alteram partem*).[71] An unusual example of *ultra vires* action quashed on judicial review was *The State (Walshe) v Murphy*,[72] in which the High Court held that the respondent, who had all the appearances of being a judge of the District Court, had not met the formal qualification requirements to be appointed to that position in the first place and was thus not empowered to convict the prosecutor on a charge under the Road Traffic Acts.

Procedure in judicial review[73]

[10.57] The application for judicial review is in two stages. The first stage involves an *ex parte* application to a High Court judge for leave to proceed, where the applicant sets out the grounds on which relief is being sought. This application is granted if the judge considers that the case discloses some ground for claiming relief, though no decision is made at this stage as to whether the applicant is likely to be ultimately successful. The applicant must then serve notice on the other party, called the 'respondent'. The second stage is the application for judicial review itself, where the court determines whether the order sought by the applicant should issue. One of the major changes introduced in 1986 was that the court may grant other remedies, such as an award of damages or a declaration on judicial review.[74]

---

[70] See para **15.47**.

[71] See para **8.29**.

[72] *State (Walshe) v Murphy* [1981] IR 275: see paras **4.82–4.85**.

[73] In its *Report on Judicial Review Procedure* (LRC 71-2004) the Law Reform Commission made recommendations for changes to procedure in judicial review. A number of these were implemented in the Planning and Development (Amendment) Act 2010, s 32; and in the Rules of the Superior Courts (Judicial Review) 2011 (SI 691/2011) (which made relevant amendments to Ord 84 of the Rules of the Superior Courts 1986).

[74] See further Delany, *Judicial Review of Administrative Action* (2nd edn, 2008); de Blacam, *Judicial Review* (2nd edn, 2009); and Hogan and Morgan, *Administrative Law in Ireland* (4th edn, 2010).

Chapter 11

Law Reform

[1]   Introduction 463
[2]   Law Reform and A Legislative Code 463
[3]   Law Reform Commission 466
[4]   Other Law Reform Bodies 472
[5]   Judicial Decisions 474

[1]   INTRODUCTION

[11.01] It is clear from earlier chapters that substantial and ongoing reform of Irish law by the Oireachtas has become much more prevalent since the 1960s than was the case in the early years of the state's existence. This book has focused on the reforms that directly concern the legal system. These include reform within both branches of the legal profession,[1] in the management of the court service,[2] increases in the number of judges appointed to the courts,[3] changes in the jurisdiction of the different courts,[4] changes in court procedure,[5] reform of the appeals system[6] and significant changes to the state-assisted civil legal aid system.[7] These changes have reflected reform within state institutions generally.[8] We have also noted that these reforms have been accompanied by changes in substantive law, including criminal law and the law of civil liability.[9] In this chapter, we examine the issue of law reform in its wider sense, including the statutory codification of Irish law. We also discuss the bodies with a specific remit to review the law with a view to its reform.

[2]   LAW REFORM AND A LEGISLATIVE CODE

[11.02] Law reform, in its widest sense, includes the changes in Irish law made by every Act of the Oireachtas. We discuss elsewhere the procedures followed in the Oireachtas

---

1   See Ch 3.
2   See Ch 4.
3   See Ch 4.
4   See Ch 5.
5   See para **6.127**.
6   See Ch 7.
7   See para **9.45**.
8   See para **8.40**.
9   See paras **5.13–5.30**.

for the enactment of primary legislation (Acts of the Oireachtas), including the use of *ad hoc* committees of inquiry and the publication of Green Papers and White Papers prior to presentation of a Bill. We also note that most Acts derive from proposals initiated by government departments. In that respect, law reform is, as the Constitution provides, exclusively a matter for the Oireachtas (subject to those areas where the European Union has competence to legislate).[10]

[11.03] We also note elsewhere the role of the Parliamentary Counsel to the government (in the Attorney General's office) in proposing consolidation legislation.[11] A Consolidation Act, such as the Taxes Consolidation Act 1997, can be enacted in a relatively speedy manner through the Oireachtas because it has been certified by the Attorney General as involving no actual change in the existing law. A Consolidation Act also involves one version of codification of the relevant law, that is, bringing the relevant text together, which facilitates accessibility of the law.

[11.04] Many common law states have moved a significant step beyond the statutory consolidation of individual areas of law, and have moved towards another type of statutory codification, that is, putting into statutory form virtually all their law, including those areas originally developed by the courts through case law, such as contract law, commercial law, criminal law, the law of evidence and land law. In the United States of America, this form of statutory codification has been in train since the late 19th century, both at federal level and individual state level. In the digital era, it is possible to access the full text of the federal United States Code (USC)[12] and the legislative codes of the individual states.[13] These legislative codes in common law states indicate that a code-based approach to the law is not the exclusive preserve of the civil law family of legal systems, such as France and Germany, although the civil law states are often cited as the originators in the (relatively) modern era of such codes from the early 19th century onwards. It may be that, historically, there has been some antipathy in the United Kingdom towards a code-based approach to law because of the association of codes with the French Revolution and their championing by Napoleon.[14] In any event, in the early 21st century, it is clear that common law states have moved in the direction of legislative codes in one form or another.

[11.05] In Ireland, the influence of almost 40 years' membership of the European Union, in which legislative codes are the norm, may further influence the movement towards the eventual development of a legislative code. This has been greatly facilitated by the

---

10   See paras **13.53–13.57**.
11   See para **13.39**.
12   See www.gpoaccess.gov/uscode/index.html.
13   See, for example, www.michie.com/.
14   See the discussion in Keane, 'Law Reform in Ireland—the European Experience' (1987) 22 Irish Jurist (ns) 1 and Keane, 'Thirty Years of Law Reform 1975–2005' (Dublin, 23 June 2005), a lecture to mark the 30th anniversary of the Law Reform Commission, available at www.lawreform.ie.

enactment of the Statute Law Revision Act 2007. As we note elsewhere,[15] the 2007 Act contains a definitive list of 1,364 pre-1922 Acts that remained on the Irish statute book as of 2007; and since 2007 about 200 of these pre-1922 Acts have, in turn, been repealed and replaced.[16] Prior to the enactment of the 2007 Act, the precise number of pre-1922 Acts that remained in force was somewhat unclear. It is now possible to track the in-force state of all Acts, whether those pre-1922 Acts retained by the 2007 Act or the post-1922 Acts enacted since the foundation of the state. This is because all of these are documented in the Legislation Directory (formerly the Chronological Tables of the Statutes), which tracks the amendments made to all Acts.[17] Of the Acts passed between 1922 and 2014, less than 2,000 remain in force. Combined with the list of pre-1922 Acts, this provides a total of about 3,200 Acts that constitute the Irish statute book. This makes more manageable the preparation of a legislative code, arranged on the lines of the major subject-matter headings used, for example, at both federal and state level in the United States.

[11.06] The Law Reform Commission has, since 2010, published and updated on a regular basis a Classified List of In-Force Legislation.[18] The Classified List comprises a list of all post-1922 Acts that remain in force (and over 100 pre-1922 Acts), organised under 36 general subject-matter headings. These 36 headings derive from: (a) some near-universal and conventional headings, such as civil liability, commercial law, criminal law and taxation; (b) some of the Titles in US federal and state legislative codes; (c) the legislative codes developed in European civil law jurisdictions; and (d) headings unique to Ireland, such as the Heading 'Irish Language and Gaeltacht'.

[11.07] In addition to the process of consolidation of legislation, such as in the taxation context already referred to, it is notable that the government has published policy documents on 'better regulation',[19] which include commitments to ongoing statute law

---

15   See para **13.100**.
16   More than 150 pre-1922 Acts listed in the 2007 Act were repealed when the Land and Conveyancing Law Reform Act 2009 came into force in 2009. A number of other Acts enacted since 2007, have also repealed pre-1922 Acts listed in the Statute Law Revision Act 2007 so that the number of pre-1922 Acts remaining in force is, at the time of writing (September 2014), closer to 1,100.
17   The Legislation Directory is available on the electronic Irish Statute Book (eISB), at irishstatututebook.ie. In 2007, the ongoing compilation of the Legislation Directory was transferred to the Law Reform Commission by the Office of the Attorney General. Since 2011, the Legislation Directory has tracked all amendments made to pre-1922 Acts that were retained by the Statute Law Revision Act 2007. Prior to 2011, the Legislation Directory had tracked all changes made to pre-1922 Act by post-1922 Acts, but had not tracked changes made prior to 1922 to pre-1922 Acts.
18   Available at www.lawreform.ie/classification-list-of-legislation-in-ireland.361.html. See generally Law Reform Commission, *Consultation Paper on a Classified List of Legislation in Ireland* (LRC 62-2010).
19   See the government's 2013 Policy Statement *Regulating for a Better Future*, available at www.taoiseach.ie.

revision and consolidation. This involves a general commitment to streamlining the statute book. In specific settings, 'mini-codes' have already been enacted or are proposed.[20]

[11.08] In the remainder of this chapter, we outline some of the specific mechanisms used to assist in this wider purpose of law reform.

[3] LAW REFORM COMMISSION

1962 Programme of Law Reform

[11.09] In the early years after the state's establishment in 1922, law reform could be described as involving a number of elements. First, a series of legislative changes to adapt to the post-independence era much of the pre-1922 legislation carried over from the United Kingdom. This was followed by legislative changes which had a distinctive Irish aspect, some reflecting particular Irish mores of the 1920s and 1930s. The 1940s and 1950s saw some increase in legislation with a distinct reforming element, but it was not until the late 1950s and early 1960s that some real momentum built up behind the concept of a planned and consistent approach to law reform which led to the enactment of important reforming legislation such as the Civil Liability Act 1961. The most significant development at that time was the publication in 1962 by the Department of Justice of a government White Paper entitled *Programme of Law Reform*.[21] The 1962 Programme set out a detailed list of over 20 specific topics on which the Department stated it intended to bring forward law reform Bills. During the 1960s, this resulted in the enactment of important reforming legislation such as the Guardianship of Infants Act 1964, the Extradition Act 1965 and the Succession Act 1965.

[11.10] The impetus for implementing the reform proposals set out in the 1962 Programme waned towards the end of the 1960s, although some of the topic areas referred to in it were, ultimately, implemented many years later, notably the reform to the insanity defence which was enacted as the Criminal Law (Insanity) Act 2006. Some of the law reform proposals in the 1962 Programme remain unimplemented at the time of writing (September 2014), such as the suggestion that the common law rules of contract law be codified in statutory form, while others have been taken up by other law reform bodies established since then. In any event, it would appear that the exigencies of more immediate legislative priorities within the Department of Justice meant that some proposals in the 1962 Programme simply remained at the end of a long waiting list.

---

[20] For example, the Land and Conveyancing Law Reform Act 2009. 'Mini-codes' is also the phrase used in the 2004 *Report of the Expert Group on Codifying the Criminal Law* to describe those Acts dealing with elements of the 'Special Part' of the criminal law, such as the Criminal Damage Act 1991, the Non-Fatal Offences against the Person Act 1997 and the Criminal Law (Theft and Fraud Offences) Act 2001. These formed the basis for the inaugural Criminal Code Bill published in 2011 by the Criminal Law Codification Advisory Committee: see www.criminalcode.ie.

[21] *Programme of Law Reform* (Pr 6379, 1962).

The establishment of the Law Reform Commission

[11.11] By the early 1970s the government had decided that, in order to bring fresh momentum to law reform, in particular those areas of the law that might otherwise not receive political priority within a busy government department, it was necessary to have in place a permanent body whose only focus was law reform. This led to the establishment of the Law Reform Commission[22] under the Law Reform Commission Act 1975.[23] This may also have been influenced by the establishment in 1967 of two law commissions in the United Kingdom, the Law Commission for England and Wales[24] and the Scottish Law Commission,[25] under the [UK] Law Commissions Act 1965. In the wake of devolution in Northern Ireland, the Northern Ireland Law Commission was established in 2007 under the [UK] Justice (Northern Ireland) Act 2002.[26] Many other common law states have also adopted the model of establishing a Law Commission.[27]

[11.12] The Irish Commission, like its counterparts in other states, has an extremely wide-ranging law reform mandate under the Law Reform Commission Act 1975.

The Commission

[11.13] The Commission comprises five persons, the President of the Law Reform Commission and four Commissioners. In effect, these five persons comprise the policy-making board of the Commission. They are appointed by the government for up to a five-year term, which may be renewed. The 1975 Act provides that the Commissioners must be suitably qualified by the holding of judicial office (defined as a judge of the High Court or Supreme Court, serving or retired), by experience as a barrister or solicitor or as a teacher of law or by reason of such other special experience, qualification or training as, in the opinion of the government, is appropriate having regard to the functions of the Commission. Since the establishment of the Commission, the President has always been a High Court or Supreme Court judge.[28] The other four Commissioners typically include leading public sector or practising lawyers, members of the law schools and other professionals.

Functions of Commission

[11.14] The 1975 Act requires the Commission to keep the law generally under review and to undertake examinations and conduct research with a view to making proposals

---

22   The Commission's website is www.lawreform.ie.
23   For a detailed discussion of the background to the Commission, see O'Connor, 'The Law Reform Commission and the Codification of Irish Law' (1974) 9 Ir Jur (ns) 14.
24   See www.lawcom.gov.uk.
25   See www.scotlawcom.gov.uk.
26   See www.nilawcommission.gov.uk.
27   The websites of the Commissions in the UK and Ireland contain links to these other Commissions in the common law world. In many civil law states, the comparable functions are performed in Ministries of Justice and Legislative Councils attached to their parliaments.

for law reform, the development of law, its codification (including in particular its simplification and modernisation) and the revision and consolidation of statute law. The 1975 Act requires the Commission to prepare, in consultation with the Attorney General, specific programmes for the examination of different branches of the law with a view to their reform. As we will see, four such programmes have been prepared since the Commission's establishment. The Attorney General may also, under the 1975 Act, request the Commission to examine specific areas of law.

Consultative documents and Reports

[11.15] The Commission may, under the 1975 Act, employ researchers (either on a full-time salaried basis or part-time contract basis). The researchers usually have legal qualifications and a proven record in legal research. The Commission publishes consultative documents (variously described since the Commission was established as working papers, consultation papers and issues papers) on specific areas of law. A consultative document such as an issues paper is published on the Commission's website. It typically contains a relatively brief analysis of a specific area of law or areas of law, including a summary of Irish law and reference to relevant law in other jurisdictions, followed by a series of questions on which consultees are asked for their views and submissions. Having considered these, the Commission publishes a report which sets out its final recommendations on the topic. This usually contains: a more detailed account of Irish law on the topic; comparative analysis by reference to other jurisdictions (generally, but not confined to, other common law jurisdictions); and final proposals by the Commission for reform of the law (or in some instances that reform is not required). Since 2000, the Commission invariably publishes a draft Bill with a report, containing the relevant recommendations in legislative form.[29]

Commission recommendations and implementation

[11.16] Since the establishment of the Commission, its consultative documents and reports have dealt with a wide range of legal issues, both procedural and substantive. Of course, the ultimate responsibility for implementing any recommendations for law

---

28   Walsh J, the first President, was then senior ordinary judge of the Supreme Court. Keane J, the second President, was then a High Court judge (afterwards appointed to the Supreme Court and, who was, between 2000 and 2004, Chief Justice). O'Hanlon J was a senior judge of the High Court when appointed, though he withdrew as President a short time after his appointment: see para **4.164,** fn 351. Hederman J was the then senior ordinary judge of the Supreme Court on his appointment. The next two Presidents, Lavan and Budd JJ, were both High Court judges on their appointment. The next President, McGuinness J, was a Supreme Court judge on her appointment as President of the Commission. The current (July 2014) President, Quirke J, was a recently retired senior High Court judge on his appointment in 2012.

29   Some comparable Commissions in other common law states have, in recent years, moved away from publishing draft Bills with their reports.

reform rests with the government and the Oireachtas.[30] At the same time, failure to take account of the Commission's work would negate its purpose. In the early years of its existence, there had been some criticism of the failure by the government to bring legislation to the Oireachtas to implement proposals for reform made by the Commission.[31] By the late 1980s, there had been a significant change in general terms[32] and, in line with more active law reform generally, the work of the Commission has resulted in the enactment of a considerable body of reforming legislation.[33]

[11.17] In general, about 70 per cent of the Commission's recommendations for reform have been implemented in the sense that about 70 per cent have influenced the content of later legislation, which is similar to the rate of implementation for comparable law reform bodies.[34] Inevitably, there are delays of varying duration between the making of proposals and their implementation. In addition, proposals for reform may be overtaken by intervening events or political considerations, and the legislation ultimately enacted may differ from the Commission's proposals. Like proposals for reform from other bodies, some Commission reports seem unlikely to receive legislative time, even in the overall context of an active record of implementation. Thus the 1994 *Report on Contempt of Court* (LRC 47-1994) has not yet been implemented at the time of writing (September 2014).[35]

[11.18] Between 1977 and 1999, the Commission worked on its *First Programme of Law Reform* as well as on specific requests from the Attorney General in that period. This resulted in the publication of over 60 documents, across a wide range of topics. The following is a selection of the areas reviewed and the implementing legislation:[36]

---

30 See para **13.47**. Between 1992 and 1997, a Minister for Equality and Law Reform held a cabinet position. The Ministry and Department were subsumed within the Department of Justice and Equality in 1997. This department now has the principal role in implementing proposals from the Commission.

31 See Kerr, 'Is there Anybody Out There Listening?' (1983) 1 ILT 100.

32 See, eg, the statement by the then President of the Commission, Keane J, in (1987) 5 ILT 123.

33 *An Expenditure Review of the Law Reform Commission (a Value for Money Review)* was completed by the Office of the Attorney General in 2007 and published on its website: www.attorneygeneral.ie/pub/other_publications.html. The review contains the results of a questionnaire completed by a number of government and non-governmental stakeholders. It also noted the internal changes which the Commission had put in place to monitor the effectiveness of its research work. The review also contains a comparative analysis of the effectiveness and efficiency of the Commission, and concluded that the Commission remained an effective means of achieving the overall objectives of law reform.

34 See Law Reform Commission, *Third Programme of Law Reform 2008–2014* (LRC 86-2007), p 21, available at www.lawreform.ie. The Commission's website also contains a regularly updated Table of Implementation of its recommendations.

35 The Commission is again examining contempt of court as part of its current Fourth Programme of Law Reform. On contempt of court generally see also para **10.49**.

36 A fuller listing is available on the Commission's website, www.lawreform.ie.

- Administrative law: *Judicial Review of Administrative Action* (Working Paper 8-1979), which resulted in changes to the judicial review procedure in Ord 84 of the Rules of the Superior Courts 1986;

- Criminal law: *Report on Vagrancy and Related Offences* (LRC 11-1985), which resulted in the enactment of the Criminal Justice (Public Order) Act 1994;

- Criminal procedure: *Report on an Examination of the Law of Bail* (LRC 50-1995), which, after a constitutional referendum, influenced the Bail Act 1997;[37]

- Family law: *Report on Divorce a Mensa Et Thoro and Related Matters* (LRC 8-1983), which influenced the Judicial Separation and Family Law Reform Act 1989;

- Tort law (occupiers' liability): *Report on Occupiers' Liability* (LRC 46-1994), which resulted in the enactment of the Occupiers' Liability Act 1995.

[11.19] The Commission's *Second Programme of Law Reform 2000–2007*, as its title indicates, differed from the *First Programme* in a significant respect, a specific time period within which the topics in the programme were to be completed. By the end of 2007, the Commission had completed work (by publishing consultation papers and reports) on almost all the 30 projects in the *Second Programme*.[38] As in the longer period 1977 to 1999, this also resulted in the publication of over 60 documents across a wide range of topics. The following is a selection of the areas reviewed and the implementing legislation.[39]

- Criminal procedure: *Report on the Establishment of a DNA Database* (LRC 78-2005), implemented in the Criminal Justice (Forensic Evidence and DNA Database System) Act 2014;

- Family law: *Report on the Rights and Duties of Cohabitants* (LRC 82-2006), implemented in Pt 15 of the Civil Partnership and Certain Rights and Obligations of Cohabitants Act 2010;

- Land law: *Report on Reform and Modernisation of Land Law and Conveyancing Law* (LRC 74-2005), implemented by the Land and Conveyancing Law Reform Act 2009;

- Legislation in general: *Report on Statutory Drafting and Interpretation: Plain Language and the Law* (LRC 61-2000), which greatly influenced the Interpretation Act 2005 and the increased use of some plain language principles in legislation.[40]

---

[37] See para **6.107**.
[38] See Ch 5 of the Commission's *Annual Report 2007*, available at www.lawreform.ie, which comprises an audit of completion of the *Second Programme*. Some projects were carried over for completion under the Commission's *Third Programme of Law Reform 2008–2014*.
[39] A fuller listing is available on the Commission's website, www.lawreform.ie.
[40] See para **13.104**.

[11.20] The Commission's *Third Programme of Law Reform 2008–2014*,[41] like the *Second Programme*, was completed over a definite time period.[42] It contained 37 topics and by 2014 the Commission had completed work on 23 of the projects, many of the remaining projects having been overtaken by developments since 2008 (including planned or enacted legislation in those areas).[43] The following is a selection of the areas reviewed and the current (July 2014) position on their implementation:

- Alternative dispute resolution: *Report on Alternative Dispute Resolution: Mediation and Conciliation* (LRC 98-2010), due to be implemented in a Mediation Bill (expected to be published by end 2014);

- Bioethics: *Report on Bioethics: Advance Care Directives* (LRC 94-2009), to be implemented in the Assisted Decision-Making (Capacity) Bill 2013;

- Commercial law (personal debt): *Report on Personal Debt Management and Debt Enforcement* (LRC 100-2010), implemented in the Personal Insolvency Act 2012;

- Family law: *Report on Legal Aspects of Family Relationships* (LRC 101-2010), due to be implemented in a Children and Family Relationships Bill (expected to be published by end 2014).

[11.21] The Commission's current *Fourth Programme of Law Reform*[44] was agreed with government in 2013 and contains 11 projects because the Commission intended that these would, if possible, be completed in a short timeframe of two to three years (by comparison with the length projected for its two previous programmes).[45] The 11 projects include the following:

- corporate offences and regulatory enforcement;
- cybercrime affecting personal safety, privacy and reputation, including cyber-bullying;
- aspects of succession law;
- domestic implementation of international obligations;
- codification, consolidation and simplification of legislation.

---

[41] Law Reform Commission, *Third Programme of Law Reform 2008–2014* (LRC 86-2007), available at www.lawreform.ie.

[42] On the different timeframes used by law reform bodies for programmes of law reform, see Law Reform Commission, *Seminar Paper on Third Programme of Law Reform* (SP3-2007), available at www.lawreform.ie.

[43] Law Reform Commission, *Annual Report 2011*, ch 6, which contains a mid-term review of the Third Programme and which led the Commission to begin preparatory work in 2012 on the Fourth Programme of Law Reform.

[44] Law Reform Commission, *Fourth Programme of Law Reform* (LRC 110-2013), available at www.lawreform.ie.

[45] The two-year timeframe was chosen to coincide with 'the remainder of the term of the current Commission': see Law Reform Commission, *Fourth Programme of Law Reform* (LRC 110-2013), para 2.10.

The topics in the *Fourth Programme*, like their predecessors, involve the Commission examining some areas of law long in need of reform and others which reflect the need to respond to new challenges in the context of a rapidly changing society. It is notable in this respect that the *Fourth Programme* contains a project that reflects the general remit of the Commission as set out in the 1975 Act, the need to address the codification of legislation. When combined with the previous work of the Commission, the picture presented by Irish law on completion of the *Fourth Programme* might bring closer the kind of codified systems in place in other common law states, discussed above.[46]

[4] OTHER LAW REFORM BODIES

[11.22] In addition to the Law Reform Commission, we outline here other institutions that have contributed to law reform generally.

Committee on Court Practice and Procedure

[11.23] In 1962, as proposed in the 1962 *Programme of Law Reform*, the Minister for Justice established a Committee on Court Practice and Procedure with a view to making recommendations concerning reform in the administration of the courts. Up to 2004, the Committee had published 29 reports concerning a wide range of topics.[47] Many of these

---

46 The 2009 (McCarthy) *Report of the Special Group on Public Service Numbers and Expenditure Programmes*, available at www.finance.gov.ie (which contained wide-ranging proposals to reduce public sector expenditure by over €4 billion in order to return the state to sustainable borrowing levels) recommended that a number of state agencies should be abolished, amalgamated or their functions absorbed by a government department. In this context it recommended that the Law Reform Commission should no longer be convened on a permanent basis (vol 1 of the Report, p 71) but should be 're-convened as required to address government mandated reform agendas' (vol 2, p 207). The proposal to discontinue the Commission as a permanent body was described by the then Director of Public Prosecutions, James Hamilton, as 'a highly retrograde step': see (2009) *The Irish Times*, 22 July. Many of the recommendations in the McCarthy Report have been implemented, notably through the abolition and amalgamation of a number of states agencies (see para **8.40**): this has sometimes been referred to as 'the bonfire of the quangos' (a phrase developed in the context of comparable reforms that occurred at the same time in the United Kingdom). A number of the McCarthy Report's recommendations have not been implemented and it appears at the time of writing (September 2014) that the government has decided not to implement the recommendation to discontinue the Law Reform Commission. This is evident from the government's appointment of a new President and Commissioners in 2012 and its decision in 2013 to approve the Commission's Fourth Programme of Law Reform.

47 See O'Malley, *Sources of Law: An Introduction to Legal Research and Writing* (2nd edn, 2001) for a list of the Committee's reports to 2001. The *27th Report* (Commercial Court: 2002), *28th Report* (Rules of Court Committees: 2003) and *29th Report* (Personal Injuries Litigation: 2004) of the Committee are available on the website of the Courts Service, www.courts.ie. The Committee has not published any reports between 2004 and the time of writing (September 2014).

reports have been implemented, both by legislation[48] and by non-legislative changes in the administration of the courts.[49] Of course, as with the work of the Law Reform Commission, not all recommendations of the Committee have been accepted.[50]

Working Group on a Courts Commission

[11.24] We discuss elsewhere the role of the Working Group on a Courts Commission, which led to the establishment of the Courts Service under the Courts Service Act 1998.[51]

Working Group on the Jurisdiction of the Courts

[11.25] We discuss elsewhere the role of the Working Group on the Jurisdiction of the Courts.[52]

Competition Authority

[11.26] We describe elsewhere the important reforms arising from the Competition Authority's 2006 *Report on the Legal Profession*, and from its predecessor, the Fair Trade Commission, in its 1990 *Report into Restrictive Practices in the Legal Profession*.[53]

The Constitution Review Group and Oireachtas Committee on the Constitution

[11.27] We refer elsewhere to the 1996 *Report of the Constitution Review Group* and the later *Reports of the Oireachtas Committee on the Constitution*.[54]

---

48   The Courts Act 1971, which conferred rights of audience on solicitors, implemented the recommendations in the *Thirteenth Interim Report of the Committee on Court Practice and Procedure* (1971): see para **3.71**. Section 24 of the Courts and Court Officers Act 1995, which increased the powers of the Master of the High Court, implemented the principal recommendations in the *Sixteenth Interim Report of the Committee on Court Practice and Procedure* (1972): see para **4.197**.

49   The appointment of research assistants to the judges, begun in 1993, had been recommended in the *Eleventh Interim Report of the Committee on Court Practice and Procedure* (1970): see para **4.64**.

50   In the *Twenty-Fourth Report of the Committee on Court Practice and Procedure: Preliminary Examination of Indictable Offences* (1997), the Committee recommended the retention of the preliminary examination procedure. This view was rejected, and the preliminary examination procedure was abolished in 2001, when Pt III of the Criminal Justice Act 1999 came into force: see para **6.106**.

51   See para **4.217**.

52   See para **5.134**.

53   See paras **3.05–3.16**.

54   See para **15.196**.

[5] JUDICIAL DECISIONS

[11.28] The process of judicial decision-making in this jurisdiction involves the application of existing legal principles, whether common law or statutory, to particular factual situations.[55] While this process does not constitute a formal element of law reform, its effect is similar. Thus, a decision of the High Court applying established common law principles of negligence in a new setting, such as the question of the liability of a solicitor to persons other than his client, establishes a precedent for subsequent similar cases.[56] The application in a new setting is equivalent to law reform. Similarly, a judicial interpretation of a statutory provision may lead to a clearer understanding of what until then was unclear.[57] In some instances, the judicial clarification may require amending legislation to remedy a defect in the existing statutory provisions[58] or to remove an unwanted interpretation.[59] A decision of the courts that certain statutory provisions are in conflict with a provision of the Constitution may be followed by legislation to remedy the difficulty,[60] or it may require an amendment to the Constitution.[61] Such law reform, while significant, is limited by the fact that it is largely reactive and *ad hoc*.[62] The more significant reforms effected in recent years, outlined earlier in this chapter, have been preceded by considered debate and discussion of the areas of law being reformed.

---

[55] See generally, Ch 12.

[56] See *Wall v Hegarty* [1980] ILRM 124; *Doran v Delaney* [1998] 2 IR 61: paras **12.158–12.166**.

[57] See, eg *Nestor v Murphy* [1979] IR 326, para **14.46**.

[58] For example, the decision in *Rafferty v Crowley* [1984] ILRM 350 (para **14.54**), which the judge in the case accepted was an unsatisfactory result, led to the enactment of the Building Societies (Amendment) Act 1983 to remedy the problem highlighted by the decision. Similarly, *The State (Clarke) v Roche* [1986] IR 619 (para **4.17**) resulted in the passing within a matter of weeks of the Courts (No 3) Act 1986.

[59] Many decisions of the courts on taxation legislation are followed by amending legislation to 'close tax loopholes', eg the decision in *C McCann Ltd v Ó Cúlacháin* [1986] IR 196 (para **14.68**), the 'banana ripening' case, and other similar cases resulted in amendment to the statutory provisions concerning tax allowances for manufacturing.

[60] For example, the decision in *de Búrca v Attorney General* [1976] IR 38 hastened the enactment of the Juries Act 1976: see para **6.143**. Similarly, the decision in *McCann v Judge of Monaghan District Court* [2009] IEHC 276 (see para **10.23**) led to the speedy enactment of the Enforcement of Court Orders (Amendment) Act 2009.

[61] For example, comments in *M v An Bord Uchtála* [1977] IR 287 resulted in a referendum which approved an amendment to Article 37 of the Constitution: see para **4.19**.

[62] For an analysis of judicial decision-making as law-making, see, for example, Posner, *How Judges Think* (2008), written by the highly-influential US Court of Appeals judge Richard A Posner, who is also author of over 40 texts, including *Economic Analysis of Law* (7th edn, 2007).

Chapter 12

Precedent

[1]   Introduction 475
[2]   *Stare Decisis* in the Irish Courts 485
[3]   The *Ratio Decidendi* and *Obiter Dictum* 519
[4]   Precedent in Action: an Example 542

[1] INTRODUCTION

[12.01] Appeals to precedent, that is, the seeking of guidance for current practice from past events, are common in many walks of life. Children pleading with their parents frequently claim parity with their perceived equals ('every other boy in my class was allowed stay up to watch the football match'); in the world of business the case-study method provides exemplars to be imitated in decision-making and planning; and within bureaucracies the repetition of practices eventually establishes models of expected conduct. In this regard legal systems are similar, with precedent being invoked to ensure the consistent application of the law.[1]

[12.02] In seeking consistency, two objectives of justice are pursued. The first is that the law is applied equally, as similar cases are treated similarly. The second is that the law becomes predictable and one can determine in advance the legal quality of a proposed course of action. Those who are subjected to regulation are entitled to fair notice of that which is required of them – a feature of authoritarianism is that one is uncertain of the laws that govern one's conduct. In this respect, if courts were afforded discretion as to whether to follow an earlier case the perceived danger is that different courts would identify and apply different rules. That is not to say that judges would exhibit favouritism or bias, but the risk is that through the application of different judicial

---

1   See generally, Goldstein (ed), *Precedent in Law* (1987); Cross and Harris, *Precedent in English Law* (4th edn, 1991); Stone, *Precedent and Law* (1985); Duxbury, *The Nature and Authority of Precedent* (2008); Harris, *Legal Philosophies* (2nd edn, 1997), Ch 13; Harris, *An Introduction to Law* (5th edn, 1997), pp 188–199; Wijffels (ed), *Case Law in the Making* (1997); Perry, 'Judicial Obligation, Precedent and the Common Law' (1987) 7 OJLS 217; Levenbook, 'The Meaning of a Precedent' (2000) 6 *Legal Theory* 185; Lamond, 'Do Precedents Create Rules?' (2005) 11 *Legal Theory* 1; Marmor, 'Should Like Cases be Treated Alike?' (2005) 11 *Legal Theory* 27; Emmert, '*Stare Decisis*: a Universally Misunderstood Idea" (2012) 6 *Legisprudence* 207; Carnwath, 'Judicial Precedent – Taming the Common Law' (2012) 12 OUCLJ 261.

standards conflicting and contradictory rules might emerge. Thus, to ensure consistency the practice developed whereby courts followed earlier relevant decisions.

[12.03] This feature is shared by civil law and common law systems alike but in the case of common law systems precedent, encapsulated in the principle of *stare decisis* ('let the decision stand'), has a greater significance.[2] Since common law systems, unlike their civilian equivalents, by and large lack authoritative codes, their rules are to be found in the decisions of courts which are assigned the task of applying them. As a result judicial decisions are a source of law, loosely called 'case law', to which lawyers have recourse – they enjoy the force of law and are not simply examples to be imitated. The practice of following earlier cases has become so prevalent that its correctness is now beyond dispute and can be considered to be the principal rule of judicial decision-making in common law systems.[3]

[12.04] The operation of a system of precedent depends on a number of implicit conditions.[4] The first is that a hierarchy of courts exists which readily facilitates the evaluation of the force of any particular precedent.[5] The second is that prior decisions are recorded in a reasonably accurate and accessible manner, thus providing the material which will govern future cases. A third condition is that the legal community acknowledges the binding force of precedent and is prepared to accept that propositions of law are validated by decided cases. Moreover, a system of precedent functions on the basis of a general acceptance that consistency, certainty and predictability are values worth pursuing and are to be preferred to competing values such as flexibility and the search for individual justice.

[12.05] The nature of a system of precedent is such that it restricts an adjudicator and denies him or her discretion which other decision-makers, such as government officials and legislators, might enjoy. The judge must decide a case on the basis of prior decisions even though he or she believes that a better solution might be reached, or justice better

---

2   See Cross and Harris, *Precedent in English Law* (4th edn, 1991), pp 10–15, comparing precedent in England and France.

3   However, it must be noted that the application of precedent varies in different common law jurisdictions; see Tunc, 'The not so Common Law of England and the United States, or, Precedent in England and in the United States, a field study by an outsider' (1984) 47 MLR 150.

4   See Miers, 'Review of Stone, *Precedent and Law* (1985)' (1986) 6 LS 331.

5   Murray CJ delivering the judgment of the Court of Criminal Appeal in *The People (DPP) v Keane* [2007] 12 JIC 1901, explained the constitutional context:

'As in virtually every country, the Courts established by and in accordance with the Constitution have a hierarchal structure. This permits, *inter alia*, access to the Courts at first instance and on appeal to a higher Court whose decision is then final and binding. Exceptionally there may be a further appeal to a higher Court again, usually in limited circumstances, in one form or another, such as an appeal from this Court to the Supreme Court pursuant to s 29 of the Courts of Justice Act 1924 ... That is the structure which we are constitutionally bound to respect.'

done, by ignoring those decisions. While a system of precedent might constrain a judge, it also operates to legitimise his or her decisions and, it is expected, preserve confidence in the judiciary. Decisions reached are not attributable to the preferences or whims of judges but to the preceding body of law which moulded them.

[12.06] When we speak of following cases it should be realised that the process is neither simple nor mechanical. On the contrary, it is complicated and involves the use of skills and techniques which are acquired through exposure to, and experience of, the methods and devices employed by courts. In one sense no two cases are similar, in that each case presents a unique set of circumstances which differentiates it from any other. The task of the courts is to identify cases which can be considered to be similar and to reach similar conclusions in those cases. To this extent the system is flexible in that courts are in essence required to place cases in conceptual categories from which the legal issues involved are analysed. But once two cases are placed in the same category, and thus considered to be similar, the expectation that earlier cases be followed strives to ensure consistency in the application of the law. In this respect the system of precedent establishes a methodology within which relevant legal principles are extracted from earlier decisions and are developed and expanded through their being applied in later cases.

[12.07] Although we have spoken so far of courts being expected to follow earlier decisions, it should not be assumed that a court is required to follow every relevant decision which preceded it. A distinction is drawn between *binding authority* and *persuasive authority*. A court is required to follow the former, but in respect of the latter it enjoys discretion as to whether or not it should adopt the decision. The principal rule which has emerged is that a court must follow the prior decisions of courts superior to it in the judicial hierarchy. This rule is so well established that it has rarely been questioned, in this jurisdiction at least. In addition, a court is generally expected to follow the earlier decisions of courts of coordinate, or equal, jurisdiction. The latter is not an inflexible rule and courts, from time to time, have declared a freedom to depart from their own earlier decisions.

[12.08] On the other hand, a court is not bound by the decisions of an inferior court. Likewise, Irish courts are not bound by the decisions of foreign courts, as that would amount to a derogation from Irish sovereignty. However, the decisions of both inferior and foreign courts are of persuasive authority and as such may be followed at the option of the court. The decisions of foreign courts are regularly cited in and adopted by Irish courts, especially where there is an absence of relevant Irish authority.

[12.09] When a court is said to be bound by an earlier decision it does not follow that everything which the earlier court said is binding. Judges do not adopt a uniform format when writing their judgments, but a number of elements may be identified in each judgment. It will contain a recitation of the material facts of the case coupled, if necessary, with comments on and an evaluation of the evidence which was adduced by the parties. A discussion and analysis of the relevant law will follow, and finally the law will be applied to the facts of the case. The part of the judgment which is binding is called the *ratio decidendi*. For present purposes it can be defined as being the reason for the decision; it consists of the principle of law applied to the facts of the case.[6] Other statements of law which are contained in the case are called *obiter dicta*. They are not of direct relevance to the decision and, consequently, are not binding. They are, however, of persuasive authority and may be adopted at the option of the later court.

[12.10] Several terms ought to be explained at this stage. When an appeal is successful the appellate court is said to have *reversed* the inferior court. The effect is that the decision of the lower court is replaced by that of the higher court and the party who initially lost the case now finds that he or she has won. However, once a decision becomes final and is no longer subject to the possibility of being appealed, the principle of *res judicata* applies and the parties to the case are bound by the decision and may not, in general, seek to have it re-opened. When an appellate court in a later case considers the earlier decision of a lower court to be erroneous, it may *overrule* that decision. Its effect, however, is prospective only in that it does not affect the position of the parties to the earlier case. In other words, by overruling a case a court states that it is not to be followed in the future.

[12.11] Courts do not often overrule decisions of courts of coordinate jurisdiction, preferring instead to *distinguish* them. A decision is said to be distinguished when a later court decides that, for one reason or another, it is not relevant to the case before it. A case might be distinguished because the later court discovers a material factual difference between the two cases or because different legal issues are involved. In essence, the subject matter of the two cases is perceived to differ and they are placed in separate conceptual categories. However, in practice, the effect of distinguishing a case can be equivalent to overruling it. By distinguishing it, a court can confine an earlier case to a very precise situation such that it becomes marginal and of limited importance. It will state that the decision was confined to its particular facts and is of no assistance in other cases. Moreover, if one court distinguishes a particular decision other courts might be more prepared to follow suit.

[12.12] In some cases a court might have reached a decision in ignorance of a relevant statutory provision or binding authority. In that event the decision is said to have been reached *per incuriam*.[7] The consequence is that no valid proposition of law is established by the decision and a later court is not bound to follow it. Where it appears that a court decided a point without its being specifically argued or mentioned in the judgment, it is said to have been decided *sub silentio* and, once again, a later court is not required to follow it.

---

[6]   See further, paras **12.88–12.120**.

[7]   See *DPP v Freeman* [2009] IEHC 179 *per* MacMenamim J: 'Clearly the concept of a decision which is reached *per incuriam* is an essential part of the doctrine of *stare decisis*. A court may conclude that a previous court of the same jurisdiction reached a decision without taking into account a relevant argument, an important judicial precedent, or a relevant statutory provision. In such circumstance the decision of such a court may be disapproved in a later case by a court of concurrent or superior jurisdiction.'

[12.13] A difference of judicial opinion is evident on the question of a judge considering a point which was not specifically addressed in counsel's argument. In *G v An Bord Uchtála*[8] Walsh J spoke both of the right to life of the unborn and the constitutionality of certain decisions which were made by the Adoption Board. His brethren expressly reserved their opinions on those points as they had not been the subject of argument. In like fashion, O'Higgins CJ and Griffin J did not join McCarthy J in commenting on the appropriate judicial evaluation of foreign cases in *Irish Shell Ltd v Elm Motors Ltd*.[9]

Law reporting[10]

[12.14] Access to reliable documents that accurately report judicial decisions is essential to the effective operation of a system of precedent.[11] The earliest records of legal proceedings are the *plea rolls* that were compiled on a systematic basis by court officials in the Royal Courts at Westminster from the late 12th century until the reign of Queen Victoria. The plea rolls were highly formal documents that recorded the various stages of the proceedings, and they were maintained for reasons of internal court administration rather than as a public record. Indeed, the final verdict of a case was often not recorded because either the litigation was abandoned or the successful party did not bother to have it enrolled. The purpose of recording the outcome seems principally to have been to support a plea of *res judicata* if the losing party sought to re-open an issue that had already been legally resolved. The plea rolls did not include details of the arguments advanced by the parties or of the reasoning of the judges. As far as providing knowledge of the substantive law they proved to be a meagre resource: as one commentator aptly observed, 'many miles of parchment may yield only a few inches of law'.[12]

[12.15] The first documents to record the arguments and reasoning employed in the courts were the *year books*. Anonymously authored, these works purported to reproduce verbatim accounts of what transpired in court. The year books were written in Law French, which at the time was the language of the common law. It is unlikely that the year books were contemporaneous accounts and it is probable that they contained truncated versions of what the writer remembered. Nevertheless, their value lay in the fact that they recorded vital legal information that was missing from the plea rolls and in this respect they can be seen as early predecessors to modern law reports. The year

---

8   *G v An Bord Uchtála* [1980] IR 32.

9   *Irish Shell Ltd v Elm Motors Ltd* [1984] IR 511.

10   See generally, O'Malley, *Sources of Law: An Introduction to Legal Research and Writing* (2nd edn, 2001); Grossman, *Legal Research: Historical Foundations of the Electronic Era* (1994); Dane and Thomas, *How to Use a Law Library* (4th edn, 2001); Holborn, *Butterworths Legal Research Guide* (2nd edn, 2001); Hall, *The Superior Courts of Law: 'Official' Law Reporting in Ireland 1866-2006* (2007)

11   Neuberger, 'Law Reporting and the Doctrine of Precedent: the Past, the Present and the Future' in *Halsbury's Laws of England Centenary Essays* (2007), p 69.

12   Baker, 'The Common Law Courts of Medieval England: Year Books and Plea Rolls' in Wijffels (ed), *Case Law in the Making* (1997), p 42.

books date from the middle of the 13th century and their original purpose appears to have been pedagogic. However, while they might have been originally produced to facilitate legal education, they came to be compiled on a regular basis and were relied on by practitioners and judges as a valuable resource containing the common law. The term 'year book' reflects the practice that had developed by which these reports were compiled in annual volumes. They were initially drafted in manuscript form but were later to be published retrospectively in printed form in the 15th and 16th centuries. The last year book to be published in this manner covers the years 1535–1536. In more recent times the year books have been reproduced, primarily for reasons of scholarly interest, in the *Rolls Series* and in various volumes published by the Selden Society.

[12.16] The striking innovation of the year books was that they recorded what transpired in court, but their major disadvantage lay in the manner in which they were organised. In the main, cases were recorded chronologically without being indexed and as the volume of recorded material grew, the usefulness of the year books diminished. A mechanism of recording that was devised in the early days of the common law had become cumbersome two centuries later when the number of cases to be recorded had grown exponentially. This left a gap that was filled by the publication of *abridgments*.[13] The latter consisted of consolidated case notes which were arranged by topic rather than chronologically. By their nature abridgements were likely to be bulkier than individual year books and with the passage of time they tended to increase in size. In the era of the manuscript this inhibited their production but, with the advent of printing, abridgments eventually surpassed the year books as a legal resource. The early classic is *La Grande Abridgment* by Anthony Fitzherbert, which was published in 1516. Fitzherbert's *Abridgment* arranged material by topic, but its real value lay in two novel features: the first was the inclusion of catchwords in the margins to aid browsing; and the second was a 'tabula' that listed all the topics, along with subtopics, with a numbering scheme to individual notes. The advantage of an accurate and detailed indexing system is obvious and although it was eventually superseded by later, more detailed works, Fitzherbert's *Abridgment* is still considered a masterpiece.

[12.17] The era of the year book was succeeded in the middle of the 16th century by that of the nominate report which lasted until the 19th century. *Nominate reports* were privately compiled series of law reports that were published under the name or names of the reporter. They varied greatly in quality and accuracy but at their best they were considered to be highly authoritative and on occasion are still cited. Early English series were published by prominent lawyers and judges: Plowden (still considered to be an exemplar of the genre); Dyer (Chief Justice of the Court of Common Pleas 1559–1582); and Coke (Attorney General and later Chief Justice of the Court of Common Pleas 1606–1616). Most series of nominate reports have been republished in the *English Reports*, consisting of 176 volumes of reports and a two-volume index. The first Irish series of nominate reports was probably *Irish Equity Cases* (1604–1612), published in 1615 by Sir John Davies, the then Attorney General for Ireland. As was the case in

---

13   Winfield, 'Abridgements of the Year Books' (1923) 37 Harv L Rev 214.

England, more series of nominate reports were published subsequently but many covered only short periods of time.

[12.18] From 1827 to 1866 the commercial publication of Irish law reports was more organised and a number of series appeared in that time: *the Law Recorder*; *Law Recorder (new series)*; *Irish Law Reports*; *Irish Equity Reports*; *Irish Common Law Reports*; and *Irish Chancery Reports*.[14]

[12.19] The modern era of law reporting is marked by the establishment of the Incorporated Council of Law Reporting for Ireland in 1866 (its English equivalent was set up one year earlier). The Council is made up of representatives of the judiciary and both branches of the legal profession and is responsible for the publication of the *Irish Reports* (cited as IR), the principal series of law reports that is published in the jurisdiction. A report usually contains the judgment or judgments delivered, a synopsis of the arguments of counsel and a headnote, which is prepared by the reporter, who by convention is a practising barrister. For this reason newspaper reports which are written by journalists, though illustrative, are not considered to be authoritative. Before being reproduced in the law reports the judgments are corrected by the judges who delivered them and it is the corrected text which is authoritative. The headnote is not part of the case, but is prepared principally for the purposes of reference; it allows the reader to know the contents of the case at a glance. It is important to realise that the headnote is not law, nor is it an authoritative interpretation of the decision.[15]

[12.20] The other general series of law reports that is currently published is the *Irish Law Reports Monthly* (ILRM), published on a commercial basis by Thomson Round Hall Ltd. The *Irish Reports* enjoy a 'semi-official' status and are preferred to the *Irish Law Reports Monthly* where a conflict arises between the two. Since March 1989 these series have been supplemented by the *Irish Times Law Reports* which are published each Monday in *The Irish Times*. Whilst the latter merely contain synopses of the judgments delivered, they may be cited in court as they are reported by practising barristers. It should be noted that there are series of reports that are no longer published but are still referred to and cited on a regular basis, principal amongst them being the *Irish Law Times Reports* (ILTR) and the *Irish Jurist Reports* (Ir Jur Rep). Several series of specialist reports are currently published, most notably the *Irish Tax Reports*[16] and *Employment Law Reports*.[17] The judgments of the Court of Criminal Appeal have been collated and published commercially in three volumes which bear the title Frewen, the late registrar of that court who compiled the first two volumes.

---

14 Most of these series were republished in reprint form.
15 However, note the observations in *Copeland v Smith* [2000] 1 All ER 457 at 459, *per* Buxton LJ: 'The purpose of cases being reported is, amongst other things, to assist the court and advocates by means of listing the cases that have been referred to ... *and also by means of the very helpful headnotes that are provided*' (emphasis added).
16 Published by Bloomsbury Professional.
17 Published by Thomson Round Hall Ltd.

[12.21] As the number of reported cases in this country runs into thousands, if not tens of thousands, locating the appropriate case law can be a time-consuming and troublesome exercise. To this end recourse is had to digests of cases, which contain abstracts of cases, and enable the reader to locate the relevant cases on a particular topic and allow him or her to trace the subsequent history of any given case.[18] Due to lack of resources, amongst other things, it was not possible to report all cases in this country and, in consequence, the superior courts adopted the practice of circulating *unreported judgments*, which consist of the judicially corrected version of the judgment delivered in the case, to the principal law libraries in the country.[19] However, they do not contain the arguments of counsel, nor are they accompanied by a headnote. The advantage of the practice of circulating unreported judgments was that it provided lawyers with the complete jurisprudence of the Irish superior courts and it made decisions available before they were eventually, if ever, reported. It became accepted that unreported judgments could be cited in Irish courts provided that they had been judicially corrected and approved for circulation,[20] a position that contrasted with the more restrictive approach taken by English courts.[21] At the time this was necessary to supplement the tardy and incomplete reporting of Irish case law, but matters have improved in the last two decades with developments in both paper and electronic reporting. The *Irish Reports* currently run to four volumes annually and two annual volumes of the *Irish Law Reports Monthly* are published.[22]

[12.22] Since the 1980s the traditional paper-based sources have been supplemented by a variety of electronic sources.[23] In Ireland, the longest established is the LEXIS online legal database, a full text system which holds materials from a number of national

---

18   Murray and Dixon (eds) *The Irish Digest 1867–1893*; Maxwell (ed), *The Irish Digest 1894–1918*; Ryland (ed), *The Irish Digest 1919–1928*; Ryland (ed), *The Irish Digest 1929–1938*; Harrison (ed), *The Irish Digest 1939–1948*; Harrison (ed), *The Irish Digest 1949–1958*; Ryan (ed), *The Irish Digest 1959–1970*; de Blaghd (ed), *The Irish Digest 1971–1983*; Clancy and Ryan (eds), *The Irish Digest 1984–1988*; Clancy (ed), *The Irish Digest 1989–1993*; Clancy (ed), *The Irish Digest 1994–1999*; see also O'Malley, *Sources of Law: An Introduction to Legal Research and Writing* (2nd edn, 2001), pp 24–29.

19   Three indexes of unreported judgment have been compiled: Aston et al (eds), *Index to Unreported Judgments of the Irish Superior Courts 1966–1975* (1990); Aston and Doyle (eds), *Index to Irish Superior Court Written Judgments 1976–1982* (1984); Aston (ed), *Index to Irish Superior Court Written Judgments 1983–1989* (1991). The indexes are commonly known as the *Green Index*, the *Red Index* and the *Blue Index* respectively.

20   See *O'Brien v Mirror Group Newspapers Ltd* [2001] 1 IR 1 at 45, *per* Geoghegan J: 'It is unfortunate that the transcript of the *ex-tempore* ruling [in *Campbell-Sharpe v Independent Newspapers* (11 February 1998, unreported), SC] remains unapproved and it would therefore be inappropriate to cite passages from it …'.

21   See *Roberts Petroleum Ltd v Bernard Kenny Ltd* [1983] 2 AC 192; *Practice Note* [1996] 3 All ER 382; see also *Michaels v Taylor Woodrow* [2000] 4 All ER 645.

22   Since January 1995 the *Irish Current Law Monthly Digest* contains headnotes of all Superior Court decisions.

23   See Holmes and Venables, *Researching the Legal Web* (2nd edn, 1999).

jurisdictions together with European and international legal sources. At present, the Irish material on LEXIS consists of the *Irish Reports* since 1950 and unreported judgments of the superior courts since 1985. Although LEXIS holds an abundance of comparative material, with the commonwealth material being especially useful, there has been a noticeable deterioration in the quality of its Irish library. The *Irish Law Reports Monthly* were withdrawn from LEXIS in early 2001 and other recently decided cases are stored in unreported form without annotation, arguments of counsel and other information that is typically included in a law report. A more recent development is westlaw.ie, which is similar to the Westlaw database in the United States. Westlaw.ie can now claim to be the most comprehensive and authoritative Irish online subscription-based legal research service: it provides a search facility to extensive collections of reported and unreported case law, legislation, journals and legal news. With customised search engines it facilitates easy and reliable legal research. The content of westlaw.ie includes:

- *Irish Law Reports Monthly*, full archive dating back to 1976;
- *Irish Law Times Reports*, 1871–1980;
- *Tottel Irish Tax Reports*, 1923–date;
- unreported judgments – full transcripts of unreported judgments starting from October 2002;
- *Employment Law Reports*, full archive dating back to 1990;
- consolidated legislation;
- annotated legislation;
- complete archive of most Irish law journals (with the important exceptions of the *Irish Jurist* and the *Northern Irish Law Quarterly*);
- current awareness;
- case digests from the *Irish Law Times*, with full archive dating back to 1983;
- *Irish Current Law Monthly Digest* (ICLMD) – provides digests of all cases from the Superior Courts with full archive dating back to 1995;
- *Irish Current Law Statutes Annotated* (ICLSA), which provides a range of Irish statute law from 1984 with expert commentary and analysis;
- European Human Rights Reports, by volume dating back to 1979;
- Human Rights Law Reports, from 2000;
- Legislation Fastcheck, which provides an overview of legislation cross referenced with relevant case law.

FirstLaw[24] is a web-based subscription legal information service in Ireland for practitioners, academics and students. It provides subscribers access to case digest journals – Employment Law Review; Local Government Review; Appeal Commissioners Decisions; Arbitration & ADR Review; Irish Intellectual Property Law Quarterly; Road Traffic Review; and Civil Practice and Procedure.

---

[24] www.firstlaw.ie.

[12.23] The advantages associated with such electronic sources are several: material can be searched and retrieved at much greater speed electronically than manually; the full text of materials is available, a matter of considerable importance to lawyers; and in an under-resourced jurisdiction like Ireland they afford access to a wide range of comparative materials that might not otherwise be available but which is a necessary complement to the relatively small body of indigenous case law. On the other hand, these databases can prove expensive and in some cases a user is charged search costs each time the database is accessed.

[12.24] The superior courts in many jurisdictions have set up websites where their judgments appear, in some case within hours of having been delivered. Typically these sites contain the bare unannotated text of the judgment and indexing, such as it is, is elementary.[25] Nevertheless, a service of this type has the advantage of providing speedy (almost immediate) access to court judgments and is relatively cost-effective.[26] The Courts Service was established in November 1999 by the Courts Service Act 1998. It is an independent corporate organisation and its functions include: the management of the courts and the provision of support services for judges. The Courts Service website[27] provides free access to judgments of the superior courts.

[12.25] Justis Publishing Ltd publishes the Electronic Irish Reports and Digests on the internet.[28] This product, which is issued in association with the Incorporated Council of Law Reporting for Ireland, stores Irish and Northern Irish case law reports and digests since 1838. It is updated eight times per year. Justis also offers subscribers access to Irish case law emanating from the Supreme Court, the High Court, the Court of Criminal Appeal, the Employment Appeal Tribunals and other courts, such as the Central Criminal Court and Circuit Court. This is one of the most comprehensive collections of online case law in Ireland. Subscription to Irish Case Law also includes access to Justis Irish Legislation, a fully searchable database of over 18,000 Acts of the Oireachtas and 9,000 statutory instruments since 1998.

---

[25] The situation is rapidly improving. The website managed by the Australian Legal Information Institute (AustLII) at austlii.edu.au is considered a model in this regard: see Dayal, *LDL Online Laying Down the Law: Computer Assisted Legal Research* (1996). A further challenge presented by the proliferation is to develop a uniform citation system: see Leith, 'Legal Citations' 2000(3) The Journal of Information, Law and Technology (JILT) elj.warwick.ac.uk/jilt/00-3/leith.html; Foster, 'Obstacles to Citation Reform' 2000(3) The Journal of Information, Law and Technology (JILT) elj.warwick.ac.uk/jilt/00-3/foster.html; Rozenberg, 'Referencing and Citation of Internet Resources—"The Truth is out There"' 2000(1) *The Journal of Information, Law and Technology* (JILT) elj.warwick.ac.uk/jilt/00-1/rozenberg.html; Donnelly, 'Towards Uniformity in Legal Citation in Ireland' (2007) 25 ILT 256.

[26] Brooke, 'The Use of Technology in the Courts' (2004) 4 JSIJ 169.

[27] www.courts.ie.

[28] www.justis.com/data-coverage/irish-law-home.aspx. Justis also stores legal material from other jurisdictions, including EU and international law materials; see www.justis.com. Justis is a subscription service.

[12.26] Since the earliest days the accumulation of case law has been a recurring issue. Lawyers were, and continue to be, concerned that the reporting of ever-increasing amounts of case law is potentially overwhelming and the belief is that the system of precedent is compromised by this phenomenon. As more and more cases are reported it becomes increasingly difficult to locate the relevant materials and there is a correspondingly greater danger that important precedents will be overlooked. In short, the perennial complaint is that there is too much law. Indeed the major developments in law reporting can be seen as responses to these concerns. More comprehensive indexing and digesting has been devised to address the problem of access. This has been matched by the growth of a large secondary literature consisting of encyclopaedias, commentaries, treatises and, in the modern era, textbooks written by academic lawyers. Ironically the advent of computerisation, which, it might have been thought, would greatly enhance the management of common law materials, now poses the same challenge.

[12.27] Electronic recording systems overcome constraints of storage space and time and hence facilitate the speedier recording of even greater volumes of material. At the same time lawyers have more immediate access to a large range of sources from other common law jurisdictions. Legal scholars and academic commentators should welcome this development but its advantages are not as obvious to practising lawyers. It is perhaps such considerations that caused the English courts to impose the restrictions noted earlier on the citation of unreported judgments (most of which are now recorded electronically).[29] Different considerations arise in Ireland where the circulation and citation of unreported judgments is a well-established practice. To this end their availability via databases and, websites can be viewed as an improvement. However, Irish courts have yet to decide whether the unreported judgments of other jurisdictions, which are now readily available by various electronic means, can be cited. With regard to the latter, the caution shown by their foreign counterparts might find favour with Irish courts: the added expense in searching for such materials, coupled with difficulties in authentication, arguably outweigh any possible advantage.[30]

[2] *STARE DECISIS* IN THE IRISH COURTS[31]

[12.28] As stated earlier, the principle of *stare decisis* reflects the expectation that earlier cases be followed. Given the hierarchical structure of the court system there are two dimensions to the system of precedent. The first, which might be considered vertical, is that a lower court is bound by the decisions of higher courts. The second, which might be considered horizontal, concerns the extent to which a court is bound by

---

[29] See para **12.21**.

[30] See the extra-judicial remarks of Clarke J noted in para **12.86**.

[31] See Dowrick, 'Precedent in Modern Irish Law' (1953) 69 LQR 25; Henchy, 'Precedent in the Irish Supreme Court' (1962) 25 MLR 544; Gavan Duffy, 'A Note on the Limitation of the Doctrine *Per Quod Servitium Amisit* and *Stare Decisis* in the Republic of Ireland' (1965) 14 ICLQ 1382.

the decisions of courts of coordinate jurisdiction. A general issue is whether a strict or liberal approach should be adopted in relation to precedent. The strict approach, which was favoured during the 19th century and lasted well into the 20th century, was set out by the Lord Halsbury in *London Tramways Co v London County Council*:

> "Of course I do not deny that cases of individual hardship may arise, and there may be a current of opinion in the profession that such and such a judgment was erroneous; but what is that occasional interference with what is perhaps abstract justice, as compared with the inconvenience – the disastrous inconvenience – of having each question subject to being re-argued and the dealings of mankind rendered doubtful by reason of different decisions, so that in truth and in fact there would be no real final Court of Appeal."[32]

[12.29] The difficulties associated with that approach are that it leads to the fossilisation of the law; it inhibits legal development and frustrates the possibility of doing justice in individual cases. On the other hand the concerns with a flexible approach are that it unsettles the law, results in an unwarranted degree of uncertainty and upsets legitimate expectations which are based on the earlier law. The resulting tension between the demands of certainty and the desire for adaptability form a recurring theme in considerations of the system of precedent.

Lower courts should follow the decisions of higher courts

[12.30] The principal rule is that an inferior court must follow the earlier decisions of superior courts. Accordingly, the High Court must follow the Supreme Court and presumably the Court of Appeal when it is established, while the Circuit Court must follow the High Court, the Court of Appeal and the Supreme Court. This rule is so well settled that it has seldom been questioned by an Irish court. Thus, in *The State (Harkin) v O'Malley*[33] O'Higgins CJ observed that Gannon J, in the High Court, was bound to follow an earlier Supreme Court decision[34] which the Supreme Court then overruled on the grounds that it was erroneously decided and was a *per incuriam* decision. And in

---

[32]   *London Tramways Co v London County Council* [1898] AC 375 at 380. The law report incorrectly lists the appellant as 'London Street Tramways'; see Cross and Harris, *Precedent in English Law* (4th edn, 1991), p 102. See Pugsley, 'London Tramways (1898)' (1996) 17 J Leg Hist 172 on the background to *London Tramways* establishing that the House of Lords had articulated the inflexible rule for at least the previous 70 years.

[33]   *State (Harkin) v O'Malley* [1978] IR 269; see *Minister for Justice, Equality and Law Reform v Adams* [2011] IEHC 366 *per* Edwards J: '[w]hile the respondent has sought to argue that [*Minister for Justice, Equality and Law Reform v*] *Stapleton* [2006] 3 IR 26 was wrongly decided, this Court is obliged by the doctrine of *stare decisis* to follow *Stapleton* where the circumstances indicate that it is apposite to do so. *Stapleton* represents a binding precedent handed down by the highest court in the land and this Court must apply it unless and until the Supreme Court says otherwise in some future case. In any event, this Court does not agree with the suggestion that *Stapleton* was wrongly decided.' See also *Harlequin Property (SVG) Ltd v O'Halloran* [2013] 1 ILRM 124, *per* Clarke J: '[t]he High Court is bound by the jurisprudence of the Supreme Court.'

[34]   *The People (Attorney General) v Doyle* (1964) 101 ILTR 136.

Carron v McMahon[35] Finlay CJ noted that at the time of the decision under appeal the High Court was bound by *Russell v Fanning*,[36] a case which the Supreme Court itself then overruled in *Carron*. The strength of the rule is evident in *Director of Public Prosecutions (Walsh) v Cash*,[37] where the High Court noted that it was bound to follow the Supreme Court decision in *The People (DPP) v Kenny*[38] despite entertaining some reservations about the principle established by the latter case. In *Walsh*, Charleton J stated:

> "I have difficulty in accepting that the separation of powers doctrine allows the courts to invent rules whereby juries, or judges as triers of fact in criminal cases, are deprived, on a non-discretionary basis, of considering evidence which is inherently reliable. I am bound by the decision in *The People (DPP) v Kenny*. A rule which remorselessly excludes evidence obtained through an illegality occurring by a mistake does not commend itself to the proper ordering of society which is the purpose of the criminal law."

[12.31] In the rare event that the High Court departs from a Supreme Court decision, a differently constituted High Court is not bound to follow that approach. Thus, in *PC v Director of Public Prosecutions*[39] Geoghegan J stated:

> "In those circumstances I consider that I am bound by the decision of the Supreme Court in *De Róiste v The Minister for Defence and Ors*[40] and insofar as the approach of Gilligan J in *K(S) v Director of Public Prosecutions*[41] may differ from that in *De Róiste*, I should not follow same."

However, the High Court is not bound to adopt a statement of law by the Supreme Court where that statement is *obiter*. In *A O'Gorman & Co Ltd v JES Holdings Ltd*[42] Peart J declined to adopt the dictum of O'Flaherty J in *Metropolitan Properties Ltd v O'Brien*[43] to the effect that a 'flying freehold' could be the subject of a right to acquire the fee simple under the Landlord and Tenant (Ground Rents) (No 2) Act 1978. The other members of the Supreme Court preferred not to make any comment which they considered unnecessary for the purpose of their decision. Peart J stated:

> "For my own part, and since they are not binding comments upon me, I would take a different view with the greatest possible respect for the views of such a learned judge of the Supreme Court."

And in *Lopes v Minister for Justice, Equality and Law Reform* Clarke J drew a distinction between the decision of the higher court, which the lower court is bound to follow, and the views of individual judges in the higher court:

---

35   *Carron v McMahon* [1990] 1 IR 239, 267.
36   *Russell v Fanning* [1988] IR 505.
37   *Director of Public Prosecutions (Walsh) v Cash* [2007] IEHC 108.
38   *The People (DPP) v Kenny* [1990] 2 IR 110.
39   *PC v Director of Public Prosecutions* [2005] IEHC 103.
40   *De Róiste v The Minister for Defence* [2001] 1 IR 190.
41   *K(S) v Director of Public Prosecutions* (26 February 2004, unreported), HC, Gilligan J.
42   *A O'Gorman & Co Ltd v JES Holdings Ltd* [2005] IEHC 168.
43   *Metropolitan Properties Ltd v O'Brien* [1995] 1 IR 467 at 482.

"It is true that lower courts, in our system and in many others, are bound by the decisions of higher courts. It is, however, the actual decision of the higher court itself (rather than the views of individual judges of those higher courts – where the court concerned consists of more than one member) to which that principle applies. A judge of a lower court is not, in any way, bound by the views of a judge of a higher court which does not represent the majority view of that court (and thus form part of the decision of that court)."[44]

[12.32] Unlike the position in which the House of Lords has found itself in the past – see, for instance, *Cassell & Co Ltd v Broome*[45] – the Supreme Court has rarely had to admonish the High Court for failure to follow one of its decisions. This problem occurred in a 1978 case, *McDonnell v Byrne Engineering Co Ltd*, of which only a newspaper report is available:

"The Chief Justice said that under the Constitution, the Supreme Court was the final court of appeal. As such, it had the duty, when necessary, to declare what legal principles should apply to cases that were reviewed by the Court. Where necessary it had the duty to lay down guidelines for all courts and all judges as to the manner in which such cases were to be tried. It was equally the duty of all other courts and judges to follow directions as to law and procedures as given by the Supreme Court ...

The Chief Justice said that following this clear and concise statement it became the duty of all judges trying such cases to follow this directive. 'It is with real concern that this Court notes that despite being asked by counsel to leave the question ... in accordance with the directions of this court, the trial judge, Mr Justice Murnaghan, expressly refused to do so. Not only did he refuse to do so, but he has indicated it is his intention to disregard this in other cases.' The Chief Justice continued: 'This Court will not permit this situation to continue and will insist that its directions be respected and obeyed.'"[46]

[12.33] The situation might arise where a lower court is required to follow a decision of a higher court even though it is firmly believed to be erroneous and it is correctly anticipated that the decision will subsequently be overruled by the Supreme Court. For instance, the High Court and courts of trial are bound by decisions of the Court of Criminal Appeal. In *O'B v Patwell*[47] the Supreme Court noted that the High Court was bound to follow two decisions of the Court of Criminal Appeal,[48] which it then proceeded to overrule as having been incorrectly decided. In *The People (DPP) v Rock*[49] a Circuit Court judge followed a decision of the Court of Criminal Appeal[50] in

---

44   *Lopes v Minister for Justice, Equality and Law Reform* [2014] IESC 21 at 6.11.
45   *Cassell & Co Ltd v Broome* [1972] AC 1027.
46   *The Irish Times*, 4 October 1978.
47   *O'B v Patwell* [1994] 2 ILRM 465.
48   *The People (Attorney General) v Dermody* [1956] IR 307; *The People (Attorney General) v Coughlan* (1968) 1 Frewen 325.
49   *People (DPP) v Rock* [1994] 1 ILRM 66.
50   *The People (Attorney General) v Mills* (1955) 1 Frewen 153.

preference to a conflicting decision of the High Court.[51] While it overruled the former decision, the Supreme Court in *Rock* noted that the trial judge was bound to follow it:

"While ... the decision of the Court of Criminal Appeal should be overruled it represented at the date of the Circuit Court hearing, in the hierarchy of courts, a decision of a court of final jurisdiction which the Court of Criminal Appeal is except where, in certain circumstances, the matter might be brought with the appropriate certificate by way of appeal to the Supreme Court ... In those circumstances, the learned trial judge was bound to follow the decision of the Court of Criminal Appeal if he considered that there was a conflict between it and a decision of the High Court."[52]

The Supreme Court[53]

[12.34] In the mid-1960s the Supreme Court began to move away from the strict rule of *stare decisis* which had been adopted in England and preferred a more relaxed approach. The first departure from the strict rule occurred in *The State (Quinn) v Ryan*[54] where the prosecutor challenged the constitutionality of s 29 of the Petty Sessions (Ireland) Act 1851. That section facilitated the 'backing of warrants', a mechanism by which warrants issued in one part of the former United Kingdom of Great Britain and Ireland would be enforced in another part without judicial intervention or supervision. That system had been established prior to Independence, but an arrangement that suited the old legal order would not necessarily be appropriate in the post-1922 environment. If s 29 still operated it would in effect circumvent the usual extradition process that operates between sovereign states where British warrants were concerned. Nevertheless, the validity of that provision had been upheld in two earlier Supreme Court decisions, *The State (Dowling) v Kingston (No 2)*[55] and *The State (Duggan) v Tapley*.[56] It was argued on behalf of the respondent that the court was bound by those decisions. In holding the section to be unconstitutional, the Supreme Court declared its freedom to depart from a strict adherence to *stare decisis*.

[12.35] The new approach and the reasons which underlie it were explained by Walsh J:

"It has been urged upon this Court on behalf of the Attorney General and on behalf of the respondents that these sections have already been held to be not inconsistent with the Constitution of Saorstát Éireann in *The State (Dowling) v Kingston (No 2)*[57] and not inconsistent with the provisions of the present Constitution in *The State (Duggan) v Tapley*.[58] It has been further urged that these decisions are binding upon this Court. It is unnecessary in this case to explore the consequences of the fact that this Court is not the Court which decided either of those cases; this Court was established in 1961. It is also

---

51 *The State (Foley) v Carroll* [1980] IR 150.
52 [1994] 1 ILRM 66 at 72.
53 See Walsh, 'Precedent in the Former Irish Superior Courts' (2005) 40 IR Jur (ns) 160.
54 *State (Quinn) v Ryan* [1965] IR 110.
55 *State (Dowling) v Kingston (No 2)* [1937] IR 699.
56 *State (Duggan) v Tapley* [1952] IR 62.
57 *The State (Dowling) v Kingston (No 2)* [1937] IR 699.
58 *The State (Duggan) v Tapley* [1952] IR 62.

unnecessary to express any final view upon the constitutionality of subjecting this Court (as distinct from all other Courts set up under the Constitution) to the rule of *stare decisis*. Neither is it necessary to discuss in detail the question of whether in the case of a Court of final appeal *stare decisis* can ever be anything more than judicial policy, albeit strong judicial policy. However, in view of the implications in the submissions advanced in this Court on behalf of the Attorney General and of the respondents it must be clearly stated, though one would have hoped it should not have been necessary to do so, that this Court is the creation of the Constitution and is not in any sense the successor in Ireland of the House of Lords. The jurisdiction formerly enjoyed by the House of Lords in Ireland is but part of the much wider jurisdiction which has been conferred upon this Court by the Constitution. I reject the submission that because upon the foundation of the State our Courts took over an English legal system and the common law that the Courts must be deemed to have adopted and should now adopt an approach to Constitutional questions conditioned by English judicial methods and English legal training which despite their undoubted excellence were not fashioned for interpreting written constitutions or reviewing the constitutionality of legislation. In this State one would have expected that if the approach of any Court of final appeal of another State was to have been held up as an example for this Court to follow it would more appropriately have been the Supreme Court of the United States rather than the House of Lords. In this context it is not out of place to recall that in delivering the judgment of the Supreme Court in *In the Matter of Tilson Infants*[59] Murnaghan J stated at p 32: 'It is not a proper method of construing a new constitution of a modern state to make an approach in the light of legal survivals of an earlier law.'

So far as the provisions of the Constitution itself bear upon the place of *stare decisis* in constitutional cases the provisions of Article 34.3.3°, which is an amendment to the Constitution as enacted by the People, appear to me to clearly indicate that it is only in the case of a law or a provision of a law, the Bill for which had been referred to the Supreme Court by the President under Article 26 of the Constitution, that there is no longer jurisdiction in any Court to question the constitutional validity of that law or that provision of that law. It has been submitted on behalf of the Attorney General and the respondents that this amendment to the Constitution was designed only to meet a possible argument that because it was a Bill which *had been* approved by the Court that the law when enacted would be open to challenge again once it was signed by the President and that it was to be inferred from this provision that the Constitution impliedly imposed the rule of *stare decisis* in respect of constitutional cases. In my view this contention is quite unsustainable and it would be strange indeed if the Constitution in making such an express provision for Bills only would leave unexpressed but to be inferred a provision in similar terms applicable to Acts. To my mind the absence of such an express provision is an indication that the People in enacting this Constitution and the Oireachtas in amending it within the period limited by the transitory provisions of the Constitution, which have since expired, had no intention of creating by inference only a situation in which a decision of this Court upon the interpretation of the Constitution could be altered only by way of a national referendum for the purpose of amending the Constitution. Far from being daunted by this formidable but inescapable conclusion arising from their submissions counsel for the Attorney General and for the respondents urged that this was the position envisaged by the Constitution. Having regard to the express provision of the Constitution I have no hesitation in rejecting the

---

[59]   *In the Matter of Tilson Infants* [1951] IR 1.

submissions which lead to such a conclusion. This is not to say, however, that the Court would depart from an earlier decision for any but the most compelling reasons. The advantages of *stare decisis* are many and obvious so long as it is remembered that it is a policy and not a binding unalterable rule."[60]

[12.36] A strict reading of *The State (Quinn) v Ryan*[61] would confine the court's relaxation of the principle of *stare decisis* to cases which involve the constitutionality of legislation. However, the wider application of the new approach was confirmed by the Court's decision in *Attorney General v Ryan's Car Hire Ltd*.[62] Again the Court refused to follow two of its earlier decisions.[63] Kingsmill Moore J restated the Court's view on *stare decisis*:

"[T]he first question, then, is whether this Court is to accept and lay down the principle that it is to be bound irrevocably by an earlier decision, the so-called rule of '*stare decisis*'. The merits and demerits of this rule have been widely canvassed and there is no consensus of opinion among academic jurists or serving judges. The practice of Courts of ultimate resort varies, the United States Supreme Court and the ultimate Courts of most European countries and of Canada, South Africa and Australia holding themselves free, where they think requisite, to refuse to follow an earlier decision; while the House of Lords, somewhat uncomfortably, abides by the principle laid down by Lord Halsbury in *London Street Tramways Co v London County Council*,[64] that a decision of the House on a question of law is conclusive and binds it in all subsequent cases until (if ever) it is upset by legislative enactment. Not all the Law Lords have been content to be confined within the strait-jacket of an earlier case. Lord Denning has broken loose (*London Transport Executive v Betts (Valuation Officer)*;[65] *Ostime v Australian Mutual Provident Society*;[66] *Close v Steel Company of Wales*).[67] Lord Reid clearly strains at the bonds (*London Transport Executive v Betts (Valuation Officer)*;[68] *Midland Silicones Ltd v Scruttons Ltd*).[69] Lord Wright would like the House of Lords to have the same freedom as the United States Supreme Court: 8 Camb LJ 144. In *R v Taylor*[70] Lord Goddard, giving the judgment of a Court of Criminal Appeal, consisting of seven judges, refused to follow the decision of an earlier Court of Criminal Appeal where the subsequent Court unanimously considered the former decision to be wrong and where an accused person had been sentenced and imprisoned on the assumption that such earlier decision was correct. In *The State (Quinn) v Ryan*,[71] Mr Justice Walsh in his judgment, to which the other members of the Court assented, refused to accept

---

60 *The State (Quinn) v Ryan* [1965] IR 110 at 125–127.
61 *The State (Quinn) v Ryan* [1965] IR 110.
62 *Attorney General v Ryan's Car Hire Ltd* [1965] IR 642.
63 *Minister for Finance and Attorney General v O'Brien* [1949] IR 91; *Attorney General and Minister for Posts and Telegraphs v CIE* (1956) 90 ILTR 139.
64 *London Street Tramways Co v London County Council* [1898] AC 375.
65 *London Transport Executive v Betts (Valuation Officer)* [1959] AC 213, 247.
66 *Ostime v Australian Mutual Provident Society* [1960] AC 459, 489.
67 *Close v Steel Company of Wales* [1962] AC 367, 388.
68 *London Transport Executive v Betts (Valuation Officer)* [1959] AC 213, 232.
69 *Midland Silicones Limited v Scruttons Limited* [1962] AC 466, 475–477.
70 *R v Taylor* [1950] 2 KB 368.
71 *State (Quinn) v Ryan* [1965] IR 110.

'*stare decisis*' as universally binding in constitutional cases, adding at p 127: 'This is not to say, however, that the Court would depart from an earlier decision for any but the most compelling reasons. The advantages of *stare decisis* are many and obvious so long as it is remembered that it is a policy and not a binding, unalterable rule.

This Court is a new court, set up by the Courts (Establishment and Constitution) Act 1961, pursuant to the Constitution and it is free to consider whether it should adopt the rule which prevails in the House of Lords or any of the less restrictive rules which have found favour in other jurisdictions. It seems clear that there can be no legal obligation on this Court to accept '*stare decisis*' as a rule binding upon it just because the House of Lords accepted it as a rule binding upon their Lordships' house. A decision which only purported to affect the House of Lords could not, by virtue of Article 73 of the Constitution of 1922, have been carried over into our law so as to bind the Supreme Court set up by that constitution; and if that Supreme Court in fact adopted the rule (as it would seem to have done in *Attorney General and Minister for Posts and Telegraphs v CIÉ*) any such determination could only bind that Court and would not under Article 50 of our present Constitution be binding on the new Supreme Court created by Article 34.4, of our present Constitution and the Courts (Establishment and Constitution) Act 1961.

[Counsel] has properly drawn a distinction between the general principle of following precedent and the strict rule of *stare decisis*. The law which we have taken over is based on the following of precedents and there can be no question of abandoning the principle of following precedent as the normal, indeed almost universal, procedure. To do so would be to introduce into our law an intolerable uncertainty. But where the Supreme Court is of the opinion that there is a compelling reason why it should not follow an earlier decision of its own, or of the Courts of ultimate jurisdiction which preceded it, where it appears to be clearly wrong, is it to be bound to perpetuate the error?

If it could safely be assumed that all members of a Supreme Court were perfectly endowed with wisdom and completely familiar with all branches of law, to treat their judgments as infallible would need but little justification. Judicial modesty has refrained from putting forward such a claim and to most jurists such a Court appears a Platonic rather than a practical ideal. Lord Halsbury in the *London Street Tramways Case* takes his stand on more pragmatic grounds: '… what is that occasional interference with what is perhaps abstract justice as compared with the inconvenience – the disastrous inconvenience – of having each question subject to being re-argued and the dealings of mankind rendered doubtful by reason of different decisions, so that in truth and in fact there would be no real final Court of Appeal.'

This argument from inconvenience would come more suitably from the mouth of an executive official than from that of a judge. The plea that 'it is expedient that one man should die for the multitude' must always be met uncompromisingly by a judge with the words, 'I find no fault in this just man,' and he must not falter in his determination. However desirable certainty, stability, and predictability of law may be, they cannot in my view justify a Court of ultimate resort in giving a judgment which they are convinced, for compelling reasons, is erroneous. Lord Halsbury himself was forced to make some modification. Faced with the hypothesis that a case might have been decided in ignorance of the existence of some relevant statutory provision or in reliance on some statutory provision which was subsequently discovered to have been repealed, he suggested that it would not be a binding authority because it was founded on a mistake of fact. The same reasoning would be applicable if the decision were given in ignorance of an earlier authority of compelling validity. Where a point has been entirely overlooked, or conceded without argument, the authority of a decision may be weakened to vanishing point. In my opinion the rigid rule of *stare decisis* must in a Court of ultimate resort give place to a more elastic formula. Where such a Court is clearly of opinion that an earlier decision was erroneous it should be at liberty to refuse to follow it at all events in exceptional cases. What are exceptional cases? I have already given some examples of cases which I would consider exceptional, but I do not suggest that these close the category and I do not propose to attempt to make a complete enumeration. It is sufficient to consider whether the present case should fall within the exception."[72]

[12.37] The judgments in those cases show that, while in general the Supreme Court will follow its own decisions, it reserves a freedom to depart from them where there are 'compelling reasons'. *Stare decisis* is now considered by the Court to be a policy, not an inflexible rule. It should be noted that when those cases were decided the House of Lords was considered to be strictly bound by its earlier decisions, a position which was relaxed two years later.[73] The circumstances in which the Court would be prepared to depart from an earlier decision are further outlined in *McNamara v Electricity Supply Board*.[74] In that case the Court, holding that an occupier of property owes a duty of reasonable care to a trespasser, declined to follow the older rule which was set out by the House of Lords in *Robert Addie and Sons (Collieries) Ltd v Dumbreck*.[75] The latter decision had been adopted by the Supreme Court in *Donovan v Landy's Ltd*,[76] which in turn was followed by the Court in *O'Leary v Wood Ltd*.[77] Despite this settled body of authority, the Court felt that it was justified in departing from it. Walsh J declined to follow *Donovan v Landy's Ltd* on the grounds that it was wrongly decided.[78]

[12.38] Henchy J set out his reasons for not following *Donovan v Landy's Ltd*:

"The degree of certainty, continuity and predictability that judicial decisions should have, to enable people to arrange their conduct so as to avoid legal liability, would normally dictate that this Court should follow its own decisions in *O'Donovan v Landy's Ltd* and *O'Leary v Wood Ltd* which restated the law as laid down in *Addie's case*. But there are exceptional and compelling reasons for not doing so.

Modern judicial decisions in jurisdictions in different parts of the common-law world show a widespread desire to escape from *Addie's case* on the ground of its unsuitability to modern social conditions and, perhaps more so, because a test of liability based on that case, whatever its original validity, runs counter to the principle that pervades the law of

---

72 [1965] IR 642, 652–654.
73 See *Practice Note* [1966] 1 WLR 1234; see generally Zander, *The Law Making Process* (6th edn, 2004), pp 217–224.
74 *McNamara v Electricity Supply Board* [1975] IR 1.
75 *Robert Addie and Sons (Collieries) Ltd v Dumbreck* [1929] AC 358.
76 *Donovan v Landy's Ltd* [1963] IR 441.
77 *O'Leary v Wood Ltd* [1964] IR 269.
78 [1975] IR 1 at 15.

negligence since *Donoghue v Stevenson*[79] which is that a man is liable to damages if he has failed to take all reasonable steps to avoid injuring those whom he ought reasonably to have foreseen as likely to be injured by his conduct. In particular, the House of Lords (where the *Addie* test was originally laid down) has now ruled that *Addie's case* was wrongly decided and that an occupier is liable to a trespasser if, by the standards of common sense and common humanity, he could be said to be culpable in failing to take reasonable steps to avoid a danger to which the trespasser was likely to be exposed: see *Herrington v British Railways Board*[80]...

In my opinion such a test correctly represents the law. Whether on the ground of juridical consistency, the social obligations of occupiers of property, or plain justice, I think it should be preferred to the principle of liability enunciated by *Addie's case* and last restated by this Court in *O'Leary v Wood*."[81]

Griffin J agreed, stating:

"If, by reason of its rigidity or harshness, a rule is found to be unsatisfactory, it is undesirable that efforts to circumvent it should be made rather than that it should be reconsidered."[82]

[12.39] In *McNamara*[83] the Supreme Court refused to be unnecessarily constrained by precedent and was prepared to adapt the law in the light of changing social conditions and legal thinking. It is striking that the decisions which it declined to follow were themselves decided only a decade earlier. However, in other cases the court has acted more cautiously and has manifested a reluctance to interfere with precedent.

[12.40] A strong desire to maintain 'judicial order and continuity' is evident in Henchy J's judgment in *Mogul of Ireland Ltd v Tipperary (North Riding) County Council*:

"A decision of the full Supreme Court (be it the pre-1961 or the post-1961 Court), given in a fully-argued case and on a consideration of all the relevant materials, should not normally be overruled merely because a later Court inclines to a different conclusion. Of course, if possible, error should not be reinforced by repetition or affirmation, and the desirability of achieving certainty, stability, and predictability should yield to the demands of justice. However, a balance has to be struck between rigidity and vacillation, and to achieve that balance the later Court must at the least, be *clearly* of opinion that the earlier decision was erroneous. In *Attorney General v Ryan's Car Hire Ltd*[84] the judgment of the Court gave examples of what it called exceptional cases, the decisions in which might be overruled if a later Court thought them to be clearly wrong. While it was made clear that the examples given were not intended to close the category of exceptional cases, it is implicit from the use in that judgment of expressions such as 'convinced' and 'for compelling reasons' and 'clearly of opinion that the earlier decision was erroneous' that the mere fact that a later

---

79   *Donoghue v Stevenson* [1932] AC 562.
80   *Herrington v British Railways Board* [1972] AC 877.
81   *McNamara v Electricity Supply Board* [1975] IR 1, 23–24.
82   [1975] IR 1 at 32.
83   [1975] IR 1.
84   *Attorney General v Ryan's Car Hire Ltd* [1965] IR 642.

Court, particularly a majority of the members of a later Court, might prefer a different conclusion is not in itself sufficient to justify overruling the earlier decision. Even if the later Court is clearly of opinion that the earlier decision was wrong, it may decide in the interests of justice not to overrule it if it has become inveterate and if, in a widespread or fundamental way, people have acted on the basis of its correctness to such an extent that greater harm would result from overruling it than from allowing it to stand. In such cases the maxim *communis error facit jus* applies …"[85]

[12.41] The point was reiterated in *Hynes-O'Sullivan v O'Driscoll*[86] when Henchy J stated his reasons for not overruling earlier decisions on qualified privilege as a defence to defamation:

"[T]his Court is being asked to hold that the communication sent by the defendant to the IMA [Irish Medical Association] is protected by qualified privilege because, although the IMA in fact had no duty or interest in the matter, the defendant honestly and reasonably believed that it had. However, such a version of the law would run counter to two Supreme Court decisions: *Reilly v Gill*[87] and *Kirkwood Hackett v Tierney*.[88] While the point does not seem to have been specifically argued in those cases, it is clear from the observations made in the judgments that the court in each of those decisions was firmly of the opinion that an occasion of qualified privilege cannot exist unless the person making the communication has a duty or interest to make it and the person to whom it is made has a corresponding duty or interest to receive it. It would require exceptional circumstances before this Court should overrule such a clearly held and repeatedly expressed opinion …

Despite the obvious attractiveness of the suggested formulation of the law of qualified privilege, I am not prepared to support the overruling of *Reilly v Gill* and *Kirkwood Hackett v Tierney*, to the extent required by the defendant's submission …

Secondly, I consider that a previous decision of this Court, be it the court established by the Courts (Establishment and Constitution) Act 1961, or the court in its earlier form, should not be overruled unless the point at issue has been duly raised and adequately argued. The formulation now suggested was first advanced to this Court by counsel for the defendant when replying to the submissions of counsel for the plaintiff. The latter did not find it necessary to deal with this point, relying as he was on the law as stated in *Reilly v Gill* and *Kirkwood Hackett v Tierney*. The result is that we are being asked to overrule part of those decisions, on what has turned out to be an *ex parte* argument. I find that unsatisfactory, particularly having regard to the possible but unknown ramifications of the suggested change in the law.

Thirdly, I am of the opinion that the suggested radical change in the hitherto accepted law should more properly be effected by statute. The public policy which a new formulation of the law would represent should more properly be found by the Law Reform Commission or by those others who are in a position to take a broad perspective as distinct from what is discernible in the tunnelled vision imposed by the facts of a single case. That is particularly

---

[85]   [1976] IR 260, 272–273; see Ervine, 'The Supreme Court, *Stare Decisis* and the Malicious Injuries Code' (1975) 10 Ir Jur (ns) 93.
[86]   *Hynes-O'Sullivan v O'Driscoll* [1989] ILRM 349.
[87]   *Reilly v Gill* (1951) 85 ILTR 165.
[88]   *Kirkwood Hackett v Tierney* [1952] IR 185.

so in a case such as this, where the law as to qualified privilege must reflect a due balancing of the constitutional right to freedom of expression and the constitutional protection of every citizen's good name. The articulation of public policy on a matter such as this would seem to be primarily a matter for the Legislature.

Finally and perhaps most crucially, the suggested restatement of the law should in my opinion not be made in this case because it is not necessary for the purpose of doing justice … If the law as to qualified privilege as stated in *Reilly v Gill* and *Kirkwood Hackett v Tierney* were to be overruled, it would be of no consequence for the purpose of this case. As was stated by this Court in *Mogul of Ireland v Tipperary (NR) County Council*[89] an overruling of a previous decision of this Court, whether it be the pre-1961 Act or the post-1961 Act court, should take place only when it is necessary for the purpose of doing justice. That requirement is absent in this case. Even if the court were to restate the law as requested, such restatement would be only *obiter* …

I respectfully adopt [the statement of law] … which was expressly approved by O'Byrne J in *Kirkwood Hackett v Tierney*. Since the judgment of O'Byrne J was the effective judgment of the court in that case, even if I disagreed with that version of the law I would not be free to refuse to follow it."[90]

[12.42] In *Ó Machín v Ireland*[91] Hardiman J, in his dissenting judgment, noted that '*Mogul* laid down restrictive criteria on which a previous case or line of previous cases can be departed from' and went on to observe that he had been 'unable to trace any case where a long established line of authority was departed from … without addressing the *Mogul* criteria.' In *Doyle v Hearne*[92] Griffin J (dissenting) cited Henchy J's judgment in *Mogul* and went on to indicate that '[s]o far as I have been able to ascertain, there is no case in which a previous decision of this Court was overruled by other than a unanimous decision of a court of five.'[93] However, the force of that observation is diluted by the fact that a divided Supreme Court overruled *Corley v Gill*,[94] an earlier decision of a three-judge Supreme Court.[95]

[12.43] The Supreme Court continues to express its approval of the *Mogul* philosophy. In *O'Brien v Mirror Group Newspapers Ltd*[96] the court declined the invitation to overrule *De Rossa v Independent Newspapers*,[97] a decision which it delivered only one

---

89   *Mogul of Ireland v Tipperary (NR) County Council* [1976] IR 260.

90   [1989] ILRM 349, 360–362.

91   *Ó Machín v Ireland* [2014] IESC 12.

92   *Doyle v Hearne* [1987] IR 601.

93   [1987] IR 601 at 614.

94   *Corley v Gill* [1975] IR 313.

95   See criticism of the decision in Hogan, 'Precedent and Statutory Interpretation' (1989) 11 DULJ (ns) 196. Griffin J's remarks must be qualified. In *McNamara v Electricity Supply Board* [1975] IR 1 FitzGerald CJ did not join his colleagues in departing from the 'old' law on occupiers' liability; however, the judgment which appears in the law report is brief and was not approved by FitzGerald CJ before he died.

96   *O'Brien v Mirror Group Newspapers Ltd* [2001] 1 IR 1.

97   *De Rossa v Independent Newspapers* [1999] 4 IR 432.

year previously. Keane CJ considered the observations in *Mogul* to be of general application and not confined to questions of statutory interpretation. An earlier decision would not be overruled unless it was shown to be 'clearly erroneous' or there are 'compelling reasons' so to act. The majority concluded that *De Rossa* was not deficient in this regard and, in words that echo the judgment in *Mogul*, Keane CJ noted:

> "[A] different view could legitimately be taken from that expressed by Hamilton CJ and assented to by the majority [in *De Rossa*]. However … I have no doubt that that fact of itself could not justify this court in overruling the decision."[98]

[12.44] This again demonstrates the discipline that is imposed by the doctrine of *stare decisis*. A difference in judicial opinion or the fact that the later court might have reached another conclusion had the matter been *res integra* does not, of itself, justify overruling the earlier case. The greater goal of legal certainty would be jeopardised were an unduly flexible approach to prevail:

> "The court, moreover, was invited to overrule the decision less than a year after it was pronounced. There is, of course, no guarantee whatever, that were it to be so overruled, within a relatively short period of time the court might not be persuaded that this decision in turn was 'clearly wrong' and must itself be overruled. The stage would have been reached at which the doctrine of *stare decisis* in this court would have been seriously weakened and the certainty, stability and predictability of law on which it is grounded significantly eroded."[99]

[12.45] However, it should not be thought that the Supreme Court is returning to the inflexible regime that characterised its approach prior to the decisions in *The State (Quinn) v Ryan*[100] and *Ryan's Car Hire*.[101] In *SPUC v Grogan (No 5)*,[102] both Denham and Keane JJ indicated that the court should be prepared to revise its earlier decisions where constitutional matters are concerned and the observations in *Mogul* were to be read subject to this modification. On this view the protection of citizens' constitutional rights is more important than adhering to an erroneous precedent: in those circumstances the case for preserving a ruling that 'has become inveterate'[103] loses its appeal. They were in a minority on the particular issue, namely whether *Attorney General (SPUC) v Open Door Counselling Ltd*[104] should be overruled, but the majority did not disagree with their more general observations. However, the judgment of MacMenamin J in *Ó Machín v Ireland*[105] suggests that the freedom identified by Keane J should be confined to 'truly exceptional cases': the fact that the applicant raised

---

98   [2001] 1 IR 1 at 18. Denham J dissented on this point and enumerated 'compelling reasons' in support of her conclusion that *De Rossa* should be reconsidered. It is perhaps significant that Denham J also delivered a dissenting judgment in the earlier decision.

99   [2001] 1 IR 1 at 16.

100   *State (Quinn) v Ryan* [1965] IR 110.

101   *Ryan's Car Hire* [1965] IR 642.

102   *SPUC v Grogan (No 5* [1998] 4 IR 343.

103   *Mogul of Ireland Ltd v Tipperary (North Riding) County Council* [1976] IR 260 at 273.

104   *Attorney General (SPUC) v Open Door Counselling Ltd* [1988] IR 593.

105   *Ó Machín v Ireland* [2014] IESC 12.

an issue of 'great importance [to] himself' did not warrant a relaxation of the *Mogul* doctrine.

[12.46] A cautious approach is also evident in Keane J's judgment in *DPP v Best*[106] where he observed that the balance of judicial opinion is to the effect that the court is bound 'by the *ratio decidendi* of judgments arising from a reference to the court under Article 26 references.'[107] He qualified these remarks with the observation that this is:

"... subject to the power of the court, being a court of final appeal, to depart from the *ratio* where it is wrong in law, first established as a legal principle in *Attorney General v Ryan's Car Hire*.[108] However, as was pointed out in *Mogul of Ireland Ltd v Tipperary (NR) County Council*,[109] the court must be clearly of the opinion that the earlier decision was erroneous before invoking that power and, undoubtedly, a significant degree of judicial restraint must always be exercised in this area."[110]

[12.47] In the event, Keane J went on to argue that the decision in question, *In Re Article 26 and the School Attendance Bill 1942*,[111] should be overruled. However, his remarks in *DPP v Best*[112] are closer in tone to the judgment in *Mogul*[113] than those which he uttered in *SPUC v Grogan (No 5)*.[114] It is improbable that he intended to establish a stricter rule of *stare decisis* where Article 26 references are concerned than would be the case in respect of other constitutional decisions – it must be that the same standard applies irrespective of the nature of the constitutional ruling. This is not to suggest that Keane J is being especially inconsistent by seeming to urge flexibility in one case and a stricter approach in the other. The two judgments are not necessarily irreconcilable and the difference might be more apparent than real. Nevertheless, there is a notable shift in emphasis, but that is probably unavoidable where questions of judicial methodology are concerned. Moreover, it must be noted that, while the two judgments are phrased in a manner that suggests contrasting approaches, Keane J's conclusion in both instances was that the earlier decision should be overruled. The same destination can often be reached by different routes.

[12.48] The potentially conflicting concerns of maintaining 'judicial order and continuity' and ensuring consistency with developments in judicial thinking are evident in *The State (Lynch) v Cooney*.[115] Commenting on the High Court's approach to the

---

106   *DPP v Best* [2000] 2 ILRM 1.
107   [2000] 2 ILRM 1, 33.
108   *Attorney General v Ryan's Car Hire* [1965] IR 642.
109   *Mogul of Ireland Ltd v Tipperary (NR) County Council* [1976] IR 260.
110   [2000] 2 ILRM 1, 33.
111   *Re Article 26 and the School Attendance Bill 1942* [1943] IR 334.
112   *DPP v Best* [2000] 2 ILRM 1.
113   *Mogul* [1976] IR 260.
114   *SPUC v Grogan (No 5)* [1998] 4 IR 343.
115   *State (Lynch) v Cooney* [1982] IR 337.

earlier decision in *Re Offences against the State (Amendment) Bill, 1940*,[116] Henchy J stated:

"... I would agree that the doctrine of *stare decisis* would have obliged the judge to follow it – even though the Supreme Court which gave that judgment was the Supreme Court which was empowered to function as such under the transitory provisions of the Constitution of Ireland, 1937, and was not the Supreme Court which was required by Article 34.1 of the Constitution to be established by law and which was eventually so established by the Courts (Establishment and Constitution) Act 1961. The maintenance of judicial order and continuity would support such a conclusion."[117]

[12.49] Further on, Henchy J considered the Supreme Court decision in *Re Ó Laighléis*[118] which he was prepared to overrule:

"What was merely *obiter* in [*Re Offences against the State (Amendment) Bill 1940*] thus became part of the *ratio decidendi* in the *Ó Laighléis case*. The question, then, is whether that ruling should be still adhered to. In my opinion it should not. It should be overruled in the exercise of the power of this Court to do so as stated in *Attorney General v Ryan's Car Hire* and in *Mogul of Ireland v Tipperary (NR) County Council*.

While it might be argued that the opinion of the then Supreme Court expressed in those decisions of 1939 [*recte* 1940] and 1957 was part of what was then current judicial thinking, that could not be said if the same opinion were expressed today. Decisions given in recent years in this and other jurisdictions show that the power of the Courts to subject the exercise of administrative powers to judicial review is nowadays seen as having a wider reach than that delimited by those decisions of 1939 [*recte* 1940] and 1957."[119]

[12.50] Similar reasoning underlies the contention in Keane J's judgment in *DPP v Best*[120] to the effect that In *Re Article 26 and the School Attendance Bill 1942*[121] should be overruled. In his view, which was not shared by the majority in *Best*, the School Attendance Bill reference was inconsistent with more recent decisions that stressed the right of the child to be educated.[122] Furthermore, he observed that 'the *ratio decidendi* of [that decision] is, in another and vital respect irreconcilable with decisions of this Court',[123] namely the presumption in *East Donegal Co-operative Livestock Mart v Attorney General*[124] that statutory procedures will be conducted in a manner that is consistent with the Constitution. Like the decision in *McNamara v Electricity Supply*

---

116 *Re Offences against the State (Amendment) Bill 1940* [1940] IR 470.
117 [1982] IR 337 at 376.
118 *Re Ó Laighléis* [1960] IR 93.
119 [1982] IR 337 at 380.
120 *DPP v Best* [2000] 2 ILRM 1.
121 *Re Article 26 and the School Attendance Bill 1942* [1943] IR 334.
122 Citing *G v An Bord Uchtála* [1980] IR 32; *Crowley v Ireland* [1980] IR 102; *O'Donoghue v Minister for Health* [1996] 2 IR 20.
123 [2000] 2 ILRM 1 at 33.
124 *East Donegal Co-operative Livestock Mart v Attorney General* [1970] IR 317.

Board,[125] Keane J's judgment demonstrates that an earlier decision might be overtaken by later juridical developments so that it can no longer stand and must be overruled.

[12.51] In *Finucane v McMahon*[126] the concern of judicial consistency manifested itself in a somewhat unusual fashion. A majority of the Supreme Court refused to follow its earlier decision in *Russell v Fanning*,[127] believing it to have been wrongly decided. Finlay CJ and Griffin J thought that that decision was correct and acceded to the majority view reluctantly. Noting the view of the majority Finlay CJ stated:

> "In these circumstances, having regard to the fundamental nature of the issues which arise in extradition cases, I am satisfied that it would be consistent with the jurisprudence of this Court that I should accept this view so that the basic principles underlying it may clearly represent the decision of this Court."[128]

[12.52] Griffin J was like-minded:

> "Notwithstanding, and with due respect to [Walsh J's] views, as expressed in his judgment [in *Finucane* itself], I remain of the opinion that *Russell v Fanning* was correctly decided. But as I am aware that the principles stated and the conclusions reached by him are supported by [Hederman and McCarthy JJ], thus forming a majority of the Court, I do not propose to elaborate on my opinion. However, as this is a court of final appeal, although it may not be necessary to do so, I should like to say, having regard to the importance of precedent in our system of jurisprudence as providing a degree of certainty upon which members of the public are entitled to rely in the conduct of their affairs, the principles established in and the conclusions reached by the majority of the Court, are those which should now be applied in all cases in which the [point of law in question] is in issue."[129]

[12.53] The stance adopted by Finlay CJ and Griffin J in acceding to the majority viewpoint was not required by the principle of *stare decisis*. They would, like all other judges, be bound by it in future cases, since it is the decision of the Supreme Court,[130] but they were entitled to deliver dissenting judgments in the instant case. In declining to do so, and thus ensuring that the court was unanimous, their conduct was commendably statesmanlike. They ensured that an important point of law was resolved definitively, albeit not in the manner they would have preferred, and that it would not be open to question in later cases. Since the majority had refused to follow an earlier Supreme Court decision, a dissent by two judges would potentially have weakened the authority with which the court spoke. The existence of a strong dissent would have invited the overruling of that decision by a later court, especially since it had ignored an earlier decision of the court. Apart from leaving a particular point of law intolerably uncertain,

---

125 [1975] IR 1; see para **12.37**.
126 *Finucane v McMahon* [1990] 1 IR 165.
127 *Russell v Fanning* [1988] IR 505.
128 [1990] 1 IR 165, 207.
129 [1990] 1 IR 165, 218.
130 See *Carron v McMahon* [1990] 1 IR 239 at 271, *per* Griffin J that the Supreme Court is now bound by *Finucane v McMahon*; see Humphreys, 'Reflections on the Role and Functioning of the Supreme Court' (1990) 12 DULJ (ns) 127.

that would invite judicial chaos, in that it would suggest that any particular majority of the court would be entitled to overrule a differently constituted majority. If that approach became commonplace the system of precedent would be undermined to the point of collapse.[131]

[12.54] It appears that the court when composed of five judges will more readily reconsider the decision of a three-judge Supreme Court. This point was alluded to by Henchy J in *Hamilton v Hamilton*,[132] where he considered a prior decision of a three-judge Supreme Court to be law 'unless and until a different conclusion is reached by a full Court'.[133] This was amplified by McCarthy J in *Doyle v Hearne*[134] where he commented on that suggestion:

> "I do not take this expression of opinion as being one that invites reconsideration of and possible disagreement with any particular triumvirate of this Court, but it lends support to the view that decisions of this court constituted of less than its full complement may be reviewed."[135]

[12.55] While these observations are somewhat tentative, they could assume a greater significance given the expansion of the Supreme Court and its authority to sit in two or more divisions at any given time.[136] The court now sits in divisions and the growing number of three-judge decisions increases the potential for the emergence of divergent judicial views.

The High Court

[12.56] Until recently there had been comparatively scant judicial opinion on the question of *stare decisis* in the High Court but that changed in the early 2000s. An initial indication of the appropriate stance was provided in the extra-judicial views of Black J in a lecture, 'The Doctrine of Precedent in Modern Irish Law', which he delivered in 1953.[137] While such opinions are valuable, it would be mistaken to attribute too much weight to them or to equate them with similar views delivered in a judicial capacity. Moreover, Black J opined that the Supreme Court would adopt the strict rule of *stare decisis* which then pertained in the House of Lords, a stance which, of course, was to be rejected some years later by the Supreme Court. In this respect he got it wrong, which might be taken to detract from the force of his views. He also took the view that pre-1922 House of Lords decisions are binding in Ireland, a view which coincided with

---

[131] See the remarks of Keane CJ in *O'Brien v Mirror Group Newspapers Ltd* [2001] 1 IR 1 at paras **12.43–12.44**.

[132] *Hamilton v Hamilton* [1982] IR 466.

[133] [1982] IR 466 at 484.

[134] *Doyle v Hearne* [1987] IR 601.

[135] [1987] IR 601 at 617.

[136] Courts (Supplemental Provisions) Act 1961, s 7(3) as amended by Courts and Court Officers Act 1995, s 7; see para **4.55**.

[137] The lecture is noted in Dowrick, 'Precedents in Modern Irish Law' (1953) 69 LQR 25.

prevailing judicial opinion but which is no longer sustainable.[138] Nevertheless, with these caveats in mind Black J's views still merit attention.

[12.57] The question of *stare decisis* in the High Court depends, in part, on the capacity in which that court sits. It may sit as a Divisional Court consisting of two or more judges, as a single judge court of first instance in Dublin, as an appellate court hearing appeals from the Circuit Court, or as the High Court on Circuit, hearing Circuit appeals and cases at first instance.

[12.58] The High Court infrequently sits as a Divisional Court, but the general view is that it is bound by its prior decisions in that capacity. This certainly was Black J's view which he based on the practice adopted by the English Court of Appeal.[139] Moreover, it is probable that a Divisional Court binds the High Court when it sits in its more usual single-judge capacity, although there is no authoritative decision to that effect.[140] This conclusion is reached by analogy with the view that a five-judge Supreme Court binds that court when it consists of three judges.[141]

[12.59] Black J stated his preference for following the decisions of a court of coordinate jurisdiction thus:

> "If I were confronted with a decision of a court of co-ordinate jurisdiction, which appeared to me of merely doubtful soundness, I none the less applied the rule of comity and followed it, leaving it for an appellate court to settle the matter, and the longer the other decision had remained unchallenged, the more ready I was to follow it. But if I was presented with a decision of a court of co-ordinate jurisdiction, my dislike of which went beyond mere doubt, and amounted to a firm conviction that it was wrong, then I declined to follow it. Thus, in the important case of charities, *Re Nolan*[142] the late Mr Justice Gavan Duffy refused to follow a decision of Mr Justice Barton in *Dwyer (deceased)*;[143] but later in *Re Clancy*[144] I refused to follow the last-mentioned decision of Mr Justice Gavan Duffy. My example was followed by Mr Justice Overend in *Re Morrissey*[145] and our view was eventually upheld by the Supreme Court in *Re Solomons*."[146]

---

138 See para **12.72**.

139 See Dowrick, 'Precedents in Modern Irish Law' (1953) 69 LQR 25 at 26. The application of *stare decisis* in the English Court of Appeal is set out in *Young v Bristol Aeroplane Co Ltd* [1944] KB 718 where it held itself, in general, to be bound by its prior decisions. This approach was confirmed by the House of Lords in *Davis v Johnson* [1979] AC 317. There are certain exceptions to the strict rule: see Zander, *The Law-Making Process* (6th edn, 2004), pp 240–245; see also Pugsley, 'Precedent in the Court of Appeal' (1983) 2 CJQ 48.

140 See *Wavin Pipes Ltd v Hepworth Iron Co Ltd* [1982] 8 FSR 32 (at para **14.173**) where Costello J would have 'felt constrained' to follow a rule of statutory interpretation which had been affirmed by a divisional court but for a conflicting decision of the Supreme Court.

141 See para **12.54**.

142 *Re Nolan* [1939] IR 388.

143 *Dwyer (deceased* (1908) 46 ILTR 147.

144 *Re Clancy* [1943] IR 23.

145 *Re Morrissey* [1944] IR 361.

146 *Re Solomons* [1949] IR 3; Dowrick, 'Precedents in Modern Irish Law' (1953) 69 LQR 25 at 26–27.

[12.60] Black J's commitment to *stare decisis* is evident in other High Court decisions where the matter was considered. In *Kearns v Manresa Estates Ltd*[147] Kenny J, in holding a 'name and arms' clause to be invalid, followed two earlier High Court decisions to the same effect.[148] In the course of his judgment he alluded to the fact that prior decisions are acted upon and in a sense create expectations of legal validity:

> "There is another argument to which I attach considerable weight. Since the decisions in *re Montgomery decd* and *re de Vere decd*, titles to property included in the ... estate and in other estates have been accepted on the basis that names and arms clauses are void for uncertainty in Ireland. A decision now that the clauses involved were valid would render those titles bad. Although I am not bound by decisions of other judges of the High Court, the usual practice is to follow them unless I am satisfied that they were wrongly decided."[149]

[12.61] In *Irish Trust Bank Ltd v Central Bank of Ireland*[150] Parke J was reluctant to depart from an earlier High Court decision. He felt that unless an earlier decision could be clearly shown to have been wrongly decided, a court of coordinate jurisdiction should follow it; the decision not to follow it should normally be made by an appellate court which enjoys the power to overrule it. Parke J was invited to overrule the prior decision of Gannon J in *Dunne v O'Neill*.[151] The matter was complicated by the fact that the Taxing Master, whose decision was the subject of review by Parke J, had refused to adopt *Dunne v O'Neill*.

[12.62] According to Parke J:

> "I think it might be said that the propriety of a Taxing Master reporting to a judge of the High Court that another judge of that Court was wrong in law is very much open to question. The situation would have been even more anomalous had this case, as it might very well have done, come on for hearing before Gannon J. Be that as it may I have no doubt that this portion of the Taxing Master's report provided a useful and well researched brief for counsel on behalf of the defendants.

> [Counsel] on behalf of the defendants urged me that I should not follow or apply the principles quoted from the judgment of Gannon J. I fully accept that there are occasions in which the principle of *stare decisis* may be departed from but I consider that these are extremely rare. A Court may depart from a decision of a Court of equal jurisdiction if it appears that such a decision was given in a case in which either insufficient authority was cited or incorrect submissions advanced or in which the nature and wording of the judgment itself reveals that the judge disregarded or misunderstood an important element in the case or the arguments submitted to him or the authority cited or in some other way departed from the proper standard to be adopted in judicial determination. It is clear that none of these elements can be detected in *Dunne v O'Neill*[152] or the judgment therein delivered. [Counsel] does not in fact contend any such thing but his argument rests solely on the fact that the

---

147   *Kearns v Manresa Estates Ltd* (25 July 1975, unreported), HC.
148   *Re Montgomery Decd* (1953) 89 ILTR 62; *Re de Vere Decd* [1961] IR 224.
149   *Kearns v Manresa Estates Ltd* (25 July 1975, unreported), HC.
150   *Irish Trust Bank Ltd v Central Bank of Ireland* [1976–7] ILRM 50.
151   *Dunne v O'Neill* [1974] IR 180.
152   *Dunne v O'Neill* [1974] IR 180.

decision is contrary to previous authorities and that I am therefore not obliged to follow it. Whatever may be the case in Courts of final appellate jurisdiction a Court of first instance should be very slow to act on such a proposition unless the arguments in favour of it were coercive. If a decision of a Court of first instance is to be challenged I consider that the appellate Court is the proper tribunal to declare the law unless the decision in question manifestly displays some one or more of the infirmities to which I have referred. The principle of *stare decisis* is one of great importance to our law and few things can be more harmful to the proper administration of justice, which requires that as far as possible lay men may be able to receive correct professional advice, than the continual existence of inconsistent decisions of Courts of equal jurisdiction. The present case affords an interesting example of what ought to be avoided. [Counsel for the plaintiffs] appeared for the applicants in *Dunne v O'Neill*. Not only are his arguments set out in detail in the judgment but they are adopted and made part of the *ratio decidendi* in a manner in which counsel is seldom gratified to experience. [He] appeared for the plaintiffs in the present case and it would be an ironic comment on the state of the law if counsel could find his arguments adopted and applied in one Court and yet be told in another Court of equal jurisdiction that they were fundamentally wrong and inconsistent with the authorities.

I find nothing to convince me that the judgment of Gannon J shows such disregard or inconsistency with previous authorities to justify me in departing from it. Although the report is scanty in information as to the authorities cited by counsel it is clear from a perusal of the judgment that almost all of the cases cited to me in argument and set out in the Taxing Master's report were considered by the learned judge. Indeed many of the passages relied upon by [counsel for the defendants] and cited in the Taxing Master's report are also cited and relied upon by the learned judge. I therefore take the view that the only grounds upon which I could properly be asked to descend from or fail to follow *Dunne v O'Neill* have not been established to my satisfaction.

I would like, however, to make it clear that I have not formed my view merely as a reluctant adherent to the doctrine of *stare decisis*. My decision is not in the words of Bowen LJ 'a sacrifice made upon the altar of authority': *Montagu v Earl of Sandwich*.[153] I think that the argument on behalf of the defendants suffers from two disabilities."[154]

[12.63] The stance adopted in *Irish Trust Bank v Central Bank of Ireland* has been reinforced by the judgment of Clarke J in *Re Worldport Ireland Ltd*.[155] In the latter case Clarke J concluded that he was bound by the earlier High Court decision[156] and articulated the underlying considerations:

"It is well established that, as a matter of judicial comity, a judge of first instance ought usually follow the decision of another judge of the same court unless there are substantial reasons for believing that the initial judgment was wrong ... Amongst the circumstances where it may be appropriate for a court to come to a different view would be where it was clear that the initial decision was not based upon a review of significant relevant authority, where there is a clear error in the judgment, or where the judgment sought to be revisited

---

153 *Montagu v Earl of Sandwich* (1886) 32 Ch D 525 at 549.
154 [1976–7] ILRM 50 at 53–54.
155 *Re Worldport Ireland Ltd* [2005] IEHC 189.
156 *Re Industrial Services Ltd* [2001] 2 IR 118.

was delivered a sufficiently lengthy period in the past so that the jurisprudence of the court in the relevant area might be said to have advanced in the intervening period. In the absence of such additional circumstances it seems to me that the virtue of consistency requires that a judge of this court should not seek to second guess a recent determination of the court which was clearly arrived at after a thorough review of all of the relevant authorities and which was … based on forming a judgment between evenly balanced argument. If each time such a point were to arise again a judge were free to form his or her own view without proper regard to the fact that the point had already been determined, the level of uncertainty that would be introduced would be disproportionate to any perceived advantage in the matter being reconsidered. In the absence of a definitive ruling from the Supreme Court on this matter I do not, therefore, consider that it is appropriate for me to consider again the issue so recently decided … "[157]

It is notable that this passage from Clarke J's judgment has been frequently cited in subsequent High Court judgments:[158] the commitment of the High Court to this version of the principle of *stare decisis* is beyond doubt. Dunne J captures the prevailing mood: '[i]t goes without saying that certainty in the law is not just a desirable concept but a necessary one. Parties to litigation are entitled to reasonable certainty as to the applicable legal principles in any given area of law.'[159] The powerful appeal of precedent is especially evident in the judgment of Hogan J in *AG v Residential Institutions Board*[160] where he would have decided the case differently had the issue in question been *res integra*. However, the matter was 'covered by recent authority' which 'effectively compelled [him] to resolve this issue adversely to the applicant'. Nevertheless, Hogan J stated that he reached this conclusion 'with deep personal reluctance'.

[12.64] The tone of the jurisprudence invites the conclusion that the gravitational pull of precedent is stronger in the High Court than in the Supreme Court: and while there is no definitive articulation of this point it is certainly the case that the language of the judgments in the respective courts lends credence to this observation. The net outcome is that the High Court is more reluctant to depart from its earlier decisions than the Supreme Court is with respect to its own decisions. This is a welcome state of affairs. The values of certainty and predictability trump the desire for flexibility where a court of first instance, such as the High Court, is concerned: the option of an appeal is available to a disappointed litigant. As a matter of judicial discipline it is better that an earlier case be overruled by an appellate court, which decision will bind the court of first

---

[157] *Re Worldport Ireland Ltd* [2005] IEHC 189.
[158] See eg *Brady v Director of Public Prosecutions* [2010] IEHC 231; *McAteer v Sheahan* [2013] IEHC 417; *GE Capital Woodchester Homeloans Ltd v Faulkner Madden* [2013] IEHC 540; *Kimpton Vale Developments Ltd v An Bord Pleanala* [2013] IEHC 442; *Brennan v Mullane* [2014] IEHC 61. See also *Pullen and ors v Dublin City Council* [2008] IEHC 379; *Lynch and ors v HSE* [2010] IEHC 346; *Environmental Protection Agency v Neiphin Trading Ltd* [2011] IEHC 6, citing *Irish Trust Bank v Central Bank of Ireland* [1976–7] ILRM 50.
[159] *GE Capital Woodchester Homeloans Ltd v Faulkner Madden* [2013] IEHC 540, para 24.
[160] *AG v Residential Institutions Board* [2012] IEHC 492.

instance and at the same time bring finality to the issue.[161] However, matters assume a different complexion in the case of a court of final appeal where, of course, the option of further appeal is not available: in those circumstances a wider range of considerations is involved. This consideration arose in the Supreme Court decision *Kadri v Governor of Wheatfield Prison*[162] where Clarke J, by now a member of the Supreme Court, observed that the High Court jurisprudence, exemplified by *Irish Trust Bank v Central Bank of Ireland* and *Re Worldport Ireland Ltd*, 'correctly states the proper approach' for the High Court to adopt. He went on to observe that while the High Court judge was correct to follow the earlier High Court decision:

"... it does not, of course, follow that this Court [ie the Supreme Court], now that the matter has come before it and been fully argued, is likewise constrained. This Court must consider the issue on the merits while of course having proper regard both to the relevant High Court cases and to the one previous decision of this Court on the point ..."

In a similar vein MacMenamin J in the same case observed that: '[t]his court is not bound by the High Court jurisprudence, and may look at the question anew.'[163]

[12.65] There are circumstances in which the High Court has felt it necessary to depart from an earlier decision. In *Walsh v President of the Circuit Court and DPP*[164] Murphy J remarked that his decision to depart from an earlier High Court decision was reached with 'considerable hesitation'. Again he emphasised the desirability of maintaining the convention of following decisions of courts of coordinate jurisdiction, but felt compelled by a Supreme Court decision to depart from the earlier High Court case. The remarks of Laffoy J in *L v Minister for Justice, Equality and Law Reform*[165] are in a similar vein when she held that a refusal on particular grounds by the High Court to grant leave to apply for judicial review bound every other judge of the High Court:

"I consider that I am bound by the decision of O'Sullivan J. If the applicant was dissatisfied with that decision, her remedy was to seek a certificate under s 5(3)(a) of the Illegal Immigrants (Trafficking) Act 2000 for leave to appeal to the Supreme Court."

---

161 See *People (DPP) v Keane* [2007] 12 JIC 1901 *per* Murray CJ: '[c]ourts of appeal have long been seen as an important and essential element in calibrating the scales of justice and thus ensuring confidence in the judicial process. Legal systems provide for an appeal from Courts of first instance not least because it is not assumed that Courts of first instance are infallible no more than it is assumed Courts of Appeal are. There is no human institution that enjoys such a brave assumption ... Moreover, an appeal by a party who, rightly or wrongly is dissatisfied with a decision of a Court of first instance, in addition to providing the party with the benefit of a case being heard or examined a second time by another Court, also brings finality to individual disputes before the Courts which is one of the objects of the administration of justice.'

162 *Kadri v Governor of Wheatfield Prison* [2012] IESC 27.

163 *Kadri v Governor of Wheatfield Prison* [2012] IESC 27.

164 *Walsh v President of the Circuit Court and DPP* [1989] ILRM 325.

165 *L v Minister for Justice, Equality and Law Reform* [2004] IEHC 81.

[12.66] There is no definitive judicial pronouncement on the question of *stare decisis* when the High Court sits in an appellate capacity dealing with appeals from the Circuit Court or when it sits as the High Court on Circuit. Clearly it binds the Circuit Court in question and, on the basis of the judicial hierarchy, all other Circuit Courts. Whether it enjoys the same precedential force in courts of coordinate jurisdiction, however, is uncertain. The authority of a Circuit Court, being a court of 'limited and local jurisdiction', is confined to its own circuit and by extension it might be argued that circuit matters determined in the High Court should be likewise circumscribed. On the other hand the High Court, unlike the Circuit Court, enjoys 'full original jurisdiction' and thus the authority of its decisions extends beyond that which is 'local and limited'. It would follow from this that its authority when it sits in these capacities is no different from that which it enjoys when it sits as a court of first instance in Dublin.

The Court of Criminal Appeal

[12.67] The Court of Criminal Appeal has also declared its freedom to depart from its earlier decisions. In *The People (Attorney General) v Moore*[166] the Court refused to follow its earlier decision in *The People (Attorney General) v O'Neill.*[167]' Davitt P outlined the Court's views:

"There remains the question whether we are bound to accept and apply the principle enunciated in *O'Neill's case* even though we differ from it to the extent which we have indicated. We have not been referred to, nor are we aware of, any case in which the question whether this court is bound to follow its previous decisions has arisen. [Counsel], on behalf of the Attorney General, cited the case of *R v Norman*[168] in which the Court of Criminal Appeal in England expressly over-ruled its previous decision in *R v Stanley.*[169] In *Stanley's* case the Court consisted of the usual number of three judges; in *Norman's Case* there was a full court of thirteen, four of whom dissented. The constitution of the Court of Criminal Appeal in England is not dissimilar from ours; and its jurisdiction is much the same as ours except that they cannot direct a new trial where they reverse a conviction. An appeal lies from them to the House of Lords in the same circumstances as an appeal lies from us to the Supreme Court. This Court, as at present constituted, certainly claims no jurisdiction to *over-rule* the decision in *O'Neill's case.* We are, however, encouraged by the decision in *Norman's case* to take the course which we now propose to adopt. We are not unmindful of the principle of *stare decisis* and of the desirability of having uniformity in judicial decisions interpreting the law. We think, however, that the interests of justice will best be served by giving effect to our own opinions, even though they differ from some of those expressed in *O'Neill's case* ..."[170]

[12.68] The Court upheld the conviction but certified two questions of law of exceptional public importance for the Supreme Court. However, the applicant

---

[166] *People (Attorney General) v Moore* [1964] Ir Jur Rep 6.
[167] *People (Attorney General) v O'Neill* [1964] Ir Jur Rep 1.
[168] *R v Norman* [1924] 2 KB 315.
[169] *R v Stanley* [1920] 2 KB 235.
[170] [1964] Ir Jur Rep 6 at 12–13.

abandoned his appeal to the Supreme Court, thus depriving that court of the opportunity to comment, *inter alia*, on the question of precedent in the Court of Criminal Appeal. The less strict approach of the English Court of Criminal Appeal was based on a concern for personal liberty; the court would not uphold a conviction on the basis of a prior decision which it considered to be erroneous.[171] That approach is understandable, and it would require an unusual commitment to the maintenance of judicial continuity to uphold a conviction on the basis of a precedent which is considered to have been wrongly decided. However, in *Moore* the reverse occurred. The Court of Criminal Appeal upheld a conviction despite its earlier decision which would have warranted an acquittal. It might be argued that the libertarian concerns which informed the English decisions did not apply here and the court's refusal to follow the earlier case could be considered to be questionable.

The new Court of Appeal

[12.69] As noted elsewhere the Constitution has been amended to facilitate the creation of a Court of Appeal.[172] At the time of writing the relevant legislation has been enacted by the Oireachtas but we await the government order appointing the 'establishment day'.[173] The new Court of Appeal will, *inter alia*, assume the jurisdiction of the Court of Criminal Appeal, and the latter court will be abolished. An issue that will arise is what stance the court should take with regard to *stare decisis*: should it adopt the relatively strict approach that is favoured in the High Court or the more flexible approach that is suggested by the Supreme Court jurisprudence. There is much to be said in favour of the stricter approach. In general, decisions of the new court will be 'final and conclusive'[174] but there will be a limited right of further appeal to the Supreme Court where the case involves a matter of great public importance or where the interests of justice necessitate an appeal.[175] While finality would suggest a more flexible approach for the reasons alluded to by Murray CJ in *The People (DPP) v Keane*,[176] the circumstances in which an appeal will lie from the Court of Appeal to the Supreme Court are typically those that will satisfy the *Mogul* criteria. In other words, the need for flexibility to meet the demands of justice will be satisfied through the appellate jurisdiction of the Supreme Court and consequently the values of certainty and predictability should retain greater weight in the Court of Appeal. Moreover, the Court of Appeal will sit in divisions and practical considerations urge the adoption of the stricter approach. A more relaxed regime could result in a multiplicity of inconsistent decisions which would introduce an

---

171   *R v Taylor* [1950] 2 KB 368.
172   See para **2.90**.
173   Court of Appeal Act 2014.
174   Provided by the new Article 34.4.3° of the Constitution, which will be inserted on the establishment of the Court of Appeal.
175   Provided by the new Article 34.5.3° of the Constitution, which will be inserted on the establishment of the Court of Appeal.
176   See *The People (DPP) v Keane* [2007] 12 JIC 1901 at fn 161.

unwarranted level of uncertainty and would pose particular difficulties for the High Court where it is faced with conflicting decisions of the Court of Appeal.

[12.70] The effective transfer of the functions of the Court of Criminal Appeal to the new Court of Appeal raises the question of the status of Court of Criminal Appeal decisions and whether the Court of Appeal should be bound by them. The Court of Appeal is not in any sense a successor of the old Court of Criminal Appeal and it follows that decisions of the old court are not its decisions. However, the better view probably is that the Court of Appeal ought to treat those decisions as it would its own and, thus, be bound by them unless there are compelling reasons not to follow them. This stance would contribute to maintaining judicial continuity and an established body of authority would not be unsettled.

Pre-1961 decisions

[12.71] Some questions have arisen as to the status of pre-1961 Irish decisions and pre-1922 decisions of the House of Lords. With respect to the former, although Article 34 of the Constitution deals with the courts, it was conceded in *The State (Killian) v Minister for Justice*[177] that the text of that Article envisaged their being established by statute. As noted earlier, this was achieved by the Courts (Establishment and Constitution) Act 1961.[178] While the courts thus established are identical to the earlier courts, technically they are new courts and decisions of the pre-1961 courts are not decisions of those courts. That point was adverted to by Walsh J in *The State (Quinn) v Ryan*[179] and was elaborated on by Kingsmill Moore J in *Attorney General v Ryan's Car Hire Ltd*, where he was of the view that a pre-1961 decision of the Supreme Court, to the effect that it should adopt a rigid practice of *stare decisis,* could not bind the 'new' Supreme Court. In contrast, Henchy J in *Mogul of Ireland v Tipperary (North Riding) County Council*[180] considered that neither pre- nor post-1961 decisions should be overruled unless they were clearly shown to be erroneous. He was unprepared to overrule a 1949 decision of the Supreme Court which, had the matter been previously undecided, he would have decided the other way. And in *The State (Lynch) v Cooney*[181] the same judge expressed similar views regarding pre-1961 decisions.

Pre-1922 House of Lords decisions

[12.72] Prior to 1922 the House of Lords was the court of final appeal for Ireland and, accordingly, Irish courts were bound by its decisions. After 1922 the question was whether those decisions still bound the Irish courts. In *Exham v Beamish*[182] Gavan Duffy J suggested that only those decisions which had been accepted as being part of

---

[177]   *State (Killian) v Minister for Justice* [1954] IR 207.
[178]   See paras **4.46–4.48**.
[179]   *State (Quinn) v Ryan* [1965] IR 110.
[180]   *Mogul of Ireland v Tipperary (North Riding) County Council* [1976] IR 260.
[181]   *State (Lynch) v Cooney* [1982] IR 337.
[182]   *Exham v Beamish* [1939] IR 336.

Irish law before 1922 were binding. On the other hand, Maguire CJ and Black J in *Boylan v Dublin Corporation*[183] and Murnaghan J in *Minister for Finance and Attorney General v O'Brien*[184] considered all pre-1922 decisions to be binding. In the light of the subsequent relaxation by the Supreme Court of the practice of *stare decisis*, it can be presumed that those decisions are no longer to be considered to be binding. Indeed, it is interesting to note that in *Attorney General v Ryan's Car Hire Ltd*[185] the Supreme Court refused to follow its earlier decision in *Minister for Finance and Attorney General v O'Brien*. This issue was also touched on by McCarthy J in his judgment in *Irish Shell Ltd v Elm Motors Ltd*.[186] In a similar vein, Davitt P, in *Attorney General v Simpson*,[187] rejected the submission that an advice of the Privy Council in an Australian appeal, given before Irish appeals thereto were abolished, bound the Irish courts.

Decisions of inferior courts

[12.73] The decisions of inferior courts do not bind superior courts, but they are of persuasive authority. A superior court is free to ignore such decisions and enjoys the power to overrule them. The manner in which this freedom should be exercised has not been the subject of judicial consideration in Ireland but several tentative observations can be made. The first is that it can be presumed that a court enjoys at least the same measure of freedom in relation to inferior decisions as it does in respect of decisions of courts of coordinate jurisdiction. Secondly, as it is the court of final appeal the Supreme Court is expected to provide authoritative rulings for all other courts to adopt and it must possess the corresponding freedom to overrule the prior decisions of inferior courts.

[12.74] Where there are conflicting decisions the Supreme Court inevitably is required to select the body of authority which it considers to be appropriate.[188] However, the tendency is not to unsettle an established line of authority, and the Supreme Court usually overrules a case only where it considers it to be wrongly decided or no longer appropriate. Thus, in *Finlay v Murtagh*[189] the Supreme Court overruled the earlier High Court decision *Somers v Erskine*[190] on the grounds that it was wrongly decided and was incompatible 'with modern developments in the law of torts'.[191] These grounds are similar to those which have been considered by the court to afford a compelling reason to overrule its own decisions and this suggests that the court will be as scrupulous in its treatment of High Court decisions as it would be in the case of its own decisions.

---

[183] *Boylan v Dublin Corporation* [1949] IR 60.
[184] *Minister for Finance and Attorney General v O'Brien* [1949] IR 91.
[185] *Attorney General v Ryan's Car Hire Ltd* [1965] IR 642.
[186] *Irish Shell Ltd v Elm Motors Ltd* [1984] IR 200; see para **12.76**.
[187] [1959] IR 105 at 129.
[188] See, eg, *UF (orse UC) v JC* [1991] 2 IR 330 where the Supreme Court had to choose between conflicting High Court decisions.
[189] *Finlay v Murtagh* [1979] IR 249.
[190] *Somers v Erskine* [1943] IR 348.
[191] [1979] IR 249 at 255, 262.

Foreign decisions

[12.75] A court is not bound to follow the decisions of foreign courts. However, those decisions are of persuasive authority and may be followed at the option of the court. Decisions of other common law countries are frequently cited and adopted by Irish courts, particularly where there is no Irish authority governing the issue in question. Given the origin of the Irish legal system and the traditional links between the two systems, it is not surprising to find that English decisions are the most commonly cited foreign decisions. But that is not to suggest that those decisions should be adopted uncritically by Irish courts.

[12.76] In *Irish Shell Ltd v Elm Motors Ltd*[192] McCarthy J criticised an observation by Costello J that English decisions should be followed unless they were shown to be erroneous:

"I do not necessarily agree or disagree with the analysis made by the learned trial judge but I deem it proper to comment on his observation that 'The High Court is not bound to follow the decisions and judgments to which I have referred if there are compelling reasons for rejecting them'. I do not believe that the true inference from this observation is that, in the absence of compelling reasons for rejection, the High Court is bound to follow decisions and judgments of the House of Lords, the Court of Appeal in England, or the Judicial Committee of the British Privy Council, but lest any such view should be entertained, I would unequivocally deny the existence of any such principle or the propriety of any such practice. Of the decisions of those courts decided prior to 1922, it is proper to say that they are part of the corpus of jurisprudence and law that was taken over on the foundation of Saorstát Éireann being the laws in force in Saorstát Éireann at the date of the coming into operation of the Constitution of the Irish Free State (Saorstát Éireann), subject to that Constitution and to the extent to which they were not inconsistent therewith. Similarly Article 50 of the Constitution provides:

'1. Subject to this Constitution and to the extent to which they are not inconsistent therewith, the laws in force in Saorstát Eireann immediately prior to the date of the coming into operation of this Constitution shall continue to be of full force and effect until the same or any of them shall have been repealed or amended by enactment of the Oireachtas.

2. Laws enacted before, but expressed to come into force after, the coming into operation of this Constitution, shall, unless otherwise enacted by the Oireachtas come into force in accordance with the terms thereof.'

Article 50 was stated by Kingsmill Moore J in *The Educational Company of Ireland Ltd v Fitzpatrick (No 2)*[193] as relating to 'statutes or law carried forward into our corpus juris' but that view has been questioned by Walsh J (with whom O'Higgins CJ agreed) in *Gaffney v Gaffney*[194] where he said at p 151 of the report: 'Contrary to what appears to have been the view of Kingsmill Moore J I do not think that Article 50 of the Constitution refers to any law other than statute law, and in my view the text of Article 50 makes that clear'. Walsh J

---

[192]   *Irish Shell Ltd v Elm Motors Ltd* [1984] IR 200.
[193]   *Educational Company of Ireland Ltd v Fitzpatrick (No 2)* [1961] IR 323.
[194]   *Gaffney v Gaffney* [1975] IR 133.

may well have been echoing the observations of Gavan Duffy J in *Exham v Beamish*[195] where at pp 348–9 of the report he stated:

'As a matter of practice, we constantly refer to judgments in the English Courts and such judgments, as every lawyer will recognise, have often proved to be of great service to us; but let us be clear. In my opinion when Saorstát Éireann, and afterwards Eire, continued the laws in force, they did not make binding on their courts anything short of law. In my opinion, judicial decisions in Ireland before the Treaty, and English decisions which were followed here, are binding upon this Court only when they represent a law so well settled or pronounced by so weighty a juristic authority that they may fairly be regarded, in a system built up upon the principle of *stare decisis,* as having become established as part of the law of the land before the Treaty; and to bind, they must, of course, not be inconsistent with the Constitution ... In my opinion, this Court cannot be fettered in the exercise of the judicial power by opinions of very different courts under the old regime, unless those opinions must reasonably be considered to have had the force of law in Ireland, so that they formed part of the code expressly retained ... If, before the Treaty, a particular law was administered in a way so repugnant to the common sense of our citizens as to make the law look ridiculous, it is not in the public interest that we should repeat the mistake. Our new High Court must mould its own *cursus curiae;* in so doing I hold that it is free, indeed bound, to decline to treat any such absurdity in the machinery of administration as having been imposed on it as part of the law of the land; nothing is law here which is inconsistent with derivation from the People.'

Whilst observations of judges of the former Supreme Court in *Boylan v Dublin Corporation*[196] and *Minister for Finance v O'Brien*,[197] appear to support the view that decisions of the House of Lords upon law common to England and Ireland, given before the coming into operation of the Constitution of 1922, are a binding force in our courts, in my view the decision of this Court in *Attorney General v Ryan's Car Hire Ltd*[198] and *The State (Quinn) v Ryan*,[199] wherein the rigidity of the principle of stare decisis was denied, must now call into question the binding force of any such pre-1922 decision. Since 26 July 1966, the House of Lords has recognised that too rigid an adherence to precedent may lead to injustice of a particular case and also unduly restrict the proper development of the law. It stated its right, while treating former decisions of the House as normally binding, to depart from a previous decision when it appears right to do so: Practice Note.[200] Such a statement of principle by the House of Lords inevitably makes even weaker any case for following the decisions of that House whether they are in cases before or after the year 1922. There are many other jurisdictions like to our own where the corpus juris includes the common law such as the United Stated, Canada, Australia and New Zealand. These are nations where, in addition, there are written and, consequently, rigid Constitutions, unlike that of the United Kingdom. Whilst the judgments in cases decided in the English Courts at all levels will, on a great many occasions, provide convenient and, indeed, convincing statements of principle

---

[195] *Exham v Beamish* [1939] IR 336.
[196] *Boylan v Dublin Corporation* [1949] IR 60.
[197] *Minister for Finance v O'Brien* [1949] IR 91.
[198] *Attorney General v Ryan's Car Hire Ltd* [1965] IR 642.
[199] *State (Quinn) v Ryan* [1965] IR 110.
[200] [1966] 1 WLR 1234.

and attractive arguments in favour of such principles, they are no more than that and must be examined and questioned in the light of a jurisprudence whose fundamental law is radically different in its denial of a supremacy of parliament and its upholding of three co-equal organs of government, in the Legislature, the Executive and the Judiciary. In no sense are our courts a continuation of or successors to the British courts. They derive their powers from a Constitution enacted by the people and would, in my view, find more appropriate guidance in the decisions of courts in other countries based upon a similar constitutional framework than in what at times, appears to be an uncritical adherence to English precedent, which itself, appears difficult to reconcile from time to time …"[201]

[12.77] In that case O'Higgins CJ and Griffin J declined to express an opinion on the points raised by McCarthy J. In *Tromso Sparebank v Beirne (No 2)*[202] Costello J again stated that an Irish court should be reluctant to refuse to follow a firmly established principle in English law:

"I think the High Court should be slow to refuse to follow a principle established in English law since 1883. But if high legal authority *in England* questions the validity of the principle so that it appears it may well be changed either by judicial decision or by the legislature, then it seems to me that the Irish court is justified in not following it, should it consider it to be erroneous."[203]

[12.78] In *MMcC v JMcC*[204] Costello J declined to follow a series of English cases, but again emphasised the strong persuasive weight of English authority and implicit in his judgment is the view that such authority should be followed unless it is shown to be wrongly decided:

"I think I have liberty to give effect to this opinion even though it is contrary to the decisions of the English courts on the subject. These decisions are of persuasive weight and should not lightly be ignored. But the Irish courts are not bound by them and I think I am not required to follow decisions which I think misconstrued the effect of an earlier decision of the House of Lords which I would be prepared to follow."[205]

[12.79] In recent years Irish courts have been willing to rely on decisions of jurisdictions other than England. In constitutional matters the courts pay special attention to decisions

---

[201] [1984] IR 200 at 225–227.

[202] *Tromso Sparebank v Beirne (No 2)* [1989] ILRM 257.

[203] [1989] ILRM 257 at 261 (emphasis added). See also *Re United Bars Ltd* [1991] 1 IR 396 at 401 *per* Murphy J: 'it seems to me of the utmost importance in dealing with commercial matters to maintain some measure of consistency, and to proceed on the footing that parties to commercial transactions have organised their affairs on the basis of the law as they understand and believe it to be for many years, and any change to or any revision or correction of that law should be made preferably by the Oireachtas or at any rate by the final court of appeal in this country. In the circumstances, it seems to me that I must apply the law as it was interpreted in *In re Lewis Merthyr Consolidated Collieries* [1929] 1 Ch 498 originally and more recently in *In re GL Saunders Ltd (in liquidation)* [1986] 1 WLR 215 notwithstanding any reservations that I might have had based on the strength of the arguments brought forward by counsel on behalf of the defendants.'

[204] *MMcC v JMcC* [1994] 1 IR 293.

[205] [1994] 1 IR 293 at 303.

of courts in the United States, especially the federal Supreme Court, as the Constitutions of both countries bear broad similarities and are rooted in similar legal philosophies. Recourse to decisions of the courts of the nearest common law jurisdiction, Northern Ireland, has been quite rare since 1922. The citation of decisions from other common law jurisdictions, such as Australia, Canada and New Zealand, has become more common in recent years. This trend seems likely to continue in the future, particularly in view of greater availability by electronic means of the case law of those countries. However, decisions of the English courts will still feature prominently for the foreseeable future. In this context, we note the findings of a study conducted in 1983 by Professors Boyle and Greer, which analysed the headnotes of reported cases between 1921 and 1975 (see Figure 12.1).[206]

[12.80] The breakdown of the cases referred to in the headnotes of decisions of the courts in the Republic of Ireland was:

Origin of Decision	Number	%
English or Scottish Cases	1,058	50
Pre-1920 Irish Cases	356	17
Post-1920 Irish Cases	654	31
Post-1920 Northern Ireland Cases	23	1
Other	6	1

Cases cited in Irish decisions 1921–1975
Figure 12.1

[12.81] The equivalent data for decisions of the courts of Northern Ireland are outlined in Figure 12.2:

Origin of Decision	Number	%
English or Scottish Cases	180	61
Pre-1920 Irish Cases	55	19
Post-1920 Irish Cases	9	3
Post-1920 Northern Ireland Cases	45	15
Other	8	3

Cases cited in Northern Irish decisions 1921–1975
Figure 12.2

[12.82] For purposes of approximate comparison we have compiled a different table in respect of decisions of the courts in the Republic of Ireland reported in 1995 (see Figure

---

[206] Boyle and Greer, *The Legal Systems, North and South* (1983), p 46.

12.3).[207] These figures reveal the following breakdown of cases judicially considered in the course of the reported judgments:

Origin of Decision	Number	%
Post-1920 Irish Cases	336	56.5
English or Scottish Cases	197	33
Pre-1920 Irish Cases	18	3
Post-1920 Northern Ireland Cases	2	0.4
European Court of Justice	19	3.2
United States	14	2.4
Australia	7	1.2
Canada	1	0
New Zealand	1	0

Cases judicially considered in Irish decisions 1995
Figure 12.3

[12.83] The number and origin of cases judicially considered in decisions reported in the 2005 and 2011 Irish Reports are outlined in Figures 12.4 and 12.5, respectively.

Origin of Decision	Number	%
Post-1920 Irish Cases	698	61.8
English or Scottish Cases	327	28.9
Pre-1920 Irish Cases	1	0.08
Post-1920 Northern Ireland Cases	4	0.35
European Court of Justice	56	4.96
United States	8	0.70
Australia	10	0.88
Canada	14	1.24
New Zealand	4	0.35
Others	8	0.70

Cases judicially considered in Irish Reports 2005
Figure 12.4

---

[207] These figures are based on the cases cited judicially in the judgments reported in [1995] 1 IR, [1995] 1 ILRM and [1995] 2 ILRM. Decisions which were reported both in IR and ILRM were counted once only for the purpose of the table. The percentages have been rounded up and down for convenience.

Origin of Decisions	Number	%
Post-1920 Irish Cases	729	55.5
English or Scottish Cases	372	28.3
Pre-1920 Irish Cases	26	2
Post-1920 Northern Ireland Cases	6	0.45
EU Cases	43	3.2
United States	30	2.3
Australia	28	2.1
Canada	9	0.68
New Zealand	8	0.61
European Court of Human Rights	62	4.7

Cases judicially considered in Irish Reports 2011
Figure 12.5

[12.84] These data provide a broad indication of the pattern of citation. The current position is that, in Ireland, the citation of post-1920 Irish decisions has overtaken reference to English and Scottish precedents. This no doubt reflects the increase in judicial output in Ireland since 1975. However, it is also clear that English and Scottish decisions remain very important as sources of persuasive authority. Of the other common law jurisdictions listed, few Northern Irish authorities have been considered, while the citation of authorities for the old Commonwealth (Australia, Canada and New Zealand) has grown slowly but steadily since 1995. One major change since the Boyle and Greer study is the increased importance of the decisions of the European Court of Justice, a consequence of membership of the European Union. Moreover, a striking increase in the citation of European Court of Human Rights decisions since 2005 is obvious, reflecting the enhanced position in domestic law of the European Convention in Human Rights since the enactment of the European Convention on Human Rights Act 2003. Finally, we may note that, in general, the courts in the Republic of Ireland are still reluctant to refer to authority from civil law systems.[208]

---

[208] An exception is *Murphy v Attorney General* [1982] IR 241 where the High Court and Supreme Court referred to decisions of the Constitutional Courts of Germany and Italy. No doubt, a difficulty in translation may account for the absence of more references to such decisions. Whether an increased facility in languages will alter this pattern remains to be seen.

[12.85] Where the decisions of different jurisdictions lead to different conclusions an Irish court is not bound to prefer any particular line of authority and may choose to adopt one or other or neither.[209] McCarthy J in *Irish Shell Ltd v Elm Motors Ltd*[210] anticipated that decisions from a variety of jurisdictions might be cited in and relied on by Irish courts. However, in *The MV 'Kapitan Labunets'*[211] Barr J expressed caution in regard to accepting foreign authority:

> "[I] apprehend that judges in this jurisdiction would have no difficulty in concurring with the view expressed by Lord Diplock on the subject of decisions of foreign courts in the course of his judgment in the House of Lords in *Fothergill v Monarch Airlines*[212] that 'the persuasive value of a particular court's decision must depend upon its reputation and its status, the extent to which its decisions are binding upon courts of co-ordinate and inferior jurisdiction in its own country and the coverage of the national law reporting system'."[213]

[12.86] Barr J's caution is particularly appropriate in relation to the citation of jurisprudence from civil law countries, where a system of binding precedent is unknown and prior decisions are primarily of illustrative value. This stance was reinforced by Clarke J in an extra-judicial address that was reported in the *Irish Times*.[214] He accepted the value of being aware of foreign authority but he emphasised the importance of having a proper understanding of the issue that confronted the foreign court:

> "[He] did stress the importance of being aware of authority from other jurisdictions: it makes sense for a small country to at least consider the views of the major courts in countries with comparable legal systems …

> Furthermore, upon gaining Independence in 1922, Ireland chose to maintain the existing legal system provided it was consistent with the Free State Constitution and, later, Bunreacht na hÉireann.

> So it followed that the country would look to other common law jurisdictions – Britain in particular – for influence …

> 'However,' he added, 'it does need to be strongly emphasised that careful consideration needs to be given to the issue of whether the foreign court concerned was answering the same question as the Irish court is now being asked to address.'

> He added that he had 'sometimes seen paragraphs plucked out of foreign authority and included in written submissions to the Irish courts [where] the foreign court was answering a very different question or was addressing issues of principle which were significantly influenced by its own legislation or constitutional provisions'.

---

[209] See, eg *The People (Attorney General) v O'Dwyer* [1972] IR 416; *Re Keenan Brothers Ltd* [1985] IR 401.

[210] *Irish Shell Ltd v Elm Motors Ltd* [1984] IR 200.

[211] *MV 'Kapitan Labunets'* [1995] 1 IR 164.

[212] *Fothergill v Monarch Airlines* [1981] AC 251.

[213] [1995] 1 IR 164 at 168.

[214] 'Judge Concerned about Foreign Jurisprudence' *Irish Times*, 5 May 2014.

This sort of large-scale citation of isolated paragraphs from foreign jurisprudence was a 'real danger' … It was one that he predicted would continue to get worse because of the ease of access to international legal databases."

Clarke J then considered the relevance of European decisions in Irish law and noted the parallels between European human rights instruments and the rights protected by the Irish Constitution:

"The rights guaranteed under the Irish Constitution were broadly similar to those guaranteed under the European Convention on Human Rights, he said. Thus, the jurisprudence of the European Court of Human Rights remained an important source of persuasive authority when the Irish courts are called upon to consider the Constitution.

He also expected the EU Charter of Fundamental Rights (which lists civic, political, social and economic rights) to play an increasingly relevant role in Irish law in the future.

This formal charter came about as a result of the Lisbon Treaty and the precise extent of its influence remained a matter for legal debate, 'at least at the edges'.

Whatever the precise boundaries of the charter's applicability, its treaty status along with Ireland's obligations as a member state of the European Union means, it was now part of the Irish constitutional structure, 'at least in some areas'.

Although a significant part of the influence of those two EU documents came from a civil law world, with a different legal culture, 'I think it is fair to say that Ireland has … assimilated well' …"

Secondary sources

[12.87] In some cases a court might be faced with an absence of authority, whether binding or persuasive. In those circumstances it might rely on the writings of jurists and reference has often been made to recognised textbooks and learned articles.[215] The traditional rule was that such materials could be cited only if the author was dead, an event which was considered to confer an authoritative status that living authors lack. This rule has been relaxed and the courts now permit the citation of the works of living authors.[216] These sources are secondary in that they are not produced by a law-making agency and, unlike case law and legislation, they lack the force of law. Nevertheless, such works can be of highly persuasive authority and often their reasoning is 'adopted'

---

[215] See, eg *Kirby v Burke and Holloway* [1944] IR 207; *The People (DPP) v Lynch* [1982] IR 64; *Hynes Ltd v Independent Newspapers Ltd* [1980] IR 204; *Desmond v Brophy* [1985] IR 449.

[216] See, eg *Metropolitan Properties Ltd v O'Brien* [1995] 2 ILRM 383 citing Wylie, *Irish Conveyancing Law* (1978); *Johnson and Kelly v Horace* [1993] ILRM 594 citing Wylie, *Irish Land Law* (2nd edn, 1986); *Iarnród Éireann v Ireland* [1995] 2 ILRM 161 citing McMahon and Binchy, *Irish Law of Torts* (2nd edn, 1990); *Gleeson v Feehan* [1993] 2 IR 113 citing Brady, *Succession Law in Ireland* (1989); *Simon and Tadea v Governor of Cloverhill Prison* [2004] IEHC 392 citing Byrne and McCutcheon, *Irish Legal System* (4th edn, 2001); (contd.../)

by courts. Moreover, in some cases a court might adopt a secondary source in preference to a persuasive precedent.[217]

[3] THE *RATIO DECIDENDI* AND *OBITER DICTUM*

[12.88] As has been already stated, not every part of an earlier decision must be followed by a later court. In the course of a judgment it is probable that the judge will consider a number of propositions of law, some of which bear on the point in question and others of which are tangential. The discussion of law in which the judge engages will typically set out reasons in support of accepting certain arguments and drawing a particular conclusion. In this respect the reasoning operates to justify the decision and to establish that it has been reached in accordance with the pre-existing law. Once decided, a case becomes authority for a certain proposition of law and the part which is binding is called the *ratio decidendi*. Briefly stated it can be said to encapsulate a proposition of law for which the decision is authority. Black J stated that he would treat as part of the *ratio decidendi* 'any assertion of principle that its author believed and intended to be part of his *ratio decidendi*' and contrasted this with 'a principle which is not required for the decision or intended to be part of it'.[218] Cross and Harris have commented that: '[t]he *ratio decidendi* of a case is any rule of law expressly or impliedly treated by the judge as a necessary step in reaching his conclusion, having regard to the line of reasoning adopted by him, or a necessary part of his direction to the jury.'[219]

[12.89] In *Considine v Shannon Regional Fisheries Board*[220] Costello J stated:

"The doctrine of judicial precedent provides that a principle of law which is the basis for an actual decision of the Supreme Court must be followed by the lower courts. Like many general principles, the principle of judicial precedent can be easily stated but may be difficult to apply in practice. And undoubtedly there may be instances where the *ratio* of a case is not always easy to discover. Again, the principle is clear. The *ratio* of a case is discovered by determining what proposition of law justified the decision in the light of the material facts which the court decided."[221]

---

[216] (\...contd) *People (DPP) v Davis* [2001] 1 IR 146 citing McAuley and McCutcheon, *Criminal Liability* (2000); *Director of Public Prosecutions v PH* [2007] IEHC 335 citing O'Malley, *Sentencing Law and Practice* (2nd edn, 2006); *Weston v An Bord Pleanala* [2008] IEHC 71 citing Scannell, *Environmental and Land Use Law* (2006); *Min for Agriculture and Food v Barry* [2009] 1 IR 215 citing Redmond, *Dismissal Law in Ireland* (2nd edn, 2007); *Ugbelase v Min Justice, Equality and Law Reform* [2010] 4 IR 233 citing Hogan and Whyte, *JM Kelly: The Irish Constitution* (4th edn, 2003).

[217] In *Kirby v Burke and Holloway* [1944] IR 207 Gavan Duffy J adopted the extra-judicial writings of Oliver Wendell Holmes in preference to the House of Lords decision in *Donoghue v Stevenson* [1932] AC 562.

[218] Dowrick, 'Precedents in Modern Irish Law' (1953) 69 LQR 25 at 27.

[219] *Precedent in English Law* (4th edn, 1991), p 72.

[220] *Considine v Shannon Regional Fisheries Board* [1994] 1 ILRM 499.

[221] [1994] 1 ILRM 499 at 501. See further, para **12.116**.

[12.90] In *Ugbelase v Minister for Justice, Equality and Law Reform* Cooke J explained the matter thus:

> "a previous judgment can only be said to be a precedent by reference to its *ratio decidendi* namely, the essential principle upon which the concrete decision in the case is based, abstracted from the specific peculiarities of the case. It is the *ratio* alone which has force of law. As has been observed, it is always dangerous to take one or two observations out of a long judgment and treat them as if they gave the *ratio decidendi* of a case."[222]

It followed, in his view, that he was not bound by observations 'that cannot be taken as statements of reason or principle which were necessary to the legal basis upon which the decision' was made.

[12.91] From the foregoing, several points in relation to the *ratio decidendi* emerge – it is based on the facts of the case, it is a necessary part of the decision ('required' or 'the basis for') and it is treated as such by the court which decided the case. Moreover, subsequent courts play a vital role in identifying the *ratio decidendi* and the scope for flexibility, indeed judicial creativity, that this allows will become clear. The manner in which later courts treat the matter is equally important in determining the *ratio decidendi* of the earlier case. In this latter respect the observations of O'Donnell J in *Pringle v Government of Ireland* are pertinent:

> "judgments are not to be read in the same way as statutes. A single sentence in a judgment rarely encapsulates the essence of a lengthy judgment, and a judgment of one judge, even one as eminent and influential as Walsh J., is not to be taken, in isolation, as stating the *ratio decidendi* of a case. There is always a danger of substituting the invocation of a vivid and memorable phrase for the analysis of the substance of a judgment."[223]

Instead he insisted that the later court must strive for a 'fair reading of the case as a whole'.

[12.92] A proposition of law contained in the judgment which is not binding is termed *dictum* or *obiter dictum* (*dicta* and *obiter dicta* being the plural forms respectively). The two expressions tend to be used interchangeably but, strictly speaking, there is a difference between them. When the point relates to a matter that was in issue in the case, *dictum* is the expression used, whereas *obiter dicta* refer to other, more peripheral matters.[224] It is unusual for a court expressly to state the *ratio decidendi* of its decision, preferring instead to leave it concealed in its reasoning. This does not reflect a judicial predilection for obfuscation but rather a desire not to hinder or fetter future courts. A

---

[222] *Ugbelase v Minister for Justice, Equality and Law Reform* [2010] 4 IR 233 at 245. See also *Minister for Agriculture and Food v Barry* [2008] IEHC 216 *per* Edwards J: '[t]he *ratio decidendi* in any particular case consists of the general reasons given for the decision or the general grounds upon which it is based, detached or abstracted from the specific peculiarities of the particular case which gives rise to the decision.'

[223] *Pringle v Government of Ireland* [2012] IESC 47.

[224] See Zander, *The Law-Making Process* (6th edn, 2004), p 268. See also *The People (DPP) v Shaw* [1982] IR 1 at 47, *per* Griffin J '… I consider those *dicta* to have been *obiter*.'

court is concerned with deciding the particular case before it and not potential future cases, which will be the task of later courts. Discovery of the *ratio decidendi*, therefore, is largely a matter of interpretation for later courts, a matter that is occasionally reflected by judges in phrases such as 'it seems to me that the *ratio decidendi* is ...' or 'in my view the *ratio decidendi* is ...' Thus in *CC v Ireland*[225] the Supreme Court considered the interpretation of s 2(2) of the Criminal Law Amendment Act 1935 in an earlier case, *Attorney General (Shaughnessy) v Ryan*.[226] In *CC*, Denham J expressly identified a particular proposition as being the *ratio decidendi* of the earlier decision:

> "The *ratio decidendi* of this case [*Shaughnessy*] is the issue of the consent of the girl. Thus I would distinguish the case. Its rationale related to consent of the girl, not to the *mens rea* of the defendant. Consequently it has no bearing on the matter for determination in this case. Indeed it illustrates confusion between the issue of the mind of the girl and her consent, and the *mens rea* of a defendant."

It should be noted that in this instance the *Shaughnessy ratio* was stated so as to distinguish it, thereby rendering it inapplicable to the instant case.

[12.93] It must be emphasised that when a court searches for the *ratio decidendi* of an earlier decision it is looking for the rule or principle which underlies the decision and for which the decision is authority. The task is essentially one of classifying statements of law as being *ratio decidendi* or *obiter dictum*.[227] In this context, it should be realised that judges do not necessarily employ the expression '*ratio decidendi*' and often speak of the 'rule' or 'principle' which is contained in the earlier decision or the reason for the decision. In this respect the terms are largely synonymous and are used interchangeably. Given the nature of the exercise no precise formula for the extraction of the *ratio decidendi* has evolved, it being a matter of art rather than science. Despite that, several points can be made.

Ratio decidendi is based on the facts of the case

[12.94] Because courts decide actual cases, and not moot points, the *ratio decidendi* is based on the facts of the case rather than on any hypothetical set of circumstances. It is the rule which was applied as limited by those facts. A court's discussion of the case is normally confined to the actual facts and a decision, by its very nature, concerns those facts and no others. This is sometimes reflected in the observation that a case is authority only for that which it decides. Unfortunately this does not provide the simple solution that at first sight it might suggest. Every case can be read as presenting an individual set of facts which will never be repeated. Details such as the identity of the

---

[225] *CC v Ireland* [2006] 4 IR 1.

[226] *Attorney General (Shaughnessy) v Ryan* [1960] IR 181.

[227] Occasionally the distinction between the two is blurred; see, eg *Elwyn (Cottons) Ltd v Master of the High Court* [1989] IR 14 at 16, *per* O'Hanlon J: 'I therefore adopt the decision of my learned colleague on this issue and the *ratio decidendi* underlying the said decision, although in the nature of *obiter dicta*.' *Wall v Hegarty* [1980] ILRM 124 at 127, *per* Barrington J: '... the *dicta*, whether they were of the *ratio* or not, are clearly of high authority.'

parties, the time and location of the event, and the event itself are unique to the particular case. However, to read cases in such a narrow manner would be so restrictive as to destroy the system of *stare decisis*. No two cases would be alike and, in consequence, no decision would be binding. But as it is authority for a particular proposition of law, it is necessarily understood that a case is capable of being applied beyond its own particular facts.

[12.95] It follows that courts are required to identify similarities and dissimilarities between cases and to adjudicate accordingly. Thus, if adequate reasons cannot be found to justify distinguishing the instant case from the earlier case, the latter must be followed. In general, therefore, the individual details, or 'specific peculiarities',[228] of a case do not limit its scope. For example, the fact that the victorious plaintiff in the earlier case was injured by a car does not, of itself, preclude that case from being applied to a case which involves injury caused by a train. The function of the later court is to identify the categories into which the earlier court sought to place the particular individual facts. When the court decides that the earlier case is a relevant authority which must be followed, it is placing the different sets of individual facts in the same category. To draw on the example already used, if the court in the case involving injury by the train decides that it is bound by the earlier case involving the car it, in effect, states that for the purposes of the rule there is no difference between a car and a train. In other words, the *ratio decidendi* of the earlier case allows recovery whether the injury is caused by a car or by a train.

[12.96] Thus, one must realise that facts can be stated at different levels of generality. It is in the identification of the appropriate level that the *ratio decidendi* is discovered. The agent of harm in the example under discussion can be described variously as a car, a motorised vehicle, a mechanical vehicle, a vehicle which might or might not be mechanical, or a tangible thing. In equating, and for that matter differentiating, cases the court selects a level of generality to apply to the instant case. The irrelevance of certain factual differences will be obvious to all. For instance, injury caused by a Ford is not perceived to differ from injury caused by a Rolls Royce. However, different factors might enter into consideration when one asks whether injury caused by a car is to be equated with that caused by a runaway horse, a leakage of chemicals or the carelessness of a surgeon. The answer will depend on the level of generality which is selected. In searching for the appropriate level the later court is attempting to identify the rule which was invoked in the earlier decision. And that, in turn, requires the court to examine the earlier decision with a view to determining how it was reached.

Relevance of reasoning and arguments

[12.97] When it examines an earlier case the later court searches for indications in the judgment as to the rule which was invoked. The earlier court will usually have commented on the individual facts concerned and have defined the category that it had in mind. However, that in itself is not conclusive as the later court might ignore the

---

228 *Ugbelase v Minister for Justice, Equality and Law Reform* [2010] 4 IR 233 at 245.

stated category and redefine it. This is particularly so where the category has been drawn in especially broad, or especially narrow, terms. Thus, although the earlier court might have spoken of the agent of harm as being a tangible thing, the later court might decline to employ that level of generality, saying that the earlier case concerned cars or vehicles and not tangible things in general. In so explaining the earlier decision the later court is, to an extent, refashioning the *ratio decidendi*.

[12.98] The earlier court will also have considered any relevant cases which preceded it. For instance, the court concerned with the injury caused by a car might have felt itself bound by, and have followed, a precedent involving injury caused by a galloping horse. In that instance the category would have to include both galloping horses and cars and the appropriate level of generality is thereby defined, in part at least. The question which the later court will face is whether the new agent of harm, a train, falls into that category. In other words, it will be required to identify, for the purposes of the rule, the characteristics which are shared by galloping horses and cars and determine whether a train possesses those properties.

[12.99] Again, the later court will examine the earlier judgments in its attempt to ascertain the nexus between them. It might be that those cases indicate that galloping horses and cars are dangerous objects which are liable to cause serious personal injury and which should be kept under control. If that is the common characteristic identified by the court it is probable that a train, which also is a dangerous object, would come within the rule. But, by the same token, injury caused by a stationary horse might be distinguished as the latter might be considered not to possess the degree of danger shared by the other objects.

[12.100] This, of course, is to assume that the earlier courts will have commented on the categories which they had in mind. It is, however, not uncommon that a court will confine its discussion of the case to the particular facts. This, in part at least, is motivated by a desire to restrict consideration of the legal issues to the case in hand and a wish not to engage in speculation which is thought to be the more suitable subject of future litigation. In this respect, the later court is left to interpret the earlier court's silence. Thus, the later court might conclude that nothing has been said in the earlier case which prevents its application to the new case. McCarthy J's remarks in *Ó Domhnaill v Merrick*[229] show an appreciation that judicial silence might be so construed when he expressed his disagreement with certain propositions which had been advanced in argument '… lest my silence on the topics might be considered to denote agreement …'.[230] Equally, a court might rely on the silence of its predecessor to exclude the application of the precedent to the new case, saying that there is no indication in the earlier case that suggests that it should apply to the later.

[12.101] The earlier court's discussion of the relevant law might also indicate the rule which it had in mind. That court will have considered cases which preceded it and will have subjected them to the same form of analysis to which it will be subject in later

---

[229] *Ó Domhnaill v Merrick* [1984] IR 151.
[230] [1984] IR 151 at 167.

cases. That analysis of earlier cases and the evaluation of their scope and effect will be taken into account by the later court in its efforts to discover the *ratio decidendi*. The earlier court will have expressed its reasons for choosing to follow, or not to follow, a preceding case, thereby stating a relationship between the two which indicates the rule which was applied. This is to state the rule in a somewhat oblique manner, but occasionally a court will in clear terms state the rule which it intends to apply. However, even where that occurs it does not dispose of the issue. The later court might not accept the stated rule as being the *ratio decidendi* of the earlier decision. That court might state that the purported rule was too broad for the particular decision and that a less expansive rule would have sufficed. Likewise, if the rule is expressed in narrow terms, which would suggest that the later case lies outside its scope, the court might conclude that the rule was so expressed as a particular application of a more general rule.

[12.102] It has been noted that the *ratio decidendi* of a case is based on its actual facts rather than on a hypothesis. A further characteristic is that a decision rests on the arguments which were advanced in the case. It is said that a point not argued is a point not decided.[231] For instance, a claim based on contract does not provide a binding rule in respect of tortious liability. The *ratio decidendi* of that case consists of some rule which forms part of the law of contract, not the law of torts. A further decision in a case on the same facts will be necessary to arrive at a binding rule which governs liability in tort. Once again, when this matter is being considered the later court will be required to examine the judgment in the earlier case in order to discover the basis on which the earlier case was decided. And in *Re Hetherington*[232] Browne-Wilkinson VC stated that a court is not bound by a proposition the correctness of which was assumed by the earlier court without its having been specifically considered. A related feature, which has already been observed, is a *per incuriam* decision.[233] That is a decision that has been made in ignorance of a relevant statute or binding authority and, in consequence, is itself not binding. Although the earlier court will, in all probability, have thought that it was reaching a binding decision, its ignorance of the earlier law deprives it of that quality. A relevant point has not been argued and, therefore, has not been decided.

[12.103] So far our consideration of this topic has proceeded on the assumption that a case consists of one judgment which advances one reason for the decision reached. Matters are more complicated where a judge advances several reasons in support of the decision or where a number of judgments are delivered. In respect of the former, it has been stated by Budd J in *Brendan Dunne Ltd v FitzPatrick*[234] that where a judge gives two reasons for the decision both are part of the *ratio decidendi*.[235] Thus, to return to our

---

231 See *The State (Quinn) v Ryan* [1965] IR 110 at 120, *per* Ó Dalaigh CJ.
232 *Re Hetherington* [1990] Ch 1 at 10, citing *Baker v The Queen* [1975] AC 774; *Berns v Bethell* [1982] Ch 294, *Ashville Investments Ltd v Elmer Contractors Ltd* [1989] QB 488.
233 See para **12.12**.
234 [1958] IR 29 at 45.
235 See *Considine v Shannon Regional Fisheries Board* [1994] 1 ILRM 499 at 501, *per* Costello J: 'It is, of course, clear that there may be more than one *ratio* in a decided case.' See further, para **12.116**.

example of the injury caused by a car, were the court to hold the car owner liable on the grounds that a car is a dangerous object *and* that its situation on the highway increases the risk of injury to other road users, the *ratio decidendi* would include both those factors. This rule would incorporate injuries caused by cars and by runaway horses as both share the characteristics identified in the judgment. But it would exclude injury caused by trains, as the latter do not pose additional threats to users of the highway.

Ratio decidendi and multiple judgments

[12.104] Special considerations apply with regard to multi-judge courts, such as the Supreme Court, the new Court of Appeal and, less frequently, a Divisional Court of the High Court. It is a convention of the common law that each judge in a multi-judge court may (but not necessarily must) deliver a separate judgment indicating his or her reasons for the decision arrived at by the court. Thus, where the Supreme Court sits as a court of five judges it is possible for a decision to be arrived at by a majority of 3:2, with each judge expressing his or her views in quite different ways. The delivery of separate judgments may pose difficulties in determining the precise point established by the decision, but the analysis of the different reasons given by the judges exposes the subtle distinctions inherent in the legal process. The dilemma presented by multiple judgments was alluded to in the Supreme Court in *Garvey v Minister for Justice, Equality and Law Reform and another*, where the court considered the *ratio* of *McGrath v The Commissioner of An Garda Síochána*.[236] In *Garvey*, Geoghegan J stated:

> "The leading judgment [in *McGrath*] was delivered by Hederman J. but in order to discover the agreed *ratio decidendi* it is necessary to read and parse the two other written judgments delivered by Finlay CJ and McCarthy J respectively."[237]

It is also important to appreciate that while in a particular case the judgment delivered by a judge who finds himself in a minority in the case is at best a consolation for the disappointed litigant, such dissenting judgments have, in some important instances, proved highly influential in subsequent cases.[238]

---

236 *McGrath v The Commissioner of An Garda Síochána* [1991] 1 IR 69.

237 *Garvey v Minister for Justice, Equality and Law Reform* [2006] 1 IR 548.

238 For example the dissenting judgment of Denning LJ (later Lord Denning MR) in *Candler v Crane, Christmas & Co* [1951] 2 KB 164 was largely adopted in *Hedley, Byrne & Co Ltd v Heller & Partners Ltd* [1964] AC 465: see further para **12.150**. Similarly, the dissenting speech of Lord Atkin in *Liversidge v Anderson* [1942] AC 206, in which he had criticised the views of the majority by comparing their attitude to interpretation of statutory language with that adopted by Humpty Dumpty in Lewis Carroll's *Alice Through the Looking Glass*. The speech was (much later) adopted as correctly setting out fundamental principles of administrative law: see *Anisminic Ltd v Foreign Compensation Tribunal* [1969] 2 AC 147.

[12.105] The practice of delivering separate, and dissenting, judgments was defended extra-judicially by McCarthy J, who had found himself in a minority in the Supreme Court on a number of occasions:

> "At the centre of the common law, the genius of its dynamism, is the interplay of judicial rationale – the multiple judgment system. Let it flourish. It has a proud history; it should continue to have a historical pride. It is for this reason that we write judgments – we may want to indulge in some semantic exercise; we may wish to polish our literary style; we may wish to temper the rigor of some decision; but most of all we wish to see the interpretation and growth of the law continue."[239]

[12.106] Consistent with this view, and echoing reservations that others have shared, McCarthy J has criticised the restrictions imposed on the Supreme Court by Article 34.4.5° which at the time required the court to deliver a single judgment where the constitutional validity of legislation enacted by the Oireachtas is in question – the so-called 'one judgment rule'.[240] This rule will be abolished on the establishment of the new Court of Appeal.[241] A similar restriction applies where the court delivers judgment in a reference to it under Article 26.[242] The practice of the Supreme Court has been to confine the application of the one judgment rule to cases concerning the validity of post-1937 Acts.[243] Separate judgments may be delivered where a constitutional question arises concerning pre-1937 Acts,[244] where post-1937 secondary legislation is challenged[245] or where no statutory provision is at issue in a constitutional claim.[246] Supreme Court judges are also free to deliver separate judgments in cases concerning judge-made rules, such as those concerning the duty of care in negligence,[247] or in cases concerning statutory interpretation.[248]

---

[239] Mr Justice McCarthy, 'Una Voce Poco Fa', in O'Reilly (ed), *Human Rights and Constitutional Law* (1992), p 162. McCarthy J's last judgment in *Attorney General v Hamilton* [1993] 2 IR 250, a dissenting judgment, has been compared with that of Lord Atkin in *Liversidge*: see obituary (1992) 14 DULJ (ns).

[240] 'Una Voce Poco Fa', in O'Reilly (ed), *Human Rights and Constitutional Law* (Essays in Honour of Brian Walsh) (1992), pp 164–165. The title of McCarthy J's article refers to the aria from Rossini's *The Barber of Seville*.

[241] Thirty-third Amendment to the Constitution Act 2013, s 5(2)(g).

[242] See para **5.88**.

[243] *The State (Sheerin) v Kennedy* [1966] IR 379. See generally, Hogan and Whyte, *JM Kelly: The Irish Constitution* (4th edn, 1994), pp 968–972.

[244] For example *McGee v Attorney General* [1974] IR 284, para **15.109**; *Norris v Attorney General* [1984] IR 36, para **15.110**.

[245] For example *Meagher v Minister for Agriculture and Food* [1994] 1 IR 329, paras **16.128–16.141**, in which the court delivered a single judgment on the issue of the constitutional validity of the European Communities Act 1972, s 3, but delivered separate judgments on the validity of Regulations made pursuant to the power conferred by s 3.

[246] For example *Attorney General v X* [1992] 1 IR 1.

[247] See paras **12.144–12.173**.

[248] See Ch 14.

[12.107] Thus, in many cases, each member of the court may deliver a separate judgment. Where one judgment attracts the concurrence of the other members of the court, or where a majority of the judgments delivered agree on the reasons for the decision, few additional problems are created. The reasoning which attracts the unanimous, or at least majority, support of the court would form the basis of the *ratio decidendi*. However, where the court is unanimous but different reasons are advanced, none of which attracts the support of a majority, two possible approaches exist. One is that the *ratio* would consist of the sum of the reasons advanced. Thus, if two judges opt for reason A and one each for reasons B, C, and D, the *ratio* of the case would consist of reasons A, B, C, and D. While this approach might entail an element of desirable compromise, the difficulty with it is that it results in the selection of the narrowest possible *ratio* which accommodates all the judgments delivered. This would come close to stating that the case is an authority only for that which it decides and it would lack any real binding quality except in identical cases.

[12.108] With this in mind Professor Cross presented an alternative approach which he thought was probably closer to actual judicial practice.[249] He suggested that one should think of the case as comprising of a number of *rationes decidendi* and select that which can be said to attract the support of a majority. Therefore, if reasons A and B are not mutually incompatible but are inconsistent with reasons C and D, the *ratio* would embrace A and B, thus attracting at least the partial support of three judges. But it should be recognised that this approach is of little avail in the, fortunately rare, case where five judges advance five separate and incompatible reasons. In that event, a later court is very much left to its own devices and can select any of the five different *rationes* or, indeed, a sixth of its own construction.

[12.109] As Professor Cross noted, dissenting judgments can be relevant when it comes to ascertaining the *ratio decidendi*. It is all too tempting to ignore those judgments in the, possibly mistaken, belief that they shed no light on the subject. Dissents can be relevant for several reasons. A dissent might be based on a different interpretation of the evidence or a different evaluation of legal issues which the case presents, but nevertheless support the propositions of law advanced by the majority. Thus, the dissenting judgment of Walsh J in *The People (DPP) v Walsh*[250] was based largely on his evaluation of the evidence, but his statement of the law is considered to be authoritative.[251] Moreover, in some cases the majority might agree on the result but for conflicting reasons and recourse must then be had to the dissenting judgments.

---

249 'The *Ratio Decidendi* and a Plurality of Speeches in the House of Lords' (1977) 93 LQR 378.
250 *People (DPP) v Walsh* [1980] IR 294.
251 See *The People (DPP) v Kenny* [1990] 2 IR 110 at 131, *per* Finlay CJ: 'The judgment of Walsh J in that case was a dissenting judgment, but not by reason of the principles of law enunciated in it, but rather by reason of the view taken as to whether on the facts of the case the detention of the applicant was or was not unlawful.'

[12.110] This can be illustrated by an example where three reasons, A, B and C, are advanced in the judgments. The majority is composed of two judges who opt for reason A and one who opts for reason B but expressly disapproves of reason A. The dissenting judges advance reason C and also express their disapproval of reason A. The third judge of the majority also expresses support of reason C but considers it inapplicable in the instant case (see Figure 12.6).

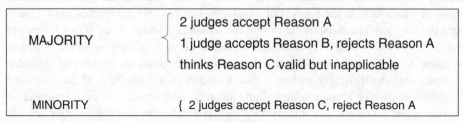

MAJORITY	2 judges accept Reason A
	1 judge accepts Reason B, rejects Reason A
	thinks Reason C valid but inapplicable
MINORITY	{ 2 judges accept Reason C, reject Reason A

Figure 12.6

[12.111] In this event it is difficult to conclude that reason A is the *ratio* of the case as three judges, the two dissidents and one member of the majority, have expressed their disapproval of it. Nor can the *ratio* be said to be based on reason B as it enjoys the support of only one judge, namely the third majority judge. Thus, the available alternatives are that the *ratio* is based on reason C, which as a proposition of law was acceptable to three judges, or that the case possesses no discernible *ratio* and is merely authority for that which it decided. But the first alternative presents the difficulty of elevating the reasoning of a minority into the *ratio* of the case and it would seem that we are left with the second.

[12.112] Another example which was considered by Professor Cross also concerns a case where there is a 3:2 majority. Two judges opt for reason A, one for reason B and the two dissidents opt for reason C, but this time each of the judges in the majority expresses disapproval of reason C (see Figure 12.7).

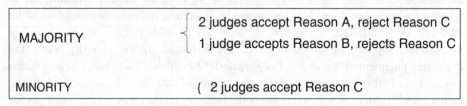

MAJORITY	2 judges accept Reason A, reject Reason C
	1 judge accepts Reason B, rejects Reason C
MINORITY	{ 2 judges accept Reason C

Figure 12.7

[12.113] In these circumstances, Professor Cross suggested that reason A forms the *ratio decidendi* of the case. It cannot be reason B as it is supported by only one judge and reason C, having been condemned by three judges, could not be the *ratio* of the case. It could be said that reason A is acceptable as being that which is least objectionable and formed part of the majority reasoning – in fact, it was supported by a 'majority of the majority'. To some extent, this issue is determined by later decisions, as can be illustrated by recent judicial practice in the Supreme Court and High Court concerning the decision in *The People (DPP) v O'Shea*.[252] In *O'Shea*, it was held by a 3:2 majority of the Supreme Court, comprising O'Higgins CJ, Walsh and Hederman JJ, with Finlay P and Henchy J dissenting, that the prosecution may appeal to the Supreme Court from an acquittal in the Central Criminal Court. In the course of the judgments two members of the majority, O'Higgins CJ and Walsh J, suggested that the Supreme Court could order a retrial in the event of a successful appeal (reason A) while the remaining member of the majority, Hederman J, reserved his opinion on that question, merely holding that an appeal lay (reason B). The two dissenting judges, Finlay P and Henchy J, held that the prosecution does not enjoy a right of appeal (reason C). In *The People (DPP) v O'Shea (No 2)*[253] the Supreme Court, comprising the same judges, unanimously held that the DPP's appeal should be dismissed on the ground that the acquittal, which had been directed by the trial judge, had been correct as there was insufficient evidence presented by the prosecution to justify putting the case to the jury. Thus, the question whether a retrial could or should be ordered did not arise. However, on Professor Cross's analysis, part of the *ratio* of *O'Shea* is that the Supreme Court may order a retrial following a successful prosecution appeal.[254]

[12.114] Just over five years later, in *The People (DPP) v Quilligan and O'Reilly (No 2)*[255] the court, again comprising five judges but with two changes in personnel, had to consider that very issue. Walsh and McCarthy JJ considered that *O'Shea* had dealt with the matter authoritatively in favour of the proposition that the court had the power to order a retrial (reason A). This is consistent with Professor Cross's analysis. By contrast Henchy J, with whom Griffin J agreed, observed that only two of the judges in *O'Shea* had supported that proposition and concluded that the point was still undecided, an approach which is at odds with Professor Cross's analysis. Henchy and Griffin JJ concluded that the court did not possess the power to order a retrial following a successful prosecution appeal (reason C). The fifth judge in *The People (DPP) v Quilligan and O'Reilly (No 2)*, Hederman J, again reserved his opinion on this issue, merely holding that a retrial should not be ordered in the case, but without considering the issue further (reason B).

[12.115] One of two alternative conclusions can be drawn from this. The first is that Henchy and Griffin JJ in *Quilligan and O'Reilly (No 2)* misinterpreted the *ratio* of

---

252 *People (DPP) v O'Shea* [1982] IR 384.

253 *People (DPP) v O'Shea (No 2)* [1983] ILRM 592.

254 See also Hogan, 'Criminal Appeals – a New Departure' (1983) 5 DULJ (ns) 254, fn 2 considering another aspect of the *ratio decidendi*, namely the type of acquittals which are capable of being appealed, and applying Professor Cross's analysis.

255 *People (DPP) v Quilligan and O'Reilly (No 2)* [1989] IR 46. In *The People (DPP) v Quilligan and O'Reilly* [1986] IR 495, the Supreme Court had held that the acquittals in that case, again directed by the trial judge, had been based on an incorrect interpretation of the law. The trial judge had held that the defendants' arrests under s 30 of the Offences against the State Act 1939 were invalid since the crimes of which they were suspected did not involve a subversive element. The Supreme Court held that s 30 was sufficiently wide to include non-subversive crime.

O'Shea and, applying the analysis of Professor Cross, ought to have adopted the remarks of O'Higgins CJ and Walsh J, as was done by Walsh and McCarthy JJ in *Quilligan and O'Reilly (No 2)*. The other is that Professor Cross's analysis does not reflect the position in Ireland and that to acquire the status of *ratio* a proposition must secure the support of an outright majority of the judges who decided the case, not just a majority of the majority. Judicial support for this proposition can be found in in *Pringle v Government of Ireland*.[256]

[12.116] In a later decision of the High Court, *Considine v Shannon Regional Fisheries Board*,[257] *O'Shea* was considered again. In *Considine*, Costello J rejected a constitutional challenge to the validity of s 310 of the Fisheries (Consolidation) Act 1959, which provides for an appeal against an acquittal in a summary prosecution under the Act. The Shannon Regional Fisheries Board had issued a summons against the plaintiff under the 1959 Act, alleging various breaches of the Act. The summons was dismissed in the District Court and the Board appealed to the Circuit Court under s 310. The plaintiff argued that s 310 was invalid on the ground that it was in conflict with Article 38.1 of the Constitution, which provides that '[n]o person shall be tried on any criminal charge save in due course of law', and contended that a trial in the Circuit Court after an acquittal in the District Court would not be conducted 'in due course of law'. In support of s 310, it was urged that Article 38.1 should be read in conjunction with Article 34.3.4° of the Constitution, which provides that '[t]he courts of first instance shall also include courts of local and limited jurisdiction with a right of appeal as determined by law' and that this contemplated the form of appeal in s 310 of the 1959 Act. It was also argued that one of the *rationes* of *O'Shea* was that Article 38.1 should not be interpreted as limiting the appellate jurisdiction of the courts, and that this was binding on Costello J as a High Court judge. Costello J accepted this latter argument.

[12.117] We have already noted that Costello J referred in *Considine* to the difficulty of determining the *ratio* or *rationes* of a particular decision.[258] In relation to *O'Shea* itself, he noted two points which distinguished it from *Considine*. First, *O'Shea* had concerned Article 34.4.3°, which dealt with the appellate jurisdiction of the Supreme Court, whereas Article 34.3.4°, which was at issue in *Considine*, concerns, *inter alia*, appeals to the Circuit Court from the District Court. Second, *O'Shea* dealt with the right of appeal from a verdict of a jury in a criminal trial in the Central Criminal Court, whereas *Considine* involved an appeal from a summary trial in the District Court. Despite these differences, he held that a number of legal principles laid down by the Supreme Court were binding on him. For present purposes, we refer only to the issue raised in *O'Shea*

---

[256] *Pringle v Government of Ireland* [2012] IESC 47 *per* Hardiman J: '[i]t will also be necessary to distil if possible a single *ratio* from the three majority judgment'; *per* O'Donnell J: '[t]he *ratio decidendi* of a decision made by a collegiate court is in my view to be determined by that proposition, or reason, which decides the particular case and on which, it can be said, a majority of the court is agreed.'

[257] *Considine v Shannon Regional Fisheries Board* [1994] 1 ILRM 499.

[258] See para **12.89**.

as to whether Article 34.4.3° (as it then was)[259] was limited by Article 38.1. Costello J noted that O'Higgins CJ and Walsh J had expressly rejected this point, as indeed they had rejected the suggestion that Article 34.4.3° was limited by Article 38.5. Costello J also noted in *Considine* that the judgment of Hederman J, which he described as '[t]he third judgment making up the majority of the court', had not expressly dealt with this point, but Costello J commented that 'by implication, he must have agreed with the conclusion of his colleagues'. In light of Hederman J's continued reservations on *O'Shea* as expressed in *Quilligan and O'Reilly (No 2)*, this comment is surprising.

[12.118] Nonetheless, Costello J concluded his judgment as follows:

"It seems to me that the decision of the Supreme Court is that Article 38.1 of the Constitution does not constitute an exception to the right of the appellate jurisdiction of the Supreme Court conferred by Article 34.4.3°. It is true that the Supreme Court was not dealing with Article 34.3.4° and was not dealing with an appeal from the District Court to the Circuit Court. However, it seems to me that the principle of law established by the Supreme Court's decision must apply with equal force to the provisions of that Article and I must therefore hold that in the light of the *O'Shea* case it has now been established that Article 38.1 would not prohibit an appeal under Article 34.3.4° from the District Court to the Circuit Court. Bound as I am by the principle established in the *O'Shea* case, I must therefore dismiss the plaintiff's claim."[260]

[12.119] It is difficult to say with any certainty whether Costello J's judgment in *Considine* supports or rejects Professor Cross's analysis of the *ratio decidendi* in a multiple judgment case such as *O'Shea*. While Costello J accepted that the point at issue had been dealt with expressly only by O'Higgins CJ and Walsh J, he sought to add a third judge, Hederman J, to make a majority of three. Ultimately, perhaps the most that can be said is that *O'Shea* – and any case like it – is authority only for the particular point that it decided, but what that point actually is remains a matter for later courts to determine. In *Considine*, Costello J in effect held that *O'Shea* had determined at least four issues definitively: that an appeal against an acquittal in the Central Criminal Court lay to the Supreme Court; that Article 34.4.3° is not limited by Article 38.5; that Article 34.4.3° is not limited by Article 38.1; and that Article 34.3.4° is not limited by Article 38.1. The last point was, of course, not addressed in *O'Shea*, but Costello J nonetheless felt bound to come to that conclusion and to hold that s 310 of the Fisheries (Consolidation) Act 1959 was not invalid. To the extent that discussion of the *ratio decidendi* is descriptive, in that it attempts to focus on actual judicial practice, it would seem best to bear in mind Costello J's comment in *Considine* that 'the principle of precedent can be stated easily but may be difficult to apply in practice'.

[12.120] A final point about multi-judge decisions concerns the very rare case where the court divides evenly. This can occur when one of the judges dies during the course of the

---

[259] Article 34.4.3° has been deleted following the establishment of the Court of Appeal. A new provision, Article 34.4.1°, sets out the jurisdiction of the Court of Appeal while the jurisdiction of the Supreme Court is outlined in the new Article 34.5.3°.
[260] [1994] 1 ILRM 499 at 503.

hearing or must absent himself or herself for some other unavoidable reason. Where an appellate court divides evenly the decision of the lower court stands. The problem, however, of determining the *ratio* in such an event remains. It would be tempting to select the reasoning of the judges who voted to dismiss the appeal as their judgments prevailed, but that would be to allow an external event, which inadvertently deprived the court of the ability to form a majority, to shape the *ratio* of the decision. A solution which was proposed by Ó Dálaigh CJ in *Rexi Irish Mink Ltd v Dublin County Council*[261] is that in such a case the question of law is still undecided and the later court must determine which of the two views suggested should be adopted.

Significance of *obiter dicta*

[12.121] As noted earlier, a statement of law which is not binding is called an *obiter dictum*. It consists of anything said by the earlier court which is not considered to be directly relevant or essential to the decision. However, although *obiter dicta* are not binding they are significant as they are of persuasive authority. They may be adopted or followed at the option of the later court. The weight, or value, of an *obiter dictum* depends on a variety of factors, including the court in which it was delivered, the reputation of the judge who delivered it,[262] how it has been dealt with in subsequent cases and its closeness to the instant case.

[12.122] It is not unusual for a statement which was *obiter* in one case to be adopted as a correct statement of law in, and thus to form the *ratio* of, a subsequent case. In effect, the later court adopts the statement and bases its decision on it. In *A v Governor of Arbour Hill Prison*,[263] a Supreme Court decision that involved consideration of the retrospective effect of a declaration that an Act of the Oireachtas is unconstitutional, Murray CJ stated:

> "Although the Court, in the majority judgment [*The State (Byrne) v Frawley*], clearly considered that it was not necessary to address the general question of retrospectivity given the particular facts of the case it nonetheless thought it important enough to state, even by way of *obiter dicta*, that there may be limitations on the retrospective effect of a declaration that an Act is unconstitutional, particularly as concerns previous decided cases ... Notwithstanding the allusion to a similar approach in the United States it is clearly intended to be a statement, albeit *obiter*, of the position in Irish law. I have no doubt it is a correct one."

---

[261] [1972] IR 123, 130.
[262] See, eg the remarks of Fennelly J in *The People (DPP) v Gilligan (No 3)* [2006] 3 IR 273, 294: 'The judgment of Walsh J is, therefore, *obiter*. It does not constitute a binding precedent for the interpretation of section 29. Nonetheless, like any pronouncement of that great judge, it deserves respect and careful consideration.'
[263] *A v Governor of Arbour Hill Prison* [2006] 4 IR 88.

Likewise, in *Clinton v An Bord Pleanála*[264] an *obiter* statement of Walsh J concerning the right of appeal under s 29 of the Courts of Justice Act 1924 was consistently applied as stating the law. Denham J stated:

"In *People (Attorney General) v Giles*[265] Walsh J held that although the granting of the certificate gives the right of appeal the certificate does not limit the scope of the appeal. While the words of Walsh J were *obiter dicta* they have been accepted and acted upon for decades."

In *The State (Raftis) v Leonard*[266] Murnaghan J followed two pre-1922 decisions, which he was otherwise reluctant to do, as they had been approved of, *obiter*, by the Supreme Court in *Walsh v Minister for Local Government*.[267] He did not feel free to adopt his own interpretation as the views of the Supreme Court should, in his opinion, be 'given the weight of an opinion of the Court and, as such, an acceptance that the law was as stated therein'.[268]

[12.123] On the other hand, it should be noted that the classification of a statement of law as being *obiter* could be contentious. In some cases a court's declaration that an earlier judicial opinion is *obiter* frees it from following what might otherwise be thought to be binding. This, in essence, is what occurred in *The People (DPP) v Shaw*[269] where Griffin J (in whose judgment three other judges concurred) argued that the remarks of Walsh J on the inadmissibility of unconstitutionally obtained evidence in *The People (Attorney General) v O'Brien*,[270] which had been followed in a number of cases, were in essence *obiter*. He stated that:

"the test for the admissibility of such statements, in so far as it was propounded in *O'Brien's case*, was in terms which went beyond the issue presented to the Court in that case; it therefore lacks the authoritativeness that it would possess if it were a necessary element of the *ratio decidendi* of that decision."[271]

[12.124] And later he argued that:

"the *ratio decidendi* of *O'Brien's case* goes no further than to lay down that where real evidence has been procured by illegal means, it falls within the discretion of the trial judge to decide whether public policy, based on a balancing of public interests, requires that such evidence be excluded. The specific and narrow issue involved in the case prevented its decision from being a vehicle in which to convey an authoritative and binding ruling on the

---

[264] *Clinton v An Bord Pleanála* [2007] 1 IR 272.
[265] *People (Attorney General) v Giles* [1974] IR 422, 430.
[266] *State (Raftis) v Leonard* [1960] IR 381, 419.
[267] *Walsh v Minister for Local Government* [1929] IR 377.
[268] See also *The State (Lynch) v Cooney* [1982] IR 337 at 380, *per* Henchy J cited at para **12.49**.
[269] *People (DPP) v Shaw* [1982] IR 1.
[270] *People (Attorney General) v O'Brien* [1965] IR 142.
[271] [1982] IR 1 at 58.

test for the admission in evidence of oral, written, or other forms of statements tendered as confessions or admissions."[272]

[12.125] In *The People (DPP) v Lynch*[273] a differently constituted Supreme Court took issue with these remarks. O'Higgins CJ disagreed with Griffin J's interpretation of the decision in *O'Brien*:

"I fear that I cannot agree with these views, either in relation to the ambit of the decision in *O'Brien's case* or in relation to the generality of the test which he suggests for the admission or exclusion of statements."[274]

[12.126] In the same case Walsh J in effect classified Griffin J's remarks as being themselves *obiter* when he observed that:

"It was not submitted in *Shaw's case*, nor was it the subject of any argument addressed to the Court, that *O'Brien's case* did not apply to statements or admissions made by an accused person."[275]

In other words, a point not argued is a point not decided.

[12.127] The Supreme Court returned to this issue some years later. In *The People (DPP) v Healy*[276] McCarthy J observed that Griffin J's remarks were 'not necessary for the decision in *Shaw*'.[277] Griffin J in turn re-iterated his earlier opinion:

"I have had the advantage of reading in advance the judgment which McCarthy J is about to deliver. In it he expresses the opinion that the examination of *The People (Attorney General) v O'Brien* in *The People (DPP) v Shaw*, and its reasoning, was not necessary for the decision in *Shaw's case*. I respectfully disagree. As in this case, the admissibility of the statements made by the defendant was directly in issue in *Shaw's case*. In the court of trial, the Court of Criminal Appeal, and in this Court the arguments advanced rested substantially on the principles enunciated by Kingsmill Moore J and Walsh J, who respectively delivered the leading majority and minority judgments in that case. It therefore became necessary for this Court to consider the extent to which the principles enunciated in the judgments in that case constituted a binding decision as to the tests to be applied in relation to the admissibility of statements made by the defendant. That was then my opinion and that of my colleagues who concurred in my judgment, and I see no reason to resile from what I said on the issue in *Shaw's case*. Further, although in this appeal substantial extracts from the judgments in *Shaw's case* were cited by counsel for both parties at no time was there any argument or submission from counsel on either side that the examination of *O'Brien's case* or its reasoning was not necessary for the decision in that case."[278]

---

272 [1982] IR 1 at 60.
273 *People (DPP) v Lynch* [1982] IR 64.
274 [1982] IR 64 at 77.
275 [1982] IR 64 at 83.
276 *People (DPP) v Healy* [1990] 2 IR 73.
277 [1990] 2 IR 73 at 90.
278 [1990] 2 IR 73 at 85.

[12.128] When the majority in *The People (DPP) v Kenny*[279] took a different view to that enunciated in *Shaw*, Griffin J remained unmoved:

"My judgment in *The People (DPP) v Shaw*[280] had the support of Henchy J, Kenny J and Parke J. Having carefully considered all the arguments advanced in this case I can see no reason why I should resile from what I said in that case."[281]

[12.129] Another difference of opinion emerged between the judges in *Shaw*. Griffin J suggested that observations which were made in *The People (Attorney General) v Conmey*[282] to the effect that an appeal would lie from the Central Criminal Court directly to the Supreme Court were *obiter*.[283] Walsh J disagreed, stating:

"I do not think that any judge would wish any statement which he might have made casually and as mere *obiter* to be treated as necessarily being an authority on the subject in question. However, when, as in *Conmey's case*, a fundamental issue is elaborately and substantially argued and the Court thinks it necessary for the purpose of the case to make an exhaustive and deliberate examination of the law and of the relevant constitutional provisions and, in the result, to state the law, the authority of such a statement of the law cannot be got rid of simply by claiming that it was not really necessary for the actual decision of the case ... Of course, some members of any court may from time to time be less than happy with some particular decision, but any such feeling cannot acceptably warrant either ignoring the decision so elaborately argued and decided or treating it as only 'a remark by the way'."[284]

[12.130] The different evaluations of *Conmey* were considered by Professor Casey:

"This judicial controversy is unusual, and does not appear to have any parallel in the earlier case-law of the Supreme Court. Further, the techniques employed are curious. It is perfectly understandable that the *Shaw* majority – three of whom did not sit in *Conmey's case* – should wish to reconsider that decision. And it can hardly be thought inappropriate that, even by way of *dictum,* they should serve advance notice of their desire to do so. But, with respect, it seems very odd to stigmatise the majority conclusion of *Conmey's case* as *obiter* ... only on the most restrictive view could it be so considered; I might add that I know of no precedent in the common law world for the adoption of so restrictive an approach.

The desire to categorise the *Conmey* majority's conclusion as *obiter* is most interesting from the standpoint of judicial psychology. As is well known, the Supreme Court has power to overrule its own previous decisions (as well as those of its predecessors as final courts of appeal). And the present court has indicated that it is quite prepared to invoke this power in constitutional cases, as it has already done in others. But the court nonetheless seems to prefer to eschew overruling, and to rely instead on traditional, less direct methods to avoid following its earlier decisions. Thus in *State (Harkin) v O'Malley*[285] the court was at pains to

---

[279] *People (DPP) v Kenny* [1990] 2 IR 110.
[280] *The People (DPP) v Shaw* [1965] IR 142.
[281] [1990] 2 IR 110 at 137.
[282] *People (Attorney General) v Conmey* [1975] IR 341.
[283] [1982] IR 1 at 47.
[284] [1982] IR 1 at 44.
[285] *State (Harkin) v O'Malley* [1978] IR 269.

show that *The People (Attorney General) v Doyle*[286] was not binding because (a) it was given without jurisdiction, and (b) it was a decision *per incuriam*.

It is doubtful, however, whether such an oblique approach is available in regard to *Conmey's case*. It can scarcely be categorised as a precedent *sub silentio,* since that term is employed only where a point appears to have been decided, though without argument or specific mention in the judgment(s). Nor can it properly be regarded as a decision *per incuriam;* this refers only to decisions given in ignorance of a statute or previous case in point. In *Morelle Ltd v Wakeling*[287] the English Court of Appeal declined to extend the *per incuriam* rule to cases in which the argument was not as full as it might have been. Now it is into this category, if any, that *Conmey's case* falls, since a number of relevant points do not appear to have been raised. Among these are: that "no appeal against acquittal" was so familiar a principle in 1937 that the Constitution must be taken to have assumed its continuance in force; that for the Supreme Court to enter a conviction in an appeal against acquittal would deny the accused the jury trial required by Article 38.5; and that a Constitution which guarantees equal protection should not be construed so as to subject one class of acquitted defendants to a form of double jeopardy. These considerations would justify reconsidering *Conmey's case* and, perhaps, overruling it; but they cannot justify anything short of this."[288]

[12.131] Different views of the *ratio decidendi* are implicit in the various remarks in *Shaw* and *Lynch*. Griffin J emphasised the role of the later court, in effect stating that it is for that court to determine what was necessary for the decision. On the other hand, Walsh J highlighted the controlling role of the court which decided the case and its views of what was necessary for the decision. Correspondingly, there is a difference in their views on the freedom of a later court to treat a proposition of law as *obiter*. Nevertheless, the cases demonstrate the emergence of different bodies of judicial opinion on the particular rules involved and the willingness of each 'side' to interpret earlier cases in a manner which denies authority to conflicting propositions of law. In this respect, a cynic could be led to the conclusion that the attribution of that status of *obiter dictum* to a proposition of law is little more than a device to evade the application of a statement of law which the court dislikes.[289]

Evolution of principles

[12.132] So far we have been considering how the *ratio decidendi* of an earlier decision can be discovered and it is clear that a significant role is played by later courts. In this

---

[286] *People (Attorney General) v Doyle* (1964) 101 ILTR 136.

[287] *Morelle Ltd v Wakeling* [1955] 2 QB 379.

[288] 'Criminal Appeals: the Confusion Persists' (1981) 16 Ir Jur (ns) 271 at 273–274; see by the same author 'Confusion in Criminal Appeals: the Legacy of *Conmey*' (1975) 10 Ir Jur (ns) 300.

[289] The remarks attributed to Lord Asquith (1950) 1 JSPTL 359 seem apposite: 'The rule is quite simple, if you agree with the other bloke you say it is part of the *ratio*; if you don't you say it is *obiter dictum*, with the implication that he is a congenital idiot.'

respect, the expression '*ratio decidendi*' can be understood in two senses and, indeed, some writers have suggested that it has two meanings. Professor Montrose wrote that:

"(1) The phrase sometimes signifies the rule of law propounded by the judge as the basis of his ultimate decision of the case ... (2) The phrase is sometimes used to mean the rule of law for which the case is of binding authority."[290]

[12.133] Professor Stone wrote of a distinction between:

"that use of the term *ratio decidendi* which describes the process of reasoning by which decision was reached (the 'descriptive' *ratio decidendi*) and that which identifies and delimits *the* reasoning which a later court is bound to follow (the 'prescriptive' or 'binding' *ratio decidendi*) ... This descriptive *ratio decidendi* may, of course, itself be sought at various levels; it may for instance be limited to the verbal behaviour of the judge, or it may seek to embrace the level of his total behaviour. Prescriptively used, on the other hand, the phrase *ratio decidendi* refers to a normative judgment requiring us to choose a particular *ratio decidendi* as legally required to be drawn from the prior case, that is, the binding *ratio decidendi*."[291]

[12.134] Professor Glanville Williams wrote:

"The phrase 'the *ratio decidendi* of a case' is slightly ambiguous. It may mean either (1) the rule that the judge who decided the case intended to lay down and apply to the facts, or (2) the rule that a later court concedes him to have had the power to lay down. The last sentence is rather clumsy, but what I mean is this. Courts do not accord to their predecessors an unlimited power of laying down wide rules ... One circumstance that may induce a court to adopt [a] niggling attitude towards an earlier decision is the necessity of reconciling that decision with others. Or again, the court in the earlier case may have enunciated an unduly wide rule without considering all its possible consequences, some of which are unjust or inconvenient or otherwise objectionable. Yet another possibility is that the earlier decision is altogether unpalatable to the court in the later case, so that the latter court wishes to interpret it as narrowly as possible."[292]

[12.135] Not all commentators agree with these observations,[293] but nevertheless they do contain an essential truth, namely that the formulation of the *ratio decidendi* is the combined result of that which occurs in the court which decided the case and later courts. In a sense what is said by the court deciding the case is the raw material which is used by later courts to assemble the *ratio decidendi*. When a later court attempts to extract a binding proposition from an earlier case it examines the reasoning of the earlier court. The rule which is divined from the earlier case is the product of the reasoning in that case. This dimension to the *ratio decidendi* has been noted by O'Donnell J in *Gillen v Commissioner of An Garda Síochána*:

"An analysis of [*McNeill v The Commissioner of An Garda Síochána, Ireland and the Attorney General*][294] and its subsequent treatment by the Superior Courts would be a modest

---

290   'The *Ratio Decidendi* of a Case' (1957) 20 MLR 587 at 588.
291   'The *Ratio* of the *Ratio Decidendi*' (1959) 22 MLR 597 at 600–601 (reference omitted).
292   *Learning the Law* (12th edn, 2002), p 103.
293   See, eg Cross and Harris, *Precedent in English Law* (4th edn, 1991), pp 72–74.
294   *McNeill v The Commissioner of An Garda Síochána, Ireland and the Attorney General* [1997] 1 IR 469.

but illuminating topic for an undergraduate class on legal systems and the doctrine of precedent. However, it does not seem that the specific issue raised here – whether the obligations imposed by the Regulations are mandatory or directory – was argued in that case. That is apparent not only from the report of the argument of counsel in the official reports, but also from the fact that the issue was not addressed either in the dissenting judgment of Denham J. (as she then was) or in the concurring judgment of O'Flaherty J. The mandatory/directory issue in statutory interpretation is well recognised, and if it was the dispositive issue in the case, it is impossible that it would not have been addressed specifically by both judges. Even though Hamilton C.J. referred to the provisions as 'mandatory' it is open to considerable doubt as to whether he had the mandatory/directory distinction in mind. In other words, although one judge used the term 'mandatory', it cannot be said that the *ratio decidendi* of the case – in the sense of the reasons given by the court for its decision – was that the Regulations were mandatory rather than directory. At yet another level, however, the *ratio* of a case is to be determined by an analysis of what the court did, rather than what it said. In this regard, I accept that it is possible to analyse the case as necessarily involving a conclusion that the requirements of Regulation 8 were mandatory. Even at that level, however, the fact that the issue was not explicitly expressed in argument, and was not to the forefront of the minds of the court deciding the case, robs the case of much of its precedential effect. At a still further level, the *ratio* of any case, and its binding effect, is determined not by what the court itself decides, or indeed any independent analysis of the decision, but rather the manner in which subsequent courts treat the decision. It is accordingly necessary to consider the subsequent case law."[295]

[12.136] As more cases are decided the rule becomes more detailed and, in effect, the courts are engaged in the process of adding flesh to what initially was a skeletal rule. Rules are not static but evolve through the course of litigation. In this way, the operation of the system of precedent does not result in the stagnation of rules. The process of adjudication as much involves the creation of law as it does the application of law.[296] The system possesses a flexibility which requires later courts to make choices. The later court must select a binding proposition from a range of canvassed alternatives. As those choices are made rules are defined and redefined, their scope being expanded and contracted. This is not to say that later courts are presented with unrestricted choices or that the process results in a form of judicial anarchy. Whilst a case might present choices, the freedom of the later court is constrained within parameters set by the reasoning in the earlier case from which the relevant legal principle is extracted. If, in categorising that principle, the court makes unreasonable distinctions or is irrational in its analysis, it runs the risk that its decision will in turn be ignored; indeed such reasoning would support the conclusion that the decision is 'clearly erroneous', thus providing a 'compelling reason' to overrule it. For instance, were a court to disregard the earlier case on the grounds that it governed injuries caused by a Rolls Royce and not by

---

[295] *Gillen v Commissioner of An Garda Síochána* [2012] IESC 3.

[296] See Fernandez and Ponzetto, '*Stare Decisis*: Rhetoric and Substance' (2012) 28 JLE&O 313: 'Thus, *stare decisis* serves two seemingly contradictory purposes: on the one hand, it endows case law with consistency and predictability; on the other, it provides for its gradual evolution.'

other cars it would not be followed in later cases – we would all agree that the manufacture of the car which caused injury is immaterial to a rule which governs injuries caused by cars.

[12.137] By identifying similarities and placing cases in the same category, the law develops through a process of reasoning by analogy, a point which was acknowledged by Costello J in *D v C*.[297] Moreover, although courts, by interpreting cases, can revise rules, they are not entitled to ignore precedents or, where binding, to overrule them. A court must accept the rule which has been determined in earlier cases and is permitted to define its scope in a manner which is reasonable and is not spurious or arbitrary. Developments in new cases must be consistent with earlier cases and the pattern which emerges is one of the law gently ebbing and flowing rather than of sudden tempestuous alterations which depend on the whims of particular judges.[298]

[12.138] When we speak of the law evolving gradually, it must be realised that its development does not follow a planned or predetermined course. In exercising choice courts select the directions in which the law should develop. The system of precedent operates to channel that development within certain constraints. The requirement that earlier cases be followed ensures that new developments are accommodated within the pre-existing law. Thus, a court's reasoning is both retrospective and prospective. In the former sense the court attempts to justify a new decision as being consistent with the old law. It invokes earlier cases in support of its decision. In this context *stare decisis* operates as a standard by which to evaluate the legitimacy, or permissibility, of new decisions. A decision which is perceived as being unsupported by preceding cases will itself be rejected in later cases. At the same time, however, the court's reasoning is prospective in that it contains a set of options from which later courts will choose. And later courts will repeat the exercise when they come to consider the legal issues which are raised by that decision. Thus, as old questions are settled new ones are raised and the process continues unabated, surviving as the central feature of our legal system.

Precedent and legislation

[12.139] It is clear that the operation of the principle of *stare decisis* is sufficiently flexible to allow for the development of rules through the process of adjudication. The system operates in a manner which validates new developments which are capable of being considered to be warranted or authorised by the old law. Nevertheless, the potential for judicially engineered change is limited and in many instances other law-

---

[297] *D v C* [1984] ILRM 173, 189. See also *UF (orse UC) v JC* [1991] 2 IR 330 at 357, *per* Finlay CJ approving Costello J's reasoning and use of analogy.

[298] See Bartholomew, 'Unreported Judgments in the House of Lords' (1983) 133 NLJ 781: 'The somewhat amoeboid principles of the common law grow or are restrained by their application, re-application or non-application to various fact situations. They are re-phrased, re-stated and re-iterated over and over again, and what eventually emerges is often startlingly different from that from which one started. The great principle of the common law in this context is that "great oaks from little acorns grow" this is the *leitmotif* of the judicial process.'

making mechanisms, most notably legislation, must be employed to effect the change sought. The expansion of liability for negligence is probably the most significant common law development of the 20th century and might be attributed to judicial reaction to changing social and economic conditions. But the development that occurred was consistent, or could be construed as being consistent, with the pre-existing law of civil liability. Thus, for instance, the common law retained the principle that liability should be based on fault and it would probably have been beyond the judicial capacity to have replaced it with a system of recovery based on welfare principles. That latter development would have involved too fundamental a change from the old law to have been validly undertaken through the adjudicative system.

[12.140] Moreover, certain common law rules proved to be incapable of amendment or elimination by judicial action. The doctrine of common employment relieved employers of vicarious liability when an employee was injured by the negligence of a fellow employee[299] – in other words a worker injured in those circumstances could not recover damages from his employer, a rule which was rightly condemned as being a 'nefarious judicial ploy'.[300] The doctrine was developed at common law, proved resistant to judicial change and was ultimately abandoned by legislation.[301] Likewise, at common law contributory negligence on the part of the plaintiff was an absolute defence to recovery. This rule was incorporated into Irish law[302] and while it was judicially modified[303] its eventual reform was effected by statute.[304] On the other hand, the rule which limited an occupier's duty of care to a trespasser was altered by the Supreme Court in *McNamara v Electricity Supply Board*;[305] that decision resulted in such an expansion of occupiers' liability that it was later curtailed by statute.[306]

[12.141] It is by no means clear why some common law rules resist judicial change while others are freely altered by the courts. It might have been thought that the old rules on common employment, contributory negligence and occupiers' liability enjoyed a similar degree of immutability yet, as we have seen, the latter was altered by the courts, but the first two were not. The explanation lies in a variety of factors which cumulatively facilitated judicial alteration in one case but not the others – developments in other neighbouring branches of the law, the willingness of courts to adapt in the light of changing social circumstances, the strictness of judicial adherence to *stare decisis* and,

---

[299] See McMahon and Binchy, *Law of Torts* (3rd edn, 2000), pp 479–480; the origin of the doctrine is attributed to an English decision *Priestly v Fowler* (1837) 3 M & W 1 and was adopted by the Irish courts; see, eg *Waldson v Junior Army and Navy Stores* [1910] 2 IR 318; *Feeney v Pollexfen & Co Ltd* [1931] 589.

[300] Fleming, *The Law of Torts* (9th edn, 1998), p 570.

[301] Law Reform (Personal Injuries) Act 1958, s 1.

[302] See, eg *Butterly v Mayor of Drogheda* [1907] 2 IR 134.

[303] See, eg *Logan v O'Donnell* [1925] 2 IR 211; *McGlynn v Clark* [1945] IR 495.

[304] Civil Liability Act 1961, s 34.

[305] *McNamara v Electricity Supply Board* [1975] IR 1; see para **12.37**.

[306] Occupiers' Liability Act 1995.

indeed, the judicial values and preferences of the judges involved. It is hardly an accident of fate that the alteration of the law on occupiers' liability occurred after the Supreme Court had relaxed its rule on *stare decisis* and was occupied by 'activist' judges to whom a commitment to expanding the judicial role can be attributed. Nevertheless, the precise dividing line between that which may be achieved through adjudication and that which is properly the preserve of legislation is difficult to draw and is no doubt mobile. That which at one time is considered an appropriate subject for legislation might at another be thought suitable for reform by judicial means.

[12.142] However, it is not unusual for a court, in refusing to expand the law, to express the view that the relief sought is more appropriately achieved through legislation. In *UF (orse UC) v JC*[307] Keane J, in the High Court, refused to expand the grounds of nullity of marriage stating:

> "[I]f the judgments to which I have already referred correctly state the law, we have moved with remarkable abruptness to a position where a decree of nullity can now be granted in any case where the court concludes that a spouse because of an emotional disability or incapacity at the time of the marriage was unable to enter into and sustain a normal marital relationship. And all this, although the Oireachtas has studiously and for whatever reasons declined to implement in any way the report of the Attorney General on *The Law of Nullity in Ireland*[308] recommending that legislation should be introduced to deal with unfitness for marriage arising from mental disorder existing at the date of the solemnisation of the marriage and the report of the Law Reform Commission[309] recommending changes in the law, including a change relating to homosexuality which would enable the petitioner in this case to obtain relief. I am forced to the conclusion, which I reach with all respect to the High Court judges who have taken a different view, that to formulate new grounds for nullity in the manner suggested constitutes an impermissible assumption of the legislative function which Article 15.2.1° of the Constitution vests exclusively in the Oireachtas. I take that view mindful of the admonition of Fitzgerald CJ in *Maher v Attorney General*[310] at p 148 of the report that:
>
>> 'The usurpation by the judiciary of an exclusively legislative function is no less unconstitutional than the usurpation by the legislature of an exclusively judicial function.'
>
> Or as McMahon J put it with characteristic terseness in *M (orse G) v M*[311] when declining to entertain a new ground of nullity (of a far more confined and specific nature):
>
>> 'For the courts to add new grounds would be to engage in legislation'."[312]

---

307 *UF (orse UC) v JC* [1991] 2 IR 330.

308 Prl 5626, 1976.

309 *Report on Nullity in Marriage* (LRC 9-1984).

310 *Maher v Attorney General* [1973] IR 140.

311 *M (orse G) v M* [1986] ILRM 515.

312 [1991] 2 IR 330, 347–48; see also *Hynes-O'Sullivan v O'Driscoll* [1989] ILRM 349, *per* Henchy J cited at para **12.40**; *McNamara v Electricity Supply Board* [1975] IR 1 at 8, *per* FitzGerald CJ: 'If the law concerning occupiers' liability is to change, it is not our function to change it; that would be the function of the legislature.'

[12.143] In the event Keane J was overruled by the Supreme Court with Finlay CJ (for the majority) stating that their decision was 'a necessary and permissible development of the law of nullity'.[313] What to one judge is 'impermissible legislation' is to another a 'permissible development'. This discloses the existence of different views of the scope of the judicial role and its potential for creativity or what is sometimes called 'judicial activism'. It cannot be said that one approach, be it 'conservative' or 'activist', is better or more correct than another and a view which prevails at any one time itself is susceptible to being replaced by a competing approach. But it cannot be denied that, irrespective of the approach adopted by a court, the adjudicative process involves the making of choices and hence the creation of law. The declaratory theory, prevalent especially in the 19th century, that judges apply law and do not make law is no longer seriously advanced. The interpretation of a case, the effort to extract its *ratio decidendi* and the range of choice afforded to the court which is bound by it clearly demonstrate the creative potential which judges possess.

[4] PRECEDENT IN ACTION: AN EXAMPLE

[12.144] In order to put what has already been examined in context and to place it on a somewhat more understandable basis, it is helpful to see how a particular rule has developed through a series of cases. The area which we have chosen is the law governing the liability in tort of professional persons, such as doctors, solicitors and accountants. This is an area which has occupied the attention of the Irish courts in recent decades and will, no doubt, continue to do so for many years to come. First, however, some background explanation is required.

[12.145] In 1932 the House of Lords, by a 3:2 majority, delivered a landmark decision in *Donoghue v Stevenson*[314] in which it was held that a consumer, who was injured as a result of eating a contaminated food product, could sue the manufacturer in negligence. The decision is significant in that it established that the existence of a contract between the plaintiff and defendant was not necessary in order to maintain an action in negligence. In the course of his speech Lord Atkin enunciated his now-famous neighbour principle:

> "The rule that you are to love your neighbour becomes in law: You must not injure your neighbour and the lawyer's question: Who is my neighbour? receives a restricted reply. You must take reasonable care to avoid acts or omissions which you can reasonably foresee would be likely to injure your neighbour. Who then, in law, is my neighbour? The answer seems to be – persons who are so closely and directly affected by my act that I ought reasonably to have them in contemplation as being so affected when I am directing my mind to the acts or omissions which are called in question."[315]

---

[313] [1991] 2 IR 330 at 357.
[314] *Donoghue v Stevenson* [1932] AC 562.
[315] [1932] AC 562 at 580.

[12.146] Despite the broad terms in which that principle was expressed Lord Atkin also formulated the somewhat narrower proposition that:

"[A] manufacturer of products which he sells in such a form as to show that he intends them to reach the ultimate consumer in the form in which they left him, with no reasonable possibility of intermediate examination, and with the knowledge that the absence of reasonable care in the preparation or putting up of the products will result in an injury to the consumer's life or property, owes a duty to the consumer to take reasonable care."[316]

[12.147] Some years later the Irish High Court was called on to consider the very same question in *Kirby v Burke and Holloway*.[317] A woman bought some jam which was subsequently eaten by members of her family, but not by her. The jam was contaminated and those who ate it became ill. They brought an action against the vendor and the manufacturer of the jam. The action against the vendor was dismissed, but damages were awarded against the manufacturer. An interesting feature of the decision is that although the plaintiffs cited *Donoghue v Stevenson* in support of their claim, Gavan Duffy J did not adopt it but reverted to first principles:

"... the question at once arises on what principle is the alleged liability of the maker, who intended no injury and made no contract with the consumers, to be determined? The inquiry involves the ascertainment of the foundation, upon the authorities, of liability for tort at common law.

In 1869, an Irish Court, following English decisions, held on demurrer that, in the absence of fraudulent misrepresentation, the law could give no redress against the manufacturers to a man (the purchaser's servant) injured by the explosion of a boiler in a steam engine, upon an allegation that the boiler was unsafe by reason of negligence in its construction: *Corry v Lucas*.[318] The confusion and conflict in later cases in England left the basis of liability in tort at common law so uncertain that at the time of the Treaty [ie of 1922] nobody could find in case law any sure guide to the actual legal position, and I have no Irish decision to guide me.

I am thus thrown back upon first principles in the endeavour to ascertain where the line is drawn at common law between conduct resulting in unintended hurt which entails liability for damage, and conduct resulting in unintended hurt which entails no liability.

In the quandary produced by the baffling inconsistencies among the pre-Treaty judicial pronouncements, I turn from the Courts to one of the outstanding juristic studies of the 19th century, *The Common Law* by Oliver Wendell Holmes, afterwards Mr Justice Holmes of the Supreme Court of the United States. The work was published in London in 1887. The law which I apply to this case is taken from his penetrating Lectures III and IV on torts and the theory of torts.

That master of the common law shows that the foundation of liability at common law for tort is blameworthiness as determined by the existing average standards of the community; a man fails at his peril to conform to those standards. Therefore, while loss from accident generally lies where it falls, a defendant cannot plead accident if, treated as a man of

---

[316] [1932] AC 562 at 599.

[317] *Kirby v Burke and Holloway* [1944] IR 207.

[318] *Corry v Lucas* (1869) IR 3 CL 208.

ordinary intelligence and foresight, he ought to have foreseen the danger which caused injury to his plaintiff ...

The much controverted 'Case of the Snail in the Bottle', while leaving subsidiary questions open, has settled the principle of liability on a similar issue finally against the manufacturer in Great Britain. But the House of Lords established that memorable conclusion only twelve years ago in *Donoghue v Stevenson*, by a majority of three Law Lords to two, 'a Celtic majority', as an unconvinced critic ruefully observed, against an English minority. Where lawyers so learned disagreed, an Irish judge could not assume, as I was invited to assume, as a matter of course, that the view which prevailed must of necessity be the true view of the common law in Ireland. One voice in the House of Lords would have turned the scale; and it is not arguable that blameworthiness according to the actual standards of our people depends upon the casting vote in a tribunal exercising no jurisdiction over them. Hence my recourse to the late Mr Justice Holmes. His classic analysis supports the principle of Lord Atkin and the majority. And to that principle I humbly subscribe."[319]

[12.148] A certain nationalist fervour is discernible in that judgment, especially in the somewhat tongue-in-cheek remarks in the last paragraph. This might be attributed to a desire to develop an indigenous body of jurisprudence that is independent of that of the neighbouring island. In this regard, the reference to the uncertain state of English law on the matter in 1922 echoes the same judge's observations in *Exham v Beamish*[320] on the applicability of pre-1922 decisions in Ireland.[321] Despite Gavan Duffy J's refusal to adopt *Donoghue v Stevenson*, Irish courts have subsequently accepted that that decision is applicable in Ireland.

[12.149] While *Donoghue v Stevenson* dealt with the relatively narrow issue of the liability of a manufacturer, Lord Atkin's neighbour principle has been developed by later courts, and it now applies to a wide range of categories beyond that of defective products. In general, courts have focused on that principle and used it as a guide in the development of the tort of negligence.[322] By using it as a guide the courts have tended to avoid categorising the neighbour principle as being either *ratio* or *obiter*. Consideration of the development of the tort of negligence is beyond our scope and can be traced in any reputable textbook.[323]

---

[319] [1944] IR 207, 214–215.

[320] *Exham v Beamish* [1939] IR 336.

[321] See para **12.72**.

[322] See, eg *Home Office v Dorset Yacht Co Ltd* [1970] AC 1004; *Anns v London Borough of Merton* [1978] AC 728; *McNamara v Electricity Supply Board* [1975] IR 1; *Keane v Electricity Supply Board* [1981] IR 44.

[323] See McMahon and *Binchy, Law of Torts* (4th edn, 2013); Peel and Goudkamp, *Winfield and Jolowicz on Tort* (19th edn, 2014); Heuston and Buckley, *Salmond and Heuston on The Law of Torts* (21st edn, 1996); Quill, *Torts in Ireland* (3rd edn, 2009). Of the myriad of articles which *Donoghue v Stevenson* has generated we might, somewhat selectively, recommend Heuston, '*Donoghue v Stevenson* in Retrospect'(1957) 20 MLR 1; Smith and Burns, '*Donoghue v Stevenson*—the Not So Golden Anniversary' (1983) 46 MLR 147; Stapleton, 'The Gist of Negligence'(1988) 104 LQR 213 and 389; Dolding and Mullender, 'Tort Law, Incrementalism and the House of Lords' (1996) 47 NILQ 12.

[12.150] With regard to professional liability a crucial development was the decision of the House of Lords in *Hedley Byrne & Co Ltd v Heller and Partners Ltd*,[324] where it overruled the earlier Court of Appeal decision in *Candler v Crane, Christmas & Co*[325] and extended *Donoghue v Stevenson* to negligently performed professional services where there was a contractual relationship or a relationship 'equivalent to contract' between the plaintiff and defendant. Liability would arise where the defendant was aware that the plaintiff relied on his or her skill and competence. In essence, the principle applies where the plaintiff is dependent on the defendant's expertise or specialist knowledge. The decision in *Hedley Byrne* was adopted by the Irish High Court in *Securities Trust Ltd v Hugh Moore & Alexander Ltd*.[326] In that case a shareholder in the defendant company held the shares on trust for the plaintiff company. The defendant company was unaware of this arrangement. The shareholder applied to the defendant company for a copy of their memorandum and articles of association. The copy delivered contained an error, on the basis of which the plaintiff company bought shares in the defendant company at a price in excess of their market value. The investment was lost when the defendant company was wound up. The plaintiff company sued for damages for negligent misrepresentation. Davitt P considered the matter:

> "The proposition that circumstances may create a relationship between two parties in which, if one seeks information from the other and is given it, that other is under a duty to take reasonable care to ensure that the information given is correct, has been accepted and applied in the case of *Hedley Byrne & Co Ltd v Heller and Partners Ltd*, recently decided by the House of Lords. Counsel for the defendant Company did not seek to dispute the proposition."[327]

[12.151] Despite the endorsement of the decision in *Hedley Byrne* the plaintiffs were unsuccessful. In the circumstances the court held that the shareholder received the memorandum and articles of association in his capacity as a member of the company and not as agent for the plaintiffs. The defendant company was unaware of the arrangement under which the shares were held and, consequently, there was no relationship between the plaintiffs and defendant on which a duty of care could be based. The court emphasised the restricted nature of the *Hedley Byrne* duty:

> "It seems to me that there was no relationship between the parties in this case other than such as would exist between the defendant Company and any person (other than [the shareholder]) who might chance to read the copy supplied to him; or, indeed, between that Company and any member of the community at large, individual or corporate, who chanced to become aware of the last sentence in Article 155 of the defective reprint of the Memorandum and Articles. It can hardly be seriously contended that the defendant Company owed a duty to the world at large to take care to avoid mistakes and printers' errors in the reprint of their Articles. In my opinion, counsel is correct in his submission that in this case the defendant Company owed no duty to the plaintiff Company to take care to

---

[324] *Hedley Byrne & Co Ltd v Heller and Partners Ltd* [1964] AC 465.
[325] *Candler v Crane, Christmas & Co* [1951] 2 KB 164.
[326] *Securities Trust Ltd v Hugh Moore & Alexander Ltd* [1964] IR 417.
[327] *Securities Trust Ltd v Hugh More & Alexander Ltd* [1964] IR 417 at 421–422.

ensure that the copy of the Articles supplied to [the shareholder] was a correct copy. For these reasons there must, in my opinion, be judgment for the defendant Company."[328]

Application to negligent solicitors[329]

[12.152] The general principle has been applied to the case of a solicitor who neglected to initiate litigation within the statutory limitation period in *Finlay v Murtagh*.[330] The plaintiff engaged the defendant to act as his solicitor in proceedings which he sought to institute against a third party. The defendant failed to bring the proceedings within the statutory limitation period and, consequently, they became time-barred. The issue in this case was whether the plaintiff could sue in tort for negligence or whether he was confined to suing for breach of contract. At the time, tort actions in the High Court were tried by jury whereas contract actions were tried by judge alone[331] and it might have been considered that the plaintiff's prospects would be enhanced by a jury trial. The Supreme Court (O'Higgins CJ, Henchy, Griffin, Parke and Kenny JJ) unanimously held that an action in tort would lie for the negligence of a solicitor. Henchy J reviewed the earlier authorities that supported the view that the client's remedy was confined to an action for breach of contract but concluded, echoing his judgment in *McNamara v ESB*,[332] that they had been overtaken by modern developments in the law:

"In my opinion, the conclusion that an action by a client against a solicitor for damages for breach of his professional duty of care is necessarily and exclusively one in contract is incompatible with modern developments in the law of torts and should be overruled.

'... it does not follow that the client, because there is privity of contract between him and the solicitor and because he may sue the solicitor for breach of the contract, is debarred from suing also for the tort of negligence. Since the decision of the House of Lords in *Hedley Byrne & Co Ltd v Heller & Partners Ltd* and the cases following in its wake, it is clear that, whether a contractual relationship exists or not, once the circumstances are such that a defendant undertakes to show professional care and skill towards a person who may be expected to rely on such care and skill and who does so rely, then if he has been damnified by such default that person may sue the defendant in the tort of negligence for failure to show such care and skill. For the purpose of such an action, the existence of a contract is merely an incident of the relationship. If, on the one side, there is a proximity of relationship creating a general duty and, on the other, a reliance on that duty, it matters not whether the parties are bound together in contract. For instance, if the defendant in the present case had not been retained for reward but had merely volunteered his services to the plaintiff, his

---

[328] [1964] IR 417 at 422.

[329] See generally McMahon and Binchy, *Law of Torts* (4th edn, 2013), pp 574–605; O'Callaghan, *The Law of Solicitors in Ireland* (2000); Holohan and Curran, *Lawyers' Professional Negligence and Insurance* (2012); Crowley, 'Professional Negligence: the Liability of Solicitors in Negligence' (1987) 5 ILT 94; Dee, 'Professional Negligence of Solicitors' (2001) 19 ILT 282.

[330] *Finlay v Murtagh* [1979] IR 249.

[331] Jury trial in High Court civil cases was subsequently abolished in most instances; see para **4.60**.

[332] *McNamara v Electricity Supply Board* [1975] IR 1; see para **12.38**.

liability in negligence would be the same as if he was to be paid for his services. The coincidence that the defendant's conduct amounts to a breach of contract cannot affect either the duty of care or the common-law liability for its breach, for it is the general relationship, and not any particular manifestation such as a contract, that gives rise to the tortious liability in such a case: see *per* Lord Devlin in the *Hedley Byrne Case* at p 530 of the report ...

'I am satisfied that the general duty of care created by the relationship of solicitor and client entitles the client to sue in negligence if he has suffered damage because of the solicitor's failure to show due professional care and skill, notwithstanding that the client could sue alternatively in contract for breach of the implied term in the contract of retainer that the solicitor will deal with the matter in hand with due professional care and skill. The solicitor's liability in tort under the general duty of care extends not only to a client for reward, but to any person for whom the solicitor undertakes to act professionally without reward, and also to those (such as beneficiaries under a will, persons entitled under an intestacy, or those entitled to benefits in circumstances such as a claim in respect of a fatal injury) with whom he has made no arrangement to act but who, as he knows or ought to know, will be relying on his professional care and skill. For the same default there should be the same cause of action. If others are entitled to sue in tort for the solicitor's want of care, so also should the client; that is so unless the solicitor's default arises not from a breach of the general duty of care arising from the relationship but from a breach of a particular and special term of the contract in respect of which the solicitor would not be liable if the contract had not contained such a term. Thus, if the client's instructions were that the solicitor was to issue proceedings within a specified time, or to close a sale by a particular date or, generally, to do or not to do some act, and the solicitor defaulted in that respect, any resulting right of action which the client might have would be in contract only unless the act or default complained of falls within the general duty of care owed by the solicitor.

The modern law of tort shows that the existence of a contractual relationship which impliedly deals with a particular act or omission is not, in itself, sufficient to rule out an action in tort in respect of that act or omission. For instance, in *Northern Bank Finance Corporation Ltd v Charlton*[333] it was unanimously held by this Court that a customer of a bank can sue the bank for the tort of deceit where the deceit arises from fraudulent misrepresentations made by the bank in the course of carrying out the contract between the bank and the customer. The existence of a contract, for the breach of which he could have sued, did not oust the customer's cause of action in tort."[334]

[12.153] In his concurring judgment in *Finlay v Murtagh* Griffin J also reviewed the relevant cases including the principal Irish authority:

"Quite apart from the fact that *Somers v Erskine*[335] was decided without the citation of relevant authorities and on an incorrect application of the test laid down by Greer LJ in the *Jarvis Case*,[336] the decision is inconsistent with developments in the law of tort since the case was decided. It is now settled law that whenever a person possessed of a special

---

[333] *Northern Bank Finance Corporation Ltd v Charlton* [1979] IR 149.
[334] [1979] IR 249 at 255–258.
[335] *Somers v Erskine* [1943] IR 348.
[336] *Jarvis v Moy, Davies, Smith, Vanderell and Co* [1936] 1 KB 399.

knowledge or skill undertakes, quite irrespective of contract, to apply that skill for the assistance of another person who relies on such skill, a duty of care will arise: see the speech of Lord Morris of Borth-y-Gest at p 502 of the report of *Hedley Byrne and Co Ltd v Heller & Partners Ltd*.[337] At p 538 of the report Lord Pearce said:

'In terms of proximity one might say that they are in particularly close proximity to those who, as they know, are relying on their skill and care although the proximity is not contractual.'

See also Lord Hodson at p 510 and Lord Devlin at p 530 of the report. Where damage has been suffered as a result of want of such skill and care, an action in tort lies against such person, and this applies whether a contractual relationship exists or not. This doctrine applies to such professional persons as solicitors, doctors, dentists, architects and accountants. Although in the *Hedley Byrne Case* the claim was in respect of a non-contractual relationship, the statements of the Law Lords were general statements of principle, and it is clear from their speeches that they did not in any way mean to limit the general principle and that their statements were not to be confined to voluntary or non-contractual situations.

Therefore, where a solicitor is retained by a client to carry out legal business (such as litigation) on his behalf, a general relationship is established, and 'Where there is a general relationship of this sort, it is unnecessary to do more than prove its existence and the duty follows' – *per* Lord Devlin at p 530 of the report of the *Hedley Byrne Case*. If, therefore, loss and damage is caused to a client owing to the want of such care and skill on the part of a solicitor as he ought to have exercised, there is liability in tort even though there would also be a liability in contract. Even if the relationship between the solicitor and the client was a non-contractual or voluntary one, the same liability in tort would follow."[338]

[12.154] The inclusion by Griffin J of doctors, dentists, architects and accountants[339] in his judgment in *Finlay v Murtagh* indicates the broad scope of the principle which the court had in mind. It was concerned with professional advisors generally, not just solicitors. This point was reiterated by Griffin J in *Rohan Construction Ltd v Insurance Corporation of Ireland plc*:

"[I] find it difficult to see how the fact that the same act amounted to both a tort and a breach of contract could enable the insurers to avoid liability under a Professional Indemnity Policy on the basis that it was a mixed claim – if that were the true legal position, such a policy would be of little avail to a professional man, such as a solicitor, accountant, architect, engineer, doctor, dentist etc, as the same act of negligence causing damage to the client is almost invariably a breach of contract also – see for example *Finlay v Murtagh* …"[340]

---

[337] *Hedley Byrne and Co Ltd v Heller & Partners Ltd* [1964] AC 465.

[338] [1979] IR 249 at 262–263.

[339] See, eg *Kelly v Haughey Boland & Co* [1989] ILRM 373 holding, on the basis of *Hedley Byrne*, that auditors owe a duty of care to third parties who they know or ought to know might wish to invest in the company, but dismissing the claim on the facts.

[340] *Rohan Construction Ltd v Insurance Corporation of Ireland plc* [1988] ILRM 373 at 379. See also *O'Donnell v Kilsaran Concrete Ltd* [2001] 4 IR 183 at 187 *per* Herbert J, applying the principle to builders engaged to construct a dwelling house: (contd.../)

Negligently performed property transactions

[12.155] A significant proportion of a solicitor's business involves acting for clients in a variety of property transactions. Given the complexity of our land law it is highly probable that errors will occur and will be the subject of litigation by disappointed clients. *Desmond v Brophy*[341] is one such case where the two plaintiffs independently retained the first defendant as solicitor to act for them in the purchase of two flats. They informed him of their concern that deposits paid by them should not pass to the builders until completion of the flats. Both believed that he would arrange matters so that the deposits would not pass to the builders until completion of the flats. The first defendant sent the clients' deposit cheques to the builders' solicitors, intending that they hold them as stakeholder rather than as agent for the builders. He did not make this clear to the builders' solicitors who, in accordance with custom and their instructions, endorsed the cheque in favour of their clients. Before the contract was signed the builders went into liquidation and the plaintiffs lost their deposits. They sued the first defendant for negligence. The builders' solicitors were joined as defendants, by order of the Master of the High Court, and the plaintiffs made an alternative claim against them for the return of the deposits as moneys had and received. The claim against the second defendants was dismissed.

[12.156] However Barrington J held the first defendant liable:

"For many years the Incorporated Law Society had been aware of the practice of builders demanding and receiving booking deposits and of the risks which purchasers who paid such booking deposits were running. The *Solicitors' Gazette* for January/February 1977 (Vol. 71, p. 17) contained an item under the heading 'Purchasers at risk on Deposits' where the problem was discussed. This item contained the following paragraph:

'The purpose of this memorandum is to emphasise to solicitors the importance of putting on record to their clients the risks which they are taking. Clients in our experience are under the mistaken impression that once the monies are paid to a solicitor or through a solicitor they have the full protection as if their own solicitor was a stakeholder. It does, of course, seem quite unfair that the purchasers should be at risk in this way as while transactions like this might be a commercial risk to the builder, it could hardly be so described from the point of view of the purchasers.'

A similar warning was issued by Mr Wylie at para 10.133 of his book on *Irish Conveyancing Law*.[342]"

---

[340] (\...contd) '[t]he plaintiffs ... plead a cause of action in negligence as an alternative plea against the [builders]. Counsel for the defendants did not argue, and in my judgment correctly so, having regard to the statement of the law in this jurisdiction expounded by the Supreme Court in *Finlay v. Murtagh* [1979] IR 249, that the existence of a contractual relationship between parties precludes the injured party from seeking a remedy in tort on the same facts.'

[341] *Desmond v Brophy* [1985] IR 449.

[342] Wylie, *Irish Conveyancing Law* (1st edn, 1978).

... [Counsel for Mr Brophy] relied, in particular, on the dissenting judgment of Lord Justice Denning in *Burt v Claude Cousins & Co*[343] which judgment was approved of by the House of Lords when they overruled *Burr v Claude Cousins & Co* in *Sorrell v Finch*.[344]

In his judgment in *Burt v Claude Cousins & Co* Lord Justice Denning distinguishes three situations in relation to a deposit. One is where a deposit is received 'as agent for the vendor', another is where a deposit is received 'as stakeholder' and a third is where nothing is said. It may be significant that in the first two cases Lord Justice Denning refers to 'an estate agent or a solicitor' but in the third case he refers only to an estate agent. Referring to the third case he says at p 615:

'If an estate agent, before any binding contract is made, asks for and receives a deposit, giving the receipt in his own name without more, the question arises: in what capacity does he receive it? As agent for the vendor? or as stakeholder? I cannot believe that he receives it as 'agent for the vendor', for, if that were so, the estate agent would be bound to pay it over to the vendor forthwith, and the vendor alone would be answerable for its return. That cannot be right. Seeing that no contract has been made, the vendor is not entitled to a penny piece. If the estate agent should pay it over to the vendor, he does wrong; and if the vendor goes bankrupt, the estate agent is answerable for it.'

It seems to me doubtful if this kind of reasoning can be applied to the case of a solicitor. But, more important, I do not think that the present case can be resolved by such general considerations. I think the same applies to evidence which the court received concerning the practice of some solicitors who act for builders and whose practice, in the absence of clear instructions, is guided by admirable considerations of what they consider to be fair as between their builder clients and prospective purchasers in relation to the payment of booking deposits. In the present case [the builders] had formulated a clear policy in relation to booking deposits and stage payments. These deposits and payments, whether received by the estate agent or the solicitor, were to go to the builder and the solicitor had no authority to accept these deposits except as agent for the builder. The fact that these deposits would go to the builder was explained by Mr. Lynch to [the plaintiffs] when they first showed interest in buying the flats.

... It is always unfortunate when, as in the present case, the court has to decide which of two innocent persons must bear a loss. I do not think there was any lack of concern on the part of Mr Brophy for his clients' interests but unfortunately, in this case, it appears to me that he did not show reasonable professional skill in defending those interests and the clients as a result, are at a loss."[345]

[12.157] A solicitor's failure to take account of new legislation which affects his client's case has been held to amount to negligence,[346] as has a failure to advise a client of the financial implications involved in purchasing the freehold of a premises.[347] However, the mere fact that a solicitor made what in retrospect transpires to be a mistake does not

---

[343] *Burt v Claude Cousins & Co* [1971] 2 QB 426.
[344] *Sorrell v Finch* [1977] AC 728.
[345] [1985] IR 449, 452–457.
[346] *McMullen v Farrell* [1993] 1 IR 123.
[347] *Kehoe v CJ Louth & Son* [1992] ILRM 282.

render him or her liable. In *Park Hall School Ltd v Overend*[348] it was held that, given the uncertain state of the relevant law at the time, the defendant solicitors were not necessarily negligent when they made an erroneous assumption regarding the validity of a transaction in which their clients were involved. In *Fallon v Gannon*[349] the Supreme Court held that the duty of a solicitor in a case where counsel is engaged is to brief appropriate and competent counsel, to instruct counsel properly and to provide for the attendance of witnesses and other proofs. Moreover, the court stated that a solicitor does not incur vicarious responsibility for the conduct of counsel, a matter of some significance given that negligence on the part of an advocate has traditionally been considered not to attract liability.[350]

Solicitor's duty to third parties

[12.158] *Finlay v Murtagh*[351] was concerned with the duty owed by a solicitor to a paying client, but *dicta* in the case suggest that a duty would also be owed to non-paying clients and, possibly, others who are not clients but can be expected to rely on the solicitor's skill and expertise. This was an issue in *Wall v Hegarty*,[352] where the principle in *Finlay v Murtagh* was extended. The plaintiff was named as both executor and a beneficiary under a will which was prepared on behalf of the deceased by the defendants, a firm of solicitors. In the will the testator had left him a legacy of £15,000. The will was insufficiently attested and, on discovering the flaw, the next of kin challenged the validity of the will. The plaintiff had to concede that the will was invalid and accordingly he lost his legacy and incurred certain expenses as executor. He sued the defendants for negligence claiming, in essence, that the defendants owed him a duty to take care in its preparation, despite their not being in a solicitor–client relationship.

[12.159] The defendant relied on an 1861 decision of the House of Lords, *Robertson v Fleming*[353] which dismissed the idea that a solicitor would owe a duty of care to a

---

[348]   *Park Hall School Ltd v Overend* [1987] IR 1.

[349]   *Fallon v Gannon* [1988] ILRM 193.

[350]   In *Rondel v Worsley* [1969] 1 AC 191 the House of Lords held on public policy grounds that liability would not attach for negligence of a barrister in the course of litigation; this immunity was extended to solicitors who engage in advocacy; *Saif Ali v Sydney Mitchell & Co* [1980] AC 198. The is no direct Irish authority on the question of advocates' liability but observations in the case law suggest that *Rondel v Worsley* represents the Irish position: see, in particular, *W v Ireland (No 2)* [1997] 2 IR 141. The House of Lords has departed from *Rondel v Worsley* and it is now established in England that an advocate may be sued in respect of negligently conducted litigation: *Hall (Arthur JJ) & Co v Simons* [2000] 3 All ER 673. Will the Irish courts follow suit? See generally Holohan and Curran, *Lawyers' Professional Negligence and Insurance* (2012), pp 600–621. The issue was alluded to in *Beatty v Rent Tribunal* [2006] 2 IR 191 at 212 where Fennelly J observed that '[f]ormerly, barristers enjoyed complete immunity from suit by their clients in respect of their conduct of proceedings.'

[351]   *Finlay v Murtagh* [1979] IR 249.

[352]   *Wall v Hegarty* [1980] ILRM 124.

[353]   *Robertson v Fleming* (1861) 4 Macq 167.

disappointed legatee, with Lord Campbell LC memorably stating that: 'this is not the law of Scotland, nor of England, and it can hardly be the law in any country where jurisprudence has been cultivated as a science.' [354] Barrington J, in the High Court, was not persuaded and observed that the law had developed since that decision was delivered:

"Traditionally, English law did not regard a solicitor as owing any such duty to a legatee named in a testator's will and, so far as I am aware, the law of Ireland was no different in this respect. A passage which appears on p 184 of the 1961 edition of Cordery's *Law Relating to Solicitors,* puts the matter as follows:

'Since the solicitor's duty to his client is based on the contract of retainer, he owes no duty of care to anyone other than his client, save where he is liable as an officer of the court.'

The chief authority relied on, in support of that proposition was *Robertson v Fleming.*[355] That was a decision of the House of Lords in a Scottish case. It is arguable that the central question in that case was whether an issue which had been settled in the Second Division of the Court of Session properly raised the question of fact in dispute between the parties. But it is also arguable that this question of fact would have been irrelevant if a solicitor owed a duty, not only to his client, but also to the person for whose benefit his services had been retained. In any event, as Sir Robert Megarry has stated in the recent case of *Ross v Caunters,*[356] at p 304, the *dicta* whether they were of the *ratio* or not are clearly of high authority.

In that case [ie *Robertson v Fleming*], Lord Campbell LC rejected in the strongest possible terms, the suggestion that a solicitor retained by a testator might owe any duty to a legatee who was a stranger to him ...'

However, since *Robertson v Fleming* was decided, there have been two major advances in the law, material to the consideration of the present question. First was the development of negligence as an independent tort and the line of authority running from *Donoghue v Stevenson*[357] to *Hedley Byrne & Co Ltd v Heller & Partners Ltd.*[358] In particular was the famous passage in Lord Atkin's speech in *Donoghue v Stevenson*, where he stressed the duty to take reasonable care to avoid injuring one's neighbour, and went on to inquire:

'Who, then, in law is my neighbour? The answer seems to be – persons who are so closely and directly affected by my act that I ought reasonably to have them in contemplation as being so affected when I am directing my mind to the acts or omissions which are called in question.'

Lord Atkin went on to stress that the concept of 'neighbour' did not include merely persons in close physical proximity to the alleged tortfeasor; but also, all such persons as stood in such direct relationship with him, as to cause him to know that they would be directly affected by his careless act: see [1932] AC 562 at p 580.

---

354 *Robertson v Fleming* (1861) 4 Macq 167 at 177.
355 *Robertson v Fleming* (1861) 4 Macq 167.
356 *Ross v Caunters* [1980] Ch 297.
357 *Donoghue v Stevenson* [1932] AC 562.
358 *Hedley Byrne & Co Ltd v Heller & Partners Ltd* [1964] AC 465.

The second important legal development which has taken place since *Robertson v Fleming*, is that it is now finally established, so far at any rate, as the law of Ireland is concerned, that a solicitor owes two kinds of duties to his client. First, is his duty in contract to carry out the terms of his retainer. Second is a duty in tort to show reasonable professional skill in attending to his client's affairs. It is clear that this duty in tort arises simply because he is purporting to act as a solicitor for his client and is independent of whether he is providing his professional services voluntarily or for reward: see the judgment of the Supreme Court in *Finlay v Murtagh*[359] and also the judgment of Oliver J in *Midland Bank v Hett, Stubbs & Kemp*.[360]

The Supreme Court in *Finlay v Murtagh* was merely dealing with a net point of law as to whether a solicitor owed a duty to a client in tort as well as in contract, but it is quite clear that the court, in holding that he did, derived the duty from the proximity principle outlined by Lord Atkin in *Donoghue v Stevenson* '

Indeed, Henchy, J, in a passage in his judgment, appears to anticipate the situation which has arisen in the present case. He says (at p 257):

> 'The solicitor's liability in tort under the general duty of care extends not only to a client for reward, but to any person for whom the solicitor undertakes to act professionally without reward, and also to those (such as beneficiaries under a will, persons entitled under an intestacy, or those entitled to benefits in circumstances such as a claim in respect of a fatal injury) with whom he has made no arrangement to act but who, as he knows or ought to know, will be relying on his professional care and skill. For the same default there should be the same cause of action. If others are entitled to sue in tort for the solicitor's want of care, so also should the client.'

Since the decision of the Supreme Court in *Finlay v Murtagh*, the specific question which arises in the present case arose for consideration in the English High Court in the case of *Ross v Caunters*[361]...

In the present case, [counsel for] the plaintiff has relied strongly on *Ross v Caunters*. [Counsel for] the defendants has drawn the distinction that in *Ross v Caunters* there was a valid will – only the bequest was invalid – whereas in the present case there was no valid will. He has also stated that I should not, by following *Ross v Caunters*, extend the traditional boundaries of the law of negligence in this country. However, it appears to me that the decision of the English High Court in *Ross v Caunters* was already anticipated by the decision of our own Supreme Court in *Finlay v Murtagh* and, for my own part, I find the reasoning of Sir Robert Megarry in *Ross v Caunters* unanswerable ...'

The authorities are, as I said, analysed by Sir Robert Megarry with consummate ability in his judgment in *Ross v Caunters*, and it would be otiose for me to repeat here the exercise which he has carried out in his judgment. Suffice it to say that I am satisfied on the basis of the decision in *Finlay v Murtagh* that a solicitor does owe a duty to a legatee named in a draft will, to draft the will with such reasonable care and skill as to ensure that the wishes of the testator are not frustrated and the expectancy of the legatee defeated through lack of reasonable care and skill on the part of the solicitor."[362]

---

[359] *Finlay v Murtagh* [1979] IR 249.
[360] *Midland Bank v Hett, Stubbs & Kemp* [1979] Ch 384.
[361] *Ross v Caunters* [1980] Ch 297.
[362] *Wall v Hegarty* [1980] ILRM 124 at 126–129.

[12.160] In *Wall v Hegarty*[363] Barrington J went on to consider the question of the plaintiff's losses. He held that the lost bequest was not too remote and that the plaintiff could recover damages accordingly. In addition, the plaintiff was entitled to recover the probate costs he incurred as executor before being put on notice of the irregularity in the will:

> "Even therefore, if the plaintiff's loss in getting involved in legal proceedings to prove the will did not flow directly from the original carelessness in drafting the will on the principle of *Donoghue v Stevenson,* it appears to me that the loss would still be recoverable because of the fact of the circumstances in which the will was sent to the plaintiff on the principles of the *Hedley Byrne case*."[364]

Barrington J also held that the plaintiff should be entitled in principle, as executor, to recover the interest which would have been payable on the legacy, although he sought to hear further argument on its particular application in the instant case.

[12.161] The question of a solicitor's duty to a third party arose again in *Doran v Delaney*[365] where it was contended in the context of a sale of land that the vendors' solicitors owed a duty of care to the purchaser, who was represented by a different firm of solicitors. In the course of the sale of a site with planning permission the purchasers' solicitor raised a requisition enquiring whether any litigation concerning the plot was pending and whether any claims had been made in relation to the land. The vendors' solicitors, having inquired of their clients, replied 'vendor says none'. In fact, there had been an on-going dispute between the vendors and a neighbouring landowner over the ownership of a strip of land that purportedly formed part of the site being sold. The vendors' solicitors had been instructed by their clients that the matter had been settled. However, the solicitors did not inquire as to the terms of the supposed settlement either from their clients or from the law firm that had acted for the neighbour in this matter.

[12.162] As things transpired the dispute had not been resolved and it re-emerged after the sale had been completed and the purchaser had commenced building on the land. It was eventually conceded that the neighbour was owner of the disputed strip of land and as a result the purchasers were left with a landlocked site. They later sold the land to another neighbour at a loss. The purchasers sued their own solicitor, the vendors and the vendors' solicitors. In the High Court[366] Hamilton P held the purchasers' solicitors liable for negligence and breach of contract and the vendors liable for negligence, misrepresentation and breach of warranty. However, he dismissed the claim against the vendors' solicitors, which finding was appealed to the Supreme Court by the purchasers.

[12.163] The central issue on appeal was whether in the circumstances the vendors' solicitors owed a duty of care to the purchasers, who after all were represented by their own professional advisers in the matter. It was argued, however, that the vendors'

---

[363] *Wall v Hegarty* [1980] ILRM 124.

[364] [1980] ILRM 124, 130.

[365] *Doran v Delaney* [1998] 2 IR 61.

[366] [1996] 1 ILRM 490.

solicitors owed a duty to exercise reasonable care in the making of statements that they knew would be acted on by the purchasers and their solicitor. The latter, being unaware of the boundary dispute, would rely on the answers to the relevant requisitions. The counter argument was that a solicitor could not become liable to a third party simply by reason of the fact that he or she in good faith passed on information that had been supplied by his or her client. The vendors' solicitors had worded their replies in such a way as to indicate that they were doing no more than conveying their clients' instructions. It was argued that to hold the vendors' solicitors liable in these circumstances would 'be extending the duty of solicitors to third parties further than was warranted by principle or authority'.[367]

[12.164] A unanimous Supreme Court (Barrington, Keane and Barron JJ) ruled in favour of the purchasers and held the vendors' solicitors liable. Keane J outlined the applicable law:

"Again, while the primary duty of the solicitor acting for the vendor in circumstances such as arose here, is, under common law and by virtue of contract, to protect his own client, that obligation is perfectly consistent with the existence of a duty of care in certain circumstances to the purchaser.

It is also clear that the transmission by a solicitor to a third party of information which turns out to be inaccurate and upon which the third party relied to his detriment does not, of itself, afford a cause of action in negligence to the injured third party. The factors necessary to give rise to liability were set out by Jauncey LJ in the passage so frequently referred to in the present case in *Midland Bank v Cameron, Thom Peterkin and Duncans*[368] as follows at p 616:

'In my opinion four factors are relevant to a determination of the question whether in a particular case a solicitor, while acting for a client, also owed a duty of care to a third party: (1) the solicitor must assume responsibility for the advice or information furnished to the third party; (2) the solicitor must let it be known to the third party expressly or impliedly that he claims, by reason of his calling, to have the requisite skill or knowledge to give the advice or furnish the information; (3) the third party must have relied upon that advice or information as a matter for which the solicitor has assumed personal responsibility; and (4) the solicitor must have been aware that the third party was likely so to rely.'

It is clear that at least in cases where those four factors are present, a solicitor may be held liable in negligence to a third party under the more general principle laid down in *Hedley Byrne & Co Ltd v Heller & Partners Ltd*.[369] An example of a case in which they were clearly met is the New Zealand decision of *Allied Finance and Investments Ltd v Haddow*,[370] to which we were also referred …

---

367 [1998] 2 IR 61, 72.
368 *Midland Bank v Cameron, Thom Peterkin and Duncans* 1988 SLT 611.
369 *Hedley Byrne & Co Ltd v Heller & Partners Ltd* [1964] AC 465.
370 *Allied Finance and Investments Ltd v Haddow* [1983] NZLR 22.

Finally, it should always be borne in mind, in considering whether a particular statement amounts to a negligent misstatement, that the omission of significantly relevant facts may be sufficient to convert a literally accurate statement into a misstatement."[371]

[12.165] Keane J was satisfied that the four factors that were identified in *Midland Bank plc v Cameron, Thom Peterkin and Duncan*[372] were also present in *Doran v Delaney*.[373] He concluded that the vendors' solicitors owed the purchaser a duty to exercise reasonable care in answering the requisition and that they were in breach of that duty. In a brief concurring judgment Barron J tersely observed that:

"A solicitor is not a conduit pipe. Once he is acting professionally he warrants that so far as his own acts are concerned he has taken the care and applied the skill and knowledge expected by a member of his profession. He cannot therefore accept his client's instructions without question when it is reasonable to query them. That is the difference between innocent and negligent misstatement. It is not enough that the solicitor was acting *bona fide*."[374]

[12.166] The decision in *Doran v Delaney*[375] can be seen as an extension of the proposition that was established in *Wall v Hegarty*,[376] namely that in some circumstances a solicitor owes a duty of care to a third party.[377] It is interesting to note that while the latter decision was cited by counsel it did not feature in the reasoning of the Supreme Court. Instead the court invoked the general principle set out by the House of Lords in *Hedley Byrne*[378] and relied on two other decisions, one from Scotland and the other from New Zealand. The issues raised in those two cases were, of course, closer to that which arose in *Doran v Delaney* than those in *Wall v Hegarty*. However, another court might have reached the same conclusion by reasoning from *Wall v Hegarty* and concluding that it reflects a broader principle of liability that embraces the facts of the present case.

[12.167] It is also worth observing that the court adopted *Hedley Byrne* 'as applied in a number of decisions in this jurisdiction', but did not feel it necessary to cite Irish jurisprudence.[379] The latter body of case law might be considered merely to have applied, but not to have added to, the general principle established in *Hedley Byrne* and, in that respect, to be of lesser significance. Some decisions of the House of Lords, including *Hedley Byrne* and *Donoghue v Stevenson*, are attributed a weight that

---

[371] [1989] 2 IR 61 at 73–75.

[372] *Midland Bank plc v Cameron, Thom Peterkin and Duncan* 1988 SLT 611.

[373] *Doran v Delaney* [1998] 2 IR 61.

[374] [1998] 2 IR 61 at 78.

[375] *Doran v Delaney* [1998] 2 IR 61.

[376] *Wall v Hegarty* [1980] ILRM 124.

[377] See Phelan, '*Doran v Delaney* – a New Duty of Care on Conveyancers?' (1998) 3(2) CPLJ 26.

[378] *Hedley Byrne* [1964] AC 465.

[379] See, in contrast, *Hazylake Fashions Ltd v Bank of Ireland* [1989] IR 601 at 604 *per* Murphy J: '[i]t seems to me that it would be impossible to extend the decision in *Hedley Byrne & Co Ltd v Heller & Partners Ltd* [1964] AC 465 or indeed the subsequent Irish decision in *Securities Trust Ltd v Hugh Moore & Alexander Ltd* [1964] IR 417 to the facts of the present case.'

surpasses their status as 'persuasive authority' and are invariably followed by superior courts throughout the common law world.

Developing the standard of care

[12.168] The standard of care which a professional person must exercise was considered by the Supreme Court in *O'Donovan v Cork County Council*.[380] In general, it is sufficient that the defendant adopted the approved practices of the profession, provided however that those practices are not themselves defective. The matter was stated by Walsh J in the following terms:

> "A medical practitioner cannot be held negligent if he follows general and approved practice in the situation in which he is faced: see *Daniels v Heskin*,[381] and the cases referred to therein.

> That proposition is not, however, without qualification. If there is a common practice which has inherent defects, which ought to be obvious to any person giving the matter due consideration, the fact that it has been shown to have been widely and generally adopted over a period of time does not make that practice any the less negligent. Neglect of duty does not cease by repetition to be neglect of duty."[382]

[12.169] *Roche v Peilow*[383] provides an example of an approved professional practice which the Supreme Court considered to be inherently defective.[384] The appellants engaged the respondent solicitors to act for them in the purchase of a new house from a building company. The latter had created an equitable charge in favour of a bank on the land on which the house was to be built. The charge was registered in the Companies Office but not in the Land Registry. When they came to investigate title the defendants made the usual requisitions on the title, but they did not make a search in the Companies Office. Only the latter search would have disclosed the existence of the charge. The building company went into liquidation, by which stage the appellants had paid £8,000 towards the purchase price. The liquidator was prepared to complete the contract, but the bank was unprepared to release the charge unless the appellants paid £6,000. The appellants sued the respondents alleging that they were negligent in that they failed to discover the existence of the charge in favour of the bank. The respondents denied that they were negligent as they had followed the common practice of the profession.

[12.170] The Supreme Court (Walsh, Henchy, Griffin, Hederman and McCarthy JJ) held that the respondents were negligent. Walsh J explained the matter thus:

> "The question in this case is whether such a common practice has such inherent defects that they ought to be obvious to any person giving the matter due consideration ...'

---

380 *O'Donovan v Cork County Council* [1967] IR 173.
381 *Daniels v Heskin* [1954] IR 73.
382 [1967] IR 173, 193.
383 *Roche v Peilow* [1985] IR 232.
384 See Doyle, 'In Defence of *Roche v Peilow*' (1986) 4 ILT 183.

It is quite clear on the evidence in the case that this method of financing building was well known to solicitors and they also knew the risks inherent in it. In a case where the builder was a limited company, as well as making a search in the Land Registry it would also be clearly necessary to make a search in the Companies Office. It may well be that the general practice of solicitors not making these searches until the time has arrived for completion was based upon the experience that in most cases nothing goes wrong. However, that practice does not obviate the risk clearly inherent in such a practice. The whole object of a search is to discover these matters and no solicitor can permit his client to purchase lands or to commit himself irrevocably financially in the purchase or development of lands unless he has first of all ascertained whether or not the land is free from encumbrances. If it is not he must bring the fact to the notice of his client and allow the client, after proper advice to decide whether or not he should take the risk of accepting the transaction with the risk posed by the existence of the encumbrance.

In his judgment the learned President of the High Court cited a passage from the decision of this Court in *O'Donovan v Cork County Council*.[385] In my view the last paragraph of that passage governs this case. The learned President in deciding against the plaintiffs relied upon a passage in an English judgment, *Simmons v Pennington & Son*.[386]

A number of observations may be made about that particular case. The first is that the conditions of sale were not particularly candid and the second is that it could scarcely be regarded as negligence to give a truthful answer to a requisition. It may well have been thought that a solicitor might not reasonably foresee that telling the truth in what was a stock answer to a stock question would fail to satisfy a purchaser. However, in my view, the case is totally different from the present case. The risk in the present case cannot be neutered by describing it as a stock risk. It is a very substantial and real risk. The fact that it was frequently undertaken does not in any way diminish the danger to which it gives rise. The consequences of the risk materialising could not be said to be unforeseeable as the evidence in this case indicates that it was a well known risk and the consequences were obvious if it should materialise. In my view, the decision in *Simmons v Pennington & Sons* is not applicable.

I have had the advantage of reading the judgments delivered by the then President of the High Court in *Taylor v Ryan*[387] and the judgment of Mr Justice Murphy in *Dermot C Kelly & anor v Finbarr J Crowley*.[388] The principles enunciated in those cases confirm, in my view, that the defendants were guilty of a failure in the duty they owed to the plaintiffs to the extent that they were negligent in law."[389]

[12.171] Henchy J, concurring in *Roche v Peilow* stated:

"When the plaintiffs engaged the defendants to act as their solicitors in the purchase of a house, they were entitled to believe that their interests would be protected by the defendants with the degree of care to be expected from a reasonably careful and competent solicitor. That duty of care may be said to arise either as a matter of contract, by reason of an implied

---

385 *O'Donovan v Cork County Council* [1967] IR 173.
386 *Simmons v Pennington & Son* [1955] 1 WLR 183.
387 *Taylor v Ryan* (10 March 1983, unreported), HC.
388 *Dermot C Kelly v Finbarr J Crowley* [1985] IR 212.
389 [1985] IR 232 at 249–252.

term to that effect in the contract of retainer, or alternatively, as an aspect of the tort of negligence arising out of the proximity of the relationship between solicitor and client: see *Finlay v Murtagh*.[390] ...

The plaintiffs' plea of negligence rests on the complaint that before they bound themselves contractually, the defendants as their solicitors should have made a search in the Companies Office to ascertain if a charge on the site had been registered by the building company under the Companies Act 1963. If such a search had been made it would have shown that the building company had given a charge to a bank, by deposit of title deeds, on the lands on Folio 58474 to secure all moneys due by the building company to the bank. Had that position been thus disclosed, the defendants would doubtless have informed the plaintiffs that the bank were equitable mortgagees and have warned them of the perils involved in making stage payments to the building company, who had not the beneficial title and against whom there would be no effective redress in case of insolvency ...

The general duty owed by a solicitor to his client is to show him the degree of care to be expected in the circumstances from a reasonably careful and skilful solicitor. Usually the solicitor will be held to have discharged that duty if he follows a practice common among the members of his profession: see *Daniels v Heskin*[391] and the cases therein referred to. Conformity with the widely accepted practice of his colleagues will normally rebut an allegation of negligence against a professional man, for the degree of care which the law expects of him is no higher than that to be expected from an ordinary reasonable member of the profession or of the speciality in question. But there is an important exception to that rule of conduct. It was concisely put as follows by Walsh J in *O'Donovan v Cork County Council*:

> 'If there is a common practice which has inherent defects, which ought to be obvious to any person giving the matter due consideration, the fact that it is shown to have been widely and generally adopted over a period of time does not make the practice any the less negligent. Neglect of duty does not cease by repetition to be neglect of duty.'[392]

The reason for that exception or qualification is that the duty imposed by the law rests on the standard to be expected from a reasonably careful member of the profession, and a person cannot be said to be acting reasonably if he automatically and mindlessly follows the practice of others when by taking thought he would have realised that the practice in question was fraught with peril for his client and was readily avoidable or remediable. The professional man is, of course, not to be judged with the benefit of hindsight, but if it can be said that if at the time, on giving the matter due consideration, he would have realised that the impugned practice was in the circumstances incompatible with his client's interests, and if an alternative and safe course of conduct was reasonably open to him, he will be held to have been negligent.

I consider it to be beyond doubt that it was inimical to the plaintiffs' interests for the defendants to allow them to enter into contractual relations with the building company, and in particular to bind themselves to make stage payments, without first making a search in the Companies Office, which would have shown that the beneficial owner of the site was

---

[390] *Finlay v Murtagh* [1979] IR 249.
[391] *Daniels v Heskin* [1954] IR 73.
[392] *O'Donovan v Cork County Council* [1967] IR 173 at 193.

the bank. Because of the defendants' default in that respect, the plaintiffs were left open to disappointment and financial disaster if, as happened, the building company proved to be unable to discharge their indebtedness to the bank. As the evidence in the High Court showed, in not making that search the defendants were following a conveyancing practice common at the time among solicitors. However, adherence to that practice can avail as a defence only if it be shown that a reasonable solicitor, giving consideration at the time to the interests of the client, would have justifiably concluded that a search in the Companies Office was unnecessary or undesirable. Having regard to the fact that no undue delay, expense or difficulty was involved in making such a search, and bearing in mind that financial disaster of the kind actually sustained by the plaintiffs was reasonably foreseeable by the defendants as a risk for the plaintiffs, I consider that, notwithstanding that the defendants in not carrying out a search were conforming to a practice widespread at the time in the profession, they were nevertheless wanting in the duty of care owed by them to the plaintiffs. It is to avoid detectable pitfalls of the kind that beset the plaintiffs that prospective purchasers engage solicitors to act for them."[393]

[12.172] The inherent risk to the client featured prominently in the judgments in *Roche v Peilow*. The Court was satisfied that the risk in question was, or ought to have been, obvious to solicitors. It followed that adhering to the then common professional practice (of not conducting a search in the Companies Office) did not eliminate that inherent risk. Accordingly, it was the solicitor's duty to conduct the search and to advise the client of the risk involved in the purchase so that the client 'after proper advice' could decide whether to accept that risk.

[12.173] In the High Court decision *ACC Bank plc v Brian Johnston & Co*[394] the defendant solicitor acted for the plaintiff bank in a series of transactions that involved a borrower providing security in the form of a charge on his land for loans advanced by the bank. The solicitor accepted undertakings from the solicitors acting for the borrowers rather than requiring direct evidence that the charges had been put in place. It transpired that the charges were not executed and the bank was left without security for the loans it had advanced. The court found that the bank had not authorised the defendant to accept undertakings and the issue was whether it was negligent on his part to accept the undertakings in question. The defendant contended that he acted in accordance with common practice and therefore was not liable in negligence. The issue of risk again featured in Clarke J's judgment in *ACC Bank plc v Brian Johnston & Co* where his concern was the exposure of clients to 'unnecessary' risks:

"While the duty of care of a professional person is often described by reference to the standards that would normally be applied by a professional of equivalent experience, it is clear from *Roche v Peilow* that the mere fact that a practice is universal does not, of itself, immunise the professional concerned from potential liability, if it is a practice which, on reasonable consideration, the professional concerned ought to have identified as giving rise to a significant risk. In that context, it is apposite to note the reference of Walsh J to a 'stock' risk. There is risk in everything. Professionals cannot remove risk from the equation.

---

393   [1985] IR 232 at 252–255.
394   *ACC Bank plc v Brian Johnston & Co* [2010] 4 IR 605.

However, professionals are normally employed to minimise risk or advise clients on relevant risks. Professionals should not expose their clients to unnecessary risk without, at a minimum, advising their clients of the risk involved and inviting their clients' instructions. The mere fact that there may be a common practice to expose clients to a particular type of risk will not necessarily provide a defence. The ordinary duty of care, therefore, extends not merely to ensuring that the relevant professional person carries out his or her duties in the way in which other suitably qualified members of the relevant profession do, but also extends to considering whether common practices may so obviously involve unnecessary risks which can be eliminated that such practices should not be engaged in. It might be said that such practices are more honoured in the breach than in the observance in the proper sense of that quote."[395]

In the circumstances Clarke J concluded that the bank retained the solicitor to avoid the very risk which was inherent in closing by undertaking: 'it does not seem to me to be appropriate for that solicitor to take it on him or herself to expose the financial institution concerned to the very risks which it has sought to avoid by employing him in the first place.'[396]

---

[395] *ACC Bank plc v Brian Johnston & Co* [2010] 4 IR 605 at 639–640.
[396] *ACC Bank plc v Brian Johnston & Co* [2010] 4 IR 605 at 640.

Chapter 13

Legislation

[1]   Introduction 563
[2]   Legislative Process 570
[3]   Legislative Product 586
[4]   Delegated Legislation 604

[1]   INTRODUCTION

[13.01] The source of law known as 'legislation' consists of measures which are enacted or adopted by a legislative organ in a manner which is prescribed by a constitutional formula. In other words it is the product of a legislative or law-making process. In Ireland legislative authority is conferred on the Oireachtas by Article 15.2.1° of the Constitution which states that '[t]he sole and exclusive power of making laws for the State is hereby vested in the Oireachtas; no other legislative authority has power to make laws for the State.'

[13.02] Legislation falls into two categories. The first, *primary legislation*, consists of Acts of the Oireachtas, also called statutes,[1] which are enacted by the Oireachtas in a particular manner which is outlined later.[2] Acts of the Oireachtas are of three types; *Acts to amend the Constitution*; *public general Acts* which create law for the public at large; and *private Acts* which create law for particular individuals or groups of individuals, such as companies or local authorities.

[13.03] The second category, variously known as *secondary*, *subordinate* or *delegated* legislation, consists of measures enacted by a person or body to whom the Oireachtas has delegated legislative authority. In general, delegated legislation establishes detailed rules while the Act under which it is made contains general principles. Like primary legislation, delegated legislation is a source of law and the two share many characteristics. The extent to which legislative power may be delegated, the relationship between primary and delegated legislation and the special features of delegated legislation are considered below.[3]

---

[1]   The term 'statute', which is now used synonymously with 'Act of the Oireachtas', originally referred to all the Acts passed in a particular parliamentary session; see *R v Bakewell* (1857) 7 E & B 848, *per* Lord Campbell CJ.

[2]   The legislative process is considered at paras **13.18–13.45**.

[3]   See paras **13.109–13.158**.

[13.04] At this stage it is sufficient to observe that both species of legislation are regulatory measures which enjoy the force of law. It should be realised that they form part of a wider regulatory environment which comprises a variety of mechanisms, both legal and non-legal, created by either public institutions or private bodies and/or individuals (see Figure 13.1). In this chapter we will also consider briefly other regulatory mechanisms which have some of the appearances of legislation but which are not legislative in nature and lack the force of law.[4] These devices, which are sometimes called *quasi-legislation*, include codes of practice, administrative rules and circulars.

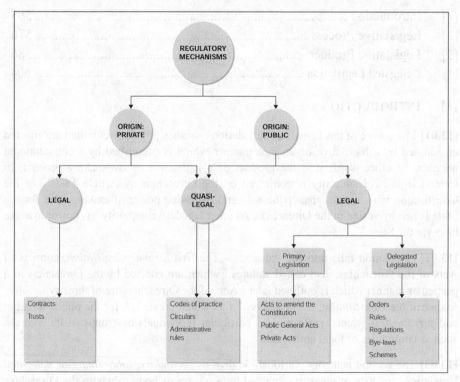

Figure 13.1

Comparison with other sources of law

[13.05] The process of legislating connotes the activity of deliberate law-making. Unlike adjudication, which is the concern of the judicial process, the primary purpose of legislation is the creation of rules which will apply to future events, rather than with the resolution of individual disputes. In this respect, the process is prospective and abstract – it establishes standards to be adopted in circumstances which have yet to occur.

---

4   See paras **13.09–13.13**.

However, it should be realised that some legislative measures regulate past events, although this tends to be an exception to the general practice. Moreover, private Acts apply to individual sets of circumstances, a feature which is shared by adjudication.[5] It is the regulatory nature of such instruments which allows them to be characterised as legislation. In contrast, adjudication is retrospective and concrete, being concerned with the resolution of past events according to pre-existing rules. Nevertheless, as we have seen in the preceding chapter, the adjudicative process does possess a creative dimension and, of course, the product of the adjudicative process is a source of law – the common law is often referred to as 'judge-made' law. However, the creative character of adjudication is of a different order to that of legislation.

[13.06] Common law rules emerge from their being identified from an existing body of law and applied by the adjudicator to the dispute which he or she is charged with resolving. The creative scope afforded to a judge is constrained by the pre-existing law and, in this respect, the law-making dimension is incidental to the adjudicative function. On the other hand, legislators are not so constrained, being confined only by the constitutional formula which confers legislative capacity on them. Thus, despite their both being creative, the general distinction between legislation and adjudication is based on their respective functions, that of the former being law-making and that of the latter being law application. Nevertheless, whatever their differences legislation and common law both enjoy the force of law.

[13.07] The private law of contract might also provide a regulatory mechanism of a different type. A contract is brought about by agreement of the parties rather than the act of a legislative body. The parties create the law which is to govern their relationship rather than having it imposed on them by an external agency. That difference aside, however, contract shares the regulatory purpose of legislation. It seeks at the outset to establish the rules by which the parties are to be governed. Significant sectors of the economy now tend to be regulated through the mechanism of standard form contracts. The entitlements of those who engage, say, dry cleaners are governed primarily by such contracts, the contents of which are predominantly determined by the dry cleaning industry. The customer is typically presented with a 'take it or leave it' choice and, in practice, is not in a position to negotiate.[6] Like legislation, contractual regulation is legally enforceable and, in this sense, it enjoys the force of law.

[13.08] Nevertheless, despite these similarities, contract is a very different phenomenon to legislation. Lying at the heart of contract law is the theory, realistic or otherwise, of

---

[5]   Parliamentary procedure in relation to the enactment of private acts shares some features with litigation; see paras **13.40–13.45**.

[6]   It should be noted that legislation increasingly regulates contractual freedom especially in the area of consumer contracts; see Sale of Goods and Supply of Services Act 1980; European Communities (Unfair Terms in Consumer Contracts) Regulations 1995 (SI 27/1995); European Communities (Unfair Terms in Consumer Contracts) (Amendment) Regulations 2000 (SI 307/2000); European Communities (Unfair Terms in Consumer Contracts) (Amendment) Regulations 2013 (SI 160/2013).

contract as a bargain which is freely entered into by two equally situated parties. The law thereby created is the consequence of a voluntary act of the parties. Legislation is the act of an agency external to those who are subjected to it.[7] Legislation might also be contrasted with the trust, a legal device which facilitates arrangements governing the ownership and management of property. Like contract, the trust is a creature of private law, having been created by the act of a private party known as the settlor, and is legally enforceable. Although trusts and contracts are different types of legal instrument,[8] they share a similar regulatory potential which is different in origin from legislation but which might be every bit as effective.

Quasi-legislation

[13.09] In addition to those sources of law a range of regulatory instruments are promulgated by various governmental agencies, in particular government departments. Administrative rules, circulars, codes of practice[9] and the like are frequently issued by these agencies and seek to govern significant areas of government business. In some, but by no means all, circumstances their introduction is governed or provided for by statute.[10] To a large extent much of this administrative rule-making is routine in nature, setting out the administration's interpretation and implementation of various schemes and powers. Viewed thus, their purpose is to remove matters of detail from the text of statutes; in the main they are beneficial to the public and pose few legal difficulties. Often the relevant statute expressly provides that the code of practice or administrative rule lacks legal status and does not impose legal liabilities.

[13.10] However, in some circumstances administrative rules seek to establish norms and standards which are expected to be adopted and their purpose, like that of

---

[7] However, in some instances a court might be prepared to treat a contract as being equivalent to legislation; see *McCord v ESB* [1980] ILRM 153; see further, para **13.119**.

[8] See Delany, *Equity and the Law of Trusts in Ireland* (5th edn, 2011), pp 58 *et seq*; Keane, *Equity and the Law of Trusts in the Republic of Ireland* (2nd edn, 2011), p 10.

[9] See Campbell, 'Codes of Practice as an Alternative to Legislation' [1985] Stat LR 127; Samuels 'Codes of Practice and Legislation' [1986] Stat LR 29.

[10] For example, Health and Safety Authority, *Code of Practice for Employers and Employees on the Prevention and Resolution of Bullying at Work* (2007), provided for by the Safety, Health and Welfare at Work Act 2005, s 60; Department of Enterprise, Trade and Employment, *Code of Practice: Grievance and Disciplinary Procedures* (2002) for which provision was made under the Industrial Relations Act 1990, s 42 and which was brought into effect by the Industrial Relations Act 1990 (Code of Practice on Grievance and Disciplinary Procedures) (Declaration) Order 2000 (SI 146/2000); the *Rules of the Road* (2006) are referred to in the Road Traffic Act 1961, s 3(4); the *Rules and Programme for Secondary Schools 1987/88 to 1994/ 95* (Pn 0983) are made under the Intermediate Education (Ireland) Acts 1878 to 1924. The Irish Sports Council Act 1999, s 6(1)(c) authorises the promulgation of guidelines and codes of practice to 'facilitate … standards of good conduct and fair play' in sport. Statutory sanction for the issuing of codes of practice is also contained in the National Disability Authority Act 1999, s 10.

legislation, is regulatory. Such rules are often used by the government as an alternative to, or surrogate for, legislation. These measures mimic legislation and are formulated with the intention that they should be followed.[11] This form of law-making has been termed 'quasi-legislation'[12] or 'ersatz legislation'.[13] Significant areas of public administration are governed in this fashion rather than by legislation, prompting the observation that:

> "there is some evidence that some government departments issue administrative rules and circulars in preference to legislation almost as a matter of policy ... It is quite remarkable, for example, that there is often no legislation underpinning the various schemes administered by the Department of Agriculture."[14]

These remarks are matched by increasingly frequent expressions of judicial disapproval of non-statutory schemes,[15] but the courts have stopped short of nullifying the general practice and quasi-legislation exists in legal limbo.[16]

[13.11] Although quasi-legislation might lack the force of law, the norms it seeks to establish are capable of being enforced by a variety of informal mechanisms which include the conferring, or possible withholding, of discretionary entitlements and benefits, official pressure, appeals to the conscience or sense of national good and making compliance a condition of government contracts and the like. A major difficulty associated with such rules is that they are enunciated without being subjected to parliamentary scrutiny and they operate beyond the legislative domain in a manner which is hardly compatible with the minimum demands of democracy. Moreover, in as much as they purport to confer rights and impose obligations, additional legal difficulties are encountered.

---

11   See, eg, the Department of Education's *Procedures for Dealing with Allegations or Suspicions of Child Abuse* (M41/92) and *Guidelines on Countering Bullying Behaviour in Primary and Post-Primary Schools* (1993).

12   Megarry, 'Administrative Quasi-legislation' (1944) 60 LQR 125; see also Ganz, *Quasi-Legislation* (1987); Zander, *The Law Making Process* (6th edn, 2004), pp 445–448; Rawlings, 'Quasi-Legislative Devolution: Powers and Principles' (2001) 52 NILQ 54.

13   Ferguson, 'Legislation' in *Stair Memorial Encyclopaedia of the Laws of Scotland* (1987) Vol 22, para 224.

14   Hogan and Morgan, *Administrative Law in Ireland* (4th edn, 2010), pp 59–60.

15   See, eg, *McCann v Minister for Education* [1997] 1 ILRM 1, 15; *O'Neill v Minister for Agriculture* [1997] 2 ILRM 435 at 442, *per* Keane J; *Kylemore Bakery Ltd v Minister for Trade, Commerce and Tourism* [1986] ILRM 529 at 530, *per* Costello J; *McKerring v Minister for Agriculture* [1989] ILRM 82 at 84. However, in *Rooney v Minister for Agriculture and Food* [1991] 2 IR 539 the Supreme Court endorsed the application of a non-statutory scheme; see para **13.78**.

16   See Hogan, 'The Legal Status of Administrative Rules and Circulars' (1987) 22 Ir Jur (ns) 194; Baldwin and Houghton, 'Circular Arguments: the Status and Legitimacy of Administrative Rules' [1986] PL 239; see also Hyland, 'Legal Status of Notices issued by the Competition Authority' (1993) 11 ILT 240.

[13.12] For example, corporal punishment in schools was initially abolished by means of a ministerial circular.[17] At that time it might have been argued, with some force, that the abolition should have been effected by formal legislation, thus facilitating parliamentary scrutiny. However, the circular did not, and could not, alter the legal position of a pupil who was so punished – until its abolition by s 24 of the Non-Fatal Offences against the Person Act 1997 the common law defence of reasonable chastisement was available to defeat both a criminal prosecution of, and a civil action against, an offending teacher.[18] Thus, until 1997 a teacher was administratively prohibited from so acting, and presumably liable to discipline in the context of his or her employment, but he or she committed no legal wrong in resorting to corporal punishment as long as the force used did not exceed the bounds of reasonable chastisement. A further difficulty with quasi-legislation is that there is no provision for its formal promulgation and publication and the very real possibility exists that citizens to whom it is directed will be ignorant of its content.

[13.13] Regulatory mechanisms might also be created by private arrangements.[19] Many industries, especially in the service sector, establish voluntary codes of conduct to which members subscribe. In some cases, the regimes established by these measures are identical to the equivalent statutory schemes. The advertising industry, for instance, is voluntarily regulated by the Advertising Standards Authority for Ireland. The Authority has created codes of practice which it implements and which are universally followed by the industry.[20] In many respects the codes resemble legislation. The mandatory language in which they are drafted is similar to that of legislation; they provide for a complaints procedure, a system of adjudication by an independent committee and an enforcement mechanism. But despite their similarity to legislation the codes are, by their very nature, voluntary, and compliance with them relies on the internal dynamics of the particular industry and the willingness of individuals to accept them as being binding. They might prove to be as effective, and indeed in some cases are more effective, than legislation enforced by a state agency, but unlike legislation they lack the force of law and compliance cannot be coerced.

---

17 In January 1982 the Minister for Education issued two circulars 9/82 and M5/82, which respectively abolished corporal punishment in primary and post-primary schools; see 333 *Dáil Debates,* cols 1430–1431.

18 *Cleary v Booth* [1893] 1 QB 465; see Children Act 1908, s 37 preserving the right of a teacher to administer punishment; see also Law Reform Commission, *Report on Non-Fatal Offences Against the Person* (LRC 45-1994), pp 23–24.

19 See, eg, Electro-Technical Council of Ireland, *National Rules for Electrical Installations* (4th edn, 2008), and Updates (Amendments, Corrigenda and Errata) 06/2009 (Revised 21.04.2011).

20 See *Manual of Advertising Self-Regulation with the Code of Standards for Advertising, Promotional and Direct Marketing in Ireland* (6th edn, 2007).

Characteristics of legislation

[13.14] Having distinguished legislation from other regulatory instruments, the characteristics of legislation may now be considered. The principal characteristic of legislation is that it reduces rules to a written and fixed verbal form. A legislative rule is stated in an inflexible manner and no linguistic variations can be substituted. This contrasts with common law rules which, as has been seen, are unwritten and unfixed, in the sense that a variety of verbal formulae can, with equal accuracy, be employed to state them. A judge's articulation of a rule in the course of a decision is but an explanation or approximation of the rule. An example will demonstrate this characteristic of legislation. The prohibition on 'drug dealing', contained in s 15(1) of the Misuse of Drugs Act 1977, is stated thus:

> "Any person who has in his possession, whether lawfully or not, a controlled drug for the purpose of selling or otherwise supplying it to another in contravention of regulations under section 5 of this Act shall be guilty of an offence."

[13.15] The section cannot be stated in any other verbal form and an alternative statement of the rule can only amount to an explanation of it. It should, however, be noted that the rule stated in s 15(1) also contains an unwritten element. It is sufficient to note at this stage that the criminal law defences of insanity and infancy apply to the offence. Thus 'any person' does not include those who are below the age of criminal responsibility or who suffer from a mental disorder. This theme will be returned to later.[21]

[13.16] A second characteristic of legislation is that rules tend to be stated in a precise rather than a general form. This is not a universal characteristic and some legislative rules are stated in open-ended terms. However, that does not detract from the general observation. Several factors contribute to this characteristic. The subject matter of many, if not most, statutes is such that detailed provisions are required; this is especially true of statutes dealing with economic and social matters. For instance, in order to be workable a tax statute must specify with great precision the details of the tax which is to be levied. To state the subject matter in general terms would result in a degree of vagueness which could undermine the purposes of the tax. Moreover, the desire for certainty in the law, whereby those who are affected by it are in a position to know exactly that which is required of them and to plan their activities accordingly, contributes to the relative precision of statutory rules.

[13.17] Related to this is an attempt by the legislature to provide for every eventuality which might arise or, in other words, to cover all conceivable loopholes. A further factor is a desire on the part of the legislature to limit judicial discretion. If legislators were confident that judicial decisions would reflect the legislative view of things, they could compose statutes in more general terms, secure in the knowledge that the courts would decide doubtful cases in the desired manner. On the other hand, some statutes are

---

[21]   See para **14.37**.

expressed in comparatively general terms, leaving their detailed operation to be supplied by judicial interpretation. This is achieved by the inclusion of a provision that broadly defines the objects of the legislation[22] and the use of open-ended phrases such as 'in the opinion of the court' or 'reasonable'.[23] A point which should be made is that legal provisions which are contained in legislation need not necessarily be stated in precise terms, the law-maker being free to employ general terms. The degree of precision employed will depend largely on the subject matter of the statute.

[2] LEGISLATIVE PROCESS

[13.18] A description of the rules and procedures which are followed by a law-making body in the enactment of primary legislation explains the legislative process in a formal sense. This embraces the constitutional and other provisions which govern the way statutes are enacted and, in the main, we are concerned with the parliamentary stage. However, the formal process is surrounded by informal procedures, practices and influences which are every bit as vital to the enactment of legislation as the formal mechanisms. It should be noted that, in practice, informal factors contribute so significantly to the enactment of legislation that they can be considered to be controlling. These factors are, of course, not expressed in the formal rules but are necessarily understood to provide the context in which those rules operate.

[13.19] At this stage it is sufficient to observe that the determination of the legislative programme (that is, the selection of proposals for enactment) is governed by concerns which exist beyond the formal process but which are accommodated by it.[24] Likewise, while the Oireachtas debates proposals and enacts legislation, the formulation of policy and its translation into legal form occurs elsewhere. Most statutes are drafted not by the Oireachtas or any of its members but by legislative drafters, officials in the Office of Parliamentary Counsel to the government who are employed for that purpose. Thus, while the Oireachtas formally enacts a statute, its text is usually the handiwork of a specialist legislative drafter.[25] An appreciation of the interaction between the formal and informal is necessary for an understanding of the legislative process. The formal rules establish the mechanism through which proposals, which derive from a variety of sources, become law.

---

22   For example, Education Act 1998, s 6.
23   However, some recent statutes contain non-exhaustive lists of factors to be taken into account when evaluating such open-ended concepts: eg the Schedule to Sale of Goods and Supply of Services Act 1980 sets out factors to be considered when determining whether a contract term is 'fair and reasonable'; Occupiers' Liability Act 1995, s 4(2) enumerates factors to be considered when determining whether an occupier acted with 'reckless disregard'.
24   See paras **13.46–13.57**.
25   See paras **13.58–13.64**.

Formal process: constitutional arrangements

[13.20] In Ireland the legislative organ established by the Constitution is the Oireachtas, which consists of two Houses and the President. Legislation is passed by both Houses of the Oireachtas, Dáil Éireann and Seanad Éireann, and is signed into law by the President. The relationship between the two Houses is regulated by the Constitution, which preserves the supremacy of the Dáil, the popularly elected House. While primary legislation other than a Money Bill may be initiated in either House, when the proposed Act is known as a 'Bill', the Dáil enjoys the power, in effect, to overrule the Seanad. Where the Seanad rejects or amends a Bill which has been passed by the Dáil, Article 23 provides that the Dáil may pass a resolution within 180 days which deems the Bill to have passed through both Houses.[26] Moreover, if a Bill which was initiated in and passed by the Seanad is amended by the Dáil it is deemed to have been initiated in the Dáil, thus requiring fresh consideration by the Seanad. Article 23 has been invoked on two occasions only but this should not be taken to suggest that the Dáil's supremacy is thereby diluted or undermined. Its possible invocation is a constraint within which the Seanad operates and its mere existence has proved to be sufficient to ensure that the Seanad does not challenge the primacy of the lower House.

[13.21] The relative weakness of the Seanad is amplified in two further provisions.[27] The first, contained in Article 21, is that Money Bills[28] may be initiated in the Dáil only and are sent to the Seanad for 'recommendations'. The Seanad has a 21-day period in which to make its recommendations, which then may be accepted or rejected by the Dáil. Echoing the proposition that there be 'no taxation without representation', this provision of course ensures that financial matters fall within the exclusive preserve of the popularly elected House.

[13.22] The second provision, in Article 24, provides a procedure for the abridgement of time allowed to the Seanad to consider a particular Bill. The rather cumbersome

---

26   Article 23.1.1°.

27   See Quinn, 'The Role of the Seanad in the Legislative Process' (2006) 24 ILT 46. The Department of Public Expenditure and Reform's *Programme for Government* (March 2010), p 17 envisaged the abolition of the Seanad (Seanad Reform Bill 2013) as part of a broader programme of constitutional reform but the proposal was rejected in a referendum on the matter in October 2013 by 51.7% to 48.3%; see Ruane, 'Proposed Abolition of the Seanad and the Implications of Judicial Independence' (2013) 18 BR 46; Whelan, 'House of a Different Colour' (2013) 107 LSG 38; Lawlor, 'Anachronistic Seanad Should be Abolished' (2013) 107 LSG 18; Bergin-Cross, 'Can We Fix It? Yes, We Can!' (2013) 107 LSG 20

28   Article 22.1.1°: 'A Money Bill means a Bill which contains only provisions dealing with all or any of the following matters, namely, the imposition, repeal, remission, alteration or regulation of taxation; the imposition for the payment of debt or other financial purposes of charges on public moneys or the variation or repeal of any such charges; supply; the appropriation, receipt, custody, issue or audit of accounts of public money; the raising or guarantee of any loan or the repayment thereof; matters subordinate and integral to these matters or any of them.'

procedure which involves an interplay of the government, the Dáil and the President is set out in Article 24.1:

> "If and whenever on the passage by Dáil Éireann of any Bill, other than a Bill expressed to be a Bill containing a proposal to amend the Constitution, the Taoiseach certifies by messages in writing to the President and the Chairman of each House of the Oireachtas that, in the opinion of the Government, the Bill is urgent and immediately necessary in the preservation of the public peace and security, or by reason of the existence of a public emergency, domestic or international, the time for the consideration of such Bill by Seanad Éireann shall, if Dáil Éireann so resolves and if the President, after consultation with the Council of State, concurs, be abridged, to such period as shall be specified in the resolution."

[13.23] In effect, once Article 24 is invoked the Bill is deemed to have passed through both Houses on the expiration of the specified time. The nature of the emergency envisaged by Article 24 is not specified and one commentator has suggested that it 'is wide enough to encompass a nuclear attack or, at the other extreme, an outbreak of smallpox in one town'.[29] A Bill thus passed remains in force for 90 days only unless within that time it is extended for a further period by resolutions of the both Houses. In practice, the Seanad has tended to facilitate the speedy passage of urgent legislation and Article 24 has not been invoked to date.

[13.24] On its being passed by both Houses of the Oireachtas a Bill is presented to the President to be signed into law. In the ordinary course of events the Bill is signed between five and seven days of its being passed.[30] The President may sign the Bill earlier than the fifth day at the request of the government and with the concurrence of the Seanad.[31] An Article 24 Bill must be signed by the President on the day it is presented to him or her for signature.[32] A Bill becomes law, that is, an Act of the Oireachtas, on the day it is signed by the President, who is required to promulgate it by the publication of a notice that it has become law in *Iris Oifigiúil* (the Official Gazette).[33] A different procedure is established in relation to Bills containing a proposal to amend the Constitution. Such proposals must be submitted to a national referendum[34] pending which, of course, it may not be signed by the President. On its being approved by the

---

[29] Morgan, *Constitutional Law of Ireland* (2nd edn, 1990), p 95; see also Hogan and Whyte, *Kelly: The Irish Constitution* (4th edn, 2003), pp 371–372.

[30] Article 25.2.1°.

[31] Article 25.2.2°. The provision, somewhat strangely, makes no reference to the Dáil in this regard. The Seanad passed motions for early signature to facilitate the speedy enactment of the Insurance (No 2) Act 1983, the Offences Against the State (Amendment) Act 1985 and the Anglo-Irish Bank Corporation Act 2009, each of which was required as matters of urgency; see 102 *Seanad Debates*, cols 218–259; 107 *Seanad Debates*, cols 362–364; and 193 *Seanad Debates*, cols 325–327, respectively.

[32] Article 25.3.

[33] Article 25.4.2°.

[34] Article 46.2.

People it must be signed 'forthwith' and 'duly promulgated' by the President.[35] The importance of ensuring a formal announcement that a law has been enacted, thereby bringing it to the attention of the public, hardly needs to be emphasised and the process is vital to maintaining the rule of law.[36] A copy of the text of the Act signed by the President is enrolled for record in the office of the Registrar of the Supreme Court.[37] This latter measure is not merely a matter of exaggerated protocol. It formalises the record and in the unlikely event of a dispute arising as to the text of an Act (as opposed to its interpretation) the text thus enrolled is conclusive evidence of its provisions.

Article 26

[13.25] In two circumstances the President may decline to sign a Bill. Under Article 26 he or she may, after consultation with the Council of State, refer a Bill to the Supreme Court for a decision on its constitutionality.[38] Pending the decision of the Supreme Court, the Bill must not be signed. If the court upholds the constitutionality of the Bill the President is then required to sign it into law. If the court decides that any provision of the Bill is repugnant to the Constitution, the President must decline to sign it into law. The value of Article 26 is that it provides a mechanism by which an advance ruling on the constitutionality of proposed legislation might be obtained. This can be a matter of some importance where the constitutionality of a proposed law has been questioned or where it is constitutionally or politically desirable to clarify doubts in advance of its being implemented. While the power has been exercised a number of times by different Presidents it is generally believed that it is better that it is used sparingly, given its associated difficulties.[39] Once a law has passed scrutiny under Article 26 its constitutionality may not be further questioned in legal proceedings.[40]

Article 27

[13.26] Article 27 establishes a procedure under which the President may decline to sign a Bill, deemed under Article 23 to have passed through both Houses of the Oireachtas, which contains a proposal of 'national importance' until the will of the People has been sought. The purpose of the procedure is to allow the People the opportunity to veto a legislative proposal, rather than seeking their affirmative support for the measure. On being presented with a petition, signed by a majority of the Seanad and not less than

---

[35] Article 46.5.

[36] Different provisions exist for publicising the enactment of delegated legislation; see para **13.117**. One criticism of quasi-legislation (administrative rules and codes of practice, etc) is that there is no prescribed mechanism of formal publication and thus the public is liable to be unaware of its existence and application.

[37] Article 25.4.5°.

[38] Article 26 is considered more fully at paras **5.84–5.88**.

[39] These include the abstract nature of Article 26 proceedings, the fact that invalidity of a minor provision will defeat the entire Bill and the immunity from further challenge enjoyed by Bills which pass scrutiny; see Casey, *Constitutional Law in Ireland* (3rd edn, 2000), pp 333–338.

[40] Article 34.3.3°.

one-third of the Dáil, the President may, after consulting the Council of State, decline to sign the Bill until the popular will has been ascertained in one of two ways. The first is that the Bill is submitted to a national referendum, thus directly canvassing the view of the People on the matter. The second is that the Bill is passed by a resolution of the Dáil after a dissolution and re-assembly of the Dáil, thus indirectly discerning popular sentiment on the measure. In that case a general election will have been held at which it can be assumed that the proposal in question will have featured prominently in the campaign. If the parties supporting the Bill are returned to power, it may properly be inferred that the proposal is supported by the electorate or, at least, that it is not opposed by it: in either case there will be a popular mandate for the measure.

[13.27] Article 27 is designed to redress the imbalance between the Dáil and the Seanad by providing a mechanism where the Dáil has overruled the Seanad. Underlying it is an assumption that the government is in a minority in the Seanad, a position which does not often arise in practice. Moreover, the Dáil has rarely found it necessary formally to overrule the Seanad under the provisions of Article 23 and, hence, it is not surprising that Article 27 has yet to be invoked.

Formal process: parliamentary procedure

[13.28] The internal workings of the Oireachtas are governed by the Standing Orders of Dáil Éireann relative to Public Business (2011) and the Standing Orders of Seanad Éireann relative to Public Business (2011).[41] The Standing Orders regulate, *inter alia*, the manner in which legislation is introduced and processed through the House. Although most Bills may be initiated by any member of either House, in the majority of cases they are initiated in the Dáil by the government minister who has responsibility for the subject matter in question. In recent years, however, the government has initiated a number of Bills in the Seanad, a measure necessitated by the demands placed on Dáil time. To this end the Constitution provides that members of the government enjoy the right to attend and be heard in both Houses.[42] The passage of a Bill through the House occurs in five stages in the initiating House.[43] When it passes through that House it is sent to the other House where the first stage is ignored.

[13.29] At the first stage the Minister responsible obtains the permission of the House to circulate the Bill. At this stage the House will know little or nothing of the proposal and thus is unlikely to oppose the measure. As an alternative to this somewhat formal device, the Standing Orders of each House allow for the introduction of a Bill by way of presentment, rather than requiring the prior consent of the House. This right is confined

---

[41] Hereafter DSO and SSO respectively. Their enactment is provided for by Article 15.10 of the Constitution.

[42] Article 28.8.

[43] See Morgan, *Constitutional Law of Ireland* (2nd edn, 1990), pp 97–103; Coakley and Gallagher (eds), *Politics in the Republic of Ireland* (5th edn, 2010), p 210; McGowan Smyth, *The Houses of the Oireachtas* (4th edn, 1979), pp 41–47.

to Ministers, Ministers of State, private members who are supported by seven TDs or five Senators, and the leader of the Seanad.

[13.30] At the second stage the general provisions of the Bill are debated. The general philosophy and principles of the Bill are debated, rather than its details. The sponsoring Minister introduces the Bill, outlines its principal provisions and presents the government's case for its being enacted into law. The spokesmen for the other parties speak in response to the Minister and may either support or oppose the proposal. Other members, from both sides of the House, frequently contribute at this stage, the number and duration of contributions having been agreed in advance by the whips, the parties' business managers. At this stage the House is entitled to reject the Bill in its entirety and the opposition is presented with the opportunity to defeat the measure, if it can muster sufficient support in the House. This rarely occurs in the case of government Bills.

[13.31] At the third, or committee, stage the details of the Bill are debated. At this stage the general principles of the Bill have been accepted and debate proceeds on that basis. The desirability or wisdom of the Bill cannot now be questioned. The committee goes through the Bill clause by clause, and amendments to its provisions, which are consistent with its general principles, can be made. In some cases the entire House sits as a committee with the result, of course, that it is unable to deal with other matters, thus limiting the volume of parliamentary business which can be transacted. As an alternative, the Bill could be sent to either a special or a select committee, which consists of a number of members chosen on the basis of party representation in the House as a whole. A select committee, unlike a special committee, enjoys the power to send for persons, papers and records, which was thought not to be of any great use in legislative debates.[44] In practice, therefore, a special committee is likely to be considered to be the more appropriate forum. Two principal advantages may be associated with using committees at the third stage: they will typically consist of members with a special interest or expertise in the subject matter and their use frees up parliamentary time to deal with other business. In the past decade or so parliamentary reform has acquired a greater prominence on the political agenda. This has resulted in the establishment of a somewhat more effective committee system. Until recently it has been the exception to refer legislation, as opposed to other parliamentary business, to a committee. However, the establishment of Joint Committees with the specific brief to consider Bills affords some opportunities in this regard.

[13.32] The restructuring of the Oireachtas committees after the 1997 general election has streamlined the system in a way that should facilitate their greater use in the process of law-making.[45] The potential of committees can be seen from the parliamentary history of the Courts and Court Officers Act 1995. Crucial amendments, including the

---

44   But see Brooke, 'Special Public Bill Committees' [1995] PL 351 discussing an experiment in the UK parliament where committees could hear evidence and discuss submissions.

45   See Coakley and Gallagher (eds), *Politics in the Republic of Ireland* (5th edn, 2010), pp 218–221.

appointment of an additional High Court judge and the qualification of solicitors for judicial appointment, were introduced on the basis of a unanimous view of the committee. This is a welcome development and it is to be hoped that the committee system will be strengthened by the operation of more assertive committees which display a greater independence of party managers. On completion of its deliberations the committee, of whatever type, reports to the House.

[13.33] The fourth stage is the report stage and its purpose is to review the work which has been conducted at the committee stage. Amendments may be made if they arise out of the committee proceedings. In practice it is not unusual for the Minister to undertake to consider suggested amendments at the third stage and to table them at the report stage. In the meantime the Minister has presumably consulted his civil servants and other advisers on the matter and, where the amendment is moved by the Minister, the drafters.

[13.34] The fifth or final stage completes the process. Usually it is taken immediately after the fourth stage and is primarily a formal matter. Only verbal amendments are permissible at this stage. After all stages are completed typographical errors can be changed by order of the Clerk of the Dáil or Seanad.[46]

Private members' Bills

[13.35] A Bill which is not sponsored by a Minister, Minister of State, the Attorney General or the leader of the Seanad is known as a private member's Bill. With some slight variations it undergoes the same legislative process as that for government-sponsored bills. Each party may have one such Bill before the House at a given time, the second stage is limited to six hours and the Bill is sent to a special or select committee rather than a committee of the whole House. Otherwise private members' Bills are treated no differently to government Bills. However, given the government's traditional domination of the Oireachtas, there was little prospect of a private members' Bill being enacted. It has not been the practice of members of the government parties to introduce such legislation and government parties have tended at the second stage to vote down a private member's Bill which is initiated by opposition members. Nevertheless, the initiation of a private member's Bill can serve to focus public and political attention on a particular topic and the device is sometimes resorted to with that purpose in mind rather than in the expectation that it might be enacted. Moreover, in some instances the government, despite voting against an opposition-sponsored Bill, might be forced into introducing its own legislation on the matter in question. And, of course, on rare occasions a private member's Bill might be successfully steered through the Oireachtas and become law. This has become somewhat more common in recent years.

[13.36] One important measure, the Judicial Separation and Family Law Reform Act 1989, was introduced as a private member's Bill sponsored by Deputy Alan Shatter TD, then an opposition backbencher. Its success was no doubt aided by the fact that at the

---

46   DSO 140; SSO 136.

time the government was in a minority position in the Dáil and could not be assured of sufficient support to ensure its defeat. The Landlord and Tenant (Amendment) Act 1994 was also introduced as a private member's Bill, again sponsored by Deputy Shatter. More recent measures that began life as private members' Bills include the Sexual Offences (Jurisdiction) Act 1996, the Electoral (Amendment) Act 1996 and the Statute of Limitations (Amendment) Act 2000.

[13.37] A Bill which has not passed through both Houses before a general election lapses. However, after the election the House may pass a resolution which restores the Bill to the Order Paper and it commences in the re-convened House at the stage it had reached before the election. In this way the House has the option of restoring a Bill which was before it prior to the election and is likely to be invoked where the Bill was uncontroversial and enjoyed general cross-party support. This device allows the Oireachtas to keep 'alive' Bills which would otherwise have terminated and it saves parliamentary time by avoiding the necessity of repeating the stages which had been successfully completed prior to the election.

[13.38] The five-stage process outlined above is adopted in relation to public general Acts which, of course, count for the bulk of legislation. Somewhat different procedures are adopted in relation to consolidation legislation and private legislation.

Consolidation legislation

[13.39] A consolidation Act is one which re-enacts in one instrument all the statute law on a particular topic. Its purpose is not to alter the law but to collate it in one statute.[47] An abbreviated procedure is adopted to facilitate the passage of such legislation. Three conditions must be satisfied for a proposal to be considered to be a consolidation measure: (i) it must declare in its long title that its purpose is to consolidate the law; (ii) the Attorney General must certify that this is the purpose of the legislation; and (iii) notice of intention to introduce the Bill must be accompanied by a memorandum which sets out the legislation which is repealed by it and the sections of the Bill in which the law is reproduced. Once these conditions are met, the procedure which is followed differs in several respects from that which is adopted generally. Time limits between the stages are specified. The only amendment permissible at the second stage is one which states a reason for challenging the Attorney General's certificate. In other words, the opposition is confined to questioning whether the Bill is in fact a consolidation measure. With the consent of both Houses the third stage is heard by the Standing Joint Committee on Consolidation Bills. The only amendments which are permissible at this stage are those which remove ambiguity or bring the Bill into conformity with existing law. Once the Bill has passed through the initiating House it proceeds to the fourth stage in the other House.

---

[47]   See further para **13.106**.

Private legislation

[13.40] Private Bills are subjected to a very different procedure which is partially judicial in character, reflecting the fact that such legislation principally affects individual rights and interests.[48] Their origin lies in the medieval practice of petitioning the king for some special privilege or dispensation which he granted in the form of a statute.[49] Nowadays petitions are brought on the basis that the legislation is necessary to ameliorate an individual set of circumstances which is not adequately provided for by existing statute law or common law. Until the end of the 18th century private legislation occupied a considerable portion of parliamentary time and during the 19th century it was the preferred instrument to deal with, amongst other things, the provision of public utilities and transport.

[13.41] The eclectic range of matters which have been the subject of private legislation since the foundation of the state includes public utilities,[50] harbours,[51] railways,[52] the Bank of Ireland,[53] the Methodist Church,[54] a sports field in Bagnalstown, Co Carlow,[55] the affairs of private institutions,[56] the composition of the Board of Trinity College, Dublin,[57] the Royal College of Surgeons[58] and individual property settlements.[59] Another species of private legislation, known as a Provisional Order Confirmation Bill, is enacted to confirm provisional orders which have been made under statute by a Minister at the behest of a local authority or statutory body. Most commonly these measures have involved the extension of city boundaries[60] or matters relating to harbours.[61]

---

[48] See generally, Morgan, *Constitutional Law of Ireland* (2nd edn, 1990), pp 103–104; McGowan Smyth, *The Theory and Practice of the Irish Senate* (1972), pp 70–80.

[49] See McDonald, *Parliament at Work* (1989), pp 178–180.

[50] For example, Sligo Lighting and Electric Power Act 1924.

[51] For example, Dundalk Harbour and Port Act 1925; Limerick Harbour Act 1926; Cork Harbour Act 1933; Galway Harbour Act 1935.

[52] For example, Dublin United Tramways (Lucan Electric Railway) Act 1927; Limerick Harbour Tramways Act 1931.

[53] Bank of Ireland Act 1929; Bank of Ireland Act 1935.

[54] Methodist Church in Ireland Act 1928.

[55] Daniel McGrath Foundation Act 1945.

[56] For example, Erasmus Smith Schools Act 1938; Convalescent Home Stillorgan (Charter Amendment) Act 1958; Royal College of Surgeons in Ireland (Charter Amendment) Act 1965; Institute of Chartered Accountants in Ireland (Charter Amendment) Act 1966; Royal College of Physicians of Ireland (Charter and Letters Patent Amendment) Act 1979.

[57] The Trinity College, Dublin (Charters and Letters Patent Amendment) Act 2000.

[58] The Royal College of Surgeons in Ireland (Charters Amendment) Acts 1965 and 2003.

[59] For example, Poë Name and Arms (Compton Domvile Estates) Act 1936; The Altamont (Amendment of Deed of Trust) Act 1993.

[60] For example, Local Government and Public Health Provisional Order Confirmation Act 1953 confirming City of Dublin (Extension of Boundaries) Order 1953.

[61] For example, Pier and Harbour Provisional Order Confirmation Act 1932 confirming Limerick Harbour Order 1932.

[13.42] Private Bills are introduced in the Seanad at the initiative of a promoter who appears before the House as a suitor. The process is governed by the Standing Orders of the Dáil and the Seanad relative to Private Business and is supervised by the Examiner of Private Bills, an official of the Oireachtas who is jointly appointed by the Ceann Comhairle and Cathaoirleach of the Seanad, to ensure compliance therewith. Notice of the Bill setting out its principal subject matter must be published in newspapers and a copy of the Bill must be deposited for inspection in the Private Bill Office of the Houses of the Oireachtas, the purpose being to bring the proposal to the attention of those who might in some way be affected by it. Those who believe that their interests are affected by the legislation may be admitted as adverse parties to contest the proposal. The parties are represented by a parliamentary agent and counsel. When the Examiner of Private Bills has reported that the promoter has complied with Standing Orders or where they have been dispensed with by both Houses, the Bill is deemed to have passed the first stage in the Seanad. The second stage reading in the Seanad is usually something of a formality since there is a general reluctance to reject a measure of this nature without a full consideration of its merits.

[13.43] After the second stage reading in the Seanad the Bill is referred for the third stage to a joint committee consisting of members of both Houses. At this stage the quasi-judicial character of the process is evident in the composition of the joint committee, the nature of the proceedings and the onus which is placed on the promoter to establish the necessity and justification for the measure. However, it is probably the case that the process is not amenable to judicial review, thus distinguishing it from quasi-judicial proceedings in other domains.[62] The joint committee consists of three members from each House and a Chairman, who may be a member of either House. Members must sign a declaration that they, and in the case of TDs their constituents, have no personal interest in the Bill; moreover, they must also declare that they will not vote on any issue without having attended and heard the relevant evidence. (In contrast, neither undertaking is expected in the case of public legislation.) The joint committee, being a select committee, has the power to call witnesses and hear evidence. It hears counsel for both the promoters and objectors, and considers submissions put to it by relevant government departments.

[13.44] In essence, the promoter is required to establish a case for the proposed legislation with those opposed being given the opportunity to contest the case. The facts on which the promoter seeks the legislation and the reasons for it must be set out in the preamble to the Bill. When the preamble has been proved the parties withdraw and the committee continues to consider the Bill clause by clause in the normal manner. The

---

[62]   The remarks of Deputy O'Malley are apposite: '[i]n dealing with Private Bills, the Oireachtas acts in a quasi-judicial capacity. Rules such as hearing both parties, giving reasons for decisions and no person acting as a judge in his own case are important. There is the added problem that our decisions probably are not justiciable and that the courts will not hear cases against them except in so far as passed legislation infringes the Constitution' *Dáil Debates*, col 42, 26 October 2000.

committee reports back, with or without amendment, to both Houses. The fourth and fifth stages follow in the Seanad, after which it is sent for consideration to the Dáil where the first three stages are waived.

[13.45] Resorting to private legislation as a means to remedy individual cases can prove to be both time-consuming and expensive. While this might prove to be irritating and cumbersome for corporate bodies, it assumes a greater significance for individuals whose affairs have to be settled by this mechanism. The enactment of The Altamont (Amendment of Deed of Trust) Act 1993 was necessary to allow certain amendments to be made to a trust which was established in respect of Lord Altamont's properties. It was introduced as a Bill in 1990 and did not become law until 1993. In the interim the promoter, and no doubt his family, were left in a state of some uncertainty – anticipated dealings with his property would have to be postponed. The cost of private legislation is usually borne by the promoter and thus it is largely the preserve of the comparatively wealthy. Nevertheless, private legislation is the only mechanism by which some legal instruments, such as certain deeds of trust and charters, may be altered and unless general legislation which provides an alternative mechanism is enacted recourse thereto will prove necessary.[63]

Informal process

[13.46] The preceding sections have concentrated on the formal rules and practices which govern the legislative process. They focused on the constitutional and legal parameters within which the process is constrained. However, that only presents part of the picture and the process operates in the context of informal practices, conventions and understandings which are at least as important in shaping the enactment of legislation. The day-to-day operation of the legislature, the selection of legislative priorities and the adoption and implementation of a legislative programme are governed by factors which exist and function beyond the formal constitutional conventions. To this extent we find ourselves in the political realm and our inquiry takes in an area of overlap between law and political science. Nevertheless, an understanding of the legislative process would be incomplete without alluding to these extra-legal factors.[64]

[13.47] The almost complete control exercised by the government over the business of the Oireachtas has already been noted. The government is usually assured of the support of a majority in the Dáil – either the government parties enjoy an absolute majority or the government has enlisted the support of a sufficient number of independent deputies to allow it to function. This, coupled with the Taoiseach's power to nominate 11 members to the Seanad (out of a total complement of 60), ensures that the government will rarely be defeated on a vote in either House. The government's numerical strength is reinforced by a relative lack of independence amongst backbenchers. The latter is the product of an amalgam of factors – a highly inflexible system of party discipline from

---

63   In this regard see the remarks of Senator O'Toole 134 *Seanad Debates*, col 1127.

64   See generally Chubb, *The Government and Politics of Ireland* (3rd edn, 1992), Chs 9–11; Coakley and Gallagher (eds) *Politics in the Republic of Ireland* (5th edn, 2010), Ch 7.

which members rarely deviate, the political ambitions of members who aspire to promotion to government in the future, a general unwillingness to rock the boat and the direction of members' energies to other tasks, especially constituency work.

[13.48] In addition, the adversarial culture of our political system has tended to assign a confrontational role to the opposition. Politics is perceived as being concerned with the acquisition and exercise of power and the conventions by which it operates are almost pugilistic. On this view, defeating the other side, or at least dealing it a body blow, is as important as influencing the enactment of legislation. It follows that active participation by the Oireachtas in formulating the legislative programme is almost non-existent and even the role it plays in scrutinising government proposals is slight.

[13.49] Nowhere is the relative weakness of the Oireachtas more evident than in the paucity of private members' Bills which have been enacted. At the time the enactment of the Judicial Separation and Family Law Reform Act 1989 was exceptional and owed its success to a combination of the tenacity of the sponsoring member and the fact that the government, being in a minority position in the Dáil, was reluctant to take the political risk of opposing the measure outright. Before that, the most recent private members' Bill to be successful was in 1965[65] and in the history of the state fewer than 25 such measures have been enacted. It is difficult to disagree with the observation that the Oireachtas has proved itself to be 'sadly ineffective'[66] in making laws. However, gradual change is evident in the enactment of a number of private members' proposals and the influence wielded by the Joint Committee on Legislation and Security in the passage of the Courts and Court Officers Act 1995.[67] These efforts might prove to be a basis for the adoption of a more assertive legislative role by the Oireachtas and are to be welcomed, but it remains to be seen whether the momentum will be maintained.

[13.50] Although the role the Oireachtas plays in formulating legislation is minimal, it would be a mistake to conclude that it exists merely to rubber-stamp proposals which are presented to it by the government. While the government dominates the Oireachtas and dictates its business, the relationship between the two bodies is more subtle than might first appear. In practical political terms the requirement of presenting legislation before and steering it through the Oireachtas imposes a discipline on the government. As a minimum it must ensure that a proposal secures the assent, or at least avoids the dissent, of its own supporters. This process, of course, does not occur on the floor of the House where it is exposed to the glare of publicity but in the privacy of the party meeting. Nevertheless, it acts as a negative check in the sense that a measure which is unacceptable will not be initiated. In this regard the government's supporters are presented with the opportunity to filter or modify proposals before they are formally initiated in the Oireachtas.

---

[65]   Protection of Animals (Amendment) Act 1965.

[66]   Chubb, *The Government and Politics of Ireland* (3rd edn, 1992), p 199.

[67]   See paras **13.35** and **13.39**.

[13.51] Once the Bill is initiated party ranks usually close but still the (admittedly slight) possibility exists that the government will withdraw or amend a proposal in the light of opposition which it attracts. In that circumstance the government's action might well be motivated by a concern to maintain its popularity with the electorate rather than by a fear of parliamentary defeat or a re-evaluation of the merits of the proposal. The significant point is that the Oireachtas becomes the forum in which the measure is brought to public attention and acts as a catalyst for wider debate.

[13.52] The role of the Oireachtas is also significant in that its procedures formalise the process of law-making. This is not simply an arcane ritual that functions as a piece of constitutional theatre. It both legitimises that which it produces and facilitates its recognition as law. Legislation is identified and assured the force of law by its having undergone the process of enactment by the Oireachtas. In contrast, other instruments which seek to regulate, such as ministerial circulars, lack that status and the accompanying force of law because they have not been subject to that process. In short, the process of enactment by the Oireachtas, in accordance with the governing constitutional formula, distinguishes legal from non-legal measures.

Sources of and influences on legislation

[13.53] Apart from the annual enactment of a Finance Act and an Appropriation Act, giving effect to the budget and allocating government expenditure respectively, the selection of measures to be included in the legislative programme is primarily determined by the government.[68] It decides which proposals will be presented to the Oireachtas for enactment and the priority to be accorded to each. This is largely a matter of political choice, but it will have been preceded by a complex policy-making process which acts as a constraint within which the choice is exercised. Legislative proposals derive from a variety of sources which include the policies of the party in government, bargaining between parties which make up a coalition government, negotiation with the social partners and lobbying by a myriad of interest groups representing different sectors of society. The workings of the process and the manner in which the various participants interact and compete are primarily of interest to political scientists and students of policy-making.[69] While the outcome of this process, namely legislation, is of interest to lawyers, its operation is of less immediate practical concern. Nevertheless, events which precede and influence the enactment of a measure might prove to be important when it comes to the lawyer's task of statutory interpretation. In this regard a number of documents are relevant, in that they might assist in identifying the purpose of the legislation or the intent with which it was enacted.

[13.54] The relative weakness of the Oireachtas does not mean that the parliamentary debates on a measure are irrelevant and should be ignored. While the government might be assured that a Bill will pass through the Oireachtas with relative ease, the discipline

---

68 The detailed procedures that are followed are set out in the *Cabinet Handbook* (2006).
69 See, eg Chubb, *The Government and Politics of Ireland* (3rd edn, 1992), Ch 9; Coakley and Gallagher (eds), *Politics in the Republic of Ireland* (5th edn, 2010), Ch 11.

of debate forces the Minister to justify the measure and to explain what it seeks to achieve. Thus, the legislative proceedings as reported in the Dáil Debates and Seanad Debates might merit scrutiny.[70] In addition, many Bills are published with an accompanying explanatory memorandum which briefly explains the reasons behind the proposal. Prior to initiating a Bill the government might publish a Green Paper or White Paper on the subject. This follows the British practice of issuing such documents, which are consultative in nature, but the distinction between the two is unclear.[71] A Green Paper is somewhat more discursive in that sets out various ideas and approaches without committing the government to any particular course of action. A White Paper tends to be more definitive in that it typically sets out a clear governmental view on the matter.

[13.55] While the government enjoys a near monopoly in selecting the contents of the legislative programme, particular proposals might owe their origin to the deliberations and activities of non-governmental bodies. The Law Reform Commission[72] is charged with examining various areas of the law with a view to their reform. Its reports will typically set out the existing law, identify its deficiencies, examine alternative approaches, compare the law of other jurisdictions and make the recommendations it considers to be appropriate.[73] Indeed the Commission has adopted the practice of appending a draft Bill to its reports. From time to time *ad hoc* committees are established to examine a particular topic and report to the government, the Dáil or both Houses of the Oireachtas. The composition of such bodies is usually representative of the various interests that are affected by the topic in question and their deliberations often result in recommendations for legislation.[74]

---

70 Whether a court may refer to parliamentary proceedings as an aid to interpreting a statute is considered at paras **14.170–14.187**.

71 See Sandford, 'Open Government: the Use of Green Papers' [1980] *British Tax Review* 351; Jordan, 'Grey Papers' (1977) 48 *Political Quarterly* 30.

72 See further paras **11.02–11.14**.

73 For example, The Statute of Limitations (Amendment) Act 1991 had its origin in the Commission's *Report on the Statute of Limitations: Claims in respect of Latent Personal Injuries* (LRC 21-1987); the Larceny Act 1990 enacted some, but not all, of the recommendations of the *Report on Receiving Stolen Property* (LRC 23-1987); the Non-Fatal Offences against the Person Act 1997 was for the most part based on recommendations in the *Report on Non-Fatal Offences Against the Person* (LRC 45-1994); the Criminal Justice (Theft and Fraud Offences) Act 2001 had its origin in the Commission's *Report on the Law Relating to Dishonesty* (LRC 43-1992); Child Care Act 1991, Criminal Evidence Act 1992, Criminal Law (Sexual Offences) Act 1993, Domestic Violence Act 1996, Criminal Justice (Miscellaneous Provisions) Act 1997, Protection for Persons Reporting Child Abuse Act 1998, and Criminal Justice (Withholding Information on Crimes against Children and Vulnerable Persons) Act 2012, all had their origin in the Commission's *Report on Child Sexual Abuse* (LRC 32-1990).

74 For example, *Report of the Commission of Inquiry on Safety, Health and Welfare at Work* (Pl 1868), published in 1983 led to the enactment of the Safety, Health and Welfare at Work Act 1989. (contd.../)

[13.56] An alternative is to nominate an individual, often a judge, to report on a topic again with a view to recommending improvements. In some instances the report of a tribunal of inquiry established under the Tribunals of Inquiry Acts 1921–2004 might contain recommendations for legislation. Legislation might also derive from the state's international obligations, whether they be contained in a treaty,[75] which is frequently accompanied by preparatory documents (*travaux préparatoires*), or result from a judicial decision which must be incorporated into domestic law.[76] In recent years a large volume of legislation has resulted from obligations which have accrued from membership of the European Communities.[77]

[13.57] Much of the foregoing suggests that a desirable and welcome element of deliberation precedes legislation. In some cases, however, the enactment of legislation is prompted by unanticipated events which require immediate attention. In the past security and economic matters have necessitated the speedy introduction of legislation and in some cases legislation has been enacted in less than 24 hours.[78] Judicial decisions can also prove to be the source of unforeseen difficulties which require legislative redress.[79]

---

74 (\...contd) The provisions of the Criminal Justice (Public Order) Act 1994, ss 20–22 derive in the main from the recommendations in the *Report of the Committee on Public Safety and Crowd Control* (Pl 7107). On the other hand the recommendations in the *Report of the Committee to Enquire into Certain Aspects of Criminal Procedure* were only partially enacted in the Criminal Procedure Act 1993.

75 For example, Geneva Conventions Act 1962 giving effect to the Conventions on Prisoners of War, etc; Genocide Act 1973, based on the UN Genocide Convention; Pt II of the Extradition Act 1965, based on European Convention on Extradition.

76 In consequence of the decision of the European Court of Human Rights in *Norris v Ireland* (1988) 13 EHRR 186 male homosexual conduct was decriminalised by the Criminal Law (Sexual Offences) Act 1993.

77 See Donelan, 'The Role of the Office of the Parliamentary Draftsman in the Implementation of European Union Directives in Ireland' (1997) 18 Stat LR 1.

78 The Anglo-Irish Bank Corporation Act 2009 passed through all stages in both Houses of the Oireachtas in one day: this swift action was deemed necessary to secure the bank's stability and, by extension that of the Irish financial sector – 672 *Dáil Debates* 1 (20 Jan 2009); the Insurance (No 2) Act 1983 was enacted to deal with the impending collapse of a major insurance company. The Offences Against the State (Amendment) Act 1985 was enacted to provide the government with the power to 'freeze' bank accounts which were suspected to contain terrorist funds. Both were passed in the space of a few hours; in both cases the opposition facilitated the enactment of the measure – see 345 *Dáil Debates*, cols 189–190 and 356 *Dáil Debates*, col 138 respectively. The Seanad did not impede the Bills' progress.

79 For example, the Solicitors (Amendment) Act 1960, which was enacted in consequence of *Re Solicitors Act 1954* [1960] IR 239. The Building Societies (Amendment) Act 1983 was enacted to deal with an anomaly which resulted from the decision of the High Court in *Rafferty v Crowley* [1984] ILRM 350; in fact the trial judge had anticipated the likelihood of legislation and directed that a copy of his judgment be sent immediately to the relevant Minister.

Drafting of legislation[80]

[13.58] Given the government's virtual monopoly over the legislative programme, individual proposals for legislation are formulated by the various Departments of State and are presented by the relevant Minister to the government for approval. By this time the advice of the Attorney General will usually have been obtained. Once a proposal has secured government approval and is scheduled on its legislative programme, the Bill which is to be initiated in the Oireachtas must be drafted. That task is undertaken by the Office of the Parliamentary Counsel to the Government,[81] which is attached to that of the Attorney General. The Office employs a number of parliamentary drafters, barristers or solicitors of four years' standing who specialise in the art of legislative drafting.

[13.59] The protocol involved in securing the drafting of a measure is described succinctly by a member of the Office:

"The decision to introduce legislation is made on foot of a document known as a 'Memorandum for Government'. The Memorandum sets out in detail the background to the Bill and the view of the Ministers concerned with the bill. The Memorandum includes an outline draft of the Bill prepared by the civil servants in the department concerned with promoting the bill. This draft is known in Ireland as 'heads'."[82]

[13.60] Once a decision has been taken by the government approving the 'heads' (with or without qualification), the Secretary of the Government sends the Attorney General a note of the decision. A letter requesting that the Parliamentary Counsel be directed to draft legislation in accordance with the Memorandum and the 'heads' is sent by the Department concerned to the Attorney General. A drafter is then nominated to draft the bill.

[13.61] In this manner the drafter is instructed as to the contents and objectives of the proposed legislation and he or she, in effect, converts those instructions into a legally intelligible form. In the course of drafting the drafter is likely to liaise with the civil servants who are involved in promoting the Bill as well as lawyers on the advisory side of the Attorney General's office. It is also conceivable that the Attorney General's advice will be sought on particular difficulties which were not foreseen when the measure was presented to government.

[13.62] A cardinal feature of the drafting process is its centralised nature. Those who have been involved in the determination and development of the policy are not directly engaged in the drafting of the law which is to implement it although, as stated, liaison between them and the drafter is likely to occur. Nevertheless, the point is that the

---

[80] See Hunt, 'Office of the Parliamentary Draftsman: A Secret History' (2004) 9 BR 167; Donelan, 'The Role of the Parliamentary Draftsman in the Preparation of Legislation in Ireland' (1992) 14 DULJ 1.

[81] Until 30 September 2000 its title was Office of the Parliamentary Draftsman.

[82] Donelan, 'The Role of the Parliamentary Draftsman in the Preparation of Legislation in Ireland' (1992) 14 DULJ 1, 3.

drafting of the law is transferred from the department which sponsors the legislation to Parliamentary Counsel. This might be justified on the basis that it brings uniformity to the process and ensures that laws are drafted in a standard format, style and language.[83] On this view it is better to employ a 'house style' than to have a different style for each sponsoring department.

[13.63] Moreover, it is argued that drafting is a specialist art, or indeed science, for which few possess the aptitude and which requires considerable experience to perfect. As one writer put it:

> "What makes a good legislative draftsman is a good basic legal knowledge, a feeling for the proper use of the English language, a critical ability, lots of imagination and plenty of practice. Experience has shown that general legal ability by itself is not sufficient and that a competent lawyer without practical experience in legislative draftsmanship cannot perform the craft satisfactorily."[84]

[13.64] The amount of experience which is believed to be necessary is uncertain, with estimates varying from five to 10 years. However, most legislative drafters will endorse the view that experience and practice at the task are essential to acquiring the necessary drafting skills. On the other hand it might be argued that the assignment of the function of drafting to specialists is itself the source of many of the problems associated with the quality of legislation. In particular, it is said that it has resulted in legislation which is opaque, complex and overly elaborate where clarity and simplicity would better serve the public.[85]

[3] LEGISLATIVE PRODUCT

The format of statutes

[13.65] The format of statutes is governed by a combination of constitutional and statutory provisions and conventional practices.

Language

[13.66] Most Bills are introduced and passed in the English language, bilingual and Irish language Bills being rare exceptions.[86] Article 25.4.4° requires that an official translation of laws passed in one language be provided.[87] When published and made

---

83 In some jurisdictions the matter is institutionalised through the adoption of formal guidelines for the draftsman.

84 Kolts, 'Observations on the Proposed New Approach to Legislative Drafting in Common Law Countries' [1980] Stat LR 144, 146–147.

85 See further, para **13.98**.

86 Examples are the Údarás na Gaeltachta (Amendment) Act 1999 and the Údarás na Gaeltachta (Amendment) (No 2) Act 1999; part of the British-Irish Agreement Act 1999 was enacted in Irish (ss 24–30) with the English language text being set out in a table at the end of those sections; the rest of the Act was passed in English.

87 Article 25.4.4°: 'Where the President signs the text of a Bill in one only of the official languages, an official translation shall be issued in the other official language.'

generally available, Acts should appear in both languages with the respective texts printed side by side. In fact, matters are somewhat in arrears and there can be a considerable delay in ensuring the bilingual publication of statutes. The failure to produce an official translation of statutes was considered in *Ó Beoláin v Fahy*[88] where the Supreme Court, by a 2:1 majority, granted a declaration to the effect that the state has a constitutional duty to make official translations of Acts of the Oireachtas available to the public. By the time of the proceedings, the applicant had been provided with Irish language versions of the relevant statutes, namely the Road Traffic Acts 1994 and 1995, and thus it was arguable that the question of translation had become moot. Moreover, the declaration granted was drafted in terms that were almost identical to the text of Article 25.4.4° and some would think it unnecessary to make such an order that states the obvious.

[13.67] However, the majority considered it necessary to grant the declaration given the state's continued disregard of its constitutional obligation. McGuinness J observed that:

> "The Respondents' argument for a reasonable time to be allowed for translation would ring more sincerely were it not for the fact that virtually no official translations of statutes have been provided for the past twenty years. That could not be described as 'a reasonable time'."[89]

Hardiman J took a similar view:

> "This failure is at its grossest in the most recent times. Anyone with access to the printed statutes will be aware that since 1980 there has been a departure from the previous policy of preparing official translations of the great majority of bills which are passed in English as they progress through the constitutional stages ending with their promulgation as law … It must be stressed that this policy of inertia is in clear and obvious breach of the express constitutional requirement contained in Article 25.4.4°."[90]

[13.68] In the light of this decision it is clear that the existing arrangements for the translation of statutes will have to be revised and appropriate resources allocated to the task. At present the task of translation is assigned to the Clerk of the Dáil,[91] but it would appear that staff shortages and an increased workload had resulted in the state of affairs that led to the proceedings in *Ó Beoláin*.[92]

---

[88] *Ó Beoláin v Fahy* [2001] 2 IR 279.

[89] [2001] 2 IR 279 at 307–308.

[90] [2001] 2 IR 279 at 346.

[91] DSO 18(3): 'The Clerk shall cause to be made an official translation into English of every law enacted by the Oireachtas in Irish, and an official translation into Irish of every law enacted by the Oireachtas in English.'

[92] The court also held that the applicant was entitled to an Irish language version of the District Court Rules 1997 (SI 93/1997); this right was, in essence, an aspect of the right to conduct legal proceeding in Irish; see *Delap v Minister for Justice* [1980–1998] IR Special Reports 46, where it was held that there is an obligation to provide a translation of the Rules of the Superior Courts. (contd.../)

Short and long title

[13.69] A statute has a short title, by which it is generally known and cited, and a statutory number.[93] For instance, the Misuse of Drugs Act 1977 is the short title, its statutory number being Number 12 of 1977. A statute also has a long title, which appears at the head of the document in which it is contained. The long title of the Misuse of Drugs Act 1977 is:

> "An Act to prevent the misuse of certain dangerous or otherwise harmful drugs, to enable the Minister for Health to make for that purpose certain regulations in relation to such drugs, to enable that Minister to provide that certain substances shall be poisons for the purposes of the Pharmacy Acts, 1875 to 1962, to amend the Pharmacopoeia Act 1931, the Poisons Act 1961, the Pharmacy Act 1962, and the Health Acts 1947 to 1970, to repeal the Dangerous Drugs Act 1934 and section 78 of the Health Act 1970 and to make certain other provisions in relation to the foregoing" [16 May 1977].

[13.70] The long title states in very general terms the purpose and objectives of the statute. In the example given it can be seen that the object is to deal with dangerous and harmful drugs, to provide the Minister for Health with the power to make regulations on the matter and to amend various earlier statutes accordingly.

Preamble

[13.71] In the past it was the practice to include a preamble which appeared after the long title, but before the main body of the Act. The preamble would typically recite the factual assumptions on which the legislation was based. The preamble to the Criminal Law (Ireland) Act 1828 reads:

> "Whereas it is expedient, with a View to improve the Administration of Justice in Criminal Cases in Ireland, to define in what Circumstances Persons may be admitted to Bail in cases of Felony; and to make better Provision for taking Examinations, Informations, Bailments, and Recognizances, and returning the same to the proper Tribunals; and to relax in some Instances the technical Strictness of Criminal Proceedings, so as to ensure the Punishment of the Guilty without depriving the Accused of any just Means of Defence; and to abolish the Benefit of Clergy and some Matters of Form which impede the due Administration of Justice; and to make better Provision for the Punishment of Offenders in certain Cases."

[13.72] A number of Acts of the Oireachtas which were passed in 1922, 1923 and 1924 contain a preamble, but the practice has been all but abandoned in the case of public Acts as more extensive long titles tend to recite the statutory purpose.[94] Preambles are still included in private Acts. In that case the preamble recites the facts that the promoter

---

92   (\...contd) There is no constitutional or statutory obligation to translate statutory instruments; see generally O'Malley, *The Status of the Irish Language—a Legal Perspective* (1990).

93   See Interpretation Act 2005, s 14(1).

94   See Xanthaki, *Thornton's Legislative Drafting* (5th edn, 2013), p 235. Preambles are commonplace in civil law jurisdictions and often precede European Community Directives. However, the Financial Emergency Measures in the Public Interest Act 2009 contains both a long title and a preamble, with the latter reciting the economic background to the Act.

of the Bill seeks to establish and are found to be proved by the joint committee which conducts the third reading.[95] Preambles to private statutes can be lengthy and often exceed the actual text of the statute. For example, the Poë Name and Arms (Compton Domvile Estates) Act 1936, which contains two brief sections consisting of seven lines of text,[96] is preceded by a five-page preamble setting out the factual background which the sponsors were required to prove.

[13.73] The practice of including a section setting out the objects or purpose of the legislation has been adopted in some recent statutes. Such sections tend to be drafted in general terms and are designed to state the principles that inform the policy contained in the legislation.[97] An example is provided by s 6 of the Education Act 1998 which sets out a 13-paragraph list of objects 'in pursuance of which the Oireachtas has enacted this Act'; the provision also commands '[e]very person concerned in the implementation' of the Act to have regard to those objects. Interestingly, the terms of s 6 are broadly similar to those of the long title to the Act: many of the objects listed in that section mirror the purposes outlined in the long title.

Dates of commencement

[13.74] The date which appears at the conclusion of the long title is that on which the Bill as passed by both Houses of the Oireachtas was signed into law by the President. Thus, the Misuse of Drugs Act 1977 became law on 16 May 1977. However, it should be noted that a statute might not come into effect until a later date, which is called the date of commencement. A statute which contains no provision concerning its commencement comes into force immediately.[98] For several reasons, however, it might be preferred to delay the commencement of a statute and one of a variety of devices might be employed in this regard. The commencement date might be stated expressly in the statute; or the statute might give the government or a particular minister power to make an order bringing the Act into force at any time; or within a stated time; or not before a stated time. An increasingly common formula is to provide that the Act is to come into force at a specified time (often one month) after its being passed.[99] On the other hand, s 43(2) of the Misuse of Drugs Act 1977 deals with its commencement thus:

---

95   See para **13.44**.
96   The Act reads:

>   1. From and after the passing of this Act and thenceforward continuously the Name and Arms of the said Sir Hugo Compton Domvile Poë to be borne and used by him shall as regards the Name be Hugo Compton Domvile Poë Domvile and as regards the Arms be the Arms of Domvile quartered with the Arms of Poë.
>   2. This Act may be cited as the Poë Name and Arms (Compton Domvile Estates) Act 1936.

97   See Samuels, 'Statements of Purpose and Principle in British Statutes' (1998) 19 Stat LR 63.
98   Article 25.4.1°.
99   For example, Criminal Justice (Public Order) Act 1994, s 1(3).

"Subsection 1 of this section and section 41(2) of this Act shall come into operation on the passing hereof and the other purposes and provisions shall come into operation on such day or days as may be fixed therefor by any order or orders of the Minister [for Health] either generally or with reference to any particular such purpose or provision and different days may be so fixed for different such purposes and different such provisions of this Act."

[13.75] Thus, with the exceptions of s 41(2) and s 43(1) which came into force immediately, the effective operation of the Act was delayed until the appropriate order was made by the Minister. Moreover, the Minister was given power to bring either the whole Act or selected parts thereof into operation at a later date. The Act was eventually brought into operation by the Misuse of Drugs Act 1977 (Commencement) Order 1979[100] A variant on the formula used in the Misuse of Drugs Act 1977 is contained in s 2 of the Succession Act 1965 which deals with the commencement of that Act thus:

"This Act shall come into effect on such day, not earlier than the 1st day of July 1966, as the Minister [for Justice] by order appoints."

In this case the Minister was given power to bring the entire Act into force, but not before the specified date. That Act was brought into effect by the Succession Act 1965 (Commencement) Order 1966.[101]

[13.76] One reason for delegating the power to order the commencement of an Act to a Minister is to allow the necessary financial and administrative changes to be made before the legislation is brought into force. It should be noted that in both examples above the respective Ministers were invested with the power to bring the Act into force but were not expressly obliged to do so. In this context the decision of the Supreme Court in *The State (Sheehan) v The Government of Ireland*[102] is instructive. Section 60(1) of the Civil Liability Act 1961 makes local authorities liable for injuries suffered through their failure adequately to maintain public roads. However, s 60(7) provides that the section 'shall come into operation on such day, not earlier than the 1st day of April 1967, as may be fixed therefor by order made by the Government'. At the time of the proceedings no such order had been made and the prosecutor sought an order of *mandamus* directing the government so to order. In rejecting his claim the court noted that the wording of the section is enabling, or permissive, not mandatory. The only limit imposed was that the provision could not come into effect before the specified date and the government's discretion is not otherwise fettered. The absence of limiting words such as 'as soon as convenient' or 'as soon as may be' confirmed the court's view that the power is unlimited.

[13.77] The view of the majority was expressed by Henchy J:

"The uses of 'shall' and 'may', both in the sub-section and the section as a whole, point to the conclusion that the radical law-reform embodied in the section was intended not to come into effect before the 1st April 1967, and thereafter only on such day as may be fixed by an

---

[100] SI 28/1979.
[101] SI 168/1966.
[102] *The State (Sheehan) v The Government of Ireland* [1987] IR 550.

order made by the Government. Not, be it noted, on such date as *shall* be fixed by the Government. Limiting words such as 'as soon as may be' or 'as soon as convenient', which are to be found in comparable statutory provisions, are markedly absent. If the true reading of s 60, sub-s 7 were to the effect that the Government were bound to bring the section into operation, it would, of course, be unconstitutional for the Government to achieve by their prolonged inactivity the virtual repeal of the section.

In my opinion, however, s 60, sub-s 7 by vesting the power of bringing the section into operation in the Government rather than in a particular Minister, and the wording used, connoting an enabling rather than a mandatory power or discretion, would seem to point to the parliamentary recognition of the fact that the important law-reform to be effected by the section was not to take effect unless and until the Government became satisfied that, in the light of factors such as the necessary deployment of financial and other resources, the postulated reform could be carried into effect. The discretion vested in the Government to bring the section into operation on a date after the 1st April 1967, was not limited in any way, as to time or otherwise."[103]

[13.78] The question of the courts' power to direct a Minister to make an order for the commencement of a statutory provision arose again in *Rooney v Minister for Agriculture and Food*.[104] The plaintiff's cattle, which were affected with bovine tuberculosis, were slaughtered. He was offered compensation assessed on the basis of a non-statutory scheme which was administered by the defendant. At the time the relevant compensation provisions contained in the Diseases of Animals Act 1966 had not been brought into effect. The plaintiff argued that the defendant ought to have brought those provisions into effect rather than administer the non-statutory scheme which provided a less generous quantum of compensation. It was contended on the Minister's behalf that the non-statutory scheme provided a better safeguard of public funds and that it would be more expensive to implement the statutory scheme.

[13.79] O'Flaherty J spoke for a unanimous Supreme Court:

"I need only look at the provisions as regards the various steps that would have to be taken if s 20 and s 58 were in operation to realise that it would be vastly more expensive than the scheme which is at present in operation and no one has ever suggested that that, itself, ever represented anything but a huge cost to the exchequer …

The court would be entitled to review such a decision [that is, not to implement the statutory scheme] and course of action (embodied in the scheme) if it were satisfied that the decision and course of conduct was *mala fides* – or, at the least, that it involved an abuse of power: see *Pine Valley Developments v Minister for the Environment*.[105] It may be that the court has no power to enjoin the Minister to make orders under s 20 (*cf The State (Sheehan) v Government of Ireland*)[106] in any circumstances but it certainly has no power to do so in the absence of proof of *mala fides* or abuse of power ... I hold that the Minister is not obliged to operate [the Act] since he has in place a reasonable scheme for providing a measure of

---

[103]   [1987] IR 550 at 561 (emphasis in original).
[104]   *Rooney v Minister for Agriculture and Food* [1991] 2 IR 539.
[105]   *Pine Valley Developments v Minister for the Environment* [1987] IR 23.
[106]   *The State (Sheehan) v The Government of Ireland* [1987] IR 550.

assistance to herd-owners of diseased cattle. That it is not the ideal scheme that the plaintiff would wish to see in place is neither here nor there."[107]

[13.80] The decision in *Rooney*[108] might require reconsideration in the light of more recent judicial utterances that have questioned the use of non-statutory schemes in preference to those that are statutorily founded.[109] For present purposes the significance of the decision lies in the conclusion that the Minister could not be compelled to order the commencement of the statute. Many would consider the policy reason that was advanced in support of the non-implementation of the relevant provision, namely controlling public expenditure, acceptable and in this respect *Rooney* might be thought to differ from *Sheehan*. In this context it should be noted that in *Sheehan* Finlay CJ and Griffin J reserved their opinions on the question whether a court could direct the making of a commencement order where the implementation of the legislation would impose a burden on the public finances. *Rooney* differs somewhat in emphasis from *Sheehan* in that the court acknowledged the possibility that the implementation of a statute might be judicially ordered.

[13.81] However, the circumstances in which judicial intervention might be successfully sought are exceedingly rare and a plaintiff would bear a heavy burden of proof. In practice, it is unlikely that, unless express limits are imposed on the power to order the commencement of an Act, the person or body so empowered would be compelled to bring the statute into force. This, in effect, would allow a Minister to postpone indefinitely the implementation of Acts passed by the Oireachtas, subject only to the infrequently invoked device of parliamentary accountability. The commencement of individual provisions, as was the case in *Sheehan*[110] and *Rooney*,[111] and of entire statutes, has been delayed in this fashion. The Health (Mental Services) Act 1981 was never brought into operation and it was eventually repealed by the Mental Health Act 2001.

Internal organisation of statutes

[13.82] An Act is divided into consecutively numbered sections, and a section may be further subdivided. In practice subsections, paragraphs and sub-paragraphs are the principal subdivisions employed. In general, a section deals with one point while sub-sections elaborate on or supplement the main point of the section. Sections may be grouped into consecutively numbered Parts or chapters. Division into Parts, each of which concerns a particular aspect, is common in Acts which deal with a large general subject and makes the Act less cumbersome. For instance, the Succession Act 1965 consists of 12 Parts. In some cases an Act will contain one or more Schedules which

---

107 *Rooney v Minister for Agriculture and Food* [1991] 2 IR 539, 546.
108 [1991] 2 IR 539.
109 For example, *McCann v Minister for Education* [1997] 1 ILRM 1; see Hogan and Morgan, *Administrative Law in Ireland* (4th edn, 2010), p 37, citing *O'Neill v Minister for Agriculture* [1997] 2 ILRM 435; see paras **13.09–13.12**.
110 *The State (Sheehan) v The Government of Ireland* [1987] IR 550.
111 *Rooney v Minister for Agriculture and Food* [1991] 2 IR 539.

appear at the end of the document. A Schedule, in effect, is an appendix which contains material which is too unwieldy to list in the main body of the Act. The Misuse of Drugs Act 1977 has one Schedule which lists controlled drugs, of which there are in excess of 120. The Succession Act 1965 has two Schedules. The first sets out the rules as to the application of a deceased's assets and the second lists earlier legislation which is repealed, amended or otherwise altered by the Act.

[13.83] Apart from its provisions, an Act is usually accompanied by material which is inserted to assist the reader. An Act contains an arrangement of sections at the start. This states briefly the subject matter of each section and it operates as a list of contents. This brief listing is repeated in the margin beside the main body of the Act, section by section, and in that context is referred to as marginal notes.[112] Marginal notes sometimes contain a reference to an earlier statute or common law rule which is affected by the section. For example, the marginal note to s 124 of the Succession Act 1965 reads, in part, 'New. Overrules Rice v Begley [1920] 1 IR 243'. By scanning the margin a user can quickly locate the provision sought. However, s 18(g) of the Interpretation Act 2005 provides that marginal and shoulder notes are not part of the text of the statute and may not 'be construed or judicially noticed in relation to the construction or interpretation of the enactment'.[113]

The state of the statute book

[13.84] The immediate publication of legislation in an accessible form is, it might be thought, crucial to the rule of law. It is vital, from the perspective both of the government and the individuals affected, that the provisions relevant to a particular issue are capable of being identified and obtained. To this end the act of promulgating legislation operates as a formal certification of its enactment and, therefore, its applicability. Nevertheless, the practical task of locating the law still remains. The manner in which legislation is published and made available is important and, ideally, the law should be published in such a manner as to facilitate its being identified and located by members of the public. Hence the significance of the state of the statute book. If the legislation is enacted and organised in a haphazard manner the task of locating the law will tax even the most adroit of lawyers, not to speak of ordinary citizens. Until recently little practical attention was given to the state of the Irish statute book, but matters have improved since the early 2000s.

[13.85] An initial problem faced by someone searching for the legislative provisions on a particular subject is that they are not necessarily to be found in one Act. In many cases the relevant provisions are contained in a number of statutes, sometimes supplemented

---

[112] See further, Stewart, 'Legislative Drafting and the Marginal Note' (1995) 16 Stat LR 21.

[113] Section 18(g) is qualified by s 7 of the 2005 Act which potentially allows a court to take account of marginal and shoulder notes in certain, albeit limited, circumstances. In *Rowe v Law* [1978] IR 55 at 66 O'Higgins CJ, dissenting, took the marginal note into consideration when interpreting the Succession Act 1965, s 90; at the time the equivalent provision, s 11(g) of the Interpretation Act 1937, prohibited that course of action.

by ministerial orders or other species of delegated legislation. The problem is aggravated in this jurisdiction by the fact that Acts of a number of different parliaments stretching over a period in excess of 700 years are still in operation. The range of statutes currently in force embraces:

- Acts of the English Parliament (pre-1707);
- Acts of Parliaments sitting in Ireland (pre-1800);
- Acts of the British Parliament (1707–1800);
- Acts of the Parliament of Great Britain and Ireland (1801–1922);
- Acts of the Oireachtas of the Irish Free State (1922–1937);
- Acts of the Oireachtas (post-1937).

[13.86] The British practice of publishing statutes in annual volumes has been adopted in Ireland since 1922, with Acts of the Oireachtas being published by the Stationery Office. Each volume of Acts of the Oireachtas begins with Acts to amend the Constitution followed by the public general Acts arranged in the order of their enactment. Private legislation is published separately at the end of each volume. The volumes are not updated or revised. Thus, the Acts passed since 1922 are contained in more than 100 volumes, arranged chronologically rather than on a subject basis. Statutes which are later repealed, become spent or otherwise lose force, are not excised. Likewise, amended statutes are not revised and republished. Since 1922 no general revision of the statute book, along the lines of the British Statutes Revised or Statutes in Force,[114] has been published. As the number of operative statutes runs into thousands, the difficulty of researching the applicable legislative provisions on a particular topic can be appreciated. Someone who seeks to rely on a provision must check to see whether, and to what extent, it has been affected by later legislation.

[13.87] The task of researching legislation is physically difficult and mentally demanding, and requires time, resources and enthusiasm. In the past this task was lightened by having recourse to the Index of Statutes, which indexes post-1922 Irish statutes and was published approximately every 10 years. The Index has been overtaken by the *Legislation Directory*, an electronic database that is now prepared by the Law Reform Commission.[115] Likewise, the re-publication of Cullinan's 1885 revised edition of the pre-Union Irish Statutes[116] is of some benefit in that it is reasonably

---

114 As to these measures see Miers and Page, *Legislation* (2nd edn, 1990), pp 149–150.

115 The current version of the Legislation Directory is hosted on the Irish Statute Book online website at www.irishstatutebook.ie/legislation_directory.html; see Law Reform Commission, *Report on Legislation Directory* (LRC 102-2010); Law Reform Commission, *Consultation Paper on the Legislation Directory: Towards a Best Practice Model* (LRC CP 49-2008); Ferriter, 'The Irish Statute Book Database' (1999) 4 (4) BR 217.

116 *The Irish Statutes 1310–1800*, originally published under the authority of the Irish Office at Westminster in 1885, re-published by Round Hall Press in 1995; Professor Osborough's introductory essay to the current volume outlines the history of the various efforts to revise the Irish statutes.

comprehensive, but unfortunately it is probably not entirely accurate.[117] The more recent publication of statutes in various electronic formats is also of assistance and is a welcome development.[118]

[13.88] Matters are further complicated by the fact that many pre-1922 statutes which have subsequently been repealed in Britain, but not in Ireland, are not published by the Stationery Office. This problem has been somewhat alleviated in recent years by increased legislative activity in Ireland which has resulted in the enactment of statutes which supersede pre-1922 legislation. However, a number of important pre-1922 statutes, to one extent or another, remain in force and frequently their availability depends on the efforts of private publishers. In this way access to vital areas of the law is impeded and it is impossible to justify the failure to ensure the official publication of legislation which is currently in force in the state.[119]

Amendments

[13.89] Another source of difficulty is that the text of a provision might not actually be found in the statute of which it is part. Statutes frequently amend, alter or repeal earlier provisions. However, as noted above the text of those earlier provisions remains unaltered in the printed version since statutes are not revised or reprinted to take account of subsequent changes. A relatively straightforward example was provided by the offence of robbery which, until 2001,[120] was contained in s 23 of the Larceny Act 1916. That section was amended by s 5 of the Criminal Law (Jurisdiction) Act 1976 which provided:

> "The Larceny Act 1916, is hereby amended by the substitution for section 23 of the following section:
>
> (1)   A person is guilty of robbery if he steals, and immediately before or at the time of doing so, and in order to do so, he uses force on any person or puts or seeks to put any person in fear of being then and there subjected to force.
>
> (2)   A person guilty of robbery, or of an assault with intent to rob, shall be liable on conviction on indictment to imprisonment for life."

[13.90] But it was the old unaltered version of s 23 which appeared in the Larceny Act 1916. Thus, to locate the offence prohibited by the 1916 Act one was forced consult the 1976 Act. That form of amendment, known as a textual amendment, involves the direct substitution of one form of words for another. The amendment is integrated into the existing law in much the same manner that a new part is put into an engine in place of the old. A non-textual amendment operates indirectly. It does not alter the text of the old

---

117   *The Irish Statutes 1310–1800*. It is probably impossible to be assured of the reliability of the records of older statutes given the haphazard arrangements for their publication in the medieval period; see further Grossman, *Legal Research: Historical Foundations of the Electronic Era* (1994), Ch 3.

118   See further para **13.108**.

119   See remarks of Senator Costello at 124 *Seanad Debates*, cols 929–931.

120   The offence of robbery is now governed by Criminal Justice (Theft and Fraud Offences) Act 2001, s 14.

law but consists of a discursive statement or narrative of the effect of the amendment on the old law.

[13.91] Examples of non-textual amendments include s 1(4) of the Infanticide Act 1949, which states:

> "Section 60 of the Offences Against the Person Act 1861 shall have effect as if the reference therein to the murder of any child included a reference to infanticide."

And s 8 of the Criminal Damage Act 1991, which provides:

> "No rule of law ousting the jurisdiction of the District Court to try offences where a dispute as to title to property is involved shall preclude that court from trying offences under this Act."

[13.92] The supposed advantage of a non-textual amendment is that it should make sense when standing alone, although that is hardly the case in the example cited from the Infanticide Act 1949. The reader should be in a position to discern the effect of the amendment, a matter of convenience which is said to be important from a legislator's perspective. Non-textual amendments have the practical advantage of effecting, in one measure, the blanket amendment of a number of different provisions. Thus, s 8 of the Criminal Damage Act 1991 manages to amend each statutory provision which concerns the jurisdiction of the District Court to try offences – every such provision is now read subject to that provision. This alleviates the necessity of enacting a separate textual amendment of each relevant provision and in this way it saves time and avoids potential legislative oversight. In some cases non-textual amendments are unavoidable.

[13.93] General adaptations of the law are often a necessary consequence of constitutional change. Following independence it was necessary to adapt pre-1922 legislation, which would be carried over under Article 73 of the Constitution of the Irish Free State, to the circumstances of the new legal order. This was achieved by the Adaptation of Enactments Act 1922 which in fact was the first measure to be passed by the Oireachtas after the 1922 Constitution itself. It would have been difficult to the point of impossibility to effect the necessary amendments to each pre-1992 statute by the textual method. Likewise, following the 'decimalisation' of the currency it was necessary to convert all statutory references to 'old' money. This was achieved by s 9(1) of the Decimal Currency Act 1970 which provided a general formula for amending existing references to the now-outmoded shillings and pence. Similarly, the Euro Changeover (Amounts) Act 2001 achieved the same purpose with the introduction of the euro as the replacement for the Irish pound (the 'decimalised' currency).

[13.94] A consequence of over-reliance on the method of non-textual amendment is that a set of cross-references, interpretations and qualifications develops which adds to the complexity and lack of intelligibility of legislation – it becomes exceedingly difficult to collect the text of legislation on a particular topic in a single instrument. For this reason the current view is that textual amendments are to be preferred for their relative simplicity.[121] For instance, s 1(4) of the Infanticide Act 1949 would have been as

---

[121] Xanthaki, *Thornton's Legislative Drafting* (5th edn, 2013), p 501; Miers and Page, *Legislation* (2nd edn, 1990), pp 195–196.

effective had it simply amended the text of s 60 of the Offences Against the Person Act 1861. A textual amendment in that case would have provided:

"Section 60 of the Offences Against the Person Act 1861 is hereby amended by the insertion of the words 'or infanticide' after the words 'murder of any child'."

[13.95] This would have been a tidier method of amendment and would have facilitated the collation of the legislative text. As things stand at present, s 60 is read as if the words 'or infanticide' are to be implied into the section but they do not form part of its text. Like its English counterpart, the Irish statute book contains a curious mixture of textual and non-textual amendments and the observation of one commentator applies here with equal force:

["The traditional style] produced a pottage comprising direct amendments, indirect amendments and provisions incorporating both techniques. The effect, at least to one not nurtured from his early years on English statutes, is confusing, particularly so as it rests on a stream of consistently invidious and inevitably inconsistent decisions as to which amendments should properly be effected by one method, which by the other, and which by both."[122]

Statutory language

[13.96] The intelligibility of legislation might also be impeded by the manner in which it is drafted. A frequent criticism directed at legislation is that it is drafted in obscure and complex language which lacks clarity and frustrates a proper understanding of its meaning. The expressed desire is for statutes to be drafted in 'plain English', in such a manner as to be capable of being readily understood by those who are affected by it.[123] In this regard the object is to ensure that statutes are reasonably intelligible to the general public. Plain language, it has been argued, 'makes the text leaner and cleaner and therefore easier to read and understand.'[124] The English drafting style has been compared unfavourably with that which is adopted in various continental jurisdictions.[125] In particular, it is said that the English style involves complex sentences

---

[122] Xanthaki, *Thornton's Legislative Drafting* (5th edn, 2013), p 501.

[123] See Thomas, 'Plain English and the Law' [1985] Stat LR 139; Staughton, 'Plain English for Lawyers' (Bracton Law Society Annual Lecture 1999) (1999) 31 Bracton Law Journal 86; Hathaway, 'An Overview of the Plain English Movement in the Law: 15 Years Later' (2000) 79 Michigan Bar Journal 30; Hunt, 'Plain Language: The End of the Road for Recondite Legislation?' (2001) 7 *Bar Review* 47; Macdonald, 'Plain English in the Law: A New Model for the 21st Century' (2004) 30 Commonwealth Law Bulletin 922; Barnes, 'The Continuing Debate About "Plain Language" Legislation: A Law Reform Conundrum' (2006) 27 Stat LR 83; Watson-Brown, 'Defining Plain English as an Aid to Legal Drafting' (2009) 30 Stat LR 85; Watson-Brown, 'In Search of Plain English: The Holy Grail or Mythical Excalibur of Legislative Drafting' (2012) 33 Stat LR 7.

[124] Turnbull, 'Legislative Drafting in Plain Language and Statements of General Principle' (1997) 18 Stat LR 21, 23.

[125] See, eg, Dale, *Legislative Drafting: a New Approach* (1977); Dale, 'A London Particular' [1985] Stat LR 11; (contd.../)

and sections, prefers detail to statements of principle and is prone to qualification and subtraction. These criticisms might also be directed at the Irish drafting style, which is largely derived from its English counterpart, although in some instances Irish legislation has departed significantly from its progenitor.[126]

[13.97] Some criticisms of the supposed lack of intelligibility are overstated. In the first place there is probably no generally agreed criterion to be applied in this regard.[127] To say that legislation should be intelligible to the ultimate user or to those to whom it is directed begs the question. The community to whom statutes are directed is not itself homogeneous but is made up of various elements each of whose demands may differ in this respect. Nor is it obvious that a statute should necessarily be intelligible to an average member of the public. It has been correctly observed that '[a] legislative text is a legal text, not just a guide to effective action'.[128] It might therefore be contended, with some force, that the real consumers of legislation are the regulators, lawyers and other professionals whose activities are affected by it. The individual citizen's desire to be addressed in a simple, uncomplicated and straightforward manner often has to yield to a competing goal of legal effectiveness. Other measures, such as explanatory leaflets and guides, can be adopted to achieve the goal of explaining the law to members of the public.[129]

[13.98] In the second place, it might be argued that copious detail in statutes is often unavoidable.[130] By its nature legislation tends to deal with complex and intricate subject

---

[125] (\...contd) Clarence Smith, 'Legislative Drafting: English and Continental' [1980] Stat LR 14; Millet 'A Comparison of British and French Legislative Drafting (with particular reference to their respective Nationality Law)' [1986] Stat LR 130; Tanner, 'Clear, Simple and Precise Legislative Drafting: Australian Guidelines Explicated Using an EC Directive' (2004) 25 Stat LR 223; Greenberg, 'The Nature of Legislative Intention and Its Implications for Legislative Drafting' (2006) 27 Stat LR 15; Tanner, 'Clear, Simple, and Precise Legislative Drafting: How Does a European Community Directive Fare?' (2006) 27 Stat LR 150.

[126] See Morris, 'The Road to Brussels—Two Routes Compared' [1988] Stat LR 33 contrasting the quite different Irish European Communities Act 1972 and the UK European Communities Act 1972.

[127] See Miers, 'Legislation, Linguistic Adequacy and Public Policy' [1986] Stat LR 90.

[128] Miers, 'Legislation, Linguistic Adequacy and Public Policy' [1986] Stat LR 90, 95.

[129] For instance, the Department of Enterprise, Trade and Employment has published a number of documents outlining the principal provisions of a number of employment statutes. The Department of Social and Family Affairs has published a similar booklet on social welfare entitlements.

[130] See Wilson, 'The Complexity of Statutes' (1974) 37 *MLR* 497; Turnbull, 'Legislative Drafting in Plain Language and Statements of General Principle' (1997) 18 Stat LR 21 disputes the view that precision and clarity are necessarily to be seen as competing goals; in his opinion the drafter's task is usually one of balancing degrees of precision against degrees of simplicity. This, however, is not appreciably different from the view that precision and simplicity are competing goals. Either way the drafter is often forced to choose between a precision and simplicity.

matter, a phenomenon which is likely to continue as the regulatory function of the state is ever expanding. The necessary, or at least desirable, detail of legislation invites a degree of precision which tends to render it less simple. This stems partly from a wish to plan for an uncertain future and to anticipate every conceivable contingency. Moreover, since language is a relatively imprecise instrument, elaboration, qualification and definition is inevitable in an effort to reduce possible ambiguity; that, in itself, adds to the complexity of legislation.

[13.99] A related complaint is that there is too much legislation. To question the quantity of legislation raises the much broader issue of the extent to which the state should be involved in the governance of society. This is principally a question of political philosophy rather than legal policy. But even then efforts to 'roll back the state' have often been accompanied by an increased volume of legislation. The privatisation of functions which were previously assigned to the central agencies of state, or their delegation to semi-state bodies, is achieved by means of legislation. Thus, it has sometimes proved to be the case that to reduce the involvement of the state more, not less, legislation has been required. With these observations in mind the desire for simplicity, while understandable, is misplaced and fails to appreciate the context in which legislation is enacted and its purposes.

Tidying the statute book

[13.100] The untidy state of the statute book is notorious and the desirability of tackling the matter has been officially acknowledged.[131] To this end a number of measures may be adopted. One is to enact statute law revision legislation which clears the statute book of its dead wood. Such legislation repeals those statutes which have become obsolete and are of no practical effect. The general practice adopted with such measures was expressly to provide in the Act that the revisions contained in it do not affect any existing rules or principles. Statute Law Revision Acts were enacted in 1962, 1983, 2005, 2007, 2009 and 2012.[132] The most comprehensive measure adopted is the Statute Law Revision Act 2007, which repealed all pre-1922 statutes except those that were specifically preserved by the 2007 Act itself. To this end the 2007 Act contains two Schedules, one of which lists the pre-1922 statutes that are retained (and therefore still enjoy the force of law) and those that are specifically repealed. In the course of preparing the 2007 Act, the Office of the Attorney General conducted a survey of 26,370 pre-1922 statutes. Of these, 9,219 were already wholly repealed prior to 2007 and 12,562 were not applicable to Ireland. This left 4,589 pre-1922 statutes still in force, of which 3,225 were repealed by the 2007 Act, and 1,364 were retained for the time being (listed in Schedule 1 to the 2007 Act). It would have been impossible in the context of a Statute Law Revision Act to repeal all pre-1922 legislation, but the 2007

---

[131] *Report of the Review Group on the Law Offices of the State* (1997), Ch 6.

[132] Statute Law Revision (Pre-Union Irish Statutes) Act 1962; Statute Law Revision Act 1983; Statute Law Revision (Pre-1922) Act 2005; Statute Law Revision Act 2007; Statute Law Revision Act 2009; Statute Law Revision Act 2012.

Act has ensured that for the first time there is a publicly available catalogue of all pre-1922 measures that still form part of Irish law. While this is an important achievement it must be realised that statute law revision is only a partial solution as old statutes which are still in operation are left untouched. Moreover, the physical state of the statute book remains intact – the old statutes that have been repealed, and therefore no longer form part of the law, remain in the official volumes of statutes. The user still has to check whether a particular provision is in force or not.

[13.101] That difficulty points to a second measure, namely the periodic re-publication of the statute book in its revised form, purged of the repealed and spent provisions that no longer enjoy the force of law. To this end the Statute Law (Restatement) Act 2002 facilitates the publication of statutory restatements in both print and electronic formats. Restatement involves the publication of a statute, or series of statutes, in a single updated text that takes account of any amendments and alterations. The Act provides that the Attorney General may certify the text so published to be a statement of the law contained in the relevant statutory provisions. It is important to note that a restatement is simply a means of publishing existing legislation, not the enactment of new legislation: the process is administrative not legislative and it follows that parliamentary time, at best a scarce resource, is not used. While a restatement does not have the force of law, it is prima facie evidence of the law contained in the provision to which it relates. In 2006 the government requested that the Law Reform Commission carry out a restatement programme. The Commission adopted its First Programme of Statute Law Restatement 2008–2009''.[133] To date the Commission has published over 200 revised Acts.[134] Each revised Act contains the updated text of the Act including textual and non-textual amendments, and relevant statutory instruments made under the Act. Annotations to the revised Acts outline the source of the amending and modifying provisions.

[13.102] A third method of alleviating the problem is to enact consolidating legislation.[135] A consolidating Act is one which re-enacts all the relevant provisions on a particular subject in one statute, making, at most, only minor amendments to the existing law. The special parliamentary procedure to expedite the enactment of such legislation[136] has been employed on several occasions – the Fisheries (Consolidation) Act 1959, the Income Tax Act 1967, the Social Welfare (Consolidation) Act 1981, the Social Welfare (Consolidation) Act 1993, the Taxes Consolidation Act 1997, the Stamp Duties Consolidation Act 1999, the Capital Acquisitions Tax Consolidation Act 2003, the Social Welfare Consolidation Act 2005 and the Value-Added Tax Consolidation Act 2010. The Taxes Consolidation Act 1997 exemplifies the benefits associated with consolidation. It collated the law on income tax, capital gains tax and corporation tax, in the process reducing its bulk: provisions that were contained in 40 separate statutes are

---

133 See Law Reform Commission, *Report on Statute Law Restatement* (LRC 91-2008).
134 The revised Acts are available at http://www.lawreform.ie/revised-acts.84.html.
135 See Lord Simon of Glaisdale and Webb, 'Consolidation and Statute Law Reform' [1975] PL 285.
136 See para **13.39**.

now found in one Act; over 2000 different sections have been compressed into 1104 sections; and material that occupied 50 Schedules is now contained in 32 Schedules.[137] Moreover, the consolidated law was drafted and structured with the user, principally tax practitioners, in mind; its more coherent format eases the task of finding the law. Nevertheless, given the frequency with which taxation and social welfare provisions are amended, the useful life of consolidating legislation in those fields is comparatively short and it is good practice to enact fresh consolidating legislation on a regular basis. Thus, within the space of 12 years the Social Welfare (Consolidation) Act 1993 (containing 304 sections and six Schedules) was repealed in its entirety and replaced by the Social Welfare Consolidation Act 2005 (containing 364 sections and seven Schedules).

[13.103] A fourth method is a codifying statute which enacts in one statute all the relevant provisions on a topic, often making major changes to the existing law. The general hostility in common law jurisdictions to codification has been reflected to some extent in Ireland, but the Succession Act 1965 can be cited as an example of a codifying measure. More recently, the enactment of a criminal code, containing all the principal provisions of the criminal law in one statute, has become a real possibility.[138] Since the 1990s the Oireachtas has pursued a discernible policy of enacting what have been called 'mini-codes'. These measures, which contain the exclusive provisions on a particular topic and typically abolish the pre-existing common law, include the Criminal Damage Act 1991, the Criminal Justice (Public Order) Act 1994, the Non-Fatal Offences against the Person Act 1997, the Criminal Justice (Theft and Fraud Offences) Act 2001 and the Criminal Law (Insanity) Act 2006. This stock of legislation provides the potential basis for a criminal code and the incremental enactment of such a code has been recommended by the Expert Group on the Codification of the Criminal Law.[139] Following the Expert Group's report a Criminal Law Codification Advisory Committee was established, as provided for by s 167 of the Criminal Justice Act 2006. The Committee's function was to oversee the development of a programme for codification and to advise the Minister for Justice, Equality and Law Reform on the future maintenance of a criminal code. The Committee produced a draft Criminal Code in 2010 that includes a general part, which restates some of the general principles of criminal liability, and a special part that incorporates the existing mini-codes.[140] The Committee aptly described the draft as a 'form of enhanced restatement': the code does not propose any significant reform of the law, other than that which is inherent in the

---

[137] Hennessy and Moore, *Taxes Consolidation Act 1997: the Busy Practitioner's Guide* (1997), p 3.

[138] See generally McCutcheon and Quinn 'Codifying Criminal Law in Ireland' (1998) 19 Stat L Rev 131; Byrne, 'Codification of the Criminal Law of Ireland' (2005) 15 ICLJ 15; Ferguson, 'Constructing a Criminal Code' (2009) Crim L Forum 139.

[139] *Codifying the Criminal Law* (2004).

[140] Criminal Law Codification Advisory Committee, *Draft Criminal Code and Commentary* (2010).

codification process itself.[141] The Draft Code could not be described as being comprehensive, and considerable additional work would be required before it could be enacted. However, the usefulness of the Committee's work is that it demonstrates the feasibility of drafting a criminal code and provides a workable template and methodology for a future code.

Improving the quality of legislation

[13.104] The difficulties currently associated with legislation prompt a number of measures that might be adopted with a view to improving the quality of legislation. One is to modify the linguistic style in which statutes are drafted. Although complexity is likely to remain as an inevitable feature of legislation, attention to the drafting style might make it somewhat more intelligible. Shorter sentences, better organisation and division of sections and less obscure language should go some way to securing this goal. To this end the Law Reform Commission has recommended a number of improvements that might be adopted.[142] These include the use of what it calls 'familiar vocabulary'; the use of shorter, less complex sentences; the avoidance of redundant language; and structural and typographical innovations, including the use of diagrams and examples.

[13.105] A second measure is to scrutinise the quality of Bills with greater vigour. Unlike the position in other countries,[143] pre- and post-legislative scrutiny is virtually unknown in Ireland, which is a matter of some concern given the weak role which is played by the Oireachtas in relation to the enactment of legislation. This might be achieved either by creating a special review body such as a 'law council',[144] or by expanding and strengthening the role of Oireachtas committees.

[13.106] A third set of measures is to alleviate the disorganised state of the statute book by enacting codifying, consolidating and statute law revision legislation, thus reducing the number of statutes in force. These initiatives, of course, would involve a commitment of financial and human resources (through, for instance, the recruitment of additional legislative drafters) which historically governments have been notoriously reluctant to approve. Moreover, it would require the allocation of time on the legislative

---

[141] Criminal Law Codification Advisory Committee, *Draft Criminal Code and Commentary* (2010), p 4.

[142] *Report on Statutory Drafting and Interpretation: Plain Language and the Law* (LRC 61-2000). See also *The Preparation of Legislation: Report of a Committee Appointed by the Lord President of the Council* (Cmnd 6053) (the 'Renton Report'), an influential document which considered the state of statute law in the UK and made various recommendations.

[143] See, eg, Bennion, 'How They do Things in France' (1995) 16 Stat LR 90; Iles, 'The Responsibilities of the New Zealand Legislative Advisory Committee' (1992) 13 Stat LR 11.

[144] The establishment of such a body in England, modelled on the French *Conseil d'Etat*, was proposed by Dale, *Legislative Drafting: a New Approach* (1977); but see criticism in Kolts, 'Observations on the Proposed New Approach to Legislative Drafting in Common Law Countries' [1980] Stat LR 144. On the operation of the Conseil d'Etat see Bell, 'What is the Function of the Conseil d'Etat in the Preparation of Legislation' (2000) 49 ICLQ 661.

programme, when other proposals might be considered by the government to be more desirable or of greater political importance. Nevertheless, there is evidence of some change in official thinking in this regard. Following the review of the state's law offices, a Statute Law Revision Unit was established within the Office of the Attorney General, devoted to statute law reform and consolidation.[145] Moreover, the drafting of parts of the Taxes Consolidation Act 1997 was undertaken by consultants hired for the purpose, thus saving time and effort expended by the state's legislative drafters.

[13.107] Fourthly, the manner in which legislation is published should be addressed. Legislative reform and statute law revision in itself does not reduce the actual physical size of the volumes of statutes which retain amended and repealed legislation. The user's requirement is to be provided with the up-to-date text of legislation, not to be presented with the challenge of navigating through volume after volume of statutes. The publication of legislation in its current as well as its historical form is crucial and to this end the production on a regular basis of a revised statute book is desirable. The publication on a commercial basis of the loose-leaf Irish Current Law Statutes Annotated had some potential to improve matters, but since it only dates from 1984 much remains to be done. The Statute Law (Restatement) Act 2002 is significantly more important. As noted earlier, the Act allows for the publication of official statutory restatements which should, in time, result in a body of up-to-date legislative texts.

[13.108] The potential represented by information technology, which has been embraced in other jurisdictions,[146] has now been realised in Ireland. Irish statutes and statutory instruments from 1922 to 2008 are available on the web and in CD-ROM format.[147] The Oireachtas website also contains this information along with more recent statutes in PDF format and Bills and explanatory memoranda since 1997.[148] These measures have a number of advantages: they are readily accessible and are comparatively easy to search. However, the legislation is published in its historic, unrevised form and, as is the case with the hard copy version of the statutes, a user must check the subsequent legislative history of a provision to ensure accurate up-to-date information. The Statute Law (Restatement) Act 2002 addresses this issue by authorising the publication of restatements in electronic format. The Oireachtas website also contains Irish language translations of many recent statutes. While this might not satisfy the concerns of the Supreme Court in *Ó Beolain v Fahy*,[149] it marks a considerable improvement on the state of affairs from the early 1980s to the mid-1990s.[150]

---

[145] *Report of the Review Group on the Law Offices of the State* (1997), para 6.21.

[146] See Hudson, 'The Scope of Computers' [1983] Stat LR 35; Campbell and McGurk, 'Revising Statutes with Computer Support' [1987] Stat LR 104. UK legislation is now available on the LEXIS database; see Harrison, 'The Statutes on LEXIS' [1982] Stat LR 51; Editorial, 'Surfing the Statutes' (1998) 19 Stat LR v.

[147] www.irishstatutebook.ie.

[148] www.oireachtas.ie.

[149] *Ó Beolain v Fahy* [2001] 2 IR 279.

[4] DELEGATED LEGISLATION

[13.109] Delegated legislation consists of instruments enacted by a subordinate body or official to which or to whom law-making power is devolved by a legislative organ. Despite the apparently absolute terms in which Article 15.2.1° ('sole and exclusive') confers legislative power on the Oireachtas it is clear that, within certain limits, power may be delegated by it to subordinate bodies. It has been accepted by the courts that power may be delegated to supply the necessary detail to facilitate the implementation of the principles and policies which have been enacted by the Oireachtas. As long as the delegation satisfies this requirement it is not considered to usurp the legislative function, which remains the exclusive preserve of the Oireachtas. An Act of the Oireachtas must expressly confer legislative power on the delegate since the latter does not possess an inherent law-making capacity. The exercise of delegated power is governed by the parent statute, which establishes the extent and scope of the delegation, the purposes for which the power may be exercised and the procedures, if any, to be followed in exercising the power.

[13.110] The exigencies of managing and regulating the modern state have resulted in an ever-increasing volume of delegated legislation as opposed to primary legislation.[151] In practice, power is delegated to a variety of bodies including government ministers, statutory boards, semi-state bodies and the like. By virtue of s 22(3) of the Interpretation Act 2005 such power includes a power to revoke or amend the instrument and to replace it with another.

[13.111] An indication of the balance between primary legislation and delegated legislation can be gleaned from a comparison of the number of public general Acts and statutory instruments which were enacted in recent years (see Figure 13.2).

---

[150] See para **13.66–13.67**.

[151] See Tudor, 'Secondary Legislation: Second Class or Crucial?' (2000) 21 Stat LR 149.

Year	Public General Acts	Statutory Instruments
2000	42	495
2001	55	658
2002	33	654
2003	46	741
2004	44	924
2005	34	926
2006	42	712
2007	42	628
2008	25	607
2009	46	595
2010	40	689
2011	41	741
2012	53	592
2013	51	585

Primary and Secondary Legislation 2000–2013
Figure 13.2

[13.112] The importance of delegated legislation is clear from the number of statutory instruments enacted each year. Statutory instruments are supplemented by a variety of measures which are local or private in character and which are created by local authorities, statutory boards, semi-state bodies and the like. The figures in Figure 13.2 are for statutory instruments only and do not take into account delegated legislation which is enacted in other forms and thus the data underestimate the quantity and range of delegated legislation.

[13.113] Several reasons can be identified for the use of delegated legislation rather than primary legislation. The first is that the constraints on parliamentary time would make it impossible for all necessary measures to be enacted as statutes. Accordingly, the Oireachtas is content to sketch the broad outline of the legislative scheme and to delegate its detailed implementation and application to the appropriate official or body. A second reason for enacting delegated legislation is that its contents tend to be of a technical or administrative nature, so it is often preferable that those who possess the appropriate expertise be given the law-making function. Thus, where a Minister is given power to make regulations he or she will be advised by the relevant experts in his or her department. This also facilitates consultation with relevant interest groups which might be affected by the measure. In some instances power is delegated to a regulatory authority, an expert body or one on which various interests are represented. Examples are the power of the Law Society of Ireland to regulate the admission and training of trainee solicitors;[152]" the power of Bord na gCon to regulate greyhound race tracks;[153] and the power of local authorities to make bye-laws for the good government of their functional areas.[154] A third reason is that delegated legislation facilitates flexible and timely responses to rapidly changing social and technical circumstances, which are not afforded by the constraints on parliamentary time."

[13.114] Much delegated legislation is enacted in the form of statutory instruments which affect the public at large. Statutory instruments are governed by the Statutory Instruments Act 1947, s 1(1) of which defines 'statutory instrument' as being an 'order, regulation, rule, scheme or bye-law' which is made in pursuance of a statutory power. Differences exist between those categories of delegated legislation but they are not mutually exclusive. An 'order' tends to be made in respect of a single exercise of a delegated power, such as a compulsory purchase order, a commencement order bringing a statute into effect and an order assigning functions to a particular official or body. 'Rules' and 'regulations' are clearly legislative in nature. Regulations tend to contain detailed provisions pertaining to the general matters which are contained in the parent statute. An example is the Safety, Health and Welfare at Work (Signs) Regulations 1995[155] which are made under the Safety, Health and Welfare at Work Act 1989. The term 'rule' is typically reserved for the instruments which govern court practice and procedure, such as the Rules of the Superior Courts 1986.[156]

[13.115] 'Bye-laws' possess similar legislative characteristics to rules and regulations. In *The State (Harrington) v Wallace*[157] the Supreme Court adopted Lord Russell's definition of a bye-law in *Kruse v Johnson* as being:

> "an ordinance affecting the public, or some portion of the public, imposed by some authority clothed with statutory powers ordering something to be done or not to be done, and accompanied by some sanction or penalty for its non-observance."[158]

[13.116] 'Schemes' tend to be of an administrative nature and often consist of numerical material such as scales of fees and charges. Hence the Central Bank is empowered by s 15(5)(a) of the Central Bank Act 1989 to make 'schemes for granting pensions, allowances and gratuities on retirement or death' of its employees.

[13.117] The Statutory Instruments Act 1947 provides for the printing and publishing of certain statutory instruments, their deposit in certain designated libraries and the publication of notice of their enactment in *Iris Oifigiúil*. The instruments affected are

---

152 Solicitors Acts 1954 to 1994.
153 Greyhound Industry Act 1958, ss 13, 25 and 48.
154 Municipal Corporations Act 1840, ss 125–127; Local Government (Ireland) Act 1898, s 16.
155 SI 132/1995.
156 SI 15/1986.
157 *The State (Harrington) v Wallace* [1988] IR 290 at 294.
158 *Kruse v Johnson* [1898] 2 QB 91 at 96.

those which are enacted by one of a number of designated authorities[159] and which must either be laid before one of the Houses of the Oireachtas or which affect the public generally or a section of the public and whose publication in *Iris Oifigiúil* is not otherwise required by statute. The Act establishes a systematic method of bringing the existence of statutory instruments to the public attention, a matter of obvious importance to the rule of law. In this respect the Act does for statutory instruments what the publication provisions of the Constitution do for primary legislation.

[13.118] Like statutory instruments other forms of delegated legislation are legislative in nature and depend for their validity on the parent statute. However, there is no established standard for their publication and a variety of arrangements are prescribed by different parent statutes.

Contracts of adhesion

[13.119] In some instances the courts might be willing to treat contracts, especially those issued in standard form by public utilities which enjoy a monopoly, as being equivalent to delegated legislation. The words of Henchy J in *McCord v ESB*[160] are apposite:

> "[I]t is important to point out that the contract made between the plaintiff and the Board (incorporating the General Conditions Relating to Supply) is what is nowadays called a contract of adhesion: it is a standardised mass contract which must be entered into, on a take it or leave it basis, by the occupier of every premises in which electricity is to be used. The would-be consumer has no standing to ask that a single iota of the draft contract presented to him be changed before he signs it. He must lump it or leave it. But, because for reasons that are too obvious to enumerate, he cannot do without electricity, he is invariably forced by necessity into signing the contract, regardless of the fact that he may consider some of its terms arbitrary, or oppressive, or demonstrably unfair. He is compelled from a position of weakness and necessity vis-à-vis a monopolist supplier of a vital commodity, to enter into what falls into the classification of a contract and which, as such, according to the theory of the common law which was evolved in the *laissez-faire* atmosphere of the 19th century, is to be treated by the courts as if it had emerged by choice from the forces of the market place, at the behest of the parties who were at arm's length and had freedom of choice. The real facts show that such an approach is largely based on legal fictions. When a monopoly supplier of a vital public utility—which is what the Board is—forces on all its customers a common form of contract, reserving to itself sweeping powers, including the power to vary the document unilaterally as it may think fit, such an instrument has less affinity with a freely negotiated interpersonal contract than with a set of bye-laws or with any other form of autonomic legislation. As such its terms may have to be construed not simply as contractual elements but as components of a piece of delegated legislation, the validity of which will depend on whether it has kept within the express or implied confines of the statutory

---

[159] The designated authorities are the President, the government, a member of the government, a Minister of State, a body exercising a governmental or administrative function throughout the state and authorities having power to make rules of court; see Statutory Instruments Act 1947, s 2(1)(b).

[160] *McCord v ESB* [1980] ILRM 153.

delegation and, even if it has, whether the delegation granted or assumed is now consistent with the provisions of the Constitution of 1937."[161]

[13.120] The significance of these observations is that they indicate a judicial willingness to subject contracts of adhesion to the same forms of judicial control as any formal instrument which implements a power of delegated legislation. Thus, it would appear that they will be subject to similar tests of constitutional validity and compliance with the parent statute under which the public utility operates.

Delegated legislation and the Constitution

[13.121] As noted at the beginning of this chapter, Article 15.2.1° of the Constitution vests exclusive legislative power in the Oireachtas. On a literal reading of that provision any delegation of legislative power would seem to be invalid. However, the courts have recognised that delegated legislation is a feature of the legal environment and that it is not per se impermissible to delegate legislative power. The matter was alluded to by Hanna J in *Pigs Marketing Board v Donnelly*:[162]

> "It is axiomatic that powers conferred upon the Legislature to make laws cannot be delegated to any other body or authority. The Oireachtas is the only constitutional agency by which laws can be made. But the Legislature may, it has always been conceded, delegate to subordinate bodies or departments not only the making of administrative rules and regulations, but the power to exercise, within the principles laid down by the Legislature, the powers so delegated and the manner in which the statutory provisions shall be carried out. The functions of every Government are now so numerous and complex that of necessity a wider sphere has been recognised for subordinate agencies, such as boards and commissions. This has been specially so in this State in matters of industry and commerce. Such bodies are not law makers; they put into execution the law as made by the governing authority and strictly in pursuance therewith, so as to bring about, not their own views but the result directed by the Government."[163]

[13.122] One might take issue with the assertion that subordinate bodies do not make law (although by 'law' Hanna J probably meant primary legislation)[164] and there appears to be some confusion between the executive and legislative roles. Nevertheless, Hanna J's judgment anticipated the direction in which the law was to develop. He held the power of the Board to fix hypothetical prices under the Pigs and Bacon Act 1937 to be in accord with the Constitution:

> "What is the legislative power which it is suggested the Pigs Marketing Board exercises? It is the fixing of the hypothetical price. It has been submitted that, while the Pigs Marketing Board has constitutional power to fix the appointed price because they are directed to consider certain matters in determining it, as there is no schedule of topics to be considered by the Pigs Marketing Board in fixing the hypothetical price, they are in the position of legislators in that respect. But I cannot accept this view of the duties of the Pigs Marketing

---

[161]   [1980] ILRM 153 at 161.
[162]   *Pigs Marketing Board v Donnelly* [1939] IR 413.
[163]   [1939] IR 413 at 421.

Board in reference to the hypothetical price, for the Legislature has directed them to fix not any price, but the price which, in their opinion, would be the proper price under normal conditions. That is the statutory direction. It is a matter of such detail and upon which such expert knowledge is necessarily required, that the Legislature being unable to fix such a price itself, is entitled to say: 'We shall leave this to a body of experts in the trade who shall in the first place determine what the normal conditions in the trade would be apart from the abnormal conditions prescribed by the statute, and then form an opinion as to what the proper price in pounds, shillings and pence would be under such normal conditions.' The Pigs Marketing Board in doing so, is not making a new law; it is giving effect to the statutory provisions as to how they should determine that price.

It would be futile to ask the Legislature to fix the normal price in pounds, shillings and pence, and in my view that duty has been properly placed upon the Pigs Marketing Board."[165]

[13.123] The question, therefore, is one of identifying the extent to which delegation is constitutionally permissible, and the test which has been adopted was established by the Supreme Court in *Cityview Press Ltd v An Chomhairle Oiliúna*:[166]

"[T]hat which is challenged as an unauthorised delegation of parliamentary power is more than a mere giving effect to principles and policies which are contained in the statute itself. If it be, then it is not authorised; for such would constitute a purported exercise of legislative power by an authority which is not permitted to do so under the Constitution. On the other hand, if it be within the permitted limits – if the law is laid down in the statute and details only are filled in or completed by the designated Minister or subordinate body – there is no unauthorised delegation of legislative power."[167]

That test preserves a balance between the role of the Oireachtas as exclusive law-maker and its competence to delegate legislative power. The power to enact 'principles and policies' lies within the sole preserve of the Oireachtas and if the delegation purports to

---

[164] See also the more recent remarks of the Supreme Court in *McGowan v Labour Court* [2013] IESC 21: 'Finally, it may be worth considering the use of terminology in this area. The term "delegated legislation" is, as a description, perhaps unexceptional. It has entered our law from the law of the neighbouring jurisdiction. In a constitutional regime where a parliament is supreme, any provision may be made including presumably, the delegation to others of part of its law making function. But it is worth recalling however, that in the constitutional dispensation created in 1922 and extended in 1937, the position is somewhat different. As Hanna J. observed in the *Pigs Marketing Board* case ... if in truth any piece of regulation amounted to truly delegated *legislation*, it would offend Article 15, since it is plain from the very language thereof, and indeed the constitutional structure, that the function of legislation is one that cannot be delegated by the Oireachtas to any other body. Indeed the case law since that time can be understood as an attempt to seek to delineate the boundary between permissible subordinate regulation, and the abdication, whether by delegation or otherwise, of the lawmaking authority conferred on the Oireachtas by the People, through the Constitution.'

[165] *Pigs Marketing Board v Donnelly* [1939] IR 413 at 421–422.

[166] *Cityview Press Ltd v An Chomhairle Oiliúna* [1980] IR 381.

[167] [1980] IR 381 at 399.

confer that power on a subordinate body or official it is invalid.[168] *Cityview Press* was considered in *John Grace Fried Chicken Ltd v Catering JLC*[169] where the plaintiffs challenged the constitutionality of ss 42, 43 and 45 of the Industrial Relations Act 1946 and s 48 of the Industrial Relations Act 1990, on the grounds that the Acts failed to provide any guidance as to the principles or policies that were to be applied in the making of employment regulation orders. The High Court held that Ireland's system for setting minimum employment standards for many low-paid workers violates the 'principles and policies' test. The Industrial Relations Act 1946 gave the Labour Court the power to fix statutory minimum rates of pay and working conditions. The Act allowed the Labour Court to establish a Joint Labour Committee (JLC) for a given class of workers. A JLC prepared draft regulations setting minimum pay and conditions. Once the Labour Court adopted the JLC's proposal, it became law without any supervision by the Oireachtas. The 1946 Act barred judicial review 'on any matters within [the Labour Court's] jurisdiction'. In concluding that the impugned provisions involved an unconstitutional delegation of legislative authority Feeney J stated:

> "This is a case where the delegated power is excessive. Such a delegation would be lawful if the Act delegating the power had either in 1946 or by subsequent amendment provided policies or principles to guide, inform and direct the Labour Court or the joint labour committees established under the Act of 1946. If that had occurred then those expert bodies could have used their expertise and knowledge to fill in the details, on an on-going basis, based upon principles or policies identifying standards, goals, factors and purposes laid down by statute. As that did not occur, the delegation in issue in this case amounts to a transfer of power. The legislation in issue in this case permits not even the Executive to be at large but the Labour Court and permits that body to make laws."[170]

---

[168] Maddox, 'Legislation by Delegation: The Principles and Policies Test in Irish Law' (2004) 22 ILT 293; Fahey, 'Reconsidering the Merits of the 'Principles and Policies' Test: A Step Towards the Reform of Article 29.4.10° of the Constitution' (2006) 24 ILT 70; *Cf* Carolan, 'Democratic Accountability and the Non-Delegation Doctrine' (2011) 18 DULJ 220.

[169] *John Grace Fried Chicken Ltd v Catering JLC* [2011] 3 IR 211.

[170] *John Grace Fried Chicken Ltd v Catering JLC* [2011] 3 IR 211 at 238. The state did not appeal the High Court decision. The latter decision considered Part IV of the 1946 Act and similar provisions in Part III of the 1946 Act were declared unconstitutional by the Supreme Court in *McGowan v Labour Court* [2013] IESC 21, again on the grounds that they involved an impermissible delegation of legislative authority:

There is not here a grant of a limited power to a subordinate body subject to review as there was for example in the *Cityview Press* case. Instead there is a wholesale grant, indeed abdication, of lawmaking power to private persons unidentified and unidentifiable at the time of grant to make law in respect of a broad and important area of human activity and subject only to a limited power of veto by a subordinate body. ... The process permitted by Part III cannot be said to be merely the filling in of gaps in a scheme already established by the Oireachtas: in truth the Oireachtas which enacted the 1946 Act could have no idea of even those areas which may be subject to regulation in an employment agreement sought to be registered under the Act, and no conception still less control of the possible range of regulation that might be made in respect of each such matter. (contd.../)

[13.124] A related matter is that it is impermissible to delegate power to enact regulations which conflict with other statutory provisions, even where the delegation per se satisfies the 'principles and policies' test. The concern in this respect is to deny the delegate the power to amend, either directly or indirectly, provisions which have been enacted by the Oireachtas, thus preserving the legislative exclusivity of the latter. It follows, of course, that the enactment of so-called 'Henry VIII clauses' which authorise the delegate to amend an Act by secondary legislation would be unconstitutional.[171]

[13.125] The foregoing must be considered in the light of other constitutional provisions and the presumption of constitutionality. With regard to the former, the Oireachtas may not confer a power to act in breach of the Constitution. Thus, in *East Donegal Co-Operative Livestock Mart Ltd v Attorney General*[172] the delegation of a power to exempt particular individuals from the operation of the parent statute was held to be invalid as it violated the constitutional guarantee of equality in Article 40.1.

[13.126] A consequence of the presumption of constitutionality[173] is that a post-1937 statute must where possible be interpreted in a manner which is consonant with the Constitution. In practice the courts have proved to be willing to avoid declaring a provision which delegates power to be unconstitutional and have tended to focus instead on the particular exercise of the delegated power. Thus, where a power is delegated in ambiguous terms the courts are prepared to construe it in as narrow a manner as is reasonably possible in order to preserve its constitutionality. In particular, a delegation of legislative power which appears to be too broad may be construed narrowly in order to preserve its constitutionality. This is demonstrated by the Supreme Court decision in *Cooke v Walsh*[174] where s 72 of the Health Act 1970 was interpreted in a manner that excluded an unconstitutional delegation of legislative power.

---

[170] (\...contd) Nor did the Oireachtas retain any capacity for review either by the Oireachtas or by a member of the Executive responsible to it, of the agreements actually made. Whatever may be thought of a scheme which permits parties to an agreement to clothe that agreement with certain legal consequences including the possibility of enforcement by criminal proceedings, once such an agreement purports to become binding on non-parties pursuant to s.30 of the Act, it passes unmistakably into the field of legislation which by Article 15 is the sole and exclusive preserve of the Oireachtas.

The Industrial Relations (Amendment) Act 2012, which was enacted after the decision in *John Grace Fried Chicken Ltd* but before that in *McGowan*, effected significant changes that are designed to cure the deficiencies identified in the earlier legislation.

[171] See Morgan, *Constitutional Law of Ireland* (2nd edn, 1990), p 108; but note the position regarding European Communities Act 1972, s 3 where ministerial regulations may alter, amend or repeal other law, the constitutionality of which was upheld in *Meagher v Minister for Agriculture* [1994] 1 IR 329; see further, paras **16.121–16.134**.

[172] *East Donegal Co-Operative Livestock Mart Ltd v Attorney General* [1970] IR 317.

[173] See further paras **14.78–14.87**.

[174] *Cooke v Walsh* [1984] IR 710.

[13.127] A distinction between a constitutionally impermissible delegation of power and an unconstitutional exercise of a valid power is evident in *Harvey v Minister for Social Welfare*.[175] There, s 75 of the Social Welfare Act 1952 was held to be constitutional on the strength of the presumption of constitutionality, although the particular regulation made under that provision was held to be unconstitutional on the ground that it invaded the legislative domain. By virtue of s 75 the Minister was authorised to make regulations governing the case of a person who was in receipt of two or more stated social welfare payments and to disallow one payment. The power to cancel certain social welfare payments is, it was contended, legislative and thus confined to the Oireachtas.

[13.128] The Supreme Court invoked the presumption of constitutionality to save the provision, concluding that it would be unconstitutional only if the exercise of the delegated power would necessarily or inevitably trespass on the legislative domain:

"The impugned section having been enacted in 1952 is entitled to the presumption of constitutional validity which has been laid down by this Court, and in particular falls to be construed in accordance with the principles in the decision of this Court pronounced in *East Donegal Co-Operative Livestock Mart Ltd v Attorney General*[176] ... it must be implied that the making of regulations by the Minister as is permitted or prescribed by s 75 of the Act of 1952 is intended by the Oireachtas to be conducted in accordance with the principles of constitutional justice and, therefore, that it is to be implied that the Minister shall not in exercising the power of making regulations pursuant to that section contravene the provisions of Article 15.2 of the Constitution. The Court is satisfied that the terms of s 75 of the Act of 1952 do not make it necessary or inevitable that a Minister for Social Welfare making regulations pursuant to the power therein created must invade the function of the Oireachtas in a manner which would constitute a breach of the provisions of Article 15.2 of the Constitution. The wide scope and unfettered discretion contained in the section can clearly be exercised by a Minister making regulations so as to ensure that what is done is truly regulatory or administrative only and does not constitute the making, repealing or amending of law in a manner which would be invalid having regard to the provisions of the Constitution."[177]

[13.129] However, although s 75 was held to be constitutionally valid the court went on to hold that the impugned regulation – Social Welfare (Overlapping Benefits) Regulations 1953,[178] art 38[179] – was invalid on the grounds that it conflicted directly with a statutory provision, namely s 7 of the Social Welfare Act 1979 and the terms of the social welfare code generally. The view of a unanimous Supreme Court was expressed by Finlay CJ:

"The ... submission made on behalf of the applicant is that the provisions of Article 38 ... are in direct contradiction to the provisions of s 7 of the Social Welfare Act 1979, and, as

---

175 *Harvey v Minister for Social Welfare* [1990] 2 IR 232.
176 *East Donegal Co-Operative Livestock Mart Ltd v Attorney General* [1970] IR 317.
177 [1990] 2 IR 232 at 240–241.
178 SI 14/1953.
179 Inserted by Social Welfare (Overlapping Benefits) (Amendment) Regulations 1979 (SI 118/1979), art 4.

such, are an impermissible intervention by the Minister pursuant to the powers of making regulations vested in him by s 75 of the Act of 1952, in the legislative function and is, therefore, an unconstitutional exercise of that power which breaches Article 15.2 of the Constitution. I accept that this submission is correct. The very terms themselves of Article 38 [of the Regulations] ... make clear what its effect is and is intended to be, and that is that where a woman would, but for that article be entitled to two pensions she shall be entitled to one only. The situation which made her a person, at the time of the passing of those regulations, entitled to two pensions, was a situation created either by the direct provisions of s 7 of the Act of 1979 or by the statutory provisions contained throughout the social welfare code prohibiting, for the purposes of the means test, the taking into consideration of the payment of social welfare pensions or allowances. If the effect of Article 38 is to be construed as terminating the widow's non-contributory pension, after pensionable age has been reached then it is in direct breach of s 7 and the expressed purpose of s 7. If, on the other hand, it is to be taken as abolishing the old age or blind (non-contributory) pension, then it is doing so by reason of the receipt of the social welfare pension or allowance and is in direct contradiction of the provisions which prevent that occurring. Quite clearly, for the Minister to exercise a power of regulation granted to him by these Acts so as to negative the expressed intention of the legislature is an unconstitutional use of the power vested in him."[180]

[13.130] As far as the constitutionality of delegated legislative power is concerned, the approach in *Harvey*[181] is more accommodating, from the perspective of the delegate, than that in *Cityview Press*.[182] Legislation delegating such power, on the *Harvey* analysis, should be considered unconstitutional only if it is 'necessary or inevitable' that the function of the Oireachtas would be usurped through the exercise of that power. This interpretation would save most legislative provisions that purport to delegate legislative power, leaving the courts to decide whether individual items of secondary legislation involved a breach of Article 15.2.1°, a position that would represent a significant modification of the 'principles and policies' test in *Cityview Press*.

[13.131] The issue arose in *Laurentiu v Minister for Justice*,[183] where the Supreme Court endorsed the *Cityview Press* 'principles and policy' test in preference to the approach in *Harvey*. The case concerned the constitutionality of s 5(1)(e) of the Aliens Act 1935 which authorised the making of orders that 'make provision for the exclusion or the deportation and exclusion of ... aliens from [the State] and provide for and authorise the making by the Minister of orders for that purpose.' The Aliens Order 1946[184] provided that:

"Subject to the restriction imposed by the Aliens Act 1935 the Minister may, if he deems it to be conducive to the public good so to do, make an order (in this Order referred to as a deportation order) requiring an alien to leave and to remain thereafter out of the State."

---

180 *Harvey v Minister for Social Welfare* [1990] 2 IR 232 at 244–245.
181 *Harvey* [1990] 2 IR 232.
182 *Cityview Press* [1980] IR 381.
183 *Laurentiu v Minister for Justice* [1999] 4 IR 26.
184 SR&O 395/1946.

It was contended by the applicant that the Act entailed an impermissible delegation of legislative power to the Minister, a contention that was accepted by a majority of the Supreme Court. In general, the power to admit or exclude aliens from the state is executive in nature and may be exercised in the absence of legislation. However, in the instant case, since the Oireachtas chose to regulate the matter by statute the question was whether the delegation of legislative power in s 5(1)(e) was excessive. The respondent relied on the decision in *Harvey* contending that the delegation would be unconstitutional only if its exercise would necessarily or inevitably involve usurping the function of the Oireachtas.

[13.132] In rejecting this argument the majority accepted that the relevant test was that established in *Cityview Press*. Denham J explained the matter in terms of the separation of powers:

> "There are limits to permissible delegation by the organs created by the Constitution. The Oireachtas may not abdicate its power to legislate. To abdicate would be to impugn the constitutional scheme. The scheme envisages the powers (legislative, executive, judicial) being exercised by the three branches of government – not any other body. The framework of the Constitution, the separation of powers, the division of power, retains a system which divides by function the powers of government to enable checks and balances to benefit democratic government. Also, in accordance with the democratic basis of the Constitution, it is the people's representatives who make the law, who determine the principles and policies. The checks and balances work as between the three branches of government – not elsewhere. Thus Article 15.2 must not be analysed in isolation but as part of the scheme of the separation of powers in the Constitution.
>
> According to the Constitution and the law it is for the Oireachtas to establish the principles and policies of legislation. It may delegate administrative, regulatory and technical matters. The principles and policies test has been part of Irish law since 1939 ..."[185]

[13.133] Keane J also saw Article 15.2 as being, *inter alia*, 'an essential component in the tripartite separation of powers'.[186] He accepted that the 'principles and policies' test governed the question of permissible delegation, in the process revising views he had expressed in an earlier case.[187] His more thorough analysis led him to observe that:

> "it is helpful to examine more closely the expression 'principles and policies'. The 'policy' of a particular legislative provision is presumably an objective of some sort which parliament wishes to achieve by effecting an alteration in the law. ... as use of the expression 'principles and policies' in the plural by O'Higgins CJ [in *Cityview Press*]

---

[185] [1999] 4 IR 26 at 61.

[186] [1999] 4 IR 26 at 83.

[187] [1999] 4 IR 26 at 88: 'To the extent that my judgment in *Carrigaline [Community Television Broadcasting] Company Ltd v Minister for Transport* [1997] 1 ILRM 241, suggests that the decision in *Harvey v Minister for Social Welfare* [1990] 2 IR 232, is universally applicable to such cases, it was clearly wrong, and should not in my view be followed. I should add that the judgment was not delivered following a uniquely elaborate scrutiny in two separate hearings of the relevant constitutional provisions, as happened in this case.'

indicates ... one can have different policies underlying various provisions in the same legislation or legislative code."[188]

[13.134] Applied to the Aliens Act 1935 he concluded that:

"the objective of s 5(1)(e) was to enable the Minister to exercise, at his absolute and uncontrolled discretion, the power of deporting individual aliens or categories of aliens or, if he considered it a preferable course, to spell out in the form of regulations the restrictions or qualifications which should be imposed on the exercise of the power ...

That was certainly an alteration in the law; but to describe it as a 'policy' begs the question, since it assumes that such an alteration can properly be so described. The *policy* of the legislation was not to enable the State to deport aliens at its pleasure, subject only to whatever qualification, by legislation or otherwise, it elected to impose on the exercise of the power: that power was already vested in the State. The effect of the alteration was to enable the Minister, and not the Oireachtas, to determine, not merely the aliens or classes of aliens who should be deported, but also the modifications, if any, to which the exercise of the power should be subjected. Undoubtedly the designation of categories of aliens as being either immune from, or subject to, deportation at the discretion of the State and the delineation in legislative form of modifications on the exercise by the State of its powers in the area of deportation were policy decisions: but they were decisions which could henceforth be taken by the Minister. The Oireachtas had, in effect, determined that policy in this area should be the responsibility of the Minister ...

The Oireachtas may properly decide as a matter of policy to impose specific restrictions on the manner in which the executive power in question is to be exercised: what it cannot do, in my judgment, is to assign their policy making role to a specified person or body, such as a Minister."[189]

[13.135] It is significant that the decision in *Harvey* was distinguished. In Keane J's view the Supreme Court in *Harvey* did not address itself to the 'principles and policies' test and, in Denham J's opinion, the application of that decision is confined to questions concerning the validity of purported delegations of the power to amend primary legislation, the notorious Henry VIII clauses. It is abundantly clear from the decision in *Laurentiu* that the extent of permissible legislative delegation is governed by the 'principles and policies' test, a matter that was not disputed by the dissenting judges, Barrington and Lynch JJ. The Supreme Court again considered the question of delegated legislation under the Aliens Act 1935 in *Leontjava v Director of Public Prosecutions*.[190] The Court identified that the delegation was lawful in that the law making power was constrained by the provisions in s 5(1) of the Aliens Act 1935, where registration, change of abode, travelling, employment, occupation and other like matters were set out. In that case, an order had to be referable to the matters identified in s 5(1). That statutory framework resulted in the Supreme Court identifying principles and policies sufficient

---

188 *Laurentiu v Minister for Justice* [1999] 4 IR 26 at 90.

189 [1999] 4 IR 26 at 92–93 (emphasis in original).

190 *Leontjava v Director of Public Prosecutions* [2004] 1 IR 591; see Fanning, 'Reflections on the legislative process following *Leontjava v Director of Public Prosecutions & Others*' (2004) 39 Ir Jur (ns) 286.

to ensure that an order did not contravene Article 15.2.1° of the Constitution. *Laurentiu* makes it clear that the principles and policies test is to be applied in accordance with constitutional presumptions regarding the interpretation of legislation and that the actions of Ministers and officials are to be presumed to be constitutional. For a delegation to be unlawful the power delegated must exceed the mere giving effect to principles and policies contained in the statute.

[13.136] The reiteration of the 'principles and policies' test in *Laurentiu*[191] reinforces the contention that the apparently extensive delegation of power by s 1 of the Imposition of Duties Act 1957 is unconstitutional. That section authorises the government to make orders imposing, altering or terminating customs, excise and stamp duties. By virtue of s 2 of the Act such orders have 'statutory effect' but cease to have effect by the end of the following year unless they are confirmed by an Act of the Oireachtas. In essence, the Act permits the government to impose or increase (or, less likely, reduce or abolish) a significant area of taxation without having recourse to the Oireachtas in the first place. The usefulness of such a mechanism to the government is obvious – it allows for immediate changes in the rates of duty, thus facilitating revenue-raising, and it avoids the necessity of bringing the matter before the Oireachtas in the first place. The role of the Oireachtas, at best, is reduced to one of confirming such measures the following year in order to give them permanent effect. In the meantime, however, the order enjoys full force of law.

[13.137] The constitutionality of s 1 was touched on in *McDaid v Sheehy*[192] where the order in question had been confirmed by s 46 of the Finance Act 1976. In the High Court Blayney J took the view that s 1 involved an unconstitutional delegation of power on the grounds that it did not pass the 'principles and policies' test:

> "I have no doubt that the only conclusion possible is that such provisions [that is, of the 1957 Act] constitute an impermissible delegation of the legislative power of the Oireachtas. The question to be answered is: Are the powers contained in these provisions more than a mere giving effect to the principles and policies contained in the Act itself? In my opinion they clearly are. There are no principles and policies contained in the Act. Section 1 states baldly that 'the Government may by order' do a number of things one of which is to impose a customs duty or an excise duty of such amount as they think proper on any particular description of goods imported into the State. In my opinion the power given to the Government here is the power to legislate. It is left to the Government to determine what imported goods are to have a customs or excise duty imposed on them and to determine the amount of such duty. And the Government is left totally free in exercising this power. It is far from a case of the Government filling in only the details. The fundamental question in regard to the imposition of customs or excise duties on imported goods is first, on what goods should a duty be imposed, and secondly, what should be the amount of the duty? The decision on both these matters is left to the Government. In my opinion, it was a proper subject for legislation and could not be delegated by the Oireachtas."[193]

---

[191] *Laurentiu* [1999] 4 IR 26.
[192] *McDaid v Sheehy* [1991] 1 IR 1.
[193] [1991] 1 IR 1 at 9.

[13.138] Nevertheless, Blayney J went on to hold that the (initially invalid) order was saved by its statutory confirmation the following year as there was no doubt in his opinion but 'that the intention of the Oireachtas was that the order should be part of the law of the State'.[194] On appeal the Supreme Court declined to confirm Blayney J's holding that this delegation of legislative power was unconstitutional. It agreed that the order was saved by s 46 of the Finance Act 1976 and, thus, was valid at the time of the proceedings. Accordingly, the court concluded that it was unnecessary to consider the constitutionality of s 1 of the Imposition of Duties Act 1957 and observed that Blayney J's remarks in this respect were *obiter*. As a result s 1 is left in something of a constitutional limbo but most commentators consider that the delegation of power is impermissibly wide.[195]

Judicial scrutiny

[13.139] Constitutional questions aside, the validity of delegated legislation is tested within the framework of the parent statute. In this context, the courts examine the terms in which the power has been delegated, which is principally a matter of statutory interpretation. If the exercise of the power exceeds those terms it is said to be *ultra vires* and, therefore, the measure is invalid. In many cases, however, the delegated power is conferred in broad open-ended terms and the question of validity is by no means self-evident. Thus, in *The State (Sheehan) v The Government of Ireland*[196] it was held that the absence of a qualification on the power to order the commencement of s 60 of the Civil Liability Act 1961 entitled the government to defer its implementation.[197] But where a power is exercised the courts examine the scope of the Act, the purpose of the power, consider whether the regulation is 'unreasonable' and, in some cases, review the procedure adopted in enacting the regulation.

[13.140] In a number of cases the courts have intervened and found delegated legislation to be deficient for various reasons. A somewhat strict approach was adopted in *Minister for Industry and Commerce v Hales*[198] where a regulation which purported to bring insurance agents engaged under contracts for services within the Holidays (Employees) Act 1961 was held to be *ultra vires* – the Act was interpreted as being confined to those engaged under contracts of service and did not extend to those engaged under contracts for services.

[13.141] In *Cooke v Walsh*[199] a regulation was impugned both on constitutional and statutory grounds. The regulation (art 6 of the Health Services Regulations 1971),[200]

---

194 [1991] 1 IR 1 at 11.
195 See Hogan, 'A Note on the Imposition of Duties Act 1957' (1985) 7 DULJ 134; Casey, *Constitutional Law in Ireland* (3rd edn, 2000), p 225.
196 *The State (Sheehan) v The Government of Ireland* [1987] IR 550.
197 See para **13.76**.
198 *Minister for Industry and Commerce v Hales* [1967] IR 50.
199 *Cooke v Walsh* [1984] IR 710.
200 SI 105/1971.

which was enacted under s 72 of the Health Act 1970, purported to exclude a category of persons which was otherwise fully eligible for health care. By construing s 72 narrowly, the Supreme Court preserved the constitutionality of the delegation, but it went on to hold that the regulation exceeded the terms of the delegation as so construed.

[13.142] O'Higgins CJ spoke for the court on both points:

"The defendant has challenged the validity of the regulation. He mounts this challenge on two distinct grounds. In the first place he questions whether the regulation is properly made within the powers conferred on the Minister by s 72. Obviously, if he succeeds on this ground the regulation will be held to be *ultra vires* the Minister and on that account to be void. If, on the other hand, the regulation is held to be within the apparent authority conferred on the Minister by the section, then the court must consider whether the section itself is valid having regard to the provisions of the Constitution …

The interpretation of the section is a prerequisite to a determination of whether what purports to be done by the regulation is, in fact, within the Minister's powers under the section. What then is permitted by s 72? The first subsection applies only to health boards and clearly relates to the manner in which these boards are to administer the health services provided for under the section. While it refers to the making of regulations 'regarding the manner in which and the extent to which the board or boards shall make available services', this must not be taken as meaning that such regulations may remove, reduce or otherwise alter obligations imposed on health boards by the Act. To attach such a meaning, unless compelled to do so by the words used would be to attribute to the Oireachtas, unnecessarily, an intention to delegate in the field of law making in a manner 'which is neither contemplated nor permitted by the Constitution'. (See this Court's judgment in *Cityview Press v An Chomhairle Oiliúna*).[201] Accordingly, these words must be taken as applying only to standards, periods, places, personnel or such other factors which may indicate the nature and quality of the services which are to be made available. However, it is not so much on this subsection as on subs 2 that reliance was placed in justification of the regulation. I again quote this subsection:

'Regulations under this section may provide for any service under this Act being made available only to a particular class of the persons who have eligibility for that service.'

Here, again, it is necessary to seek a meaning for these words which absolve the National Parliament from any intention to delegate its exclusive power of making or changing the laws. Needless to say, if such a meaning is not possible then the invalidity of the subsection would be established. *Prima facie,* therefore, these words are to be interpreted in such a manner as to authorise only exclusions which the Act itself contemplates … I am, however, satisfied that the subsection is not to be interpreted as permitting by regulation the cancelling, repeal or alteration of anything laid down in the Act itself unless such is contemplated by the Act.

Having said this, I turn to what the Regulation purports to do. It, in effect, seeks to add new subsections to ss 52 and 56 of the Act which exclude, from the benefit of these sections and the statutory entitlement thereby afforded, a category of persons whose exclusion is in no way authorised or contemplated by the Act. Included in this category must, necessarily, be

---

[201]   *Cityview Press v An Chomhairle Oiliúna* [1980] IR 381 at 399.

persons who by the Act are given full eligibility and full statutory entitlement to avail of the services provided for by the two sections without charge. This is, in reality, an attempt to amend the two sections by Ministerial regulation instead of by appropriate legislation. In my view, the National Parliament could not and did not intend to give such a power to the Minister for Health when it enacted s 2 of the Health Act 1970. Accordingly, in my view, the Regulation is *ultra vires* the Minister and is void."[202]

Statutory purpose

[13.143] The exercise of delegated power must be confined to the purposes for which it is conferred. If regulations are purportedly made for another purpose they will be held to be *ultra vires*. In *Cassidy v Minister for Industry and Commerce*[203] the Supreme Court tested a ministerial order, *inter alia*, in relation to the purpose which it sought to achieve. Under s 22A of the Prices Act 1958, as amended, the Minister enjoyed the power to regulate the maximum prices of certain commodities including alcohol. An offence was committed where a commodity was sold in excess of the maximum stipulated price. A voluntary arrangement was relied on by which publicans agreed to give the Minister notice of proposed price increases in order to allow him to consider their appropriateness. Publicans in Dundalk refused to abide by this informal price control mechanism. Accordingly, the Minister made orders which set maximum prices for the Dundalk area by which, *inter alia*, the price of a half pint bottle of lager was set at 14 pence (approximately 18 cent!). The plaintiffs sought a declaration that the orders were invalid. The first ground of challenge was that the orders were made for a purpose which was not authorised by the Act, namely to compel publicans to abide by the voluntary scheme.

[13.144] The Supreme Court considered that point against the general background of price control by the state. It was satisfied that the Minister's purpose in making the orders was to control alcohol prices in Dundalk and thus the orders were valid. Their validity was unaffected by the 'secondary' purpose of enforcing the voluntary scheme. O'Higgins CJ and Griffin J concurred with Henchy J's judgment:

"The evidence is coercive of the conclusion that the Minister, in making these orders, was primarily concerned to restore the stability of prices that had existed in the retail drink trade before the unilateral decision of the Dundalk publicans to award themselves price increases. In other words, in making these orders the Minister was exercising his statutory powers so as to achieve the object set by the legislature.

However, I think that the Minister had a secondary purpose which is not covered by the judge's findings. It would seem from the correspondence and the oral evidence that the Minister, as well as wiping out the unwarranted price increases, hoped that the threat of making maximum-price orders would force the Dundalk publicans and their organisation to return to the system of voluntary price control. He was not authorised by statute to make maximum-price orders for such a purpose, but it seems to me clear from the evidence that this further purpose behind the making of the orders was very much a secondary or

---

[202] *Cooke v Walsh* [1984] IR 710 at 727.
[203] *Cassidy v Minister for Industry and Commerce* [1978] IR 297.

subordinate purpose. The evil which the Minister wished to eliminate by making the orders was the unwarranted increase in drink prices in the Dundalk area. Having regard to the scale of those increases, he would have been wanting in the exercise of his statutory powers if he had ignored them. It is true that in correspondence he complained of those increases as being 'unauthorised price increases' and as having been made 'without ... prior approval.' So they were. But for the Minister to label them as such is a far cry from proclaiming it to be his sole or primary intention to compel the Dundalk publicans to return to the system of voluntary price control. If price increases had been justifiable because of increased costs but had been made without prior notice to the Minister, there is nothing to suggest that he would have wiped them out by making maximum-price orders.

The evidence forces me to the conclusion that the primary and dominant purpose of the Minister in making these orders was to eliminate unwarranted price increases and that, while he also had as his aim the return of the publicans to the voluntary practice of not making price increases without giving him prior notice, that aim was merely subsidiary and consequential to the dominant and permitted aim. I would hold that the Minister did not act *ultra vires* in this respect. Where a power to legislate for a particular purpose is delegated and the power is exercised *bona fide* and primarily for that purpose, I consider that the exercise of the power is not vitiated if it is aimed also at the attainment of a subsidiary or consequential purpose which is not inconsistent with the permitted purpose. If the law were otherwise, many delegated powers would be unexercisable, for the permitted purpose frequently encompasses of necessity the attainment of other purposes. In my opinion the first ground of appeal fails."[204]

Reasonableness

[13.145] Delegated legislation might also be rendered invalid by virtue of its being considered to be unreasonable. Although the exercise of a power might be for a purpose which is authorised by the parent Act, the terms of the delegated legislation might be such as to lead to the conclusion that it is unreasonable. In this context a regulation is considered to be unreasonable if its terms are so arbitrary, oppressive or unjust that it could not be said to enjoy parliamentary authority. It is unlikely that the parent Act will expressly prohibit an unreasonable exercise of the delegated power and, in effect, the courts imply this requirement into the Act. The issue arose in *Cassidy v Minister for Industry and Commerce*[205] where the Supreme Court held it to be unreasonable to set the same maximum price for alcohol sold in lounge bars[206] and public bars.

---

[204] [1978] IR 297 at 306.

[205] [1978] IR 297.

[206] The distinction between a lounge bar and a public bar, a regular feature of the licences trade at the time, was explained by the Court: 'The lounge bar is a well-recognised and widespread feature of the licensed trade in this country. A member of the public would probably recognise the term as meaning a secluded or segregated area, usually within or annexed to a public bar, where in consideration of prices somewhat higher than those charged in a public bar, patrons are provided with amenities such as seclusion, comfortable seating and tables and, varying from premises to premises, extras such as a carpeted floor, waiter service, television, service of food, and the like.' *Cassidy v Minister for Industry and Commerce* [1978] IR 297 at 309.

[13.146] The court's reasoning on this point was explained by Henchy J:

"If, on the other hand, it be the legislative policy that lounge bars should no longer exist as areas of licensed premises where prices higher than those in a public bar are charged, that policy should be implemented in a statute duly made in conformity with the Constitution. The change cannot be effected by Ministerial orders made under the Prices Acts. The purpose of such orders is 'to maintain stability of prices generally' (s 22A, sub-s 1, of the Prices Act 1958) and not to devalue or disrupt, unnecessarily or unfairly, property, trade or industry. The Minister has not been empowered by Parliament to do more than what is necessary to maintain the stability of prices generally.

The general rule of law is that where Parliament has by statute delegated a power of subordinate legislation, the power must be exercised within the limitations of that power as they are expressed or necessarily implied in the statutory delegation. Otherwise it will be held to have been invalidly exercised for being *ultra vires*. And it is a necessary implication in such a statutory delegation that the power to issue subordinate legislation should be exercised reasonably. Diplock LJ has stated in *Mixnam's Properties Ltd v Chertsey Urban District Council*:

'Thus, the kind of unreasonableness which invalidates a by-law [*or, I would add, any other form of subordinate legislation*] is not the antonym of 'reasonableness' in the sense of which that expression is used in the common law, but such manifest arbitrariness, injustice or partiality that a court would say: 'Parliament never intended to give authority to make such rules; they are unreasonable and *ultra vires*'.'[207]

I consider that to be the correct test. Applied here it produces the conclusion that Parliament could not have intended that licensees of lounge bars would be treated so oppressively and unfairly by maximum-price orders. If the Minister had made a maximum-price order which forbade hotel owners to sell drink in their hotels at prices higher than those fixed for public bars, it would be generally accepted that such an order would be oppressive and unfair. The capital outlay and overhead expenses necessarily involved in the residential and other features of hotels are such that to force their drink prices down to those chargeable in a public bar would in many cases be ruinously unfair. Understandably, the Minister expressly excluded the application of the Dundalk maximum-price orders to hotels. To have done otherwise would have been unreasonable. But if the orders are construed as not distinguishing lounge bars in any way, and as forcing their prices down to those of public bars, they fail unreasonably to have regard to the fact that owners of lounge bars, like hoteliers, are entitled, because of capital outlay and overhead expenses, to separate treatment in the matter of drink prices, at least to the extent of not requiring them to sell at prices which may cause them serious economic hardship. For that reason the application of the orders to lounge bars is unjustifiable.

For another reason, these maximum-price orders are inapplicable to lounge bars. They apply, be it noted, only to sales of liquor in the urban district of Dundalk; we have been told that 17 such orders have been made for other localities throughout the State. In so far as these two impugned orders apply to public bars, their object and effect is, broadly speaking, to bring drink prices in Dundalk into line with drink prices elsewhere. The combination of the statutory price control, as effected by these orders, and the voluntary price control

---

[207] *Mixnam's Properties Ltd v Chertsey Urban District Council* [1964] 1 QB 214 at 237.

operating elsewhere results in a general standardisation of maximum prices for drink sold in public bars. Licensees of public bars, whether the bars are inside or outside the urban district of Dundalk, cannot generally point to unequal treatment in the matter of maximum prices; but there would be unequal treatment if the orders applied to lounge bars. Licensees of lounge bars would have their prices depressed to the level of the maximum prices fixed for public bars; that would be the result if the lounge bar happened to be situated in the urban district of Dundalk. If the lounge bar happened to be situated outside that urban district, the maximum-price orders would not apply so that, in such a lounge bar, prices in excess of the maximum prices in public bars might be charged. This would amount to unfair, unequal and arbitrary treatment. It would be plainly unjust and inequitable if, merely because his lounge bar is situated within the urban district, a licensee were compelled to charge no more than public-bar prices while his competitor, who might be trading only a short distance away, is not subject to such price control because his lounge bar happens to be outside the urban district. Discrimination of that kind would be justifiable only if it were based on some distinguishing economic factor; but there is none. The distinction would rest entirely on the haphazard circumstance of different locations.

Parliament cannot have intended that the Minister would exercise in such an arbitrary and unfair way the legislative powers of price control vested in him. That being so, it must be held that the orders would be *ultra vires* if they were to be applied to lounge bars ... [i]f the Minister wishes to fix maximum prices for drinks sold in lounge bars, he may do so by exercising the powers vested in him by the Prices Acts but, to be valid, any maximum-prices orders so made should not be flawed by unfair and unjustifiable discrimination."[208]

Bad faith

[13.147] Related to the question of unreasonableness is that of bad faith. It has been held that an otherwise valid exercise of delegated power will be deemed to be *ultra vires* if it is established that it was exercised in bad faith. This was confirmed by the Supreme Court in *Listowel Urban District Council v McDonagh*[209] where Ó Dálaigh CJ (with the concurrence of Walsh and FitzGerald JJ) observed that there is a:

> "distinction between an *ultra vires* act done *bona fide* and an act, on the face of it regular, which will be held to be null and void if *mala fides* is discovered and brought before the court ... a discretionary statutory power, if exercised in bad faith, can be condemned as invalid and ... *mala fides* is a well-recognised ground of challenge ... [t]he answer to the principal question put in the Case Stated, whether the court in deciding the appeal is entitled to enquire into 'whether or not the said opinion (ie of the Urban Council) was arrived at *bona fide*' will therefore be 'Yes'."[210]

[13.148] To assist in determining whether or not the power was exercised in bad faith the court further held that it would be permissible to enquire into what transpired at the council meeting which passed the bye-law, the views of the council members and council officials concerning the bye-laws and the veracity of the opinions they expressed.

---

[208] [1978] IR 297, 309.
[209] *Listowel Urban District Council v McDonagh* [1968] IR 312.
[210] [1968] IR 312 at 318–319.

Compliance with procedures

[13.149] Procedural issues arose in *Burke v Minister for Labour*[211] where the order in question was held to be invalid due to the failure of the designated rule-making body to observe basic fairness in its enactment. At the time the Industrial Relations Act 1946 empowered Joint Labour Committees (JLCs) to make recommendations to the Labour Court to fix minimum wages to be paid to certain categories of workers. Unless the court referred the proposal back to the JLC it was required either make an order in accordance with the proposals or refuse to make the order sought. An employer was obliged to pay the minimum rates set by the order, failure to comply with which was a criminal offence and the employer was also liable to pay arrears.[212] A JLC considered a proposal to set a new minimum wage for workers in the hotel industry to give effect to a national wage agreement. The proposal did not contain an adjustment in respect of the value of board and lodgings provided to workers. An amendment was tabled by the employers' representatives, which sought to have their submissions on that matter considered and adopted, but it was defeated by a vote at one of the JLC meetings. At subsequent meetings it became clear that the JLC would not consider the submissions although no formal vote was taken.

[13.150] The Labour Court ultimately made an order which implemented the JLC's proposal. The Supreme Court held that the failure to consider the employers' submission amounted to a denial of basic fairness and rendered the order invalid. O'Higgins CJ, Griffin, Parke and Kenny JJ concurred in Henchy J's judgment:

> "Where Parliament has delegated functions of that nature, it is to be necessarily inferred as part of the legislative intention that the body which makes the orders will exercise its functions, not only with constitutional propriety and due regard to natural justice, but also within the framework of the terms and objects of the relevant Act and with basic fairness, reasonableness and good faith. The absoluteness of the delegation is susceptible of unjust and tyrannous abuse unless its operation is thus confined; so it is entirely proper to ascribe to the Oireachtas (being the Parliament of a State which is constitutionally bound to protect, by its laws, its citizens from unjust attack) an intention that the delegated functions must be exercised within those limitations.
>
> Here the Committee undertook the task of making a statutory instrument fixing minimum rates of remuneration for certain workers in the hotel industry. The representatives of employers in the hotel industry, as members of the Committee, wished the Committee to give consideration, before such an order was made, to the actual cost to employers of board and lodging supplied to workers. That was an eminently reasonable proposal. It was not

---

[211] *Burke v Minister for Labour* [1979] IR 354.

[212] The relevant provisions of the Industrial Relations Act 1946 were eventually found to involve an unconstitutional delegation of legislative authority: *John Grace Fried Chicken Ltd v Catering JLC* [2011] 3 IR 211; also *McGowan v Labour Court* [2013] IESC 21; see para **13.123**. The subsequent fate of the legislation does not detract from the significance of *Burke v Minister for Labour* [1979] IR 354, which as the court emphasised did not involve a challenge to the order on constitutional grounds.

possible to assess a fair and reasonable figure for minimum remuneration until a fair and reasonable assessment was made of the gross value of cash remuneration plus board and lodging. By the self-denying restraint by which the Committee debarred themselves from looking at the data necessary to determine the true cost to the employer of board and lodging, the Committee left themselves open to the charge that the consequent minimum remuneration order may be unjust and unfair.

It is no answer to that charge to say that the Committee were following the practice adopted previously before such orders were made. Two wrongs do not make a right; but in this case there was the difference that the Committee were specifically and repeatedly asked to receive and have regard to evidence as to the cost of the benefits which the workers were getting in the form of board and lodging. Nor is it a good answer to say that, if the Committee had taken into account the true, rather than the estimated, cost of board and lodging, the figures fixed as minimum rates of remuneration would not have been materially affected. As the Committee did not hear such evidence, it is impossible to say what effect such evidence would have had on them. Even if such evidence would have made no difference, the Committee, by rejecting it unheard and unconsidered, left themselves open to the imputation of bias, unfairness and prejudice. Such accusations, if made, would be unmerited; the members of the Committee were, no doubt, all acting in good faith and to the best of their abilities.

However, the fact is that the Committee, in formulating the proposals for the order of 1978, were acting as an unelected body, functioning behind closed doors, to produce a statutory order fixing minimum rates of remuneration; and that order could not be varied for at least six months, and non-compliance with it could lead to criminal responsibility and civil compellability. Elementary fairness required that the employers as well as the employees, both of whom were represented on the Committee, should have been allowed to present and to see consideration given to material which was crucially relevant to the question of minimum rates of remuneration.

By failing to receive and consider that evidence, the Committee failed to keep within the confines of their statutory terms of reference as those must necessarily be inferred. In other words, the order of 1978 was made in excess of jurisdiction to that extent.

I would allow the plaintiffs' appeal and declare that the Employment Regulation Order (Hotels Joint Labour Committee) 1978, was and is void in so far as it purported to substitute new minimum rates of remuneration payable to hotel workers in receipt of board, or in receipt of board and lodging, and to revoke that part of the order of 1977 which dealt with minimum rates of remuneration payable to hotel workers in receipt of board, or in receipt of board and lodging."[213]

Parliamentary scrutiny

[13.151] While the Oireachtas has no direct role in the enactment of delegated legislation, parliamentary control is achieved by a variety of mechanisms. In many cases the parent statute expressly retains the right of the Oireachtas, or one of its Houses, to annul, or less frequently to approve, the instruments made thereunder. Thus, the Act will provide that instruments be 'laid before' one or other or both Houses of the Oireachtas,

---

[213]   [1979] IR 354 at 358–363.

who may within a stated time annul it. The 'laying before' procedure, which is governed by the Houses of the Oireachtas (Laying of Documents) Act 1966 and standing orders,[214] is largely symbolic but is nevertheless important in that it formalises the parliamentary role in relation to delegated legislation. However, as Keane J remarked 'even in the hands of a vigilant deputy or senator, [the power of annulment] is something of a blunt instrument, since it necessarily involves the annulment of the entire instrument, although parts of it only may be regarded as objectionable.'[215] Moreover, given the fact that most delegated legislation is enacted by Ministers and that the government in effect controls the Oireachtas, it is highly improbable that a particular measure will be annulled in this fashion.

[13.152] There is no parliamentary body which deals specifically with delegated legislation, although scrutiny is facilitated by the existence of the Oireachtas Joint Committees within whose remit such matters would fall. Nevertheless, this state of affairs is indicative of the sense of priority which is attached to the issue. In the past scrutiny was achieved through the workings of the Seanad Select Committee on Statutory Instruments. That committee issued a number of reports over the years and identified problems with various instruments. Amongst the faults noted were overbroad provisions, delay in the publication or 'laying before' of instruments, lack of explanatory memoranda accompanying instruments, lack of citation of statutory authority under which instruments are enacted and poor drafting. The power of the Seanad Committee was simply to report to both Houses of the Oireachtas, and the validity of the instruments complained of remained unaffected. Moreover, it was probably inevitable given the technical nature of its remit that its reports were rarely, if ever, debated in either House. However, as technical exercises the reports proved to be worthwhile and they were effective in that government departments tended to take account of the observations and criticism contained in them.[216]

Domestic measures deriving from European Community law

[13.153] The large volume of European Community measures which are implemented into domestic law by means of statutory instrument is noted elsewhere.[217] A special regime of parliamentary scrutiny of such measures was envisaged from the outset. At first, s 4 of the European Communities Act 1972 provided that ministerial regulations would lapse after six months unless confirmed by statute. This mechanism proved to be problematic for a number of reasons and only one such statute – the European Communities (Confirmation of Regulations) Act 1973 – was enacted. Subsequently, the European Communities (Amendment) Act 1973 amended s 4 of the 1972 Act to provide an annulment mechanism rather than a confirmation procedure. The current position is

---

[214] DSO 171; SSO 152.

[215] *Laurentiu v Minister for Justice* [1999] 4 IR 26, 93.

[216] See Joseph, 'Delegated Legislation in New Zealand' (1997) 18 Stat LR 85, 99–103 outlining the processes of parliamentary and executive scrutiny in New Zealand.

[217] See para **16.218**.

that ministerial regulations enjoy permanent statutory effect unless they are annulled by a resolution of both Houses of the Oireachtas on the recommendation of the Joint Committee on European Affairs.[218]

[13.154] The Joint Committee acts as a filter and the Oireachtas is confined to annulling regulations on its recommendation. The Joint Committee established a sub-committee to monitor European Community law and its function in regard to legislation is twofold: it reviews domestic regulations which implement Community measures and it reports on draft European measures prior to their adoption at Community level. Previously this task was undertaken by the Oireachtas Joint Committee on the Secondary Legislation of the European Communities, which produced numerous reports since its establishment in 1973.[219] That Committee was especially critical of the manner in which European Community measures were incorporated into national law on a number of grounds.[220] These included the manner of implementation, poor drafting, unusual or excessive use of power, the appropriateness of penalties, the failure to cite the authority for regulations and the lack of uniformity in language. In its Thirtieth Report, the First Joint Committee recommended that statutory instruments should be detailed and comprehensive so that the user is provided with all the necessary information in the one instrument.[221]

[13.155] The extensive powers to make regulations which are conferred on Ministers by s 3 of the European Communities Act 1972 were held to be constitutional in *Meagher v Minister for Agriculture*.[222] It is clear that the scope of delegated legislative power in respect of matters 'necessitated' by Community membership far exceeds that which would be permitted in domestic law. Dicta in *Meagher* envisaged that some measures might require implementation into national law by means of primary legislation, but most exercises of ministerial regulatory power are in effect immunised. Thus, the government enjoys discretion as to whether to implement its Community obligations by primary or secondary legislation. In a number of cases where domestic law would be significantly affected by the Community measure primary legislation has been the chosen mechanism:[223] examples are the Central Bank Act 1989, the Liability for Defective Products Act 1991, the Animal Remedies Act 1993, the Package Holidays and Travel Trade Act 1995 and the Consumer Credit Act 1995.

---

[218] European Communities Act 1972, s 4, amended by European Communities (Amendment) Act 1995, s 1.

[219] See *Seventh Report of the Sixth Oireachtas Joint Committee on the Secondary Legislation of the European Communities*.

[220] See Robinson, 'Irish Parliamentary Scrutiny of European Community Legislation' (1979) 16 CML Rev 9; Walsh, 'Irish Parliamentary Scrutiny of EU Measures on the Free Movement of Persons: Going Through the Motions' (2005) 40 Ir Jur 261.

[221] Prl 5419, p 7.

[222] *Meagher v Minister for Agriculture* [1994] 1 IR 329. See further, para **16.128**.

[223] See *Second Report of First Oireachtas Joint Committee on the Secondary Legislation of the European Communities* (Prl 3841), p 17 recommending that company law matters be implemented by primary rather than secondary legislation.

[13.156] On the other hand, while regulations have tended to implement measures which are principally technical or administrative in nature, secondary legislation has been resorted to in some cases which have entailed significant alterations to domestic law. For instance, the European Communities (Unfair Terms in Consumer Contracts) Regulations 1995[224] implement Council Directive 93/13/EEC on unfair terms in consumer contracts.[225] This measure, which has a major significance for the law governing consumer contracts, co-exists with the existing national legislation on the matter, in particular the Sale of Goods and Supply of Services Act 1980, and the two must be read side by side.

[13.157] The choice of delegated legislation to implement a measure of this magnitude might be criticised on several grounds.[226] One is that the diluted form of parliamentary scrutiny, which exists in the case of delegated legislation, is inappropriate for a measure which has such far-reaching consequences. Another is that it results in an important body of law being governed by two sets of measures which overlap and might potentially be in conflict. Moreover, the usual supremacy of primary legislation is inverted: the measures which are contained in the primary legislation (being domestic) are subordinate to those which are contained in secondary legislation (being European in origin). In contrast, Council Directives 87/102/EEC and 90/80/EEC are implemented by the Consumer Credit Act 1995, which also made the appropriate alterations to existing domestic legislation and this, it is argued, conforms to a better legislative policy.

[13.158] The implementation of European Community measures by non-legislative means (such as departmental circulars and administrative schemes)[227] has also attracted criticism.[228] Although such domestic measures are permitted by Community law, the point is that parliamentary scrutiny is only possible when they are implemented in legislative form, be it primary or secondary.

---

[224] SI 27/1995.

[225] [1993] OJ L95/29–34.

[226] See also Murphy, 'The Unfair Contract Terms Regulations 1995: A Red Card for the State' (1995) 13 ILT (ns) 156, questioning their constitutionality.

[227] See observations on quasi-legislation at paras **13.09–13.13**.

[228] See *Eleventh Report of First Oireachtas Joint Committee on the Secondary Legislation of the European Communities* (Prl 4669), p 5.

Chapter 14

Interpretation of Legislation

[1]   Introduction 629
[2]   The Principal Approaches 640
[3]   Aids to Interpretation 664
[4]   External Sources 694

[1] INTRODUCTION

[14.01] In this chapter we examine the interpretation of legislation.[1] In the main we are concerned with the rules, principles, practices and techniques which are currently employed to determine the meaning of statutory provisions, which have aptly been called the 'conventions of interpretation'.[2] Some preliminary observations are warranted.

[14.02] We have noted that one of the characteristics of legislation is that it addresses its commands in a fixed verbal format.[3] It is that which, of course, falls to be interpreted. By its nature language is an imprecise instrument of communication. Interpretation is a necessary part of communication, not only in the case of difficult or doubtful linguistic constructions, but in every case where one wishes to understand that which is written or spoken by another. Words do not have settled, definite and uniform meanings – they are surrounded by uncertainty and doubt and usage adapts and evolves over time. For instance, does the term 'motor car' include a mechanically propelled three-wheeled vehicle or is that a 'motor tricycle'? Is a ruined castle a 'building'? Is a tomato 'vegetable' or 'fruit'?

[14.03] In most cases we experience few difficulties but it is worth reflecting for a moment on the variety of ways in which we attribute meaning to language. The expression 'feed the dog' is a much more complex statement than its terseness might

---

1   See generally Dodd, *Statutory Interpretation in Ireland* (2008); *Craies on Legislation: A Practitioner's Guide to the Nature, Process, Effect and Interpretation of Legislation* (10th edn, 2012); *Maxwell on the Interpretation of Statutes* (12th edn, 1969); *Bennion on Statutory Interpretation* (6th edn, 2013); Bennion, *Understanding Common Law Legislation: Drafting and Interpretation* (2001); Cross, *Statutory Interpretation* (3rd edn, 1995); Law Reform Commission, *Consultation Paper on Statutory Drafting and Interpretation* (CP 14-1999); Law Reform Commission, *Report on Statutory Drafting and Interpretation* (LRC 61-2000).

2   Miers and Page, *Legislation* (2nd edn, 1990), p 160.

3   See para **13.14**.

suggest. We can take it that the person to whom those words are addressed understands whether the words contain a command or a request, knows which dog is to be fed, what food is to be provided, whether water is to be included, where the task is to be performed and the consequences in the event of his or her not complying with the direction. The context and manner in which the words are addressed, the relationship between the parties, the unstated assumptions which they make and their shared beliefs and understandings are among the factors that contribute to the interpretation of the seemingly simple expression. All this is to state the obvious, but it helps to place the process of the interpretation of legislation in context.[4]

[14.04] While much of the foregoing applies with equal force to the interpretation of legislation, problems become more pronounced. The meaning to be attributed to many, if not most, legislative provisions will prove to be uncontroversial either because it is sufficiently clear or because the community to which it is addressed attributes an agreed meaning to it. Nevertheless, problems of interpretation are apt to be exacerbated in the case of legislation for a variety of reasons. In the preceding chapter we noted the problems with the state of the statute book[5] and the intelligibility of legislation[6] and these factors have an obvious bearing on the difficulties encountered when interpreting legislation. The location of provisions in a number of disparate sources, coupled with opaque drafting, adds to the complexity of legislation and hence accentuates the problems associated with its interpretation. Any of a number of difficulties might be encountered by interpreters. One is that of ascertaining which of a variety of provisions contained in different statutes applies to the particular case in hand.

[14.05] A second is that some provisions are drafted in opaque terms. This is compounded where the statute is drafted in archaic language or is the product of a number of drafters over the years. A striking example of a convoluted[7] provision is s 63(1) of the Settled Land Act 1882:

"Any land, or any estate or interest in land, which under or by virtue of any deed, will, or agreement, covenant to surrender, copy of court roll, Act of Parliament, or other instrument or any number of instruments, whether made or passed before or after, or partly before or partly after, the commencement of this Act, is subject to a trust or direction for sale of that land, estate or interest, and for the application or disposal of the money to arise from the sale, or the income of that money, or the income of the land until sale, or any part of that money or income, for the benefit of any person for his life, or any other limited period, or for the benefit of two or more persons concurrently for any limited period, and whether absolutely, or subject to a trust for accumulation of income for payment of debts or other purposes, or to any other restriction, shall be deemed to be settled land, and the instrument or instruments under which the trust arises shall be deemed to be a settlement; and the person for the time being beneficially entitled to the income of the land, estate, or interest

---

4   See eg *Health Service Executive v Carroll* [2012] 3 IR 1 in the context of the Public Health (Tobacco) Act 2002.
5   See paras **13.84–13.88**.
6   See paras **13.96–13.99**.
7   See Wylie, *Irish Land Law* (5th edn, 2013), p 509.

aforesaid until sale, whether absolutely or subject as aforesaid, shall be deemed to be tenant for life thereof, and the persons, if any, who are for the time being under the settlement trustees for sale of the settled land, or having power to consent to, or approval of, or control over the sale, or if under the settlement there are no such trustees, then the persons, if any, for the time being, who are by the settlement declared to be trustees thereof for the purposes of this Act are for purposes of this Act trustees of the settlement."

[14.06] A third difficulty lies in the fact that, since the main statutes are drafted with a view to regulating future events, the drafters of legislation attempt to anticipate every possible contingency. This, in itself, adds to the complexity of legislation, yet it is virtually inevitable that unforeseen cases will arise. In those circumstances the question to be determined is whether the provision should be interpreted to include or exclude the unforeseen event. Fourthly, technical and social change can overtake legislation. Provisions that were drafted in the 19th century often require a strained interpretation to be applied to modern conditions.

The role of the courts

[14.07] The role of the courts in the interpretation of statutes was outlined with great clarity by Lord Nicholls in *R v Secretary of State for the Environment, Ex p Spath Holme Ltd*:[8]

> "Statutory interpretation is an exercise which requires the court to identify the meaning borne by the words in question in the particular context. The task of the court is often said to be to ascertain the intention of Parliament expressed in the language under consideration. This is correct and may be helpful, so long as it is remembered that the 'intention of Parliament' is an objective concept, not subjective. The phrase is a shorthand reference to the intention which the court reasonably imputes to Parliament in respect of the language used. It is not the subjective intention of the minister or other persons who promoted the legislation. Nor is it the subjective intention of the draftsman, or of individual members or even of a majority of individual members of either House. These individuals will often have widely varying intentions. Their understanding of the legislation and the words used may be impressively complete or woefully inadequate. Thus when the courts say that such-and-such a meaning 'cannot be what Parliament intended', they are saying only that the words under consideration cannot reasonably be taken as used by Parliament with that meaning."[9]

While the task of interpreting statutes falls primarily on the courts, it should be noted that a number of others bodies, agencies and individuals might be involved in the interpretation of the legislation. These include civil servants and administrative agencies charged with implementing the legislation, tribunals involved in its application and lawyers and other specialists who advise clients affected by the legislation. To an extent these non-judicial bodies will lend to their interpretation a perspective and range of experience which is not necessarily shared by the courts.[10] For example, a lawyer or an

---

8   [2001] 2 WLR 15.

9   [2001] 2 WLR 15 at 37.

10   Indeed one of the reasons for establishing tribunals is to bring a wider range of experience to the function of adjudication.

accountant who advises a client on a new revenue statute will examine it from the client's perspective and the interpretation canvassed will be coloured accordingly; the adviser in that case will seek to interpret the statute in a manner which minimises the client's liability. By the same token, a civil servant who has the function of collecting the new tax might wish to maximise the taxpayer's liability.

[14.08] Put simply, competing interests dictate the manner in which different participants approach the issue and this leads to competing interpretations. Although the interpretations suggested by different bodies might be influenced by their different perspectives, account must be taken of the likely interpretation that will be adopted by the courts. Interpretation by the courts differs from that by others in two respects. The first is that by their very nature the courts, unlike other interpreters, are impartial since they lack an interest in the outcome of the case. Secondly, interpretation by the courts enjoys the formal force of law. The courts are, therefore, the ultimate interpreters of legislation and their probable response to the statute operates as a parameter within which others will present competing interpretations. Because the courts have the last word on the subject, an interpretation by another agency will in part amount to a prediction of or attempt to anticipate their decision.

[14.09] The primacy of the courts' role in the interpretation of legislation was asserted by Barr J in *Shannon Regional Fisheries Board v An Bord Pleanála*,[11] where it was argued that a court should not interfere with the interpretation of a tribunal unless it was shown to be irrational:

> "I reject this proposition. Statutory interpretation is solely a matter for the courts and no other body has authority to usurp the power of the court in performing that function ... In the present case the meaning [of the provision] is not free from doubt and, therefore, it is a matter for the court to interpret the regulation."[12]

[14.10] In practice, the bulk of legislation is implemented with little difficulty and without recourse to the courts. However, given the primacy of the courts as interpreters of legislation, it is necessary to focus on the manner in which they operate in this regard.

Intention of the legislature

[14.11] The stated objective of the courts is to discover 'the intention of the legislature'. In this respect, the exercise is one of unravelling the meaning which the Oireachtas expected the words to bear. However, to an extent the phrase is devoid of meaning. It is pointless to speak of the intention of a group of people in the sense that the group had a

---

11   *Shannon Regional Fisheries Board v An Bord Pleanála* [1994] 3 IR 449.
12   [1994] 3 IR 449 at 456; see also *Maher v An Bord Pleanála* [1999] 2 ILRM 198, 201–202, per Kelly J: 'It does not appear to me that ... the attitude adopted by the board in relation to [previous planning applications] has any bearing on the legal questions in suit ... As the judgment proceeds it will become apparent that the board has not been consistent in its interpretation and application of the relevant statutory provisions. Again that is not a factor which has a bearing upon this application since it falls for me to decide whether or not in the present case the board adopted the correct approach or not.'

collective intent. One can hardly say that all the members of the Oireachtas intended the statute to bear one meaning to the exclusion of all other possibilities. The reality is that few members will, in all probability, have considered the meaning of the statute. Moreover, of those who did consider the matter it is conceivable that they had different intentions in mind and, indeed, the variety of intentions might not be recorded in a reliable form. The intention of the Minister who introduced the Bill and who, therefore, was most closely associated with its drafting, cannot be ascribed to the Oireachtas[13] – amendments to the Bill might have been made during its passage through the Oireachtas despite opposition from the Minister. By the same token, even were it known, the intention of the drafter who was responsible for drafting the measure cannot be equated with that of the legislature. The drafter is not the lawmaker nor does he or she act as agent for the lawmaker.[14]

[14.12] As a concept 'the intention of the legislature' is nebulous and can best be regarded as a linguistic formula which reveals the nature of the exercise of legislative interpretation. It points to a constitutional arrangement based on the relationship between the legislature and the judiciary. It recognises that the function of legislating is given to the Oireachtas and that that function should not be undermined by the courts. The intention of the Oireachtas is expressed in legislation and the courts are required to give effect to that duly expressed intention. It conveys the idea that the principal constraint on statutory interpretation is that the courts are required to act in a manner which does not usurp the legislative function.

[14.13] The restrained role which this arrangement assigns to the courts is most evident in the view that a court is confined to interpreting the text of a provision. The primacy of the text was emphasised by Blayney J in *Howard v Commissioners of Public Works*[15] where he reiterated the fundamental proposition that the intention of the legislature is found in the words in which that body expressed itself. It follows that a court may not add to the text even where this would lead to a more equitable result or one which better

---

13   See *Re National Irish Bank* [1999] 3 IR 145 at 164, *per* Shanley J: '[I]t does not appear to me, on a perusal of the debate, that [the Minister's] contribution to that debate had the effect of indicating a legislative intention to preserve the privilege against self-incrimination. His contribution represented Dáil material more evidencing his own personal view of the effect of section 10 than material disclosing the legislative intention behind the section.'

14   See *Crilly v Farrington* [2001] 3 IR 251 at 295–296, Murray J quoted with approval Lord Nicholls' statement in *R v Secretary of State for the Environment, ex p Spath Holme Ltd* [2001] 2 WLR 15 at 37: 'The phrase [ie intention of the legislature] is a shorthand reference to the intention which the courts reasonably impute to parliament in respect of the language used. It is not the subjective intention of the minister or other persons who promoted the legislation. Nor is it the subjective intention of the draftsman, or of individual members or even of a majority of individual members of either house. These individuals will often have had widely varying intentions. Their understanding of the legislation and the words used may be impressively complete or woefully inadequate.'

15   *Howard v Commissioners of Public Works* [1994] 1 IR 101 at 151, citing *Craies on Statute Law* (7th edn, 1971) and *Maxwell on the Interpretation of Statutes* (12th edn, 1969).

corresponds to the known or presumed legislative purpose since that, it is said, would involve the court in law-making.[16] Barr J explained the matter in *PJ v JJ*:

"A court is entitled to interpret legislation so as to resolve any ambiguity or obvious error therein. However, where the statute is clear in its terms, the court has no power to extend its provisions to make good what is perceived to be a significant omission. If the court took that course it would entail going beyond statutory interpretation and into the realm of law-making, a function which under the Constitution is reserved to the Oireachtas. Occasionally circumstances arise where the court is powerless to avoid injustice ..."[17]

[14.14] Thus, where an unanticipated event arises or where an obvious oversight on the part of the legislature is identified, a court is powerless to supply the omission through interpretation. This arose in *McGrath v McDermott*[18] where the Supreme Court had to consider a 'loophole' in the Capital Gains Tax Act 1975. Taxpayers entered into a series of transactions which involved the purchase and disposal of shares in certain companies. The purpose of the transactions was to enable the taxpayers to become 'connected' with the companies so that they could claim allowable losses under the Act. While the transactions were not 'shams', their sole purpose was tax avoidance and no real losses were incurred by the taxpayers. It was argued that the transactions should be regarded as 'fiscal nullities' and should be disregarded for tax purposes. This argument had prevailed in similar cases before the US Supreme Court[19] and the House of Lords[20] but was rejected by the Supreme Court.

[14.15] Finlay CJ, expressing the view of the majority, advanced both constitutional and practical grounds for the restrained approach:

"It is, however, contended on behalf of the Revenue that this Court should introduce into the application of these statutory provisions a rule or principle which renders them inoperative unless the taxpayer can establish a real loss. It is with some hesitation conceded on their behalf that it is difficult to avoid the logical conclusion that a similar precondition would have to apply to the computation of a gain under the subsection. Such a principle, it is suggested, would be justified by the general undesirability and unfairness of tax avoidance and by the necessity for the courts to look on such schemes with disfavour ...

The function of the courts in interpreting a statute of the Oireachtas is, however, strictly confined to ascertaining the true meaning of each statutory provision, resorting in cases of doubt or ambiguity to a consideration of the purpose and intention of the legislature to be inferred from other provisions of the statute involved, or even of other statutes expressed to be construed with it. The courts have not got a function to add to or delete from express statutory provisions so as to achieve objectives which to the courts appear desirable. In rare and limited circumstances words or phrases may be implied into statutory provisions solely for the purpose of making them effective to achieve their expressly avowed objective. What

---

[16] See *H v H* [1978] IR 138; *Trustees of Kinsale Yacht Club v Commissioner of Valuation* [1994] 1 ILRM 457 at 464.

[17] *PJ v JJ* [1993] 1 IR 150 at 154–155.

[18] *McGrath v McDermott* [1988] IR 258.

[19] *Knetch v United States* (1960) 364 US 361.

[20] *WT Ramsey Ltd v IRC* [1982] AC 300; *Furniss v Dawson* [1984] AC 474.

is urged upon the Court by the Revenue in this case is no more and no less than the implication into the provisions of either s 12 or s 33 of the 1975 Act of a new sub clause or subsection providing that a condition precedent to the computing of an allowable loss pursuant to the provisions of s 33(5) is the proof by the taxpayer of an actual loss, presumably at least coextensive with the artificial loss to be computed in accordance with the subsection.

... for this Court to avoid the application of the provisions of the 1975 Act to these transactions could only constitute the invasion by the judiciary of the powers and functions of the legislature, in plain breach of the constitutional separation of powers.

Such an approach appears to me to be entirely consistent with the decision of the former Supreme Court in *Revenue Commissioners v Doorley*[21] and with the decision of this Court in *Inspector of Taxes v Kiernan*.[22]

Apart from the special constitutional rights vested in Dáil Éireann in regard to taxation legislation in their character as Money Bills, the acceptance by the Oireachtas of its special powers and duties in regard to tax legislation, with particular reference to the desirability of preventing the success of tax avoidance schemes, is exemplified (as was pointed out by counsel for the taxpayer) by the fact that since 1973 there have been 8 Finance Acts containing chapters especially headed with the words 'anti-avoidance' or similar words.

Not only am I quite satisfied that it is outside the functions of the courts to condemn tax avoidance schemes which have not been prohibited by statute law, but I would consider it probable that such a role would be undesirable even if it were permissible. It is the Revenue Commissioners (whose advice is available to the Oireachtas in enacting taxation legislation) who have the practical expertise and experience to know the most likely types of avoidance to be anticipated and prohibited, and most importantly of all, the predictable consequences and side-effects of the terms of any prohibiting enactment."[23]

[14.16] It is fair to assume that had the Oireachtas considered the point when it enacted the legislation, an anti-avoidance provision would have been inserted. Indeed, after the decision a provision to that effect was inserted in s 86 of the Finance Act 1989. Despite this, and its acceptance that tax avoidance schemes might result in unfair burdens to other taxpayers, the court was unwilling to adopt an interpretation which had commended itself to courts in the US and England.

[14.17] The primacy of the text is further evident in *The State (Murphy) v Johnson*[24] where the Supreme Court declined to correct an obvious error in the text of the statute. The prosecutor had been charged with the offence of driving a vehicle with an unlawful concentration of alcohol in his body, contrary to s 49 of the Road Traffic Act 1961. At

---

[21]   *Revenue Commissioners v Doorley* [1933] IR 750.

[22]   *Inspector of Taxes v Kiernan* [1981] IR 117.

[23]   *McGrath v McDermott* [1988] IR 258 at 275–277. Denham J alluded to the constitutional dimension in *Lawlor v Flood* [1999] 3 IR 107 at 136: 'In applying the ordinary meaning of the words the Court is enforcing the clear intention of the legislature. This aspect of statutory construction is an essential part of the separation of powers. Further, it is an illustration of appropriate respect by one organ of government to another ...'

[24]   *The State (Murphy) v Johnson* [1983] IR 235.

his trial in the District Court, a certificate of alcohol level provided by the Medical Bureau of Road Safety under s 23 of the Road Traffic (Amendment) Act 1978 was produced in evidence. Section 23 of the 1978 Act provided that this certificate was to be regarded as evidence of compliance by the Bureau with the requirements laid down in Pt III of the 1978 Act 'or under Part III of the Act of 1968', ie the Road Traffic Act 1968. It was agreed that the reference to Pt III of the 1968 Act was erroneous, since that Part dealt with driving licences, whereas a reference to Pt V of the 1968 Act would have been more appropriate since it dealt with road traffic offences. The District Court judge held that, since this was an obvious error, he was entitled to read 'Part III of the 1968 Act' as meaning 'Part V of the 1968 Act' and he convicted the prosecutor.

[14.18] The prosecutor relied on the error in s 23 of the 1978 Act in seeking to have his conviction under s 49 of the 1961 Act quashed on *certiorari*. He was successful, the Supreme Court holding that although the error in s 23 of the 1978 Act was obvious, the section clearly and unambiguously referred to Pt III of the 1968 Act and to read it as something other than this would be to amend the section, a course of action that was not within the competence of the courts. Griffin J accepted that the courts proceed on the 'strong presumption' that the legislature does not make mistakes and that where possible statutory words 'must be construed so as to give a sensible meaning to them *ut res magis valeat quam pereat.*'[25] Nonetheless, in the instant case, he agreed that any attempt to substitute 'Part V of the Act of 1968' for 'Part III of the Act of 1968' would amount to amendment of s 23 of the 1978 Act rather than interpreting it, and this was a function reserved solely to the Oireachtas.[26]

The traditional rules of interpretation

[14.19] In interpreting legislation the courts adopt a number of canons, or general rules, of interpretation. These are supplemented by a number of maxims and presumptions that exist in respect of linguistic usage and subject matter of the statute. The canons of interpretation are not rules in the sense that the courts are bound to apply any or all of them and are better regarded as general guides that describe different approaches which can legitimately be taken by the courts. Moreover, they are not written in stone and may be adapted by the courts. Murray J provided a succinct overview in *Crilly v Farrington*:[27]

> "The judicial aids to the construction of statutes … were formulated as a matter of judicial policy in the light of experience and with a view to enabling the courts to ascertain, as far as possible, in a useful, efficient and objective manner the true meaning of the statute in issue. They are not fundamental principles. They are a methodology of approach to the interpretation of statutes. They may be changed or adapted … There is no rule of law which prohibits a review of a rule of construction."

---

[25] [1983] IR 235 at 240, citing *Maxwell on the Interpretation of Statutes* (12th edn, 1969), p 230.
[26] See also *The State (Rollinson) v Kelly* [1984] IR 248 where the Supreme Court also declined to 'correct' an error, though in that instance this conclusion was arrived at by a 3:2 decision.
[27] *Crilly v Farrington* [2001] 3 IR 251 at 288.

Traditionally, the options open to the courts have been expressed in the form of three rules of interpretation: the *literal rule*, the *golden rule* and the *mischief rule*.

The literal rule

[14.20] The literal rule was thought of as being the primary canon of interpretation. Briefly stated, it required the court to attribute to a provision its literal meaning, which has been described variously as the ordinary, commonplace or grammatical sense in which the words are normally used.[28] The literal rule reflected a growing acceptance by the courts of Parliament's supremacy and a classic articulation was that of Tindal CJ in the *Sussex Peerage Case*:

"The only rule of construction of Acts of Parliament is that they should be construed according to the intent of the Parliament which passed the Act. If the words of the statute are in themselves precise and unambiguous, then no more can be necessary than to expound those words in that natural and ordinary sense. The words themselves alone do, in such cases, best declare the intention of the lawgiver. But if any doubt arises from the terms employed by the legislature, it has always been held a safe means of collecting the intention, to call in aid the ground and cause of making the statute, and to have recourse to the preamble ..."[29]

[14.21] A more recent expression of the rule appears in the judgment of Budd J in *Rahill v Brady*:[30]

"In the absence of some special technical or acquired meaning, the language of a statute should be construed according to its ordinary meaning and in accordance with the rules of grammar. While the literal construction generally has *prima facie* preference, there is also a further rule that in seeking the true construction of a section of an Act the whole Act must be looked at in order to see what the objects and intention of the legislature were; but the ordinary meaning of words should not be departed from unless adequate grounds can be found in the context in which the words are used to indicate that a literal interpretation would not give the real intention of the legislature."[31]

And in *Crilly v Farrington Ltd*,[32] Murray J observed that regard should be had to the statute as a whole:

"Manifestly, however, what the courts in this country have always sought to ascertain is the objective intent or will of the legislature. This is evident for example from the rule of construction according to which when the meaning of the statute is clear and definite and

---

[28] See eg *Walsh v Minister for Justice, Equaliy and Law Reform* [2010] 2 IR 463, where the High Court *per* Laffoy J held that the Criminal Justice (Legal Aid) (Tax Clearance Certificate) Regulations 1999 were neither obscure nor ambiguous, nor did a literal interpretation of it provide an absurd result or fail to reflect the plain intention of the Regulations as a whole, in the context of the Criminal Justice (Legal Aid) Act 1962. To imply the words suggested by the plaintiff would change the meaning of the provision.

[29] *Sussex Peerage Case* (1844) 11 Cl & Fin 85 at 143.

[30] *Rahill v Brady* [1971] IR 69.

[31] [1971] IR 69 at 86.

[32] *Crilly v Farrington Ltd* [2001] 3 IR 251.

open to one interpretation only in the context of the statute as a whole, that is the meaning to be attributed to it."[33]

[14.22] Underlying the literal rule was the view that the intention of the legislature is to be derived predominantly, if not exclusively, from the words in which it chose to express its commands. In this regard primacy was attached to the text of the legislation, and the rule was associated with the principle that a court may not add words to the text of an Act.[34] Parke J outlined the connection between the two in *H v H*:[35]

"Such a construction would not be in conformity with one of the fundamental rules of interpretation ie that words may not be interpolated into a statute unless it is absolutely necessary to do so in order to render it intelligible or to prevent it from having an absurd or wholly unreasonable meaning or effect. No such necessity arises here. The words [of the provision] are clear and intelligible as they stand."[36]

The same point is found in the judgment of Denham J in *DPP (Ivers) v Murphy*[37] where she observed:

"The rules of construction are part of the tools of the court. The literal rule should not be applied if it obtains an absurd result which is pointless and which negates the intention of the legislature. If the purpose of the legislature is clear and may be read in the section without rewriting the section then that is the appropriate interpretation for the court to take."

[14.23] It is clear, therefore, that if the provision was unambiguous on its face it was to be accorded its literal meaning even where this might have led to an undesirable or unjust result. The judicial role was to interpret that which the legislature had expressed, not to remedy its supposed defects. Nevertheless, most formulations of the literal rule (as can be seen in the quotations above) accepted that a secondary or modified meaning might be adopted where the words are not clear and unambiguous. It is to the competing rules that we now turn our attention.

The golden rule

[14.24] A court was permitted to invoke the golden rule if the application of the literal rule would have led to an absurdity or inconsistency.[38] In this case the provision would be attributed a modified or secondary meaning rather than that which was urged by the literal rule. An early articulation of the rule is that of Burton J in *Warburton v Loveland*[39] where he stated:

---

[33]   [2001] 3 IR 251 at 295–296.

[34]   See *McGrath v McDermott* [1988] IR 258; see para **14.14**.

[35]   *H v H* [1978] IR 138.

[36]   [1978] IR 138 at 147.

[37]   *DPP (Ivers) v Murphy* [1999] 1 IR 98 at 159–160.

[38]   See eg *The People (AG) v Bell* [1969] IR 24.

[39]   *Warburton v Loveland* (1828) 1 Hud & B 623; see also *Grey v Pearson* (1857) HL Cas 61 at 106, *per* Lord Wensleydale adopting Burton J's formulation; *DPP v Flanagan* [1979] IR 265 at 277, *per* O'Higgins CJ.

"I apprehend it is a rule in the construction of statutes, that, in the first instance, the grammatical sense of the words is to be adhered to. If that is contrary to, or inconsistent with any expressed intention, or any declared purpose of the statute; or if it would involve any absurdity, repugnance, or inconsistency in its different provisions, the grammatical sense must then be modified, extended, or abridged, so far as to avoid such inconvenience, but no farther."[40]

[14.25] Budd J's treatment of the matter in *The People (Attorney General) v McGlynn* is somewhat more complete:[41]

"What has been described as the golden rule in the construction of statutes is that the words of a statute must *prima facie* be given their ordinary meaning. That literal construction has, however, but *prima facie* preference. As Lord Shaw said in *Shannon Realties v St Michel (Ville de)*[42] at p 192 of the report:

'... where alternative constructions are equally open, that alternative is to be chosen which will be consistent with the smooth working of the system which the statute purports to be regulating; and that alternative is to be rejected which will introduce uncertainty, friction or confusion into the working of the system.'

It might be that when regard is had to what the law was before the statute was enacted and to the defect in the law which the Oireachtas had the intention of remedying by the change in the law effected by the section, the conclusion would be reached that the real meaning of the words used was something different to their apparent literal meaning. Assuming for the moment that an alternative construction of the section is open, the question is whether that alternative construction ... is consistent with the smooth working of the system which the statute purports to regulate."[43]

[14.26] When adopting the golden rule a court was not confined to examining the provision in isolation. The long title, the preamble and other provisions in the statute could be considered in an effort to discern the legislative intention. However, while the court could examine the statute 'as a whole' it was precluded from taking extrinsic materials or the parliamentary history of the provision into account.[44]

The mischief rule

[14.27] The other rule which competed with the literal rule was the mischief rule, which was the oldest of the three rules. It allowed a court to examine the pre-existing common law in order to determine the defect, or mischief, which the statute was designed to remedy. The statute was interpreted in a manner which was sufficient to deal with that defect. This rule was devised by the common law courts in the 16th century and was outlined in *Heydon's* case:[45]

---

40 (1828) 1 Hud & B 623 at 648.
41 *The People (Attorney General) v McGlynn* [1967] IR 232.
42 *Shannon Realties v St Michel (Ville de)* [1924] AC 185.
43 *The People (Attorney General) v McGlynn* [1967] IR 232 at 242.
44 See *Minister for Industry and Commerce v Hales* [1967] IR 50.
45 *Heydon's case* (1584) 3 Co Rep 7a.

"And it was resolved by them that for the sure and true interpretation of all statutes in general (be they penal or beneficial, restrictive or enlarging of the common law) four things are to be discerned and considered:

　1st　What was the common law before the making of the Act,

　2nd　What was the mischief and defect for which the common law did not provide,

　3rd　What remedy the Parliament hath resolved and appointed to cure the disease of the Commonwealth, and

　4th　The true reason of the remedy

and then the office of all the judges is always to make such construction as shall suppress the mischief, and advance the remedy, and to suppress subtle inventions and evasions for the continuance of the mischief, and *pro privato commodo*, and to add force and life to the cure and the remedy, according to the true intent of the Act, *pro bono publico*."[46]

[14.28] The mischief rule was devised by the common law courts at a time when they manifested a suspicion of statute law and sought to preserve the predominance of the common law; hence the concentration on the defect which the statute was designed to cure. An example of the application of the mischief rule is the decision in *Gorris v Scott*.[47] The plaintiff sought damages for the loss of his sheep which drowned having been washed overboard from the defendant's ship. The defendant was in breach of a statutory duty to equip the ship with pens and had they been provided the sheep would not have been lost. The action failed since the purpose of the duty (that is, the mischief towards which the statute was directed) was to avoid the spread of disease amongst animals during transportation, not to prevent their being lost overboard. At the time it was formulated, the mischief rule was the principal alternative to a literal interpretation but over time it was, to a large extent, overtaken by the golden rule.

[14.29] A certain degree of overlap existed between the three rules. The literal rule facilitated the taking into account of the context in which the words appeared. Like the mischief rule, the golden rule sought to discover the legislative purpose, although it tended to focus on the text of the legislation. The mischief rule was minimalist, in the sense that the provision was construed only as widely as was considered to be necessary to cure the defect in the common law. Whether, and to what extent, the principles of interpretation survive in those forms is open to question. But however they might be stated, two main issues remain – how expansive the task of interpretation should be and whether account should be taken of the statutory context and purpose as opposed to reading the words in isolation.

[2]　THE PRINCIPAL APPROACHES

[14.30] The canons of interpretation which are currently invoked by the courts can be stated in the form of two broad approaches, the literal approach and the schematic or

---

46　(1584) 3 Co Rep 7a at 7b.
47　*Gorris v Scott* (1874) LR 9 Ex 125.

teleological approach.[48] Before considering those approaches some preliminary points should be noted. The first is that the interpretation of legislation is now governed by the Interpretation Act 2005. That Act replaced the Interpretation Acts of 1889, 1923, 1937 and the Interpretation (Amendment) Act 1993. The 2005 Act also dispensed with obsolete provisions, which are no longer necessary for the interpretation of legislation. Furthermore, the Act updated the wording of the provisions of the repealed statutes and has also expanded the scope of certain provisions so as to provide for broader application. The 2005 Act also contains new provisions that were inspired by the Law Reform Commission Report on *Statutory Drafting and Interpretation: Plain Language and the Law.*[49] The latter provisions relate to the enactment of future legislation and eliminate the need to include in each Act specific provisions that govern references to other statutes, including amendments to those enactments. While many of these new provisions are effectively a restatement of the common law principles governing the interpretation of legislation, they were included in order to remove any doubt in the interpretative process. In addition, the 2005 Act provides for the interpretation of statutory powers and duties and the meaning of particular words and expressions as well as containing a schedule in which 40 frequently used words and phrases are defined. Thus, s 18(a) of the 2005 Act provides that words which import the singular should include the plural, and vice versa, unless a contrary intention appears;[50] s 18(b) provides that a word which imports the masculine should be interpreted as including the feminine, unless the contrary intention appears and the reverse proposition applies to enactments passed after 22 December 1993;[51] s 18(c) provides that the word 'person' includes corporate bodies unless the contrary intention appears.[52] The Interpretation (Amendment) Act 1997 applies to provisions that abolish a common law offence; in effect, it facilitates the continuation of criminal proceedings for such offences that were committed prior to the repeal and in this respect the 1997 Act is a self-contained measure.[53]

---

[48] See the similar views of the Law Reform Commission, *Report on Statutory Drafting and Interpretation* (LRC 61-2000), p 6: 'we shall use the terms "literal" and "purposive" rules of interpretation … we are referring to two ends of a spectrum …'

[49] LRC 61-2000.

[50] See *The People (DPP) v Kelly (No 2)* [1983] IR 1, applying the Interpretation Act 1937, s 11(a) to the same effect.

[51] See *Lonergan v Morrisey* (1947) 81 ILTR 130, dealing with Interpretation Act 1937, s 11(b). The proposition that words importing the feminine should be interpreted to include the masculine unless there is a contrary intention was initially established by the Interpretation (Amendment) Act 1993; in effect statutes drafted since that time have been 'gender-proofed'. See further Petersson, 'Gender Neutral Drafting: Historical Perspective' (1998) 19 Stat LR 93.

[52] See *Truloc Ltd v McMenamin* [1994] 1 ILRM 151; *DPP v Wexford Farmers' Club* [1994] 1 IR 546.

[53] See Donlan and Kennedy, 'A Flood of Light? Comments on the Interpretation Act 2005' (2006) 6 JSIJ 92; Dodd, 'The Interpretation Act 2005' (2006) 11(3) BR 100; Hunt, 'A Matter of Interpretation' (2006) 100 LSG 32.

[14.31] Secondly, many statutes contain sections which define particular expressions used in the Act or which guide its interpretation. For example, s 1 of the Misuse of Drugs Act 1977 defines 25 words and phrases which appear in the Act. In this sense an interpretation section acts as a glossary of terms or mini-dictionary for the statute and its provisions are governing, a point which was acknowledged by Murnaghan J in *Mason v Levy*:[54]

> "Where a statute ... defines its own terms and makes what has been called its own dictionary, a court should not depart from the definitions given by the statute and the meanings assigned to the words used in the statute."

Accordingly, when faced with interpreting a provision a court will have first recourse to both the Interpretation Act 2005 and the interpretation section, if any, of the Act in which the provision in question appears.

[14.32] As noted, the Interpretation Act 2005 has replaced earlier Interpretation Acts. The Interpretation (Amendment) Act 1997, which was passed to deal with the case where a statute abolishes a common law offence, was not affected.[55] In the main the 2005 Act updates and re-enacts the provisions of the earlier legislation. In addition, s 6 of the Act enables new measures to be enacted within the need for specific interpretation provisions in each such instrument. A novel feature in the Act is s 5, which authorises the departure from the literal meaning of a provision in certain circumstances. While this does no more than reflect the general practice adopted by the courts and does not create new law, it is significant in that it represents the first occasion that statutory provision is made in respect of a canon of interpretation.[56] The canons have traditionally been considered to be 'part of the tools of the court'[57] that have been developed by the courts rather than the legislature.

The literal approach

[14.33] The literal approach is the modern articulation of the old literal rule which emerged in the 19th century as the preferred method of interpretation. It is still considered to be the primary principle of construction. Thus, in *Cork County Council v Whillock*[58] O'Flaherty J stated:

> "[I]t is clear to me that the first rule of construction requires that a literal construction must be applied. If there is nothing to modify, alter or qualify the language which the statute contains, it must be construed in the ordinary and natural meaning of the words and sentences."[59]

---

54   *Mason v Levy* [1952] IR 40 at 47.
55   Problems associated with 1997 Act are considered at para **14.139** *et seq.*
56   See further, para **14.56**.
57   *DPP (Ivers) v Murphy* [1999] 1 IR 98, 111, *per* Denham J.
58   *Cork County Council v Whillock* [1993] 1 IR 231.
59   [1993] 1 IR 231 at 237.

[14.34] While the literal approach requires a court to attribute the ordinary and natural meaning to the words, it is acknowledged that that meaning is to be derived from the context in which they appear. The authoritative statement of the literal approach is that of Henchy J in *Inspector of Taxes v Kiernan*[60] where the Supreme Court was required to consider whether the expression 'cattle' in the Income Tax Act 1967 included pigs:

"There is no doubt that at certain stages of English usage and in certain statutory contexts, the word 'cattle' is wide enough in its express or implied significance to include pigs. That fact, however, does not lead us to a solution of the essential question before us. When the legislature used the word 'cattle' in the [Income Tax] Act of 1918 and again in the Act of 1967, without in either case giving it a definition, was it intended that the word should comprehend pigs? That the word has, or has been held to have, that breadth of meaning in other statutes is not to the point. A word or expression in a given statute must be given meaning and scope according to its immediate context, in line with the scheme and purpose of the particular statutory pattern as a whole, and to an extent that will truly effectuate the particular legislation or a particular definition therein. For example, s 1 of the Towns Improvement (Ireland) Act 1854, defines the word 'cattle' as including 'horse, mare, gelding, foal, colt, filly, bull, cow, heifer, ox, calf, ass, mule, ram, ewe, wether, lamb, goat, kid, or swine.' Unlike such an instance, the question posed here is whether the word 'cattle' includes pigs in a taxing Act when the word is left undefined.

Leaving aside any judicial decision on the point, I would approach the matter by the application of three basic rules of statutory interpretation. First, if the statutory provision is one directed to the public at large, rather than to a particular class who may be expected to use the word or expression in question in either a narrowed or an extended connotation, or as a term of art, then, in the absence of internal evidence suggesting the contrary, the word or expression should be given its ordinary or colloquial meaning. As Lord Esher MR put it in *Unwin v Hanson*[61] at p 119 of the report:

'If the Act is directed to dealing with matters affecting everybody generally, the words used have the meaning attached to them in the common and ordinary use of language. If the Act is one passed with reference to a particular trade, business, or transaction, and words are used which everybody conversant with that trade, business, or transaction, knows and understands to have a particular meaning in it, then the words are to be construed as having that particular meaning, though it may differ from the common or ordinary meaning of the words.'

The statutory provisions we are concerned with here are plainly addressed to the public generally, rather than to a selected section thereof who might be expected to use words in a specialised sense. Accordingly, the word 'cattle' should be given the meaning which an ordinary member of the public would intend it to have when using it ordinarily.

Secondly, if a word or expression is used in a statute creating a penal or taxation liability, and there is looseness or ambiguity attaching to it, the word should be construed strictly so as to prevent a fresh imposition of liability from being created unfairly by the use of oblique or slack language: see Lord Esher MR in *Tuck & Sons v Preister*;[62] Lord Reid in *Director of*

---

[60] *Inspector of Taxes v Kiernan* [1981] IR 117.
[61] *Unwin v Hanson* [1891] 2 QB 115.
[62] *Tuck & Sons v Preister* (1887) 19 QBD 629 at 638.

Public Prosecutions v Ottewell[63] and Lord Denning MR in *Farrell v Alexander*.[64] As used in the statutory provisions in question here, the word 'cattle' calls for such a strict construction.

Thirdly, when the word which requires to be given its natural and ordinary meaning is a simple word which has a widespread and unambiguous currency, the judge construing it should draw primarily on his own experience of its use. Dictionaries or other literary sources should be looked at only when alternative meanings, regional usages or other obliquities are shown to cast doubt on the singularity of its ordinary meaning, or when there are grounds for suggesting that the meaning of the word has changed since the statute in question was passed. In regard to 'cattle', which is an ordinary and widely used word, one's experience is that in its modern usage the word, as it would fall from the lips of the man in the street, would be intended to mean and would be taken to mean no more than bovine animals. To the ordinary person, cattle, sheep and pigs are distinct forms of livestock."[65]

[14.35] The principles outlined by Henchy J have received general judicial endorsement. In *McGrath v McDermott*[66] Finlay CJ stated:

"The function of the courts in interpreting a statute of the Oireachtas is, however, strictly confined to ascertaining the true meaning of each statutory provision, resorting in cases of doubt or ambiguity to consideration of the purposes and intention of the legislature to be inferred from other provisions of the statute involved, or even of other statutes expressed to be construed with it. The courts have not got a function to add to or delete from express statutory provisions so as to achieve objectives which to the courts appear desirable."[67]

Likewise, McCarthy J's observations in *Texaco (Ireland) Ltd v Murphy*:

"[T]he first rule of statutory construction remains that the words be given their ordinary literal meaning. True it is that one should seek to construe a statute as a whole, a principle perhaps less relevant to the construction of revenue legislation than, for instance, that with a social purpose ... the legal principle appears clearly to be that if the claim for allowance falls within the express wording of the permitting section, it must be upheld. Arguments based upon the application or otherwise of other sections, proximate or not, appear to me to be unsound in law."[68]

[14.36] A similar view was expressed in the much-cited judgment of Blayney J in *Howard v Commissioners of Public Works*,[69] where he endorsed the proposition outlined in *Craies on Statute Law*:

"The cardinal rule for the construction of Acts of Parliament is that they should be construed according to the intention expressed in the Acts themselves. If the words of the statute are themselves precise and unambiguous, then no more can be necessary than to expound those

---

[63] *Director of Public Prosecutions v Ottewell* [1970] AC 642 at 649.
[64] *Farrell v Alexander* [1975] 3 WLR 642 at 650–651.
[65] [1981] IR 117 at 121–122.
[66] *McGrath v McDermott* [1988] IR 258.
[67] [1988] IR 258 at 276.
[68] *Texaco (Ireland) Ltd v Murphy* [1991] 2 IR 449 at 456–457.
[69] *Howard v Commissioners of Public Works* [1994] 1 IR 101.

words in their ordinary and natural sense. The words themselves alone do in such a case best declare the intention of the law giver.'[70]

In the same case Denham J remarked:

'Statutes should be construed according to the intention expressed in the legislation. The words used in the statute best declare the intent of the Act. Where the language of the statute is clear we must give effect to it, applying the basic meaning of the words. There is well established case law on this aspect of statutory construction.'[71]

This passage has subsequently been approved in the Supreme Court as the cornerstone for the interpretation of statutes in a number of decisions including *DB v Minister for Health*[72] and *Minister for Justice v Dundon*.[73]

[14.37] The literal approach emphasises the ordinary use of language, which is to be attributed to statutory provisions in the first instance. It is significant that Henchy J noted that the context has a bearing on the interpretation of a provision. At one level this is to acknowledge that the meaning of language in ordinary communication is contextually derived. The remarks made earlier on the expression 'feed the dog' are apposite.[74] In relation to statutory interpretation the context facilitates the invocation of concepts which are unexpressed but are generally understood to apply. For example, a section in a penal statute which provides for the punishment of a 'person' who commits a defined act will not apply to underage persons or those with serious mental disorders – the defences of infancy and insanity will apply despite the statute's silence on the matter. In other words, the general principles of criminal capacity, which exclude children and the criminally insane from liability, form the context in which the word is to be understood. This states the obvious and it follows that a word or expression might bear different 'literal' meanings in different statutory contexts.

Technical meanings

[14.38] The literal approach has a special application in two instances, each of which draws on its particular context. The first is where the words in the statute are legal terms of art they will bear that meaning rather than their ordinary meaning. This arose in *Minister for Industry and Commerce v Pim Brothers Ltd*,[75] regarding the interpretation of the Hire Purchase and Credit-Sale (Advertising) Order 1961 which applied to

---

[70]   [1994] 1 IR 101 at 151. See *Lawlor v Flood* [1999] 3 IR 107 at 136, *per* Denham J: 'The words of the statute are clear and unambiguous. Thus the ordinary sense of the words should be applied ... As plain words make clear the meaning and intent of the section it is unnecessary to apply any further canon of construction.' See also *DPP v Doyle* [1996] 3 IR 579; *Hegarty v Labour Court* [1999] 3 IR 603; *Montex Holdings Ltd v Controller of Patents* [2000] 1 IR 577.

[71]   [1994] 1 IR 101 at 162.

[72]   *DB v Minister for Health* [2003] 3 IR 12.

[73]   *Minister for Justice v Dundon* [2005] 1 IR 261.

[74]   See para **14.03**.

[75]   *Minister for Industry and Commerce v Pim Brothers Ltd* [1966] IR 154.

advertisements that offered goods for sale by way of hire purchase or credit-sale agreement. The defendants attached an advertisement to a coat which was displayed for sale in their premises. If the Order applied to the notice it was deficient in a number of respects.

[14.39] At issue was whether the display amounted to an 'offer'. In answering the question in the negative Davitt P, on a case stated to the High Court, opted for the legal rather than the ordinary sense of the words 'offer for sale':

> "In one sense it could be described as an offer to sell. In popular terms the coat could properly be said to be on offer to the public. In the strictly legal sense, however, the advertisement was merely a statement of the cash price at which the defendants were prepared to sell the goods, with an indication that certain credit facilities, the exact nature of which were unspecified, would be available. This would not constitute an offer to sell which could be made a contract of sale by acceptance; *Harvey v Facey*[76]... If the expression 'offered for sale' ... is to be construed in the strict legal sense then the learned District Justice was clearly correct in his decision. In my opinion, it should be so construed."[77]

[14.40] The second special application of the literal approach is where the statute is directed at a particular class rather than the public at large, in which case the words are assigned the meaning which would be understood by that class. This is what occurred in *Minister for Industry and Commerce v Hammond Lane Metal Co Ltd*[78] where the expression 'scrap lead' was assigned the meaning which it would bear in the scrap metal business, that being the class to which the relevant measure was directed.

[14.41] Judge Shannon, in the Circuit Court, expressed the matter thus:

> "The question for my determination is whether Article 3 of the Emergency Powers (Scrap Lead) (Maximum Prices) Order 1945, should be construed in its ordinary acceptation or its acceptation in the particular trade to which the Order was, in my opinion, intended primarily to apply. If I accept [counsel for the Minister's] submission I would hold the commodity in question to be 'scrap lead'. There is no doubt that it is 'scrap' and that it is in the main 'lead'. I think that the submission on behalf of the defendants is correct, and that I should look to the aims of the Order and consider the people to whom it was meant to apply. The Order was meant to apply to a particular trade and the control of certain sales in that trade. I must have regard to the meaning of words as accepted by that trade. The commodity in this sale was invoiced as 'battery lead'. There is a distinction in the trade between the meaning of 'scrap lead' and 'battery lead', and in view of that distinction I hold that the defendants did not sell 'scrap lead'."

[14.42] The technical meanings of the words 'embarking' and 'disembarking' an aircraft were adopted by the High Court in *Burke v Aer Lingus plc*.[79] Relying on the Warsaw Convention (on international carriage by air) it was concluded that those terms were not limited to the acts of entering and leaving an aeroplane but, in the instant case,

---

[76] *Harvey v Facey* [1893] AC 552.
[77] [1966] IR 154 at 160.
[78] *Minister for Industry and Commerce v Hammond Lane Metal Co Ltd* [1947] Ir Jur Rep 59.
[79] *Burke v Aer Lingus plc* [1997] 1 ILRM 148.

included a passenger's being transported by shuttle bus to the terminal building. Barr J observed that the terms 'have a wider connotation than their ordinary meaning in common parlance. They relate to a particular activity – air travel – and have a quasi-technical significance.'[80]

The schematic or teleological approach

[14.43] Where the application of the literal approach leads to an 'absurdity' the courts have recourse to alternative approaches, which in the past, as we have seen, were articulated as the golden and mischief rules. ''Where the possibility of an absurdity arises a court may reject the literal interpretation and attribute to the words a secondary, modified meaning which they are capable of bearing. In adopting an alternative the court may examine the provision in its wider statutory context and take into account the perceived defect of the pre-existing law.

[14.44] In recent years the courts have tended to avoid using the terms 'golden' and 'mischief' rules,[81] preferring to invoke the scheme and purpose of the statute. An early instance of the latter is provided by *Frescati Estates Ltd v Walker*[82] where the Supreme Court was called on to interpret the word 'applicant' in relation to the planning permission provisions of the Local Government (Planning and Development) Act 1963. The defendant submitted that the word should bear its literal meaning, that is, anyone that applies, while the plaintiffs argued that it should be interpreted in a modified sense to mean a person who applies with the consent of the owner (thus excluding the defendant).

[14.45] The Supreme Court accepted the plaintiffs' contention despite the Act being silent on the question of owners' consent. In the course of his judgment (in which his brethren concurred) Henchy J observed:

> "The fundamental rule that a statute must be construed so as to keep its operation within the ambit of the broad *purpose* of the Act rules out such an interpretation; otherwise it would be possible for persons, by means of frivolous or perverse applications, to cause the imposition of duties and liabilities which would be wholly unnecessary for the operation of the Act in the interests of the common good … I find nothing in the *scheme* of the Act that would allow interfering, if well-intentioned, outsiders to intrude into the rights of those with a legal interest …"[83]

---

80 [1997] 1 ILRM 148 at 159.
81 However the mischief rule appears not to have been entirely expunged and occasional reference is still made to the 'mischief' against which particular measures are directed; see *Jones v Gunn* [1997] 3 IR 1 at 17, per McGuinness J; *DPP (Ivers) v Murphy* [1999] 1 IR 98 at 110–111, *per* Denham J; *An Blascaod Mór Teo v Commissioners for Public Works* [2000] 1 IR 1 at 4, *per* Budd J.
82 *Frescati Estates Ltd v Walker* [1975] IR 177.
83 [1975] IR 177 at 189–190 (emphasis added).

[14.46] This hints at the emerging 'schematic or teleological' approach, the classic articulation of which is to be found in the judgment of Henchy J in *Nestor v Murphy*:[84]

"The two defendants are a married couple. Their family home is in Lucan in the county of Dublin. It is held by them under a long lease and they are joint tenants of the leasehold interest. In July, 1978, they agreed to sell their interest to the plaintiff. They each signed a contract to sell to the plaintiff for £18,500. In form it is a binding and enforceable contract. However, they refuse to complete the sale. The reason they give is that the contract is void under s 3(1), of the Family Home Protection Act 1976, because the wife did not consent in writing to the sale before the contract was signed. That is the net point in this claim by the plaintiff for the specific performance of the contract.

A surface, or literal, appraisal of s 3(1), might be thought to give support to the defendants' objection to the contract. That sub-section states: 'Where a spouse, without the prior consent in writing of the other spouse, purports to convey any interest in the family home to any person except the other spouse, then, subject to subs (2) and (3) and s 4, the purported conveyance shall be void.' Sub-sections 2 and 3 of s 3, and s 4, are not applicable to this case. By reason of the definition in s 1(1), the contract signed by the defendants is a 'conveyance'. Therefore, the argument runs, the provisions of s 3(1), make the contract void because a spouse (the husband), without the prior consent in writing of the other spouse, 'conveyed' an interest in the family home to the plaintiff.

The flaw in this interpretation of s 3(1), is that it assumes that it was intended to apply when both spouses are parties to the 'conveyance'. That, however, is not so. The basic purpose of the sub-section is to protect the family home by giving a right of avoidance to the spouse who was not a party to the transaction. It ensures that protection by requiring, for the validity of the contract to dispose and of the actual disposition, that the non-disposing spouse should have given a prior consent in writing. The point and purpose of imposing the sanction of voidness is to enforce the right of the non-disposing spouse to veto the disposition by the other spouse of an interest in the family home. The sub-section cannot have been intended by Parliament to apply when both spouses join in the 'conveyance'. In such event no protection is needed for one spouse against an unfair and unnotified alienation by the other of an interest in the family home. The provisions of s 3(1), are directed against unilateral alienation by one spouse. When both spouses join in the 'conveyance', the evil at which the sub-section is directed does not exist.

To construe the sub-section in the way proposed on behalf of the defendants would lead to a pointless absurdity. As is conceded by counsel for the defendants, if their construction of s 3(1), is correct then either the husband or the wife could have the contract declared void because the other did not give a prior consent in writing. Such an avoidance of an otherwise enforceable obligation would not be required for the protection of the family home when both spouses have entered into a contract to sell it. Therefore, it would be outside the spirit and purpose of the Act.

In such circumstances we must adopt what has been called a schematic or teleological approach. This means that s 3(1), must be given a construction which does not overstep the limits of the operative range that must be ascribed to it, having regard to the legislative scheme as expressed in the Act of 1976 as a whole. Therefore, the words of s 3(1), must be

---

[84]   *Nestor v Murphy* [1979] IR 326.

given no wider meaning than is necessary to effectuate the right of avoidance given when the non-participating spouse has not consented in advance in writing to the alienation of any interest in the family home ...

Because it is evident from the pattern and purpose of the Act of 1976 that the primary aim of s 3(1), is to enable a spouse who was not a party to a 'conveyance' of the family home, and did not give a prior consent in writing to it, to have it declared void, and because an extension of that right of avoidance to spouses who have entered into a joint 'conveyance' would not only be unnecessary for the attainment of that aim but would enable contracts to be unfairly or dishonestly repudiated by parties who entered into them freely, willingly and with full knowledge, I would hold that the spouse whose 'conveyance' is avoided by the provisions of s 3(1), is a spouse who has unilaterally (ie, without the other spouse joining), purported to 'convey' an interest in the family home without having obtained the prior consent in writing of the other spouse. It is only by thus confining the reach of the subsection that its operation can be kept within what must have been the legislative intent."[85]

[14.47] When this approach is invoked a court examines the general purpose and scheme of the statute.[86] In ascertaining the statutory purpose the court may examine the long title to the Act, its subject matter and the pre-existing law which it was designed to alter.[87] Once the statutory purpose is identified the provision in question is interpreted in a manner which is consistent with it and which avoids the absurdity. In effect, the courts read words into the provision.

[14.48] There is no doubt that the Supreme Court envisaged that the approach outlined in *Nestor v Murphy*[88] would facilitate the adoption of a non-literal meaning, but it is uncertain whether this approach should be called 'schematic *or* teleological' or 'schematic *and* teleological'. The two expressions have been used interchangeably but the case might be made that a schematic interpretation is different to one that is teleological. On this latter view a schematic approach, by and large, involves a consideration of the statutory context in which the provision in question appears in order to determine its meaning: the overall structure of the legislation, comparable and contrasting provisions contained in it, the long title and preamble (if any) and the interpretation of similar statutes might feature in the interpretative exercise. On the other

---

85 [1979] IR 326 at 328–330.

86 See eg *Mulcahy v Minister for the Marine* (4 November 1994, unreported) HC, where Keane J, having examined the relevant statutory provisions stated: 'While the court is not, in the absence of a constitutional challenge, entitled to do violence to the plain language of an enactment in order to avoid an unjust or anomalous consequence, that does not preclude the court from departing from the literal construction of an enactment and adopting in its place a teleological or purposive approach, if that would more faithfully reflect the true legislative intention gathered from the Act as a whole.'

87 See *Minister for Industry and Commerce v Hales* [1967] IR 50; *Charles McCann Ltd v Ó Culacháin* [1986] IR 196; *Weekes v Revenue Commissioners* [1989] ILRM 165; *Madden v Minister for the Marine* [1997] 1 ILRM 136; *Lawlor v Flood* [1999] 3 IR 107, *per* Hamilton CJ.

88 *Nestor v Murphy* [1979] IR 326.

hand, teleological interpretation, which is also referred to as 'purposive interpretation', expressly involves the consideration of the legislative purpose in order to determine the meaning of the measure under scrutiny.[89]

[14.49] On the foregoing basis the schematic and teleological approaches differ in terms of the methodology employed and could be considered to have replaced the golden and mischief rules, respectively. Some judicial support for this view of the rules of interpretation is discernible, in particular in the judgment of Denham J in *DPP (Ivers) v Murphy*,[90] but it probably does not represent the preponderance of judicial opinion. Nevertheless, the methodological differences should not be allowed to obscure the main point which is that in certain circumstances it is permissible to reject the literal interpretation of a provision and to adopt a modified meaning.

[14.50] The attribution of a modified meaning to a measure is premised on the court's having concluded that an absurdity would result from the literal interpretation. But there is no clear or concrete definition of what constitutes an absurdity. Various broadly synonymous expressions, which are employed by the courts to justify the adoption of a non-literal meaning, are little more definite. The schematic approach is adopted where the literal meaning is said to be repugnant, to render the statute unworkable or meaningless or to be grossly unreasonable. On the other hand, the mere fact that the literal meaning would lead to an unfair, unreasonable or inequitable result is insufficient to warrant its rejection. Something more is required and an absurdity is considered to arise where the literal interpretation leads to a conclusion which, it is thought, could not have been intended by the Oireachtas. It is this factor, the failure to give effect to the assumed intention of the Oireachtas, which justifies the invocation of the schematic approach. This point is evident in the judgment of Denham J in *DPP (Ivers) v Murphy* where she also emphasised the limits of the teleological approach:

"... [n]o method of interpretation may be such as to encroach on the constitutional role of the Oireachtas as the legislative organ of the State. The rules are applied to interpret the Act passed by the legislature and in so doing afford the respect appropriate from the judicial organ of Government to the legislature.

The rules of construction are part of the tools of the court. The literal should not be applied if it obtains an absurd result which is pointless and which negates the intention of the legislature. If the purpose of the legislature is clear and may be read in the section without re-writing the section then that is the appropriate interpretation for the court to take."[91]

[14.51] Another example of circumstances where a departure from the literal interpretation is warranted is *DPP (Ivers) v Murphy*[92] where the Supreme Court was faced with the interpretation of s 6(1) of the Criminal Justice (Miscellaneous Provisions)

---

89   See eg *O'Dwyer v Keegan* [1997] 2 IR 585.
90   *DPP (Ivers) v Murphy* [1999] 1 IR 98 at 109–111.
91   *DPP (Ivers) v Murphy* [1999] 1 IR 98 at 111; see also *Cork County Council v Shackleton and Murphy Construction* [2008] 1 ILRM 185 at 209.
92   *DPP (Ivers) v Murphy* [1999] 1 IR 98.

Act 1997. That provision allowed for the giving of evidence by certificate of the circumstances of an arrest (where it was made 'otherwise than under a warrant') when an accused first appears in the District Court. Prior to its enactment that evidence would have been given *viva voce* by the arresting garda and the new measure was clearly designed to save police time by relieving members of the force of the burden of personally appearing in the District Court to testify on what was essentially a technical matter of procedure that would have little bearing in the eventual outcome of the case. However, s 6(1) did not expressly provide that evidence of the condition which authorised the reception of the certificate evidence, namely that the arrest had been made 'otherwise than under a warrant', could also be contained in the certificate.

[14.52] Relying on a literal reading of the section the accused contended that the arresting garda would be required to testify in person that the arrest had been made without warrant before the remaining evidence could be provided by certificate. The Supreme Court rejected this argument and held that the certificate could also include the assertion that the arrest had been made without warrant. The literal interpretation would have rendered the provision redundant and, as Denham J observed, it would lead to 'the absurd result that the garda is required to be in court to prove that his presence is not required!'[93]

[14.53] In the ordinary course of events the modification by the courts of statutory language is considered to be a usurpation of the legislative function, but it is permitted where it is done to implement the 'true' or 'real' intention of the Oireachtas. Nevertheless, the identification of an absurdity leaves an element of discretion to the courts and, to this extent, they are in the position of exercising choice as to the meaning to be attributed to the provision. What to one court is considered to be absurd might not be so viewed by another.

[14.54] In *Rafferty v Crowley*[94] Murphy J refused to adopt the schematic approach and to read an exception into the definition of 'prior mortgage' in s 80 of the Building Societies Act 1976 on the grounds that if the Oireachtas intended to create that exception it could easily have done so:

"Counsel on behalf of the vendor plaintiff has sought to adopt a schematic or teleological approach to the Act and in particular s 80 thereof. She says that the purpose of the Act, and in particular Pt VI thereof, is to ensure that advances made by building societies are fully and properly secured for the benefit of the society and its members. That being the intent of the Act – or so the argument goes – no purpose would be served and no benefit would be achieved by preventing or prohibiting a society from lending on the security of part of the lands comprised in and demised by a lease where the owner of that part (or his predecessor) had charged it with the payment of the rent apportioned to that part as such a charge does not reduce, in any way, the value of the leasehold interest. Again, it is pointed out that the 1976 Act expressly recognises the right of a building society to advance money on the security of leasehold property. Every person holding any part of lands demised by a lease is

---

[93]   [1999] 1 IR 98 at 111.
[94]   *Rafferty v Crowley* [1984] ILRM 350.

651

on risk for the payment of the entire of the rent thereby reserved. Accordingly, the mutual covenants and cross-charges benefit rather than prejudice the holders of any part of leasehold land and through him any person holding a mortgage or charge on such lands. Accordingly, there is nothing to be gained and no purpose served by interpreting the words 'a prior mortgage' in s 80 so as to include cross-charges of this nature.

Whilst I have every sympathy with the case made by the plaintiff and indeed I believe that it would be in the public interest generally to uphold this construction of s 80 of the 1976 Act I do not believe that the accepted canons of construction would permit me to support that view.

Reference was made to the decision of the Supreme Court in *Nestor v Murphy*[95] as an example of a case in which the schematic approach might be adopted. However, it appears clearly from the judgment of Henchy J, that the approach was justified so as to avoid 'a pointless absurdity'. Again, Henchy J pursued 'the pattern and purpose' of the legislation then under consideration where he was satisfied that by doing otherwise 'would not only be unnecessary for the attainment of that aim but would enable contracts to be unfairly or dishonestly repudiated by parties who entered into them freely, willingly and with full knowledge'. It would appear that the schematic approach is justified where – in the words of Lord Reid in *Luke v The Inland Revenue Commissioners*:

> 'To apply the words literally is to defeat the obvious intention of the legislation and to produce a wholly unreasonable result.'[96]

It is clear that by s 80 the legislature set its face against a building society making a loan on the security of a property which was subject to any prior mortgage. It would have been a relatively easy task to restrict the operation of the section to cases where the prior mortgage or charge exceeded specified amounts or perhaps a particular percentage of the value of the property in question. Alternatively, what could have been done was to exclude the various categories of prior charge as was done by s 32 of the United Kingdom Building Societies Act 1962. If that precedent did not commend itself to the draftsman he could have adopted the formula used in s 99 of the Companies Act 1963 which, having provided for the registration of (among other things) a charge on land wherever situate or any interest therein, goes on to provide:

> 'but not including a charge for any rent or other periodical sum issuing out of land.'

In fact it does not require reference to examples or precedents confidently to infer that the legislature in enacting s 80 in its existing form was conscious of that fact that it could have exempted from the scope of the prohibition certain prior mortgages or charges and deliberately chose not to do so. In these circumstances it seems to me that I am precluded from interpreting s 80 so as to achieve an effect – however desirable – not intended by the Oireachtas."[97]

[14.55] It is obvious that Murphy J considered the plaintiff's suggestion to conform to better legal policy and realised the inconvenience of a literal interpretation of the Act. Indeed, given the far-reaching economic and social consequences which his decision

---

[95]   *Nestor v Murphy* [1979] IR 326.
[96]   *Luke v The Inland Revenue Commissioners* [1963] AC 557 at 577.
[97]   [1984] ILRM 350 at 352–353.

entailed he directed that copies of his judgment be sent immediately to the Minister for the Environment and the Registrar of Friendly Societies. Nevertheless, he still felt constrained by his role as an interpreter to adopt the literal meaning. Within a short time of his judgment being delivered the Oireachtas passed the Building Societies (Amendment) Act 1983 to create the exception which had been omitted from the original Act, thus confirming Murphy J's view of the need for urgent legislative action. One conclusion to be drawn from this sequence of events is that in this case the schematic approach would have reflected the intention of the legislature since it acted almost immediately to 'correct' the decision. On the other hand, it might be said that the enactment of an amending statute merely amounts to a legislative recognition of oversight on its part and is not a reflection on the decision in *Rafferty v Crowley*.[98]

[14.56] Section 5 of the Interpretation Act 2005 permits a departure from the literal meaning where the provision under scrutiny is 'obscure or ambiguous' or 'on a literal interpretation would be absurd or would fail to reflect the plain intention of the Oireachtas' or of 'the parliament concerned' before the coming into operation of the Constitution. In those circumstances 'the provision shall be given a construction that reflects the plain intention of the Oireachtas or parliament concerned, as the case may be, where that intention can be ascertained from the Act as a whole.' However, this does not apply to the construction of a provision of legislation 'that relates to the imposition of a penal or other sanction'. The approach outlined in s 5 was referred to in the Explanatory Memorandum accompanying the Interpretation Bill 2000 as a 'more purposive approach'. It is clear that this measure, which had been endorsed by the Law Reform Commission,[99] does not alter existing practice and the circumstances in which the adoption of a non-literal meaning are permitted are defined in terms that closely reflect the balance of judicial pronouncements on the matter. It should be noted that s 5 speaks of discerning the legislative intent from the 'Act as a whole' and is silent on the question of using external sources to that end.[100]

Purposive interpretation of EU measures

[14.57] The schematic approach has been adopted with especial enthusiasm in cases where the provision in question is contained in an EU legal measure or a national measure which derives from the obligations of EU law. This is not unexpected since purposive interpretation is particularly associated with continental jurists and is often adopted in the interpretation of EU law. The connection was drawn by Murphy J in *Lawlor v Minister for Agriculture*,[101] which concerned the interpretation of the European Communities (Milk Levy) Regulations 1985[102] which implemented Art 5(1) and (2) of Council Regulation 1371/84/EEC into domestic law.

---

[98]   *Rafferty v Crowley* [1984] ILRM 350.
[99]   *Report on Statutory Drafting and Interpretation* (LRC 61-2000), pp 3, 10.
[100] See further, paras **14.154–14.190**.
[101] *Lawlor v Minister for Agriculture* [1990] 1 IR 356.
[102] SI 416/1985.

[14.58] In the course of his judgment upholding the validity of the regulations, Murphy J considered the schematic approach and its application to legislative measures which implement EC regulations:

"Attention was drawn to the appropriate canons of interpretation of EEC legislation. In particular reference was made to the second edition of HG Schermers, *Judicial Protection in the European Communities* (1979) at pp 15–23 and the comments to be found therein on the teleological and schematic approaches to interpretation. With respect, it seems to me that the principles of interpretation were most helpfully and authoritatively dealt with in the paper read by Professor Kutscher, the President of the Chamber at the Court of Justice in Luxembourg in 1976 on *Methods of Interpretation as seen by a Judge at the Court of Justice*. I may quote at some length a passage from page 1.36 of that paper as follows:

'It would be superfluous to point out once more what importance schematic interpretation has in the case law of the Court of Justice. Its application corresponds to the special features which characterise the legal system of the community. If this legal system takes the form of a broadly conceived plan and if it confines itself essentially to setting aims and directions as well as to establishing principles and programmes for individual sectors, and if in addition there is no legislature which fills in the framework drawn up by the treaties within a reasonable time ... the judge is compelled to supplement the law on his own and to find the detailed rules without which he is unable to decide the case brought before him. The judge can succeed in this task only by having recourse to the scheme the guidelines and the principles which can be seen to underlie the broad plan and the programme for individual sectors. Without recourse to these guidelines and principles it is not even possible to give precise definition to the significance and scope of the general rules and concepts of which the treaties make such abundant use ... It is plain that such a schematic interpretation which sees the rules of community law in their relationship with each other and with the scheme and principles of the plan, cannot escape a certain systemisation and therefore on occasion demand that solutions of a problem be inferred by deduction from general principles of law.'

It is interesting to note from his decision in *Buchanan & Co v Babco Ltd*[103] that Lord Denning MR was equally impressed by Judge Kutscher's paper and he explained the European method of interpretation in the following terms:

'They adopt a method which they call in English by strange words – at any rate they were strange to me – the schematic and teleological method of interpretation. It is not really so alarming as it sounds. All it means is that the judges do not go by the literal meaning of the words or by the grammatical structure of the sentence. They go by the design or purpose which lies behind it. When they come upon a situation which is to their minds within the spirit – but not the letter – of the legislation, they solve the problem by looking at the design and purpose of the legislature – at the effect which it was sought to achieve. They then interpret the legislation so as to produce the desired effect. This means that they fill in gaps, quite unashamedly, without hesitation. They ask simply: what is the sensible way of dealing with this situation so as to give effect to the presumed purpose of the legislation?'

---

[103] *Buchanan & Co v Babco Ltd* [1977] QB 208 at 213.

It is proper to say, however, that the House of Lords on appeal from the Court of Appeal in *Buchanan & Co v Babco Ltd*[104] made it clear that they did not share Lord Denning's enthusiasm for the schematic or teleological approach nor did they find any justification for incorporating it in the English legal system.

It seems to me that in construing EEC regulations I am bound to apply the canons of interpretation so clearly adumbrated by Judge Kutscher in his paper and with regard to domestic legislation it does seem to me that similar principles must be applicable at least insofar as it concerns the application of Community regulations to this State. Moreover, it does seem to me that the teleological and schematic approach has for many years been adopted in this country – though not necessarily under the description – in the interpretation of the Constitution. The innumerable occasions in which the preamble to the Constitution has been invoked and in particular the desire therein expressed 'to promote the common good with due observance of prudence, justice and charity so that the dignity and freedom of the individual may be assured, true social order attained, the unity of our country restored and concord established with other nations' in seeking to 'fill the gaps' in the Constitution is itself an obvious example of the teleological approach. Indeed in somewhat more mundane circumstances arising in the interpretation of the Family Home Protection Act 1976 in *Nestor v Murphy*[105] Henchy J expressly decided that the court 'must adopt what has been called a schematic or teleological approach'.'[106]

[14.59] This was reiterated in *Bosphorus Hava v Minister for Transport*[107] where Murphy J considered the interpretation of Council Regulation 990/93/EEC, and of the domestic regulations[108] which were made on foot of it, by virtue of which aircraft owned by Serbian nationals were to be impounded. An aeroplane which was leased by the plaintiffs, a Turkish airline, from Yugoslav Airlines was seized in Dublin Airport. Murphy J outlined the principles of interpretation thus:

"Counsel for each party is in agreement with the general principle that the regulations in question should be interpreted purposively. That is to say that the court should take a teleological or schematic approach to these regulations. Those rules of interpretation were referred to by me at some length in *Lawlor v Minister for Agriculture*[109] where I traced this rule of interpretation from the exciting paper read in 1976 by Professor Kutscher, then a judge of the Court of Justice in Luxembourg, and entitled *Methods of Interpretation as seen by a judge at the Court of Justice* through to the adoption and incorporation of the said principles in Irish domestic law by the Supreme Court in *Nestor v Murphy*[110] but their rejection by the House of Lords as part of the English legal system in *Buchanan (James) Ltd*

104 *Buchanan & Co v Babco Ltd* [1978] AC 141.
105 *Nestor v Murphy* [1979] IR 326.
106 [1990] 1 IR 356 at 374–376; see Murphy J's judgment to the same effect in *O'Brien v Ireland* [1991] 2 IR 387; see also, *Greene v Minister for Agriculture* [1990] 2 IR 17.
107 *Bosphorus Hava v Minister for Transport* [1994] 2 ILRM 551.
108 European Communities (Prohibition of Trade with the Federal Republic of Yugoslavia (Serbia and Montenegro)) Regulations 1993 (SI 144/1993).
109 *Lawlor v Minister for Agriculture* [1990] 1 IR 356.
110 *Nestor v Murphy* [1979] IR 326.

v Babco Forwarding Shipping (UK) Ltd.[111] At any rate, there is no doubt that the schematic and teleological approach is a fundamental principle of interpretation to be applied to EC regulations and directives.

Occasionally, in both European and Irish law, difficulty is encountered in identifying the precise purpose or end which the legislation under consideration is intended to achieve. No such problem arises in the present case. The express purpose of the harsh commercial regime imposed by the regulations is to deter the Federal Republic from engaging in or continuing with activities which will lead to further unacceptable loss of human life and material damage. It is clear, beyond debate, that these regulations are intended to operate as a punishment, deterrent or sanction against the people or government of that troubled republic. Conversely, it is equally clear that the regulations are not intended to punish or penalise peoples or countries who have not in any way caused or contributed to these tragic events. Between these two propositions there may be some grey areas."[112]

[14.60] Applying those principles, Murphy J concluded that it was not the purpose of the regulation to cause hardship to innocent parties unless that was necessary to effect the sanction imposed on Yugoslavia (or Serbia and Montenegro) and he ordered the release of the aeroplane. Although the European Court of Justice[113] overruled that decision this does not detract from the general remarks on the interpretation of European measures by Irish courts which have been judicially reiterated on a number of occasions.[114]

[14.61] This approach was also adopted, in somewhat different circumstances, in *Murphy v Bord Telecom Éireann.*[115] Article 119 (now Art 157 TFEU) of the EEC Treaty contains the principle of equality of pay for men and women engaged in equal work. The Anti-Discrimination (Pay) Act 1974 provides for equal pay where a man and a woman are engaged in 'like work', which includes work of equal value. The applicant did work which was of greater value than that performed by the male employee with whom she compared herself. Initially, it was held on the basis of the literal approach that that did not amount to 'like work'.[116] The matter was referred to the European Court of Justice which ruled, *inter alia*, that:

"Article 119 of the EEC Treaty must be interpreted as covering the case where a worker who relies on that provision to obtain equal pay within the meaning thereof is engaged in work of higher value than that of a person with whom a comparison is to be made."[117]

---

[111] *Buchanan (James) Ltd v Babco Forwarding Shipping (UK) Ltd* [1978] AC 141.

[112] *Bosphorus Hava v Minister for Transport* [1994] 2 ILRM 551 at 557–558.

[113] [1996] ECR 569; the ECJ concluded that the aims of regulation justified the imposition of negative consequences on some individuals; the impounding of the aircraft was not disproportionate.

[114] *Shannon Regional Fisheries Board v An Bord Pleanála* [1994] 3 IR 449; *Nathan v Bailey Gibson* [1998] 2 IR 162; *Maher v An Bord Pleanála* [1999] 2 ILRM 198; *Coastal Line Container Terminal Ltd v SIPTU* [2000] 1 IR 549.

[115] *Murphy v Bord Telecom Éireann* [1989] ILRM 53.

[116] See [1986] ILRM 483.

[117] [1989] ILRM 53 at 56.

[14.62] The case was remitted to the High Court where Keane J employed the schematic approach to bring the 1974 Act within that ruling:

"In the present case, counsel seemed to agree that treating the national law as inapplicable meant that the relevant provisions of the Act of 1974 were of no effect and that the rights of the appellants under Article 119 could be protected only in proceedings in this Court. [Counsel] ... on behalf of the appellants submitted that the applicability of the national law could and should be preserved by giving a purposive interpretation to the relevant sections rather than the literal construction which would normally be demanded.

In my view, it does not follow that, if the national law is inapplicable, the rights of the appellants under Article 119 can be protected only by proceedings in this Court. The Oireachtas has provided in the Act of 1974 a statutory machinery intended to give effect to the principle of equal pay for equal work and has entrusted the arbitral role between employers and employees in this area to the Labour Court. That tribunal in discharging its statutory function is as much bound to apply the law of the Community as is this court. Similarly, where national law and Community law conflict, it must give precedence to Community law. It is accordingly entirely appropriate in the light of the ruling of the Court of Justice of the EC in the present case to remit the matter to the Labour Court with a direction that the issues between the parties should be determined on the basis that the appellants and the male employee are employed in "like work". The statutory adjudication must, in other words, be arrived at by applying the relevant principle of Community law enunciated by the Court of Justice of the EC rather than the words of ss 2 and 3 of the Act of 1974 literally construed as our principles of statutory construction require. This seems to me entirely in accordance with the judgments of the Court of Justice in *Simmenthal*[118] and in the present case.

There are other considerations which indicate that remitting the case to the Labour Court with such a direction is the appropriate course. The Act of 1974 is presumed to be constitutional until the contrary is shown and it is a necessary corollary of that presumption that the Oireachtas is presumed not to legislate in a manner which is in breach of rights protected under Community law. Those rights already existed in our domestic law by virtue of s 2 of the European Communities Act 1972 when the Act of 1974 was passed by the Oireachtas. In the present case, in the light of the ruling of the Court of Justice of the EC, this court should seek if possible to adopt a teleological construction of the relevant sections of the Act of 1974, [that is] one which looks to the effect of the legislation rather than the actual words used by the legislature.

It should be pointed out, in this context, that [counsel] on behalf of the respondents did not press the court at the resumed hearing to adhere to the literal construction and reject the teleological construction relied on by [counsel for the appellants]. There were of course practical considerations which made this a sensible course for the respondents to adopt. If, however, a party in a case such as the present were to press for a literal construction of the Act which necessitated a finding that the Oireachtas had legislated in contravention of Community law and hence in a manner which appeared to violate the primacy given to Community law under the Constitution, I would have thought it desirable that the Attorney General should be joined in the proceedings before that issue was resolved. In the present

---

[118] *Amministrazione della Finanze dello Stato v Simmenthal* [1978] ECR 629.

case, however, that course is unnecessary since, having regard to the stance adopted by the parties, a teleological construction of the sections, if such is available, should be adopted.

Such a construction was urged upon me both at the original and the resumed hearing by [counsel] on behalf of the appellants. This requires reading into the wording of ss 2 and 3 a proviso that, in cases where the work is of unequal value and the worker doing the work of greater value is in fact being paid less than the other worker, the work is to be treated as though it were of equal value, and reading s 3(c) as though the words 'at least' appeared before the words 'equal in value'. Such a construction necessarily involves a departure from the ordinary and natural meaning of the words 'equal in value'. In the light of the interpretation of Article 119 laid down by the Court of Justice of the EC, however, it is this approach, rather than the literal approach adopted in my earlier judgment, which must be adopted by the court.

In my earlier judgment, I indicated that this approach does not in the present case bring about a situation of equal pay for equal work, but rather one of equal pay for unequal work. It has not been contended on behalf of the appellants that the Act can be interpreted so as to enable their remuneration to be increased to a level which would reflect the superiority of their work over the work of the male employee. They have confined their claim to the raising of their remuneration to the level of the male employee. However, while this matter is not specifically addressed in the judgment of the court, I think it is implicit in their judgment that the principle enshrined in Article 119 is sufficiently respected by the national legislation if it ensures that workers of one sex engaged in work of superior value to that of work of the opposite sex are not paid a lower wage than the latter on grounds of sex.

I am satisfied, accordingly, that the teleological construction of the relevant sections in the present case ensures the primacy of Community law and the efficacy of Article 119, as interpreted by the Court of Justice of EC, in this State.

I should, however, add one rider. In my earlier judgment, I said that:

> 'This teleological or schematic approach, which was adopted by the Supreme Court in *Nestor v Murphy*[119] is not appropriate in a case such as the present where the legislature could by the use of apt language have provided for a particular situation but has failed to do so, whether intentionally or by an oversight. For the same reason, it is not possible to pray in aid the provisions of the EEC Treaty or the council directive on equal pay in the absence of any ambiguity, patent or latent, in the language used by the legislature.'[120]

This passage appears to me, on further consideration, to be misleading. While it is true that the language used by the Oireachtas, literally interpreted, yields a result which is at variance with the law of the Community, it does not follow, as this passage might have suggested, that the literal construction is the only construction available. On the contrary, in the light of the judgment of the Court of Justice of the EC, it is clear that it must give way in the present case to the teleological construction, for the reasons I have already given."[121]

---

[119] *Nestor v Murphy* [1979] IR 326.
[120] [1986] ILRM 483 at 487.
[121] [1989] ILRM 53 at 59–62.

The approaches compared

[14.63] Few problems surround the terms in which the literal and schematic or teleological approaches are formulated. It is when those approaches are to be applied that difficulties are encountered. It is clear the literal approach may be abandoned only where its adoption would lead to an absurdity, but the question which remains is how that condition can be identified. It is equally clear that judicial preference or a belief that a non-literal meaning would make for better policy or would improve the terms of the statute does not justify the conclusion that an absurdity arises. This is illustrated by *Rafferty v Crowley*[122] where the court was satisfied that the failure of the legislature to include an exemption for the case in question precluded its being supplied by judicial interpretation – it was satisfied that if the Oireachtas had wished there to be an exemption it would have written it into the statute.

[14.64] However, the very same reasoning could have been adopted by the Supreme Court in *Nestor v Murphy*[123] where it invoked the schematic approach and exempted certain conveyances from the prior written consent requirement of the Family Home Protection Act 1976. It might have been argued that if the Oireachtas wished to exempt those conveyances from the ambit of the Act it could easily have done so by inserting an express provision to that effect. In other words, a set of reasons that prevailed in one case was unsuccessful in the other, and *vice versa*. Nevertheless, this shows that there is an element of choice left to the courts and this could have resulted in both those cases having been decided in the opposite way. This is not to suggest that one or other decision was 'wrong'. Given the element of choice, both decisions can be said to be 'correct' in that they are based on generally accepted principles of interpretation. The arguments that won the day in each case were themselves plausible and fit within an accepted range of reasons that may properly be invoked by a court faced with the task of interpretation.

[14.65] To this extent, the interpretation of legislation, despite its purpose being to give effect to the legislative expression of choice, involves a creative dimension not unlike the position which pertains in respect of common law decision-making. Ultimately the decision to prefer one approach to the other is a matter of choice which is based on the judicial perception of the legislative intention which motivated the statute.

[14.66] It should not be assumed that the literal and schematic approaches inevitably lead to different conclusions or that a provision is susceptible to being interpreted on the basis of one approach only. The nature of some statutes is such that different interpreters might adopt different approaches while directing their efforts to the same end, namely that of discovering the legislative intention. Moreover, the adoption of the different approaches might in some instances lead to the same conclusion. For example, two judgments were delivered in the unanimous Supreme Court decision in *Lawlor v Flood*.[124]

---

122 *Rafferty v Crowley* [1984] ILRM 350.
123 *Nestor v Murphy* [1979] IR 326.
124 *Lawlor v Flood* [1999] 3 IR 107.

[14.67] Hamilton CJ emphasised the statutory 'scheme or design' and invoked the 'objectives' of the legislation in question, language that is redolent of the schematic approach. At the same time the terms of Denham J's judgment were framed in the terminology of the literal approach:

> "[T]he plain and unambiguous words render the interpretation of [the provision] clear ... as the plain words make clear the meaning and intent of the section it is unnecessary to apply any further canons of construction."[125]

Yet despite adopting different approaches both judges reached the same conclusion on the interpretation of the provision in question.

[14.68] These points are illustrated by a series of decisions that involve the interpretation of the phrase 'manufactured goods' in various revenue statutes – typically the provisions in question allowed for relief from tax for producers of manufactured goods. In *Charles McCann Ltd v Ó Culacháin*[126] the appellants imported unripened bananas into the state and subjected them to an artificial ripening process. They contended that the ripened bananas were manufactured goods within the meaning of s 54 of the Corporation Tax Act 1976. In the High Court Carroll J, applying *Inspector of Taxes v Kiernan*,[127] rejected that argument and concluded that an ordinary person would not attribute the term 'manufacture' to the ripening process.[128]

[14.69] The Supreme Court, in overturning that decision, invoked the scheme and purpose of the statute. McCarthy J's judgment enjoyed the concurrence of Finlay CJ and Hederman J:

> "At first sight, it might be thought that 'manufactured' is a simple word which has a widespread and unambiguous currency; closer examination, however, reveals the use of the word in many differing ways; in some instances the word implies virtual creation, in others alteration of appearance rather than make-up, of shape rather than substance. I doubt if true guidance can be obtained from the application of the third basic rule [in *Inspector of Taxes v Kiernan*]. The second [rule in *Kiernan*] is clearly to be applied and depends for its application upon there being ambiguity or doubt as to the meaning of the word, and certainly there is that. Since the decision of the High Court in this case Murphy J, in construing somewhat like legislation, the Finance Act, 1980, s 41(2) (as amended by the Finance Act, 1982, s 26 and Schedule 2 thereof) in *Cronin (Inspector of Taxes) v Strand Dairy Ltd*[129] having adverted to the judgment of Carroll J in the instant case, and that of Lord MacDermott LCJ in *McCausland v Ministry of Commerce*,[130] expressed his own view as follows:
>
> > 'It seems to me, therefore, that one must look at the goods alleged to have been manufactured and consider what they are; how they appear, what qualities they

---

125 [1999] 3 IR 107 at 136.

126 *Charles McCann Ltd v Ó Culacháin* [1986] IR 196.

127 *Inspector of Taxes v Kiernan* [1981] IR 117.

128 See [1985] IR 298 at 305–306.

129 *Cronin (Inspector of Taxes) v Strand Dairy Ltd* (18 December 1985, unreported), HC.

130 *McCausland v Ministry of Commerce* [1956] NI 36.

possess, what value attaches to them. One then looks at the process and seeks to identify to what extent that process conferred on the goods the characteristics which they are found to possess. It is obvious – as indeed Lord MacDermott pointed out (at p 43) that the question is to a large extent one of degree. Nobody would doubt that well made and fully finished furniture would constitute manufactured goods but it is unlikely that the ordinary man would accept that the trunk of a tree which had been felled and provided a convenient seat constituted a manufactured article.'

I agree with the approach as so stated, subject to the qualification that one must also, in aid of construction of the particular word *as used in the statute,* look to the scheme and purpose as disclosed by the statute or the relevant part thereof. It is true that one may eventually put the question, as stated by Carroll J – whether an ordinary person would attribute the word 'manufacture' to the ripening process, not whether the ordinary person in the street would describe the bananas which have been subjected to the ripening process as 'manufactured goods', but one must ensure that the ordinary person, as so contemplated, is one adequately informed as to those matters identified in the judgment of Murphy J which I have cited. The scheme and purpose of the relevant part of the statute appear to me to be the very context within which the word is used and the requirements of which must be examined in order to construe it. It is manifest that the purpose of Pt IV of the Act of 1976 was, by tax incentives, to encourage the creation of employment within the State and the promotion of exports –naturally outside the State – objectives of proper, social and economic kind which the State would be bound to encourage. Employment is created by labour intensive processes and exports by the creation of saleable goods. The operation described in the case stated clearly comes within both categories; in my judgment, it is then a matter of degree, itself a question of law, as to whether or not what the company has done to the raw material makes it goods within the definition in s 54. Applying that test, I am satisfied that the ripened bananas, having been subjected to the process as described, constitute a commercially different product and one within the definition.'[131]

[14.70] The interpretation of s 42(2) of the Finance Act 1980, which allowed relief for goods manufactured within the state in the course of a trade carried on by a company, was considered in *Ó Culacháin v Hunter Advertising Ltd.*[132] An advertising agency produced video tapes, photographic negatives and posters and sold them to its clients for use during their advertising campaigns. The company argued that the goods were their creation and that, amongst other things, blank film which is of minimal value is, through the editing process, converted into something of substantial value. Murphy J expressed his doubts as to whether an ordinary person would consider the respondents' activities to constitute a manufacturing process and continued:

"[I]t is not sufficient to have regard to the views of the ordinary person as to what constitutes a manufacturing process or manufactured goods. In addition one must postulate the judgment of an ordinary person who is adequately informed as to the relevant legal

---

[131] *Charles McCann v Ó Culacháin* [1986] IR 196 at 200–201.
[132] *Ó Culacháin v Hunter Advertising Ltd* [1990] 2 IR 431.

principles involved and in addition one must look to the scheme and purpose disclosed by the statute in question."[133]

[14.71] Thus echoing the decision in *McCann*[134] he concluded that the purpose of the statute was to assist the manufacturing industry, not the services sector, into which latter category the respondents fell, and accordingly relief was denied.[135]

[14.72] In *Irish Agricultural Machinery Ltd v Ó Culacháin*[136] the appellants assembled agricultural machines from component parts. They claimed relief under s 31 of the Finance Act 1975 on the grounds, *inter alia*, that their trading operations consisted wholly or mainly of the manufacture of goods. The Supreme Court adopted *McCann* in relation to the interpretation of 'manufacture' but without express reference to the scheme or purpose of the statute. Griffin J, speaking for the court, stated:

"[I]t seems to me that an ordinary adequately informed person would attribute the word 'manufacture' to the process carried on by the appellant. All the machines have a utility, a quality and a value entirely distinct from the component parts which comprise the whole. Instead of a confusing array of innumerable components ... which would be of no use or value whatever to anyone engaged in agriculture, each of the machines is of immense utility and value, and it seems to me that the fact that they have been 'assembled' rather than fabricated begs the question. It does not necessarily follow that it cannot be described as manufacture."[137]

[14.73] A difference in approach is evident in *Ó Laochdha v Johnson and Johnson (Ireland) Ltd*.[138] The respondents produced nappy liners and 'J cloths' by placing bales of fabric through sophisticated machines which rapidly cut, folded, and in the case of the 'J cloths' packaged them. The employees required special training to operate the machinery and while the process did not alter the nature of the cloth it did enhance its financial value significantly. Carroll J held that the items in question amounted to

---

[133] *Ó Culacháin v Hunter Advertising Ltd* [1990] 2 IR 431 at 435. See also *Brosnan v Leeside Nurseries Ltd* [1998] 2 IR 304 at 310, *per* Murphy J: '... I think that a properly informed observer asking himself the question whether or not these out of season dwarfed chrysanthemums were goods manufactured by the tax payer, could only conclude that such was not the case' (emphasis added). The Supreme Court, on appeal, observed *per* Barrington J (at 316) '... I think that the ordinary man, however well informed about the plants and the process to which they had been subjected and the scheme and purposes of [the legislation], would be startled to hear them described as "manufactured" goods.'; *per* Keane J (at 319) '[c]hrysanthemums, whether of the dwarfed variety or otherwise, are not objects capable of being produced by what would be described in ordinary language as a manufacturing process ...'

[134] *Charles McCann v Ó Culacháin* [1986] IR 196.

[135] See *Denis Coakley & Co Ltd v Commissioner of Valuation* [1991] 1 IR 402 (HC); [1996] 2 ILRM 90 (SC), in which the High Court had adopted *McCann* in relation to the interpretation of the Annual Revision of Rateable Property (Ireland) Amendment Act 1860, s 7.

[136] *Irish Agricultural Machinery Ltd v Ó Culacháin* [1990] 1 IR 535.

[137] *Irish Agricultural Machinery Ltd v Ó Culacháin* [1990] 1 IR 535 at 543.

[138] *Ó Laochdha v Johnson and Johnson (Ireland) Ltd* [1991] 2 IR 287.

manufactured goods under s 42 of the Finance Act 1980 but in doing so distinguished *McCann* and the earlier cases on the basis of the difference in the respective manufacturing processes:

"The present case differs from *Charles McCann Ltd v Ó Culacháin*[139] and *W Cronin (Inspector of Taxes) v Strand Dairies Ltd*[140] in that no change is effected in the raw material. The fabric in the J cloths and nappy liners is identical to the bulk fabric on the bale. The case differs from Irish *Agricultural Machinery Ltd v Ó Culacháin*[141] in that nothing is added so that there is no aggregation of component parts. The appellant [the Inspector of Taxes] therefore claims that all that has occurred is a sophisticated cutting, folding and packaging process where the quality of the bulk fabric has not changed.

However the machinery which produces the two products is an expensive, sophisticated and fast machine. Looking at the end product one can immediately say that it is commercially different from the bales of fabric. The process adds more than 70% in value to the J cloths and 40% to the nappy liners according to the manufacturing costs set out in the case stated.

It seems to me that the reduction in size and ease of handling combined with the inherent quality of the raw material has a utility, quality and worth which are due to, and cannot be dissociated from, the process carried out by the respondent. The fact that the process does not bring about any change in the raw material does not of itself prevent the process from being a manufacturing process. I can think of other products where the raw material is unchanged. A toothpick is part of a tree which has been cut and packaged but it has an intrinsic quality given to it by the process, namely size and convenience and being tailored to a purpose. Confetti is another. You can throw confetti where you could not throw bulk paper.

Even though the raw material is unchanged the quality of the end product is commercially enhanced by the process. I am quite sure that an ordinary person, even if he or she did not know how the actual process was carried out, would consider the process to be a manufacturing process."[142]

[14.74] Given the ambiguity attaching to an expression such as 'manufactured goods', the abundance of decisions on its interpretation can hardly be a matter of surprise.[143] By the same token it is unobjectionable that the courts view the matter as being one of degree, with the determination to be made based on the circumstances of particular cases. What is interesting is that in determining which side of the line any particular case falls a variety of methods of interpretation have been adopted in relation to the same provision. In *Charles McCann Ltd v Ó Culacháin*[144] the scheme and purpose of the

---

[139]   *Charles McCann v Ó Culacháin* [1986] IR 196.

[140]   *Cronin (Inspector of Taxes) v Strand Dairy Ltd* (18 December 1985, unreported), HC.

[141]   *Agricultural Machinery Ltd v Ó Culacháin* [1990] 1 IR 535.

[142]   [1991] 2 IR 287 at 289–290.

[143]   See *McNally v Ó Maoldomhnaigh* [1990] 2 IR 513 where the Finance Act 1971, s 22 was said to be ambiguous, thus allowing the object of the statute to be considered. In *Cullen v Wicklow County Manager* [1996] 3 IR 474 the term 'information' was considered to be so broad as to require reference to the purpose of the legislation.

[144]   *Charles McCann v Ó Culacháin* [1986] IR 196.

statute was expressly referred to and influenced the ultimate resolution of the issue. The scheme and purpose was also considered in *Ó Culacháin v Hunter Advertising Ltd*,[145] although in this case it convinced the court that the goods were not 'manufactured'.

[14.75] *McCann*[146] was cited in *Irish Agricultural Machinery Ltd v Ó Culacháin*[147] but the court also referred to the first principle in Henchy J's judgment in *Inspector of Taxes v Kiernan*.[148] This confuses matters somewhat since, while there are references to both approaches, the court was silent as to which, if either, it was adopting. All that can safely be said is that the court accepted the *McCann* definition of 'manufactured goods' and the decision might well do little more than illustrate the application of *stare decisis* to statutory interpretation. In *Ó Laochdha v Johnson and Johnson (Ireland) Ltd*[149] Carroll J's concluding words ('an ordinary person ... would consider the process to be a manufacturing process') seem to amount to a return by her to her initial position in *McCann*. In the latter case she stated the criterion to be whether an ordinary person would consider the artificial ripening of bananas to be a manufacturing process, an approach which was overturned by the Supreme Court.[150]

[3] AIDS TO INTERPRETATION

[14.76] The general approaches to interpretation which have been considered in the preceding section are supplemented by a variety of devices which are invoked in the course of interpretation. It should be noted that these devices, which are often expressed in the form of maxims and presumptions, do not supplant the general approaches but complement them. The devices in question include presumptions which derive from the nature of the legislation and what have been called 'linguistic canons of construction'[151] which exist in respect of statutory language.

[14.77] Like the general approaches they reflect judicial attitudes and practices adopted in the exercise of interpreting legislation and are invoked on the assumption that their application best identifies the intention of the legislature. In other words it is assumed that the Oireachtas intended the words to bear the meaning which the particular device would attribute to them. By the same token a drafter will be aware of their existence and the courts' employment of them and it may be presumed that he or she will take them into account when drafting legislation. Thus, if a particular object is sought to be achieved by legislation the drafter might be directed towards a particular form of words to secure that objective.

---

145 *Ó Culacháin v Hunter Advertising Ltd* [1990] 2 IR 431.
146 *McCann* [1986] IR 196.
147 *Irish Agricultural Machinery Ltd v Ó Culacháin* [1990] 1 IR 535.
148 *Inspector of Taxes v Kiernan* [1981] IR 117.
149 *Ó Laochdha v Johnson and Johnson (Ireland) Ltd* [1991] 2 IR 287.
150 See para **14.69**.
151 Bennion, *Statute Law* (3rd edn, 1990), p 187.

Presumption of constitutionality

[14.78] It is presumed that all statutes enacted by the Oireachtas are constitutional until the contrary is established.[152] This is based on an assumption that the Oireachtas intends to abide by the provisions of the Constitution. The presumption was outlined by the Supreme Court in *East Donegal Co-operative Livestock Mart Ltd v Attorney General*:[153]

> "[A]n Act of the Oireachtas, or any provision thereof, will not be declared to be invalid where it is possible to construe it in accordance with the Constitution; and it is not only a question of preferring a constitutional construction to one which would be unconstitutional where they both may appear to be open but it also means that an interpretation favouring the validity of an Act should be given in cases of doubt. It must be added, of course, that interpretation or construction of an Act or any provision thereof in conformity with the Constitution cannot be pushed to the point where the interpretation would result in the substitution of the legislative provision by another provision with a different context, as that would be to usurp the functions of the Oireachtas. In seeking to reach an interpretation or construction in accordance with the Constitution, a statutory provision which is clear and unambiguous cannot be given an opposite meaning. At the same time, however, the presumption of constitutionality carries with it not only the presumption that the constitutional interpretation or construction is the one intended by the Oireachtas but also that the Oireachtas intended that proceedings, procedures, discretions and adjudications which are permitted, provided for, or prescribed by an Act of the Oireachtas are to be conducted in accordance with the principles of constitutional justice. In such a case any departure from those principles would be restrained and corrected by the Courts."[154]

[14.79] It is also presumed that statutes passed by the Oireachtas of the Irish Free State accord with the Constitution under which they were enacted. A number of consequences flow from the presumption. One is that in cases where the validity of a statute is challenged it assigns the burden of proof to the party who alleges invalidity. Secondly, the presumption has a bearing on the interpretation of post-1937 statutes. Those statutes must, where possible, be interpreted in a manner which would render them constitutional, an approach that has been called the 'double construction' rule.[155] Thus, where a court is faced with two reasonable interpretations, one of which would result in the statute bearing a constitutional meaning and the other of which would render the statute unconstitutional, the former must be adopted.[156]

---

[152] See Foley, 'Presuming the Legislature Acts Constitutionally: Legislative Process and Constitutional Decision-Making' (2007) 29 DULJ 141.

[153] *East Donegal Co-operative Livestock Mart Ltd v Attorney General* [1970] IR 317.

[154] [1970] IR 317 at 341.

[155] Hogan and Whyte, *JM Kelly: The Irish Constitution* (4th edn, 2003), pp 853–856. See also *Shirley v A O'Gorman & Co Ltd* [2012] 2 IR 170; *Damache v DPP* [2012] 2 IR 266.

[156] See, eg, *Croke v Smith (No 2)* [1998] 1 IR 101; *Eastern Health Board v McDonnell* [1999] 1 IR 174.

[14.80] Moreover, it has been suggested that a court should reject an interpretation that carries the 'risk' that it would render the provision unconstitutional.[157]

[14.81] A third consequence associated with the presumption is that it is also presumed that all powers and procedures created by the statute will be exercised in a manner which accords with the dictates of the Constitution. It follows that where a statute confers a power in open-ended terms it will be construed as authorising only those exercises of the power which are compatible with the Constitution.[158]

[14.82] On the other hand there are limits to the presumption. It is accepted that the presumption should not be invoked to save the validity of a statute where the effect would be to amend or substitute the provision in question.[159] It has also been suggested that the presumption does not require a court to interpret a statute in a manner that is least restrictive of a constitutional right, provided of course that the alternative interpretation does not involve an unlawful infringement of the right in question.

[14.83] O'Sullivan J considered the last point in *Colgan v Independent Radio and Television Commission*,[160] where he observed:

> "In my view it is only in cases of doubt that an interpretation favouring the validity of an Act must be given … a court is compelled to adopt the interpretation which most favours the validity of a statute only if there is a doubt about the constitutional validity of another meaning … I do not think that I am compelled to reject the otherwise correct meaning simply because it is more invasive of the applicant's guaranteed right of free speech and because a less intrusive meaning is available. I am compelled to do this, as I understand it, only if there is a doubt about the otherwise correct meaning."[161]

[14.84] The decision in *Colgan* concerned the limitation of the right of free speech that resulted from the prohibition on political and religious advertising contained in s 10(3) of the Radio and Television Act 1988 but the general tenor of the judgment points to a broader issue that is rooted in the separation of powers. An element of judicial restraint is necessary and the courts must be cautious to ensure that they do not invade the legislative domain under the guise of exercising their duty to protect constitutional rights. There is a constitutionally vital difference between interpreting legislation in such a way as to ensure that it does not improperly invade a citizen's rights and adopting a restrictive construction of a valid measure that curtails rights in a lawful manner. The

---

[157] *Madden v Minister for the Marine* [1997] 1 ILRM 136 at 146, *per* Blayney J (Hamilton CJ and Barrington J concurring): 'It seems to me that a court should be reluctant to give the section such a construction, as there would clearly be the risk that it is unconstitutional, and accordingly it should be rejected unless the wording of the section is incapable of any other meaning.'

[158] See discussion of the constitutionality of exercise of powers of delegated legislation, paras **13.121–13.138**.

[159] *Dowling v Ireland* [1991] 2 IR 379.

[160] *Colgan v Independent Radio and Television Commission* [1999] 1 ILRM 22.

[161] [1999] 1 ILRM 22 at 39.

former is a necessary consequence of the duty to protect rights but the latter is improper usurpation of the legislative function.

[14.85] The presumption has determined the interpretation of a number of provisions. In *Quinn v Wren*[162] the Supreme Court interpreted 'political offence' and 'offence connected with a political offence' in s 50 of the Extradition Act 1965 to exclude offences which were committed on behalf of the Irish National Liberation Army (INLA). In his judgment Finlay CJ invoked the presumption:

> "The Act ... having been passed since the coming into force of the Constitution, the first and fundamental rule which governs that interpretation is that it must be presumed that the Oireachtas intended an interpretation which will not offend any express or implied provision of the Constitution ...

> The plaintiff states that he committed the offence charged for the purposes of the INLA, the aims and objectives of which are the establishment of a 32 county workers' republic by force of arms. The achievement of that objective necessarily and inevitably involves the destruction and setting aside of the Constitution by means expressly or impliedly prohibited by it: see Articles 15.6 and 39. To interpret the words 'political offence' contained in s 50 of the Act of 1965 so as to grant immunity or protection to a person charged with an offence directly intended to further that objective would be to give the section a patently unconstitutional construction. The Court cannot, it seems to me, interpret an Act of the Oireachtas as having an intention to grant immunity from extradition to a person charged with an offence, the admitted purpose of which is to further or facilitate the overthrow, by violence, of the Constitution and of the organs of State established thereby."[163]

[14.86] The decision in that case is not beyond dispute[164] but, for present purposes, its interest lies in the fact that the presumption determined the interpretation which was adopted. Similarly, in *Re JH*[165] the Supreme Court construed s 3 of the Guardianship of Infants Act 1964 as involving a constitutional presumption, based on Article 42.1, that the best interests of a child are protected within the family unit unless there is compelling evidence to the contrary. Concerns of constitutionality arose in somewhat different circumstances in *National Union of Journalists v Sisk*.[166] There, ss 2, 3 and 4 of the Trade Union Act 1975, which governed the transfer of engagements, were interpreted in a fashion which facilitated the enjoyment of the freedom of association guaranteed by Article 40.6.1°(iii). In the absence of an express statutory limitation of the enjoyment of that right the court refused to interpret it as containing an implied restriction.

---

[162] *Quinn v Wren* [1985] IR 322.

[163] *Quinn v Wren* [1985] IR 322 at 337.

[164] Its 'rather artificial reasoning' (Hogan and Whyte, *JM Kelly: The Irish Constitution* (4th edn, 2003), p 1242) was endorsed in *Russell v Fanning* [1988] IR 505 but was subsequently departed from in *Finucane v McMahon* [1990] 1 IR 165.

[165] *Re JH* [1985] IR 375.

[166] *National Union of Journalists v Sisk* [1992] 2 IR 171.

[14.87] It should, however, be realised that the interpretation of a word need not necessarily be confined to the meaning which it bears in the Constitution, provided that a different meaning does not lead to the statute's being unconstitutional. Thus, in *Jordan v O'Brien*[167] the word 'family' in the Rent Restrictions Act 1946 was given a wider interpretation than that which it bears in Article 41 of the Constitution – the point is that the narrower meaning which the word bears in the Constitution was not necessary to ensure the validity of the Act.

Presumption of compatibility with EU law

[14.88] It is an accepted principle that EU secondary legislation, such as Regulations and Directives, should be interpreted in a manner which preserves its compatibility with the provisions of the Treaties.[168] In *Dowling v Ireland*[169] Murphy J recognised the similarity between that proposition and the presumption of constitutionality. In principle, it should follow from the applicability of EU law in national legal systems and its precedence over domestic law that as a matter of domestic law a court should interpret legislation, be it EU or national, in a manner which is consistent with the Treaties. This is evident in *Murphy v Minister for the Marine*[170] where Shanley J observed that:

> "the court is obliged to refrain from interpreting ... legislation in a manner inconsistent with the provisions of community law. The principle of the supremacy of community law also involves member states being obliged not to do any act which offends that state's general treaty obligations and that national courts, in construing national legislation, must do so having regard to those same general obligations ..."[171]

Moreover, Shanley J expressed the view that this obligation applied irrespective of whether the EU obligation pre-dated or post-dated the national legislation.

[14.89] The so-called doctrine of 'indirect effect' requires a court to interpret its domestic legislation in conformity with EU law, in so far as it enjoys the discretion so to do.[172] Thus, cognisance should be taken of EU measures which are not directly effective when interpreting the national implementing legislation. In *Navan Tanker Services Ltd v Meath County Council*[173] the extent of the discretion allowed under the national regulations was determined by reference to the purpose of the Directive on which they were based. And although the matter was not expressed in those terms, *Murphy v Bord*

---

167 *Jordan v O'Brien* [1960] IR 363.
168 *Blottner v Bestuur van de Niewe Algemene Bedrijfsvereniging* [1977] ECR 1141; *Statens Control v Larsen* [1978] ECR 1543; *Klench v Secretaire d'état à l'Agriculture et à la Viticulture* [1986] ECR 3477.
169 *Dowling v Ireland* [1991] 2 IR 379.
170 *Murphy v Minister for the Marine* [1997] 2 ILRM 523.
171 [1997] 2 ILRM 523 at 536.
172 *Von Colson and Kamann v Land Nordrhein-Westfalen* [1984] ECR 1891; see Hartley, *Foundations of European Community Law* (4th edn, 1998), pp 211–215.
173 *Navan Tanker Services Ltd v Meath County Council* [1998] 1 IR 166.

Telecom Éireann[174] illustrates the point where the demands of European law overrode a literal reading of a domestic measure. The Anti-Discrimination (Pay) Act 1974 was interpreted in such a way as to preserve its validity under the Treaty of Rome.

[14.90] The expectation that national measures are interpreted in a manner that takes account of the state's EC obligations will probably override more traditional principles such as the strict construction of penal statutes. This was suggested by Kelly J in *Byrne v Conroy*,[175] a case in which the extradition of the appellant to the United Kingdom was sought on charges of conspiracy to defraud the British Intervention Board of monetary compensatory amounts payable under the Common Agricultural Policy. It was argued that the offences in question were revenue offences which were excluded by s 50 of the Extradition Act 1965.

[14.91] In the event Kelly J held that, as a matter of Irish law, the offences were not revenue offences. However, he observed that even if they were to be considered revenue offences under national law the exclusion under the 1965 Act might not apply:

"[G]iven the European dimension to the instant case, the appropriate way to construe the relevant provisions of the Extradition Act is to do so in a manner which is consistent with the obligations of the State to the European Union. The obligation of this country as a Member State of the European Union is, *inter alia*, to protect the financial interests of that Union and this obligation would be impeded, in the case of ambiguity, by construing the relevant provisions of the Extradition Act in a manner which would conclude that the offence charged against the applicant here is a revenue one and thereby prevent his extradition.

It would follow from this approach that, in the case of ambiguity in the legislation, the strict constructionist approach would have to give way to an interpretation which would comply with the State's obligations in European Law."[176]

Presumption of compatibility with international law

[14.92] The nature of international law and its status is considered elsewhere.[177] While international law does not apply within the domestic legal system (unless it is specifically incorporated by a domestic legal measure) it can prove to be of assistance in statutory interpretation.[178] In addition to having recourse to international legal

---

174 *Murphy v Bord Telecom Éireann* [1989] ILRM 53; see para **14.61**.

175 *Byrne v Conroy* [1998] 3 IR 1.

176 *Byrne v Conroy* [1998] 3 IR 1 at 23.

177 See generally Ch 17.

178 For instance, the European Convention on Human Rights Act 2003 incorporated he European Convention on Human Rights and Fundamental Freedoms into Irish domestic law. Section 2 of the 2003 Act requires that Courts when 'interpreting and applying' law must, as far as is possible, do so in a manner compatible with the state's obligations under the Convention provisions; see eg *O'Donnell v South Dublin County Council* [2011] 3 IR 417.

instruments[179] there is a general presumption that the Oireachtas intended to abide by its international legal obligations when it enacted domestic legislation.[180]

[14.93] The latter presumption was considered in *Ó Domhnaill v Merrick* where the extent of its operation was subject to different interpretations. In his majority judgment Henchy J stated:

"[O]ne must assume that the statute was enacted (there being no indication in it of a contrary intention) subject to the postulate that it would be construed and applied in consonance with the State's obligations under international law, including any relevant treaty obligations. The relevance of that rule of statutory interpretation in this case lies in the fact that Article 6(1) of the Convention for the Protection of Human Rights and Fundamental Freedoms (1950), provides – 'In the determination of his civil rights and obligations or of any criminal charge against him, everyone is entitled to a fair hearing *within a reasonable time* by an independent and impartial tribunal established by law.' I have supplied the emphasis.

While the Convention is not part of the domestic law of the State, still, because the Statute of Limitations 1957, was passed after this State ratified the Convention in 1953, it is to be argued that the Statute, since it does not show any contrary intention, should be deemed to be in conformity with the convention and should be construed and applied accordingly."[181]

[14.94] However, in his dissenting judgment McCarthy J took a different approach. He agreed with the principle of interpretation in accordance with international law but was reluctant to invoke the Convention on the ground that it had not been enacted into domestic law:

"I accept, as a general principle, that a statute must be construed, so far as possible, so as not to be inconsistent with the established rules of international law and that one should avoid a construction which will lead to a conflict between domestic and international law ... but since the Convention is not part of the domestic law of the State (*Re Ó Laighléis*),[182] I cannot subscribe to the view that the Statute of Limitations ... is to be limited by Article 6(1) of the Convention."[183]

---

179 See further para **14.162**.

180 The courts have also been prepared to construe common law rules in the light of international obligations; see *The State (DPP) v Walsh* [1981] IR 412; *Desmond v Glackin (No 2)* [1993] 3 IR 67.

181 *Ó Domhnaill v Merrick* [1984] IR 151 at 159.

182 *Re Ó Laighléis* [1960] IR 93. See further para **17.64**.

183 *Ó Domhnaill v Merrick* [1984] IR 151 at 166. This argument is based in part on Article 29.6 of the Constitution which provides that '[n]o international agreement shall be part of the domestic law of the State save as may be determined by the Oireachtas'; see also *Croke v Smith and ors* (31 July 1995, unreported), HC, *per* Budd J at pp 34–35: '... while this Court can look to the European Convention and the United Nations principles as being influential guidelines with regard to matters of public policy ... [where] there is a challenge to the constitutionality of [legislation] such Conventions may not be used as a touchstone with regard to constitutionality.'

Presumption that all words bear a meaning

[14.95] It is assumed that the legislature intended that each word in a provision should contribute to its meaning. It is taken that the legislature did not intend words to be redundant and provisions are to be construed accordingly. The matter was alluded to by the Supreme Court in *Cork County Council v Whillock* where O'Flaherty J stated that 'a construction which would leave without effect any part of the language of a statute will normally be rejected'.[184]

Egan J explained the matter thus:

"There is abundant authority for the presumption that words are not used in a statute without a meaning and are not tautologous or superfluous, and so effect must be given, if possible, to all the words used, for the legislature must be deemed not to waste its words or say anything in vain."[185]

The reluctance to avoid rendering a provision redundant is also evident in *Greene v Minister for Defence*[186] where Lavan J construed the Civil Liability (Assessment of Hearing Loss) Act 1998 in a manner that 'distinguishes the legislative intent in enacting s 4 from that of s 3 sufficiently to overcome the concerns ... that s 4 could be rendered nugatory'.[187]

Presumption that a statute should be given an 'updated' meaning

[14.96] A large amount of the statute law which currently applies have been inherited from previous generations.[188] Frequent updating is not practicable with the result that legislation which was drafted in the language of earlier generations is to be applied to changed times. If the interpretation of such legislation were to be governed by the historical context in which it was enacted, its adaptability to new circumstances would be appreciably retarded. The words of Lavery J in *The State (O'Connor) v Ó Caomhanaigh*[189] are pertinent:

"Many statutes ... were conditioned by the political, economic, religious and social sentiments of the time of their enactment or establishment but it is the provisions themselves which are to be looked at and examined—not the motives of those who enacted them."[190]

[14.97] Bennion has suggested that statutes should be given an 'updated' meaning, that is one that facilitates their being applied to new conditions.[191] This is based on the notion that an Act is 'always speaking' and that the legislature intended that the law should

---

184 *Cork County Council v Whillock* [1993] 1 IR 231 at 237.
185 [1993] 1 IR 231 at 239.
186 *Greene v Minister for Defence* [1998] 4 IR 464.
187 [1998] 4 IR 464 at 492.
188 See Hurst, 'The Problem of the Elderly Statute' (1983) 3 LS 21.
189 *The State (O'Connor) v Ó Caomhanaigh* [1963] IR 112.
190 [1963] IR 112 at 118.
191 *Statute Law* (3rd edn, 1990), pp 181–186; see also Cross, *Statutory Interpretation* (3rd edn, 1995), p 51.

apply to future circumstances. An interpreter should, accordingly, make allowances for changes in the law and in social and technological conditions. Thus, in *Attorney General v Edison Telephone Co*[192] the word 'telegraph' in the Telegraph Act 1863 was interpreted to include a telephone, despite the fact that that instrument had not been invented, nor it would appear to have been contemplated, in 1863.

[14.98] Broad but qualified support for the principle of 'updated' interpretation was expressed by Murphy J in *Keane v An Bord Pleanála*:[193]

> "I have no difficulty in accepting the desirability and, in general, the necessity for giving to legislation an 'updating construction'. Where terminology used in legislation is wide enough to capture a subsequent invention, there is no reason to exclude it from the ambit of the legislation. But a distinction must be made between giving an updated construction to the general scheme of the legislation and altering the meaning of particular words used therein."[194]

[14.99] Murphy J appears to be less enthusiastic about updated construction than Bennion, and would adopt that construction only if it could be shown to be within the general intent of the statute, as might be the case if wide terminology is employed. His explanation of the decision in *Edison Telephone* was that the language in the Telegraph Act 1863 was sufficiently wide in that it 'anticipated every form of communication whether by signal or sound conveyed by means of electric currents of varying intensities along wires'.[195] In *Keane* the question was whether an electronic navigation aid, known as the Loran-C system, was a 'lighthouse, buoy or beacon' within the meaning of s 638 of the Merchant Shipping Act 1894.

[14.100] In answering in the negative, Murphy J took account both of the general scheme of the legislation and the terms in which it was drafted:

> "It is submitted on behalf of the respondents that the 'great object' of Part II of the 1894 Act was and remains to enable the Commissioners [of Irish Lights], in the interests of the safety of mariners, to provide all necessary aids for navigation.
>
> I do not accept that it is possible to interpret this legislation or ascertain the statutory powers of the [Commissioners of Irish Lights] by reference to such a wide general principle. The history of the [Commissioners] was based on legislation conferring jurisdiction on the different bodies within particular geographical areas of the then United Kingdom. The powers given to the different Commissioners [in Britain and Ireland] in relation to navigation were defined by reference to precise equipment, that is to say, lighthouses, buoys and beacons and not by reference to navigational aids in general terms. The area of operations would appear to have been local rather than international and the means of signalling was identified, and as a result limited, to procedures which were visual or aural. What the authorities establish is that if a suitable formula had been used by the draftsman

---

[192] *Attorney General v Edison Telephone Co* (1886) 6 QBD 244.
[193] *Keane v An Bord Pleanála* [1997] 1 IR 184.
[194] [1997] 1 IR 184 at 193.
[195] [1997] 1 IR 184 at 194.

foreseeing scientific development or speculating in science fiction, it might have been possible to define a 'lighthouse' in the 1894 Act so as to include any structure or device emitting or radiating any wave motion, particle or source of energy which could be utilised to make contact with or provide warnings to vessels, vehicles or craft of any description and in any part of the world for the purpose of alerting them to potential danger or enabling them to fix their position. That course was not adopted ... It does not seem to me that the general scheme of the Act or more particularly the range of the powers and duties expressly or implicitly conferred on the Commissioners or the particular words used in the 1894 Act would permit them to engage in the construction, maintenance or operation of a navigational aid system based on the transmission by and reception (on equipment which had not been invented) of a wave motion or impulse which had not then been identified."[196]

[14.101] This decision was upheld on appeal by the Supreme Court. Hamilton CJ endorsed Murphy J's observations on the principle of updated construction but concluded that at the time of the enactment 'buoys' and 'beacons' were regarded as visual aids to navigation and this precluded bringing the Loran-C system within the scope of the legislation. In a concurring judgment Barrington J observed that had the expression 'aids to navigation' been employed in the legislation he would have been 'happy to conclude that the Loran-C system of navigation was an "aid to navigation" ... even though it had not been invented when the Act was passed'.' The difficulty was that the provision used terms that 'tie[d] the Act to the technology of the times'.[197]

[14.102] In a strong dissenting judgment O'Flaherty J expressed concern that the legislature should be expected constantly to be prepared to update legislation in the light of new developments. He continued:

"When we deal with an old statute we do no injustice to anyone if we allow it to operate in the light of new discoveries in science or elsewhere which can be taken to be within the ambit of what that particular Act seeks to achieve ... I hold that it is asking too much of the legislature to be on the alert to amend old legislation to take account of every new development."[198]

[14.103] The caution expressed in *Keane*[199] does not inhibit the adoption of an updated construction where that is considered appropriate and more recent decisions have accommodated technological developments that were unknown at the time of the enactment in uestion.[200] Nevertheless, the approach which is evident in *Keane* is commendable. It is possible to foresee that social and technological change will occur

---

[196] [1997] 1 IR 184 at 197–198.

[197] [1997] 1 IR 184 at 234.

[198] [1997] 1 IR 184 at 219.

[199] [1997] 1 IR 184.

[200] *Universal City Studios Incorporated v Mulligan (No 1)* [1999] 3 IR 381: videotape held to be a 'cinematograph film' within the Copyright Act 1963; *Mandarim Records Ltd v Mechanical Copyright Protection Society (Ireland) Ltd* [1999] 1 ILRM 154: Power CD held to be a 'record' within Copyright Act 1963. In both cases the judgments in Keane were cited.

and legislation can be drafted in terms which embrace that possibility.[201] Where it is not drafted in that manner it is reasonable to conclude that such change was not intended to come within the scope of the legislation and that the legislature reserved the matter for further legislation. The application of the updated construction technique to unanticipated change is more difficult to justify, since in this case it is not possible to impute an intention in that regard to the legislature or the drafter. Moreover, it is very often change of that nature that raises the profound ethical, moral and social dilemmas which require express consideration by lawmakers.

Presumption against unclear changes in the law

[14.104] The effect of this presumption is that a change in the law must be achieved unambiguously, either by express terms or by a clear implication. In the event of an ambiguity a court should decline to interpret the provision as changing the law. The presumption dates from the time when the bulk of the law consisted of common law rules and statute law played a comparatively unimportant role, in the main curing its defects or mischief.[202] Given the current importance of legislation as a source of law, the presumption probably enjoys lesser significance than heretofore.

[14.105] Moreover, it overlaps with a number of other rules of interpretation (especially those urging strict construction) which insist that a desired statutory objective must be achieved clearly and unambiguously. Hence the presumption is unlikely to prove to be crucial in questions of interpretation. Nevertheless, a version of the presumption, that against implicit alteration of the law, was expressly endorsed by Henchy J in *Minister for Industry & Commerce v Hales*.[203] Applying the presumption he avoided an interpretation which would result in 'radical and far-reaching changes in the law of contract'.[204]

Presumption that penal statutes be construed strictly

[14.106] Based on a concern to protect individual liberty, it is presumed that if the Oireachtas wishes to impose penal liability it will do so expressly in clear and unambiguous terms.[205] The corollary is that penal statutes should be construed strictly,

---

201 Interpretation Act 2005, s 6 now provides a statutory basis for this principle: 'In construing a provision of any Act or statutory instrument, a court may make allowances for any changes in the law, social conditions, technology, the meaning of words used in that Act or statutory instrument and other relevant matters, which have occurred since the date of the passing of that Act or the making of that statutory instrument, but only in so far as its text, purpose and context permit.'

202 See Cross, *Statutory Interpretation* (3rd edn, 1995), pp 167–168.

203 *Minister for Industry & Commerce v Hales* [1967] IR 50 at 76.

204 *Minister for Industry and Commerce v Hales* [1967] IR 50 at 77; see also *DPP v McCreesh* [1992] 2 IR 239.

205 See *DPP v Tivoli Cinema Ltd* [1999] 2 IR 260 at 268, *per* Barron J: 'The sections are penal in that they provide a criminal sanction. Accordingly, before a criminal sanction can be applied the defendant is entitled to know by clear and unambiguous language that such sanction will be applied in specified circumstances.'

in a manner which leans against the creation or extension of penal liability by implication. One of the reasons advanced in *Frescati Estates Ltd v Walker*[206] for the schematic interpretation which was adopted was that a literal reading of the provision would have led to the imposition of penal duties and liabilities on landowners. In *CW Shipping Co Ltd v Limerick Harbour Commissioners*[207] a tug was held not to come within the licensing requirements of s 53(1) of the Harbours Act 1946 on the basis, *inter alia*, that:

> "... a penal provision in a statute must be construed strictly, and this rule is a further constraint on giving to the terminology of [the section] the wide interpretation necessary if the use of tugs are to be brought within its ambit."[208]

The same view was expressed by Kearns P in *Health Service Executive v Carroll*:[209]

> "The creation of criminal offences must be by language which is clear and certain. Where a statutory provision gives rise to a plausible range of constructions, one wide and one narrow, the narrow construction must always be preferred where a penal statute is involved."[210]

[14.107] Given its concern with individual liberty it is hardly surprising that the principle of strict construction is applicable in relation to statutes which confer police powers. In *The People (DPP) v Farrell*[211] it was stated that s 30 of the Offences Against the State Act 1939 must be strictly construed; the Court of Criminal Appeal refused to assume in the absence of evidence to that effect that the procedural requirements of that section had been complied with by the gardaí. The same approach is taken in relation to the admissibility of evidence in criminal proceedings. Clear and unambiguous language is required to render admissible evidence that would otherwise be excluded.[212] Likewise, road traffic legislation is to be construed strictly.[213] Extradition provisions are also to be construed strictly on the same basis that they constitute a 'penal statutory code involving penal sanctions on an individual'.[214]

[14.108] In some instances, however, legislation which imposes criminal sanctions, especially in the regulatory sphere, is subject to an 'intermediate' approach. Industrial legislation, such as the Factories Act 1955 and its successor the Safety, Health and

---

[206] *Frescati Estates Ltd v Walker* [1975] IR 177.

[207] *CW Shipping Co Ltd v Limerick Harbour Commissioners* [1989] ILRM 416.

[208] [1989] ILRM 416 at 424.

[209] *Health Service Executive v Carroll* [2012] 3 IR 1.

[210] [2012] 3 IR 1 at 17.

[211] *The People (DPP) v Farrell* [1978] IR 13; see *Re Emergency Powers Bill 1976* [1977] IR 159 at 173: 'A statutory provision of this nature which makes such inroads upon the liberty of the person must be strictly construed.'

[212] *DPP v Keogh* [1998] 1 ILRM 72.

[213] *DPP v Corcoran* [1996] 1 ILRM 182.

[214] *Aamand v Smithwick* [1995] 1 ILRM 61 at 67. But see *Byrne v Conroy* [1998] 3 IR 1 at 23 suggesting that a less strict approach might be necessary where the offence alleged involved an infringement of EC law; para **14.89**.

Welfare at Work Act 1989 attracts an expansive interpretation in respect of some of its provisions while a stricter approach is taken in the interpretation of others.[215]

Presumption that revenue statutes be construed strictly

[14.109] This presumption, which is analogous to that requiring strict construction of penal provisions, is stated as the second proposition in Henchy J's judgment in *Inspector of Taxes v Kiernan*[216] and has received frequent judicial endorsement.[217] In his authoritative pronouncement on the matter in *Revenue Commissioners v Doorley*, Kennedy CJ equated the question of the imposition of tax with that of its exemption:

"The duty of the Court, as it appears to me, is to reject an *a priori* line of reasoning and to examine the text of the taxing Act in question and determine whether the tax in question is thereby imposed expressly and in clear and unambiguous terms, on the alleged subject of taxation, for no person or property is to be subjected to taxation unless brought within the letter of the taxing statute, ie within the letter of the statute as interpreted with the assistance of the ordinary canons of interpretation applicable to Acts of Parliament so far as they can be applied without violating the proper character of taxing Acts to which I have referred.

I have been discussing taxing legislation from the point of view of the imposition of tax. Now the exemption from tax, with which we are immediately concerned, is governed by the same considerations. If it is clear that a tax is imposed by the Act under consideration, then exemption from that tax must be given expressly and in clear and unambiguous terms, within the letter of the statute as interpreted with the assistance of the ordinary canons for the interpretation of statutes … [t]he Court is not, by greater indulgence in delimiting the area of exemptions, to enlarge their operation beyond what the statute, clearly and without doubt and in express terms, except for some good reason from the burden of a tax thereby imposed generally on that description of subject-matter. As the imposition of, so the exemption from, the tax must be brought within the letter of the taxing Act as interpreted by the established canons of construction so far as applicable."[218]

While the presumption is more often invoked to prevent the imposition of a tax, it is clear from this passage that it works both ways and it can provide the basis on which a court will refuse to extend an exemption. The latter point is illustrated by the decision in

---

[215] Compare *Franklin v Gramaphone Ltd* [1948] 1 KB 542 at 557 with *Harrison v National Coal Board* [1951] 1 All ER 1102 at 1107.

[216] *Inspector of Taxes v Kiernan* [1981] IR 117; see para **14.34**.

[217] See, eg, *Kellystown Co v Hogan* [1985] ILRM 200; *Charles McCann Ltd v Ó Culacháin* [1986] IR 196; *Texaco (Ireland) Ltd v Murphy* [1991] 2 IR 449; *Trustees of Kinsale Yacht Club v Commissioner of Valuation* [1994] 1 ILRM 457. Of course, in many cases the literal approach will coincide with this presumption as *Inspector of Taxes v Kiernan* [1981] IR 117 demonstrates. The relationship between the presumption and the literal approach was considered in *Kearns v Dilleen* [1997] 3 IR 286 at 297, *per* Barron J: 'Undoubtedly taxation statutes are construed strictly. I regard this as meaning that when the literal construction is being sought, the courts will be stricter in their endeavours to find a literal interpretation than they might be in other forms of legislation.'

[218] [1933] IR 750 at 765–766.

Saatchi & Saatchi Advertising Ltd v McGarry.[219] The appellants, an advertising agency that *inter alia* produced advertising films for television, sought to avail of a statutory exemption that had been enacted, in effect, to reverse the decision in *Ó Culacháin v Hunter Advertising Ltd.*[220] However, s 41(8) of the Finance Act 1980 provided that a company is not entitled to tax relief unless a claim is made before the date on which its tax assessment for a particular accounting period becomes final. In this case the appellants had not made the claim within that period but argued that the intention of the Oireachtas was to allow companies in its line of business the relief in question and they contended that their claim should not be defeated by a procedural provision. The Supreme Court rejected that argument and, adopting the reasoning in *Revenue Commissioners v Doorley,* concluded that the literal wording of s 41(8) of the 1980 Act barred the claim.

Presumption against retrospective effect

[14.110] Article 15.5 of the Constitution provides that '[t]he Oireachtas shall not declare acts to be infringements of the law which were not so at the date of their commission'. This clearly prohibits the enactment of retrospective penal legislation and, probably, legislation which imposes a civil or revenue liability.[221] The philosophy underlying that provision is that it is inherently unjust to declare acts to be unlawful which were lawful at the time of their commission. Similar sentiments infuse the common law presumption that legislation does not operate retrospectively.[222]

[14.111] The presumption was considered by the Supreme Court in *Hamilton v Hamilton*[223] where O'Higgins CJ examined its history and underlying concern:

"This brings me to the subject of retrospectivity; it is necessary to state with some precision what I regard as such in a statute. Many statutes are passed to deal with events which are over and which necessarily have a retrospective effect. Examples of such statutes, often described as *ex post facto* statutes, are to be found in Acts of immunity or pardon. Other statutes having a retroactive effect are statutes dealing with the practice and procedure of the Courts and applying to causes of action arising before the operation of the statute. Such statutes do not and are not intended to impair or affect vested rights and are not within the type of statute with which, it seems to me, this case is concerned. For the purpose of stating what I mean by retrospectivity in a statute, I adopt a definition taken from *Craies on Statute*

---

[219] *Saatchi & Saatchi Advertising Ltd v McGarry* [1998] 2 IR 562.

[220] *Ó Culacháin v Hunter Advertising Ltd* [1990] 2 IR 431; see para **14.70**. The provision in question is Finance Act 1990, s 41(1)(b).

[221] See *Doyle v An Taoiseach* [1986] ILRM 693; *Magee v Culligan* [1992] 1 IR 223; *Re Hefferon Kearns Ltd (No 1)* [1993] 3 IR 177; see also Hogan and Whyte, *JM Kelly: The Irish Constitution* (4th edn, 2003), pp 274–284.

[222] See eg *The People (DPP) v Cawley* [2003] 4 IR 321; *Enright v Ireland* [2003] 2 IR 321; *Minister for Social, Community and Family Affairs v Scanlon* [2001] 1 IR 64; *Kelly v Scales* [1994] 1 IR 42; *Caulfield v Bourke* [1980] ILRM 223.

[223] *Hamilton v Hamilton* [1982] IR 466.

Law[224] which is, I am satisfied, based on sound authority. It is to the effect that a statute is to be deemed to be retrospective in effect when it 'takes away or impairs any vested right acquired under existing laws, or creates a new obligation, or imposes a new duty, or attaches a new disability in respect to transactions or considerations already past' …

Retrospective legislation, since it necessarily affects vested rights, has always been regarded as being *prima facie* unjust. In the early 17th century Coke sought to establish the principle that the common law could control such Acts and adjudge them void as being contrary to 'the natural law' or 'common right and reason' – see *Dr Bonham's Case*.[225] In this view he was supported by Lord Hobart in *Day v Savadge*[226] and by Lord Holt in *City of London v Wood*.[227] However, with the recognition by the English courts of the sovereignty of Parliament in the eighteenth century, this view was no longer maintained and Blackstone[228] was able to declare in his commentaries: 'If Parliament would positively enact a thing to be done which is unreasonable, there is no power in the ordinary forms of the Constitution that is vested with the authority to control it.' And further, that an Act of Parliament is 'the exercise of the highest authority that the Kingdom acknowledges on earth.'

It is, therefore, in the light of the existence of a sovereign parliament, entitled to legislate both retrospectively and prospectively, that the English courts have laid down the principles on which a statute should be examined for retrospectivity. The result is a rule of construction which leans against such retrospectivity and which, according to Maxwell, is based upon the presumption 'that the legislature does not intend what is unjust'[229] …

Having referred, perhaps unnecessarily, to the past and to the manner in which the courts (both in England and in Ireland) considered the question of retrospectivity in relation to the Acts of a sovereign parliament, I must now come to the present and to the examination of an Act of the Oireachtas for the same purpose. Our Oireachtas, or legislature, is subject to the Constitution – like all other organs of the State. Its powers are circumscribed by constitutional limitations. In considering and interpreting Acts of the Oireachtas we must assume, in the first instance, that what the legislature has done was not intended to contravene the Constitution … [O'Higgins CJ noted the effect of the presumption of constitutionality on interpretation and continued] … This approach to the interpretation and construction of Acts of the Oireachtas is required by the Constitution. While it may not replace the common-law rule, it certainly supersedes it once a question of the possible infringement of the Constitution arises."[230]

[14.112] In the same case Henchy J put the issue thus:

"From a wide range of judicial decisions I find the relevant canon of interpretation at common law to be this. When an Act changes the substantive, as distinct from procedural, law then, regardless of whether the Act is otherwise prospective or retrospective in its operation, it is not to be deemed to affect proceedings brought under the pre-Act law and

---

[224] *Craies on Statute Law* (7th edn, 1971), p 387.
[225] *Dr Bonham's Case* (1610) 8 Co Rep 114(a).
[226] *Day v Savadge* (1614) Hob 85.
[227] *City of London v Wood* (1701) 12 Mod Rep 669.
[228] 1 Comm 91.
[229] See *Maxwell on the Interpretation of Statutes* (12th edn, 1969), p 215.
[230] [1982] IR 466 at 473–475.

pending at the date of the coming into operation of the Act, unless the Act expressly or by necessary intendment provides to the contrary."[231]

[14.113] It is clear from *Hamilton v Hamilton* that the presumption does not apply to every provision which operates retrospectively; its principal concern is with statutes which alter substantive law or which affect vested rights.[232] A difference in emphasis is evident in *Dublin County Council v Grealy*[233] where Blayney J spoke of a presumption that a statute should apply prospectively and continued:

"[T]he Act must express a clear and unambiguous intention to [operate retrospectively], or there must be some circumstances rendering it inevitable that the court should conclude that the Act is retrospective, or the change effected by the statute must be purely procedural."[234]

[14.114] The constitutional dimension to the presumption was noted in *Re Hefferon Kearns Ltd (No 1)*[235] where Murphy J observed that an intention not to legislate retrospectively can be imputed to the Oireachtas given the 'particular obligations imposed upon it by the Constitution'.[236] In this manner he saw a harmony between the presumption and the relevant constitutional provisions. In that case the question was whether s 33 of the Companies (Amendment) Act 1990, which imposes civil liability for reckless trading, applied to transactions which occurred prior to its enactment. Murphy J was satisfied that there was nothing in the Act to indicate an intention that it should apply retrospectively and concluded that, "… having regard to the common law principles and constitutional requirements … it is the absence of an intention indicated expressly or at any rate unambiguously implied that is decisive …'.[237] Moreover, he also concluded that retrospective application of the reckless trading provisions would violate Article 15.5. They made such conduct 'an infringement of the law' which was not necessarily the case at the time the acts were committed.[238]

[14.115] The presumption was rebutted in *Chestvale Properties Ltd v Glackin*[239] where Murphy J concluded that the provisions governing the appointment and functioning of inspectors under the Companies Act 1990 were intended to operate retrospectively. In particular, he held that an inspector was authorised to demand the production of

---

231 *Hamilton v Hamilton* [1982] IR 466 at 480–481.
232 See also *O'H v O'H* [1990] 2 IR 558, holding the Judicial Separation and Family Law Reform Act 1989, s 29 not to apply to transactions completed prior to its enactment.
233 *Dublin County Council v Grealy* [1990] 1 IR 77.
234 [1990] 1 IR 77 at 82.
235 *Re Hefferon Kearns Ltd (No 1)* [1993] 3 IR 177.
236 [1993] 3 IR 177 at 184.
237 [1993] 3 IR 177 at 186.
238 See also *Jones v Gunn* [1997] 3 IR 1 where McGuinness J refused to apply s 297A of the Companies Act 1963 retrospectively despite her view (at 17) that it was not 'a particularly attractive proposition that a director of a company, who may have treated his creditors in a fraudulent manner, should be able to avoid personal liability simply by ceasing to trade and by not winding up the company.'
239 *Chestvale Properties Ltd v Glackin* [1993] 3 IR 35.

documents which came into existence before the enactment of the Act despite the absence of an express provision to that effect. The 1990 Act repealed the inspection provisions of earlier legislation and in their absence the only way an inspector could carry out his duties was if the 1990 powers were to operate retrospectively.

Presumption against extra-territorial effect

[14.116] It is accepted both in national[240] and international[241] law that the state may legislate with extraterritorial effect, that is, with effect beyond its geographical boundaries. At the same time it is presumed that the operation of an Act is intended to be confined to the territory of the state unless a contrary intention is evident. This presumption was applied in *Chemical Bank v McCormack*[242] where the Bankers' Books Evidence Acts 1879 and 1959 were held not to apply to documents held by an Irish bank in its New York branch – the Acts lacked clear words indicating an intention to legislate extraterritorially.

Expressio unius est exclusio alterius

[14.117] This maxim, which can be broadly translated as meaning 'to express one thing is to exclude another', has been alluded to in several Irish cases. It was invoked by Henchy J in construing the Social Welfare (Insurance Appeals) Regulations 1952[243] in *Kiely v Minister for Social Welfare*:

> "The fact that Article 11(5) [of the Regulations] allows a written statement to be received in evidence in specified limited circumstances means that it cannot be received in other circumstances; *expressio unius est exclusio alterius*."[244]

The maxim was also invoked in *Fanning v University College Cork*,[245] a decision in which Gilligan J noted the similarity between a university statute and primary legislation:

> "[A]lthough not actually enacted by the Oireachtas, NUI Statute 86 (1951) has much in common with a piece of legislation. Much of the language used in the statute is of a legal nature and many of the procedures set out therein are so precise and technical that it appears probable that its drafters had a legal background. It is to be noted that although NUI Statute 86 (1951) was not enacted by the Oireachtas itself, the Universities Act 1908 expressly vested power in the Dublin Commissioners, and subsequently the Senate, to create it. As a result, I am satisfied that it is correct for this court to apply the maxim *expressio unius est exclusio alterius* when interpreting the statute."

---

240 *Re Criminal Law (Jurisdiction) Bill 1975* [1977] IR 129; *McGimpsey v Ireland* [1990] 1 IR 110: see also para **15.07**.
241 *Lotus case* (1927), PCIJ Ser A No 10.
242 *Chemical Bank v McCormack* [1983] ILRM 350.
243 SI 376/1952.
244 *Kiely v Minister for Social Welfare* [1977] IR 267, 279.
245 *Fanning v University College Cork* [2007] 18 ELR 301.

[14.118] The limits of the maxim are evident in *Inspector of Taxes v Arida Ltd*[246] which concerned the question whether the Circuit Court has jurisdiction to award costs in the event of a successful appeal from the Appeal Commissioners on an assessment of tax. Order 58, r 1 of the Rules of the Circuit Court 1950[247] states that the question of costs lies within the discretion of the judge 'save as otherwise provided by statute'. Section 428(6) of the Income Tax Act 1967 allows the High Court to award costs on a case stated to it by the Appeal Commissioners. It was argued that that provision limited the general power to award costs – that on the basis of *expressio unius*, it should be inferred from the conferring of power on the High Court that a Circuit Court judge has no such power.

[14.119] In rejecting that contention Murphy J expressed the view that an exception from the general law (in this case the power to award costs) should, if not expressly stated, be implied with clarity and he believed that this was not so in this case. He referred to an earlier decision, *The State (Minister for Lands and Fisheries) v Judge Sealy*,[248] which throws some light on the matter. In some circumstances a statutory reference might amount to no more than a particular statement of a more general and widely accepted principle, in which case the particular statutory reference is superfluous and cannot be considered to be an expression of one thing to the exclusion of all others.

Ejusdem generis rule

[14.120] This rule is conveniently summarised by Carroll J in *Cronin v Lunham Brothers Ltd*:[249]

> "The *ejusdem generis* rule as applied to the interpretation of statutes means that where a general word follows particular and specific words of the same nature as itself, it takes its meaning from them and is presumed to be restricted to the same genus as those words. The rule applies to general words following words which are less general."

[14.121] Most commonly, the preceding limited words consist of a list of individual items establishing a particular genus followed by a general residual clause. That clause is typically inserted by the drafter to ensure that items which might be inadvertently omitted from the preceding list are nonetheless included in the category. The effect of the rule is to apply a restricted meaning derived from the statutory context to words which would otherwise be unrestricted. For example, in the expression 'dogs, cats and other animals' the general words are to be interpreted in the light of the preceding specific items and thus an 'other animal' will be interpreted as falling into the same genus as, and to share the characteristics of, dogs and cats – it would be construed to mean domestic animals of some type.

---

[246] *Inspector of Taxes v Arida Ltd* [1992] 2 IR 155.
[247] SI 179/1950.
[248] *The State (Minister for Lands and Fisheries) v Judge Sealy* [1939] IR 21.
[249] [1986] ILRM 415 at 417 (reference omitted).

[14.122] The *ejusdem generis* rule has been invoked in a number of cases. In *The People (DPP) v Farrell*[250] it was applied to the interpretation of 'a Garda Síochána station, a prison or other convenient place' in s 30 of the Offences Against the State Act 1939 where a police car was held not to be a 'convenient place'. Applying the rule the Court of Criminal Appeal held that those general words must at least mean a convenient building of some type. In *Irish Commercial Society Ltd v Plunkett*[251] the expression 'other misconduct' in s 14(8) of the Industrial and Provident Societies (Amendment) Act 1978 was interpreted in the light of the immediately preceding words 'fraud' and 'misfeasance', thus limiting its meaning to misconduct which was of the same type as fraud and misfeasance.

[14.123] In *CW Shipping Co Ltd v Limerick Harbour Commissioners*[252] O'Hanlon J applied the rule in considering whether a tug is a 'lighter, ferry-boat or other small boat' in s 53(1) of the Harbours Act 1953:

> "I consider that the words 'or other small boat' should be construed as being *ejusdem generis* with the specific descriptive words which immediately precede them, and I do not regard a tug as being of the same genus as a lighter or a ferry-boat. It is a very specialised type of craft designed for carrying out towing (or occasionally pushing) of much larger vessels, and not for the carriage for hire of persons or goods."[253]

[14.124] There are cases where the *ejusdem generis* rule will not apply. One is where only one specific item is mentioned before the general words[254] – the enumeration of a single item does not establish a discernible class that would facilitate the application of the rule. Another arises where the specific words do not create a genus to which the general words might be limited. In *Kielthy v Ascon Ltd*[255] it was held that the genus must be established by a number of specific categories and thus the enumeration of one specific category is insufficient to bring the rule into operation. Moreover, a listing of a number of specific items might be incapable of establishing a single genus as is evident in *Dublin Corporation v Dublin Cinemas Ltd* where the words in question were held to be 'too incongruous to constitute a genus'.[256]

[14.125] It is also established that the general words must succeed the specific words and thus the rule will not apply where the general term precedes the enumeration of specifics. This point was noted by Griffin J in *Application of Quinn*:

> "Where in a statute there are general words following particular and specific words, as a rule it is correct to say that the general words must be confined to things of the same kind as those specified; but the *ejusdem generis* rule is one to be applied with caution as it is a mere

---

250   *The People (DPP) v Farrell* [1978] IR 13.
251   *Irish Commercial Society Ltd v Plunkett* [1986] IR 258.
252   *CW Shipping Co Ltd v Limerick Harbour Commissioners* [1989] ILRM 416.
253   [1989] ILRM 416 at 424.
254   *Royal Dublin Society v Revenue Commissioners* [2000] 1 IR 270.
255   *Kielthy v Ascon Ltd* [1970] IR 122.
256   [1963] IR 103 at 109.

presumption which applies in the absence of any other indications of the legislature. Before the rule can apply the general words must *follow* specific words; in the present case the general words *precede* the specific words ... [i]n my opinion, the general words ... are not in any way limited by the words which subsequently appear in the sub-section ..."[257]

Apart from the particular point concerning general words which appear before specific words, Griffin J's judgment discloses a degree of caution in the application of the rule.[258]

Noscitur a sociis

[14.126] The *ejusdem generis* rule can be considered to be a manifestation of a wider principle or practice by which meaning is attributed to a word by reference to the context in which it appears.[259] That practice is sometimes encapsulated in the Latin maxim *noscitur a sociis* (a thing is known by its associates). Henchy J's judgment in *Inspector of Taxes v Kiernan*[260] acknowledges the significance of context in general but in some cases the courts have specifically invoked the *noscitur a sociis* principle. Like the *ejusdem generis* rule it can be invoked to give a restricted meaning to otherwise general words.

[14.127] In *The People (Attorney General) v Kennedy*[261] it was held that an appeal by the Attorney General to the Supreme Court was not authorised by s 29 of the Courts of Justice Act 1924, despite the 'ordinary' meaning of the words in that provision. The appropriate mode of interpretation was explained by Black J:

"[W]e have an express grant of a right of appeal without any express limitation of parties, and it is said that as the words are clear, there can be no limitation. I am satisfied that to look at the provision in that way is to adopt an erroneous method of final approach.

A small section of a picture, if looked at close-up, may indicate something quite clearly; but when one stands back and examines the whole canvas, the close-up view of the small section is often found to have given a wholly wrong view of what it really represented.

If one could pick out a single word or phrase and, finding it perfectly clear in itself, refuse to check its apparent meaning in the light thrown upon it by the context or by other provisions, the result would be to render the principle of *ejusdem generis* and *noscitur a sociis* utterly meaningless; for this principle requires frequently that a word or phrase or even a whole

---

257 [1974] IR 19 at 30–31 (emphasis in original).
258 See *O'Dwyer v Cafolla Ltd* (1950) 84 ILTR 44; *Attorney General v Leaf Ltd* [1982] ILRM 441 where the rule was not applied; see contra *O'Sullivan v Leitrim County Council* [1953] IR 71; *Kenny v Quinn* [1981] ILRM 385; *Irish Nationwide Building Society Ltd v Revenue Commissioners* (2 October 1990, unreported), HC applying the rule.
259 See Cross, *Statutory Interpretation* (3rd edn, 1995), p 138; also Bennion, *Statute Law* (3rd edn, 1990), p 196.
260 *Inspector of Taxes v Kiernan* [1981] IR 117.
261 *The People (Attorney General) v Kennedy* [1946] IR 517; see also *Application of Quinn* [1974] IR 19 at 22.

provision which, standing alone, has a clear meaning must be given quite a different meaning when viewed in the light of its context."[262]

[14.128] In *Dillon v Minister for Posts and Telegraphs*[263] the Supreme Court was required to consider whether the plaintiff, a candidate in a Dáil election, was entitled to avail of the free postage facilities provided to candidates by s 50 of the Prevention of Electoral Abuses Act 1923. The defendant contended, *inter alia*, that the plaintiff's election material was 'grossly offensive' under the provisions of the Inland Postal Warrant 1939[264] and thus could not be conveyed in the post. In rejecting that contention Henchy J invoked the principle:

"Assuming (without necessarily so holding) that that Act and those regulations have application to this case, one notes that Article 6 of the relevant regulations (The Inland Post Warrant 1939), prohibits the posting, conveyance, or delivery by post of 'any postal packet ... having thereon, or on the cover thereof, any words, marks, or designs of an indecent, obscene or grossly offensive character'. Again assuming (without necessarily so deciding) that this brochure falls within the definition of 'postal packet' given in the 1908 Act, or within the more restricted definition of 'postal packet' given in the 1939 regulations, I would find it impossible to hold that the brochure is debarred from the benefit of free post because of the passage in it to which the Minister takes exception. That passage, and it is the only passage relied on for the purpose of this point, runs as follows:

'Today's politicians are dishonest because they are being political and must please the largest number of people.'

I am far from saying that even if the prohibition were simply against words of a grossly offensive character, I would have held that that sentence would offend against such a prohibition. And I venture to think that those who practise what is often dubbed the art of the possible would not feel grossly offended by such an expression of opinion which, denigratory and cynical though it might be thought by some, is no more than the small coinage of the currency of political controversy. Some of the most revered and successful politicians who have lived have failed at least in the eyes of reputable historians, to align great political acumen and success with moral or intellectual honesty. A charge of dishonesty is one that rarely penetrates the epidermis of any seasoned politician.

But the embargo is not simply against words of a grossly offensive character. So I do not have to reject the Minister's objection on that ground. The embargo is against 'any words, marks or designs of an indecent, obscene or grossly offensive character'. That assemblage of words gives a limited and special meaning to the expression 'grossly offensive character'. As Stamp J said in *Bourne v Norwich Crematorium Ltd*:[265]

'English words derive colour from those which surround them. Sentences are not mere collections of words to be taken out of the sentence, defined separately by reference to

---

[262] [1946] IR 517 at 536.

[263] *Dillon v Minister for Posts and Telegraphs* (3 June 1981, unreported), SC; see also *United States Tobacco International Inc v Minister for Health* [1990] 1 IR 394.

[264] SR&O 202/1939.

[265] *Bourne v Norwich Crematorium Ltd* [1967] 2 All ER 576 at 578.

the dictionary or decided cases, and then put back again into the sentence with the meaning which you have assigned to them as separate words ...'

Applying the maxim *noscitur a sociis*, which means that a word or expression is known from its companions, the expression 'grossly offensive character' must be held to be infected in this context with something akin to the taint of indecency or obscenity. Much of what might be comprehended by the expression if it stood alone is excluded by its juxtaposition with the words 'indecent' and 'obscene'. This means that the Minister may not reject a passage as disqualified for free circulation through the post because it is apt to be thought displeasing or distasteful. To merit rejection it must be grossly offensive in the sense of being obnoxious or abhorrent in a way that brings it close to the realm of indecency or obscenity. The sentence objected to by the Minister, while many people would consider it to be denigratory of today's politicians, is far from being of a 'grossly offensive character' in the special sense in which that expression is used in the Act.'[266]

Generalia specialibus non derogant

[14.129] The proposition in this maxim is that a statute containing general subject matter is taken not to affect one which applies to a specific topic. Its effect is to prevent the unintentional repeal or qualification of a specific provision by a later one which is general in nature.[267] The general provision may appear either in a subsequent enactment or later in the same instrument.[268] In *McGonagle v McGonagle*[269] O'Byrne J explained the maxim thus:

"It is a general rule of construction that a prior statute is held to be repealed, by implication, by a subsequent statute which is inconsistent with and repugnant to the prior statute. This

---

[266] *Dillon v Minister for Posts and Telegraphs* (3 June 1981, unreported), SC. See also *Li v Governor of Cloverhill Prison* [2012] 2 IR 400 at 410 *per* Hogan J:

This case at hand also presents another textbook example of where *noscitur a sociis* as a principle of statutory interpretation comes into its own. The very fact that the reference to 'public order' is juxtaposed beside the words 'national security' in s. 9(8)(a) of the [Refugee Act 1996] means that the former words take on their traditional and somewhat more restricted meaning in the sphere of immigration law. Adapting the language of Henchy J. at p. 6 in *Dillon v. Minister for Posts and Telegraphs* to the present case, '[t]hat assemblage of words gives [the words "public order"] a limited and special meaning.' In that context, the words 'public order' do not simply mean conduct which involves a breach of our immigration laws, but rather connote a situation where the *personal conduct* of the immigrant poses a real and immediate threat to fundamental policy interests of the State. In that sense, the concept of public order at issue here is but another variant of the concept of national security *albeit* wider and somewhat more flexible in its scope and reach than that of national security properly so called.

[267] See eg *Keane v Western Health Board and Ann Meehan* [2007] 2 IR 555; *National Authority for Occupational Safety and Health v Fingal County Council* [1997] 2 IR 547.

[268] See *The People (DPP) v Kelly* [1982] IR 90 at 114; *Welch v Bowmaker (Ireland) Ltd* [1980] IR 251.

[269] *McGonagle v McGonagle* [1951] IR 123.

rule, however, does not apply where, as in the present case, the prior statute is special and the subsequent statute general."[270]

[14.130] In *DPP v Grey*[271] the Supreme Court held that s 27 of the Excise Management Act 1827 (dealing with penalties for excise offences) was unaffected by s 8 of the Criminal Justice Act 1951 (which allows other offences to be taken into consideration when sentencing). Henchy J expressly invoked the maxim:

"There is therefore brought into application the rule of statutory interpretation that when Parliament has provided specifically by statute for a limited set of circumstances, there is a presumption that general words in a later statute are not to be taken as overriding the earlier specific provision, unless an intention to do so is clearly expressed."[272]

[14.131] McCarthy J, dissenting, took a different view:

"The Court has not been referred to any case in which this principle has been extended to the criminal law or the construction of a criminal statute which, of its nature, is subject to the canon of construction appropriate to a penal Act, in which the more lenient of two reasonable constructions must be given."[273]

While McCarthy J does identify the not uncommon phenomenon of two rules leading to conflicting interpretations, his remarks on the application of the maxim to criminal cases should be qualified. In *McGonagle v McGonagle*[274] the maxim was applied to a criminal evidence statute, to which the principle of strict construction might otherwise have applied. It would thus appear that there is nothing in principle to preclude its application to penal provisions. Nevertheless, the general application of the maxim to other statutes is beyond question.[275]

Conjunctive and disjunctive meanings

[14.132] An issue which sometimes arises is whether the word 'and' should be interpreted as bearing a disjunctive meaning, in other words whether 'and' should be interpreted as meaning 'or'. The issue arose in *Duggan v Dublin Corporation*.[276] The applicant was the owner of a jewellery shop which had been raided by a three-man gang. The gang committed extensive property damage inside the shop, struck the applicant on the arm with a baseball bat and stole a number of trays of rings and other items of jewellery. The gang escaped in a car driven by a fourth member. The jewellery stolen was valued at £10,650. The applicant claimed damages against the Corporation under s 6 of the Malicious Injuries Act 1981, which provides that a malicious injuries claim for stolen property can be made arising from a situation in which 'three or more persons ...

---

[270] [1951] IR 123 at 127; see *The People (DPP) v T* (1988) 3 Frewen 141.
[271] *DPP v Grey* [1986] IR 317.
[272] [1986] IR 317 at 327.
[273] [1986] IR 317 at 330.
[274] *McGonagle v McGonagle* [1951] IR 123.
[275] See *Duffy v Dublin Corporation* [1974] IR 33; *Short v Dublin County Council* [1982] ILRM 117; *The People (DPP) v Kelly* [1982] IR 90 at 114, per Henchy and Kenny JJ.
[276] *Duggan v Dublin Corporation* [1991] 1 IR 275.

are tumultuously and riotously assembled together ...' The applicant's claim was dismissed in the Circuit Court, the judge deciding that, while the gang's actions amounted to 'riotous assembly' they did not constitute a 'tumultuous assembly'.

[14.133] On a case stated, the Supreme Court (Finlay CJ, McCarthy and O'Flaherty JJ) upheld that decision. The court concluded that to construe the word 'and' in s 6 of the 1981 Act either in a disjunctive sense or as being 'mere surplusage' would be to amend the section, and such an interpretation was impermissible having regard in particular to s 5 of the Act (which dealt with claims for damage to property as opposed to stolen property), which had used the phrase 'unlawfully, riotously or tumultuously'.

[14.134] McCarthy J noted that counsel for the applicant:

"... has been unable to identify any case in which the word 'and' has been read as 'or', whereas there are a number in which the converse has been the case ... To me, in its ordinary sense, riotously differs from tumultuously in the measure of activity, noise, alarm and so on ... they are not mutually exclusive and, consequently, there is no requirement that the word 'and' is to be read as 'or'."[277]

Repealed provisions

[14.135] In *The People (DPP) v Gilligan*,[278] the Court of Criminal Appeal considered the effect of a statutory provision which substituted a new section in existing law. In *Gilligan* the court was concerned with s 3 of the Larceny Act 1990, which provided that the Larceny Act 1916 should be amended by the substitution for s 33 of the 1916 Act of the section set out in s 3 of the 1990 Act. The 1990 Act replaced the old offence of receiving stolen property with an offence of handling stolen property. The applicant had been charged with receiving stolen property, contrary to s 33 of the 1916 Act as originally enacted. The offence was alleged to have taken place in January 1988. The 1990 Act had come into force in August 1990 and the applicant was put on trial in November 1990. It was argued that the applicant could not have been tried in November 1990 with the receiving offence since this had been abolished by the 1990 Act.

[14.136] The case turned on s 21(1)(e) of the Interpretation Act 1937, which provided that the 'repeal' of statutory provisions would not affect pending civil or criminal proceedings. The applicant argued that s 3 of the 1990 Act had not repealed s 33 of the 1916 Act but had merely substituted a new section for the original s 33.

[14.137] The Court of Criminal Appeal (O'Flaherty, Keane and Barron JJ) rejected this argument. The court concluded that since the 1990 Act had altered the legal meaning of the 1916 Act, this amounted to a repeal of s 33 of the 1916 Act. Thus, s 33 was regarded as still extant for the purposes of the charge against the defendant. The court therefore dismissed the application on this ground. This view of s 21 of the Interpretation Act

---

[277] *Duggan v Dublin Corporation* [1991] 1 IR 275, 283; see *H v H* [1978] IR 138 and *Dillon v Minister for Posts and Telegraphs* (3 June 1981, unreported), SC where 'or' was interpreted as being conjunctive.

[278] *The People (DPP) v Gilligan* [1992] ILRM 769.

1937 is important given the proliferation of the 'repeals by substitution' in the statute book.[279]

[14.138] Different considerations arise where a statute abolishes a common law offence and replaces it with a statutory alternative. In these circumstances it is good drafting practice to include a transitional provision in the amending legislation. Typically, a provision of this nature will contain a formula that allows prosecutions to be brought on the basis of the old common law in respect of offences committed before the new legislation came into effect. To this extent, the old law is kept in being for the purpose of prosecutions in respect of conduct that was committed prior to the new enactment. However, no such provision is contained in the Non-Fatal Offences Against the Person Act 1997, a measure that abolished the common law offences of assault, battery, kidnapping and false imprisonment and replaced them with statutory alternatives.

[14.139] The question that has arisen is whether it is possible to try an accused after the Act came into force for offences committed before that date. The difficulty is that the old common law offences have been abolished and the argument is that to try an accused for such offences after the date of their abolition is to try a person for an offence that is not known to the law. On the other hand, the prohibition on retrospective penalisation prevents the bringing of charges on the basis of the new law since the impugned conduct occurred prior to the change in the law.

[14.140] It was these considerations that persuaded the Special Criminal Court in *The People (DPP) v Kavanagh*[280] to dismiss charges of false imprisonment allegedly committed by the accused prior to the 1997 Act but prosecuted after that date. The Oireachtas responded by enacting the Interpretation (Amendment) Act 1997 which contains a general transitional provision and became law on 4 November 1997.

[14.141] The issue arose again in *Quinlivan v Governor of Portlaoise Prison*[281] which involved a charge of false imprisonment committed prior to the date the Act came into force. It was accepted that the Interpretation (Amendment) Act 1997 did not apply and in the absence of a transitional provision in the Non-Fatal Offences Against the Person Act 1997 the court was required to 'draw such inferences as to the intended transitional arrangements as it considered Parliament to have intended'.[282] McGuinness J took a different view to that which prevailed in *Kavanagh* and concluded that in amending the law 'the intention of the Oireachtas was to act prospectively and not to interfere with prosecutions under common law ... *of which the courts were already seised*'.[283] The fact that the applicant had been charged with the offence at the time that the Act became law was significant. At that stage the case had fallen within the judicial domain and for the legislation to have the effect of terminating proceedings would, in McGuinness J's

---

[279] The effect of repeals is now governed by the Interpretation Act 2005, s 27.

[280] *The People (DPP) v Kavanagh* (29 October 1997, unreported), SCC.

[281] *Quinlivan v Governor of Portlaoise Prison* [1998] 2 IR 113.

[282] [1998] 2 IR 113 at 132.

[283] [1998] 2 IR 113 at 146 (emphasis added).

opinion, have entailed an unconstitutional interference with the administration of justice.[284]

[14.142] In *Mullins v Hartnett*[285] O'Higgins J was faced with the same issue in relation to a charge of assault contrary to common law. Applying 'all the canons of interpretation'[286] he concluded that the proper construction of the Non-Fatal Offences Against the Person Act 1997 was that the offence was not abolished for pre-existing charges. As in *Quinlivan* proceedings had been initiated prior to the coming into force of the Non-Fatal Offences Against the Person Act 1997 but the fact that the courts were seised of the case at the time of its enactment did not feature in O'Higgins J's reasoning. To this extent the decision in *Mullins v Hartnett* purported to establish a broader principle than that in *Quinlivan* and it would have applied whether or not the case had begun at the time the Act came into force. However, those decisions have now been overtaken by the more recent Supreme Court decisions in *Grealis v DPP; Corbett v DPP*.[287]

[14.143] In the joined cases of *Grealis v DPP* and *Corbett v DPP* the Supreme Court was presented with the opportunity to consider the consequences of the abolition of the common law offences by the Non-Fatal Offences Against the Person Act 1997, its effect on charges that were pending before the courts at that time, and the scope of the Interpretation (Amendment) Act 1997. In *Grealis* the applicant had been summoned on two charges of assault and one of assault occasioning actual bodily harm contrary to s 47 of the Offences Against the Person Act 1861. In *Corbett* the applicant faced charges of assault and assault contrary to s 47. All the alleged offences had been committed prior to the enactment of the Non-Fatal Offences Against the Person Act. Moreover, the *Corbett* summonses had been issued before that Act was passed, thus raising the argument that the legislation could not affect proceedings of which the courts were seised, the point that was central to the decision in *Quinlivan*.

[14.144] The Supreme Court unanimously held that the absence of a transitional provision in the Non-Fatal Offences Against the Person Act was fatal to the continuing of the prosecutions. The court accepted the contention that the effect of a statutory abolition of an offence is that the latter ceases to exist *for all purposes* unless legislation specifically provides otherwise. This proposition was supported by a well-established body of authority[288] and was to be preferred to the principles of construction that

---

284 Citing *Buckley v Attorney General* [1950] IR 67.

285 *Mullins v Hartnett* [1998] 4 IR 426.

286 [1998] 4 IR 426 at 435.

287 *Grealis v DPP; Corbett v DPP* [2001] 3 IR 144.

288 Citing *Miller's Case* (1764) 1 Black W 451; *R v MacKenzie* (1820) Russ & Ry 429; *Kay v Goodwin* (1830) 6 Bing 576; *R v Swann* (1849) 4 Cox CC 108; *The General Pickney: Yeaton v United States* (1809) 9 US 281; *Commonwealth v Cooley* (1830) HF & N 36; *United States v Tynen* 11 Wall 88; *Massey v United States* (1934) 291 US 608.

prevailed in *Quinlivan* and *Mullins v Hartnett*. The abolition was effected in clear terms and Keane CJ observed:

"Section 28(1) of the [Non-Fatal Offences Against the Person Act 1997] is, however, clear and unambiguous. The only construction of which it is capable is that the common law offences to which it applies are abolished from the coming into force of the section. They cease to exist in law with all the consequences that flow from their abolition spelled out in the authorities to which I have referred. Counsel in the present case have been unable to put forward any construction of the provision in question which displaces the plain and unambiguous words the draughtsman has used."[289]

[14.145] The court also concluded that the provisions of the Interpretation (Amendment) Act 1997 did not save the prosecutions. Section 1 of that Act contains a general transitional provision in respect of the statutory abolition of common law offences and its effect is that the abolition of an offence will not prevent the bringing of charges in respect of conduct committed prior to that abolition. However, the Interpretation Act was enacted after the Non-Fatal Offences Against the Person Act and, no doubt with this in mind, s 1(3) of the former sought to ensure retrospective effect by providing that '[t]his section applies to an offence which is an offence at common law, abolished, abrogated or otherwise repealed before or after the passing of this Act'. Given the obvious constitutional issues that might arise, s 1(4) stipulates that:

"If, because of all or any of its provisions, this section would, but for the provisions of this subsection conflict with the constitutional rights of any person, the provisions of this section shall be subject to such limitations as are necessary to secure that they do not so conflict, but shall otherwise be of full force and effect."

The High Court in *Grealis* concluded that the Interpretation (Amendment) Act 1997 was unconstitutional, but on appeal the applicants in effect abandoned the constitutional argument and the Attorney General's appeal against the finding of unconstitutionality was successful.

[14.146] Nevertheless, the Supreme Court was alive to the issue and it held that the purpose of s 1(4) was to act as a constitutional safety net. Given the potential constitutional difficulties involved with the retrospective application of a penal provision, the court concluded that the Act, despite the wording of s 1(3), should only apply prospectively. Keane CJ took the view that s 1(4) was 'intended to preserve the constitutionality of the section as a whole by excluding prosecutions initiated before the commencement of the 1997 Interpretation Act from the ambit of the Act'. Denham J also expressed the view that the retrospective operation of the transitional provision in the Interpretation (Amendment) Act 1997 might cause constitutional difficulties:

"A purported validation retrospectively of the law may be a breach of the Constitution. An application retrospectively of s 1 of the Interpretation (Amendment) Act 1997 would conflict with [an accused's] right to be tried for an offence at law, in due process of law, in circumstances where the actions had ceased to be an offence and so remained at the time of

---

[289]   [2001] 3 IR 144 at 158–159.

the issuing of the summons. A vacuum was created at which time the actions were no longer an offence under the law. A *lacuna* was left by the legislature. Any prosecution of [an accused] after the abolition of the offence and prior to the coming into effect of the Interpretation (Amendment) act 1997 was a nullity. A purported validation retrospectively of the new law would be a breach of the rule of law, due process and fundamental constitutional principles. The general validation would not apply to criminal proceedings such as these issued [in the instant cases] ... the respondents may not rely on s 1 of the Interpretation (Amendment) Act 1997. It is an Act which, in accordance with constitutional principles, applies prospectively."[290]

[14.147] The court also held by a majority, with Keane CJ dissenting on this point, that assault occasioning actual bodily harm was a common law offence. As it too had been abolished by the Non-Fatal Offences Against the Person Act 1997, proceedings against the applicants for that offence were prohibited.

[14.148] The decisions in *Grealis v DPP; Corbett v DPP*[291] can be summarised. The abolition by the Non-Fatal Offences Against the Person Act 1997 of the old common law offences, including assault occasioning actual bodily harm under s 47 of the Offences Against the Person Act 1861, operated for all legal purposes. It followed that prosecutions for offences that were allegedly committed prior to their abolition could not be brought after that time in the absence of specific statutory authority. No such transitional provision was contained in the Non-Fatal Offences Against the Person Act, with the result that prosecutions for the offences in question were no longer possible. The subsequent enactment of the Interpretation (Amendment) Act 1997, with its general transitional provision, was of no avail since, for constitutional reasons, it could only apply prospectively. As a consequence, where legislation abolishes a common law offence it is crucial to ensure that it includes a transitional provision to facilitate further prosecutions for the abolished offence. However, as far as non-fatal offences are concerned a serious lacuna resulted from the enactment of the Non-Fatal Offences Act and the broader consequence of *Grealis v DPP; Corbett v DPP* was to prohibit prosecutions for many assaults committed prior to the enactment of that Act.

Mandatory and directory provisions

[14.149] A statute might require a course of conduct to be adopted or an act to be performed, yet its omission might not be of great significance. Such provisions might be considered to be directory (or discretionary)[292] rather than mandatory. Failure to comply with a directory provision does not affect the validity of other matters which are connected with it. The identification of a provision as being mandatory or directory is based on the intent of the legislation, with the provision being examined in relation to the overall statutory scheme.

---

[290] *Corbett v DPP* [2001] 3 IR 144 at 187–188.

[291] *Grealis v DPP; Corbett v DPP* [2001] 3 IR 144.

[292] The term 'discretionary' was employed by the Supreme Court in *Bakht v The Medical Council* [1990] 1 IR 515, holding the requirement in the Medical Practitioners Act 1978, s 27(2)(d) to make qualification rules for non-EC-trained medical practitioners to be mandatory.

[14.150] In general, the less important the provision the greater the likelihood that it will be held to be directory. The test is set out in Henchy J's judgment in *The State (Elm Developments) v An Bord Pleanála*:[293]

"Whether a provision in a statute or statutory instrument, which on the face of it is obligatory (for example, by the use of the word 'shall'), should be treated by the courts as truly mandatory or merely directory depends on the statutory scheme as a whole and the part played in that scheme by the provision in question. If the requirement which has not been observed may fairly be said to be an integral and indispensable part of the statutory intendment, the courts will hold it to be truly mandatory, and will not excuse a departure from it. But if, on the other hand, what is apparently a requirement is in essence merely a direction which is not of the substance of the aim and scheme of the statute, non-compliance may be excused."

[14.151] The Supreme Court held that the requirement, in Art 36 of the Local Government (Planning and Development) Regulations 1977,[294] to include the grounds of appeal in a notice of appeal to An Bord Pleanála is directory. Henchy J explained:

"The decision of a planning authority to grant a development permission, while not necessarily final, will become final if an appeal is not lodged within the time fixed by the Act. Since an extension of that time is not provided for, the requirement as to time is mandatory, so that a departure from it cannot be excused. The requirement that the appeal be in writing is so obviously basic to the institution of an appeal that it too must be considered mandatory. So also must the requirement that the written appeal state the subject matter of the appeal, for the absence of such identification could lead to administrative confusion. The lodgement of a deposit of £10 with the appeal (perhaps not necessarily physically or contemporaneously with the appeal) would also seem to be an essential part of the statutory scheme, so as to discourage frivolous, delaying or otherwise, worthless appeals.

The requirement that the appeal should state the grounds of appeal seems to me to rest on different considerations. Even when the appeal contains a full statement of the grounds of appeal, that statement is not conclusive as to the grounds that will be considered on the hearing of the appeal. That is because s 17 of the 1976 Act says this:

'The Board in deciding a reference or appeal may take into account matters other than those raised by the parties to the reference or appeal if the matters either relate to the proper planning and development of the area of the relevant planning authority or are matters to which by virtue of s 24(2) of this Act the Board may have regard, provided that the matters are brought to the notice of those parties and they are accorded an opportunity of making observations thereon to the Board or, in the case of an oral hearing, the person conducting the hearing.'

The effect of that provision is that the Board may always treat the grounds lodged with the appeal as merely interim or provisional grounds. Even if the objector in this case had lodged a set of grounds of appeal with his appeal, the Board would be entitled to entertain further or other grounds at any stage up to the determination of the appeal, provided those further or

---

[293] [1981] ILRM 108 at 110.
[294] SI 65/1977.

other grounds relate to the proper planning and development of the area, or are matters to which by virtue of s 24(2) of the 1976 Act the Board may have regard, and provided the developer is given an opportunity of making observations thereon.

Because of that, the grounds of appeal required to be stated in the appeal are not to be equated with pleadings in court proceedings, or with a notice of appeal from one court to a superior court. They cannot circumscribe or identify the issues on which the appeal will be decided. The Board (or the person holding the oral hearing, if there is one) may go outside them. They cannot be treated with any confidence by the developer as indicative of the scope of the case he will have to meet on the hearing of the appeal. I deduce that the primary purpose of the requirement of stating grounds of appeal in a case such as this is to inform the Board as to the primary matters relied on, so that the procedure for the disposition of the appeal may be decided on. Whether that deduction be correct or not, I am satisfied that the grounds of appeal required are essentially informative. To hold that they must be given as part of, or contemporaneously with, the notice of appeal, would be to attribute a conclusiveness to them which the statute clearly shows they cannot have … [i]t would be unduly legalistic, and unfair, if laymen who may have no skill in such matters, but who may be vitally affected by the permission which they wish to appeal against, were to be shut out from appealing merely because their notice of appeal did not state their grounds of appeal, particularly when those grounds of appeal can never be anything more than an opening salvo in the appellate battle. In such circumstances, the requirement of stating the grounds of appeal is essentially informative and directory, and therefore not mandatory. When the appellant in this case furnished grounds of appeal, within a few weeks of his appeal, to the satisfaction of the Board, it did not lie in the mouth of the developer to say that he had been in any way wrong-footed or damnified, or that the spirit or purpose of the Acts and regulations had been breached. In seeking an order of prohibition against the Board, he is endeavouring to benefit from what is no more than a technical breach of a regulation, which breach has been put right by the appellant and has been therefore rightly overlooked by the Board in the interests of justice."[295]

[14.152] The distinction between mandatory and directory provisions operates to prevent a party from relying on a minor breach of a statutory requirement to invalidate a procedure or an administrative act.[296] In general, a comparatively unimportant provision in relation to the overall scheme will be held to be directory, thereby avoiding the unfortunate consequences which would otherwise attend its non-observance. On the other hand it is clear that a provision which is of greater importance should be held to be directory, breach of which will affect the validity of an act that is dependent on it.

[14.153] However, the distinction between mandatory and directory provisions was blurred in *The State (D & D) v Groarke*.[297] There it was held that the obligation to specify the religious persuasion of a child in a fit person order, under s 23 of the Children Act 1908, is mandatory, on the basis that something connected with the welfare

---

[295] *The State (Elm Developments) v An Bord Pleanála* [1981] ILRM 108 at 111–112.
[296] See Hogan and Morgan, *Administrative Law in Ireland* (4th edn, 2010), pp 504–508; see also *Irish Refining plc v Commissioner of Valuation* [1990] 1 IR 568.
[297] *The State (D & D) v Groarke* [1990] 1 IR 305.

of a child was a 'very fundamental matter'.[298] While failure to obey that requirement would render the order 'incomplete' that alone would not affect the validity of the order by virtue of the 'intention and purpose of the statutory provisions ... namely, the urgent protection the welfare of the child ...'.[299] In so ruling, the court attached to the breach of a mandatory requirement the consequence (or, more accurately, non-consequence) which could be expected had it decided that the provision is directory.

[4]   EXTERNAL SOURCES

[14.154] The rules and principles which we have examined in the preceding sections focus on the contents and context of the statute and as such a court which invokes them is concerned primarily with the internal materials of the statute. Traditionally, the courts refused to seek assistance in material which lies outside the statute, but over time that reluctance has abated and in some circumstances a court might have recourse to external materials.

Prior statutes

[14.155] The interpretation of an earlier statute might be applied to a later statute in either of two cases. The first is where the later statute expressly states that it should be construed with the earlier. This device is often employed where a series of successive statutes on a particular subject form what in essence is an inchoate code. Thus, s 1(1) of the Health Act 2008 provides that it and the Health Acts 1947 to 2007 'shall be construed together as one'. In a similar vein, s 1(3) of the Merchant Shipping Act 1992 provides:

> "This Act shall be construed as one with the Merchant Shipping Acts 1894 to 1983 and may be cited together therewith as the Merchant Shipping Acts 1894 to 1992."

[14.156] In some cases a statute might provide for collective construction only in respect of certain of its provisions, as is evident in s 1(2) of the Child Abduction and Enforcement of Custody Orders Act 1991:[300]

> "The Courts (Supplemental Provisions) Acts, 1961 to 1988 and this Act, insofar as it affects the jurisdiction and procedure of any court in the State, shall be construed together as one."

The effect of such provisions is to require that all the sections of the relevant statutes should be interpreted as if they were contained in the one statute. Accordingly the interpretation of the earlier statute will apply to the later unless there is some 'manifest discrepancy'.[301]

---

[298]   [1990] 1 IR 305 at 315.

[299]   *The State (D & D) v Groarke* [1990] 1 IR 305.

[300]   See also the more elaborate Worker Protection (Part-Time Employees) Act 1991, s 8 providing for its being construed with a number of different series of statutes.

[301]   See *Canada Southern Ry Co v International Bridge Co* (1883) 3 App Cas 723, 727.

[14.157] Secondly, even in the absence of an express provision a statute might be construed in the light of a prior statute.[302] If words or expressions which have been used in the earlier legislation are repeated in a subsequent Act in a similar context they are liable to be given the meaning which was previously attributed to them. This is especially so where the words or expressions have been judicially interpreted or have a clear and settled meaning.[303] This is based on an assumption that when it employed terms whose meaning was known or had been judicially determined, the Oireachtas intended to adopt that meaning. If it had sought to change the law it could be expected that different words would have been used.

[14.158] This proposition applies only where the statutes are *in pari materia*, that is, their context is similar.[304] Henchy J explained the matter in *The State (Sheehan) v Government of Ireland*[305] where he stated that 'in construing a particular statutory provision no provision of another statute may be used as an aid or a guide unless that other statutory provision is *in pari materia*, that is forming part of the same statutory context'.[306]

[14.159] Thus, in *Mogul of Ireland Ltd v Tipperary (North Riding) County Council*[307] s 1 of the Malicious Injuries (Ireland) Act 1853 was interpreted in the light of s 135 of the Grand Jury (Ireland) Act 1836 as both formed part of the same legislative scheme. Likewise, the Redundancy Payments Act 1967 and the Minimum Notice and Terms of Employment Act 1973 have been construed as being *in pari materia*;[308] so too the phrase 'total income brought into charge' in the Corporation Tax Act 1976 was considered to be *in pari materia* with 'profits or gains brought into charge' in the Income Tax legislation.[309] On the other hand, the Finance Act 1975 and the Value Added Tax Act 1972 were held not to be *in pari materia*[310] nor were the Labourers Act 1936 and the Landlord and Tenant Act 1931.[311]

[14.160] In *Murphy v Dublin Corporation*[312] the Supreme Court was invited to read together the Housing Act 1966 and the Local Government (Planning and Development)

---

[302] However, there is a manifest reluctance to interpret a provision in the light of a subsequent amendment; see *Cronin v Cork and County Properties Ltd* [1986] IR 559; *Dublin County Council v Eighty Five Developments Ltd (No 1)* [1993] 2 IR 378.

[303] See *Cronin v Youghal Carpets (Yarns) Ltd* [1985] IR 312.

[304] The qualified nature of this proposition is evident in *Inspector of Taxes v Kiernan* [1981] IR 117 where the Supreme Court refused to adopt *Phillips (Inspector of Taxes) v Bourne* [1947] KB 533 on the interpretation of the word 'cattle' in a similar statute.

[305] *The State (Sheehan) v Government of Ireland* [1987] IR 550.

[306] [1987] IR 550 at 562.

[307] *Mogul of Ireland Ltd v Tipperary (North Riding) County Council* [1976] IR 260.

[308] *Irish Leathers Ltd v Minister for Labour* [1986] IR 177.

[309] *Cronin v Youghal Carpets (Yarns) Ltd* [1985] IR 312.

[310] *Irish Agricultural Machinery Ltd v Ó Culacháin* [1990] 1 IR 535.

[311] *Gough v Kinsella* (1971) 105 ILTR 116.

[312] *Murphy v Dublin Corporation* [1976] IR 143.

Act 1963 in order to achieve legislative harmony. The court refused, holding that the Acts are not *in pari materia* since, in the words of Henchy J, 'they lack a common subject matter or purpose. So it would be a breach of a fundamental rule of statutory interpretation to treat them as a statutory whole.'[313]

Legislative history

[14.161] The legislative process, which was outlined in the previous chapter,[314] is liable to result in the production of a variety of materials which might be cited as external assistance in the interpretation of a measure. ''

The common law's traditional approach was to avoid examining the legislative history of a measure. This reluctance is evident in *Minister for Industry and Commerce v Hales*[315] where correspondence between the Minister who initiated the legislation and a citizen, which indicated the Minister's views on the meaning of the provision in question, was held to be inadmissible.

[14.162] Both in the terms of his judgment and the authorities cited, McLoughlin J was unequivocal in his rejection of such material:

> "[T]he statute should be construed principally by the words of the statute itself which we should only modify or alter so far as it may be necessary to avoid some manifest absurdity or incongruity, [and] it would be departing very far from this canon of interpretation if we were to admit evidence of contemporaneous circumstances which would result in giving an interpretation to a section of the statute … which would be repugnant to the intentions of the legislature as indicated by the Act in question, construed as a whole."[316]

[14.163] Nevertheless, since the late 1970s the courts on occasion have departed from this absolutist position. In *Rowe v Law*[317] O'Higgins CJ, dissenting, considered the parliamentary history of s 90 of the Succession Act 1965, including various different drafts which had been mooted.[318] In *Finucane v McMahon*[319] Walsh J reviewed the political and historical background to extradition legislation when interpreting s 50 of the Extradition Act 1965. In *An Blascaod Mór Teo v Commissioners of Public Works (No 2)*[320] Budd J was prepared to admit a Bill in evidence to assist in determining the purpose of the Act in question. While these cases may be invoked in support of the proposition that it is permissible to have recourse to the legislative history of a provision and to relevant external materials, they must be construed in the light of the more recent decision of the Supreme Court in *Crilly v Farrington*, which is considered below.[321]

---

313 [1976] IR 143 at 149.
314 See paras **13.18–13.64**.
315 *Minister for Industry and Commerce v Hales* [1967] IR 50.
316 [1967] IR 50 at 68.
317 *Rowe v Law* [1978] IR 55.
318 See Power, 'Parliamentary History as an Aid to Statutory Interpretation' [1984] Stat LR 38.
319 *Finucane v McMahon* [1990] 1 ILRM 505.
320 *An Blascaod Mór Teo v Commissioners of Public Works (No 2)* [2000] 1 IR 1.
321 *Crilly v Farrington* [2001] 3 IR 251; see further at paras **14.186–14.187**.

International treaties

[14.164] Where domestic legislation is based on an international treaty it is accepted that a court may examine the treaty and its associated preparatory materials (the so-called *travaux préparatoires*) as an aid to interpreting the domestic provision. This can be linked to the presumption of compatibility with international law[322] and it reinforces the assumption that the Oireachtas intended to abide by its international obligations.

[14.165] The propriety of looking at those materials was confirmed by the Supreme Court in *Bourke v Attorney General*[323] where it examined the *travaux préparatoires* of the European Convention on Extradition, on which s 50 of the Extradition Act 1965 was based. The wide range of materials which was evaluated by the court included the article of the European Convention on which s 50 was indirectly based, earlier drafts of that article, various working documents, the Belgian Extradition Law (of 1833) which was cited in those documents, the Norwegian Extradition Law (of 1908) and the German–Turkish Extradition Treaty of 1930. The force of this judgment might be thought to be somewhat diluted by Ó Dálaigh CJ's statement that he would have arrived at the same conclusion without reference to the *travaux préparatoires*, but the propriety of having recourse to such materials is beyond question.[324] The rationale underlying this approach was cogently explained by Murray J in *Crilly v Farrington*:

"For a very long time principles of common law concerning the interpretation of statutes which give effect to international treaties permit the courts to interpret such a statute in the light of the meaning of relevant provisions of the treaty concerned. No doubt this is in part because the intention of the national legislature is clear – to give effect to provisions of the treaty in domestic law – and the objective consequence of that intent can be clarified or ascertained, where necessary, by reference to the meaning of the relevant provisions of the treaty, itself a legal instrument. There is also the consideration that contracting parties to international agreements should seek, as far as possible, to give uniform effect to its provision in domestic law. Furthermore, with this latter objective in mind, international treaties are interpreted in accordance with the principles of international law according to which the *travaux préparatoires* may be consulted for the purposes of their interpretation (unless such an approach is excluded, expressly, or by implication by the terms of the treaty itself or if there are no *travaux préparatoires* available)." [325]

EC materials

[14.166] As the volume of domestic legislation that is based on EC law increases it is likely that the interpretation which the EC measure attributes to the provision will be adopted in relation to its domestic counterpart. This is evident in the decision in *Deane v Voluntary Health Insurance Board*[326] where the Supreme Court considered whether the

---

[322] See para **14.91**.
[323] *Bourke v Attorney General* [1972] IR 36.
[324] See also *Aamand v Smithwick* [1995] 1 ILRM 61.
[325] *Crilly v Farrington* [2001] 3 IR 251 at 291.
[326] *Deane v Voluntary Health Insurance Board* [1992] 2 IR 319.

defendants were an 'undertaking' within the meaning of the Competition Act 1991. That Act defined 'undertaking' to mean a person or body 'engaged for gain in the production, supply or distribution of goods or the provision of a service'. The defendants provided health insurance on a non-profit-making basis and it was contended that accordingly they were not 'engaged for gain'.

[14.167] The Supreme Court held that 'gain' was not confined to pecuniary gain or profit and that the defendants amounted to an 'undertaking'. While the court appeared to have been satisfied that the term 'gain' was not ambiguous, it was nevertheless prepared to adopt the interpretation of the EC measures on which the Competition Act 1991 is based. According to Finlay CJ:

"... it is stated that the purposes of the Act include the prohibition by analogy with Articles 85 and 86 [now Arts 81 and 82] of the Treaty establishing the EEC and in the interests of the common good the prevention, restriction or distortion of competition and the abuse of dominant positions in trade in the State. Articles 85 and 86 undoubtedly apply to a body corporate engaged in the supply of services even if it does not have as its object the making of commercial profits."[327]

[14.168] The analogy between the domestic legislation and the equivalent treaty provisions was expressed in the long title to the Competition Act 1991, thus facilitating the adoption of the EC interpretation of the measure. However, there is nothing in principle to preclude having recourse to the interpretation of EC measures where such a link exists, although it might not be explicitly stated.

Pre-parliamentary materials

[14.169] A significant number of official materials fall into this category: Green and White Papers, reports of special commissions and tribunals of inquiry, Law Reform Commission reports, explanatory memoranda which accompany Bills. In *Maher v Attorney General*[328] the Supreme Court, in considering the constitutionality of s 44(2) of the Road Traffic Act 1968, examined a commission report on which the legislation in question was based. In *McLoughlin v Minister for the Public Service*[329] the explanatory memorandum that accompanied the Bill, which eventually became the Act in question, was examined and influenced the interpretation adopted by the Supreme Court. That material declared the purpose of the legislation and thus facilitated its interpretation accordingly.

[14.170] In the light of this decision it can be taken that, in general, pre-parliamentary materials may be employed as external assistance at least where they are official in origin. Those materials are accessible and are published in a reliable form, they contain the deliberations and/or conclusions of bodies which are established to consider legislative proposals and, having been submitted to public scrutiny, they form part of the

---

[327] *Deane v Voluntary Health Insurance Board* [1992] 2 IR 319 at 331.
[328] *Maher v Attorney General* [1973] IR 140.
[329] *McLoughlin v Minister for the Public Service* [1985] IR 631.

informal legislative process.[330] As an indication of legislative intent or the purpose of legislation their usefulness is obvious.

[14.171] However, the same might not be said of other non-official or private documents which might be offered as evidence of legislative intent. For instance, private briefing documents, correspondence of the type in *Minister for Industry and Commerce v Hales*, written submissions by interested parties in the course of lobbying and political party manifestos lack the qualities of 'official' documents and it is difficult to envisage circumstances which would justify their reception by a court of interpretation.

Parliamentary materials

[14.172] Parliamentary materials include the proceedings of both Houses of the Oireachtas, reported in the *Dáil Debates* and *Seanad Debates*, and reports of the various parliamentary committees. The traditional approach was that such materials could not be cited in court nor used as an aid to interpretation. This was based, in part, on constitutional considerations which are conveniently summarised by Miers:

> "First, the primary constitutional duty of a judge is to give effect to the intention of Parliament as expressed in the words of the statute: the statute alone is the uniquely authoritative statement of that intention. Second, 'the rule of law as a constitutional principle requires that the citizen, before committing himself to any course of action, should be able to know in advance what are the legal consequences that will flow from it. Where those consequences are regulated by a statute, the source of that knowledge is what the statute says' ... the citizen is entitled to rely on the words of the statute alone, or where it is judicially interpreted, on an interpretation based upon what he might reasonably understand by those words ... as a constitutional ground rule the law which establishes ... rights and duties should be what passes as law, and not what a representative of the executive thinks it is. Under the rule of law, ministerial glosses expressed during debate 'cannot affect the matter. Parliament ... is sovereign only in respect of what it expresses by the words used in the legislation it has passed.' Thus the corollary of the proposition that what Parliament says (at least in the form of primary legislation) goes, is that it is only the judiciary, and no other person, who has the authority finally and compellingly to say what those laws mean."[331]

[14.173] Another consideration was the belief that to open parliamentary debates in court was to subject parliament's actions to judicial scrutiny, a course of action prohibited by the principle of parliamentary privilege.[332]

[14.174] In as much as they were based on a view of parliamentary supremacy it was arguable that the foregoing concerns were of lesser force in Ireland, where judicial review of legislation, that is, of parliament's handiwork, is a central feature of the legal environment.[333] Eventually, some Irish courts displayed a willingness to depart from the

---

[330] See paras **13.46–13.57**.

[331] 'Taxing Perks and Interpreting Statutes: Pepper v Hart' (1993) 56 MLR 695, 702 (references omitted).

[332] *McLoughlin v Minister for Public Service* [1985] IR 631 at 703.

[333] See Casey, 'Statutory Interpretation – a New Departure' (1981) 3 DULJ (ns) 110, 114–115.

absolute rule and adopted the practice of courts in other countries to consider parliamentary proceedings when interpreting legislation.

[14.175] The revised approach was first adopted in *Wavin Pipes Ltd v Hepworth Iron Co Ltd*[334] where Costello J held that a court is permitted to consider the parliamentary debates on the provision in question. He justified his departure from that approach on the strength of the Supreme Court decision in *Bourke v Attorney General*:[335]

"… I should briefly here set out the reasons by which I have concluded that in certain circumstances a court is entitled to have regard to the parliamentary history of an Act to assist in its interpretation because to avoid overburdening an already long judgment I did not state them in my judgment in *Beecham Group Limited v Bristol Myers Company*.[336] The rules for the interpretation of statutes are judge-made. As long ago as 1769 it was established in England that 'the sense and meaning of an Act of Parliament must be collected from what it says when cast into law; and not from the history of changes it underwent in the House where it took its rise' (Willes J in *Millar v Taylor*,[337] quoted in Cross, *Statutory Interpretation* at p 134) and this rule has been applied ever since both in England and in this country. It should, however, be pointed out that this rule is not one followed in civil law jurisdictions, or in the United States of America, or in the European Court of Human Rights. I would have felt constrained to follow it, however, particularly as it has been re-affirmed by a divisional court in this country (see *Minister for Industry and Commerce v Hales*[338] in which the court refused to consider the legislative history of the Holidays (Employees) Act 1961) but for the decision of the Supreme Court in the *Bourke* case to which I have already referred.

There is no strict rule of construction which requires the court to examine only the words of the statute it is construing. In *McMahon v Attorney General*[339] the Supreme Court considered the Report of a Special Committee on electoral systems which preceded the Ballot Act 1872 on which provisions of the Electoral Act 1923 dealing with secrecy of the ballot were based. In *Maher v Attorney General*[340] the court found assistance in the interpretation of the Road Traffic Act 1968 in the Report of a Commission which had been established to consider the law relating to driving whilst under the influence of drink.

In the *Bourke* case the Supreme Court was called upon to interpret the phrase 'offence connected with a political offence' in s 50, Pt III, of the Extradition Act 1965. Part III of the Act dealt with the special arrangements for extradition between this country and the United Kingdom; Part II with extradition generally. The Act made it clear that Part II enacted as part of the municipal law of the State certain provisions of the Council of Europe Convention on Extradition signed on the 13 December 1957 and Part II contained a prohibition against extradition in respect of a political offence 'or an offence connected with a political offence' (s 11). In interpreting the phrase 'offence connected with a political

---

334 *Wavin Pipes Ltd v Hepworth Iron Co Ltd* [1982] 8 FSR 32.
335 *Bourke v Attorney General* [1972] IR 36.
336 *Beecham Group Limited v Bristol Myers Company* (13 March 1981, unreported), HC.
337 *Millar v Taylor* (1769) 4 Burr 2303, 2332.
338 *Minister for Industry and Commerce v Hales* [1967] IR 50.
339 *McMahon v Attorney General* [1972] IR 69.
340 *Maher v Attorney General* [1973] IR 140.

offence' in Pt III of the Act the Supreme Court took the view that as s 11 and s 50 speak of the same thing, as the Convention could be examined to discover the meaning of s 11, the court was entitled to look at the Convention for the purpose of interpreting s 50. But the court not only examined the text of the Convention for the purpose of interpreting the meaning of the phrase 'offence connected with a political offence' used in s 50 of the Irish statute, it also examined the *travaux préparatoires* of the Convention. In the course of this examination it reached conclusions as to the meaning of the phrase and based these conclusions on the fact that the original draft of the Convention had been amended in the course of its consideration by the organs of the Council of Europe and on the reasons disclosed in the *travaux préparatoires* for such amendments.

In doing so the Supreme Court extended considerably the existing rules as to the use of treaties in the interpretation of statutes (*Salomon v Commissioners of Customs and Excise*;[341] *Post Office v Estuary Radio Ltd*).[342] Parenthetically I think that it is relevant to note that not only had the House of Lords recently sanctioned the limited use of the *travaux préparatoires* of an international convention in the interpretation of a statute (see: *Fothergill v Monarch Airlines Ltd*),[343] but the Master of the Rolls, emboldened he said, by remarks of the Lord Chancellor in a debate in the House of Lords on 26 March of this year, has made use of the parliamentary history of the Employment Act 1980 for the purpose of interpreting some of its provisions (see: *Hadmor Productions Ltd v Hamilton*).[344] The arguments against the use by the courts of the parliamentary history of a statute for the purpose of its construction must apply with equal force to the history of the adoption of an international convention by an international organisation. And so, if the courts can properly look at the history of the adoption of an international convention for the purpose of ascertaining the meaning of the words used in it there would appear to be no reason in principle why in appropriate cases they should not be free when construing the words of a statute to obtain assistance from the history of its enactment by parliament. As I do not find persuasive the arguments against the use of the legislative history in the interpretation of statutes (which are helpfully brought together in the Report of the Law Commission and the Scottish Law Commission, *The Interpretation of Statutes*), as I believe I am entitled to seek assistance from the legislative history in appropriate cases, as in the present the legislative history greatly assists in construing the meaning of 'available to the public' as used in the Patents Act, 1964, I have used it in support of the construction of the 1964 Act which I have already given …"[345]

[14.176] In *Wavin Pipes* it was clear that an evaluation of the parliamentary history of the somewhat ambiguous provision would indicate the intention of the Oireachtas. The interpretation urged by the defendants formed the basis of an opposition amendment which would have inserted express words into the section. That amendment was

---

[341] *Salomon v Commissioners of Customs and Excise* [1967] 2 QB 306.
[342] *Post Office v Estuary Radio Ltd* [1968] 2 QB 740.
[343] *Fothergill v Monarch Airlines Ltd* [1980] 3 WLR 209.
[344] *Hadmor Productions Ltd v Hamilton* [1981] 3 WLR 139.
[345] *Wavin Pipes Ltd v Hepworth Iron Co Ltd* [1982] 8 FSR 32.

defeated and the fact that it was rejected and the reasons given for its rejection indicated that the words should not be construed in the manner sought by the defendants.[346]

[14.177] It was uncertain from the terms of the judgment in *Wavin Pipes*[347] when it would be considered permissible to have recourse to the parliamentary debates on a provision, the only qualification being that it could be done 'in appropriate cases'. In *FF v CF*,[348] which concerned the interpretation of s 2 of the Statute Law Revision (Pre-Union Irish Statutes) Act 1962, Barr J referred to the second stage speech of the Minister for Justice and deduced the legislative intention from it. However, the conclusion was not especially controversial and the point in question was conceded by both parties. Subsequent decisions lent weight to the view that a more cautious approach should be adopted and, in particular, that parliamentary materials should not be considered if the provision is clear and unambiguous.

[14.178] In *Wadda v Ireland*,[349] concerning the interpretation of the Child Abduction and Enforcement of Court Orders Act 1991, Keane J stated:

"It was also submitted that I should have regard in construing the provisions of the Act ... to statements made during the debates on the Bill in the Dáil by the minister responsible for introducing the measure. In this context, counsel relied on the decision of Costello J in *Wavin Pipes Ltd v Hepworth Iron Co Ltd* in which he held that the court could in defined circumstances have regard to its parliamentary history in order to ascertain the intention of the legislature in enacting a particular measure ...

The question does not arise, however, in the present case, for two reasons ... [i]n the second place, there is no obscurity, ambiguity or potential absurdity in the relevant provisions which would justify the court having recourse to what was said in the Oireachtas in order to ascertain the legislative intention."[350]

[14.179] Similar caution was evident in *Flynn and Village Crafts v Irish Nationwide Building Society Ltd*[351] where Lavan J cited Keane J's remarks and, being satisfied that the provisions in question were plain and unambiguous, refused to consult the *Dáil Debates*. Likewise, in *Re National Irish Bank*[352] Shanley J relied on the plain wording of the provision in question and observed that he considered a ministerial comment made during the relevant parliamentary proceedings to be unhelpful.

---

[346] It might also be observed that Costello J was ideally situated to examine the history of the provisions, having at the time been the deputy who moved the unsuccessful amendment; see Hogan and Whyte, *JM Kelly: The Irish Constitution* (4th edn, 2003), pp 877–884.

[347] *Wavin Pipes Ltd v Hepworth Iron Co Ltd* [1982] 8 FSR 32.

[348] *FF v CF* [1987] ILRM 1.

[349] *Wadda v Ireland* [1994] ILRM 126.

[350] [1994] ILRM 126 at 136–137; see also *CK v CK* [1993] ILRM 535.

[351] *Flynn and Village Crafts v Irish Nationwide Building Society Ltd* (31 July 1995, unreported), HC.

[352] *Re National Irish Bank* [1999] 1 ILRM 321.

[14.180] The High Court cases decided after *Wavin Pipes* showed a distinct lack of enthusiasm for consulting parliamentary materials, a position that may be contrasted with emerging developments in England.[353] This judicial reticence, together with the reiteration by the Supreme Court in *Howard v Commissioners of Public Works*[354] of the primacy of the text, lead to the conclusion that such materials (and, indeed, other external materials) should be consulted only as a last resort.

[14.181] There are several considerations to commend a restricted approach.[355] If a statute is plain and unambiguous, or can be interpreted by using the established canons of interpretation, examining the parliamentary history of the measure will at best be unnecessary and at worst be a source of uncertainty. If parliamentary materials merely confirm the conclusion that the court would have reached in any event, consideration of them is redundant since that would add nothing, as was arguably the case in *FF v CF*.[356]

[14.182] Moreover, where the parliamentary debates suggest a conclusion which is different from that which the ordinary canons of interpretation would suggest, their being consulted makes uncertain that which would otherwise have a settled meaning. Thus, those materials are liable to become a source of confusion, not of clarification. Hence, the importance of excluding consideration of parliamentary debates where the provision is plain and unambiguous or where the intention of the Oireachtas can be discerned by applying the conventional canons of interpretation.

[14.183] The unanimous decision of the Supreme Court in *The People (DPP) v McDonagh*[357] in which the court examined the history of s 2(1) of the Criminal Law (Rape) Act 1981, and the parliamentary history of the (British) Rape Act 1976 on which

---

[353] See *Pepper v Hart* [1993] 1 All ER 42 where the House of Lords has ruled that a court could consult Hansard (the House of Commons debates) in interpreting a statute. In a number of subsequent cases parliamentary materials have been used: *R v Warwickshire County Council, ex parte Johnson* [1993] 1 All ER 299; *Stubbings v Webb* [1993] 2 WLR 120; *Chief Adjudication Officer v Foster* [1993] 2 WLR 292. The decision in *Pepper v Hart* has resulted in an appreciable body of academic literature; see, eg Bennion, 'Hansard—Help or Hindrance? A Draftsman's View of *Pepper v Hart*' [1993] Stat LR 149; Lyell, '*Pepper v Hart*: The Government Perspective' [1994] Stat LR 1; Lester, '*Pepper v Hart* Revisited' [1994] Stat LR 10; Jenkins, '*Pepper v Hart*: A Draftsman's Perspective' [1994] Stat LR 23; Styles, 'The Rule of Parliament: Statutory Interpretation after *Pepper ? Hart*' (1994) 14 OJLS 151; Steyn, '*Pepper v Hart*: A Re-examination' (2001) 21 OJLS 59; Vogenauer, 'A Retreat from *Pepper v Hart*: A Reply to Lord Steyn' (2005) OJLS 629.

[354] *Howard v Commissioners of Public Works* [1994] 1 IR 101; see also *The People (DPP) v Quilligan* [1986] IR 496 at 511, *per* Walsh J: 'Whatever may have been in the minds of the members of the Oireachtas when the legislation was passed, in so far as their intention can be deduced, as it must be, from the words of the statute ...' (emphasis added).

[355] See also Law Reform Commission, *Report on Statutory Drafting and Interpretation* (LRC 61-2000), pp 63–69.

[356] *FF v CF* [1987] ILRM 1.

[357] *The People (DPP) v McDonagh* [1996] 1 IR 565. The only judgment was delivered by Costello P, who had delivered judgment in *Wavin Pipes*.

the 1981 Act was modelled, was thought to lend support to the view that there are instances where recourse to parliamentary materials is appropriate. However, in that case the court examined the legislative history of the provision, not the Oireachtas debates which have been referred to as 'parliamentary history'. The former refers to the legal antecedents to the legislation, while the latter consists of the history of the measure as it passed through the Oireachtas. The distinction between legislative and parliamentary history was highlighted by Murray J in *Crilly v Farrington*:

> "Perhaps at this point I should expressly refer to a distinction between *'legislative history'* and *'parliamentary history'* of a statute … In some writings and judgments the former term is used so as to include the latter but in classic common law tradition that is not the case. As the seventh edition of *Craies* observes at p 126:
>
> > 'The cause and necessity of the Act may be discovered, first, by considering the state of the law at the time when the Act was passed. In innumerable cases the courts, with a view to construing an Act, have considered the existing law and reviewed the history of legislation upon the subject.'[358]
>
> *Craies* also observed that it was hardly necessary to cite authorities for this proposition. This is an approach which permits an Act to be interpreted in the light of its legal historical context and with regard to the provisions of other Acts *in pari materia*. This long established approach of looking at *legislative history* is entirely distinct from that of *parliamentary history* where the latter refers to parliamentary debates and what occurred in the passage of a Bill through parliamentary procedures prior to its enactment."[359]

[14.184] Pragmatic considerations could also be invoked to support a restricted approach. In some instances parliamentary materials might themselves reflect doubts as to the meaning of the proposal or at least not help to solve the problem. That aside, it is open to question whether it is reasonable or practical to expect a citizen (or more probably his or her legal advisers) as a matter of routine to consult these materials in order to ascertain the meaning of a statute. If the courts had frequent recourse to parliamentary materials the inevitable result would be that it would become standard practice to consult such materials. Lawyers are liable to feel compelled to consult parliamentary materials on a regular basis both to improve the service to their clients and to avoid the possibility of an action for negligence.

[14.185] This consideration has become especially important as the quantity of cases involving questions of statutory interpretation has increased significantly. In some, possibly many, instances access to parliamentary materials will prove to be problematic. This will be particularly so where the legal adviser does not enjoy access to a properly stocked library. The availability of Oireachtas debates and other relevant materials on the internet[360] represents an improvement but that development is not such as to urge a more liberal approach to the admissibility of parliamentary materials.

---

[358] Edgar (ed), *Craies on Statute Law* (7th edn, 1971).

[359] *Crilly v Farrington* [2001] 3 IR 251 at 291–292.

[360] See http://oireachtasdebates.oireachtas.ie/.

[14.186] Even where lawyers have access to parliamentary materials, as would be the case for most practising barristers who subscribe to the Law Library, it does not follow that it is reasonable to expect consultation of parliamentary materials, since that would extend the research time involved, with the accompanying expense to clients. In addition, there is a fear that valuable court time will be wasted by needless reference to parliamentary materials.

[14.187] On the other hand, it might have been argued that these pragmatic concerns were over-estimated. The annotations in *Irish Current Law Statutes Annotated* often refer to the relevant portions of the parliamentary proceedings, thus providing a reasonably convenient point of reference in respect of post-1984 statutes. Moreover, a lawyer is expected to consult and read the relevant case law concerning the interpretation of the provision, a task which is not necessarily less onerous than that of consulting the relevant parliamentary materials. Of course, from the perspective of the authority they enjoy, a crucial distinction is to be drawn between case law, which has the force of law, and parliamentary materials which at most can provide guidance to the interpreter.

[14.188] Many of the foregoing concerns were raised in the judgments in *Crilly v Farrington*.[361] In that case the Supreme Court refused to take account of the Oireachtas debates surrounding the enactment of s 2(1) of the Health (Amendment) Act 1986, the particular provision that fell to be interpreted. Instead, the court relied on the traditional methods of interpretation, which included a consideration of the provision's legislative, as opposed to parliamentary, history. The court was unanimous in rejecting the use of Oireachtas debates as an aid to interpretation. A number of considerations drove the court to this conclusion. It was suggested that if such material were admissible it would undermine the traditional canons of interpretation and the presumptions that have been developed by the courts. The potential adverse consequences for the Oireachtas were also considered important: there was a fear that members of Oireachtas, especially those promoting a measure, would feel constrained in their choice of language when the 'cut and thrust' of parliamentary debate favours a freer debating style.[362] In any event, the ministerial speech that introduced the Bill could not be considered a reliable guide to intention of the Oireachtas as such statements are not 'sufficiently neutral'[363] and the measure might have been amended significantly during the course of its passage through the Oireachtas.[364] The consequences for the courts were also considered relevant. If parliamentary material were admissible it would increase legal costs since lawyers would be obliged to research such materials when advising clients[365] and such

---

[361] *Crilly v Farrington* [2001] 3 IR 251.
[362] [2001] 3 IR 251 at 297 *per* Murray J.
[363] [2001] 3 IR 251 at 301 *per* Murray J.
[364] [2001] 3 IR 251 at 282 *per* Denham J.
[365] [2001] 3 IR 251 at 311 *per* Fennelly J.

material would be introduced in every contentious case.[366] The general thrust of the court's views is captured in the judgment of Murray J:

"The intent of the Oireachtas is imputed to it on the basis of the text of an Act adopted and promulgated as law in accordance with the Constitution.

Any proposal that the courts should go behind the constitutionally expressed will of the Oireachtas so as to rely on the statement of one member of one House, whatever his or her status, must be approached with circumspection and constitutional prudence. To go behind a will so expressed so as to look at such statement and impute an intent expressed by one member to the Oireachtas as a whole may, and I use that word guardedly, risk compromising the legislative process and the role of other members of the Oireachtas. Thus the question as to whether reliance should be placed by the courts on the parliamentary history of an Act raises considerations which in my view render the issue *sui generis* and not to be equated with reliance on other external aids such as reports of commissions which give a contextual background to legislative history. The use of such external aids has a different provenance, gives rise to different considerations and although they too must be relied on with circumspection, we are not concerned with them in this case.

It is in the context of the constitutional role of the courts to ascertain the will of the Oireachtas as constitutionally expressed that the question of judicial policy concerning recourse to parliamentary history, and in particular statements of a minister or other member of the House, for interpretative purposes falls to be considered. I think it can be fairly said that the primary duty of the Houses of the Oireachtas is to express the legislative will in the constitutionally prescribed manner in an Act which they adopt. Such a duty would reflect the universal constitutional principle in a democratic society: men, and women, may intend what they will; but it is only the laws which they enact which bind us.

Of course the Oireachtas may, subject to the Constitution, adopt by law rules governing the interpretation of statutes which are the fruits of the legislative process ...

A minister or promoter of a Bill may feel constrained when intervening in the cut and thrust of parliamentary debate to choose *her* or *his* words carefully for fear of giving rise to any misunderstanding as to her or his intent on a subsequent parsing of those words in a court of law. On the other hand it has been suggested that a clear and deliberate statement on the part of the minister or other promoter of the Bill as to the purpose for which it is been introduced could be a helpful aid to interpretation. Apart from other considerations which I will refer to, there is the foreseeable risk that the promoter of the Bill would feel constrained to make statements calculated specifically for interpretative purposes, something which has occurred in the United States. Even if a minister did not feel so constrained, the fact remains that ministers or other promoters of Bills do routinely inform the House in question of the general purposes of the Bill and the reasons for its introduction. Statements, calculated or otherwise, promoting a Bill passing through a politically contentious process would not necessarily constitute a neutral aid to construction. If the courts were to go behind an Act and look at the proceedings in the Houses of the Oireachtas and statements made by the promoter of a Bill for the purposes of interpreting the Act adopted, it would place an onus on other members of the Oireachtas to examine his or her spoken words for its implications

---

[366] [2001] 3 IR 251 at 298 *per* Murray J.

as to the ultimate effect of a Bill when it becomes law. They would have to do so from a perspective which they have never had to do and which does not currently arise.

As the legislative organ of State the Oireachtas has, subject to the Constitution, exclusive responsibility for the conduct of its proceedings so I refer to these general considerations primarily for the purpose of indicating that any decision to rely on statements made in one or other House as an aid to the construction of an Act could have implications for the conduct of the legislative process which is another reason for the courts to consider this question with prudence ...

On practical grounds alone this is too broad a portal through which to allow parliamentary material to enter into consideration in the interpretation of Acts of the Oireachtas. It would seem unavoidable that recourse to ministerial statements to confirm, contradict, verify, strengthen, qualify, even nuance a particular construction argued for would enter into most if not every contentious case. Account would have to be taken of amendments in one or other House subsequent to a statement. It would be a foolhardy if not negligent lawyer who didn't at least trawl through the parliamentary interventions of ministers in one House or both in order to check whether there was something which supported one interpretation or another. Similar considerations could arise when lawyers, accountants or other professionals are advising clients, private or corporate, concerning the implications and effect of an Act. This would be a complex and burdensome exercise—evaluating what weight the courts might attach to this or that sentence or passage in a minister's speech. It would add to legal costs. It is difficult to envisage that a ministerial statement could always be divorced from the context of a debate as a whole particularly if a different perception of the Bill was expressed by other members who nonetheless supported the passage of the Bill. That is a situation that one could not exclude. The option of having recourse to ministerial statements generally in the interpretation of Acts must at least risk introducing uncertainty where none may have existed ... At best, recourse to ministerial statements as an aid to interpretation would have limited value in a limited number of cases. The disadvantages of permitting recourse to ministerial statements greatly outweigh potential benefits. For these reasons I think the submissions on behalf of the appellants should fail. They should also fail for other reasons.

The disadvantages concerning complexity and uncertainty, to which reliance generally on ministerial statements could give rise would not, to my mind, be greatly ameliorated by limiting such reliance only to cases where there is ambiguity in the statute or the need to avoid a patent absurdity and the ministerial statement is clear and unequivocal. First of all I would recall that there are a wide range of canons of construction and presumptions available which are more sophisticated than neutral aids to the resolution of such interpretative problems. Also available are methods of interpretation such as the purposive or teleological approach to statutory construction."[367]

[14.189] McGuinness J's explanation in her concurring judgment was succinct and to the point:

"In this short *addendum* to the judgments of my learned colleagues, I wish to stress that I entirely share Murray J's concerns as to the constitutional impropriety of blurring the

---

[367] [2001] 3 IR 251 at 296–299.

distinction between the legislative task of the Oireachtas in forming and enacting the law and the judicial task of the courts in interpreting the law as it has been enacted.

Apart from these concerns of principle, it seems to me that there are very real practical difficulties in the way of such reliance on either ministerial statements or parliamentary debates in the construction of statutes.

The process of legislation by the Oireachtas is essentially collective. It is the Oireachtas *as a whole* which legislates. It would in my view be a misleading oversimplification of this process to rely, in interpreting a statute, on ministerial statements alone. Particularly in the case of more complex statutes, which pass through a lengthy committee stage, contributions come from all sides of both Houses of the Oireachtas. The statute as finally enacted may well have been extensively amended and may differ crucially from the Bill as introduced by the minister's initial introductory statement at the second stage. For the courts to rely on ministerial statements in interpreting statutes would not, therefore, reflect the will of the Oireachtas as a whole. Yet to search the entire parliamentary debates for indications as to the proper interpretation of statutes would be both complex, time consuming and extremely difficult in practice …

The actual issue between the parties in the present proceedings can be decided without this court making a decision in principle on the use of parliamentary proceedings as an aid to the construction of statutes. I am, however, clear in my view that in the present proceedings the statement of the minister should not have been considered. The issue of admissibility of parliamentary debates is of considerable importance and will, no doubt, arise again in the future. As a matter of general judicial policy, however, I share the view of Murray J that at present insufficient grounds have been established for abolishing or gratifying the established exclusionary rule."[368]

[14.190] In reaching its decision in *Crilly v Farrington* the Supreme Court observed that the statement by Costello P in *People (DPP) v McDonagh*[369] that Oireachtas debates are admissible was *obiter*. The Court also distinguished the position outlined in *Bourke v Attorney General*[370] where the *travaux préparatoires* to an international treaty were consulted: 'international treaties are a different and specific matter.'[371] The court expressed its views on the question of using Oireachtas debates as an aid to interpretation in forthright terms but it stopped short of establishing an unequivocal rule that such materials may never be consulted: instead the proposition was expressed in relation to the present case. By the same token the court did not formally overrule the earlier decisions, such as *Wavin Pipes*, that considered Oireachtas debates. Nevertheless, the force of the judgments in *Crilly v Farrington* is such that there can be few doubts as to the current position in Irish law. It remains to be seen whether that position might change in the future.

---

368 [2001] 3 IR 251 at 302–303.
369 *People (DPP) v McDonagh* [1996] 1 IR 565.
370 *Bourke v Attorney General* [1972] IR 36.
371 [2001] 3 IR 251 at 282, *per* Denham J.

Dictionaries and reference works

[14.191] The third proposition in Henchy J's judgment in *Inspector of Taxes v Kiernan*[372] is that the ordinary meaning of a word should be derived primarily from the judge's own experience of its use. Dictionaries and other sources should be employed only when 'alternative meanings, regional usages or other obliquities are shown to cast doubt on the singularity of its ordinary meaning'[373] or where the meaning of the word might have changed since the enactment of the Act.

[14.192] This reluctance to resort to dictionaries was not shared by the Supreme Court in *Rahill v Brady*[374] where reference was made to the *Shorter Oxford Dictionary*. Ó Dálaigh CJ took the view that:[375]

"… reference to the better dictionaries does afford either by definition or illustration some guide to the use of a term in a statute … dictionaries are not to be taken as authoritative exponents of the meaning of words used in Acts of Parliament, it is nevertheless a well-known rule of courts of law that words should be taken in their ordinary sense and we are therefore sent for instruction to these books; *per* Lord Coleridge in *R v Peters*."[376]

Based on current practice this is a more accurate statement of the law, as dictionaries are frequently cited and used in statutory interpretation.[377]

---

[372] *Inspector of Taxes v Kiernan* [1981] IR 117.

[373] [1981] IR 117 at 122.

[374] *Rahill v Brady* [1971] IR 69 at 82.

[375] [1971] IR 69 at 82.

[376] *R v Peters* (1886) 16 QBD 636 at 641.

[377] See, eg, *Flynn v Denieffe* [1989] IR 722; *McGurrin v The Campion Publications Ltd* (15 December 1993, unreported), HC; *Trustees of Kinsale Yacht Club v Commissioner of Valuation* [1993] ILRM 393; *Carl Stuart Ltd v Biotrace Ltd* [1993] ILRM 633; *Shannon Regional Fisheries Board v An Bord Pleanála* [1994] 3 IR 449; *Keane v An Bord Pleanála* [1997] 1 IR 184; *Maher v An Bord Pleanála* [1999] 2 ILRM 198.

Chapter 15

The Constitution and its Interpretation

[1]   Introduction 711
[2]   The 1937 Constitution 712
[3]   Fundamental Rights and Constitutional Judicial Review 723
[4]   Principles of Constitutional Interpretation 752
[5]   Report of Constitution Review Group and Reports of Oireachtas
      Committee on Constitution 776
[6]   The Constitution and the European Convention on Human Rights 779

[1]   INTRODUCTION

[15.01] In this chapter, we discuss the provisions of the Constitution of Ireland 1937, Bunreacht na hÉireann,[1] which replaced the 1922 Constitution of the Irish Free State.[2] The 1937 Constitution provides, in effect, that it is superior to the sources of law described in previous chapters, namely common law and legislation. In particular, the High Court and Supreme Court (and the Court of Appeal which, it is expected, is to be established in 2014[3]) are empowered to declare invalid any common law or legislative rule which is in conflict with the text of the 1937 Constitution. In this respect, we discuss the distinctive principles of constitutional interpretation and the development in recent years of significant case law concerning the fundamental rights which the Constitution recognises and supports. We end the chapter by considering the effect on constitutional law of the incorporation into Irish law of the rights in the European Convention on Human Rights brought about by the European Convention on Human Rights Act 2003.

---

[1]   The leading texts are: Casey, *Constitutional Law in Ireland* (3rd edn, 2000); Doyle, *Constitutional Law: Texts, Cases and Materials* (2008); Forde, *Constitutional Law of Ireland* (3rd edn, 2011); Hogan and Whyte, *JM Kelly: The Irish Constitution* (4th edn, 2003); and Morgan, *Constitutional Law of Ireland* (2nd edn, 1990) (the latter focusing on the institutions of state only).

[2]   See para **2.58**.

[3]   On the establishment of the Court of Appeal see para **4.34**ff.

[2] THE 1937 CONSTITUTION

[15.02] As discussed elsewhere,[4] the text of the 1937 Constitution has been described as both 'law and manifesto', since it contains not only statements of basic legal principles but also general aspirations. In the original version, Article 2 asserted that the 'national territory' of Ireland includes the entire island of Ireland, a provision that was to remain politically controversial until its alteration in 1998.[5] Other provisions contained overtly religious statements which appeared to reflect the religious teachings of the Roman Catholic Church to the exclusion of other religious faiths and the views of those with no religious beliefs.

[15.03] The opening words of the Preamble recite that the Constitution is enacted by the people of Ireland 'In the Name of the Most Holy Trinity'. Article 41, which contains guarantees of support for the family in society, has been criticised for its statement that women should not be required 'to engage in labour to the neglect of their duties in the home' and for the prohibition on divorce that was not removed until 1995.[6] In this chapter, we discuss the overall ethos of the Constitution and its impact on constitutional judicial review.[7]

Right to self-determination

[15.04] Not all provisions of the 1937 Constitution contain controversial elements. For example, Article 1 proclaims a simple and clear declaration of independence and right to self-determination, which is common to many constitutional texts:

> "The Irish nation hereby affirms its inalienable, indefeasible, and sovereign right to choose its own form of Government, to determine its relations with other nations, and to develop its life, political, economic and cultural, in accordance with its own genius and traditions."

This clear assertion was to be expected from a constitutional text seeking to mark out a new 'Basic Law' (*Bunreacht*).

The national territory: the 'original' Articles 2 and 3

[15.05] More controversial, however, were the original versions of Articles 2 and 3, which remained in the Constitution until 1998 when they were replaced as a result of the Good Friday Agreement. The original text of Article 2 contained an assertion that the national territory of Ireland 'consists of the whole island of Ireland, its islands and the territorial seas'. This claim was slightly modified by the original text of Article 3 which provided that '[p]ending the re-integration of the national territory' the laws enacted by the Parliament established by the 1937 Constitution 'shall have the like area and extent

---

4 See para **2.78**.
5 Nineteenth Amendment of the Constitution Act 1998; see further, para **15.11**.
6 Fifteenth Amendment of the Constitution Act 1996: see para **15.150**. See also Scannell, 'The Constitution and the Role of Women' in Farrell (ed), *De Valera's Constitution and Ours* (1988).
7 See paras **15.45–15.195**.

of application as the laws of Saorstát Éireann and the like extra-territorial effect'. This appeared to limit the laws of Ireland to the 26 counties that constituted the Irish Free State.[8] However, this modification was itself stated to be 'without prejudice to the right of the Parliament and the Government established by this Constitution to exercise jurisdiction over the whole' of the national territory.

[15.06] Two issues thus arose concerning the original Articles 2 and 3: whether they involved political aspirations only or had a legal significance; and whether the Oireachtas could enact laws applicable in the six counties of Northern Ireland. On the second point the courts were in agreement that the Oireachtas was prohibited from enacting legislation applicable in Northern Ireland, but quite different views had been expressed on the first point.

[15.07] In *Re the Criminal Law (Jurisdiction) Bill 1975*,[9] the Supreme Court indicated that the original Articles 2 and 3 belonged in the realm of political rhetoric. The court stated:

> [T]he Constitution ... expresses not only legal norms but basic doctrines of social and political theory ... the Constitution contains more than legal rules: it reflects, in part, aspirations and aims and expresses the political theories on which the people acted when they enacted the Constitution.

> One of the theories held in 1937 by a substantial number of people was that a nation, as distinct from a state, had rights; that the people living in what is now described as the Republic of Ireland and in Northern Ireland together formed the Irish Nation; that a nation has a right to unity of territory in some form, be it as a unitary or federal state; and that the Government of Ireland Act 1920, though legally binding, was a violation of that natural right to unity which was superior to positive law.[10]

> This national claim to unity exists not in the legal but in the political order and is one of the rights which are envisaged in Article 2; it is expressly saved by Article 3 which states that the area to which the laws enacted by the parliament established by the Constitution apply.[11]

[15.08] This view of the original text of Articles 2 and 3 was, at first sight, plausible and arguably sensitive to those in Northern Ireland with a Unionist viewpoint who did not share the 'Irish nation' theory referred to by the Supreme Court. However, in *McGimpsey v Ireland*[12] the Supreme Court rejected the view that the original Articles 2 and 3 involved political aspirations only. Finlay CJ stated that the correct interpretation of the original Articles 2 and 3 was as follows:

> "1. The re-integration of the national territory is a constitutional imperative (*cf* Hederman J in *Russell v Fanning*).[13]

---

8   As provided for in the Government of Ireland Act 1920, as amended: see para **2.46**.
9   *Re the Criminal Law (Jurisdiction) Bill 1975* [1977] IR 129.
10   On natural law and positive law, see para **15.152**.
11   [1977] IR 129, 147. The judgment of the court was delivered by O'Higgins CJ.
12   *McGimpsey v Ireland* [1990] 1 IR 110.
13   *Russell v Fanning* [1988] IR 505, 537.

2. Article 2 of the Constitution consists of a declaration of the extent of the national territory as a claim of legal right.

3. Article 3 of the Constitution prohibits, pending the re-integration of the national territory, the enactment of laws with any greater area or extent of application or extra-territorial effect than the laws of Saorstát Éireann and this prohibits the enactment of laws applicable in the counties of Northern Ireland.

4. The restriction imposed by Article 3 pending the re-integration of the national territory in no way derogated from the claim as a legal right to the entire national territory."[14]

[15.09] This interpretation of the original Articles 2 and 3 confirmed that the territorial application of legislation enacted by the Oireachtas was limited to the 26 counties of Ireland. Moreover, in *McGimpsey*[15] the Supreme Court dismissed a challenge to the Anglo-Irish Agreement 1985,[16] Art 1 of which provided that the United Kingdom and Irish governments:

"(a) affirm that any change in the status of Northern Ireland would only come about with the consent of a majority of the people of Northern Ireland;

(b) recognise that the present wish of a majority of the people of Northern Ireland is for no change in the status of Northern Ireland ..."

[15.10] The Supreme Court concluded that these provisions were not in conflict with the constitutional imperative to seek the reintegration of the national territory, particularly since Article 29 committed the state to peaceful settlement of international disputes.[17] However, the view that reintegration of the national territory was a 'constitutional imperative' and that Article 3 was a 'claim of legal right' continued to attract considerably more publicity than this conclusion. Amendments to Articles 2 and 3 remained a key element in discussions during the 1990s concerning future political relationships on the island of Ireland and the relationships between the two jurisdictions in Ireland and that in the United Kingdom. The culmination, in 1998, was the Good Friday Agreement.

The Good Friday Agreement and the current Articles 2 and 3[18]

[15.11] The British–Irish Agreement signed in Belfast on Good Friday, 10 April 1998, committed the United Kingdom and Irish governments to implement the provisions of the Multi-Party Agreement also signed in Belfast on the same date and which was annexed to the British–Irish Agreement. The Multi-Party Agreement, commonly known as the Good Friday or Belfast Agreement, was the result of two years of discussions

---

14   [1990] 1 IR 110, 119. The other members of the court concurred in this interpretation.

15   [1990] 1 IR 110.

16   The Anglo–Irish Agreement 1985 was replaced by the Belfast Agreement 1998, which led to the approval of the new Articles 2 and 3.

17   See generally para **16.98**.

18   See Humphreys, 'Constitutional Contradictions: Accommodating Multiple Identities After the Good Friday Agreement' in Carolan and Doyle, *The Irish Constitution: Governance and Values* (2008), pp 114–120.

between the political parties in Northern Ireland and the two governments, chaired by former US Senator and federal judge George Mitchell. These discussions aimed at agreeing a comprehensive framework for the so-called three strands: the future governance of Northern Ireland, its relationship with the rest of the United Kingdom and its relationship with Ireland (which for convenience will be referred to as the Republic of Ireland[19] below where necessary).

[15.12] A number of provisions of the Multi-Party Agreement necessitated amendments to the Constitution, in particular Articles 2 and 3, in order to recognise on a formal basis the new relationships on the island of Ireland.[20] The new versions of Articles 2 and 3 of the Constitution, which came into effect in 1999 when the Northern Ireland executive established under the Multi-Party Agreement took office, involved a major recasting of the constitutional relationship between (the Republic of) Ireland and Northern Ireland.

[15.13] The claim in the original Article 2 that the national territory of Ireland (the Republic of Ireland) comprised the whole island of Ireland, including Northern Ireland, was replaced by a recognition of the reality that Northern Ireland forms part of the United Kingdom of Great Britain and Northern Ireland and is a separate jurisdiction from the Republic of Ireland. As Hogan and Whyte note, 'the focus of attention in the new provisions shifts from a definition of national territory to an attempt to define the nation by reference to its people'.[21] The acceptance in the original version of Article 3 that the laws of the Republic of Ireland did not apply in Northern Ireland was replaced by provisions dealing with cross-border institutions established under the two Good Friday Belfast Agreements.

[15.14] In addition to the establishment of the Northern Ireland executive, the Multi-Party and the British–Irish Agreements envisaged the establishment of a number of cross-border (extra-territorial) institutions:

  (a) a North–South Ministerial Council, that is a council comprising Ministers from the Northern Ireland executive formed after the Multi-Party Agreement and Ministers from the Republic of Ireland;

  (b) implementation bodies implementing on an all-island and cross-border basis policies agreed by that Council;

  (c) a British–Irish Council; and

  (d) a British–Irish Intergovernmental Conference.

---

[19] On the distinction between 'Ireland' and 'the Republic of Ireland' see para **15.30**.

[20] See Ryan, 'The Ian Paisley Question: Irish Citizenship and Northern Ireland' (2003) 10(1) DULJ 145.

[21] Hogan and Whyte, *JM Kelly: The Irish Constitution* (4th edn, 2003), p 71.

[15.15] The British-Irish Agreement Act 1999 gave legislative effect to the provisions concerning the North-South Ministerial Council,[22] the implementation bodies[23] and the British-Irish Council.[24]

[15.16] Article 1 of the British-Irish Agreement also contains the shared understanding of the two governments on constitutional issues in relation to Northern Ireland. To a large extent, these reflected the principles contained in the 1985 Anglo–Irish Agreement, whose constitutional validity had been upheld in *McGimpsey v Ireland.*[25] With the entry into force of the British–Irish Agreement in 1999, the 1985 Anglo-Irish Agreement and its associated Anglo–Irish Intergovernmental Conference and Secretariat (the latter located in Northern Ireland, a highly contentious point for Northern Ireland Unionist parties) ceased to exist and was replaced by the institutions established under the 1998 Agreement.

[15.17] Article 2 now reads:

"It is the entitlement and birthright of every person born in the island of Ireland, which includes its islands and seas, to be part of the Irish Nation. That is also the entitlement of all persons otherwise qualified in accordance with law to be citizens of Ireland. Furthermore, the Irish nation cherishes its special affinity with people of Irish ancestry living abroad who share its cultural identity and heritage."

This post-1998 Article 2 contains three elements:

(a)   a statement that it is the entitlement and birthright of every person born in the island of Ireland to be part of the Irish nation;

(b)   a statement that this is also the entitlement of persons otherwise qualified in accordance with law to be citizens of Ireland; and

(c)   a statement that the nation cherishes its affinity with people of Irish ancestry living abroad.

[15.18] The first of these elements effectively substitutes a statement defining the Irish nation in terms of territory (the whole island of Ireland) with a statement identifying an entitlement to membership of the nation and to citizenship of the state. It places on a constitutional basis the right of every person born in the island of Ireland, including persons born in Northern Ireland, to Irish nationality and hence citizenship; this was already provided for on a statutory basis in the Irish Nationality and Citizenship Act 1956. Because this post-1998 Article 2 is based on the terms of the British–Irish

---

[22]   The North–South Ministerial Council deals with the areas of executive responsibility devolved to the Northern Ireland executive.

[23]   The implementation bodies deal with: food safety, trade and business development, language, aquaculture and marine, inland waterways and special EU programmes.

[24]   The British–Irish Council deals with areas of mutual concern between the UK and Irish governments not dealt with by the North–South Ministerial Council or the implementation bodies.

[25]   *McGimpsey v Ireland* [1990] 1 IR 110: see para **15.08**.

Agreement, the United Kingdom government formally recognised the state's assertion of the right of persons born anywhere in Ireland to be regarded as Irish citizens.

[15.19] The post-1998 Article 2 was discussed by the Supreme Court in *AO v Minister for Justice*.[26] In the Supreme Court, McGuinness and Hardiman JJ stated that the post-1998 Article 2 had altered the nature of the entitlement to citizenship for everyone born in Ireland from a statutory right to a constitutional right.[27] This led to concern that some might re-locate to Ireland with the intention of having children who would be Irish citizens. As a consequence, following a referendum in 2004, new Articles 9.2.1° and 9.2.2° were inserted into the Irish Constitution, which provide:

"1° Notwithstanding any other provision of this Constitution, a person born in the island of Ireland, which includes its islands and seas, who does not have, at the time of the birth of that person, at least one parent who is an Irish citizen or entitled to be an Irish citizen is not entitled to Irish citizenship or nationality, unless provided for by law.

2° This section shall not apply to persons born before the date of the enactment of this section."

The phrase 'notwithstanding any other provision of this Constitution' means that Article 9 takes precedence over Article 2.[28] The phrase 'unless provided for by law' has allowed the Oireachtas to provide for more far-reaching rights than those contained in Article 9. The Irish Nationality and Citizenship Act 2004 provides that a person born in Ireland to a non-Irish parent, but who has been residing in Ireland for in excess of three out the previous four years is entitled to Irish citizenship.

[15.20] Returning to the post-1998 Article 2 of the Constitution, the second element includes those who are otherwise entitled to citizenship to be regarded as part of the nation; this is a recognition of the increasing plurality of those who live on the island of Ireland. The third element is a constitutional acknowledgement of the national diaspora and it reflects the realities of forced emigration in the past, and the more recent phenomenon towards the end of the 20th century of voluntary emigration by a sizeable number of persons born in Ireland. It recognises the influence of such expatriates on the developments in Northern Ireland and on the wider debate concerning their continued contribution to the state.

[15.21] The post-1998 Article 3 is divided into two sections and reads:

"1. It is the firm will of the Irish Nation, in harmony and friendship, to unite all the people who share the territory of the island of Ireland, in all the diversity of their

[26] *AO v Minister for Justice* [2003] 1 IR 1.

[27] *AO v Minister for Justice* [2003] 1 IR 1. See the comments of McGuinness J at 99–100 and Hardiman J (*obiter*) at 132. See also Doyle, *Constitutional Law: Texts, Cases and Materials*, (2008), pp 4–5 and Hogan and Whyte, *JM Kelly: The Irish Constitution* (4th edn, 2003), pp 74–75.

[28] Doyle, *Constitutional Law: Texts, Cases and Materials* (2008), pp 4–5 and Doyle and Feldman, 'Constitutional Law' in Byrne and Binchy (eds), *Annual Review of Irish Law 2004* (2005).

identities and traditions, recognising that a united Ireland shall be brought about only by peaceful means with the consent of a majority of the people, democratically expressed, in both jurisdictions in the island. Until then, the laws enacted by the Parliament established by this Constitution shall have the like area and extent of application as the laws enacted by the Parliament that existed immediately before the coming into operation of this Constitution.

2. Institutions with executive powers and functions that are shared between those jurisdictions may be established by their respective responsible authorities for stated purposes and may exercise powers and functions in respect of all or any part of the island."

[15.22] Taking these two sections separately, Article 3.1 contains the following elements:

(a) a statement that it is the firm will of the Irish nation, in harmony and friendship, to unite all the people who share the territory of the island of Ireland;

(b) a recognition of the diversity of the identities and traditions of the people who share the island;

(c) a recognition that a united Ireland shall be brought about only by peaceful means with the consent of a majority of the people, democratically expressed, in both the jurisdictions in the island; and

(d) a recognition that until Irish unity comes about, the area of jurisdiction of the State is the same as that which existed prior to 1937.

[15.23] Provision for the state's extra-territorial jurisdiction, which was found in the old Article 3, has been 'moved' to Article 29, a more appropriate 'home' since Article 29 deals with international relations generally.

[15.24] By comparison with the original Article 3, the first three elements of the post-1998 Article 3.1 are entirely new. These three elements in the post-1998 Article 3.1 have the following effect. They recognise that the establishment of a unitary state on the island of Ireland (in nationalist terms, the reunification of the national territory) can come about only by peaceful means and with the consent of a majority of the people in both the existing jurisdictions. Thus, the current status of Northern Ireland within the United Kingdom is expressly recognised for the first time in the Irish Constitution and this status will continue while a majority of its population wishes this to be the case. A corollary is that the establishment of a unitary state on the island of Ireland can be brought about with the consent of a majority of people, democratically expressed, in both parts of the island. It also describes for the first time the manner in which unity might be achieved.[29]

[15.25] The fourth element of the post-1998 Article 3.1 involves a complete recasting of the original Article 3. The wording reflected the recommendations of the All-Party Committee on the Constitution (1967), whose membership included the former

---

[29] Hogan and Whyte, *JM Kelly: The Irish Constitution* (4th edn, 2003), p 75.

Taoiseach, Seán Lemass, who had been responsible for an attempted rapprochement with the then Northern Ireland government in the 1960s. The changes effected by the new Article 3.1 are substantial. In particular:

- the original Article 3 contained no recognition of the existence, let alone the separate status, of Northern Ireland;

- the original Article 3 contained no acknowledgement that the current position was that a majority of the people of Northern Ireland wished to remain part of the United Kingdom;

- the original Article 3 contained no reference to the principle of obtaining the consent of the people of Northern Ireland to establishing a unitary state on the island of Ireland; and

- the original Article 3 contained no reference to achieving a unitary state by peaceful means, though this was implied by the Supreme Court in *McGimpsey v Ireland*. [30]

[15.26] Turning to the second part of the post-1998 Article 3, Article 3.2, this is also new. This enabled the creation of institutions with executive powers and functions that are shared between the two jurisdictions on the island of Ireland and enable them to exercise powers and functions in respect of all or any part of the island. The focus in the post-1998 Article 3.2 is to enable the exercise of executive power in the island as a whole, notwithstanding the limiting provisions in the post-1998 Article 3.1 on the exercise of jurisdiction outside the Republic of Ireland.

[15.27] There is a link between Article 3.2 and the post-1998 Article 29.7.2°, which reads:

"Any institution established by or under the [British–Irish] Agreement may exercise the powers and functions thereby conferred on it in respect of all or any part of the island of Ireland notwithstanding any other provision of this Constitution conferring a like power or function on any person or any organ of State appointed under or created or established by or under this Constitution. Any power or function conferred on such an institution in relation to the settlement or resolution of disputes or controversies may be in addition to or in substitution for any like power or function conferred by this Constitution on any such person or organ of State as aforesaid."

[15.28] This permits all-Ireland institutions to operate in the Republic of Ireland notwithstanding the existing constitutional provisions conferring legislative, executive and judicial powers exclusively on the organs of government established under the Constitution. In particular, where disputes arising from the exercise of the North–South bodies require mediation, this may be done without infringing the exclusive jurisdiction of the courts under Article 34 to administer justice.

---

[30]   *McGimpsey v Ireland* [1990] 1 IR 110: see para **15.08**.

[15.29] The final component of the constitutional changes made after the Good Friday Agreement is the insertion of a new Article 29.8. This reads:

"The State may exercise extra-territorial jurisdiction in accordance with the generally recognised principles of international law."

This effects a relocation of the provision on extra-territoriality from the original Article 3 to Article 29, where it more properly belongs. Again, this proposal is in line with recommendations of the *Report of the All-Party Committee on the Constitution* (1967). In the original Article 3, the provision seemed merely to operate as an exception to the limitation of the jurisdiction of the state with respect to Northern Ireland. The relocation to Article 29 clarifies that the exercise of this jurisdiction must be in accordance with the generally recognised principles of international law.

Ireland and the Republic of Ireland

[15.30] Article 4 of the 1937 Constitution provides:

"The name of the State is *Éire*, or, in the English language, Ireland."[31]

The text of Art 4 has given rise to some difficulties concerning the name of the state,[32] but in the English language the correct name is 'Ireland'.[33]

Article 5 provides:

"Ireland is a sovereign, independent, democratic State."

[15.31] While the Constitution created, to all intents and purposes, a republic,[34] there is no explicit reference to this in the constitutional text. By 1936, the sole remaining function of the British Crown concerned the accreditation of foreign diplomats, acting on the advice of the Executive Council of the Irish Free State under the Executive Authority (External Relations) Act 1936. Article 29.4.1° of the 1937 Constitution provides that the executive power of the state in connection with external relations shall be exercised by the government. Thus, effective power rests with the government.

[15.32] However, Article 29.4.2° provides that the government is empowered (though not required) to continue the position as at 1936 by adopting any 'method of procedure used or adopted ... by the members of any group or league of nations with which the State is or becomes associated for the purpose of international co-operation in matters of common concern.'[35] Between 1937 and 1948, Irish diplomats continued to be accredited

---

31 The Irish language version reads: 'Éire is ainm don Stát, nó sa Sacs-Bhéarla, Ireland'.
32 On the difficulties with the use of the word 'Éire' in the English language text, see paras **2.95**.
33 To simplify matters, the *Report of the Constitution Review Group* (Pn 2632, 1996) (see para **15.196**), p 11, recommended that the English language text of Article 4 be amended to read thus: 'The name of the State is Ireland,' with the Irish language text to read thus: 'Éire is ainm don Stát.
34 There are references to republican rhetoric in the judgment of Walsh J in *Byrne v Ireland* [1972] IR 241: para **15.38**.
35 See para **16.100**.

in the name of the Crown acting on the advice of the government. During this time, the state also continued its membership of the British Commonwealth, inherited from the Irish Free State.

[15.33] In 1948, the then government announced its intention to withdraw from the Commonwealth. The Republic of Ireland Act 1948 gave effect to this decision. Section 2 of the 1948 Act provides:

"It is hereby declared that the description of the State shall be the Republic of Ireland."[36]

This 'description' of the state as the Republic of Ireland does not, of course, amend the name of the state, as contained in Article 4 of the Constitution. Section 3 of the 1948 Act provides that:

"[T]he President, on the authority and on the advice of the Government, may exercise the executive power or any executive function of the State in or in connection with its external relations."

[15.34] While s 3 provided for the formal transfer from the British Crown to the President of the executive power in external relations,[37] it was and remains the government which in practice exercises this power.

Sovereignty of the people and liability of the state

[15.35] The Preamble to the Constitution provides, in part:

"We, the people of Éire ... Do hereby adopt, enact and give to ourselves this Constitution."[38]

This enacting formula marks a clear break from the 1922 Constitution where, from an Irish legal perspective,[39] the Third Dáil enacted that Constitution as a Constituent Assembly. The 1937 Constitution ensured that the People of Ireland were the source of all legal authority. As with Articles 2 and 3 of the Constitution, this enacting formula is not simply a matter of political rhetoric but has important practical implications. Article 5 provides that 'Ireland is a sovereign, independent, democratic State' and Article 6.1 states:

"All powers of government, legislative, executive and judicial, derive, under God, from the people, whose right it is to designate the rulers of the State and, in final appeal, to decide all questions of national policy, according to the requirements of the common good."

---

[36] The 1948 Act was enacted in both the English and Irish languages; in the Irish language text of s 2, 'Republic of Ireland' reads 'Poblacht na hÉireann'.

[37] The 1948 Act also repealed the Executive Authority (External Relations) Act 1936.

[38] The English language version of the Preamble is in italics. The Irish language version was originally published in roman type, but later versions have appeared in italics.

[39] See para **2.71**.

[15.36] The Constitution contains three practical instances of popular sovereignty: the power to elect their political representatives to Dáil Éireann in a general election; the power to elect the President; and the power to amend the Constitution itself.

[15.37] Another aspect of the sovereignty of the people emerged in *Byrne v Ireland*.[40] In that case, the plaintiff had suffered personal injuries when she fell into a trench which had been dug by employees of what was then the Department of Posts and Telegraphs. The evidence seemed to indicate that, in refilling the trench, these employees had been negligent and that this was the cause of the plaintiff's injuries. On this basis, the plaintiff appeared to have a simple task in claiming damages against the Minister for Posts and Telegraphs.[41] However, it was argued that, since those alleged to have been negligent were employees of the state, the latter was immune from any claim on the basis that it had inherited the pre-1922 sovereign immunity from suit of the Crown and its servants.

[15.38] While this was accepted in the High Court, the Supreme Court held that any such immunity had not been carried over into Irish law under the 1937 Constitution. Thus the state was held vicariously liable for the injuries sustained by the plaintiff. The court traced the historical development of the concept of sovereign immunity, and also explained how the Constitution created an entirely new legal order in the state. This explains, for example, the view expressed in the judgment of Walsh J (which reflected the views of four of the five Supreme Court judges in *Byrne*) that decisions of English courts might not be relevant to an understanding of the principles contained in the 1937 Constitution. Nonetheless, English precedent continues to play a significant role in the development of Irish law generally.[42]

[15.39] The effect of *Byrne v Ireland* may be described in different ways. In one respect, it merely established that personal injuries cases involving the state should be treated no differently from personal injuries actions involving private individuals. However, the implications of the decision are more profound. In his judgment, Walsh J noted that in the United Kingdom the Crown Proceedings Act 1947 (as amended) regulates claims against the Crown, ministries and government departments. Under s 40 of the 1947 Act, such claims may in general be brought only in respect of liability arising in the United Kingdom. After *Byrne*, no legislation was enacted to regulate the position of the state in civil proceedings so that the question of liability in respect of acts occurring outside the state is a matter for the Irish courts to determine.

[15.40] In *Ryan v Ireland*,[43] the plaintiff had been on active service with the Irish Army in Lebanon as part of a United Nations peacekeeping force when his post came under mortar attack from hostile forces. He instituted proceedings against the Department of Defence, claiming that there had been a failure to protect his position adequately against such attacks. The High Court and Supreme Court held that the Department owed a duty

---

40   *Byrne v Ireland* [1972] IR 241.
41   On negligence generally, see para **12.144**.
42   See para **12.84**.
43   *Ryan v Ireland* [1989] IR 177.

of care to the plaintiff while he was on active service and that, although the conditions in the Lebanon were not like those of a factory or other 'ordinary' place of work, they were in breach of that duty of care.[44]

[15.41] The *Ryan* case was thus dealt with solely on the basis of judge-made principles. A comparable claim in the United Kingdom might not proceed to court, arising from restrictions on claims against the British Ministry of Defence contained in the Crown Proceedings Act 1947, as amended by the Crown Proceedings (Armed Forces) Act 1987. In this respect, *Byrne v Ireland* introduced a dramatic change in the liability of the state in tort.

[15.42] In *Webb v Ireland*,[45] the High Court and Supreme Court affirmed the central conclusion in *Byrne* that Crown immunities or prerogatives did not survive the enactment of the Constitution. In *Webb*, the court held that the prerogative concerning treasure trove had not been carried forward. However, the court also held that in certain instances the Constitution substituted new versions of the old prerogatives and in the case of ancient treasure, the court held that these became the property of the People of Ireland. *Webb* indicates, therefore, that the pre-1922 prerogatives may in some instances be transformed into 'constitutional' variants.

[15.43] It remains to be seen whether other aspects of the royal prerogative were carried over in a new form into Irish law,[46] such as the power to establish entities by royal charter, as was originally the case with the Honorable Society of the King's Inns,[47] or the power to grant letters patent to senior counsel.[48] The Executive Powers (Consequential Provisions) Act 1937, enacted after the 1937 Constitution had been approved by referendum but before it came into effect, empowers the government to adapt any pre-1922 charters and letters patent by substituting the government for the Crown.[49]

[3] FUNDAMENTAL RIGHTS AND CONSTITUTIONAL JUDICIAL REVIEW

[15.44] We have noted that the 1937 Constitution may be divided into two components, those Articles which describe the institutions of state and those which describe the fundamental rights of persons. We turn now to discuss these fundamental rights

---

[44] For criticism, see Byrne and Binchy, *Annual Review of Irish Law 1989* (1990), pp 410–418.

[45] *Webb v Ireland* [1988] IR 353.

[46] See Kelly, 'Hidden Treasure and the Constitution' (1988) 10 DULJ (ns) 5; Morgan, 'Constitutional Interpretation: Three Cautionary Tales' (1988) 10 DULJ (ns) 24; Hogan and Whyte, *JM Kelly: The Irish Constitution* (4th edn, 2003), pp 2113–2116.

[47] See para **3.78**.

[48] See para **3.100**.

[49] In *Geoghegan v Institute of Chartered Accountants in Ireland* [1995] 3 IR 86, the Royal Charter of the Institute of Chartered Accountants in Ireland, as amended in 1966 by an Act of the Oireachtas, was upheld as constitutionally valid: see para **4.16**.

provisions and the connected power of the courts to require the executive and legislature to comply with these provisions by means of constitutional judicial review.

Restrictions on law-making authority of Oireachtas

[15.45] The 1937 Constitution places limits on the legislative authority of the Oireachtas. Article 15.2.1° appears to confer unlimited authority on the Oireachtas by providing:

"The sole and exclusive power of making laws for the State is hereby vested in the Oireachtas: no other legislative authority has power to make laws for the State."

However, this must be read in conjunction with Article 15.4, which provides:

"1°   The Oireachtas shall not enact any law which is in any respect repugnant to this Constitution or any provision thereof.

2°   Every law enacted by the Oireachtas which is in any respect repugnant to this Constitution or to any provision thereof, shall, but to the extent only of such repugnancy, be invalid."

[15.46] Article 15.4 deals with laws enacted by the Oireachtas after 1937. For laws in place prior to this, Article 50.1 states:

"Subject to this Constitution and to the extent to which they are not inconsistent therewith, the laws in force in Saorstát Éireann immediately prior to the date of the coming into operation of this Constitution shall continue to be of full force and effect until the same or any of them shall have been repealed or amended by enactment of the Oireachtas."

This ensured continuity with laws enacted prior to the 1937 Constitution, and echoes Article 73 of the 1922 Constitution.[50] However, Article 34 of the 1937 Constitution added a new dimension to these provisions.

The basis for constitutional judicial review

[15.47] Article 34 of the 1937 Constitution expressly confers on the High Court and Supreme Court (and the Court of Appeal which, it is expected, is to be established in 2014[51]) the power to determine whether any law is valid having regard to the Constitution.

[15.48] Article 34.3.2° provides:

"Save as otherwise provided by this Article,[52] the jurisdiction of the High Court shall extend to the question of the validity of any law having regard to the provisions of this Constitution, and no such question shall be raised (whether by pleading, argument or otherwise) in any Court established under this or any other Article of this Constitution other than the High Court, the Court of Appeal[53] or the Supreme Court."

---

50   See para **2.64**.
51   On the establishment of the Court of Appeal see para **4.33*ff***.
52   This refers to the exclusive jurisdiction of the Supreme Court in referrals of Bills under Art 26: see para **5.84**.

[15.49] Article 34.4 and 34.5 provide that the Court of Appeal and the Supreme Court shall subject to such regulations as may be prescribed by law, have appellate jurisdiction from all decisions of the High Court and that no law may be enacted to exclude the Court of Appeal or Supreme Court from having appellate jurisdiction in cases which involve questions as to the validity of any law having regard to the provisions of this Constitution. [54]

[15.50] Thus, the High Court, the Court of Appeal[55] and the Supreme Court have exclusive jurisdiction to determine whether laws are valid or invalid on the ground that they are in conflict with any provision of the Constitution. The most significant provisions in this respect are those which recognise basic or fundamental rights, similar to the Bill of Rights in the Constitution of the United States of America.

Fundamental rights

[15.51] Many of the fundamental rights provisions are contained in Articles 40 to 44 of the 1937 Constitution, though other Articles also confer important rights. Among the rights explicitly recognised and supported by the Constitution are the following:

- retrospective criminal laws are prohibited (Art 15.5);
- sittings of the Oireachtas must, in general, be in public (Art 15.8);
- the right to vote at Dáil elections is given equally to men and women (Art 16.1.2°);
- voting at Dáil elections must be by secret ballot (Art 16.1.4°);
- each Dáil constituency must be equally proportioned in terms of the proportion between Dáil deputies and population (Art 16.2.3°);[56]
- courts must, in general, sit in public (Art 34.1);[57]
- criminal trials must be held in due course of law (Art 38.1);[58]
- trial by jury is in general required in the case of serious offences (Art 38.5);[59]
- all citizens must be held equal before the law, but account may be taken of differences in capacity and of social function (Art 40.1);
- no titles of nobility may be conferred (Art 40.2);
- no person may be deprived of his or her liberty save in accordance with law (Art 40.4);

---

[53] The reference to the Court of Appeal was added by the Thirty-Third Amendment of the Constitution (Court of Appeal) Act 2013, which provided for the establishment of the Court of Appeal and which was approved by a referendum held in 2013: see para **4.33**ff.

[54] See para **4.36**.

[55] On the establishment of the Court of Appeal see para **4.33**ff.

[56] See *Murphy and McGrath v Minister for the Environment* [2007] IEHC 185.

[57] See para **4.24**.

[58] See para **15.65**.

[59] See para **5.90**.

- the dwelling of every citizen is inviolable and may not be entered forcibly, save in accordance with law (Art 40.5);

- liberty to express freely one's convictions and opinions, to assemble peacefully and without arms and to form associations and unions is guaranteed, subject to public order and morality (Art 40.6);

- the institution of the family is recognised as the fundamental unit group of society (Art 41);

- parents have the right to educate their children, subject to limited rights of the state (Art 42);

- the rights of children are recognised (Art 42A);[60]

- the right to own private property is recognised, but may be limited by the state (Art 43); and

- freedom of conscience and the free practice of religion are guaranteed, subject to public order and morality (Art 44).

Many of these provisions echo comparable Articles in the 1922 Constitution, but others, such as those on the family, were new in the 1937 Constitution.

[15.52] It is notable that many rights are subject to certain limitations or qualifying words. In general, it may be said that few constitutional rights are absolute in nature; to some extent, the function of the courts in constitutional judicial review is to determine the precise meaning of the general limits placed on such rights.[61]

Unenumerated personal rights

[15.53] In addition to these rights, Article 40.3 has, since the 1960s, proved a source of an additional tranche of rights. In its original form,[62] Article 40.3 provided:

"1°   The State guarantees in its laws to respect, and, as far as practicable, by its laws to defend and vindicate the personal rights of the citizen.

2°   The State shall, in particular, by its laws protect as best it may from unjust attack and, in the case of injustice done, vindicate the life, person, good name and property rights of every citizen."

[15.54] Between 1937 and 1963, it was not considered that Article 40.3 contained any additional rights beyond those already listed in the remainder of the constitutional text. This view was radically transformed by the decision in *Ryan v Attorney General*,[63] which marked a watershed in the development of constitutional judicial review. The

---

60   To be inserted into the Constitution after a referendum held in 2012. In *Jordan v Attorney General* [2013] IEHC 625, the High Court rejected a challenge to the validity of this referendum under the Referendum Act 1994. At the time of writing (September 2014) this decision is under appeal to the Supreme Court, pending which the constitutional amendment does not take effect.

61   On the interpretative techniques used, see paras **15.127–15.148**.

62   On its amendment, see para **15.175**.

63   *Ryan v Attorney General* [1965] IR 294: see para also **15.134**.

plaintiff challenged the constitutionality of the Health (Fluoridation of Water Supplies) Act 1960. The Act had been introduced after the government had appointed a Consultative Council comprising a representative group of experts to recommend proposals for the treatment of dental caries, particularly in children. Having consulted widely on the matter, the council presented a lengthy report to government, in which it recommended that the addition of limited quantities of sodium fluoride in water supplies (up to four parts per million) would contribute substantially to the elimination of dental caries and that this would greatly outweigh any possible risk to public health, such as a possible risk to older persons of 'brittle bone' due to deposits of fluorine forming on the skeletal frame.

[15.55] On foot of this report, the 1960 Act authorised local authorities to add specified quantities of sodium fluoride to public water supplies in the state. Although the Consultative Council's report had been based on the most recently available scientific data concerning safe levels of fluoride in water, the addition of fluoride to public water supplies was surrounded with some controversy, including the question whether the improvement in children's teeth was justified by the risks for older persons and also the general question of whether such a mass public health measure should be 'imposed' by legislation.

[15.56] As to the constitutional issues raised, the plaintiff in *Ryan* claimed that the 1960 Act infringed a number of her constitutional rights, including the right to bodily integrity. Her counsel defined this as the right to be free from any process imposed by the state which might be harmful to her life or health. The plaintiff faced considerable difficulty in asserting that the 1960 Act was unconstitutional on this ground, since a right to bodily integrity is not mentioned in the text of the Constitution. Nonetheless, it was argued that such a right was implicit in Article 40.3. Crucially, this argument was accepted by the High Court and, on appeal, by the Supreme Court. The plaintiff was ultimately unsuccessful in her challenge to the 1960 Act, since the High Court and Supreme Court held that it had not been established that the 1960 Act was in fact harmful to the plaintiff's health and, in any event, she could filter any fluoride out of her own personal water supply without great expense.

[15.57] The courts also stated that they would be reluctant to interfere with legislation that involved finely balanced judgments on social policy, unless it was clearly established that there was a breach of a constitutional right. This cautious approach to constitutional judicial review has been echoed many times since the *Ryan* case. Nonetheless, the decision in *Ryan* that Article 40.3 contains a guarantee to protect a catalogue of unspecified rights in addition to those expressly referred to in the constitutional text has been of great importance in the development of Irish constitutional law.[64]

[15.58] These unspecified personal rights are referred to as 'unenumerated' rights, since there is no complete list of the rights guaranteed under the general terms of Article

---

[64] See further paras **15.166–15.195**.

40.3.[65] Since the *Ryan* case, the following rights have been recognised as unspecified personal rights:[66]

- the right to bodily integrity: *Ryan v Attorney General*;[67]

- the right not to be tortured or ill-treated: *The State (C) v Frawley*;[68]

- the right to travel within the state: *Ryan v Attorney General*;

- the right to travel outside the state: *The State (M) v Attorney General*;[69]

- the right to communicate: *AG v Paperlink Ltd*;[70]

- the right to marry: *Ryan v Attorney General*;

- the right to marital privacy: *McGee v Attorney General*;[71]

- the right to individual privacy: *Kennedy v Ireland*;[72]

- the right to procreate: *Murray v Ireland*;[73]

- the rights of an unmarried mother concerning her child: *G v An Bord Uchtála*;[74]

- the rights of a child: *Re the Adoption (No 2) Bill 1987*;[75]

- the right to independent domicile and to maintenance: *CM v TM (No 2)*;[76]

- the right of access to the courts: *Macauley v Minister for Posts and Telegraphs*;[77]

- the right to legal representation in certain criminal cases: *The State (Healy) v Donoghue*;[78]

- the right to fair procedures: *Re Haughey*;[79]

- the right to earn a livelihood: *Murphy v Stewart*;[80] and

- the right to know the identity of one's natural mother: *O'T v B*.[81]

---

[65] In *McGee v Attorney General* [1974] IR 284, Henchy J stated that any attempt to compile a full list of such rights would be 'difficult, if not impossible'.

[66] See *Report of the Constitution Review Group* (Pn 2632, 1996), p 246.

[67] *Ryan v Attorney General* [1965] IR 294: see para **15.166**.

[68] *State (C) v Frawley* [1976] IR 365.

[69] *State (M) v Attorney General* [1979] IR 73.

[70] *Attorney General v Paperlink Ltd* [1984] ILRM 343.

[71] *McGee v Attorney General* [1974] IR 284: see para **15.169**.

[72] *Kennedy v Ireland* [1987] IR 587.

[73] *Murray v Ireland* [1985] IR 532 (HC), [1991] ILRM 465 (SC).

[74] *G v An Bord Uchtála* [1980] IR 32.

[75] *Re the Adoption (No 2) Bill 1987* [1989] IR 656.

[76] *CM v TM (No 2)* [1991] ILRM 268.

[77] *Macauley v Minister for Posts and Telegraphs* [1966] IR 345: see also para **9.02**.

[78] *State (Healy) v Donoghue* [1976] IR 325: see also para **9.19**.

[79] *Re Haughey* [1971] IR 217.

[80] *Murphy v Stewart* [1973] IR 97.

[81] *O'T v B* [1998] 2 IR 321.

[15.59] It is clear that the unspecified personal rights guaranteed protection by Article 40.3 cover a wide range of matters. However, like many of the rights expressly stated in the constitutional text, they are not absolute, but are to some extent limited by the requirement that the state must respect and defend them 'as far as practicable'. Thus, in the *Ryan* case, while the courts accepted that the right to bodily integrity was guaranteed protection by Article 40.3, they also concluded that it had not been established that the state had failed to protect it 'as far as practicable' in the Health (Fluoridation of Water Supplies) Act 1960.

[15.60] Some Supreme Court judges have expressed caution about the continuing elucidation of further unenumerated constitutional rights under Article 40.3. In *O'T v B*,[82] Keane J called for 'judicial restraint ... in identifying new rights'.[83] As Keane CJ, he repeated this in *TD v Minister for Education*[84] and stated that he had the gravest doubts whether the courts should assume responsibility for declaring socio-economic rights to be unenumerated rights protected by Article 40.3. One commentator has suggested that:

> "it seems unlikely that Art 40.3.1° will in future play any role other than a location for rights that could reasonably be said to be implicit in other constitutional provisions. Perhaps the unenumerated rights doctrine was a necessary constitutional device that has done its job and now can be gracefully abandoned."[85]

Example of declaration of invalidity

[15.61] A common method by which constitutional cases are brought before the courts is for a person to issue a High Court plenary summons seeking a declaration that a specified statutory provision is not valid on the ground that it is in conflict with a provision, or provisions, of the Constitution.[86] However, constitutional points may also arise by way of 'ordinary' judicial review, that is, through an application for *certiorari* seeking to quash a District Court decision.[87] A combination of both may also be involved.[88]

[15.62] In *King v Attorney General*,[89] the plaintiff had been convicted in the District Court of certain offences under s 4 of the Vagrancy Act 1824. That provision created a large number of offences, broadly associated with persons suspected of being in public places with a view to committing criminal offences. For example, it created the offence of being in possession of implements, such as a crowbar, with the intention of breaking into a house or other building. It also created more wide-ranging offences, including the quintessential vagrancy offences of being a 'person wandering abroad ... not having any

---

82 *O'T v B* [1998] 2 IR 321.
83 [1998] 2 IR 321, 370.
84 *TD v Minister for Education* [2001] 4 IR 259, 281: see also para **4.22**.
85 Doyle, *Constitutional Law: Texts, Cases and Materials* (2008), p 108.
86 For example, *Norris v Attorney General* [1984] IR 36: see para **15.110**.
87 For example, *The State (Healy) v Donoghue* [1976] IR 326: see para **9.19**.
88 See Collins and O'Reilly, *Civil Proceedings and the State in Ireland* (2003), p 104.
89 *King v Attorney General* [1981] IR 233.

visible means of subsistence, and not giving a good account of himself', that is being poor in public,[90] and 'wandering abroad and endeavouring by the exposure of wounds or deformities to obtain or gather alms', that is begging in public.[91]

[15.63] As amended, s 4 of the 1824 Act also created the offence of being a 'suspected person or reputed thief' who was 'loitering about or in' public places with the intention of committing a felony. Section 15 of the Prevention of Crimes Act 1871 provided that, to convict a person as a 'suspected person', it was not necessary to establish any act tending to show a criminal intent and a conviction could be based on the person's 'known character'. The courts had held that 'known character' could include past convictions; thus a person could be convicted under s 4 merely on the ground that a judge considered that he or she intended to commit a felony because he or she had a previous conviction.

[15.64] The plaintiff in the *King* case had been convicted in the District Court under s 4 of the 1824 Act on a number of charges, including the following: that, being a suspected person, he had been loitering on a public road between 8.30 pm and 9.30 pm on a particular date with intent to commit a felony, namely to housebreak and steal; and that, on the same date, and at the same time and place, he had in his possession housebreaking implements, namely two screwdrivers, a tyre lever, hacksaw, haversack, shifting spanner and a candle, with intent to commit a felony, namely to steal. He sought a declaration that the relevant parts of s 4 of the 1824 Act concerning 'loitering with intent' were invalid on the ground that they were in conflict with various provisions of the Constitution and he also sought orders of *certiorari* quashing the convictions.

[15.65] The High Court and Supreme Court held that the 'loitering with intent' offence did not comply with a number of constitutional provisions. It was in conflict with the right to a trial in due course of law in Article 38.1, particularly because evidence of past convictions could be used to convict a person and no evidence of an act involving criminal intent, or *mens rea*, was required. Section 4 was in conflict with the right to be held equal before the law in Article 40.1, since a person could be convicted of something which it was lawful for another person to do, such as to 'walk slowly, dawdle or stop altogether in a public street'.[92] The courts also considered that s 4 failed to meet the requirements of Article 40.4, that a person may only be deprived of liberty in accordance with law.

---

90 This provision was repealed by the Housing Act 1988 which now regulates homelessness.

91 The provisions of s 4 concerning possession of housebreaking implements remain in place. Those on public begging were held to be invalid in *Dillon v DPP* [2008] 1 IR 383 as they breached the applicant's right to freedom of expression of opinions and convictions under Articles 40.3 and 40.6.1° of the Constitution. As a result of the *Dillon* case the Criminal Justice (Public Order) Act 2011 was enacted to prohibit begging that also involves intimidation.

92 [1981] IR 233, 242–3, *per* McWilliam J (High Court).

[15.66] The courts considered that Article 40.4 requires that a person should only be convicted of an offence if it is established beyond reasonable doubt that he has broken a clearly stated rule, whereas the language of s 4 was so vague and unclear that it conferred an arbitrary and overbroad power to charge and convict a person. In these circumstances, the High Court, and the Supreme Court granted a declaration that the 'loitering with intent' elements of s 4 were invalid and it quashed the appellant's convictions on *certiorari*.[93]

Effect of declaration of invalidity

[15.67] Where a declaration of invalidity concerning a statutory provision is granted, this amounts to a 'judicial death certificate'.[94] If the statutory provision in question is not replaced,[95] it is no longer a law capable of being enforced, despite having being enacted by the Oireachtas or other pre-1937 legislative authority. The courts thus have a negative power to declare a law invalid, but do not have the power to declare what might be enacted to replace the invalid law.

[15.68] However, the reasons given for declaring legislation invalid may, in effect, point the way for the Oireachtas where a replacement law is required. Thus, in *de Burca v Attorney General*,[96] the Supreme Court found the Juries Act 1927 unconstitutional on the grounds that it effectively excluded women and non-property owners from sitting on juries and this amounted to invalid discrimination under Article 40.1. The legislative response, the Juries Act 1976,[97] provides that jurors be drawn primarily from the electoral roll, thus removing the discriminatory aspects of the 1927 Act found invalid in the *de Burca* case.

[15.69] The courts have also occasionally provided more positive indications of what legislative provisions might be required to fill the gap created by a finding of

---

93 See the text of the orders made: [1981] IR 233, 244. Where the courts consider a non-statutory rule of law, as in *Byrne v Ireland* [1972] IR 241, there is no statutory provision to be declared invalid. In such circumstances, the High Court or Supreme Court grants a declaration concerning the person's rights without anything more.

94 *Murphy v Attorney General* [1982] IR 241, 307, *per* Henchy J.

95 In many instances, a replacement may not be deemed either necessary or constitutionally permissible. Thus, the 'loitering with intent' provisions of the Vagrancy Act 1824, s 4 declared invalid in *King v Attorney General* [1981] IR 233 (see para **15.62**) were not replaced by any broadly comparable provision. Rather, the Criminal Justice (Public Order) Act 1994, s 8 requires a person in a public place to 'move on' when so requested by a garda.

96 *de Burca v Attorney General* [1976] IR 38: see para **6.143**.

97 The 1976 Act also involved belated implementation of the detailed recommendations for reform of the 1927 Act (including removal of the effective ban on women jurors) in the Second and Fourth Reports of the Committee on Court Practice and Procedure, *Jury Service* (Pr 8328, 1965) and *Jury Challenges* (Pr 8577, 1965). On the need for reform of the 1976 Act to reflect demographic changes in Ireland's population since the 1970s see the Law Reform Commission's 2013 *Report on Jury Service* (LRC 107-2013) discussed at para **6.147**.

unconstitutionality.[98] Indeed, even where it is found that legislation is not invalid, the courts may nonetheless indicate that there is a strong case for amending the law, but that this is a matter for the Oireachtas.[99]

[15.70] Not all 'successful' constitutional cases involve declarations of invalidity. Thus, in *The State (Healy) v Donoghue*[100] the Supreme Court identified the need to interpret the Criminal Justice (Legal Aid) Act 1962 in a manner that coincided with the constitutional dimension of the right to legal representation identified in the case, but no textual alterations to the 1962 Act were required.

Effect in cases involving common law rule

[15.71] Where a constitutional action involves a challenge to a common law rule rather than legislation, a 'successful' action has a different impact. In *Byrne v Ireland*,[101] the plaintiff established that the supposed immunity of the state from suit had not been carried forward by Article 50 of the 1937 Constitution. We have seen that, since *Byrne*, no legislation has been enacted to regulate proceedings against the state, and they are dealt with simply by reference to the principles in *Byrne*.[102] By contrast with constitutional cases involving legislation, *Byrne* involved the creation of constitutional judge-made principles regulating this area in a positive manner.[103]

Retrospective or prospective effect of invalidity

[15.72] In *Murphy v Attorney General*,[104] the question arose as to whether a declaration of invalidity has full retrospective effect or applies prospectively only, from the date of the decision of the court. The plaintiffs were a married couple and were both earning salaries as teachers. They were taxed under ss 192 to 196 of the Income Tax Act 1967, which at the time provided for an 'aggregation' of the incomes of married couples; that is, where husband and wife were both earning, their incomes were added together, counted as one income and taxed on that basis.

[15.73] Under ss 192 to 196 of the 1967 Act, a married couple could opt for separate taxation of their incomes, but in such a case they would not be given two tax-free allowances and their total income tax would be same as if their incomes were aggregated. The plaintiffs pointed out that, if they had remained unmarried but had

---

[98] See the comments of the Supreme Court in *Blake v Attorney General* [1982] IR 117, 141–2. See also the Supreme Court's jurisdiction under Article 26: para **5.84**.

[99] See the comments of Henchy J in *Cahill v Sutton* [1980] IR 269, 288: see para **15.89**. See also his comments in *Norris v Attorney General* [1984] IR 36, 78–79. A similar approach is evident where the courts are forced to an unsatisfactory interpretation of legislation: see *Rafferty v Crowley* [1984] ILRM 350, discussed at para **14.54**.

[100] *State (Healy) v Donoghue* [1976] IR 325: see para **9.19**.

[101] *Byrne v Ireland* [1972] IR 241.

[102] See paras **15.37–15.39**.

[103] See also *McKinley v Minister for Defence* [1992] 2 IR 333.

[104] *Murphy v Attorney General* [1982] IR 241.

decided to cohabit, they could be taxed separately, would be entitled to a tax-free allowance each and their total tax bill would be less than that of a married couple.

[15.74] They sought declarations that the aggregation system in the 1967 Act failed to comply with the guarantee by the state in Article 41 to protect the family. The High Court and Supreme Court accepted this argument and declared invalid ss 192 to 196 of the 1967 Act. The question then arose as to whether that decision had retrospective effect to the date when the 1967 Act was enacted; and, if so, whether the state was required to refund all tax collected from married couples between 1967 and 1980 (when the decision in *Murphy* was given), or at least the excess they paid over and above what unmarried couples would have paid.

[15.75] Ultimately, while the Supreme Court concluded that the declaration of invalidity was retrospective, it also held that only persons who had already initiated proceedings could seek compensation arising from the unconstitutionally collected taxes. This, in effect, restricted the retrospective benefit of the decision to the plaintiffs in the *Murphy* case.[105] The Finance Act 1980, enacted in the wake of the *Murphy* case, inserted 'new' ss 192 to 196 into the Income Tax Act 1967, introducing double income tax allowances for married couples, whether only one or both spouses have an income.[106] To that extent, of course, all married couples benefited, at least prospectively, from the *Murphy* case. Indeed, by introducing measures applicable to married couples with one income only, the *Murphy* case produced tangible benefits for a wider category of persons than those envisaged by the outcome in the case. It has been suggested that *Murphy* should be overruled and instead the courts should provide that, as in the United States, statutes are void only from the time they are declared unconstitutional.[107] This matter came into stark relief in *A v Governor of Arbour Hill Prison*.[108]

[15.76] In *CC v Ireland (No 2)*,[109] the Supreme Court had declared unconstitutional s 1(1) of the Criminal Law Amendment Act 1935, which criminalised on a strict liability basis sexual intercourse with a girl under the age of 17, commonly called 'statutory rape'. The decision was based primarily on the ground that it failed to afford the defence of honest mistake as to the age of the girl to an accused. The court considered that the effect of the provision was to 'criminalise in a serious way a person who is mentally innocent' and that this amounted to a failure of the state protect and vindicate the rights to liberty and good name of the accused.[110] The accused had been convicted of the offence of unlawful carnal knowledge of a girl under the age of 15.[111]

---

[105] See generally, Hogan and Whyte, *JM Kelly: The Irish Constitution* (4th edn, 2003), generally and pp 480–487. For a different retrospection problem, see para **4.188,** fn 406.

[106] See now the Taxes Consolidation Act 1997.

[107] Doyle and Feldman, 'Constitutional Law' in Byrne and Binchy, *Annual Review of Irish Law 2006* (2007), pp 184–185.

[108] *A v Governor of Arbour Hill Prison* [2006] IEHC 169; [2006] IESC 45; [2006] 4 IR 88.

[109] *CC v Ireland (No 2)* [2005] IESC 48, [2006] 4 IR 1.

[110] [2006] 4 IR 1, 78–9.

[111] In response to the decision the Oireachtas enacted the Criminal Law (Sexual Offences) Act 2006, which includes a 'reasonable mistake' defence to the offences previously contained in the 1935 Act. (contd.../)

[15.77] Three days after the Supreme Court decision in *CC*, the applicant in *A v Governor of Arbour Hill Prison*[112] applied to the High Court for an order of *habeas corpus* directing his release from prison on the grounds that his conviction under s 1(1) of the Criminal Law (Amendment) Act 1935 was unlawful. The primary issue was whether the declaration of unconstitutionality in *CC* affected orders made prior to the declaration of unconstitutionality. In the High Court, Laffoy J ordered Mr A's release on the ground that his conviction and sentence pursuant to an invalid statute were null and void.[113] This was immediately appealed to the Supreme Court, which gave an *ex tempore* judgment three days after the decision of the High Court allowing the state's appeal and ordering the re-arrest and detention of Mr A. He was arrested later that evening and returned to custody.

[15.78] The Supreme Court later delivered reserved judgments setting out the reasons for overturning the High Court decision.[114] The Supreme Court held that the invalidity of a law does not automatically confer a remedy on those who have been convicted under its provisions. The court stated that 'the Constitution permits, if not requires, a distinction to be made between a declaration of invalidity and the retrospective effects of such a declaration on previous and finally decided cases'.[115] The Supreme Court rejected the contention that cases which had been decided on the basis of a statute which had subsequently been declared unconstitutional must be set aside as having no legal effect. This allowed it to hold that the courts can give effect to actions taken on foot of legislation subsequently declared unconstitutional and, more importantly, that the courts can give effect to those actions even after the legislation has been declared unconstitutional.[116] In this respect, Murray CJ stated:[117]

"In a criminal prosecution where the State relies in good faith on a statute in force at the time and the accused does not seek to impugn the bringing or conduct of the prosecution, on any grounds that may in law be open to him or her, including the constitutionality of the statute, before the case reaches finality, on appeal or otherwise, then the final decision in the case must be deemed to be and to remain lawful notwithstanding any subsequent ruling that the statute, or a provision of it, is unconstitutional. That is the general principle.

I do not exclude, by way of exception to the foregoing general principle, that the grounds upon which a court declares a statute to be unconstitutional, or some extreme feature of an individual case, might require, for wholly exceptional reasons related to some fundamental

---

[111] (\...contd) At the time of writing (September 2014), the substantive criminal law concerning sexual offences involving persons under the age of 17 remains under review and it is expected that a Sexual Offences Bill to consolidate the law relating to sexual offences involving children will be published by the end of 2014.

[112] *A v Governor of Arbour Hill Prison* [2006] IEHC 169; [2006] IESC 45, [2006] 4 IR 88.

[113] [2006] IEHC 169, [2006] 4 IR 88.

[114] [2006] IESC 45, [2006 4 IR 88.

[115] [2006] IESC 45, [2006] 4 IR 88, 142.

[116] Doyle, *Constitutional Law: Texts, Cases and Materials* (2008), p 453.

[117] *A v Governor of Arbour Hill Prison* [2006] IESC 45, [2006] 4 IR 88, 143.

unfairness amounting to a denial of justice, that verdicts in particular cases or a particular class of cases be not allowed to stand."

[15.79] The decision of the Supreme Court has been criticised on the basis that it did not directly deal with the primary issue before it: the prospective detention of Mr A and not his historic detention.[118] Nonetheless, the case demonstrates the difficulties caused by the judgment in *Murphy* that post-1937 statutes declared to be unconstitutional are void *ab initio*. The suggestion that *Murphy* be overruled and replaced with a view that unconstitutional statutes are void only from the time they are declared unconstitutional seems sensible.[119]

Representative actions

[15.80] The restriction of the benefit of a 'test' case such as *Murphy*[120] to a small group of persons can be avoided by the institution of a representative action, in which a large group or class of persons may be represented by one or more persons who actually conduct the litigation.[121] This form of multi-party action (called a 'class action' in the United States) has become more common in recent years.[122]

Amendments to 1937 Constitution[123]

[15.81] Article 51 of the Constitution authorised amendments by ordinary legislation for a three-year period after the entry into office of the first President of Ireland, that is, until 25 June 1941. Since then, a referendum of the entire electorate has been required. Unlike the comparable provision in Article 50 of the 1922 Constitution, Article 51 was hedged around with a number of restrictions which prevented its extension beyond 1941. Prior to 1941, two Acts were enacted amending the text of the 1937 Constitution by means of ordinary legislation.

[15.82] The First Amendment of the Constitution Act 1939 was enacted immediately after the invasion of Poland by Germany at the beginning of World War II and it extended the provisions of Article 28.3.3° of the Constitution to include a state of emergency where no actual invasion of the state had occurred. Article 28.3.3° provides, in effect, that legislation enacted under its terms is exempt from challenge for being in

---

118 Fanning, 'Hard Case: Bad Law? The Supreme Court decision in *A v Governor of Arbour Hill Prison*' (2005) 40 Ir Jur 188.

119 Doyle and Feldman, 'Constitutional Law' in Byrne and Binchy, *Annual Review of Irish Law 2006* (2007), pp 184–185.

120 *Murphy v Attorney General* [1982] IR 241.

121 See Collins and O'Reilly, *Civil Proceedings and the State in Ireland* (2003), pp 188–189.

122 For example, *Tate v Minister for Social Welfare* [1995] 1 IR 419 (para **16.205**); *Abrahamson v Law Society of Ireland* [1996] 1 IR 403 (para **3.56**) and *Duff v Minister for Agriculture (No 2)* [1997] 2 IR 22. See also Law Reform Commission, *Report on Multi Party Litigation* (LRC 76-2005).

123 O'Neill, 'The Referendum Process in Ireland' (2000) 35 Irish Jurist 305 and Oireachtas Committee on the Constitution, *Sixth Progress Report: The Referendum* (2001).

conflict with the Constitution. The extension of Article 28.3.3° in 1939 facilitated the establishment of military tribunals comparable to those provided for under Article 2A of the 1922 Constitution and the conferring of emergency powers on Ministers for the duration of World War II.

[15.83] The Second Amendment of the Constitution Act 1941 was enacted just before the expiry of the three-year limitation period for amendment by 'ordinary' legislation. By contrast with the First Amendment, this contained over 20 amendments to 16 Articles. Some were of a technical or drafting type, but others involved substantive change. Among these were changes to Article 24.2 concerning Bills deemed to have been passed by both Houses of the Oireachtas;[124] Article 25.4 concerning the signature of Bills by the President;[125] the requirement that one judgment only be delivered by the Supreme Court in judgments given under Articles 26 and 34 on the constitutionality of Bills or post-1937 Acts (which was removed in 2013 in the referendum that also established the Court of Appeal);[126] an immunity from further constitutional challenge of any Bill approved by the Supreme Court on a reference to it under Article 26;[127] a further extension of Article 28.3.3°; clarification that the High Court only had original jurisdiction in cases seeking to challenge the constitutional validity of legislation;[128] and allowing the High Court to state a case to the Supreme Court after an inquiry under Article 40.4.2°.[129]

[15.84] Between 1959 and 2012, referenda have been held to consider over 30 amendments to the Constitution. Each has involved a separate vote to approve an amendment to a constitutional provision, though some referenda have been combined with a General Election and up to three separate constitutional amendments have been voted on in a single referendum held on the same date. Of these proposed constitutional amendments, more than 20 have been approved and less than 10 rejected. A number of recent referenda have provoked substantial and sometimes heated debate, particularly those concerning the right to life of the unborn, the two referenda proposing the introduction of divorce, the 2001 Nice Treaty referendum and the 2008 Treaty of Lisbon referendum.

[15.85] As a result of these amendments the text of the 1937 Constitution has been altered considerably and, indeed, the pace of amendment has greatly accelerated in recent years. Since 1996, some of these have emerged from the recommendations of the *Report of the Constitution Review Group* and of the Oireachtas Committee on the Constitution.[130]

---

124 See para **13.22**.
125 See para **13.24**.
126 See para **12.106**.
127 See para **5.83**.
128 See para **15.49**.
129 See para **10.54**.
130 See para **15.196**.

Rules of self-restraint in constitutional judicial review

[15.86] In an attempt to ensure that the courts do not overstep the boundaries between the judicial power and the other two branches of government, the executive and the legislature, some 'rules of self-restraint' have been developed.[131] These include the requirement that only justiciable matters may be litigated, rather than political controversies;[132] that constitutional issues will be avoided where a case may be decided on a narrower ground, for example, that ministerial regulations were *ultra vires* an Act;[133] that a litigant must establish personal standing or *locus standi* to raise a constitutional point;[134] that a presumption of constitutionality is applicable to post-1937 legislation;[135] and that the least amount of legislative text is declared invalid or severed, thus leaving intact as much legislative text as is possible.[136]

Locus standi

[15.87] It is a fundamental requirement of public law litigation, of which constitutional cases form part, that the person initiating the claim establish that he or she has an identifiable personal interest in the point at issue.[137] This is referred to as *locus standi* or standing.[138] In *Byrne v Ireland*,[139] the plaintiff's *locus standi* or standing was clear: the reliance by the defendants on the supposed immunity from suit of the state was a direct bar to her claim against the Department of Posts and Telegraphs. However, in a number of instances, constitutional actions have failed because the plaintiff has been unable to establish any direct or personal connection with the operation of the legal rule being challenged.[140]

[15.88] The leading case on *locus standi* in constitutional cases is *Cahill v Sutton*.[141] In that case, the plaintiff had initiated an action against the defendant, a doctor, in respect of certain medical treatment she had received. Her action was initiated four years after she became aware of the facts she alleged were the basis for her claim. Her claim was based on an alleged breach of contract, and s 11(2)(b) of the Statute of Limitations

---

[131] See Hogan and Whyte, *JM Kelly: The Irish Constitution* (4th edn, 2003), p 883.

[132] See para **4.20**.

[133] See para **13.126**.

[134] See para **15.87**.

[135] See para **14.78**.

[136] *Maher v Attorney General* [1973] IR 140; *Desmond v Glackin (No 2)* [1993] 3 IR 67.

[137] See Hogan & Whyte, *JM Kelly: The Irish Constitution* (4th edn, 2003), pp 807–832; Doyle, *Constitutional Law: Texts, Cases and Materials* (2008), pp 431–436; Keating and Lowry, 'Pacifying Turbulent Water: The Case for Greater Clarity in Constitutional Standing Rules' (2003) 21 ILT 166, 183.

[138] See para **6.07**.

[139] *Byrne v Ireland* [1972] IR 241: see para **15.37**.

[140] For example see *Dunne v Minister for the Environment* [2004] IEHC 304, [2007] 1 IR 194 (SC) and *Grace v Attorney General* [2007] 2 ILRM 283.

[141] *Cahill v Sutton* [1980] IR 269.

1957[142] specified that such claims must be initiated within three years from the date of the events or facts on which the claim is based. The plaintiff was thus statute-barred and, apparently, precluded from initiating her claim.

[15.89] However, she then raised a constitutional point, claiming that s 11(2)(b) of the 1957 Statute was invalid because it failed to contain any saver allowing an extension of time for a person who did not become aware of the facts on which a claim would be based until after the expiration of the specified time limit and, on that basis, was in breach of Article 40.3 for failing to uphold the right of access to the courts.[143] Although the absence of such a saver, to deal with cases of 'latent' injury, was a justifiable criticism of s 11(2)(b), the question in *Cahill* was whether the plaintiff should be allowed to raise this point when she did not fall into this category of person – after all, she had known of the facts well within the three-year time limit in s 11(2)(b).

[15.90] In those circumstances, the Supreme Court refused to allow her raise the constitutional point. Henchy J explained this in the following passage:

"At all material times she [the plaintiff] was aware of all the facts necessary for the making of a claim against Dr Sutton. Her present claim is founded on breach of contract. Within weeks of the commencement of her treatment in 1968 she knew of the facts which, according to her, constituted a breach of contract, and of their prejudicial effect on her. Yet she did not bring her action within the three-year period. It is clear—indeed, it is admitted— that the plaintiff would still be shut out from suing after the three-year period of limitation even if the suggested saving provision had been included in the Act of 1957.

That being the legal predicament in which the plaintiff finds herself, the argument formulated on her behalf is not that she is unjustly debarred from suing because of the alleged statutory defect but that a person to whom the suggested saving provision would apply if it had been enacted could claim successfully in the High Court a declaration that s 11, sub-s 2(b), is unconstitutional because the suggested saving provision is not attached to it. Therefore, the plaintiff is seeking to be allowed to conjure up, invoke and champion the putative constitutional rights of a hypothetical third party, so that the provisions of s 11, sub-s 2(b), may be declared unconstitutional on the basis of that constitutional *jus tertii*— thus allowing the plaintiff to march through the resulting gap in the statute. The question which the Court has to consider is whether such an indirect and hypothetical assertion of constitutional rights gives the plaintiff the standing necessary for the successful invocation of the judicial power to strike down a statutory provision on the ground of unconstitutionality ...

While a cogent theoretical argument might be made for allowing any citizen, regardless of personal interest or injury, to bring proceedings to have a particular statutory provision declared unconstitutional, there are countervailing considerations which make such an approach generally undesirable and not in the public interest. To allow one litigant to present and argue what is essentially another person's case would not be conducive to the administration of justice as a general rule. Without concrete personal circumstances

---

[142] See generally, para **6.09**.
[143] See para **9.02**.

pointing to a wrong suffered or threatened, a case tends to lack the force and urgency of reality. There is also the risk that the person whose case has been put forward unsuccessfully by another may be left with the grievance that his claim was wrongly or inadequately presented ...

There is also the hazard that, if the Courts were to accord citizens unrestricted access, regardless of qualification, for the purpose of getting legislative provisions invalidated on constitutional grounds, this important jurisdiction would be subject to abuse. For the litigious person, the crank, the obstructionist, the meddlesome, the perverse, the officious man of straw and many others, the temptation to litigate the constitutionality of a law, rather than to observe it, would prove irresistible on occasion.

In particular, the working interrelation that must be presumed to exist between Parliament and the Judiciary in the democratic scheme of things postulated by the Constitution would not be served if no threshold qualification were ever required for an attack in the Courts on the manner in which the Legislature has exercised its law-making powers. Without such a qualification, the Courts might be thought to encourage those who have opposed a particular Bill on its way through Parliament to ignore or devalue its elevation into an Act of Parliament by continuing their opposition to it by means of an action to have it invalidated on constitutional grounds. It would be contrary to the spirit of the Constitution if the Courts were to allow those who were opposed to a proposed legislative measure, inside or outside Parliament, to have an unrestricted and unqualified right to move from the political arena to the High Court once a Bill had become an Act. It would not accord with the smooth working of the organs of State established by the Constitution if the enactments of the National Parliament were liable to be thwarted or delayed in their operation by litigation which could be brought at the whim of every or any citizen, whether or not he had a personal interest in the outcome."

General locus standi principle

[15.91] The judgment of Henchy J in *Cahill*[144] indicates that, in general, only a person with a personal interest in the point at issue will be regarded as having sufficient standing or *locus standi* to initiate a constitutional claim. Among the reasons given was that, with the exception of references to the Supreme Court under Article 26 of the Constitution,[145] the courts generally deal with cases based on concrete sets of facts rather than considering points of law in a vacuum. This is supported by the distinction in the doctrine of precedent between the binding nature of the *ratio decidendi* of a case and the non-binding nature of *obiter dicta*.[146] This general approach in *Cahill* has been followed in subsequent cases. Thus, in *King v Attorney General*,[147] the plaintiff was restricted to challenging only those parts of s 4 of the Vagrancy Act 1824 in respect of which he had been convicted, notwithstanding some doubts cast on s 4 as a whole.

---

[144] *Cahill v Sutton* [1980] IR 269.
[145] See para **5.84**.
[146] See para **12.88**.
[147] *King v Attorney General* [1981] IR 233: see para **15.62**.

[15.92] In exceptional circumstances, the normal *locus standi* requirement will be waived in order to ensure the protection of constitutional rights. Thus, the courts have relaxed the requirement in cases involving the rights of the unborn, since an unborn person clearly cannot sue.[148] He also referred to cases where an executive or legislative action affects 'a grouping which includes the challenger, or with whom the challenger may be said to have a common interest.' This relaxation of the rule has been applied in the case of a challenge to the Single European Act,[149] the Anglo–Irish Agreement 1985[150] and the conduct of the government surrounding the proposed Fifteenth Amendment to the Constitution.[151] The *locus standi* of representative bodies in actions has also been upheld.[152]

The growth of constitutional judicial review

[15.93] A second justification for the *locus standi* rule referred to by Henchy J in *Cahill*[153] was the risk of abuse, whereby 'the crank, the obstructionist ... the officious man of straw' might be tempted to litigate the constitutionality of a law. In the context of the appropriate relationship between the legislative and judicial branches, he considered that the absence of a *locus standi* rule might be interpreted as encouraging those who had opposed legislation during its debate in the Oireachtas to continue their opposition

---

148 See *Society for the Protection of Unborn Children Ltd v Coogan* [1989] IR 734.

149 *Crotty v An Taoiseach* [1987] IR 713.

150 *McGimpsey v Ireland* [1990] 1 IR 110. In this case, the plaintiffs, both members of the Ulster Unionist Party, challenged the validity of the 1985 Agreement on the ground that it was in conflict with Articles 2 and 3 of the Constitution. In the High Court, the defendants argued that the plaintiffs lacked *locus standi* to invoke Article 2 because, as members of a unionist party, they did not believe that the national territory consists of the whole island of Ireland and were only invoking Article 2 as a 'tactical manoeuvre' to have the 1985 Agreement declared invalid. This was rejected by Barrington J in the High Court on the basis that the plaintiffs were deeply concerned about the present state of Northern Ireland and of all Ireland; were opposed to any form of sectarianism; had participated in peace movements seeking to accommodate the various traditions living on the island of Ireland; and sincerely believed that the 1985 Agreement had aggravated the problems on the island rather than solving them. In those circumstances, he concluded 'it would be inappropriate ... to refuse to listen to their complaints'. He also indicated that, as the plaintiffs had been born in Ireland, they were Irish citizens, although no evidence to that effect had been introduced. In the Supreme Court, these conclusions were not challenged by the defendants, and the court proceeded to deal with the case. However, Finlay CJ expressed considerable doubt as to whether the plaintiffs had established that they were Irish citizens and, if so, whether a citizen would have *locus standi* to challenge an executive or legislative act 'for the specific and sole purpose of achieving an objective directly contrary to the purpose of the constitutional provision invoked'. See also *Iarnród Éireann v Ireland* [1996] 2 ILRM 500.

151 *McKenna v An Taoiseach* [1995] 2 IR 10.

152 See for example, *Irish Penal Reform Trust v Governor of Mountjoy Prison* [2005] IEHC 305 and Kirwan, 'Locus Standi and Representative Bodies' (2005) 23 ILT 98.

153 *Cahill v Sutton* [1980] IR 269.

to the legislation by a constitutional action, that is, 'to move from the political arena to the High Court'.

[15.94] Despite this and the other 'rules of self-restraint',[154] cases involving politically charged matters have been debated with increasing frequency in the courts. There has been a significant growth in constitutional litigation, particularly since the 1960s; indeed this reflects a growth in litigation generally.[155] It has been suggested that the emergence of constitutional judicial review in the 1960s is characteristic of the emergence of Irish society generally from the economic and intellectual isolationism associated with earlier decades, the introduction of television and general awareness of civil rights movements, particularly in the United States and Northern Ireland.[156]

[15.95] While no official statistics are available on the growth, Figure 15.1 lists the number of Irish cases cited in successive editions of Professor John Kelly's textbooks on Irish constitutional law between 1967 and 1994.[157]

Year	Irish cases
1967	130
1980	480
1984	650
1987	850
1994	1,100

Irish cases cited in *Kelly*, 1967–1994
Figure 15.1

[15.96] Figure 15.1 indicates that, between 1922 and 1967, there were in the region of 130 decisions of the Irish courts (primarily of the High Court and Supreme Court) worthy of comment in a text dealing with Irish constitutional law. By 1980, almost 350 more cases were referred to, and between 1980 and 1984 another 270 decisions of note required discussion. In the 10 years between 1984 and 1994, the total number of cases almost doubled, growing from 650 to 1,100. It is hardly surprising that commentators have referred to an 'explosion of constitutional litigation'.[158] This is not merely a

---

154 See para **15.86**.
155 See paras **4.206** and **5.07**.
156 Casey, 'Changing the Constitution: Amendment and Judicial Review', in Farrell (ed), *de Valera's Constitution and Ours* (1988), p 156. See also the comments of Walsh J, para **4.92**, fn 243.
157 Sources for material in Figure 15.1: table of cases in Kelly, *Fundamental Rights in the Irish Law and Constitution* (2nd edn, 1967); Kelly, *The Irish Constitution* (2nd edn, 1984), p xxx, and Supplement (1987), iii; table of Irish cases in Kelly, *The Irish Constitution*, (3rd edn, 1994), Hogan and Whyte (eds).
158 Hogan and Whyte, *JM Kelly: The Irish Constitution* (4th edn, 2003), p i of Preface.

question of volume but also of the range of important matters dealt with. The following sample of cases may help illustrate this.

The Constitution and the legal system

[15.97] Constitutional litigation has involved issues of direct importance to the legal system. In 1963, in *The People (Attorney General) v O'Brien*,[159] the Supreme Court held that evidence obtained in conscious and deliberate violation of constitutional rights was automatically inadmissible in court. In 1966, in *The People (Attorney General) v O'Callaghan*,[160] the Supreme Court held that the right to a trial in due course of law in Article 38.1 and the right to liberty under Article 40.4 required that bail could only be refused in very limited circumstances. The limitations thus imposed on the Oireachtas led for calls to amend the Constitution in order to reverse the effect of the *O'Callaghan* case, and this occurred in 1996.[161]

[15.98] In 1975, in *de Burca v Attorney General*,[162] the Supreme Court declared invalid the Juries Act 1927 for its discriminatory exclusion, contrary to Article 40.1, of women and non-property owners from sitting on juries. Many decisions of the courts have also defined the meaning of the judicial function within Article 34, thus determining whether certain persons and bodies are empowered to exercise powers conferred on them by statute.[163] Similarly, constitutional provisions have been central to many decisions determining the extent of the original jurisdiction of the courts[164] and the appellate jurisdiction of the Supreme Court.[165]

In 2006, the Supreme Court decisions in *CC v Ireland (No 2)*[166] and *A v Governor of Arbour Hill Prison*,[167] discussed above, were significant not only in terms of the legal issues raised but also in terms of their indirect impact on general public discussion of sexual activity by persons under the age of 17.

The legislative power

[15.99] Many constitutional cases have required consideration of the limits to the legislative power in areas with a political dimension. In 1961, in *O'Donovan v Attorney General*,[168] the High Court held the Electoral Act 1959 invalid because it failed to respect the proportionality requirement for Dáil constituencies in Article 16.2. The decision of the Supreme Court in 1964 in *Ryan v Attorney General*[169] established that the

---

[159] *The People (Attorney General) v O'Brien* [1965] IR 142.

[160] *People (Attorney General) v O'Callaghan* [1966] IR 501.

[161] See para **6.107**.

[162] *de Burca v Attorney General* [1976] IR 38: see para **6.143**.

[163] See para **4.15**.

[164] See para **5.59**.

[165] See para **7.26**.

[166] *CC v Ireland (No 2)* [2005] IESC 48, [2006] 4 IR 1.

[167] *A v Governor of Arbour Hill Prison* [2006] IEHC 169, [2006] IESC 45, [2006] 4 IR 88.

[168] *O'Donovan v Attorney General* [1961] IR 114.

[169] *Ryan v Attorney General* [1965] IR 294: see para **15.54**.

legislature was restricted not only by the rights expressly stated in the constitutional text but also by the unspecified personal rights in Article 40.3. In 1971, the Supreme Court held in *McMahon v Attorney General*[170] that various provisions of the Electoral Act 1963 had failed to respect the requirement of a secret ballot in Article 16.1.4°.

[15.100] In 1976, in *Re the Emergency Powers Bill 1976*,[171] a reference to the Supreme Court under Article 26, the court imposed procedural limitations on what became the Emergency Powers Act 1976, which had been enacted on foot of a declaration of emergency by the Oireachtas under Article 28.3.3°. The political fallout from the Article 26 reference led to the resignation of the then President.[172] In 1980, in *Cityview Press Ltd v An Chomhairle Oiliúna*,[173] the court upheld the validity of wide-ranging delegation of powers by the Oireachtas to Ministers and other bodies to promulgate secondary legislation, subject to certain restrictions.

[15.101] Earlier in 1980, in *Murphy v Attorney General*,[174] the Supreme Court declared invalid ss 192 to 196 of the Income Tax Act 1967 concerning the taxation of married couples for being in breach of Article 41. The decision indicated that one of the central features of the legislature's powers, tax collection, was subject to constitutional judicial review. Another major aspect of taxation policy, the collection of rates on agricultural land under the Valuation (Ireland) Act 1852, was declared invalid by the Supreme Court in 1984 in *Brennan v Attorney General*[175] for being in breach of the property rights in Article 43. Both these issues had previously been the subject of unsuccessful political campaigns to amend the statutory provisions in question. Notwithstanding the views of Henchy J in *Cahill v Sutton*,[176] therefore, *Murphy* and *Brennan* both involved a 'move from the political arena to the High Court'.

[15.102] In 1981, in *Blake v Attorney General*,[177] the Supreme Court declared invalid the Rent Restrictions Acts 1946 and 1960, which had placed artificial limits on the rent chargeable by landlords in certain private rented dwellings.[178] In 1997, in *Re the Employment Equality Bill 1996*[179] and *Re the Equal Status Bill 1997*[180] the Supreme Court found two important legislative proposals on employment equality and equal

---

170 *McMahon v Attorney General* [1972] IR 69.
171 *Re the Emergency Powers Bill 1976* [1977] IR 159.
172 President Cearbhall Ó Dálaigh had previously been Chief Justice and the first Irish judge of the Court of Justice of the EU.
173 *Cityview Press Ltd v An Chomhairle Oiliúna* [1980] IR 381: see para **13.123**.
174 *Murphy v Attorney General* [1982] IR 241: see para **15.72**.
175 *Brennan v Attorney General* [1983] ILRM 449 (HC), [1984] ILRM 355 (SC).
176 *Cahill v Sutton* [1980] IR 269.
177 *Blake v Attorney General* [1982] IR 117.
178 This necessitated the enactment of the Housing (Private Rented Dwellings) Act 1982, by which the state in effect subsidises those unable to afford the market rents now payable in such dwellings.
179 *Re the Employment Equality Bill 1996* [1997] 2 IR 321.
180 *Re the Equal Status Bill 1997* [1997] 2 IR 387.

status to be unconstitutional, at least in part, with the result that modified legislation was required.[181]

[15.103] It should be noted that not all such constitutional challenges are successful,[182] and in 1996, in *Heaney v Ireland*[183] the Supreme Court found to be constitutional statutory restrictions on the common law right to silence and in 1998, in *Donnelly v Ireland*[184] it upheld the validity of legislation authorising evidence to be taken in certain criminal cases using a live television link. In 2000, in *Re the Illegal Immigrants (Trafficking) Bill 1999*[185] the Supreme Court upheld the validity of detention and deportation powers in respect of the asylum system in the state.[186] On the same date, the court, in *Re the Planning and Development Bill 1999*[187] upheld the validity of planning legislation which requires private building developers to set aside up to 20 per cent of their building land for social housing purposes.[188] While these latter decisions indicate that not all legislation is prone to constitutional challenge, the rate of increase in constitutional litigation in recent years reflects a greater tendency to challenge legislative measures.

The executive power

[15.104] In 1971, in *Byrne v Ireland*,[189] the Supreme Court held that the state could be sued, thus sweeping away the former immunity from suit based on the royal prerogative. On Christmas Eve 1986, in *Crotty v An Taoiseach*,[190] the High Court granted the plaintiff an interim injunction preventing the government from depositing the instrument of ratification of the Single European Act. The Supreme Court ultimately held in *Crotty* that certain provisions of the Single European Act were in conflict with the Constitution as it then stood, necessitating the holding of a referendum to amend the Constitution. The decision in *Crotty* amounted to a legal interpretation of the relevant provisions, but the result was to cause considerable political embarrassment to the then government.

---

[181] The Employment Equality Act 1998 and the Equal Status Act 2000 were subsequently enacted, taking account of the Supreme Court decisions.
[182] *Madigan v Attorney General* [1986] ILRM 136 (unsuccessful challenge to residential property tax in Finance Act 1984); *Browne v Attorney General* [1991] 2 IR 58 (unsuccessful challenge to 'benefit in kind' tax on cars in Finance Act 1982).
[183] *Heaney v Ireland* [1996] 1 IR 580. The provisions were subsequently found to be in breach of the European Convention on Human Rights.
[184] *Donnelly v Ireland* [1998] 1 ILRM 401.
[185] *Re the Illegal Immigrants (Trafficking) Bill 1999* [2000] 2 IR 360.
[186] The Bill became the Illegal Immigrants (Trafficking) Act 2000. See also *FP v Minister for Justice* [2002] 1 IR 164.
[187] *Re the Planning and Development Bill 1999* [2000] 2 IR 321.
[188] The Bill became the Planning and Development Act 2000.
[189] *Byrne v Ireland* [1972] IR 241: see para **15.37**.
[190] *Crotty v An Taoiseach* [1987] IR 713: see further, para **16.105**.

[15.105] In 1993, in *Meagher v Minister for Agriculture and Food*,[191] the Supreme Court saved the executive's blushes by upholding the constitutionality of the wide ministerial powers in s 3 of the European Communities Act 1972 to amend primary legislation by means of delegated legislation where this was done to implement European Community laws. By contrast, in 2000 the High Court came close to finding three government Ministers in contempt of court for failing to provide adequate facilities for children with difficult emotional problems.[192]

[15.106] In 2001, in *Sinnott v Minister for Education*[193] the Supreme Court held that the state was obliged by Article 42.4 to provide primary educational facilities to persons with conditions such as autism up to the age of 18 years, though not beyond that age. The result, hotly debated in the media in the wake of the decision, left the state free to determine the level of financial support it would provide to such persons. The boundaries between the executive and the judiciary again came to the forefront in *TD v Minister for Education*.[194] In the High Court, Kelly J had made a mandatory order requiring the Minister for Education to implement the stated government policy of providing a secure detention unit for the applicants, young persons who had been repeatedly in trouble with the law. On appeal to the Supreme Court, the Minister accepted that the applicants had a right to such accommodation but questioned whether the judicial arm of the state should make such far-reaching orders requiring public expenditure. The Supreme Court agreed with this view and overturned the mandatory order made in the High Court. The Supreme Court held that such an order should only be made in the most exceptional of circumstances, and the applicants had failed to meet the high threshold involved.

[15.107] The decisions in *Sinnott* and *TD* have provoked considerable academic debate.[195] Hardiman J has expressed the view judicially[196] and extra-judicially[197] that it is

---

[191] *Meagher v Minister for Agriculture and Food* [1994] 1 IR 329: see para **16.121**.

[192] See the discussion of *TD v Minister for Education* [2000] 3 IR 62: para **4.22**.

[193] *Sinnott v Minister for Education* [2001] 2 IR 545. In the High Court decision in the case, Barr J had held that the constitutional obligation continued to apply after the age of 18.

[194] *TD v Minister for Education* [2001] 4 IR 259. See also the comments on the decision in Doyle, *Constitutional Law: Texts, Cases and Materials* (2008), p 436.

[195] For example see Whyte, *Social Inclusion and the Legal System* (2002); Ruane, 'The Separation of Powers and the Grant of Mandatory Orders to Enforce Constitutional Rights' [2000] 5 *Bar Review* 416; Hogan, 'Directive Principles, Socio-Economic Rights and the Constitution' (2001) 36 Ir Jur (ns) 174; Keating and Lowry, 'The Supreme Court's Approach to Affirmative Duties' [2003] 21 ILT 103 and [2003] 21 ILT 118; Hardiman, 'The Role of the Supreme Court in our Democracy' in Mulholland (ed), *Political Choice and Democratic Freedom in Ireland: 40 Leading Thinkers* (2004) 32; De Blacam, 'Children, Constitutional Rights and the Separation of Powers' (2002) IR Jur 113; Whyte, 'The Role of the Supreme Court in our Democracy: A Response to Mr Justice Hardiman' (2006) 13(1) DULJ 1; and Langwallner, 'Separation of Powers, Judicial Deference and the Failure to Protect the Rights of the Individual' in Carolan and Doyle (eds), *The Irish Constitution: Governance and Values* (2008), p 256.

[196] *Sinnott v Minister for Education* [2001] 2 IR 545, 711.

not the proper function of the judiciary to involve themselves in questions of public policy. On the other hand Whyte has argued that the judiciary should ensure that the political system takes account of marginalised groups.[198] The debate about the appropriate respective roles of the judicial and other branches is likely to continue, especially in the context of socio-economic rights. The relevance to this debate of the rights contained in the European Convention on Human Rights (ECHR) may have an impact in this respect. For example, in *O'Donnell v South Dublin County Council*[199] the High Court invoked the protection of family life in Article 8 of the ECHR in making an order requiring suitable accommodation to be provided by the respondent local authority for a family who had been living in sub-standard accommodation.[200]

[15.108] In the politically sensitive area of relations between the state and the United Kingdom, the courts dealt with numerous extradition cases in the 1980s and 1990s. Whether extradition was refused or granted in such cases, the courts were inevitably involved in some element of controversy.[201] In a connected area in 1990, the Supreme Court in *McGimpsey v Ireland*[202] considered Articles 2 and 3 of the Constitution and upheld the validity of the Anglo–Irish Agreement 1985.

Sexual privacy and the right to life

[15.109] A long sequence of constitutional cases has concerned various aspects of sexuality and the right of privacy, sometimes referred to as the 'right to be let alone' or the 'right to choose'. In 1973, in *McGee v Attorney General*,[203] the Supreme Court, by a 4:1 majority, declared invalid s 17 of the Criminal Law Amendment Act 1935, which had prohibited the importation into the state of most forms of contraception on the ground that it conflicted with the plaintiff's right to marital privacy under Articles 40.3 and 41. The decision caused political concern at the time,[204] and it was not until 1979 that legislation was enacted to regularise the statutory position.[205]

---

[197] Hardiman, 'The Role of the Supreme Court in our Democracy' in Mulholland (ed), *Political Choice and Democratic Freedom in Ireland: 40 Leading Thinkers* (2004) 32.

[198] Whyte, 'The Role of the Supreme Court in our Democracy: A Response to Mr Justice Hardiman' (2006) 13(1) DULJ 1.

[199] *O'Donnell v South Dublin County Council* [2007] IEHC 204.

[200] Also see *EF v Minister for Education* [2007] IEHC 36 where Smyth J indicated that courts should approach these cases dealing with distribution of resources with 'self restraint'.

[201] See generally Forde, *Extradition Law in Ireland* (2nd edn, 1995).

[202] *McGimpsey v Ireland* [1988] IR 567 (HC); [1990] 1 IR 110 (SC): see para **15.08**.

[203] *McGee v Attorney General* [1974] IR 284: see para **15.169**.

[204] See McMahon, 'The Law Relating to Contraception in Ireland', in Clarke (ed), *Morality and the Law* (1982).

[205] Health (Family Planning) Act 1979. The Act required that spermicidal jellies and condoms could lawfully only be obtained on the prescription of a doctor for '*bona fide* family planning purposes'. The then Minister for Health described this as 'an Irish solution to an Irish problem'. The Health (Family Planning) (Amendment) Act 1985, also highly contentious at the time, removed the prescription requirement. (contd.../)

[15.110] In 1983, in *Norris v Attorney General*,[206] the Supreme Court rejected, by a 3:2 majority, a challenge to ss 60 and 61 of the Offences against the Person Act 1861 which made buggery a criminal offence in all cases, including those where the act occurred between consenting adults. The plaintiff had claimed that ss 60 and 61 of the 1861 Act were in conflict with his right to privacy as a homosexual male. While this case was unsuccessful, it was part of a wider campaign to replace ss 60 and 61 with legislation which would remove consensual sexual acts involving male homosexuals from the realm of the criminal law.[207]

[15.111] In light of the acceptance by the courts of the right of privacy, concern was expressed that the right to choose methods of contraception could be extended to the right to choose to terminate a pregnancy, in effect a right to abortion. This led to a series of constitutional referenda and litigation in the 1980s and 1990s concerning abortion and the right to life of the unborn. These included the 1992 case *Attorney General v X*, in which the Supreme Court held that Article 40.3.3° of the Constitution permitted abortions where the right to life of the mother was in immediate danger.

[15.112] In 1995, the Supreme Court delivered two decisions involving the right to life. *In Re the Regulation of Information (Services Outside the State for the Termination of Pregnancies) Bill 1995*,[208] the court found that the Bill in question, which authorised giving information to pregnant women on abortion services abroad, was not repugnant to the Constitution.[209] The Supreme Court held that the Bill was constitutional because, following the *X* case, the Fourteenth Amendment to the Constitution had inserted into the Constitution a qualification on the right to life of the unborn to allow for the provision of information about abortion services lawfully available abroad. In another 'right to life/right to die' case, *Re a Ward of Court (No 2)*,[210] the court authorised the

---

[205]   (\...contd) The Health (Family Planning) (Amendment) Act 1992 and the Health (Family Planning) (Amendment) Act 1993 removed virtually all restrictions on the sale of condoms (and femidoms). Indeed, by 1993, in the context of the use of condoms in AIDS-awareness campaigns, there was little political opposition to treating condoms as instruments of public health.

[206]   *Norris v Attorney General* [1984] IR 36: see para **15.172**.

[207]   The Criminal Law (Sexual Offences) Act 1993 repealed ss 60 and 61 of the Offences against the Person Act 1861, replacing them with provisions concerning sexual offences with persons under the age of 17 and those otherwise incapable of giving informed consent. The 1993 Act was enacted in the wake of the decision of the European Court of Human Rights in *Norris v Ireland* (1988) 13 EHRR 186: see para **17.67**. It is worth noting that, in the wake of *CC v Ireland (No 2)* [2005] IESC 48, [2006] 4 IR 1 the provisions of the 1993 Act dealing with buggery were repealed and replaced by gender neutral offences of engaging or attempting to engage in a sexual act with a child under 15 or 17: see ss 2 and 3 of the Criminal Law (Sexual Offences) Act 2006.

[208]   *Attorney General v X* [1992] 1 IR 1: see para **15.177**.

[209]   The Bill was enacted as the Regulation of Information (Services Outside the State for the Termination of Pregnancies) Act 1995.

[210]   *Re a Ward of Court (No 2)* [1996] 2 IR 79. The case was known as the 'right to die' case: see para **15.185**.

withdrawal of nourishment from a woman in a near-permanent vegetative state (near-PVS) who had been on life support for over 20 years. All these decisions have been subjected to considerable public discussion and have fuelled media interest in the judiciary. A pregnant woman who challenged her deportation on the ground that this would fail to vindicate the right to life of her unborn child was rejected by both the High Court and Supreme Court.[211] In *R v R*,[212] the High Court considered whether embryos created in vitro were protected by the right to life of the unborn. The court held that frozen fertilised embryos did not come within meaning of 'unborn' for the purposes of the Constitution, being of the view that the people voting in favour of the Eighth Amendment to the Constitution (which provides for the right to life of the unborn and the equal right to life of the mother) would have had in mind only a foetus or child within the womb as being 'unborn' for the purposes of the Constitution.

Marital breakdown and divorce

[15.113] A series of important decisions in 1995 and 1996 concerned marital breakdown. In *TF v Ireland*,[213] the Supreme Court rejected claims that the Judicial Separation and Family Law Reform Act 1989 was in conflict with Article 41 of the Constitution. This was important at that time because a referendum to remove the constitutional prohibition on enacting divorce legislation had been proposed with government support. The 1989 Act had been enacted as a model for any proposed divorce legislation. Just one week before the divorce referendum took place, the Court held in *McKenna v An Taoiseach*[214] that Dáil Éireann and the government had acted in excess of their respective powers, in the case of the former by authorising the spending of money in support of the changes proposed in the divorce referendum and in the case of the latter by spending that money.[215]

[15.114] The *McKenna* case produced further litigation in 1996 in the wake of the narrow approval in the 1995 referendum of the removal of the ban on divorce. In *Hanafin v Minister for the Environment*,[216] the Supreme Court dismissed a referendum petition under the Referendum Act 1994 in which it had been argued that the unconstitutional spending by the government in support of the divorce referendum had invalidated the referendum result. This decision to uphold the referendum result, while primarily a matter of legal interpretation of the 1994 Act, also removed the final

---

211 *O v Minister for Justice* [2002] 2 IR 169.

212 *R v R* [2006] IEHC 359.

213 *TF v Ireland* [1995] 1 IR 321.

214 *McKenna v An Taoiseach* [1995] 2 IR 10.

215 See also *Coughlan v Broadcasting Complaints Committee* [2000] 3 IR 1 where the Supreme Court held that RTE had breached its statutory duty under s 18 of the Broadcasting Act 1960 to be impartial and objective in its duty by broadcasting 42.5 minutes of uncontested coverage to the yes side in the divorce referendum but only 10 minutes of uncontested coverage to the no side. See also Houses of the Oireachtas Joint Committee on the Constitution, *First Report Article 40.6.1.i – Freedom of Expression* (2008) available at www.oireachtas.ie.

216 *Hanafin v Minister for the Environment* [1996] 2 IR 321.

obstacle to the introduction in the Oireachtas of the detailed legislation concerning divorce, the Family Law (Divorce) Act 1996.

Criticisms of and limits to constitutional judicial review

[15.115] These decisions indicate the increasing importance of constitutional judicial review. By the 1970s, the courts had begun to develop this jurisdiction to such an extent that one Taoiseach commented that 'it would be a brave man who would predict, these days, what was or was not contrary to the Constitution'.[217] This has raised questions as to whether such a power is consistent with a democratic state.

[15.116] The simplest form of objection is that it is fundamentally undemocratic for 'unelected judges' to declare invalid laws enacted by the elected representatives of the people. This argument finds some support in writings on United States constitutional law, where constitutional judicial review is regarded as highly politicised.[218] One US commentator has argued that 'judicial review of legislation is inappropriate as a mode of final decision-making in a free and democratic society'.[219] However, the 1937 Constitution expressly provides for constitutional judicial review, whereas this power was inferred by the United States courts from the text of the United States Constitution.[220]

[15.117] However, the development by the Irish courts of the concept of unspecified or implied personal rights under Article 40.3 raises issues comparable to those made in the United States context. The question thus arises whether constitutional judicial review means 'government by judges' and whether it can be said that '[w]e are under a Constitution, but the Constitution is what the judges say it is, and the judiciary is the safeguard of our liberty and of our property under the Constitution'.[221]

[15.118] The most recent comprehensive analysis of the 1937 Constitution has described constitutional judicial review as 'conspicuously successful'.[222] This may have been influenced by the feeling that, for many years, the judiciary had been 'forced' to deal with matters which, for whatever reason, the Oireachtas had simply ignored and

---

217 Quoted in Kelly, *The Irish Constitution* (4th edn, 1994), (Hogan and Whyte eds), in the Preface to the First Edition.

218 See generally, Hogan, 'Unenumerated Personal Rights: *Ryan's* Case Re-Evaluated' (1990–1992) 25–27 Ir Jur (ns) 95.

219 Waldron, 'The Core of the Case against Judicial Review' (2006) 115 Yale Law Review 1346, 1348.

220 In particular the judgment of Marshall CJ in *Marbury v Madison* (1803) 1 Cranch 137. This was alluded to by Walsh J in *Byrne v Ireland* [1972] IR 241: see generally para **15.37**.

221 Charles Evans Hughes, later a judge of the US Supreme Court, speech before the Chamber of Commerce, Elmira, New York, May 3 1907. See *Addresses and Papers of Charles Evans Hughes, Governor of New York* 1906–1908 (1908), p 139.

222 *Report of the Constitution Review Group* (Pn 2632, 1996), p 159.

that the results of their judicial efforts were largely 'beneficial, rational, progressive and fair'.[223]

[15.119] Since the mid-1990s the executive and the Oireachtas have become noticeably active in law reform generally.[224] The Constitution itself and the principles established by the courts in constitutional cases impose a limitation on certain executive and legislative measures, but it must also be borne in mind that the judicial function is limited to those cases initiated in the courts and by the 'rules of self-restraint' which the courts themselves have adopted.

[15.120] In a characteristic flourish, Professor John Kelly had commented, in 1967, that, in any event:

"If they [the people] allow villains into Government, a piece of paper will not protect them from the consequences, nor must they expect a few learned men in wigs and gowns to save the fools from the knaves they have elected."[225]

[15.121] Another commentator summarised the relative position of constitutional judicial review thus:

"Though the courts play a significant role under the Constitution they are far from being the ultimate policy-makers in our society. There are obvious limits on their powers, especially since so many policy choices involve public expenditure priorities. The courts have no power to decree a new social welfare or health service scheme, a more progressive taxation system, or a new policy for full employment. Such policy choices remain the prerogative of the Government and Oireachtas. The electorate, of course, retains the ultimate policy choice of whether to keep judicial review or abolish it. It is noteworthy that no government – no matter how irritated by a particular decision – had proposed its abolition. This suggests that judicial review, as it has now developed, has come to be accepted – indeed to be prized – as a valuable constitutional safeguard."[226]

[15.122] The reality that the judiciary does not control national budgets or plan national policies places constitutional judicial review in context. Indeed, as part of the 'rules of restraint', the courts have emphasised a number of times that they do not wish to become involved in such policy choices. Thus, in *O'Reilly v Limerick Corporation*[227] Costello J rejected the plaintiff's contention that he had a constitutional right to be provided with a serviced halting site. He referred to the distinction between commutative justice and distributive justice first adopted by the pre-Christian Greek philosopher Aristotle. Commutative justice refers to the obligations arising from

---

[223] Professor John Kelly, 'Preface' to Hogan and Whyte, *JM Kelly: The Irish Constitution* (4th edn, 2003).

[224] See paras **5.13–5.29**.

[225] Kelly, *Fundamental Rights in the Irish Law and Constitution* (2nd edn, 1967), p 73.

[226] Casey, 'Changing the Constitution: Amendment and Judicial Review', in Farrell (ed), *de Valera's Constitution and Ours* (1988), pp 160–161.

[227] *O'Reilly v Limerick Corporation* [1989] ILRM 181.

dealings or transactions involving individuals and the state, which Costello J considered was the ambit of the judicial function.

[15.123] Distributive justice, by contrast, refers to the relationship between the individual and the state concerning the distribution and allocation of state resources, which in the *O'Reilly* case Costello J considered was a matter outside the judicial function. If he held in the plaintiff's favour, he noted that this:

> "would be the imposition by the Court of its view that there had been an unfair distribution of national resources. To arrive at such a conclusion, it would have to make an assessment of the validity of the many competing claims on those resources, the correct priority to be given to them and the financial implications of the plaintiff's claim."[228]

[15.124] Costello J declined to engage in this process. This provides some general guide as to the limits of the judicial power; however, the distinction between commutative and distributive justice is no easier to draw than the distinction between justiciable matters and political controversies, despite recent judicial pronouncements appearing to endorse this distinction.[229]

[15.125] This distinction between commutative justice and distributive justice was also applied by the Supreme Court in the *Sinnott*[230] and *TD*[231] decisions discussed above. Thus, it is only where another organ of state is deliberately or with bad faith ignoring declaratory orders that the mandatory type of relief sought in both of these cases would be granted. The courts in these cases were not prepared to become involved in the distribution of resources and dictate to the government how public expenditure should be directed. It has been argued that in *TD*[232] the judges 'enthusiastically endorsed the distinction between distributive and commutative justice'.[233] One commentator has pointed out that this distinction does not necessarily coincide with the separation between the judicial and the executive or legislative powers:

> "The question raised by the judgments in *O'Reilly* and *Sinnott* is whether there is any necessary relationship between these two concepts of justice and the separation of powers. The answer ... is that clearly there is not. Of course it is true that in many instances the issue before a judge may be characterised as one of commutative justice and that before the legislator as one of distributive justice, but it is manifestly not the case that judges are concerned only with the former and legislators with the latter ..."[234]

[15.126] In 2004, the Supreme Court endorsed the view that there is no constitutional right to free residential medical care for older persons or the infirm and therefore it

---

[228] [1989] ILRM 181, 192.
[229] See para **4.20**.
[230] *Sinnott v Minister for Education* [2001] 2 IR 545: see para **5.107**.
[231] *TD v Minister for Education* [2001] 4 IR 259: see also para **5.107**.
[232] *TD v Minister for Education* [2001] 4 IR 259.
[233] Doyle, *Constitutional Law: Texts, Cases and Materials* (2008), p 377.
[234] de Blacam, 'Children, Constitutional Rights and the Separation of Powers' (2002) 37 Ir Jur 113, 131.

would be constitutionally permissible to impose charges for such residential medical care.[235] However, the Supreme Court was not prepared to accept the argument that such charges could be retrospectively charged without legislative authority as to allow such retrospective charges would infringe the property rights of those affected.

[4] PRINCIPLES OF CONSTITUTIONAL INTERPRETATION

[15.127] Having outlined the general development of constitutional judicial review since the 1960s, it remains to discuss the principles of interpretation developed by the courts in the elucidation of constitutional principles. In general terms, developments have to some extent mirrored those in the interpretation of legislation.[236] Thus, in some cases, the courts have applied a literal or grammatical rule of interpretation to the Constitution while in others they have developed an historical approach. More recently, a purposive or harmonious approach has emerged as a competing approach to constitutional interpretation.

[15.128] The text of some constitutional provisions renders it impossible to make a simple comparison between legislation and the Constitution. This arises in particular from references in some Articles to natural law and natural rights. This necessitated the development of particular rules of constitutional interpretation in order to reflect this intellectual influence.[237] While the influence of natural law may now be less strong, it would appear that it remains in some instances as an important interpretative aid alongside the harmonious approach to interpretation.

The literal or grammatical approach

[15.129] In a number of cases, a literal approach to the constitutional text has been applied by the courts. This approach may be compared with the approach taken in the interpretation of legislation. The literal approach, whether used in a statutory or constitutional context, can be supported on the basis that the courts remain faithful to the text of the material being examined and are thus not open to the criticism that they have substituted their own personal or subjective judgment for a more objective determination. Nonetheless, as with statutory interpretation,[238] a literal approach to the constitutional text can prove problematic. This is particularly evident where provisions of the Constitution come into conflict.[239]

[15.130] A literal approach to Article 34.4.3°, which prior to 2013 set out the appellate jurisdiction of the Supreme Court, had proved controversial in some instances. Article 34.4.3° provided: 'The Supreme Court shall, with such exceptions and subject to such

---

235 *Re Article 26 and the Health (Amendment) (No 2) Bill 2004* [2005] 1 IR 105.
236 See para **14.19**.
237 See para **15.147**.
238 See para **14.23**.
239 Clarke, 'Interpreting the Constitution: Essentially Contested Concepts' in Carolan and Doyle, *The Irish Constitution Governance and Values* (2008), p 103.

regulations as may be prescribed by law, have appellate jurisdiction from all decisions of the High Court ...' While this provision had not, in general, proved difficult to interpret,[240] the Supreme Court held, in *The People (DPP) v O'Shea*,[241] that the court's appellate jurisdiction extended to appeals against acquittals in the Central Criminal Court.

[15.131] The decision in *O'Shea* was by a majority of 3:2. The majority, O'Higgins CJ, Walsh and Hederman JJ, relied primarily on a literal interpretation of Article 34.4.3°. This was criticised by the two minority judges, Finlay P and Henchy J, on two grounds. First, it failed to have regard to the historical principles of double jeopardy and *autrefois acquit* which regarded an acquittal as a final verdict and that these principles were consistent with various other constitutional provisions such as the right to a trial in due course of law under Article 38. Second, the minority suggested that a literal approach to one constitutional provision was inappropriate and that it must be seen in the light of the Constitution as whole.

[15.132] At a narrow level, the minority considered that a literal interpretation of Article 34.4.3° failed to recognise that various determinations of the High Court were not amenable to appeal, such as the quasi-administrative allocation of judicial duties by the President of the High Court.[242] However, Henchy J also articulated a more general objection to the literal approach:

> "Any single constitutional right or power is but a component in an ensemble of interconnected and interacting provisions which must be brought into play as part of a larger composition, and which must be given such an integrated interpretation as will fit it harmoniously into the general constitutional order and modulation. It may be said of a constitution more than of any other legal instrument, that 'the letter killeth, but the spirit giveth life'. No single constitutional provision (particularly one designed to safeguard personal liberty or the social order) may be isolated and construed with undeviating literalness."[243]

[15.133] This passage anticipates our discussion below of the purposive or harmonious approach to constitutional interpretation. Henchy J seemed to link this approach with that in statutory interpretation because he immediately went on to quote with approval the following comments of Black J in *The People (Attorney General) v Kennedy*,[244] a case involving statutory interpretation:[245]

> "A small section of a picture, if looked at close-up, may indicate something quite clearly; but when one stands back and views the whole canvas, the close-up view of the small

---

[240] See para **7.26** which sets out the provisions concerning the Supreme Court's appellate jurisdiction after the establishment of the Court of Appeal, now set out in Article 34.5.

[241] *The People (DPP) v O'Shea* [1982] IR 384: see para **7.57**. See paras **12.113** on the status of *O'Shea* as a precedent.

[242] See para **4.63**.

[243] [1982] IR 384, 426.

[244] *The People (Attorney General) v Kennedy* [1946] I R 517: see also para **14.127**.

[245] In *Kennedy*, the Supreme Court had considered the Courts of Justice Act 1924, s 29, which gave jurisdiction to the court to hear an appeal from the Court of Criminal Appeal. (contd,,,.)

section is often found to have given a wholly wrong view of what it really represented. If one could pick out a single word or phrase and, finding it perfectly clear in itself, refuse to check its apparent meaning in the light thrown upon it by the context or by other provisions, the result would be to render the principle of *ejusdem generis* and *noscitur a sociis* utterly meaningless; for this principle requires frequently that a word or phrase or even a whole provision which, standing alone, has a clear meaning must be given a quite different meaning when viewed in the light of its context."[246]

Although Henchy J was in a minority in the *O'Shea* case, these comments on the limitations of the literal approach to interpretation, whether in a statutory or constitutional setting, carry great weight.[247]

[15.134] A variation on the literal approach was used in *Ryan v Attorney General*,[248] in which the High Court and Supreme Court held that Article 40.3 contained a guarantee to protect an unspecified number of personal rights. In the High Court, Kenny J conducted a literal or grammatical analysis of Article 40.3.1° and 2°, which provide:

"1° The State guarantees in its laws to respect, and, as far as practicable, by its laws to defend and vindicate the personal rights of the citizen.

2° The State shall, in particular, by its laws protect as best it may from unjust attack and, in the case of injustice done, vindicate the life, person, good name and property rights of every citizen."

Commenting on these, Kenny J stated:

"The words 'in particular' show that sub-s 2° is a detailed statement of something which is already contained in sub-s 1° which is the general guarantee. But sub-s 2° refers to rights in connection with life and good name and there are no rights in connection with these two matters specified in Article 40. It follows, I think, that the general guarantee in sub-s 1° must extend to rights not specified in Article 40."[249]

[15.135] While the grammatical analysis involved here was described as 'logically faultless', it has been criticised for introducing an element of uncertainty which is

---

[245] (\...contd) Section 29 provided that such appeal lay where a certificate that the case involved points of law of exceptional public importance was granted by the Court of Criminal Appeal or the Attorney General (or now also the Director of Public Prosecutions). The defendant's conviction had been quashed on appeal to the Court of Criminal Appeal and the Attorney General then sought to bring an appeal to the Supreme Court under s 29. The court concluded that, notwithstanding a literal reading of s 29 by which an appeal seemed to lie, the correct meaning was that no appeal lay from the decision by the Court of Criminal Appeal quashing a conviction. The effect of the decision was (belatedly) reversed by s 22 of the Criminal Justice Act 2006: see also para **7.56**.

[246] [1946] IR 517, 536.

[247] On the abolition of appeals against acquittals and modification of the double jeopardy rule, see paras **7.57–7.60**.

[248] *Ryan v Attorney General* [1965] IR 294: see para **15.54**.

[249] [1965] IR 294, 312.

repugnant to the concept of the rule of law itself.[250] Despite this criticism, the courts have continued to develop the unspecified unenumerated rights under Article 40.3, though the grammatical approach of Kenny J in *Ryan* has been replaced by the purposive or harmonious approach.[251]

Historical approach and 'original understanding'

[15.136] In *The People (DPP) v O'Shea*,[252] Finlay P and Henchy J criticised the majority's conclusion that appeals to the Supreme Court lay from acquittals in the Central Criminal Court on the ground that this ignored the common law's historical double jeopardy rule. Similar references to well-established principles of law or the state of the law in 1937 when the Constitution was passed are to be found in other cases.[253] Indeed, this echoes an approach of the United States Supreme Court by which it seeks to find an 'original understanding' of the text of the Constitution, based on the views of those who drafted its text in 1787.[254] This approach has been associated in recent years with commentators and judges who disapprove of the judicial activism and liberalism of the United States Supreme Court in the 1960s.[255] While references to the historical state of the law in 1937 are likely to continue, they are unlikely to prove decisive in many instances.

[15.137] The approach of the courts to the interpretation of legislation is instructive in this context; while in some instances an original or historical meaning may be required to interpret some statutory language, in others the language may develop a somewhat different meaning over time.[256] Similarly, the courts have developed common law principles, such as the duty of care in negligence, to accommodate new situations.[257] It should come as no surprise that in constitutional interpretation a similar pragmatic approach is evident.

[15.138] In the High Court judgment in *McGee v Attorney General*,[258] O'Keeffe P rejected the plaintiff's claim that s 17 of the Criminal Law Amendment Act 1935, which prohibited the importation of contraceptive items, conflicted with the plaintiff's right to marital privacy by preventing her and her husband from using such items. O'Keeffe P

---

[250] Kelly, *Fundamental Rights in the Irish Law and Constitution* (2nd edn, 1967), p 42. See also Hogan, 'Unenumerated Personal Rights: *Ryan's* Case Re-Evaluated' (1990–1992) 25–27 Ir Jur (ns) 95.

[251] See para **15.142**.

[252] *People (DPP) v O'Shea* [1982] IR 384: see para **15.131**. See also *DPP v Independent Newspapers (Ireland) Ltd* [2009] IESC 20.

[253] See Hogan and Whyte, *JM Kelly: The Irish Constitution* (4th edn, 2003), pp 18–30.

[254] Such texts include *The Federalist Papers*.

[255] For example, Bork, *The Tempting of America: The Political Seduction of the Law* (1990). For an overview of the debates in the US regarding constitutional interpretation, see, for example, Posner, *How Judges Think* (2008).

[256] See para **14.96**.

[257] See para **12.144**_ff._

[258] *McGee v Attorney General* [1974] IR 284: see para **15.169**.

rejected the idea that the right to marital privacy existed at all, since this would suppose that those who voted to enact the 1937 Constitution had, in effect, also voted to create a right of marital privacy and to repeal s 17 of the 1935 Act. O'Keeffe P doubted that this was the intention of the people in 1937. This, undoubtedly accurate, historical analysis of the state of public opinion in 1937 was rejected by the Supreme Court who declared s 17 of the 1935 Act invalid. In this respect, Walsh J commented that 'no interpretation of the Constitution is intended to be final for all time. It is given in the light of prevailing ideas and concepts.' This approach has been adopted in a number of subsequent cases. This approach has, on occasion, been questioned. Thus, in *Gilligan and Zappone v Revenue Commissioners*[259] the High Court noted that difficulties could arise ascertaining or determining the nature of these prevailing ideas and concepts.[260]

[15.139] Thus, between 1937 and 1975, juries were composed almost exclusively of men; nonetheless, in *de Búrca v Attorney General*,[261] the Supreme Court found the consequent exclusion of women to be discrimination prohibited by Article 40.1 of the Constitution. Similarly, between 1937 and 1984 legislation required unanimous jury verdicts in criminal trials; in *O'Callaghan v Attorney General*[262] the Supreme Court held that the introduction of majority verdicts by the Criminal Justice Act 1984 was not in conflict with the Constitution. It would seem from these cases that there is no 'original understanding' of the Irish Constitution.[263]

[15.140] The historical mode of constitutional interpretation has also re-emerged in a number of Supreme Court decisions, which may also reflect the similar US approach in terms of the 'original meaning' of the US federal Constitution. In *Sinnott v Minister for Education*[264] Murray J examined the understanding of the term 'primary education' in practice in the educational system in 1937 (when the Constitution came into force) to determine whether primary education could extend beyond the age of 18. He concluded that the state's obligations in relation to free primary education under Article 42.4 extended to children only and not adults.

[15.141] In *Maguire v Ardagh*[265] the Supreme Court considered the historical context of the 1922 and 1937 Constitutions in order to determine the scope of power of the Oireachtas to establish investigative committees. Similarly, the High Court referred also to the intention of the framers of the Constitution in *Gilligan and Zappone v Revenue Commissioners*[266] which concerned the recognition of same-sex marriages from outside Ireland for tax purposes. Dunne J accepted the traditional common law definition of

---

[259] *Gilligan and Zappone v Revenue Commissioners* [2008] 2 IR 417.
[260] [2008] 2 IR 417, 505.
[261] *de Búrca v Attorney General* [1976] IR 38: see para. **6.143**.
[262] *O'Callaghan v Attorney General* [1993] 2 IR 17: see para **6.159**.
[263] See also Whyte, 'Constitutional Adjudication, Ideology and Access to the Courts' in Whelan (ed), *Law and Liberty in Ireland* (1993).
[264] *Sinnott v Minister for Education* [2001] 2 IR 545.
[265] *Maguire v Ardagh* [2002] 1 IR 385: see para **8.59**.
[266] *Gilligan and Zappone v Revenue Commissioners* [2008] 2 IR 417.

marriage as being between one man and one woman and that this would have been relevant in the context of the framers of the Constitution. She rejected the argument that societal consensus had changed between 1937 and 2008 to the extent that marriage could have evolved beyond its traditional definition. Similarly, in *R v R*,[267] discussed above, McGovern J examined the political and historical context in which the Eighth Amendment in 1983 – which inserted Article 40.3.3° into the Constitution – had arisen in his consideration of whether an embryo outside the womb constituted an 'unborn' for the purposes of Article 40.3.3°. He concluded that the primary aim of the Eighth Amendment was to deal with the issue of termination of pregnancy and that there was no evidence that the People in voting on the Eighth Amendment would have considered that 'unborn' meant anything other than a foetus or child within the womb.

Purposive or harmonious approach

[15.142] We have seen that, in *The People (DPP) v O'Shea*,[268] Henchy J stated that the courts should avoid examining a constitutional provision in isolation and should ensure that each provision is given an 'integrated interpretation as will fit it harmoniously into the general constitutional order'. This harmonious approach requires the courts to interpret a provision in a way that is consistent with the 'general scheme' of the Constitution.[269] In that respect the harmonious approach is also a purposive approach and it seeks to avoid any internal inconsistency in the Constitution.

[15.143] The rationale for the purposive approach was set out by Keane CJ in *Maguire v Ardagh*[270] as follows:

> "The Constitution is a political charter, using the adjective in its broadest sense. One does not expect to find in it the level of detail which, in our legislative tradition, we associate with Acts, regulations and by-laws."[271]

[15.144] This approach was applied by the Supreme Court in *Tormey v Ireland*.[272] The plaintiff had been returned for trial to the Circuit Criminal Court, but wished to be tried in the High Court, the Central Criminal Court. Prior to 1981, he was entitled to elect for trial in the Central Criminal Court, but that right had been removed by s 31 of the Courts Act 1981. The issue raised was whether this was consistent with Article 34.3.1°, which provides that 'the High Court [is] invested with full original jurisdiction in and power to determine all matters and questions, whether of fact or law, civil or criminal'. The High Court and, on appeal, the Supreme Court, rejected the plaintiff's claim. The Supreme Court held that Article 34.3.1° should not be given a literal meaning.

---

267 *R v R* [2006] IEHC 359.
268 *The People (DPP) v O'Shea* [1982] IR 384: see para **15.131**.
269 See also *DPP v Independent Newspapers (Ireland) Ltd* [2009] IESC 20.
270 *Maguire v Ardagh* [2002] 1 IR 385.
271 [2002] 1 IR 385, 504.
272 *Tormey v Ireland* [1985] IR 289: see para **5.103**.

[15.145] Using the harmonious approach, the court pointed out that the High Court retained an original jurisdiction under Article 34.3.1° through its power to order judicial review of trials in the Circuit Criminal Court or through its power to make declaratory orders.[273] Delivering the judgment of the Court, Henchy J stated:

> "It is to be pointed out at the outset that the terms in which original jurisdiction is vested in the High Court by Article 34, s 3, sub-s 1 cannot be read literally. To do so would produce absurdity and bring Article 34, s 3, sub-s 1 into conflict with other constitutional provisions. At first view it might be thought that there is given to the High Court jurisdiction to determine 'all matters and questions', but that cannot be so, for in the nature of things there are matters and questions which are not amenable to determination by any court. They are not justiciable. Consequently, 'all matters and questions' must be read as confined to 'all justiciable matters and questions'. But even 'all justiciable matters and questions' expresses too widely the jurisdiction conferred by Article 34, s 3, sub-s 1, for other constitutional provisions show that an original jurisdiction in certain justiciable matters and questions shall, or may, be exercised by other courts, tribunals, persons or bodies. For example, it is implicit in Article 26 that no court other than the Supreme Court shall have jurisdiction to rule on the constitutionality of a Bill referred by the President under that Article; Article 34, s 3, sub-s 3 debars the High Court from considering the constitutionality of a statutory provision declared constitutional by the Supreme Court in a reference under Article 26; and Article 34, s 4, sub-s 6 provides more generally that the High Court cannot entertain any question which has been determined by the Supreme Court. Furthermore, an original jurisdiction may be exercised by courts of summary jurisdiction to try minor offences (Article 38, s 2), by special courts to try offences of the kind specified in Article 38, s 3, sub-s 1, by military tribunals to try offences against military law (Article 38, s 4, sub-s 1), and by persons or bodies exercising limited functions and powers of a judicial nature in matters other than criminal matters, duly committed to them under Article 37. The jurisdiction to try thus vested by the Constitution in courts, tribunals, persons or bodies other than the High Court must be taken to be capable of being exercised, at least in certain instances, to the exclusion of the High Court, for the allocation of jurisdiction would otherwise be overlapping and unworkable."[274]

[15.146] Henchy J states that a literal approach would produce 'absurdity' and that this should be avoided. This is reminiscent of the golden and teleological rules of statutory interpretation.[275] The harmonious approach goes further, ensuring that the Constitution is internally consistent and is not contradictory. The harmonious approach was summed up in *Tormey* thus:

> "As indicated earlier in this judgment, Article 34, s 3, sub-s 1, despite its unqualified and unambiguous terms, cannot be given an entirely literal construction. The rule of literal interpretation, which is generally applied in the absence of ambiguity or absurdity in the text, must here give way to the more fundamental rule of constitutional interpretation that the Constitution must be read as a whole and that its several provisions must not be looked at in isolation, but be treated as interlocking parts of the general constitutional scheme. This

---

273 See paras **10.18** and **10.53**.
274 [1985] IR 289, 294.
275 See para **14.43**.

means that where two constructions of a provision are open in the light of the Constitution as a whole, despite the apparent unambiguity of the provision itself, the Court should adopt the construction which will achieve the smooth and harmonious operation of the Constitution. A judicial attitude of strict construction should be avoided when it would allow the imperfection or inadequacy of the words used to defeat or pervert any of the fundamental purposes of the Constitution. It follows from such a global approach that, save where the Constitution itself otherwise provides, all its provisions should be given due weight and effect and not be subordinated one to the other. Thus, where there are two provisions in apparent conflict with one another, there should be adopted, if possible, an interpretation which will give due and harmonious effect to both provisions. The true purpose and range of a Constitution would not be achieved if it were treated as no more than the sum of its parts."[276]

[15.147] In summary, the harmonious approach entails the proposition that the Constitution cannot contradict itself; where there appears to be a conflict, the harmonious approach requires the courts to interpret provisions in a manner that ensures internal consistency. In *Tormey* this was achieved by concluding that, although the High Court does not hear all cases at first instance, it retains a 'full' jurisdiction under Article 34.3.1° by means of judicial review and the power to issue declaratory orders. The harmonious approach has been applied in a number of cases in recent years, and it would appear that it has now been accepted as the dominant canon of interpretation.[277]

European influence on harmonious approach

[15.148] The harmonious approach is virtually identical to the approach adopted by the Court of Justice of the European Union in its interpretation of the treaties which form the basis for European Union law.[278] Seen in conjunction with the emergence in recent years of the teleological approach to the interpretation of legislation,[279] it is evident that European Union law has had an important influence on Irish interpretative techniques. The courts have also given a cautious indication that, in limited circumstances, international conventions to which Ireland is a party might have a persuasive authority.[280]

Natural law and constitutional interpretation

[15.149] We have already referred to the Constitution as 'manifesto', a mixture of law and political aspiration, as in the case of Articles 2 and 3.[281] Some Articles also allude to

---

[276] [1985] IR 289, 295.

[277] For example, *Attorney General v X* [1992] 1 IR 1; *Re the Regulation of Information (Services Outside the State for the Termination of Pregnancies) Bill 1995* [1995] 1 IR 1: see paras **15.177–15.184**.

[278] See paras **16.81***ff*.

[279] See para **14.46**.

[280] See paras **14.92**.

[281] See para **15.02**.

concepts that require further explanation. For example, Article 41, which deals with the family, provides:

"1.1° The State recognises the Family as the natural primary and fundamental unit group of Society, and as a moral institution possessing inalienable and imprescriptible rights, antecedent and superior to all positive law.

2° The State, therefore, guarantees to protect the Family in its constitution and authority, as the necessary basis of social order and as indispensable to the welfare of the Nation and the State.

2.1° In particular, the State recognises that, by her life within the home, woman gives to the State a support without which the common good cannot be achieved.

2° The State shall, therefore, endeavour to ensure that mothers shall not be obliged by economic necessity to engage in labour to the neglect of their duties in the home.

3.1° The State pledges itself to guard with special care the institution of Marriage, on which the Family is founded, and to protect it against attack.

2° A Court designated by law may grant a dissolution of marriage where, but only where, it is satisfied that:

i. at the date of the institution of the proceedings, the spouses have lived apart from one another for a period of, or periods amounting to, at least four years during the previous five years,

ii. there is no reasonable prospect of a reconciliation between the spouses,

iii. such provision as the Court considers proper having regard to the circumstances exists, or will be made for the spouses, any children of either of them and any other person prescribed by law, and

iv. any further conditions prescribed by law are complied with. No law shall be enacted providing for the grant of a dissolution of marriage.[282]

3° No person whose marriage has been dissolved under the civil law of any other State but is a subsisting valid marriage under the law for the time being in force within the jurisdiction of the Government and Parliament established by this Constitution shall be capable of contracting a valid marriage within that jurisdiction during the lifetime of the other party to the marriage so dissolved."

[15.150] Article 41 encapsulates many of the difficulties inherent in the interpretation of the Constitution. Thus, from the literal and historical approach, Article 41.2 may appear to reflect the view that 'a woman's place is in the home'. This interpretation has been rejected as incorrect,[283] but in any event it appears dated and has been criticised for failing to reflect the increase from 5.6% to 32.4% in the proportion of married women who work outside the home, the absence of any reference to those who care for elderly

---

[282] The original text of Article 41.3.2°, prohibiting divorce, was: 'No law shall be enacted providing for the grant of a dissolution of marriage.' This was replaced by the text of Article 41.3.2° in the main body after its terms had been approved in the 1995 divorce referendum and which became the Fifteenth Amendment of the Constitution Act 1996.

[283] Mr Justice Walsh, 'The Constitution and Constitutional Rights' in Litton (ed), *The Constitution of Ireland, 1937–1987* (1988).

relatives in the home and the failure to refer to any role for husbands and fathers.[284] Article 41.3 presents another problem for the historical approach. Prior to 1996, Article 41.3.1°, by which the state pledges itself to guard with special care the institution of marriage, was followed by a ban on divorce in Article 41.3.2°. This ban was replaced in 1996 by the 'new' Article 41.3.2° quoted above, which permits divorce in certain circumstances.

[15.151] The creation of a divorce jurisdiction must of necessity involve a re-appraisal of the pledge to guard the family in Article 41.3.1°. In addition, pre-1996 decisions concerning annulment of marriages, which had emphasised that the Constitution supports marriage as an institution involving a lifelong commitment, would also require re-assessment.[285] These problems of interpretation can be resolved, however, by the rules of interpretation already referred to, which require that Article 41 is interpreted in accordance with changes in its own text, in the light of changes in society and also by avoiding any interpretation that would produce an internal contradiction.

Natural law and positive law

[15.152] Article 41.1 refers to the family as 'a moral institution possessing inalienable and imprescriptible rights, antecedent and superior to all positive law'. This is an allusion to the concept or theory of natural law that individuals are endowed with certain rights by virtue of their human personality and that these are superior to positive law, that is, the law of human institutions, such as a legislature. These rights, called natural rights, are inalienable in the sense that they may not, in general, be given away by the individual; they are imprescriptible in that they may not, in general, be taken away by the state; and they are antecedent to positive law in that they pre-date positive law, that is, exist in some pre-existing form. The concept of natural law and natural rights originated with philosophers of Ancient Greece such as Aristotle.[286] However, it was also adopted by Christian philosophers, beginning in medieval times with St Thomas Aquinas, and its inclusion in the 1937 Constitution has been attributed largely to the Christian, and in particular Roman Catholic, influence on the drafters of the 1937 text.

[15.153] In general terms, the natural law theory begins with the assumption that some natural authority confers rights on human beings. For the pre-Christian Greek philosophers, the ultimate authority was a metaphysical or absolute state of nature. For Christian philosophers, the ultimate authority is, of course, a metaphysical divine being, God.

---

[284] The *Report of the Constitution Review Group* (Pn 2632, 1996), pp 333–334, recommended that Article 41.2 might be revised to read: 'The State recognises that home and family life gives to society a support without which the common good cannot be achieved. The State shall endeavour to support persons caring for others within the home.'

[285] For example, *N(K) v K* [1985] IR 733.

[286] See also paras **1.38–1.57**.

[15.154] All natural law philosophers have in common the concept that the moral validity of any laws enacted by human institutions (positive law) depends on its compliance with the basic principles of natural law and natural rights. Thus, natural law is a 'higher law' and superior to positive law, a concept expressly referred to in Article 41.1. Natural law philosophers are thus engaged in a discussion about the moral standing of laws enacted by human institutions.

[15.155] One of the consequences of such 'moral disagreement' over the content of laws is that a law which does not comply with natural law is morally wrong or bad and that, in general, one would be entitled to disregard such a law. In the 16th and 17th centuries, this concept gave rise to the suggestion by some English judges, such as the 17th century English Chief Justice Sir Edward Coke, that legislation enacted in conflict with natural law, or the law of God, could be declared invalid by the courts. However, this suggestion was not acted on and later judges and writers on English law ultimately accepted the view that the English legislature was entirely free to enact any form of legislation and the courts were obliged to give effect to it.[287]

[15.156] Until the enactment of the UK Human Rights Act 1998, which incorporated the Council of Europe Convention on Human Rights into UK law, moral disagreement in the UK over the content of laws was a matter for political debate rather than judicial decision. Confining the moral evaluation of laws to the political realm is also manifested in the concept of 'civil disobedience', which involves the refusal to accept the political or moral legitimacy of a law but realises its legal validity (in a positivist sense) may result in criminal prosecution and punishment. The political campaigns of Mahatma Gandhi in India in the 1930s and of Martin Luther King in the United States of America in the 1960s are examples.

[15.157] Among the rights regarded as part of natural law theory are the right to life, which is referred to in Article 40.3 of the 1937 Constitution, and to equality before the law, referred to in Article 40.1. A difficulty with the natural law theory is that the precise scope of natural rights may either be difficult to discern or the views of philosophers may change over time. Thus, in ancient Greece, the concept of equality was effectively reserved for citizens of Athens; other persons were excluded from the political process and the concept of slavery was also 'accommodated' within the general equality guarantee. Some philosophers have criticised the natural law tradition for its lack of specificity. In addition, the long association of the natural law theory with Christian philosophy, and in particular the Roman Catholic Church, has resulted in a negative response from philosophers who espouse a secular approach to the content of law.

Natural law and utilitarianism

[15.158] The theory of utilitarianism is associated with the 19th-century writings of the English philosophers Jeremy Bentham and John Stuart Mill. Utilitarianism developed in part by way of opposition to what was seen as the vagueness of the natural law theory

---

287   See generally, para **2.10**.

and its insistence that a 'higher' law determined whether positive law was valid. Utilitarians begin by rejecting the concept that law can include a 'higher' law. They are also associated with rejecting the notion of individual rights or natural rights.

[15.159] For utilitarians, therefore, English law comprises the common law and statute law and there is no question of such laws being declared invalid for being in conflict with a 'higher' law as Lord Coke had suggested. Nonetheless, Bentham's theory requires that positive law conform with the principle of utility, which requires that laws meet the 'happiness' (or needs) of the community as a whole. This is sometimes inaccurately summarised as a crude assertion of 'majority rule', but Bentham acknowledged that the interests of the community may sometimes best be served by laws which respect the needs of a minority in the community even though this might marginally diminish the 'happiness' of the majority. Thus utilitarianism may be used in support of laws which respect minority interests. In that respect, it is not necessarily opposed in practice to a theory of rights.[288] Many important legal reforms of the 19th century have been attributed to utilitarianism, such as the reform of the court system and rationalisation of legal procedures.[289]

[15.160] Indeed, Mill, a utilitarian, may be regarded as a founder of the 'liberal' movement, in particular the concept that the law should not concern itself with matters of private morality unless these conflicted with the common good of society. Thus, where a person engaged in an activity in private, Mill had argued that this ought not necessarily be regulated by law even if the majority in society found such activity morally wrong. In the 20th and 21st centuries this principle has been adopted in a number of states as the basis for much law reform. It has been resisted by many supporters of the natural law theory, particularly in areas concerning sexual freedom. This may be attributed in part to the fact that many who support natural law theory do so from a theological or religious standpoint.

[15.161] Thus, in many states, moral disagreement over the content of laws has focused on what is sometimes referred to as the 'liberal agenda'. In Ireland, this has included calls for legislation liberalising access to contraception, legislation for divorce (which required a prior amendment of the Constitution); decriminalisation of homosexual sexual acts; the right to choose (that is, the right of women to control their fertility through access to abortion); and, to a lesser extent, the right to die in dignity (described by its opponents as a euphemism for euthanasia). Many of these calls have been resisted by those who support the natural law theory on the ground that such matters are contrary to natural law or are 'unnatural' and are not matters of rights or liberty but merely of 'licence'.

[15.162] Thus, the natural law theory, while supporting the concept of rights, has been portrayed by some as 'conservative' and inimical to individual liberty, while

---

[288] Kelly, 'The Constitution: Law and Manifesto' in Litton (ed), *The Constitution of Ireland, 1937–1987* (1987), p 216.

[289] See para **2.23**.

utilitarianism has been portrayed as 'liberal' and progressive even though it does not necessarily use the language of rights.

[15.163] In the second half of the 20th century, there was a resurgence of interest in natural law and utilitarianism. While natural law and utilitarianism remain quite different theories, both are moral theories in that they subject positive laws to a test of whether they are morally good or bad. In addition, it may be said that, in recent years, many of those who have developed the natural law theory cannot always be categorised as 'conservative'.[290]

The Constitution, natural law and utilitarianism

[15.164] The 1937 Constitution clearly rejects the basic premise of utilitarianism that natural rights do not exist. However, the Constitution also reflects some elements of utilitarianism by subjecting the exercise of rights to the requirements of the common good, as in the case of property rights under Article 43. Nonetheless, the dominant influence, as indicated by Article 41, is that individuals have rights which are anterior and superior to positive law.

[15.165] A crucial question in this respect is whether the Constitution, by invoking natural law principles, established natural law as a 'higher' law by which the Constitution itself is bound. This has two implications. First, it has been argued that the courts must interpret the Constitution consistently with natural law. Second, and more profoundly, it has been suggested that the Constitution may not be amended in a manner that would be in conflict with natural law. This argument, which has been associated with those who oppose many elements of the 'liberal agenda', arose with particular vigour in the immediate aftermath of the decision of the Supreme Court in *Attorney General v X*,[291] in which the court held that Article 40.3.3° permitted abortions where the right to life of the mother was in immediate danger.[292] To place this debate in context, it is necessary to refer back to earlier decisions of the courts on Article 40.3.

Ryan v Attorney General

[15.166] In *Ryan v Attorney General*,[293] Kenny J had stated that, in addition to discerning a list of unenumerated rights from a grammatical analysis of Article 40.3, such rights were also implicit in the 'Christian and democratic nature of the State' as indicated by the overall text of the 1937 Constitution. He instanced the right to marry as a personal right implicit in the Christian nature of the state, while the right to travel freely within the state was mentioned as a right implicit in the democratic nature of the state.[294]

---

[290] See the discussion of law and morality at paras **1.45–1.57**.

[291] *Attorney General v X* [1992] 1 IR 1: see para **15.177**.

[292] For example, O'Hanlon, 'Natural Rights and the Irish Constitution' (1993) 11 ILT 8 (see also para **4.164**). See also the essays in Quinn (ed), *Justice and Legal Theory in Ireland* (1993).

[293] *Ryan v Attorney General* [1965] IR 294: see para **15.54**.

[294] See also *King v Attorney General* [1981] IR 233 on the right to 'dawdle': see para **15.65**.

[15.167] In concluding that the right to bodily integrity was also a right guaranteed protection under Article 40.3, Kenny J cited with approval a reference to the right in a papal encyclical written by Pope John XIII, *Pacem In Terris*. This encyclical was written by a Pope who was regarded as a reforming and 'liberal' influence within the Roman Catholic Church, evidenced in particular by the establishment of the Second Vatican Council during his reign. Nonetheless, the impression might have been created that 'Christian' equalled 'Roman Catholic' as far as the 'Christian and democratic' nature of the state was concerned.[295]

[15.168] Thus, the general question arose as to whether any existing, or more significantly, any proposed law, that was in conflict with the 'Christian' nature of the Constitution would be declared invalid. This question came to prominence in the late 1960s and early 1970s when law reform proposals were initiated in the Oireachtas. In the late 1960s, private members' Bills seeking to legalise the importation of contraceptive devices, a criminal offence under s 17 of the Criminal Law Amendment Act 1935, were introduced by Senator Mary Robinson,[296] but were overwhelmingly defeated. The issue was shortly to become a matter for the courts.[297]

McGee v Attorney General

[15.169] After *Ryan v Attorney General*,[298] the next major decision concerning Article 40.3 was in 1973, *McGee v Attorney General*.[299] The plaintiff, a married woman, had been advised by her doctor that to have any more children would seriously endanger her life. Together with her husband, she took the decision to use a form of contraception to avoid further pregnancy. Her doctor advised a particular method which required her to import spermicidal jelly into the state. This was impounded by the Revenue Commissioners pursuant to the powers conferred by s 17 of the Criminal Law Amendment Act 1935, which made the importation of such material a criminal offence. The plaintiff sought a declaration that s 17 was in conflict with her right to privacy. By a 4:1 majority, the Supreme Court accepted that s 17 of the 1935 Act was in conflict with the plaintiff's right to marital privacy under Articles 40.3 and 41.

[15.170] In his judgment in *McGee*, Walsh J alluded to the principles of natural law in concluding that s 17 of the 1935 Act had breached the plaintiff's rights under Articles 40.3 and 41. By contrast, in his judgment in *McGee* Henchy J avoided any reference to natural law but took an approach consistent with the later emergence of the harmonious approach in concluding that the plaintiff's rights under Article 40.3 had been violated.

---

[295] At this time the Roman Catholic Church was acknowledged as having a 'special position': see para **2.78**.

[296] President of Ireland between 1990 and 1997, she became UN High Commissioner for Human Rights in 1997.

[297] Thus involving, in one sense, the transfer from the Oireachtas to the Courts referred to by Henchy J in *Cahill v Sutton* [1980] IR 269: see para **15.90**.

[298] *Ryan v Attorney General* [1965] IR 294.

[299] *McGee v Attorney General* [1974] IR 284.

[15.171] In the *McGee* case, Walsh and Henchy JJ took different approaches but they reached the same conclusion, namely that the prohibition of the importation of contraceptives breached the plaintiff's right to marital privacy. In referring to the natural law,[300] Walsh J noted that the courts were not bound by the theological views expressed by one particular faith in determining whether the natural rights of a person under the Constitution had been violated, thus suggesting that the constitutional vision of natural law was not linked to a particular theological teaching. As Henchy J later pointed out in *Norris v Attorney General*,[301] this use of the natural law theory by Walsh J resulted in a finding that was, in fact, prohibited by the teachings of the Roman Catholic Church, which clearly prohibit the use of contraceptive devices in any circumstances as a means of birth control. However, the differences between the natural law and harmonious approaches were to appear in the *Norris* case.

Norris v Attorney General

[15.172] In 1983, in *Norris v Attorney General*,[302] the Supreme Court rejected, by a 3:2 majority, a challenge to ss 60 and 61 of the Offences against the Person Act 1861 which made buggery a criminal offence in all cases, including those where the act occurred between consenting adults. The plaintiff had claimed that ss 60 and 61 of the 1861 Act were in conflict with his right of privacy as a homosexual male. O'Higgins CJ (with whom Finlay P and Griffin J concurred) pointed out that buggery had been condemned as gravely sinful by St Paul and all Christian churches and that this should inform the court's interpretation of Article 40.3 of the Constitution. By contrast, Henchy and McCarthy JJ in *Norris* pointed out that positive law in Ireland did not criminalise all the seven deadly sins and that it was inappropriate to use natural law in the manner suggested by the majority.

[15.173] The majority in *Norris* clearly took a 'conservative' natural law approach and rejected John Stuart Mill's view that the law should not concern itself in the area of private morality except to the extent necessary to protect public order and to guard citizens against injury and exploitation.[303] The majority also rejected the comparable view of the English Wolfenden Committee on Homosexual Offences and Prostitution in 1957 that there were certain matters of private morality and immorality that were 'not the law's business' (the 1957 Report led to the enactment of the British Sexual Offences Act 1967 which repealed in Britain ss 60 and 61 of the 1861 Act). The majority's reference to St Paul is reminiscent of Kenny J's allusion to the papal encyclical in *Ryan v Attorney General*,[304] and overall the majority judgment is more conservative in tone than

---

[300] He did not expressly refer to the views on natural law of Kennedy CJ in *The State (Ryan) v Lennon* [1935] IR 170: see para **2.70**.

[301] *Norris v Attorney General* [1984] IR 36.

[302] *Norris v Attorney General* [1984] IR 36.

[303] On Mill generally, see paras **1.45–1.57**.

[304] *Ryan v Attorney General* [1965] IR 294: see para **15.166**.

that of Walsh J in *McGee*.[305] Although Walsh J was not a member of the Supreme Court in *Norris*,[306] he agreed with the essential conclusion that, while the right of privacy under natural law prohibited the state from interfering with the right of married couples to use contraceptives, the state was entitled to prevent homosexual men from engaging in consensual sexual acts.[307] Thus, Walsh J's natural law approach was not as extensive as the purposive and harmonious approach favoured by Henchy J in *Norris*, which appeared to involve a more secular interpretation of the Constitution.

[15.174] Despite the emphasis by the majority in *Norris* on a 'conservative' view of natural law, the earlier acceptance by the Supreme Court in *McGee* of the right of privacy led to concern that the right to choose methods of contraception could be extended to the right to choose the termination of a pregnancy, that is, a right to abortion,[308] even though this had been expressly disavowed by some of the judges in *McGee* and by others in later cases.[309]

---

[305] *McGee v Attorney General* [1974] IR 284.

[306] He was, at the time, full-time President of the Law Reform Commission and thus an additional judge of the Supreme Court had been appointed (see para **4.53**, fn 114) so that Walsh J was not a member of the Court in the *Norris* case.

[307] See his dissenting judgment as a judge of the European Court of Human Rights in *Norris v Ireland* (1988) 13 EHRR 186, a successful claim by the plaintiff in *Norris v Attorney General* that the state was in breach of the European Convention on Human Rights in continuing to maintain ss 60 and 61 of the 1861 Act on the statute books. This confirmed its earlier decision in *Dudgeon v United Kingdom* (1981) 4 EHRR 149 (referred to by both O'Higgins CJ and Henchy J in *Norris v Attorney General*), in which it had also held that ss 60 and 61 of the Offences against the Person Act 1861 were in breach of the Convention. In his judgment in *Norris v Ireland*, Walsh J reviewed in some detail the views expressed by Mill, Devlin and Hart (see paras **1.45–1.57**) on the role of the law in areas of personal morality. He concluded that Ireland was entitled to take a different view on homosexual sexual acts from that of other states, and on the basis of this 'margin of appreciation' should not have been found in breach of the Convention. In the wake of the majority decision, the Criminal Law (Sexual Offences) Act 1993 repealed ss 60 and 61 of the 1861 Act and replaced them with provisions which no longer make buggery between consenting adults a criminal offence.

[308] Abortion, the procuring of a miscarriage, was a criminal offence under the Offences Against the Person Act 1861, ss 58 and 59, the sections immediately preceding those which made buggery a criminal offence and which were discussed in *Norris v Attorney General* [1984] IR 36. Sections 58 and 59 of the 1861 Act were repealed and replaced by the Protection of Life During Pregnancy Act 2013: see para **15.180**, fn 318.

[309] For example, Walsh J in *G v An Bord Uchtála* [1980] IR 32. In the *Norris* case, McCarthy J (who was one of the two judges in the minority of the view that ss 60 and 61 of the 1861 Act were inconsistent with the Constitution) stated, *obiter*, that he would not declare invalid ss 58 and 59 of the Offences against the Person Act 1861 if the issue were to arise. He was aware at the time (1983) that the campaign to insert Article 40.3.3° was nearing fruition.

Despite this comment from a judge who would have been regarded as the most 'liberal' on the Supreme Court at that time, those who feared that the right to privacy would lead, at some time, to a 'test' case on abortion pointed out that this had happened in the United States Supreme Court in 1972 in *Roe v Wade* (1972) 410 US 113, a year before the decision in *McGee v Attorney General*. (contd.../)

[15.175] The campaign to ensure that abortion would not be introduced by a constitutional 'test case' on the right to privacy culminated in the insertion of Article 40.3.3° into the Constitution in 1983, which provides:

> "The State acknowledges the right to life of the unborn and, with due regard to the equal right to life of the mother, guarantees in its laws to respect, and, as far as practicable, by its laws to defend and vindicate that right."

[15.176] Those supporting its wording intended that it would prohibit abortion, while also preserving existing arrangements to protect the life of the mother. These included surgical interventions in ectopic pregnancies, that is where the foetus is outside the womb and is not viable but where the mother's life may be at risk unless the foetus is removed. However, the intention to ensure that such interventions would not be prohibited produced a wording that some commentators, including the then Attorney General, considered could be open to the interpretation that abortion was being made lawful in some limited circumstances.[310] The insertion of Article 40.3.3° was followed by a series of cases which prohibited the distribution of information concerning abortion services abroad, including the addresses of abortion clinics in Britain.[311]

Attorney General v X

[15.177] In 1992, in *Attorney General v X*,[312] the High Court granted the Attorney General an injunction prohibiting the defendant, a 14-year-old girl who had become pregnant having been raped, from leaving the state with a view to obtaining an abortion. The girl had stated that she would commit suicide if she were required to bring the pregnancy to full term. In the High Court Article 40.3.3° was interpreted to mean that abortion was prohibited in such circumstances. However, on appeal, the Supreme Court held, by a 4:1 majority, that Article 40.3.3° permitted abortions where, as here, the right to life of the mother was in immediate danger. The majority reached this conclusion by a textual analysis of Article 40.3.3° and accepted that it should adopt the harmonious approach to the constitutional text. The court accepted that, in certain circumstances, there could be a conflict between 'the right to life of the unborn' and 'the equal right to life of the mother'; that where such conflict of rights could not be avoided, the Constitution required that its provisions be interpreted harmoniously and that the rights

---

309 (\...contd) See generally Kelly, *The Irish Constitution*, (3rd edn, 1994), (Hogan and Whyte eds), pp 1495–1533 on the connection between *McGee* and the abortion referenda and litigation between 1983 and 1993.

310 See generally Hesketh, *The Second Partitioning of Ireland?* (1990).

311 For example, *Attorney General (Society for the Protection of Unborn Children Ltd) v Open Door Counselling Ltd* [1988] IR 593; *Society for the Protection of Unborn Children Ltd v Coogan* [1989] IR 734.

312 *Attorney General v X* [1992] 1 IR 1.

thereby guaranteed should be interpreted in concert in accordance with the concepts of prudence, justice and charity. Finlay CJ stated:

> "I accept the submission made on behalf of the Attorney General, that the doctrine of the harmonious interpretation of the Constitution involves in this case a consideration of the constitutional rights and obligations of the mother of the unborn child and the interrelation of those rights and obligations with the rights and obligations of other people and, of course, with the right to life of the unborn child as well.
>
> Such a harmonious interpretation of the Constitution carried out in accordance with concepts of prudence, justice and charity, as they have been explained in the judgment of Walsh J in *McGee v Attorney General*[313] leads me to the conclusion that in vindicating and defending as far as practicable the right of the unborn to life but at the same time giving due regard to the right of the mother to life, the court must, amongst the matters to be so regarded, concern itself with the position of the mother within a family group, with persons on whom she is dependent, with, in other instances, persons who are dependent upon her and her interaction with other citizens and members of society in the areas in which her activities occur. Having regard to that conclusion, I am satisfied that the test proposed on behalf of the Attorney General that the life of the unborn could only be terminated if it were established that an inevitable or immediate risk to the life of the mother existed, for the avoidance of which a termination of the pregnancy was necessary, insufficiently vindicates the mother's right to life.
>
> I, therefore, conclude that the proper test to be applied is that if it is established as a matter of probability that there is a real and substantial risk to the life, as distinct from the health, of the mother, which can only be avoided by the termination of her pregnancy, such termination is permissible, having regard to the true interpretation of Article 40.3.3° of the Constitution."[314]

[15.178] The acceptance by the Supreme Court of the harmonious approach and the submission by counsel for the Attorney General in the *X* case that Article 40.3.3° authorised abortion in limited circumstances seemed to confirm the views expressed in 1983 that the text might authorise abortion in certain circumstances. The decision was sharply criticised on the ground that it disregarded the apparent intention of those who voted for the insertion of Article 40.3.3° into the Constitution less than 10 years earlier.[315]

[15.179] It was in the context of this conclusion that the debate then arose in 1992 as to whether the courts were obliged to interpret the Constitution in the light of the natural law, that is, whether natural law took priority over the text of the Constitution.

[15.180] In response to the *X* case, three further proposed amendments to Article 40.3.3° were put to a referendum in late 1992. The first of these concerned the

---

[313] *McGee v Attorney General* [1974] IR 284: see para **15.169**.
[314] [1992] 1 IR 1, 53.
[315] This was noted by the dissenting judge, Hederman J. See also the extensive critique in Byrne and Binchy, *Annual Review of Irish Law 1992* (1994), pp 159–185.

'substantive' issue of abortion, and proposed to insert an additional clause into Article 40.3.3° authorising abortion where the life of the mother was at risk, though excluding the risk of suicide.[316] This was rejected by the electorate,[317] but two further clauses were approved, and these provide that Article 40.3.3° 'shall not limit freedom to travel between the State and another state' and 'shall not limit freedom to obtain or make available, in the State, subject to such conditions as may be laid down by law, information relating to services lawfully available in another state'.

Regulation of Information Bill 1995 case

[15.181] The clause concerning information resulted in the Oireachtas passing the Regulation of Information (Services Outside the State for the Termination of Pregnancies) Bill 1995. In *Re the Regulation of Information (Services Outside the State for the Termination of Pregnancies) Bill 1995*,[318] the court found that the Bill was not repugnant to the Constitution.[319] In the course of argument in the case, it was suggested that the 1995 Bill was repugnant to the Constitution since it was in conflict with natural law.

[15.182] The judgment of the court, delivered by Hamilton CJ, stated:

"These arguments raise the question of the role of the natural law in the development of constitutional jurisprudence with regard to the identification 'of the personal rights of the citizen' referred to in Article 40.3.1° of the Constitution and the guarantee therein set forth on the part of the State to respect, and as far as practicable, by its laws to defend and vindicate such rights.

---

[316] The proposed clause was: 'It shall be unlawful to terminate the life of the unborn unless such termination is necessary to save the life, as distinct from the health, of the mother where there is an illness or disorder of the mother giving rise to a real and substantial risk to her life, not being a risk of self-destruction.'

[317] The rejection of the 'substantive' amendment has led to continuing debate since 1992 on the abortion topic. In 1999, the government published a *Green Paper on Abortion* which outlined seven possible options on the matter, ranging from the inclusion of a ban on abortion in the Constitution to provision for a liberal abortion regime in the state. In 2000, the Oireachtas All-Party Committee on the Constitution, in its *Fifth Progress Report* dealt with abortion and also outlined possible options. In 2002 the Twenty-Fifth Amendment to the Constitution Bill proposed to deal with the right to life of the unborn and at the same time replace the relevant provisions of the 1861 Act on procuring a miscarriage with statutory provisions that would be aligned with an amended version of Article 40.3.3°. This proposal was rejected in the referendum on the Bill, so that the legal position at the time of writing (September 2014) remains as set out in the *X* case. Legislation to given effect to the analysis in the X case was, ultimately, enacted in the Protection of Life During Pregnancy Act 2013, which also repealed and replaced ss 58 and 50 of the Offences Against the Person Act 1861.

[318] *Re the Regulation of Information (Services Outside the State for the Termination of Pregnancies) Bill 1995* [1995] 1 IR 1.

[319] The Bill was enacted as the Regulation of Information (Services Outside the State for the Termination of Pregnancies) Act 1995.

It is fundamental to this argument that, what is described as 'the natural law' is the fundamental law of this State and as such is antecedent and superior to all positive law, including the Constitution and that it is impermissible for the people to exercise the power of amendment of the Constitution by way of variation, addition or repeal, as permitted by Article 46 of the Constitution unless such amendment is compatible with the natural law and existing provisions of the Constitution and if they purport to do so, such amendment would have no effect.

The court does not accept this argument."

[15.183] For the first time, the Supreme Court was required to consider whether natural law was superior to the Constitution. The court rejected this argument, and concluded that the Constitution was the supreme law in the state. Having reviewed various provisions of the Constitution limiting the powers of the executive and legislative branches and the case law on Article 40.3, the court commented:

"From a consideration of all the cases which recognised the existence of a personal right which was not specifically enumerated in the Constitution, it is manifest that the court in each such case had satisfied itself that such personal right was one which could be reasonably implied from and was guaranteed by the provisions of the Constitution, interpreted in accordance with its ideas of prudence, justice and charity. The courts, as they were and are bound to, recognised the Constitution as the fundamental law of the State to which the organs of the State were subject and at no stage recognised the provisions of the natural law as superior to the Constitution.

The people were entitled to amend the Constitution in accordance with the provisions of Article 46 of the Constitution and the Constitution as so amended by the fourteenth amendment is the fundamental and supreme law of the State representing as it does the will of the people."

[15.184] While the decision of the court establishes that natural law cannot take priority over the text of the Constitution, it nonetheless remains that the Constitution invokes 'higher law' principles which require elucidation in order to interpret its meaning. Thus, it would seem wrong to conclude that the *Regulation of Information Bill 1995* case signalled the 'death of natural law'.[320] This can be supported by referring to one other decision of the court.

Ward of Court case

[15.185] Just over two months after its decision in the *Regulation of Information Bill case*, the Supreme Court was faced with another difficult issue. In *Re a Ward of Court (No 2)*,[321] the family of a woman who had suffered irreversible brain damage during surgery in April 1972, and who had subsequently been made a ward of court,[322] applied

---

[320] See Twomey, 'The Death of the Natural Law?' (1995) 13 ILT 270.
[321] *Re a Ward of Court (No 2)* [1996] 2 IR 79.
[322] On the impending replacement of the wardship jurisdiction by the Assisted Decision-Making (Capacity) Bill 2013, see para **15.79**.

for an order that all artificial nutrition and hydration of her should cease. The woman was described as being in a near-persistent or permanent vegetative state (near-PVS); she appeared to have minimal cognitive capacity but seemed to recognise her family and the nursing staff who cared for her and reacted to strangers by showing distress. Her heart and lungs functioned normally, but she was unable to speak, was spastic, could not swallow, was incontinent and bedridden. She received nutrition through a gastronomy tube, which had been inserted under general anaesthetic into her stomach (commonly known as a peg tube).

[15.186] It appeared that her condition was unlikely to improve. The institution in which she received medical treatment and care refused her family's request to remove the gastronomy tube. The issue raised for the court was whether, after 22 years in this condition, it was permissible to order that the nutrition and hydration provided by the gastronomy tube be removed. This in turn raised the question of the extent of the right to life and whether any circumstances existed in which the courts could, in effect, decide not to prolong life.

[15.187] In approaching the case, the court agreed with the distinction drawn by Taylor LJ (later Lord Taylor LCJ) in *Re J (A Minor)*[323] between terminating life, which he had stated was unlawful, and not prolonging life, which might be permissible in certain circumstances. Having quoted the distinction drawn by Taylor LJ, Hamilton CJ stated:

> "Having regard to the provisions of Article 40.3.2° of the Constitution, this statement of the law applies with even greater force in this jurisdiction. Even in the case of the most horrendous disability, any course of action or treatment aimed at terminating life or accelerating death is unlawful."

[15.188] The court went on to consider whether the order sought by the woman's family was permissible. By a majority of 4:1, the court accepted that it was. Hamilton CJ referred to the decision of the Court in the *X* case and its use of the harmonious approach of constitutional interpretation where, as in that case, the right to life of the unborn and the right to life of the mother appeared to conflict. Hamilton CJ commented:

> "I am satisfied that in this case, if there was an interaction of constitutional rights which I was not capable of harmonising, the right to life would take precedence over any other rights. The nature of the right to life and its importance imposes a strong presumption in favour of taking all steps capable of preserving it save in exceptional circumstances. The problem is to define such circumstances. The definition of such circumstances must, of necessity, involve a determination of the right to life acknowledged by the Constitution."

[15.189] He referred to the judgment of Walsh J in *G v An Bord Uchtála*,[324] in which he had stated that the right to life involved certain ancillary rights. In the context of the woman in the *Ward of Court* case, Hamilton CJ continued:

> "These rights include the right to live life in its fullest content, to enjoy the support and comfort of her family, to social contact with her peers, to education, to the practice of her

---

[323] *Re J (A Minor)* [1991] Fam 33.
[324] *G v An Bord Uchtála* [1980] IR 32.

religion, to work, to marry and have children, to privacy, to bodily integrity and to self-determination. These rights are not, however, unqualified: they may be subject to the constitutional rights of others and to the requirements of the common good. They, however, spring from the right to life which is recognised by the Constitution.

As the process of dying is part, and an ultimate inevitable consequence, of life, the right to life necessarily implies the right to have nature take its course and to die a natural death and, unless the individual concerned so wishes, not to have life artificially maintained by the provision of nourishment by abnormal artificial means, which have no curative effect and which are intended merely to prolong life.

This right, as so defined, does not include the right to have life terminated or death accelerated and is confined to the natural process of dying. No person has the right to terminate his or her life or to accelerate or have accelerated his or her death.

In this case, the [woman's] life is being artificially maintained by the provision of life sustaining nourishment through a gastronomy tube inserted in her body. Such treatment is in no way, nor intended to be, curative and she will continue to be in the condition in which she now is, and has been for over twenty years, if she continues to be provided with nourishment in this manner."

[15.190] Hamilton CJ thus accepted that, in limited circumstances, the right to life included the right to die, to 'let nature take its course'. He concluded that the particular circumstances of this case involved such exceptional circumstances. He stated: 'The true cause of the [woman's] death will not be the withdrawal of [the] nourishment but the injuries which she sustained on 26 April 1972 [during her surgery].'

[15.191] Although the judgment of Hamilton CJ in the *Ward of Court* case would appear to support the overriding importance of the harmonious approach to the exclusion of any natural law or religious component, this may be an inaccurate view. Indeed, in the *Ward of Court* case, Hamilton CJ referred to the right of the woman to the practice of her religion, that the woman's family had approached the case from a religious viewpoint seeking to ensure that her religious faith would be upheld and had introduced evidence from moral theologians who had advised the family that withdrawal of the gastronomy tube was not contrary to their religious beliefs. Moreover, in a concurring judgment, Denham J quoted with approval the comment of Walsh J in *Quinn's Supermarket Ltd v Attorney General*,[325] that the Constitution 'reflects a firm conviction that we are a religious people'. She commented:

"This foundation is an aid in interpreting the law and the Constitution. In regard specifically to the right to life, it enables the interpretation to be inclusive of a spiritual or religious component. This approach is signalled in the first words of Article 40.3.1° where the unqualified 'respect' for life is stated. In respecting a person's death, we are also respecting their life – giving to it sanctity. That concept of sanctity is an inclusive view which recognises that in our society persons, whether members of a religion, or not, are all under the Constitution protected by respect for human life. A view that life must be preserved at

---

[325] *Quinn's Supermarket Ltd v Attorney General* [1972] IR 1.

all costs does not sanctify life. A person, and/or her family, who have a view as to the intrinsic sanctity of the life in question are, in fact, encompassed in the constitutional mandate to protect life for the common good; what is being protected (and not denied or ignored or overruled) is the sanctity of that person's life. To care for the dying, to love and cherish them, and to free them from suffering rather than simply to postpone death, is to have fundamental respect for the sanctity of life and its end."

[15.192] Thus, while the harmonious interpretation may be said to represent the most significant canon of interpretation of the Constitution, the religious or spiritual or natural law component remains as an aid to its interpretation.[326] The judgment of Denham J in the *Ward of Court* case indicates that it would be inaccurate to describe contemporary constitutional interpretation as comprising an exclusively secular approach; thus a 'liberal' version of natural law may be relevant in some instances.[327]

The Fleming case

[15.193] The High Court and Supreme Court returned to complex end-of-life questions in *Fleming v Ireland*.[328] The plaintiff was 59 years of age at the time of the case and had been living with the effects of multiple sclerosis since her early 30s. Her neurological condition was that she was unable to walk or to use her lower or upper limbs, she often had difficulty swallowing and was beginning to lose her ability to communicate. It was agreed that she was in the final stage of the disease and was experiencing a rapid deterioration of her condition but that her condition did not, however, affect her decision-making capacity. She wished to be allowed to have the assistance of her partner in ending her life at a time and place of her choosing, with her children also present, but did not wish to leave a legacy behind her whereby her partner or her children could be prosecuted for the offence of assisting her suicide under s 2 of the Criminal Law (Suicide) Act 1993. Her partner, while willing to help her, would only do so if it was lawful. The plaintiff sought an order that s 2 of the 1993 Act was unconstitutional.

[15.194] The case thus turned on whether the Constitution recognised a "right to die" in extreme circumstances and whether the absolute terms of s 2 of the 1993 Act was in breach of such a right. While both the High Court and, on appeal, the Supreme Court, expressed considerable sympathy for the plaintiff, her claim was dismissed. The courts accepted that the 1993 Act interfered with an individual's autonomy but that this was justified in particular because of the State's duty under Article 40.3.2° of the Constitution to protect the right to life. The courts also noted that in *Pretty v United*

---

[326] Natural law has also been considered in *North Western Health Board v HW* [2001] 3 IR 622 and *AO v Minister for Justice, Equality and Law Reform* [2003] 1 IR 1.

[327] On the complex medical ethical and legislative issues arising from the *Ward of Court* case, which was widely reported in the media as the 'right to die' case, see Tomkin and Hanafin, 'Medical Treatment at Life's End: The Need for Legislation' (1995) 1 Medico-Legal Journal of Ireland 3.

[328] *Fleming v Ireland* [2013] IEHC 2, [2013] IESC 19.

Kingdom[329] the European Court of Human Rights had held that the comparable prohibition on assisted suicide in the English Suicide Act 1961 (on which the 1993 Act was modelled) did not breach the applicant's right to privacy under Article 8 of the European Convention on Human Rights, and that this remained essentially a matter for individual states to determine. The High Court and Supreme Court accepted that while a number of jurisdictions such as Switzerland and the Netherlands had made provision for assisted suicide under certain circumstances, they also noted that there remained prevailing doubts in the literature and in the evidence presented in the case as to the adequacy of the legal safeguards in those jurisdictions. On this basis, the Supreme Court concluded that "there is no constitutional right to commit suicide or to arrange for the determination of one's life at a time of one's choosing."[330] The Supreme Court added, nonetheless, that this would not preclude the Oireachtas from reconsidering the complex policy issues involved in determining whether to make provision for assisted suicide:[331]

> "Nothing in this judgment should be taken as necessarily implying that it would not be open to the State, in the event that the Oireachtas were satisfied that measures with appropriate safeguards could be introduced, to legislate to deal with a case such as that of the appellant. If such legislation was introduced it would be for the courts to determine whether the balancing by the Oireachtas of any legitimate concerns was within the boundaries of what was constitutionally permissible. Any such consideration would, necessarily, have to pay appropriate regard to the assessment made by the Oireachtas both of any competing interests and the practicability of any measures thus introduced."

[15.195] The plaintiff had also sought an order to compel the Director of Public Prosecutions to publish guidelines on assisted suicide, pointing out that the English Director of Public Prosecutions had published guidelines specific to assisted suicide as a result of the decision in *R (Purdy) v Director of Public Prosecutions*[332] (which was, in effect, a follow-up to the *Pretty* case, discussed above). The High Court accepted that while in Ireland the Director had published *Guidelines for Prosecutors* which assisted prosecutors in the implementation of the prosecuting process, they were general in nature and were not offence-specific. The High Court also held that there was no statutory duty on the Director to publish the type of offence-specific guidelines sought by the plaintiff, and also considered that such guidelines would be in breach of the separation of powers in Article 15.2 of the Constitution because they might have the effect of placing a gloss on the legislative intent of the Oireachtas in enacting the 1993 Act. The High Court nonetheless concluded its judgment by noting that counsel for the Director had confirmed to the Court that, in the context of exercising her discretion whether to prosecute in an individual case, "full and careful consideration would have to be given to evidence of compliance with a list of factors such as those that followed the *Purdy* case."[333] The plaintiff did not appeal this aspect of the High Court decision and, as

---

[329]   *Pretty v United Kingdom* (2002) 35 EHRR 1.

[330]   *Fleming v Ireland* [2013] IESC 19, para 137.

[331]   *Fleming v Ireland* [2013] IESC 19, para 108.

[332]   *R (Purdy) v Director of Public Prosecutions* [2009] UKHL 45, [2010] 1 AC 435.

[333]   *Fleming v Ireland* [2013] IEHC 2, para 175.

the High Court itself noted this undertaking by the Director provided "a measure of comfort"[334] to the plaintiff and her family.[335]

[5] REPORT OF CONSTITUTION REVIEW GROUP, REPORTS OF OIREACHTAS COMMITTEE ON CONSTITUTION AND REPORTS OF CONSTITUTIONAL CONVENTION

[15.196] In 1995,[336] a Constitution Review Group was established with a general remit to review the terms of the 1937 Constitution 'to establish those areas where constitutional change may be desirable or necessary, with a view to assisting the all-Party Committee on the Constitution, to be established by the Oireachtas'. The group was precluded from examining Articles 2 and 3, divorce, the right to bail, cabinet confidentiality and votes for emigrants, which were the subject of separate consideration.[337] The group published its final report, running to over 700 pages, in 1996.[338] Aside from those matters on which it was prevented by its terms of references from commenting, the report was a comprehensive analysis of the 1937 Constitution and contained wide-ranging proposals for the amendment of the Constitution.

[15.197] In general terms, the group recommended reform of the 1937 Constitution rather than its replacement. Indeed, the essential distribution of powers between the three arms of government, executive, legislative and judicial, would remain intact if the group's recommendations were enacted by the People. However, the report recommended a full review of the role and functions of the Senate.[339] It also proposed a specific reference be included concerning membership of the United Nations.[340] As to

---

334 *Fleming v Ireland* [2013] IEHC 2, para 175.

335 It was reported that Ms Fleming subsequently died peacefully in her own home: see Buckley "Right-to-die campaigner Marie Fleming had 'peaceful death'", Irish Examiner, 21 December 2013.

336 A Committee on the Constitution had previously been established in the 1960s: *Report of the Committee on the Constitution* (Pr 9817, 1967). One of the few recommendations of this Committee actually implemented was the deletion by the Fifth Amendment of the Constitution Act 1972 of the reference to the 'special position' of the Roman Catholic Church. Its recommendations on amending Articles 2 and 3 of the Constitution ultimately formed the basis for the changes effected in 1998 in the wake of the Good Friday Agreement: see para **15.11**.

337 Articles 2 and 3 were amended in 1998 in the wake of the Good Friday Agreement: see para **15.11**. A referendum on divorce was held in 1995, resulting in the removal of the ban on divorce in Article 41: see para **15.150**. A referendum on bail was held in 1997, resulting in changes to the basis on which it may be refused: see para **6.107**. A referendum on cabinet confidentiality was also held in 1997 which amended Article 28.4 to allow for cabinet discussions to be disclosed in court proceedings and tribunals of inquiry.

338 *Report of the Constitution Review Group* (Pn 2632, 1996).

339 *Report of the Constitution Review Group* (Pn 2632, 1996), pp 65–71.

340 *Report of the Constitution Review Group* (Pn 2632, 1996), p 113.

the courts, the group recommended the retention of the existing integrated court system and it did not recommend any change to Article 34 concerning the delineation of the judicial power.[341] However, the report made influential recommendations on judicial conduct and ethics.[342] In connection with fundamental rights, a number of significant changes were proposed. Thus, the group recommended that Article 40.3 be amended to provide a comprehensive list of fundamental rights to take account of those identified to date as well as those contained in the European Convention on Human Rights and Fundamental Freedoms and the United Nations International Covenant on Civil and Political Rights.[343]

[15.198] In 1996, the group's report was referred to an All-Party Oireachtas Committee on the Constitution, which was mandated to deal with all aspects of the Constitution. Between 1997 and 2006, the Committee published 10 reports:[344]

- First Progress Report (1997);[345]
- Second Progress Report: Seanad Éireann (1998);
- Third Progress Report: the President (1999);
- Fourth Progress Report: the Courts and the Judiciary (1999);
- Fifth Progress Report: Abortion (2000);
- Sixth Progress Report: The Referendum (2001);
- Seventh Progress Report: Parliament (2002);
- Eighth Progress Report: Government (2003);
- Ninth Progress Report: Private Property (2004);
- Tenth Progress Report: The Family (2006).

[15.199] From these reports, a constitutional amendment to recognise the place of local government, recommended in the *First Progress Report*, was approved in 1999.[346] The recommendations in the *Fourth Progress Report* to amend the provisions on judicial impeachment and for the establishment of a judicial council were accepted by government, but a proposed referendum was withdrawn in 2001.[347] The *Fifth Progress Report*, dealing with abortion, remains a highly contentious issue as does the *Tenth Progress Report on the Family*. In the *Tenth Progress Report*, the Committee

---

[341] *Report of the Constitution Review Group* (Pn 2632, 1996), pp 146–57.

[342] See paras **4.138–4.160** on the proposed Judicial Council.

[343] *Report of the Constitution Review Group* (Pn 2632, 1996), pp 245–64.

[344] These are all available at www.constitution.ie.

[345] The *First Progress Report* dealt with: constitutional reviews generally; the referendum process; the power to dissolve Dáil Éireann; constitutionality of Bills and Laws; local government; the Electoral and Ethics Commission; the Ombudsman; 'woman in the home' and gender-proofing; and technical amendments.

[346] See para **8.40** on the reduction of the number of local authorities under the Local Government Reform Act 2014.

[347] See para **4.149**. It appears that a Judicial Council will be established without the need for a constitutional amendment: see para **4.155**!

recommended against constitutional change to the definition of family and instead recommended legislative change for the positions of cohabiting heterosexual couples and same-sex couples.[348] Other aspects of the work of the Review Group and of the Oireachtas Committee are not politically controversial and involve changes of a technical or drafting character.

[15.200] In 2007, a new Joint Committee on the Constitution was established in succession to the Committee that had been in place since 1997. This Committee has continued to examine areas in which constitutional change may be desirable or necessary. Its *First Report* (2008) was on Article 40.6.1°.i, which concerns freedom of expression.[349] The Committee concluded that the current provision is unsatisfactory as limitations on free speech are afforded undue prominence. It recommended that Article 40.6.1°.i be amended to align it with Art 10 of the ECHR, which would ensure greater emphasis on freedom of expression. The Committee's *Second Report* (2009) considered the referendum process, in particular the current manner in which information is imparted by the media to the public during the course of referendum campaigns.[350] It recommended the enactment of legislation to deal with political broadcasting during the course of referendum campaigns to ensure that the diverse views are given a fair hearing.

[15.201] In 2012, a Convention on the Constitution was established by Dáil Éireann. It comprised 100 members: a Chairperson appointed by the Government, 66 citizens randomly selected from the electoral register so as to be broadly representative of Irish society, with the remaining 32 comprising a member from each of the political parties in the Northern Ireland Assembly and members of the Houses of the Oireachtas, so as to be impartially representative of the Houses. The Convention's terms of reference required it to examine the following issues in connection with amendment and reform of the Constitution: (i) reducing the seven-year Presidential term of office to five years and aligning it with the local and European elections; (ii) reducing the voting age from 18; (iii) review of the Dáil electoral system; (iv) giving citizens resident outside the State the right to vote in Presidential elections at Irish embassies, or otherwise; (v) provision for same-sex marriage; (vi) amending the clause on the role of women in the home in Article 41 and encouraging greater participation of women in public life; (vii) increasing the participation of women in politics; (viii) removal of the offence of blasphemy from Article 40.6 the Constitution; and (ix) following completion of the above reports, such other relevant constitutional amendments that may be recommended by it. Between 2012 and 2014, when the Convention's term ended, it published nine

---

[348] The Civil Partnership and Certain Rights and Obligations of Cohabitants Act 2010 contains the legislative response to this.

[349] Houses of the Oireachtas Joint Committee on the Constitution, *First Report Article 40.6.1.i – Freedom of Expression* (2008) available at www.oireachtas.ie.

[350] Houses of the Oireachtas Joint Committee on the Constitution, *Second Report: Articles 46 and 47 Amendment of the Constitution and Referendum* (2009), available at www.oireachtas.ie.

Reports on these issues.[351] While neither the government or Dáil Éireann was bound by any recommendations in these reports, it appears at the time of writing (September 2014) that a number of referendums arising from its deliberations will be held in the foreseeable future, including three in 2015 concerning: reducing the voting age to 16, reducing the age barrier for presidential candidates from the current 35, and allowing same-sex marriage.

[6] THE CONSTITUTION AND THE EUROPEAN CONVENTION ON HUMAN RIGHTS

[15.202] We have noted that the Constitution Review Group recommended that Article 40.3 be amended to provide a comprehensive list of fundamental rights to take account of those identified to date as well as those contained in the European Convention on Human Rights and Fundamental Freedoms.[352] Separately, as part of the 1998 Good Friday agreement,[353] the state committed itself to bringing forward proposals to incorporate the Convention into domestic law. This was done by the European Convention on Human Rights Act 2003. The 2003 Act incorporates the European Convention on Human Rights on a sub-constitutional level, in other words it is subject to the Constitution and should there be any conflict, the Constitution will prevail. This approach mirrors the United Kingdom's Human Rights Act 1998. Section 2(1) of the European Convention on Human Rights Act 2003 provides:

> "In interpreting and applying any statutory provision or rule of law, a court shall, in so far as possible, subject to the rules of law relating to such interpretation and application, do so in a manner compatible with the State's obligations under the Convention provisions."

The Supreme Court sees the purpose of the Act of 2003 as follows:

> "[T]o enable further effect to be given, subject to the Constitution, to certain provisions of the European Convention for the Protection of Human Rights and Fundamental Freedoms 1950."[354]

[15.203] In *Foy v An t-Ard Chlaraitheoir*[355] the High Court (McKechnie J) clarified the precise status of the ECHR in Irish law:

> "It is a misleading metaphor to say that the Convention was incorporated into domestic law. It is not. The rights contained in the Convention are now part of Irish law. They are so by reason of the Act of 2003. That is their source. Not the Convention."

---

[351] *The Ninth Report of the Convention on the Constitution: Conclusions and Final Recommendations* (2014) contains an overview of the Convention's work and a summary of the recommendations made in its Reports. The reports are available at www.constitution.ie.

[352] See para **15.197**.

[353] See para **15.11**.

[354] *Dublin City Council v Fennell* [2005] 1 IR 604. See also *Byrne v Dublin City Council* [2009] IEHC 122.

[355] *Foy v An t-Ard Chlaraitheoir* [2007] IEHC 470: see para **17.71**.

It has been argued that the introduction of the European Convention on Human Rights into Irish law was probably the most important human rights development to emerge from the signing of the Good Friday Agreement.[356] However, in many areas the Constitution either provides for greater rights or similar rights to the ECHR. For example, from a survey of the impact of the ECHR on criminal law, McDermott and Murphy conclude from the case law that the Irish experience in incorporating the ECHR into our criminal law has been one of adaptation rather than upheaval.[357] Nonetheless, it has been equally argued that:

> "[T]he values and norms it [the Constitution] shares with the ECHR are in places better articulated and better conceptualised at present in the Convention case law. In addition, there are elements of the Irish constitutional system of rights protection which have grown stale. Incorporation of the ECHR with its subtly different value systems has the potential to trigger a reassessment of fundamental rights and how they should be respected and upheld in contemporary Ireland."[358]

A good example of this is the resurgence of the jurisdiction of the courts to strike out claims for want of prosecution owing to delay.[359] The courts have used jurisprudence under the ECHR as an additional factor in cases, thereby building on case law already in place on the issue using constitutional jurisprudence.[360] In relation to the delay cases, Hogan makes the following observation on the impact of the ECHR:

> "Perhaps the only real tangible effect this far has been that the ECHR case-law on delay has prompted the courts to take a more interventionist line so far as litigant delay is concerned, although the constitutional principles on fair procedures meant that the court were already moving in this direction in any event."[361]

As with constitutional claims, cases invoking the Convention have been dismissed. For example in *Grace v Ireland*[362] the applicant unsuccessfully argued that provisions of the Bankruptcy Act 1988 were incompatible with the ECHR. The excessive rigours of the

---

[356] O'Connell, 'Watched Kettles Boil (Slowly): The Impact of the ECHR Act 2003' in Kilkelly (ed), *ECHR and Irish Law* (2nd edn, 2009), p 1.

[357] McDermott and Murphy, 'No Revolution: The Impact of the ECHR Act 2003 on Irish Criminal Law' (2008) 15(1) DULJ 1, 40. On the impact of the ECHR on criminal law see also Ní Raifeartaigh, 'The Convention and Irish Criminal Law: Selected Topics' in Kilkelly (ed), *ECHR and Irish Law* (2nd edn, 2009), p 247.

[358] O'Cinneide, 'The European Convention on Human Rights and the Irish Constitutional System of Rights Protection: Complementary or Divergent' in Carolan and Doyle (ed), *The Irish Constitution Governance and Values* (2008), p 510.

[359] See Browne, 'Article 6 and Civil Cases' in Kilkelly (ed), *ECHR and Irish Law* (2nd edn, 2009), pp 118–123.

[360] For example see *DF v McGarry* [2007] IEHC 215.

[361] Hogan, 'The Value of Declarations of Incompatibility and the Rule of Avoidance' [2006] DULJ 408, 411–412.

[362] *Grace v Ireland* [2007] 2 ILRM 283.

1988 Act have subsequently been substantially ameliorated by the Personal Insolvency Act 2010.[363]

[15.204] Section 2 of the 2003 Act requires the courts when interpreting and applying statutory provisions or rules of law to do so in a manner compatible with the Convention. Section 3 of the 2003 Act requires every organ of state to perform its functions in a manner compatible with the Convention and allows persons who have suffered loss and damage arising out of the state's failure to do so to sue for damages. Courts, the President, the Oireachtas or either House of the Oireachtas or a Committee of either of the Houses of the Oireachtas are excluded from the definition of organ of the state within the 2003 Act.[364] However, this does not appear to have prevented the application of the ECHR to the courts themselves.[365] Nor does it prevent an applicant from bringing proceedings against Ireland in the European Court of Human Rights.[366]

[15.205] Article 13 of the ECHR provides that each person whose rights have been violated under the ECHR is entitled to an effective remedy. This article is included in the Schedule to the 2003 Act setting out the relevant Convention provisions. The UK Human Rights Act 1998 omitted this provision, as concerns were expressed that its inclusion might lead the courts to develop a new range of remedies previously unknown to the law, together with a sense that it was unnecessary in view of the range of remedies available under the 1998 Act.[367] The effect of the inclusion of Art 13 within the remit of the 2003 Act was considered by the High Court in *Byrne v Dublin City Council*.[368] In this case Murphy J held that he would grant an interlocutory injunction restraining the eviction of the applicant and her husband from their property as this would amount to a breach of s 3 of the 2003 Act. Having considered a number of academic commentaries,[369] which argued that the reference in s 3 to damages did not exclude other remedies, he concluded that s 3 of the 2003 Act permitted him to grant an interlocutory injunction to order to enforce the duty in that section. He distinguished the previous case of *Donegan v Dublin City Council*[370] in which Laffoy J refused to grant an injunction merely on the basis that a law itself is incompatible with the Convention as in that case

---

363 The 2012 Act implemented recommendations in the Law Reform Commission's *Report on Personal Debt Management and Debt Enforcement* (LRC 100-2010).

364 European Convention on Human Rights Act 2003, s 1(1).

365 O'Connell, 'Watched Kettles Boil (Slowly): The Impact of the ECHR Act 2003' in Kilkelly (ed), *ECHR and Irish Law* (2nd edn, 2009), p 10.

366 Forde, *Constitutional Law* (2nd edn, 2004), p 275.

367 Lord Irvine, Hansard, House of Lords, col 475, 18 November 1997.

368 *Byrne v Dublin City Council* [2009] IEHC 122, [2012] IESC 18 and see the response to the Supreme Court decision discussed at para **17.72**.

369 Byrne and Binchy, *Annual Review of Irish Law 2003* (2004), p 277; Collins and O'Reilly, *Civil Proceedings and the State* (2003), paras 11–25; and Doyle, 'Procedures, Remedies and the Place of the ECHR Act within the Existing Constitutional System' delivered on 20 November 2007 to the Irish Centre for European Law.

370 *Donegan v Dublin City Council* [2008] IEHC 288, [2012] IESC 18 (and see the response to the Supreme Court decision discussed at para **17.72**).

there was no breach of s 3 because the injunction was sought before the issue of a warrant for possession. In *Byrne*, the High Court held that the only circumstances in which it is appropriate for an applicant to seek an injunction is to restrain a breach of the s 3 duty. The court held that it is not sufficient to show a breach of Convention rights which is inherent in the statutory provision or rule of law itself. The availability of an injunction to restrain a breach by an organ of state of its s 3 duty is thus a very powerful remedy for applicants.

[15.206] Section 5 of the 2003 Act empowers the High Court and, on appeal, the Supreme Court, to make a declaration of incompatibility that a provision or rule is incompatible with the Convention 'where no other legal remedy is adequate and available', thereby suggesting that other remedies such as a declaration of unconstitutionality should be determined first. However, in *Carmody v Minister for Justice, Equality and Law Reform*[371] Laffoy J held that the issue of ECHR compatibility should be decided first. Hogan is critical of this approach[372] and he prefers the approach taken by O'Neill J in *Law Society of Ireland v Competition Authority*[373] where he dealt with the constitutional issue first and, after granting an order quashing a decision of the Competition Authority, found that any issue of compatibility with the ECHR was unnecessary. Indeed, the Supreme Court in *Carmody* also took this approach. It therefore appears the courts are more willing to consider the constitutional issues first and, if necessary, then the ECHR issue. For example in *TH v DPP*[374] the accused alleged his constitutional and ECHR rights had been infringed by a delay of 22 months in prosecution of the offence with which he had been charged. The High Court found that the delay had been unreasonable and this breached the accused's constitutional rights to a reasonably expeditious trial. As a result of this finding, the High Court found it unnecessary to deal with the ECHR issue. In *McCann v Judge of Monaghan District Court*,[375] Laffoy J acknowledged that it was inappropriate for the court to express any view on the ECHR issue as she had found that the relevant provision was incompatible with the Constitution. The approach to this issue thus seems settled: the courts will consider the Constitution first and then if necessary the ECHR.

[15.207] It is notable that a s 5 declaration does not affect the continued enforcement or operation of the provision. Hogan and Whyte describe s 5 as a 'limping provision' and argue that that it will cause difficulties.[376] As is evident from *Foy v An t-Ard Chlaraitheoir*,[377] although the Irish system of registration of births was declared

---

371 *Carmody v Minister for Justice Equality and Law Reform* [2005] IEHC 10, [2009] IESC 91, [2009] 1 IR 635: see also para **9.22**.

372 Hogan, 'The Value of Declarations of Incompatibility and the Rule of Avoidance' [2006] DULJ 408.

373 *Law Society of Ireland v Competition Authority* [2006] 2 IR 262.

374 *TH v DPP* [2004] IEHC 76.

375 *McCann v Judge of Monaghan District Court* [2009] IEHC 276: see para **10.23**.

376 Hogan and Whyte, *JM Kelly: The Irish Constitution* (4th edn, 2003), p 1320.

377 *Foy v An t-Ard Chlaraitheoir* [2002] IEHC 116; [2007] IEHC 470. See para **17.71**.

incompatible with the ECHR, the legislative response has been inadequate. At the time of writing (September 2014) a General Scheme of a Gender Recognition Bill has been published and while this is expected to be enacted in 2014 or 2015 the pace of legislative response to the *Foy* decision has been extremely slow. Four declarations of incompatibility have been made at the time of writing. By contrast, in the UK a 2006 report on the implementation of the Human Rights Act 1998 found that up to July 2006 there had been 15 declarations of incompatibility of UK legislation with the ECHR and all of these had been remedied by primary legislation or remedies were being considered.[378] Section 5 provides that the Taoiseach shall cause a copy of the court order containing a declaration of incompatibility to be laid before each House of the Oireachtas within 21 days on which the House has sat after the making of the order. Section 5 also permits an *ex gratia* payment to be made to the party who is the subject of the order of declaration upon the application of that party to the Attorney General. The Supreme Court has held that the ECHR cannot be relied upon to challenge acts done by the organs of state prior to the implementation of the 2003 Act.[379] Therefore, the jurisprudence on the effect of the incorporation of the ECHR will take time to emerge.

---

[378] Department for Constitutional Affairs, *Review of the Implementation of the Human Rights Act* (2006). The Department for Constitutional Affairs is now known as the Ministry of Justice. The report is available at www.justice.gov.uk.

[379] *Dublin City Council v Fennell* [2005] 2 ILRM 288.

Chapter 16

European Union Law

[1] Introduction 785
[2] European Integration after 1945 788
[3] The Three European Communities 789
[4] From European Community to European Union 796
[5] The Nature of European Union Law 812
[6] Institutions of the European Union 828
[7] The Form of European Union Laws 840
[8] Implementation of European Union Law in Ireland 846

[1] INTRODUCTION

[16.01] On 1 January 1973, Ireland became a member state of what was then the European Communities. This involved the amendment of Article 29 of the Constitution to enable the state to ratify a treaty of accession to three international organisations: the European Coal and Steel Community (ECSC),[1] the European Atomic Energy Community (EAEC or Euratom) and the European Economic Community (EEC). Each Community had been established by a separate treaty signed by six states in the 1950s; the effect of the referendum was that these three treaties were incorporated into Irish law. The three original treaties were later amended, notably by the Single European Act, the Treaty on European Union, the Treaty of Amsterdam, the Treaty of Nice, and the Treaty of Lisbon, with the Irish Constitution being amended on each occasion.

[16.02] The original treaties have been significantly amended since their adoption in the 1950s. In consequence of the Treaty of Lisbon, which came into effect in 2009, the principal constitutional instruments governing the European Union are the Treaty on the European Union (TEU) and the Treaty on the Functioning of the European Union (TFEU). The Treaty on European Union established the European Union as a legal entity in itself, incorporating what until then had been the separate entities of the European Communities and the European Union. The Treaty of Rome[2] which

---

1   The ECSC expired in 2002, see para **16.14**.
2   The Treaty of Rome was initially titled 'Treaty Establishing the European Economic Community', was renamed 'Treaty Establishing the European Community' by the Maastricht Treaty in 1992, and became the 'Treaty on the Functioning of the European Union' in 2009. In this chapter we use the term 'Treaty of Rome' when referring to the Treaty in its pre-2009 guise. We use the TFEU title when referring to the Treaty in its current post-Lisbon version.

established the European Economic Community in 1957 had been much amended and, in 2009, was renamed the Treaty on the Functioning of the European Union by the Treaty of Lisbon. Since its foundation, the European Union has grown from six original member states[3] to 28, with the accession of Croatia on 1 July 2013. Further expansion of the EU is anticipated and accession negotiations are currently under way with several countries. The Former Yugoslav Republic of Macedonia, Turkey, Iceland, Montenegro and Serbia have been granted the status of official candidate for membership. Albania, Bosnia and Herzegovina and Kosovo are currently engaged in the stabilisation and association process and have the status of potential candidate countries.

[16.03] This chapter deals primarily with the legal effects of the state's membership of the European Union.[4] Membership required the state to subscribe to a new legal order, thus creating a new source of law in Ireland, namely European Union law.[5] One of the most significant aspects of this new source of law is that it derives from an institutional structure that operates outside the state, in contrast with the sources of law discussed in previous chapters.

Financial and economic context

[16.04] There are a number of reasons why Ireland joined what were then known as the European Communities in 1973. Since the establishment of the Irish Free State in 1922, the United Kingdom (and in particular England) remained a major trading partner for

---

[3]   The six founding members in 1957 were Belgium, France, Germany, Italy, Luxembourg and the Netherlands.

[4]   See generally Pech, *The European Union and its Constitution: From Rome to Lisbon* (2008); Keville and Lucey, *Irish Perspectives on EC Law* (2003); Fahey, *EU Law in Ireland* (2010); McMahon and Murphy, *European Community Law in Ireland* (1989); Fennelly, *International Law in the Irish Legal System* (2014); Kapteyn and Van Themaat, *Introduction to the Law of the European Communities* (3rd edn, 1998); Craig and de Búrca, *EU Law: Text, Cases and Materials* (5th edn, 2011); Weatherill and Beaumont, *EU Law: The Essential Guide to the Legal Workings of the European Union* (3rd edn, 1999); *Wyatt and Dashwood's European Union Law* (6th edn, 2011); Kapteyn, McDonnell, Mortelmans, Timmermans (eds), *The Law of the European Union and the European Communities* (2008); Hartley, *The Foundations of European Union Law* (7th edn, 2010); Kaczorowska, *European Union Law* (3rd edn, 2013); Berry, Homewood and Bogusz, *Complete EU Law: Text, Cases, and Materials* (2013); Barnard, *The Substantive Law of the EU: The Four Freedoms* (2013), Barnard and Peers, *European Union Law* (2014); Chalmers, Davies and Monti, *European Union Law: Text and Materials* (2014); Hartley, 'The Constitutional Foundations of the European Union' (2001) 117 LQR 225. For an overview of the impact prior to the Treaty on European Union, see McCutcheon, 'The Legal System', in Keatinge (ed), *Ireland and EC Membership Evaluated* (1991), pp 209–229.

[5]   On 1 December 2009, the date on which the Treaty of Lisbon entered into force, the European Union gained legal personality and acquired the competences previously conferred on the European Community. Community law has therefore become European Union law. In this chapter we prefer the term 'EU law' but occasionally we use the term 'Community law' when referring to that body of law in a historical context or when quoting directly.

the state. When, in the 1960s, the United Kingdom began negotiations to join the European Communities, it was necessary for Ireland to do likewise. In addition, it was considered that membership would open up new markets for Irish companies and thus lessen dependency on the British market in the long term. The European Communities had also already established policies which it was considered would benefit certain sectors, in particular agriculture and associated industries. With the growing globalisation of trade in the 1980s and 1990s, membership continued to be of increased significance

[16.05] In an international trading context, the European Union has become a single trading entity, with a combined population of over 506 million people. By 2012, the combined Gross Domestic Product (GDP) of the member states exceeded that of the United States of America, Japan, Russia and China. And while the EU has only seven per cent of the world's population, its trade with the rest of the world accounts for approximately 20 per cent of the global total.

[16.06] The European Union is financed from three principal sources: customs duties imposed on goods imported into the Union, a percentage of each EU country's Value Added Tax receipts and contributions from the member states themselves. In 2008, just under 20 per cent of this annual income was contributed by Germany, with France being the next major contributor at 17 per cent of the total, followed by Italy at 13 per cent and the United Kingdom at 11.5 per cent. This income is then re-distributed among the member states under the various laws and policies adopted by the Union. By far the largest single item of expenditure is in the area of agriculture, which in 2008 accounted for more than €53bn, with regional policy at €36bn forming the second largest item of expenditure.[6]

[16.07] Ireland's contribution in 2008 came to €1.5bn, about 1.5 per cent of the total national contributions. However, since joining the European Communities, Ireland has received approximately €60bn in funding, principally in the area of agriculture and structural funds.

[16.08] It is clear that, in financial terms, Ireland has been a net beneficiary of European Union membership. Of course, membership is not simply a one-way street, and it involves certain responsibilities as well as entitlements. For example, the state is required to allow virtually unrestricted access to the Irish market for goods and services from other member states and may not enact any protectionist laws to shield industry in Ireland from foreign competition. The political arguments about the benefits and costs of membership have been debated in the years prior to and since 1973. In general terms, it may be said that the arguments for membership have been supported by a majority of the state's population, although enthusiasm for deepening European integration is at best lukewarm, judged by the results of the first referenda on the Nice and Lisbon Treaties.

---

6   [2008] OJ L 71: eur-lex.europa.eu/JOHtml.do?uri=OJ:L:2008:071:SOM:EN:HTML.

[2] EUROPEAN INTEGRATION AFTER 1945

[16.09] The history of the European Union begins in the aftermath of the Second World War. The widespread devastation throughout Europe in 1945, the effect of the Holocaust, the virtual economic ruin of the Allied and Axis states and the breakdown of the pre-war monarchies, brought home the need for complete restructuring of European, and world, institutions. In this context the establishment of the United Nations Organisation in 1945[7] can be seen as the first move in the direction of establishing a new world order. In Europe, it was recognised that institutional change was necessary to avoid future wars on the European mainland. A number of 'grand ideas' for closer cooperation between all the Allied powers was presented, some leading to the creation of enduring organisations, others remaining as ideas and little more.

[16.10] On the military front, the establishment of the North Atlantic Treaty Organisation (NATO) brought military cooperation between the United States and the major European Allied states, acting as a counterpoint in the Cold War to the Warsaw Pact alliance of the states of Central and Eastern Europe. The European allies also formed an organisation called the Western European Union (WEU), with slightly less overt Cold War connotations of military cooperation and mutual defence.

[16.11] In terms of human rights protection, the Convention for the Protection of Human Rights and Fundamental Freedoms, signed in 1950 by the states of the Council of Europe, established a basis for the protection of those rights that had been so clearly negated during the Second World War. A novel feature of the Convention, in the context of the early 1950s, was that it established a Commission on Human Rights with power to hear complaints from individuals concerning human rights violations.[8] Before the 1950 Convention, such international agreements tended to confer rights only on states to lodge complaints against other states. The Convention also established a Court of Human Rights to operate as decision-maker on whether the Convention itself had been violated.[9]

[16.12] On the economic front, the end of the Second World War presented two major problems. One was the need to rebuild the economies of Europe and the other was the desire to prevent future wars. The general need for the states of Europe to cooperate to achieve these aims was recognised, and continues to be recognised, but bringing that idea to fruition was more difficult. What later became the enormously influential trading bloc, the European Union, began in 1952 in modest circumstances.

---

[7]   See generally, on international law, Ch 17.

[8]   See Quinn, 'The European Union and the Council of Europe on the Issues of Human Rights: Twins Separated at Birth?' (2001) 46 McGill LJ 849.

[9]   See further, para **17.21**.

[3]   THE THREE EUROPEAN COMMUNITIES

The European Coal and Steel Community

[16.13] The European Coal and Steel Community (ECSC), was established by a treaty signed in Paris in April 1951 by the six original member states: France, Germany, Italy, Belgium, the Netherlands and Luxembourg. This treaty became known as the 'Treaty of Paris'. The ECSC Treaty, which came into effect in July 1952, aimed at ensuring the peaceful and cooperative development of the coal and steel industries of the six member states, especially those of France, Germany and Italy. These were the industries that had formed the basis for the industrial development of those states, but to some extent also the two World Wars of the 20th century. The ECSC Treaty provided that the coal and steel industries in the six member states would be developed and coordinated on an agreed basis by a full-time ECSC High Authority acting in conjunction with a Council of Ministers representing the governments of the member states. It also established an Assembly to represent the peoples of the member states and a Court of Justice to ensure the observance of the legal rules that were to be agreed by the ECSC institutions.

[16.14] The ECSC was to prove a success and the institutional framework it established became the model for two further Communities established in 1957 by the same six member states. These Communities, the European Atomic Energy Community (EAEC or Euratom) and the European Economic Community (EEC), were established by two treaties signed on the same day in Rome in March 1957. Although there are, therefore, two Treaties of Rome, the title 'Treaty of Rome' is usually taken to refer to the treaty establishing the EEC. The treaty establishing the European Coal and Steel Community (ECSC) was designed to last for 50 years. It was signed on 18 April 1951 in Paris, entered into force on 23 July 1952 and expired on 23 July 2002.

The European Atomic Energy Community

[16.15] The EAEC or Euratom Treaty, which came into force in January 1958, followed the pattern of the ECSC Treaty in that it was confined to a relatively narrow sector of economic activity, in this instance the development of the civil nuclear energy industry (the military side of the industry being excluded).

The European Economic Community

[16.16] The European Economic Community was established by the Treaty of Rome, which also came into force in January 1958. The Treaty followed the pattern of the other two treaties in terms of the institutional structures it established: a Commission (the equivalent of the ECSC High Authority) sharing decision-making powers with a Council representing Ministers from the governments of the member states. An Assembly and Court of Justice were also established. Legislative mechanisms for the enforcement of Community rules were also included in the Treaty. In that context, the Commission and the Court of Justice were the focus of procedures for the enforcement of the legal obligations created by the Treaty. It is also important to note that the Treaty differed from the other two treaties in that it had the potential to apply to virtually all aspects of economic activity.

[16.17] The Treaty of Rome dealt with the organisation of virtually all commercial and economic activity, including agriculture, manufacturing and services, whether in the public sector or private sector. The overall aim of the Treaty was to ensure that the member states create a single trading entity, within which any obstacles to free trade would be eliminated.

[16.18] The first words of the Preamble to the Treaty of Rome, provided that the original six signatory member states were:

"DETERMINED to lay the foundations of an ever closer union among the peoples of Europe."

[16.19] It must be said that, even after the substantial amendments made by subsequent treaties, these words remain in place, indicating that the 'ever closer union' remained an objective rather than a concrete achievement. Indeed, an enduring debate since the 1950s has been the extent to which what is now the European Union should be confined to economic cooperation or whether it should extend to closer political cooperation and union. While some states would wish to see the European Union restricted to economic cooperation, the history of events since the 1950s indicates a gradual, if piecemeal, movement in the direction of closer political integration. However, this remains a controversial issue of political debate that has raised its head in recent Irish referenda.

Common market

[16.20] The creation of a single European economic area based on a common market was the fundamental objective of the Treaty of Rome. Article 2 of Treaty set out that objective as follows:

"The Community shall have as its task, by establishing a common market and progressively approximating the economic policies of Member States, to promote throughout the Community a harmonious development of economic activities, a continuous and balanced expansion, an increase in stability, an accelerated raising of the standard of living and closer relations between the States belonging to it."

It was clear that the common market was not an end in itself, but a means to achieve economic and political goals. The phrase 'common market' came to encompass the three European Communities. However, the concept of a 'common market' evolved since 1957, in particular, in the light of the movement towards 'an ever closer union'. While the terms 'common market', 'single market' and 'internal market' were used interchangeably they are not exact synonyms. The common market is a stage in the multinational integration process, which, in the words of a Court of Justice ruling, aims to remove all the barriers to intra-Community trade with a view to the merger of national markets into a single market giving rise to conditions as close as possible to a genuine internal market. The most recent treaty, the Treaty of Lisbon, ignores the terms 'single market' and 'common market'. It abandoned the phrase 'common market', preferring the term 'internal market', which according to art 26 TFEU comprises 'an area without internal frontiers in which the free movement of goods, persons, services and capital is ensured in accordance with the provisions of the Treaties'.

[16.21] In 1957, art 7 of the Treaty of Rome stated:

"The common market shall be progressively established during a transitional period of twelve years."

This transitional period, which art 7 divided into three stages of four years each, was to end in January 1970 when the common market should have been fully in place. The target date proved impossible to meet, for reasons which included an insistence that the legal measures needed to achieve the common market be arrived at by unanimous agreement of the member states.[10]

[16.22] The Single European Act 1986 inserted a new provision, art 7a, into the Treaty, setting a further target date of 31 December 1992 for achieving the 'internal market'. Even that date proved somewhat ambitious, though certainly the vast bulk of what constitutes a single market had been put in place or was at an advanced stage by the end of 1992.

[16.23] In 1957, art 3 of the Treaty of Rome listed some of the specific activities of the Community in order to achieve the task established in art 2. Among these activities were:

"... the elimination, as between Member States, of customs duties and quantitative restrictions on the import and export of goods, and of all other measures having equivalent effect;

... the abolition ... of obstacles to the free movement of goods, persons, services and capital;

... the approximation of the laws of Member States to the extent required for the functioning of the common market."

The four freedoms and the internal market

[16.24] As well as the 'common market', the idea of 'the four freedoms' (from the reference in art 3 to free movement of goods, persons, services and capital) became key objectives of the European Economic Community. It is notable that the 'four freedoms' appeared again in the amendments introduced by the Single European Act 1986. In setting the end of 1992 as the date for achieving an 'internal market', art 7a of the Treaty of Rome (inserted by the Single European Act) stated:

"The internal market shall comprise an area without internal frontiers in which the free movement of goods, persons, services and capital is ensured in accordance with the provisions of this Treaty."

---

10 See the discussion of the Luxembourg Accords, para **16.40**.

[16.25] As we have seen, art 3 also indicated that the intention of the original member states was to eliminate customs duties and other restrictions on the import and export of goods so that free trade could occur. This would involve the dismantling of many existing national laws of a protectionist nature. Article 3 also recognised that, to do this, the laws of the member states would require 'approximation' to the extent required for the functioning of the common market. The term 'approximation' indicated that there were differences between the laws of the member states in a number of areas and that these would need to be ironed out to achieve a true common market for the four freedoms.

Subsidiarity and the Community

[16.26] A further refinement of the activities of the European Community, the principle of subsidiarity, was added in 1992 by the Maastricht Treaty. This added a new art 3b, which specified:

"In areas which do not fall within its exclusive competence the Community shall have due regard to the principle of subsidiarity ..."

[16.27] This broad provision was supplemented by the addition (*via* the Treaty of Amsterdam) of a Protocol on the Principles of Subsidiarity and Proportionality. Shortly stated, the principle of subsidiarity required the Community to take into account that certain areas of economic activity might best be regulated by each member state through its own national laws. In essence, subsidiarity required the Community to refrain from taking action in some areas, thus allowing for some continued diversity or differences between the laws of the member states. The concept of subsidiarity can be compared to that of decentralisation and in terms of political structures it overlaps with federalism although the two are not necessarily connected. The immediate origin of the notion of subsidiarity lies in Catholic social thinking, articulated in the Papal encyclicals *Rerum Novarum* (1891) and *Quadragessimo Anno* (1931). In short, subsidiarity proposes that functions of government should be as local as possible, with central government confined to acting where individuals or private groups lack the necessary capacity.

[16.28] It should be noted, however, that while subsidiarity was mentioned in the Treaty on European Union, it would be inaccurate to describe the European Union as a federation. Indeed, while some member states might wish to see a federal union, other member states would regard this as unacceptable. In this respect, the inclusion of subsidiarity in the Treaty on European Union is seen primarily as a brake on excessive interference by the Union in certain sensitive issues of national concern. To that extent, it reflects continuing tension about the future direction of the European Union, with some member states willing to engage in deeper integration, including further political integration, while others would wish to see developments being confined primarily to trade and economic issues.

[16.29] The Treaty of Lisbon amplified the principle of subsidiarity in art 5(3) TFEU:

"Under the principle of subsidiarity, in areas which do not fall within its exclusive competence, the Union shall act only if and in so far as the objectives of the proposed action cannot be sufficiently achieved by the Member States, either at central level or at regional and local level, but can rather, by reason of the scale or effects of the proposed action, be better achieved at Union level.

The institutions of the Union shall apply the principle of subsidiarity as laid down in the Protocol on the application of the principles of subsidiarity and proportionality. National Parliaments ensure compliance with the principle of subsidiarity in accordance with the procedure set out in that Protocol."

The rights of national parliaments were increased in order to reinforce accountability in addition to enhancing respect for the principle of subsidiarity. National parliaments will be permitted to give reasoned opinions as to whether a draft legislative proposal is in compliance with the principle of subsidiarity. The Commission will then be obliged to review or re-examine the proposal in view of concerns expressed by national parliaments. Thus, the role of national parliaments has, for the first time, been recognised as of the formal decision-making structure of the European Union.[11]

Detailed activities of the Community

[16.30] The Treaty of Rome contained much more than merely a statement of general objectives. It details many aspects of the activities of the Community, which in 1957 included:

- the gradual establishment during the 'transitional period' of a Customs Union between the member states, effectively banning custom duties on imports and exports between the member states;

- the gradual establishment of a common customs tariff to lay down a common set of customs duties for imports and exports from and to 'third countries', that is trade with non-member states;

- the gradual elimination of quantitative restrictions (quotas) on imports and all measures having equivalent effect between member states;

- the gradual establishment of a common agricultural policy (CAP), by which the member states would have an agreed strategy for the development of this sector;

- the gradual securing of the right of establishment, that is, the freedom of movement of workers and of services, including the right of self-employed persons to pursue their careers and of service organisations to set up in any member state;

---

11   See Conte, 'Reinforcing Democracy, Sovereignty and Union Efficacy: Supremacy and Subsidiarity in the European Union' (2004) 26 DULJ 1; Vause, 'The Subsidiarity Principle in European Union Law: American Federalism Compared' (1995) 27 *Case Western Reserve Journal of International Law* 61; Verbeek, 'The Politics of Subsidiarity in the European Union' (1994) 32 *Journal of Common Market Studies* 215; Kiiver, 'The Treaty of Lisbon, the National Parliaments and the Principle of Subsidiarity' (2008) 15 *Maastricht Journal of European and Comparative Law* 77.

- the progressive abolition of restrictions on movement of capital;
- the gradual establishment of a common transport policy, which, like the CAP, would require the member states to agree a common strategy for the development of transport and its infrastructure;
- the development of general rules concerning competition between undertakings, including restrictions on price-fixing, the abuse by an undertaking of a dominant position within the common market and limits on state aid to undertakings;
- provision for the 'approximation of the laws of the Member States' in order to achieve the objectives of the common market;
- the development of a Community social policy, including improvement of working conditions for workers and the principle of equal pay for men and women;
- the institutional arrangements for the Community, including the Council, the Commission, the European Assembly (now called the European Parliament), the Court of Justice and the Court of Auditors;
- legislative mechanisms for the detailed implementation of the general aims of the Treaty;
- financial provisions, including the adoption of the Budget;
- the conferral of legal personality on the Community;
- the conclusion of the Treaty for an unlimited period.

[16.31] This partial listing of the provisions of the Treaty of Rome indicates the ambitious scope of the original six member states of the Community. It is hardly surprising that all these objectives were not met in the 12-year transitional period initially set in 1957. It should also indicate how, in some respects, the Treaty resembles a Constitution, setting out general principles and an institutional framework for the Community.

Obstacles to the aims of the Treaty of Rome

[16.32] In 1957, there were many obstacles to achieving a common market for the four freedoms and the other aims and objectives of the European Economic Community. It may be helpful to itemise these to indicate the task faced by the original member states.

[16.33] In relation to free movement of goods, many member states' laws imposed quotas ('quantitative restrictions') on the amount of goods of various types that they would permit into their state. Other obstacles to free trade were the high import duties or tariffs imposed by member states. Many such quotas, duties and tariffs were intended to protect native companies from outside competition. More restrictions came in the form of laws that imposed specific national standards to which imported goods (from television sets to major items of industrial machinery) would be required to comply before they could be brought into the member state. Many of these restrictions have been removed since 1957, largely through the process of approximating the laws of the member states. In relation to quotas, duties and tariffs, the member states have established the Customs Union and the Common Customs Tariff envisaged by the Treaty of Rome. In relation to standards, many national standards have been replaced by harmonised standards so that goods manufactured in one member state can be sold in any other member state if they meet technical criteria laid down in the harmonised law.

[16.34] In connection with free movement of persons, there was the need to deal with the fact that most member states imposed restrictions on the number of foreign workers they would allow to enter their workforce. Other problems included the non-recognition of qualifications of foreign workers, including such diverse examples as hairdressers, veterinary surgeons, dentists and lawyers. Many of these rights of establishment issues have since been resolved.[12] But, once these initial problems were overcome, others arose in this area of social policy, such as ensuring equal social security and pension rights for workers who have worked in different member states.

[16.35] As to free movement of services, once again many member states in the 1950s imposed severe restrictions on the establishment and operation of services. For example, the provision of water, electricity, transport (especially rail and air transport), postal and telecommunication services were operated by state bodies that held virtual monopolies of such services. In the 1950s, very few states saw privatisation or the de-regulation of such services as either desirable or realistic. In the private sector, services such as insurance and banking were again subject to restrictions that, in effect, prevented foreign companies competing with local companies. And, in relation to non-recognition of qualifications, there was an overlap with the freedom of workers. Again, many though not all of these areas have been subject to an approximation of laws intended to create a level playing field.

[16.36] In relation to the free movement of capital, most states also operated restrictions, by means of exchange control laws, on the extent to which money could be invested in projects outside the state. This was not just a question of limiting the amount people could bring with them on foreign holidays, but extended to restricting the use of large sums for foreign speculation or investment in foreign industrial projects.

[16.37] Other obstacles to trade covered all aspects of the four freedoms. For example, many states operated different forms of entities for conducting business. What in Britain or Ireland would be described as a limited liability company might find an equivalent in France or Italy, but the legal consequences of forming the equivalent in those countries might be very different. Another source of difficulty was the abuse by undertakings (whether in the public sector or the private sector) of powerful monopoly positions to prevent others from competing in the same area of trade. As noted, the Treaty of Rome also contained provisions to prevent certain anti-competitive activities. Again, a large effort at Community level was required to remove these obstacles to free trade.

---

12   See para **3.145** for the arrangements concerning lawyers.

[4] FROM EUROPEAN COMMUNITY TO EUROPEAN UNION

[16.38] As has been noted already, the original three treaties, in particular the Treaty of Rome, were significantly overhauled since the 1950s. The consequence is that the scope of the original treaties has been considerably expanded. The initial focus was on achieving a 'common' or 'internal' market where economic-related activities were to the forefront. However, later developments went far beyond purely economic matters and reflect a broader range of deeper political concerns.

Merger Treaty

[16.39] In institutional terms, the first significant move was what is commonly called the Merger Treaty of April 1965, which established a common set of institutions for the three Communities. Until the Merger Treaty, there had been separate Commissions and Councils for each of the three Communities, with a single Assembly and Court of Justice. From the time the Merger Treaty came into effect in July 1967, the three Communities have been subject to a single Commission, Council, Assembly, now called the European Parliament, and Court of Justice.

Luxembourg Accords

[16.40] At about the same time, there was unease in some member states, in particular in France, that vital national interests would be threatened if, as was scheduled under the third stage of the transitional period in the Treaty of Rome, certain decisions could be made by majority voting rather than unanimous agreement. Under a series of arrangements in 1966 known as the Luxembourg Accords (or the 'Luxembourg Compromise'), it was agreed that any member state could, in effect, block a proposed Community law where it was deemed by that member state to conflict with a vital national interest. This procedure became known as the 'veto'. Although no amendment to the Treaty of Rome was made to incorporate these arrangements, they became part of the understanding between the member states in the late 1960s and into the 1970s when Ireland became a member state. The effect of the Luxembourg Accords was that relatively little progress was made in the 1970s in achieving the original aims of the Treaty. It became clear to the member states in the 1980s that the unanimity requirement could lead to the economic collapse of the Communities in the face of growing global competition.

Single European Act

[16.41] Ultimately, the Single European Act, which was signed in February 1986 and came into force in July 1987, re-affirmed and also extended the provisions contained in the Treaty of Rome that many approximating laws could be made on the basis of a form of majority voting known as qualified majority voting (QMV). It also set the end of 1992 as the target date for achieving what became known as the 'single market'. The Single European Act also extended the scope of the Communities to include areas such as political and monetary cooperation, research and technological development and environmental policy. In addition, the Single European Act recognised the fact that the member states had, informally, been engaged in cooperation concerning the wider political aspects of the Community. For many years, the member states had acknowledged that, internationally, the Community needed to speak with one voice and to agree a common trade and foreign policy where this was possible. The Single European Act provided formal mechanisms for this European Political Co-operation (EPC) to be developed, although this was to occur outside the legal enforcement mechanisms (such as through the Court of Justice) specified in the treaties. To this extent, the Single European Act acknowledged that certain aspects of the European Community had more of a political than a legal importance.[13]

Treaty on European Union

[16.42] Further extensions to the original treaties, and in particular the Treaty of Rome, were agreed in the Treaty on European Union (TEU), which was signed in the city of Maastricht in February 1992, hence the popular reference to 'the Maastricht Treaty'. The Treaty, which came into effect in October 1993, also created a new entity, the European Union, that was designed to take the process of European integration beyond the then-existing confines of the European Community structure.

[16.43] The Maastricht Treaty also dealt with certain aspects of economic and monetary union, including the establishment of a European Central Bank (ECB) and the creation of a single currency for member states.[14] In addition, important new areas of competence were inserted into the existing treaties. The amended text of art 2 of the Treaty of Rome to include the following as part of the overall task of the European Community indicates the wide scope of the Maastricht Treaty:

- economic and monetary union;
- balanced development;
- sustainable and non-inflationary growth respecting the environment;
- a high degree of convergence of economic performance;
- a high level of employment and of social protection;
- the raising of the standard of living and quality of life; and
- economic and social cohesion and solidarity among member states.

---

13 Note, however, that while elements of the European Union may operate primarily in the political sphere, this may still involve legal consequences in Irish law: see *Crotty v An Taoiseach* [1987] IR 713, para **16.105** *et seq.*

14 The euro currency was introduced in December 1998, when exchange rates between the euro and national currencies in the eurozone became fixed. Euro notes and coins were introduced and the national currencies withdrawn in 2002. However, the euro is not the currency of all member states: Denmark and the United Kingdom agreed an opt-out clause in the Treaty exempting them from participation, while the remaining member states have not to date satisfied the criteria for adopting the single currency. The euro is managed and administered by the European Central Bank (ECB) based in Frankfurt, and the euro system which comprises the central banks of the eurozone countries. The ECB is an independent central bank with exclusive authority to set monetary policy for the eurozone.

[16.44] The most significant amendments made by the Maastricht Treaty were made to the Treaty of Rome, including the provisions that concerned monetary union. These amendments were so numerous and extensive that the full title of the EEC Treaty was changed from 'Treaty establishing the European Economic Community' to 'Treaty establishing the European Community'. After the Treaty came into effect in 1993, the EEC became the European Community.

[16.45] The reach of European integration beyond primarily economic matters is evident in the provisions in the Maastricht Treaty concerning closer cooperation in defence and foreign policy matters. These were influenced by the collapse in 1989 and 1990 of the Soviet-dominated Communist Governments in the states of Central and Eastern Europe. In that respect, the Maastricht Treaty represented a response by the states of Western Europe to these major political changes. The Treaty added to the existing provisions on foreign policy cooperation first introduced in the Single European Act and introduced new procedures concerning what was renamed Common Foreign and Security Policy (CFSP). It also introduced the first reference in a treaty to cooperation on Justice and Home Affairs (JHA), which included cooperation between the Justice Ministers on matters such as immigration and drug-related activity. In this respect, the Maastricht Treaty in fact formalised for the first time the cooperation that in practice existed between the Justice Ministers in this regard.

[16.46] The outcome of the Maastricht Treaty was two overlapping but separate organisations, the European Community and the European Union, each tasked with separate areas of competence. While the EU was a separate entity, from the perspective of enforceable rules of law, it depended on the European Community. Thus, the Maastricht Treaty stated that the Union should 'maintain in full the *acquis communautaire* and build on it'. The '*acquis communautaire*' encompassed the legal principles established by the Treaties, EC legislation and case law. Adopting the analogy of a Greek temple, the Maastricht Treaty was conceived of as establishing 'Three Pillars', namely:

1. The Treaties establishing the ECSC, Euratom and the EC;
2. Common Foreign and Security Policy (CFSP); and
3. Police and Judicial Co-operation in Criminal Matters (PJCC).

A different balance was struck between Community activity and inter-governmental cooperation in respect of each of the Three Pillars. In terms of the *political* development of the European Union, each of these Three Pillars carried equal weight. However, from a *legal* perspective, the First Pillar was the most important. This is because the amendments made to the existing Treaties, and in particular Treaty of Rome, were legally enforceable under the mechanisms established by the Treaties. In contrast, not all the member states were willing to commit themselves to legally enforceable policies and cooperation or to allow a role for the Community institutions in relation to the Second and Third Pillars. For that reason, the Treaty provided that CFSP and JHA were not to come under the enforcement mechanisms established by the Treaties. At that stage, therefore, those Pillars of the European Union remained matters for voluntary cooperation between the member states, guided but not legally bound by the *acquis communautaire*. The Pillar structure remained in place until 2009 when it was eliminated by the Treaty of Lisbon.

The Treaty of Amsterdam

[16.47] The process of European integration reached a further stage with the coming into force of the Treaty of Amsterdam on 1 May 1999. That Treaty was designed to consolidate existing development and to streamline the parallel European Community and European Union processes. Nevertheless, it effected a number of piecemeal, but important, changes to both the Maastricht Treaty and the Treaty of Rome. In addition, it made amendments that were designed to tidy up the treaties including a renumbering of their titles, articles and sections.[15]

[16.48] Concerns with the democratic image of the European Union are met by the Treaty of Amsterdam, which amended the Maastricht Treaty in a number of respects. Article 1 was amended to provide that decisions would to be taken 'as openly as possible and as closely as possible to the citizen'. Article 6 of the TEU declared that the Union is founded on 'the principles of liberty, democracy, respect for human rights and fundamental freedoms, and the rule of law'. The same article stated that the Union 'shall respect' the fundamental rights that are guaranteed by the European Convention for the Protection of Human Rights and Fundamental Freedoms. Respect for these principles was made a condition for applicant countries that might in the future seek to join the EU (art 49). Moreover, art 7 provided that the Council may suspend some of a member state's rights where that state is guilty of a 'serious and persistent' breach of the principles set out in art 6. However, it was also stated in art 7 that a state whose rights are suspended in this manner remains bound by its obligations under the TEU. The Treaty of Lisbon preserved these provisions.

[16.49] The Treaty of Amsterdam expanded the scope of the EC in a number of respects. New objectives were added to those listed in art 2 of the Treaty of Rome. In particular, the promotion of gender equality and environmental protection became goals in themselves rather than mere consequences of economic development. This was amplified in further additions to the Treaty. Article 6 provided that '[e]nvironmental protection requirements must be integrated into the definition and implementation' of Community policies. Article 13 invested the Community with legislative competence 'to combat discrimination based on sex, racial or ethnic origin, religion or belief, disability, age or sexual orientation'. A new Title on Employment was added to allow the Community to adopt what are referred to as 'soft law' instruments, in the form of guidelines, recommendations and incentive measures, to complement national unemployment strategies. Alterations were also made to the provisions on social policy, public health and consumer protection.

---

[15]   See Editorial, 'Renumbering the Treaties: Another Fine Mess' (1999) 24 EL Rev 443.

[16.50] One of the principal substantive changes brought about by the Treaty of Amsterdam was an alteration to the Pillar structure by the transfer to the European Community of certain functions in relation to Justice and Home Affairs that until that time been the province of the European Union. In particular, the European Community acquired competence in the areas of visas, asylum, immigration and judicial cooperation in civil matters and a new title, the aim of which was described as being the establishment of 'an area of freedom, security and justice', was inserted into the Treaty of Rome.[16] This development reflected the progressive abolition of border controls and the corresponding free movement of persons within the Community.[17] The effect of the transfer of this area of competence from the Third Pillar to the First, was a focus on criminal matters within the reformulated Third Pillar – hence its amended heading 'Police and Judicial Co-operation in Criminal Matters' (PJCC).[18] Moreover, the Treaty marked a crucial shift from the intergovernmentalism that characterised the Third Pillar in its pre-Amsterdam version to a form of communitarianism in which Community institutions were assigned a role in PJCC matters. However, while the legal arrangements surrounding the revised Third Pillar, in particular the introduction of a Community dimension, were designed to enhance the effectiveness of that Pillar, this was achieved at the expense of fragmenting the constitutional structure within which it operated.[19]

[16.51] The Treaty of Amsterdam also provided for what, in effect, was differentiated integration although it was not expressed in those terms. It amended art 11 of the Treaty of Rome which, together with Title VII of TEU, provided a mechanism by which the

---

[16] Fennelly, 'The Area of "Freedom, Security and Justice" and the European Court of Justice – a Personal View' (2000) 49 ICLQ 1. See also Ferola, 'The Fight against Organized Crime in Europe Building an Area of Freedom, Security and Justice in the EU' (2002) *International Journal of Legal Information* 53; Lodge, 'Sustaining Freedom, Security and Justice: From Terrorism to Immigration' (2002) 24 Liverpool LR 41; Walker, 'Europe's area of Freedom, Security and Justice' (2005) 16 King's College LJ 234; Callewaert, 'The European Court of Human Rights and the Area of Freedom, Security and Justice' (2007) 8 *ERA Forum* 511.

[17] Ireland and the United Kingdom secured an opt out from these provisions although they may opt in at a later stage. Title IV was complemented by the integration of the 'Schengen *acquis*' into the framework of the European Union by means of a Protocol that was added by the Treaty of Amsterdam. Again Ireland and the United Kingdom, not being parties to the original Schengen Treaty, will not be bound by this *acquis* unless and until they so choose. The 'Schengen *acquis*' refers to the accumulated body of law that has grown out of the Schengen Treaty which provides for the abolition of border checks between member states; the Treaty was not signed by Ireland and the United Kingdom. See Crowe, 'The Schengen Acquis in Police Cooperation: Implementation in an Enlarged Europe" (2005) 3 *ERA Forum* 415; Schutte, 'The Incorporation of the Schengen Acquis in the European Union' (1998) 6 *Hume Papers on Public Policy* 124.

[18] See Regan, *The New Third Pillar: Cooperation against Crime in the European Union* (2000); Collins, 'Freedom through Security? The Third Pillar' (1998) IJEL 36.

[19] Monar, 'Judicial and Home Affairs in the Treaty of Amsterdam; Reform at the Price of Fragmentation' (1998) 23 EL Rev 320.

Council, acting by a qualified majority, could authorise 'closer cooperation' between member states. The significant point is that such cooperation was integrated into the Community system and the member states in question could use Community institutions and procedures to this end. However, it was provided that closer cooperation could not exceed the limits of the powers conferred by the Treaty.

[16.52] It was also stipulated that closer cooperation could not involve subject matter that fell within the 'exclusive competence' of the Community nor could it affect Community policies, actions and programmes; equally it could not discriminate between nationals of member states, nor discriminate against or restrict trade between member states or distort competition between them. Moreover, an individual member state was given a right to veto the grant of an authorisation for important reasons of national policy. Nevertheless, the inclusion of these provisions was a recognition of a desire for flexibility and an acceptance that not all member states will necessarily be committed to full participation in an increasingly complex process of integration.[20]

The Treaty of Nice

[16.53] The Treaty of Nice[21] was designed to deal with the unfinished business of the Treaty of Amsterdam. Its general purpose was to facilitate the process of enlargement of the European Union to 27 states.[22] The general belief underlying the Treaty of Nice was

---

[20] See Byrne, 'Legal Aspects of the Treaty of Amsterdam' (1998) 7 IJEL 7; Liston, 'The Amsterdam Treaty: A Glance at the Main Substantive Provisions' (1998) 3 BR 243; O'Connor, 'Ireland's Neutrality under the Amsterdam Treaty' (2000) 18 ILT 283.

[21] See *Treaty of Nice White Paper* Pn 9544 (2001); Regan, 'The Treaty of Nice' (2001) 6 BR 205; Tillitson, 'The Nice Treaty: Some First Impressions' (January 2001) Euro CL xi.

[22] The Treaty of Nice facilitated the accession of Bulgaria, Cyprus, Czech Republic, Estonia, Hungary, Latvia, Lithuania, Malta, Poland, Romania, Slovakia and Slovenia. The position of Iceland, Liechtenstein and Norway, who fall outside the current enlargement process, should be noted. In 1992, the Agreement on the European Economic Area, the EEA Agreement, was signed between the 12 member states of the European Union and the then seven states of the European Free Trade Association (EFTA), *viz* Austria, Finland, Iceland, Liechtenstein, Norway, Sweden and Switzerland. The effect of the EEA Agreement was that, within the EEA, which consists of the member states of the European Union and those of EFTA (apart from Switzerland, which ultimately decided in a referendum not to join the EEA), many of the core elements of EU law apply as they do in the member states of the Union. For example, much of the law on the free movement of persons, services, capital and goods as well as those on competition, social policy, the environment, education, research and development were, in effect, extended to the EEA. Three EFTA states, namely Austria, Finland and Sweden, became full member states of the European Union in 1995, thus superseding the provisions of the EEA that applied to them. This has considerably limited the scope of the EEA, though it remains of considerable importance in terms of the relationship between the Union and the remaining EEA states, Norway (whose citizens have twice rejected membership of the European Union in referenda), Iceland and Liechtenstein. For an analysis of the background to and effect of the EEA Agreement, see Whelan 'Annotation to the European Communities (Amendment) Act 1993' *Irish Current Law Statutes Annotated.*

that institutional change was necessary to prevent the Union from collapsing under the weight of that expansion. It was initially expected that the process of ratification would be completed by December 2002. As was the case with similar treaties in the past, the method of ratification in Ireland involved an amendment to the Constitution. However, the electorate (by a majority of 54 per cent to 46 per cent with approximately 35 per cent of those so entitled actually voting) rejected a proposal to amend the Constitution to authorise ratification of the Treaty of Nice in referendum held in June 2001.

[16.54] The 2001 vote is the first time that a referendum to ratify a European Treaty was defeated, and the state was prevented from ratifying the Nice Treaty until another referendum on the matter was held. Renegotiating the substance of the Treaty of Nice was politically impossible. Many Irish voters believed that smaller member states would be marginalised by the Treaty, and issues also surfaced regarding Irish neutrality. In response to this, the Irish government obtained the 'Seville Declaration' from the European Council regarding Ireland's policy of military neutrality, which contained two important safeguards. First, enhanced cooperation under the Treaty would require the consent of Dáil Éireann and, second, that Ireland would be exempt from joining an EU common defence policy. A second referendum was held in October 2002. The Treaty was approved by a majority of voters (approx 63 per cent).

[16.55] The Treaty resulted in the institutional reform that was considered necessary to ensure that an enlarged Union was workable. Amongst the principal changes that were effected were an alteration of voting weights at the Council of Ministers, the extension of qualified majority voting to a wider range of areas, changes in the numbers of seats in the European Parliament, a system of rotation to cap the number of Commissioners and an increase in the powers of the President of the Commission. Important changes were also made in relation to the jurisdiction and operation of the Court of First Instance (subsequently renamed the 'General Court' by the Treaty of Lisbon) and to the functioning of the European Court of Justice.

[16.56] The 'closer cooperation' provisions that were introduced by the Treaty of Amsterdam were altered by the Treaty of Nice. As was the case previously, cooperation was to be consistent with the basic principles of the Union but the procedures attending the grant of an authorisation were simplified. A proposal for closer cooperation would require a minimum of eight member states irrespective of the size of the Union. The grant of authorisation by the Council would be decided by qualified majority, with an individual member state's right of veto being confined to cases of closer cooperation in the area of foreign and security policy.

[16.57] It was widely accepted that the Treaty of Nice failed to address the issue of institutional reform adequately, in view of the fact that the institutions of the European Union were regarded as being excessively complicated. Further, it also failed to deal with the incorporation of the Charter of Fundamental Rights into the Treaty. It was generally agreed that the Pillar structure was excessively complicated, and that the separate Treaties of the European Union should be fused into a single Treaty. Furthermore, there was a widely shared view that the European Community and the

European Union should be merged, with the result that the European Union, as the consolidated entity, would be endowed with legal personality.

The Treaty of Lisbon

[16.58] Although the case for reforming the treaties may have seemed obvious, achieving that goal has proved difficult. A proposed Treaty Establishing a Constitution for Europe was adopted by the Heads of State and governments at the Brussels European Council in June 2004, and subsequently signed in Rome in October 2004; however, it was never ratified.[23]

[16.59] The Treaty of Lisbon, which entered into force on 1 December 2009, is a lengthy and complex document that amends the existing treaties and changes the means by which decisions are made.[24] The principal objectives of the Treaty of Lisbon include: promoting a more democratic EU and ensuring high standards of accountability, openness, transparency and participation. The Treaty seeks to make the EU more efficient and to enhance its ability to deal with global challenges including security, climate change, and sustainable development, which is fundamental given the current global economic climate.[25] The Treaty identifies the areas of competence belonging to the EU itself; the areas which are exclusive to national governments; and areas involving cooperation between the EU and national governments. Although the Treaty does not give the EU any new areas of exclusive competence, it gives the EU a role in several new areas of competence including tourism, energy and sport, which is shared with national governments.

[16.60] The Treaty of Lisbon abolished the Pillar structure that had been in place since the Maastricht Treaty. In doing this it brought the remaining Second and Third Pillar areas within the competence of the EU. The intergovernmental method continues to apply to the Common Foreign and Security Policy. However, many decisions relating to judicial and police cooperation in criminal matters are subject to the 'ordinary legislative procedure' under which the Council and European Parliament jointly adopt the relevant measures.[26] The TFEU envisages the harmonisation of both criminal

---

[23] See, eg Shaw and Monnet, 'Legal and Political Sources of the Treaty Establishing a Constitution for Europe' (2004) 55 NILQ 214.

[24] The Twenty-eighth Amendment of the Constitution permitted the state to ratify the Treaty of Lisbon. This was effected by the Twenty-eighth Amendment of the Constitution (Treaty of Lisbon) Act 2009, which was approved by referendum on 2 October 2009 (known as the 'Lisbon II referendum').

[25] Crowe, 'The Treaty of Lisbon: A Revised Legal Framework for the Organisation and Functioning of the European Union' (2008) 9 *ERA Forum* 163; Maganza, 'The Lisbon Treaty: A Brief Outline' (2008) 31 *Fordham International Law Journal*, 1603; Craig, 'The Treaty of Lisbon: Process, Architecture and Substance' (2008) 33 Eur L Rev 137; Barret, *Final Impact: The Treaty of Lisbon and the Final Provisions of the Treaty Establishing the European Community and the Treaty on European Union*, UCD Dublin European Institute Working Paper 08-1, May 2008.

[26] TFEU, arts 82–89.

procedure rules and the definition of criminal offences that have a cross-border dimension: terrorism, trafficking in human beings and sexual exploitation of women and children, illicit drug trafficking, illicit arms trafficking, money laundering, corruption, counterfeiting of means of payment, computer crime and organised crime. The methods prescribed involve closer cooperation between national police forces and customs authorities, both directly and through the medium of Europol.[27]

[16.61] The Treaty of Lisbon made a number of changes to the EU institutions:

- the European Commission;
- the European Council (abolition of the rotating Presidency; the appointment of a permanent President of the Council; the holding of some decision-making meetings of the Councils in public);
- the European Parliament (increase in the number of areas over which it will make joint decisions with the Council);
- the European Court of Justice (proposed changes mainly involve renaming parts of the Court and reorganising it).

The Treaty of Lisbon gives the Charter on Fundamental Rights the same legal standing as the Treaties. Although there were no mechanisms in existing governing treaties for a member state to leave the EU, the Lisbon Treaty provides such a procedure. The rules on enhanced cooperation (also referred to as flexibility), which involves a number of member states using the institutions of the EU to agree particular actions and promote closer cooperation between themselves, were streamlined with the ratification of the Treaty.[28]

The protection of fundamental rights[29]

[16.62] Questions of fundamental human rights were originally thought to lie beyond the scope of the European Communities. In their original versions the Treaties establishing the three Communities omitted any reference to human rights, a position that was undoubtedly based on the view, prevalent in the late 1950s, that European

---

27   The Maastricht Treaty (1992) envisaged the establishment of a European police force. In 1995 the member states signed the Convention on the Establishment of a European Police Office (the Europol Convention), which was enacted into Irish law by the Europol Act 1997: see Byrne and Binchy, *Annual Review of Irish Law 1997* (1998), pp 376–379; Walsh, 'The Europol Act 1997', *Irish Current Law Statutes Annotated*; Murray, 'An Overview of the Europol Act 1997' (1998) 16 ILT 73.

28   TEU, art 20 and TFEU, arts 328–334.

29   See Douglas-Scott, 'The European Union and Human Rights after the Treaty of Lisbon' (2011) 11(4) *Human Rights Law Review* 645; Weiß, 'Human Rights in the EU: Rethinking the Role of the European Convention on Human Rights after Lisbon' (2011) 7(1) *European Constitutional Law Review* 64; Sánchez, 'Fundamental Rights and Citizenship of the Union at the Crossroads: A Promising Alliance or a Dangerous Liaison? (2014) 20 ELJ 464; von Bogdandy, 'The European Union as a Human Rights Organisation? Human Rights and the Core of the European Union' (2000) 37 CMLRev 1307; (contd.../)

integration was best confined to the economic domain. Even then certain provisions of the treaties, especially the four freedoms, were susceptible to a rights interpretation: they could be construed as being based on the right to earn a livelihood, which right attracted legal and constitutional protection in many West European states. However, that right is itself economic in nature and is consistent with the economic concerns that dominated the early stages of the European Community development.

[16.63] This restrictive view was reflected in a series of decisions of the Court of Justice to the effect that fundamental rights provisions in national constitutions could not be invoked in relation to questions of Community law and that the treaties did not contain general principles that guaranteed 'vested' rights.[30] The initial reluctance to accommodate fundamental rights concerns within the mosaic of Community law abated somewhat in the late 1960s. In *Stauder v City of Ulm*[31] the court recognised the significance of fundamental rights within the EU legal order and observed that they are integrated into EU law as general principles. One year later in *Internationale Handelsgesellschaft mbH v Einfuhr-und Vorratsstelle für Getreide und Futtermittel*[32] the court held that EU law is supreme to the extent that its provisions take precedence over fundamental right clauses in a national constitution. Nevertheless, in the same case it also acknowledged the importance of fundamental rights stating that:

> "Respect for fundamental rights forms an integral part of the general principles of law protected by the Court of Justice. The protection of such rights whilst inspired by the constitutional traditions common to the Member States, must be ensured within the framework of the structure and objectives of the Communities."[33]

[16.64] Several years later, in *Nold v Commission*[34] the court indicated that it would draw inspiration from the constitutional traditions common to member states in guaranteeing the protection of fundamental rights. In later decisions, the court indicated that it would be guided by international conventions that were ratified by member states, especially the European Convention on the Protection of Human Rights and

---

[29]   (\...contd) Fennelly, 'Pillar Talk: Fundamental Rights Protection in the European Union' (2008) 8 JSIJ 95; Ní Raifeartaigh, 'The European Convention on Human Rights and the Irish Criminal Justice System' (2001) 7 BR 111; Murphy and Wills, 'The European Convention on Human Rights and Irish Incorporation: Adopting a Minimalist Approach: Part II' (2001) 7 BR 41; Murphy and Wills, 'The European Convention on Human Rights and Irish Incorporation: Adopting a Minimalist Approach: Part I' (2001) 7 BR 41; Ahmed and de Jesus Butler, 'The European Union and Human Right: An International Law Perspective' (2006) 17 *European Journal of International Law* 771; Stever, 'Protecting Human Rights in the European: Union: An Argument for Treaty Reform' (1996) 20 *Fordham International Law Journal* 919.

[30]   *Stork v High Authority* [1959] ECR 17; *Geitling v High Authority* [1960] ECR 423; *Sgarlatta v Commission* [1965] ECR 215.

[31]   *Stauder v City of Ulm* [1969] ECR 419.

[32]   *Internationale Handelsgesellschaft mbH v Einfuhr-und Vorratsstelle für Getreide und Futtermittel* [1970] ECR 1125: see para **16.91**.

[33]   [1970] ECR 1125 at 1134.

[34]   *Nold v Commission* [1974] ECR 941.

Fundamental Freedoms. In *Rutili v Minister for the Interior*,[35] for example, the court stated that various rights that had been guaranteed by Community legislation were based on a more general principle found in several articles of the Convention.

[16.65] The potential of the rights regime recognised by the court can be seen in a number of its decisions. In *Johnston v Chief Constable for the Royal Ulster Constabulary*[36] the applicant challenged a decision not to renew her contract as a full-time police reserve constable which had in turn been based on a policy decision not to allow female reservists to be armed. The Secretary of State issued a certificate stating that the refusal to renew the contract was done to safeguard national security and to protect public safety and public order. Under the applicable national legislation the certificate was conclusive and it precluded the applicant's case in domestic law. She contended that this was in breach of the EC Equal Treatment Directive 76/207, which prohibits sex discrimination and contains a right to pursue claims 'by judicial process'.

[16.66] The Court of Justice agreed and held that the national provision infringed Community law. It observed that:

> "The requirement of judicial control stipulated by [the Directive] reflects a general principle of law which underlies the constitutional tradition common to the Member States. That principle is also laid down in Articles 6 and 13 of the European Convention [on Human Rights] ... and as the Court has recognised in its decisions, the principles on which that Convention is based must be taken into consideration in Community law."[37]

[16.67] In *Cowan v Trésor public*[38] the Court of Justice held that a UK national who was assaulted while visiting Paris as a tourist was entitled to claim under the French criminal injuries compensation system. French law had confined the right to claim to French citizens (and certain categories of foreigner that did not include the plaintiff) but the court concluded that the protection of a person's integrity by a member state on the same basis as its citizens is a corollary of the freedom of movement that is guaranteed by EU law. Significantly, the court rejected the argument that the issue fell outside the scope of the Treaty of Rome since the right of compensation was part of the French law of criminal procedure. Although that body of law is normally a matter of national competence the court noted that it has 'consistently held that Community law sets certain limits' to a member state's power in this regard.

[16.68] In *Commission v Germany*[39] the court ruled that a Community regulation on the rights of migrant workers was to be interpreted 'in the light of the requirement of respect for family life set out in art 8 of the [European Convention] ... [which] is one of the

---

[35] *Rutili v Minister for the Interior* [1975] ECR 1219.

[36] *Johnston v Chief Constable for the Royal Ulster Constabulary* [1986] ECR 1651; followed in *Lommers v Minister van Landbouw, Natuurbeheer en Visserij* [2002] ECR I-2891; and applied in *Kreil v Bundesrepublik Deutschland* [2000] ECR I-69.

[37] *Johnston v Chief Constable for the Royal Ulster Constabulary* [1986] ECR 1651 at 1682.

[38] *Cowan v Trésor public* [1989] ECR 195.

[39] *Commission v Germany* [1989] ECR 1263.

fundamental rights which, according to the Court's settled case-law, restated in the preamble to the Single European Act, are recognized by Community law.'[40]

[16.69] Despite the frequent assertions in principled terms of the importance of fundamental rights the actual impact is probably less dramatic. In particular, the Court of Justice has resisted claims based on the terms of the European Convention on Human Rights where there was no discernible Community law dimension. In *Demirel v Stadt Schwäbisch Gmünd*[41] it observed that 'although it is the duty of the Court to ensure observance of fundamental rights in the field of Community law, it has no power to examine the compatibility with the European Convention on Human Rights of national legislation lying outside the scope of Community law'.[42] Of course what constitutes the 'scope of Community law' is a fluid concept that is liable to be re-interpreted by the court[43] but decisions like *Demirel* mark a limit to the court's fundamental rights jurisdiction.

[16.70] Another limit is that while the court has been prepared to employ the Convention as a guide it has rejected the view that the latter had in some way been incorporated into Community law or that it had acquired the status of being a formal source of Community law. To this end rights were recognised as matters of Community law and not by virtue of their being guaranteed by the European Convention. As one commentator has observed, '[i]n practice there is a gulf between "the general principles of Community law" and the guarantees of the Convention.'[44] Moreover, in 1996 the Court of Justice held that the Community lacked the competence to accede to the Convention since no provision of the Treaty of Rome conferred the power to enact rules concerning human rights or to conclude international agreements in this area.[45] Nevertheless, in the same case the court reiterated its general view on the importance of fundamental rights and it noted that that the Convention has a 'special significance' in this regard.

[16.71] The growing recognition of the significance of fundamental rights by the court has been matched by the introduction of a number of treaty provisions over the years. The preamble to the Single European Act referred, *inter alia*, to the European Convention on Human Rights, the European Social Charter and, more vaguely, to 'equality and social justice'. Those aspirational statements were principally symbolic and would have had slight impact, if any, on the actual contents of Community law. More substantial provisions were introduced in 1992 by the Maastricht Treaty by making development cooperation conditional on respect for the rule of law and human rights. The Treaty also provided that the European Union would respect the rights

---

[40]   [1989] ECR 1263 at 1290.
[41]   *Demirel v Stadt Schwäbisch Gmünd* [1981] ECR 3719.
[42]   [1987] ECR 3719 at 3754.
[43]   See, eg *ERT v Dimotiki Etairia Pliorforissis* [1991] ECR I-2925.
[44]   Gallagher, 'The Treaty of Amsterdam and Fundamental Rights' (1998) 7 IJEL 21.
[45]   *Opinion pursuant to Article 228(6) of the EC Treaty* [1996] ECR I-1759.

guaranteed by the European Convention and by national constitutional traditions. Respect for fundamental rights was also stated to be an aspect of the Second and Third Pillars. At the time TEU matters, unlike the provisions of the Treaty of Rome, fell outside the competence of the Court of Justice. Nevertheless, their inclusion in the Treaty invested them with the status of 'hard' law, representing a transition from political desideratum to legal obligation.

[16.72] A significant development was implemented by the Treaty of Amsterdam which amplified these fundamental rights provisions in art 6 of the TEU. That article declared that the Union is founded on the principles of liberty, democracy, respect for human rights and the rule of law.[46] It continued:

> "The Union shall respect fundamental rights, as guaranteed by the European Convention for the Protection of Human Rights and Fundamental Freedoms signed in Rome on 4 November 1950 and as they result from the constitutional traditions common to the Member States, as general principles of Community law."

[16.73] This provision was reinforced by art 7 of TEU which provided a form of enforcement mechanism; the Council was authorised to suspend the rights of a member state that is found to be in breach of the principles enumerated in art 6. The Treaty of Nice strengthened this provision by facilitating the suspension of a Member State where there is a 'clear risk' of such a breach occurring. The Treaty of Amsterdam also provided that accession to the Union by new member states would be conditional on respect for these principles. Significantly the Court of Justice acquired the competence, albeit restricted in scope, to consider TEU matters. This might have been of especial importance where Third Pillar issues relating to police and judicial cooperation in criminal matters were concerned. Moreover, the transfer of a large part of the Third Pillar to the EC Treaty brought the general principles of Community law into play. Given the subject matter that has been transferred (namely asylum, visas, immigration and judicial cooperation in civil matters) the importance of fundamental rights is obvious. The Treaty of Amsterdam also added a provision to the Treaty of Rome in the form of art 13 which invests the Community with the competence to legislate against discrimination.[47]

[16.74] It should not be supposed that fundamental rights protection at EU level is comprehensive. The treaties lacked a catalogue or listing of rights[48] and a sceptic might see the amendments that were made to the treaties as window-dressing designed to lend a measure of political acceptability to the expansion of Community power and a corresponding encroachment on national sovereignty. At the same time, the Court of Justice is open to the criticism that it has been eager to invoke the rhetoric of rights but has delivered little in terms of real protection. It has been argued that the court has

---

46   See para **16.48**.
47   See para **16.49**.
48   See Riley, 'A Human Rights Charter for the European Union?' (September 2000) Euro CL xi.

treated fundamental rights on an equal footing to economic freedom. On this view the key element in the decision in *Cowan v Trésor public*[49] is that the plaintiff succeeded in his claim on the basis of his being the recipient of services. In consequence, it has been contended that 'the high rhetoric of human rights protection can be seen as no more than a vehicle for the court to extend the scope and impact of European law.'[50]

[16.75] These criticisms probably overstate the case and at the same time expect too much. The context in which the Court of Justice has found itself must be understood. Its initial concern was to assert the supremacy of what was then known as Community law and to ensure its uniform application. Moreover, given the origin of the Communities it is hardly surprising that Community law should initially recognise economic rights, a position that is lent support by the text of the treaties. Indeed, had the court taken a more activist approach at the outset it might have attracted the equally damning criticism that it was exceeding its role by acting without explicit Treaty authorisation. However, the court has been prepared to interpret economic rights expansively. Thus, in *Cowan v Trésor public*[51] the protection of Community citizens from harm on the same basis as nationals was seen to be a corollary of the freedom of movement guaranteed by the Treaties. In speaking of a right to equal treatment in that case the court, in effect, adopted a broad construction of the prohibition against discrimination in what was then art 7 of the Treaty of Rome.

[16.76] Experience has shown that the judicial evolution of rights is a slow process and that developments occur incrementally over a long period. Little by little, particular rights are augmented through their being interpreted and re-interpreted in one case after another. Moreover, decisions on rights are liable to be expressed in broad statements of principle that are subsequently qualified by finely tuned detail. The same is true of legal instruments protecting fundamental rights: the general terms are typically shrouded by exceptions and qualifications that are either expressed in the text or are recognised by courts as being 'implicit' in the text or as 'general principles of law'.

[16.77] That said, as things currently stand the rights provisions of national law coupled with the regime established by the European Convention on Human Rights afford more complete protection. Indeed, it might be argued with some force that it is both unrealistic and inappropriate to expect the Court of Justice to assume a jurisdiction that more properly belongs to its counterpart in Strasbourg. Nevertheless, the growing recognition of the importance of fundamental rights at European Union level, both in the jurisprudence of the Court of Justice and the successive amendments to the Treaties, marks the emergence of a process whose potential has yet fully to be realised.

---

49   *Cowan v Trésor public* [1989] ECR 195.
50   Coppel and O'Neill, 'The European Court of Justice: Taking Rights Seriously' (1992) 29 CML Rev 669; see also Phelan, 'Right to Life of the Unborn v Promotion of Trade in Services: The European Court of Justice and the Normative Shaping of the European Union' (1992) 55 MLR 670.
51   *Cowan v Trésor public* [1989] ECR 195.

[16.78] As against this it must be observed that some initiatives in the area of fundamental rights were designed with political objectives in mind. The EU Charter of Fundamental Rights was drafted by a convention made up of representatives of the European Parliament, national parliaments, national governments and the Commission.[52] Initially the status of the Charter was shrouded in ambivalence and it was not clear whether it was intended to be legally binding or to create new principles. Viewed thus its purpose appeared to be to raise the profile of the existing regime of rights protection amongst the citizenry of Europe.[53] However, matters were clarified by the Treaty of Lisbon which recognised the Charter as having the same 'legal value' as the Treaties. [54]

[16.79] The Charter of Fundamental Rights deals with civil, political, social and economic rights listed under the following headings:

- Dignity (human dignity, the right to life, the right to integrity of the person, the prohibition of torture and inhuman or degrading treatment or punishment, and the prohibition of slavery and forced labour);

- Freedoms (right to liberty and security; respect for private and family life; the protection of personal data; the right to marry and have a family; freedom of thought, conscience and religion; freedom of expression and information; freedom of assembly and association; freedom of the arts and sciences; the right to education; the freedom to choose an occupation and the right to engage in work; the freedom to conduct a business; the right to property; the right to asylum; and protection in the event of removal, expulsion or extradition);

- Equality (equality before the law; non-discrimination; cultural, religious and linguistic diversity; equality between women and men; the rights of the child; the rights of older people; the integration of people with disabilities);

- Solidarity (workers' right to information and consultation within the undertaking; the right of collective bargaining and action; the right of access to

---

52   See de Búrca, 'The Drafting of the European Union Charter of Fundamental Rights' (2001) 26 EL Rev 126.

53   Hence the two-page 'public information supplement' sponsored by the European Parliament Office in Ireland and published in (2001) *The Irish Times*, 9 May; this supplement contains the full text of the Charter.

54   See TEU, art 6(1):

   The Union recognises the rights, freedoms and principles set out in the Charter of Fundamental Rights of the European Union of 7 December 2000, as adapted at Strasbourg, on 12 December 2007, which shall have the same legal value as the Treaties.

   The provisions of the Charter shall not extend in any way the competences of the Union as defined in the Treaties.

   The rights, freedoms and principles in the Charter shall be interpreted in accordance with the general provisions in Title VII of the Charter governing its interpretation and application and with due regard to the explanations referred to in the Charter, that set out the sources of those provisions.

placement services; protection in the event of unjustified dismissal; fair and just working conditions; the prohibition of child labour and the protection of young people at work; family and professional life; social security and social assistance; health care; access to services of general economic interest; environmental protection; and consumer protection);

• Citizens' rights (right to vote and to stand as a candidate at elections to the European Parliament; the right to vote and to stand as a candidate at local elections; the right to good administration; the right of access to documents; the European Ombudsman; the right to petition the European Parliament; freedom of movement and of residence; and diplomatic and consular protection);

• Justice (right to an effective remedy and to a fair trial; the presumption of innocence and the right of defence; the principles of the legality and proportionality of criminal offences and penalties; and the right not to be tried or punished twice in criminal proceedings for the same criminal offence).

The sources for these rights originate in the European Convention on Human Rights, European Union law, the Social Charters of the EU and the Council of Europe, and the constitutional traditions of the member states.

[16.80] The European Convention on Human Rights has been ratified by all member states. The Treaty of Lisbon deepens the protection of human rights by providing for the European Union to accede to the ECHR, thus conferring on it the same legal standing as various other treaties. Such provision would also apply the Charter of Fundamental Rights to the EU institutions and to the member states when implementing European Union law.[55] Under the Treaty of Lisbon the ECHR is incorporated by reference and given legal status without forming part of the treaties.[56] The EU must act and legislate consistently with the Charter and EU courts will strike down EU legislation which

---

[55] De Burca, 'The Domestic Impact of the EU Charter on Fundamental Rights' (2013) 48 Ir Jur (ns) 49; Mahoney, 'The Charter of Fundamental Rights of the European Union and the European Convention on Human Rights from the Perspective of the European Convention' (2002) 23 *Human Rights Law Journal* 300; Ergun, 'The EU Charter of Fundamental Rights: An Alternative to the European Convention on Human Rights' (2004) 8 *Mediterranean Journal of Human Rights* 91; Douglas-Scott, 'The Charter of Fundamental Rights as a Constitutional Document' (2004) *European Human Rights Law Review*, 37; Eriksen, 'Why a Charter of Fundamental Human Rights in the EU?' (2003) 16 *Ratio Juris* 352; Eicke, 'The European Charter of Fundamental Rights: Unique Opportunity or Unwelcome Distraction' (2000) *European Human Rights Law Review*, 280; Ferigo, 'The Charter of Fundamental Rights in the Work of the European Convention on the Future of the Union' (2005) 9 *Mediterranean Journal of Human Rights*, 257; Young, 'The Charter, Constitution and Human Rights is this the Beginning or the End of Human Rights Protections by Community Law?' (2005) 11 *European Public Law*, 219; Hogan, 'The Belfast Agreement and the Future Incorporation of the European Convention of Human Rights in the Republic of Ireland' (1999) 4 BR 205.

[56] TEU, art 6(2).

contravenes it. The Charter only applies to member states as regards their implementation of EU law and does not extend the competences of the EU beyond its competences as defined in the treaties.

[5] THE NATURE OF EUROPEAN UNION LAW

[16.81] The Court of Justice, a central institution of the European Communities from the beginning, is charged with ensuring that, 'in the interpretation and application of the Treaties the law is observed.'[57] In two of the earliest cases decided by the Court of Justice, it made clear that 'the law' created by the Treaties was of a different nature to any other form of international agreement.

[16.82] In *Van Gend en Loos v Nederlandse Belastingenadministratie*[58] the Court of Justice was required to consider whether the Treaty of Rome had created legal rights for companies such as Van Gend en Loos and whether any such legal rights could be enforced in national courts. The court answered these questions in the affirmative, and in the process held that the Treaty had 'direct effect'. In other words, the court held that the Treaty was also part of the domestic law of the member states.

[16.83] The Court of Justice held that, in analysing the provisions of the Treaty of Rome, it should consider 'the general scheme and wording of those provisions'. This is similar to the harmonious approach later adopted by the Irish courts in the interpretation of the 1937 Constitution.[59] The court then referred to the Preamble to the Treaty, noting that it referred not only to the member states but also to the 'peoples of Europe'.[60] It also pointed out that the powers exercised by the Community institutions would affect not only the member states but also their citizens. In addition, the court referred to art 177 [now art 267 of TFEU] , which confers jurisdiction on it to give rulings concerning the interpretation of the Treaty and the validity of an act of the Community institutions '[w]here such a question is raised before any court or tribunal of a Member State'.

[16.84] In the court's view, this provision thus acknowledged that an issue of Community law could be dealt with in national courts. In a passage that has been quoted many times, the court continued:

"The conclusion to be drawn from this is that the [European Economic] Community constitutes a new legal order of international law, for the benefit of which the States have limited their sovereign rights, albeit within limited fields, and the subjects of which comprise not only Member States but also their nationals. Independently of the legislation of Member States, Community law therefore not only imposes obligations on individuals but is also intended to confer upon them rights which become part of their legal heritage. These rights arise not only where they are expressly granted by the Treaty, but also by

---

[57] TEU, art 19(1).
[58] *Van Gend en Loos v Nederlandse Belastingenadministratie* [1963] ECR 1.
[59] See para **15.142**.
[60] See para **16.18**.

reason of obligations which the Treaty imposes in a clearly defined way upon individuals as well as upon Member States and upon the institutions of the Community."[61]

[16.85] The Court of Justice did not conclude that all treaty provisions were legally enforceable in this way. In fact, a three-part test was established in this respect:

1. the provision in question must be clear and precise;

2. it must be unconditional; and

3. it must be such that no further action is required by the Community institutions or the member states or, if the provision requires the Member States to amend their laws, it leaves no discretion to the member states about the content of those amendments.

[16.86] In *Van Gend en Loos*, the government of the Netherlands had, in 1960, re-classified a particular chemical substance that was imported by Van Gend en Loos in such a way that it attracted a higher import duty than had applied on 1 January 1958, when the Treaty of Rome had come into effect. Article 12 of the Treaty provided that:

"Member states shall refrain from introducing between themselves any new customs duties on imports or exports or any charges having equivalent effect, and from increasing those which they already apply in their trade with each other."[62]

[16.87] The company argued that the article prohibited the re-classification of the chemical substance as it had the effect of increasing the import duty. The Court of Justice agreed, concluding that art 12 had 'direct effect' in Dutch law, preventing the state from imposing the higher duty on the plaintiff company and allowing the plaintiff to raise that point in the Dutch national courts.

[16.88] The following year, in *Costa v ENEL*,[63] the Court of Justice expanded on the general approach it laid down in *Van Gend en Loos*. In *Costa*, the plaintiff objected to the Italian law which had nationalised the Italian electricity industry to the extent of refusing to pay his electricity bill. When he was sued for non-payment in the Italian courts, his defence was that the Italian law was contrary to a number of provisions of Community law, including arts 92 to 94 of the Treaty of Rome [now arts 107 to 109 TFEU] concerning state aids to industry.[64] The Italian court referred the question

---

[61] *Van Gend en Loos v Nederlandse Belastingadministratie* [1963] ECR 1 at 12.

[62] The equivalent measure in TFEU, art 30 states: 'Customs duties on imports and exports and charges having equivalent effect shall be prohibited between Member States. This prohibition shall also apply to customs duties of a fiscal nature.'

[63] *Costa v ENEL* [1964] ECR 585.

[64] See, eg Travers, 'Some Reflections on Recent Developments in European Community Law Concerning State Aid' (1999) 34 Ir Jur (ns) 31.

whether Community law could be raised in such circumstances. The Court of Justice answered emphatically in the affirmative:

> "By contrast with ordinary international treaties, the EEC Treaty has created its own legal system, which, on the entry into force of the Treaty, became an integral part of the legal system of the Member States and which their courts are bound to apply.
>
> By creating a Community of unlimited duration, having its own institutions, its own personality, its own legal capacity and capacity of representation on the international plane and, more particularly, real powers stemming from a limitation of sovereignty or a transfer of powers from the States to the Community, the Member States have limited their sovereign powers, albeit within limited fields, and have thus created a body of law which binds both their nationals and themselves.
>
> It follows from these observations that the law stemming from the Treaty, an independent source of law, could not, because of its special and original nature, be overridden by domestic legal provisions, however framed, without being deprived of its character as Community law and without the legal basis of the Community itself being called into question."[65]

[16.89] Although the challenge to the Italian law was ultimately unsuccessful, this passage has been quoted many times in subsequent cases.

[16.90] *Van Gend en Loos* and *Costa v ENEL* remain the key decisions that assert the supremacy of EU law over national law. However, one further point of particular importance for Ireland was added by the decision of the Court of Justice in *Internationale Handelsgesellschaft mbH v Einfuhr-und Vorratsstelle für Getreide und Futtermittel.*[66]

[16.91] In *Internationale Handelsgesellschaft,*[67] the plaintiff company had obtained an export licence for maize under a European Community Regulation, one of the detailed legal instruments provided for in the Treaties aimed at achieving the 'common market'.[68] The regulation required the deposit of a sum of money with the relevant German licensing authority as a condition to the obtaining of a licence. This was designed to act as a guarantee that the licensee would comply with the terms laid down in the licence, in particular that it would export the quantity of maize to which it had committed itself by a given time. The company failed to export the quantity of grain within the agreed time limit and it was notified, again in accordance with the Community Regulation, that the deposit would be forfeited. The company then instituted proceedings in which it claimed that the forfeiture provisions of the

---

65 [1964] ECR 585 at 593.
66 *Internationale Handelsgesellschaft mbH v Einfuhr-und Vorratsstelle für Getreide und Futtermittel* [1970] ECR 1125.
67 *Internationale Handelsgesellschaft mbH v Einfuhr-und Vorratsstelle für Getreide und Futtermittel* [1970] ECR 1125.
68 On the making of a Community Regulation, see para **16.190** *et seq.*

Community Regulation were in conflict with its fundamental rights under certain provisions of the German Basic Law, in effect the German Constitution.

[16.92] These fundamental rights were described as the principles of freedom of action and disposition, of economic liberty and of proportionality. Echoing the language of the *Van Gend en Loos*[69] and *Costa v ENEL*[70] the Court of Justice rejected the plaintiff company's argument, stating:

> "Recourse to the legal rules or concepts of national law in order to judge the validity of measures adopted by the institutions of the Community would have an adverse effect on the uniformity and efficiency of Community law. The validity of such measures can only be judged in the light of Community law. In fact, the law stemming from the Treaty, an independent source of law, cannot because of its very nature be overridden by rules of national law, however framed, without being deprived of its character as Community law and without the legal basis of the Community itself being called in question. Therefore, the validity of a Community measure or its effect within a Member State cannot be affected by allegations that it runs counter to either fundamental rights as formulated by the constitution of that State or the principles of a national constitutional structure."[71]

[16.93] The court went on to state that, while the fundamental rights provisions of the German Basic Law could not take priority over Community law, similar though not necessarily identical fundamental rights were part of the *corpus* of Community law. The court stated:

> "However, an examination should be made as to whether or not any analogous guarantee [*that is, analogous to those in the German Basic Law*] inherent in Community law has been disregarded. In fact, respect for fundamental rights forms an integral part of the general principles of law protected by the Court of Justice. The protection of such rights, whilst inspired by the constitutional traditions common to the Member States, must be ensured within the framework of the structure and objectives of the Community. It must therefore be ascertained ... whether the system of deposits has infringed rights of a fundamental nature, respect for which must be ensured in the Community legal order."[72]

[16.94] As with the general approach of the court in *Van Gend en Loos* and *Costa v ENEL*, the decision in *Internationale Handelsgesellschaft* can be compared with developments in constitutional interpretation in Ireland. The concept of fundamental rights as being 'inherent' in EU law is similar to the jurisprudence concerning the unenumerated personal rights under Article 40.3 of the Constitution.[73]

[16.95] The key points emerging from these three leading cases are:

- in contrast with ordinary international treaties, the Treaties establishing the European Communities have created a new legal order;

---

[69] *Van Gend en Loos* [1963] ECR 1.
[70] *Costa v ENEL* [1964] ECR 585.
[71] [1970] ECR 1125 at 1134.
[72] [1970] ECR 1125 at 1134.
[73] See para **15.53**.

- by signing the Treaties, the member states had permanently limited their sovereign powers and transferred them to the new legal order, even if only in relation to the subjects covered by the Treaties;
- this legal order has become an integral part of the legal systems of the member states, and national courts are required to apply its rules;
- the legal order may be relied on in the national courts by the citizens of the member states;
- the law stemming from the Treaty may not be overridden by any domestic law of a member state, including the national Constitutions of the member states, since this would call into question the legal basis of the EU; and
- although EU law takes priority over provisions in national constitutions, respect for fundamental rights formed an integral part of EU law, inspired by the constitutional traditions common to the member states.

[16.96] The clear effect of the three decisions was that, in the event of a conflict, the new legal order took priority over national legal rules, even those contained in national constitutions.

[16.97] When the government of Ireland entered into negotiations with a view to joining the European Communities, it was clear that certain provisions of the Constitution were in direct conflict with the views of the Court of Justice in these cases. In order to join the new legal order, it was therefore necessary to amend the Constitution so that Community law would take priority over Irish law, including the 'basic law' (*Bunreacht*) contained in the Constitution.

The Constitution and international agreements

[16.98] The Constitution establishes the main institutions of state and places limits on their powers. Article 6 of the Constitution specifies that the executive, legislative and judicial powers of government can only be exercised by the organs of state established by the Constitution. This Article makes clear that no international organisation can exercise these powers. Article 15.2 provides that the Oireachtas has exclusive law-making powers, while Article 34 requires that justice be administered only in courts established by the Constitution and that the Supreme Court is the court of final appeal.[74]

[16.99] These provisions are underlined by Article 29 of the Constitution, which deals with the international relations of the state. Article 29.4.1° specifies:

"The executive power of the State in ... connection with its external relations shall ... be exercised by or on the authority of the Government."

[16.100] In other words, external relations, or what would now be described as international relations or foreign affairs, are a matter for the executive appointed under Article 28 of the Constitution. Many aspects of international relations are dealt with by

---

[74] See paras **15.47–15.50**.

way of treaties or other agreements between states. Article 29.4.2° also provides that, for this purpose, the government may adopt any 'method of procedure used or adopted ... by the members of any group or league of nations with which the State is or becomes associated for the purpose of international co-operation in matters of common concern.'

[16.101] Article 29.4 makes clear that the government is responsible for conducting the state's international relations. However, the effect of any international agreement adopted by the government on behalf of the state is also important. Article 29.3 deals with this point and provides:

"Ireland accepts the generally recognised principles of international law as its rule of conduct in its relations with other States."

[16.102] This provision acknowledges that the government should conduct relations with other states on the basis of generally recognised principles of international law.[75] One of the principles of international law accepted by most states is that agreements between states do not generally form part of the national, or domestic, law of those states unless they are specifically enacted into law by the parliaments of the states in question. This requirement to have two legal instruments (an international agreement followed by separate implementing national legislation, in turn leading back to ratification of the agreement) before the agreement becomes part of national law, is known as the dualist approach to international law. Article 29.6 of the Constitution adopts this approach by providing:

"No international agreement shall be part of the domestic law of the State save as may be determined by the Oireachtas."

[16.103] This preserves the role of the Oireachtas under Article 15.2 as the exclusive law-making body for the state. While Article 29.4 authorises the government to enter into international agreements, Article 29.6 ensures that only the Oireachtas can incorporate such agreements into Irish law. International agreements do not therefore have any legal force in the domestic law of Ireland unless they have been incorporated into law by means of an Act of the Oireachtas. As we note elsewhere, the dualist approach has been confirmed a number of times by the courts in Ireland.

Adapting the Constitution to the EU legal order

[16.104] It was clear that as things stood prior to Irish accession to the European Communities the provisions of the Constitution, and in particular Article 29, were in direct conflict with the primacy of EU law, as established by the Court of Justice in *Van Gend en Loos*,[76] *Costa v ENEL*[77] and *Internationale Handelsgesellschaft*.[78] In order to

---

75 It may be queried whether there is an agreed body of generally accepted principles of international law. However, in *Crotty v An Taoiseach* [1987] IR 713 the High Court and Supreme Court referred to the Vienna Convention on the Interpretation of Treaties of 1963 as containing some significant generally accepted principles of international law.

76 *Van Gend en Loos* [1963] ECR 1.

77 *Costa v ENEL* [1964] ECR 585.

78 *Internationale Handelsgesellschaft* [1970] ECR 1125.

comply with the requirements of the new legal order, a new subsection, Article 29.4.3°, was added to the Constitution:

> "The State may become a member of the European Coal and Steel Community (established by Treaty signed at Paris on the 18th day of April, 1951), the European Economic Community (established by Treaty signed at Rome on the 25th day of March, 1957) and the European Atomic Energy Community (established by Treaty signed at Rome on the 25th day of March, 1957). No provision of this Constitution invalidates laws enacted, acts done or measures adopted by the State necessitated by the obligations of membership of the Communities or prevents laws enacted, acts done or measures adopted by the Communities, or institutions thereof, from having the force of law in the State."

[16.105] In the wake of the Single European Act, a further constitutional amendment was required in 1987, though only after the Supreme Court had held in *Crotty v An Taoiseach*[79] to that effect. In December 1986, the Oireachtas had enacted the European Communities (Amendment) Act 1986 to give effect in Irish law to the relevant provisions of the Single European Act. However, before the government had deposited the formal instruments of ratification with the Italian government, as required by the Single European Act, the High Court granted to the plaintiff in *Crotty* an interlocutory injunction prohibiting the government from depositing the instrument of ratification. The injunction could hardly have been granted in more dramatic circumstances; Barrington J heard legal argument in his home on Christmas Eve 1986 and delivered judgment after a short adjournment to consider the matter.

[16.106] In 1987, a Divisional High Court (Hamilton P, Barrington and Carroll JJ) upheld the validity of the 1986 Act on the ground that it came within the scope of Article 29.4.3°. The High Court held that, in connection with Title III of the Single European Act, which concerned European Political Cooperation (EPC),[80] it had no function since EPC had been kept outside the scope of enforceable Community law and had thus not been incorporated into Irish law by the 1986 Act.

[16.107] On appeal, the Supreme Court in *Crotty* accepted that the 'licence' contained in the first sentence of Article 29.4.3° authorising the state to join the Communities contained an acknowledgement that it had joined a 'moving train'. Delivering the judgment of the Supreme Court, Finlay CJ stated that Article 29.4.3° was:

> "... an authorisation given to the State not only to join the Communities as they stood in 1973, but also to join in amendments of the Treaties so long as such amendments do not alter the essential scope or objectives of the Communities."[81]

[16.108] The court considered whether the amendments to the existing treaties, including the extension of the aims of the Communities to include protection of the

---

79   *Crotty v An Taoiseach* [1987] IR 713.
80   See para **16.41**.
81   *Crotty v An Taoiseach* [1987] IR 713 at 767.

environment, the introduction of qualified majority voting (QMV) in the Community institutions,[82] or the establishment of a Court of First Instance attached to the Court of Justice[83] involved an alteration to the essential scope or objectives of the Communities. The Supreme Court concluded that they did not, noting that the Communities which the state joined in 1973 constituted 'a developing organism'. The court thus agreed with the High Court in upholding the validity of the 1986 Act which had incorporated these provisions into Irish law. This aspect of the case acknowledges that not every change to the Treaties requires a constitutional amendment.

[16.109] However, the Court held, by a 3:2 majority (Walsh, Henchy and Hederman JJ; Finlay CJ and Griffin JJ dissenting) that the provisions of Title III were unconstitutional. The majority concluded that the commitment by the state in Title III to endeavour to agree a common foreign policy with other member states restricted its freedom to formulate an independent foreign policy, and this was inconsistent with the sovereignty of the state under Article 5 of the Constitution. This conclusion necessitated a referendum to amend the Constitution.[84]

[16.110] The decision in *Crotty* was considered in *Pringle v Ireland*,[85] which involved a challenge by independent TD Thomas Pringle to the ratification of the ESM (European Stability Mechanism) Treaty by the Irish Government. His argument that provisions of the ESM Treaty were incompatible with the Constitution and that a referendum was required to validate Irish ratification was rejected in the Supreme Court (with Hardiman J dissenting). The view of the majority is captured in in the judgment of Denham CJ where she distinguished the transfer of power that was at issue in *Crotty* from the instant case:

> "The State has not ceded policy making for the future. The State has not ceded power to another institution to enable the creation of policy in the future. Nor has the State ceded to elsewhere the power to increase the State's financial contributions. Consequently, there has been no transfer of sovereignty to any degree which is incompatible with the Constitution. To refer to the analysis by Walsh J. in *Crotty*, there has not been an abdication of freedom of action or to bind the State in its freedom of action in its formulation of foreign policy. Nor, in reference to the judgment of Henchy J. in *Crotty*, has there been any attempt by the Government to make a binding commitment to alienate to other States the conduct of foreign relations. Nor has there been any attempt at a fundamental transformation or diminution of sovereignty, such as arose in the *Crotty* case. Nor, in reference to the judgment of Hederman J. in *Crotty*, is this an agreement to subordinate or submit the exercise of the powers bestowed by the Constitution to the interests of other States. Rather,

---

82 See para **16.41**.

83 See para **16.178**.

84 See McCutcheon, 'The Irish Supreme Court, European Political Co-operation and the Single European Act' [1988/2] LIEI 93, replying to some of the criticisms of the majority decision in *Crotty*.

85 *Pringle v Ireland* [2012] IESC 47. See O'Gorman, 'Thomas Pringle v Government of Ireland, Ireland and the Attorney General' (2013) 48 Ir Jur (ns) 221.

it is an election by the Government of a policy in union with other States in pursuit of an identical policy."[86]

Denham CJ concluded that:

"… applying the principles stated in *Crotty* to the facts of the case, I am satisfied that the Government did not abdicate, alienate, cede, or subordinate its power to another. The decision of the Government to enter into the ESM Treaty was a policy decision within its executive power, pursuant to the Constitution, and so did not involve an impermissible transfer of sovereignty."[87]

The Court held that the ESM did not involve ceding sovereignty to such an extent that it amounted to a breach of the Constitution, and instead viewed it as an agreement to pursue a defined policy of the government rather than an inappropriate transfer of executive powers.

[16.111] Further amendments to Article 29.4 were made to facilitate the ratification of the Maastricht Treaty, the Treaty of Amsterdam, the Treaty of Nice and the Treaty of Lisbon. A certain amount of re-positioning of the relevant provisions of the Constitution resulted from this so that they currently read:

"3° The State may become a member of the European Atomic Energy Community (established by Treaty signed at Rome on the 25th day of March, 1957).

4° Ireland affirms its commitment to the European Union within which the member states of that Union work together to promote peace, shared values and the well-being of their peoples.

5° The State may ratify the Treaty of Lisbon amending the Treaty on European Union and the Treaty establishing the European Community, signed at Lisbon on the 13th day of December 2007 ('Treaty of Lisbon'), and may be a member of the European Union established by virtue of that Treaty.

6° No provision of this Constitution invalidates laws enacted, acts done or measures adopted by the State, before, on or after the entry into force of the Treaty of Lisbon, that are necessitated by the obligations of membership of the European Union referred to in subsection 5° of this section or of the European Atomic Energy Community, or prevents laws enacted, acts done or measures adopted by—

    i   the said European Union or the European Atomic Energy Community, or institutions thereof,

    ii the European Communities or European Union existing immediately before the entry into force of the Treaty of Lisbon, or institutions thereof, or

    iii bodies competent under the treaties referred to in this section,

from having the force of law in the State.

---

86 [2012] IESC 47, para 17.xii.
87 [2012] IESC 47, para 26.

7° The State may exercise the options or discretions—

    i   to which Article 20 of the Treaty on European Union relating to enhanced cooperation applies,

    ii   under Protocol No. 19 on the Schengen acquis integrated into the framework of the European Union annexed to that treaty and to the Treaty on the Functioning of the European Union (formerly known as the Treaty establishing the European Community), and

    iii under Protocol No. 21 on the position of the United Kingdom and Ireland in respect of the area of freedom, security and justice, so annexed, including the option that the said Protocol No. 21 shall, in whole or in part, cease to apply to the State,

but any such exercise shall be subject to the prior approval of both Houses of the Oireachtas.

8° The State may agree to the decisions, regulations or other acts—

    i   under the Treaty on European Union and the Treaty on the Functioning of the European Union authorising the Council of the European Union to act other than by unanimity,

    ii   under those treaties authorising the adoption of the ordinary legislative procedure, and

    iii under subparagraph (d) of Article 82.2, the third subparagraph of Article 83.1 and paragraphs 1 and 4 of Article 86 of the Treaty on the Functioning of the European Union, relating to the area of freedom, security and justice,

but the agreement to any such decision, regulation or act shall be subject to the prior approval of both Houses of the Oireachtas.

9° The State shall not adopt a decision taken by the European Council to establish a common defence pursuant to Article 42 of the Treaty on European Union where that common defence would include the State.

10° The State may ratify the Treaty on Stability, Coordination and Governance in the Economic and Monetary Union done at Brussels on the 2nd day of March 2012. No provision of this Constitution invalidates laws enacted, acts done or measures adopted by the State that are necessitated by the obligations of the State under that Treaty or prevents laws enacted, acts done or measures adopted by bodies competent under that Treaty from having the force of law in the State."

[16.112] What is now Article 29.4.6° of the Constitution allowed the state to comply with the terms of *Van Gend en Loos*, *Costa v ENEL* and *Internationale Handelsgesellschaft*. Article 29.4.6° has two major effects. The first is that nothing in the Constitution can prevent laws enacted, acts done or measures adopted by the European Union, or by their institutions, from having the force of law in the state. The second is that nothing in the Constitution can invalidate laws enacted, acts done or measures adopted by the state where these were necessitated by membership of the European Union or its predecessor European Communities. The principal area of doubt was the scope of that which is 'necessitated' by membership of the European Union.

This gave rise to a number of cases in the courts in Ireland.[88] However, it is clear that Article 29.4.6° permits all laws enacted by the EU institutions to have priority over laws enacted by the institutions established by the Constitution itself, notably laws enacted by the Oireachtas.

[16.113] In summary, therefore, the effect of Article 29.4.6° is that EU law is part of the domestic law of Ireland and, where there is a conflict between EU law and any provisions of the Constitution (or any other domestic laws), EU law takes priority. In *Doyle v An Taoiseach*,[89] it was observed that EU law 'has the paramount force and effect of constitutional provisions'. In essence, Article 29.4.6° has created a set of fundamental European provisions that take priority over Irish constitutional provisions.

Incorporating the Treaties and Community Acts

[16.114] In addition to the amendments made to Article 29.4 of the Constitution, the incorporation of EU law into Irish law was completed by the European Communities Act 1972 (the 1972 Act). This brief, but highly important, measure has been the vehicle for the implementation in the law of the state of many of the detailed laws that have emerged from the European Union.

[16.115] Section 1 of the 1972 Act contains the definition of the expression 'the Treaties governing the European Communities'. This definition has been amended many times since 1972 to incorporate amending treaties to the three original treaties of the ECSC, Euratom and the EC Treaty. The most recent amendment to the definition of 'the Treaties governing the European Communities' was effected by s 1 of the European Communities (Amendment) Act 2012.

[16.116] Section 2 of the 1972 Act, amended to reflect the replacement of the European Communities by the European Union, lists the Treaties and acts that bind the state:

"(1) The following shall be binding on the State and shall be part of the domestic law thereof under the conditions laid down in the treaties governing the European Union:

    (a)   the treaties governing the European Union;

    (b)   acts adopted by the institutions of the European Union (other than acts to which the first paragraph of Article 275 of the Treaty on the Functioning of the European Union applies);

    (c)   acts adopted by the institutions of the European Communities in force immediately before the entry into force of the Lisbon Treaty; and

    (d)   acts adopted by bodies competent under those treaties (other than acts to which the first paragraph of the said Article 275 applies)."[90]

The exclusion of art 275 of the EU Treaty reflects the fact that the Court of Justice lacks jurisdiction in respect of acts done under the EU common foreign and security policy.[91]

---

[88]   See *Meagher v Minister for Agriculture and Food* [1994] 1 IR 329 at para **16.121** *et seq.*

[89]   *Doyle v An Taoiseach* [1986] ILRM 693.

[90]   Inserted by European Union Act 2009, s 3.

[16.117] In some respects, it might be said that s 2 of the 1972 Act merely repeats in another form what is already contained in Article 29.4.6° of the Constitution. Nonetheless, it does provide an explicit statement that the Treaties and the acts of the EU institutions are part of the domestic law of the state. This includes confirmation that decisions of the Court of Justice concerning EU law are binding on all courts in Ireland, including the Supreme Court. It also confirms in Irish law the enforcement procedures provided for by the Treaties, including references by Irish courts and tribunals of points of EU law to the Court of Justice under art 267 TFEU.

[16.118] This explicit incorporation of EU law is also relevant to ss 3 and 4 of the 1972 Act, which deal with the precise manner in which the detailed rules of EU law could be incorporated into Irish law. Section 3 in part provides:

"(1) A Minister ... may make Regulations for enabling section 2 of this Act to have full effect.

(2) Regulations under this section may contain such incidental, supplementary and consequential provisions as appear to the Minister making the Regulations to be necessary for the purposes of the Regulations (including provisions repealing, amending or applying, with or without modification, other law, exclusive of this Act)."

[16.119] Section 4 of the 1972 Act, as originally enacted in 1972, provided that ministerial regulations under s 3 would have statutory effect but would cease to do so unless confirmed by an Act of the Oireachtas passed within six months of their making. The European Communities (Confirmation of Regulations) Act 1973 was the only Act made under this original version of s 4 of the 1972 Act. Later that year the European Communities (Amendment) Act 1973 amended s 4 of the 1972 Act by providing that regulations under the 1972 Act 'shall have statutory effect' unless annulled by resolutions passed by both Houses of the Oireachtas on the basis of a report from what is now the Joint Committee on European Affairs.[92] The effect was to transform the parliamentary role from one of confirmation to one of annulment. Since 1973, no such annulling resolutions have been passed by the Houses of the Oireachtas so that, in practice, regulations made under s 3 of the 1972 Act have had full statutory effect.

[16.120] The effect of ss 3 and 4 of the 1972 Act is to authorise a Minister to make regulations in order to implement in domestic law any act of the EU institutions, where that EU act required effect to be given to them in this way. The scope of s 3, particularly when read in conjunction with the amended form of s 4, has been criticised, *inter alia*,

---

[91] TFEU, art 375: 'The Court of Justice of the European Union shall not have jurisdiction with respect to the provisions relating to the common foreign and security policy nor with respect to acts adopted on the basis of those provisions.'

[92] The reference to the Joint Committee on European Affairs, a Joint Committee of the Houses of the Oireachtas, was inserted by the European Communities (Amendment) Act 1995.

on the ground that it conferred a power to amend an Act of the Oireachtas, primary legislation, by means of regulations, secondary legislation.[93]

[16.121] Despite these criticisms, the validity of s 3 of the 1972 Act was, in large measure, upheld by the 1993 decision of the Supreme Court in *Meagher v Minister for Agriculture and Food*.[94] In *Meagher*, the applicant unsuccessfully challenged the validity of the European Communities (Control of Oestrogenic, Androgenic, Gestagenic and Thyrostatic Substances) Regulations 1988[95] and the European Communities (Control of Veterinary Medicinal Products and their Residues) Regulations 1990.[96] These regulations had implemented a number of Community Directives[97] aimed at prohibiting the use of certain hormone growth promoters in farm animals, including clembuterol (commonly known as 'angel dust').

[16.122] The 1988 Regulations provided that search warrants could be issued to authorised officers of the Department of Agriculture and Food and to members of An Garda Síochána to enter lands and other premises with a view to taking samples from animals to ascertain whether growth promoters prohibited under the regulations were being used. Pursuant to a warrant issued under the 1988 Regulations, officers entered the applicant's farm and took relevant samples. The applicant was later served with 20 summonses alleging offences under the 1988 and 1990 Regulations. The applicant initiated judicial review proceedings in which he claimed that the 1988 and 1990 Regulations were *ultra vires* the 1972 Act and also that s 3 of the 1972 Act was invalid.

[16.123] Both the 1988 and 1990 Regulations provided that, notwithstanding the six-month time limit for initiating summary criminal prosecutions in s 10 of the Petty Sessions (Ireland) Act 1851,[98] prosecutions under the 1988 and 1990 Regulations could be initiated within two years of the date of the alleged offence. This, in effect, amounted to an amendment of s 10 of the 1851 Act by means of delegated legislation.

[16.124] The applicant contended that the general power in s 3 of the 1972 Act to implement Community acts by ministerial regulations was not 'necessitated' by membership of the Communities under Article 29.4 of the Constitution and was thus in conflict with the exclusive law-making power of the Oireachtas. It was clear that, if s 3 was not 'saved' by Article 29.4.5° [now Article 29.4.6°], it was in conflict with the limited power of delegation granted to the Oireachtas by Article 15 of the Constitution[99]

---

93   See McCutcheon, 'The Legal System', in Keatinge (ed), *Ireland and EC Membership Evaluated* (1991), pp 213–214; Hogan and Morgan, *Administrative Law in Ireland* (3rd edn, 1998) pp 15–19; but see *contra* Curtin, 'Some Reflections on European Community Law in Ireland' (1989) 11 DULJ (ns) 207.

94   *Meagher v Minister for Agriculture and Food* [1994] 1 IR 329.

95   SI 218/1988.

96   SI 171/1990.

97   See para **16.195**.

98   See para **6.10**.

99   *Cityview Press Ltd v An Chomhairle Oiliúna* [1980] IR 38; see para **13.123**.

and that the only appropriate legislative mechanism would have been an Act of the Oireachtas implementing the Directives, which could have provided for the required extension to the time limit in the 1851 Act.

[16.125] The Minister contended that the power in s 3 of the 1972 Act was 'necessitated' by membership of the Community and was thus immune from challenge. The Minister referred to art 189 [now art 288 TFEU] which provides that, while a Directive is binding on each member state, 'it shall leave to the national authorities the choice of form and methods'.[100] The Minister therefore argued that under both EU law and Irish law the amendment of the 1851 Act by the 1988 Regulations was valid since it was open to the national authorities to choose how to give effect to the Directives. The Minister also contended that the particular use of the power under s 3 was justified in this instance and that the two-year time limit was required in order to ensure effective implementation of the Directives: the complex sampling and testing of animals that is required to detect the presence of the prohibited substances made a lengthier period necessary.

[16.126] In the High Court, Johnson J rejected the Minister's argument on the immunity of s 3. He concluded that, by virtue of Treaty the Minister was obliged to consider the appropriate method by which to implement the Directives in question. He did not consider that Article 29.4.5° [now Article 29.4.6°] of the Constitution conferred an absolute discretion in this respect but that, in certain cases, an Act would be the appropriate choice for the implementation of Directives. Since s 3 of the 1972 Act conferred what appeared to be an unfettered discretion, Johnson J held it was invalid.[101] The decision of Johnson J was ultimately overturned by the Supreme Court, thus breathing life back into the many pre-1993 Regulations made under s 3 of the 1972 Act, over 400 in total, which had effected changes to primary legislation.

---

[100] See para **16.195**.

[101] Following the High Court decision, two Acts were passed to reverse its effects. In the immediate context of the case, the Animal Remedies Act 1993 now provides the statutory basis for control of growth promoters in animals. At the wider level of the many regulations which had effected changes to primary legislation, s 5(1) of the European Communities (Amendment) Act 1993 provided that all pre-1993 Regulations were 'hereby confirmed' from the date on which they purported to come into operation. However, in view of the then pending Supreme Court appeal, s 5(2) provided that this was subject to its being in accordance with the Constitution. Since the Supreme Court ultimately upheld the validity of s 3 of the 1972 Act, the confirmation in the 1993 Act became moot. However, s 5(4) of the 1993 Act remains important as it provided for a blanket extension of the time limit for initiating prosecutions to two years in respect of all regulations made under s 3 of the 1972 Act, including those which had originally provided, for example, a 12-month time limit. Such a blanket extension may be open to question.

[16.127] In the course of delivering the judgment of the Supreme Court, Finlay CJ stated:

> "The Court is satisfied that, having regard to the number of Community laws, acts done and measures adopted which either have to be facilitated in their direct application to the law of the State or have to be implemented by appropriate action into the law of the State, the obligation of membership would necessitate facilitating of these activities in some instances at least, and possibly in a great majority of instances, by the making of ministerial Regulations rather than legislation of the Oireachtas.
>
> The Court is accordingly satisfied that the power to make Regulations in the form in which it is contained in s 3(2) of the Act of 1972 is necessitated by the obligations of membership by the State of the Communities, and now of the Union, and is therefore ... immune from constitutional challenge."[102]

[16.128] The Court in *Meagher* accepted that there might be particular instances where the making of regulations under s 3 of the 1972 Act would not be 'necessitated' in this sense and that an Act of the Oireachtas would therefore be required. However, the court held that the presumption of constitutionality[103] made it inappropriate to consider this question as a hypothetical matter and that, therefore, each exercise of the s 3 power should be considered on its own merits. Having reached this conclusion, members of the court delivered separate judgments on the question of the validity of the regulations in the instant case.

[16.129] Blayney J examined the Directives on which the regulations were based as well as the nature of EU law. He accepted that a fundamental prerequisite of membership was the supremacy of EU law over domestic law. He cited in this context the decision of the Court of Justice in *Francovich v Italian Republic*.[104] He noted that Directive 85/358/EEC, one of the Directives implemented by the 1988 Regulations, was mandatory and required member states to make arrangements for taking official and random on-the-spot samples on farms in order to detect prohibited substances in farm animals; this justified the authorisation of searches under the 1988 Regulations.

[16.130] On the question of criminal offences, Blayney J noted that the applicant accepted that the 1985 Directive required the creation of offences for breaches of the principles contained in the Directive. On the time limit for prosecutions, the uncontroverted evidence was that, in view of the complexities involved in taking and analysing samples from a farm, it was necessary to extend the six-month time limit in s 10(4) of the Petty Sessions Act 1851. Blayney J held that this supported the view that

---

[102] *Meagher v Minister for Agriculture and Food* [1994] 1 IR 329.
[103] See para **14.78**.
[104] *Francovich v Italian Republic* [1991] ECR 1-5357: see para **16.200**. *Francovich* was followed in *Evans v Secretary of State for the Environment Transport and the Regions* [2003] ECR I-14447, and applied in *R v Ministry of Agriculture, Fisheries and Food, ex p Hedley Lomas (Ireland) Ltd* [1996] ECR I-2553; *Dillenkofer v Germany* [1996] ECR I-4845; *Riksskatteverket v Gharehveran* [2001] ECR I-7687.

the extension was required so that effective sanctions were in place to ensure that the Directive was implemented, as required by the Treaty. Since the state was obliged to implement the 1985 Directive, Blayney J upheld the validity of the 1988 Regulations because they correctly implemented the requirements of the directive; the fact that the Regulations had also amended an Act was irrelevant.

[16.131] In a concurring judgment, Denham J rejected the argument that an Act of the Oireachtas was required where a Directive lays down a set of rules and principles that must be implemented by the member states. She stated:

> "The role of the Oireachtas in such a situation would be sterile. To require the Oireachtas to legislate would be artificial. It would be able solely to have a debate as to what has already been decided, which debate would act as a source of information. Such a sterile debate would take up Dáil and Senate time and act only as a window on Community directives for the members of the Oireachtas and the nation. That is not a role envisaged for the Oireachtas in the Constitution."[105]

[16.132] Denham J thus underlined the extent to which law-making authority has been transferred from the Oireachtas to European Union institutions. While her comments are confined to Directives that prescribe mandatory rules and principles,[106] most Directives fall into this category. *Meagher* thus involved the recognition of a major exception to the principle established in *Cityview Press Ltd v An Chomhairle Oiliúna*,[107] at least where implementation of EU law is concerned.

[16.133] In *Meagher*, the court accepted that the power contained s 3 of the European Communities Act 1972 had been validly exercised, particularly because the Directives in question left no discretion to the member states as to whether the rules contained in them would be implemented. Since the rules in the Directives were mandatory, they were 'directly applicable' and were legally enforceable in the state irrespective of any domestic implementing legislation. On that basis, the legislative method chosen by the Minister was not open to challenge and the 1988 and 1990 Regulations were upheld.

[16.134] The Supreme Court's interpretation of Article 29.4.5° [now Article 29.4.6°] in *Meagher* has been criticised by some commentators.[108] While it was welcomed in government circles on the ground that it did not invalidate the hundreds of regulations made by many different Ministers under s 3 of the 1972 Act, it also upheld the situation where primary legislation may be amended by secondary legislation. Although there is some visibility in the implementation of Directives by ministerial regulations, the process is less transparent than that involved in the enactment of Acts of the Oireachtas. The volume of EU acts implemented by ministerial regulations has grown substantially

---

[105] [1994] 1 IR 329.

[106] Denham J repeated this view in *Laurentiu v Minister for Justice* [1999] 4 IR 26, 50–51.

[107] *Cityview Press Ltd v An Chomhairle Oiliúna* [1980] IR 38: see para **13.123**.

[108] See eg Walsh, 'The Democratic Deficit in Criminal law and Criminal Justice in Title VI of the Treaty on European Union' (2002) 12 ICLJ 7; Hogan, 'The Implementation of European Union Law in Ireland: the Meagher Case and the Democratic Deficit' (1994) 3 IJEL 190.

in recent years,[109] and since many of these involve amendments to primary legislation, this has further complicated the state of the statute book in Ireland.[110]

[6] INSTITUTIONS OF THE EUROPEAN UNION

[16.135] We turn to examine EU law-making procedures. The functions of the various institutions have evolved considerably over the years and their powers have been altered in many ways as the process of European integration developed. This process culminated with the adoption of the Treaty of Lisbon which introduced significant innovations that are intended to make the EU institutions more efficient. The underlying objective is to enable the institutions to work more effectively in continually enlarging Union, and to make them more democratic and accountable.[111]

[16.136] Article 13 TEU sets out the EU's institutional framework:

- the European Parliament;
- the European Council;
- the Council;
- the European Commission;
- the Court of Justice of the European Union;
- the European Central Bank;
- the Court of Auditors.

[16.137] The institutions of the European Union resemble in some respects those of member states, in that they were invested with executive, legislative and judicial powers. However, any comparison between the EU institutions and those of the member states breaks down when the detailed powers are examined. Executive powers were conferred by the Treaties, but these are shared between a full-time EU institution, the Commission, and ministerial representatives of the governments of the member states, the Council. The major decision-making powers were given to the Council while the Commission was given the main power to initiate proposals to implement the aims of the Treaties.

[16.138] The Treaties have progressively increased the legislative power of the European Parliament. That said, however, the Commission and Council of Ministers remain the dominant institutions in this regard. The Treaties also created a Court of Justice which has the power to issue authoritative rulings on EU law. The court is also a key component of the enforcement mechanisms provided for in the Treaties. The Court of Auditors performs functions for which parallels are found in all member states, namely ensuring that funds have been properly spent by EU institutions. What follows is a description of the powers and functions of the main institutions of the European Union.

---

109 See para **16.218**.
110 See para **13.84** on the different sources of primary legislation in Ireland.
111 *Cf* Voermans, Hartman and Kaeding, 'The Quest for Legitimacy in EU Secondary Legislation' (2014) 2 *Theory and Practice of Legislation* 5.

The Commission

[16.139] The European Commission has been described as an embryonic government of the Community. The broad role of the Commission is set out in art 18(1) TEU:

"The Commission shall promote the general interest of the Union and take appropriate initiatives to that end. It shall ensure the application of the Treaties, and of measures adopted by the institutions pursuant to them. It shall oversee the application of Union law under the control of the Court of Justice of the European Union. It shall execute the budget and manage programmes. It shall exercise coordinating, executive and management functions, as laid down in the Treaties. With the exception of the common foreign and security policy, and other cases provided for in the Treaties, it shall ensure the Union's external representation. It shall initiate the Union's annual and multiannual programming with a view to achieving interinstitutional agreements."

Although the Treaties confer final decision-making powers in most areas on the Council and the European Parliament, in many cases those institutions cannot act without an initial proposal from the Commission. Thus, art 18(2) TEU provides:

"Union legislative acts may only be adopted on the basis of a Commission proposal, except where the Treaties provide otherwise. Other acts shall be adopted on the basis of a Commission proposal where the Treaties so provide."

This has the effect of empowering the Commission to set the agenda for large areas of action in the EU. In the context of the jurisdiction of the Court of Justice, the Commission is empowered by art 258 TFEU to bring proceedings to the court where there has been a failure by member states to implement Treaty obligations.[112]

[16.140] In practice, the Commission and Council (and, increasingly, the European Parliament) are involved in a power-sharing arrangement, which state of affairs has been reinforced by the Lisbon Treaty. Nevertheless, the Commission retains its central role in European governance.

[16.141] The Commission, which is expected to act as a collegiate body, at present consists of 28 members, usually called Commissioners. The Commissioners are nominated by the governments of the member states on a full-time basis for a period of five years. Currently, each member state nominates one member of the Commission. The Treaty of Lisbon initially proposed that from 2014 the number of the Commissioners would be reduced so as to make the Commission more efficient. However, following Irish rejection of the Treaty in the 2008 referendum, it was agreed that member states would retain their right to nominate one Commissioner each. The incoming Commission President was selected on the nomination of the largest political group in the European Parliament (the Christian Democrats) following the 2014 elections.

---

[112] See para **16.166**.

[16.142] The head of the Commission is called the President. He or she is initially chosen by the governments of the member states but must also be approved by the European Parliament.[113] The President then allocates each Commissioner a particular area of responsibility and the Commissioner takes charge of what is the equivalent of a Government Department. While an undoubted degree of political influence and authority attached to the office, the President did not initially enjoy any additional legal powers to reflect his or her position. However, the more recent Treaties, especially Nice and Lisbon, strengthened the position of the President who now enjoys the authority to decide on the internal organisation of the Commission; to allocate tasks amongst the Commissioners and to re-allocate portfolios; with the approval of the Commission to appoint Vice-Presidents; and to require a Commissioner to resign. The person holding the new post of High Representative of the Union for Foreign Affairs and Security Policy automatically becomes a Vice-President of the Commission.[114]

[16.143] The effect of the various Treaty provisions conferring the power of initiation on the Commission is that it is involved in the initiation of most proposals designed to implement the aims of the Union. The Commission will present such proposals to the governments of the member states for final decision by the Council and the European Parliament. Having heard initial comments from these other institutions the Commission may, and in some instances must, reformulate the proposals. This process can take some time, depending on the political sensitivities involved in the proposal in question. While the Commission's functions include the initiation of policies and the drafting of proposals to achieve the objectives of the Treaties, the final decision on ordinarily rests with the Council and the Parliament. However, in many areas the Council has 'delegated back' to the Commission the day-to-day implementation of Council functions, further reinforcing the central role of the Commission.

[16.144] In addition to forwarding proposals to the member states and to the other EU institutions, the Commission is assisted in its functions by a large number of advisory and specialist committees representative of governments, employers, the farming community and workers. These include the Economic and Social Committee (ECOSOC) and the Committee of the Regions established under art 300 TFEU, which must be consulted by the Council, the Commission and the European Parliament in certain cases. Numerous other advisory committees, consisting of national experts in particular areas, have also been established under the Treaties and these are consulted where proposals are initiated by the Commission within their areas of expertise.

[16.145] We have already observed that the Commission may bring proceedings in the Court of Justice against member states who fail to implement their Treaty obligations. Another area in which the Commission has been given important powers by the TFEU is to enforce or 'police' the implementation of EU policies. For example, in relation to competition policy, this includes the power to impose fines on individuals or companies

---

[113] TEU, art 18(7).
[114] TEU, art 18(4).

for breaches of EU rules on competition. This has become particularly important in recent years as the EU has developed more detailed rules in this area. Thus, in addition to its executive functions under the Treaty, the Commission exercises a semi-judicial function that would ordinarily be associated with a court only.[115]

The Council of the EU

[16.146] The Council of the EU, colloquially known as the Council of Ministers, is governed by art 16 TEU. The Council consists of a representative of each member state at ministerial level, authorised to take decisions on behalf of the government of that member state. The Council of Ministers therefore currently consists of 28 Ministers from the governments of the member states. Each area of EU activity has its own separate Council. For example, the Council of Agriculture Ministers consists of the Agriculture Ministers from the member states. This Council deals with the largest area of expenditure of the European Union, the common agricultural policy. The Council of Finance Ministers deals with customs and other taxation issues.

[16.147] The various Councils of Ministers meet on a regular basis and the agenda for such meetings are prepared by the Committee of Permanent Representatives (COREPER), who in effect are the ambassadors of the Member States to the EU. The existence of COREPER allows for permanent liaison between the Ministers and the Commission so that there is no lack of continuity between Council meetings. The function of COREPER is to ensure that, where possible, agreement over matters of concern can be dealt with before Council meetings.[116]

[16.148] The Presidency of the Council rotates among the member states on an agreed cycle. Under this arrangement, Ireland held the Presidency of the Council of Ministers for the period January to June 2013. While the Presidency does not involve any additional decision-making powers, the member state in question is involved in advance preparation of the agenda for Council meetings and in ensuring that Council meetings are as successful as possible. This agenda-setting power confers considerable informal power on the member state holding the Presidency of the Council, particularly in the context of summit meetings and meetings at foreign ministerial level.

[16.149] The compromise brought about by the Luxembourg Accords of 1966 in effect required unanimity in all Council decisions[117] but that has now been abandoned. Article 238(1) TFEU states that 'where it is required to act by a simple majority, the Council shall act by a majority of its component members'. However, the Treaties still preserve the situation where, certain decisions continue to require unanimity and other specified matters are decided by qualified majority voting (QMV).

---

[115] See generally, McMahon and Murphy, *European Community Law in Ireland* (1989), pp 435–438.

[116] Bustock, 'Coreper Revisited' (2002) 40 *Journal of Common Market Studies* 215.

[117] See para **16.40**.

[16.150] The move towards QMV is worth noting. The vote of each Minister is given a certain weighting. The Treaty of Nice brought about a re-weighting of votes to take account of enlargement and to compensate the member states that lost the right to nominate a second Commissioner. QMV requires a majority of all member countries (55 per cent) who represent a majority of all EU citizens (65 per cent) to vote in favour of a proposal. However, when the Council is not acting on a proposal from the Commission, the majority of all member countries required increases to 72 per cent although the population requirement does not change. At least four member states have to vote against a proposal to block it. The effect of introducing the QMV procedure has been the acceleration of the decision-making process, since the option of vetoing a proposal is no longer available in respect of most matters. For this reason, although relatively few decisions at Council meetings involve a vote, the QMV procedure has had a significant impact. The Treaty of Nice provisions were overtaken when the Treaty of Lisbon came into force.

[16.151] It should, however, be borne in mind that certain key decisions at Council level still require unanimity. Thus, any changes in the Treaties themselves require a unanimous decision of the Council; art 48 TEU requires that any such amendments be reached by 'common accord'. Similarly, any changes in the decision-making procedures, such as extension of the QMV arrangement must be unanimous. Decisions in certain politically sensitive areas such as agricultural policy and taxation continue to require unanimity, thus continuing the possibility of a veto in Council by a single member state in order to prevent a decision being made. However, in practice, as with QMV, the actual use of the veto is quite rare, and compromise decisions are in many instances the outcome.

The European Council

[16.152] In addition to Council meetings involving Ministers responsible for particular areas of Community policy, two other 'unofficial' Councils began meeting in the late 1960s. The first consisted of meetings between the Heads of State and heads of government of the member states. These 'summit' meetings became known, somewhat confusingly, as the 'European Council'. Meetings between the Foreign Ministers of the member states also emerged to coordinate responses to the foreign policy of the Community. Neither of these meetings was formally recognised until the adoption of the Single European Act in 1986.[118]

[16.153] The European Council has now been recognised as a key EU institution in its own right. Its role, defined in art 15(1) TEU, is to provide the 'necessary impetus for its development and [it] shall define the general political directions and priorities thereof.' Significantly the European Council does not exercise a legislative function: law-making

---

[118] It was the inclusion of provisions on a common foreign policy in the Single European Act that led the Supreme Court in *Crotty v An Taoiseach* [1987] IR 713 to hold that certain aspects of the SEA went beyond the original terms of Article 29.4.3° of the Constitution, thus requiring a further amendment to ratify the SEA: see para **16.105** *et seq*.

is the preserve of the other EU institutions. The European Council is comprised of the heads of government of the member states and the President of the European Commission. A new post of President of the European Council was created by the Treaty of Lisbon, and the President would henceforth be elected (by qualified majority) by the European Council for two and a half years (renewable once). The role of the President is primarily to chair and coordinate the European Council's work, and to represent the European Union worldwide. The President does not have any decision-making powers.

The European Parliament

[16.154] The general role of the European Parliament is outlined in art 14(1) TEU:

"The European Parliament shall, jointly with the Council, exercise legislative and budgetary functions. It shall exercise functions of political control and consultation as laid down in the Treaties. It shall elect the President of the Commission."

[16.155] The composition of the European Parliament is also governed by art 14 TEU. Representation is 'degressively proportional': it is not directly proportional to member states' populations, and smaller states are assigned more MEPs per head of population than the larger ones. An upper limit of 751 MEPs, has been set with a minimum threshold of six MEPs per country and a maximum of 96. Thus Germany, with a population of over 80 million people, is assigned 96 MEPs; the United Kingdom, whose population is approximately 63 million, is allocated 73 MEPs; Ireland, with a population of 4.5 million, has 11 MEPs; Luxembourg, with a population of about 537,000, is allocated 6 MEPs. MEPs are directly elected for a five-year term of office.

[16.156] The powers initially conferred on the Parliament by the Treaty of Rome were confined primarily to two matters: to approve (or disapprove) the proposed members of the Commission and to pass (or refuse to pass) the annual budget for the Community. The power to approve the Commission members was limited to voting *en bloc* for or against the entire Commission, and objection could not be taken to a particular Commissioner. At first this considerably limited the impact of this power as it was thought to be embarrassing to refuse to approve the entire list of Commissioners. However, this state of affairs changed with the resignation of the Commission in 1999, an event replete with the potential to redress the imbalance between the Commission and the Parliament.[119]

[16.157] Despite allegations of inefficiency and corruption the Commission survived a vote of censure by the Parliament in January 1999, largely as a result of political wrangling amongst the various groups in the Parliament. However, a committee of experts was appointed to investigate the allegations and the resulting report was highly critical of the Commission. Faced with the possibility of a second vote of censure that it would surely lose, the Commission resigned *en masse* in March 1999. This represented

---

[119] See Dinan, 'Governance and Institutions 1999: Resignation, Reform and Renewal' (2000) *Journal of Common Market Studies Annual Review of the EU 1999/2000* 25–30.

an important institutional advance for the Parliament, not least in that it was seen to assert its authority over a Commission that was perceived to be corrupt. In relation to the Community's annual budget, the Parliament's power of veto has proved important, as on occasion it has held back its implementation until certain requirements were met.

[16.158] As is already clear, the European Parliament was not the main law-making body in the European Union, and in this respect it differs from most national Parliaments. In terms of law-making, the Parliament was, initially, a consultative body, with some powers of influence but with no power to amend legislative proposals from the Commission. For many years, MEPs have called for additional legislative powers to be conferred on the Parliament. The case for additional powers was strengthened when a procedure for direct elections was agreed in the 1970s.

[16.159] Under the Single European Act, the role of the Parliament was significantly increased through the introduction of a mechanism which is called the 'Cooperation Procedure'. This procedure ensured that, in many cases, legislative proposals originating in the Commission were sent to the Parliament for its views, with the former usually taking the comments of the latter into account before sending amended proposals to the Council of Ministers for final decision. In certain situations, only a unanimous decision of the Council could block a Parliament objection, with the result that Parliament acquired a measure of legislative influence.

[16.160] The cooperation procedure has been largely overtaken by the 'co-decision procedure' which was introduced in 1992 by the Maastricht Treaty. Under the latter procedure the Parliament is empowered to enact certain legislation jointly with the Commission or Council. Where this procedure applies, both the Council and Parliament are named in the legislative title. A consequence of the procedure is that if the Parliament votes against a legislative proposal from the Commission in the areas covered by co-decision the effect is the blocking, or vetoing, of the proposal.

[16.161] Where the Parliament indicates its rejection of a Commission or Council proposal, an effort to resolve the conflict must be made through a 'conciliation committee'. If the conciliation committee fails to resolve a problem, the proposed law cannot be passed, even by a unanimous vote of the Council of Ministers. The range of policy areas that are subject to the co-decision procedure was expanded by the Treaty of Amsterdam and further extended by the Treaty of Nice. The latter Treaty also gave the Parliament the right to initiate action to deal with situations where there is the risk of a breach of the EU's fundamental principles, which in this context includes human rights. Moreover, Parliament was given the right to refer certain cases to the Court of Justice. While the European Parliament still remains the lesser partner *vis-à-vis* the Council and Commission, the incremental increase in its powers can be seen to enhance its role in the governance of the European Union.

[16.162] The Treaty of Lisbon has further strengthened the role of the European Parliament in several areas of competence. The co-decision process with the Council of Ministers, which has been renamed the 'ordinary legislative procedure', has been expanded to include other areas such as agriculture, energy policy, immigration, and judicial cooperation in criminal and civil matters, giving the Parliament an increased law-making role. In the few remaining areas the European Parliament now has the right of consent to a Council measure, except in the limited cases where the old *consultation procedure* still applies, under which the Council will only need to consult the European Parliament before voting on the Commission proposal. In these circumstances, the Council is not bound by the Parliament's position but only by the obligation to consult it. Parliament would need to be consulted again if the Council deviated too far from the initial proposal.

[16.163] The European Parliament has a role in the selection of the President of the Commission. Parliament elects the President of the Commission on foot of a proposal from the European Council. If the proposed candidate does not secure majority support from the Parliament the European Council is required within one month to propose a new candidate. Although the balance of power in selecting the Commission President still lies with national governments, acting in the form of the European Council, the enhanced role of Parliament is of considerable political significance.

The Court of Justice of the European Union

[16.164] The Court of Justice of the European Union (the CJEU) is the highest court in the EU system. Provision is made for the Court of Justice in art 19 TEU which states that it: 'shall ensure that, in the interpretation and application of this Treaty, the law is observed'.[120] The CJEU is comprised of three levels:

(i)   the Court of Justice;

(ii) the General Court; and

(iii) specialised courts, which may be attached to the General Court to determine cases brought in specific areas.

[16.165] In the wake of *Van Gend en Loos*, *Costa v ENEL* and *Internationale Handelsgesellschaft*,[121] the court has established that its decisions on the interpretation of EU law are binding on all courts in the member states, including the Supreme Court in Ireland. It should be noted, however, that the binding nature of EU law only applies to the areas of law with which the European Union is concerned. There are certain areas of the law of the member states that remain largely unaffected by EU law, such as areas of criminal law and family law as well as most aspects of national court procedure. The TFEU assigns three principal areas of jurisdiction to the court.

---

120 The Court of Justice interprets EU law to make sure it is applied in the same way in all EU member states. It also settles legal disputes between EU governments and EU institutions. Individuals, companies or organisations can also bring cases before the Court if they feel their rights have been infringed by an EU institution. To help the Court cope with the large number of cases brought before it, and to offer citizens better legal protection, a 'General Court' deals with cases brought forward by private individuals, companies and some organisations, and cases relating to competition law.

121 See paras **16.81–16.97**.

[16.166] Article 258 TFEU empowers the Commission to initiate proceedings in the Court of Justice against a member state if it considers that 'a Member State has failed to fulfil an obligation under the Treaties'. The most common form of such proceedings is that the Commission alleges that a member state has failed to implement in national law an EU Directive.[122] Originally, the Court of Justice could only make a 'finding' that the member state had failed to fulfil its obligations but art 260 now authorises the court to impose a fine on a member state that does not comply with a decision of the court to the effect that it has failed to fulfil its Treaty obligations. It should also be noted that art 259 TFEU provides that a member state may also initiate similar proceedings against another member state for failure to implement a Treaty obligation. Such proceedings are quite rare, reflecting the fact that the Commission is seen as the primary guardian of the Treaty.

[16.167] Under art 263 TFEU the court may review the legality of any acts, other than recommendations and opinions, adopted by the Commission, the Council, the European Central Bank and the Parliament, as well as acts of the European Council that are 'intended to produce legal effects *vis-à-vis* third parties'. The Article also provides that:

> "[The Court of Justice] shall for this purpose have jurisdiction in actions brought by a Member State, the European Parliament, the Council or the Commission on grounds of lack of competence, infringement of an essential procedural requirement, infringement of the Treaties or of any rule of law relating to their application, or misuse of powers.

> The Court shall have jurisdiction under the same conditions in actions brought by the Court of Auditors, by the European Central Bank and by the Committee of the Regions for the purpose of protecting their prerogatives."

[16.168] Article 264 TFEU provides that, if the action under art 263 is well founded, 'the Court of Justice shall declare the act concerned to be void'. Thus, actions under art 263 are generally referred to as *actions for annulment*. Article 265 TFEU provides for a complementary form of action, the action for failure to act, where a Community institution has failed to carry out its functions. The jurisdiction of the Court of Justice under these articles may be compared with the process of judicial review in Irish public law, where decisions, including legislative acts, may be declared invalid for being *ultra vires*, whether on the basis that ministerial regulations are unauthorised by the parent statute or where any legislative act is challenged for being in conflict with the Constitution.

[16.169] The third basis for the court's jurisdiction arises from proceedings brought before it by natural or legal persons. In this respect, art 263 TFEU also provides that any natural or legal person may, under the same conditions as already described for member states and EU institutions, institute proceedings against a decision addressed to that person or against any other Community act that 'is of direct and individual concern' to the person. Again, this is comparable to the requirement of *locus standi* in Irish public law.[123]

---

[122] See para **16.190**.

[123] See para **15.87**.

[16.170] However, even more significant is art 267 TFEU, which provides a direct link between the Court of Justice and the national courts and tribunals of the member states. Article 267 stipulates:

"Where such a question [that is, interpretation of the Treaty or the validity or interpretation of acts of the Community institutions] is raised before any court or tribunal of a Member State, that court or tribunal may, if it considers it necessary to enable it to give judgment, request the Court to give a ruling thereon."

The majority of cases that come before the Court of Justice involve references under art 267 TFEU and thus originate in the member states. In the case of Ireland, most cases originate in civil proceedings initiated in the High Court.[124] Thus, in a series of such references in the 1980s and 1990s, the court held that the state had, in effect, failed to fulfil its obligations to implement a 1979 Directive on equality in social welfare.[125] Any court or tribunal may refer any point of EU law arising in the case to the Court of Justice under art 267 for what it describes as a 'preliminary' ruling.

[16.171] This procedure is similar to the case stated appeal on a point of law, in that, having dealt with the point of EU law, the case will be returned by the Court of Justice to the court or tribunal which will then dispose of the case in accordance with the Court of Justice's preliminary ruling.[126] The decisions of the court, while preliminary in that sense, involve definitive determinations on the application and scope of EU law. Many of the court's most significant decisions, including those in *Van Gend en Loos*, *Costa v ENEL* and *Internationale Handelsgesellschaft*,[127] involved such references from domestic courts or tribunals.

[16.172] We should also mention at this stage a further refinement of the court's jurisprudence on the effect of EU law in the national laws of the member states. As noted earlier, under art 258 TFEU, the Commission may initiate proceedings against the member state before the Court of Justice, which may lead to the imposition of a fine. However, the Court of Justice has also been required, in art 267 proceedings, to consider the effect on individuals and other legal persons in such a member state of the failure to implement Treaty obligations, such as the failure to implement a Directive. In this context, the decision of the Court in *Francovich v Italian Republic*,[128] where the court held that individuals might be entitled to claim damages from the defaulting state for such failures, is relevant.[129]

---

124 See para **7.68**.
125 See para **16.204**.
126 On the case stated procedure, see para **7.14**. On the issue of whether, and to what extent, Irish courts are obliged to refer points of EU law to the Court of Justice, see paras **7.74–7.80**.
127 See paras **16.81–16.97**.
128 *Francovich v Italian Republic* [1991] ECR I-5357: see para **16.200**.
129 See, eg Barrington, 'State Liability for Breach of EC Law: Francovich Developed Upon' (1996) 1 BR 22.

[16.173] The Court of Justice is composed of 28 judges (one from each member state)[130] and eight Advocates General.[131] The qualification for appointment as a judge (and as an Advocate-General) is the same as that for appointment to the highest judicial office in the appointing member state, which in the case of Irish appointees means the qualifications for appointment to the superior courts. The Court may sit as a full court of 28 judges, as a Grand Chamber of 13 judges, or in chambers of five and three judges. Advocates General assist the Court in presenting opinions on a case assigned to them. The detailed workings of the Court are amplified in the Statute of the Court of Justice of the European Union, which is enacted under art 281 TFEU.

[16.174] Article 253 TFEU provides for the appointment of judges for six-year terms with that half of the judges being required to retire every three years. Article 253 also provides that judges thus retiring are eligible for re-appointment. In practice, many of the judges remain on the court, by means of the re-appointment mechanism, until the retirement age laid down for senior judges of the state from which they were nominated (which in the case of Irish appointees is 70 years of age). Article 253 also provides that the court is to be presided over by a President of the Court, who is elected by the judges of the court for a three-year term, and to which the President may be re-elected. The judges are assisted by legal research assistants, called *référendaires*, who may prepare draft judgments and engage in related research.

[16.175] The court may form chambers, each consisting of three or five judges, and the court can decide cases as a Grand Chamber of 13 judges in accordance with the Statute of the Court of Justice and its own Rules of Procedure. The full court sitting in plenary session is reserved for a limited range of highly important cases.

[16.176] Article 19 TEU and art 252 TFEU provides that the Court of Justice shall be assisted by Advocates General, currently totalling eight in all. Equivalents of these Advocates General are a feature of many of the civil law legal systems of the member states, but are found only by way of exception in common law jurisdictions.[132] Article 252 TFEU requires an Advocate General to make 'reasoned submissions' on cases brought before the court. These reasoned submissions typically consist of a summary of the factual circumstances of the case, the legal issues arising, an analysis of previous decisions of the court and a recommendation to the court on how it should decide the case. In most cases, the court will, in fact, decide the case in accordance with the Advocate General's reasoned submission.

[16.177] The positions of Advocate General are rotated among the larger and smaller member states on an agreed system. The effect of this system for a small member state such as Ireland was that it did not become 'eligible' to nominate an Advocate General until 1995, more than 22 years after acceding to the European Communities.[133]

---

130   TEU, art 19(2).
131   TFEU, art 252.
132   For example, the guardian *ad litem* in wardship proceedings.
133   See Fennelly, 'Reflections of an Irish Advocate General' (1996) 5 IJEL 5.

General Court

[16.178] By the 1980s it had become clear that the Court of Justice was unable to cope with its rapidly increasing caseload. To alleviate the burden the Single European Act provided for the establishment of a Court of First Instance (renamed the General Court by the Treaty of Lisbon) with power to determine certain issues of EU law, subject to a right of appeal on points of law only to the Court of Justice: art 256 TFEU. The Court came into being in 1989.[134] Reflecting the composition of the Court of Justice, the General Court consists of 28 judges, with each member state nominating a judge. Unlike the Court of Justice, the General Court is not assisted by Advocates General, but a judge of the court itself may be selected to act as Advocate General for a particular case. The judges of the General Court may sit as a full Court, as a Grand Chamber of 13 judges, in chambers of 5 or 3 judges, or in certain cases may sit as a single judge.[135] The General Court may hear, as a first instance court:

- actions for annulment of EU acts (art 263 TFEU);
- actions for failure to act against an EU institution (art 265 TFEU);
- actions for damages against the EU (arts 268 and 340 TFEU).

A decision of the General Court in these cases may be appealed to the Court of Justice on a point of law.

[16.179] The categories of cases which the General Court may hear are determined from time to time by the Council under art 256 TFEU on foot of a request by the Court of Justice and after consultation with the Commission and Parliament. However, art 256 TFEU also specifies that the Court may hear questions referred for a preliminary ruling under art 267 TFEU in specific areas 'laid down' the Statute of the Court of Justice.

[16.180] The progressive restructuring of the European Court involved a transfer of competence from the Court of Justice to the General Court and a corresponding enhancement of the role of the latter tribunal. Overall it was anticipated that the revised system would result in a faster rate of disposing of cases that 'clogged up' the European court system.

Specialised Courts

[16.181] Article 257 TFEU provides that the European Parliament and the Council may establish specialised courts attached to the General Court to hear at first instance certain classes of cases in specific areas. Decisions of specialised courts may be appealed to the General Court. A specialised court, known as the Civil Service Tribunal, has been established to hear cases involving disputes within the civil service of the EU (art 270 TFEU). The specialised court consists of seven judges and usually sits as a panel of three judges, although it may also sit as a full panel, or as a single judge.[136] The General

---

[134] On foot of Council Decision 88/591/ECSC, EEC, Euratom.
[135] Cases handled by the General Court are coded with the letter 'T'.
[136] Cases handled by the Civil Service Tribunal are coded with the letter 'F'.

Court acts as an appeal court for decisions given by the specialised courts (art 256 TFEU).

The Court of Auditors

[16.182] Article 285 TFEU provides that the Court of Auditors shall carry out the audit of the European Union. The Court of Auditors is not a court in the same sense as the Court of Justice or the General Court and its functions are broadly similar to those performed by the Comptroller and Auditor General under the Constitution of Ireland.[137] It is thus responsible for ensuring that the Community budget is properly spent by the other EU institutions and by any body established under the Treaties.

[16.183] The Court of Auditors is also required by art 287 TFEU to assist the Parliament and Council in exercising their powers of control over the implementation of the budget. The Court of Auditors currently consists of 28 members, each member state being entitled to nominate one member to the court. Anticipating the potential problems that might beset a court of 28 members the Treaty also made provision for the adoption of a system of internal chambers. The term of office of a member of the Court of Auditors is six years, though members are eligible for re-appointment.

[7]   THE FORM OF EUROPEAN UNION LAWS

[16.184] As we have already seen, the Court of Justice has established the supremacy of EU law over national laws. The form of that *corpus* of EU laws is ultimately based on the treaties establishing the Union and the legal instruments that the Union institutions are authorised to make under the treaties.

The Treaties

[16.185] As well as setting out the institutional structure, the text of the Treaties establishing the three European Communities, as amended since the 1950s, prescribed detailed arrangements and timetables concerning the establishment of the 'common market' and 'internal market'. Like the Constitution, some of these provisions could be described as aspirational in nature and lack the mandatory element typical of legally enforceable rules. However, other provisions of the Treaties in particular have all the hallmarks of a legally enforceable rule, as the Court of Justice first made clear in *Van Gend en Loos*,[138] where art 12 of the Treaty of Rome [now art 30 TFEU] was found to have 'direct effect' in national law.[139]

[16.186] Similarly, art 157 TFEU provides:

"Each Member State shall ensure that the principle of equal pay for male and female workers for equal work or work of equal value is applied."

---

[137]   See para **2.82**.

[138]   *Van Gend en Loos* [1963] ECR 1.

[139]   See para **16.82**.

[16.187] In this context, 'pay' means the ordinary basic or minimum wage or salary and any other consideration, whether in cash or in kind, which the worker receives, directly or indirectly, in respect of employment from his employer. The article also states that:

"Equal pay without discrimination based on sex means:

(a) that pay for the same work at piece rates shall be calculated on the basis of the same unit of measurement;

(b) that pay for work at time rates shall be the same for the same job."

This provision has formed the basis for many cases on equal pay that have been considered both by the Court of Justice and by courts in the member states.[140]

[16.188] However, more significantly, art 288 TFEU also empowers the EU institutions to approve legally binding instruments in order to implement the general principles contained in the treaties. There are three types of legally binding instruments provided for in art 288: Regulations, Directives and Decisions. The article also authorises the making of recommendations and opinions, measures that are not legally binding.

[16.189] Article 289 TFEU stipulates that: 'the ordinary legislative procedure shall consist in the joint adoption by the European Parliament and the Council of a regulation, directive or decision on a proposal from the Commission.' However, the Council and Parliament can also delegate certain power to the Commission to adopt 'non-legislative acts of general application to supplement or amend certain non-essential elements of [a] legislative act'.[141]

Regulations

[16.190] Article 288 TFEU states:

"A regulation shall have general application. It shall be binding in its entirety and directly applicable in all Member States."

[16.191] Article 288 TFEU does not provide much information on the precise form of a Regulation. In essence, it is law in the sense that it will set out certain legally enforceable rules. It is important not to confuse an EU regulation with domestic measures that bear the same title: the latter are a species of secondary or delegated legislation made under the authority of an Act of the Oireachtas.[142] In accordance with the decisions of the Court of Justice in *Van Gend en Loos*, *Costa v ENEL* and *Internationale Handelsgesellschaft*,[143] once an EU Regulation is made under the powers conferred by the Treaty, it automatically becomes law in all member states. Like the legally enforceable provisions of the treaties, a Regulation made under art 288 TFEU is a clear instance of the 'direct effect' of EU law. The Oireachtas has no formal function

---

140 See McMahon and Murphy, *European Community Law in Ireland* (1989), pp 492–503: and *Murphy v Bord Telecom Éireann* [1989] ILRM 53, para **14.61**.

141 TFEU, art 290.

142 On domestic delegated or secondary legislation, see para **13.109** *et seq*.

143 See paras **16.80–16.97**.

whatever in its enactment and the Regulation thus by-passes the normal law-making procedure prescribed by the Constitution.

[16.192] A Regulation differs from a directive in that it has legal force in the member states without the need for any further domestic legislative act. All necessary legislative acts have taken place once the procedures provided for in the Treaty have been completed. This means that, in relation to a Regulation, there will usually be no Irish law to implement it, because there is simply no need. The Regulation is already law once it is made.

[16.193] Each Regulation is given an official number. The full text of a Regulation is published in the L (Legislative) Series of the *Official Journal of the European Union* (OJ), which is the official daily gazette of European Union laws and other important information.[144] In recent years, well in excess of 3,000 Regulations have been made each year and published in the *Official Journal*, and this provides some indication of the level of legislative activity at European level. By way of contrast, about 30 to 40 Acts of the Oireachtas and 600 to 700 statutory instruments are enacted in a typical year in Ireland.[145]

[16.194] A Regulation is generally employed as the appropriate legislative vehicle where the topic covered does not overlap with any existing national laws. For example, the detailed provisions of the common agricultural policy (CAP), such as intervention prices, milk quotas and the like are dealt with by means of regulations. In connection with the CAP, the Council and Parliament make Regulations concerning CAP. However, day-to-day aspects of the implementation of EU policy, including the CAP, are typically delegated to the Commission. Such delegation will include the power to make regulations concerning the implementation of the CAP, such as the detailed administrative arrangements for payment of subsidies. Indeed, Commission Regulations of this type form a large part of the 3,000 annual entries for regulations in the L Series of the *Official Journal*.

Directives

[16.195] Article 288 TFEU states:

> "A directive shall be binding, as to the result to be achieved, upon each Member State to which it is addressed, but shall leave to the national authorities the choice of form and methods."

---

[144] The *Official Journal* is published in two series. The 'L' (Legislation) Series contains the text of Regulations, Directives and Decisions. The 'C' (Information and Notices) Series contains other significant pieces of information, including proposals for the more important proposed regulations and directives. The Journal is published in the different official languages of the Community. Since 1 March 2000 it is available in electronic format only, publishing in hard copy having been abandoned from that date. The Official Journal is available on CD-Rom, on the JUSTIS database and on the web: eur-lex.europa.eu/JOIndex.do.

[145] See para **13.111**.

[16.196] A Directive is the legal mechanism employed where existing national laws are in place and there is a need to approximate or harmonise them in order to fulfil the general aims of the Treaties. Unlike a Regulation, a Directive is not 'directly applicable' immediately. Instead, it will set out the basic rules which must be implemented by all the member states on a particular topic. The member states are then left to decide how best to implement the requirements of the directive so that it fits into the existing law of the state in question. Apart from this difference, Directives resemble Regulations in terms of setting down legislative rules in a format that is similar to domestic legislation. Frequently, a Directive sets a time limit within which a member state must implement its requirements. This can range from a number of months to a number of years, though a period of two to three years is common.

[16.197] Like Regulations, a Directive is given an official number. The full text of a Directive is also published in the *Official Journal of the European Union*. The number of Directives agreed each year is relatively small by comparison with the number of Regulations. The total number of Directives that Ireland was required to implement between the time it became a member state in 1973 and the end of 1993 was 1,148.[146] Despite the fact that this would not represent half the number of regulations made in any given year, Directives have tended to have a higher profile as EU legislation since, in practice, they generally require the enactment of domestic legislation to implement them.

[16.198] In addition, Directives also tend to require the amendment of existing domestic legislation. Although this should increase their visibility, the problems arising from the implementation of Directives by means of domestic delegated or secondary legislation should be noted.[147] As with a Regulation, any significant Directive must be made by the Council and Parliament. However, the Commission is also empowered by various Council Directives to make Directives involving minor adjustments or updating of Council Directives: these are usually known as Directives involving adaptations to technical progress (ATPs).

[16.199] Two problems might arise in relation to the implementation of a Directive. One is that a member state does not comply with the specified deadline for implementation. The other is encountered where there is an incomplete implementation of the Directive. In either case, the Commission may initiate proceedings against the member state under art 258 TFEU.[148] However, the tardy implementation of Directives has also been discussed in a number of cases by the Court of Justice where individual citizens have claimed that their rights have been affected by the failure of a member state to fulfil treaty obligations. In this respect, the court has confirmed the approach in *Van Gend en*

---

146 See para **16.212**.
147 See para **16.134**.
148 See para **16.166**.

Loos[149] and *Costa v ENEL*[150] that EU law, whether in the form of the treaties or of Directives, can have 'direct effect' in domestic law.

[16.200] In *Francovich v Italian Republic*,[151] the court reiterated that 'direct effect' arises where a Directive is clear and unconditional and is intended to create individuals rights, leaving no discretion to member states except as to the method by which it is to be implemented. In *Francovich*, the court considered its well-established jurisprudence in the rather novel context of the impact on individuals of the failure of the Italian state to implement in Italian law Directive 80/987/EEC of 20 October 1980 on the protection of employees in the event of an insolvency ([1980] OJ L 283/23).

[16.201] The 1980 Directive required member states to put in place specific measures by 23 October 1983 to guarantee, *inter alia*, the payment of salary arrears to employees whose employers have become insolvent. This had not been done by the relevant date. The plaintiffs were Italians whose employer had become insolvent and at the time they were owed substantial arrears. The liquidator informed them that they were unlikely to receive any payment for salary arrears. The plaintiffs then brought proceedings against the Italian state claiming the amounts that would have been due to them had the Directive been implemented domestically.

[16.202] The Court of Justice concluded that a member state might be required to make good any damage suffered by individuals as a result of infringements of EU law attributable to the member state. The court stated such state liability would arise if three conditions are satisfied:

- the result required by the Directive must involve the granting of rights to private individuals;

- the contents of these rights must be identified by reference to the provisions of the Directive;

- there must be cause and effect relationship (or causative link) between the breach of the member state's obligation and the damage suffered by the persons concerned.[152]

[16.203] The Court of Justice concluded that if these conditions are met a private individual has a right to claim compensation arising directly from EU law. The court held that the exact procedures by which such a claim would be processed was a matter for national law. Although the decision in *Francovich* was in some respects new, it could also be seen as a development of the 'direct effect' approach of earlier cases.[153] It also

---

149 *Van Gend en Loos* [1963] ECR 1.

150 *Costa v ENEL* [1964] ECR 585.

151 *Francovich v Italian Republic* [1991] ECR I-5357.

152 See Hyland, 'State Liability for Non-implementation of Directives: Further and Better Particulars' (1997) 3 BR 40; Brown, 'State Liability to Individuals in Damages: An Emerging Doctrine of European Union Law' (1996) 31 Ir Jur (ns) 7.

153 See generally, Collins, 'Community Law as a Source of Rights and Remedies in the Irish Legal Order' (1994) 2 IJEL 173. *Francovich* was cited with approval in *Meagher v Minister for Agriculture and Food* [1994] 1 IR 329: see para **16.129**.

indicates that the court's role in the development of EU jurisprudence is not confined to the early decisions of the 1960s.

[16.204] The effect of *Francovich* was dramatically felt in Ireland arising from the failure to implement Directive 79/7/EEC on equal treatment for men and women in social security by the 1984 deadline specified in the Directive. The Social Welfare Act 1984 formally implemented the Directive, but the 1984 Act did not come into effect until 1986, a delay that at the time was defended on grounds of the potential cost involved. A series of cases was initiated in the High Court by a number of married women who claimed damages arising from the failure to implement the Directive. In effect, the plaintiffs sought to be paid the relevant social welfare benefit due in the period between 1984, when the Directive should have been implemented, and 1986, when it finally was implemented. The state defended the proceedings to the full, and a number of references under art 177 of the Treaty of Rome [now art 267 TFEU] were made to the Court of Justice.[154]

[16.205] The Court of Justice concluded that the Directive came within the test laid down in *Francovich* and held that full payment should be made to the women involved. Eventually, in a representative action or final 'test case' on behalf of the women affected, *Tate v Minister for Social Welfare*,[155] the High Court concluded that the state was fully liable. The government finally announced in 1995 that up to £265m in arrears would be paid to the 70,000 married women affected.[156] The need to pay that large sum brings home the importance in some instances of implementing Directives within agreed time limits.[157]

Decisions

[16.206] Article 288 TFEU states:

> "A Decision shall be binding in its entirety upon those to whom it is addressed."

This indicates that, unlike a Regulation or Directive, a decision usually has limited scope and does not necessarily apply in all member states. However, it is legally binding on those concerned with it. The text of decisions is also published in the *Official Journal of the European Communities*. For example, when the Irish government proposed in 1993

---

[154] *McDermott and Cotter v Minister for Social Welfare* [1987] ECR 1453; *Cotter and McDermott v Minister for Social Welfare* [1991] ECR I-1155; *Emmott v Minister for Social Welfare* [1991] ECR I-4269.

[155] *Tate v Minister for Social Welfare* [1995] 1 IR 419.

[156] See Cousins, 'Equal Treatment in Social Welfare: The Final Round?' (1995) 4 IJEL 195 at 203.

[157] In the British context, the *Factortame case* gave rise to a similar obligation to pay compensation arising from a failure to implement correctly a directive concerning access to British fishing waters: see *Brasserie du Pêcheur SA v Federal Republic of Germany/Reg v Secretary of State for Transport, ex p Factortame Ltd* [1996] 2 WLR 506, discussed in Flynn, 'State Liability in Damages for Failure to Observe EC Law' (1996) 14 ILT 170.

to provide £175m to the Irish state airline Aer Lingus as part of the rescue plan for the airline, approval from the European Commission was required in view of its responsibility to ensure that this did not breach European competition law. The eventual approval of the Commission came in the form of Commission Decision 94/118/EC of 21 December 1993 ([1994] OJ L 54/30). If the cash injection had been rejected by the Commission, this would also have been in the form of a decision.

[16.207] Where the Commission finds that there is a breach of EU competition policy, it is also empowered to conduct investigations of any such breach and if it finds a company or member state in breach of EU law, it can also take a decision declaring the activity illegal. Such a decision would be similar to a court judgment and could even include the imposition of a fine: some decisions made by the Commission have involved fines of tens of millions of euro.

Recommendations and Opinions

[16.208] Article 288 TFEU also specifies that recommendations can be made or opinions delivered. However, the terms of the article provide that these measures 'shall have no binding force'. It goes without saying that recommendations and opinions need not be implemented in national laws even when made or delivered by the Council or Commission. However, they may have some important effects notwithstanding. Thus, in the context of child care facilities for women in paid employment, the 1992 Council Recommendation of 31 March 1992 on child care, 92/241/EEC ([1992] OJ L 123/16), may form the basis for discussion at national level in the member states on the provision of child care facilities to ensure equal participation by women in the workforce. Although not legally binding, the recommendation may be influential in the formation of domestic policy.

[8] IMPLEMENTATION OF EUROPEAN UNION LAW IN IRELAND

Self-executing treaties and Regulations

[16.209] The combination of Article 29.4.6° of the Constitution and the European Communities Act 1972 has given effect in general terms to the EU treaties.[158] As to the detailed legislative acts of the institutions adopted under art 288 TFEU, EU Regulations are largely self-executing, are 'directly applicable' and in general do not require domestic implementing measures. As noted, the bulk of legislative activity at EU level involves the enactment of Regulations[159] and, since no domestic implementing measures are required, the effect of these Regulations on Irish law is largely 'invisible'. In this respect, many aspects of what might be described as the 'law of agriculture' are to be found in the *Official Journal of the European Communities* rather than in the annual volumes of Acts of the Oireachtas or of Irish statutory instruments.

---

[158] See paras **16.104–16.113**.
[159] See para **16.193**.

EU Regulations requiring domestic enforcement procedures

[16.210] There are some exceptions to the general rule that EU Regulations need not be implemented by domestic legislation. An example is provided by the European Communities (Rules on Competition) Regulations 1993,[160] made under s 3 of the European Communities Act 1972. The domestic regulations were designed to facilitate the full implementation in Ireland of Council Regulation 17/62 and Council Regulation 4064/89/EEC, dealing, *inter alia*, with investigations into anti-competitive practices carried out by the European Commission.

[16.211] While it is true that the EU Regulations are in most respects self-executing, the 1993 Irish Regulations enable designated officers of the Department of Enterprise, Trade and Employment to assist European Commission officials in the carrying out of their functions by investing the department officers with powers of entry and inspection. The 1993 Regulations specify that it is an offence to obstruct any investigations being carried out and a maximum penalty of £1,000 and/or imprisonment of 12 months is specified. This domestic element to the directly applicable EU laws was enacted to ensure the effective implementation of those EU provisions.

EU Directives requiring domestic enforcement measures

[16.212] The principal need for domestic implementing measures arises from the requirement to implement or 'transpose' Directives in accordance with art 288 TFEU. At the end of 1993, there were 1,148 Directives which Ireland was due to have implemented in domestic law, of which 1,019 (or 88.7% of the total) had in fact been implemented.[161] It is clear from this total that the implementation of Directives over the years has required a significant amount of domestic legislative activity in Ireland. Not only has EU membership required the amendment and updating of existing law, but it has also created entirely new areas of legal regulation where domestic law made no provision before.

[16.213] It is virtually impossible to provide a comprehensive list of the wide range of areas of law affected by the implementation of Directives, even if one were to leave aside the creation of entirely new subjects of legal regulation arising from the directly applicable provisions of EU law. However, the areas involved include the following:

– agriculture and fisheries;

– chemical safety, including pharmaceuticals and pesticides;

– coal and steel industries;

– company law, including disclosure of financial information and insolvency;

– competition, including state aids to industry, public procurement and competition between private undertakings;

---

160 SI 124/1993.

161 See Eleventh Annual Report by the Commission to the European Parliament on monitoring the application of Community law [1993] 1993 OJ C 154/7.

- contract law, in particular consumer protection;
- customs duties;
- educational qualifications (recognition and the right of establishment);
- employment and labour law, including equal access to employment, equal pay, maternity leave, employment protection and movement of migrant workers;
- environmental protection;
- exchange control and capital movements;
- financial services, including banking and other credit provision;
- food safety;
- insurance;
- intellectual property, including copyright, patents and trade marks;
- international enforcement of civil judgments;
- international relations;
- manufacturing standards for products;
- nuclear/radiological safety;
- occupational pensions;
- social security equality;
- taxation, especially indirect taxation such as VAT;
- telecommunications and other media;
- transport.

Areas not affected by EU law

[16.214] Hardly any area of domestic law has *not* been affected by EU law. Even areas such as criminal law and family law that lay far beyond the competence of the Union at the time of Irish accession in 1972 have been affected to some extent.[162] At a simple level, many domestic implementing provisions involve the creation of criminal offences. At first, the power to create such offences by means of domestic regulations under s 3 of the European Communities Act 1972 was limited to summary offences. However, the European Communities Act 2007 amended s 3 of the 1972 Act to facilitate the creation of indictable offences by means of Ministerial regulation, thus increasing the impact of EU law on domestic criminal law. Moreover, the TFEU provisions on judicial cooperation in criminal matters have the potential to bring about common definitions of certain criminal offences.[163] In relation to family law, many areas of domestic family law remain untouched by the treaties, though some elements of employment law have an indirect impact, for instance in relation to equality of access to employment and to child care facilities.[164] Even an area as contentious in the Irish context as abortion has been the

---

[162] *Cf* Peers, 'The European Union and Criminal Law: An Overview' (2002) 12 ICLJ 2.
[163] See para **16.60**.
[164] See the Recommendation on Child Care at para **16.208**.

subject of litigation in the Court of Justice and in the negotiation of the Treaty on European Union.[165]

National implementing measures

[16.215] Article 288 TFEU specifies that the form and method of implementation of Directives is a matter for each member state to decide. We have seen that, in Ireland, the European Communities Act 1972 empowers a government Minister to implement Directives by means of regulations made under s 3 of the 1972 Act. The majority of Directives have been implemented into Irish law in this way but some have been implemented by means of an Act of the Oireachtas or via regulations made under an Act other than the European Communities Act 1972.[166] Nor has the same form been used consistently for the same areas of the law.

[16.216] For example, in the area of company law, a number of Directives were implemented by means of Companies Acts, amending the principal Act in this area, the Companies Act 1963. The Companies (Amendment) Act 1977, the Companies (Amendment) Act 1983 and some provisions of the Companies Act 1990 implemented a number of Directives in this way. But other Directives in this area were implemented by the European Communities (Companies) Regulations 1973, the European Communities (Companies: Group Accounts) Regulations 1992 and the European Communities (Accounts) Regulations 1993, these three sets of regulations being made under s 3 of the European Communities Act 1972. This poses some difficulties for those attempting to assemble a complete list of the relevant legislative provisions on company law.[167]

[16.217] In relation to Directives, some have been implemented by means of regulations made under the European Communities Act 1972, others under relevant Acts where these exist. Thus, a number of Directives in the area of safety and health at work have been implemented through regulations made under the Safety, Health and Welfare at Work Act 1989; the Safety, Health and Welfare at Work (General Application) Regulations 1993 implemented seven Directives in the area of safety and health at work. On the environmental front, regulations under the Air Pollution Act 1987 and the Environmental Protection Agency Act 1992 also implement Directives.

---

[165] See Byrne and Binchy, *Annual Review of Irish Law 1992* (1994), p 208.

[166] See generally Donelan, 'The Role of the Office of the Parliamentary Draftsman in the Implementation of European Union Directives in Ireland' (1997) 18 Stat LR 1; see also Samuels, 'Incorporating, Translating or Implementing European Union Law into UK Law' (1998) 19 Stat LR 80.

[167] In the area of company law, there are happily some excellent collections of the legislative materials: see MacCann and Courtney, *The Companies Acts 1963–2009* (2009) which includes the relevant regulations implementing Directives in this area.

[16.218] To indicate the scale of the domestic legislative activity involved, Figure 16.1 notes the number of Acts of the Oireachtas and statutory instruments in 1993, 1994, 2007 and 2008, which involved implementation of EU law obligations.[168]

Year	Total No of Acts	Acts with EU element
1993	40	6
1994	34	6
2007	42	13
2008	25	12

Year	Total No of SIs	SIs with EU element
1993	422	73
1994	464	116
2007	871	179
2008	598	123

Volume of Legislation Implementing EU Obligations
Figure 16.1

[16.219] The reliance on delegated legislation in preference to Acts of the Oireachtas as the principal mechanism to implement EU law obligations is clear. In the years surveyed between 17% and 25% of statutory instruments implement EU obligations. The data in Figure 16.1 reveal the growing significance of EU law in Irish domestic legislation. Nevertheless, it is worth noting that the proportion of statutes (as opposed to statutory instruments) that in some way or another incorporate an EU dimension has increased significantly, from 15% in 1994 to 33% in 2007 and 50% in 2008. While these raw figures do not reveal the full picture a trend towards using primary legislation as the means of translating EU obligations into domestic law is discernible.

[16.220] In many instances, the statutory instruments involved the repeal and revocation of existing statutory provisions on the topics they covered, including primary legislation, while in others entirely new domestic legislative provisions were involved. Were it not for the effective constitutional immunity granted to such statutory instruments,[169] they would otherwise have required primary legislation.

[16.221] The indirect effect of EU law on domestic legislative activity should be noted. An example is afforded by the Competition Acts 1991 and 1996, which contain legal provisions which are based on the competition provisions of the Treaties (now arts 101

---

[168] Source: European Community chapters in Byrne and Binchy, *Annual Review of Irish Law 1993* (1996); Byrne and Binchy, *Annual Review of Irish Law 1994* (1996).

[169] See para **16.121** *et seq.*

and 102 TFEU). The 1991 Act was not 'necessitated' by membership, but the rules contained in it owe their form and substance to those articles.

Effects on interpretative approaches

[**16.222**] We have already discussed the *Francovich*[170] case in connection with the effects of delayed implementation of a Directive.[171] A connected issue arises where a treaty provision or Directive is not fully implemented in domestic law or is implemented in language that contains some ambiguity. Again, the concept of 'direct effect' is relevant here. In this respect, an Irish court will refer back to the text of the relevant Directive or treaty provision. In a case of ambiguity, the text of the Directive takes priority over any implementing domestic law.

[**16.223**] An example is the decision in *Murphy v Bord Telecom Éireann*.[172] In that case, the statutory words contained in the Anti-Discrimination (Pay) Act 1974 were interpreted by reference to art 119 of the Treaty of Rome (now art 157 TFEU) concerning equal pay on which the 1974 Act was based. The decision in this case also illustrates the influence in Irish law of the teleological approach to statutory interpretation that is a feature of civil law systems.[173] Similarly, the harmonious approach to constitutional interpretation was largely influenced by the similar approach adopted by the Court of Justice to interpretation of the Treaties.[174]

---

[170] *Francovich* [1991] ECR I-5357.

[171] See para **16.200**.

[172] *Murphy v Bord Telecom Éireann* [1989] ILRM 53: see also *Murphy v Minister for the Marine* [1997] 2 ILRM 523; *Byrne v Conroy* [1998] 3 IR 1; and para **14.61**.

[173] See also *Tate v Minister for Social Welfare* [1995] 1 IR 419: para **16.205**.

[174] See para **16.83**.

Chapter 17

International Law

[1]   Introduction 853
[2]   Sources of International Law 854
[3]   Ireland in International Law 856
[4]   The Council of Europe 858
[5]   The United Nations Organisation 862
[6]   The World Trade Organisation 869
[7]   International Law in Ireland 873
[8]   Private International Law 880

[1] INTRODUCTION

[17.01] In this chapter, we discuss public international law, the body of rules and principles that determines the rights and duties of states, principally in their relationships with one another. It is also sometimes referred to simply as international law or, in more archaic terms, as the *jus gentium*, that is, the law of nations. International law has existed as long as there have been relations between nations, and classical international law, dating from the Late Middle Ages, recognises the nation state as the primary participant in the international legal order. Since the end of World War II in 1945, other participants have emerged onto the stage, and modern international law permits international organisations and non-state actors such as individuals, groups and other entities to play an ever-increasing role.

[17.02] The body of international law includes a vast range of rules and principles governing the relationships between states. It includes rules in relation to all matters which require international cooperation, including commerce, criminal and civil jurisdiction, the use of the oceans, the protection of the environment, the protection of human rights, the use of force and the conduct of hostilities. Rules relating to statehood, sovereign and diplomatic immunities, state responsibility, nationality and the interpretation of treaties allow this cooperation to take place in an ordered way. International law contains both hard law (legally binding rules and principles) and soft law (principles which are more in the nature of normative guides).

[17.03] In order to foster international cooperation and maintain international security, the community of states has established many international organisations. These include global organisations, such as the United Nations Organisation (UN) and the World Trade

Organisation (WTO), as well as 'regional' organisations such as the Council of Europe and the European Union (EU).

[17.04] In practice, international law and international agreements have become increasingly influential in the domestic law of most states, including Ireland. In this chapter we discuss the effect of international law on the Irish legal system as well as membership of the Council of Europe, the UN and the WTO. We also discuss briefly the connected area of private international law, or the conflict of laws.[1]

[2]   SOURCES OF INTERNATIONAL LAW

[17.05] Irish domestic law receives its force and authority from the sovereignty of the people, whose will is expressed through the Oireachtas. The community of states, however, has no over-arching sovereign. Indeed, it is composed of nearly 200 sovereign and equal states, of which Ireland is just one. For this reason, the sources of international law are very different to those in domestic, national, law. The most authoritative statement of the sources of international law appears in art 38(1) of the Statute of the International Court of Justice, the main judicial organ of the UN:

> "1. The Court, whose function is to decide in accordance with international law such disputes as are submitted to it, shall apply:
>
> a.   international conventions, whether general or particular, establishing rulers expressly recognised by the contesting states;
>
> b.   international custom, as evidence of a general practice accepted as law;
>
> c.   the general principles of law recognised by civilised nations;
>
> d.   subject to the provisions of Article 59, judicial decisions and teachings of the most highly qualified publicists of the various nations, as subsidiary means for the determination of rules of law."[2]

International custom[3]

[17.06] Of these sources, perhaps the source of international law that least resembles the sources of law discussed in the previous chapters of this book (the Constitution, legislation and precedent) is international custom. International custom is a major source of international rules. Some rules of customary law, such as the inviolability of diplomatic personnel, have evolved over centuries. Others, such as the rules governing the activities of states in outer space, have evolved very quickly. The existence of a rule of international customary law is evidenced by (i) a general practice among states and (ii) an acceptance on the part of states that the practice is in conformity with a rule of international law (this subjective element is known as *opinio juris*). The wider the acceptance of a practice among states and the longer its duration, the greater the force of the rule. All states are bound by international customary law, the force of which comes

---

1   See paras **17.82–17.89**.

2   Statute of the International Court of Justice, art 38(1).

3   See Brownlie, *Principles of Public International Law* (2008), pp 6–12.

chiefly from the self-interested inclination of states to maintain the international legal order and from the pressure to conform that states exert on each other.

Treaties

[17.07] As a rule, states are free to vary the rules of customary international law by agreement between themselves.[4] Such agreements, usually in the form of treaties, are binding between the parties only. Treaties may be bilateral (between two states only) or multilateral (between more than two states). Usually, international treaties do not entail any surrender of sovereignty; rather, the parties agree to exercise their sovereignty in a particular way, usually by way of creating for themselves positive or negative obligations (the EU Treaties, which as we have seen have direct effect in the domestic laws of EU member states, are exceptions to this general rule). It is a fundamental principle of international law that treaty commitments must be observed – a principle often expressed in Latin as *pacta sunt servanda*. Many international organisations, such as the United Nations and the Council of Europe, derive their law-making power from their establishing treaties. For example, the binding nature of United Nations Security Council Resolutions comes from the agreement of the members of the United Nations to exercise their sovereignty in accordance with the 1947 UN Charter. Some treaties even establish courts and tribunals to determine conflicts between states and, more recently, between individuals and states (as in the case of the Council of Europe's 1950 Convention on Human Rights and Fundamental Freedoms). Judicial enforcement is, however, the exception rather than the rule, so that the force of any treaty, like the force of customary international law, comes primarily from peer-pressure and self-interest operating at an intergovernmental political level.

General principles of law applied by civilised nations

[17.08] A third source of international law is the general principles of law recognised by civilised nations. These include the rules of natural justice and doctrines such as estoppel and proportionality which, though they have never been codified by treaty and may be called by many different names, are applied every day in the courts of all states subject to the rule of law. This source recognises that the international legal system is intimately connected with national legal systems the world over.

Subsidiary sources of international law

[17.09] In seeking to identify and determine rules of international law from treaties, international custom and general principles of law recognised by civilised nations, lawyers may also have recourse to judicial decisions, both from international tribunals and national courts and to the writings and teachings of the most qualified jurists from the various nations. Of course, such sources are often used to inform understandings of

---

4   Certain peremptory norms of international law – such as the prohibitions on slavery and torture – cannot be varied even by treaty. These are known as rules of *jus cogens* (compelling law).

law in the domestic setting, but the diffuse nature of international law makes them much more influential on the international plane.

[17.10] It is worth noting also that international organisations and their institutions have an increasingly active role in the creation and propagation of international rules and principles. This will be discussed in more detail below in the sections dealing with specific organisations.

[3] IRELAND IN INTERNATIONAL LAW

[17.11] Since the foundation of the state, Ireland has been an enthusiastic player on the world stage. Article 29.1 to 29.3 of the Constitution commit the state to the rule of international law and the peaceful settlement of international disputes, and Ireland has become a party to most multilateral treaties of international importance. In addition, Ireland has entered into many bilateral agreements with other states on matters such as taxation and extradition. Most such agreements involve the application of an established body of international rules and principles, though some affect crucial domestic constitutional issues, as was the case with the Good Friday Agreement 1998, entered into between Ireland and the United Kingdom.[5]

[17.12] As a matter of international law, the mere signature of a treaty does not establish consent on the part of a state to be bound by it. Such consent is established by ratification, which usually involves deposit of an instrument of ratification with an entity nominated by the treaty.[6] In Ireland, Article 29.4.1° of the Constitution provides that the executive power of the state in or in connection with its external relations shall be exercised by or on the authority of the government, and because the conclusion of international agreements involves an exercise of executive power, the authority to conclude such agreements is usually exercised by the Minister for Foreign Affairs. Although it is not required by Article 29, in practice, all treaties are laid before the Dáil before the state becomes a party.

[17.13] By virtue of Article 29.4, the state cannot be compelled to ratify a treaty, even where it has already signalled an intention to ratify by way of signature. In *Hutchinson v Minister for Justice*,[7] the High Court rejected the proposition that the state was in any way bound simply by its having signed an international agreement on the transfer of prisoners. The applicant was a British national serving a life sentence for murder, imposed in 1980, in an Irish prison. He wished to be transferred to an English prison to serve the remainder of his term. His case centred on whether the state had committed itself to be bound by the 1983 Council of Europe Convention on the Transfer of Prisoners. Article 18.2 of the Convention provided that it would enter into force one month following ratification of the Convention by three states. Article 18.3 provided that, subsequently, the Convention would enter into force in any other state one month

---

5   See para **15.11**.
6   See Brownlie, *Principles of Public International Law* (2008), pp 609–612.
7   *Hutchinson v Minister for Justice* [1993] ILRM 602.

after it had ratified the Convention. France, Spain and Sweden ratified the Convention in 1985, and the Convention entered into force in July 1985. In 1986, the Convention was signed on behalf of Ireland by the Minister for Foreign Affairs. The government had not, at any time up to 1992, ratified the Convention, but the applicant sought an order to the effect that the government's signature placed it under an obligation to ratify the Convention. The High Court referred to a number of the leading textbooks on international law, and rejected the applicant's argument that such a proposition formed part of the generally accepted principles of international law. The applicant had argued that the concept of 'good faith' in international law required that the state ratify an international agreement to which it was signatory. The textbooks to which the High Court referred, however, had all rejected this proposition.[8]

[17.14] Many of the treaties to which Ireland is a party establish international organisations. At a global level, it has been a member of the UN since 1955 (when the then Soviet Union lifted its veto on membership). In the European context, the state was a founder member of the Council of Europe in 1949. In 1973, Ireland was among a group of three states to become the first new members of the European Economic Community (EEC) (now the European Union, EU) since it had been established in 1958 by its original six member states. Ireland is also a member of the Organisation for Security and Co-operation in Europe (OSCE), the successor to the Conference for Security and Co-operation in Europe (CSCE), which has emerged in the aftermath of the Cold War (which ended in the wake of the fall of the Berlin Wall and related developments in Central and Eastern Europe in 1989 and 1990) as a major influence in seeking to establish agreed principles on security, arms control, human rights and cooperation on economic, social and cultural matters in Europe.

[17.15] International organisations play an increasingly important role in world trade. The state is a member of the World Trade Organisation (WTO), established in 1994 as successor to the organisation called the General Agreement on Tariffs and Trade (GATT). Since the 1940s, international rules have been influential in the removal of many protectionist barriers to trade. For the most part, Ireland is today represented at the WTO through the EU. Ireland is also a member of the Organisation for Economic Co-operation and Development (OECD).

[17.16] In light of the state's policy of military neutrality,[9] it has not sought membership of the North Atlantic Treaty Organisation (NATO), which would involve a mutual defence commitment.[10] However, in the 1990s the state joined the NATO-affiliated Partnership for Peace, which involved no such commitment; and, through EU membership and its enhanced functions in defence cooperation (notably when the 2001

---

[8]   The 1983 Convention was ultimately implemented by the Transfer of Sentenced Prisoners Act 1997.

[9]   See para **16.54**.

[10] See para **16.10**.

EU Treaty of Nice merged the Western European Union (WEU), an intergovernmental defence and security organisation, into EU intergovernmental structures).[11]

[17.17] It would be impossible in this chapter to provide an overview of all the organisations of which the state is a member. Having already addressed the state's membership of the European Union in Chapter 16, we now proceed to examine three organisations of which the state is a member: the Council of Europe, the UN and the WTO.

[4] THE COUNCIL OF EUROPE

[17.18] In 1949, Ireland was a founder member of the Council of Europe. Each of the 28 member states of the EU is also a member. Since the fall of the Communist regimes in Central and Eastern Europe in 1989 and 1990, membership of the Council of Europe has, like that of the EU, expanded considerably and now includes 47 states,[12] incorporating virtually all the states of Central and Eastern Europe, including the Russian Federation.

[17.19] The Council of Europe was one of the first institutions established after World War II (1939–1945) in an attempt to prevent repetition of the mass violation of human rights which had occurred during the war. Since its establishment, its aims have expanded beyond this initial vision to include the promotion of pluralist democracy, the rule of law and an awareness of Europe's cultural identity and diversity. The Council of Europe also seeks solutions to problems such as discrimination against minorities, xenophobia, intolerance, environmental degradation, AIDS, drug abuse and organised crime. It has also helped to consolidate democratic stability in Central and Eastern Europe by supporting political, legislative and constitutional reform.

[17.20] The three main institutions of the Council are the Committee of Ministers, the Parliamentary Assembly and the European Court of Human Rights. All of the institutions of the Council of Europe are based in Strasbourg, France. The Council's first major initiative was the drafting of the Convention for the Protection of Human Rights and Fundamental Freedoms 1950 (usually known as the European Convention on Human Rights or the ECHR), which provided for the establishment of the European Court of Human Rights.

The European Convention on Human Rights

[17.21] The Convention, as amended and expanded by later Protocols, contains provisions guaranteeing the following rights:
-   the right to life (art 2);
-   freedom from torture or inhuman or degrading treatment or punishment (art 3);
-   freedom from slavery and forced or compulsory labour (art 4);

---

11   See para **16.10**.
12   At the time of writing (September 2014), the most recent member state is Montenegro (2007).

- the right to liberty and security of person (art 5);
- the right to a fair and public hearing within a reasonable time by an independent and impartial tribunal established by law (art 6);
- freedom from retrospective criminal and penal legislation (art 7);
- the right to respect for private and family life, home and correspondence (art 8);
- the right to freedom of thought, conscience and religion (art 9);
- the right to freedom of expression (art 10);
- the right to freedom of assembly and of association with others (art 11);
- the right to marry and found a family (art 12);
- the right to an effective remedy before a national authority (art 13);
- the right to equality, that is, a prohibition on discrimination on any ground such as sex, race, colour, language, religion, political or other opinion, national or social origin, association with a national minority, property, birth or other status (art 14);
- the right to peaceful enjoyment of possessions (First Protocol, art 1);
- the right to education (First Protocol, art 2);
- the right to free elections at reasonable intervals by secret ballot (First Protocol, art 3);
- freedom from deprivation of liberty due to inability to fulfil a contractual obligation (Fourth Protocol, art 1);
- the right of a national of a contracting state to choose a place of residence in that state and to move within and beyond the territory of that state (Fourth Protocol, art 2);
- the right of a national of a contracting state to enter the territory of that state and freedom from expulsion from that state (Fourth Protocol, art 3);
- freedom of aliens from collective expulsion from a contracting state (Fourth Protocol, art 4);
- freedom from the death penalty in peacetime (Sixth Protocol, art 1);
- the right not to be expelled from the territory of a contracting state save in compliance with the law and fair procedures (Seventh Protocol, art 1);
- the right of appeal against conviction or sentence in a criminal matter (Seventh Protocol, art 2);
- the right to receive compensation owing to a miscarriage of justice (Seventh Protocol, art 3);
- freedom from double jeopardy in criminal matters (Seventh Protocol, art 4);
- the right of spouses to equal treatment in family law proceedings (Seventh Protocol, art 5).

[17.22] While some of the rights provided for in the ECHR are absolute – the prohibitions on torture and slavery, for instance – the majority may be subject to restriction where this is prescribed by law and is necessary in a democratic society to protect such values as national security, public health or public morals. When the European Court of Human Rights assesses whether a restriction to a right is legitimate, it asks whether the limitation on the right of the individual is proportionate to the end desired by the state. In addition, pursuant to art 15, states may legitimately derogate from their obligations under the Convention in time of war or public emergency. The ECHR has proved to be a model for many other international human rights conventions, including the American Convention on Human Rights 1969 and the African Charter on Human and Peoples' Rights 1981.

The European Court of Human Rights

[17.23] As an international treaty, the ECHR is unusual because it contains concrete mechanisms for its enforcement, both horizontally (that is, between states) and vertically (between states and individuals). States parties to the ECHR are entitled to bring cases against another state party to the court where that other state is suspected of violating the human rights protected by the Convention. This was the case in *Ireland v United Kingdom*,[13] where the United Kingdom was found by the court to have subjected internees in Northern Ireland to inhuman and degrading treatment in the early 1970s, contrary to art 3 ECHR.

[17.24] Individuals are also permitted to make bring cases against member states to the European Court of Human Rights, provided they have exhausted all domestic remedies but have not found redress. Under the system which applied between 1953 and 1998, complaints were first examined as to their admissibility by the European Commission of Human Rights.[14] If the Commission found them admissible, it attempted to secure a friendly settlement, failing which it established the facts to see whether there had been a violation. The case could then be referred for final decision to the court, which delivered final judgments binding on the states concerned, and could award a remedy in damages and the costs of the proceedings. Neither the Commission nor the court sat permanently up to 1998, but they convened regularly to consider cases. Until 1998, cases not referred to the court were determined by the Committee of Ministers of the Council of Europe, whose decisions, like the court's judgments, were final and binding. The Committee of Ministers supervised the implementation of the court's judgments and its own decisions. The European Commission of Human Rights examined over 40,000 individual cases under the Convention between 1953 and 1998 and the court had delivered over 1,000 judgments in that time.

[17.25] Because of the increasing caseload of the court from the 1980s, a radical revision of the procedure was necessitated.[15] This gave rise to Protocol No 11, which came into force in 1998. It established a single permanent court in place of the

---

13   *Ireland v United Kingdom* (1979–1980) 2 EHRR 25.
14   This body should be distinguished from the Commission of the EU: para **16.139**.
15   See O'Boyle, 'The Reconstruction of the Strasbourg Human Rights System' (1992) 14 DULJ (ns) 41.

Convention's previous protection machinery. The new European Court of Human Rights is directly accessible to the individual and its jurisdiction is compulsory for all member states of the Council of Europe. It sits on a permanent basis, and deals with all the preliminary stages of a case, as well as delivering judgments. The increased accessibility of the court led to a significant increase in its caseload, to the extent that a new, and even larger, backlog of cases developed. Protocol No 14 to the ECHR, which came into force in 2010 when the Russian Federation ratified it, further streamlined the admissibility procedure in order to reduce delays in administering judgments. Nonetheless at the end of 2013, approximately 99,900 applications were pending before the Court, more than half of which had been lodged against one of four countries: the Russian Federation, Italy, Ukraine and Serbia. In recent years, the Court has delivered around 1,000 judgments annually, which may be contrasted with the fact that, between 1959 and 1998, it had delivered about 1,000 judgments in total in that 40-year period'.

[17.26] The court consists of 47 judges, equal to the number of Council of Europe member states. Candidates are initially put forward by each government, but the selection procedure is monitored by the Committee of Ministers. Judges are elected by the Parliamentary Assembly. They do not represent the states which proposed them, and enjoy complete independence in the performance of their duties.

[17.27] Any cases that are 'manifestly unfounded' are deleted from the register of cases at an early stage by a unanimous decision of the court, sitting as a three-judge committee. In the vast majority of cases, the court sits as a seven-judge chamber. If applications are then judged admissible, the chamber may attempt to reach a friendly settlement with the parties. If this is not possible, the chamber delivers its judgment. In cases raising a serious issue concerning the interpretation or application of the European Convention on Human Rights, a case may be referred to a Grand Chamber of 17 judges. The court's judgments are final and binding on the states concerned. The Committee of Ministers no longer deals with the merits of cases, although it has maintained its important role of ensuring that states comply with the court's judgments. A judgment by the court against a state implies an obligation on the part of that state to avoid any future violations similar to those found by the court.

[17.28] The jurisprudence of the European Court of Human Rights has had a very significant effect on the development of Irish law, and this effect is discussed below in relation to the role of international law in the domestic legal order.

Other Council of Europe Conventions

[17.29] In addition to the ECHR, a number of other Conventions have been signed since 1950 under the auspices of the Council of Europe. These include:

- the European Convention on the Suppression of Terrorism 1977, implemented in Irish law by the Extradition (European Convention on the Suppression of Terrorism) Act 1987;

–   the Convention for the Protection of Individuals With Regard to the Automatic Processing of Data 1982, implemented in Irish law by the Data Protection Act 1988;

–   the Convention on the Transfer of Sentenced Prisoners 1983, implemented in Irish law by the Transfer of Sentenced Prisoners Act 1997;[16]

–   the Convention on Cybercrime 2001, not yet implemented in Irish law.[17]

[5]   THE UNITED NATIONS ORGANISATION

[17.30] The United Nations Organisation (UNO, or UN) was established in San Francisco in 1945 in the aftermath of World War II as a successor to the League of Nations. The Charter of the United Nations, which established the organisation, emphasises that it is a grouping of sovereign States.[18] Article 1 of the Charter states the purposes of the UN:

"1.   To maintain international peace and security, and to that end: to take effective collective measures for the prevention and removal of threats to the peace, and for the suppression of acts of aggression or other breaches of the peace, and to bring about by peaceful means, and in conformity with the principles of justice and international law, adjustment or settlement of international disputes or situations which might lead to a breach of the peace;

2.   To develop friendly relations among nations based on respect for the principle of equal rights and self-determination of peoples, and to take other appropriate measures to strengthen universal peace;

3.   To achieve international co-operation in solving international problems of an economic, social, cultural, or humanitarian character, and in promoting and encouraging respect for human rights and for fundamental freedoms for all without distinction as to race, sex, language, or religion; and

4.   To be a centre for harmonising the actions of nations in the attainment of these common ends."[19]

[17.31] Article 2 provides that, in pursuit of the purposes stated in art 1, the UN and its members must act in accordance with the following principles:

"1.   The Organisation is based on the principle of the sovereign equality of all its Members.

2.   All Members, in order to ensure to a of them the rights and benefits resulting from membership, shall fulfil in good faith the obligations assumed by them in accordance with the present Charter.

---

16   See para **17.13**.

17   At the time of writing (September 2014), the *Government Legislation Programme Autumn Session 2014*, available at www.taoiseach.ie, states that a Criminal Justice (Cybercrime) Bill intended to implement the 2001 Convention is under preparation.

18   At the time of writing (September 2014), there are 193 states parties to the Charter of the UN (South Sudan being the most recent member, admitted in 2011).

19   UN Charter, art 1.

3. All Members shall settle their international disputes by peaceful means in such a manner that international peace and security, and justice, are not endangered.

4. All Members shall refrain in their international relations from the threat or use of force against the territorial integrity or political independence of any state, or in any other manner inconsistent with the Purposes of the United Nations.

5. All Members shall give the United Nations every assistance in any action it takes in accordance with the present Charter, and shall refrain from giving assistance to any state against which the United Nations is taking preventive or enforcement action.

6. The Organisation shall ensure that states which are not Members of the United Nations act in accordance with these Principles so far as may be necessary for the maintenance of international peace and security.

7. Nothing contained in the present Charter shall authorise the United Nations to intervene in matters which are essentially within the domestic jurisdiction of any state or shall require the Members to submit such matters to settlement under the present Charter; but this principle shall not prejudice the application of enforcement measures under Chapter VII [which empowers the Security Council to authorise armed measures to maintain peace and security]."[20]

[17.32] Article 2 makes clear that the UN may not, in general, take any action which interferes with the internal domestic sovereignty of states. In essence, therefore, the UN provides a political framework to help find solutions to international problems or disputes, and to deal with other global concerns. The Charter establishes a number of institutions to carry out the functions of the UN, and these are discussed below. In addition, a large number of specialised agencies, working in areas such as health, finance, agriculture, civil aviation and telecommunications have also been established under the UN umbrella.[21]

The principal organs of the UN

[17.33] According to Chapter III of the Charter, the principal organs of the UN are the General Assembly, the Security Council, the Economic and Social Council (ECOSOC), the Secretariat and the International Court of Justice (ICJ). The General Assembly, the Security Council and the ECOSOC meet at the organisation's headquarters in New York. The ICJ has its seat in the Peace Palace in The Hague, the Netherlands.

The General Assembly

[17.34] The General Assembly is the main deliberative body of the UN. All member states are represented in it and each has one vote. Decisions on ordinary matters are taken by simple majority, but some require a two-thirds majority. The Assembly has the power to discuss and make recommendations on all matters within the scope of the UN Charter. As is the case with most international bodies, it has no power to compel action by any government, but its recommendations carry political weight. The Assembly also

---

20 UN Charter, art 2.
21 See para **17.40**.

sets policies and determines programmes for the UN Secretariat, directs activities for development, and approves the UN budget, including peacekeeping operations. It also appoints the UN Secretary-General.

The Security Council

[17.35] The Security Council is the institution to which the UN Charter gives primary responsibility for maintaining peace and security. It can be convened at any time, whenever peace is threatened. The basic structure of the Security Council is set out in Chapter V of the Charter: it has 15 members, five permanent and ten elected. The permanent members are a modern reflection of the balance of power at the end of World War II: the People's Republic of China, France, the Russian Federation, the United Kingdom and the United States. The other 10 are elected by the General Assembly for two-year terms. Decisions require nine votes, but with the exception of votes on procedural questions, a decision cannot be taken if there is a negative vote by a permanent member (known as the 'veto'). Under Chapter VI of the Charter, the Security Council may recommend measures such as mediation or judicial settlement – to ensure the pacific settlement of disputes between states. Under Chapter VII, the Security Council has wide powers to decide measures to be taken in situations involving threats to international peace and security. It may authorise peace-keeping operations in post-conflict situations. These operations are then conducted by the armed forces of member states under the auspices of the UN. Irish troops have played an important role in peace-keeping missions all over the world. It may also authorise measures – including economic sanctions and the use of force – against breaches of the peace, threats to the peace and acts of aggression by states.[22] Resolutions of the Security Council made under Chapter VII are binding on all states, but because the provisions of the Charter to give the UN an army of its own have never been activated, the organisation relies on states to implement its decisions, and cooperation is not always forthcoming.

[17.36] Notwithstanding this, states often take Security Council Resolutions very seriously, as illustrated when in 1991 economic sanctions were imposed by the Security Council against the Federal Republic of Yugoslavia (FRY) because of its behaviour in the Balkan civil wars of the time. Security Council Resolution 820 (1993) required all states to impound Yugoslav aircraft, and an EC Council Regulation was adopted to give effect to this resolution. When in 1993 a Yugoslav aircraft operated by a Turkish company landed in Dublin for maintenance, it was seized by the state. Its operators sued the state unsuccessfully in the Irish courts and then took a case to the European Court of Human Rights for violation of their property rights as protected by art 1 of Protocol 1 to

---

22   The Charter forbids the use of force between states except in two circumstances: firstly, a state may use force in self defence in accordance with art 51 of the Charter where an armed attack has occurred against it; secondly, under Chapter VII, the Security Council may authorise the use of military force against breaches of the peace, threats to the peace and acts of aggression in order to maintain and restore international peace and security. It was under Chapter VII that the UN authorised the use of force against Iraq when it invaded Kuwait in 1991 and against Afghanistan in the wake of the terrorist attacks of 11 September 2001 ('9/11').

the ECHR. In *Bosphorus v Ireland*,[23] the European Court of Human Rights accepted Ireland's contention that it had been bound by Community law and by international law as expressed in the Security Council Resolution to seize the aircraft, and found that there had been no violation.

The Economic and Social Council

[17.37] The Economic and Social Council (ECOSOC) is the primary forum for the discussion of economic and social issues at the UN. It consists of 54 states elected from and by the General Assembly. Its primary role is to advise the General Assembly on economic and social matters and to make recommendations with respect to these matters, particularly in relation to development.

The Secretariat

[17.38] The Secretariat, in effect the civil service of the UN, works for the other organs of the UN and administers their programmes. At its head is the UN Secretary-General. The Secretary-General plays a central role in peace-making and may bring to the attention of the Security Council any matter which appears to threaten international peace and security. To help resolve disputes, the Secretary-General may use what are described as 'good offices' to carry out mediation in order to resolve disputes.

The International Court of Justice

[17.39] The ICJ, sometimes colloquially referred to as the World Court, is the main judicial organ of the UN.[24] The Statute of the ICJ is annexed to the UN Charter. Its jurisdiction falls under two headings: it hears disputes between member states and it provides advisory opinions to the UN and its agencies. It consists of 15 judges, elected by the General Assembly and the Security Council. Only states or UN agencies may be parties in cases brought before the ICJ; there is no right of individual petition comparable to that which exists at the European Court of Human Rights. Another significant difference from the Council of Europe is that a UN member state need not accept the court's jurisdiction, and, indeed, may withdraw from proceedings even after they have begun.[25] Thus, the jurisdiction of the ICJ is dependent on the consent of parties. Nonetheless, like other international judicial institutions, its caseload has increased dramatically in recent years. The court's judgments in cases referred to it by states have addressed disputes over land frontiers and maritime boundaries, territorial sovereignty, the use of force, interference in the internal affairs of states, diplomatic relations, hostage-taking, the right of asylum, nationality, guardianship, rights of passage, economic rights and genocide. Its Advisory Opinions have concerned such diverse issues as admission to United Nations membership, reparation for injuries suffered in the service of the United Nations, the territorial status of South-West Africa (now Namibia) and the Western Sahara, the legality of the threat or use of nuclear

---

[23] *Bosphorus v Ireland* (2006) 42 EHRR 1. The EU Council Regulation in question was 990/93.
[24] The court's website is www.icj-cij.org.
[25] See the *Norwegian Loans case* [1957] ICJ Rep 9.

weapons and the status of a wall erected by the state of Israel in the Occupied Palestinian Territories. Judgments and Advisory Opinions of the ICJ carry great weight as statements of the state of international law.

The UN agencies

[17.40] A number of autonomous agencies also operate under the auspices of the UN to promote international cooperation in relation to particular issues. These agencies conduct research which is widely publicised and used to formulate national policies and relevant legislation. They engage in the dissemination of standards which are applied internationally. These agencies include the International Labour Organisation (ILO), the Food and Agriculture Organisation (FAO), the UN Educational, Scientific and Cultural Organisation (UNESCO), the World Health Organisation (WHO), the International Civil Aviation Organisation (ICAO), the Universal Postal Union (UPU), the International Telecommunication Union (ITU), the World Meteorological Organisation (WMO), the International Maritime Organisation (IMO), the World Intellectual Property Organisation (WIPO), the International Fund for Agricultural Development (IFAD) and the International Atomic Energy Agency (IAEA).

The influence of the UN on international law

[17.41] Although many UN decisions do not have the force of law in themselves, their influence can be significant in the development of the law. The General Assembly has adopted a number of treaties, many of which have been influential in setting national political agendas and which have developed novel monitoring and enforcement mechanisms.

[17.42] For example, the UN facilitated the conclusion of the Convention on the Law of the Sea 1982 (UNCLOS) which defines the rights and responsibilities of states in their use of the world's oceans. The treaty came into force in 1994 and was ratified by Ireland in 1996. UNCLOS established the International Tribunal for the Law of the Sea (ITLOS) to adjudicate on disputes arising between states parties on issues covered by the treaty. The tribunal has its seat in Hamburg, Germany. In a dispute with the United Kingdom over the Mixed Oxide (MOX) Plant at Sellafield, Ireland instituted proceedings at the ITLOS alleging that the United Kingdom had breached its environmental obligations under the treaty. As a result, the European Commission complained to the EU Court of Justice, which held that, because EU law requires that disputes between member states should be resolved within the EU legal order rather than by recourse to international mechanisms, Ireland's case against the United Kingdom in Hamburg was in violation of its obligations under EU treaty law.[26] The case before the ITLOS was therefore abandoned.

[17.43] A number of UN treaties have been aimed at reducing arms proliferation, both nuclear and conventional weapons. These have included treaties to ban nuclear weapons from outer space, the seabed and ocean floor; to prohibit the development, production

---

26 *Commission v Ireland*, Case C-459/03, [2006] ECR I-4635.

and stockpiling of chemical and biological weapons and to ban nuclear testing. Ireland is a party to all of these treaties. Indeed, the Nuclear Test Ban Act 2008 gives effect in Irish law to the comprehensive Nuclear Test Ban Treaty adopted by the General Assembly in 1996. Ireland has also become a party to the Ottawa Convention prohibiting the use of land mines and the Oslo Convention banning cluster munitions.

[17.44] Other key UN documents have focused on human rights and equality issues. In 1948, the General Assembly adopted the Universal Declaration of Human Rights, a proclamation of basic rights and freedoms. These include the rights which would become part of the European Convention on Human Rights in 1950, including the right to life, liberty and nationality, to freedom of thought, conscience and religion, to work, to be educated and to take part in government. Unlike the ECHR, the Universal Declaration is largely aspirational and is not legally binding on states. Nonetheless, it has led to the adoption by the General Assembly of more specific UN documents, such as the International Covenant on Civil and Political Rights 1966 (ICCPR) and the International Covenant on Economic, Social and Cultural Rights 1966 (ICESCR). The UN has also been instrumental in the conclusion of human rights treaties such as the Convention on the Rights of the Child (CRC), the Convention on the Elimination of All Forms of Discrimination (CERD), the Convention against Torture (CAT), the Convention on the Elimination of Discrimination against Women (CEDAW) and the Convention on the Rights of Persons with Disabilities (CRPD).

[17.45] States parties to many human rights treaties are subject to period review by committees established under their terms. The most high profile of these committees is the Human Rights Committee, which is established under the ICCPR. The Human Rights Committee comprises an independent body of lawyers and other experts in the field of human rights protection. The Committee monitors the compliance of states with their obligations under the Covenant. To facilitate this, states submit periodic reports to the Committee on their compliance with the Covenant. Ireland has submitted periodic reports to the Human Rights Committee on its implementation of the Covenant. These reports are considered by the Committee in public hearings. The Committee also hears submissions from other interested parties, including the Irish Human Rights and Equality Commission and non-governmental organisations (NGOs) involved in monitoring human rights such as the Irish Council for Civil Liberties and the Irish Penal Reform Trust. While the Committee has usually expressed general approval for the record of the state in promoting its obligations under the ICCPR, it has also expressed disquiet about a number of matters, including the continued existence of the Special Criminal Court, the detention of asylum seekers and the absence of legal recognition of Travellers as an ethnic minority group.

[17.46] States may also allow their citizens to make individual communications to the Human Rights Committee by ratifying the Optional Protocol to the ICCPR. Ireland ratified both the ICCPR and the Protocol in 1989. In 1998, Joseph Kavanagh, an Irish citizen sent a communication to the Human Rights Committee alleging that his imminent trial by the Special Criminal Court contravened his right to equal protection under the law pursuant to art 26 of the ICCPR. In *Kavanagh v Ireland*, the Human Rights Committee agreed with him that Ireland had violated art 26 ICCPR, but his trial in Dublin went ahead regardless.[27] His unsuccessful attempt to have his conviction by the Special Criminal Court overturned on the basis of the Human Rights Committee's views in *Kavanagh v Governor of Mountjoy Prison* is discussed below in the context of international law in the Irish legal system. A subsequent attempt by Mr Kavanagh to obtain relief from the Human Rights Committee on the grounds of absence of an effective remedy was deemed inadmissible because he had suffered no new damage.[28]

[17.47] In 1951 the Geneva Convention on the Status of Refugees was agreed to provide protection for people fleeing persecution in their countries of origin. The implementation of the treaty is monitored by the UN High Commissioner for Refugees (UNHCR). The UN has also established the position of UN High Commissioner for Human Rights to coordinate the human rights activities of the UN, investigate abuses and work with governments in resolving violations. The General Assembly has also established the UN Human Rights Council as a subsidiary body. The Council conducts public meetings on human rights abuses brought to its attention and reviews the human rights performance of all UN member states. This enforcement mechanism is less specific than those provided under the ICCPR, and the members of the Council are states rather than independent experts. The Human Rights Council replaced the Commission on Human Rights, which had been the subject of sustained criticism because it was dominated by states with poor human rights records such as China, Libya and Cuba.[29]

[17.48] The UN has also been instrumental in the development of international criminal law. This body of law asserts that some crimes, such as genocide, crimes against humanity and war crimes are so serious that all states are under a duty to suppress them. These duties arise under treaties such as the Genocide Convention 1948, the four Geneva Conventions of 1949 (dealing with the protection of treatment of the wounded and sick in time of war as well as prisoners of war and civilians) and the UN Convention against Torture as well as under customary international law. Where states fail to take action against the perpetrators of international crimes, the international community may supply the means of investigation and prosecution. Building on the legacy of the International Military Tribunal in Nuremburg which tried Nazi war criminals after World War II, the Security Council established international criminal tribunals in The Hague and in Arusha, Tanzania, to try persons accused of war crimes during the 1990s

---

27 *Kavanagh v Ireland*, UN Human Rights Committee, Communication No 819/1998, 4 April 2001.

28 *Kavanagh v Ireland*, UN Human Rights Committee, Communication No 1114/2002, 25 October 2002.

29 For criticism of the Council, however, see Boyle, 'The United Nations Human Rights Council' (2009) 60 NILQ 121.

in the conflicts in the former Yugoslavia[30] and Rwanda.[31] Other war crimes tribunals have been established by states with international assistance, such as the Special Court for Sierra Leone and the Extraordinary Chambers of the Courts of Cambodia. In Ireland, the International War Crimes Tribunals Act 1998 enables the state to fulfil its international obligations to cooperate with the work of these tribunals. Many senior government officials and military commanders from the former Yugoslavia, Rwanda, Sierra Leone, Liberia and Cambodia have been convicted of genocide, war crimes and crimes against humanity by these tribunals.

[17.49] The trend set by the UN tribunals has continued outside the UN umbrella. In 1998, the Statute of the International Criminal Court (ICC) was agreed in Rome. Over 100 states are now parties to the Rome Statute which gives the ICC jurisdiction to try individuals for genocide, war crimes and crimes against humanity committed by nationals of, or on the territory of, states parties.[32] The establishment of the ICC can be seen as a tentative step towards ensuring that there is global accountability for grave breaches of international humanitarian and human rights law. At the time of writing, situations in four states have been referred to the Court for investigation, and prosecutions are underway in seven cases.[33] The International Criminal Court Act 2006 facilitates Ireland's cooperation with the court and provides for the punishment of genocide, war crimes and crimes against humanity in Irish law.

[6] THE WORLD TRADE ORGANISATION

[17.50] The World Trade Organisation (WTO) is the main global organisation concerning international trade and was established in 1995. The WTO succeeds the General Agreement on Tariffs and Trade (GATT) of 1947. The WTO has its headquarters in Geneva, Switzerland.

---

[30] The International Tribunal for the Prosecution of Persons Responsible for Serious Violations of International Humanitarian Law Committed in the Territory of the Former Yugoslavia (ICTY).

[31] The International Criminal Tribunal for the Prosecution of Persons Responsible for Genocide and Other Serious Violations of International Humanitarian Law Committed in the Territory of Rwanda (ICTR).

[32] The Twenty-Third Amendment of the Constitution Act 2001 amended Article 29 of the Constitution to enable the state ratify the 1998 Rome Convention establishing the International Criminal Court.

[33] On the strengths and weaknesses of the ICC, see Murphy, 'The Permanent International Criminal Court—solving the missing link in the international legal system?' (2000) 18 ILT 319.

The origins of the WTO

[17.51] The GATT organisation originated in meetings held towards the end of World War II at Bretton Woods, New Hampshire. In effect, these were the international trade meetings that mirrored those being held to deal with the establishment of the United Nations. The Bretton Woods Agreement 1944 provided for the establishment of the International Monetary Fund (IMF) and the International Bank for Reconstruction and Development (also known as the World Bank), which formally came into effect in 1945. It also envisaged the creation of an International Trade Organisation (ITO), but this did not materialise at the time. Instead, the GATT was established in 1947. This organisation existed on a 'provisional' basis until the establishment in 1995 of the World Trade Organisation (WTO). Ireland joined the GATT in 1967 and remains a member of the WTO.

[17.52] GATT had many of the hallmarks of an international body, though it was not established as a separate entity in international law. The Articles of GATT 1947 set out a number of significant principles by which the states parties were to be bound. These were aimed mainly at reducing tariffs and avoiding the protectionist policies which were regarded as having contributed to the length of the Great Depression of the 1930s. The principles agreed in GATT 1947 resulted in 45,000 tariff concessions affecting $10bn of trade, estimated to have been about one-fifth of the world's total at that time. GATT 1947 also established important mechanisms by which those principles could be enforced, in particular by means of references to GATT Panels, which in effect acted as arbitration panels on multilateral and bilateral disputes. The GATT 1947 was amended a number of times by means of multilateral trade negotiations, or Rounds, negotiated by the contracting states.

[17.53] In 1994, the Uruguay Round of multilateral trade negotiations was completed in Marrakesh, Morocco. As well as achieving agreement on a significant number of international trade issues and updating the GATT 1947, the Marrakesh Agreement also provided for the establishment of the World Trade Organisation (WTO) as a successor to GATT and as a separate legal entity in international law. The principles contained in the GATT 1947 and its enforcement mechanisms were brought under the aegis of the WTO. The WTO is currently (September 2014) involved in the Doha Round of multilateral negotiations aimed at the equitable participation of poorer states in the world economy, though, at the time of writing, agreement remains elusive in this process that began in 2001.

The founding principles

[17.54] A key element of the GATT was a prohibition on trade discrimination between the states parties. This remains a pillar of the WTO. Each state is required to accord the same trading privileges as it accords to its most-favoured nation to all states parties. This is known as the most-favoured nation (MFN) principle. Furthermore, once foreign goods are imported into one member state from another, they must be treated in the same manner as domestic goods (the national treatment rule). It is conceded that customs unions and free trade agreements are an acceptable means of liberalising trade provided that they do not, in general, discriminate against other member states. This clearly included such 'regional' trade organisations as the EU.[34] A number of exceptions to these general principles were also contained in GATT 1947 and survive today in the WTO. These include balance of payments imbalances, unexpected damage to domestic production, the need to promote economic development, and the need to protect domestic national security and public health.

The WTO System

[17.55] As mentioned, the 1994 Marrakesh Agreement provided for the establishment of the World Trade Organisation (WTO). In addition, it involved the conclusion of multilateral agreements on a number of major issues. These are contained in lengthy Annexes to the Agreement establishing the WTO and include:

– General Agreement on Tariffs and Trade 1994 (including various Understandings between the contracting states on the provisions of GATT 1947);

– Agreement on Agriculture;

– Agreement on Trade-Related Investment Measures (TRIMS);

– General Agreement on Trade in Services (GATS);

– Agreement on Trade-Related Aspects of Intellectual Property Rights (TRIPS); and

– Understanding on Rules and Procedures Governing the Settlement of Disputes.

[17.56] In summary, the WTO agreements cover goods, services and intellectual property. They spell out the principles governing the liberalisation of trade and the permitted exceptions. They include individual states' commitments to lower customs tariffs and other trade barriers, and to open and keep open services markets. The range of topics indicates that international trade rules are no longer confined to trade in goods, though the Agreement on Agriculture indicates that trade in primary goods continues to be of major importance. The TRIPS Agreement brought intellectual property rights, such as copyright, trademarks and patents, into the WTO system for the first time.[35] This is an increasingly important part of international trade, but one that is not uncontroversial. The TRIPS Agreement was criticised for favouring developed drug-

---

[34] See Ch 16. Many other regional and sectoral trading entities have also been established. The Organisation of Petroleum Exporting States (OPEC) represents most, though not all, of the major oil exporting states of the Middle East. The 1992 North American Free Trade Agreement (NAFTA) involves the United States, Canada and Mexico. In Latin America trade pacts such as MERCUSOR (Mercado Comun del Sur, formed in 1991) have been established. In Africa, the African Economic Community is built on the many regional trade blocs. The Asian Pacific Economic Co-operation (APEC) was founded in 1989 and involves many of the states on the Pacific Rim, including Australia, China, Indonesia, Japan, Malaysia, the Philippines, Singapore, South Korea, Taiwan, Canada, Mexico and the United States.

exporting states to the detriment of developing countries in need of cheap generic antiretroviral medicines to combat HIV/AIDS. Since the 1990s, bilateral private agreements outside the TRIPS Agreement between, for example, multinational pharmaceutical companies and private foundations such as the Clinton Global Initiative, have mitigated to some extent the effects of the rules in the TRIPS Agreement.

[17.57] The WTO is now the primary international structure governing international trade relations. Its main institutions are:

– a Ministerial Conference, comprising representatives of all the states parties;[36]

– a Secretariat, headed by the Director General of the WTO, appointed by the Ministerial Conference; and

– a General Council, also made up of representatives of all member states.

The WTO Dispute Settlement Mechanism

[17.58] The provisional system under which GATT had operated since 1947 had many weaknesses, not least being its mechanism for the resolution of disputes between states parties. GATT 1947 provided for disputes between contracting states to be referred to GATT Panels, in effect a system of arbitration, whose reports would then be referred back to the GATT permanent secretariat. However, GATT 1947 provided that a consensus of the relevant contracting states was required for the adoption of 'panel reports'. The Marrakesh Agreement, which includes a 'dispute settlement understanding', sought to remedy that defect through the creation of a comprehensive dispute settlement system.

[17.59] Typical WTO dispute settlement proceedings proceed through a number of stages. The parties must first attempt to resolve their differences through consultations. If consultations fail, the parties may avail themselves of the WTO's conciliation or mediation services. Alternatively, a panel may be established to hear the dispute. The panel's terms of reference are then set and a hearing is convened. The panel then issues its report which is considered by the Dispute Settlement Body. The Dispute Settlement Body then either adopts or rejects the report.

[17.60] A new procedure introduced by the 1994 Understanding allows for the possibility of an appeal of the Dispute Settlement Body's finding to the WTO Appellate Body by any party to the dispute. This procedure can result in the imposition of trade sanctions. The dispute settlement procedure is clearly based on the mediation and conciliation model rather than on an adversarial template that characterises court-based adjudication. However, the changes effected in the GATT 1994 indicate that the WTO member states were prepared to move from the previous voluntary system to one which involves something closer to binding arbitration.

---

35 For an example of how the TRIPS Agreement impacted on Irish law, see *Allen & Hanbury Ltd v Controller of Patents, Designs and Trade Marks and Clonmel Healthcare Ltd* [1997] 1 ILRM 416.

36 At the time of writing (September 2014), there are 159 member states.

[17.61] For the most part, Ireland's interests at the WTO are advanced through the EU. The EU has been involved in many cases in the WTO dispute settlement mechanism which have had wide implications for Irish trade, particularly in relation to agriculture and food standards. [37]

[7] INTERNATIONAL LAW IN IRELAND

[17.62] Domestic legal systems may be monist, dualist, or a combination of both in their relationship with international law. In monist systems, international custom and all treaties ratified by the state are directly effective in domestic law. Dualist systems require that international rules be incorporated into domestic law before they have legal effect on the national level. Some national legal systems are monist in respect of some types of international rules and dualist in respect of others. The Irish legal system belongs in the dualist category.

Treaties in Irish law

[17.63] Ireland's Constitution places it squarely in the dualist camp in so far as treaties are concerned. Article 29.6 of the Constitution provides that no international agreement may form part of the domestic law of the state except as provided for by the Oireachtas. Ireland's membership of the European Union, discussed in Chapter 16, requires that this provision be amended regularly to allow the state to ratify the various EU treaties and to permit European Community law to have direct effect in Ireland. Most treaties to which Ireland becomes a party are never incorporated because they relate solely to the state's rights and duties with respect to other states or, in the case of human rights treaties, because the rights they confer are already protected in Irish law. Where incorporation takes place, it is, for the most part, achieved indirectly: the Oireachtas gives carefully defined effect to a treaty by mirroring the most important of its provisions in the body of an Act. This is the case, for example, with respect to the Refugee Act 1996 and its indirect incorporation of the Refugee Convention 1951. [38] International agreements that have not been incorporated into Irish law create important obligations between Ireland and other states, but to the extent that they confer rights on individuals, these are not justiciable in Irish courts.

[17.64] The ECHR is the international agreement which has given rise to the most litigation in the Irish courts. Until 2003, it had not been incorporated into Irish law in any form. The seminal case on the role of treaties not incorporated into the Irish legal system arose in relation to a litigant's attempt to rely on the ECHR in Irish law before its incorporation. In *Re Ó Laighléis,* the applicant, who had been interned under the Offences Against the State (Amendment) Act 1940, sought an inquiry into the legality of his detention under Article 40.4.2° of the Constitution. He asserted that the

---

[37] For discussion of a number of disputes dealt with by the WTO, including the long-running trade disputes between the USA and the European Union over the EU 'banana regime', see Gardiner, 'US and EC Banana Split at the World Trade Organisation' (1999) 17 ILT 199.

[38] See *NS v Anderson* [2008] 3 IR 417.

internment power provided for under the Act was in conflict with his right to liberty under art 5 ECHR and his right to a fair trial pursuant to art 6 ECHR.[39] The Supreme Court, in a judgment delivered by Maguire CJ, rejected the suggestion that the Convention was in any respect relevant to the validity of the 1940 Act:

"The Court cannot accept the idea that the primacy of domestic legislation is displaced by the State becoming a party to the Convention ... The insuperable obstacle to importing the provisions of the Convention ... into the domestic law of Ireland—if they be at variance with that law is, however, the terms of the Constitution of Ireland. By Article 15, s 2, sub-s 1 of the Constitution it is provided that 'the sole and exclusive power of making laws for the State is hereby vested in Oireachtas: no other legislative authority has power to make laws for the State'. Moreover, Article 29, the Article dealing with international relations, provides at s 6 that 'no international agreement shall be part of the domestic law of the State save as may be determined by the Oireachtas'.

The Oireachtas has not determined that the Convention of Human Rights and Fundamental Freedoms is to be part of the domestic law of the State, and accordingly this Court cannot give effect to the Convention if it be contrary to domestic law or purports to grant rights or impose obligations additional to those of domestic law.

No argument can prevail against the express command of section 6 of Article 29 of the Constitution before judges whose declared duty it is to uphold the Constitution and the laws.

The Court accordingly cannot accept the idea that the primacy of domestic legislation is displaced by the State becoming a party to the Convention for the Protection of Human Rights and Fundamental Freedoms. Nor can the Court accede to the view that in the domestic forum the Executive is in any way estopped from relying on the domestic law. It may be that such estoppel might operate as between the High Contracting Parties to the Convention, or in the court contemplated by Section IV of the Convention [that is, the European Court of Human Rights] if it comes into existence, but it cannot operate in a domestic Court administering domestic law. Nor can the Court accept the contention that the Act of 1940 is to be construed in the light of, and so as to produce conformity with, a Convention entered into ten years afterwards."[40]

[17.65] Having had no success in the Irish courts, Mr Ó Laighléis then took his case to the European Court of Human Rights, making international legal history as the first person to take a case against a state to an international tribunal. In *Lawless v Ireland*, the European Court of Human Rights held against the applicant, finding that Ireland had legitimately derogated from its obligations under the Convention because of a public emergency related to the troubles in Northern Ireland.

[17.66] The decision in *Ó Laighléis* was applied by the Supreme Court in *Norris v Attorney General*.[41] The Supreme Court held, by a 3:2 majority, that ss 61 and 62 of the Offences Against the Person Act 1861 – which criminalised consensual sexual relations

---

[39]   *Re Ó Laighléis* [1960] IR 93.
[40]   *Re Ó Laighléis* [1960] IR 93, 125.
[41]   *Norris v Attorney General* [1984] IR 36: see para **15.172**.

between males – were not unconstitutional. In the course of his judgment for the majority, O'Higgins CJ pointed out that the 1981 ruling of the European Court of Human Rights in *Dudgeon v United Kingdom*[42] to the effect that the same provisions, then still in force in Northern Ireland, were in breach of the right to privacy under art 8 ECHR was not relevant to a decision on the constitutional validity of ss 60 and 61 of the 1861 Act. He expressly followed *Ó Laighléis* in this respect:

"The Convention is an international agreement to which Ireland is a subscribing party. As such, however, it does not and cannot form part of our domestic law, nor affect in any way questions which arise thereunder. This is made quite clear by Article 29, s 6 of the Constitution which declares: 'No international agreement shall be part of the domestic law of the State save as may be determined by the Oireachtas' ... Neither the Convention on Human Rights nor the decision of the European Court in *Dudgeon v United Kingdom* is in any way relevant to the question which we have to consider in this case."[43]

[17.67] In his dissenting judgment, Henchy J pointed out that ss 60 and 61 seemed to be 'doomed to extinction' in view of the *Dudgeon* ruling, and this was confirmed nearly six years later in *Norris v Ireland* when the European Court of Human Rights ruled that ss 61 and 62 of the 1861, as they operated in Ireland, were in conflict with art 8 ECHR.[44]

[17.68] The judgment of the European Court of Human Rights in the *Norris* case led, eventually, to the decriminalisation of consensual sexual acts between males in the Criminal Law (Sexual Offences) Act 1993. Prior to 2003, because Ireland accepted only those rulings of the court in proceedings to which it was a party, the whole corpus of European jurisprudence on human rights was of very limited application to litigants in Ireland. Nonetheless, cases taken against Ireland by Irish citizens to the European Court of Human Rights led to the establishment of, for example, the civil legal aid scheme (ultimately placed on a statutory footing in the Civil Legal Aid Act 1995), the right of a natural father to be consulted in relation to his child's adoption and the periodic review of the detention of persons detained in mental institutions.[45]

[17.69] Since the enactment by the Oireachtas of the European Convention on Human Rights Act 2003, the legal landscape has changed dramatically, and the Convention and jurisprudence of the European Court of Human Rights have come to be extensively relied upon by parties to litigation in all areas touching on fundamental rights.[46] Although the rights protected by the Convention are, to a large extent, already protected by the Constitution, there is an increasing cross-fertilisation between constitutional and European human rights law, especially in the fields of equality, housing, immigration and criminal procedure.

---

[42]   *Dudgeon v United Kingdom* (1981) 4 EHRR 149.

[43]   [1984] IR 36, 66.

[44]   *Norris v Ireland* (1988) 13 EHRR 186.

[45]   *Airey v Ireland* (1979) 2 EHRR 305; *Keegan v Ireland* (1994) 18 EHRR 342; *Croke v Ireland*, European Court of Human Rights, 21 December 2000 (friendly settlement).

[46]   See Kilkelly (ed), *ECHR and Irish Law* (2nd edn, 2009).

[17.70] The European Convention on Human Rights Act 2003 incorporates the Convention rights into Irish law on a sub-constitutional level. Section 2 of the 2003 Act obliges the courts to interpret and apply all Irish laws in a manner compatible with the state's obligations under the Convention. Section 3 of the 2003 Act requires that the organs of the state perform their functions in a manner compatible with the rights protected by the Convention. Section 3 also provides for a remedy in damages against the state for failure to respect Convention rights where no other remedy in damages is available.[47] Section 4 of the 2003 Act requires the Irish courts to take judicial notice of judgments and decisions of the European Court of Human Rights in the interpretation of the Convention provisions. Section 5 empowers Irish courts to make 'declarations of incompatibility' in respect of statutory provisions or rules of law which are incompatible with the state's obligations under the ECHR. Such declarations may be granted only where no other legal remedy is adequate and available. They do not affect the validity or continuing operation of the impugned provision or rule, though copies of declarations of incompatibility must be laid before the Dáil so that the incompatibility can be addressed by the Oireachtas.

[17.71] The High Court decisions in *Foy v An t-Ard Chlaraitheoir*[48] illustrate the significant influence of the ECHR and case law of the European Court of Human Rights on Irish jurisprudence since incorporation of the Convention by the 2003 Act. In 2002, the applicant, a post-operative male-to-female transsexual, sought an order of the High Court correcting the record of her gender in the register of births from male to female. She argued that, if no such finding were attainable, the legal regime for the registration of births infringed her constitutional rights to privacy, dignity and equality. The High Court refused the reliefs sought and found no breach of Article 40.1 of the Constitution. Two days later, the European Court of Human Rights held, in *Goodwin v United Kingdom*[49] and *I v United Kingdom*,[50] that the British system for the registration of births, which was, broadly speaking, comparable to the Irish system, failed to respect the applicants' rights to privacy and marriage and that the interference in those rights was disproportionate. The *Foy* case was appealed to the Supreme Court, and, following the passage of the 2003 Act, it was remitted to the High Court so that the Convention issues could be addressed. In the light of the *Goodwin* and *I* cases, the High Court granted a declaration in the applicant's favour that the system for the registration of births in Ireland was incompatible with the Convention.[51] At the time of writing (September 2014), a draft Scheme of a Gender Recognition Bill has been published but has not yet been enacted.[52]

---

[47] For an example of a case in which damages were awarded for a failure to respect Convention rights, see *O'Donnell v South Dublin County Council* (11 January 2008, unreported), HC.

[48] *Foy v An t-Ard Chlaraitheoir* [2002] IEHC 116 and [2007] IEHC 470.

[49] *Goodwin v United Kingdom* (2002) 35 EHRR 447.

[50] *I v United Kingdom* (2003) 36 EHRR 53.

[51] *Foy v An t-Ard Chlaraitheoir (No 2)* [2007] IEHC 470.

[52] See also para **15.203**.

[17.72] Local authority tenants have also been affected by case law of the European Court of Human Rights. Section 62 of the Housing Act 1966, as amended by s 13 of the Housing Act 1970, provided a special summary eviction procedure for tenants in local authority housing. In 2002, the European Court of Human Rights had decided, in *Connors v United Kingdom*,[53] that there was an absence of fair procedures in an English local authority's summary eviction of a gypsy family from their home to the extent that the eviction interfered disproportionately with the family's right to privacy, family and home as guaranteed by art 8 of the ECHR. In the wake of the *Connors* decision, the High Court and on appeal, the Supreme Court has granted declarations that s 62 of the 1966 Act is incompatible with the requirement of fair procedures implicit in art 6 of the ECHR: see *Donegan v Dublin City Council*,[54] *Dublin City Council v Gallagher*[55] and *Pullen v Dublin City Council*.[56] In response, Part 2 of the Housing (Miscellaneous Provisions) Act 2014 repealed s 62 of the 1966 Act and replaced it with a notice-based termination process.

[17.73] The jurisprudence of the European Court of Human Rights is also regularly referred to by applicants in immigration and asylum cases. For instance, in *Izevbekhai v Minister for Justice Equality and Law Reform*,[57] the High Court accepted that the practice of female genital mutilation (FGM) constituted torture for the purposes of art 3 of the ECHR and granted leave to the applicants to challenge by judicial review the decision of the respondent Minister to deport them. When the substantive case was heard, the High Court refused to quash the deportation orders on the grounds that the Minister had adequately addressed his duty not to deport persons facing a real risk of mistreatment such as that proscribed by art 3 ECHR.[58] Such a duty had been identified by the European Court of Human Rights in *Chahal v United Kingdom*.[59]

[17.74] Subsequently, in *Izevbekhai v Ireland*[60] the applicants unsuccessfully challenged the deportation order in the European Court of Human Rights. The court held that the information presented by the government with respect to the documents relied upon by Ms Izevbekhai gave strong reasons to question the veracity of the applicants' core factual submission concerning the death of a child in Nigeria as a result of FGM. The court considered the applicants' response to the core issue of credibility to be unsatisfactory. Having considered country of origin information with respect to the

---

53   *Connors v United Kingdom* (2002) 35 EHRR 691.
54   *Donegan v Dublin City Council* [2008] IEHC 288, [2012] IESC 18.
55   *Dublin City Council v Gallagher* [2008] IEHC 354, [2012] IESC 18 (joined case with *Donegan*).
56   *Pullen v Dublin City Council* [2008] IEHC 379. See also *Byrne v Dublin City Council* [2009] IEHC 122.
57   *Izevbhekhai v Minister for Justice Equality and Law Reform* (10 November 2006, unreported), HC.
58   *EPI v Minister for Justice, Equality and Law Reform* [2008] IEHC 23.
59   *Chahal v United Kingdom* (1997) 23 EHRR 413.
60   *Izevbekhai v Ireland* App No 43408/08, European Court of Human Rights, 17 May 2011.

incidence of FGM in Nigeria and the particular circumstances of the applicants, the court held that Ms Izevbekhai and her husband could protect their daughters from FGM if they returned to Nigeria. The court therefore found that the applicants had failed to substantiate that Ms Izevbekhai's daughters would face a real and concrete risk of mistreatment contrary to Article 3 of the Convention upon return to Nigeria.[61]

[17.75] While the ECHR is now incorporated into Irish law by virtue of the 2003 Act, litigants seeking to rely on international agreements that have not been incorporated into Irish law, such as the ICCPR or the UN Convention on the Rights of the Child, encounter the same difficulty faced in 1957 by the applicant in *Re Ó Laighléis*.[62]

[17.76] Thus, in *Kavanagh v Governor of Mountjoy Prison*,[63] the applicant sought to rely on a decision of the UN Human Rights Committee to the effect that his trial by the Special Criminal Court would be in contravention of his rights to a equal protection of the law under art 26 of the ICCPR. When he was nevertheless tried and convicted by that court, he sought to have his conviction quashed on the grounds that the trial had been incompatible with his rights under the ICCPR. He argued that Ireland's ratification of the ICCPR created a legitimate expectation that the state would respect the terms of the ICCPR itself in its substance and, more particularly, that it would take steps to give effect to the views of the Committee. The Supreme Court disagreed, and held that although the state may, by entering into an international agreement, create a legitimate expectation that its agencies will respect its terms, such an expectation could not affect either the provisions of a statute or the judgment of a court without coming into conflict with Article 29.6 of the Constitution.

[17.77] It is important to note that there exists nevertheless a presumption that Irish law is in conformity with international law. This presumption arises out of Article 29.3 of the Constitution, which provides that:

> "Ireland accepts the generally recognised principles of international law as its rule of conduct in its relations with other States."

[17.78] The presumption means that, where there is ambiguity in any Irish law, it should be interpreted in a manner consistent with Ireland's international obligations. Thus, international treaties to which Ireland is a party may legitimately be used to inform our understanding of Irish law, even where these treaties have not been incorporated.

International custom in Irish law

[17.79] The influence of international custom in domestic legal systems tends to be quite limited and this is borne out in the Irish legal system. In the *Kavanagh*[64] case, the

---

61 As a result, the applicants were deported to Nigeria in July 2011: see McDonald, '€1m legal bill after Pamela and girls finally deported' *Irish Independent*, 20 July 2011.
62 *Re Ó Laighléis* [1960] IR 93.
63 *Kavanagh v Governor of Mountjoy Prison* [2002] 3 IR 97.
64 *Kavanagh v Governor of Mountjoy Prison* [2002] 3 IR 97.

applicant also argued that the principle of equality before the law was a generally recognised principle of international law such that it was 'constitutionalised' by Article 29.3 of the Constitution. The Supreme Court concluded that Article 29.3 applied only to Ireland's relations with other states and did not confer any rights on individuals. This line of reasoning, which was first laid down in *Re O Laighléis*,[65] was followed in *Horgan v An Taoiseach*.[66] In *Horgan*, the applicant sought declarations that the state's decision to allow Shannon Airport to be used as a stop-over by United States aircraft engaged in attacks on Iraq was in contravention of the Hague (V) Convention on the Rights and Duties of Neutral Powers 1907, which, although Ireland was not a party to it, was expressive of obligations of a customary nature. The High Court accepted that there existed a rule of customary international law prohibiting neutral powers from permitting the movement of troops and materials through their territory. On the status of such a rule in the Irish legal system, the court held that it entered domestic law only to the extent that no constitutional, statutory or judge-made law was inconsistent with it, and that, where a conflict arose, the rule of international law must in every case yield to domestic law. The High Court then followed the precedents set by the Supreme Court in *Re O Laighléis*[67] and *Kavanagh*[68] in finding that Article 29 conferred no individual rights but rather referred only to relations between states, and declined to order the reliefs sought by the applicant.

[17.80] Other cases, such as those dealing with sovereign immunity, suggest that customary international law plays a part in the Irish legal system far in excess of that described by the High Court in *Horgan*[69] even to the extent that it may limit constitutional rights. For example, in *Government of Canada v Employment Appeals Tribunal and Burke*,[70] the government of Canada relied on Article 29.3 in asserting sovereign immunity in the Irish courts against Mr Burke, who had been employed as chauffeur for the Ambassador by the Canadian Embassy in Ireland and who had instituted proceedings under the Unfair Dismissals Act 1977 when he had been dismissed from his post. The Canadian government argued that the Employment Appeals Tribunal had no jurisdiction to hear the matter, claiming that the government of Canada was entitled to rely on the customary law doctrine of sovereign immunity. In upholding this contention, the Supreme Court acknowledged that Article 29.3 had imported the doctrine of sovereign immunity into Irish law and that the modern doctrine of sovereign immunity attached to the public business and policy of states, but not to their private commercial relationships.[71] In the case before it, the court found that the contract between Mr Burke and the embassy to act as chauffeur to the Ambassador was

---

[65] *Re Ó Laighléis* [1960] IR 93.

[66] *Horgan v An Taoiseach* [2003] 2 IR 468.

[67] *Re Ó Laighléis* [1960] IR 93.

[68] *Kavanagh v Governor of Mountjoy Prison* [2002] 3 IR 97.

[69] *Horgan* [2003] 2 IR 468.

[70] *Government of Canada v Employment Appeals Tribunal and Burke* [1992] 2 IR 484.

[71] The court followed the general approach of Lord Wilberforce in the House of Lords decision *I Congreso del Partido* [1983] 1 AC 244.

not a commercial contract in the ordinary sense because it involved an element of trust and confidentiality which was connected with the government of Canada's public business and interests. Accordingly the Supreme Court upheld the government of Canada's plea of sovereign immunity notwithstanding Mr Burke's invocation of his constitutional right of access to the courts.[72]

[17.81] Irish jurisprudence on international custom and general principles of law suggests a divergence in approach to the role of Article 29.3 in our legal system depending on whether a right is being asserted by an individual or by another state. This is not an easy distinction to maintain, and the future development of the law in this area is therefore uncertain.

[8] PRIVATE INTERNATIONAL LAW

[17.82] Private international law, or the 'conflict of laws', refers to the rules which are intended to resolve the conflicts between laws of different countries in domestic courts. These rules deal primarily with two issues: which state has jurisdiction to deal with the matter, and which state's laws apply (choice of laws). Private international law is not part of international law in the sense discussed above because each state has its own domestic body of private international law by which it seeks to regulate disputes that arise in its national courts.[73] There have however been significant efforts on the international level to harmonise these domestic rules. Private international law is largely concerned with civil law disputes, rather than criminal liability, though there have been some significant recent developments in this area also which indicate that global corporate governance laws may emerge in the future.

Jurisdiction

[17.83] When a conflict of laws arises, a court must decide whether it has jurisdiction to hear the case. The traditional rule is that the appropriate court to hear the case is the one which is most convenient. This will usually mean that jurisdiction lies with the state which has most connection to the dispute. A court has discretion not to hear a case if it concludes that it is not a convenient forum – that it is *forum non conveniens* – and that the case would be better heard elsewhere.

[17.84] The doctrine of *forum non conveniens* was considered in *Doe v Armour Pharmaceutical Inc*,[74] in which plaintiffs who had haemophilia claimed that they had

---

72. See also *O'Shea v Italian Embassy* [2002] 13 ELR 276 where sovereign immunity was held to apply and *Geraghty v Embassy of Mexico* [1998] ELR 310 where sovereign immunity was held not to apply. Both concern employment issues. In 2014 the Department of Foreign Affairs published a non-statutory code of conduct on the employment protections of embassy staff in embassies located in the State.

73. See generally Binchy, *Irish Conflict of Laws* (1988).

74. *Doe v Armour Pharmaceutical Inc* [1994] 1 ILRM 416. For a critical analysis, see Cole and Tomkin 'Doe v Armour – Forum Non Conveniens or Political Decision?' (1994) 12 ILT 267. The litigation was ultimately settled in 2001.

become HIV positive arising from the use of a blood-clotting agent manufactured by the defendant, a United States company. They alleged that the defendant had been negligent in the manufacture of the agent and they instituted proceedings seeking damages in the New York courts. In New York, their actions had been dismissed on the grounds of *forum non conveniens*, albeit with the proviso that the defendant company consented to allowing the plaintiffs return to the US courts if the Irish courts declined to accept jurisdiction in the actions. The plaintiffs then applied to the High Court in Ireland seeking a declaration that the actions could more conveniently be dealt with in the US courts. In the High Court, it was held that the appropriate forum was Ireland, and this was upheld in the Supreme Court.

Choice of laws

[17.85] The choice of jurisdiction does not necessarily determine the law that is applied in the determination of the action. While procedural issues are decided based on the law of the forum, substantive rights and duties may be determined with reference to foreign law. Different rules apply to different substantive areas of law such as tort and contract. In relation to tort, common law jurisdictions usually favour the application of the law of the forum, the *lex fori*, while civil law jurisdictions tend to apply the *lex loci delicti*, that is, the law of the place in which the tort occurred. Another theory, sometimes called 'the proper law of tort' suggests that the law to be applied should be determined based on the particular circumstances of the individual case. In the context of actions based on contract, the traditional approach of the common law was to favour the *lex loci contractus*, the law of the place in which the contract was made. More recently, there has been a tendency toward an approach comparable to that of 'the proper law of tort', known, somewhat predictably, as 'the proper law of contract'.

The influence of the EU on private international law in Ireland

[17.86] Within the EU, the traditional rules of private international law have been supplanted by Community law. For instance, Council Regulation 44/2001 (Brussels II Regulation) applies uniform rules across the EU in relation to jurisdiction and enforcement of judgments concerning almost all civil and commercial matters. The 2001 Regulation largely replicates the provisions of the Brussels Conventions of 1968 and 1982 but gives them direct effect. The general rule, set out in art 2 of the 2001 Regulation is that persons domiciled in a member state shall, whatever their nationality, be sued in the courts of that member state. Choice of law in relation to contracts is also governed by Community law. The Rome Convention on the Law Applicable to Contractual Obligations sets out the rules in respect of choice of law for contractual disputes in member states of the EU. This treaty has been incorporated into Irish law by the Contractual Obligations (Applicable Law) Act 1980.

International codification of private international law

[17.87] In 1966, the UN General Assembly established the United Nations Commission on International Trade Law (UNCITRAL) with a remit of proposing conventions and uniform laws on international trade law. The work of UNCITRAL has resulted in a number of important Conventions, such as the 1980 Vienna Convention on Contracts for the International Sale of Goods and the 1985 Model Law on International Arbitration. The 1985 Convention was incorporated into Irish law by the Arbitration (International Commercial) Act 1998. The 1998 Act was repealed and replaced by the Arbitration Act 2010, which now applies the Model Law to both domestic and international arbitrations.[75]

[17.88] Other similar bodies are the Rome Institute for the Unification of Private Law (UNIDROIT) and the Hague Conference on Private International Law. The UNIDROIT 1980 Convention on the Law Applicable to Contractual Obligations was implemented in Irish law by the Contractual Obligations (Applicable Law) Act 1991.[76] The work of the Hague Conference has included a 1993 Convention on Protection of Children, incorporated into Irish law by the Protection of Children (Hague Convention) Act 2000, and a 1996 Convention on inter-country adoption, incorporated into Irish law by the Adoption Act 2010.[77]

[17.89] Other Conventions involve a combination of 'private' elements and 'public' enforcement by contracting states. These include some of the Conventions concerning the environment, such as the International Convention for the Prevention of Pollution from Ships (MARPOL) 1973 (the 'London Convention'). This was implemented in Irish law by the Sea Pollution Act 1991.

---

[75] See para **8.21**.

[76] In this instance, the 1991 Act followed accession by the European Union to the Rome Convention.

[77] In these instances, incorporation of the Hague Conference Conventions followed Law Reform Commission Reports recommending this.

Bibliography

Books

Abrahamson, W, Dwyer, J and Fitzpatrick, A, *Discovery and Disclosure* 2nd edn Dublin, Round Hall, 2013

Akehurst's Modern Introduction to International Law (Malanczuk, P ed) 7th edn London, Routledge, 1997

Allott, A, *The Limits of Law* London, Butterworths, 1980

Ashworth, A, *Principles of Criminal Law* 6th edn Oxford, Oxford University Press, 2009

Aston, J (ed), *Index to Irish Superior Court Written Judgments 1983–1989* Dublin, Irish Association of Law Teachers, 1991

Aston, J and Doyle, M (eds), *Index to Irish Superior Court Written Judgments 1976–1982* Dublin, Irish Association of Law Teachers, 1984

Aston, J et al (eds), *Index to Unreported Judgments of the Irish Superior Courts 1966–1975* Dublin, Irish Association of Law Teachers, 1990

Austin, J, *The Province of Jurisprudence Determined* (1832) Aldershot, Ashgate, 1998

Ball, FE, *The Judges in Ireland, 1221–1921* (1921) Dublin, Round Hall Press, 1993 (reprint)

Banville, J, *The Book of Evidence* London, Martin Secker & Warburg, 1992

Barnard, C, *The Substantive Law of the EU: The Four Freedoms* 4th edn Oxford, Oxford University Press, 2013

Barnard, C and Peers, S, *European Union Law* Oxford, Oxford University Press, 2014

Barrett, G, *Final Impact: The Treaty of Lisbon and the Final Provisions of the Treaty Establishing the European Community and the Treaty on European Union* Dublin, UCD European Institute Working Paper 08–1, May 2008

Barrett, J, and Barrett, J *A History of Alternative Dispute Resolution* San Francisco, Jossey-Bass, 2004

Barron, J, *Practice and Procedure in The Master's Court* 2nd edn Dublin, Round Hall Press, 1998

Bartholomew, P, *The Irish Judiciary* Dublin, Institute of Public Administration, 1971

Bellomo, M, *The Common Legal Past of Europe 1000–1800* Washington DC, Catholic University of America Press, 1995

Bennion on Statutory Interpretation 6th edn London, Butterworths, 2013

Bennion, F, *Statute Law* 3rd edn Harlow, Longman, 1990

Bennion, F, *Understanding Common Law Legislation: Drafting and Interpretation* Oxford, Oxford University Press, 2001

Bentham, J, *Of Laws in General* (1782) London, Athlone Press, 1970

Berry, E, Homewood, M and Bogusz, B, *Complete EU Law: Text, Cases and Materials* Oxford, Oxford University Press, 2013

Biehler, H, *Judicial Review of Administrative Action* 3rd edn, Dublin, Round Hall, 2013

Binchy, D, *Corpus Iuris Hibernici* Dublin, Institute for Advanced Studies, 1979

Binchy, W, *Irish Conflict of Laws* Dublin, Butterworth Ireland, 1988

Blackstone, W, *Commentaries on the Laws of England* 4 vols (1765–1769)

Blondel, J, *Thinking Politically* Harmondsworth, Penguin, 1978

Bork, R, *The Tempting of America: The Political Seduction of the Law* New York, Free Press, 1990

Boyle, K, and Greer, D *The Legal Systems, North and South* Dublin, Stationery Office, 1983

Brand, P, *The Making of the Common Law* London, Hambledon, 1992

Breathnach, L, *Uraicecht na R'ar: the Poetic Grades in Early Irish Law* Dublin, Dublin Institute for Advanced Studies, 1987

Brownlie, I, *Principles of Public International Law* Oxford, Oxford University Press, 2008

Byrne, R and Binchy, W, *Annual Review of Irish Law 1988* Dublin, Round Hall Press, 1989

Byrne, R and Binchy, W, *Annual Review of Irish Law 1989* Dublin, Round Hall Press, 1990

Byrne, R and Binchy, W, *Annual Review of Irish Law 1992* Dublin, Round Hall Press, 1994

Byrne, R and Binchy, W, *Annual Review of Irish Law 1993* Dublin, Round Hall Sweet & Maxwell, 1996

Byrne, R and Binchy, W, *Annual Review of Irish Law 1994* Dublin, Round Hall Sweet & Maxwell, 1996

Byrne, R and Binchy, W, *Annual Review of Irish Law 1997* Dublin, Round Hall Sweet & Maxwell, 1998

Byrne, R and Binchy, W, *Annual Review of Irish Law 1998* Dublin, Round Hall Sweet & Maxwell, 1999

Byrne, R and Binchy, W, *Annual Review of Irish Law 1999* Dublin, Round Hall Ltd, 2000

Byrne, R and Binchy, W, *Annual Review of Irish Law 2012* Dublin, Round Hall, 2013

Byrne, R, *Safety, Health and Welfare at Work Law in Ireland* 2nd edn, Cork, Nifast, 2008

Byrne, R, Hogan, G and McDermott, P, *Prisoners' Rights* Dublin, Co-op Books, 1981

Cane, P, *Atiyah's Accidents, Compensation and the Law* 6th edn London, Butterworths, 1999

Canny, M, *Limitation of Actions* Dublin, Round Hall, 2010

Carolan, E and Doyle, O, *The Irish Constitution: Governance and Values* Dublin, Thomson Round Hall, 2008

Casey, J, *The Irish Law Officers: Roles and Responsibilities of the Attorney General and Director of Public Prosecutions* Dublin, Round Hall Sweet & Maxwell, 1996

Casey, J, *Constitutional Law in Ireland* 3rd edn Dublin, Round Hall Sweet & Maxwell, 2000

Cassidy, C, *The Licensing Acts 1833–1995* Dublin, Round Hall Sweet & Maxwell, 1996

Chalmers, D, Davies, G and Monti, G, *European Union Law: Text and Materials* 3rd edn Cambridge, Cambridge University Press, 2014

Charles-Edwards, T and Kelly, F (eds), *Bechbretha: an Old Irish Law Tract on Beekeeping* Dublin, Dublin Institute for Advanced Studies, 1983

Charleton, P, *Controlled Drugs and the Criminal Law* Dublin, An Cló Liúir, 1986

Charleton, P, *Offences Against the Person* Dublin, Round Hall Press, 1992

Chubb, B, *The Government and Politics of Ireland* 3rd edn Harlow, Longman, 1992

Clark, R, *Contract Law in Ireland* 6th edn Dublin, Thomson Round Hall, 2008

Clarke, D (ed), *Morality and the Law* Dublin, RTÉ/Mercier Press, 1982

Coakley, J and Gallagher, M (eds), *Politics in the Republic of Ireland* 5th edn London, Routledge, 2010

Coke, E, Institutes of the Law of England 4 vols (1628–1644)

Collins, A and O'Reilly, J, *Civil Proceedings and the State in Ireland* Dublin 2nd edn, Dublin, Round Hall Press, 2004

Connelly, A (ed), *Gender and the Law in Ireland* Dublin, Oak Tree Press, 1993

Connery, N and Hodnett, D, *Regulatory Law in Ireland* Dublin, Bloomsbury Professional, 2009

Coonan, G and O'Toole, K, *Criminal Procedure in the District Court* Dublin, Round Hall, 2011

Cousins, M, *The Irish Social Welfare System: Law and Social Policy* Dublin, Round Hall Press, 1995

Craies on Statute Law 7th edn London, Sweet & Maxwell, 1971

Craies on Legislation: A Practitioner's Guide to the Nature, Process, Effect and Interpretation of Legislation 10th edn London, Sweet & Maxwell, 2012

Craig, P and De Búrca, G, *EU Law: Text, Cases and Materials* 5th edn Oxford, Oxford University Press, 2011

Cross, R and Harris, J, *Precedent in English Law* 4th edn Oxford, Clarendon Press, 1991

Cross, R, *Statutory Interpretation* 3rd edn London, Butterworths, 1995

Crotty, R, *A Radical's Response* Swords, Poolbeg, 1988

Curtin, D and O'Keeffe, D (eds), *Constitutional Adjudication in European Community and National Law* Dublin, Butterworth Ireland, 1992

Dale, W, *Legislative Drafting: a New Approach* London, Butterworths, 1977

Dane, J and Thomas, P, *How to Use a Law Library* 4th edn London, Sweet & Maxwell, 2001

Dashwood, A et al, *Wyatt and Dashwood's European Union Law* 6th edn Oxford, Hart Publishing, 2011

Dawson, N and Ors (eds), *One Hundred and Fifty Years of Irish Law* Belfast, SLS Publications, 1996

Dayal, S, *LDL Online Laying Down the Law: Computer Assisted Legal Research* Sydney, Butterworths, 1996

de Blacam, M, *Drunken Driving and the Law* 3rd edn Dublin, Thomson Round Hall, 2003

de Blacam, M, *Judicial Review* 2nd edn, Dublin, Tottel Publishing, 2009

Deale, K, *Beyond any Reasonable Doubt?* 2nd rev ed Dublin, Gill and Macmillan, 1990

Delany, H, *Equity and the Law of Trusts in Ireland* 5th edn Dublin, Round Hall, 2011

Delany, H, *The Courts Acts 1924–1997* 2nd edn, Dublin, Round Hall Press, 2000

Delany, H and McGrath, D, *Civil Procedure in the Superior Courts* 3rd edn, Dublin, Round Hall, 2012

Delany, VTH, *Christopher Palles* Dublin, Allen Figgis & Co, 1960

Delany, VTH, *The Administration of Justice in Ireland*, 4th edn Dublin, Institute of Public Administration, 1975 (Lysaght, C ed)

Denning, A, *My Family Story* London, Butterworths, 1981

Devlin, P, *The Enforcement of Morals* Oxford, Oxford University Press, 1965

Devlin, P, *The Judge* Oxford, Oxford University Press, 1979

Dickson, B, *The Legal System of Northern Ireland* 5th edn Belfast, SLS Publications, 2005

Dodd, D, *Statutory Interpretation* Dublin, Bloomsbury Professional, 2008

Donaldson, A, *Some Comparative Aspects of Irish Law* Durham NC, Duke University Press, 1957

Dowling, K and Savage, B, *Civil Procedure in the District Court* Dublin, Round Hall, 2009

Dowling, S, *The Commercial Court* 2nd edn, Dublin, Thomson Round Hall, 2012

Dowling-Hussey, A and Dunne, D, *Arbitration Law* Dublin, Thomson Round Hall, 2008

Doyle, O, *Constitutional Law: Texts, Cases and Materials* Dublin, Clarus Press, 2008

Duignan, S, *One Spin on the Merry-Go-Round* Dublin, Blackwater Press, 1996

Duncan W (ed), *Law and Social Policy* Dublin, Dublin University Law Journal, 1987

Dunne, D and Kerrigan, G, *Round Up the Usual Suspects* Dublin, Magill, 1984

Durcan, P, *Daddy, Daddy* Belfast, Blackstaff, 1990

Dworkin, R, *Taking Rights Seriously* London, Duckworth, 1977

Fahey, E, *EU Law in Ireland* Dublin, Clarus Press, 2010

Fahey, E, *Practice and Procedure in Preliminary References to Europe: 30 years of Article 234 EC Caselaw from the Irish Courts* Dublin, First Law, 2007

Farrell, B, *Coroners: Practice and Procedure* Dublin, Round Hall Sweet & Maxwell, 2000

Farrell, J, *Irish Law of Specific Performance* Dublin, Butterworth Ireland, 1994

Farrell, R and Hanrahan, A, *The European Arrest Warrant in Ireland* Dublin, Clarus Press, 2011

Feinberg, J, *The Moral Limits of the Criminal Law* Vol 1: *Harm to Others* Oxford, Oxford University Press, 1984; Vol 2: *Offense to Others* Oxford, Oxford University Press, 1985; Vol 3: *Harm to Self* Oxford, Oxford University Press, 1986; Vol 4: *Harmless Wrongdoing* Oxford, Oxford University Press, 1990

Fennell, C, *Law of Evidence in Ireland* 3rd edn, Dublin, Bloomsbury Professional, 2009

Finnis, J, *Natural Law and Natural Rights* Oxford, Clarendon Press, 1980

Friel, J, The Suspect: The Story of Rachel O'Reilly's Murder Maverick House, 2007

Fleming, J, *The Law of Torts* 9th edn North Ryde, NSW, LBC Information Services, 1998

Forde, M, *Constitutional Law of Ireland* 3rd edn, Dublin, Bloomsbury Professional, 2013

Forde, M, *Industrial Relations Law* Dublin, Round Hall Press, 1991

Forde, M, *Employment Law* Dublin, Round Hall Press, 1992

Forde, M, *Arbitration Law and Procedure* Dublin, Round Hall Press, 1994

Forde, M, *Extradition Law in Ireland* 2nd edn Dublin, Round Hall Sweet & Maxwell, 1995

Foxton, D, *Revolutionary Lawyers: Sinn Féin and the Crown Courts in Ireland and Britain 1916–1923* Dublin, Four Courts Press, 2008

Free Legal Advice Centres, *The Closed Door; A Report on Civil Legal Aid Services in Ireland* Dublin, FLAC, 1987

Free Legal Advice Centres, *Access to Justice: a Right or Privilege? A Blueprint for Civil Legal Aid in Ireland* Dublin, FLAC, 2009

Friel, R, *The Law of Contract* 2nd edn Dublin, Round Hall Press, 2000

Fuller, L, *The Morality of Law* New Haven, Yale University Press, 1969

Galligan, E and McGrath, M, *Compulsory Purchase and Compensation: Law and Practice in Ireland* 2nd edn Dublin, Bloomsbury Professional, 2013

Ganz, G, *Quasi-Legislation* London, Sweet & Maxwell, 1987

Geldart, W, *Introduction to English Law* 11th edn Oxford, Oxford University Press, 1995

George, R (ed), *Natural Law Theory* Oxford, Clarendon Press, 1992

Golding, G, *George Gavan Duffy* Dublin, Irish Academic Press, 1982

Goldstein, L (ed), *Precedent in Law* Oxford, Clarendon Press, 1987

Goodrich, P, *Reading the Law* Oxford, Basil Blackwell, 1986

Griffith, JAG, *The Politics of the Judiciary* 5th edn London, Fontana, 1997

Grossman, G, *Legal Research: Historical Foundations of the Electronic Era New York*, Oxford University Press, 1994

Hale, M, *The History of the Pleas of the Crown* 2 vols (1736)

Hall, E, *The Superior Courts of Law: 'Official' Law Reporting in Ireland 1866–2006* Dublin, Incorporated Council of Law Reporting for Ireland, 2007

Hand, G, *English Law in Ireland, 1290–1324* Cambridge, Cambridge University Press, 1967

Hanly, C, *An Introduction to Irish Criminal Law* 2nd edn, Dublin, Gill & MacMillan, 2006

Harris, J, *Legal Philosophies* 2nd edn London, Butterworths, 1997

Harris, P, *An Introduction to Law* 5th edn London, Weidenfeld and Nicolson 1997

Hart, HLA, *The Concept of Law* Oxford, Clarendon Press, 1961

Hart, HLA, *Law, Liberty and Morality* Oxford, Oxford University Press, 1963

Hartley, T, *Foundations of European Community Law* 7th edn Oxford, Oxford University Press, 2014

Healy, M, *The Old Munster Circuit* (1939) Cork, Mercier Reprint, 1981

Hennessy, L and Moore, P, *Taxes Consolidation Act 1997: the Busy Practitioner's Guide* Dublin, Institute of Taxation, 1997

Hesketh, T, *The Second Partitioning of Ireland?* Dun Laoighaire, Brandsma, 1990

Heuston, R and Buckley, R, *Salmond and Heuston on the Law of Torts* 21st edn London, Sweet & Maxwell, 1996

Hobbes, T, *Leviathan* (1651) London, Penguin Classics, 1985

Hogan, D and Osborough WN (eds), *Brehons, Sergeants and Attorneys: Studies in the History of the Irish Legal Profession* Dublin, Irish Academic Press/Irish Legal History Society, 1990

Hogan, D, *The Legal Profession in Ireland 1789–1922* Dublin, Incorporated Law Society of Ireland, 1986

Hogan, G and Morgan, D *Administrative Law in Ireland* 4th edn Dublin, Round Hall, 2010

Hogan, G and Walker, C *Political Violence and the Law in Ireland* Manchester, Manchester University Press, 1989

Hogan, G and Whyte, G *JM Kelly: The Irish Constitution* 4th edn, Dublin, LexisNexis, 2003

Holborn, G, *Butterworths Legal Research Guide* London, Butterworths, 1993

Holmes, N and Venables, D, *Researching the Legal Web* 2nd edn London, Butterworths, 1999

Holohan, B and Curran, D, *Lawyers' Professional Negligence and Insurance* Dublin, Round Hall, 2012

Honourable Society of King's Inns, *Rules of the Honourable Society of King's Inns* Dublin, 2000

Honourable Society of King's Inns, *Education Rules of the Honourable Society of King's Inns* Dublin, 2006

Joyce, J and Murtagh, P, *Blind Justice* Swords, Poolbeg, 1984

Kaczorowska, A, *European Union Law* 3rd edn, Oxford, Routledge, 2013

Kapteyn, P et al, *The Law of the European Union and the European Communities* Kluwer Law International, 2008

Kapteyn, P and Van Themaat, V, *Introduction to the Law of the European Communities* 3rd edn London, Kluwer Law, 1998

Keane, A, and McKeown, P, *The Modern Law of Evidence* 10th edn Oxford, Oxford University Press, 2014

Keane, R, *Equity and the Law of Trusts in the Republic of Ireland* 2nd edn Dublin, Bloomsbury Professional, 2011

Keatinge, P (ed), *Ireland and EC Membership Evaluated* London, Pinter, 1991

Kelly, F, *A Guide to Early Irish Law* Dublin, Dublin Institute for Advanced Studies, 1988

Kelly, F, *Early Irish Farming: a Study Based Mainly on the Law Texts of the 7th and 8th Centuries AD Dublin*, Dublin Institute for Advanced Studies, 1998

Kelly, J, *Orders for the Captain?* Dublin, Kelly, 1971

Kelly, JM, *Fundamental Rights in the Irish Law and Constitution* 2nd edn Dublin, Hodges Figgis, 1967

Kelly, JM, *The Irish Constitution* 2nd edn Dublin, Jurist Publishing, 1984

Kelsen, H, *General Theory of Law and State* (1945) New York, Russell & Russell, 1961

Kelsen, H, *The Pure Theory of Law* Berkeley, California University Press, 1967

Kenny, C, *King's Inns and the Kingdom of Ireland: the Irish 'inn of court' 1541–1800* Dublin, Irish Academic Press, 1992

Keogh, D, *The Vatican, the Bishops and Irish Politics 1919-39* Cambridge, Cambridge University Press, 1986

Keogh, D, Ireland and the Vatican: the Politics of Church-State Diplomacy Cork, Cork University Press, 1995

Kerrigan, G, *Nothing But the Truth* Dublin, Tomar, 1990

Keville, M and Lucey, C, *Irish Perspectives on EC Law* Dublin, Thomson Round Hall, 2003

Kilkelly, U, *ECHR and Irish Law* 2nd edn, Bristol, Jordans, 2009

Kirwan, B, *Injunctions Law & Practice* Dublin, Thomson Round Hall, 2008

Kohn, L, *The Constitution of the Irish Free State* London, G Allen & Unwin, 1932

Kotsonouris, M, *Retreat from Revolution* Dublin, Irish Academic Press, 1994

Lee, J, *Ireland 1912–1985* Cambridge, Cambridge University Press, 1990

Lee, S, *Judging Judges* London, Faber, 1988

Lee, S, *Law and Morals* Oxford, Oxford University Press, 1986

Lindsay, P, *Memories* Dublin, Blackwater Press, 1992

Litton, F (ed), *The Constitution of Ireland 1937–1987* Dublin, Institute of Public Administration, 1988

MacCann, L and Courtney, T, *The Companies Acts 1963–2009* Dublin, Bloomsbury Professional, 2009

MacCormick, N, *Legal Right and Social Democracy* Oxford, Oxford University Press, 1982

Mackey, R, *Windward of the Law* London, WH Allen, 1965

MacNeill, E, *Early Irish Law and Institutions* Dublin, Burns, Oates and Washbourne, 1935

Malleson, K and Moules, R, *The Legal System* 4th edn, Oxford, Oxford University Press, 2010

Mathews, A (ed), *Immediate Man: Cuimhní ar Chearbhall Ó Dálaigh* Mountrath, Dolmen Press, 1983

Maxwell on the Interpretation of Statutes (St Langan, P ed) 12th edn London, Sweet & Maxwell, 1969

McArdle, *Irish Legal Anecdotes* Dublin, Gill & Macmillan, 1995

McAuley, F and McCutcheon, JP, *Criminal Liability* Dublin, Round Hall Sweet & Maxwell, 2000

McCafferty, N, *In the Eyes of the Law* Ward River Press, 1981

McCarthy, P, *'A Favourite Study' Building the King's Inns* Dublin, Gill & MacMillan, 2006

McCutcheon, JP, *The Larceny Act 1916* Dublin, Round Hall Press, 1988

McDermott, P, *Prison Law* Dublin, Round Hall Sweet & Maxwell, 2000

McDonald, O, *Parliament at Work* London, Methuen, 1989

McGonagle, M, *A Textbook on Media Law* Dublin, 2nd edn, Gill and Macmillan, 2003

McGowan Smyth, J, *The Theory and Practice of the Irish Senate* Dublin, Institute of Public Administration, 1972

McGowan Smyth, J, *The Houses of the Oireachtas* 4th edn Dublin, Institute of Public Administration, 1979

McGrath, D, *Evidence* Dublin, Thomson Round Hall, 2005

McGreal, C, *The Criminal Law (Theft and Fraud Offences) Act 2001* Dublin, Thomson Round Hall, 2003

McHugh, D, *Small Claims Court in Ireland: A Consumer Guide* Dublin, First Law, 2003

McIntyre, T, *Through the Bridewell Gate* London, Faber & Faber, 1971

McLeod, N, *Early Irish Contract Law* Sydney, Centre for Celtic Studies University of Sydney, 1996

McMahon, B and Binchy, W, *A Casebook on the Irish Law of Torts* Abingdon, Professional Books, 1983

McMahon B and Binchy, W, *Law of Torts* 4th edn Dublin, Bloomsbury Professional, 2013

McMahon, B and Murphy, F, *European Community Law in Ireland* Dublin, Butterworth Ireland, 1989

Miers, D and Page, A, *Legislation* 2nd edn London, Sweet & Maxwell, 1990

Mill, JS, *On Liberty* (1859) Cambridge, Cambridge Texts in the History of Political Thought, 1989

Miller, C, *Contempt of Court* 3rd edn Oxford, Clarendon Press, 2000

Morgan, D, *Constitutional Law of Ireland* 2nd edn Dublin, Round Hall, 1990

Mulholland, J (ed), *Political Choice and Democratic Freedom in Ireland: 40 Leading Thinkers* Glenties, MacGill Irish Summer School, 2004

Ó Cearúil, M, *Bunreacht na hÉireann: a Study of the Irish Text* Dublin, Stationery Office, 1999

O'Callaghan, J, *The Red Book* Dublin, Poolbeg Press, 1992

O'Callaghan, P, *The Law of Solicitors in Ireland* Dublin, Butterworth Ireland, 2000

O'Connell, D, *International Law* 2nd edn London, Stevens & Son, 1970

O'Flaherty, M and Heffernan, L, *The International Covenant on Civil and Political Rights: International Human Rights Law in Ireland* Dublin, Brehon, 1995

O'Flanagan, J, *Lives of the Lord Chancellors of Ireland*, 2 vols London, Longmans Green, 1870

O'Higgins, T, *A Double Life* Dublin, Town House, 1996

O'Mahony, P, *Crime and Punishment in Ireland* Dublin, Round Hall Press, 1993

O'Malley, T, *The Criminal Process* Dublin, Round Hall, 2009

O'Malley, T, *The Status of the Irish Language – a Legal Perspective* Dublin, Bord na Gaeilge, 1990

O'Malley, T, *The Round Hall Guide to Sources of Law* Dublin, Round Hall Press, 1993

O'Malley, T, *Sentencing Law and Practice* Dublin 2nd edn, Thomson Round Hall 2006

O'Reilly J (ed), *Human Rights and Constitutional Law* Dublin, Round Hall Press, 1992

Oppenheim, L, *International Law* (McNair, A ed) 4th edn London, Longmans Green, 1928

Pech, L, *The European Union and its Constitution: From Rome to Lisbon* Dublin, Clarus Press, 2008

Peel, E and Goudkamp, J, *Winfield and Jolowicz on Tort* 19th edn London, Sweet & Maxwell, 2014

Penner, J and Melissaris, E, *McCoubrey & White's Textbook on Jurisprudence* 5th edn Oxford, Oxford University Press, 2012

Pierse, R, *Road Traffic Law* 2nd edn Dublin, Butterworth Ireland, 1995

Posner, R, *Economic Analysis of Law* 7th edn, Wolters Kluwer, 2007

Posner, R, *How Judges Think* Harvard University Press, 2008

Prawlisch, H, *Sir John Davies and the Conquest of Ireland* Cambridge, Cambridge University Press, 1985

Quigley, P and Binchy, W (eds), *The Personal Injuries Assessment Board: Implications for Legal Practice* Dublin, First Law, 2004

Quill, E, *Torts in Ireland* 3rd edn, Dublin, Gill & Macmillan, 2009

Quinn, G, Ingram, A and Livingstone, S (eds), *Justice and Legal Theory in Ireland* Dublin, Oak Tree Press, 1995

Raz, J, *The Concept of a Legal System* 2nd edn Oxford, Clarendon Press, 1980

Redmond, M, *Dismissal Law in Ireland* 2nd edn, Dublin, Tottel Publishing, 2007

Reddy, T, *Murder Will Out: A Book of Irish Murder Cases* Dublin, Gill & Macmillan, 1990

Regan, E, *The New Third Pillar: Cooperation against Crime in the European Union* Dublin, Institute for European Affairs, 2000

Richardson, H and Sayles, G, *The Irish Parliament in the Middle Ages* Philadelphia, University of Pennsylvania Press, 1952

Ryan, E and Magee, P, *The Irish Criminal Process* Dublin, Mercier Press, 1983

Scannell, Y, *Environmental and Planning Law in Ireland* Dublin, Round Hall Press, 1995

Schermers, HG, *Judicial Protection in the European Communities* 2nd edn Deventer, Kluwer, 1979

Schwarzenberger, G, *A Manual of International Law* 6th edn Abingdon, Professional Books, 1976

Shavell, S, *Foundations of Economic Analysis of Law* Cambridge, Harvard University Press, 2004

Slapper, G and Kelly, D, *The English Legal System* 15th edn London, Routledge, 2014

Smith De Bruin, M, *Transnational Litigation: Jurisdiction and Procedure* Dublin, Round Hall, 2008

Stephens, JF, *Liberty, Equality, Fraternity* London, Smith, Elder & Co, 1873

Stewart, E, *Arbitration: Commentary and Sources* Dublin, First Law, 2003

Stone, J, *Precedent and Law* Sydney, Butterworths, 1985

Sturgess, G and Chubb, P (ed), *Judging the World* London, Butterworths, 1988

Susskind, R, *The End of Lawyers? Rethinking the Nature of Legal Services* rev edn, Oxford, Oxford University Press, 2010

Susskind, R, *The Future of Law: Facing the Challenges of Information Technology* Oxford, Clarendon Press, 1998

Susskind, R, *Tomorrow's Lawyers: An Introduction to Your Future* Oxford, Oxford University Press, 2013

Tapper, C, *Cross and Tapper on Evidence* 12th edn London, LexisNexis, 2010

Thurneysen, R, *Studies in Early Irish Law* Dublin, Hodges Figgis & Co, 1936 van Caenegem, R, Judges, *Legislators and Professors: Chapters in European Legal History Cambridge*, Cambridge University Press, 1987

Van den Wyngaert, C et al, *Criminal Procedure Systems in the European Community* London, Butterworths, 1993

Walker, R and Walker, M, *English Legal System* 7th edn London, Butterworths, 1994

Walsh, D and Sexton, P, *An Empirical Study of Community Service Orders in Ireland* Dublin, Stationery Office, 1999

Walsh, D, *Criminal Procedure* Dublin, Thomson Round Hall, 2002

Walsh, D, *Juvenile Justice* Dublin, Thomson Round Hall, 2005

Weatherill, S and Beaumont, P, *EU Law* 3rd edn London, Penguin, 1998

Whelan A (ed), *Law and Liberty in Ireland* Dublin, Oak Tree Press, 1993

Whyte, J, *Church and State in Modern Ireland, 1923–1979* 2nd edn Dublin, Gill & Macmillan, 1980

Whyte, G, *Social Inclusion and the Legal System: Public Interest Law in Ireland* Dublin, IPA, 2002

Wijffels, A (ed), *Case Law in the Making* Berlin, Duncker & Humblot 1997

Williams, G, *Learning the Law* 12th edn London, Stevens, 2002

Williams, P, *The General* O'Brien Press, 1994

Woodward, B and Armstrong, S, *The Brethern* New York, Simon and Schuster, 1979

Wylie, JCW, *Irish Land Law* 5th edn, Dublin, Bloomsbury Professional, 2013

Wylie, JCW, *Landlord and Tenant Law* 2nd edn Dublin, Butterworth Ireland, 1998

Xanthaki, H, *Thornton's Legislative Drafting* 5th edn Haywards Heath, Bloomsbury Professional, 2013

Zander, M, *The Law-Making Process* 6th edn London, Butterworth Ireland, 2004

Articles and Chapters

Ahmed, T and de Jesus Butler, I, 'The European Union and Human Rights: An International Law Perspective' (2006) 17 *European Journal of International Law* 771

Baker, J, 'The Common Law Courts of Medieval England: Year Books and Plea Rolls' in Wijffels, A (ed) *Case Law in the Making* Berlin, Duncker & Humblot, 1997

Baldwin, R and Houghton, J, 'Circular Arguments: the Status and Legitimacy of Administrative Rules' [1986] PL 239

Barnes, J, 'The Continuing Debate About "Plain Language" Legislation: A Law Reform Conundrum' (2006) 27 Stat LR 83

Barthelomew, G, 'Unreported Judgments in the House of Lords' (1983) 133 NLJ 781

Bell, J, 'What is the Function of the Conseil d'Etat in the Preparation of Legislation' (2000) 49 ICLQ 661

Bennion, F, 'Hansard – Help or Hindrance? A Draftsman's View of *Pepper v Hart*' [1993] Stat LR 149

Bennion, F, 'How They do Things in France' (1995) 16 Stat LR 90

Bergin-Cross, C, 'Can We Fix It? Yes, We Can!' (2013) 107 *Law Society Gazette* 20

Boyle, 'The United Nations Human Rights Council' (2009) 60 NILQ 121

Brooke, H, 'Special Public Bill Committees' [1995] PL 351

Brooke LJ, 'The Use of Technology in the Courts' (2004) 4 JSIJ 169

Bruton, C, 'Law Reform Commission Consultation Paper on Consolidation and Reform of the Courts Acts' (2007) 12 (5) *Bar Review* 176

Bruton, C, 'Court in the Act' (2007) 101 (9) *Law Society Gazette* 34

Burke-Murphy, E, 'Delay in Irish Courts as Viewed from Strasbourg: *McFarlane v Ireland*' (2011) 29 ILT 30

Bustock, 'Coreper Revisited' (2002) 40 *Journal of Common Market Studies* 215

Byrne, JP, 'Codification of the Criminal Law of Ireland' (2005) 15 ICLJ 15

Byrne, R, 'The Criminal Justice Act 1999' (2000) 18 ILT 190

Cahillane, L, 'Need for Sentencing Guidelines in Ireland?' (2013) 23(1) ICLJ 11

Callewaert, J, 'The European Court of Human Rights and the Area of Freedom, Security and Justice' (2007) 8 *ERA Forum* 511

Carey, G, 'Concurrent Liability in Contract and Tort Part I' (2001) 8(8) CLP 183

Carey, G, 'Concurrent Liability in Contract and Tort Part II' (2001) 8(9) CLP 214

Campbell of Alloway, Lord, 'Codes of Practice as an Alternative to Legislation' [1985] Stat LR 127

Campbell, C and McGurk, J, 'Revising Statutes with Computer Support' [1987] Stat LR 104

Carnwath, L, 'Judicial Precedent – Taming the Common Law' (2012) 12 OUCLJ 261

Carolan, B, 'Economic Analysis and the Law: An Introduction' (1995) 13 ILT 162

Carolan, E, 'Democratic Accountability and the Non-Delegation Doctrine' (2011) 18 DULJ 220

Carroll, J, 'The Right Stuff ' (2007) 101 (7) *Law Society Gazette* 32.

Carroll, 'You Be the Judge: A Study of the Backgrounds of Superior Court Judges in Ireland in 2004 Part I' [2005] 10 (5) *Bar Review* 153

Carroll, 'You Be the Judge Part II' [2005] 10(6) *Bar Review* 182

Casey, G, 'Jury Reform' (2000) 18 ILT 122

Casey, J, 'Confusion in Criminal Appeals: the Legacy of *Conmey*' (1975) 10 Ir Jur (ns) 300

Casey, J, 'Criminal Appeals: the Confusion Persists' (1981) 16 Ir Jur (ns) 271

Casey, J, 'Statutory Interpretation – a New Departure' (1981) 3 DULJ (ns) 110

Casey, J, 'Changing the Constitution: Amendment and Judicial Review', in Farrell, B (ed), *de Valera's Constitution and Ours* Dublin, Gill and Macmillan, 1988

Cassidy, P, 'Hole in my Bucket' [2008] 101(5) *Law Society Gazette* 32

Clarence Smith, 'Legislative Drafting: English and Continental' [1980] Stat LR 14

Coffee, '"No Soul to Damn, no Body to kick": an Unscandalised Inquiry into the Problem of Corporate Punishment' (1981) 79 Mich L Rev 386

Coggans, 'The *in camera* rule: time for change?' (2001) 4 (1) IJFL 1

Collins, A, 'Community Law as a Source of Rights and Remedies in the Irish Legal Order' (1994) 2 IJEL 173

Collins, A, 'Freedom through Security? The Third Pillar' (1998) 7 IJEL 36

Conroy, B and Gunning, P, 'Introducing the Irish Sentencing Information System' [2009] 11(1) *Courts Service News* 15

Conte, F, 'Reinforcing Democracy, Sovereignty and Union Efficacy: Supremacy and Subsidiarity in the European Union' (2004) 26 DULJ 1

Coonon, 'The Role of Judicial Research Assistants in Supporting the Decision Making Role of the Irish Judiciary' [2006] 6(1) *Judicial Studies Institute Journal* 171

Coppal, J and O'Neill, A, 'The European Court of Justice: Taking Rights Seriously' (1992) 29 CMLRev 669

Coulter, C, 'The Child Care Act in Practice: Some Emerging Issues from the Child Care Law Reporting Project' (2014) 17(2) IJFL 35

Cousins, M, 'Access to the Courts' (1992) 14 DULJ (ns) 51

Cousins, M, 'Equal Treatment in Social Welfare: The final round?' (1995) 4 IJEL 195

Cox, N, 'Dismissal of an Action on the Grounds of Delay or Want of Prosecutions: Recent Developments' (2012) 19(1) DULJ 121

Craig, P, 'The Treaty of Lisbon: Process, Architecture and Substance' (2008) 33 Eur L Rev 137

Cross, R, 'The *Ratio Decidendi* and a Plurality of Speeches in the House of Lords' (1977) 93 LQR 378

Crowe, R, 'The Schengen Acquis in Police Cooperation: Implementation in an Enlarged Europe' (2005) 3 *ERA Forum* 415

Crowe, R, 'The Treaty of Lisbon: A Revised Legal Framework for the Organisation and Functioning of the European Union' (2008) 9 *ERA Forum* 163

Curtin, D, 'Some Reflections on European Community Law in Ireland' (1989) 11 DULJ (ns) 207

Cusack, D, 'The Coroner's Court' (1995) 1 *Medico-Legal Journal of Ireland* 82

Dale, W, 'A London Particular' [1985] Stat LR 11

Daly, Y, 'Does the Buck Stop Here? An Examination of the Right to Pre-Trial Legal Advice in the Light of *O'Brien v DPP*' (2006) 28 DULJ 345

de Blacam, M, 'Children, Constitutional Rights and the Separation of Powers' (2002) 37 Ir Jur 113

De Burca, G, 'The Drafting of the European Union Charter of Fundamental Rights' (2001) 26 EL Rev 126

Delany, H, 'Joining Co-Defendants and Amici Curiae – Recent Developments' (2007) 25 ILT 237

Delany, H, 'The Obligation on the Courts to Deal with Cases within a "Reasonable Time"' (2004) 22 ILT 249

Delany, H, 'Regulation of the Supreme Court's Appellate Jurisdiction Must be Clear and Unambiguous' (2002) 20 ILT 73

Devlin, A, 'Law and Economics' 45 Ir Jur (ns) 165

Devlin, A, 'Questioning the Sole-Trader Rule in the Barrister Profession' (2009) 44(1) Irish Jurist 123

Dinan, D, 'Governance and Institutions 1999: Resignation, Reform and Renewal' *Journal of Common Market Studies Annual Review of the EU* 1999/2000

Dodd, D, 'The Interpretation Act 2005' (2006) 11(3) *Bar Review* 100

Dolding, L and Mullender, R, 'Tort Law, Incrementalism and the House of Lords' (1996) 47 NILQ 12

Donelan, E, 'The Role of the Parliamentary Draftsman in the Preparation of Legislation in Ireland' (1992) 14 DULJ 1

Donelan, E, 'The Role of the Office of the Parliamentary Draftsman in the Implementation of European Union Directives in Ireland' (1997) 18 Stat LR 1

Donlan, S and Kennedy, R, 'A Flood of Light? Comments on the Interpretation Act 2005' (2006) 6 JSIJ 92.

Donnelly, L, 'Towards Uniformity in Legal Citation in Ireland' (2007) 25 ILT 256

Dowrick, F, 'Precedent in Modern Irish Law' (1953) 69 LQR 25

Douglas-Scott, S, 'The Charter of Fundamental Rights as a Constitutional Document' (2004) *European Human Rights Law Review* 37

Dworkin, G, 'Devlin was Right: Law and the Enforcement of Morality' (1999) 40 Wm and Mary L Rev 927

Editorial, 'Renumbering the Treaties: Another Fine Mess' (1999) 24 ELRev 443

Editorial, 'Surfing the Statutes' (1998) 19 Stat LR v

Egan, A, 'The *In Camera* Rule: A Barrier to Transparency or a Necessity in Irish Family Law?' (2012) 15(3) IJFL 59

Emmert, F, '*Stare Decisis*: a Universally Misunderstood Idea' (2012) 6 *Legisprudence* 207

English, R, 'Forensic Immunity Post-Osman' (2001) 64 MLR 300

Ergun, CE, 'The EU Charter of Fundamental Rights: An Alternative to the European Convention on Human Rights' (2004) 8 *Mediterranean Journal of Human Rights* 91

Eriksen, E, 'Why a Charter of Fundamental Human Rights in the EU?' (2003) 16 *Ratio Juris* 352

Ervine, W, 'The Supreme Court, *Stare Decisis* and the Malicious Injuries Code' (1975) 10 Ir Jur (ns) 93

Fahey, E, 'Reconsidering the Merits of the 'Principles and Policies' Test: A Step Towards the Reform of Article 29.4.10° of the Constitution' (2006) 24 ILT 70

Fanning, R, 'Hard Case: Bad Law? The Supreme Court decision in *A v Governor of Arbour Hill Prison*' (2005) 40 Ir Jur 188

Fanning, R, 'Reflections on the legislative process following *Leontjava v Director of Public Prosecutions & Others*' (2004) 39 Ir Jur (ns) 286

Feenan, D, 'Judicial Appointments in Ireland in Comparative Perspective' (2008) 8(1) JSIJ 37

Fennelly, N, 'Pillar Talk: Fundamental Rights Protection in the European Union' (2008) 8 JSIJ 95

Fennelly, N, 'Reflections of an Irish Advocate General' (1996) 5 IJEL 5

Fennelly, N, 'The Area of "Freedom, Security and Justice" and the European Court of Justice – a Personal View' (2000) 49 ICLQ 1

Ferguson, P, 'Constructing a Criminal Code' (2009) Crim L Forum 139

Ferguson, 'Legislation' in Stair Memorial Encyclopedia of the Laws of Scotland (1987) Vol 22 par 224

Ferigo, M, 'The Charter of Fundamental Rights in the Work of the European Convention on the Future of the Union' (2005) 9 *Mediterranean Journal of Human Rights* 257

Fernandez, P and Ponzetto, G, '*Stare Decisis*: Rhetoric and Substance' (2012) 28 JLE&O 313

Ferola, L, 'The Fight against Organized Crime in Europe Building an Area of Freedom, Security and Justice in the EU' (2002) *International Journal of Legal Information* 53

Ferriter, C, 'The Irish Statute Book Database' (1999) 4(4) *Bar Review* 217

Finlay, T, 'Criminal Defence Advocacy' (1981) 1 ICLJ 1

Fottrell, D, 'Reporting to the UN Human Rights Committee – A Ruse by Any Other Name?' (2001) 19 ILT 61

Flynn, L, 'State Liability in Damages for Failure to Observe EC Law' (1996) 14 ILT 170

Fitzgerald, 'The Compo Culture', *Business and Finance*, 16 May 1996

Foster, L, 'Obstacles to Citation Reform' 2000(3) *The Journal of Information, Law and Technology (JILT)* http://elj.warwick.ac.uk/jilt/

Fottrell, D, 'Reporting to the UN Human Rights Committee – A Ruse by Any Other Name?' (2001) 19 ILT 61

Gallagher, P, 'The Treaty of Amsterdam and Fundamental Rights' (1998) 7 IJEL 21

Gavan Duffy, C, 'A Note on the Limitation of the Doctrine *Per Quod Servitium Amisit* and *Stare Decisis* in the Republic of Ireland' (1965) 14 ICLQ 1382

Greenberg, D, 'The Nature of Legislative Intention and Its Implications for Legislative Drafting' (2006) 27 Stat LR 15

Greer, D ,'Legal Services and the Poor in Ireland' (1969) 4 Ir Jur (ns) 270

Greer, D, 'The Development of the Civil Bill Procedure in Ireland' in McEldowney, J and O'Higgins, P, *The Common Law Tradition: Essays in Irish Legal History* Dublin, Irish Academic Press, 1990

Gwynn Morgan, D, 'Selection of Superior Court Judges' [2004] ILT 42

Harcourt, B, 'The Collapse of the Harm Principle' (1999) 90 J Crim L & Criminology 109

Harlow, C, '"Public" and "Private" Law: Definition without Distinction' (1980) 43 MLR 1

Harrison, R, 'The Statutes on LEXIS' [1982] Stat LR 51

Hartley, T, 'The Constitutional Foundations of the European Union' (2001) 117 LQR 225

Henchy, S, 'Precedent in the Irish Supreme Court' (1962) 25 MLR 544

Heuston, R, '*Donoghue v Stevenson* in Retrospect' (1957) 20 MLR 1

Hogan, G, 'Criminal Appeals – a New Departure' (1983) 5 DULJ (ns) 254

Hogan, G, 'A Note on the Imposition of Duties Act 1957' (1985) 7 DULJ 134

Hogan, G, 'Directive Principles, Socio-Economic Rights and the Constitution' (2001) 36 Ir Jur (ns) 174

Hogan, G, 'The Legal Status of Administrative Rules and Circulars' (1987) 22 Ir Jur (ns) 194

Hogan, G, 'Precedent and Statutory Interpretation' (1989) 11 DULJ (ns) 196

Hogan, G, 'The Implementation of European Union Law in Ireland: the *Meagher* case and the Democratic Deficit' (1994) 3 IJEL 190

Hogan, G, 'Unenumerated Personal Rights: *Ryan's* Case Re-Evaluated' (1990–1992) 25–27 Ir Jur (ns) 95

Hogan, G, 'The European Convention on Human Rights Act 2003' (2006) 12(3) Eur PL 331.

Hogan, G, 'The Value of Declarations of Incompability and the Rule of Avoidance' [2006] DULJ 408

Horgan, R, Shannon, G and Gallagher, B, 'Reform of the *In Camera* Rule – A Sensitive Balancing Act' (2002) *Bar Review* 278

Hudson, H, 'The Scope of Computers' [1983] Stat LR 35

Humphreys, R, 'Reflections on the Role and Functioning of the Supreme Court' (1990) 12 DULJ (ns) 127

Humphreys, R, 'Annotation to the Irish Land Commission (Dissolution) Act 1992' *Irish Current Law Statutes Annotated* (1992)

Hunt, B, 'A Matter of Interpretation' (2006) 100 *Law Society Gazette* 32

Hunt, B, 'Office of the Parliamentary Draftsman: A Secret History' (2004) 9 *Bar Review* 167

Hunt, B, 'Plain Language: The End of the Road for Recondite Legislation?' (2001) 7 *Bar Review* 47

Hurst, 'The Problem of the Elderly Statute' (1983) 3 LS 21

Iles, W, 'The Responsibilities of the New Zealand Legislative Advisory Committee' (1992) 13 Stat LR 11

Jenkins, J, '*Pepper v Hart*: A Draftsman's Perspective' [1994] Stat LR 23

Johnson, W, 'The First Adventure of the Common Law' (1920) 36 LQR 9

Johnston, W, 'The English Legislature and the Irish Courts' (1924) 40 LQR 91

Jordan, G, 'Grey Papers' (1977) 48 *Political Quarterly* 30

Joseph, P, 'Delegated Legislation in New Zealand' (1997) 18 Stat LR 85

Keane, R, 'The Irish Courts System in the Twenty-first Century: Planning for the Future' (2001) 6 *Bar Review* 321

Keating, A and Lowry, A, 'Pacifying Turbulent Water: The Case for Greater Clarity in Constitutional Standing Rules' (2003) 21 ILT 166, 183

Keating, A and Lowry, A, 'The Supreme Court's Approach to Affirmative Duties' [2003] 21 ILT 103 and [2003] 21 ILT 118

Kelleher, D, 'The Courts and Court Officers Act 1995 – The Main Provisions' (1996) 14 ILT 18

Kelly, P, 'The Commercial Court' (2004) 9(1) *Bar Review* 4

Kelly, JM, 'Hidden Treasure and the Constitution' (1988) 10 DULJ (ns) 5

Kelly, JM, 'The Constitution: Law and Manifesto', in Litton, F (ed), *The Constitution of Ireland, 1937–1987* Dublin, Institute of Public Administration, 1988

Kennedy, R, 'Extra Judicial Comments by Judges' (2005) JSIJ 5 (1) 199

Kenny, C, 'The Exclusion of Catholics from the Legal Profession in Ireland, 1537–1829' (1987) 25(100) Ir Hist Stud 337

Keogh, D, 'The Constitutional Revolution: An Analysis of the Making of the Constitution', in Litton, F (ed), *The Constitution of Ireland 1937–1987* Dublin, Institute of Public Administration, 1988

Kerr, A, 'Is there Anybody Out There Listening?' (1983) 1 ILT 100

Kerr, A, 'Annotation to the Courts Act 1988' *Irish Current Law Statutes Annotated* (1988)

Kiiver, P, 'The Treaty of Lisbon, the National Parliaments and the Principle of Subsidiarity' (2008) 15 *Maastricht Journal of European and Comparative Law* 77

Kirwan, B, '*Locus Standi* and Representative Bodies' (2005) 23 ILT 98.

Kolts, 'Observations on the Proposed New Approach to Legislative Drafting in Common Law Countries' [1980] Stat LR 144

Lambert, 'Cues, Cameras and Courtroom Actors: Resisting the Temptation of Courtroom Television Cameras' (1996) 14 ILT 13

Lambert, 'Free Press – Fair Trial: a Comment' (1997) 15 ILT 176

Lamond, G, 'Do Precedents Create Rules?' (2005) 11 *Legal Theory* 1

Lawlor, M, 'Anachronistic Seanad Should be Abolished' (2013) 107 *Law Society Gazette* 18

Leith, PG, 'Legal Citations' 2000(3), *The Journal of Information, Law and Technology (JILT)* http://elj.warwick.ac.uk/jilt/

Lester of Herne Hill, Lord, '*Pepper v Hart* Revisited' [1994] Stat LR 10

Lodge, D, 'Sustaining Freedom, Security and Justice: From Terrorism to Immigration' (2002) 24 Liverpool LR 41

Loftus, C, 'Establishment of office of Chief Prosecution Solicitor' (2002) *Bar Review* 348

Lyall, A, 'The Irish House of Lords as a Judicial Body 1783–1800' (1993–1995) 28-30 Ir Jur (ns) 314

Lyell, N, '*Pepper v Hart*: The Government Perspective' [1994] Stat LR 1

Lysaght, C, 'Competition Authority Report on Solicitors and Barristers' (2008) 8(2) JSIJ 159

Macklem, T, 'Entrenching Bills of Rights' (2006) 26 OJLS 197

Maddox, N, 'Legislation by Delegation: The Principles and Policies Test in Irish Law' (2004) 22 ILT 293

Maguire, C, 'The Personal Injuries Assessment Board' [2001] 7(1) *Bar Review* 39

Maitland, FW, 'Notes and Documents: The Introduction of English Law into Ireland' (1889) 4 *English Historical Review* 516

Maganza, G, 'The Lisbon Treaty: A Brief Outline' (2008) 31 *Fordham International Law Journal* 1603

Mahoney, P, 'The Charter of Fundamental Rights of the European Union and the European Convention on Human Rights from the Perspective of the European Convention' (2002) 23 *Human Rights Law Journal* 300

Marmor, A, 'Should Like Cases be Treated Alike?' (2005) 11 *Legal Theory* 27

McAleese, 'Reporting Restrictions' *Gazette, Law Society of Ireland*, May 2000

McCarthy, N, 'Una Voce Poco Fa', in O'Reilly, J (ed), *Human Rights and Constitutional Law* Dublin, Round Hall Press, 1992

McCutcheon, JP, 'The Irish Supreme Court, European Political Co-operation and the Single European Act' [1988/2] LIEI 93

McCutcheon, JP, 'The Legal System', in Keatinge, P (ed) *Ireland and EC Membership Evaluated* London, Pinter, 1991

McDermott, PA and Murphy, MW, 'No Revolution: The Impact of the ECHR Act 2003 on Irish Criminal Law' (2008) 15(1) DULJ 1

McEldowney, J and O'Higgins, P, 'Irish Legal History and the Nineteenth Century' in McEldowney, J and O'Higgins, P, *The Common Law Tradition: Essays in Irish Legal History* Dublin, Irish Academic Press, 1990

Macdonald, R, 'Plain English in the Law: A New Model for the 21st Century' (2004) 30 *Commonwealth Law Bulletin* 922

MacEochaidh, C, 'Eurowatch' (The New Establishment Directive) (1998) 3 *Bar Review* 193

McMahon, B, 'The Law Relating to Contraception in Ireland', in Clarke, D (ed), *Morality and the Law* Dublin, RTE/Mercier Press 1982

Megarry, R, 'Administrative Quasi-legislation' (1944) 60 LQR 125

Miers, D, 'Review of Stone, *Precedent and Law* (Butterworths, 1985)' (1986) 6 LS 331

Miers, D, 'Legislation, Linguistic Adequacy and Public Policy' [1986] Stat LR 90

Miers, D, 'Taxing Perks and Interpreting Statutes: *Pepper v Hart*' (1993) 56 MLR 695

Mee, M, 'The Changing Nature of the Presidency: The President and the Government should be Friends' (1996) 14 ILT 2, 30

Millet, T, 'A Comparison of British and French Legislative Drafting (with particular reference to their respective Nationality Law)' [1986] Stat LR 130

Monar, J, 'Judicial and Home Affairs in the Treaty of Amsterdam; Reform at the Price of Fragmentation' (1998) 23 EL Rev 320

Montrose, J, 'The Ratio Decidendi of a Case' (1957) 20 MLR 587

Moran, F, 'The Migration of the Common Law: Republic of Ireland' (1960) 76 LQR 69

Morgan, D, 'Constitutional Interpretation: Three Cautionary Tales' (1988) 10 DULJ (ns) 24

Murphy, F, 'The Unfair Contract Terms Regulations 1995: A red card for the State' (1995) 13 ILT (ns) 156

Murphy, J, 'Moral Reasons and the Limitation of Liberty' (1999) 40 Wm and Mary L Rev 947

Murphy, R, 'The Permanent International Criminal Court – Solving the Missing Link in the International Legal System?' (2000) 18 ILT 319

Morris, D, 'The Road to Brussels – Two Routes Compared' [1988] Stat LR 33

Muchlinski, P, 'Corporations in International Litigation: Problems of Jurisdiction and the United Kingdom Asbestos Cases (2001) 50 ICLQ 1

Murdoch, H, 'Bell, Book and Candle' (December 2004) *Law Society Gazette* 8

Murphy, R and Wills, S, 'The European Convention on Human Rights and Irish Incorporation: Adopting a Minimalist Approach: Part I' (2001) 7 *Bar Review* 41

Murphy, R and Wills, S, 'The European Convention on Human Rights and Irish Incorporation: Adopting a Minimalist Approach: Part II' (2001) 7 *Bar Review* 41

Newark, F, 'The Bringing of English Law to Ireland' (1972) 23 NILQ 1

Ní Raifeartaigh, U, 'The European Convention on Human Rights and the Irish Criminal Justice System' (2001) 7 *Bar Review* 111

Noctor, C, 'The Presence of McKenzie Friends in *in Camera* Proceedings' (1999) 17 ILT 214

Nolan, D, 'The Personal Injuries Assessment Board Act 2003: A Critical Analysis' (2004) 9(1) *Bar Review* 7

O'Boyle, M, 'The Reconstruction of the Strasbourg Human Rights System' (1992) 14 DULJ (ns) 41

O'Dowd, J, 'Judges in Whose Cause? The Irish Bench after the Judges' Pay Referendum' (2012) 47(2) Irish Jurist 102

O'Dwyer, C, 'Procedures for Personal Injuries Claims' [2004] 9(6) *Bar Review* 199

O'Flaherty, M, 'Implementation of the International Covenant on Civil and Political Rights – Ireland before the Human Rights Committee' (1993) 11 ILT 225

O'Halloran, S, 'Barristers' Immunity in the Twenty First Century' (2008) 26 ILT 304

O'Hanlon, R, 'Natural Rights and the Irish Constitution' (1993) 11 ILT 8

O'Mahony, P, 'The Proposed Constitutional Referendum on Bail: An Unholy Grail?' (1995) 13 ILT 234

O'Neill, A, 'The Effect of a Finding that Legislation is Unconstitutional: The Approach of the Irish Supreme Court' (2007) 36 *Common Law World Review* 220

Osborough, WN, 'The Irish Legal System, 1796–1877' in Costello, C (ed), *The Four Courts: 200 Years* Dublin, Incorporated Council of Law Reporting for Ireland, 1996

Osborough, WN, 'Introduction' *The Irish Statutes 1310–1800* rev edn Dublin, Round Hall Press, 1995

Peers, S, 'The European Union and Criminal Law: An Overview' (2002) 12 ICLJ 2

Petersson, S, 'Gender Neutral Drafting: Historical Perspective' (1998) 19 Stat LR 93

Phelan, D, 'Right to Life of the Unborn v Promotion of Trade in Services: The European Court of Justice and the Normative Shaping of the European Union' (1992) 55 MLR 670

Phelan, S, 'The Civil Legal Aid Bill 1995: A Critique' (1995) 13 ILT 109

Phillips, J, 'The Concurrence of Remedies in Contract and Tort' (1977) 12 Ir Jur (ns) 234

Posner, R, 'Law and Economics in Common-Law, Civil-Law and Developing Nations' (2004) 17 Ratio Juris 166.

Pye, S, 'Appeals to the Supreme Court in Planning Compensation Cases' (1987) 5 ILT 252

Pugsley, D, 'London Tramways (1898)' (1996) 17 J Leg Hist 172

Pugsley, D 'Precedent in the Court of Appeal' (1983) 2 CJQ 48

Quinn, 'F, The Role of the Seanad in the Legislative Process' (2006) 24 ILT 46

Quinn, P, 'Keynote Address to 1993 Conference of Irish Association of Law Teachers' (1994) 12 ILT 18

Rawlings, R, 'Quasi-Legislative Devolution: Powers and Principles' (2001) 52 NILQ 54

Regan, E, 'The Treaty of Nice' (2001) 6 *Bar Review* 205

Power, V, 'Parliamentary History as an Aid to Statutory Interpretation' [1984] Stat LR 38

Riley, A, 'A Human Rights Charter for the European Union?' September 2000 Euro CL xi

Riley, A, 'The Nice Court Reforms: A Major Gain' February 2001 Euro CL xi

Robinson, M, 'Irish Parliamentary Scrutiny of European Community Legislation' (1979) 16 CMLRev 9

Rothwell, 'Lord Phillips attacks expensive litigation and pledges to resist politicians' (2005) *Law Society Gazette*, 13 October

Rozenberg, P, 'Referencing and Citation of Internet Resources – "The Truth is out There"' 2000(1) *The Journal of Information, Law and Technology (JILT)* http://elj.warwick.ac.uk/jilt/

Ruane, B, 'The Separation of Powers and the Grant of Mandatory Orders to Enforce Constitutional Rights' [2000] 5 *Bar Review* 416

Ruane, B, 'Proposed Abolition of the Seanad and the Implications of Judicial Independence' (2013) 18 BR 46

Ryan, B, 'The Ian Paisley Question: Irish Citizenship and Northern Ireland' (2003) 10(1) DULJ 145

Ryan, D and Ryan, R, 'A Bar to Recovery? Barristers, Public Policy, and Immunity from Suit' [2005] 10 (6) *Bar Review* 209

Samuels, A, 'Codes of Practice and Legislation' [1986] Stat LR 29

Samuels, A, 'Incorporating, Translating or Implementing European Union Law into UK Law' (1998) 19 Stat LR 80

Samuels, A, 'Statements of Purpose and Principle in British Statutes' (1998) 19 Stat LR 63

Sandford, 'Open Government: the Use of Green Papers' [1980] *British Tax Review* 351

Shaw, J and Monnet, J, 'Legal and Political Sources of the Treaty Establishing a Constitution for Europe' (2004) 55 NILQ 214

Sheehy, M, 'English Law in Medieval Ireland' (1960) 22 *Archivum Hibernicum* 167

Simon of Glaisdale, Lord and Webb, J 'Consolidation and Statute Law Reform' [1975] PL 285

Sinder, J, 'Irish Legal History: an Overview and Guide to the Sources' (2001) 93 *Law Library Journal* 231

Smith, J and Burns, P, '*Donoghue v Stevenson* – the Not So Golden Anniversary' (1983) 46 MLR 147

Stapleton, J, 'The Gist of Negligence' (1988) 104 LQR 213 and 389

Stewart, G, 'Legislative Drafting and the Marginal Note' (1995) 16 Stat LR 21

Steyn, J, '*Pepper v Hart*: A Re-examination' (2001) 21 OJLS 59

Stone, J, 'The Ratio of the Ratio Decidendi' (1959) 22 MLR 597

Tanner, E, 'Clear, Simple and Precise Legislative Drafting: Australian Guidelines Explicated Using an EC Directive' (2004) 25 Stat LR 223

Tanner, 'Clear, Simple, and Precise Legislative Drafting: How Does a European Community Directive Fare?' (2006) 27 Stat LR 150

Temple Lang, J and Gallagher, E, 'The Commission, the "Community Method," and the Smaller Member States' (2006) 29 *Fordham International Law Journal* 1009

Thomas, R, 'Plain English and the Law' [1985] Stat LR 139

Tillitson, J, 'The Nice Treaty: Some First Impressions' January 2001 Euro CL xi

Tomkin, D and Hanafin, P, 'Medical Treatment at Life's End: The Need for Legislation' (1995) 1 *Medico-Legal Journal of Ireland* 3

Tottenham, M, 'Justice Should be Seen to be Done – On Television' (2003) 21 ILT 138

Tudor, P, 'Secondary Legislation: Second Class or Crucial?' (2000) 21 Stat LR 149

Tunc, A, 'The not so Common Law of England and the United States, or, Precedent in England and in the United States, a field study by an outsider' (1984) 47 MLR 150

Turnbull, I, 'Legislative Drafting in Plain Language and Statements of General Principle' (1997) 18 Stat LR 21

Twomey, A, 'The Death of the Natural Law?' (1995) 13 ILT 270

Vogenauer, S, 'A Retreat from *Pepper v Hart*: A Reply to Lord Steyn' (2005) OJLS 629

von Bogdandy, A, 'The European Union as a Human Rights Organisation? Human Rights and the Core of the European Union' (2000) 37 CMLRev 1307

Waldron, J, 'The Core of the Case against Judicial Review' (2006) 115 Yale LR 1346

Walker, 'Europe's area of Freedom, Security and Justice' (2005) 16 King's College LJ 234

Walsh, B, 'The Constitution and Constitutional Rights', in Litton, F (ed), *The Constitution of Ireland, 1937–1987* Dublin, Institute of Public Administration Dublin, Institute of Public Administration, 1988

Walsh, D, 'Annotation to The Europol Act 1997' *Irish Current Law Statutes Annotated* (1997)

Walsh, D, 'Irish Parliamentary Scrutiny of EU Measures on the Free Movement of Persons: Going Through the Motions' (2005) 40 Ir Jur 261

Walsh, D, 'The Democratic Deficit in Criminal law and Criminal Justice in Title VI of the Treaty on European Union' (2002) 12 ICLJ 7

Walsh, K, 'Privacy's New Paradigm: The Rise and Reform of the *In Camera* Rule', (2005) 8(1) IJFL 10

Walsh, I, 'Precedent in the Former Irish Superior Courts' (2005) 40 IR Jur (ns) 160

Ward, T, 'Independence, Accountability and the Irish Judiciary' (2008) 8(1) JSIJ 1

Watson-Brown, A, 'Defining Plain English as an Aid to Legal Drafting' (2009) 30 Stat LR 85

Watson-Brown, A, 'In Search of Plain English: The Holy Grail or Mythical Excalibur of Legislative Drafting' (2012) 33 Stat LR 7

Whelan, A, 'Annotation to the European Communities (Amendment) Act 1993' *Irish Current Law Statutes Annotated* (1993)

Whelan, N, 'House of a Different Colour' (2013) 107 *Law Society Gazette* 38

Whyte, G, 'And Justice for Some' (1984) 6 DULJ (ns) 88

Whyte, G, 'Constitutional Adjudication, Ideology and Access to the Courts', in Whelan, A (ed), *Law and Liberty in Ireland* Dublin, Oak Tree Press, 1993

Whyte, G, 'The Future of Civil Legal Aid in Ireland' (2005) 10 (4) *Bar Review* 111

Whyte, G, 'The Role of the Supreme Court in our Democracy: A Response to Mr Justice Hardiman' (2006) 13(1) DULJ 1

Wilson, 'The Complexity of Statutes' (1974) 37 MLR 497

Young, AL, 'The Charter, Constitution and Human Rights is this the Beginning or the End of Human Rights Protections by Community Law?' (2005) 11 *European Public Law* 219

Official Publications

European Commission for the Efficiency of Justice, *European Judicial Systems Edition 2008 (2006): Efficiency and Quality of Justice* Council of Europe, 2008

Eurostat, *Statistics in Focus: Economy and Finance*, 1996, No 1 (published by the Commission of the European Communities)

Ireland, All Party Oireachtas Committee on the Constitution, *Fourth Progress Report: The Courts and the Judiciary* (Pn 7831) Dublin, Stationery Office, 1999

Ireland, Attorney General, *The Law of Nullity in Ireland* (Prl 5626) Dublin, Stationery Office, 1976

Ireland, Central Statistics Office *Statistical Abstracts 1966 1976, 1982-85, 1986, 1995* (all published by the Stationery Office, Dublin)

Ireland, Commission of Inquiry on Safety, Health and Welfare at Work, *Report of the Commission of Inquiry on Safety, Health and Welfare at Work* (Pl 1868) Dublin, Stationery Office, 1983

Ireland, Committee on Civil Legal Aid and Advice, *Committee on Civil Legal Aid and Advice: Report to Minister for Justice* (Prl 6862) Dublin, Stationery Office, 1977

Ireland, Committee on Court Practice and Procedure, *Eleventh Interim Report of the Committee on Court Practice and Procedure* Dublin, Stationery Office, 1970

Ireland, Committee on Court Practice and Procedure, 29th Interim Report Inquiry to Examine All Aspects of Practice and Procedure Relating to Personal Injuries Litigation Dublin, Stationery Office, 2004

Ireland, Committee on Court Practice and Procedure, *Seventeenth Interim Report of the Committee on Court Practice and Procedure: Court Fees* (Prl 2699) Dublin, Stationery Office, 1972

Ireland, Committee on Court Practice and Procedure, *Seventh Interim Report of the Committee on Court Practice and Procedure* Dublin, Stationery Office, 1966

Ireland, Committee on Court Practice and Procedure, *Sixteenth Interim Report of the Committee on Court Practice and Procedure* Dublin, Stationery Office, 1972

Ireland, Committee on Court Practice and Procedure, *Sixth Interim Report of the Committee on Court Practice and Procedure* Dublin Stationery Office, 1966

Ireland, Committee on Court Practice and Procedure, *Thirteenth Interim Report of the Committee on Court Practice and Procedure* Dublin, Stationery Office, 1971

Ireland, Committee on Court Practice and Procedure, *Twenty-fourth Report of the Committee on Court Practice and Procedure: Preliminary Examination of Indictable Offences* Dublin, Stationery Office, 1997

Ireland, Committee on Court Practice and Procedure, *Twenty-Seventh Interim Report, A Commercial Court in Ireland* Dublin, Stationery Office, 2003

Ireland, Committee to Enquire into Certain Aspects of Criminal Procedure, *Report of the Committee to Enquire into Certain Aspects of Criminal Procedure* Dublin, Stationery Office, 1990

Ireland, Committee on Judicial Conduct and Ethics, *Report* (Pn 9449) Dublin, Stationery Office, 2000

Ireland, Committee on the Constitution, *Report of the Committee on the Constitution* (Pr 9817) Dublin, Stationery Office, 1967

Ireland, Committee on Public Safety and Crowd Control, *Report of the Committee on Public Safety and Crowd Control* (Pl 7107) Dublin, Stationery Office, 1990

Ireland, Committee to Review the Offences Against the State Acts 1939–1998 and Related Matters, *Report of the Committee to Review the Offences Against the State Acts 1939–1998 and Related Matters* Dublin, Stationery Office, 2002

Ireland, Constitution Review Group, *Report of the Constitution Review Group* (Pn 2632) Dublin, Constitution Review Group, 1996

Ireland, Criminal Legal Aid Review Committee, *First Report of the Criminal Legal Aid Review Committee* (2000) www.justice.ie

Ireland, Dáil Éireann, *Standing Orders Relative to Public Business* Dublin, Stationery Office, 1997

Ireland, Competition Authority, *Study of Competition in Legal Services: Preliminary Report* (February 2005)

Ireland, Competition Authority, *Competition in Professional Services: Solicitors and Barristers* (December 2006)

Ireland, Comptroller and Auditor General, *Special Report 63: Tribunals of Inquiry* (December 2008)

Ireland, Department of Education and Science, *Rules and Programme for Secondary Schools 1987/88 to 1994/95* (Pn 0983) Dublin, Stationery Office

Ireland, Department of Education, *Guidelines on Countering Bullying Behaviour in Primary and Post-Primary Schools* Dublin, Stationery Office, 1993

Ireland, Department of Education, *Procedures for Dealing with Allegations or Suspicions of Child Abuse* (M41/92)

Ireland, Department of Enterprise, Trade and Employment, *Code of Practice: Grievance and Disciplinary Procedures* Dublin, 2002

Ireland, Department of Enterprise, Trade and Employment, *Final Report of the Motor Insurance Advisory Board* (2002)

Ireland, Department of Enterprise, Trade and Employment *Second Report of the Special Working Group on Personal Injury Compensation* (2001) www.entemp.ie/

Ireland, Department of Finance, McCarthy, *Report of the Special Group on Public Service Numbers and Expenditure Programmes* Dublin, Department of Finance, 2009

Ireland, Department of Health, *A New Mental Health Act* (Pn 1824) Dublin, Stationery Office, 1995

Ireland, Department of Justice, Equality and Law Reform, *Working Together: an Integrated Approach to Victims of Crime* Dublin, Stationery Office, 1998

Ireland, Department of Justice, *Programme of Law Reform* (Pr 6379) Dublin, Stationery Office, 1962

Ireland, Department of Justice, Equality and Law Reform, *Report of Legal Costs Working Group* (2005)

Ireland, Department of Justice, Equality and Law Reform, *Report of the Legal Costs Implementation Advisory Group* (Pn A7/0027) 2006

Ireland, Department of Justice, Equality and Law Reform, *Criminal Legal Aid Review Committee: Final Report* (2002)

Ireland, Department of Justice, *Equality and Law Reform, Redmond and Nexus Research Co-operative, Imprisonment for Fine Default and Civil Debt: Report to the Department of Justice, Equality and Law Reform* (2002)

Ireland, Department of Justice, *Review of the Coroner Service* (2000) www.justice.ie

Ireland, Department of Justice, *Scheme of Civil Legal Aid and Advice* (Prl 8543) Dublin, Stationery Office, 1979

Ireland, Department of Justice, *Towards Gender Parity in Decision-Making* (2013) www.justice.ie

Ireland, Department of Labour, *Code of Practice: Dispute Procedures, including Procedures in Essential Services* (1992)

Ireland, Department of the Taoiseach, *Cabinet Handbook* Dublin, Stationery Office, 1998

Ireland, Director of Public Prosecutions, *Annual Report of the Director of Public Prosecutions 1999* Dublin, Stationery Office, 2000

Ireland, Director of Public Prosecutions, *Annual Report of the Office of the Director of Public Prosecutions 2013* Dublin, www.dppireland.ie, 2014

Ireland, Director of Public Prosecutions, *Strategy Statement of the DPP 2013–2015* Dublin, www.dppireland.ie, 2013

Ireland, Fair Trade Commission, *Report of Study of Restrictive Practices in the Legal Profession* Dublin, Stationery Office, 1990

Ireland, *Green Paper on Abortion* Dublin, Stationery Office, 1999

Ireland, Health and Safety Authority, *Code of Practice for Employers and Employees on the Prevention and Resolution of Bullying at Work* Dublin, Health and Safety Authority, 2007

Ireland, Law Reform Commission, *Annual Report 2011*, Dublin, Law Reform Commission, 2012

Ireland, Law Reform Commission, *The Court Poor Box: Probation of Offenders* (LRC 75–2005) Dublin, Law Reform Commission, 2005

Ireland, Law Reform Commission, *Report on Prosecution Appeals and Pre-Trial Hearings* (LRC 81–2006) Dublin, Law Reform Commission, 2006

Ireland, Law Reform Commission, *Consultation Paper on a Classified List of Legislation in Ireland* (LRC 62–2010) Dublin, Law Reform Commission, 2010

Ireland, Law Reform Commission, *Consultation Paper on Alternative Dispute Resolution* (LRC CP 50–2008) Dublin, Law Reform Commission, 2008

Ireland, Law Reform Commission, *Consultation Paper on the Consolidation and Reform of the Courts Acts* (LRC CP 46–2007) Dublin, Law Reform Commission, 2007

Ireland, Law Reform Commission, *Consultation Paper on Prosecution Appeals in Cases brought on Indictment* (LRC CP 19–2002) Dublin, Law Reform Commission, 2002

Ireland, Law Reform Commission, *Consultation Paper on Public Inquiries Including Tribunals of Inquiry* (LRC CP 22–2003) Dublin, Law Reform Commission, 2003

Ireland, Law Reform Commission, *Consultation Paper on Statutory Drafting and Interpretation* (CP14–1999) Dublin, Law Reform Commission, 1999

Ireland, Law Reform Commission, *Fourth Programme of Law Reform* (LRC 110–2013) Dublin, Law Reform Commission, 2013

Ireland, Law Reform Commission, *Judicial Review of Administrative Action: The Problem of Remedies* Working Paper No 8–1979 Dublin Law Reform Commission, 1979

Ireland, Law Reform Commission, *Report on Alternative Dispute Resolution: Mediation and Conciliation* (LRC CP 98–2010) Dublin, Law Reform Commission, 2010

Ireland, Law Reform Commission, *Report on Child Sexual Abuse* (LRC 32–1990) Dublin, Law Reform Commission, 1990

Ireland, Law Reform Commission, *Report on Consolidation and Reform of the Courts Acts* (LRC 97–2010) Dublin, Law Reform Commission, 2010

Ireland, Law Reform Commission, *Report on Contempt of Court* (LRC 47–1994) Dublin, Law Reform Commission, 1994

Ireland, Law Reform Commission, *Report on Family Courts* (LRC52–1996) Dublin, Law Reform Commission, 1996

Ireland, Law Reform Commission, *Report on Indexation of Fines* (LRC 37–1991) Dublin, Law Reform Commission, 1991

Ireland, Law Reform Commission, *Report on Judicial Review Procedure* (LRC 71–2004) Dublin, Law Reform Commission, 2004

Ireland, Law Reform Commission, *Report on Jury Service* (LRC 107–2013) Dublin, Law Reform Commission, 2013

Ireland, Law Reform Commission, *Report on Legislation Directory* (LRC 102–2010) Dublin, Law Reform Commission, 2010

Ireland, Law Reform Commission, *Report on Limitation of Actions* (LRC 104–2011) Dublin, Law Reform Commission, 2011

Ireland, Law Reform Commission, *Report on Mandatory Sentences* (LRC 108–2013) Dublin, Law Reform Commission, 2013

Ireland, Law Reform Commission, *Report on Multi Party Litigation* (LRC 76–2005) Dublin, Law Reform Commission, 2005

Ireland, Law Reform Commission, *Report on Non-Fatal Offences Against the Person* (LRC 45–1994) Dublin, Law Reform Commission, 1994

Ireland, Law Reform Commission, *Report on Nullity in Marriage* (LRC 9–1984) Dublin, Law Reform Commission, 1984

Ireland, Law Reform Commission, *Report on Oaths and Affirmations* (LRC 34–1990) Dublin, Law Reform Commission, 1990

Ireland, Law Reform Commission, *Report on Personal Debt Management and Debt Enforcement* (LRC 100–2010) Dublin, Law Reform Commission, 2010

Ireland, Law Reform Commission, *Report on Public Inquiries Including Tribunals of Inquiry* (LRC 73–2005) Dublin, Law Reform Commission, 2005

Ireland, Law Reform Commission, *Report on Rape and Allied Offences* (LRC 24–1988) Dublin, Law Reform Commission, 1988

Ireland, Law Reform Commission, *Report on Receiving Stolen Property* (LRC 23–1989) Dublin, Law Reform Commission, 1989

Ireland, Law Reform Commission, *Report on Statute Law Restatement* (LRC 91–2008) Dublin, Law Reform Commission, 2008

Ireland, Law Reform Commission, *Report on Statutory Drafting and Interpretation* (LRC61–2000) Dublin, Law Reform Commission, 2000

Ireland, Law Reform Commission, *Report on Vulnerable Adults and the Law* (LRC 83–2006) Dublin, Law Reform Commission, 2006

Ireland, Law Reform Commission, *Report on the Establishment of a DNA Database* (LRC 78–2005) Dublin, Law Reform Commission, 2005

Ireland, Law Reform Commission, *Report on the Implementation of the Hague Convention on Protection of Children and Co-operation in respect of Intercountry Adoption, 1993* (LRC 58–1998) Dublin, Law Reform Commission, 1998

Ireland, Law Reform Commission, *Report on the Law Relating to Dishonesty* (LRC 43–1992) Dublin, Law Reform Commission, 1992

Ireland, Law Reform Commission, *Report on the Rule against Hearsay in Civil Cases* (LRC 25–1988) Dublin, Law Reform Commission, 1988

Ireland, Law Reform Commission, Report on the Statute of Limitations: Claims in respect of Latent Personal Injuries (LRC 21–1987)

Ireland, Law Reform Commission Law Reform Commission, *Third Programme of Law Reform 20082014* (LRC 86–2007) Dublin, Law Reform Commission, 2007

Ireland, Legal Aid Board, *Annual Report of the Legal Aid Board 1999* Dublin, 2000

Ireland, Ministerial Policy Directive No 1 of 1991 (Pl 7936), *Iris Oifigiúil*, 22 March 1991

Ireland, National Authority for Occupational Safety and Health, *Annual Report of the National Authority for Occupational Safety and Health 1994* Dublin, National Authority for Occupational Safety and Health, 1995

Ireland, Office of the Director of Public Prosecutions, *Report on Prosecution Policy on the Giving of Reasons for Decisions* Dublin, Office of the Director of Public Prosecutions, 2008

Ireland, Office of the Ombudsman, *Annual Report of the Ombudsman 1995* (Pn 2590) Dublin, Stationery Office, 1996

Ireland, Office of the Ombudsman, *Annual Report of the Ombudsman 2000* www.gov.ie/en/publications/AnnualReports/AnnualReportof theOmbudsman2000

Ireland, Oireachtas, Joint Committee on the Secondary Legislation of the European Communities, *Eleventh Report* (Pr 4669)

Ireland, Oireachtas, Public Accounts Committee, *Final Report of Sub-Commitee on Certain Revenue Matters: Parliamentary Inquiry into DIRT* 2001

Ireland, Oireachtas, All-Party Committee on the Constitution, *Fourth Progress Report of the All-Party Oireachtas Committee on the Constitution: The Courts and the Judiciary* Dublin, Stationery Office, 1999

Ireland, Oireachtas, Joint Committee on the Secondary Legislation of the European Communities, *Second Report of First Oireachtas Joint Committee on the Secondary Legislation of the European Communities* (Prl 3841)

Ireland, Oireachtas, Joint Committee on the Secondary Legislation of the European Communities, *Seventh Report of the Sixth Oireachtas Joint Committee on the Secondary Legislation of the European Communities*

Ireland, Oireachtas, Joint Committee on the Secondary Legislation of the European Communities, *Thirtieth Report of the First Oireachtas Joint Committee on the Secondary Legislation of the European Communities* (Prl 5419)

Ireland, Oireachtas, *Report of the Sub-Committee on Legislation and Security* (Pn 1478) 1995

Ireland, Oireachtas, *Select Committee on Legislation and Security*, L5, No 11, 7 December 1995

Ireland, Public Prosecution System, Study Group, *Report of the Public Prosecution System Study Group* 1997 www.gov.ie/ag

Ireland, *Report of the Department of Justice, Equality and Law Reform Arising from the Early Release from Prison of Philip Sheedy*, 1999

Ireland, *Report of the Judiciary Committee* 1923

Ireland, *Report on the role of the judiciary* prepared by the then Chief Justice, Hamilton CJ, 14 April 1999

Ireland, Review Group of the Law Offices of the State, *Report of the Review Group on the Law Offices of the State* (1997)

Ireland, *Rules of the Road* Dublin, Stationery Office, 1992

Ireland, *Scheme of Compensation for Personal Injuries Criminally Inflicted* (Prl 3658) Dublin, Stationery Office, 1974

Ireland, Seanad Éireann, *Standing Orders Relative to Public Business* Dublin, Stationery Office, 1996

Ireland, *Treaty of Nice White Paper* (Pn 9544) Dublin, Stationery Office, 2001

Ireland, Tribunal of Inquiry, *Report of the Tribunal of Inquiry into 'The Kerry Babies Case'* (Pl 3514) Dublin, Stationery Office, 1985

Ireland, Tribunal of Inquiry, *Report of the Tribunal of Inquiry into Payments to Politicians (Dunnes Stores)* (Pn 4199) Dublin Stationery Office, 1997

Ireland, Tribunal of Inquiry, *Report of the Tribunal of Inquiry into the Beef Processing Industry* (Pn 1007) Dublin, Stationery Office, 1994

Ireland, Tribunal of Inquiry, *Report of the Tribunal of Inquiry into the Blood Transfusion Service Board* (Pn 3695) Dublin, Stationery Office, 1997

Ireland, Tribunal of Inquiry, *Report of the Tribunal of Inquiry on the Fire at the Stardust, Artane*, Dublin (Pl 853) Dublin Stationery Office, 1982

Ireland, Tribunal of Inquiry, *Report on the Disaster at Whiddy Island, Bantry, Co Cork* (Prl 8911) Dublin, Stationery Office, 1980

Ireland, Working Group on a Courts Commission, *First Report: Management and Financing of the Courts* (Pn 2690), Dublin, Stationery Office, 1996

Ireland, Working Group on a Courts Commission, *Second Report of the Working Group on a Courts Commission: Case Management and Court Management* (Pn 3070) Dublin, Stationery Office, 1996

Ireland, Working Group on a Courts Commission, *Sixth Report: Conclusion with Summary* (Pn 2690) Dublin, Stationery Office, 1999

Ireland, Working Group on a Courts Commission, *Third Report: Towards the Courts Service* (Pn 3273) Dublin, Stationery Office, 1996

Ireland, Working Group on a Courts Commission, *Working Paper: Conference on Case Management* (1997) www.courts.ie

Ireland, Working Group on the Jurisdiction of the Courts, *The Criminal Jurisdiction of the Courts* Dublin, Stationery Office, 2003

Ireland, Working Group on Qualifications for Appointment as Judges of the High Court and Supreme Court, *Report of the Working Group on Qualifications for Appointment as Judges of the High Court and Supreme Court* Dublin, Stationery Office, 1999

Organisation of Economic Co-operation and Development, *Report on Regulatory Reform in Ireland* Paris, OECD, 2001

Organisation of Economic Co-operation and Development, *OECD Public Management Reviews: Ireland Towards an Integrated Public Service* Paris, OECD, 2008

United Kingdom, *Access to Justice, Final Report* (1996) http://www.lcd.gov.uk/civil/final/contents.htm

United Kingdom, *Access to Justice, Interim Report* (1995) http://www.lcd.gov.uk/civil/interim/contents.htm

United Kingdom, Department of the Lord Chancellor, *civil.justice.2000: A vision of the Civil Justice System in the Information Age* 2000 www.lcd.gov.uk/cj2000/cj2000fr.htm

United Kingdom, *Emerging Findings – an early evaluation of the Civil Justice Reforms* (2001) http://www.lcd.gov.uk/civil/emerge/emerge.htm

United Kingdom, Office of Fair Trading, *Competition in Professions* (OFT328) London, 2001

United Kingdom, Office of Fair Trading, *Employed Barristers' Rights to Conduct Litigation* (OFT333) London, 2001

United Kingdom, Ministry of Justice, *Civil Court Fees 2008: Consultation Paper* London, 2008

United Kingdom, *Report of the Committee on Homosexual Offences and Prostitution* (Cmnd 257) London, HMSO, 1957

United Kingdom, Department for Constitutional Affairs, Clementi, *Review of the Regulation System for Legal Services in England and Wales: Final Report*, 2004

United Kingdom, Department for Constitutional Affairs, Peysner and Semeviratne, *The Management of Civil Cases: The Courts and Post-Woolf Landscape*, 2005

United Kingdom, *Legal Services Review Group, Legal Services in Northern Ireland: Complaints, Regulation, Competition* TSO, 2006

United Kingdom, The Preparation of Legislation: *Report of a Committee Appointed by the Lord President of the Council* (Cmnd 6053) (1975) London, Sweet & Maxwell, 1981

Other Publications

Advertising Standards Authority for Ireland, *Code of Advertising Standards for Ireland* 4th edn Dublin, 1995

Advertising Standards Authority for Ireland, *Code of Sales Promotion Practice* 2nd edn Dublin, 1995

Advertising Standards Authority for Ireland, *Manual of Advertising Self-Regulation with the Code of Standards for Advertising, Promotional and Direct Marketing in Ireland* 6th edn, Dublin, 2007

Clancy, J (ed), *The Irish Digest 1989–1993* Dublin, Incorporated Council of Law Reporting for Ireland, 1995

Clancy, J (ed), *The Irish Digest 1994–1999* Dublin, Incorporated Council of Law Reporting for Ireland, 2001

Clancy, J and Ryan, E (eds), *The Irish Digest 1984–1988* Dublin, Incorporated Council of Law Reporting for Ireland, 1991

De Blaghd, E (ed), *The Irish Digest 1971–1983* Dublin, Incorporated Council of Law Reporting for Ireland [1987]

Electro-Technical Council of Ireland, *National Rules for Electrical Installations* 4th edn Dublin, 2008

Irish Business and Employers Confederation, *Employer/Public Liability Claims for Personal Injury* 1993 Dublin, IBEC, 1993

Irish Business and Employers Confederation, *IBEC National Survey of Personal Injuries Claims 2000* 2001 Dublin, IBEC, 2001

Irish Council for Civil Liberties, *Interrogation Endangers the Innocent* Dublin, Irish Council for Civil Liberties, 1993

Irish Council for Civil Liberties, *Justice Matters: Independence, Accountability and the Irish Judiciary* Dublin, ICCL, 2007

Harrison, R (ed), *The Irish Digest 1939–1948* Dublin, Incorporated Council of Law Reporting for Ireland, 1952

Harrison, R (ed), *The Irish Digest 1949–1958* Dublin, Incorporated Council of Law Reporting for Ireland [no date]

Maxwell, T (ed), *The Irish Digest 1894–1918* Dublin, John Falconer, 1921

Murray, R and Dixon, G (eds), *The Irish Digest 1867–1893* Dublin, Edward Ponsonby, 1899

Ryan, E (ed), *The Irish Digest 1959–1970* Dublin, Incorporated Council of Law Reporting for Ireland, 1972

Ryland, R (ed), *The Irish Digest 1919–1928* Dublin, John Falconer, 1930

Ryland, R (ed), *The Irish Digest 1929–1938* Dublin, John Falconer, 1940

Index

All references are to *paragraph* numbers

Absolute discharge
  sentencing, and, 10.36
Academic writings
  sources of law, and, 1.22
Access to law
  access to courts
    assistance of party by lay person,
      9.10
    generally, 9.02–9.04
    McKenzie friends, 9.10–9.12
    parties representing themselves,
      9.05–9.08
    persons lacking capacity, 9.09
    self-representation, 9.05–9.08
    young persons, 9.09
  assistance of party by lay person, 9.10
  constitutional setting, 9.02–9.12
  costs, 9.71–9.72
  court fees, 9.66–9.70
  habeas corpus, and, 9.02
  introduction, 9.01
  legal aid
    And see **Legal aid**
    civil cases, 9.37–9.65
    criminal cases, 9.17–9.36
    introduction, 9.13–9.16
  legal costs
    generally, 9.71–9.72
    protective costs orders, 9.73–9.77
  McKenzie friends, 9.10–9.12
  parties representing themselves,
    9.05–9.08
  persons lacking capacity, 9.09
  protective costs orders, 9.73–9.77
  self-representation, 9.05–9.08
  young persons, 9.09
Accusatorial approach
  evidence, and, 6.138–6.141
Acquittal
  criminal appeals, and, 7.57–7.60

Act of Union 1803
  historical development of legal
    system, and, 2.20–2.21
Acts
  And see **Legislation**
  generally, 13.02
  overview, 1.09
Adjectival law
  divisions of the law, and, 1.23
Adjudicative bodies
  agriculture, 8.46
  appeals, and, 7.61
  criminal injuries compensation, 8.47–
    8.48
  disciplinary tribunals, 8.61
  employment, 8.49–8.53
  generally, 8.45
  government, and
    audi alteram partem, 8.29
    development of government, 8.30–
      8.31
    fair procedures, 8.29
    introduction, 8.26–8.27
    ministerial adjudicative powers,
      8.41–8.44
    natural justice, 8.28
    nemo judex in causa sua, 8.29
    obligation to act judicially, 8.28–
      8.29
    organisation of government, 8.32–
      8.37
    recent reforms in government,
      8.38–8.40
  inspectorates, 8.54–8.55
  intellectual property, 8.56–8.57
  introduction, 8.26–8.27
  obligation to act judicially, 8.28–8.29
  Oireachtas committees, 8.58–8.59
  planning and development, 8.60
  privatised industries regulators, 8.73–
    8.64

Adjudicative bodies (contd)
  professional body tribunals, 8.61
  public contracts, 8.62
  public utilities, 8.63–8.64
  rating and valuation, 8.65
  reform proposals, 8.69
  refugees, 8.66
  revenue, 8.67
  social welfare, 8.68
Administration of justice system
  characteristic features, 4.13–4.19
  Constitutional provisions, 4.08–4.12
  introduction, 4.08–4.12
  justiciable controversies, 4.20–4.23
  political controversies, 4.20–4.23
  public, in, 4.24–4.32
  structure of courts, 4.33–4.45
Administrative law
  adjudicative functions exercised by
  government
    audi alteram partem, 8.29
    development of government, 8.30–
    8.31
    fair procedures, 8.29
    introduction, 8.26–8.27
    ministerial adjudicative powers,
    8.41–8.44
    natural justice, 8.28
    nemo judex in causa sua, 8.29
    obligation to act judicially, 8.28–
    8.29
    organisation of government, 8.32–
    8.37
    recent reforms in government,
    8.38–8.40
  divisions of the law, and, 1.24
  introduction, 8.26–8.27
  obligation to act judicially, 8.28–8.29
  other adjudicative bodies
    agriculture, 8.46
    criminal injuries compensation,
    8.47–8.48
    disciplinary tribunals, 8.61
    employment, 8.49–8.53
    generally, 8.45

    inspectorates, 8.54–8.55
    intellectual property, 8.56–8.57
    introduction, 8.26–8.27
    obligation to act judicially, 8.28–
    8.29
    Oireachtas committees, 8.58–8.59
    planning and development, 8.60
    privatised industries regulators,
    8.73–8.64
    professional body tribunals, 8.61
    public contracts, 8.62
    public utilities, 8.63–8.64
    rating and valuation, 8.65
    reform proposals, 8.69
    refugees, 8.66
    revenue, 8.67
    social welfare, 8.68
  overview, 1.24
  reforms, 8.69
Adversarial procedure
  criminal procedure, and, 6.116
Advocacy
  barristers, and, 3.105–3.106
Agriculture Appeals Office
  dispute resolution, and, 8.46
Aids to interpretation of legislation
  all words bear a meaning, 14.95
  compatibility with EU law, 14.88–
  14.91
  compatibility with international law,
  14.92–14.94
  conjunctive meanings, 14.132–
  14.134
  constitutionality, 14.78–14.87
  directory provisions, 14.149–14.153
  disjunctive meanings, 14.132–14.134
  ejusdem generis rule, 14.120–14.125
  expressio unius est exclusio alterius,
  14.117–14.119
  extra-territorial effect, 14.116
  generalia specialibus non derogant,
  14.129–14.131
  indirect effect doctrine, and, 14.89
  introduction, 14.76–14.77

Aids to interpretation of legislation (contd)
mandatory provisions, 14.149–14.153
noscitur a sociis, 14.126–14.128
penal statutes be construed strictly, 14.106–14.108
presumptions
  all words bear a meaning, that, 14.95
  compatibility with EU law, of, 14.88–14.91
  compatibility with international law, of, 14.92–14.94
  constitutionality, of, 14.78–14.87
  extra-territorial effect, against, 14.116
  penal statutes be construed strictly, that, 14.106–14.108
  retrospective effect, against, 14.110–14.115
  revenue statutes be construed strictly, that, 14.109
  statute should be given an updated meaning, that, 14.96–14.103
  unclear changes in law, against, 14.104–14.105
repealed provisions, 14.135–14.148
retrospective effect, 14.110–14.115
revenue statutes be construed strictly, 14.109
statute should be given an updated meaning, 14.96–14.103
unclear changes in law, 14.104–14.105
Alternative dispute resolution (ADR)
and see under individual headings
administrative law, and
  adjudicative functions exercised by government, 8.30–8.44
  introduction, 8.26–8.27
  obligation to act judicially, 8.28–8.29
  other bodies, 8.45–8.68
  reforms, 8.69

arbitration, 8.20–8.25
commissions of inquiry, 8.74–8.82
conciliation, 8.04–8.19
Coroners' Courts, 8.70–8.73
introduction, 8.01–8.03
judicial review, and
  adjudicative functions exercised by government, 8.30–8.44
  introduction, 8.26–8.27
  obligation to act judicially, 8.28–8.29
  other bodies, 8.45–8.68
  reforms, 8.69
mediation, 8.04–8.19
nature of procedures, 8.01–8.03
Ombudsmen, 8.83–8.95
tribunals of inquiry, 8.74–8.82
Amendments
legislation, and, 13.89–13.95
Appearance
civil procedure, and, 6.44
Appellate jurisdiction
See also **Courts of appeal**
adjudicative bodies, from, 7.61
civil cases, in
  And see **Civil appeals**
  Circuit Court, from, 7.20–7.23
  District Court, from, 7.12–7.19
  High Court, from, 7.24–7.31
constitutional setting, 7.02
Court of Appeal, 7.42–7.44
Court of Criminal Appeal, 7.41–7.44
criminal cases, in
  And see **Criminal appeals**
  acquittals, against, 7.57–7.60
  conviction, against, 7.45–7.47
  double jeopardy, and, 7.57–7.60
  leave to Supreme Court, by, 7.56
  miscarriages of justice, concerning, 7.51–7.53
  prosecution without prejudice to verdict, by, 7.54–7.55
  sentence, against, 7.48–7.50
  summary trials, from, 7.32–7.36

Appellate jurisdiction (contd)
 trials on indictment, from, 7.37–
 7.60
 de novo hearings, 7.04
 European Court of Justice, of
 discretionary references, 7.80
 introduction, 7.74–7.75
 mandatory references, 7.78–7.79
 relevant courts and tribunals, 7.76–
 7.77
 forms of appeal
 de novo hearing, 7.04
 introduction, 7.03
 point of law, 7.05–7.11
 introduction, 7.01
 point of law
 findings of primary fact, 7.07
 findings of secondary fact, 7.08–
 7.11
 generally, 7.05–7.06
 reform proposals
 Law Reform Commission Report
 (2010), 7.72–7.73
 lecture by Keane CJ (2001), 7.62–
 7.68
 Working Group on Court of Appeal,
 7.71
 Working Group on the Jurisdiction
 of the Courts, 7.70
 rehearings, 7.04
Arbitration
 See also **Alternative dispute
 resolution**
 generally, 8.20–8.25
Arraignment
 criminal procedure, and, 6.113
Article 26 of the Irish Constitution
 legislation, and, 13.25
Article 27 of the Irish Constitution
 legislation, and, 13.26–13.27
Assize Courts
 historical development of legal
 system, and, 2.50
Associations
 legal personality, and, 1.31

Attachment of earnings orders
 civil enforcement, and, 10.25
Attorney General
 generally, 3.115–3.124
Audi alteram partem
 administrative law, and, 8.29
 judicial ethical conduct, and, 4.120
Bail
 criminal procedure, and, 6.107–6.109
Bain Report
 legal profession reform, and, 3.43
Barristers
 See also **Legal profession**
 admission to profession, 3.78–3.82
 advocacy, 3.105–3.106
 chambers, and, 3.83
 conduct, 3.89–3.94
 direct access, 3.95–3.98
 discipline, 3.89–3.94
 immunity from suit, 3.107–3.111
 instructions, 3.95–3.98
 introduction, 3.77
 junior counsel, 3.99–3.104
 Law Library, 3.83–3.88
 mode of dress, 3.112–3.113
 senior counsel, 3.99–3.104
Binding authority
 precedent, and, 12.07
Binding to the peace
 sentencing, and, 10.38
Brehon law
 historical development of legal
 system, and, 2.02
Burden of proof
 procedure, and, 6.18–6.21
Canon law
 sources of law, and, 1.21
Capacity decisions
 High Court jurisdiction, 5.80
Case law (precedent)
 binding authority, 12.07
 distinguishing, 12.11
 example
 developing the standard of care,
 12.168–12.173

Case law (precedent) (contd)
  general principle, 12.144–12.151
  negligent solicitors, 12.152–12.154
  negligently performed property
    transactions, 12.155–12.157
  solicitor's duty to third parties,
    12.158–12.167
  FirstLaw database, 12.22
  introduction, 12.01–12.13
  Justis Publishing database, 12.24
  law reporting, 12.14–12.27
  LEXIS database, 12.22
  obiter dicta
    generally, 12.88–12.93
    introduction, 12.09
    significance, 12.121–12.131
  per incuriam, 12.12
  persuasive authority, 12.07
  ratio decidendi
    evolution of principles, 12.132–
      12.138
    facts of case, and, 12.94–12.96
    generally, 12.88–12.93
    introduction, 12.09
    legislation, and, 12.139–12.143
    multiple judgments, and, 12.104–
      12.120
    precedent, and, 12.139–12.143
    reasoning and argument, and,
      12.97–12.103
  res judicata, and, 12.10
  stare decisis
    Court of Appeal, and, 12.69–12.70
    Court of Criminal Appeal, and,
      12.67–12.68
    foreign decisions, 12.75–12.86
    generally, 12.28–12.29
    High Court, and, 12.56–12.66
    House of Lords decisions (pre-
      1922), and, 12.72
    House of Lords decisions (pre-
      1961), and, 12.71
    inferior court decisions, 12.73–
      12.74
    introduction, 12.03

    lower courts should follow
      decisions of higher courts, 12.30–
      12.33
    secondary sources, 12.87
    Supreme Court, and, 12.34–12.55
  sub silentio, 12.12
  Westlaw database, 12.22
Case management
  Commercial Court, 6.78–6.79
  generally, 6.66–6.77
Central Criminal Court
  criminal appeals, and
    acquittals, against, 7.57–7.60
    conviction, against, 7.45–7.47
    generally, 7.37–7.44
    miscarriages of justice, concerning,
      7.51–7.53
    prosecution without prejudice to
      verdict, by, 7.54–7.55
    sentence, against, 7.48–7.50
Central Office of the High Court
  generally, 4.198
Chancery
  High Court jurisdiction, 5.79
  historical development of legal
    system, and, 2.38
Charter of Fundamental Rights
  generally, 16.78–16.80
Chief State Solicitor
  generally, 3.124
Children's Court
  jurisdiction, 5.98
Circuit Court
  civil appeals from
    de novo hearing in High Court, 7.21
    generally, 7.20
    outline of process, 7.23
    point of law by case stated to
      Supreme Court, 7.22
  commercial claims, 5.61
  consumer claims, 5.61
  court officers, 4.202
  court sittings and vacations, 4.203
  criminal appeals from
    acquittals, against, 7.57–7.60

Circuit Court (contd)
   conviction, against, 7.45–7.47
   generally, 7.37–7.44
   miscarriages of justice, concerning, 7.51–7.53
   prosecution without prejudice to verdict, by, 7.54–7.55
   sentence, against, 7.48–7.50
  election petitions, 5.66
  environmental matters, 5.62
  equity, 5.63
  family proceedings, 5.59–5.60
  general jurisdiction, 5.55–5.57
  generally, 4.40–4.41
  historical development of legal system, and, 2.107
  intoxicating liquor licences, 5.58
  judicial composition and structure, 4.65–4.67
  land, 5.63
  landlord and tenant, 5.64
  liquor licences, 5.58
  local government election petitions, 5.66
  malicious injuries, 5.65
  modes of address and notation, 4.75
  monetary limits, 5.55–5.57
  new intoxicating liquor licences, 5.58
  original jurisdiction in civil claims
   commercial claims, 5.61
   consumer claims, 5.61
   election petitions, 5.66
   environmental matters, 5.62
   equity, 5.63
   family proceedings, 5.59–5.60
   general jurisdiction, 5.55–5.57
   introduction, 5.54
   land, 5.63
   landlord and tenant, 5.64
   local government election petitions, 5.66
   malicious injuries, 5.65
   monetary limits, 5.55–5.57
   new intoxicating liquor licences, 5.58

  original jurisdiction in criminal matters
   general, 5.102
   introduction, 5.101
   restrictions on transfer of trial, 5.103–5.104
  procedure
   And see **Civil procedure**
   generally, 6.61
   introduction, 6.01
  transfer of trial, 5.103–5.104
Civil appeals
See also **Appellate jurisdiction**
  adjudicative bodies, from, 7.61
  Circuit Court, from
   de novo hearing in High Court, 7.21
   generally, 7.20
   outline of process, 7.23
   point of law by case stated to Supreme Court, 7.22
  constitutional setting, 7.02
  de novo hearings
   appeals from Circuit Court, on, 7.21
   appeals from District Court, on, 7.13
   generally, 7.04
  District Court, from
   de novo hearing in Circuit Court, 7.13
   further appeal on point of law to Court of Appeal, 7.17–7.18
   generally, 7.12
   outline of process, 7.19
   point of law by case stated to High Court, 7.14–7.16
  forms
   de novo hearing, 7.04
   introduction, 7.03
   point of law, 7.05–7.11
  High Court, from
   generally, 7.24
   liability and quantum, 7.29–7.28
   outline of process, 7.31

Civil appeals (contd)
  point of law to Court of Appeal and
  Supreme Court, 7.25–7.28
  introduction, 7.01
  point of law, on
    Circuit Court, from, 7.22
    District Court, from, 7.14–7.17–
    7.18
    findings of primary fact, 7.07
    findings of secondary fact, 7.08–
    7.11
    generally, 7.05–7.06
    High Court, from, 7.25–7.28
  rehearings, 7.04
Civil claims
  appeals
    And see **Civil appeals**
    Circuit Court, from, 7.20–7.23
    District Court, from, 7.12–7.19
    High Court, from, 7.24–7.31
  basis of jurisdiction, 5.02–5.03
  consumer claims, 5.24
  enforcement of court orders
    attachment of earnings orders,
    10.25
    fi fa orders, 10.19
    garnishee orders, 10.20
    imprisonment, and, 10.25
    possession and sale of land, 10.21
    schedule of payments order, 10.22
    transnational basis, and, 10.26
  family law, 5.23
  first instance jurisdiction
    basis of jurisdiction, 5.02–5.03
    consumer claims, 5.24
    family law, 5.23
    original jurisdiction, 5.31–5.88
    personal injury actions, 5.13–5.22
    small claims, 5.24
  juries
    directions from judge on legal
    issues, 6.154
    directions from judge on verdict,
    6.155–6.157
    disqualified persons, 6.144–6.147

    excused persons, 6.144–6.147
    ineligible persons, 6.144–6.147
    introduction, 6.142
    majority verdicts, 6.159
    representative nature, 6.143
    scope of decision-making, 6.158
    selection, 6.148–6.153
    unqualified persons, 6.144–6.147
  legal aid
    access to the courts, and, 9.41–9.43
    Committee on Civil Legal Aid and
    Advice, 9.39–9.43
    criteria for obtaining legal advice,
    9.52
    criteria for obtaining legal aid,
    9.53–9.55
    eligibility tests, 9.48–9.51
    excluded matters, 9.57–9.58
    Free Legal Advice Centres, 9.38
    funding of system, 9.59–9.63
    introduction, 9.37
    Legal Aid Board, 9.45–9.46
    means test, 9.49–9.51
    merits test, 9.48
    non-statutory scheme, 9.44
    prescribed courts and tribunals,
    9.56
    review of scheme, 9.64–9.65
    statutory scheme, 9.45–9.51
  original jurisdiction
    And see **Original jurisdiction**
    changes in monetary limits, 5.31–
    5.34
    Circuit Court, 5.54–5.66
    costs awards, 5.37–5.41
    District Court, 5.46–5.53
    High Court, 5.68–5.81
    monetary limits, 5.31–5.41
    regulation of costs, 5.42–5.45
    relative seriousness of a claim,
    5.35–5.36
    Supreme Court, 5.82–5.89
  personal injury actions, 5.13–5.22
  procedure
    And see **Civil procedure**

Civil claims (contd)
  appearance, 6.44
  case management, 6.66–6.79
  Circuit Court, and, 6.61
  comparison with criminal
  procedure, 6.02–6.21
  compromise or settlement, 6.63–
  6.65
  defence, 6.49–6.52
  defence and counterclaim, 6.53
  District Court, and, 6.62
  evidence, 6.123–6.141
  generally, 6.22
  introduction, 6.01
  pleadings, 6.23–6.56
  pre-trial remedies, 6.57–6.60
  reply, 6.56
  statements of claim, 6.45–6.48
  summonses, 6.29–6.42
  verifying affidavits, 6.43
  remedies
    damages, 10.03–10.08
    declarations, 10.18
    enforcement, 10.19–10.26
    injunctions, 10.09–10.16
    introduction, 10.02
    specific performance, 10.17
  small claims, 5.24
  trial by judge alone, 6.160
Civil law
  divisions of the law, and, 1.28
Civil procedure
  appearance, 6.44
  burden of proof, 6.18–6.21
  case management
    Commercial Court, 6.78–6.79
    generally, 6.66–6.77
  Circuit Court pleadings, 6.61
  close of pleadings, 6.54–6.55
  comparison with criminal procedure
    burden of proof, 6.18–6.21
    compensation/punishment
    distinction, 6.03–6.05
    court types, 6.16
    description of case, 6.15

    mixed proceedings from single
    event, 6.12–6.13
    notification, 6.08
    outcome terminology, 6.17
    parties to proceedings, 6.14
    private law/public law distinction,
    6.02
    standing, 6.07
    time limits, 6.09–6.11
    titles of parties, 6.06
  compensation, and, 6.03–6.05
  compromises, 6.63–6.65
  defence, 6.49–6.52
  defence and counterclaim, 6.53
  discovery of documents, 6.58–6.59
  District Court pleadings, 6.62
  evidence
    accusatorial approach to trials, and,
    6.138–6.141
    hearsay, 6.131–6.134
    legislative amendments, 6.136
    oath, under, 6.123–6.124
    opinion, 6.135
    oral testimony, 6.125–6.127
    presumption of evidence, and,
    6.139–6.141
    rules, 6.128–6.130
    sequence of witnesses, 6.137
    written testimony, 6.125–6.127
  generally, 6.22
  indorsement of claim, 6.33–6.42
  interrogatories, 6.60
  introduction, 6.01
  juries
    directions from judge on legal
    issues, 6.154
    directions from judge on verdict,
    6.155–6.157
    disqualified persons, 6.144–6.147
    excused persons, 6.144–6.147
    ineligible persons, 6.144–6.147
    introduction, 6.142
    majority verdicts, 6.159
    representative nature, 6.143
    scope of decision-making, 6.158

Civil procedure (contd)
   selection, 6.148–6.153
   unqualified persons, 6.144–6.147
  mixed proceedings from single event,
  6.12–6.13
  notification, 6.08
  parties to proceedings, 6.14
  personal injuries summons
   appearance, 6.44
   generally, 6.32
   indorsement of claim, 6.33–6.42
   introduction, 6.31
   verifying affidavits, 6.43
  pleadings
   Circuit Court, in, 6.61
   close, 6.54–6.55
   defence, 6.49–6.52
   defence and counterclaim, 6.53
   District Court, in, 6.62
   formality, 6.26–6.27
   introduction, 6.23–6.25
   reply, 6.56
   statements of claim, 6.45–6.48
   summonses, 6.29–6.42
  plenary summons
   appearance, 6.44
   generally, 6.31
   personal injuries claims, 6.32–6.43
  pre-trial remedies, 6.57–6.60
  private law disputes, and, 6.02
  reply, 6.56
  settlements, 6.63–6.65
  special summons, 6.30
  standing, 6.07
  statements of claim, 6.45–6.48
  summary summons, 6.29
  summonses
   introduction, 6.28
   personal injuries summons, 6.32–
   6.43
   plenary summons, 6.31–6.42
   special summons, 6.30
   summary summons, 6.29
   types, 6.28
  time limits, 6.09–6.11

  title of parties, 6.06
  trial by judge alone, 6.160
  verifying affidavits, 6.43
Civil remedies
  damages, 10.03–10.08
  declarations, 10.18
  enforcement, 10.19–10.26
  injunctions, 10.09–10.16
  introduction, 10.02
  specific performance, 10.17
Close of pleadings
  civil procedure, and, 6.54–6.55
Codes of practice
  legislation, and, 12.04
Codification legislation
  And see **Legislation**
  improving quality of legislation,
  13.106
  state of the statute book, 13.103
Commentaries
  sources of law, and, 1.22
Commercial claims
  Circuit Court jurisdiction, 5.61
  District Court jurisdiction, 5.50–5.51
  High Court jurisdiction, 5.78
Commercial Court
  case management, and, 6.78–6.79
  jurisdiction, 5.78
**Commission of the European
  Communities**
  generally, 16.139–16.145
Commissions of inquiry
  alternative dispute resolution, and,
  8.74–8.82
**Committee on Civil Legal Aid and
  Advice**
  state-assisted legal aid, and, 9.39–
  9.43
**Committee on Court Practice and
  Procedure**
  law reform, and, 11.23
Common law
  historical development of legal
  system, and, 2.04–2.06
  legal systems, and

Common law (contd)
generally, 1.10–1.12
separation from civil law systems, 2.07
legislation, and, 13.06
meaning, 1.28
sources of law, and, 1.14
Common market
four freedoms
free movement of capital, 16.36
free movement of goods, 16.33
free movement of persons, 16.34
free movement of services, 16.35
generally, 16.24–16.25
obstacles to aims, 16.32–16.37
quantitative restrictions, 16.33
generally, 16.20–16.23
Community service
sentencing, and, 10.39–10.40
Compensation orders
sentencing, and, 10.41
Competition Authority Report 2006
appointment of senior counsel, 3.101
generally, 3.12–3.17
introduction, 11.26
rights of audience, 3.73
Compromises
civil procedure, and, 6.63–6.65
Comptroller and Auditor General
separation of powers, and, 2.82
Conciliation
See also **Alternative dispute resolution**
generally, 8.04–8.19
Conditional discharge
sentencing, and, 10.35
Conjunctive meanings
interpretation of legislation, and, 14.132–14.134
Consolidation legislation
And see **Legislation**
formal process, 13.39
improving quality of legislation, 13.106
state of the statute book, 13.102

Constitution of 1922
amendment, 2.66–2.75
continuity of laws, 2.64–2.65
fundamental rights, 2.63
generally, 2.58–2.59
institutions of State, 2.60–2.62
separation of powers, 2.61–2.62
sources of law, and, 1.16
Constitution of 1937
amendments, 15.81–15.85
constitutional judicial review
basis, 15.47–15.50
constitutional power, and, 15.99–15.103
criticisms, 15.115–15.126
declarations of invalidity, 15.61–15.79
executive power, and, 15.104–15.108
fundamental rights, 15.51–15.60
growth, 15.93–15.96
legal system, and, 15.97–15.98
limits, 15.115–15.126
locus standi, 15.87–15.92
representative actions, 15.80
rules of self-restraint, 15.86
standing, 15.87–15.92
content
introduction, 15.02–15.03
liability of the state, 15.35–15.43
name of the state, 15.30–15.34
national territory, 15.05–15.29
right to self-determination, 15.04
sovereignty, 15.35–15.43
continuity of laws, 2.91
cross-border institutions, and, 15.21–15.29
declarations of invalidity
common law rules, and, 15.71
effect, 15.67–15.70
generally, 15.61–15.66
prospective effect, 15.72–15.76
retrospective effect, 15.72–15.76
English language text, 2.92–2.94
EU law, and

Constitution of 1937 (contd)
 adaptation to Community legal
 order, 16.104–16.113
 incorporation of Treaties and
 Community Acts, 16.114–16.134
 international agreements, 16.98–
 16.103
 European Convention on Human
 Rights, and, 15.202–15.207
 fundamental rights
  amendments, 15.81–15.85
  basis for constitutional judicial
  review, 2.88–2.90, 15.47–15.50
  constitutional power, and, 15.99–
  15.103
  criticisms, 15.115–15.126
  declarations of invalidity, 15.61–
  15.79
  divorce, 15.113–15.114
  enumerated rights, 15.51–15.52
  executive power, and, 15.104–
  15.108
  generally 2.85, 15.44
  limits, 15.115–15.126
  marital breakdown, 15.113–15.114
  multi-party actions, and, 15.80
  representative actions, 15.80
  restrictions on law-making authority
  of Oireachtas, 2.86–2.87, 15.45–
  15.46
  right to life, 15.109–15.112
  sexual privacy, 15.109–15.112
  unenumerated personal rights,
  15.53–15.60
 further constitutional development,
 2.95–2.97
 generally, 2.76
 Good Friday Agreement, and, 15.11
 institutions of State
  generally, 2.77
  rhetoric of Constitution, 2.78
  separation of powers, 2.79–2.84
 interpretation
  And see **Interpretation of the**
  Constitution

  grammatical approach, 15.129–
  15.135
  harmonious approach, 15.142–
  15.147
  historical approach, 15.136–15.141
  introduction, 15.127–15.128
  literal approach, 15.129–15.135
  natural law, 15.148–15.195
  'original understanding', 15.136–
  15.141
  purposive approach, 15.142–
  15.146
 introduction, 15.01
 'Ireland', 15.30–15.34
 'Irish nation' assertion, and, 15.05–
 15.10
 liability of the state, 15.35–15.43
 name of the state, 15.30–15.34
 national territory
  Article 2, 15.12–15.20
  Article 3, 15.21–15.27
  Good Friday Agreement, and, 15.11
  new provisions, 15.11–15.29
  original provisions, 15.05–15.10
 personal rights
  enumerated rights, 15.51
  generally 15.44
  unenumerated personal rights,
  15.53–15.60
 position in Northern Ireland, 2.98
 religion, and, 15.02–15.03
 'Republic of Ireland', 15.30–15.34
 review
  Constitution Review Group,
  15.196–15.197
  Convention on the Constitution,
  15.201
  Oireachtas Committee on the
  Constitution, 15.198–15.200
 right to self-determination, 15.44
 separation of powers
  Comptroller and Auditor General,
  2.82
  executive, 2.81
  generally, 2.79

Constitution of 1937 (contd)
    judiciary, 2.84
    legislature, 2.83
    President of Ireland, 2.80
  sources of law, and, 1.16
  sovereignty, 15.35–15.43
  status, 15.01
Constitution Review Group
  generally, 15.196–15.197
  law reform, and, 11.27
Constitutional cases
  original jurisdiction in civil claims, and, 5.74
Constitutional judicial review
  basis, 15.47–15.50
  constitutional power, and, 15.99–15.103
  criticisms, 15.115–15.126
  declarations of invalidity
    common law rules, and, 15.71
    effect, 15.67–15.70
    generally, 15.61–15.66
    prospective effect, 15.72–15.76
    retrospective effect, 15.72–15.76
  executive power, and, 15.104–15.108
  fundamental rights
    enumerated rights, 15.51–15.52
    unenumerated personal rights, 15.53–15.60
  growth, 15.93–15.96
  legal system, and, 15.97–15.98
  limits, 15.115–15.126
  locus standi, 15.87–15.92
  representative actions, 15.80
  rules of self-restraint, 15.86
  standing, 15.87–15.92
Constitutional law
  divisions of the law, and, 1.24
Constitutionality
  interpretation of legislation, and, 14.78–14.87
Consumer claims
  first instance jurisdiction, and
    Circuit Court, 5.61
    District Court, 5.50–5.51

  generally, 5.24
Contempt of court
  civil contempt
    generally, 10.50
    procedure, 10.51
  criminal contempt
    generally, 10.50
    procedure, 10.52
  introduction, 10.49
  types, 10.50
Continuing legal education
  legal profession, and, 3.144–3.145
Continuity of laws
  Constitution of 1922, under, 2.64–2.65
  Constitution of 1937, under, 2.91
Contract law
  divisions of the law, and, 1.25
  legislation, and, 13.07–13.08
Controller of Patents, Designs and Trade Marks
  dispute resolution, and, 8.56–8.57
Convention for the Protection of Human Rights and Fundamental Freedoms
  See also **Fundamental rights**
  Constitution, and, 15.202–15.207
  generally, 16.11
  international law, and, 17.21–17.22
Convention on the Constitution, 15.201
Conveyancing
  foreign qualifications, and 3.151–3.152
  generally, 3.63–3.69
  law clerks, 3.155
  legal executives, 3.156
  reform of the profession, 3.38
Conviction
  criminal appeals, and, 7.45–7.47
Coroners' Courts
  generally, 8.70–8.73
Corporate insolvency
  High Court jurisdiction, 5.77

Corporate offences
enforcement, and, 10.46–10.47
Corporations
legal personality, and, 1.29–1.30
Costs awards
first instance jurisdiction, and
generally, 5.37–5.41
regulation, 5.42–5.45
generally, 9.71–9.72
legal profession, and, 3.27–3.37
protective costs orders, 9.73–9.77
Council of Europe
Convention on Human Rights, 17.21–17.28
generally, 17.18–17.20
other conventions, 17.29
Council of the European Communities
generally, 16.146–16.151
Counsel
admission to profession, 3.78–3.82
advocacy, 3.105–3.106
chambers, and, 3.83
conduct, 3.89–3.94
direct access, 3.95–3.98
discipline, 3.89–3.94
immunity from suit, 3.107–3.111
instructions, 3.95–3.98
introduction, 3.77
junior counsel, 3.99–3.104
Law Library, 3.83–3.88
mode of dress, 3.112–3.113
senior counsel, 3.99–3.104
County courts
historical development of legal system, and, 2.54
generally, 4.40
Court fees
access to the law, and, 9.66–9.70
Court of Appeal
appeal on point of law to
from District Court, 7.17–7.18
from High Court, 7.25–7.28
court officers, 4.195–4.201
court sittings and vacations, 4.203

criminal appeals, and, 7.42–7.44
generally, 4.35–4.39
judicial composition and structure, 4.60
modes of address and notation, 4.72–4.74
stare decisis, and, 12.69–12.70
Court of Auditors
EU law, and, 16.182–16.183
Court of Chancery
historical development of legal system, and, 2.38
Court of Common Pleas
historical development of legal system, and, 2.36
Court of Criminal Appeal
See also **Criminal appeals**
generally, 7.41–7.44
historical development of legal system, and, 2.109
stare decisis, and, 12.67–12.68
Court of Exchequer
historical development of legal system, and, 2.35
Court of First Instance
EU law, and, 16.178
Court of Justice of the European Union
discretionary references, 7.80
generally, 16.164–16.177
introduction, 7.74–7.75
mandatory references, 7.78–7.79
relevant courts and tribunals, 7.76–7.77
Court of King's Bench
historical development of legal system, and, 2.37
Court officers and offices
Central Office, 4.198
Circuit Court, in, 4.202
District Court, in, 4.202
generally, 4.193–4.194
High Court, in
Central Office, 4.198
introduction, 4.195

Court officers and offices (contd)
    Master of the High Court, 4.196–4.197
    registrars, 4.199
    Taxing Master's Office, 4.200
    Master of the High Court, 4.196–4.197
    Registrar of the Supreme Court, 4.201
    Supreme Court, in
      introduction, 4.195
      Registrar, 4.201
    Taxing Master's Office, 4.200
Court sittings and vacations
    generally, 4.203
Court system
    administration of justice system
      characteristic features, 4.13–4.19
      Constitutional provisions, 4.08–4.12
      introduction, 4.08–4.12
      justiciable controversies, 4.20–4.23
      political controversies, 4.20–4.23
      public, in, 4.24–4.32
      structure of courts, 4.33–4.45
    Circuit Court
      court officers, 4.202
      court sittings and vacations, 4.203
      generally, 4.40–4.41
      judicial composition and structure, 4.65–4.67
      modes of address and notation, 4.75
    County courts
      historical development of legal system, and, 2.54
      generally, 4.40
    court officers
      Circuit Court, in, 4.202
      District Court, in, 4.202
      generally, 4.193–4.194
      High Court, in, 4.195–4.201
      Supreme Court, in, 4.195–4.201
    court sittings and vacations, 4.203
    Court of Appeal

      court officers, 4.195–4.201
      court sittings and vacations, 4.203
      generally, 4.35–4.39
      judicial composition and structure, 4.60
      modes of address and notation, 4.72–4.74
    courts of appeal, 4.34
    courts of first instance, 4.34
    courts of local and limited jurisdiction, 4.40–4.41
    Courts Service, 4.217–4.224
    criminal matters, 4.45
    development post-1937 Constitution
      Courts (Establishment and Constitution) Act 1961, 4.47–4.48
      'former' courts, 4.49
      introduction, 4.46
    District Court
      court officers, 4.202
      court sittings and vacations, 4.203
      generally, 4.40–4.41
      judicial composition and structure, 4.68–4.70
      modes of address and notation, 4.76
    ethical conduct, 4.42
    High Court
      court officers, 4.195–4.201
      court sittings and vacations, 4.203
      generally, 4.35–4.39
      judicial composition and structure, 4.61–4.64
      modes of address and notation, 4.72–4.74
    introduction, 4.01–4.07
    judges
      appointments, 4.77–4.115
      composition and structure, 4.50–4.70
      contempt of court, 4.185
      ethical conduct, 4.120–4.160
      immunity from suit, 4.184–4.185
      independence, 4.116–4.119

Court system (contd)
   misbehaviour or incapacity, and,
      4.118–4.119
   mode of address, 4.71–4.76
   numbers, 4.52
   pensions, 4.190
   place of judiciary in society, 4.161–
      4.173
   precedence, 4.51
   remuneration, 4.174–4.183
   retirement, 4.187–4.192
   salaries, 4.174–4.183
   titles, 4.52
   vacation of office, 4.186–4.192
   judicial appointments
      class, 4.94–4.95
      formal aspects, 4.78–4.85
      informal aspects, 4.86–4.115
      introduction, 4.77
      Judicial Appointments Advisory
         Board, 4.101–4.113
      overview, 4.42
      political allegiances, 4.86–4.90
      political ideology, 4.91–4.92
      qualifications, 4.78–4.85
      the *Whelehan* affair, 4.96–4.100
   judicial composition and structure
      Circuit Court 4.65–4.67
      Court of Appeal, 4.60
      District Court, 4.68–4.70
      High Court, 4.61–4.64
      introduction, 4.50
      numbers, 4.52
      precedence, 4.51
      Supreme Court, 4.53–4.59
      titles, 4.52
   judicial conduct
      Curtin case, 4.150–4.154
      General Committee, 4.148
      generally, 4.120–4.123
      impeachment, 4.124–4.137
      Judicial Conduct and Ethics
         Committee, 4.144–4.146
      Judicial Council Bill (2010),
         4.155–4.160

   Judicial Studies Committee, 4.147
      overview, 4.42
      post-*Sheedy* fallout, 4.138–4.149
      Sheedy affair, 4.124–4.137
   Judicial Conduct and Ethics
      Committee, 4.144–4.146
   Judicial Council Bill (2010), 4.155–
      4.160
   judicial immunity, 4.184–4.185
   judicial incapacity, 4.118–4.119
   judicial independence
      generally, 4.116–4.117
      immunity from suit, and, 4.184–
         4.185
      overview, 4.42
      misbehaviour or incapacity, and,
         4.118–4.119
      place of judiciary in society, 4.161–
         4.173
   judicial numbers, 4.52
   judicial precedence, 4.51
   judicial salaries, 4.174–4.183
   Judicial Studies Committee, 4.147
   judicial titles, 4.52
   justiciable controversies, 4.20–4.23
   management
      Courts Service, 4.217–4.224
      generally, 4.204–4.205
      growth in civil and criminal cases,
         4.206–4.208
      reform, 4.209–4.216
   modes of address and notation
      Circuit Court judges, 4.75
      District Court judges, 4.76
      High Court judges, 4.72–4.74
      introduction, 4.71
      Supreme Court judges, 4.72–4.74
   Petty Sessions
      historical development of legal
         system, and, 2.51–2.53
      generally, 4.40
   political controversies, 4.20–4.23
   regulation of court business, 4.43–
      4.44
   structure

Court system (contd)
    Circuit Court 4.40–4.41
    Court of Appeal, 4.35–4.39
    courts of appeal, 4.34
    courts of first instance, 4.34
    courts of local and limited
    jurisdiction, 4.40–4.41
    criminal matters, 4.45
    District Court, 4.40–4.41
    High Court, 4.35–4.39
    introduction, 4.33
    judicial appointment, independence
    and ethical conduct, 4.42
    regulation of court business, 4.43–
    4.44
    Supreme Court, 4.35–4.39
  Supreme Court
    court officers, 4.195–4.201
    court sittings and vacations, 4.203
    generally, 4.35–4.39
    judicial composition and structure,
    4.53–4.59
    modes of address and notation,
    4.72–4.74
Courts of appeal
  appellate jurisdiction
    And see **Appellate jurisdiction**
    adjudicative bodies, from, 7.61
    civil claims, 7.12–7.31
    criminal cases, 7.32–7.60
    European Court of Justice, of,
    7.74–7.80
    introduction, 7.01–7.11
    reform proposals, 7.62–7.73
  Court of Appeal
    court officers, 4.195–4.201
    court sittings and vacations, 4.203
    generally, 4.35–4.39
    judicial composition and structure,
    4.60
    modes of address and notation,
    4.72–4.74
  introduction, 4.34
  Supreme Court
    And see **Supreme Court**

    court officers, 4.195–4.201
    court sittings and vacations, 4.203
    generally, 4.35–4.39
    judicial composition and structure,
    4.53–4.59
    modes of address and notation,
    4.72–4.74
Courts of chancery
  historical development of legal
  system, and, 2.08–2.09
Courts of first instance
  annual activity, 5.07–5.11
  basis of jurisdiction
    civil claims, 5.02–5.03
    criminal cases, 5.04–5.06
  Circuit Court
    And see **Circuit Court**
    court officers, 4.202–4.203
    generally, 4.40–4.41
    judicial composition and structure,
    4.65–4.67
    modes of address and notation,
    4.75
    original jurisdiction in civil claims,
    5.54–5.66
    original jurisdiction in criminal
    cases, 5.101–5.104
  civil claims
    annual activity, 5.09–5.10
    basis of jurisdiction, 5.02–5.03
    consumer claims, 5.24
    family law, 5.23
    original jurisdiction, 5.31–5.89
    personal injury actions, 5.13–5.22
    small claims, 5.24
  costs awards, 5.37–5.41
  criminal cases
    annual activity, 5.07–5.08
    basis of jurisdiction, 5.04–5.06
    generally 5.25–5.30
    original jurisdiction, 5.90–5.121
  development of the business of the
  courts, 5.12
  District Court
    And see **District Court**

Courts of first instance (contd)
    court officers, 4.202–4.203
    generally, 4.40–4.41
    judicial composition and structure,
    4.68–4.70
    modes of address and notation,
    4.76
    original jurisdiction in civil claims,
    5.46–5.53
    original jurisdiction in criminal
    cases, 5.90–5.99
  High Court
    And see **High Court**
    court officers, 4.195–4.201
    court sittings and vacations, 4.203
    generally, 4.35–4.39
    judicial composition and structure,
    4.61–4.64
    modes of address and notation,
    4.72–4.74
    original jurisdiction in civil claims,
    5.68–5.81
    original jurisdiction in criminal
    cases, 5.105–5.108
  generally, 4.34
  introduction, 5.01
  original jurisdiction (civil claims)
    And see **Original jurisdiction**
    changes in monetary limits, 5.31–
    5.34
    Circuit Court, 5.54–5.66
    costs awards, 5.37–5.41
    District Court, 5.46–5.53
    High Court, 5.68–5.81
    monetary limits, 5.31–5.41
    regulation of costs, 5.42–5.45
    relative seriousness of a claim,
    5.35–5.36
    Supreme Court, 5.82–5.89
  original jurisdiction (criminal cases)
    And see **Original jurisdiction**
    Circuit Court, 5.101–5.104
    District Court, 5.91–5.100
    High Court, 5.105–5.108
    introduction, 5.90

  Special Criminal Courts, 5.109–
  5.121
  reform proposals
    Law Reform Commission Report
    (2010), 5.137–5.139
    lecture by Keane CJ (2001), 5.122–
    5.133
    Working Group on the Jurisdiction
    of the Courts, 5.134–5.136
  regulation of costs, 5.42–5.45
  Special Criminal Courts
    composition, 5.119–5.121
    operation, in, 5.118
    original jurisdiction in criminal
    cases, 5.109–5.117
  Supreme Court
    original jurisdiction in civil claims,
    5.82–5.89
  taxation of costs, 5.42–5.45
Courts of local and limited
jurisdiction
  Circuit Court
    And see **Circuit Court**
    court officers, 4.202–4.203
    generally, 4.40–4.41
    judicial composition and structure,
    4.65–4.67
    modes of address and notation,
    4.75
  District Court
    And see **District Court**
    court officers, 4.202–4.203
    generally, 4.40–4.41
    judicial composition and structure,
    4.68–4.70
    modes of address and notation,
    4.76
  introduction, 4.40
Courts Service
  management of court system, and,
  4.217–4.224
Criminal appeals
  See also **Appellate jurisdiction**
  acquittals, against, 7.57–7.60
  Central Criminal Court, from

Criminal appeals (contd)
    acquittals, against, 7.57–7.60
    conviction, against, 7.45–7.47
    generally, 7.37–7.44
    miscarriages of justice, concerning, 7.51–7.53
    prosecution without prejudice to verdict, by, 7.54–7.55
    sentence, against, 7.48–7.50
  Circuit Court, from
    acquittals, against, 7.57–7.60
    conviction, against, 7.45–7.47
    generally, 7.37–7.44
    miscarriages of justice, concerning, 7.51–7.53
    prosecution without prejudice to verdict, by, 7.54–7.55
    sentence, against, 7.48–7.50
  constitutional setting, 7.02
  conviction, against, 7.45–7.47
  Court of Appeal, 7.42–7.44
  Court of Criminal Appeal, 7.41–7.44
  de novo hearings
    District Court, from, 7.33
    generally, 7.04
    summary trials, from, 7.33
  District Court, from
    de novo hearing in Circuit Court, 7.33
    further appeal on point of law to Supreme Court, 7.35
    generally, 7.32
    outline of process, 7.36
    point of law by case stated to High Court, 7.34
  double jeopardy, and, 7.57–7.60
  forms
    de novo hearing, 7.04
    introduction, 7.03
    point of law, 7.05–7.11
  High Court, from
    acquittals, against, 7.57–7.60
    conviction, against, 7.45–7.47
    generally, 7.37–7.44

    miscarriages of justice, concerning, 7.51–7.53
    prosecution without prejudice to verdict, by, 7.54–7.55
    sentence, against, 7.48–7.50
  leave to Supreme Court, by, 7.56
  miscarriages of justice, concerning, 7.51–7.53
  point of law
    findings of primary fact, 7.07
    findings of secondary fact, 7.08–7.11
    generally, 7.05–7.06
    summary trials in District Court, from, 7.34–7.35
  prosecution without prejudice to verdict, by, 7.54–7.55
  rehearings, 7.04
  sentence, against
    generally, 7.48–7.50
    miscarriages of justice, concerning, 7.51–7.53
  Special Criminal Courts, from
    acquittals, against, 7.57–7.60
    conviction, against, 7.45–7.47
    generally, 7.37–7.44
    miscarriages of justice, concerning, 7.51–7.53
    prosecution without prejudice to verdict, by, 7.54–7.55
    sentence, against, 7.48–7.50
  summary trials, from
    de novo hearing in Circuit Court, 7.33
    further appeal on point of law to Supreme Court, 7.35
    generally, 7.32
    outline of process, 7.36
    point of law by case stated to High Court, 7.34
  trials on indictment, from
    acquittals, against, 7.57–7.60
    conviction, against, 7.45–7.47
    double jeopardy, and, 7.57–7.60
    generally, 7.37–7.44

Criminal appeals (contd)
  leave to Supreme Court, by, 7.56
  miscarriages of justice, concerning,
  7.51–7.53
  prosecution without prejudice to
  verdict, by, 7.54–7.55
  sentence, against, 7.48–7.50
Criminal cases
  absolute discharge, 10.36
  access to a lwayer, 9.34–9.36
  appeals
    And see **Criminal appeals**
    acquittals, against, 7.57–7.60
    conviction, against, 7.45–7.47
    double jeopardy, and, 7.57–7.60
    leave to Supreme Court, by, 7.56
    miscarriages of justice, concerning,
    7.51–7.53
    prosecution without prejudice to
    verdict, by, 7.54–7.55
    sentence, against, 7.48–7.50
    summary trials, from, 7.32–7.36
    trials on indictment, from, 7.37–
    7.60
  binding to the peace, 10.38
  community service, 10.39–10.40
  compensation orders, 10.41
  conditional discharge, 10.35
  court system, and, 4.45
  enforcement
    absolute discharge, 10.36–10.37
    binding to the peace, 10.38
    community service, 10.39–10.40
    compensation orders, 10.41
    conditional discharge, 10.35
    Court Poor Box Payment, 10.37
    fines, 10.28–10.33
    imprisonment, 10.28–10.33
    introduction, 10.27
    probation, 10.34–10.38
    restorative justice principles,
    10.42–10.45
    transnational basis, and, 10.48
  evidence
    accusatorial approach to trials, and,
    6.138–6.141

    hearsay, 6.131–6.134
    legislative amendments, 6.136
    oath, under, 6.123–6.124
    opinion, 6.135
    oral testimony, 6.125–6.127
    presumption of evidence, and,
    6.139–6.141
    rules, 6.128–6.130
    sequence of witnesses, 6.137
    written testimony, 6.125–6.127
  fines, 10.28–10.33
  first instance jurisdiction, and
    basis of jurisdiction, 5.04–5.06
    generally 5.25–5.30
    original jurisdiction, 5.90–5.121
  imprisonment, 10.28–10.332
  juries
    directions from judge on legal
    issues, 6.154
    directions from judge on verdict,
    6.155–6.157
    disqualified persons, 6.144–6.147
    excused persons, 6.144–6.147
    ineligible persons, 6.144–6.147
    introduction, 6.142
    majority verdicts, 6.159
    representative nature, 6.143
    scope of decision-making, 6.158
    selection, 6.148–6.153
    unqualified persons, 6.144–6.147
  legal aid
    funding of system, 9.24–9.32
    judicial review, 9.33
    police custody, in, 9.34–9.36
    reforms and proposals, 9.24–9.32
    trial, at, 9.17–9.23
    introduction, 9.13–9.16
  original jurisdiction (criminal cases)
    And see **Original jurisdiction**
    Circuit Court, 5.101–5.104
    District Court, 5.91–5.100
    High Court, 5.105–5.108
    introduction, 5.90
    Special Criminal Courts, 5.109–
    5.121

Criminal cases (contd)
  probation, 10.34–10.36
  procedure
    And see **Criminal procedure**
    adversarial system, 6.116
    arraignment, 6.113
    bail, 6.107–6.109
    comparison with civil procedure
      distinction, 6.03–6.21
    District Court's role, 6.103–6.106
    evidence, 6.123–6.141
    form of indictment, 6.110–6.112
    guilty plea, 6.114–6.115
    introduction, 6.80
    prosecution on indictment, 6.94–
      6.102
    prosecution system, 6.85–6.89
    summary prosecution, 6.90–6.93
    summary trial, 6.81–6.84
    trial on indictment, 6.81–6.84
    victim's role, 6.110–6.122
Criminal Injuries Compensation
  Tribunal
  dispute resolution, and, 8.47–8.48
Criminal law
  divisions of the law, and, 1.24
Criminal procedure
  adversarial system, 6.116
  arraignment, 6.113
  bail, 6.107–6.109
  burden of proof, 6.18–6.21
  comparison with civil procedure
    burden of proof, 6.18–6.21
    compensation/punishment
      distinction, 6.03–6.05
    court types, 6.16
    description of case, 6.15
    mixed proceedings from single
      event, 6.12–6.13
    notification, 6.08
    outcome terminology, 6.17
    parties to proceedings, 6.14
    private law/public law distinction,
      6.02
    standing, 6.07

  time limits, 6.09–6.11
  titles of parties, 6.06
  District Court's role
    generally, 6.103
    indictable offences tried summarily,
      6.104
    sending indictable offences forward
      for trial, 6.105–6.106
  evidence
    accusatorial approach to trials, and,
      6.138–6.141
    hearsay, 6.131–6.134
    legislative amendments, 6.136
    oath, under, 6.123–6.124
    opinion, 6.135
    oral testimony, 6.125–6.127
    presumption of evidence, and,
      6.139–6.141
    rules, 6.128–6.130
    sequence of witnesses, 6.137
    written testimony, 6.125–6.127
  form of indictment, 6.110–6.112
  guilty plea, 6.114–6.115
  juries
    directions from judge on legal
      issues, 6.154
    directions from judge on verdict,
      6.155–6.157
    disqualified persons, 6.144–6.147
    excused persons, 6.144–6.147
    ineligible persons, 6.144–6.147
    introduction, 6.142
    majority verdicts, 6.159
    representative nature, 6.143
    scope of decision-making, 6.158
    selection, 6.148–6.153
    unqualified persons, 6.144–6.147
  mixed proceedings from single event,
    6.12–6.13
  notification, 6.08
  parties to proceedings, 6.14
  prosecution on indictment, 6.94–
    6.102
  prosecution system, 6.85–6.89
  public law, and, 6.02

Criminal procedure (contd)
  punishment, and, 6.03–6.05
  standing, 6.07
  summary prosecution, 6.90–6.93
  summary trial, 6.81–6.84
  time limits, 6.09–6.11
  titles of parties, 6.06
  trial by judge alone, 6.160
  trial on indictment, 6.81–6.84
  victim's role, 6.110–6.122
Cross-border institutions
  Constitution, and, 15.21–15.29
Custom
  sources of law, and, 1.19
Dáil courts
  historical development of legal
  system, and, 2.101–2.104
Damages
  civil remedies, and, 10.03–10.08
De novo **hearings**
  alternative dispute resolution, and,
  8.26
  civil appeals
    Circuit Court, from, 7.21
    District Court, from, 7.13
  criminal appeals, and
    District Court, from, 7.33
    summary trials, from, 7.33
  generally, 7.04
Decisions
  EU law, and, 16.206–16.207
Declarations
  civil remedies, and, 10.18
Declarations of invalidity
  common law rules, and, 15.71
  effect, 15.67–15.70
  generally, 15.61–15.66
  prospective effect, 15.72–15.76
  retrospective effect, 15.72–15.76
Defence
  civil procedure, and, 6.49–6.52
Defence and counterclaim
  civil procedure, and, 6.53
Deferred fees
  solicitors, and, 3.76

Delegated legislation
  Constitution, and, 13.121–13.138
  contracts of adhesion, 13.119–13.120
  domestic measures derived from EU
  law, 13.153–13.155
  generally, 13.03
  introduction, 13.109–13.118
  judicial scrutiny
    bad faith, 13.147–13.148
    compliance with procedures,
    13.149–13.150
    generally, 13.139–13.142
    reasonableness, 13.145–13.146
    statutory purpose, 13.143–13.144
  overview, 1.09
  parliamentary scrutiny of delegated
  legislation, 13.151–13.155
Dictionaries
  interpretation of legislation, and,
  14.191–14.192
Directions from judge
  juries, to
    legal issues, 6.154
    verdict, 6.155–6.157
Directives
  EU law, and
    generally, 16.195–16.205
    implementation in Ireland, 16.212–
    16.213
Director of Public Prosecutions
  generally, 3.125–3.128
Discovery of documents
  civil procedure, and, 6.58–6.59
Dispute resolution
  and see under individual headings
  administrative law, and
    adjudicative functions exercised by
    government, 8.30–8.44
    introduction, 8.26–8.27
    obligation to act judicially, 8.28–
    8.29
    other bodies, 8.45–8.68
    reforms, 8.69
  arbitration, 8.20–8.25
  commissions of inquiry, 8.74–8.82

Dispute resolution (contd)
conciliation, 8.04–8.19
Coroners' Courts, 8.70–8.73
introduction, 8.01–8.03
judicial review, and
  adjudicative functions exercised by
  government, 8.30–8.44
  introduction, 8.26–8.27
  obligation to act judicially, 8.28–
  8.29
  other bodies, 8.45–8.68
  reforms, 8.69
mediation, 8.04–8.19
nature of procedures, 8.01–8.03
Ombudsmen, 8.83–8.95
tribunals of inquiry, 8.74–8.82
Distinguishing previous decisions
precedent, and, 12.11
District Court
civil appeals from
  de novo hearing in Circuit Court,
  7.13
  further appeal on point of law to
  Court of Appeal, 7.17–7.18
  generally, 7.12
  outline of process, 7.19
  point of law by case stated to High
  Court, 7.14–7.16
commercial claims, 5.50–5.51
consumer claims, 5.50–5.51
court officers, 4.202
court sittings and vacations, 4.203
criminal appeals, and
  de novo hearing in Circuit Court,
  7.33
  further appeal on point of law to
  Supreme Court, 7.35
  generally, 7.32
  outline of process, 7.36
  point of law by case stated to High
  Court, 7.34
criminal procedure, and
  generally, 6.103
  indictable offences tried summarily,
  6.104

sending indictable offences forward
  for trial, 6.105–6.106
environmental matters, 5.52
'either way' offences, 5.96–5.97
equity, 5.53
extradition applications, 5.100
family proceedings, 5.49
general jurisdiction, 5.47
generally, 4.40–4.41
historical development of legal
  system, and, 2.1
'hybrid' offences, 5.96–5.97
indictable offences tried summarily,
  5.96–5.97
intoxicating liquor licences, 5.48
judicial composition and structure,
  4.68–4.70
land, 5.53
liquor licences, 5.48
minor offences, 5.92–5.95
modes of address and notation, 4.76
monetary limits, 5.47
renewal of intoxicating liquor
  licences, 5.48
original jurisdiction in civil claims,
  and
  commercial claims, 5.50–5.51
  consumer claims, 5.50–5.51
  environmental matters, 5.52
  equity, 5.53
  family proceedings, 5.49
  general jurisdiction, 5.47
  introduction, 5.46
  land, 5.53
  monetary limits, 5.47
  renewal of intoxicating liquor
  licences, 5.48
  small claims, 5.51
original jurisdiction in criminal
matters
  children, 5.98
  'either way' offences, 5.96–5.97
  extradition applications, 5.100
  'hybrid' offences, 5.96–5.97

District Court (contd)
 indictable offences tried summarily,
  5.96–5.97
 introduction, 5.91
 minor offences, 5.92–5.95
 persons under 18 years old, 5.98
 sending forward indictable offences
  for trial, 5.99
 procedure
  And see **Civil procedure**
  generally, 6.62
  introduction, 6.01
 renewal of intoxicating liquor
  licences, 5.48
 sending forward indictable offences
  for trial, 5.99
 small claims, 5.51
Divisions of the law
 common expressions, 1.28
 generally, 1.23–1.27
Divorce
 Constitution, and, 15.113–15.114
Double jeopardy
 criminal appeals, and, 7.57–7.60
Drafting
 legislation, and, 14.05
EC law
 See **EU law**
Education
 continuing legal education, 3.144–
  3.145
 exchanges between lawyers at EU
  level, 3.153
 Fair Trade Commission Report, and,
  3.133–3.143
 recognition of foreign qualifications,
  3.146–3.152
 universities, 3.129–3.132
Either way offences
 District Court jurisdiction, 5.96–5.97
Ejusdem generis **rule**
 interpretation of legislation, and,
  14.120–14.125
Election petitions
 Circuit Court jurisdiction, 5.66
 High Court jurisdiction, 5.81

Employment Appeals Tribunal
 dispute resolution, and, 8.53
Employment bodies
 dispute resolution, and, 8.49–8.53
Environmental matters
 Circuit Court jurisdiction, 5.62
 District Court jurisdiction, 5.52
Equity
 first instance jurisdiction, and
  Circuit Court, 5.63
  District Court, 5.53
  High Court, 5.79
 historical development of legal
  system, and, 2.08–2.09
Ethical conduct
 Curtin case, 4.150–4.154
 General Committee, 4.148
 generally, 4.120–4.123
 impeachment, 4.124–4.137
 Judicial Conduct and Ethics
  Committee, 4.144–4.146
 Judicial Council Bill (2010), 4.155–
  4.160
 Judicial Studies Committee, 4.147
 overview, 4.42
 post-*Sheedy* fallout, 4.138–4.149
 Sheedy affair, 4.124–4.137
EU law
 See also **European Community**
 Constitution, and
  adaptation to Community legal
   order, 16.104–16.113
  incorporation of Treaties and
   Community Acts, 16.114–16.134
  international agreements, 16.98–
   16.103
 Decisions, 16.206–16.207
 Directives
  generally, 16.195–16.205
  implementation in Ireland, 16.212–
   16.213
 form
  Decisions, 16.206–16.207
  Directives, 16.195–16.205
  introduction, 16.184
  Opinions, 16.208

EU law (contd)
Recommendations, 16.208
Regulations, 16.190–16.194
Treaties, 16.185–16.189
generally, 16.81–16.97
implementation in Ireland
Directives, 16.212–16.213
effects on interpretative approaches, 16.222–16.223
national measures, 16.215–16.221
Regulations, 16.209–16.211
treaties, 16.209
incorporation of Treaties and
Community Acts, 16.114–16.134
institutions, and
Commission of the European
Communities, 16.139–16.145
Council of the European
Communities, 16.146–16.151
Court of Auditors, 16.182–16.183
Court of First Instance, 16.178
Court of Justice of the European
Union, 16.164–16.177
European Council, 16.152–16.153
European Parliament, 16.154–16.163
General Court, 16.178–16.181
introduction, 16.135–16.138
specialised courts, 16.181
international agreements, 16.98–16.103
interpretation of legislation, and, 16.222–16.223
introduction, 16.01–16.03
nature
Constitution, 16.98–16.113
generally, 16.81–16.97
incorporation of Treaties and
Community Acts, 16.114–16.134
international agreements, 16.98–16.103
Opinions, 16.208
Recommendations, 16.208
Regulations
generally, 16.190–16.194

implementation in Ireland, 16.209–16.211
sources of law, and, 1.17–1.18
Treaties
generally, 16.185–16.189
implementation in Ireland, 16.209–16.211

EU materials
interpretation of legislation, and, 14.166–14.168
European Atomic Energy Community (EAEC)
generally, 16.15
European Coal and Steel Community (ECSC)
generally, 16.13–16.14
European Community (EC)
accession, 2.96
activities, 16.30–16.31
Charter of Fundamental Rights, 16.78–16.80
Commission of the European
Communities, 16.139–16.145
common market
four freedoms, 16.24–16.37
generally, 16.20–16.23
Council of the European
Communities, 16.146–16.151
Court of Auditors, 16.182–16.183
Court of First Instance, 16.178
Court of Justice of the European
Union, 16.164–16.177
development
introduction, 16.38
Lisbon Treaty (proposed), 16.58–16.61
Luxembourg Compromise, 16.40
Merger Treaty, 16.39
protection of fundamental rights, 16.62–16.80
Single European Act, 16.41
Treaty of Amsterdam, 16.47–16.52
Treaty on European Union, 16.42–16.46
Treaty of Nice, 16.53–16.57

European Community (EC) (contd)
  economic context, 16.04–16.08
  EU law, and
    And see **EU law**
    Constitution, and, 16.98–16.113
    Decisions, 16.206–16.207
    Directives, 16.195–16.205
    form, 16.184–16.208
    generally, 16.81–16.97
    implementation in Ireland, 16.209–16.223
    incorporation of Treaties and Community Acts, 16.114–16.134
    nature, 16.81–16.134
    Opinions, 16.208
    Recommendations, 16.208
    Regulations, 16.190–16.194
    Treaties, 16.185–16.189
  European Atomic Energy Community, 16.15
  European Coal and Steel Community, 16.13–16.14
  European Council, 16.152–16.153
  European Economic Community
    common market, 16.20–16.23
    four freedoms, 16.24–16.37
    generally, 16.16–16.19
  European integration after 1945, 16.09–16.12
  European Parliament, 16.154–16.163
  financial context, 16.04–16.08
  foreign workers, 16.34
  'four freedoms'
    free movement of capital, 16.36
    free movement of goods, 16.33
    free movement of persons, 16.34
    free movement of services, 16.35
    generally, 16.24–16.25
    obstacles to aims, 16.32–16.37
    quantitative restrictions, 16.33
  funding, 16.06–16.08
  General Court
    generally, 16.178–16.180
    specialised courts, 16.181
  incorporation of Treaties and Community Acts, 16.114–16.134
  institutions
    Commission of the European Communities, 16.139–16.145
    Council of the European Communities, 16.146–16.151
    Court of Auditors, 16.182–16.183
    Court of First Instance, 16.178
    Court of Justice of the European Union, 16.164–16.177
    European Council, 16.152–16.153
    European Parliament, 16.154–16.163
    General Court, 16.178–16.181
    introduction, 16.135–16.138
    specialised courts, 16.181
  introduction, 16.01–16.03
  Lisbon Treaty (proposed), 16.58–16.61
  Luxembourg Compromise, 16.40
  Maastricht Treaty, 16.42–16.46
  membership, 16.02
  Merger Treaty, 16.39
  obstacles to aims, 16.32–16.37
  protection of fundamental rights, 16.62–16.80
  quantitative restrictions, 16.33
  Single European Act, 16.41
  specialised courts, 16.181
  subsidiarity, 16.26–16.29
  Treaty of Amsterdam, 16.47–16.52
  Treaty on European Union, 16.42–16.46
  Treaty of Nice, 16.53–16.57
  'veto', 16.40
European Consumer Centre
  alternative dispute resolution, and, 8.13
European Convention on Human Rights (ECHR)
  See also **Fundamental rights**
  Constitution, and, 15.202–15.207
  generally, 16.11
  international law, and, 17.21–17.22

European Convention on Human Rights
 (ECHR) (contd)
overview, 1.20
ratification, 16.80
European Council
generally, 16.152–16.153
European Court of Human Rights
 (ECtHR)
generally, 17.23–17.28
overview, 1.20
European Court of Justice (ECJ)
discretionary references, 7.80
introduction, 7.74–7.75
mandatory references, 7.78–7.79
relevant courts and tribunals, 7.76–
 7.77
European Economic Community
 (EEC)
common market, 16.20–16.23
four freedoms
 free movement of capital, 16.36
 free movement of goods, 16.33
 free movement of persons, 16.34
 free movement of services, 16.35
 generally, 16.24–16.25
 obstacles to aims, 16.32–16.37
 quantitative restrictions, 16.33
generally, 16.16–16.19
European Parliament
generally, 16.154–16.163
Evidence
accusatorial approach to trials, and,
 6.138–6.141
hearsay, 6.131–6.134
legislative amendments, 6.136
oath, under, 6.123–6.124
opinion, 6.135
oral testimony, 6.125–6.127
presumption of evidence, and, 6.139–
 6.141
rules, 6.128–6.130
sequence of witnesses, 6.137
written testimony, 6.125–6.127

Executive
historical development of legal
 system, and, 2.25–2.26
separation of powers, and, 2.81
Executive power
Constitution, and, 15.104–15.108
Expressio unius est exclusio alterius
interpretation of legislation, and,
 14.117–14.119
Extradition applications
District Court jurisdiction, 5.100
Extra-territorial effect
interpretation of legislation, and,
 14.116
Fair procedures
administrative law, and, 8.29
Fair Trade Commission Report 1990
advertising by solicitors, 3.75
appointment of senior counsel, 3.101
conveyancing, 3.64
costs, 3.27–3.37
direct access to barristers, 3.98
discipline of barristers, 3.92
generally, 3.05–3.11
legal education, 3.133–3.143
legal fees, 3.27–3.37
rights of audience, 3.72
Family law
first instance jurisdiction, and, 5.23
Family Mediation Service
alternative dispute resolution, and,
 8.12
Family proceedings
Circuit Court jurisdiction, 5.59–5.60
District Court jurisdiction, 5.49
High Court jurisdiction, 5.76
mediation, and, 8.12
Fees
access to the law, and, 9.66–9.70
generally, 3.27–3.37
Fi fa **orders**
civil enforcement, and, 10.19
Fines
sentencing, and, 10.28–10.33

FirstLaw database
precedent, and, 12.22
Foreign case decisions
stare decisis, and, 12.75–12.86
Foreign qualifications
recognition, 3.146–3.152
'Four freedoms'
free movement of capital, 16.36
free movement of goods, 16.33
free movement of persons, 16.34
free movement of services, 16.35
generally, 16.24–16.25
obstacles to aims, 16.32–16.37
quantitative restrictions, 16.33
Free Legal Advice Centres
generally, 9.38
Free movement of capital
generally, 16.36
introduction, 16.24
Free movement of goods
generally, 16.33
introduction, 16.24
Free movement of persons
generally, 16.34
introduction, 16.24
Free movement of services
generally, 16.35
introduction, 16.24
Fundamental rights
Charter of Fundamental Rights,
16.78–16.80
Constitution of 1922, under, 2.63
Constitution of 1937, under
basis for constitutional judicial
review, 2.88–2.90
generally 2.85
restrictions on law-making authority
of Oireachtas, 2.86–2.87
constitutional power, and, 15.99–
15.103
criticisms, 15.115–15.126
declarations of invalidity
common law rules, and, 15.71
effect, 15.67–15.70
generally, 15.61–15.66

prospective effect, 15.72–15.76
retrospective effect, 15.72–15.76
divorce, 15.113–15.114
enumerated rights, 15.51–15.52
European Community, and
Charter of Fundamental Rights,
16.78–16.80
generally, 16.62–16.77
executive power, and, 15.104–15.108
generally 15.44
introduction, 2.63
limits, 15.115–15.126
marital breakdown, 15.113–15.114
multi-party actions, and, 15.80
representative actions, 15.80
right to life, 15.109–15.112
sexual privacy, 15.109–15.112
unenumerated rights, 15.53–15.60
Garnishee orders
civil enforcement, and, 10.20
**General Agreement on Tariffs and
Trade (GATT)**
generally, 17.50–17.53
General Court
EU law, and
generally, 16.178–16.180
specialised courts, 16.181
Generalia specialibus non derogant
interpretation of legislation, and,
14.129–14.131
Golden rule
interpretation of legislation, and,
14.24–14.26
Good Friday Agreement 1998
Constitution, and, 15.11
historical development of legal
system, and, 2.97
Government bodies
administrative law, and
audi alteram partem, 8.29
development of government, 8.30–
8.31
fair procedures, 8.29
introduction, 8.26–8.27

Government bodies (contd)
    ministerial adjudicative powers, 8.41–8.44
    natural justice, 8.28
    nemo judex in causa sua, 8.29
    obligation to act judicially, 8.28–8.29
    organisation of government, 8.32–8.37
    recent reforms in government, 8.38–8.40

Government of Ireland Act 1920
    historical development of legal system, and, 2.46–2.48

Grammatical approach
    interpretation of the Constitution, and, 15.129–15.135

Grattan's Parliament
    historical development of legal system, and, 2.19–2.21

Guilty plea
    criminal procedure, and, 6.114–6.115

Habeas corpus
    access to the law, and, 9.02

Harmonious approach
    interpretation of the Constitution, and
    European influence, 15.147
    generally, 15.142–15.146

Hearsay evidence
    generally, 6.131–6.134

High Court
    civil appeals from
        generally, 7.24
        liability and quantum, 7.29–7.28
        outline of process, 7.31
        point of law to Court of Appeal and Supreme Court, 7.25–7.28
    Central Office, 4.198
    court officers
        Central Office, 4.198
        introduction, 4.195
        Master of the High Court, 4.196–4.197
        registrars, 4.199
        Taxing Master's Office, 4.200

    court sittings and vacations, 4.203
    criminal appeals, and
        acquittals, against, 7.57–7.60
        conviction, against, 7.45–7.47
        generally, 7.37–7.44
        miscarriages of justice, concerning, 7.51–7.53
        prosecution without prejudice to verdict, by, 7.54–7.55
        sentence, against, 7.48–7.50
    generally, 4.35–4.39
    historical development of legal system, and, 2.108
    judicial composition and structure, and
        generally, 4.61–4.63
        research assistants and clerks, 4.64
    Master of the High Court, 4.196–4.197
    modes of address and notation, 4.72–4.74
    original jurisdiction in civil claims
        capacity decisions, 5.80
        chancery, 5.79
        commercial claims, 5.78
        constitutional cases, 5.74
        corporate insolvency, 5.77
        election petitions, 5.81
        equity, 5.79
        family proceedings, 5.76
        general jurisdiction, 5.72–5.73
        introduction, 5.68–5.71
        judicial review, 5.75
        monetary limits, 5.72–5.73
        Oireachtas election petitions, 5.81
        personal insolvency, 5.77
        referendum petitions, 5.81
        wardship, 5.80
    original jurisdiction in criminal matters, 5.105–5.108
    procedure
        And see **Civil procedure**
        appearance, 6.44
        case management, 6.66–6.79

High Court (contd)
   comparison with criminal procedure, 6.02–6.21
   compromise or settlement, 6.63–6.65
   defence, 6.49–6.52
   defence and counterclaim, 6.53
   generally, 6.22
   introduction, 6.01
   pleadings, 6.23–6.56
   pre-trial remedies, 6.57–6.60
   reply, 6.56
   statements of claim, 6.45–6.48
   summonses, 6.29–6.42
   verifying affidavits, 6.43
  research assistants and clerks, 4.64
  stare decisis, and, 12.56–12.66
  Taxing Master's Office, 4.200

Historical approach
  interpretation of the Constitution, and, 15.136–15.141

Historical development of the Irish legal system
  accession to European Community, 2.96
  Act of Union 1803, 2.20–2.21
  arrival of English law
   Act of Union, 2.20–2.21
   common law, 2.04–2.06
   equity in the courts of chancery, 2.08–2.09
   Grattan's Parliament, 2.19–2.21
   judges as law makers, 2.11
   Parliament as law-making institution, 2.10
   separation of common law and civil law systems, 2.07
   statutes as source of law, 2.10
   Tudor settlements or plantations, 2.17–2.28
  Brehon law, 2.02
  common law, 2.04–2.06
  Constitution of 1922
   amendment, 2.66–2.75
   continuity of laws, 2.64–2.65

   fundamental rights, 2.63
   generally, 2.58–2.59
   institutions of State, 2.60–2.62
   separation of powers, 2.61–2.62
  Constitution of 1937
   continuity of laws, 2.91
   English language text, 2.92–2.94
   fundamental rights, 2.85–2.90
   further constitutional development, 2.95–2.97
   generally, 2.76
   institutions of State, 2.77–2.84
   position in Northern Ireland, 2.98
   separation of powers, 2.79–2.84
  continuity of laws
   Constitution of 1922, under, 2.64–2.65
   Constitution of 1937, under, 2.91
  emergence of new state, 2.55–2.57
  equity in the courts of chancery, 2.08–2.09
  executive, 2.25–2.26
  fundamental rights
   basis for constitutional judicial review, 2.88–2.90
   Constitution of 1922, under, 2.63
   Constitution of 1937, under, 2.85–2.90
   generally 2.85
   introduction, 2.63
   restrictions on law-making authority of Oireachtas, 2.86–2.87
  Good Friday Agreement 1998, 2.97
  Government of Ireland Act 1920, 2.46–2.48
  Grattan's Parliament, 2.19–2.21
  Home Rule movement, 2.44–2.45
  inferior court, 2.49–2.54
  institutions of State
   Constitution of 1922, under, 2.60–2.62
   Constitution of 1937, under, 2.77–2.84
   generally, 2.77
   rhetoric of Constitution, 2.78

Historical development of the Irish legal system (contd)
separation of powers, 2.79–2.84
institutions of State in the UK, and
executive, 2.25–2.26
Government of Ireland Act 1920, 2.46–2.48
Home Rule movement, 2.44–2.45
inferior court, 2.49–2.54
judiciary, 2.27–2.29
land reform in the 19th century, 2.42–2.43
legislature, 2.24
separation of powers, 2.22–2.23
superior courts, 2.33–2.41
Supreme Court of Judicature Acts 1873 and 1877, 2.30–2.32
introduction, 2.01
judges as law makers, 2.11
judiciary, 2.27–2.29
land reform in the 19th century, 2.42–2.43
legislature, 2.24
Parliament as law-making institution, 2.10
pre-Norman period, 2.02
revised court system
Circuit Court, 2.107
Court of Criminal Appeal, 2.109
Dáil courts, 2.101–2.104
District Court, 2.106
High Court, 2.108
introduction, 2.99–2.100
judiciary committee, 2.105
Supreme Court, 2.110–2.111
separation of common law and civil law systems, 2.07
separation of powers
Comptroller and Auditor General, 2.82
Constitution of 1922, under, 2.61
Constitution of 1937, under, 2.79–2.84
executive, 2.81
generally, 2.79

institutions of State in the UK, and, 2.22–2.23
introduction, 2.61
judiciary, 2.84
legislature, 2.83
President of Ireland, 2.80
statutes as source of law, 2.10
superior courts, 2.33–2.41
Supreme Court of Judicature Acts 1873 and 1877
establishment of superior courts, 2.33–2.41
generally, 2.30–2.32
Tudor settlements or plantations, 2.17–2.28

Home Rule movement
historical development of legal system, and, 2.44–2.45

House of Lords
historical development of legal system, and, 2.39
stare decisis, and, 12.71–12.72

Hybrid offences
District Court jurisdiction, 5.96–5.97

Immunity from suit
barristers, and, 3.107–3.111
judges, and, 4.184–4.185

Impeachment
judges, and, 4.124–4.137

Imprisonment
civil enforcement, and, 10.25
criminal sentencing, and, 10.28–10.33

Incapacity
judges, and, 4.118–4.119

Incorporated practices
solicitors, and, 3.62

Indictable offences
Circuit Court jurisdiction, 5.101–5.102

Indictable offences tried summarily
District Court jurisdiction, 5.96–5.97

Indictment
criminal procedure, and, 6.110–6.112

Indirect effect doctrine
interpretation of legislation, and,
14.89
Indorsement of claim
civil procedure, and, 6.33–6.42
Inferior courts
stare decisis, and, 12.73–12.74
Information technology
legislation, and, 13.108
Injunctions
civil remedies, and, 10.09–10.16
Insolvency
High Court jurisdiction, 5.77
Inspector of Taxes
dispute resolution, and, 8.67
Inspectorates
dispute resolution, and, 8.54–8.55
Institutions of State
Constitution of 1922, under, 2.60–
2.62
Constitution of 1937, under, 2.77–
2.84
generally, 2.77
rhetoric of Constitution, 2.78
separation of powers
Comptroller and Auditor General,
2.82
executive, 2.81
generally, 2.79
judiciary, 2.84
legislature, 2.83
President of Ireland, 2.80
UK, in
executive, 2.25–2.26
Government of Ireland Act 1920,
2.46–2.48
Home Rule movement, 2.44–2.45
inferior court, 2.49–2.54
judiciary, 2.27–2.29
land reform in the 19th century,
2.42–2.43
legislature, 2.24
separation of powers, 2.22–2.23
superior courts, 2.33–2.41

Supreme Court of Judicature Acts
1873 and 1877, 2.30–2.32
Intellectual property bodies
dispute resolution, and, 8.56–8.57
Intention of legislature
interpretation of legislation, and,
14.11–14.18
International agreements
EU law, and, 16.98–16.103
International Court of Justice (ICJ)
generally, 17.39
International custom
generally, 17.06
Ireland, in, 17.79–17.81
International law
Council of Europe
Convention on Human Rights,
17.21–17.28
generally, 17.18–17.20
other conventions, 17.29
European Convention on Human
Rights, 17.21–17.22
European Court of Human Rights,
17.23–17.28
General Agreement on Tariffs and
Trade (GATT), 17.50–17.53
International Court of Justice (ICJ),
17.39
international custom
generally, 17.06
Ireland, in, 17.79–17.81
introduction, 17.01–17.04
Ireland, in
international custom, 17.79–17.81
introduction, 17.62
treaties, 17.63–17.78
Ireland's role, 17.11–17.17
private international law
choice of laws, 17.85
forum non conveniens, 17.83–17.84
influence of EU, 17.86
international codification, 17.87–
17.89
introduction, 17.82

International law (contd)
    jurisdiction, 17.83–17.84
    lex fori, 17.85
  sources
    general principles of law applied by
    civilised nations, 17.08
    international custom, 17.06
    introduction, 17.05
    subsidiary, 17.09–17.10
    treaties, 17.07
  sources of law, and, 1.20
  treaties
    generally, 17.07
    Ireland, in, 17.63–17.78
  UNCITRAL, 17.87
  UNIDROIT, 17.88
  United Nations Organisation (UN)
    agencies, 17.40
    Economic and Social Council
    (ECOSOC), 17.37
    General Assembly, 17.34
    generally, 17.30–17.32
    influence, 17.41–17.49
    International Court of Justice (ICJ),
    17.39
    principal organs, 17.33
    Secretariat, 17.38
    Security Council, 17.35–17.36
    UN Secretary-General, 17.38
    veto, 17.35
  'World Court', 17.39
  World Trade Organisation (WTO)
    Dispute Settlement Mechanism,
    17.58–17.61
    founding principles, 17.54
    introduction, 17.50
    origins, 17.51–17.53
    system, 17.55–17.57
International treaties
  interpretation of legislation, and,
  14.164–14.165
Interpretation of legislation
  aids
    all words bear a meaning, 14.95

    compatibility with EU law, 14.88–
    14.91
    compatibility with international law,
    14.92–14.94
    conjunctive meanings, 14.132–
    14.134
    constitutionality, 14.78–14.87
    directory provisions, 14.149–
    14.153
    disjunctive meanings, 14.132–
    14.134
    ejusdem generis rule, 14.120–
    14.125
    expressio unius est exclusio alterius,
    14.117–14.119
    extra-territorial effect, 14.116
    generalia specialibus non derogant,
    14.129–14.131
    indirect effect doctrine, and, 14.89
    introduction, 14.76–14.77
    mandatory provisions, 14.149–
    14.153
    noscitur a sociis, 14.126–14.128
    penal statutes be construed strictly,
    14.106–14.108
    presumptions, 14.78–14.116
    repealed provisions, 14.135–14.148
    retrospective effect, 14.110–14.115
    revenue statutes be construed
    strictly, 14.109
    statute should be given an updated
    meaning, 14.96–14.103
    unclear changes in law, 14.104–
    14.105
  canons
    golden rule, 14.24–14.26
    introduction, 14.19
    literal rule, 14.20–14.23
    mischief rule, 14.27–14.29
  conjunctive meanings, 14.132–
  14.134
  constitutionality, 14.78–14.87
  courts' role, 14.07–14.10
  dictionaries, 14.191–14.192
  drafting of legislation, and, 14.05

Interpretation of legislation (contd)
  ejusdem generis rule, 14.120–14.125
  EU law, and, 16.222–16.223
  EU materials, 14.166–14.168
  expressio unius est exclusio alterius, 14.117–14.119
  external sources
    dictionaries, 14.191–14.192
    EC materials, 14.166–14.168
    international treaties, 14.164–14.165
    introduction, 14.154
    legislative history, 14.161–14.163
    parliamentary materials, 14.172–14.190
    pre-parliamentary materials, 14.169–14.171
    prior statutes, 14.155–14.160
    reference works, 14.191–14.192
  extra-territorial effect, 14.116
  general rules
    golden rule, 14.24–14.26
    introduction, 14.19
    literal rule, 14.20–14.23
    mischief rule, 14.27–14.29
  generalia specialibus non derogant, 14.129–14.131
  golden rule, 14.24–14.26
  indirect effect doctrine, and, 14.89
  intention of legislature, 14.11–14.18
  international treaties, 14.164–14.165
  Interpretation Act 2005, and, 14.30
  introduction, 14.01–14.06
  legislative history, 14.161–14.163
  literal approach
    comparison with schematic approach, 14.63–14.75
    generally, 14.33–14.37
    technical meanings, 14.38–14.42
  literal rule, 14.20–14.23
  mischief rule, 14.27–14.29
  noscitur a sociis, 14.126–14.128
  parliamentary materials, 14.172–14.190
  penal statutes, 14.106–14.108

  pre-parliamentary materials, 14.169–14.171
  presumptions
    all words bear a meaning, that, 14.95
    compatibility with EU law, of, 14.88–14.91
    compatibility with international law, of, 14.92–14.94
    constitutionality, of, 14.78–14.87
    extra-territorial effect, against, 14.116
    penal statutes be construed strictly, that, 14.106–14.108
    retrospective effect, against, 14.110–14.115
    revenue statutes be construed strictly, that, 14.109
    statute should be given an updated meaning, that, 14.96–14.103
    unclear changes in law, against, 14.104–14.105
  principal approaches
    comparison, 14.63–14.75
    introduction, 14.30–14.32
    literal approach, 14.33–14.42
    schematic or teleological approach, 14.43–14.
  prior statutes, 14.155–14.160
  purposive interpretation of EC measures, 14.57–14.62
  reference works, 14.191–14.192
  repealed provisions, 14.135–14.148
  retrospective effect, 14.110–14.115
  revenue statutes, 14.109
  role of courts, 14.07–14.10
  schematic or teleological approach
    comparison with literal approach, 14.63–14.75
    generally, 14.43–14.56
    purposive interpretation of EC measures, 14.57–14.62
  technical meanings, 14.38–14.42
  unclear changes in law, 14.104–14.105
  updated meaning, 14.96–14.103

Interpretation of the Constitution
grammatical approach, 15.129–
15.135
harmonious approach
European influence, 15.147
generally, 15.142–15.146
historical approach, 15.136–15.141
introduction, 15.127–15.128
literal approach, 15.129–15.135
natural law
Attorney General v X, 15.177–
15.180
Constitution, and, 15.164–15.165
Fleming case, 15.193–15.195
generally, 15.148–15.151
McGee v Attorney General,
15.169–15.171
Norris v Attorney General, 15.172–
15.176
positive law, 15.152–15.157
Re a Ward of Court (No 2), 15.185–
15.192
*Re the Regulation of Information
Bill 1995*, 15.181–15.184
Ryan v Attorney General, 15.166–
15.168
utilitarianism, 15.158–15.163
'original understanding', 15.136–
15.141
purposive approach, 15.142–15.146
Interrogatories
civil procedure, and, 6.60
Intoxicating liquor licences
Circuit Court jurisdiction, 5.58
District Court jurisdiction, 5.48
Irish Constitution of 1922
amendment, 2.66–2.75
continuity of laws, 2.64–2.65
fundamental rights, 2.63
generally, 2.58–2.59
institutions of State, 2.60–2.62
separation of powers, 2.61–2.62
sources of law, and, 1.16
Irish Constitution of 1937
amendments, 15.81–15.85

constitutional judicial review
basis, 15.47–15.50
constitutional power, and, 15.99–
15.103
criticisms, 15.115–15.126
declarations of invalidity, 15.61–
15.79
executive power, and, 15.104–
15.108
fundamental rights, 15.51–15.60
growth, 15.93–15.96
legal system, and, 15.97–15.98
limits, 15.115–15.126
locus standi, 15.87–15.92
representative actions, 15.80
rules of self-restraint, 15.86
standing, 15.87–15.92
content
introduction, 15.02–15.03
liability of the state, 15.35–15.43
name of the state, 15.30–15.34
national territory, 15.05–15.29
right to self-determination, 15.04
sovereignty, 15.35–15.43
continuity of laws, 2.91
cross-border institutions, and, 15.21–
15.29
declarations of invalidity
common law rules, and, 15.71
effect, 15.67–15.70
generally, 15.61–15.66
prospective effect, 15.72–15.76
retrospective effect, 15.72–15.76
English language text, 2.92–2.94
EU law, and
adaptation to Community legal
order, 16.104–16.113
incorporation of Treaties and
Community Acts, 16.114–16.134
international agreements, 16.98–
16.103
European Convention on Human
Rights, and, 15.202–15.207
fundamental rights
amendments, 15.81–15.85

Irish Constitution of 1937 (contd)
   basis for constitutional judicial
     review, 2.88–2.90, 15.47–15.50
   constitutional power, and, 15.99–
     15.103
   criticisms, 15.115–15.126
   declarations of invalidity, 15.61–
     15.79
   divorce, 15.113–15.114
   enumerated rights, 15.51–15.52
   executive power, and, 15.104–
     15.108
   generally 2.85, 15.44
   limits, 15.115–15.126
   marital breakdown, 15.113–15.114
   multi-party actions, and, 15.80
   representative actions, 15.80
   restrictions on law-making authority
     of Oireachtas, 2.86–2.87, 15.45–
     15.46
   right to life, 15.109–15.112
   sexual privacy, 15.109–15.112
   unenumerated personal rights,
     15.53–15.60
  further constitutional development,
   2.95–2.97
  generally, 2.76
  Good Friday Agreement, and, 15.11
  institutions of State
   generally, 2.77
   rhetoric of Constitution, 2.78
   separation of powers, 2.79–2.84
  interpretation
   And see **Interpretation of the**
   Constitution
   grammatical approach, 15.129–
     15.135
   harmonious approach, 15.142–
     15.147
   historical approach, 15.136–15.141
   introduction, 15.127–15.128
   literal approach, 15.129–15.135
   natural law, 15.148–15.195
   'original understanding', 15.136–
     15.141

   purposive approach, 15.142–
     15.146
  introduction, 15.01
  'Ireland', 15.30–15.34
  'Irish nation' assertion, and, 15.05–
   15.10
  liability of the state, 15.35–15.43
  name of the state, 15.30–15.34
  national territory
   Article 2, 15.12–15.20
   Article 3, 15.21–15.27
   Good Friday Agreement, and, 15.11
   new provisions, 15.11–15.29
   original provisions, 15.05–15.10
  personal rights
   enumerated rights, 15.51
   generally 15.44
   unenumerated personal rights,
     15.53–15.60
  position in Northern Ireland, 2.98
  religion, and, 15.02–15.03
  'Republic of Ireland', 15.30–15.34
  review
   Constitution Review Group,
     15.196–15.197
   Convention on the Constitution,
     15.201
   Oireachtas Committee on the
     Constitution, 15.198–15.200
  right to self-determination, 15.44
  separation of powers
   Comptroller and Auditor General,
     2.82
   executive, 2.81
   generally, 2.79
   judiciary, 2.84
   legislature, 2.83
   President of Ireland, 2.80
  sources of law, and, 1.16
  sovereignty, 15.35–15.43
  status, 15.01
Irish legal system
  common law system, as, 1.10–1.12
  divisions of the law
   common expressions, 1.28

Irish legal system (contd)
    generally, 1.23–1.27
    historical development
      arrival of English law, 2.03–2.21
      Brehon law, 2.02
      Constitution of 1922, 2.58–2.75
      Constitution of 1937, 2.76–2.98
      emergence of new state, 2.55–2.57
      institutions of State in the UK,
      2.22–2.54
      introduction, 2.01
      pre-Norman period, 2.02
      revised court system, 2.99–2.113
    introduction, 1.01–1.06
    jurisprudential overview, 1.32–1.44
    law and laws, 1.07–1.09
    legal personality, 1.29–1.31
    morality, 1.45–1.57
    rule of law, 1.58–1.60
    sources of law
      academic writings, 1.22
      canon law, 1.21
      commentaries, 1.22
      common law, 1.14
      Constitution, 1.16
      custom, 1.19
      EU law, 1.17–1.18
      international law, 1.20
      introduction, 1.13
      legislation, 1.15

Judges
    appointments
      class, 4.94–4.95
      formal aspects, 4.78–4.85
      informal aspects, 4.86–4.115
      introduction, 4.77
      Judicial Appointments Advisory
      Board, 4.101–4.113
      overview, 4.42
      political allegiances, 4.86–4.90
      political ideology, 4.91–4.92
      qualifications, 4.78–4.85
      the *Whelehan* affair, 4.96–4.100
    composition and structure
      Circuit Court 4.65–4.67

      Court of Appeal, 4.60
      District Court, 4.68–4.70
      High Court, 4.61–4.64
      introduction, 4.50
      numbers, 4.52
      precedence, 4.51
      Supreme Court, 4.53–4.59
      titles, 4.52
    conduct
      Curtin case, 4.150–4.154
      General Committee, 4.148
      generally, 4.120–4.123
      impeachment, 4.124–4.137
      Judicial Conduct and Ethics
      Committee, 4.144–4.146
      Judicial Council Bill (2010),
      4.155–4.160
      Judicial Studies Committee, 4.147
      overview, 4.42
      post-*Sheedy* fallout, 4.138–4.149
      Sheedy affair, 4.124–4.137
    contempt of court, 4.185
    directions to juries
      legal issues, on, 6.154
      verdict, on, 6.155–6.157
    immunity from suit, 4.184–4.185
    incapacity, 4.118–4.119
    independence
      generally, 4.116–4.117
      immunity from suit, and, 4.184–
      4.185
      overview, 4.42
      misbehaviour or incapacity, and,
      4.118–4.119
      place of judiciary in society, 4.161–
      4.173
    law makers, 2.11
    law reform, and, 11.28
    misbehaviour or incapacity, 4.118–
    4.119
    modes of address and notation
      Circuit Court judges, 4.75
      District Court judges, 4.76
      High Court judges, 4.72–4.74
      introduction, 4.71

Judges (contd)
    Supreme Court judges, 4.72–4.74
  numbers, 4.52
  pensions, 4.190
  place of judiciary in society, 4.161–4.173
  precedence, 4.51
  remuneration, 4.174–4.183
  retirement, 4.187–4.192
  salaries, 4.174–4.183
  titles, 4.52
  vacation of office, 4.186–4.192
Judicial appointments
  class, 4.94–4.95
  formal aspects, 4.78–4.85
  informal aspects, 4.86–4.115
  introduction, 4.77
  Judicial Appointments Advisory Board, 4.101–4.113
  overview, 4.42
  political allegiances, 4.86–4.90
  political ideology, 4.91–4.92
  qualifications, 4.78–4.85
  the *Whelehan* affair, 4.96–4.100
Judicial composition and structure
  Circuit Court 4.65–4.67
  Court of Appeal, 4.60
  District Court, 4.68–4.70
  High Court
    generally, 4.61–4.63
    research assistants and clerks, 4.64
  introduction, 4.50
  numbers, 4.52
  precedence, 4.51
  Supreme Court
    collegiate body, as, 4.57–4.59
    generally, 4.53–4.54
    simultaneous sittings in divisions, 4.55–4.56
    titles, 4.52
Judicial conduct
  Curtin case, 4.150–4.154
  General Committee, 4.148
  generally, 4.120–4.123
  impeachment, 4.124–4.137

Judicial Conduct and Ethics Committee, 4.144–4.146
Judicial Council, 4.140–4.143
Judicial Studies Committee, 4.147
overview, 4.42
post-*Sheedy* fallout, 4.138–4.149
Sheedy affair, 4.124–4.137
Judicial Conduct and Ethics Committee
  generally, 4.144–4.146
Judicial Council
  generally, 4.140–4.143
  legislation, 4.155–4.160
Judicial decision-making
  law reform, and, 11.28
Judicial immunity
  generally, 4.184–4.185
Judicial incapacity
  generally, 4.118–4.119
Judicial independence
  generally, 4.116–4.117
  immunity from suit, and, 4.184–4.185
  overview, 4.42
  misbehaviour or incapacity, and, 4.118–4.119
  place of judiciary in society, 4.161–4.173
Judicial precedence
  generally, 4.51
Judicial remuneration
  generally, 4.174–4.183
Judicial review
  alternative dispute resolution, and
    adjudicative functions exercised by government, 8.30–8.44
    introduction, 8.26–8.27
    obligation to act judicially, 8.28–8.29
    other bodies, 8.45–8.68
    reforms, 8.69
  Constitution, and
    basis, 15.47–15.50
    constitutional power, and, 15.99–15.103
    criticisms, 15.115–15.126

Judicial review (contd)
    declarations of invalidity, 15.61–
    15.79
    executive power, and, 15.104–
    15.108
    fundamental rights, 15.51–15.60
    growth, 15.93–15.96
    legal system, and, 15.97–15.98
    limits, 15.115–15.126
    locus standi, 15.87–15.92
    representative actions, 15.80
    rules of self-restraint, 15.86
    standing, 15.87–15.92
    generally, 10.53–10.56
    High Court jurisdiction, and, 5.75
    legal aid, and, 9.33
    procedure, 10.57
Judicial salaries
    generally, 4.174–4.183
Judicial Studies Committee
    generally, 4.147
Judiciary
    historical development of legal
    system, and, 2.27–2.29
    separation of powers, and, 2.84
Judiciary committee
    historical development of legal
    system, and, 2.105
Junior counsel
    And see **Barristers**
    generally, 3.99–3.104
Juries
    directions from judge on legal issues,
    6.154
    directions from judge on verdict,
    6.155–6.157
    disqualified persons, 6.144–6.147
    excused persons, 6.144–6.147
    ineligible persons, 6.144–6.147
    introduction, 6.142
    majority verdicts, 6.159
    representative nature, 6.143
    scope of decision-making, 6.158
    selection, 6.148–6.153
    unqualified persons, 6.144–6.147

Jurisprudence
    distributive justice, 1.44
    generally, 1.32
    morality, 1.45–1.57
    natural law, 1.38–1.40
    positivism, 1.33–1.37
    rights, 1.41
    rule of law, 1.58–1.60
    utilitarianism, 1.42–1.43
Justices of the Peace
    historical development of legal
    system, and, 2.51–2.53
Justis Publishing database
    precedent, and, 12.24
Keane CJ (2001) lecture
    appellate jurisdiction reforms, and,
    7.62–7.68
    courts of first instance reforms, and,
    5.122–5.133
Labour Court
    dispute resolution, and, 8.49–8.51
Labour Relations Commission
    dispute resolution, and, 8.49–8.51
Land
    Circuit Court jurisdiction, 5.63
    District Court jurisdiction, 5.53
Land reform
    historical development of legal
    system, and, 2.42–2.43
Landlord and tenant
    Circuit Court jurisdiction, 5.64
Law clerks
    legal profession, and, 3.155
Law Library
    barristers, and, 3.83–3.88
Law Officers
    Attorney General, 3.115–3.124
    Director of Public Prosecutions,
    3.125–3.128
    introduction, 3.114
Law reform
    adjudicative bodies, and, 8.69
    appeals, and
        Law Reform Commission Report
        (2010), 7.72–7.73

Law reform (contd)
　　lecture by Keane CJ (2001), 7.62–7.68
　　Working Group on Court of Appeal, 7.71
　　Working Group on the Jurisdiction of the Courts, 7.70
　Committee on Court Practice and Procedure, 11.23
　Competition Authority, 11.26
　Constitution Review Group, 11.27
　court management, and, 4.209–4.216
　criminal legal aid, and, 9.24–9.32
　introduction, 11.01
　judicial decision-making, and, 11.28
　Law Reform Commission
　　background, 11.09–11.10
　　composition, 11.13
　　consultative documents and reports, 11.15
　　establishment, 11.11–11.12
　　functions, 11.14
　　Programmes of Law Reform, 11.18–11.21
　　recommendations, 11.16–11.21
　legal profession, and
　　Competition Authority reports, 3.12–3.17
　　EU-IMF Framework, 3.18
　　Fair Trade Commission Report 1990, 3.05–3.11
　　influences, 3.38–3.44
　　Legal Services Regulation Bill, 3.18–3.21
　legislation, and, 11.02–11.08
　Oireachtas Committee on the Constitution, 11.27
　Programme of Law Reform (1962), 11.09–11.10
　Working Group on a Courts Commission, 11.24
　Working Group on the Jurisdiction of the Courts, 11.25
Law Reform Commission
　appellate jurisdiction, and, 7.72–7.73

background, 11.09–11.10
composition, 11.13
consultative documents and reports, 11.15
courts of first instance, and, 5.137–5.139
establishment, 11.11–11.12
functions, 11.14
Programmes of Law Reform, 11.18–11.21
recommendations, 11.16–11.21
Law reporting
precedent, and, 12.14–12.27
Legal aid
civil cases
　access to the courts, and, 9.41–9.43
　Committee on Civil Legal Aid and Advice, 9.39–9.43
　criteria for obtaining legal advice, 9.52
　criteria for obtaining legal aid, 9.53–9.55
　eligibility tests, 9.48–9.51
　excluded matters, 9.57–9.58
　Free Legal Advice Centres, 9.38
　funding of system, 9.59–9.63
　introduction, 9.37
　Legal Aid Board, 9.45–9.46
　means test, 9.49–9.51
　merits test, 9.48
　non-statutory scheme, 9.44
　prescribed courts and tribunals, 9.56
　review of scheme, 9.64–9.65
　statutory scheme, 9.45–9.51
criminal cases
　funding of system, 9.24–9.32
　judicial review, 9.33
　police custody, in, 9.34–9.36
　reforms and proposals, 9.24–9.32
　trial, at, 9.17–9.23
introduction, 9.13–9.13
Legal Aid Board
generally, 9.45–9.46

Legal costs
first instance jurisdiction, and
generally, 5.37–5.41
regulation, 5.42–5.45
generally, 9.71–9.72
protective costs orders, 9.73–9.77
Legal executives
legal profession, and, 3.156–3.157
Legal personality
generally, 1.29–1.31
Legal profession
access, 3.22–3.26
Attorney General, 3.115–3.124
Bain Report, and, 3.43
barristers
admission to profession, 3.78–3.82
advocacy, 3.105–3.106
chambers, and, 3.83
conduct, 3.89–3.94
direct access, 3.95–3.98
discipline, 3.89–3.94
immunity from suit, 3.107–3.111
instructions, 3.95–3.98
introduction, 3.77
junior counsel, 3.99–3.104
Law Library, 3.83–3.88
mode of dress, 3.112–3.113
senior counsel, 3.99–3.104
branches, 3.02–3.04
Chief State Solicitor, 3.124
Competition Authority reports, and
appointment of senior counsel,
3.101
generally, 3.12–3.17
introduction, 11.26
rights of audience, 3.73
continuing legal education, 3.144–
3.145
conveyancing, and, 3.38
costs, 3.27–3.37
Director of Public Prosecutions,
3.125–3.128
education
continuing legal education, 3.144–
3.145

exchanges between lawyers at EU
level, 3.153
Fair Trade Commission Report, and,
3.133–3.143
recognition of foreign
qualifications, 3.146–3.152
universities, 3.129–3.132
EU-IMF Framework, 3.18
Fair Trade Commission Report 1990,
and
advertising by solicitors, 3.75
appointment of senior counsel,
3.101
conveyancing, 3.64
costs, 3.27–3.37
direct access to barristers, 3.98
discipline of barristers, 3.92
generally, 3.05–3.11
legal education, 3.133–3.143
legal fees, 3.27–3.37
rights of audience, 3.72
fees, 3.27–3.37
foreign qualifications, 3.146–3.152
future issues, 3.47–3.51
gender change, 3.45–3.46
introduction, 3.01
junior counsel, 3.99–3.104
law clerks, 3.155
Law Library, 3.83–3.88
Law Officers
Attorney General, 3.115–3.124
Chief State Solicitor, 3.124
Director of Public Prosecutions,
3.125–3.128
introduction, 3.114
legal executives, 3.156–3.157
Legal Services Ombudsman
background, 3.17
generally, 8.88
Legal Services Regulation Bill, 3.18–
3.21
non-lawyer professions, 3.158–3.160
numbers of practising lawyers, 3.22–
3.26

Legal profession (contd)
  recognition of foreign qualifications,
  3.146–3.152
  reform
    Competition Authority reports,
    3.12–3.17
    Fair Trade Commission Report
    1990, 3.05–3.11
    future issues, 3.47–3.51
    gender change, 3.45–3.46
    influences, 3.38–3.44
  solicitors
    admission to profession, 3.53–3.57
    advertising, 3.75–3.76
    compensation fund, 3.61
    contentious business, 3.70
    conveyancing, 3.63–3.69
    deferred fees, 3.76
    discipline, 3.58–3.61
    firms, 3.62
    incorporated practices, 3.62
    introduction, 3.52
    judicial appointments, 3.74
    'no foal, no fee' litigation, 3.76
    non-contentious business, 3.63–
    3.69
    practice, 3.62
    rights of audience, 3.71–3.73
  statutory compensation fund, 3.61
Legal rules
  generally, 1.08
Legal Services Ombudsman
  background, 3.17
  generally, 8.88
Legal Services Regulation Bill
  legal profession, and, 3.18–3.21
Legal system
  And see **Irish legal system**
  generally, 1.08–1.09
Legislation
  Acts, 13.02
  amendments, 13.89–13.95
  Article 26 of the Irish Constitution,
  13.25

Article 27 of the Irish Constitution,
13.26–13.27
categories
  primary legislation, 13.02
  secondary legislation, 13.03
characteristics, 13.14–13.17
codes of practice, 12.04
codification legislation
  improving quality of legislation,
  13.106
  state of the statute book, 13.103
common law rules, and, 13.06
comparison with other sources of law,
13.05–13.08
consolidation legislation
  formal process, 13.39
  improving quality of legislation,
  13.106
  state of the statute book, 13.102
constitutional arrangements
  Article 26, 13.25
  Article 27, 13.26–13.27
  generally, 13.20–13.24
contracts, and, 13.07–13.08
delegated legislation
  And see **Delegated legislation**
  Constitution, and, 13.121–13.138
  contracts of adhesion, 13.119–
  13.120
  domestic measures derived from EU
  law, 13.153–13.155
  generally, 13.03
  introduction, 13.109–13.118
  judicial scrutiny, 13.139–13.150
  parliamentary scrutiny, 13.151–
  13.155
drafting, 13.58–13.64
formal process
  Article 26, 13.25
  Article 27, 13.26–13.27
  consolidation legislation, 13.39
  constitutional arrangements,
  13.20–13.27
  parliamentary procedure, 13.28–
  13.45

Legislation (contd)
    private legislation, 13.40–13.45
    private members' Bills, 13.35–
    13.38
  format
    arrangement of sections, 13.83
    chapters, 13.82
    commencement dates, 13.74–13.81
    internal organisation, 13.82–13.83
    introduction, 13.65
    language, 13.66–13.68
    long title, 13.69–13.70
    margin notes, 13.83
    objects of legislation, 13.73
    parts, 13.82
    preamble, 13.71–13.73
    schedules, 13.82
    sections, 13.82
    short title, 13.69
    shoulder notes, 13.83
    statutory number, 13.69
    sub-sections, 12.86
  improving quality of legislation,
  13.104–13.108
  influences on, 13.53–13.57
  informal process, 13.46–13.57
  information technology, and, 13.108
  interpretation
    And see **Interpretation of**
    legislation
    aids, 14.76–14.153
    canons, 14.19–14.29
    external sources, 14.154–14.192
    general rules, 14.19–14.29
    intention of legislature, 14.11–
    14.18
    introduction, 14.01–14.06
    principal approaches, 14.30–14.75
    role of courts, 14.07–14.10
  introduction, 13.01–13.04
  law reform, and, 11.02–11.08
  overview, 1.09
  parliamentary procedure
    consolidation legislation, 13.39
    generally, 13.28–13.34
    private legislation, 13.40–13.45

    private members' Bills, 13.35–
    13.38
  primary legislation, 13.02
  private Acts
    generally, 13.02
    parliamentary procedure, 13.40–
    13.45
  private members' Bills
    generally, 13.35–13.38
    practice, in, 13.49
  process
    formal, 13.20–13.45
    informal, 13.46–13.57
    introduction, 13.18–13.19
  public general Acts, 13.02
  publication, 13.107
  quality of legislation, 13.104–13.108
  quasi-legislation
    generally, 13.09–13.13
    introduction, 13.04
  ratio decidendi, and, 12.139–12.143
  restatement programme, 13.101
  revision
    improving quality of legislation,
    13.106
    state of the statute book, 13.100
  secondary legislation, 13.03
  sources and influences, 13.53–13.57
  sources of law, and, 1.15
  state of the statute book
    amendments, 13.89–13.95
    codification legislation, 13.103
    consolidation legislation, 13.102
    improving quality of legislation,
    13.104–13.108
    introduction, 13.84–13.88
    pre-1922 legislation, 13.100
    restatement programme, 13.101
    statutory language, 13.96–13.99
    tidying measures, 13.100–13.103
  Statute Law (Restatement) Act,
  13.101
  Statute Law Revision Acts, 13.100
  statutes, 13.02
  statutory language, 13.96–13.99
  subordinate legislation, 13.03

Legislative history
interpretation of legislation, and, 14.161–14.163

Legislature
historical development of legal system, and, 2.24
separation of powers, and, 2.83

LEXIS database
precedent, and, 12.22

Liability of the state
Constitution, and, 15.35–15.43

Liquor licences
Circuit Court jurisdiction, 5.58
District Court jurisdiction, 5.48

Lisbon Treaty (proposed)
EU law, and, 16.58–16.61

Literal approach
comparison with schematic approach, 14.63–14.75
generally, 14.33–14.37
interpretation of the Constitution, and, 15.129–15.135
technical meanings, 14.38–14.42

Literal rule
interpretation of legislation, and, 14.20–14.23

Local government election petitions
Circuit Court jurisdiction, 5.66

Locus standi
court procedure, and, 6.07

Luxembourg Compromise
EU law, and, 16.40

Maastricht Treaty
EU law, and, 16.42–16.46

Majority verdicts
juries, and, 6.159

Malicious injuries
Circuit Court jurisdiction, 5.65

Marital breakdown
Constitution, and, 15.113–15.114

Master of the High Court
generally, 4.196–4.197

McKenzie friends
access to the law, and, 9.10–9.12

Means test
civil legal aid, and, 9.49–9.51

Mediation
See also **Alternative dispute resolution**
generally, 8.04–8.19

Merger Treaty
EU law, and, 16.39

Merits test
civil legal aid, and, 9.48

Minor offences
District Court jurisdiction, 5.92–5.95

Miscarriages of justice
criminal appeals, and, 7.51–7.53

Mischief rule
interpretation of legislation, and, 14.27–14.29

Modes of address and notation
Circuit Court judges, 4.75
District Court judges, 4.76
High Court judges, 4.72–4.74
introduction, 4.71
Supreme Court judges, 4.72–4.74

Monetary jurisdiction
changes, 5.31–5.34
Circuit Court, 5.55–5.57
costs awards, and, 5.37–5.41
District Court, 5.47
High Court, 5.72–5.73
introduction, 5.03
seriousness of a claim, and, 5.35–5.36

Morality
jurisprudence, and, 1.45–1.57

Multi-party actions
Constitution, and, 15.80

National territory
Article 2, 15.12–15.20
Article 3, 15.21–15.27
Good Friday Agreement, and, 15.11
new provisions, 15.11–15.29
original provisions, 15.05–15.10

Natural justice
administrative law, and, 8.28

Natural law
Attorney General v X, 15.177–15.180
Constitution, and, 15.164–15.165
Fleming case, 15.193–15.195
generally, 15.148–15.151
jurisprudential theories, and, 1.37–1.40
McGee v Attorney General, 15.169–15.171
Norris v Attorney General, 15.172–15.176
positive law, 15.152–15.157
Re a Ward of Court (No 2), 15.185–15.192
Re the Regulation of Information Bill 1995, 15.181–15.184
Ryan v Attorney General, 15.166–15.168
utilitarianism, 15.158–15.163
Natural persons
legal personality, and, 1.29
Nemo judex in causa sua
administrative law, and, 8.29
judicial ethical conduct, and, 4.120
'No foal, no fee' litigation
solicitors, and, 3.76
Non-jury trials
Special Criminal Courts jurisdiction, 5.110–5.113
North Atlantic Treaty Organisation (NATO)
generally, 16.10
Noscitur a sociis
interpretation of legislation, and, 14.126–14.128
Oath
evidence, and, 6.123–6.124
Obiter dicta
See also **Precedent**
generally, 12.88–12.93
introduction, 12.09
significance, 12.121–12.131
Office of the Director of Equality Investigations
dispute resolution, and, 8.52

Oireachtas
restrictions on law-making authority, 2.86–2.87
Oireachtas committees
Constitution, and, 15.198–15.200
dispute resolution, and, 8.58–8.59
law reform, and, 11.27
Oireachtas election petitions
High Court jurisdiction, 5.81
Ombudsmen
See also **Alternative dispute resolution**
Children, 8.91
Credit Unions, 8.89
Defence Forces, 8.92
Financial Services, 8.89
Garda, 8.93
Insurance, 8.89
introduction, 8.83
Legal Services, 8.88
other, 8.88–8.95
Parliamentary Commissioner, 8.84–8.87
Pension, 8.90
Press, 8.95
Opinion evidence
generally, 6.135
Opinions
EU law, and, 16.208
Oral testimony
evidence, and, 6.125–6.127
Original jurisdiction
civil claims
And see **Original jurisdiction (civil claims)**
changes in monetary limits, 5.31–5.34
Circuit Court, 5.54–5.66
costs awards, 5.37–5.41
District Court, 5.46–5.53
High Court, 5.68–5.81
monetary limits, 5.31–5.41
regulation of costs, 5.42–5.45
relative seriousness of a claim, 5.35–5.36

Original jurisdiction (contd)
   Supreme Court, 5.82–5.89
  criminal cases
   And see **Original jurisdiction**
   (criminal cases)
   Circuit Court, 5.101–5.104
   District Court, 5.91–5.100
   High Court, 5.105–5.108
   introduction, 5.90
   Special Criminal Courts, 5.109–
   5.121

Original jurisdiction (civil claims)
  capacity decisions, 5.80
  chancery, 5.79
  changes in monetary limits, 5.31–
  5.34
  Circuit Court
   commercial claims, 5.61
   consumer claims, 5.61
   election petitions, 5.66
   environmental matters, 5.62
   equity, 5.63
   family proceedings, 5.59–5.60
   general jurisdiction, 5.55–5.57
   introduction, 5.54
   land, 5.63
   landlord and tenant, 5.64
   local government election petitions,
   5.66
   malicious injuries, 5.65
   monetary limits, 5.55–5.57
   new intoxicating liquor licences,
   5.58
  commercial claims
   Circuit Court, 5.61
   District Court, 5.50–5.51
   High Court, 5.78
  Commercial Court, 5.78
  constitutional cases, 5.74
  consumer claims
   Circuit Court, 5.61
   District Court, 5.50–5.51
  corporate insolvency, 5.77
  costs awards
   generally, 5.37–5.41

   regulation, 5.42–5.45
  District Court
   commercial claims, 5.50–5.51
   consumer claims, 5.50–5.51
   environmental matters, 5.52
   equity, 5.53
   family proceedings, 5.49
   general jurisdiction, 5.47
   introduction, 5.46
   land, 5.53
   monetary limits, 5.47
   renewal of intoxicating liquor
   licences, 5.48
   small claims, 5.51
  election petitions
   Circuit Court, 5.66
   High Court, 5.81
  environmental matters
   Circuit Court, 5.62
   District Court, 5.52
  equity
   Circuit Court, 5.63
   District Court, 5.53
   High Court, 5.79
  family proceedings
   Circuit Court, 5.59–5.60
   District Court, 5.49
   High Court, 5.75
  High Court
   capacity decisions, 5.80
   chancery, 5.79
   commercial claims, 5.78
   constitutional cases, 5.74
   corporate insolvency, 5.77
   election petitions, 5.81
   equity, 5.79
   family proceedings, 5.76
   general jurisdiction, 5.72–5.73
   introduction, 5.68–5.71
   judicial review, 5.75
   monetary limits, 5.72–5.73
   Oireachtas election petitions, 5.81
   personal insolvency, 5.77
   referendum petitions, 5.81
   wardship, 5.80

Original jurisdiction (civil claims) (contd)
insolvency, 5.77
intoxicating liquor licences
Circuit Court, 5.58
District Court, 5.48
judicial review, 5.75
land
Circuit Court, 5.63
District Court, 5.53
landlord and tenant , 5.64
local government election petitions , 5.66
malicious injuries, 5.65
monetary limits
changes, 5.31–5.34
Circuit Court, 5.55–5.57
costs awards, and, 5.37–5.41
District Court, 5.47
High Court, 5.72–5.73
seriousness of a claim, and, 5.35–5.36
Oireachtas election petitions, 5.81
personal insolvency, 5.77
referendum petitions, 5.81
regulation of costs, 5.42–5.45
relative seriousness of a claim, 5.35–5.36
small claims, 5.51
Supreme Court
functions exercised by Chief Justice, 5.89
incapacity of President of Ireland, 5.83
introduction, 5.82
reference of Bills by President, 5.84–5.88
wardship, 5.80
Original jurisdiction (criminal cases)
Children's Court, 5.98
Circuit Court
general, 5.102
introduction, 5.101
restrictions on transfer of trial, 5.103–5.104

District Court
children, 5.98
'either way' offences, 5.96–5.97
extradition applications, 5.100
'hybrid' offences, 5.96–5.97
indictable offences tried summarily, 5.96–5.97
introduction, 5.91
minor offences, 5.92–5.95
persons under 18 years old, 5.98
sending forward indictable offences for trial, 5.99
'either way' offences, 5.96–5.97
extradition applications, 5.100
High Court, 5.105–5.108
'hybrid' offences, 5.96–5.97
indictable offences, 5.101–5.102
indictable offences tried summarily, 5.96–5.97
introduction, 5.90
minor offences, 5.92–5.95
non-jury trials, 5.110–5.113
persons under 18 years old, 5.98
scheduled offences, 5.114–5.117
sending forward indictable offences for trial, 5.99
Special Criminal Courts
constitutional setting, 5.110–5.113
introduction, 5.109
non-jury court, 5.110–5.113
scheduled offences, 5.114–5.117
transfer of trials, 5.114–5.117
Parliament
law-making institution, as, 2.10
Parliamentary Commissioner
alternative dispute resolution, and, 8.84–8.87
Parliamentary materials
interpretation of legislation, and, 14.172–14.190
Penal statutes
interpretation of legislation, and, 14.106–14.108
Per incuriam
precedent, and, 12.12

Personal Injuries Assessment Board
background, 5.16
costs, 5.19
jurisdiction, 5.17
limitation period, 5.21
procedure, 5.18–5.20
Personal injuries summons
appearance, 6.44
generally, 6.32
indorsement of claim, 6.33–6.42
introduction, 6.31
verifying affidavits, 6.43
Personal injury actions
first instance jurisdiction, and, 5.13–5.22
Personal insolvency
High Court jurisdiction, 5.77
Personal rights
See also **Fundamental rights**
enumerated rights, 15.51
generally 15.44
unenumerated personal rights, 15.53–15.60
Persons lacking capacity
access to the law, and, 9.09
Persons under 18 years old
District Court jurisdiction, 5.98
Persuasive authority
precedent, and, 12.07
Petty Sessions
historical development of legal
system, and, 2.51–2.53
generally, 4.40
Planning appeals board
dispute resolution, and, 8.60
Pleadings
Circuit Court, in, 6.61
close, 6.54–6.55
defence, 6.49–6.52
defence and counterclaim, 6.53
District Court, in, 6.62
formality, 6.26–6.27
introduction, 6.23–6.25
reply, 6.56

statements of claim, 6.45–6.48
summonses, 6.29–6.42
Plenary summons
appearance, 6.44
generally, 6.31
personal injuries claims, 6.32–6.43
Point of law, appeals on
civil appeals
Circuit Court, from, 7.22
District Court, from, 7.14–7.18
High Court, from, 7.25–7.28
criminal appeals, and,
summary trials in District Court,
from, 7.34–7.35
findings of primary fact, 7.07
findings of secondary fact, 7.08–7.11
generally, 7.05–7.06
Political controversies
judicial independence, and, 4.20–4.23
Police custody
access to a lawyer, and, 9.34–9.36
Possession and sale of land
civil enforcement, and, 10.21
Positivism
jurisprudential theories, and, 1.33–1.37
Precedent
binding authority, 12.07
distinguishing, 12.11
example
developing the standard of care,
12.168–12.173
general principle, 12.144–12.151
negligent solicitors, 12.152–12.154
negligently performed property
transactions, 12.155–12.157
solicitor's duty to third parties,
12.158–12.167
FirstLaw database, 12.22
introduction, 12.01–12.13
Justis Publishing database, 12.24
law reporting, 12.14–12.27
LEXIS database, 12.22
obiter dicta

Precedent (contd)
  generally, 12.88–12.93
  introduction, 12.09
  significance, 12.121–12.131
  overview, 1.09
  per incuriam, 12.12
  persuasive authority, 12.07
  ratio decidendi
    evolution of principles, 12.132–12.138
    facts of case, and, 12.94–12.96
    generally, 12.88–12.93
    introduction, 12.09
    legislation, and, 12.139–12.143
    multiple judgments, and, 12.104–12.120
    precedent, and, 12.139–12.143
    reasoning and argument, and, 12.97–12.103
  res judicata, and, 12.10
  stare decisis
    Court of Appeal, and, 12.69–12.70
    Court of Criminal Appeal, and, 12.67–12.68
    foreign decisions, 12.75–12.86
    generally, 12.28–12.29
    High Court, and, 12.56–12.66
    House of Lords decisions (pre-1922), and, 12.72
    House of Lords decisions (pre-1961), and, 12.71
    inferior court decisions, 12.73–12.74
    introduction, 12.03
    lower courts should follow decisions of higher courts, 12.30–12.33
    secondary sources, 12.87
    Supreme Court, and, 12.34–12.55
  sub silentio, 12.12
  Westlaw database, 12.22
Prejudice to verdict
  criminal appeals, and, 7.54–7.55

Pre-parliamentary materials
  interpretation of legislation, and, 14.169–14.171
President of Ireland
  separation of powers, and, 2.80
Presumptions
  aid interpretation of legislation, to
    all words bear a meaning, that, 14.95
    compatibility with EU law, of, 14.88–14.91
    compatibility with international law, of, 14.92–14.94
    constitutionality, of, 14.78–14.87
    extra-territorial effect, against, 14.116
    penal statutes be construed strictly, that, 14.106–14.108
    retrospective effect, against, 14.110–14.115
    revenue statutes be construed strictly, that, 14.109
    statute should be given an updated meaning, that, 14.96–14.103
    unclear changes in law, against, 14.104–14.105
  innocence, of, 6.139–6.141
Pre-trial remedies
  civil procedure, and, 6.57–6.60
Primary legislation
  And see **Legislation**
  generally, 13.02
Prior statutes
  interpretation of legislation, and, 14.155–14.160
Private international law
  choice of laws, 17.85
  forum non conveniens, 17.83–17.84
  influence of EU, 17.86
  international codification, 17.87–17.89
  introduction, 17.82
  jurisdiction, 17.83–17.84
  lex fori, 17.85

Private law
divisions of the law, and, 1.25–1.26
Private legislation
generally, 13.02
parliamentary procedure, 13.40–13.45
Private members' Bills
generally, 13.35–13.38
practice, in, 13.49
Probation
sentencing, and, 10.34–10.38
Procedural law
divisions of the law, and, 1.23
Professional body tribunals
dispute resolution, and, 8.61
Programmes of Law Reform
generally, 11.09–11.10
Law Reform Commission, and, 11.18–11.21
Property law
divisions of the law, and, 1.25
Prosecution on indictment
criminal procedure, and, 6.94–6.102
Prosecution system
criminal procedure, and, 6.85–6.89
Protective costs orders
access to law, and, 9.73–9.77
Public contracts
dispute resolution, and, 8.62
Public general Acts
legislation, and, 13.02
Public law
criminal procedure, and, 6.02
divisions of the law, and, 1.24
Public utilities
dispute resolution, and, 8.63–8.64
Punishment
criminal procedure, and, 6.03–6.05
Purposive approach
interpretation of the Constitution, and, 15.142–15.146
Purposive interpretation of EC measures
interpretation of legislation, and, 14.57–14.62

Quantitative restrictions
EU law, and, 16.33
Quarter Sessions
historical development of legal system, and, 2.51–2.53
Quasi-legislation
And see **Legislation**
generally, 13.09–13.13
introduction, 13.04
Rating and valuation
dispute resolution, and, 8.65
Ratio decidendi
See also **Precedent**
evolution of principles, 12.132–12.138
facts of case, and, 12.94–12.96
generally, 12.88–12.93
introduction, 12.09
legislation, and, 12.139–12.143
multiple judgments, and, 12.104–12.120
precedent, and, 12.139–12.143
reasoning and argument, and, 12.97–12.103
Recognition of foreign qualifications
generally, 3.146–3.152
Recommendations
EU law, and, 16.208
Reference works
interpretation of legislation, and, 14.191–14.192
Referendum petitions
High Court jurisdiction, 5.81
Refugees Appeal Tribunal
dispute resolution, and, 8.66
Registrar of the Supreme Court
generally, 4.201
Regulation of costs
first instance jurisdiction, and, 5.42–5.45
Regulations
And see **Legislation**
EU law, and
generally, 16.190–16.194

Regulations (contd)
    implementation in Ireland, 16.209–
    16.211
    generally, 13.03
Regulators
    enforcement, and, 10.46–10.47
Rehearings
    criminal appeals, and, 7.04
Religion
    Constitution, and, 15.02–15.03
Remedies
    civil claims, in
        damages, 10.03–10.08
        declarations, 10.18
        enforcement, 10.19–10.26
        injunctions, 10.09–10.16
        introduction, 10.02
        specific performance, 10.17
    enforcement of civil court orders
        attachment of earnings orders,
        10.25
        fi fa orders, 10.19
        garnishee orders, 10.20
        imprisonment, and, 10.25
        possession and sale of land, 10.21
        schedule of payments order, 10.22
        transnational basis, and, 10.26
    contempt of court
        civil contempt, 10.51
        criminal contempt, 10.52
        introduction, 10.49
        procedure, 10.51–10.52
        types, 10.50
    corporate offences, 10.46–10.47
    criminal offences, for
        absolute discharge, 10.36–10.37
        binding to the peace, 10.38
        community service, 10.39–10.40
        compensation orders, 10.41
        conditional discharge, 10.35
        Court Poor Box Payment, 10.37
        fines, 10.28–10.33
        imprisonment, 10.28–10.33
        introduction, 10.27
        probation, 10.34–10.38

    restorative justice principles,
        10.42–10.45
    transnational basis, and, 10.48
    introduction, 10.01
    judicial review
        generally, 10.53–10.56
        procedure, 10.57
    regulatory offences, 10.46–10.47
Repealed provisions
    interpretation of legislation, and,
    14.135–14.148
Reply
    civil procedure, and, 6.56
Representative actions
    constitutional judicial review, and,
    15.80
Research assistants and clerks
    judicial composition and structure,
    and, 4.64
Res judicata
    precedent, and, 12.10
Restatement programme
    legislation, and, 13.101
Retrospective effect
    interpretation of legislation, and,
    14.110–14.115
Revenue Commissioners
    dispute resolution, and, 8.67
Revenue statutes
    interpretation of legislation, and,
    14.109
Revision of legislation
    improving quality of legislation,
    13.106
    state of the statute book, 13.100
Right to life
    Constitution, and, 15.109–15.112
Right to self-determination
    Constitution, and, 15.044
Rights of audience
    solicitors, and, 3.71–3.73
Rule of law
    generally, 1.58–1.60
Sale of land
    civil enforcement, and, 10.21

Schedule of payments
civil enforcement, and, 10.22
Scheduled offences
Special Criminal Courts jurisdiction,
5.114–5.117
Schematic or teleological approach
comparison with literal approach,
14.63–14.75
generally, 14.43–14.56
purposive interpretation of EC
measures, 14.57–14.62
Secondary legislation
And see **Legislation**
generally, 13.03
overview, 1.09
**Sending forward indictable offences
for trial**
District Court jurisdiction, 5.99
Sentences
criminal appeals, and
generally, 7.48–7.50
miscarriages of justice, concerning,
7.51–7.53
Separation of powers
Constitution of 1922, under, 2.61
Constitution of 1937, under,
Comptroller and Auditor General,
2.82
executive, 2.81
generally, 2.79
judiciary, 2.84
legislature, 2.83
President of Ireland, 2.80
institutions of State in the UK, and,
2.22–2.23
introduction, 2.61
Seriousness of a claim
first instance jurisdiction, and, 5.35–
5.36
Settlements
civil procedure, and, 6.63–6.65
Sexual privacy
Constitution, and, 15.109–15.112
Single European Act
generally, 16.41

Small claims
alternative dispute resolution, and,
8.13
District Court, 5.51
generally, 5.24
Social welfare appeals
dispute resolution, and, 8.65
Solicitors
See also **Legal profession**
admission to profession, 3.53–3.57
advertising, 3.75–3.76
compensation fund, 3.61
contentious business, 3.70
conveyancing, 3.63–3.69
deferred fees, 3.76
discipline, 3.58–3.61
firms, 3.62
incorporated practices, 3.62
introduction, 3.52
judicial appointments, 3.74
'no foal, no fee' litigation, 3.76
non-contentious business, 3.63–3.69
practice, 3.62
rights of audience, 3.71–3.73
Sources of law
academic writings, 1.22
canon law, 1.21
commentaries, 1.22
common law, 1.14
Constitution, 1.16
custom, 1.19
EU law, 1.17–1.18
international law, 1.20
introduction, 1.13
legislation, 1.15
Sovereignty
Constitution, and, 15.35–15.43
Special Criminal Courts
criminal appeals, and
acquittals, against, 7.57–7.60
conviction, against, 7.45–7.47
generally, 7.37–7.44
miscarriages of justice, concerning,
7.51–7.53

Special Criminal Courts (contd)
    prosecution without prejudice to
      verdict, by, 7.54–7.55
      sentence, against, 7.48–7.50
    composition, 5.119–5.121
    jurisdiction
      constitutional setting, 5.110–5.113
      introduction, 5.109
      non-jury court, 5.110–5.113
      scheduled offences, 5.114–5.117
    operation, in, 5.118
    trial by judges alone, 6.160
Special summons
    civil procedure, and, 6.30
Specific performance
    civil remedies, and, 10.17
Standing
    civil procedure, and, 6.07
Stare decisis
    See also **Precedent**
    Court of Appeal, and, 12.69–12.70
    Court of Criminal Appeal, and,
      12.67–12.68
    foreign decisions, 12.75–12.86
    generally, 12.28–12.29
    High Court, and, 12.56–12.66
    House of Lords decisions (pre-1922),
      and, 12.72
    House of Lords decisions (pre-1961),
      and, 12.71
    inferior court decisions, 12.73–12.74
    introduction, 12.03
    lower courts should follow decisions
      of higher courts, 12.30–12.33
    secondary sources, 12.87
    Supreme Court, and, 12.34–12.55
State-assisted legal aid
    civil cases
      access to the courts, and, 9.41–9.43
      Committee on Civil Legal Aid and
      Advice, 9.39–9.43
      criteria for obtaining legal advice,
      9.52
      criteria for obtaining legal aid,
      9.53–9.55

      eligibility tests, 9.48–9.51
      excluded matters, 9.57–9.58
      Free Legal Advice Centres, 9.38
      funding of system, 9.59–9.63
      introduction, 9.37
      Legal Aid Board, 9.45–9.46
      means test, 9.49–9.51
      merits test, 9.48
      non-statutory scheme, 9.44
      prescribed courts and tribunals,
      9.56
      review of scheme, 9.64–9.65
      statutory scheme, 9.45–9.51
    criminal cases
      funding of system, 9.24–9.32
      judicial review, 9.33
      police custody, in, 9.34–9.36
      reforms and proposals, 9.24–9.32
      trial, at, 9.17–9.23
    introduction, 9.13–9.16
Statements of claim
    civil procedure, and, 6.45–6.48
Statute Law (Restatement) Act
    legislation, and, 13.101
Statute Law Revision Acts
    legislation, and, 13.100
Statutes
    And see **Legislation**
    generally, 13.02
    introduction 2.10
    overview, 1.09
    sources of law, and, 1.15
Statutory compensation fund
    solicitors, and, 3.61
Statutory language
    legislation, and, 13.96–13.99
Sub silentio
    precedent, and, 12.12
Subordinate legislation
    And see **Legislation**
    generally, 13.03
Subsidiarity
    EU law, and, 16.26–16.29
Substantive law
    divisions of the law, and, 1.23

Summary prosecution
criminal procedure, and, 6.90–6.93
Summary summons
civil procedure, and, 6.29
Summary trials
criminal appeals, and
de novo hearing in Circuit Court,
7.33
further appeal on point of law to
Supreme Court, 7.35
generally, 7.32
outline of process, 7.36
point of law by case stated to High
Court, 7.34
generally, 6.81–6.84
Summonses
introduction, 6.28
personal injuries summons
appearance, 6.44
generally, 6.32
indorsement of claim, 6.33–6.42
introduction, 6.31
verifying affidavits, 6.43
plenary summons
appearance, 6.44
generally, 6.31
special summons, 6.30
summary summons, 6.29
types, 6.28
Superior courts
historical development of legal
system, and, 2.33–2.41
Supreme Court
court officers
introduction, 4.195
Registrar, 4.201
court sittings and vacations, 4.203
generally, 4.35–4.39
historical development of legal
system, and, 2.110–2.111
judicial composition and structure,
and
collegiate body, as, 4.57–4.59
generally, 4.53–4.54

simultaneous sittings in divisions,
4.55–4.56
modes of address and notation, 4.72–
4.74
original jurisdiction in civil claims
functions exercised by Chief
Justice, 5.89
incapacity of President of Ireland,
5.83
introduction, 5.82
reference of Bills by President,
5.84–5.88
Registrar of the Supreme Court,
4.201
stare decisis, and, 12.34–12.55
**Supreme Court of Judicature Acts
1873 and 1877**
establishment of superior courts,
2.33–2.41
generally, 2.30–2.32
Taxation of costs
first instance jurisdiction, and, 5.42–
5.45
Taxing Master's Office
generally, 4.200
Technical meanings
interpretation of legislation, and,
14.38–14.42
Teleological approach
comparison with literal approach,
14.63–14.75
generally, 14.43–14.56
purposive interpretation of EC
measures, 14.57–14.62
Time limits
civil procedure, and, 6.09–6.11
Title to proceedings
civil procedure, and, 6.06
Torts
divisions of the law, and, 1.25
Transfer of trials
Circuit Court jurisdiction, 5.103–
5.104
Special Criminal Courts jurisdiction,
5.114–5.117

Treaties
EU law, and
generally, 16.185–16.189
implementation in Ireland, 16.209–16.211
incorporation, 16.114–16.134
international law, and
generally, 17.07
Ireland, in, 17.63–17.78
Treaty of Amsterdam, 16.47–16.52
Treaty on European Union, 16.42–16.46
Treaty of Nice, 16.53–16.57
Trials on indictment
criminal appeals, and
acquittals, against, 7.57–7.60
conviction, against, 7.45–7.47
double jeopardy, and, 7.57–7.60
generally, 7.37–7.44
leave to Supreme Court, by, 7.56
miscarriages of justice, concerning, 7.51–7.53
prosecution without prejudice to verdict, by, 7.54–7.55
sentence, against, 7.48–7.50
generally, 6.81–6.84
Tribunals of inquiry
alternative dispute resolution, and, 8.74–8.82
Tudor settlements or plantations
historical development of legal system, and, 2.17–2.28
UNCITRAL
generally, 17.87
UNIDROIT
generally, 17.88
United Nations Organisation (UN)
agencies, 17.40
Economic and Social Council (ECOSOC), 17.37
General Assembly, 17.34
generally, 17.30–17.32
influence, 17.41–17.49
International Court of Justice (ICJ), 17.39

principal organs, 17.33
Secretariat, 17.38
Security Council, 17.35–17.36
UN Secretary-General, 17.38
veto, 17.35
Utilitarianism
interpretation of the Constitution, and, 15.158–15.163
jurisprudential theories, and, 1.42–1.43
Valuation Tribunal
dispute resolution, and, 8.65
Verifying affidavits
civil procedure, and, 6.43
Veto
EU law, and, 16.40
Victims
criminal procedure, and, 6.110–6.122
Wardship
High Court jurisdiction, 5.80
Westlaw database
precedent, and, 12.22
Woolf Reforms (UK)
alternative dispute resolution, and, 8.15–8.18
case management, and, 6.66–6.77
Working Group on a Courts Commission
court officers, and, 4.194
law reform, and, 11.24
management of court system, and, 4.209–4.218
Working Group on Court of Appeal
appellate jurisdiction reforms, and, 7.71
Working Group on the Jurisdiction of the Courts
appellate jurisdiction reforms, and, 7.70
courts of first instance reforms, and, 5.134–5.136
law reform, and, 11.25
Written evidence
generally, 6.125–6.127

'World Court'
generally, 17.39
World Trade Organisation (WTO)
Dispute Settlement Mechanism,
17.58–17.61
founding principles, 17.54

introduction, 17.50
origins, 17.51–17.53
system, 17.55–17.57
Young persons
access to the law, and, 9.09